Guide to Good Food

Nutrition and Food Preparation

15TH EDITION

by

Velda L. Largen
Author of Family and Consumer Sciences
Instructional Materials

Deborah L. Bence
Family and Consumer Sciences Author
Granville, Ohio

Contributing Author

Michelle Lancaster
Family and Consumer Sciences Instructor
Bushland High School
Bushland, Texas

Publisher

The Goodheart-Willcox Company, Inc.

Tinley Park, IL

www.g-w.com

About the Authors

Velda L. Largen was a high school home economics teacher and department head in Missouri. During her career she developed a World Foods course, which later inspired her to write the *Guide to Good Food* text and its supplements.

Deborah L. Bence attended Miami University where she earned a bachelor's degree in home economics education. She taught family and consumer sciences at the middle school level before turning her focus to the writing and development of instructional materials. Deborah worked as an editor for an educational publisher for almost 20 years, applying her teaching and subject matter knowledge to creating textbooks and supplements for FCS classrooms, with an emphasis on foods and nutrition.

Deborah considers herself to be a lifelong learner as well as an educator. She enjoys the challenge of keeping up with new findings in the area of nutrition, trends in food marketing and preparation, and changes in the field of education. In addition to teaching students in various settings, Deborah has published a number of informative articles and other resources.

Michelle Lancaster attended Baylor University where she earned a bachelor of science degree in home economics. Michelle has been a family and consumer sciences teacher for over 20 years, is a certified ServSafe instructor, and also teaches culinary classes for a local college continuing education program. She has been a member of the Family and Consumer Sciences Teacher Association of Texas (FCSTAT) and an adviser for Family, Career and Community Leaders of America (FCCLA) since 1997. Michelle is also a member of the American Association of Family & Consumer Sciences (AAFCS).

In 2010, Michelle was awarded the Family & Consumer Sciences Teacher of the Year Award for the state of Texas, and the Region I Texas State Teacher of the Year Award in 2010–2011. She was also the recipient of the Johnson and Wales University Outstanding Texas State Teacher Award.

Reviewers

Goodheart-Willcox Publisher and the authors would like to thank the following instructors who reviewed selected manuscript chapters and provided valuable input into the development of this textbook program.

Sharon Baillie
Family and Consumer Sciences Instructor
Burgettstown Middle/High School
Burgettstown, PA

Victoria Blackstone
Family and Consumer Sciences Instructor
Williston-Elko High School
Williston, SC

Veronica Carmical
Family and Consumer Sciences Instructor
Whitley County High School
Williamsburg, KY

Peggy Caruso
Family and Consumer Sciences Instructor
Southwest High School
Houston, TX

Josephine Castillo
Family and Consumer Sciences Instructor
Harper Alternative High School
Houston, TX

Virginia DiPalma
Family and Consumer Sciences Instructor
Taconic Hills High School
Craryville, NY

Lara Dorner
Family and Consumer Sciences Instructor
Mascoutah High School
Mascoutah, IL

Iris Gardner
Family and Consumer Sciences Instructor
Irmo High School
Columbia, SC

Serina Gay
Family and Consumer Sciences Instructor
Central Gwinnett High School
Lawrenceville, GA

Stacey Horn
Family and Consumer Sciences Instructor
DeLand High School
DeLand, FL

Michelle Lancaster
Family and Consumer Sciences Instructor
Bushland High School
Bushland, TX

Kelly Ruud
Family and Consumer Sciences Instructor
Richland High School
Richland, WA

Ginger Sajdera
Family and Consumer Sciences Instructor
Valparaiso High School
Valparaiso, IN

Maria Scirone
Family and Consumer Sciences Instructor
Westlake High School
Westlake, CA

Eleanor A. Sicluna
Family and Consumer Sciences Instructor
Albany High School
Albany, NY

Rebecca Silvas
Family and Consumer Sciences Instructor
Monache High School
Porterville, CA

Rebecca Silvas
Family and Consumer Sciences Instructor
Monache High School
Porterville, CA

Anna Sullinger
Family and Consumer Sciences Instructor
Grant County High School
Dry Ridge, KY

Virginia Tate
Family and Consumer Sciences Instructor
East Forsyth High School
Kernersville, NC

Pamela Teems
Family and Consumer Sciences Instructor
Etowah High School
Woodstock, GA

LeeAnn Tomlinson
Family and Consumer Sciences Instructor
Ava High School
Ava, MO

Bessie Walker
Family and Consumer Sciences Instructor
Fort Dorchester High School
North Charleston, SC

Cynthia Ziemba
Family and Consumer Sciences Instructor
Hamilton Southeastern High School
Fishers, IN

Precision Exams Certification

Goodheart-Willcox is pleased to partner with Precision Exams by correlating *Guide to Good Food* to their Nutrition and Wellness standards. Precision Exams Standards and Career Skill Exams were created in concert with industry and subject matter experts to match real-world job skills and marketplace demands. Students that pass the exam and performance portion of the exam can earn a Career Skills Certification™. Precision Exams provides:

- Access to over 150 Career Skills Exams™ with pre- and post-exams for all 16 Career Clusters.
- Instant reporting suite access to measure student academic growth.
- Easy-to-use, 100% online exam delivery system.

To see how *Guide to Good Food* correlates to the Precision Exams Standards, please visit https://www.g-w.com/guide-to-good-food-2022 and click on the Correlations tab. For more information on Precision Exams, including a complete listing of their 150+ Career Skills Exams and Certificates, please visit https://www.precisionexams.com.

I earned a CAREER SKILLS™ Certificate in Nutrition and Wellness. You can earn one, too!

Career Skills Certificate

Ask your instructor how you can earn a

CAREER SKILLS™ Certificate for your resume.

800.470.1215   PRECISION EXAMS   precisionexams.com

MBI/Shutterstock.com

Brief Contents

Contents

Chinaview/Shutterstock.com

FamVeld/Shutterstock.com

conejota/Shutterstock.com

MBI/Shutterstock.com

Africa Studio/Shutterstock.com

©iStock.com/Wavebreakmedia

Feature Contents

Exploring Careers

FCCLA: *Taking the Lead*

Food Science

Global Perspective

Health and Wellness

Mini Lab

Learn About...

Culture and Social Studies

Recipe for Good Food

Ildi Papp/Shutterstock.com

Introduction

Guide to Good Food includes information on a wide range of food and nutrition topics. This practical text focuses on the latest advice about nutrition and physical activity. It offers guidelines for using appliances, setting up a food budget, and buying and storing foods. It provides help for managing resources, organizing workspace, and working effectively as part of a team. Discussions on basic cooking methods will give you the background needed to prepare a variety of foods. *Guide to Good Food* also includes several chapters on foods from around the world.

The broad scope of information in this text is intended to show you food is more than just something to eat. Food provides a source of income for millions of people. It is at the heart of scientific research. It is also a part of people's cultural identity.

You will find *Guide to Good Food* easy to read and understand. A *Reading Prep* activity, content and academic terms, and learning objectives will introduce you to the content of each chapter. As you read, hundreds of images will help you picture the many foods and techniques that are discussed. Colorful boxes will address scientific, cultural, environmental, and health issues related to food. Descriptions of an array of food industry careers detail work tasks, needed skills, and training requirements to help you think about your future options for work. Numerous recipes will give you the chance to practice food preparation methods covered in the book. Review questions at the end of each chapter will help you assess your learning of what you read. A variety of activities are suggested to help you build skills needed for success at home, at work, and in the community. All these resources are intended to add to your experience as you study the interesting and vital subject of food and nutrition.

Unit 1
Getting Started in the Kitchen

Chinaview /Shutterstock.com

Essential Questions

- Other than satisfying hunger, how does food affect daily life?
- What steps do you need to take to keep food, and the kitchen in which it is prepared, safe?
- What basic skills do you need to have before you are ready to prepare simple recipes?

FCCLA: Taking the Lead

Now is the time to establish healthy habits and attitudes about eating to last *your* lifetime. Use Chapter 1 and FCCLA *Student Body* units The Healthy You, The Fit You, The Real You, and The Resilient You and accept the challenge to learn more about helping young people make informed, responsible decisions about their health for today and in the future. Talk with your FCCLA adviser about completing a Student Body chapter project.

While studying, look for the activity icon ↗ for:
- Content and Academic Terms with e-flash cards, vocabulary games, and matching activities

These activities can be accessed at
www.g-wlearning.com/foodandnutrition/9582

Food Affects Life

MSPhotographic/Shutterstock.com

Objectives

After studying this chapter, you will be able to

- **explain** how the search for food led to the development of civilization;
- **use** the steps of the decision-making process to make food choices;
- **outline** physical, social, and psychological influences on food choices; and
- **describe** factors that affect the food supply.

Reading Prep

Write what you think each Chapter 1 Content and Academic term means. Then look up the term in the glossary and write the textbook definition.

Content Terms ↱

decision-making process
alternative
goal
wellness
hunger
appetite
culture
custom
fasting
value
lifestyle
peer pressure
fallacy
fad
functional food

stress
agriculture
environment
aquaculture
hydroponic farming
sustainability
United States Department of Agriculture (USDA)
Food and Drug Administration (FDA)
fair trade product
technology
genetically modified organism (GMO)

Academic Terms

entice
surmise
inclement

Food has different meanings for different people. People who are starving see food as a means of survival. People who are proud of their culture consider traditional foods to be part of their heritage. Members of some faiths regard certain foods as religious symbols. People who are entertaining guests view food as a sign of hospitality.

Clearly, food does much more than meet a basic physical need. It meets emotional, social, and psychological needs as well.

As long as people have walked the earth, they have searched for food and the means to produce it. Efforts to improve food resources are likely to continue as long as life exists.

The History of Food

Early people probably ate food raw. At some point, they accidentally discovered cooked food tasted better and was easier to digest. By trial and error, they learned to control fire and use it to prepare food.

Eventually, these early people found they could protect themselves and secure food more easily by living in groups. They formed tribes and began to hunt for food together.

Some hunters became herders when they discovered they could capture and domesticate animals. People also discovered they could plant seeds to produce large amounts of food. This discovery led to the beginning of farming. The advances of herding and farming made the food supply much more dependable.

As food became easier to obtain, not all people had to spend their time hunting and farming. Some were able to learn a craft. Others became merchants. Trading in its simplest form began, and with it came the development of civilization.

Making Choices About Foods

In the United States, many people are fortunate enough to have a variety of foods available to them. This requires them to make many choices about foods. They must decide when and where to eat.

Global Perspective

The Migration of Food

As civilizations grew and developed, people began searching for food in distant places. By the fifteenth century, Spanish, Portuguese, English, and Dutch sailors were traveling the world in search of tea and spices. These sailors discovered new lands as well as new foods. Thus, the search for new food sources fostered European colonization of distant continents and the growth of powerful empires.

European explorers introduced foods they carried with them in the new lands to which they traveled. In North America, Spanish explorers introduced cane sugar and wheat. English explorers brought apples and walnuts. The Europeans also carried foods from the lands they explored back to their homelands. Therefore, foods that were once native to one place are now found in many places. This type of exchange led to an increased variety of foods throughout the world.

MSPhotographic/Shutterstock.com

Apple pie would not be a U.S. national dish if English explorers had not introduced apples to the New World.

They must choose what to eat and how to prepare it. These choices require some skill in thinking and making decisions (**Figure 1.1**).

Steps of the Decision-Making Process

You can use a process to make decisions and solve problems about foods, activities, or any other topics. The **decision-making process** is a

Blend Images/Shutterstock.com

Figure 1.1   Once the decision is made what to eat, you must choose when, where, and what foods need to be purchased. You must decide how much food to buy and how much money you can spend.

method for thinking about possible options and outcomes before making a choice. It involves the following series of steps:

1. **Identify the problem or decision.** This helps you define the specific issue you are considering so you can focus your thoughts. You may want to phrase this step as a question. A decision about food might be *What should I do for lunch?*

2. **Consider your alternatives. Alternatives** are the various options you might choose. Options for your lunch decision might include making a sandwich, reheating yesterday's leftovers, and going out for fast food.

3. **Think about how your alternatives relate to your goals. Goals** are aims you try to reach. You have goals that guide your actions in all areas of your life. You want to be sure the decisions you make are in line with those goals. Suppose you have a goal to make healthy food choices. One of your other goals is to avoid wasting food. You might also have a goal to save money. Think about how your lunch options relate to each of these goals.

4. **Determine which alternatives are acceptable.** Sometimes, when measuring your options against your goals, there is only one suitable choice. Other times, there will be more than one alternative that seems to fit with your goals. All three of your lunch options could meet your goal for healthy food, depending on the specific foods you select to prepare or purchase. You can safely store the leftovers for another day. Therefore, all three of your options would fit your goal to avoid wasting food if you eat everything you prepare or purchase. Both making a sandwich and reheating leftovers would go along with your goal to save money. However, buying fast food would not. Going through this step shows you that you have two acceptable alternatives.

5. **Choose one alternative.** If you have more than one acceptable alternative, now is the time to decide which one you will choose. Perhaps you do not feel like making the effort to prepare a sandwich. In this case, reheating leftovers may seem like the best choice.

6. **Evaluate your decision.** Thinking about how happy you are with a decision can help you make decisions in the future. Perhaps after eating the leftovers, you realize you do not like eating the same food two days in a row. You determine making a sandwich would have been worth the extra effort. This evaluation will help you make a more pleasing choice the next time you are deciding what to do for lunch.

Using the Decision-Making Process

You can use the decision-making process whenever you have a problem to solve or a choice to make. It can help you with daily decisions like what to wear in the morning or how to spend your time after school. When making such routine choices, you may go through the process rather quickly without even realizing you are doing it. However, the process can also help you make major decisions, such as what to do after you graduate from high school. When making big decisions, you will find it worthwhile to take the time to carefully go through each step. This will help you make a satisfying choice that is in line with your goals.

One goal most people try to achieve through their decisions, including their decisions about food, is wellness. **Wellness** is the state of being in overall good health. It involves *physical* (relating to the body), *mental* (relating to the mind), and *social* (relating to relationships) health. Using the decision-making process can help you make choices that will benefit you in these three areas (**Figure 1.2**).

Physical Influences on Food Choices

What do you choose to eat when you are hungry? Where do you usually eat? Who is with you when you eat? When do you eat? How does food make you feel?

Your answers to all these questions reflect your food habits. Each of your friends would likely answer these questions a bit differently. This is because the factors that affect food habits are a little different for everyone.

When it comes to food, one factor that all people have in common is a basic physical need for it. Have you ever tried studying for a test when you were hungry? You may have found it hard to concentrate. Because the instinct to meet the need for food is so strong, you cannot focus on other issues until this need has been addressed.

Your body needs food to provide the energy required to maintain vital functions, such as keeping your heart beating. You also need energy from food to move your muscles so you can perform tasks like walking, bending, and climbing. Your body needs substances from food to build and repair tissues, too.

A complex system within your body senses when you need a fresh supply of the materials food provides. This system involves your digestive tract, which sends a message to your brain. Your brain receives this message and gives a signal, which you recognize as hunger. **Hunger** is the physical need for food. The hunger signal stimulates your stomach to produce hunger pangs. The hunger signal may also stimulate your **appetite**, which is a psychological desire to eat.

You can choose how you respond to the sensations of hunger and appetite. If you choose to eat, food relieves your hunger and the pangs in your stomach go away. If you choose not to eat, the pangs are likely to become more intense. You may experience other symptoms as hunger continues, such as a headache or dizziness.

michaeljung/Shutterstock.com

michaeljung/Shutterstock.com

Figure 1.2 You can use the decision-making process to help you decide if you have time to volunteer after school or should spend it studying.

Both hunger and appetite influence your food choices. When you are hungry, you will want to choose a food that will fill you up. For instance, a handful of nuts will keep you feeling full longer than a handful of pretzels. The nuts provide satisfying protein, fiber, and healthy oils, which are all missing from the pretzels.

Your appetite influences your food choices when you have a desire for a particular food. Suppose you have a taste for veggie pizza. In this case, you are not likely to choose to eat a grilled chicken sandwich. The sandwich will relieve your hunger, but your appetite will not be satisfied.

Social Influences on Food Choices

For many people, preparing and eating food are social activities. Food can bring people together. It brings family members together at the dinner table. It brings friends together at parties and picnics. When guests come to visit, the host usually offers them something to eat or drink. People often transact business over lunch. In each of these situations, food is part of the social interaction. Therefore, eating habits and food choices are affected by social influences (**Figure 1.3**).

Rido/Shutterstock.com

Figure 1.3 A business lunch is a way to build relationships and alliances.

Culture

One social influence that affects food habits is culture. **Culture** is the traditions and beliefs of a racial, religious, or social group. People of a certain race form a cultural group. Citizens of a given country and followers of a specific religion are also examples of cultural groups. Many people are part of more than one cultural group.

The United States is a *multicultural society.* People living in this nation can trace their ancestors to countries all over the world. They practice a wide range of religions. You might think of the United States as a cultural "tossed salad." A tossed salad is a single food item made up of a variety of vegetables. Each vegetable contributes a distinct flavor, color, and texture. In a similar way, each culture that is part of U.S. society contributes unique **customs** (typical ways of behaving) and beliefs to the nation.

Many cultural groups have special dishes and distinct food customs. The diverse cuisine in the United States reflects the country's multicultural society. People who identify with a particular group often make food choices based on their culture.

National Origin

Some people make food choices based on their national origin. They enjoy dishes that come from the land where they or their parents or grandparents grew up. Eating foods that have a traditional taste and familiar look can create a sense of comfort. Many restaurants and grocery stores are owned by people who want others to be able to choose flavors and ingredients of their national cuisines (**Figure 1.4**).

Religion

Religion is an important cultural influence on the food habits of many people. Some religions have certain customs regarding food and how people should eat it. For instance, Hindus will not use cattle (beef) for food because they consider cattle to be sacred. Muslims can eat only with the right hand.

Through the ages, people have used foods as symbols in religious ceremonies. The bread and wine used in Christian churches during communion represent the sacrifice of Christ's body and blood. Unleavened bread is a symbol for Jewish

Figure 1.4   This Ukranian restaurant features a Ukranian band to help establish an authentic environment.

Health and Wellness

Fasting to Cleanse the Body

Religious observances are not the only reason some people choose to fast. A number of fasting plans have attracted a lot of attention as health and diet practices. These programs are reported to cleanse the body of toxins. Fasting is often followed by consumption of a very limited diet, such as nothing but fruit and vegetable juices. These plans typically last for a set number of days and suggest followers repeat the program about once a year.

Most health and nutrition experts do not advise robbing your body of nutrients, which is what fasting does. Fasting programs and detox diets may also have risks of side effects, such as dehydration and fatigue. One aspect of fasting health providers would support is excluding foods that are high in calories, but low in nutrients.

Your liver and digestive system work to remove waste material from your body. Your body does not require any other form of internal cleansing.

people during Passover, when they remember the ancient flight of Hebrew people from Egypt. Because the Hebrews had to leave their homes so quickly, they did not have time to allow their bread to rise.

Fasting, or denying oneself food, has long been a religious custom. Some Christians fast during Lent, a 40-day period leading up to Easter. Jews fast on Yom Kippur, the Day of Atonement. Muslims fast from sunrise to sunset each day of Ramadan, the ninth month of the Islamic calendar.

Holidays

People of all cultures have special days set aside each year for celebration. The impact of culture on food choices may be most apparent on these days. Holiday celebrations abound with food traditions. Some holiday foods have special symbolism. For instance, heart-shaped chocolates are given on Valentine's Day as a symbol of love. Other holiday foods have simply become part of the customs connected with the celebration. As an example, many people eat corn on the cob and hot dogs on Independence Day.

Family

Family has a great impact on the foods people eat and how they eat them. Of course, a person's culture often comes from his or her family. In addition, food choices are often a reflection of family values. **Values** are items and ideas that a person or group considers important. For instance, a family who values the environment might choose to buy foods that are locally grown and have limited packaging. Children who grow up in this family are likely to adopt these values. They will probably continue to make similar food choices as they become adults.

Many food habits are formed around family customs. As mentioned earlier, customs are typical ways of behaving. In many families, it is a custom to eat dinner together. Holiday meal traditions are another example of family food customs. Adults often continue to follow the customs they learned at home as children (**Figure 1.5**).

Lifestyle is another way families affect food choices and eating patterns. **Lifestyle** is the way a person usually lives. Today, many families

MBI/Shutterstock.com

Figure 1.5   Families maintain traditions by teaching younger generations their food customs. What food customs does your family practice?

would describe their lifestyles as busy. Work, school, sports, and lessons keep family members running in different directions. This limits time family members have for tasks, such as grocery shopping and preparing meals.

One way busy families can respond to time constraints is to have a few family members share meal tasks. They may also try to prepare and freeze large batches of food when they have time, such as on weekends. These strategies can keep families from feeling their food choices are limited to convenience foods and takeout meals, which may be less healthy.

Busy lifestyles limit the amount of time family members have to share meals. However, most families say they want to keep family meals a priority. They realize mealtime is a great time to build relationships. Sharing a meal gives family members a chance to relax together and talk about interests and concerns.

Friends

Your friends have an effect on the foods you choose. You may feel peer pressure to eat the same foods your friends are eating. **Peer pressure** is influence that comes from people in a person's social group. For instance, suppose you are in a restaurant with friends. If they all order pizza, you are also likely to order pizza even if you would really have preferred a sandwich.

Friends may also encourage you to try new foods or preparation techniques (**Figure 1.6**). A friend could persuade you to sample a food such as squid, which might have little appeal to you. A friend might convince someone used to eating French fries to try roasted potatoes instead.

Mass Media

Mass media, such as the Internet, television, radio, and magazines, can affect your food choices. The media acquaints you with, reminds you of, and informs you about food products and nutrition issues.

News

News in the media can tell you about findings of a food's special health properties. The media can also notify you about products that are found to be unsafe. Learning this information can help you make wise food purchase decisions. However, news stories about food and nutrition are sometimes missing important points. You need to read and listen with care to help you analyze media information.

Incomplete or inaccurate information through the media may be behind many food fallacies and fads. A **fallacy** is a mistaken belief. Mistaken beliefs often lead to **fads**, or practices that are very popular for a short time. Many food

Ruslan Kainitsky/Shutterstock.com

Figure 1.6   Peer pressure can influence your eating habits in either a positive or negative way.

Learn About...

Evaluating Information in the Media

When you read news about food and nutrition, you need to decide if you want to use the information to guide your choices. You can use the AAOCC criteria to help you judge if information is reliable. This stands for *authority*, *accuracy*, *objectivity*, *currency*, and *coverage*. Looking for answers to a few questions can help you weigh information according to these measures.

Authority
- Who conducted the research? Experts in the field of the research are likely to know how to best interpret findings. The "About" page on a website can tell you about a person's background or an organization's purpose.
- Where were the results of the research published? A journal reviewed by experts in the field has more credibility than a popular magazine. A website from the government or a professional organization is likely to be more trustworthy than a personal blog.

Accuracy
- How was the study set up? A valid study needs to be conducted under carefully controlled conditions. Steps must be taken to keep unplanned variables from affecting the outcomes.
- How many people did the researchers study? A study that involves a large group of subjects may be more relevant than one that involves a small group.
- Were the results of this study similar to the results of other studies? Findings are more significant when they match those of a number of research teams.

Objectivity
- Who funded the research? You may have reason to be more skeptical if the funding party stands to gain financially from the findings.

Currency
- When was the research conducted? A study that took place years ago may or may not still be relevant.

Coverage
- How much and how often does the food or nutrient need to be consumed to experience the benefit or harmful effect? Quantities should resemble what people might normally be expected to consume. For instance, one study found eating dark chocolate could help lower blood pressure. However, the amount needed would likely cause weight gain or decreased nutrient intakes for most people.
- Do the beneficial or harmful effects of the food or nutrient build with repeated consumption? This indicates the degree to which the research findings might affect established eating habits.
- Does the food or nutrient have different effects on certain groups of people, such as children or pregnant women? This indicates how much bearing the research has for you.

Answers to these questions tell you if a news story is merely interesting or truly helpful.

Know and Apply
1. When might you use the AAOCC criteria?
2. How would you adapt these questions to help you evaluate information related to different subject matter?

---

fads and fallacies are related to nutrition, weight loss, and food safety issues.

For instance, suppose the media reports that a component in apples helps reduce some signs of aging. Although there may be some research behind this story, the information is incomplete. Nevertheless, a fallacy spreads that eating apples will help people live longer.

Suddenly, it becomes a fad to eat three or more apples a day. Apple sales soar. Apples begin to appear in every new food product that hits the market, from muffins to frozen entrees.

A few months later, the media issues a new story. This report states much more research is needed before any link between apples and the aging process becomes clear. However, studies show eating large amounts of apples will probably not change a person's life span. The fad comes to an end, and the popularity of apple products fades.

Food fads can lead to disappointment when they do not produce promised results. Some fads can even be harmful if they keep people from eating the variety of foods needed for good health.

Before jumping on the bandwagon to try a new fad, find out the facts. Take a little time to research the information on which the fad is based. The time you invest may end up saving you money and possible harm.

Advertising

Another key way the media influences your food choices is through advertising. Manufacturers spend millions of dollars to *entice* (tempt) you to try new food products. They also urge you to continue buying products you have used for years.

The first level of advertising for a food product is the product package. Clearly showing the brand as well as the name of the product is an important part of the packaging. Manufacturers want you to remember what product you are buying so you can buy it again. They also want you to remember who makes the product so you will be encouraged to look for other products from the same company.

Packaging is carefully designed to catch the eye of consumers. Most packages show an attractive photo of the prepared food. This image is intended to appeal to your appetite. Manufacturers use package coloring to send messages about their products, too. Think about how many foods promoted as being "healthy" have a package with a green background or green lettering. Green is the color of healthy, growing plants in nature. Using this color on the package sends the message that choosing the food product will help you be healthy.

Of course, manufacturers also use advertising through the media to try to sway people's choices. Companies use a number of techniques to sell their products. The *bandwagon appeal* stirs a desire to belong by saying everyone is using the product. *Celebrity association* uses famous people to sell products. Ads prompt you to link assets like fame, wealth, and beauty of actors or athletes with the products they promote. The use

of *expert testimony* leads you to buy a product because a doctor or other specialist recommends it. The *emotional appeal* urges you to connect products with the feelings you have when watching the ads. For instance, an ad might suggest drinking a certain beverage will make you feel happy.

Another common advertising practice is the use of *advertising icons*. These are characters designed to help people recognize products (**Figure 1.7**). Icons encourage people to try new products, too. For instance, suppose a box of the newest cereal bars on the market shows the smiling cow icon from your favorite yogurt. You like the yogurt, and you associate the cow with the yogurt. Therefore, seeing the cow might lead you to **surmise** (assume) you will also like the cereal bars, so you try them.

Ken Weinrich/Shutterstock.com

Figure 1.7 Advertising icons are the characters on product packages used to help shoppers quickly spot favorite brands. Can you identify the advertising icon on this food label?

Exploring Careers

Food Photographer

A food photographer arranges food and props in a studio to take photographs for commercial use. The photographer needs to adjust the lighting and camera settings to create the effect desired by the client. Then the photographer needs to review images and choose those that best show the food product.

To fully grasp the needs of the client, a food photographer must use active listening skills. Many photographers set their own schedules. They need to be dependable and able to manage their time to plan photography sessions and meet client deadlines. Producing images that show products in unique ways requires creativity and attention to detail.

A food photographer may begin training in a technical school. One way to learn about this career could be to work as an apprentice to a skilled photographer. A photographer will probably need a few years of experience to earn a name in the field and attract clients.

Manufacturers know that getting you to try a product is the key to turning you into a repeat buyer. Free samples, coupons, rebates, eye-catching displays, and special offers are tools they use to prompt you to check out food products.

Food Product Trends

Whereas fads are short lived, *trends* shape the market for an extended period. Consumer demand drives trends for new products in the marketplace. In turn, what products are available influences your consumer choices. When it comes to food products, consumers demand three main qualities. They want foods that are healthy, convenient, and great tasting.

Health

A consumer concern for health continues to fuel a trend for functional food products. **Functional foods** are foods that provide health benefits beyond the nutrients they contain. One example is *probiotic* yogurt. This product is viewed as more than just a source of protein, calcium, and potassium. It contains added yogurt cultures to aid digestive health. Nutrition bars that have ingredients linked to heart health are another example of functional foods.

Many sources report people in the United States are facing health risks from consuming too much sugar. Concern about this issue is behind a new trend in beverages. A number of companies are introducing new drinks that are less sweet. Some of these contain natural sweeteners, such as honey, which are often perceived to be healthier than sugar. Savory drinks made with yogurt or vegetables are also appearing as low-sugar options.

Many consumers want to avoid certain components in foods for health reasons. This impacts trends in product labeling. Claims such as *gluten-free*, *reduced sodium*, and *no added sugar* are seen on a wide range of product labels (**Figure 1.8**). Labels also promote qualities such as high protein and high fiber in response to consumer health goals.

Convenience

Busy consumers want food products that are convenient. They are looking for options that require minimal prep and cleanup.

Many consumers are multitaskers. They eat snacks as well as a large number of meals on the go. This has spurred a trend for portable food products. Pocket bread sandwiches and wraps that hold in ingredients are popular examples in this category. Such foods can be held in one hand while the other hand is holding a phone or navigating a computer screen.

A related convenience trend is single-serve packaging. Servings for one are handy for grab-and-go eating. They help with portion control, and they also allow groups to satisfy individual flavor preferences. Salad and snack kits are products that have evolved out of this trend.

Convenience is important to consumers even when they are not on the move. Many consumers say they enjoy cooking at home, but do not have a

Figure 1.8   Consumers wanting to avoid certain food components can look for products with claims like these on the labels.

lot of time to spend on food preparation. This has led to the growth of meal subscription services. These services allow meals to be ordered online and scheduled for regular delivery. Kits come to the home containing everything needed to prepare the ordered meal. Ingredients are premeasured. This not only saves time, it avoids the need to buy items, such as uncommon spices, that will not be used again. Preparation instructions may be in the form of step-by-step photos or online videos. Such resources allow consumers to try unfamiliar recipes with confidence.

Another convenience trend meets the need of consumers who want to dine at home, but do not feel like cooking. This is an increase in the number of restaurants that offer online ordering. Some restaurants will deliver food to your home. A larger number will prepare your order and have it ready for you to pick up at a preset time. Some foodservice operations do not have eat-in locations at all. Instead, they offer only delivered meals that are ready to heat and eat when scheduled (**Figure 1.9**).

Great Taste

Consumers are not willing to give up taste for health or convenience. That is why food manufacturers are always introducing new and improved flavors of products.

Food flavors that are growing in popularity include smoky flavors and salty-sour mixtures. Smoky flavors have long been popular with meats like ham and bacon. Other foods that are appearing with a wood-grilled taste include

peppers and cooking sauces as well as cheeses, snacks, and even some desserts.

Pickles and sauerkraut are classic examples of foods that combine the flavors of salty and sour. These foods are experiencing a renewed popularity. This flavor combination is also being added to dips, dressings, and beverages.

Many consumers seek out new flavors by trying cuisines of other cultures or regions. However, the particular cuisine that is most

Figure 1.9   Many supermarkets are trying to meet the consumer demand for ready-to-eat meals by offering buffets of hot and cold prepared foods. Some supermarkets even have seating areas where customers can dine if they choose.

trendy tends to change. In general, the trend is for flavors to be big and bold. Hot peppers, tangy vinegars, and exotic spices are being used in new ways to add distinct flavors to every type of food.

Another trend in terms of taste is a blurring of the lines between sweet and savory. Savory herbs, like tarragon and basil, are being used to tone down the sweetness of desserts. At the same time, fruit juices and purees are being used to add color, nutrients, and sweetness to savory dishes. Although popular flavors come and go, it seems fair to say that bland foods will not be trendy anytime soon.

Psychological Influences on Food Choices

Psychology has to do with how your thoughts and feelings affect your behavior. The way you think and feel about foods will influence what foods you choose. Many of your thoughts and feelings are based on memories of your experiences. Picture a monthly dinner at your aunt's house that always includes roasted chicken. If these meals are filled with laughter and fun, roasted chicken may make you think of pleasant experiences (**Figure 1.10**). You may

Brenda Carson/Shutterstock.com

Figure 1.10 Some real estate agents suggest that homeowners bake chocolate chips cookies before their home is toured by potential buyers. What influence is this sales trick employing?

choose to eat it at other times because doing so makes you feel happy. If these gatherings are filled with arguments and tension, roasted chicken may bring you bad memories. You may avoid eating it because it brings you a sense of sadness.

Odors as well as events create memories that affect food choices. Odor is a key part of flavor, and smell is more likely to trigger memories than any of the other senses. Therefore, an odor linked with a pleasant memory may lead you to choose certain foods. For instance, imagine you had a kind uncle who always used breath mints. The smell of mint may bring on happy memories of your uncle, and you may be drawn to mint-flavored foods. In the same way, an odor you connect with an unpleasant memory may cause you to reject some foods.

Psychology affects why you eat as well as what you eat. Food can please the senses and help meet people's need for social contact. Therefore, most people eat partly because eating is enjoyable. However, some people may avoid eating when they feel sad or lonely. Some people may eat too much because they find comfort in foods they like. Food psychologically makes up for such emotions as anger and regret in certain people.

In a similar way, there are those who use food to help them manage stress. **Stress** is mental and physical tension caused by change. For instance, moving to a new community creates many changes. Some of these changes may be positive, such as living in a nicer home. Some of the changes may be negative, such as seeing less of your friends in the old neighborhood. In both cases, the changes can cause stress.

Some people reach for foods that are high in fat, sugar, and calories when they are feeling stress. Mindlessly eating foods like chips and ice cream is their response to the strain they are experiencing. Unfortunately, this type of eating can lead to weight gain and other health problems, which are likely to add to stress. Other people avoid eating when they are sensing stress. They may feel too tense to eat. Yet a lack of food is likely to contribute to fatigue at a time when they are already feeling drained.

Actually, food can provide a healthy way to manage stress. When you eat the foods your body needs, you are less likely to develop certain illnesses. Illness can be a major source of stress.

Therefore, preventing illness through careful food choices can help you avoid stress and improve your mental health. Eating well can also give you the strength to face stressful situations when they arise.

Psychology even plays a role in food preparation. Cooking a meal that tastes good and looks attractive can give a person a psychological lift. It can also serve as a creative outlet. The cook who receives praise for a beautifully prepared dish feels a sense of pride and self-esteem.

Factors That Affect the Food Supply

Many factors affect the supply of foods from which you can choose when you go to the store. These factors include regional agriculture and the environment. The government, economics, and technology also play roles in food choices.

Agriculture and the Environment

Agriculture is the use of knowledge and skill to tend soil, grow crops, and raise livestock. Successful agriculture requires a suitable environment. **Environment** refers to such interrelated factors as air, water, soil, mineral resources, plants, and animals that ultimately affect the survival of life on Earth (**Figure 1.11**).

Food crops require the right air temperatures, adequate water, and fertile soil to grow.

Livestock need supplies of food and water. The specific requirements vary from one type of plant or animal to another. This is why certain crops and livestock are easier to raise in some regions than in others.

In the United States, regional agriculture does not affect the availability of foods as much as it affects their costs. This is because foods are routinely shipped from one region to another. You can easily obtain foods even if they do not grow well in your local environment. However, you may have to pay more for them due to transportation costs.

The environment can also affect food availability and costs. For instance, severe weather, such as a flood or drought, can damage crops. This results in a shortage of affected food products, which, in turn, causes prices to rise.

In some areas of the world, the regional nature of agriculture limits food choices. In these areas, the equipment needed to preserve and ship food from one region to another may not be available. People may not be able to afford food with added transportation costs. Therefore, people's food choices are restricted to crops and livestock that are produced locally.

Nontraditional Farming

In an effort to meet the demands of a growing population, food production has expanded far beyond barns and fields. One area of expansion is that of **aquaculture**. This is farming to raise animals or plants that live in water. Catfish, salmon, shrimp, and clams

Paul Orr/Shutterstock.com

Becky Sheridan/Shutterstock.com

Figure 1.11 Although a soybean farm and a cattle ranch seem quite different, both are closely intertwined with the environment.

are examples of seafood that are commonly produced through aquaculture. Some types of algae and seaweed that are used as food are raised this way, too.

Another way food is being produced is through **hydroponic farming**. This involves growing plants in a nutrient-rich liquid rather than in soil. It is often done indoors where the climate is controlled, which means food can be harvested year-round. While this method is not well suited to field crops like wheat and corn, it can be a good method for herbs and vegetables like lettuce and tomatoes (**Figure 1.12**).

Setting up a hydroponic farm can be costly, but it has a lot of advantages. It requires no pesticides or herbicides. It requires much less water than traditional farming, and it creates no pollution from farm machinery. Layers of plants in trays can be stacked vertically. This allows about four times more plants to be grown than if the same amount of space was used for horizontal field farming. Hydroponic farming can also be done in urban areas and other places that could not accommodate traditional farming. These benefits are leading a small, but growing number of farmers to consider hydroponics as a way to meet future food needs.

Sustainability

Just as the environment can affect crop growth, crop growth can affect the environment. Soil that is overworked by farmers can lose its ability to support crops in the future. Watering crops can strain water reserves in areas where there is not enough rain. In addition, chemicals used in farming sometimes get into water supplies. Tainted water affects the plants and animals that live in and around it. That is why practicing sustainable agriculture is so important.

Sustainability refers to practices that either preserve or improve societal, environmental, and economic conditions for future generations. Foods that are produced using these practices are often referred to as *green food choices*. Farmers produce the most crops and livestock possible to feed the growing population. However, they also work to protect the environment so they can keep producing crops and livestock in the future. They need to reach both of these goals in a way that is not too costly so they can still make a living.

Some people confuse farm size with sustainable practices. They believe that small family farms are sustainable and large commercial

NoRegret/Shutterstock.com

Figure 1.12 Hydroponic farming uses much less water than traditional farming, but is limited in the types of plants that can be grown and harvested.

farms are not. A *family farm* is owned and operated by people who are related by blood, marriage, or adoption. Family farms can be any size. In the United States, most farms, both small and large, are family farms. Regardless of size, all farms can, and must, use sustainable methods to ensure a safe, abundant food supply for generations to come.

Sustainability is not just an issue for farmers. It relates to all areas of society. Companies can make sustainable choices in the way they do business. For instance, they can purchase supplies from local and regional sources. This decreases the distance supplies have to be transported. This, in turn, lessens the amount of pollution created by shipping vehicles. Manufacturers can reduce the amount of material they use to package products. This will cut down on the amount of package waste that ends up in landfills.

As a consumer, you can also make sustainable choices that help care for the planet. Stock up on fresh foods when they are in season (**Figure 1.13**). Then you may freeze, can, or dry them for later use. Include more plant foods in your diet, as more energy is required to produce meat. Limit the number of trips you make to the store or carpool to the store with a friend. Choose products that are less processed and have less packaging.

AshTproductions/Shutterstock.com

Figure 1.13   Planning your menu around seasonal foods not only benefits the environment, but also leads to better tasting meals.

When choosing foods, you can buy fruits and vegetables that are grown in your region. Keep in mind that even sustainably grown foods are not environmentally friendly if they are being shipped to the other side of the planet. You might even consider planting a garden and growing some of your own food. All these steps will help reduce the impact you make on the environment.

Food Loss and Waste

Another focus of sustainability practices is to reduce food loss and food waste. Food that is ruined before it reaches the retail market is called *food loss*. For example, a large bag of flour that spills on the floor of a wheat milling plant would be food loss. Farmers, food processors, and transporters need to take steps to reduce food loss.

Food that is discarded by retailers or consumers is called *food waste*. A restaurant will throw away a tray of burned breadsticks. A grocery stock clerk would dispose of a sack of flour that gets slit with a box cutter when opening a carton. A consumer is likely to toss a box of crackers that have become stale. These are all examples of food waste.

Each year, billions of pounds of edible food go uneaten in the United States. This costs consumers hundreds of dollars each. The wasted food fills up landfills and requires resources, including water and energy. At the same time, people in need continue to go hungry.

Use care to buy only the amount of food you need, store it carefully, and prepare it properly. If you realize you will not be able to use food before it spoils, freeze it or donate it. These simple steps will help you save money and avoid food waste (**Figure 1.14**).

Government

A number of federal departments and agencies play roles that affect the food supply. Among these is the **United States Department of Agriculture (USDA)**. This sector promotes farm production that feeds people in the United States. Agencies within the USDA serve many functions. These include teaching people about nutrition and running programs to help those in need of food. One agency also enforces standards for the quality and wholesomeness of meat, poultry, and eggs.

The **Food and Drug Administration (FDA)** ensures the health and safety of all other foods. Inspecting food processing plants is one of the FDA's many roles. The agency controls product labeling and dietary supplements. The FDA also sets policies for foods exported to and imported from other countries.

DavidEwingPhotography/Shutterstock.com

Figure 1.14   Many gardeners who grow more food than they can eat, donate the excess to food pantries.

Mini Lab: Sustainability

Windowsill Gardening

Each student will need:

- A clean recycled polystyrene (number 6 plastic) container, such as a foam takeout box, produce tray, or beverage cup
- A clean recycled round metal or plastic container at least 4 inches (10.2 cm) in diameter and at least 4½ inches (11.4 cm) deep
- Soilless potting mix
- Parsley seeds

1. Break the polystyrene container into roughly 1-inch (2.5 cm) square pieces and put them in the bottom of the metal or plastic container. This will help provide drainage for your plant.
2. Add soilless potting mix to the container and lightly pack it to about ¾ inch (1.9 cm) from the top of the container. Water the surface to just moisten the potting mix.
3. Sprinkle a pinch of parsley seeds across the top of the potting mix. Then cover the seeds with a ¼-inch (0.6 cm) layer of potting mix. The container should now be filled to about ½ inch (1.3 cm) from the top.
4. Place the container on the sill of a southern- or eastern-facing window that gets at least five hours of sun each day. Be sure to keep the container away from drafts and heat vents.
5. Water regularly to keep potting mix slightly moist just beneath the surface. Avoid overwatering. Save unsalted water from cooking or steaming vegetables to use as a natural fertilizer about twice a month.
6. Sprouts should appear in two to three weeks. When sprouts are 1 to 2 inches (2.5 to 5 cm) tall, gently remove all but the one or two sturdiest seedlings.
7. Remove flowering stalks to maximize leaf growth. Parsley should be ready to harvest about 6 to 8 weeks after planting. Cut leaves from the bottom of the stalk for use in recipes and as a garnish.

Federal agencies are only in charge of foods shipped across state lines. Foods sold within the state in which they are produced are controlled by state agencies. Local health inspectors check the facilities and workers in food businesses within a community.

Economics

Economics has a great effect on the food supply. A basic economic concept is the *law of supply and demand*. This means if consumers are willing to pay for a product, producers will provide it. An example of this is a food store in a neighborhood with a large population of people with a common cultural background. Some people in this neighborhood will probably want to buy certain ingredients needed to make the dishes of their culture. Therefore, the manager of the neighborhood store will stock these ingredients. In a neighborhood that has a different demographic makeup, these ingredients may not be in demand. Stores in this neighborhood are less likely to carry these items.

Consumer demand for some food products affects much more than local stores. Some foods, such as coffee, sugar, and cacao beans (used to make chocolate) are grown in faraway places. Many of the countries where these foods are grown have large populations of people with very low income. These people have trouble affording food to feed themselves and their families. Land that might be used to grow nourishing grains and legumes is instead used to raise crops for export. The money made from the exported crops often goes to wealthy landowners rather than the poor farmers who grow the crops. Therefore, the farmers cannot earn enough to lift themselves out of poverty.

Many other factors affect the problem of world hunger. People with little money are not able to pay for quality seeds to grow hearty crops. They do not own modern farm equipment. Poor farmers often lack education. They may be unknowingly using farming methods that lead to shrinking crop yields. All these factors work together to limit the amount of food people in low-income areas can produce.

A number of organizations are working to deal with world hunger. These organizations want to make an adequate supply of safe and nutritious food available to every person on Earth. However, the hunger problem is widespread and complex. Many factors affect the degree to which hunger-relief organizations can meet their goals.

One way consumers can help break the cycle of poverty is to look for **fair trade products**. These are goods for which farmers and workers are paid a reasonable wage. Workers are also assured safe working conditions, as practices such as child and slave labor are prohibited. In addition, fair trade goods are produced through environmentally sustainable methods (**Figure 1.15**).

Fair trade items include a wide range of goods, from coffee, tea, and cocoa to cotton clothing and skin lotion. Products that have been verified to meet fair trade standards have labels stating they are Fair Trade Certified. These products may cost more than mass-produced goods. However, prices are usually competitive with those of specialty items. Many consumers feel the price of fair trade products is worthwhile to help create a more sustainable world community.

Technology

Technology affects every aspect of the food supply, from the farm to the table. **Technology** is the use of knowledge to develop improved methods for doing tasks. Researchers are using technology to help farmers produce more food in less space and in less time. Food manufacturers

stanislaff/Shutterstock.com

Figure 1.15 Bananas and pineapples make up a large percentage of the fair trade produce in the United States.

use technology to develop new products that meet consumer demands. These uses of technology affect your options when buying foods. You also use technology when you prepare many foods. For instance, your refrigerator and microwave oven help you keep foods fresh and cook them quickly. This would not be possible without technology.

In the area of technology, one hotly debated topic is that of **genetically modified organisms (GMOs)**. These are plants and animals whose DNA has been changed in a way that does not happen in nature. (*DNA* is a substance in an organism's cells that carries genetic information. It is what determines all the organism's exact traits.)

People have been creating new species of plants and animals for thousands of years through a process called *selective breeding*. Corn is a classic case of selective breeding. Early farmers chose which seeds to plant for an ancient type of edible grass. They saved and replanted seeds from the grass plants that had traits such as the biggest kernels and the best taste. Over a period of many years, these planting techniques caused the grass to develop into corn. GMOs are produced through modern technology that allows similar genetic changes to occur much faster and with more precise results (**Figure 1.16**).

In some GMOs, a gene from one species is inserted into the DNA of a completely different plant or animal. The result is known as a *transgenic organism*. For instance, a gene from a type of bacterium has been inserted into corn to produce a crop that can better tolerate drought. These transgenic GMOs seem to be the type that creates the greatest concern.

Many consumers feel there needs to be more testing to evaluate the long-term effects of GMOs. Antibiotic genes have been used to help some plants and animals resist disease. Some people fear eating such plants and animals may make antibiotic drugs less effective in the human body. GMOs can contain proteins that are not naturally found in the organisms. There are those who are afraid people will develop new allergic reactions to these proteins when they eat GMO foods containing them. These are just a few of the many concerns surrounding GMO technology.

Nutrient Content

Among the benefits researchers believe GMOs can bring are changes in the nutrient content of the food supply. Genetic engineers are working to develop crops that are more nutrient rich. They are growing grains that are higher in protein. They are finding ways to increase the vitamin and mineral content of fruits and vegetables, too.

Of course, technology is not always used at the genetic level. Food scientists use technology when they develop food products. They often reformulate foods to make them lower in calories, sugar, fat, and sodium.

Availability

Throughout the world, most of the land that can sustain crops is already being farmed. Researchers are studying ways to increase the amount of crops a given piece of land can produce. They are concerned with finding ways to feed the growing number of people on Earth. They are also worried about placing added strain on Earth's limited resources.

Genetic engineers are working to grow plants that can resist diseases and pests that destroy crops in the field. They are studying plants that grow larger and faster so more food

Photo by Scott Bauer/USDA

Figure 1.16 These scientists are checking apples that have been genetically engineered to be more resistant to rot.

can be produced in less time. Plant technologists are also raising crops that can grow in *inclement* (harsh) soil and weather conditions.

Growing healthy plants is only part of the picture when it comes to ensuring the availability of food. Large amounts of crops spoil after being harvested. Researchers are studying ways to destroy the organisms that cause this spoilage. They are also trying to develop plants that are more resistant to these organisms. All these efforts are intended to increase the food supply to better meet future needs.

Safety

The safety of the food supply is another issue that has drawn the interest of food technologists. Each year, millions of people get sick from something they ate. Researchers are trying to develop foods that are less likely to spread disease. They are working to improve packaging so foods will stay safer longer. They are also developing new ways to preserve foods. Disease is not the only food safety concern for food technologists. Researchers also want to keep the food supply relatively free of harmful substances, such as some chemicals used to grow and process foods. They are coming up with faster, less costly, and more effective ways to screen foods for these substances. They are looking for ways to limit the amounts of these substances needed to produce foods, too. Through these efforts, scientists hope to create a safer food supply.

Chapter 1 Review and Expand

Summary

In prehistoric times, people viewed food solely as a means of survival. Early humans spent most of their time and energy hunting and gathering food. As time passed, people learned to herd and farm. As food resources became more plentiful, people could spend more time in other pursuits. With the development of a more stable food supply came the development of civilization.

You can use the decision-making process to help you make choices, including choices about foods. Physical hunger will drive you to eat. However, many factors will affect your specific decisions about what foods you consume and how you consume them. These include social factors like culture, family, friends, mass media, and food product trends. Even psychological factors, such as memories and feelings, play a role in your food habits.

Of course, decisions about food are limited by the supply of foods available. Nontraditional farming methods are being used to add to the food produced by traditional agriculture. At every point in the supply chain, people need to follow sustainable practices and avoid food loss and waste. These steps will help protect the environment and ensure an ample food supply in the future.

A number of other factors also impact the food supply. Government agencies set guidelines and inspect facilities to be sure foods are safe and fit. Consumers can use their economic power to demand fair trade products. This will help make sure workers receive an honest wage for the foods they supply. Technology, including GMOs, is being used to improve the nutrient content, availability, and safety of the food supply. However, consumer concerns must be addressed when deciding the best way to use technology to meet future needs.

Vocabulary Activities

1. **Content Terms**   Select 10 terms from the list of terms that follows. Reread the sections that introduce each term. Then write down each definition in your own words. Keep your notes to prepare for the exam.

decision-making
    process
alternative
goal
wellness
hunger
appetite
culture

custom
fasting
value
lifestyle
peer pressure
fallacy
fad
functional food
stress
agriculture
environment
aquaculture
hydroponic farming
sustainability
United States Department of Agriculture (USDA)
Food and Drug Administration (FDA)
fair trade product
technology
genetically modified organism (GMO)

2. **Academic Terms**   Write each of the following terms on a separate sheet of paper. For each term, quickly write a word you think relates to the term. In small groups, exchange papers. Have each person in the group explain a term on the list. Take turns until all terms have been explained.

entice
surmise
inclement

Review

Write your answers using complete sentences when appropriate.

3. What led early people to begin farming?
4. What are the six steps of the decision-making process?
5. What is the difference between hunger and appetite?
6. How has the multicultural society in the United States affected the cuisine in this country?
7. Give two examples of religious customs regarding food.
8. Describe two ways family might influence a person's food choices.
9. How can news stories about food and nutrition lead to food fallacies and fads?
10. Describe five techniques advertisers use to encourage people to buy food products.
11. What three main trend-driving qualities do consumers demand in food products?
12. Which of the senses is most likely to trigger memories that influence food choices?
13. Describe two nontraditional farming methods.

Chapter 1 Review and Expand

14. What are three ways consumers can practice sustainability to help reduce the impact they make on the environment when choosing foods?

15. What is the difference between food loss and food waste?

16. Name two key federal agencies that oversee the food supply in the United States and identify one function of each agency.

17. How can shopping for fair trade products allow consumers to help create a more sustainable world community?

18. How does GMO technology differ from selective breeding techniques that farmers have been using for thousands of years?

Core Skills

19. **Research, Writing**   Research the types of tools used by prehistoric people. Write a report describing the tools used to hunt and prepare foods. Reread your report and revise as needed to correct grammar, spelling, and organization.

20. **Speaking, Listening, Writing**   As a class, prepare a survey to find out how students in your school make food choices in an average day. Each student should work with a partner and use the survey to interview five students outside your class. Then compile your findings into a blog post about using the decision-making process to make food choices. Be sure to edit your post for style and accuracy before posting on your class or school website.

21. **Speaking, Listening**   Talk with your grandparents or older adults in your community about family food customs they followed as children. Discuss whether those customs are still followed in families today. Share what you learned in a brief oral report to the class.

22. **Technology**   Navigate the website for *Prepared Foods* magazine to read about a food or beverage product that was recently launched (introduced to the market). Use presentation software to give a brief description of the product and explain how it offers consumers the trend-driving qualities of health, convenience, and/or great taste.

23. **Technology, Speaking**   Use the Internet to identify a hydroponic produce grower in the United States. Find out what kinds and quantities of produce they grow and where their produce is sold. Share your findings in class.

24. **Technology, Speaking, Listening**   Each student should visit the website for a different food manufacturer. Find out what steps the company is taking to promote sustainability. Compare your findings with those of your classmates. Discuss similarities and differences among the practices being followed by various companies.

25. **Career Readiness Practice**   Successful employees are also responsible citizens. As a class, plan an event in the community to raise funds for a hunger-relief organization. Imagine you are employed by the local supermarket. Put together a handout to help educate the public about how food is a physical need and a basic right of every human being. You can distribute it at the event or use it as a tool to encourage people to become involved in the event.

Critical Thinking and Problem Solving

26. **Analyze**   Analyze food customs in your community. Make a list of cultural influences that affect the foods available in local restaurants and supermarkets. Compile your list with those of your classmates and summarize your findings in a poster presentation.

27. **Evaluate**   Find a recent news report on the Internet or in print media about a food or nutrition topic. Evaluate the reliability of the information in the report using the AAOCC criteria.

28. **Evaluate**   Conduct research to evaluate the advantages and disadvantages of GMO food products. Based on your evaluation, decide whether you favor or oppose the use of GMOs. Prepare arguments to help support your viewpoint in a class debate.

Chapter 2
Safety and Sanitation

Olesya Feketa /Shutterstock.com

Content Terms 📤

foodborne illness
contaminant
microorganism
pathogen
bacteria

toxin
parasite
sanitation
cross-contamination
abdominal thrust

Academic Terms

impaired
transmission

residue
expel

Objectives

After studying this chapter, you will be able to

- **discuss** causes, symptoms, and treatment of common foodborne illnesses;
- **list** the four key steps to food safety and give examples of each;
- **give** examples of how following good safety practices can help you prevent kitchen accidents; and
- **apply** basic first aid measures.

Reading Prep

Read the chapter title and tell a classmate what you have experienced or already know about the topic. Write a paragraph describing what you would like to learn about the topic. After reading the chapter, share two things you have learned with the classmate.

Keeping foods safe to eat and making the kitchen a safe place to work are keys to good health. Improper food handling can make you ill. Kitchen accidents can cause severe injuries. You can prevent both illnesses and accidents by following safety principles.

Foodborne Illnesses

A disease transmitted by food is called a **foodborne illness**. Millions of cases of foodborne illness occur in the United States each year. Many of these cases go unreported because people mistake their symptoms for the "flu." To reduce the number of cases, it is important to know and follow advice for keeping food safe.

Food Contamination

Most foodborne illnesses are caused by contaminants. A **contaminant** is a potentially harmful substance that has accidentally been introduced to food. Many contaminants are microorganisms. A **microorganism** is a living substance so small it can be seen only under a microscope. Many contaminated foods do not look or smell spoiled, but they can still cause illness.

Microorganisms that cause disease are known as **pathogens**. One type of pathogen that causes many foodborne illnesses is **bacteria**. Bacteria are single-celled microorganisms. They live almost everywhere. They are not all pathogens. Some types of harmless bacteria are normally found in foods.

Harmful bacteria can get into food at any point from the farm to the table **(Figure 2.1)**. Soil, insects, humans, and cooking tools can all transfer bacteria to foods. Improper handling can taint food that was not affected previously. For instance, leaving food at room temperature can turn it into a breeding ground for bacteria. This is why all people who produce, process, and consume food must use care to avoid contaminating it.

Health professionals recommend avoiding foods that are often contaminated with harmful bacteria. These foods include raw and under-cooked meat, poultry, fish, shellfish, and eggs. Any dishes made with these foods should be avoided, too. Unpasteurized (raw) milk and any products made from it are also on the list of foods to avoid.

These foods present risks because animals raised for food often contain microorganisms that can be harmful to humans. This is true even if the animals are healthy. Thorough cooking will kill most harmful bacteria. However, when these foods are eaten in a raw or undercooked state, the bacteria can be passed on to the people who eat them.

Steer clear of unpasteurized juices. Fresh fruits and vegetables can be contaminated if they are fertilized with untreated manure or washed with tainted water. Pasteurization kills bacteria in juices made from fresh produce, but unpasteurized juices retain any harmful bacteria that are present. Carefully washing fresh fruits and vegetables in clean running water right before eating will help reduce risk of contamination.

T photography/Shutterstock.com; Lauren Ave/Shutterstock.com; zmkstudio/Shutterstock.com; FomaA/Shutterstock.com; FomaA/Shutterstock.com

Figure 2.1 Contaminants can get into food at any stage of production, processing, or preparation. At what point from the farm to the table do consumers play the biggest roles in keeping food safe to eat?

Learn About...

Governing Food Supply Safety

Federal, state, and local governments all play key roles in helping to keep the food supply safe. Federal laws govern food plants that process foods sold across state lines. Federal regulations require some food processors to follow a quality control system called *HACCP*. This stands for Hazard Analysis and Critical Control Point. This system involves looking at food production processes to see where hazards can occur. Processors can then take steps to prevent problems and respond to problems quickly.

State laws govern food businesses like restaurants and grocery stores. Each state sets health codes based on federal food codes. State codes may include programs like HACCP.

Local governments are in charge of sending health inspectors to visit food businesses. These inspectors make sure the businesses are following state health codes. Inspectors issue warnings when they find minor code violations. When violations are severe, inspectors may close businesses until problems are addressed.

Another federal program related to the safety of the food supply is the Total Diet Study (TDS). This is a survey conducted by the U.S. Food and Drug Administration (FDA). FDA staff purchase samples of commonly eaten foods from grocery stores. They collect samples from different cities in different regions. This assures the samples reflect the food supply of the entire nation. The FDA has the food samples made into dishes that would be eaten at the table. Then they check the foods for contaminants such as pesticide residues and industrial chemicals. This allows the FDA to track the amounts of various contaminants people are likely to consume. Most contaminants are found in amounts well below levels that are thought to be unsafe.

Know and Apply

1. Do you feel the food supply in the United States is generally safe? Why or why not?
2. What is the value of testing dishes prepared from food samples collected for the Total Diet Study rather than simply testing the samples?

Raw sprouts pose a threat, too. The conditions used to grow sprouts are also well suited for growing bacteria. Cooking sprouts will kill any bacteria they may contain.

Bacterial Illnesses

Common foodborne illnesses include *campylobacteriosis*, *listeriosis*, and *perfringens food poisoning*. All these diseases are caused by bacteria. Some other foodborne illnesses, such as *botulism* and *staphylococcal food poisoning*, are caused by **toxins** (poisons) produced by bacteria.

The bodies of most healthy people can handle small amounts of harmful bacteria. However, when the bacterial count becomes too great, illness can occur. Foodborne illnesses pose a greater risk for some groups of people. These groups include infants and young children, pregnant women, older adults, and people with *impaired* (damaged) immune systems. Extra care should be used when handling foods for people in these high-risk groups.

Symptoms of bacterial foodborne illnesses vary depending on the type of bacteria. However, most of these illnesses affect the digestive system. Symptoms may appear 30 minutes to 30 days after eating tainted food. The amount of time required for symptoms to develop often makes it hard to pinpoint the source of foodborne illness. The symptoms of botulism differ from those of most other foodborne illnesses. This disease affects the nervous system. The death rate for botulism is high. However, a doctor can treat botulism with an antitoxin if he or she diagnoses it in time.

Infants, pregnant women, older adults, and those with chronic illnesses should see a doctor about symptoms of foodborne illness. If you are not in these high-risk groups, you may not need professional treatment for foodborne illness. Resting will help you regain your strength. Drinking liquids will help replace body fluids lost due to diarrhea and vomiting. If you suspect you have botulism, or if your symptoms are severe, you should call your doctor right away.

Other Foodborne Illnesses

Bacteria are not the only microorganisms that can cause foodborne illnesses. Parasites, protozoa, and viruses transmitted by food can cause illnesses, too **(Figure 2.2)**.

Parasites are another type of microorganism that can be sources of foodborne illness. A **parasite** is a microorganism that needs another organism, called a *host*, to live. Hogs were once a common host for parasitic roundworms called *trichinae*, which cause the disease *trichinosis*. Improved standards for feeding hogs have all but eliminated this risk in pork. However, hogs and other sources of red meat are often infected with the parasite *Toxoplasma gondii*. This parasite causes the infection *toxoplasmosis*, which can damage the central nervous system. People can become infected with *Toxoplasma* by eating undercooked meat from animals infected with this parasite.

Another parasite that is becoming more of a concern is *anisakis*. This is a worm that causes an illness called *anisakiasis*. It is found in raw fish, which means there is some risk involved in eating raw fish dishes like sashimi and sushi. The larvae of this parasite can cause vomiting and diarrhea.

A couple of foodborne illnesses are caused by *protozoa* (tiny, one-celled animals). *Amebiasis* is caused by drinking polluted water or eating vegetables grown in polluted soil. *Giardiasis* can also be caused by drinking impure water.

Some foodborne illnesses are caused by viruses. (A *virus* is the smallest and simplest known type of microorganism.) For instance, common "stomach flu" can be spread by food handlers infected with *norovirus*. Symptoms include vomiting and diarrhea. To prevent spreading norovirus, wash hands before handling food and avoid handling food when symptoms are present.

The *hepatitis A* virus is found in some shellfish. It is highly heat-resistant. This makes disease prevention difficult because people often eat shellfish raw or just slightly cooked. Contaminated water and sewage are the major sources of this virus. The best way to avoid contamination is to buy shellfish that come only from commercial sources. If you gather fresh shellfish, be sure to stay safely away from any source of pollution.

A few foods have *natural toxins* that can cause illness. Certain varieties of mushrooms and leaves of the rhubarb plant are two such foods. Avoid picking wild mushrooms as well as fruits, roots, and berries unless you are knowledgeable about them. Some varieties can be poisonous. Information about the pathogens that cause the most common foodborne illnesses is shown in **Figure 2.3**.

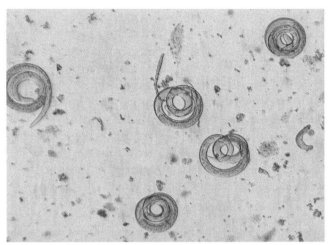

©iStock.com/dotana

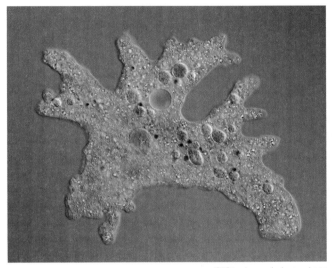

©iStock.com/micro_photo

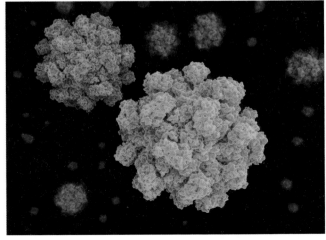

©iStock.com/selvanegra

Figure 2.2 Many pathogens such as parasites, protozoa, and viruses that cause illness cannot be seen, smelled, or tasted.

Four Steps to Food Safety

Most foodborne illnesses are spread through improper food handling. All the guidelines for keeping food safe to eat can be summed up in four basic steps—clean, separate, cook, and chill. Keep these steps in mind when you are buying, preparing, and storing food. This can help you avoid foodborne illness.

Clean

One of the key steps you can take to prevent foodborne illness is to follow good sanitation practices. **Sanitation** means maintaining conditions to prevent disease and promote good health. In some cases, this involves going beyond basic *cleaning*, which removes dirt, grease, and grime from surfaces. It is important to realize that surfaces that look clean are not necessarily free of germs. Once cleaned, some surfaces need

Foodborne Illnesses		
Pathogen and Illness	**Food Sources**	**Symptoms**
Campylobacter jejuni **causes campylobacteriosis**	Raw and undercooked beef and poultry, unpasteurized milk, and untreated water	Diarrhea, abdominal cramping, fever, bloody stools Appear: 2 to 5 days after eating Last: 2 to 5 days
Clostridium perfringens **causes** *C. perfringens* **food poisoning**	Beef, poultry, and gravy not chilled in a timely manner after cooking and/ or not thoroughly reheated	Abdominal cramping, diarrhea Appear: 6 to 24 hours after eating Last: less than 24 hours
E. coli O157:H7 **causes STEC infection**	Fresh fruits and vegetables, raw and un-dercooked ground beef, unpasteurized milk, unpasteurized juice and cider	Bloody diarrhea, vomiting, stomach cramps Appear: usually 3 to 4 days after eating Last: 5 to 7 days
Listeria monocytogenes **causes listeriosis**	Unpasteurized milk and soft cheeses, hot dogs, deli meats and protein salads, smoked fish	Diarrhea and abdominal pain followed by fever and muscle aches Appear: a few days to 2 months after eating Last: days to weeks
Norovirus **causes norovirus illness**	Any raw or cooked food handled by someone who is infected	Vomiting, stomach pain, nausea, diarrhea Appear: 12 to 48 hours after eating Last: 1 to 3 days
Salmonella **causes salmonellosis**	Fresh fruits and vegetables; raw and undercooked meat, poultry, and eggs; raw sprouts; unpasteurized milk	Abdominal pain, diarrhea, fever Appear: 12 to 72 hours after eating Last: 4 to 7 days
Staphylococcus aureus **causes staphylococcal food poisoning**	High-protein cooked foods that are handled before serving, such as sliced meats, sandwiches, protein salads, bakery products like cream pies, and dairy products like cus-tard; unpasteurized milk	Vomiting, abdominal cramping, nausea, diarrhea Appear: 30 minutes to 6 hours after eating Last: 1 to 3 days
Toxoplasma gondii **causes toxoplasmosis**	Raw or undercooked pork, lamb, and venison Also spread through contact with infected cat feces	Flu-like symptoms, including swollen glands and muscle aches Appear: possibly 10 to 20 or more days after eating Last: a month or more

Figure 2.3   Various pathogens that cause foodborne illnesses are linked with different food sources.

to be sanitized. *Sanitizing* is a process that kills pathogens and reduces the likelihood of illness.

Hand Washing and Other Hygiene

Practicing good personal hygiene, such as proper hand washing, is critical to food safety. Washing your hands may be the most important step you can take to prevent the *transmission* (spread) of harmful bacteria. Wash hands for 20 seconds, rubbing briskly with soap and warm running water before starting to work with food. (Note that using a hand sanitizer will not adequately clean your hands before food preparation.) Be sure to clean under your fingernails, too. Dry hands with paper towels or use a clean hand towel.

Follow these same hand washing steps after handling raw meat, fish, poultry, or eggs and before touching any other food. Also, wash your hands after sneezing, coughing, using the toilet, or touching your face, hair, or any unsanitary object. This will prevent the transfer of bacteria **(Figure 2.4)**.

If you have an open sore or cut on your hand, put on gloves before handling food. Open sores are a major source of staphylococcal

S_L /Shutterstock.com

Figure 2.4 Wash your hands after using your smartphone or other electronic devices. Harmful bacteria and viruses can survive on them for hours.

bacteria. Wash gloved hands while working with food just as you would wash bare hands.

In addition to hand washing, other aspects of your personal hygiene can affect the safety of the food you prepare. Bacteria can accumulate on dirty clothes. For this reason, be sure to wear clean clothes and a clean apron when working around food. Avoid loose sleeves, which can dip into foods.

Your hair is also a source of bacteria. To prevent hair from becoming an unwanted ingredient in your dish, keep long hair tied back and avoid touching hair while you work.

When you cough or sneeze, many droplets carrying bacteria are spewed far and wide. Stop the droplets from entering your food by covering coughs and sneezes with a disposable tissue. Then, dispose of tissue and wash hands immediately.

Maintain a Clean Work Area

You are practicing good personal hygiene—now apply it to the work area. A messy, unclean work area can contribute to the spread of bacteria. Be sure to wipe up spills as they happen. Regularly clean refrigerator surfaces, including meat and produce compartments, walls, and both sides of shelves, with hot water and soap **(Figure 2.5)**. This helps reduce pathogens that can live and grow at refrigerated temperatures. Be sure to keep the freezer clean, too.

Use paper towels to wipe up juices from raw meat and poultry. Then, immediately wash the area on which the juices dripped. Remove dirty utensils from your work area before proceeding to the next task. Bacteria grow quickly in spills and on dirty utensils.

Food cans are stored in warehouses, transported in trucks and trains, and handled by many people before you buy them. During this time, the cans are exposed to dirt, bacteria, and possibly chemicals. To prevent these unwanted substances from mixing with the food when you open the can, wash the tops of cans before opening them. Wash can openers after each use to prevent contaminating the food being opened with *residue* (remains) on the opener. Also, do not use the same can opener for pet products that you use for food products.

Thoroughly wash cutting boards, counters, and utensils after each use. In addition, regularly

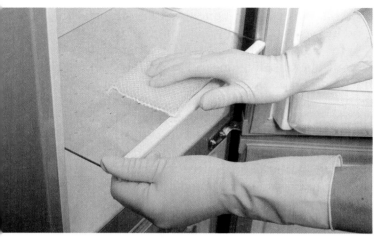

Janis Smits /Shutterstock.com

Figure 2.5 Wipe up spills right away and clean all surfaces often to help keep the refrigerator safe for storing food. What part of the refrigerator is touched most often?

use a food-safe sanitizing solution on counters and cutting boards to kill bacteria. Wash dishes promptly, using hot water and detergent. Wash dishes in the following order: glasses and cups, flatware, plates and bowls, pots and pans, and greasy utensils. Rinse dishes with scalding water and allow them to air dry. If you must dry dishes, be sure to use a clean dish towel.

If you are washing counters, dishes, and cutting boards with dirty dishcloths and sponges, you are not cleaning. It is important to wash dishcloths and sponges daily. (Sponges can be washed in a dishwasher in a covered basket designed to hold small items.) Between uses, rinse dishcloths and sponges well, wring thoroughly, and allow to air-dry. This discourages bacteria from breeding on damp surfaces.

Dispose of garbage properly and promptly. Frequent washing and air-drying of garbage pails prevents odors and bacterial growth.

Separate

A second step for preventing foodborne illness is to separate cooked and ready-to-eat foods from raw foods. Following this step will avoid the risks of cross-contamination. **Cross-contamination** occurs when harmful bacteria from one food or surface are transferred to another food. For instance, juices from a leaky package of raw chicken may contain harmful bacteria. If the juices drip on other foods in your

Exploring Careers

Dishwasher

The foodservice industry offers a number of entry-level jobs for young workers. One such job is that of dishwasher. Of course, a dishwasher's main task is to wash dishes. Some dishwashing is done by hand, but most involves the use of a commercial dishwashing system. A dishwasher may also have to clean other kitchen equipment and work areas. A dishwasher may be asked to stock food and utensils in storage areas and handle minor food preparation tasks, too.

Generally, a dishwasher does not need specific education or training. Training often comes from a coworker on the job. Therefore, being able to listen to and follow directions are key skills. A dishwasher also needs to be able to read instructions and operate equipment. In time, an experienced dishwasher may need skill in training others to do the job.

A dishwasher's most important personal qualities are attention to detail and cooperation. A successful dishwasher needs to make sure all cleaning tasks are done to accepted sanitation standards. He or she needs to get along with coworkers and show a willingness to help others.

A dishwasher with these traits may soon find opportunities to move into other positions. He or she might become a cook's assistant in the kitchen or a waiter in the front of the restaurant. Once on this path, a willing worker who enrolls in a culinary program can have a bright future in the foodservice industry.

shopping cart or refrigerator, the bacteria will be transferred to these foods. The following guidelines will help you keep foods that may be contaminated separated from other foods:

- Put raw poultry, meat, and seafood in separate plastic bags before placing them in your shopping cart.

- Store raw poultry, meat, and seafood in containers to keep them separate from other foods in the refrigerator.
- Do not wash raw meat or poultry. This can spread bacteria from these foods to other foods and surfaces.

Food can be contaminated by nonfood sources as well. Any surface or substance that comes in contact with a food can contaminate it. For instance, dirty utensils, pests, or leaky pipes are all possible sources of contamination and should be kept separate from food. The following tips prevent cross-contamination by nonfood sources:

- Use a clean tasting spoon each time you taste a dish while cooking. Use a separate spoon for stirring. Do not lick your fingers.
- Use clean utensils and containers. Never use the same utensil, cutting board, or plate for both raw and cooked meat, poultry, fish, or eggs. Utensils can transfer bacteria from raw foods to cooked foods.
- Never use a hand towel to wipe dishes. Dirty towels can transfer bacteria.
- Keep pets and insects out of the kitchen. Do not feed pets in the kitchen or wash their dishes with your dishes. Remove leftover pet food and dispose of it promptly.
- Store nonperishables, such as pasta and dry beans, in tightly sealed containers. This will keep them fresh and free from insects and rodents.
- Never store any foods under the kitchen sink or near chemicals and cleaners. Drainpipes can leak and damage or contaminate the food. Food that is tainted with chemicals or cleaners can cause illness.

Cook

Raw meat, poultry, seafood, and eggs can contain harmful bacteria. Cooking these foods to a safe internal temperature is the third step to food safety. High temperatures can kill bacteria in these and other foods.

Become familiar with the internal temperatures the USDA recommends various foods must be cooked to for safety **(Figure 2.6)**. Use a food thermometer to ensure the food is actually reaching the appropriate temperature. Once a food has reached its safe minimum internal temperature, it should be held at or above 140°F (60°C) until mealtime.

USDA Recommended Safe Minimum Internal Temperatures	
Whole cuts (steaks and roasts) of beef, veal, pork, and lamb	145°F (63°C)*
Ground beef, veal, pork, and lamb	160°F (71°C)
Ham, fresh or smoked (uncooked)	145°F (63°C)
Ham, fully cooked (reheated)	165°F (74°C)
All poultry products	165°F (74°C)
Fish	145°F (63°C)
Egg dishes	160°F (71°C)
Casseroles	165°F (74°C)
Stuffing (cooked alone or in stuffed meats, poultry, and fish)	165°F (74°C)
Leftovers	165°F (74°C)
*Measure temperature with a food thermometer before removing meat from the heat source. After removing meat from heat, allow it to rest for 3 minutes before carving or serving.	

Figure 2.6 Different foods have different safe minimum internal cooking temperatures. Why do you think these temperatures vary?

To further reduce the opportunity for foodborne illness, do not partially cook foods and then set them aside or refrigerate them to complete the cooking later. When reheating sauces, soups, and gravies, make sure they come to a full boil. Boil low-acid, home-canned foods for 10 minutes before tasting. When serving these foods at high altitudes, add one minute of boiling time for each 1,000 feet of altitude. Do not eat raw cookie dough or taste partially cooked dishes containing meat, poultry, fish, or eggs.

Chill

Chilling foods is the fourth basic step to food safety. Bacteria multiply fastest at temperatures between 40°F and 140°F (4°C and 60°C). This temperature range is called the *danger zone* and room temperature falls within this range **(Figure 2.7)**. Chilling foods promptly after buying or serving them limits time spent at room temperature and prevents harmful bacteria from multiplying. Cold foods should be stored at or below 40°F (4°C) because growth of bacteria slows or even stops at these temperatures.

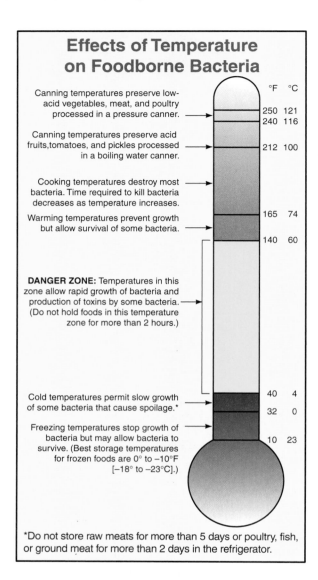

Effects of Temperature on Foodborne Bacteria

Canning temperatures preserve low-acid vegetables, meat, and poultry processed in a pressure canner. → 250 121 / 240 116

Canning temperatures preserve acid fruits, tomatoes, and pickles processed in a boiling water canner. → 212 100

Cooking temperatures destroy most bacteria. Time required to kill bacteria decreases as temperature increases.

Warming temperatures prevent growth but allow survival of some bacteria. → 165 74 / 140 60

DANGER ZONE: Temperatures in this zone allow rapid growth of bacteria and production of toxins by some bacteria. → (Do not hold foods in this temperature zone for more than 2 hours.)

Cold temperatures permit slow growth of some bacteria that cause spoilage.* → 40 4 / 32 0

Freezing temperatures stop growth of bacteria but may allow bacteria to survive. (Best storage temperatures for frozen foods are 0° to –10°F [–18° to –23°C].) → 10 23

°F °C

*Do not store raw meats for more than 5 days or poultry, fish, or ground meat for more than 2 days in the refrigerator.

Figure 2.7 Bacteria multiply rapidly at moderate temperatures. To prevent this, keep hot foods hot and cold foods cold.

Limit the time that foods are exposed to unsafe temperatures with the following practices:

- Do not allow food to be unrefrigerated for more than two hours. In warm weather when the temperature is 90°F (32°C) or higher, food should not sit out for more than one hour.

- Make the supermarket your last stop on the way home. Put perishable items in your shopping cart last. Refrigerate or freeze them as soon as you get home. If you will not be going directly home after grocery shopping, take an insulated cooler to the store with you. Use it to keep perishable foods cool until you can store them properly.

- Refrigerate leftovers promptly. Eat or freeze refrigerated leftovers within three days.

- Package refrigerated and frozen foods properly. Use moistureproof and vaporproof wraps for the freezer. For the refrigerator, store fresh meats and leftovers in tightly covered containers. Use foods within recommended storage times.

- Read labels to identify foods that need to be refrigerated after opening, such as ketchup and salad dressings. Once opened, refrigerate and use these foods within about three months.

Simply placing food in a refrigerator does not always guarantee the food is being chilled properly. Use a refrigerator thermometer to check the temperature of your refrigerator and freezer regularly. Refrigerator temperatures should be 40°F (4°C) or just slightly below. Freezer temperatures should be 0°F (–18°C) or below. Also, check the gaskets around the doors to be sure they are tight.

Refrigerators vary in the amount of food they are designed to handle. When the capacity of a refrigerator is exceeded, it may not be able to cool foods properly. Do not overfill the refrigerator. Cool air must be able to move around food to maintain safe temperatures. When large, deep containers of hot food are placed in a refrigerator, it may take longer than two hours to cool the food to a safe temperature. Instead, use shallow containers for refrigerator storage to help foods reach safe, cool temperatures faster. You can also hasten cooling by placing containers of food in an ice water bath. Remove stuffing from poultry, meat, and fish promptly after serving and refrigerate it separately. This reduces the time it takes for the stuffing to cool.

Frozen foods are already chilled, but may enter the danger zone if care is not taken during thawing. Food should not be thawed at room temperature. The following guidelines keep food safe during thawing:

- Thaw foods in the refrigerator.

- To thaw food quickly, defrost it in a microwave oven immediately before cooking.

- Food can also be wrapped in airtight packaging and submerged in cold water to defrost right before cooking.

- Do not refreeze foods unless they still contain ice crystals. Do not refreeze ice cream that has thawed. Use defrosted foods promptly.

Mini Lab: Using a Food Thermometer

Testing Doneness of Beef Patties

Each lab group will cook a beef patty as directed. All patties should be the same weight and thickness, preferably at least 4 ounces (113 g) and ½ inch (1.25 cm) thick.

During cooking, you will use an instant-read thermometer to test the internal temperature of the meat. A digital thermometer is recommended for this exercise. You will use it by inserting the thermometer's probe into the center of the patty, making sure not to touch the surface of the skillet. Wait about 10 seconds for the temperature to register. If you are using a dial thermometer, hold the patty horizontally and insert the stem of the thermometer through the side about 2 inches into the patty. Wait 15 to 20 seconds for the temperature to register. Be sure to wash the thermometer with hot soapy water after each use before using it again.

1. Create an observation sheet and write a description of the color of the uncooked patty. Also use this sheet to record the internal temperature of the patty at each of the specified intervals.

2. In a small nonstick skillet, heat 1 tablespoon cooking oil over medium heat for 5 minutes.

3. **Lab group 1**—Cook the patty, flipping it every 30 seconds. Test and record the internal temperature of the patty every 30 seconds. Be sure to wash the spatula between uses in hot soapy water and dry with a clean paper towel. Remove the patty from the pan when the internal temperature reaches 160°F (71°C). Record the total cooking time required.

   Lab group 2—Cook for 5 minutes, undisturbed. Then flip the patty and cook for another 5 minutes, or until the meat reaches an internal temperature of 160°F (71°C). Test and record the internal temperature of the patty every 30 seconds. Record the total cooking time required.

   Lab group 3—Cook the patty for 3 minutes, undisturbed. Then flip the patty and cook for another 3 minutes. This is a suggested cooking time for rare burgers. Remove the patty from the skillet. Test and record the internal temperature of the patty.

   Lab group 4—Cook the patty for 3.5 minutes, undisturbed. Then flip the patty and cook for another 3.5 minutes. This is a suggested cooking time for medium-rare burgers. Remove the patty from the skillet. Test and record the internal temperature of the patty.

   Lab group 5—Cook the patty for 4 minutes, undisturbed. Then flip the patty and cook for another 4 minutes. This is a suggested cooking time for medium burgers. Remove the patty from the skillet. Test and record the internal temperature of the patty.

   Lab group 6—Cook the patty, flipping it every 60 seconds. Test and record the internal temperature of the patty every 30 seconds. Be sure to wash the spatula between uses in hot soapy water and dry with a clean paper towel. Remove the patty from the pan when the internal temperature reaches 160°F (71°C). Record the total cooking time required.

4. Cut the cooked patty in half and write a description of the internal and external color of the meat.

5. Compare your observations with those of the other lab groups. Then answer the following questions:
   A. How does frequent flipping affect the length of time required for a burger to reach a safe internal temperature?
   B. Do rare, medium-rare, and medium burgers meet the standard for safely cooked ground beef?
   C. Does the color of cooked beef seem to accurately indicate a safe internal temperature? Why or why not?
   D. Why is it important to always use a food thermometer when cooking food?

Learn About...

The Temperature Danger Zone

Consumers are warned to limit the amount of time foods are between 40°F and 140°F (4°C and 60°C). Foodservice workers are trained to limit the amount of time foods are between 41°F and 135°F (5°C and 57°C). Both of these ranges are correctly referred to as the *temperature danger zone*.

Recommended internal temperatures for some cooked foods also differ for consumers and foodservice workers. The consumer numbers are based on older information. They were not updated because the old numbers offer a slightly greater margin of safety. So, if you follow consumer advice, you will be within commercial food safety guidelines as well.

In addition, the range of "40 to 140" is easier to remember. These temperatures are easier to maintain with the less-precise controls found on equipment used in consumer kitchens, too.

No matter which numbers you use, the key point is the same. The temperature danger zone is the range at which bacteria that cause foodborne illness multiply most rapidly. Avoiding this zone means keeping hot foods hot and cold foods cold. The only reliable way to be sure you are keeping food at safe temperatures is to use food and appliance thermometers.

This textbook is designed mainly for students in consumer food and nutrition classes. Thus, consumer temperature guidelines are used in this book.

Know and Apply

1. How much narrower is the commercial temperature danger zone than the consumer zone?

2. What is the best way to be sure foods are at safe temperatures?

Cooking for Special Occasions

Cooking for a crowd or cooking outdoor meals requires extra measures to keep food safe to eat. Before planning any big gathering, be sure your equipment can handle large amounts of food. Refrigerators must be able to chill increased quantities of warm foods without raising the temperature above 40°F (4°C). Preparing and freezing foods ahead will prevent overloading your refrigerator the day before an event. Heating appliances must be able to keep hot foods at or above 140°F (60°C) until serving time.

If using buffet service, put the food in small serving dishes, which you can refill or replace as needed. Another way to keep hot foods hot and cold foods cold is to use heated serving appliances and ice.

Large amounts of food take longer to heat and chill than do small or average amounts. Divide food and place it in small, shallow containers for quicker heating and cooling.

Be sure to thoroughly cook all foods. Then serve them promptly. Refrigerate leftovers immediately after the meal.

Eating Safely When Eating Out

Most of the foodborne illness cases reported each year occur in foodservice establishments. Restaurants have strict sanitation guidelines they must follow when preparing food for the public. State health departments inspect foodservice facilities regularly to ensure that guidelines are being met. However, occasional problems still occur.

You can take several steps when eating out to protect yourself from foodborne illness. First, look at the surroundings on your way into a restaurant. The parking lot should be free from litter. The way the outside of a restaurant is maintained can give you a clue about how the inside is maintained.

When you enter the restaurant, you should see a concern for cleanliness throughout the establishment. Tables should be wiped. Walls and floors should be clean. Restrooms should be tidy.

Observe the employees as they wait on you. They should appear to be in good health. Their clothes should be clean. If they have long hair, they should have it tied back. When they serve you, they should not touch the eating surfaces of your tableware.

When your food is served, it should look and smell wholesome. Hot foods should be hot. Cold foods should be cold.

If you have a concern about your food, do not be afraid to speak to your server. If your server cannot answer your questions or correct the problem, ask to speak to the manager.

Most servers will wrap leftovers for you if you wish to take them home. However, be sure you are going directly home and promptly put leftovers in

Health and Wellness

Picnic Food Safety

Picnic and barbecue foods present specific problems. You may carry these foods some distance before serving them. Use insulated containers to maintain these foods at the proper temperature to prevent the growth of bacteria. Wrap raw meat, poultry, and fish carefully to prevent them from leaking onto other foods. You may want to use a separate cooler for beverages. This will help you avoid repeatedly opening the cooler containing the perishable foods. Do not take perishables from the cooler until you are ready to cook or serve them.

Use sanitary procedures when preparing picnic foods. Be sure utensils are clean. Do not let hamburgers, hot dogs, or other meats sit next to the grill while the charcoal heats. Keep them in the cooler. Do not put cooked meat on the same plate that held raw meat.

AVN Photo Lab/Shutterstock.com

To keep picnic foods safe, be sure to keep meat and all perishables chilled until right before grilling. Also, use separate plates and utensils for raw and cooked meats.

the refrigerator. If you cannot refrigerate food within two hours from the time it was served, discard it.

If you choose restaurants with care, you may never have a problem with foodborne illness. However, if you get ill from something you ate at a restaurant, call local health authorities. Others should be warned they may have been exposed to the infected food also.

Storing Food for Emergencies

Most people do not want to think about hurricanes, floods, tornadoes, and earthquakes. Unfortunately, such disasters can happen. When they do, people are often stranded in their homes or forced to evacuate for days. Utilities may be cut off, and stores may be closed, unreachable, or out of merchandise. That is why safely storing food and water for emergency situations is important.

The American Red Cross recommends storing at least a three-day supply of food and water for each person. Be sure to keep special needs of those such as infants and people with diabetes in mind. Choose nonperishable foods that do not require cooking. Many canned goods make wise choices. Foods like dried fruits and beef jerky are good choices, too. They are compact and lightweight, so they will be easy to carry if there is an evacuation. Remember to store a can opener and any other tools you might need to prepare the food. Store items in a backpack or a container with wheels and a handle for pulling. This will make it easier to transport your supplies if you have to leave your home. Replace stored food and water every six months so they will be safe and fresh when you need them.

Safety in the Kitchen

Many common kitchen items may seem harmless. However, they can be dangerous if you do not take safety precautions. For instance, people can injure themselves by bumping into open cabinet doors and drawers. Keeping all kitchen cabinets and drawers closed will prevent accidental injuries **(Figure 2.8)**.

Hospital emergency room personnel see the results of thousands of kitchen accidents each year. Some kitchen accidents are due to ignorance. Many result from carelessness. Chemical poisonings, cuts, burns and fires, and falls are the most common of these accidents. Electric shocks, choking, and other types of injury can also occur in the kitchen. You can prevent many accidents by properly using and caring for equipment. Following good safety practices and keeping the kitchen clean will also help you avoid accidents.

Knowledge of basic first aid will help you provide treatment to someone involved in a kitchen accident. A simple first aid kit kept in the kitchen should include the items you need to treat minor injuries.

Preventing and Treating Chemical Poisonings

Children are especially susceptible to chemical poisonings. To many children, poisonous

Clockwise from top left: DomDew_Studio/Shutterstock.com; Robyn Mackenzie/Shutterstock.com; Olga&Elnur/Shutterstock.com; NatUlrich/Shutterstock.com; Bacho/Shutterstock.com; EM Arts/Shutterstock.com; Egor Rodynchenko /Shutterstock.com

Figure 2.8   Ordinary kitchen items can cause serious injuries if they are not handled with care. What type of danger could be posed by each of these objects?

household chemicals, such as furniture polishes, cleaners, and bleach, look like food products. To prevent chemical poisonings, store all household chemicals in a location where children cannot reach them. Be sure to keep them in the original, clearly labeled containers. Do not put them in soda bottles or other food containers. Keep all containers tightly closed. Some children can open safety caps, so do not rely on containers with safety closures to prevent access. If the phone or doorbell interrupts you while you are using a household chemical, take the product with you.

Pesticides and insecticides used on food can be poisonous. Wash all fresh fruits and vegetables thoroughly before use to remove any chemical residues. If using a pesticide in the kitchen, use care to make sure it does not contaminate food. Also make sure it does not get on anything that touches food, such as cooking and eating utensils, dish towels, and countertops.

Medication should not be stored in the kitchen and should never be referred to as candy. Keep all medicines out of a child's reach. Contact a local hospital or pharmacy to find out how to properly dispose of unused medication.

Read all warning labels, and keep a poison chart handy. This will help you know what first aid to give if someone is accidentally poisoned. It will also help you know what to tell a doctor.

In a case of poisoning, call the nearest poison control center immediately. Have the poison container with you when you call so you can accurately describe the poison taken. If the label on the poison lists first aid instructions, follow them. Keep the victim comfortable and calm until help arrives.

Preventing and Treating Cuts

Knives are an essential kitchen tool. Knives are also a frequent source of kitchen accidents. The following guidelines will prevent unnecessary injuries as well as prolong the useful life of the knife:

- Keep knives sharp. Dull blades can slip and cause cuts.
- Use knives properly. Move the blade away from your body as you cut. Never point a knife or any sharp object at another person.
- Do not try to catch a falling knife in midair. Let the knife fall to the floor and then carefully pick it up.
- Use a knife only for its intended purpose. Do not use it as a screwdriver or to pry open containers. To do so can cause serious injuries.

- Wash and store knives separately from other utensils.

However, knives are not the only source of kitchen cuts. Many appliances have sharp blades which can cause injuries. Never put fingers near beaters or the blades of blenders, food processors, or food waste disposers to dislodge foods or objects. Instead, disconnect the appliance and use a nonmetal utensil to remove items that are stuck. If you cannot dislodge an object, call a repair person.

Many food products are packaged in cans or jars. Glass tumblers and dishes are washed and stored in kitchens. When improperly handled, these can cause injuries as well. After opening cans, dispose of sharp-edged lids immediately. Never pick up broken glass with your bare hands. Wear rubber gloves to pick up large pieces. Sweep smaller pieces into a disposable dustpan and use damp paper towels to wipe up any remaining fragments. Dispose of broken glass immediately.

To treat a cut, cover the wound with a sterile cloth or clean handkerchief. Apply firm pressure to the wound to stop bleeding. If a cut is minor, wash it with soap and water. Apply a *topical antiseptic*. This product reduces the likelihood of infection by limiting the action of microorganisms on the skin. Bandage the wound with a sterile dressing. If a cut is severe, continue to apply pressure to the wound, and take the person to a doctor or the hospital emergency room.

Preventing Burns and Fires

Scalding liquids, spattering grease, and hot cooking utensils cause most kitchen burns. The majority of fires are due to malfunctioning electric appliances and carelessness around hot surfaces and open flames. The following guidelines will help you prevent burns and fires:
- Use pot holders to handle hot utensils.
- Make sure pan handles do not extend over the front edge of the cooktop to prevent accidental tipping **(Figure 2.9)**.
- To avoid a steam burn, open pan lids away from you so the steam will escape safely.
- Never open a pressure cooker before the pressure has gone down to zero. The pressurized steam within the cooker can rush out and cause a severe burn.
- Do not let children play near the range or cook without help. Teach them proper safety procedures.

Tom Begasse/Shutterstock.com

Figure 2.9 Turning a pan's handle away from the front edge of a cooktop will help avoid accidentally spilling the hot food in the pan.

- Turn off range and oven controls and disconnect small appliances when not in use.
- Use caution with liquids heated in a microwave oven. Water can reach temperatures over 212°F (100°C) without showing signs of boiling. Adding teabags, beverage mixes, or ice cubes to the water can cause sudden, rapid boiling to begin.
- Follow manufacturer's directions for use and care of all electric and gas appliances.
- Be sure to ground all electric appliances. Avoid using lightweight extension cords and multiple plug adapters.
- When working near the range, wear tight-fitting clothing. Roll up long sleeves.
- Do not hang towels, curtains, or other flammable materials near the range.
- If you must light a gas range manually, light the match first. Then turn on the gas to prevent an accidental explosion. If you smell gas, turn off the controls, leave the premises, and call the gas company.
- Never leave a pan of grease unattended; it could burst into flames.
- Use care around lit candles, canisters of cooking fuel, and other sources of open flames.
- Clean grease from exhaust hoods frequently to prevent grease fires.
- Install a smoke alarm in the kitchen. Check it monthly to be sure batteries are operating.

Putting Out a Fire

It is important to know what to do if a fire starts. If the fire is small, try to smother the flames.

First, protect your hands by putting on oven mitts. Then you might cover the flames with the lid of a pan or sheet pan, being careful not to fan the flames. You could throw a large amount of baking soda on the fire to cut off the oxygen to the flames. However, never try to put out a fire with flour, as the fine particles of flour can ignite and explode. Do not pour water on a kitchen fire. Many kitchen fires involve grease, and water can cause a grease fire to spread. If the fire does not involve grease or electricity, you could try smothering a small fire with a wet kitchen towel.

A class ABC fire extinguisher is the best choice for putting out a fire. Know where it is stored and know how to use it. Choose a storage location that is handy, but not over the range. Have the fire extinguisher checked annually to be sure it is still in working order. If you need to use the extinguisher, remember the abbreviation *P.A.S.S.*

P – Pull the pin.
A – Aim at the base of the fire, not at the flames.
S – Squeeze the trigger or handle.
S – Sweep from side to side until the fire appears to be out. Watch and repeat if the fire reignites.

If a fire starts to spread or seems too big to control, evacuate the location immediately. If your clothes should catch on fire, do not panic and run. Drop to the floor and roll over to smother the flames. Make sure everyone in your household knows escape routes to follow in case of a fire. Once everyone is safely out of the building, call 9-1-1.

Treating Burns

When someone becomes burned, place the burned area immediately under cold running water or in a cold water bath. Do not apply ointments or grease of any kind. Do not break blisters that may form. Call a physician immediately if a burn is severe or if pain and redness persist.

Preventing and Treating Falls

Most kitchen falls result from unsteady step stools and wet or cluttered floors. Many falls occur because an unstable chair or box is used to reach high places. Always use a sturdy step stool or ladder for safety.

Slips can be avoided by wiping up spills from floors immediately. Be sure no sticky or greasy residue remains. That freshly washed floor, however, is now a slip hazard. Wait until the floor dries before walking across the room. Throw rugs can also result in a slip and fall. Only use rugs with nonskid backings.

The kitchen floor should be kept free and clear of trip hazards. Remove toys, shoes, boots, sports equipment, electric cords, and other objects from kitchen traffic areas, which may result in a fall.

When someone is injured in a fall, stop bleeding if necessary. Loosen clothing around the victim's neck. If you suspect a broken bone, do not move the victim unless absolutely necessary. Make the victim as comfortable as possible. Do not give the victim anything to eat or drink. Call a physician.

Preventing and Treating Electric Shock

Faulty wiring, overloaded electrical outlets, and damaged appliances are common causes of electric shock. Electrical hazards can also be fire hazards. The following guidelines will help you prevent electric shock:

- Never stand on a wet floor or work near a wet counter when using electric appliances.
- Do not touch any electrical plugs, switches, or appliances when your hands are wet.
- Do not run electrical cords under rugs or carpeting.
- Do not use lightweight extension cords with small appliances. If possible, plug appliances directly into electrical outlets. If you must use an extension cord, choose a heavy-gauge cord that is designed to carry a heavier electrical load.
- Do not overload electrical outlets by plugging several appliances into the same outlet.
- Place safety covers over unused electrical outlets to prevent children from sticking fingers or objects into them **(Figure 2.10)**.
- Unplug the toaster before trying to pry loose food that has become stuck.
- When you disconnect appliances, hold onto the plug, not the cord. Replace all cords and plugs when they become worn.
- Do not use damaged appliances.

©iStock.com/blphotocorp

Figure 2.10 Covering electrical outlets when they are not in use will help keep children safe from electric shock. What are two other precautions you should take to improve kitchen safety for young children?

If someone receives an electric shock, immediately disconnect the appliance or turn off the power causing the shock. Do not touch the victim if he or she is connected to the power source. If you do, you will receive a shock, too. Use some nonconducting material to pull the victim away from the electrical source. A rope, a long piece of dry cloth, or a wooden pole would be suitable choices. Then immediately call your local emergency number.

Preventing and Treating Choking

Choking occurs when an object, such as a piece of food, becomes stuck in the throat. The trapped object blocks the airway, making it impossible for the victim to speak or breathe. Someone who is choking quickly turns blue and collapses. The choking victim can die of strangulation in four minutes if the airway is not cleared.

Many instances of choking can be prevented by chewing food thoroughly before swallowing. You should not talk or laugh when you have food in your mouth. Do not give children small, round pieces of food, such as grapes or slices of hot dogs or carrots. Cut slices in halves or quarters.

If someone appears to be choking, be sure they require assistance before providing aid. Someone who can cough, breathe, or talk may not need help. Encourage the person to keep coughing

to *expel* (force out) the object from his or her airway. If a choking victim cannot cough, breathe, or talk, you need to be ready to take action.

First, tell someone to call 9-1-1. Then ask the victim for permission to provide help. Once you have the victim's consent, you will follow a two-step process to provide aid. You will use a combination of five back blows and five abdominal thrusts. An **abdominal thrust** is a technique that exerts pressure on a choking victim's abdomen. This causes a trapped object to be expelled from his or her airway. The combination of five back blows and five abdominal thrusts is repeated until the object blocking the victim's airway is ejected. At this point, the person should be able to breathe again. The steps for aiding a conscious choking victim are described in **Figure 2.11**. If no help is available, you can also perform the abdominal thrust on yourself before losing consciousness.

The abdominal thrust can injure a choking victim. Therefore, the victim should see a doctor as soon as possible after the rescue.

If a choking victim loses consciousness, do not attempt to use this procedure. Instead, carefully ease the victim to the ground, paying attention to protect his or her head. Make sure 9-1-1 was called and emergency medical help is on the way.

Aiding a Conscious Choking Victim

For adults and children over one year of age:
1. Bend the victim forward at the waist, using your forearm to support his or her chest. Use the base of your other hand, between the bottom of your thumb and your wrist, to give five separate blows to the victim's back between the shoulder blades.
2. Begin abdominal thrusts by standing behind the victim. Wrap your arms around the victim's waist.
3. With your thumb toward the victim, place your fist against the victim's abdomen. Your fist should be above the navel and just below the rib cage.
4. Grasping your fist with your other hand, use a quick thrust to press upward into the victim's abdomen. Repeat the thrust five times.

Repeat these steps until the object blocking the victim's airway is ejected or the person is able to cough or breathe again.

Figure 2.11 Be sure a person is choking before using the abdominal thrust.

Chapter 2 Review and Expand

Summary

Foodborne illnesses are very common in the United States. Although bacteria cause many of these illnesses, people are often at fault for spreading the bacteria. Bacteria and other pathogens can get into food at any point during production, processing, or preparation. Most symptoms of foodborne illnesses affect the digestive system and last only a few days. However, foodborne illnesses can be deadly.

Foods often become contaminated through improper handling. It is important to keep yourself and your kitchen clean when preparing food. Make a point of separating raw foods from cooked and ready-to-eat foods. You must cook foods thoroughly and chill them promptly after purchase or serving. Be sure to take special precautions when cooking for a large group or transporting food. You need to be wary when you are eating out to avoid the risk of illness. Using care when storing supplies in a special location will ensure that you have safe food in the event of an emergency, too.

Exercising safety is another concern when you are working in the kitchen. Many kitchen injuries are the result of poisonings, cuts, burns, falls, electric shock, and choking. You can take steps to prevent common kitchen accidents. You should also learn how to provide proper treatment when minor injuries occur.

Vocabulary Activities

1. **Content Terms**   For each of the following terms, identify a word or group of words describing a quality of the term—an *attribute*. Pair up with a classmate and discuss your list of attributes. Then discuss your list of attributes with the whole class to increase understanding.

foodborne illness	toxin
contaminant	parasite
microorganism	sanitation
pathogen	cross-contamination
bacteria	abdominal thrust

2. **Academic Terms**   Individually or with a partner, create a T-chart on a sheet of paper and list each of the following terms in the left column. In the right column, list an *antonym* (a word of opposite meaning) for each term in the left column.

impaired	residue
transmission	expel

Review

Write your answers using complete sentences when appropriate.

3. Name six foods health professionals recommend avoiding due to risk of contamination.
4. For what groups of people do foodborne illnesses pose the greatest risk?
5. What are three microorganisms other than bacteria that can cause foodborne illness?
6. List the four basic steps for keeping food safe to eat and avoiding foodborne illness.
7. For how long should hands be washed before starting to work with food?
8. List eight standards for personal and kitchen cleanliness.
9. List five guidelines for keeping foods that may be contaminated separated from other foods.
10. What are the proper temperatures for holding hot and cold foods prior to serving?
11. How can large amounts of food be heated or chilled quickly?
12. Where do most foodborne illness cases reported each year occur?
13. What age group is especially susceptible to chemical poisonings?
14. Describe the correct way to pick up and dispose of broken glass in order to prevent cuts.
15. List eight safety precautions that can prevent burns and fires.
16. List three guidelines for preventing falls.
17. What should be used to pull a shock victim away from an electrical source?
18. What is the two-step process used to provide aid to conscious choking victims?

Core Skills

19. **Science, Writing**   Look at examples of parasites and protozoa under microscopes. Sketch what you see. Write a paragraph to accompany each sketch. Identify foods that are most likely to be contaminated with each microorganism. Also describe precautions consumers need to take to avoid contamination.
20. **Science**   Pour ¼ teaspoon (1.25 mL) of cooking oil on your hands. Try to remove the oil using just warm water. After a few seconds, put a couple drops of liquid soap on your hands to help remove

Chapter 2 Review and Expand

the oil. Describe what difference the soap made. Note that soap is an emulsifier that surrounds the oil droplets, keeping them suspended in the water so they can be washed away.

21. **Writing, Speaking, Technology** Write a public service ad about safe food handling. Include a jingle or slogan to help people remember a specific standard of personal or kitchen cleanliness. Be sure to demonstrate appropriate dress and personal hygiene in the video. Record your ad and obtain permission to upload the video to your school's channel on a video-sharing website.

22. **Math** With proper growth conditions, bacteria can double in number every 20 minutes. If there were 100 bacterial cells on a surface initially, calculate how many bacteria would exist on the surface after 2 hours. Then calculate how many bacteria would exist on the surface after 5 hours. Discuss what these calculations show about the importance of wiping up spills as they happen and storing leftovers promptly.

23. **Reading, Speaking, Technology** Visit the USDA Food Safety and Inspection Service website. Survey the variety of fact sheets available on food safety topics. Choose one of the topics to demonstrate. Prepare a presentation to demonstrate the fact sheet for the class. Use digital media and visual aids to add interest to your presentation.

24. **Writing** Write a first aid pamphlet for consumers. List items to keep in a first aid kit. Also describe simple first aid procedures for poisonings, cuts, burns, falls, and electric shock. Be sure to reread and revise your pamphlet to improve organization and clarity. Edit your writing for grammar and spelling. Cite any sources you used to help write the pamphlet.

25. **Career Readiness Practice** To become career ready, it will be important to learn how to communicate clearly and effectively by using reason. Imagine you are educating young children about the steps in food safety. Create an outline that includes information about the importance of cleaning, separating, cooking, and chilling. Consider your audience as you prepare the information. Using the outline, make a presentation to your class.

Critical Thinking and Problem Solving

26. **Analyze** Analyze how food might become contaminated during a specific aspect of food production, processing, or transportation. Make a diagram illustrating this operation and the possible points of contamination. Also note safeguards that are taken to prevent contamination at these points.

27. **Create** Work in a group of four to research one type of foodborne illness. Each group member should summarize a different one of the following aspects: pathogen, food sources, symptoms, or prevention. Combine your ideas to create an electronic presentation for the rest of the class.

28. **Analyze** Choose a commercial antibacterial kitchen cleaner. Identify the active ingredients in the cleaner and note the pathogens the product claims to kill. Research any concerns related to these ingredients in terms of human and environmental safety. Then investigate how distilled white vinegar can be used to effectively sanitize food preparation surfaces. Be sure to learn about effective concentrations, application temperatures, and contact time as well as safety precautions about what products to avoid mixing with vinegar. Finally, research the effectiveness of microfiber cleaning cloths, which can be used to clean with just water. Write an opinion paper comparing all your findings and stating your conclusions about when and why you would or would not choose to use each of these products in your kitchen. Be sure to revise and edit your paper to refine the organization of thoughts and the precision of your writing. Edit your writing for sentence structure, tense, and spelling. Cite your sources.

29. **Create** Plan primary and secondary emergency escape routes for your family to use in your home if there is a fire. Use approved online software to create a floor plan of your home. Illustrate your planned escape routes on your floor plan. Then print copies to post in each room of your home. Conduct a fire drill with your family members to practice getting out of your home quickly and safely.

Chapter 3
Basic Skills and Equipment

©iStock.com/RPMGsas

Content Terms ⤳

whisk
colander
serrated blade
chef's knife
saucepan

pot
double boiler
springform pan
casserole
nonstick finish

Academic Terms

pitting
alloy
fused
toxic

Objectives

After studying this chapter, you will be able to

- **measure** liquid, dry, and moist ingredients for use in recipes;
- **identify** various small kitchen utensils and **discuss** their functions;
- **demonstrate** basic knife skills;
- **explain** how to select and care for cookware and bakeware; and
- **use** various pieces of small kitchen equipment, cookware, and bakeware.

Reading Prep

Arrange a study session to read the chapter aloud with a classmate. At the end of each section, discuss any words you do not know. Take notes of words you would like to discuss in class.

Experienced chefs spend years learning a range of knowledge about preparing foods. You do not need to wait years before getting started in the kitchen. However, you do need to demonstrate a few basic skills and know how to use some common equipment.

Measuring Ingredients

Knowing how to measure ingredients correctly will help food products turn out right. The first step in measuring is choosing the correct tools for the task.

Measuring Tools

Measuring tools are essential for cooking and baking. Failing to measure ingredients accurately can result in poor quality food products.

Liquid measures are made of glass or clear plastic. Use them to measure liquid ingredients, such as milk, water, and vegetable oil. They should have handles, pouring lips, and clearly marked measurements. The most common sizes available are 1 cup, 2 cup, and 4 cup. (Metric liquid measures are 250 mL, 500 mL, and 1 L.)

Dry measures are made of metal or plastic. Use them to measure dry ingredients, such as flour and sugar, and solid ingredients such as shortening and peanut butter. They are commonly sold in sets containing ¼-cup, ⅓-cup, ½-cup, and 1-cup sizes. (Metric dry measures are 60 mL, 80 mL, 125 mL, and 250 mL.)

Measuring spoons are also made of metal or plastic. Use them to measure small amounts of liquid and dry ingredients, such as spices and flavoring extracts. A typical set includes ¼-teaspoon, ½-teaspoon, 1-teaspoon, and 1-tablespoon sizes. (Metric measures are 1.25 mL, 2.5 mL, 5 mL, and 15 mL.)

Professional kitchens often use *kitchen scales* instead of measuring cups and spoons. Scales give more precise measurements. Scales are sold for home kitchens, too **(Figure 3.1)**.

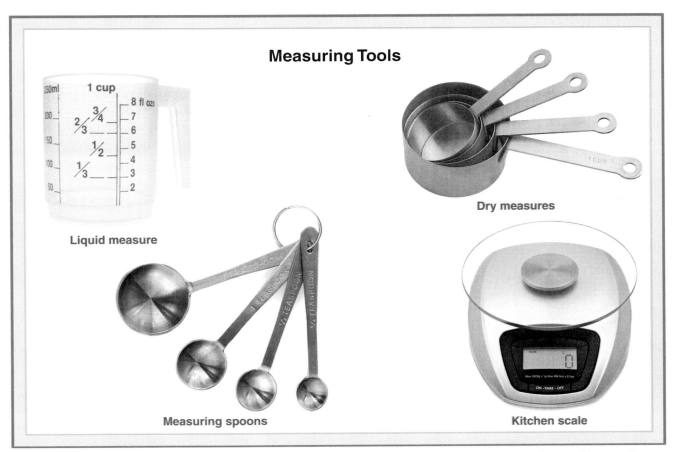

Measuring Tools

Liquid measure

Dry measures

Measuring spoons

Kitchen scale

Clockwise from top left: HomeStudio/Shutterstock.com; Hurst Photo/Shutterstock.com; Gtranquility/Shutterstock.com; Elena Elisseeva/Shutterstock.com

Figure 3.1 Using the proper tools to accurately measure ingredients helps ensure the success of a recipe.

Measuring Techniques

When preparing foods, you will need to measure different types of ingredients in different ways.

Measuring Dry Ingredients

Dry ingredients include sugar, flours, and grain products such as uncooked rice and oatmeal. Measure these ingredients in dry measuring cups. Do not dip the measuring cup into a dry ingredient. Instead, spoon the ingredient into the correct measuring cup until it is overfilled. Do not shake or tap the measuring cup or press down the ingredient as you spoon it into the cup. Hold the measuring cup over the ingredient container or a sheet of wax paper. Then use a straight-edged spatula to level off any excess. The ingredient should be even with the top edge of the measuring cup **(Figure 3.2)**.

Flour is thoroughly sifted during the milling process and usually does not need to be sifted before measuring. Just stir it lightly and measure it like other dry ingredients. However, you should not skip the sifting step when a recipe tells you to sift flour with other dry ingredients. In this case, sifting helps combine the ingredients. Also, if a recipe specifically calls for "sifted flour," you should sift the flour before you measure it.

Measure brown sugar a bit differently from other dry ingredients. Press it firmly into a dry measure with the back of a spoon. This is called *packing*. Overfill the measuring cup and then level it with a straight-edged spatula. The brown sugar should hold the shape of the measuring cup when you dump it out.

Baking soda, salt, and spices are dry ingredients that are often used in small amounts. Use measuring spoons when measuring less than ¼ cup (60 mL) of dry ingredients. Dip the correct measuring spoon into the ingredient container and level off any excess.

You may need to use combinations of dry measures to measure the amounts of ingredients you need. For instance, you would fill a ⅓-cup measure twice to measure ⅔ cup. You would fill a ¼-teaspoon measure and a ½-teaspoon measure to measure ¾ teaspoon.

Measuring Liquid Ingredients

Liquid ingredients include milk, water, oil, juices, food colorings, and extracts. Measure these ingredients in liquid measuring cups or measuring spoons. The handles and spouts on liquid measuring cups make pouring easy. The extra room at the top of the cup will help you avoid spilling.

Set the liquid measuring cup on a flat surface. Then bend down so the mark on the cup for the desired amount is at eye level. Slowly pour the ingredient into the measuring cup until it reaches the mark **(Figure 3.3)**.

Use measuring spoons when measuring less than ¼ cup (60 mL) of liquid ingredients.

Courtesy ACH Food Companies, Inc.

Figure 3.2   Level off a dry measuring cup so the ingredient is even with the top edge. For what ingredients, other than flour, would you use this measuring technique?

Courtesy ACH Food Companies, Inc.

Figure 3.3   Fill a liquid measuring cup to the appropriate mark at eye level. How much milk is being measured in the cup on the left side of the photo?

Carefully pour the ingredient into the correct spoon until it is filled to the edge.

Measuring Thick, Moist Ingredients

Thick, moist ingredients used in recipes include solid fats such as butter, margarine, and shortening. These ingredients also include foods such as jelly, sour cream, and nut butters, such as peanut butter.

Stick butter and margarine have markings on their wrappers to help you measure needed amounts. Each stick equals 8 tablespoons or ½ cup (125 mL). Use a sharp knife to cut through the wrapper at the marking for the desired number of tablespoons.

You can measure other thick, moist ingredients in dry measuring cups. Spray the inside of the measuring cup with nonstick cooking spray to help the ingredient come out of the cup easily. Use a flexible spatula to press these ingredients into the measuring cup, making sure you eliminate any air pockets. Overfill the measuring cup, and then level it with a straight-edged spatula **(Figure 3.4)**.

Solid fats like shortening can also be measured using the *water displacement method*. Fill a 2-cup (500 mL) liquid measuring cup with 1 cup (250 mL) of cold water. Then carefully spoon in the solid fat until the water level rises by the amount you need. For instance, suppose you need ½ cup (125 mL) of shortening. You would spoon the shortening into the measuring cup until the water level reached 1½ cups (375 mL). Make sure the fat is not clinging to the side of the measuring cup. Drain off the water before using the fat. (Note: This method cannot be used for any ingredient that would dissolve in water.)

Measuring by Weight

Some recipes list amounts of ingredients by weight, such as ounces or grams, rather than volume, such as tablespoons and cups. To measure ingredients by weight, you need a kitchen scale. Before you weigh an ingredient, you need to *tare* the scale. To do this, place the empty container you will use to hold the ingredient on the scale. Follow the manufacturer's directions to set the scale back to zero or tare. (This keeps you from including the weight of the container with the weight of your ingredient.) Then add the ingredient to the container until the amount needed registers on the scale.

Kitchen Utensils

Small equipment can do much to save time and increase efficiency in the kitchen. Housewares departments in many stores carry a wide variety of kitchen utensils. Many of these small tools are needed for meal preparation. Others may not really be needed, but they are helpful.

Choose tools that best meet needs and the budget. Before buying small equipment, ask the following questions.

- What kinds of kitchen tasks are performed and how often are they performed? A specialized piece of equipment may not be needed for a task that is seldom performed.
- How is the equipment designed and how does it work? Avoid complicated equipment that is hard to assemble. Choose well-designed, durable tools that are easy to operate and clean.
- What quality of materials is used to make the equipment? For example, many tools are made of stainless steel, which is a strong, rustproof material.

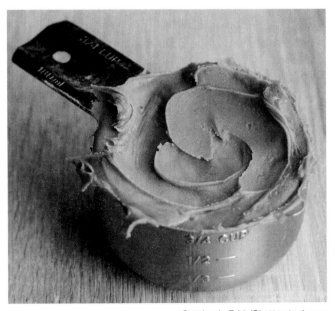

Stephanie Eddy/Shutterstock.com

Figure 3.4 When measuring thick, moist ingredients like peanut butter, press them into a dry measuring cup to make sure any air pockets are removed.

Mini Lab: Measuring Practice

Oatmeal Raisin Energy Bites

Use liquid and dry measuring cups, measuring spoons, and a kitchen scale to correctly measure ingredients listed. All group members will measure their ingredients into the same small and/or medium bowl.

1. **Group member A**—Measure ½ cup (125 mL) old-fashioned oats into the medium bowl and ½ teaspoon (2.5 mL) vanilla extract into the small bowl.

   Group member B—Measure ¼ cup (60 mL) ground flaxseed into the medium bowl and ¼ cup (60 mL) maple syrup into the small bowl.

   Group member C—Measure ¼ cup (60 mL) chopped raisins into the medium bowl and ¼ cup (60 mL) almond or peanut butter into the small bowl.

   Group member D—Measure ¼ teaspoon (1.25 mL) ground cinnamon and 1 ounce (28 g) ground walnuts into the medium bowl.
2. Use a mixing spoon to combine the ingredients in the medium bowl.
3. Use a mixing spoon to combine the ingredients in the small bowl.
4. Add the ingredients in the small bowl to the ingredients in the medium bowl and stir until thoroughly combined.
5. Cover the medium bowl with plastic wrap and place in the freezer for 20 minutes.
6. Remove the bowl from the freezer. Use teaspoons to gather dough and roll by hand into 1-inch (2.5 cm) balls. Place balls on wax paper. Store energy bites in an airtight container in the refrigerator for up to one week.

Makes about 24 energy bites

Per energy bite: 51 calories (6% from fat), 1 g protein, 6 g carbohydrate, 3 g fat, 0 mg cholesterol, 1 g fiber, 13 mg sodium

- How are the handles constructed? The handles should fit the hand comfortably. They should be sturdy enough to withstand frequent use.

To receive the most satisfaction and value from small equipment, select tools wisely. Follow manufacturers' directions for their use and care. Also, store small equipment in a convenient location.

Small kitchen utensils can make many food preparation tasks easier. Utensils can be grouped according to the types of tasks they perform.

Mixing Tools

Virtually every recipe requires ingredients to be mixed together. *Mixing spoons* are available in many sizes and shapes for stirring and mixing. Spoons made from wood, nylon, and silicone will not scratch pan surfaces, and their handles remain cool when stirring hot mixtures.

Metal spoons typically have deeper *bowls* (the round or oval part of a spoon that holds food) than nonmetal spoons. Therefore, metal spoons are a good choice when scooping mixtures out of containers. Use *slotted spoons* to remove pieces of food from a liquid, such as peas from broth.

Use a **whisk**, a mixing tool made of loops of wire attached to a handle, to incorporate air into foods. Use it for eggs, soufflés, and meringues. When preparing sauces, use a whisk to prevent lumps from forming **(Figure 3.5)**.

Baking Tools

A number of tools are used just for preparing baked goods. One such tool is a *sifter*. Use a sifter to blend dry ingredients, add air, and remove lumps from ingredients like powdered sugar.

A *pastry blender* is made of several thin, curved pieces of metal attached to a handle. Use

Mixing Tools

Mixing spoons   Slotted spoon   Whisk

L to r: Bernd Schmidt/Shutterstock.com; johnfoto 18/Shutterstock.com; ra3m/Shutterstock.com; ifong/Shutterstock.com

Figure 3.5   Choose the best tool for each mixing task—stirring, blending, or incorporating air.

it to blend solid fats such as shortening with flour when making pastry. It can also be used to blend butter and cheese mixtures.

Use *pastry brushes* to brush glazes on dough and baked goods. They can also be used to remove crumbs from a cake before frosting it. A *basting brush* is a similar tool with a longer handle. It is used to baste sauces on foods on a grill or in an oven. Basting brushes must have heat-resistant bristles, which are often made of silicone.

Use a *rolling pin* to roll dough or pastry. You may want to place the dough on a *nonstick baking mat*. These mats are made of reinforced silicone. They can keep dough from sticking to the counter while it is being kneaded or rolled. However, baking mats are especially useful for lining baking pans in the oven. Food will not stick to the mat. Therefore, pans do not need to be greased, and they are easier to clean after baking. You can also use *parchment paper* in place of a baking mat.

Spatulas can be made of plastic or metal. They come in various widths and lengths. *Bent-edged spatulas* are commonly used to remove cookies from baking trays. They can also be used to turn meats, fish, pancakes, eggs, and omelets. Use *straight-edged spatulas* to spread cake icings and meringues and to level ingredients in dry measuring cups. Use *flexible spatulas* to scrape

bowls and saucepans and to fold one ingredient into another **(Figure 3.6)**.

Thermometers

Being able to accurately measure the temperature of a food product can improve cooking success. It can also help reduce the risk of foodborne illness. Many foods contain harmful bacteria that can be killed by thorough cooking. Use a thermometer when cooking protein foods, such as meat, poultry, fish, egg dishes, and casseroles. This is the only way to be sure these foods have reached recommended internal temperatures.

Several types of thermometers are available. *Meat thermometers* are designed to be placed in meat or poultry while it is cooking. *Instant-read thermometers* are inserted into a food at the end of cooking time. This type of thermometer will provide an accurate reading in a matter of seconds.

Candy/fat thermometers usually have a clip or hook so they can be attached to the side of a pan. They are marked with the temperatures needed for making different kinds of candies. They also register oil temperatures for deep-frying foods such as doughnuts and French fries.

Two other types of thermometers are important pieces of kitchen equipment. Use a *refrigerator-freezer*

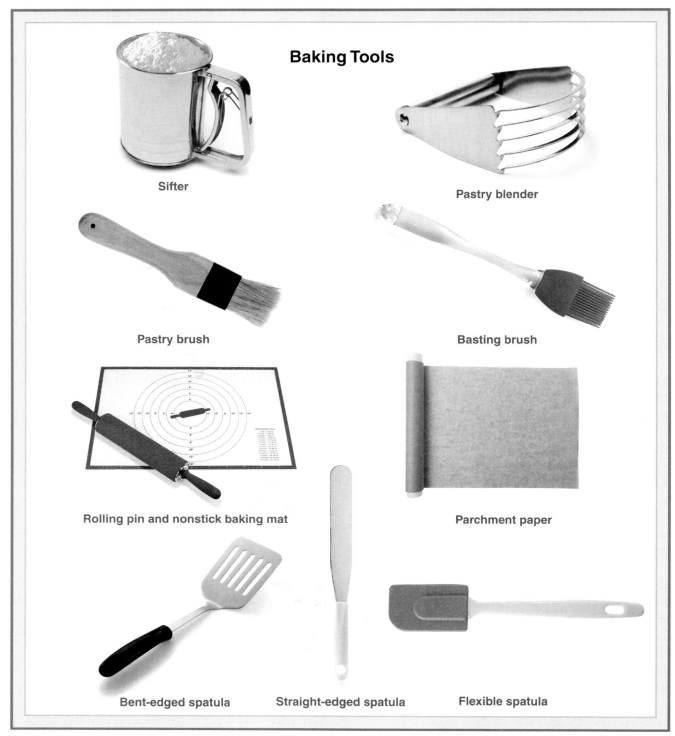

Baking Tools

Sifter

Pastry blender

Pastry brush

Basting brush

Rolling pin and nonstick baking mat

Parchment paper

Bent-edged spatula   Straight-edged spatula   Flexible spatula

Figure 3.6   Using the correct tools can improve the quality of baked products.

thermometer to keep track of the temperatures at which foods are stored. The refrigerator should not be more than 40°F (4°C). Keep the freezer at no more than 0°F (–18°C). An *oven thermometer* can help make sure an oven heats to the temperature for which it is set. An oven that overheats can cause foods to burn, whereas an oven that underheats can lengthen cooking times **(Figure 3.7)**.

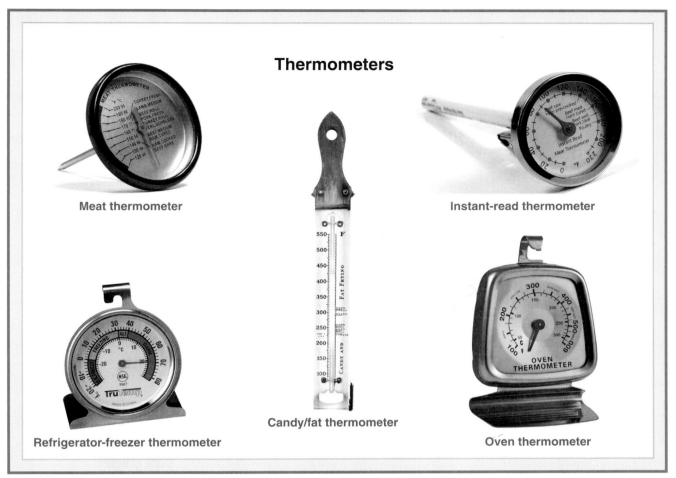

Thermometers

Meat thermometer

Instant-read thermometer

Refrigerator-freezer thermometer

Candy/fat thermometer

Oven thermometer

Clockwise from top left: de2marco/Shutterstock.com; ©iStock.com/webking; Jo De Vulder/Shutterstock.com; Belinda Pretorius/Shutterstock.com; Taylor Precision

Figure 3.7 Thermometers are essential tools for preventing foodborne illness. Which thermometer would you use when checking the temperature of a casserole?

Cutting Tools

Preparing ingredients often involves a variety of cutting tasks. Use *kitchen shears* to snip herbs and trim vegetables. They can also be used to cut meat, dough, cookies, and pizza. *Poultry shears* are heavier and sharper than ordinary kitchen shears. Use them to cut through fowl and fish bones. Use kitchen shears only for food preparation tasks to minimize cross-contamination and keep shears sharp.

Use a *peeler* to remove the outer surface of fruits and vegetables. A peeler removes only a thin layer, so nutrients lying near the surface are preserved. Peelers can also be used to make garnishes or decorative elements, such as carrot curls and chocolate shavings.

A *shredder-grater* is a four-sided metal tool with openings of different sizes on each side. It is used to shred and grate foods such as cheese and cabbage into small or large pieces. Chefs often choose to use a *plane grater* to perform these cutting tasks. This tool has a handle attached to a flat stainless steel panel that is perforated with cutting teeth. Foods such as cheese, chocolate, and vegetables are scraped against the teeth to be grated or shredded. Plane graters with very fine perforations are often used for grating spices and removing the *zest* (thin outer rind) from citrus fruits.

Cutting boards can be made of a variety of materials and are usually rectangular in shape. They are sometimes built into a cabinet or counter. Use a cutting board when cutting and chopping foods to protect tables and countertops as well as knives. Wooden and plastic cutting boards are the best choices to keep knife blades from becoming dull **(Figure 3.8)**.

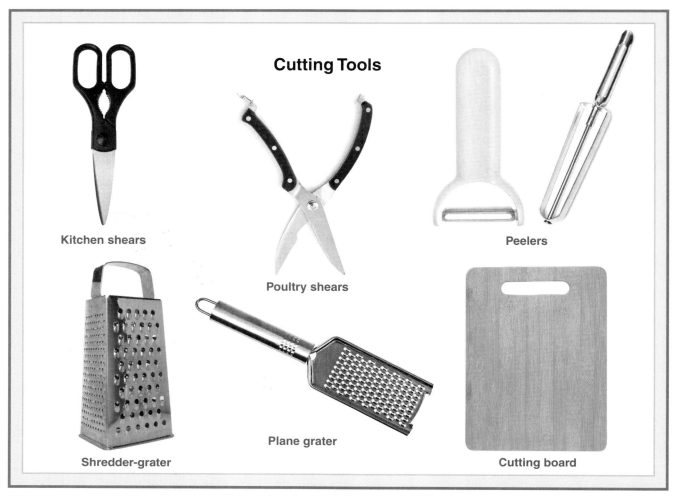

Cutting Tools

Kitchen shears

Poultry shears

Peelers

Shredder-grater

Plane grater

Cutting board

Clockwise from top left: Olga Popova/Shutterstock.com; hgphotgrapy/Shutterstock.com; raresirimie/Shutterstock.com; Edward Westmacott/Shutterstock.com; Evlakhov Valeriy/Shutterstock.com; Sebastian Radu/Shutterstock.com; PremiumVector/Shutterstock.com

Figure 3.8 A variety of cutting tools are available for cutting food into just the right size and shape for any recipe.

Other Preparation Tools

Tongs are made of metal or plastic. Use metal tongs for turning meats and fried foods. They might also be used for handling such foods as corn on the cob, hard-cooked eggs, and baked potatoes. Plastic tongs are typically used for serving cold foods, such as tossed salads and raw vegetables.

Kitchen forks are made of heavy-duty metal. Use them when transferring heavy meats and poultry. A kitchen fork can also be used to turn heavy foods.

Ladles are round cups attached to long handles. They come in different sizes for different purposes. Use a ladle for dipping and pouring. A ladle might be used to serve punches, soups, sauces, gravies, and salad dressings.

A *baster* is a long tube attached to a flexible bulb. A baster uses suction to collect juices from meat and poultry for basting (coating foods with liquid). It can also be used to skim fat from soups and gravies.

Colanders are perforated bowls used to drain fruits, vegetables, and pasta. They are available in metal and plastic and come in a variety of sizes. A colander should have heat-proof handles.

Strainers are available in several sizes. Use them to separate liquid and solid foods.

Manual *can openers* remove the tops of cans. Some have round blades that puncture the tops of cans and cut the lids off. Other can openers decrimp the tops of cans where they are attached to the sides, leaving no sharp edges. Most can openers have handles that can be squeezed. Then a key is turned, which causes the can to rotate through the mechanism of the opener **(Figure 3.9)**.

Knives and Knife Skills

Ingredients are often cut into smaller pieces before being added to a recipe. Many foods need to be cut before they are served. Therefore, knowing how to choose knives and use them to perform specific cuts are important skills.

Types of Knives

Different types of knives are used for different kitchen cutting tasks. Knife blades can be smooth or serrated. A **serrated blade** has a sawtooth edge. Some serrated knives are called *slicers*. They are especially helpful for slicing tender foods that are firm on the outside, such as tomatoes and crusty breads.

Some of the most popular kitchen knives are chef's, paring, bread, boning, and utility knives. A **chef's knife**, also known as a *French knife*, is the most versatile of all kitchen knives. It has a long, smooth blade for slicing, dicing, and mincing fresh fruits, vegetables, and herbs. A *paring knife* is one of the smallest knives used in the kitchen. It has a smooth blade for peeling and trimming fruits and vegetables. A *bread knife* has a long, serrated blade for cutting bread without squashing the loaf or shredding the slices. A *boning knife* has a thin, smooth blade to easily cut and remove bones from raw meat and poultry. A *utility knife* is a good all-around knife. It can be

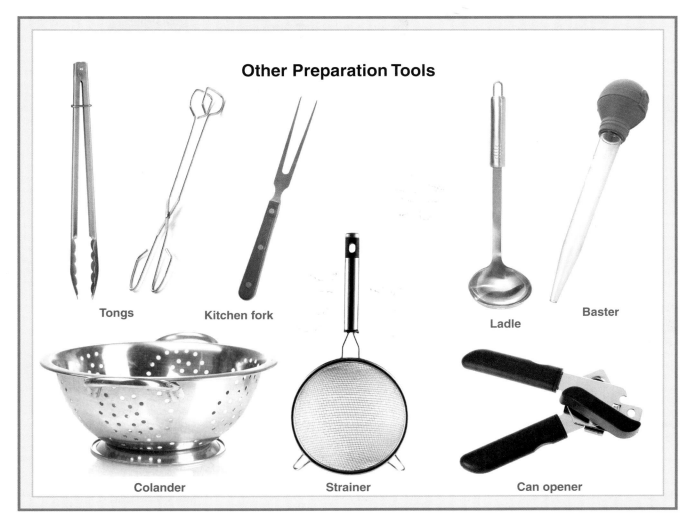

Other Preparation Tools

Tongs   Kitchen fork   Ladle   Baster

Colander   Strainer   Can opener

Figure 3.9 Small utensils are designed to perform a variety of food preparation tasks.

used to trim fat from meat and cut tender vegetables, cheese, and cold cuts **(Figure 3.10)**.

Buying Knives

Knives may be purchased individually or in sets. Quality knives can be expensive. However, you are likely to use them more than any other equipment in the kitchen. Therefore, choosing good knives is worth the investment. With proper care, your knives can last for years.

When choosing knives, look at the materials from which they are made. Knife blades are made of carbon steel, stainless steel, or ceramic. Carbon steel is easy to sharpen because it is soft.

However, it will stain and rust easily unless the knife is washed and dried soon after each use. Stainless steel is durable and will not rust, but stainless is so hard that sharpening is difficult. (Some manufacturers, however, produce a type of stainless steel that is soft enough to sharpen easily.) Ceramic blades are very hard and will hold a sharp edge for a long time. They are excellent for slicing. However, ceramic blades are not flexible and can chip or break with misuse.

Knife handles can be made of plastic, wood, metal, or bone. Regardless of the material, a knife handle should fit the hand comfortably. It should also be properly balanced and constructed for maximum safety.

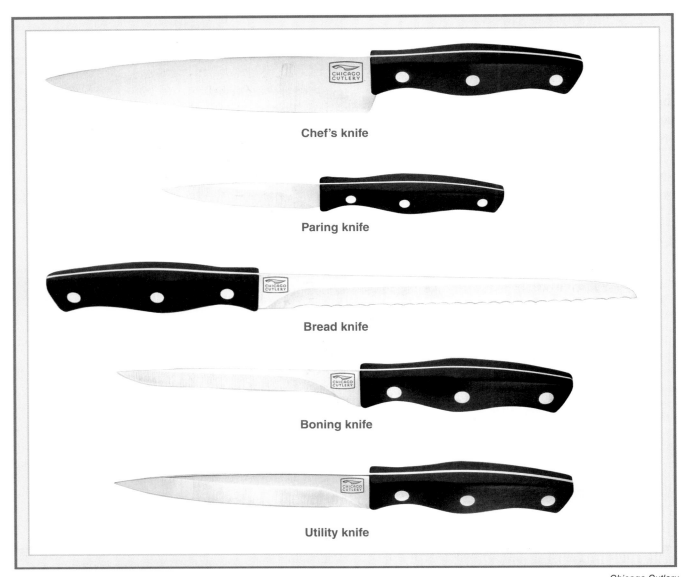

Chef's knife

Paring knife

Bread knife

Boning knife

Utility knife

Chicago Cutlery

Figure 3.10 Choose a knife that is best suited to the food preparation task.

Exploring Careers

Housewares Demonstrator

A housewares demonstrator shows people how to use and care for kitchen utensils, highlighting the special features of each product. Demonstrators may work for housewares makers. They show their products to retail business owners to urge them to offer the products for sale in their stores. Demonstrators may also work for retailers. They may need to travel to various stores and set up their display areas before demonstrating utensils to store customers. Demonstrators may pass out product brochures and samples and offer discounts to help boost sales.

Housewares demonstrators require good speaking skills as they discuss their products. They must feel comfortable working in front of people. They need good listening skills to answer questions. Reading skills will help them understand product literature so they will be informed about the items they are demonstrating. They must pay attention to details to keep their work area tidy and keep track of sales records. They have to be flexible so they can adjust their demonstrations to best suit their customers.

A housewares demonstrator needs only a high school diploma. However, a few months of on-the-job training may be required. This will allow the demonstrator to become fully familiar with all the products and techniques he or she will be using. Experience speaking in front of others may also be helpful.

The *tang* is the prong of the blade that extends into the knife's handle. For safety, the tang should extend at least one-third of the way into the handle. Better quality knives have a full tang, which extends the full length and width of the handle.

The tang is often secured to the handle with rivets. At least two rivets should join the blade and handle. Three rivets should join larger knives.

Knife Skills

You will likely use a chef's knife most often when preparing foods. Learning to use this knife correctly takes practice. However, once you acquire this skill, you will be able to work faster and more safely when cutting foods.

The first step to using a chef's knife is a proper grip. You will grip the knife using your writing hand. Place your thumb on one side of the blade near the handle. Place your index finger on the other side of the blade. Then wrap your middle finger, ring finger, and pinkie around the handle. This grip may feel a bit awkward at first. As you get used to it, you will find it gives you better control of the knife **(Figure 3.11)**.

Slicing foods into thin, flat pieces is a basic cutting technique. Begin by cutting rounded foods in half or by cutting a slice off one side to create a flat surface. Place the flat side against the cutting board so the food will not roll while you are cutting it.

You will use the hand that is not holding the knife to hold the food and guide the knife. Curl the fingers of this hand under like a claw to protect them from getting cut. Hold the food

gosphotodesign/Shutterstock.com

Figure 3.11 Using the proper grip when holding a knife will give you the control needed to cut foods quickly and safely.

item firmly between your thumb and pinkie. Rest the other three fingers on top of the food with your knuckles forward. The food should extend just slightly in front of your knuckles.

Hold the knife blade perpendicular to the cutting board with the tip pointed down. The flat side of the blade should be against the knuckle of your middle finger. Slice the blade through the food as you move the handle down toward the cutting board and forward away from your body. As the edge of the blade comes in contact with the cutting board, you should have cut completely through the food.

To continue slicing, lift the handle of the knife, keeping the tip pointed toward the cutting board. Slide the hand that is holding the food back slightly. Repeat the slicing motion. Be sure to keep the flat side of the knife blade against your knuckle to control the thickness of each slice. Try to make all the pieces the same thickness. Foods will look more appealing and cook more evenly when ingredients are cut in uniform pieces **(Figure 3.12)**.

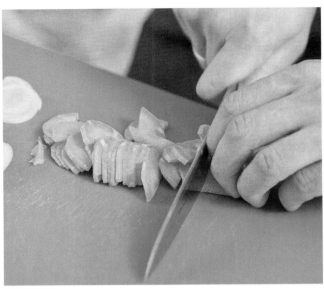

Shebeko/Shutterstock.com

Figure 3.12 Keeping the flat side of the knife blade against the knuckle will help you control the thickness of each slice of food. Why is it important to keep your fingers curled under when holding food you are cutting?

Mini Lab: Practicing Knife Skills

Cucumber and Carrot Salad

1. **Group members A and B**—Wash one carrot each. Use a peeler to peel the carrot. Use a paring knife to trim off both ends and cut the carrot in half crosswise.

   Group member C—Wash one English cucumber. Use a paring knife to trim off both ends. Cut the cucumber in half lengthwise from end to end. Then cut each piece in half crosswise through the middle so you have four pieces.

   Group member D—Whisk together 1 tablespoon (15 mL) sesame oil, 1 tablespoon (15 mL) low-sodium soy sauce, and 1 tablespoon (15 mL) rice vinegar to make dressing.

2. Each group member will take turns using a cutting board and a chef's knife to practice knife skills. Lightly trim the side of a carrot half to create a flat surface. Place the flat surface on the cutting board and cut the carrot into ¼-inch (6 mm) slices.

3. Place the flat side of a quarter of an English cucumber on the cutting board and cut into ¼-inch (6 mm) slices.

4. Place all sliced vegetables in a medium bowl.

5. Drizzle the vegetables with the prepared dressing. Toss with a serving spoon to coat. Sprinkle with 1 teaspoon (2.5 mL) toasted sesame seeds.

Makes 4 servings

Per serving: 63 calories (57% from fat), 1 g protein, 6 g carbohydrate, 4 g fat, 0 mg cholesterol, 2 g fiber, 158 mg sodium

In addition to slices, recipes call for foods to be cut in sticks and *dices* (cubes) in several common dimensions. Once you master the slicing technique, you can use the chef's knife to cut a small stack of slices into sticks. Cutting sticks crosswise will create diced foods.

Caring for Knives

Follow safety precautions as you care for your knives. This will help protect you and allow your knives to provide years of use.

Begin by keeping knives sharp so they will easily slice through foods. Dull knives are more dangerous because they can slip when extra pressure is applied. Several types of sharpeners are available. However, most chefs recommend using a *sharpening steel*, also known as a *honing steel*, to maintain a sharp edge on knife blades. This rod-shaped tool has a ridged or textured surface. The blade is stroked along the steel a few times after each use to smooth away tiny imperfections. It is important to hold the knife blade at a proper 20 degree angle and use only moderate pressure when using a steel **(Figure 3.13)**. Using a steel incorrectly can actually cause damage to a knife blade.

Knife blades that have been allowed to become dull are best sharpened using a tool called a *whetstone*. If knife blades become nicked or damaged, they may need to be professionally sharpened or repaired.

Follow proper cutting techniques and use knives only as intended. Using knives as screwdrivers or prying tools can damage blades. Cut on wooden or plastic cutting boards, which are less damaging than glass and stone boards.

The best way to clean knives is to wash and dry them individually by hand. Avoid putting knives in the sink, which creates the risk of sharp blades being hidden in soapy water. In addition, soaking can cause handles to loosen. Do not put knives in the dishwasher, as harsh detergents and contact with other utensils can cause damage. Sharp knives also present a danger when unloading a dishwasher.

Do not store knives with other utensils, which can nick and damage blades. Store knives in a separate drawer or compartment. Cover blades with protective edge guards or sheaths to prevent damage and cuts. You can also hang knives on a magnetic strip or store them in a wooden knife block.

Cooking and Baking Equipment

A well-stocked kitchen will contain a variety of cooking and baking equipment. Knowing how each item is used will help you choose the best piece for each food product you want to prepare.

Cookware

Cookware refers to the various types of saucepans and pots used for cooking foods in water or other liquids over direct surface heat. **Saucepans** generally have one handle. **Pots** have two handles. Sizes range from a 1-pint (0.5 L) saucepan to a 12-quart (12 L) *stockpot*. For maximum cooking efficiency, the bottoms of pots and pans should be about the same diameter as the heating unit. Handles should be heat-resistant and comfortable to hold. Pots and pans can often be purchased with matching lids.

A **double boiler** is a small pan that fits into a larger pan. Food is put into the smaller pan. Then a small amount of water is put in the larger pan. As the water simmers, the heat produced by the steam gently cooks the food.

Dimitry Kalinovsky/Shutterstock.com

Figure 3.13 When using a sharpening steel, hold the knife at a slight angle to the steel and apply only moderate pressure.

A *pressure cooker* cooks foods more quickly than conventional saucepans. This is because as pressure increases, temperature increases. Choose a pressure cooker that carries a safety seal. Be sure to read manufacturer's directions carefully before using a pressure cooker.

Skillets and sauté pans have wide bottoms and low sides and are used for cooking foods in a small amount of fat. *Skillets* are also called *fry pans*. They have sloping sides, which are helpful when gently tossing foods to redistribute heat during cooking. *Sauté pans* have vertical sides, which give them more cooking surface area than skillets of the same size.

Griddle, grill, and omelet pans are variations of skillets. *Griddle pans* and *grill pans* have very low or no sides. Griddles have a flat surface for cooking foods, such as French toast and pancakes. Grills have ridges that give characteristic grill marks to burgers, vegetables, and other foods. Some of these pans are reversible with a griddle on one side and a grill on the other. An *omelet pan* is an uncovered skillet with smooth, shallow, sloping sides. Use it to make omelets and crêpes (delicate French pancakes) **(Figure 3.14)**.

Bakeware

Bakeware refers to the various pieces of equipment used when cooking in an oven. When selecting bakeware, it is important to consider whether the pan's surface is shiny or dull. The outer surface of a pan affects the amount of heat the pan absorbs. A shiny or bright surface reflects

Cookware

Saucepan

Stockpot

Double boiler

Pressure cooker

Skillet

Sauté pan

Griddle pan

Grill pan

Omelet pan

Top row, l to r: MidoSemsem/Shutterstock.com; Dimitry Kalinovsky/Shutterstock.com; Pierdelune/Shutterstock.com; middle row, l to r: angelo gilardelli/ Shutterstock.com; Tatiana Popova/Shutterstock.com; mike ledray/Shutterstock.com; bottom row, l to r: Olga Popova/Shutterstock.com; twomeerkats/ Shutterstock.com; Kudla/Shutterstock.com

Figure 3.14 Cookware comes in a variety of sizes and shapes for preparing all types of dishes.

part of the heat away from the food. A dull or dark surface absorbs heat. Products baked in bright, shiny pans will have softer, lighter crusts. Products baked in dull, dark pans will have darker and crisper crusts. Reducing the oven temperature by 25°F (15°C) will help avoid over-browning when baking in dark pans.

Insulated bakeware is made from two sheets of metal. An airspace between the two sheets creates a layer of insulation. This layer helps protect baked goods from overbrowning.

Cookie sheets are often made of aluminum. They are flat sheets of metal with a low rim on one or more sides for strength. Use them for baking cookies, toasting bread, and supporting small containers, such as custard cups.

Cake, tube, springform, jelly roll, pizza, muffin, and loaf pans are usually made of aluminum. Cake and loaf pans are also available in glass, ceramic, and silicone materials. Each of these bakeware pieces is available in several sizes.

Cake pans can be round, square, or oblong. *Tube pans* are deep, round pans with smooth or fluted sides and a tube in the center. Smooth-sided pans, which may have removable bottoms, are used for baking angel food, sponge, and chiffon cakes. Fluted tube pans, often called Bundt pans, are used for other ring-shaped cakes. A **springform pan** is also round and has a removable bottom. A latch or spring makes it easy to remove the pan from cheesecakes, tortes, and other delicate desserts. A *jelly roll pan* is a large, shallow oblong pan. Use it to make sheet cakes and to bake the sponge cake for cake rolls. *Pizza pans* are large and round. They may have a narrow rim around the edge. Some have holes in the bottom to help create a crisper crust. *Muffin pans* are oblong pans with round depressions. Use them for baking muffins and cupcakes. *Loaf pans* are deep, narrow, oblong pans. These are used most often for breads and loaf cakes.

Pie plates are round with sloping sides. They are generally made of glass or aluminum. Use them when making dessert and main dish pies.

Casseroles are baking dishes with high sides. They can be made of glass, glass-ceramic, or earthenware. Some casseroles are designed for freezer-to-oven use. *Soufflé dishes* are a variation of a casserole. They have high, steep sides.

Roasting pans can be oval or oblong. They are larger and heavier than pots, pans, and skillets. Most have high, dome lids, and many have racks

Learn About...

Cookware Shapes for Microwaving

The shape of cookware can affect how evenly foods cook in a microwave oven. Round-shaped containers allow microwaves to hit food evenly. Microwaves can overlap in the corners of square cookware pieces. This causes food in the corners to overcook.

Ring-shaped pans give great results when microwaving cakes, meat loaves, and other foods. This shape accounts for the fact that foods tend to cook slower in the center of a microwave oven. The circular arrangement allows foods to cook more evenly. Ring shapes also allow microwaves to hit foods from the center as well as the top, bottom, and sides. This increased microwave penetration speeds cooking time.

Cookware pieces should correspond to the amount and kind of food being microwaved. Choose single-serving pieces when cooking small amounts of food. Use a rack with a slotted or raised surface when cooking meats so fats and juices can drain. Select deeper containers when cooking foods like milk that may boil over.

Know and Apply

1. Which would be a better choice for microwaving a casserole: an 8-inch (20 cm) round baking dish or a 9 × 5 inch (22.5 × 12.5 cm) oblong pan? Explain your choice.

2. What type of container would be a good choice for warming one cup (250 mL) of applesauce in a microwave oven?

to keep food from resting on the bottom of the pan **(Figure 3.15)**.

Buying Cookware and Bakeware

Cookware and bakeware pieces can be purchased separately or in sets. Before buying these items, think about needs and the features each piece offers. All cookware and bakeware pieces should last a long time and maintain their appearance with normal care.

Consider the following features when buying cookware and bakeware:

- Pots and pans should be sturdy and well balanced to prevent tipping. All edges should be smooth. Pan bottoms should be flat for good heat conduction. Beware of crevices where food particles can collect.

- Handles should be heat-resistant, sturdy, and securely attached.
- Lids should be well constructed and should fit tightly. Handles on lids should be heat-resistant and easy to grasp with a pot holder.
- Cookware and bakeware pieces should be light enough to handle comfortably and

Bakeware

Cookie sheet

Cake pans

Tube Bundt pan

Springform pan

Jelly roll pan

Pizza pan

Muffin pan

Loaf pan

Pie plate

Casseroles

Soufflé dish

Roasting pan

Figure 3.15   Each piece of bakeware is designed for preparing specific types of food items in an oven.

safely. They should be heavy enough to be durable and to withstand warping.

- Saucepans should be able to stack or hang from a rack for storage.

Cookware and Bakeware Materials

A chief consideration when choosing cookware and bakeware is the material from which items are made. Metal, glass, ceramic, silicone, and plastics are the most popular cookware and bakeware materials.

Metal Materials

Several metals are used for conventional cookware and bakeware. *Cast iron* is a cookware material that distributes and holds heat well. It is a magnetic-based metal and thus can be used on an induction cooktop. Its porous surface holds oils that help prevent sticking. Iron is heavy, however. It can also rust, retain food flavors, and lose its nonstick qualities unless it is cared for properly.

Aluminum is a lightweight, corrosion-resistant cookware and bakeware material. It conducts heat rapidly and is reasonably priced. It comes in several thicknesses. Cast aluminum is used for heavier pieces, such as skillets. Sheet aluminum is used for lighter items, such as cookie sheets. Aluminum is susceptible to scratches, dents, and detergent damage. Food and minerals can cause *pitting* (marking with tiny indentations). Hard water, eggs, and alkalis, such as baking soda, can cause darkening.

Copper is a good heat conductor. However, saucepans cannot be made from pure copper. When heated, copper reacts with food and forms poisonous compounds. Copper cookware must be lined with another material to make it safe for cooking. Copper must be cleaned with a special cleaner to keep it from discoloring.

Stainless steel is an **alloy** (mixture) of steel, nickel, and chromium. Most stainless steel is magnetic, making it an option for induction cooking. It resists stains, does not discolor, and is strong and durable. However, it does not distribute heat evenly, so hot spots can occur. Stainless steel may darken if overheated. It is relatively expensive.

Some stainless steel pieces have a copper or aluminum bottom to improve heat distribution. Other pieces may have a core of copper, carbon steel, or other heat-conducting metal. These materials help conduct heat across the pan bottom and up the sides. A heat-conducting core prevents scorching, conserves fuel, and allows low-temperature cooking **(Figure 3.16)**.

Glass and Ceramic Materials

Glass and ceramic materials are used for a range of cookware and bakeware pieces. These materials are attractive. However, they must be handled with care to avoid cracking, chipping, and breaking.

Glass used to make cookware and bakeware is *tempered*, or specially treated to make it stronger and more heat-resistant. Glass is transparent, which allows the food to be seen while it is cooking. This material does not react with the flavors or colors of food. However, it is a poor heat conductor.

Glass-ceramic is strong and durable. It can withstand a wide range of temperatures. This property allows glass-ceramic bakeware to be taken from the freezer and put directly in the oven. This material has the drawbacks of developing hot spots and heating unevenly.

Porcelain enamel is a glass-like material. It is **fused** (joined) to a base metal at very high temperatures. The outer surfaces of metal cookware and bakeware are often coated with

Revere®

Figure 3.16 Stainless steel is not a good heat conductor and can allow hot spots that cause scorching (left). A copper or aluminum bottom or core on a stainless steel pan promotes even heating (right).

porcelain enamel. This makes the pieces colorful and easy to clean.

Ceramic materials are made from nonmetallic minerals that are fired at very high temperatures. Ceramic materials include earthenware and terra-cotta. Many of these materials are not suitable for rangetop cooking. However, they can retain heat well. This makes them good choices for bakeware pieces.

Silicone and Plastic Materials

Silicone has a rubbery texture and comes in an array of bright colors. Many bakers like its nonstick properties for bakeware items such as cake, loaf, and muffin pans. *Plastic materials* are popular for microwave cookware. Both types of materials can be placed in the freezer and dishwasher. However, both will melt when exposed to the direct heat of a broiler or rangetop. Using nonmetal utensils will protect silicone and plastic pieces from damage.

Nonstick Finishes

Nonstick finishes prevent foods from sticking to cookware and bakeware. The coating may be applied to both the inside and outside of items for easier cooking and cleanup. The effectiveness of a nonstick finish depends on the type of finish and how it is applied.

Nonstick finishes have been associated with various health issues. If you choose to use pieces with nonstick finishes, avoid allowing them to overheat. Nonstick cookware can release *toxic* (poisonous) chemicals when heated to high temperatures. Use cooking and cleaning tools designed for nonstick cookware to prevent scratching. Avoid using pieces that have become scratched.

Microwavable Materials

The main requirement for a microwave cookware material is that microwaves must be able to pass through it. Otherwise, the microwaves will not be able to reach the food. Microwaves can pass through materials such as ceramic, plastics, glass, wood, and paper. These materials can all be used for cooking in a microwave oven **(Figure 3.17)**.

Metal cookware reflects microwaves and keeps them from cooking food in a microwave

Pyrex®

Figure 3.17   Glass material and ventable lids make these containers a good choice for microwave cooking. How does the shape of these containers affect their performance in a microwave oven?

oven. However, some microwave dishes have special metal surfaces to brown foods. Before using these or any metal items in a microwave oven, check the oven use and care guide.

Not all containers made from microwavable materials are microwave safe. For instance, cookware made from microwavable material should not be used if it has bands of metal trim. The trim can cause sparking. Foam takeout containers and disposable plastic containers from margarine and whipped toppings are not recommended for microwave cooking. They are made of materials that may melt when they come in contact with hot food. This can cause chemicals and toxins from the materials to get into the food **(Figure 3.18)**. Containers that absorb liquid, such as wooden bowls, should not be used when microwaving liquids. The moisture absorbed by such containers will attract microwave energy away from the food.

ThamKC/Shutterstock.com

Duplass/Shutterstock.com

Olha Afanasieva/Shutterstock.com

Figure 3.18 Using these materials when microwaving can introduce undesirable chemicals into the food or damage the microwave.

Use and Care of Cookware and Bakeware

To maintain cookware and bakeware, proper use and care are essential. Note the temperatures and types of cooking for which pieces are designed to be used. Certain materials tolerate only specified temperatures. For instance, many glass pieces are designed for use in the oven but cannot withstand the direct heat of a rangetop or broiler. Solid cast iron skillets can be put in an oven. However, oven heat might damage pans with plastic or wooden handles.

Cast iron skillets and some other metal cookware and bakeware pieces need to be *seasoned*, or treated in preparation for use. Seasoning helps protect pieces as well as gives them some nonstick properties and makes them easier to clean. The recommended method for seasoning varies, depending on the piece and the material. Generally, it involves washing and drying the piece, applying a thin coat of cooking oil or shortening, and heating. You need to use care to maintain seasoned surfaces, including repeating the seasoning process from time to time.

Cookware and bakeware pieces may have some special cleaning considerations. Avoid using soap on seasoned pieces, as this can remove the seasoning. Simply wash seasoned pieces in hot water using a cloth or sponge. Do not use steel wool pads or abrasive cleaners, which can scratch cookware and bakeware. A nylon scrubber can be used to remove stuck-on

food **(Figure 3.19)**. Wash stainless steel pieces by hand to avoid dulling from harsh dishwasher detergents. Drying pieces promptly with a soft towel will prevent water spots. Some pieces may require polishing to keep them looking bright and shiny.

Always read the use and care information that accompanies cookware and bakeware. Follow manufacturer's directions for use and cleaning.

Swapan Photography/Shutterstock.com

Figure 3.19 Use nylon scrubbers to preserve finishes on cookware and bakeware.

Chapter 3 Review and Expand

Summary

Getting ready to work in the kitchen begins with learning a few basic skills. You must know the correct ways to measure different types of ingredients. You need to be familiar with how to use common kitchen utensils for various measuring, mixing, baking, and cutting tasks. You will have to demonstrate the ability to safely use knives to cut foods, too.

Along with utensils, you should be able to recognize standard pieces of cookware and bakeware. In addition to knowing how these items are used, you need to learn what to look for when you buy equipment. This includes understanding some of the pros and cons of the various materials from which kitchen equipment is made. It is also important to find out how to care for equipment to help it perform well and last a long time.

Vocabulary Activities

1. **Content Terms** On a separate sheet of paper, list words that relate to each of the following terms. Then work with a partner to explain how these words are related.

whisk	pot
colander	double boiler
serrated blade	springform pan
chef's knife	casserole
saucepan	nonstick finish

2. **Academic Terms** With a partner, create a T-chart. Write each of the following academic terms in the left column. Write a *synonym* (a word that has the same or similar meaning) for each term in the right column. Discuss your synonyms with the class.

pitting	fused
alloy	toxic

Review

Write your answers using complete sentences when appropriate.

3. What types of ingredients are measured with measuring spoons?

4. True or false. When measuring a liquid ingredient, the measuring cup should be held up so the mark on the cup for the desired amount is at eye level.

5. Why do you need to tare a kitchen scale before weighing an ingredient?

6. What is the function of a whisk?

7. Which type of spatula would be used to level ingredients in dry measuring cups?

8. What type of thermometer is inserted into a food at the end of cooking time?

9. List four uses for kitchen shears.

10. A perforated bowl used to drain fruits, vegetables, and pasta is a _____.

11. What is one of the smallest knives used in the kitchen?

12. When cutting with a chef's knife, what is the function of the hand that is not holding the knife?

13. What are three recommendations for storing knives to help prevent damage and cuts?

14. What is the difference between a saucepan and a pot?

15. What piece of bakeware is used to make sheet cakes?

16. What is an advantage of transparent glass as a cookware and bakeware material?

17. Which cookware material reflects microwaves and keeps food from cooking in a microwave oven?

18. Why do cast iron skillets and some other metal cookware and bakeware pieces need to be seasoned?

Core Skills

19. **Reading, Research, Speaking, Technology** Research a kitchen utensil used in the seventeenth or eighteenth century. Prepare an oral report for the class on how the utensil was used. Be sure to explain what tool or tools would be used today to perform the functions of the antique utensil. Download a sketch or photograph of the utensil from the Internet to use as a visual aid.

Chapter 3 Review and Expand

20. **Science, Research**   Seek out reliable print or Internet sources to learn how to perform the boiling water test and the ice bath test for checking the accuracy of thermometers. Test the accuracy of several types of kitchen thermometers using both of these testing methods.

21. **Research, Speaking**   Investigate benefits and concerns associated with the various materials used as nonstick finishes on cookware and bakeware. Prepare for and participate in a class debate about whether these finishes should be used in the kitchen.

22. **Math**   Suppose you are measuring peanut butter. You begin with 1½ cups of cold water in a container. After you add the peanut butter to the water, the water level reads 2¼ cups. What is the volume of the peanut butter?

23. **Technology, Math**   Make a list of cookware and bakeware pieces a single person would need in his or her first apartment. Then visit the website of a retailer that sells cookware and bakeware. Figure how much it would cost to equip this hypothetical kitchen.

24. **Science, Writing**   Do a simple test to compare the performance of various microwavable materials. Choose three pieces of cookware with similar dimensions, each made from a different microwavable material. For instance, you might choose 2-quart (2 L) casseroles made from glass, ceramic, and stoneware. (For fire safety reasons, remember not to use any metal cookware in a microwave oven.) Test each piece of cookware individually by filling it with 2 cups (500 mL) of water. Measure and record the temperature of the water. Then place the cookware in the microwave oven and turn the oven on high power for one minute. Remove the cookware from the oven and measure and record the temperature of the water again. Repeat this test with the other two pieces of cookware. On an observation sheet, record the cookware materials, the results of the tests, and your conclusions about each material.

25. **Career Readiness Practice**   Your store manager overheard you explaining the directions for using types of thermometers to a client. The manager asks you to demonstrate the proper use, care, cleaning, and storage

of thermometers to a group of clients at the monthly cooking class. You will use the store's equipment. Be sure to consider the makeup of your audience as you prepare your demonstration and ask yourself the following questions:

- Would a formal or informal presentation style be more effective?
- How long can I expect to keep my audience's attention?
- What level of vocabulary is best suited to this audience?

Critical Thinking and Problem Solving

26. **Assess**   Measure a cup (250 mL) of flour by spooning it into a dry measuring cup until it is overfilled. Then use a straight-edged spatula to level off any excess. Measure a second cup (250 mL) of flour by filling a dry measuring cup. Tap the cup to settle the flour, and then add more flour as needed to fill the cup again. Use a kitchen scale to separately weigh the contents of each measuring cup. Explain how failure to use proper measuring techniques could affect the outcome of food products.

27. **Analyze**   Use safe and proper knife skills to cut 1 cup (250 mL) of ¾-inch (19 mm) diced potatoes. Then cut 1 cup (250 mL) of ½-inch (13 mm) diced potatoes and 1 cup (250 mL) of ¼-inch (6 mm) diced potatoes. Put each of the potato sizes in a separate identical bowl. Microwave each bowl of potatoes on high power for one minute. Compare the firmness of the three sizes of cooked potatoes. Draw conclusions about how cutting foods in uniform pieces will affect evenness of cooking.

28. **Assess**   Investigate how kitchen utensils are developed and promoted in a competitive market. Identify features and characteristics manufacturers use to encourage consumers to choose their products over similar products from other manufacturers.

Chapter 4
Recipes and Work Plans

©iStock.com/Tonygers

Objectives

After studying this chapter, you will be able to

- **identify** abbreviations and **define** cooking terms used in recipes;
- **change** the yield of a recipe;
- **determine** the cost per serving of a recipe;
- **explain** terms and techniques used in microwave recipes; and
- **plan** time-work schedules.

Reading Prep

Write what you think each Chapter 4 Content and Academic term means. Then look up the term in the glossary and write the textbook definition.

Content Terms 🔗

recipe
yield
cooking time
watt
standing time
dehydration
arcing
time-work schedule
dovetail

Academic Terms

distinctive
customary
leaching
promote

Cooking skills are not essential to satisfy hunger. You can buy foods that require little or no preparation. However, you can add unlimited variety and interest to meals when you know how to prepare foods from scratch.

Each type of food requires some specific knowledge about how to select, store, and prepare. However, some general information applies to nearly all foods. Learning how to follow a recipe and plan your use of time in the kitchen will benefit you no matter what dish you are making.

Using Recipes

A **recipe** is a set of instructions for preparing a specific food. Cookbooks are popular sources of recipes. Magazines, newspapers, appliance manuals, and recipe software can all be good places to find recipes, too. A meal manager can use these resources to help plan and prepare daily meals.

You can also explore numerous recipe websites on the Internet. Many sites allow you to search for recipes using factors such as type of dish, cuisine, and preparation method. You can easily adjust the number of servings and make a printout of any recipe. Many sites allow you to prepare food budgets, shopping lists, nutritional analyses, and adjust the number of servings. You can often save favorite recipes in a personal online recipe file as well.

Good recipes are written in a clear, concise manner. A recipe should list ingredients in the order in which you will be combining them. Amounts should be easy to measure. Directions for mixing and/or handling procedures must be complete, specifying required equipment when necessary. Baking or cooking times and temperatures and pan sizes need to be accurate. The recipe should state the **yield**, which is the average amount or number of servings a recipe makes. Many recipes include a nutritional analysis to help you evaluate how the food fits into a healthy diet. Some also include a photo of how the prepared food product should look **(Figure 4.1)**.

A recipe is your work plan for the food you are going to prepare. Read through the recipe before you begin to prepare it. This ensures that you understand the directions and have all the needed ingredients. As you read through a recipe, remember the four basic steps for keeping foods safe to eat—clean, separate, cook, and chill. Avoid recipes that include unsafe practices, such

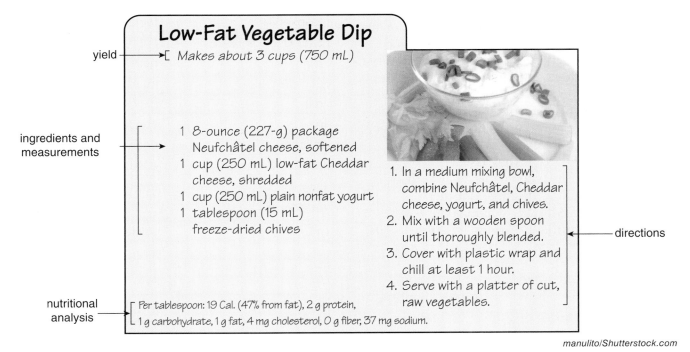

yield

Low-Fat Vegetable Dip

Makes about 3 cups (750 mL)

ingredients and measurements

1 8-ounce (227-g) package Neufchâtel cheese, softened
1 cup (250 mL) low-fat Cheddar cheese, shredded
1 cup (250 mL) plain nonfat yogurt
1 tablespoon (15 mL) freeze-dried chives

1. In a medium mixing bowl, combine Neufchâtel, Cheddar cheese, yogurt, and chives.
2. Mix with a wooden spoon until thoroughly blended.
3. Cover with plastic wrap and chill at least 1 hour.
4. Serve with a platter of cut, raw vegetables.

directions

nutritional analysis

Per tablespoon: 19 Cal. (47% from fat), 2 g protein, 1 g carbohydrate, 1 g fat, 4 mg cholesterol, 0 g fiber, 37 mg sodium.

Figure 4.1 A well-written recipe should include all the information needed to prepare a particular food. What equipment would be needed to prepare this recipe?

as marinating meat at room temperature. When you are ready to begin, reread the recipe one step at a time. Follow the directions carefully as you prepare the product.

Learn About...

Adjusting Recipes for High-Altitude Cooking

Atmospheric pressure decreases at high altitudes. At an altitude of 3,000 feet (914 m), this decrease begins to affect the outcome of food products. As the altitude increases, so does the effect on food. If you are cooking at high altitudes, you may need to make some adjustments to your recipes.

Water boils at a lower temperature at high altitudes. Therefore, most foods cooked in liquid will require more cooking time. Liquids also evaporate faster at high altitudes. You may need to add extra liquid when preparing some foods. You may need to reduce the temperature of deep fat to keep foods from overbrowning before they are thoroughly cooked.

Breads and cakes tend to rise more during baking at high altitudes. To account for this, oven temperature may need to be increased by 25°F (4°C). This will help set the batter before air cells formed by leavening gases have a chance to expand too much. A decreased baking time may be needed to keep foods from overcooking at the higher oven temperatures. Reducing the amount of leavening agents used in recipes will help compensate for excess rising. Using larger baking pans will also keep baked goods from overflowing the pans as they rise.

For best results when cooking at high altitudes, choose recipes designed for high-altitude cooking. Many commercial mixes include high-altitude directions on the package.

Know and Apply

1. In what areas of the United States would recipes need to be adjusted for high altitude?

2. Give an example of a food product that is cooked in liquid that might require an increased cooking time at high altitudes.

Abbreviations

The amounts of ingredients listed in recipes are often given as abbreviations. You must be able to interpret these abbreviations. This ensures that you include ingredients in the right proportions. Common recipe abbreviations are listed in **Figure 4.2**.

Ingredient Substitutions

When evaluating a recipe, one factor to consider is the list of ingredients. You should review the ingredients to determine if they
- sound appealing to you
- present an allergy concern for anyone who will be eating the food
- are on hand in your pantry or must be purchased

If there is an issue with any of the ingredients, you may be able to solve the problem by making a substitution.

Abbreviations Used in Recipes	
Customary	
tsp. or t.	teaspoon
tbsp. or T.	tablespoon
c. or C.	cup
pt.	pint
qt.	quart
gal.	gallon
oz.	ounce
lb. or #	pound
doz.	dozen
pkg.	package
SI (Metric)	
mL	milliliter
L	liter
g	gram
kg	kilogram

Figure 4.2 Abbreviations are often used for units of measurement in recipes.

Suppose you are looking at a recipe for potato salad. The ingredient list includes dill pickle relish, which you do not like. In this case, you have three main options. You might simply decide to look for a different recipe. You could choose to keep an open mind and try the recipe, hoping that the flavor combination will be surprisingly tasty. Your third option is to make an ingredient substitution.

When substituting an ingredient, you need to think about the functions that ingredient plays in the recipe. The dill pickle relish adds volume and consistency as well as *distinctive* (unique) flavors to the salad dressing. If there is only a small amount of relish in the recipe, you may be able to just omit it. If the relish makes up more than 10 percent of the volume of the dressing, omitting it may result in too little dressing. If you like sweet pickle relish, you could substitute an equal amount of that.

Suppose your potato salad recipe also calls for yellow mustard, but you discover that you do not have any. Although the required amount is small, you do not want to omit the flavor the mustard gives the recipe. In this case, you could substitute an ingredient such as prepared horseradish, which will give the dressing a similar bite of flavor.

You know that mayonnaise in your potato salad recipe is high in fat and provides a lot of calories. You might decide to substitute plain yogurt, which has a similar consistency but is lower in fat and calories.

A few common ingredient substitutions are shown in **Figure 4.3**. You can also find many others by searching for ingredient substitutions on the Internet.

Substituting One Ingredient for Another		
Ingredient	**Amount**	**Substitution**
Baking powder	1 teaspoon (5 mL)	¼ teaspoon (1.25 mL) baking soda plus ½ teaspoon (2.5 mL) cream of tartar
Broth, beef or chicken	1 cup (250 mL)	1 bouillon cube plus 1 cup (250 mL) boiling water or 1 tablespoon (15 mL) soy sauce plus enough water to make 1 cup (250 mL)
Brown sugar	1 cup (250 mL), packed	1 cup (250 mL) white sugar plus ¼ cup (60 mL) molasses and decrease the liquid in recipe by ¼ cup (60 mL)
Butter	1 cup (250 mL)	1 cup (250 mL) margarine or shortening 1 cup (250 mL) vegetable oil can be substituted if the recipe calls for *melted* butter
Buttermilk	1 cup (250 mL)	1 cup (250 mL) yogurt or 1 tablespoon (15 mL) vinegar or lemon juice plus milk to make 1 cup (250 mL) (Allow this mixture to stand several minutes before using.)
Chocolate, unsweetened	1 ounce (28 g)	3 tablespoons (45 mL) unsweetened cocoa powder plus 1 tablespoon (15 mL) butter or margarine
Corn syrup	1 cup (250 mL)	1 cup (250 mL) honey or 1¼ cups (310 mL) sugar plus ¼ cup (60 mL) liquid used in recipe
Cornstarch	1 tablespoon (15 mL)	2 tablespoons (30 mL) flour
Cream, heavy	1 cup (250 mL)	¾ cup (185 mL) milk plus ⅓ cup (80 mL) butter
Egg yolks	2	1 whole egg, for baking or thickening
Flour, cake	1 cup (250 mL)	⅞ cup (220 mL) all-purpose flour
Milk, fat-free	1 cup (250 mL)	1 cup (250 mL) reconstituted nonfat dry milk
Milk, whole	1 cup (250 mL)	½ cup (125 mL) evaporated milk plus ½ cup (125 mL) water

Figure 4.3 When substituting one ingredient for another, you may have to adjust the amount used.

Mini Lab: Substituting Ingredients

Breakfast Basket Scones

Each lab group will prepare the following recipe as directed. For groups making ingredient substitutions, refer to the table in Figure 4.3.

- **Lab group 1**—Prepare the recipe as written, making no ingredient substitutions.
- **Lab group 2**—Prepare the recipe with a substitution for the baking powder.
- **Lab group 3**—Prepare the recipe with a substitution for the brown sugar.
- **Lab group 4**—Prepare the recipe with a substitution for the melted butter.
- **Lab group 5**—Prepare the recipe with a substitution for the buttermilk.
- **Lab group 6**—Prepare the recipe with substitutions for the baking powder, brown sugar, melted butter, and buttermilk.

©iStock.com/fotogal

1½	cups (375 mL) all-purpose flour
1½	teaspoons (7.5 mL) baking powder
¼	teaspoon (1.25 mL) salt
3	tablespoons (45 mL) brown sugar
¼	cup (60 mL) butter, melted
⅔	cup (160 mL) buttermilk

1. Preheat oven to 425°F (220°C).
2. In a large mixing bowl, whisk together flour, baking powder, salt, and brown sugar. Stir in melted butter and buttermilk. Mix just until moistened.
3. Drop large spoonfuls of dough onto a baking sheet covered with parchment paper or a nonstick baking mat. Bake in the preheated oven for 10 to 15 minutes, or until lightly brown and fully set. Serve warm.

Place prepared scones on a plate labeled with the appropriate ingredient substitution(s). All students should sample all versions of the recipe. Compare the taste, texture, and appearance of each variation with the unaltered recipe. Also compare the taste, texture, and appearance of the recipes with a single substitution to the recipe with multiple substitutions. Note any differences you can attribute to the ingredient substitutions.

Makes 8 scones

Per scone (original recipe): 164 calories (33% from fat), 3 g protein, 24 g carbohydrate, 6 g fat, 16 mg cholesterol, 1 g fiber, 228 mg sodium

Changing Yield

Some recipes make more or less of a food product than you want. For instance, a recipe might make four dozen chocolate chip cookies. When making them for a large group, you may want twice that many. A recipe for a chicken and rice casserole might make eight servings. When preparing dinner for four, you might want only half that amount. Knowing the *measuring*

equivalents shown in **Figure 4.4** will help you *scale*, or adjust the yield of, a recipe.

Customary (usual) units of measure used in recipes are teaspoons, tablespoons, and cups. Changing the yield of a customary recipe can be tricky. You may have to convert from one unit to another. For instance, 3 teaspoons is the equivalent of 1 tablespoon. Suppose you are doubling a recipe that calls for 1½ teaspoons of baking soda. Two times 1½ teaspoons equals

Common Equivalent Measures

Customary Measure	Customary Equivalent	Approximate SI Equivalent*
¼ teaspoon	—	1.25 milliliter
½ teaspoon	—	2.5 milliliters
1 teaspoon	—	5 milliliters
3 teaspoons	1 tablespoon	15 milliliters
2 tablespoons	⅛ cup	30 milliliters
4 tablespoons	¼ cup	60 milliliters
5⅓ tablespoons	⅓ cup	80 milliliters
8 tablespoons	½ cup	125 milliliters
10⅔ tablespoons	⅔ cup	160 milliliters
12 tablespoons	¾ cup	185 milliliters
16 tablespoons	1 cup, ½ pint	250 milliliters
2 cups	1 pint	500 milliliters
4 cups	1 quart	1 liter

*Based on measures seen on standard SI equipment.

Figure 4.4 Memorizing common equivalent measures makes cooking easier. Use the information in this table to calculate how many tablespoons make one cup.

3 teaspoons, or 1 tablespoon. Likewise, ¼ cup equals 4 tablespoons. Suppose you are halving a recipe that calls for ¼ cup sugar. You can easily figure half of 4 tablespoons is 2 tablespoons. Figure the adjusted amounts of each ingredient before you begin cooking. Write the adjusted amounts on your recipe so you remember them as you work. Sample scaling calculations for some common ingredient amounts are shown in **Figure 4.5**.

The main SI (metric) unit of measure used in recipes is the milliliter. Changing the yield of a recipe with SI units is easy. You do not have to convert from one unit to another.

Cooking Terms

Recipes use a variety of terms to describe exactly how ingredients are to be handled. For instance, a recipe that includes carrots is not likely to tell you to just *cut* the carrots. This term is too general to let you know how the carrots should look in the finished product. Instead, the recipe might tell you to slice, dice, or shred the carrots. Becoming familiar with specific cooking terms will help your food products turn out as expected.

Recipe Scaling

Ingredient	Original Ingredient Amount	Double Recipe	New Amount (= Equivalent Measure)
All-purpose flour	1½ cups	× 2	3 cups
Baking powder	1½ teaspoons	× 2	3 teaspoons (= 1 tablespoon)
Salt	¼ teaspoon	× 2	½ teaspoon
Brown sugar	3 tablespoons	× 2	6 tablespoons (= 3/8 cup)
Butter, melted	¼ cup	× 2	½ cup
Buttermilk	⅔ cup	× 2	4/3 cup (= 1⅓ cup)
Ingredient	**Original Ingredient Amount**	**Halve Recipe**	**New Ingredient Amount (= Equivalent Measure)**
All-purpose flour	1½ cups	÷ 2	¾ cup
Baking powder	1½ teaspoons	÷ 2	¾ teaspoon
Salt	¼ teaspoon	÷ 2	⅛ teaspoon
Brown sugar	3 tablespoons	÷ 2	1½ tablespoons (= 4½ teaspoons)
Butter, melted	¼ cup	÷ 2	⅛ cup (= 2 tablespoons)
Buttermilk	⅔ cup	÷ 2	⅓ cup

Figure 4.5 Sometimes it is necessary to convert from one unit of measure to another to calculate ingredient amounts when scaling a recipe up or down.

Glossary of Food Preparation Terms

Bacho/Shutterstock.com

bake: To cook in the oven with dry heat.

MilanMarkovic78/Shutterstock.com

blend: To stir ingredients until they are thoroughly combined.

tlorna /Shutterstock.com

baste: To spoon pan juices, melted fat, or another liquid over the surface of food during cooking to keep the food moist and add flavor.

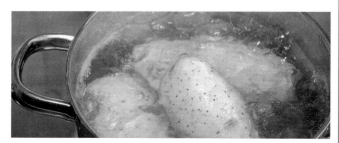

Ansebach/Shutterstock.com

boil: To cook in liquid at 212°F (100°C).

ffolas /Shutterstock.com

beat: To mix ingredients together with a circular up-and-down motion using a spoon, whisk, or electric mixer.

Anna Hoychuk/Shutterstock.com

braise: To cook in a small amount of liquid in a tightly covered pan over low heat.

kungverylucky/Shutterstock.com

blanch: To scald or parboil in water or steam.

©iStock.com/Serenethos

broil: To cook uncovered under a direct source of heat.

(Continued)

Glossary of Food Preparation Terms *(Continued)*

Shebeko/Shutterstock.com

brown: To turn the surface of a food brown by placing it under a broiler or quickly cooking it in hot fat.

IngridHS/Shutterstock.com

chill: To make a food cold by placing it in a refrigerator or in a bowl with ice.

Krzysztof Slusarczyk/Shutterstock.com

chop: To cut into small pieces.

ffolas/Shutterstock.com

coat: To thoroughly cover a food with a liquid or dry mixture.

karamysh/Shutterstock.com

combine: To mix or blend two or more ingredients.

Warren Price Photography/Shutterstock.com

core: To remove the center part of a fruit such as an apple or pineapple.

Chalermsak/Shutterstock.com

cream: To soften solid fats, often by adding a second ingredient, such as sugar, and working with a wooden spoon or an electric mixer until the fat is creamy.

Charlotte Lake/Shutterstock.com

cut in: To combine solid fat with flour using a pastry blender, two forks, or fingers.

(Continued)

Glossary of Food Preparation Terms *(Continued)*

Africa Studio/Shutterstock.com

deep-fry: To cook in a large amount of hot fat.

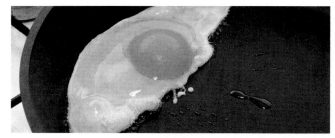

lyf1/Shutterstock.com

fry: To cook in a small amount of hot fat.

LeoWolfert/Shutterstock.com

dice: To cut into small cubes of even size.

Teri Virbickis/Shutterstock.com

grate: To reduce a food into small bits by rubbing it on the sharp teeth of a utensil.

ffolas/Shutterstock.com

flour: To sprinkle or coat with flour.

wsf-s/Shutterstock.com

grease: To rub fat on the surface of a cooking utensil or on a food itself.

gourmetphotography/Shutterstock.com

fold: To incorporate a delicate mixture into a thicker, heavier mixture with a whisk or flexible spatula using a down, up, and over motion so the finished product remains light.

WAYHOME Studio/Shutterstock.com

knead: To work dough by pressing it with the heels of the hands, folding it, turning it, and repeating each motion until the dough is smooth and elastic.

(Continued)

Glossary of Food Preparation Terms *(Continued)*

Robyn Mackenzie/Shutterstock.com

marinate: To soak meat in a solution containing an acid, such as vinegar or lemon juice, that helps tenderize the connective tissue.

Angel Simon/Shutterstock.com

mince: To cut or chop into very fine pieces.

Oleksandr Briagin/Shutterstock.com

panbroil: To cook without fat in an uncovered skillet.

Paul Vasarhelyi/Shutterstock.com

panfry: To cook larger pieces of food in a skillet in about ¼ inch of fat or oil.

StudioFI/Shutterstock.com

parboil: To boil in liquid until partially cooked.

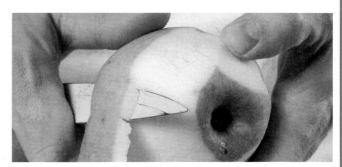

ffolas/Shutterstock.com

pare: To remove the stem and outer covering of a vegetable or fruit with a paring knife or peeler.

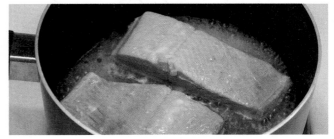

Serenethos/Shutterstock.com

poach: To cook gently in a moderate temperature liquid.

Kostenko Maxim/Shutterstock.com

preheat: To heat an appliance to a desired temperature about 15 minutes before it is to be used.

(Continued)

Glossary of Food Preparation Terms *(Continued)*

marco mayer/Shutterstock.com

puree: To put food through a fine sieve or a food mill to form a thick and smooth liquid.

Steve Cukrov/Shutterstock.com

roast: To cook uncovered in the oven with dry heat.

threerocksimages/Shutterstock.com

roll: To flatten dough to an even thickness with a rolling pin.

ffolas/Shutterstock.com

sauté: To cook small pieces of food in only enough fat or oil to coat the bottom of the pan.

imagedb/Shutterstock.com

scald: To heat liquid to just below the boiling point; to dip food into boiling water or pour boiling water over the food.

Joe Gough/Shutterstock.com

sear: To brown the surface of a food very quickly with high heat.

vvoe/Shutterstock.com

shred: To cut or break into thin pieces.

ffolas/Shutterstock.com

sift: To put through a sifter or sieve to reduce to finer particles.

(Continued)

Glossary of Food Preparation Terms *(Continued)*

Joe Belanger/Shutterstock.com

simmer: To cook slowly and gently in liquid that is below the boiling point.

Lilyana Vynogradova/Shutterstock.com

skim: To remove a substance from the surface of a liquid.

marekuliasz/Shutterstock.com

steam: To cook with vapor produced by a boiling liquid.

Stephen Gibson/Shutterstock.com

stew: To cook one food or several foods together in a seasoned liquid for a long period.

Nielskliim/Shutterstock.com

stir: To mix with a circular motion.

3445128471/Shutterstock.com

stir-fry: To cook foods quickly in a small amount of fat over high heat while stirring constantly.

Paul Hakimata Photography/Shutterstock.com

toss: To mix lightly.

kazoka/Shutterstock.com

whip: To beat quickly and steadily by hand with a whisk.

Recipe Costing

Recipe costing is a method used to find out how much it costs to prepare a recipe. Restaurant managers use recipe costing to decide how much to charge for menu items. At home, recipe costing can be used to see how a particular recipe fits into the food budget.

To figure the cost of a recipe, you will need your ingredient list and your grocery store receipt **(Figure 4.6).** You may also require some information from food product labels. You will want to have a calculator handy, too. Then follow the steps in **Figure 4.7** to learn how to complete a Recipe Costing Worksheet.

Most meal managers do not find it necessary to figure the cost of every recipe. However, costing a few favorite recipes can provide information about which ingredients tend to be most expensive. Recipe costing can also help in menu planning. A higher cost main dish can be paired with lower cost side dishes to keep meals within the household food budget.

Microwave Recipes

Many people use their microwave ovens mainly for defrosting and reheating foods and making popcorn. However, you can also cook foods in a microwave oven if you have a little specific knowledge. Understanding some terms and techniques found in microwave recipes can help you make better use of this versatile appliance.

Microwave cooking times vary, depending on the power of the microwave oven being used. **Cooking time** in a microwave recipe refers to the total amount of time food is exposed to microwave energy. Microwave cooking power is measured in units of power called **watts**. Most oven models produce a maximum of 600 to 1,200 watts. More watts mean faster cooking. For best results, you should always start with the shortest microwave cooking time stated in a recipe. Then check to see if more time is needed.

Many microwave recipes specify **standing time**. This is the time during which foods finish cooking by internal heat after being removed from a microwave oven. For instance, a recipe for baked potatoes may specify four minutes of cooking time and five minutes of standing time. Microwaving foods until they are fully cooked, without allowing for the additional cooking that takes place during standing time, can result in overcooking. Overcooking can cause **dehydration**, or drying out of foods. Wrapping foods in aluminum foil will help hold in heat during standing time.

Bruschetta Salad

Serves 2

1 tablespoon (15 mL) extra virgin olive oil
1 tablespoon (15 mL) red wine vinegar
¼ teaspoon (1.25 mL) fresh ground pepper
1 clove garlic, minced
¼ cup (60 mL) chopped onion
10 pimento-stuffed green olives, chopped
1 Roma tomato, seeded and chopped
1 heart of romaine lettuce
2 tablespoons (30 mL) grated Parmesan cheese
¼ cup (60 mL) seasoned croutons
fresh basil, chopped

©iStock.com/ilmoro100

1. In a medium glass bowl, whisk together olive oil, vinegar, pepper, and garlic. Add chopped onion, olives, and tomato and toss to coat. Allow to sit for 10 minutes.
2. Tear lettuce into bite-sized pieces and place in a large serving bowl.
3. Spoon tomato mixture over top of lettuce. Sprinkle with grated Parmesan cheese and top with seasoned croutons. Serve with fresh basil.

Per serving: 160 cal. (68% from fat), 4 g protein, 10 g carbohydrate, 12 g fat, 5 mg cholesterol, 4 g fiber, 425 mg sodium.

SAVE MART Receipt	
SEASND CROUTONS	1.59
STFD OLIVES 10 OZ.	3.29
PARM CHEESE 8 OZ.	5.99
ROM LETTUCE HRTS	2.99
ROMA TOMATO	.69
FF BASIL .75 OZ.	2.49
WHT ONION	.79

Figure 4.6 Refer to this recipe and store receipt as you follow the steps in the Recipe Costing Procedure in **Figure 4.7.**

Recipe Costing Procedure

The following steps explain how to cost a recipe, using the recipe and store receipt shown in Figure 4.6:

1. On paper or using a computer, make a Recipe Costing Worksheet (below).
2. List all the needed Ingredients and their Amounts in the first two columns.
3. Use the grocery store receipt to figure the Cost of each item.
   - If you used an entire food product, list the full price on the receipt.
   - If you used only part of a food product, divide the price on the receipt by the portion used. Write the divided cost in the table. For instance, a package of romaine hearts contains three hearts. This recipe calls for just one heart, so the price of the romaine hearts is divided by three ($2.99 ÷ 3 = $1.00).
   - For some items, you must look at the Nutrition Facts panel to see how many servings are in a package or container. Determine how many servings you used from the package. Divide the price of the product by the number of servings per container. Then multiply by the number of servings used.
   - For ingredients such as seasonings and condiments that are used in very small or variable amounts, computing specific costs may be difficult. This recipe calls for just ¼ teaspoon of black pepper. The recipe is served with chopped fresh basil. One way to account for these types of ingredients is to add a small percentage after calculating a subtotal. (Foodservice establishments call this percentage the **Q** factor, in which Q stands for questionable ingredients.) Five percent should be enough to account for these ingredients in many recipes.
4. Add all the ingredient costs you have calculated to figure a Subtotal.
5. Calculate the 5 percent Q factor by multiplying the subtotal from step 5 by 0.05. The Q factor for this recipe is $0.15 ($2.98 × 0.05 = $0.15).
6. Add the calculated Q factor to the Subtotal for the Total cost of the recipe.
7. Divide the Total cost by the number of servings to figure the Cost per Serving.

1 Recipe Costing Worksheet		
2 Ingredient	2 Amount	3 Cost
olive oil	1 tablespoon (15 mL)	$0.17
red wine vinegar	1 tablespoon (15 mL)	0.02
pepper	¼ teaspoon (1.25 mL)	*
garlic	1 clove	0.10
chopped onion	¼ cup (60 mL)	0.13
olives	10 each	0.34
Roma tomato	1 each	0.69
heart of romaine lettuce	1 each	1.00
grated Parmesan cheese	2 tablespoons (30 mL)	0.37
croutons	¼ cup (60 mL)	0.16
fresh basil	?	*
4 Subtotal		2.98
5 *Q factor (5% of subtotal)		0.15
6 Total		3.13
Number of servings (divide into total)		2
7 Cost per serving		$1.57

Figure 4.7 Match the procedure steps circled in red to the matching numbers on the worksheet.

Global Perspective

SI – The Metric System

The SI is often referred to as the metric system. SI stands for a French term that means International System of Units. This is the standard of weights and measures used by most countries around the world.

Government agencies and many industries in the United States use SI units. This aids international trade and allows U.S. companies to better compete in the global marketplace.

U.S. consumers use SI units every day. An athlete might take a 200 mg pain reliever tablet with a 450 mL bottle of juice to reduce muscle soreness after running a 5,000 m race. However, that same athlete may have listed his weight in customary pounds and his height in feet and inches on the race registration form.

In U.S. kitchens, most food products and many pieces of equipment are labeled with both SI and customary units. However, many recipes list ingredients in only customary measures, such as cups and ounces. As more products are marketed in primarily SI quantities, it is likely that more SI recipes will begin to appear. When SI recipes become the standard, cooks will be able to use conversion tables or software to easily adjust traditional recipes.

digitalreflections

Most food products include SI as well as customary units on their labels.

Covering Foods

Many microwave recipes state that you should cover foods during cooking. Covering distributes heat more evenly and helps foods retain moisture so they will not dry out. The steam held in by the cover can help speed cooking time and tenderize foods. Covers are also useful for preventing spatters inside the microwave oven.

Several materials can be used to cover foods in a microwave oven. Tight fitting casserole lids are excellent for foods that require steam for cooking. Waxed paper works well as a loose covering. Covering foods with paper towels will help absorb spatters. (Choose paper towels designed for microwave use, as they are free of materials not approved for food contact.)

Some health concerns are linked with the use of plastic wrap in microwave ovens. If you choose to cover food containers with plastic wrap, take care to keep the wrap from directly touching the food. This will help prevent the possibility of chemicals in the wrap from *leaching* (seeping) into food during heating.

Recipes often recommend *venting* food covers during microwave cooking. This means creating a small opening in the cover or allowing a slight gap between the cover and the container. A vent allows steam to escape and prevents a buildup of pressure in the food container.

Not all foods require a cover in the microwave oven. You may leave some foods uncovered to allow excess moisture to evaporate. You may need to cover other foods for only part of the cooking time. For best results, follow the directions in your recipe.

Evenness of Cooking

Microwaves are not always distributed evenly throughout the microwave oven cavity. This can cause foods to cook unevenly. Stirring foods partway through cooking will redistribute the heat and *promote* (encourage) more even cooking. Many microwave recipes also recommend rotating food at one or more intervals in the cooking period. (Turntables included in many microwave ovens rotate food automatically during the entire cooking cycle.)

Health and Wellness

Create Healthier Recipes

Recipes can easily be modified to boost nutrients that may be missing in your diet or to reduce others. Do not be afraid to use your imagination and try new combinations.

Most people in the United States do not consume enough vegetables. Experiment by adding new vegetables to your favorite casseroles. For instance, adding broccoli florets to your macaroni and cheese contributes color, texture, nutrients, and great flavor to the dish. Add vegetables, such as grated carrots, diced jalapeño peppers, or spinach, to tomato sauce for pasta. Replace some or all of the meat in a recipe with your favorite bean, such as pinto beans or chickpeas. Get creative and puree cooked beans or other vegetables to make your own signature sauces.

Bump up the whole grains in your recipes by replacing processed grains with whole grains. Use brown rice or whole-grain noodles to make casseroles. Substitute a portion of the flour in baked goods with whole-wheat flour. Sprinkle cooked grains such as faro or wheatberries on salads.

Replace butter in recipes with healthier fats such as canola and olive oils. Rather than spreading mayonnaise on your favorite sandwich, add avocado slices to supply richness, flavor, and nutrients. Try reinventing tuna salad by replacing mayonnaise with olive oil, seasonings, and a pepper relish such as giardiniera.

Foods tend to cook more slowly in the center of a container in a microwave oven. Therefore, recipes often suggest arranging individual foods, such as potatoes, in a circular pattern. They recommend placing large or dense foods, such as meats, around the edge of a dish. Arrange unevenly shaped foods, like chicken legs, with the thicker parts toward the outside of the container.

Some recipes recommend *shielding* areas of unevenly shaped foods that might overcook with small pieces of aluminum foil. Be sure to check

manufacturer's directions before using any type of metal in a microwave oven. The foil will reflect the microwaves so the covered areas will not continue to cook. However, microwaves will penetrate the uncovered areas, allowing them to finish cooking.

Use care to keep foil or any metal material away from microwave oven walls. When metal meets oven walls, **arcing**, or sparking, can occur. Intense arcing can cause oven failure. The presence of narrow bands of metal, such as wire twist ties and metal-trimmed china, can also cause arcing.

Browning Techniques

Many foods cook so quickly in a microwave oven they do not have time to brown. Lack of browning affects the appearance of a food, which in turn affects its appetite appeal.

Some microwave ovens have a convection cooking feature that circulates heated air and improves browning. If your microwave does not have such a feature, you can use gravies, sauces, or toppings to cover a lack of browning (**Figure 4.8**).

kostrez/Shutterstock.com

Figure 4.8 The appearance of foods cooked in a microwave oven can be enhanced by sauces, which hide the lack of browning. What other qualities of food products are affected by the use of sauces?

Using a Time-Work Schedule

When serving a meal, you would not want a side dish to finish cooking 20 minutes after you serve the main course. As a meal manager, you are responsible for making sure all the food is ready at the same time. You can accomplish this goal by using a **time-work schedule**. This is a written plan that lists times for doing specific tasks to prepare a meal or food product.

A time-work schedule should be specific enough to identify the order and timing of all the critical preparation steps. On the other hand, it should be flexible enough to allow you to make adjustments. If you underestimate your speed or need to substitute an ingredient, you may need this flexibility.

Preliminary Planning

Before writing your time-work schedule, you need to think about the tasks involved in preparing a meal. As you gather recipes for each menu item, think about the cooking methods required. Choosing two or more items that can be prepared by the same method can help you save time and energy. For instance, you can use the heat of the oven to roast chicken and carrots at the same time.

In addition to recipes, you will need a computer or paper and a pencil to create your schedule. You may also want a calculator to figure the total time required to prepare each food.

The following steps outline how to do some initial planning. The example shows completed plans for the meal in **Figure 4.9**.

Menu

Quinoa Egg Casserole

Melon Wedges

Milk

© 2015 Wisconsin Milk Marketing Board, Inc.

Figure 4.9   With planning, this nutritious breakfast can be prepared and served in under an hour.

1. Set up a *food preparation timetable*, as shown in **Figure 4.10**. List the menu items in the first column. Add table setting to this list because time needs to be reserved for this task.

2. Use the recipes to identify preparation tasks that must be done as you make each menu item. Remember, these tasks may appear in the ingredient list as well as in the recipe directions. For instance, a recipe might call for ½ cup (125 mL) chopped onions or 2 strips fried bacon.

Food Preparation Timetable					
Menu Item	**Preparation Time**	**Cooking Time**	**Serving Time**	**Total Time**	**Rank**
Quinoa Egg Casserole	15 minutes, divided	36 minutes	1 minute	52 minutes	1
Melon Wedges	5 minutes	—	1 minute	6 minutes	2
Milk	—	—	2 minutes	2 minutes	4
Table setting	3 minutes	—	—	3 minutes	3

Figure 4.10   A food preparation timetable helps you to prepare and serve a meal successfully.

List estimates in the table for the time required to prepare, cook, and serve each food. (Some recipes give estimated preparation and cooking times, which will help you with this step.)

3. Add the total time required to prepare each item and list these totals in the table.

4. In the last column, rank menu items in order of total time. The item ranked number *1* should be the food requiring the most time. This step will help you decide which menu items to prepare first.

Making a Schedule

Use the completed food preparation timetable to help plan the actual time-work schedule. The first decision to make when creating a time-work schedule is what time you want to begin eating the meal. Think about your daily activities and the activities of other diners when making this decision. Allow enough time to prepare the meal so you will not feel rushed. Allow other diners enough time to come to the meal leisurely. You may want to plan the serving time at least 15 minutes after a guest's intended arrival time. This will allow a time cushion for any unexpected delays.

Once you have decided when to begin eating the meal, the following steps will help you write the time-work schedule:

1. Set up a *time-work schedule* like the one in **Figure 4.11**. Write the time you plan to begin eating at the bottom of the time column. In this schedule, the plan is to begin eating at 8:00 a.m.

2. Add all the entries in the *serving time* column of the food preparation timetable. Work backward from the eating time to determine when to begin serving. A total of 4 minutes is needed to serve this meal, so serving needs to begin at 7:56 a.m.

3. Look at the *cooking time* column of the food preparation timetable. Work backward from the serving time and identify the time at which you should begin cooking each item. Be aware that some recipes include steps that will divide the cooking and preparation times.

This casserole is to be baked for 25 minutes. Then the bacon and eggs are added and it goes back into the oven for 5 more minutes. Finally, cheese is sprinkled on the casserole, and it finishes baking for 6 additional minutes. You need to add the intermediate preparation time to the cooking time to determine when to begin cooking.

Time-Work Schedule	
Time	**Tasks**
7:08 a.m.	Preheat oven. Heat broth. Rinse and drain quinoa. Wash and dry spinach. Butter baking dish. Open canned tomatoes. Grate cheese.
7:14 a.m.	Stir quinoa and cream cheese into boiling broth. Add spinach, tomatoes, and grated cheese. Pour into baking dish.
7:17 a.m.	Put casserole in oven. Fry bacon. Wash and cut melon. Set table. Start cleanup.
7:42 a.m.	Remove casserole from oven. Make 6 indentations in quinoa and place cooked bacon and raw egg into each indentation.
7:47 a.m.	Return casserole to oven. Continue cleanup.
7:52 a.m.	Remove casserole from oven. Sprinkle with remaining cheese. Return casserole to oven. Complete cleanup.
7:56 a.m.	Place melon on the table. Put glasses on the table and pour milk.
7:59 a.m.	Place casserole on the table.
8:00 a.m.	Eat.

Figure 4.11 Can you think of other areas of your life in which you could apply the time-work schedule?

Exploring Careers

Research Chef

Research chefs help develop recipes for mass production. They might work for restaurant chains to create new items that will appear on menus throughout the country. Some are employed by food manufacturers to craft products that will be prepared and eaten by millions of consumers. Research chefs are also hired by ingredient producers to come up with new ways to use and promote those ingredients.

To do their work, research chefs need more than just excellent cooking skills. They must have a scientific understanding of food products. They know how ingredients will interact to affect flavors and textures of prepared products. They can also predict how processing methods and cooking techniques will affect the characteristics of foods. Research chefs use reading skills to review consumer and industry data to keep up with current nutrition and flavor trends. They need math skills to carefully measure and adjust ingredients as they fine-tune their recipes.

Research chefs need a number of personal qualities to be successful. They must have good communication skills, as their work often involves giving presentations to clients. They need to be able to cooperate with other members of their research and development team. Research chefs are also creative, detail oriented, and patient. These traits help them repeatedly tweak their recipes until they find the version that will serve as the standard for mass production.

Research chef is one of the highest levels of success for culinary professionals. Most research chefs have attended culinary school. Some have also earned degrees in food science. This schooling is generally combined with years of experience in the foodservice industry.

This recipe has a total of 36 minutes of cooking time (25 + 5 + 6 = 36). It will take 5 minutes to add the bacon and eggs and 1 minute to sprinkle the cheese. These 6 minutes of preparation time must be added to the 36 minutes of cooking time. This tells you the casserole needs to begin cooking 42 minutes before it is to be served (36 + 6 = 42). The casserole is to be served last at 7:59 a.m. Therefore, it needs to begin cooking at 7:17 a.m. (59 − 42 = 17).

4. Use recipes to help list all the preparation tasks needed to be done. Refer to the *preparation time* column of the food preparation timetable. It will help you decide how much time to allow for these tasks.

To keep the schedule flexible, avoid listing specific times for every task. Instead, group tasks in 5- or 10-minute blocks of time. Plan to do related tasks together. For instance, you can wash the spinach at the same time you are rinsing the quinoa.

Remember to dovetail your meal preparation tasks as you plan the schedule. **Dovetail** means to overlap tasks to use time more efficiently. You can often dovetail during cooking time. For example, while the casserole is baking, you can fry the bacon and prepare the melon. You can often start cleanup tasks during cooking time, too. This will shorten cleanup time after the meal.

Another point to keep in mind is you do not have to prepare food items ranked "number 1" first. Sometimes it is helpful to get simple tasks, such as setting the table, out of the way. You may also want to prepare foods that do not need to be served hot ahead of time. This will prevent hot foods from cooling while you prepare other menu items.

Even a complete schedule is no guarantee that plans will go smoothly from start to finish. Sometimes one dish might cook in more or less time than you estimated. In these cases, you might have to keep some foods warm while you finish preparing the other foods.

As you become more skilled in the kitchen, you will be able to use less detailed schedules. Until that time, however, a schedule that is both detailed and flexible will be helpful.

©iStock.com/michaeljung

Figure 4.12   When family members work together on meals, it spreads the burden of meal preparation.

Cooperation in the Kitchen

You will not always work alone in the kitchen. At home, family members may help you prepare meals. At school, you will work with classmates to prepare food products. If you work in a professional kitchen, you will have coworkers attending to a variety of tasks. The kitchen can become a chaotic place when several people are in it at the same time. To work effectively, each person must do his or her part as a member of a team **(Figure 4.12)**.

Teams work best when one person takes a leadership role. In the kitchen, this person may be called a *meal manager, head chef,* or simply a *group leader.* No matter what this person is called, he or she will be in charge of assigning meal preparation tasks. The time-work schedule should indicate who will do each task listed. Be sure to rotate tasks from one time to the next to give everyone a range of kitchen experience.

When you are filling the leader role, consider your time frame and each person's skills before making assignments. For instance, if you are in a hurry, you may not want someone with little baking experience to make biscuits. If you have the time, however, you might want this person to help you with the biscuits. This will give him or her more baking practice. Helping team members develop their skills is another part of your role as leader.

When you are a team member, show responsibility. This means doing your assigned tasks quickly, correctly, and without needing anyone to prompt you. Accept direction from your leader and cooperate with the other members of the team. When everyone works well together, the group will be making the best use of time, space, and skills in the kitchen.

Chapter 4 Review and Expand

Summary

To prepare meals, it is necessary to know how to choose and follow recipes. You need to recognize abbreviations and cooking terms. Being familiar with ingredient substitutions and measuring equivalents will help you adjust recipes when needed. Knowing how to determine cost per serving allows you to choose recipes that fit into your food budget. Learning a few special techniques will make it easier when cooking foods in a microwave oven.

As a meal manager, you will want to be able to make a time-work schedule. This will help you plan the use of time in the kitchen. When cooking with others, it is important to understand what is expected of leaders and team members so everyone can work cooperatively.

Vocabulary Activities

1. **Content Terms** Read the text passages that contain each of the following terms. Then write the definitions of each term in your own words. Double-check your definitions by re-reading the text and using the text glossary.

   recipe   dehydration

   yield   arcing

   cooking time   time-work schedule

   watt   dovetail

   standing time

2. **Academic Terms** Individually or with a partner, create a T-chart on a sheet of paper and list each of the following terms in the left column. In the right column, list an *antonym* (a word of opposite meaning) for each term in the left column.

   distinctive   leaching

   customary   promote

Review

Write your answers using complete sentences when appropriate.

3. What are the components of a well-written recipe?

4. What happens to the boiling point of water at high altitudes?

5. Give the unit of measure for which each of the following abbreviations stands:
   A. c.
   B. oz.
   C. t.
   D. tbsp.

6. What is an important consideration when making an ingredient substitution?

7. What is the main SI unit of measure used in recipes?

8. Complete each of the following statements.
   A. To stir ingredients until they are thoroughly combined is to _____.
   B. To cut into small cubes of even size is to _____.
   C. To rub fat on the surface of a cooking utensil or on a food itself is to _____.
   D. To heat an appliance to a desired temperature about 15 minutes before it is to be used is to _____.

9. What is the Q factor in recipe costing?

10. How can dehydration occur during microwave cooking?

11. What is the purpose of venting food covers during microwave cooking?

12. Why should wire twist ties and metal-trimmed china not be used in a microwave oven?

13. Explain why time-work schedules for preparing meals need to be flexible.

14. What is the first decision that must be made when writing a time-work schedule?

15. What two things does a leader in the kitchen need to consider before assigning meal preparation tasks to members of the work team?

Core Skills

16. **Math** Each 1,000 feet increase in elevation decreases atmospheric pressure by about ½ pound and the boiling point of water by 1.9°F. At sea level, pressure is 14.7 pounds per square inch and the boiling point is 212°F. Figure the approximate atmospheric pressure and the boiling point of water at 2,000; 5,000; 7,500; and 10,000 feet.

Chapter 4 Review and Expand

17. **Technology, Math** Develop a spreadsheet with formulas that will scale ingredient measurements. One formula should scale measurements for a yield that is one-and-a- half times that of the original recipe. A second formula should scale measurements for a yield that is three times that of the original recipe. Use the spreadsheet to scale each of the following amounts:
    A. 2 tablespoons
    B. 1½ teaspoons
    C. ¾ cup
    D. 1⅔ cups

18. **Reading, Writing** Copy recipes for five types of food products. In each recipe, highlight any of the food preparation terms listed in the glossary in this chapter. Write a brief analysis noting the types of food products with which each term is used. Also note which terms appear most often. Look up the definitions of any preparation terms in your recipes that are not listed in the glossary.

19. **Speaking, Listening** Survey three people about the tasks for which they most often use a microwave oven. Ask why they do not use the microwave oven more often for cooking food products. Choose subjects of both genders and different age groups. Share your findings in class and note any similarities with the findings of your classmates.

20. **Research, Speaking, Technology** Search print or online resources for an interesting recipe from the 18th century or earlier. Gather information about the type of people who would have prepared the recipe and/or eaten the recipe. Research to learn if the ingredients were difficult to obtain or were commonplace. Identify any cooking terms that are not discussed in this chapter and learn their meaning. Analyze how the recipe is written. Rewrite the recipe in the style of a 21st century recipe. If possible, prepare the recipe. Present your findings in class. Use digital media and visual aids to add interest to your presentation. Consider dressing or speaking in the manner of the time period from which the recipe originates. Include the original recipe and your revision in your presentation.

21. **Math** As you are gathering your ingredients to bake a cake, you discover that you have only all-purpose flour. The recipe calls for 2 cups of cake flour. How much all-purpose flour should you use? (*Hint: See Figure 4.3*)

22. **Career Readiness Practice** The director of the food pantry at which you volunteer overheard you explaining the directions for cooking a low-cost chicken dish to a client. The director asks you to demonstrate your dish to a group of clients at the monthly nutrition and cooking class. She said the food pantry will supply your ingredients and equipment. You need to supply the recipe and prepare a cost list—showing the total cost and cost per portion. Your chicken dish is a one-dish meal that uses chicken, broccoli, whole-grain noodles, and grated low-fat cheese topping and makes eight portions. Think about the following content to include as you prepare your demonstration:
    - standard measuring techniques and equipment
    - thrifty substitutions to make that are equally nutritious and utilize foods from every food group
    - ways to save time during preparation
    - methods for keeping food safe and retaining nutrients
    - ways to utilize leftovers

    Video your presentation to show in class. Use the video to critique your presentation skills and identify areas you could improve.

Critical Thinking and Problem Solving

23. **Analyze** Select two types of cookbooks from your school or local library. Analyze the strengths and weaknesses of each cookbook. Write a critique stating which one you prefer and why.

24. **Evaluate** On a photocopy of a map of the United States, determine where high-altitude cooking principles would apply and color in those areas.

25. **Create** Work with your lab group to brainstorm food ideas for a meal. Choose from among the suggestions to plan a specific menu. Collect recipes for the foods you have selected. Create a food preparation timetable. Plan a time-work schedule for the members of your lab group. What factors did you consider when creating your schedule? Write a brief evaluation of the team's performance. Did all team members demonstrate cooperation and responsibility? How did this affect the team's effectiveness?

Chapter 5
Preparing Simple Recipes

MJTH/Shutterstock.com

Objectives

After studying this chapter, you will be able to

- **identify** healthy snack food options;
- **list** tips for preparing sandwiches and wraps;
- **choose** ingredient alternatives for reducing fat, salt, and calories when preparing pizza;
- **discuss** considerations for preparing cold and hot beverages; and
- **follow** a simple recipe to prepare a snack, sandwich, pizza, or beverage.

Reading Prep

Arrange a study session to read the chapter aloud with a classmate. Take turns reading each section. Stop at the end of each section to discuss what you think its main points are. Take notes of your study session to share with the class.

Content Terms ↪

snack
sandwich
wrap
flatbread
pizza
beverage
coffee blend
caffeine
decaffeinated
tea

Academic Terms

deterrent
discerning
complement
perishable

Simple recipes can make cooking an option for someone who might otherwise pick up food from the nearest drive-through. Simple recipes could be described as those that have short ingredient lists and just a few directions. Such recipes are well suited for cooks with limited experience. In addition, buying fewer ingredients helps save money. Reducing preparation steps helps save time.

Simple recipes are available for every type of food product. Search online using terms such as "15-minute meals" or "5-ingredient salads" to find dozens of results. Snacks, sandwiches, pizza, and beverages are among the most popular foods for which simple recipes abound (**Figure 5.1**).

Making Every Recipe Simpler

Some recipes are designed to be quick and easy to prepare. However, following a few tips can help simplify the preparation of any recipe.

Keep ingredients you use frequently on hand all the time. When possible, store ingredients in forms that are ready to use. For instance, many recipes call for chopped onions. Keeping whole onions in your pantry will make it possible to prepare these recipes. Keeping chopped onions in your freezer will make it easy to prepare these recipes. Other prepped ingredients you might want to keep in your kitchen include minced garlic, shredded cheeses, and premixed seasoning blends.

When getting ready to cook, begin by reading the recipe you want to prepare. Be sure you understand all the directions and have all the needed ingredients. Then gather the ingredients before you start to cook. Note whether the ingredients require any preparation. For instance, do carrots need to be sliced, or do nuts need to be toasted? Complete these tasks at the beginning of your food preparation time. Then measure the amount of each ingredient required for the recipe. Getting ingredients ready in this manner is what chefs call *mise en place* (MEEZ-ahn-plahs). Taking these steps streamlines recipe assembly.

When you are getting ready to cook, gather your equipment along with your ingredients.

Svetlana Foote/Shutterstock.com

Figure 5.1 This simple, healthy snack mix recipe consists of a variety of dried fruits, nuts, and seeds.

This will help you be sure you have all the tools you need. You do not want to be in the middle of preparing a recipe when you find out that a necessary utensil is dirty, broken, or missing.

For some people, one of the biggest *deterrents* (obstacles) to cooking is cleaning up afterward. Facing a cluttered kitchen can be discouraging, especially when you would rather be enjoying the food you made. One way to streamline cleanup is to fill your sink with soapy water and wash dirty dishes as you go. Keep counters wiped while you work, too. This will keep the amount of time you spend cleaning up after cooking to a minimum.

Snacks

When searching for simple recipes, a number of snack recipes would likely top the list. When you think of snacks, foods such as salty snacks and cookies may come to mind. However, a **snack** can more accurately be defined as a light meal. Traditionally, people thought of snacks as small amounts of food they ate between meals. In today's busy world, people are more often choosing snacks in place of regular meals. With this being the case, making healthy choices when selecting snack foods is especially important.

Many snack foods are easy to make. Some require no cooking. Others can be quickly heated in a microwave oven. Even if you are just learning your way around the kitchen, you can make simple snacks with ease.

Problems with Some Snack Foods

Popular snack foods such as chips and candy contain large amounts of sugar, fat, and salt (sodium). There is a reason why these foods are so well liked. Research shows that people tend to prefer foods with sugar over those without sugar. Fat gives foods appealing creamy and crunchy textures. Salt provides an instant burst of flavor on the tongue. Each of these components stimulates the desire to eat. When all three of these components are in a food, the food becomes more difficult to resist.

A big problem with these types of snack foods is that they provide nothing but *empty calories*, or calories with few nutrients. If you are tempted to eat large quantities of these foods, you risk gaining unhealthy weight (**Figure 5.2**).

One of the best strategies for limiting snacks that are high in sugar, fat, and salt is to simply not keep them around. You cannot snack on foods that are not in your cupboard. If you want to occasionally enjoy these types of foods, make them a treat that you must go out to get.

Smart Snack Standards

Nutrient	Smart Snack Standard	Candy Bar	Caramel Popcorn	Potato Chips
Calories	200 calories or less	250	120	160
Sodium	200 mg or less	140 mg	70 mg	150 mg
Total Fat	35% of calories or less	36%	15%	56%
Saturated Fat	Less than 10% of calories	18%	0%	9%
Sugar	35% by weight or less	39%	50%	2%

Smart Snack Standards provided by the USDA

Figure 5.2 Many popular snack foods tend to be high in sugar, fat, and sodium—nutrients for which most Americans exceed recommended limits. For which nutrients do the snack foods listed here fail to meet the Smart Snack Standard?

Choosing Healthy Snacks

Some people choose sugary snacks, like candy bars, for a quick burst of energy. These foods provide only a short-term boost. With a bit of planning, you can have snacks on hand that are nutritious and simple to prepare. Snacks that are higher in fiber, such as fresh fruits and whole grains, sustain you and help you feel full longer. Snacks that include some protein, such as nuts and cheese, can help improve mental focus, too.

When stocking up on healthier snack options, you need to be *discerning* (show good judgment). Foods such as yogurt, whole-grain crackers, and cheese slices are handy to grab when you are in a hurry. However, you should eat these snack foods in moderation. Yogurt can be high in sugar. Crackers and cheese often contain fair amounts of fat and sodium. You need to read nutrition labels to be sure the products you buy meet your goals for healthy snacking.

Look for healthy alternatives to less nutritious snack choices. Instead of buying a bag of potato chips, make homemade chips by toasting whole-grain bagels, pita bread, or tortillas. Instead of ice cream, try frozen bananas pureed in a food processor for a similar creamy texture.

Dips and spreads can be turned into snacks in no time. You can prepare them ahead and store them in the refrigerator. Keep a supply of cut fresh fruits and vegetables, and whole-grain crackers on hand to use for dipping (**Figure 5.3**). Flavorful dips can also double as sandwich spreads or even be used as the sauce for unique pizza recipes.

You can make healthier versions of dips and spreads sold in stores. For a creamy base, start with plain nonfat yogurt. This can replace higher-fat ingredients such as sour cream, mayonnaise, and cream cheese listed in many traditional recipes. Make homemade *salsa* from fresh tomatoes and onions to avoid the sodium in ready-made salsa. Use canned chickpeas, a little olive oil, and some seasonings to whip up a batch of fiber-rich *hummus*. Blend fresh herbs, garlic, and a small amount of olive oil to make a light *pesto*.

Keeping Snacks "Snack-Sized"

One important point about snacking is portion size. Remember that snacks are small amounts of food. Some researchers believe

Timolina/Shutterstock.com

Figure 5.3 Vegetables, pita chips, and hummus dip make a healthy snack that is easy to prepare. At what time of day would you enjoy this type of snack?

eating five or six small meals throughout the day instead of three larger meals can help people manage their weight. The idea is that waiting five or six hours between three daily meals causes people to get quite hungry. This makes them more likely to overeat at their next meal. Eating more frequently wards off intense hunger and reduces the chance of overeating.

The key to this advice is keeping the meals small in terms of calories. Eating too many large snacks will result in weight gain instead of weight management.

One way to control snack portions is to prepackage snack foods into small bags or containers. Make a healthy snack mix out of raisins, nuts, and whole-grain ready-to-eat cereal. Then take a few minutes to bag it into individual servings. Cut up a variety of fresh vegetables. Then pack them into small containers, perhaps with measured amounts of a low-fat dip on the side. This not only deters overeating, it saves time when you need to grab a snack on the go. When nutritious snack foods are convenient, you are less likely to choose foods that provide empty calories.

Sandwiches and Wraps

Sandwiches and wraps are other foods for which simple recipes abound. A **sandwich** is a food item in which ingredients are placed on, in, or between bread. A **wrap** is a filling rolled in some

Recipe for Good Food

Savory Toasted Chickpeas

Serves 3

1   15-ounce can chickpeas, rinsed and drained
1   tablespoon olive oil
1½   teaspoons Worcestershire sauce
½   teaspoon seasoned salt
¼   teaspoon garlic powder

1. Preheat oven to 425°F (218°C). Cover a jelly roll pan with parchment paper or a silicone baking mat.
2. Drain chickpeas on paper towels and pat dry. Discard any skins that come loose from the peas.
3. Spread the chickpeas on the prepared jelly roll pan in a single layer. Toast in preheated oven for 30 minutes, giving the pan a gentle shake about every 10 minutes.
4. Meanwhile, combine olive oil, Worcestershire sauce, seasoned salt, and garlic powder in a medium bowl.
5. At the end of the toasting time, remove the jelly roll pan from the oven. Using pot holders, gently lift the parchment paper or baking mat and slide the chickpeas into the bowl. Toss to coat with the olive oil mixture.
6. Place the parchment paper or baking mat back on the jelly roll pan. Pour the chickpeas back onto the pan and return it to the oven. Toast for 5 more minutes.
7. Allow chickpeas to cool before serving. Store leftovers in an airtight container or sealed plastic bag.

Per serving: 206 calories (31% from fat), 8 g protein, 28 g carbohydrate, 7 g fat, 0 mg cholesterol, 7 g fiber, 501 mg sodium

type of flatbread. **Flatbread** is simply flat, thin bread. Tortillas and pita bread are examples of flatbread.

Sandwiches and wraps are common choices for packed lunches because they travel well and can be eaten without utensils. These foods are also popular for parties and picnics because they are convenient to serve to a group.

There are many variations of sandwiches and wraps. A variation is a product that differs in some way from the standard form of that product. For instance, a *panini* is a sandwich variation that is made with Italian bread. It is pressed as it is toasted in a pan or special panini press. *Open-faced sandwiches* have the filling ingredients placed on a single piece of bread. *Pinwheels* are a variation of a wrap. They are made by spreading flatbread with a filling and rolling it up. Then the roll is sliced crosswise to show the bread and filling spiraled together.

Sandwich and Wrap Ingredients

All sandwiches and wraps are made with some type of bread and a filling. Any kind of bread or rolls can be used to make sandwiches. With the wide variety of breads available, the possibilities are numerous. No matter what type you choose, make sure it is fresh. Choose whole-grain breads and rolls most often.

Sandwich and wrap fillings are often protein foods. Leftover meats and poultry are good choices. Cheese, hard-cooked eggs, peanut butter, and canned fish also make good fillings. When choosing fillings, it is best to limit use of packaged luncheon meats, which tend to be high in sodium. Using lower sodium ingredients can reduce sodium content significantly without loss of flavor (**Figure 5.4**).

Lettuce, tomatoes, onions, and bell peppers *complement* (complete or make better) many

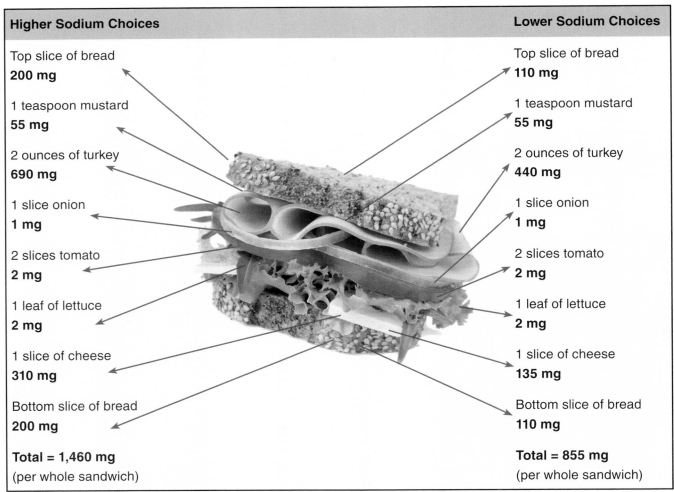

Higher Sodium Choices	Lower Sodium Choices
Top slice of bread **200 mg**	Top slice of bread **110 mg**
1 teaspoon mustard **55 mg**	1 teaspoon mustard **55 mg**
2 ounces of turkey **690 mg**	2 ounces of turkey **440 mg**
1 slice onion **1 mg**	1 slice onion **1 mg**
2 slices tomato **2 mg**	2 slices tomato **2 mg**
1 leaf of lettuce **2 mg**	1 leaf of lettuce **2 mg**
1 slice of cheese **310 mg**	1 slice of cheese **135 mg**
Bottom slice of bread **200 mg**	Bottom slice of bread **110 mg**
Total = 1,460 mg (per whole sandwich)	**Total = 855 mg** (per whole sandwich)

Robyn Mackenzie/Shutterstock.com

Figure 5.4 Consider sodium content when choosing ingredients for your sandwich.

sandwiches and wraps. These and other vegetables add fiber and nutrients. In fact, you can even skip the protein food and make a veggie sandwich filled just with tasty, colorful vegetables.

Items such as bacon, pitted olives, and pickles can add interesting flavors to sandwiches and wraps. However, use these ingredients sparingly, as they are high in fat and sodium. First choose the filling; then choose the extras.

Preparing Sandwiches and Wraps

The following guidelines will help you prepare nutritious, attractive, and flavorful sandwiches:
- Use a variety of breads and fillings (**Figure 5.5**).
- Cut sandwiches and wraps into halves to make them easier to eat. For party sandwiches that are extra interesting and attractive, cut bread into shapes, such as circles, diamonds, and hearts.
- Garnish sandwiches and wraps attractively. Garnishes can improve the appearance and food value of a sandwich or wrap.
- Keep sandwiches and wraps refrigerated until serving time. Bacteria grow quickly above 40°F (4°C). Therefore, pack sandwiches and wraps in a cooler when transporting them. Use ice, frozen gel packs, or chilled drinks to keep *perishable* (likely to spoil) ingredients safe. Place sandwiches and wraps in sealed bags or containers to prevent staling. Pack lettuce, pickles, tomatoes, and other relishes separately to keep bread and rolls from getting soggy.

Figure 5.5 Offering a variety of breads and fillings allows each person to make a sandwich that suits his or her taste.

- Make hot sandwiches and wraps just before serving. Serve them hot, not lukewarm.
- Use freshly toasted bread for sandwiches served on toast.

Pizza

Pizza is a popular food for which many simple recipes can be found. Traditional **pizza** is a dish with Italian origins. It is typically made of flattened dough, spread with flavorful sauce, covered with toppings, and baked. Popular toppings include cheese and a variety of meats and vegetables.

Like sandwiches and wraps, pizza has many variations. *Calzone* is a type of pizza with the crust folded in half over the filling before it is baked. *Dessert pizzas* are made with sweet sauces and fruit toppings.

With thick crusts, loads of cheese, and toppings like pepperoni and sausage, pizza can be a dish you should save for rare occasions. However, many recipes exist for creating flavorful pizza that is much lower in fat, sodium, and calories.

To prepare a healthier pizza, start with the crust. Choose whole-wheat crust for more fiber than crust made with white flour. Choose flatbreads such as pita bread or a tortilla for a thin, crispy crust that provides fewer calories.

Tomato sauce is a fine choice for a healthy pizza. You might also try homemade barbecue sauce, taco sauce, or salsa. Even just sliced fresh tomatoes make an appealing alternative to traditional tomato sauce. Avoid pizza variations that call for heavy sauces, like classic Alfredo, which is made with high-fat cream, butter, and cheese.

When it comes to the toppings, try grilled chicken instead of sausage and pepperoni, which are high in fat. You can also skip the meat and just load up on vegetables. Mushrooms, onions, and bell peppers are common vegetable toppings. You might also try asparagus, spinach, and broccoli for something a bit more unusual. Fruits such as figs and pineapple can be used in tasty combinations as pizza toppings, too.

Classic pizza is topped with mozzarella cheese. However, blue cheese, feta, Cheddar, and Swiss are just a few of the other cheeses that make tasty pizza toppings. Whatever cheese you choose, use it sparingly. A light sprinkle is all that is needed to give pizza a delicious cheese flavor. You can even choose to skip the cheese completely, if you prefer (**Figure 5.6**).

Beverages

A **beverage** is a drinkable liquid. People drink beverages with meals and throughout the day. Beverages can quench thirst and help meet the body's need for water. Some beverages also provide other nutrients. For instance, milk is a good source of calcium. Many fruit and vegetable juices are high in vitamin C.

Many beverages require no preparation. Those beverages that have recipes are usually simple enough for even the most inexperienced cooks to prepare.

Cold Drinks

Milk, water, carbonated beverages, fruit and vegetable juices and drinks, lemonade, smoothies, slushies, and milk shakes are popular cold drinks. Many drinks are ready to enjoy, right from the refrigerator. Make sure to serve drinks icy cold. Have plenty of ice on hand to keep drinks chilled.

Timofeev Sergey/Shutterstock.com

Figure 5.6 When making pizza, use less cheese to reduce fat and calories and allow the flavor of vegetable toppings to come through. What kinds of vegetables do you like on your pizza?

When choosing drinks, be aware that beverages can have a lot of calories. In fact, sugar-sweetened beverages are the number one source of added sugars in the U.S. diet. Some people consume a full day's worth of calories just from beverages. Soda has been linked to a number of health and environmental concerns.

Contrary to advertising hype, fruit drinks, vitamin drinks, energy drinks, and calorie-free beverages are not really healthier options. Although some drinks may offer a few vitamins, many supply

Learn About...

Preparing Beverages for a Party

When serving cold drinks for a party or picnic, you might want to fill a tub or cooler with ice. Then you can stock it with a variety of canned beverages, juice boxes, and bottled water. Guests can choose their favorite drinks whenever they get thirsty.

If you plan to make a large quantity of a special beverage recipe, consider serving it in a drink dispenser. This is a large container that will require less frequent refilling. It has a spigot that allows guests to serve themselves without lifting heavy pitchers.

To keep your special recipe cold, freeze some of it in ice cube trays. These ice cubes will not dilute drinks. You can also freeze some of your recipe in a small bowl or ring mold. This will make a large block of ice to put in a drink dispenser or punch bowl. Ice blocks take longer to melt than ice cubes, so they keep drinks cold longer.

When preparing a sparkling beverage recipe, use seltzer to add fizz without adding sugar. You can make a beverage base ahead of time by mixing all ingredients except the seltzer. Chill the base and seltzer separately. Just before the party, pour the base over an ice block in a beverage dispenser or punch bowl. Add the seltzer at the last minute to keep the drink from getting "flat."

Know and Apply

1. What is the advantage of using an ice block instead of ice cubes for chilling beverages in a drink dispenser or punch bowl?
2. Why would seltzer be a better choice than lemon-lime soda for making sparkling beverages?

nearly as much sugar as soda. Caffeine in energy drinks is linked with health risks for children and teens. Drinks and mixes made with artificial sweeteners provide few if any calories. However, some health experts believe habitual use of these products can play a role in weight gain. Studies show people who regularly consume artificial sweeteners tend to seek out sugar from other sources.

For good health, you need to drink plenty of liquids every day. To make healthful drink choices and limit calories, opt for pure water most often. Try adding lemon wedges, mint sprigs, or cucumber slices to give water a refreshing flavor twist. Drink milk to help meet your daily need for dairy foods. Then choose limited amounts of calorie- free beverages and juices. Enjoy drinks such as flavored milk and fruit smoothies less often, as they provide more calories than other options. Choose nondiet soft drinks and fruit drinks only on rare occasions. (Try a flavored sparkling water for an alternative to carbonated soft drinks you can enjoy more often.)

Milk shakes, smoothies, and fruit slushies are thick, frosty treats. Ingredients can vary, but milk shakes contain milk and ice cream. Smoothies are often made with yogurt and fruit. While shakes and smoothies provide some nutrition, they can be high in fat, sugar, and calories. Slushies do not contain dairy ingredients. If they are made with just fruits and juices, they are a lower-fat, lower-sugar treat choice.

When preparing shakes, smoothies, and slushies, have all ingredients as cold as possible. Using frozen fruit will help make drinks extra thick and cold. Combine all ingredients in a blender. Adding the liquid ingredients first will help the solid ingredients become thoroughly blended. Blend for about 20 to 30 seconds until the mixture is smooth. Pour it into tall glasses and serve with straws.

Coffee

Coffee is a popular beverage at breakfast and with desserts. However, many people drink coffee, both hot and iced, all day long.

Coffee is made from the beans of the coffee plant. The beans are dried, roasted, and packaged for shipment. The flavor of coffee beans depends on the variety and growing conditions. It also depends on the degree of roasting, which may be described as mild to dark.

You can buy a single variety of coffee beans. You can also buy **coffee blends**, which are mixtures of several varieties of coffee beans. Coffees that have added flavorings, such as hazelnut or French vanilla, are available, too.

You can choose ground or whole bean coffee. If you choose whole bean coffee, you can have it ground at the store. For freshness, however, you might prefer to grind it yourself just before brewing. You can choose the coarseness of the grind to suit your preparation method. Coffee stales quickly when exposed to moisture and air. Buy only enough coffee to last a week or two. To help maintain freshness, store both ground and whole bean coffee in opaque, airtight containers at room temperature.

Recipe for Good Food

Mix and Match Fruit Slushies

Serves 2

Select a juice:	Select one or more fruits:
Apple	Banana, sliced
Orange	Cantaloupe, cubed
Pineapple	Mango, diced
White grape	Strawberries, halved

1. Measure ½ cup of your choice of juice from the first column and pour it in a blender.
2. Measure 1½ cups of your choice of one or more types of fruit from the second column. Add fruit to the blender.
3. Add 5 or 6 ice cubes to the blender.
4. Blend 20 to 30 seconds, until smooth. For a thinner consistency, add more juice. For a thicker consistency, add more ice cubes.
5. Pour into glasses. Serve with straws.

Average per serving (varies by juice and fruits chosen): 96 calories (0% from fat), 1 g protein, 24 g carbohydrate, 0 g fat, 0 mg cholesterol, 2 g fiber, 8 mg sodium

You can purchase coffee in instant form. Instant coffee products are dry, powdered, water-soluble solids made by removing the moisture from very strong, brewed coffee. Some brands are freeze-dried. Prepare instant coffee by adding freshly boiled water to the coffee granules according to the manufacturer's directions.

Caffeine is a naturally occurring compound in coffee and some other plant products that acts as a stimulant. **Decaffeinated** coffee (and tea) is made by removing most of the caffeine. Decaffeinated coffee is available ground, whole bean, and in instant form.

Preparing Coffee

When you brew ground coffee, be sure to start with a clean pot. Thoroughly wash the inside of the coffeepot with hot, soapy water and rinse it well after each use. Oily film that collects on the inside of a coffeepot can cause coffee to be bitter.

Measuring can mean the difference between pleasing coffee and dreadful coffee. Measure fresh, cold water for the desired amount of coffee, 6 ounces (175 mL) per serving. Then measure 1 tablespoon (15 mL) ground coffee per serving for a regular strength brew. Measure 2 tablespoons (30 mL) ground coffee per serving if you prefer strong coffee.

Serve coffee as soon as possible after brewing. Heating too long can cause substances in coffee to become more soluble, giving the coffee a bitter taste. Correctly prepared coffee is clear and flavorful and has a pleasing aroma.

Coffee drinks, such as *cappuccino* and *latte* are made with a base of plain coffee or a strong type of specially brewed coffee called *espresso* (**Figure 5.7**). Milk, sweetener, flavorings, and toppings like whipped cream or cinnamon may be added, depending on the beverage. These drinks can be served cold or blended with ice until thick and creamy to prepare other popular variations.

Tea

Hot tea may be served in place of or in addition to coffee at brunches, dinners, and other occasions. Iced tea is popular at picnics and other warm-weather get-togethers.

Tea is the leaves of a small tropical evergreen used to make a beverage. Teas vary according to the age of the tea leaves and the way they are processed. *Black teas* are made from tea leaves that are fermented and dried. When brewed, black teas are amber in color and have a rich aroma and flavor. *Green teas* are made from tea leaves that are not fermented. When brewed, green teas are a greenish-yellow color. *Oolong teas* are made from partially fermented tea leaves. The color and flavor of brewed oolong teas fall between those of black and green teas. *White teas* are made from tea leaves that are gathered before they have fully opened. They are not fermented and produce a brew with a pale color and delicate flavor. All four varieties of tea are available decaffeinated.

Other Forms of Tea

Tea is available in instant form. Instant teas may be sweetened and flavored. They can be dissolved in cold or freshly boiled water.

You can buy tea with a wide range of added flavoring ingredients. Fruits like lemon, herbs like mint, and floral fragrances like jasmine are common flavorings. *Chai* is a popular drink made from black tea flavored with spices, which often include cardamom, cinnamon, ginger, and black pepper. It can be prepared with milk, sweetened with honey, and may be served hot or iced.

Herbal teas are made from a variety of plants. They come in many interesting flavors, and they do not contain caffeine. Fennel seeds, chamomile flowers, ginger root, and mint leaves are just a few of the ingredients commonly found in herbal teas.

Vitaliy Hrabar/Shutterstock.com

Figure 5.7   Latte and cappuccino are popular drinks in coffee shops and cafes.

Exploring Careers

Barista

Baristas do all the tasks involved with waiting on customers in a coffeehouse. They weigh, grind, and pack coffee. They prepare and serve coffee beverages and other menu items. Baristas order and stock supplies. They also clean work areas and equipment.

Successful baristas are friendly, helpful, and have good listening skills for accurately taking customer orders. They use speaking skills to describe menu items to customers. Baristas use math skills to make change and balance cash drawers. They need to be able to work as members of a team as they relay orders to other employees for preparation. Baristas must keep up with a fast-paced work environment when there is a rush of customers. They must see what needs to be done and take the initiative to do it.

Barista is an entry-level job. However, many coffeehouses prefer to hire people with high school diplomas. A background in foodservice is helpful but not required. Baristas will learn how to perform most tasks from coworkers and training manuals. In time, baristas may move into jobs as coffeehouse supervisors or managers. Their skills will also help them find work in other areas of the hospitality industry.

Some of the plants used in herbal teas can cause allergic reactions. Some herbal teas can also interact with certain medications. When purchasing herbal teas, choose commercial brands. Avoid herbal mixtures that claim to have special health or medicinal properties. Check with a healthcare provider if you have concerns or questions.

Red tea, also known as *rooibos* (ROY-boss), is brewed from an herb grown in South Africa. It has an amber color and is naturally caffeine-free (**Figure 5.8**).

Preparing Tea

You can purchase tea in teabags or in loose form. To prepare either form of tea, begin by rinsing a clean teapot or cup with boiling water to preheat it. Place a teabag or loose tea in the preheated pot or cup. (Place loose tea directly in the bottom of the pot or cup, in a cheesecloth bag, or in a tea infuser. A *tea infuser* is a small mesh or perforated container.) Then pour freshly heated water over the tea. Allow the tea to steep two to six minutes, until it reaches the desired strength. Remove the teabag or leaves from the pot before serving. If the tea leaves stay in contact with the water too long, the tea can become bitter. Serve cream, sugar or honey, and lemon with tea.

Prepare iced tea by first making strong hot tea. If desired, dissolve honey or sugar in the tea. Then pour the tea over ice and stir until chilled. Making the hot tea stronger than you usually drink it will keep the ice from diluting the iced tea too much.

Chocolate and Cocoa Beverages

Hot chocolate is made with chocolate, which is usually shaved or ground to help it melt when hot liquid is added. Hot cocoa is made with cocoa powder and sugar. Unlike chocolate, cocoa powder contains very little fat. Therefore, hot cocoa is less rich than hot chocolate.

Both hot chocolate and hot cocoa contain milk or cream. This means you must use low temperatures to prevent scorching. Choose nonfat milk to reduce calories.

Do not allow these beverages to boil after adding milk. Beating these beverages with a whisk until foamy will keep the milk from forming a scum layer. If desired, you may flavor either beverage with vanilla extract. Try adding flavorings like peppermint extract, orange extract, or cinnamon for tasty variations.

Africa Studio/Shutterstock.com

Figure 5.8 Each type of tea has a characteristic color and aroma. How long should tea leaves be allowed to steep in order to achieve a pleasing flavor?

Chapter 5 Review and Expand

Summary

You can put basic cooking skills to use when preparing simple recipes. Snacks, sandwiches, pizza, and beverages are good foods for beginning cooks to make. Keeping common ingredients on hand and gathering needed supplies before cooking are tips that can simplify any recipe.

Whether snacks are eaten between or in place of meals, making healthy choices is important. Using fruits, vegetables, whole grains, and low-fat dairy foods can help limit your intake of sugar, fat, and salt from snacks. Keeping portions small will help you avoid overeating.

Sandwiches and wraps are made with some type of bread and a filling. Pizza is assembled from crust, sauce, and toppings. By changing the specific components, you can create a number of healthy variations on these foods.

Popular beverages include a wide variety of cold drinks, coffee, tea, and chocolate and cocoa beverages. Balance these choices with pure water to control calories. Following a few preparation tips will result in pleasing beverages.

Vocabulary Activities

1. **Content Terms**   Working with a partner, choose two words from the following list to compare. Create a Venn diagram (see sample diagram that follows) to compare your words. Write one term under the left circle and the other term under the right circle. Where the circles overlap, write two or three characteristics the terms have in common. In the portions of the circles that do not overlap, write two or three characteristics that are not shared with the other term.

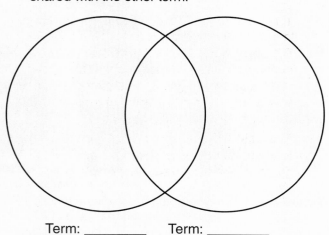

Term: _____   Term: _____

snack	beverage
sandwich	coffee blend
wrap	caffeine
flatbread	decaffeinated
pizza	tea

2. **Academic Terms**   For each of the following terms, identify a word or group of words describing a quality of the term—an *attribute*. Pair up with a classmate and discuss your list of attributes. Then, discuss your list of attributes with the whole class to increase understanding.

deterrent	complement
discerning	perishable

Review

Write your answers using complete sentences when appropriate.

3. What two characteristics are typical of recipes that can be described as "simple?"
4. When getting ready to cook, how should you begin?
5. What three components make many snack foods hard to resist?
6. What are two advantages of prepackaging snack foods into small bags or containers?
7. Give two examples of sandwich variations.
8. Give two guidelines for preparing sandwiches and wraps.
9. What is the advantage of using some type of flatbread as a crust for pizza?
10. How can you prevent cold juice drinks from being diluted by ice cubes?
11. Why should coffee be served as soon as possible after brewing?
12. Why is it important to remove the teabag or leaves from the pot before serving?

Chapter 5 Review and Expand

Core Skills

13. **Reading**   Read through six snack, sandwich, pizza, and/or beverage recipes. Make a list of at least five ready-to-use ingredients that would be helpful to have on hand if you were preparing these recipes.

14. **Research, Technology, Reading, Writing** Conduct online research to learn the meaning of the term *bliss point* and how it is used in the food industry in the development of snack foods. Summarize your findings in a one-page paper. Edit and refine your writing to ensure your ideas are presented in a logical, organized manner that is clear to the reader.

15. **Math**   Find a sandwich recipe with a yield of 8 servings or fewer. Copy the recipe and calculate how much of each ingredient would be needed to serve 40 party guests.

16. **Science**   This activity illustrates some of the characteristics of carbonated beverages. Drop a tablespoon of raisins into a clear plastic cup filled with a clear carbonated soft drink and note what happens. Note that a soft drink is a gas-in-liquid solution in which carbon dioxide gas is dispersed in water. The gas forms bubbles that attach to the raisins and raise them to the surface of the beverage. When the bubbles break, the raisins drop back to the bottom of the cup and the cycle is repeated.

17. **Research, Speaking**   In a small group, research some aspect of the traditional Japanese tea ceremony. Give a group presentation using digital media and visual displays to help convey the information and improve understanding.

18. **Math**   Suppose you are asked to make coffee for four people. How many tablespoons of ground coffee should you use to make four 6-ounce servings of regular strength coffee?

19. **Writing**   Search cookbooks or online to find a sandwich or pizza recipe that appeals to you. Read the recipe. List the tasks that you should perform before you begin preparing the recipe, also referred to as *mise en place*.

20. **Math**   Analyze your favorite sandwich to determine its sodium content. Identify ingredients that are higher in sodium and suggest alternatives that are lower in sodium. Prepare a chart comparing the sodium content of your favorite sandwich with the sodium content in your modified sandwich recipe. Calculate the percent decrease in sodium.

21. **Career Readiness Practice**   Most employers value employees that can set and achieve reasonable, attainable goals. Here are a few things you need to know about goals. Goals should

- be specific, measurable, attainable, realistic, and timely
- be positive
- have a target deadline (either short-term—several months, or long-term—several years)

Think about your snack habits and how it relates to your health. In writing, set a goal for improving the healthiness of your snacks, determine how you will measure achievement of this goal, and identify a deadline for meeting it.

Critical Thinking and Problem Solving

22. **Analyze**   Make a nutrient analysis table to compare the calorie, fat, sodium, fiber, and added sugar content of a processed snack food with that of a healthy snack alternative. In class, identify the two foods you compared and what you learned from your analysis.

23. **Create**   Following the format of the recipe for Mix and Match Fruit Slushies, construct a mix and match recipe table for pizza. Your table should have columns for Crust, Sauce, Toppings, and Cheese. List at least four healthy options in each column. When your table is complete, choose at least one option from each column to create your desired pizza variation. Give your dish a name.

24. **Evaluate**   Prepare several coffee blends. Evaluate the color, aroma, and flavor of each blend. Identify the blend you prefer and explain why you prefer it.

Unit 2
Nutrition and Wellness

FamVeld /Shutterstock.com

Essential Questions

- What nutrients do foods supply and what functions do those nutrients perform in the body?
- How do nutrient needs change through the life cycle?
- What food and activity choices will help promote health and manage weight?

FCCLA: Taking the Lead

As a *Power of One* project for the *A Better You* unit, set a goal for improving your nutritional status. You might begin by using the ChooseMyPlate.gov website to conduct personal nutrition assessments. After identifying nutrients for which your intakes are low, you can make food choices, find recipes, and write menus to plan a more healthful diet that will help you meet nutrient needs. After following the healthful diet for a set period, repeat the nutrition assessments and write an evaluation of how the dietary changes you have made have affected you physically and mentally.

While studying, look for the activity icon ⬀ for:
- Content and Academic Terms with e-flash cards, vocabulary games, and matching activities

These activities can be accessed at
www.g-wlearning.com/foodandnutrition/9582

Chapter 6
The Energy Nutrients

AnnaHoychuk /Shutterstock.com

Content Terms ➦

nutrient
nutrition
malnutrition
calorie
deficiency disease
carbohydrate
glucose
dietary fiber
artificial sweetener
fat
fatty acid
hydrogenation
trans fatty acid

cholesterol
hormone
protein
amino acid
enzyme
antibody
protein-energy
    malnutrition (PEM)
digestion
absorption
peristalsis
saliva
metabolism
diabetes

Academic Terms

regulate
toxicity

Objectives

After studying this chapter, you will be able to

- **name** the energy nutrients, **describe** their functions, and **list** important sources of each;
- **discuss** the effects of deficiencies and excesses of the energy nutrients; and
- **explain** the processes of digestion, absorption, and metabolism.

Reading Prep

Write all of the chapter terms on a sheet of paper. Highlight the words that you don't know. Before you begin reading, look up the highlighted words in the glossary and write the definitions.

The foods you eat can affect your state of health. Food provides nutrients. **Nutrients** are chemical substances from food the body needs to live.

Nutrition is the study of how the body uses the nutrients in the foods that are eaten. If you do not eat the foods your body needs, you may experience malnutrition. **Malnutrition**, in its simplest form, is a lack of the right proportions of nutrients over an extended period. Besides an inadequate diet, malnutrition can be caused by the body's inability to use nutrients from foods. In either case, the body does not receive all the nutrients it needs. Energy, growth, repair, and the regulation of various body processes can all be impaired.

Body weight is not a sign of a person's nutritional status. A person who is malnourished may be overweight or underweight. He or she can even have a healthy body weight. Eating enough food does not necessarily mean you are eating all the foods you need. The amount of food eaten is not as important as the right variety of foods.

Some of the effects of malnutrition may be long lasting. The foods a teen girl eats today may affect her pregnancy in later years. The foods a pregnant woman eats may affect her unborn child's development. The foods a child eats may affect his or her growth and resistance to disease. Each person's health and life span may be affected by his or her food choices (**Figure 6.1**).

The Nutrients

Several nutrients may be described as *nonessential nutrients*. Some of these nutrients are substances the body can make. Therefore, you do not need to get them from the foods you eat. Cholesterol is an example of this type of nutrient. Other nonessential nutrients do not meet the true definition of nutrients because they are not required to sustain life. However, they are substances from foods that have an impact on health. Carotenoids found in some plant foods are an example of this type of nutrient.

In contrast, *essential nutrients* are substances the body cannot make, at least not in a quantity needed to sustain life. These nutrients must be supplied by the foods you eat.

Monkey Business Images/Shutterstock.com

Figure 6.1 Making healthy food choices early in life improves your chances for a longer, healthier life.

Humans need over 50 essential nutrients for good health. These nutrients can be divided into six groups. The first three groups—carbohydrates, fats, and proteins—are often called *macronutrients*. They are also known as the *energy nutrients*. They provide the body with calories. **Calories** are the units used to measure the energy value of foods. The other three nutrient groups—vitamins, minerals, and water—do not give the body energy. However, they are needed to maintain cells and tissues and *regulate* (control) bodily processes.

No single food supplies all the nutrients the body needs to function. A diet that meets the body's needs contains nutrients from all six groups in the right proportions.

Failure to get enough of needed nutrients may result in a **deficiency disease**. This is an illness caused by the lack of a sufficient amount of a nutrient. There are a number of deficiency diseases, each linked to a different nutrient.

Some groups of people are more vulnerable to nutrient deficiencies than others. Pregnant women, infants, and children up to the age of two years are among those who are most at risk. The bodies of people in these life stages have high nutritional needs to support rapid growth. Nursing mothers are also more open to deficiencies. They need extra nutrients to aid in the production of milk. Older adults are at risk of certain deficiencies, too. Though their bodies have reduced energy needs, they have increased requirements for some nutrients.

Consuming too much of some nutrients can be just as harmful to your health as not getting

enough. Getting an excess of some nutrients can result in *toxicity* (poisoning). Symptoms of toxicity vary from one nutrient to another.

Exploring Careers

Registered Dietitian Nutritionist

A registered dietitian nutritionist (RDN) is a healthcare specialist who is trained to do diet analysis and counseling. Most RDNs focus on a few specific areas. Such areas include diabetes, weight control, vegetarian diets, sports nutrition, and eating disorders. Some RDNs counsel clients from private practices. Some work in hospitals planning medical diets for patients. RDNs often work in nursing homes and institutions to plan nutritious menus for residents. RDNs might also teach at universities or do research for government or industry.

An RDN must be able to assess the nutritional status of a client's current diet. This may involve listening skills when interviewing clients about their eating habits. It may also involve reading and interpreting medical records. Using analytical skills, an RDN can determine what changes a client needs to make. Then the RDN will need skills in instructing to help the client learn how to adopt new eating patterns. Among other qualifications, this work requires attention to detail and concern for others.

RDNs must graduate from a college or university program approved by the Academy of Nutrition and Dietetics (AND). After graduating, they must pass a national test. An RDN must complete an internship before beginning to work. RDNs must also take part in continuing education throughout their careers to maintain their registration.

Carbohydrates

Carbohydrates, also known as *carbs*, are the body's chief source of energy. They supply the body with 4 calories per gram. Most carbohydrates come from plant foods. Three main types of carbohydrates are important in the diet—sugars, starches, and fiber.

Types of Carbohydrates

Because of their molecular structures, sugars are sometimes called *simple carbohydrates*. The diet includes six types of sugars. At the molecular level, glucose, fructose, and galactose are made up of single sugar units, or *monosaccharides*. **Glucose** is the form of sugar carried in the bloodstream for energy use throughout the body. Therefore, it is sometimes called *blood sugar*. *Fructose*, which is also known as *fruit sugar*, is the sweetest of all sugars. A third sugar is *galactose*. It is found attached to glucose to form the sugar in milk. (References to *milk* in this text refer to cow's milk unless otherwise stated.)

Sucrose, lactose, and maltose are made up of pairs of sugar units, or *disaccharides*. *Sucrose* is ordinary table sugar. The milk of mammals contains *lactose*, or milk sugar. Grain products contain *maltose*, or malt sugar.

Starches and fiber are often called *complex carbohydrates* because they are made from many glucose sugar units that are bonded together, or *polysaccharides*. *Starch* is the storage form of energy in plants. Because humans eat an array of plant foods, starch is the most abundant carbohydrate in the diet. When people digest plant foods, they release the energy the plants have stored as starch. The body can then use the released energy for fuel.

Dietary fiber is a form of complex carbohydrates from plants that humans cannot digest. Therefore, it does not provide the body with energy like other carbohydrates. Fiber provides bulk in the diet and promotes normal bowel function (**Figure 6.2**).

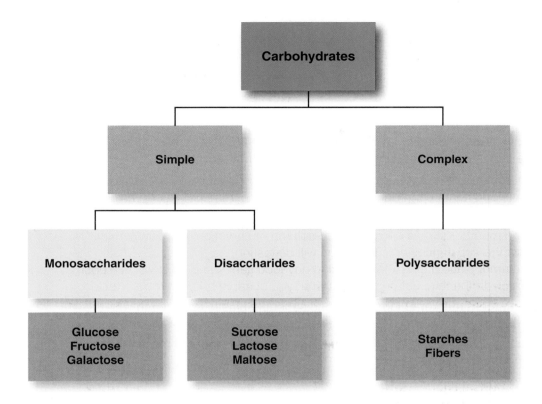

Figure 6.2 Complex carbohydrates take longer for your body to break down than simple carbohydrates.

Functions of Carbohydrates

The main function of carbohydrates is to furnish the body with energy. You will learn that fats and proteins can also provide the body with energy. However, carbohydrates are the only source of energy the brain can use. Also, the body can use carbohydrates as an energy source more readily than fats or proteins. Fats serve as long-lasting energy reserves. Proteins are mainly needed to build and repair body tissues—functions they cannot perform if they are being used for energy.

Functions performed by fiber are linked to the prevention of heart disease and some types of cancer. Fiber binds to a compound made from cholesterol and carries it out of the body. This helps lower blood cholesterol levels, which reduces the risk of heart disease. Fiber stimulates the action of the muscles in the digestive tract, helping speed food through the body. The bulk created by fiber may also help dilute *carcinogens* (cancer-causing agents) in food. Experts believe these functions may help reduce the risks of cancer. In order to receive the full range of benefits fiber provides, nearly all people need to increase their daily intake.

Sources of Carbohydrates

Many foods are rich sources of carbohydrates. Fruits and dairy products are sources of simple carbohydrates. However, the large majority of simple carbohydrates in the diets of most Americans are foods made with sugars and syrups. Such foods include sugar-sweetened drinks, candies, and most desserts. Sources of starch are breads, cereals, pasta products, and rice. Some vegetables, such as corn, potatoes, beans, peas, and lentils, are also high in starch. Whole-grain cereal products and fresh fruits and vegetables are good sources of fiber.

Carbohydrate Deficiencies and Excesses

Foods high in carbohydrates are abundant and inexpensive. Therefore, deficiencies in the United States are usually the result of self-prescribed limitations.

Mini Lab: Using an Indicator

Testing Foods for Starch

This lab involves using an indicator, which is a chemical that shows the presence of a specific substance. In this case, the indicator is an iodine solution, which will show the presence of starch. The indicator will change to a blue-black or purple color if starch is present. The indicator will not change colors if starch is not present.

The iodine solution is made with iodine tincture, which is a poisonous substance. Do not taste any food items used during this lab experience. Also use caution when handling iodine tincture, as it will stain clothing and skin.

1. Each group member should create a three-column observation sheet. In the first column, list the substances your lab group will be testing, as shown in Step 3. In the second column, place a check mark next to any food item you predict will test positive for starch. In the third column, record what you observe as each food is tested.

2. Use a permanent marker to label a set of disposable plastic cups, each with the name of one of the foods your lab group will be testing.

3. Place each of the following test foods in the appropriately labeled plastic cup:
   1 tablespoon (15 mL) all-purpose flour
   1 tablespoon (15 mL) corn oil
   1 egg white
   1 tablespoon (15 mL) granulated sugar
   2 slices unripe banana, ¼-inch (0.6 cm) thick
   1 tablespoon (15 mL) canned green peas, mashed
   ¼ slice luncheon meat, cut into ½-inch (1.2 cm) squares
   1 tablespoon (15 mL) powdered sugar
   4 pieces bite-sized toasted rice cereal
   1 tablespoon (15 mL) vanilla yogurt
   4 ½-inch (1.2 cm) cubes white potatoes
   ¼ slice whole-wheat bread, torn into ½-inch (1.2 cm) pieces

4. To make the indicator solution, use a clean glass dropper to carefully add 12 drops of iodine tincture to a clean disposable plastic cup. Add 1¼ teaspoons (6.25 mL) water to the cup and swirl gently to combine. Rinse the glass dropper thoroughly.

5. Lab group members should take turns testing the various food substances. For each test, use the glass dropper to carefully drop 4 drops of the indicator solution onto the food substance in each plastic cup. After each test, record your observations in the appropriate place on your observation sheet. Be sure to look at each food sample closely, as foods containing smaller amounts of starch may have less dramatic reactions to the indicator.

6. Carefully dispose of all test foods and indicator solution and handle glass droppers as directed by your teacher.

7. Review your observations. Then answer the following questions:
   A. Which test results surprised you? Why?
   B. What are five other foods you would like to test for starch? Explain why you think each of these foods would or would not test positive.
   C. What are three factors you think might affect the starch content of a food? Briefly describe how you could test one of these factors.

Learn About...

Added Sugars

Be aware that foods contain two types of sugars—natural and added. *Natural sugars* are found in many nutritious foods, such as fruit and milk. *Added sugars* are ingredients that are put into foods during processing. Natural sugars are not a dietary concern. However, diets high in added sugars are linked to various health risks.

Health experts recommend limiting added sugars to no more than 10% of total daily calories. This means a person who needs 2,000 calories a day should consume no more than 200 daily calories from added sugars. The Nutrition Facts label shows how food products fit with that limit. A label lists "Total Sugars" provided by a serving of the product. This includes natural and added sugars. Then the amount and % Daily Value (DV) of added sugars is listed. For instance, a carton of yogurt might list 29 grams of total sugars and 17 grams (34% DV) of added sugars. This tells you a serving of this yogurt provides one-third of the recommended daily limit for added sugars.

©iStock.com/Jaromila

Added sugars are hidden in foods you would not expect, such as ketchup.

Know and Apply

1. Why are added sugars a health concern when natural sugars are not?
2. What are three foods that are high in added sugars?

allowed to continue. If fiber is lacking in the diet, constipation may occur.

Nutrition experts recommend that most of the calories in your diet come from carbohydrates. They suggest eating a diet rich in whole grains, legumes, and fresh fruits and vegetables. These foods are fiber-rich sources of complex carbohydrates. By consuming more calories from these foods, you may consume fewer calories from foods that are low in nutrients.

Too many simple carbohydrates in the form of added sugars in the diet can be a health concern. Foods high in added sugars, such as soft drinks and candy, tend to be low in other nutrients. Eating added sugars in place of other foods may deprive the body of needed nutrients. Eating too many added sugars along with other foods increases the risk of unhealthy weight gain. In addition, consuming lots of added sugar has been associated with a higher risk of high blood pressure, diabetes, and other health issues.

Bacteria in the mouth act on sugar and starch to produce acid. This acid can erode teeth, causing tooth decay and gum disease. To help avoid these problems, dentists recommend limiting snacks between meals, especially sticky sweets. They also suggest brushing teeth after eating, flossing daily, and getting regular dental checkups.

People who want to enjoy sweet foods while limiting added sugars often turn to **artificial sweeteners**, (also called *nonnutritive sweeteners*). These are products that sweeten foods with fewer calories and less carbohydrates than sugar. Artificial sweeteners include aspartame, acesulfame K, sucralose, and saccharin. Neotame, advantame, stevia, and luo han guo (monk) fruit extract are also approved sweeteners.

Sugar alcohols, such as xylitol and sorbitol, are used as sugar substitutes, too. These products are used in a number of sugar-free foods and beverages. Many of them are also sold for home use. Keep in mind that replacing added sugar does not necessarily make a food nutritious. Make a point of reading Nutrition Facts panels to see how foods fit into a healthy diet (**Figure 6.3**).

A diet low in carbohydrates may cause the body to use protein as an energy source. This can interfere with the normal growth and repair of body tissues. It can also create a chemical imbalance in the body that could be dangerous if it is

Fats

Like carbohydrates, **fats** are important energy sources. Fats belong to a larger group of compounds called *lipids*, which include both fats and oils.

Sweetness Intensity Comparison	
Artificial Sweetener	**Sweetness Intensity Compared to Table Sugar**
Luo Han Guo (monk) fruit extracts	160–250 times sweeter
Aspartame	200 times sweeter
Acesulfame potassium	160–250 times sweeter
Steviol glycosides (stevia)	200–300 times sweeter
Saccharin	300 times sweeter
Sucralose	320–1,000 times sweeter
Neotame	7,000–13,000 times sweeter
Advantame	20,000 times sweeter

Figure 6.3   Artificial sweeteners provide varying degrees of sweetness.

Types of Fats

All lipids contain fatty acids. **Fatty acids** are chemical chains that contain carbon, hydrogen, and oxygen atoms. There are three types of fatty acids. Each type contains different amounts of hydrogen atoms.

Saturated fatty acids are fatty acids that have as many hydrogen atoms as they can hold. Fatty acids that have fewer hydrogen atoms than they can hold may be monounsaturated or polyunsaturated. *Monounsaturated fatty acids* are missing one hydrogen atom. *Polyunsaturated fatty acids* are missing two or more hydrogen atoms. Each type of fatty acids has different effects on the body.

Most fats that are high in saturated fatty acids are solid at room temperature. Most oils that are high in unsaturated fatty acids are liquid at room temperature. A process called **hydrogenation** adds hydrogen atoms to unsaturated fatty acids in liquid oils. This turns the liquid oils into more highly saturated solid fats.

Partial hydrogenation gives oils a spreadable texture. This process was once popular for making shortening and margarine. However, it creates **trans fatty acids**, or *trans* fats. These are fatty acids with odd molecular shapes. Studies have shown *trans* fats increase the risk of heart disease. Therefore, partially hydrogenated oils (PHOs) are being removed from the U.S. food supply. Very small amounts of *trans* fats will still be found in natural sources like beef and dairy products.

Oils that are fully hydrogenated have a firmer texture than PHOs. These oils do not contain *trans* fats, and they will remain on the market for use in foods. However, fully hydrogenated oils are a source of saturated fatty acids, which health experts advise limiting.

Cholesterol is a fatlike substance found in every cell in the body. Cholesterol serves several important functions. It is part of skin tissue. It aids in the transport of fatty acids in the body. It is also needed to produce **hormones**, which are chemicals that control certain body functions and processes.

Health and nutrition experts refer to *dietary cholesterol*, which is a nutrient in certain foods. These experts also refer to *blood cholesterol*, which circulates through the body in the bloodstream. A blood test can be used to check your blood cholesterol level. The test will give a score of two types of cholesterol in the blood.

Low-density lipoprotein (LDL) cholesterol is often called "bad" cholesterol. This cholesterol forms deposits, called *plaque*, on the walls of arteries. A buildup of plaque makes blood vessels narrow and less flexible. A high LDL score is a risk factor for heart disease. *High-density lipoprotein (HDL) cholesterol* is often called "good" cholesterol. It helps remove LDL cholesterol from arteries. A high HDL score is a sign of good heart health.

Functions of Fats

Fats in the diet serve a number of important roles. They provide a source of energy. They help the body absorb certain vitamins. Fats also carry flavor substances that make food taste good.

They make foods such as meats and baked goods tender, which makes these foods more appealing. Fats help you feel full after eating, too.

The body needs various fatty acids to make other important compounds, such as hormones. The body can produce some of the fatty acids it needs. These are called *nonessential fatty acids*. However, there are a few fatty acids the body cannot produce. These are called *essential fatty acids*. You must obtain these fatty acids from the foods you eat.

The body stores energy in fatty tissues. In addition to serving as energy reserves, these tissues form cushions that help protect internal organs from injury. Fat under the skin forms a layer of insulation that helps maintain body temperature. Fats are also part of the membrane that surrounds every cell in the body.

Sources of Fats

Fats and oils in foods contain mixtures of the three types of fatty acids. Learning which fats and oils contain more of each type will help you make healthier food choices. The fats in meat and dairy products are high in saturated fatty acids. Palm, palm kernel, and coconut oils are also high in saturated fatty acids. Avocados, as well as olive, canola, and peanut oils are good sources of monounsaturated fatty acids. Safflower, corn, and soybean oils are rich in polyunsaturated fatty acids (**Figure 6.4**).

Omega-3 fatty acids are a particular type of polyunsaturated fatty acids. They have been shown to be good for heart health. Fatty fish, such as salmon and trout, are good sources of these fatty acids. Flaxseeds and walnuts are also rich in omega-3 fatty acids.

Dietary cholesterol occurs only in foods of animal origin. It is not found in plant foods. Liver and egg yolks are especially high in dietary cholesterol. However, your body makes the cholesterol it needs. Therefore, you do not need to include sources of cholesterol in your diet.

Making Healthy Fat Choices

Fat deficiencies are rare in the United States. However, a diet too low in fat may result in a loss of weight and energy. Also, too little fat may cause deficiencies of essential fatty acids and fat-soluble vitamins.

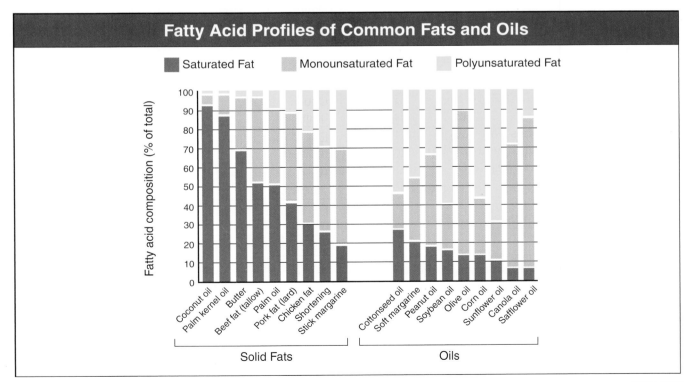

USDA/ARS

Figure 6.4 Fats and oils differ in the percents of saturated, monounsaturated, and polyunsaturated fatty acids they contain. Which of these fats has the highest percentage of saturated fat? the lowest?

Fat is a concentrated source of food energy. Fat provides 9 calories per gram. This is more than twice as many calories per gram as carbohydrates and proteins. Therefore, a diet that is high in fat may also be high in calories. Excess calories can lead to unhealthy weight gain.

Experts recommend making healthy fat choices. These recommendations are based on more than possible weight problems. Saturated and *trans* fats in the diet increase blood cholesterol. (Cholesterol in foods you eat seems to have little effect on blood cholesterol levels.) High blood cholesterol is one of several risk factors for heart disease. High-fat diets have also been linked to increased risk of diabetes, stroke, and some types of cancer.

A healthy diet begins with a variety of fruits, vegetables, and whole grain foods. For healthy fat choices, include fatty fish and other sources of omega-3 fatty acids regularly. To reduce saturated fats, limit high-fat meat and full-fat dairy products. Instead, select lean meats, skinless poultry, and low-fat and fat-free dairy products (**Figure 6.5**). Nuts, seeds, and legumes are part of a healthy diet, too.

Most of the fats in your diet should be mono- and polyunsaturated, which do not raise blood cholesterol levels. Choose fats and oils that have less than 2 grams of saturated fat per serving. Liquid and tub margarine meet this guideline. Opt for plant oils, such as olive and canola, instead of animal fat when preparing foods.

Avoid foods that contain *trans* fat as well as those that list partially hydrogenated oils on the ingredient list. Also limit commercially fried foods, such as French fries and doughnuts. These foods tend to be low in nutrients and are often fried in oils that contain *trans* fat.

Proteins

Proteins are chemical compounds that are found in every body cell. They are made up of small units called **amino acids** (the building blocks of proteins). Scientists have found 20 amino acids that are important to the human body. Nine of these amino acids are called *indispensable* or *essential amino acids*.

The body cannot make some indispensable amino acids. It can make others, but not at a rate fast enough to meet nutritional needs. Therefore, you must get the indispensable amino acids from the foods you eat. The other 11 amino acids are called

dispensable or *nonessential amino acids*. You do not have to get these amino acids from foods because your body can make them fast enough to meet its needs.

Functions of Proteins

The body needs amino acids from proteins for growth, maintenance, and repair of tissues. Proteins aid in the formation of enzymes, some hormones, and antibodies. (**Enzymes** are complex proteins produced by living cells that cause specific chemical reactions. **Antibodies** are a specific type of protein that helps fight infection.)

Another function of protein can be to provide energy. Like carbohydrates, proteins provide 4 calories per gram. (Your diet needs to

Beef Nutrition Facts			
Beef Cut (3 oz. cooked serving with no added ingredients)	Calories	Total Fat (grams)	Saturated Fat (grams)
Bottom round steak, braised	210	10	4
Brisket (whole), braised	280	21	8
Chuck arm pot roast, braised	250	16	6
Chuck blade roast, braised	290	21	8
Eye of round steak, roasted	170	8	3
Rib roast large end, roasted	300	24	10
Rib steak small end, broiled	240	17	7
Round tip roast, roasted	180	10	3.5
Sirloin steak, broiled	200	12	4.5
Tenderloin steak, broiled	220	14	6
Top loin steak, broiled	220	14	6
Top round steak, broiled	170	8	3

Adapted from USDA/ARS Beef & Veal Nutrition Facts

Figure 6.5 Cuts of beef with "round" or "loin" in the name contain less saturated fat than other cuts. Which cut of beef in the chart above would you select if you wanted to make a healthy choice?

supply enough carbohydrates and fats to meet energy needs. Otherwise, your body will use proteins for energy before using them to support growth and maintenance.) Regulation of bodily processes, such as fluid balance in the cells, is also a function of proteins.

Protein needs are based mainly on age, body size, and physical state. Children need more protein per pound of body weight than adults because they are growing so rapidly (**Figure 6.6**). Pound for pound, adult men and women need the same amount of protein. Therefore, because men generally weigh more than women, they need more protein each day. Pregnant women need extra protein to support the growth of their developing babies. Nursing women need extra protein to produce milk.

Multiplying body weight in pounds by 0.4 will tell most people how many grams of protein they need daily. Athletes need about double this amount to build and repair muscle tissue. Pregnant women should multiply weight by 0.5 to meet their increased needs. So this means, a normally active woman weighing 120 pounds would need about 48 g of protein per day (120 × 0.4 = 48). If this woman is an athlete, she would need about 96 g of protein daily (48 × 2 = 96). If she is pregnant, she would need about 60 g of protein per day (120 × 0.5 = 60). (Her daily needs would continue to increase to match her weight gain during pregnancy.)

Most people do not have to compute their protein needs and count grams of intake. On average, people in the United States consume about 15 percent of their calories from protein. This means someone who eats 2,000 calories a day gets about 75 g of protein (2,000 × 0.15 = 300; 300 ÷ 4 = 75). Therefore, protein is not a nutrient of concern in most U.S. diets.

Sources of Protein

When looking at sources of protein, some people refer to complete proteins and incomplete proteins. These terms are used to indicate the quality of the protein. *Complete proteins* are those that have ample amounts of all nine indispensable amino acids. *Incomplete proteins* are low in one or more of the indispensable amino acids.

In truth, all foods that provide protein contain some amount of each amino acid. In general, foods from animal sources might be viewed as having more complete proteins than foods from plant sources. Meat, poultry, fish, eggs, and dairy foods typically have higher levels of all the indispensable amino acids. However, dried beans, peas, nuts, grains, and vegetables provide worthwhile amounts of these amino acids, too.

Your body does not require all the indispensable amino acids to come from a single food item. In fact, all these amino acids do not even

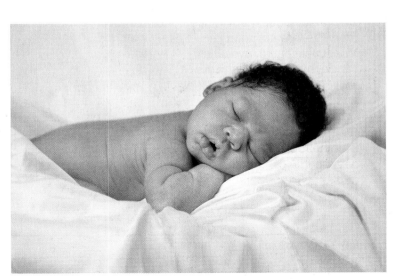

Flashon Studio/Shutterstock.com   *Gelpi JM/Shutterstock.com*

Figure 6.6 Protein needs are high during the first year of life due to the rapid growth that is occuring.

have to be provided at the same meal. As long as you consume the needed amino acids through the day, your body will have the protein it needs.

Most people who eat a variety of nutritious foods have no concern about meeting their protein needs. Different foods in the diet complement one another in terms of amino acids. One food may have a low level of a certain amino acid. However, this will be offset by a higher level of that amino acid in another food. This is true whether protein comes from animal sources or entirely from plants, as in the case of vegetarian diets.

Protein Deficiencies and Excesses

If the diet does not contain enough protein and calories, a condition called **protein-energy malnutrition (PEM)** may result. In adults, signs of this condition include fatigue and weight loss. In children, it can lead to diarrhea, infections, poor brain development, and stunted growth.

PEM is common in many low-income countries around the world. However, even higher-income nations have hungry people who are affected by PEM. People who fail to get enough food for reasons such as drug addictions or eating disorders may also experience PEM.

If the diet provides more protein than the body needs to build tissue, the excess can be used for energy. If you are already consuming enough calories to meet your energy needs, excess protein will be converted to fat. This fat is stored in the body and can contribute to unhealthy weight gain. Protein stored as fat cannot be converted back into amino acids for use in building tissues. This is why you need to consume protein sources every day.

The kidneys work to remove waste created by the breakdown of proteins in the body. Therefore, excess protein creates more work for the kidneys. This may not be a problem for people who have healthy kidneys. However, it can increase difficulties for those who have other kidney issues.

A summary of functions, sources, and recommended intakes of the energy nutrients is shown in the table in **Figure 6.7**.

Energy Nutrients			
Nutrient	**Functions**	**Sources**	**Recommended Intake**
Carbohydrates	Supply energy Provide bulk from fiber (needed for digestion) Help the body digest fats efficiently Spare proteins so they can be used for growth and regulation	Sugar: Honey, jam, jelly, molasses, sugar, sweetened drinks Fiber: Fresh fruits and vegetables, whole-grain breads and cereals Starch: Beans, breads, cereals, corn, pasta, peas, potatoes, rice	45–65% of total calories Fiber:* men–38 g/day women–25 g/day
Fats	Supply energy Help the body absorb fat-soluble vitamins Add flavor and satisfying quality to foods Serve as a source of essential fatty acids	Saturated: Coconut oil, dairy products, meats, palm kernel oil Monounsaturated: Avocados; canola, olive, and peanut oils Polyunsaturated: Corn, safflower, and soybean oils Omega-3 fatty acids: Fatty fish, such as salmon and trout, flaxseeds, walnuts	20–35% of total calories
Proteins	Build and repair tissues Help make antibodies, enzymes, hormones, and some vitamins Regulate fluid balance in the cells and other body processes Supply energy, when needed	Dairy foods, dried beans and peas, eggs, fish, grains, meat, nuts, poultry, vegetables	10–35% of total calories

*Recommended intake to age 50. Recommended intakes drop a bit for older adults.

Figure 6.7   Choose healthy sources for your energy nutrients more often.

Digestion and Absorption

The nutrients you eat in food must be digested and absorbed before they can serve their functions. **Digestion** is the bodily process of breaking food down into simpler compounds the body can use. **Absorption** is the process of taking in nutrients and making them part of the body.

These processes take place in the *digestive tract*, also called the *gastrointestinal (GI) tract*. This system of organs forms a tube that is about 30 feet (9 m) long. It extends from the mouth to the anus. It contains the esophagus, the stomach, the small intestine, and the large intestine. The pancreas, liver, and gallbladder also play important roles in these processes. These organs each perform specific functions to help the body use food **(Figure 6.8)**.

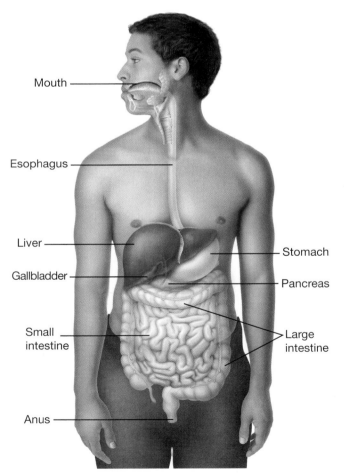

©Body Scientific International

Figure 6.8   Foods and beverages you consume are digested and absorbed as they move through the digestive tract.

Protein Drinks and Powders

Some bodybuilders and other athletes believe they need extra protein if they are trying to add muscle. This belief has fueled the sales of protein drinks and powders. These products are also used by pregnant women, vegetarians, and others who think they need to increase their protein intake.

In fact, most people in the U.S., including vegetarians, consume enough protein to meet their daily needs. Athletes and pregnant women do have increased protein needs. However, protein drinks and powders may not be the best way to meet them.

Most nutrition experts agree the best way to get nutrients is through whole foods. Foods provide a variety of nutrients that work together to support the body. Isolated protein in drinks and powders cannot offer these beneficial interactions.

Labels on protein drinks and powders often suggest consuming three or more servings daily. These amounts may provide more protein than the body can use for amino acids. The excess protein ends up getting converted to fat or being excreted. Frequent use of these protein products also gives some people diarrhea and other side effects.

Another disadvantage of protein drinks and powders is their cost. Many products cost two to three times more than foods that provide similar amounts of protein, such as eggs and chicken.

A final point to keep in mind is that protein drinks and powders are not magic potions. Athletes who are trying to bulk up will not automatically build muscle just because they consume a certain product. Building muscle requires exercise as well as a nutritious diet that meets the needs for all nutrients, not just protein.

The Digestion Process

During digestion, the body breaks down complex molecules obtained from food into simple, soluble materials. These simple materials can pass through the digestive tract into the blood and lymph systems. Vitamins and minerals go through very little chemical change during digestion. However, fats, proteins, and carbohydrates undergo many changes.

The Mechanical Phase

The digestion process involves two phases. The mechanical phase begins in the mouth. Here, the teeth chew the food and break it down into smaller pieces.

Contractions of the muscular walls of the digestive tract continue the mechanical action. These contractions mix food particles and break them into smaller pieces. With waves of contractions known as **peristalsis**, the muscles also push food through the digestive tract. Emotions such as sadness, depression, and fear can slow down peristalsis. Anger and aggression can speed up this process.

The Chemical Phase

Like the mechanical phase, the chemical phase of digestion begins in the mouth. As you chew, food is mixed with **saliva**. This is a mucus- and enzyme-containing liquid secreted by the mouth. It moistens food particles, helping them move down the esophagus into the stomach. Saliva also begins to break down starches.

In the stomach, *gastric juices* containing hydrochloric acid and several enzymes are secreted. These juices further break down the carbohydrates as well as the proteins in food. Many factors affect how long food remains in the stomach. However, it takes about four or five hours for the stomach to completely empty after an ordinary meal. Carbohydrates leave the stomach first. Proteins are second to leave the stomach, followed by fats. This is why it is good to include some protein and a little fat at every meal. Such a meal will help you feel full longer than a meal that is made up mostly of carbohydrates (**Figure 6.9**).

As the semiliquid food mass leaves the stomach, it enters the *duodenum*. This is the first section of the small intestine. *Bile*, which is produced by the liver and stored in the gallbladder, is released into the duodenum to break down fats. Enzymes from the pancreas are also released to finish the digestion of the proteins, fats, and carbohydrates.

Each type of enzyme has a specific function. An enzyme that breaks down proteins, for example, will not break down fats. As a result of all the chemical action, carbohydrates are split into monosaccharides, or single sugar units. Fats become fatty acids and an alcohol called *glycerol*. Proteins are divided into amino acids.

hungryworks/Shutterstock.com   *siamionau pavel/Shutterstock.com*

Figure 6.9 This white bread toast with jam is higher in carbohydrates and lower in fats and proteins than the egg and vegetable scramble breakfast. Which breakfast meal do you think will help you feel full longer?

The Absorption Process

The body can absorb water, ethyl alcohol, and simple sugars right from the stomach. These substances pass through the stomach walls into the bloodstream. Most nutrient absorption, however, takes place after digestion in the duodenum is complete. Food then moves into the lower sections of the small intestine, which are lined with millions of *villi*. These hairlike fingers increase the absorptive surface of the small intestine by more than 600 percent. Each villus contains a lymph vessel surrounded by a network of capillaries. Nutrients absorbed by the capillaries are carried by the bloodstream all through the body.

Undigested parts of food travel from the small intestine to the large intestine. Here, water is absorbed. Then the waste moves to the lower part of the large intestine, which is called the *rectum*. It is stored there until it is excreted as feces.

Metabolism

Metabolism is the chemical processes that take place in the cells after the body absorbs nutrients. Enzymes cause nearly all metabolic reactions. The body uses some nutrients to replace substances used for growth. It uses some nutrients to carry out bodily processes. The body breaks down some nutrients into simpler substances to release energy. The body uses part of this energy to carry out metabolic reactions. It converts the rest into heat.

Each nutrient follows a distinct metabolic path. The body converts all carbohydrates into glucose for use as an energy source (**Figure 6.10**). When glucose is absorbed into the bloodstream, the pancreas releases *insulin*. This is a hormone that signals the cells to take in glucose from the blood. If carbohydrates are not needed for immediate energy, they can be converted to *glycogen*. This is the storage form of carbohydrates in the body. Excess carbohydrates can also be stored as fat tissue.

A common disease related to carbohydrate metabolism is **diabetes**. It is caused by the body's failure to adequately produce or use insulin. This results in an inability to keep blood sugar at normal levels. There are three main types of diabetes.

In simple terms, *type 1 diabetes* occurs when the pancreas does not make insulin. This is because the body's immune system has destroyed pancreatic cells that produce it. *Type 2 diabetes*, the most common type, results when the body does not make enough insulin. It can also occur when the body is unable to use the insulin that is produced. Type 1 is most often found in children, and type 2 is more commonly diagnosed in adults who are middle-aged or older. However, both types can occur in people of any age. The third type of diabetes, *gestational diabetes*, sometimes develops in women during pregnancy. This type often goes away after delivery.

During fat metabolism, fatty acid chains are shortened. The body uses most fat for fuel.

The body can use amino acids from protein metabolism for cell maintenance or cell growth. It can also use amino acids to make enzymes, antibodies, and dispensable amino acids. The body can use amino acids as an energy source, too.

Monkey Business Images/Shutterstock.com

Figure 6.10 Carbohydrates provide the body with glucose, which is used as an energy source to fuel physical activity.

Chapter 6 Review and Expand

Summary

Food provides the body with six basic types of nutrients. Three of these—carbohydrates, fats, and proteins—provide the body with energy.

Sugars, starches, and fiber are the three types of carbohydrates in the diet. Sugars and starches serve as an energy source for the brain as well as the body. Fiber promotes normal digestion and has been shown to reduce risks of heart disease and some cancers. Whole grains, fruits, and vegetables are healthy sources of carbohydrates. However, most people in the United States also consume large amounts of simple sugars from drinks and other processed foods.

Fats and oils in foods contain mixtures of saturated, monounsaturated, and polyunsaturated fatty acids. Fats serve a number of important functions in the body. However, health experts recommend getting most fats from liquid plant oils and fatty fish. They advise limiting fats from meat and dairy products, which are high in saturated fats. They also recommend limiting processed foods that contain *trans* fats, as these two types of fat can raise blood cholesterol.

Proteins provide the body with amino acids needed to build and repair tissues. Meat, poultry, fish, eggs, dried beans, and nuts are all good sources of protein. Nearly everyone who consumes enough calories from a variety of foods meets daily protein needs.

The body must break down the foods you eat into components it can use. This happens during the digestion process. The digestion process involves both a mechanical and a chemical phase. After foods have been broken down in the digestive tract, the body absorbs the nutrients. Then nutrients are metabolized in the cells to release energy or make other compounds needed by the body.

Vocabulary Activities

1. **Content Terms**   Select 10 terms from the list of key terms at the beginning of this chapter. Re-read the sections that introduce each term. Then write down each definition in your own words. Keep your notes to prepare for the exam.

nutrient   malnutrition

nutrition   calorie

deficiency disease   protein

carbohydrate   amino acid

glucose   enzyme

dietary fiber   antibody

artificial sweetener   protein-energy

fat   malnutrition (PEM)

fatty acid   digestion

hydrogenation   absorption

trans fatty acid   peristalsis

cholesterol   saliva

hormone   metabolism

                              diabetes

2. **Academic Terms**   On a separate sheet of paper, list words that relate to each of the following terms. Then, work with a partner to explain how these words are related.

regulate   toxicity

Review

Write your answers using complete sentences when appropriate.

3. List the six groups into which nutrients are divided and their basic functions.
4. True or false. The foods a child eats can affect his or her health as an adult.
5. What is an illness caused by the lack of a sufficient amount of a nutrient called?
6. What type of carbohydrates is important to the diet even though humans cannot digest it?
7. Why is eating too many simple carbohydrates in the form of added sugars a health concern?
8. Name four functions of fats in the body.
9. What two substances can increase blood cholesterol and why is this a concern?
10. Describe the two groups of amino acids that are important to the human body.
11. How can protein-energy malnutrition (PEM) affect children?
12. Identify two food sources for each of the energy nutrients.
13. How can emotions affect digestion?
14. What is the duodenum and what role does it play in the process of digestion?

Chapter 6 Review and Expand

15. In what part of the body does most nutrient absorption take place?

16. What role does insulin play in carbohydrate metabolism?

Core Skills

17. **Listening, Writing** As a class, develop questions for a survey to determine students' general nutrition knowledge. Each class member should then survey three students from other classes. Compile the results to find the nutrition topic about which other students are least familiar. Write an informative article about this topic for your school's online newspaper. Edit your writing for grammar and spelling. Refine the article to make it concise and engaging to your readers.

18. **Technology, Math** Enrico had a glass of orange juice and two pieces of whole-wheat toast for breakfast. He had a hamburger, carrot sticks, and an apple for lunch. For dinner, he had a pork chop, mashed potatoes, and fresh broccoli spears. Use an online nutrient database to calculate Enrico's fiber intake for the day. Note the serving sizes and descriptors of the food items you select from the database. How do your findings for Enrico's daily fiber intake compare to the recommendation given in the chapter? What foods might Enrico add to his diet if he needs to increase his intake of fiber?

19. **Research, Speaking, Listening** Working in small groups, use reliable print or online resources to research protein energy malnutrition (PEM). Share what you learned through your research as you participate in a round-table discussion about this topic.

20. **Writing** Choose one of the nutrients discussed in this chapter and write a short story from its point of view. Creatively describe where you live (food sources) and your job (functions in the human body). Share your story in class.

21. **Science** Put an oyster cracker in your mouth. Wait 20 seconds without chewing or swallowing. Note any changes to the taste and texture of the cracker. Rinse your mouth with water. Then put a small piece of Cheddar cheese in your mouth. Again, wait 20 seconds without chewing or swallowing. Note any changes to the taste and texture of the cheese. You should have observed that the cracker started to get mushy, and it may have had a slightly sweet taste. This is because the enzyme amylase in your saliva started to chemically digest the starch in the cracker, breaking it down into sugars. You should have noted little change to the taste and texture of the cheese because it does not contain any starch. Therefore, it would not have been affected by the amylase.

22. **Career Readiness Practice** Use text or reliable Internet or print resources to investigate the changes that occur in the digestive system (GI tract) as people age. Compare the GI tract characteristics of a young person with that of a person in his or her later years. Develop a list of recommendations related to food intake based on changes in digestion for older adults.

Critical Thinking and Problem Solving

23. **Evaluate** Write menus for meals and snacks for one day to reflect food choices that might be made by a teenage girl. Note the portion size of each food item listed. Assume the girl follows a vegetarian diet, so your menus may include eggs and dairy products, but they cannot contain any meat, poultry, or fish. After your menus are complete, use a nutrient database to look up the number of grams of protein provided by each food item you listed. Calculate the total amount of protein provided. Evaluate how well your menus would meet the girl's daily recommended protein need of 46 grams.

24. **Analyze** Research the various enzymes involved in the digestion process. Create a table that compares the enzymes, the nutrients on which they work, and the stage in the process in which they are used.

Chapter 7
Vitamins, Minerals, and Water

AnastasiaKopa /Shutterstock.com

Content Terms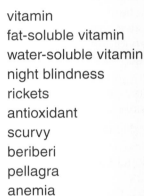

vitamin	mineral
fat-soluble vitamin	macromineral
water-soluble vitamin	trace element
night blindness	osteoporosis
rickets	hypertension
antioxidant	goiter
scurvy	dietary supplement
beriberi	fortified food
pellagra	phytonutrient
anemia	carotenoid

Academic Terms

hemorrhaging
apathy
lesion
synthetic

Objectives

After studying this chapter, you will be able to

- **identify** key vitamins and minerals, **explain** their functions, and **name** important sources of each;
- **describe** the effects of deficiencies and excesses of various vitamins and minerals;
- **discuss** the roles of water in the body; and
- **state** general advice regarding the use of dietary supplements.

Reading Prep

Review the chapter headings and use them to create an outline for taking notes during reading and class discussion. Under each heading, list any term highlighted in yellow. Write two questions that you expect the chapter to answer.

Although some nutrients do not provide energy, they are still important in your diet. Vitamins and minerals are vital for good health. You need them in small amounts, but they play big roles in the body. Water is essential for life and is part of almost every food and beverage you consume. Learning about the functions and sources of these nutrients may prompt you to meet your needs for them each day.

Vitamins

Vitamins are complex organic substances. You need them in small amounts for normal growth, maintenance, and reproduction. The body cannot produce most vitamins, at least not in large enough amounts to meet nutritional needs. The best way to get all the vitamins you need is to eat a nutritious diet.

Vitamins are either fat-soluble or water-soluble. **Fat-soluble vitamins** dissolve in fats. They are carried throughout the body by the fats in foods and can be stored in the body's fatty tissues. When consumed in excess, fat-soluble vitamins can build up in the body and may reach dangerous levels. **Water-soluble vitamins** dissolve in water. The body does not store them to any great extent. Instead, excess water-soluble vitamins are carried out of the body in the urine.

Although the body does not store large amounts of water-soluble vitamins, consuming large quantities may still be harmful. You are not likely to get harmful quantities of fat- or water-soluble vitamins from the foods you eat. However, taking large doses of vitamin supplements could put you at risk of developing symptoms of toxicity.

Vitamins A, D, E, and K are the fat-soluble vitamins. Vitamin C, the B-complex vitamins, and choline are water-soluble.

Vitamin A

The body uses vitamin A to make a chemical compound the eyes need to adapt to darkness. Vitamin A promotes normal bone growth. The health of tissues such as skin and mucous membranes also depends on the presence of vitamin A.

The body obtains vitamin A in two forms. The first form is the preformed vitamin. This form of vitamin A is in foods from animal sources like liver, egg yolk, and whole milk. It is also in fortified dairy products, butter, and fish oils.

The second form of vitamin A is *provitamin A carotenoids*. These are substances the body can convert into vitamin A. Provitamin A carotenoids are in plant foods. Deeper color indicates the presence of more provitamin A carotenoids. Therefore, orange and dark green fruits and vegetables normally have a higher vitamin A value than lighter colored produce. Carrots, cantaloupe, mangoes, spinach, and kale are high in this form of vitamin A (**Figure 7.1**).

marco mayer/Shutterstock.com   *Marie C Fields/Shutterstock.com*

Figure 7.1 Animal sources like egg yolk and whole milk supply preformed vitamin A. Deeply colored plant foods, such as spinach and carrots, provide provitamin A carotenoids. Which form of vitamin A do you include most in your diet?

If the diet contains too little vitamin A, the eyes will become sensitive to light. They may develop **night blindness**, which is a reduced ability to see in dim light. The skin will become rough, and susceptibility to disease may increase. In severe cases, stunted growth may result.

People seldom get too much vitamin A from food. However, like other fat-soluble vitamins, vitamin A can build up in the body over time. If people take too many vitamin A supplements, the accumulation may reach a dangerous level. Fatigue, headaches, nausea, vomiting, and liver damage may eventually occur. Overuse of vitamin A supplements has also been linked to an increase in bone loss, especially among older adults.

Vitamin D

The major function of vitamin D is to promote the growth and proper mineralization of bones and teeth. Vitamin D performs this function by helping the body use the minerals calcium and phosphorus.

Vitamin D occurs naturally in a few foods. These include eggs, liver, and fatty fish. In addition, vitamin D is added to most cow's milk as well as some cereals and margarine.

If the diet does not contain enough vitamin D, the body will not be able to use calcium and phosphorus as it should. In severe cases, children with vitamin D deficiencies can develop a disease called **rickets**. Symptoms of rickets include crooked legs and misshapen breastbones. Adults may develop other bone abnormalities.

If the diet contains too much vitamin D, the body will store the excess. Over an extended period, excesses of vitamin D may result in nausea, diarrhea, and loss of weight. In severe cases, kidneys and lungs may be damaged, and bones may become deformed.

Vitamin E

In humans, vitamin E functions mainly as an **antioxidant**. This is a substance that prevents or slows damage caused by chemical reactions involving oxygen. Some cells in the body, such as cells in the lungs, are constantly exposed to high levels of oxygen. Oxygen can destroy the membranes of these cells. When vitamin E is

Health and Wellness

The Sunshine Vitamin

The body can make vitamin D with exposure to sunlight. Thus, some people call vitamin D the "sunshine vitamin." Sunlight helps convert a substance found in the skin to vitamin D. Advanced age, darker skin color, sunscreen, heavy clothing, and smog all decrease the production of vitamin D in the skin.

Sun exposure is linked to about 30 percent of all cancers. However, you do not have to be in the sun for long periods to manufacture vitamin D. Therefore, you should follow advice for using sunscreens, wearing protective clothes, and avoiding dangerous exposure times. Most people who drink cow's milk and enjoy normal outdoor activities will get enough vitamin D to meet their needs.

oliveromg/Shutterstock.com

Spending time enjoying outdoor activities can help your body make the vitamin D it needs.

present, however, it combines with the oxygen before the oxygen can react with and harm the cells. Vitamin E also protects red and white blood cells, fatty acids, and vitamin A from harmful reactions with oxygen.

Vitamin E is widely distributed throughout the food supply. Sources include fats and oils, whole-grain breads and cereals, liver, eggs, whole milk dairy foods, and leafy green vegetables.

The average diet in the United States supplies sufficient amounts of vitamin E. Therefore, deficiencies are rare. However, premature infants may have deficiencies. Babies who do not reach full term fail to receive enough vitamin E from their mothers before birth. Toxicity from excess dietary vitamin E also seems to be rare. However, people who take large doses of vitamin E supplements are at increased risk of stroke from internal *hemorrhaging* (bleeding).

Vitamin K

Vitamin K is known as the blood-clotting vitamin. Vitamin K performs this function by helping the liver make a substance called *prothrombin*. Prothrombin is a protein blood needs to clot. If vitamin K is not available, the liver cannot form prothrombin and blood cannot clot properly.

Bacteria in the human intestinal tract can make vitamin K. Leafy green vegetables and cauliflower are good dietary sources of vitamin K. Additional sources include other vegetables, organ meats, and egg yolk.

Most people receive enough vitamin K from the foods they eat. Deficiencies are more likely due to a body's inability to absorb or make vitamin K. In cases where deficiency is severe, hemorrhaging can occur due to lack of blood clotting.

The amount of vitamin K consumed in a normal diet is not harmful. However, toxicity can develop through the use of vitamin K supplements. The functions and sources of the fat-soluble vitamins are summarized in **Figure 7.2.**

Vitamin C

Vitamin C, which is also known as *ascorbic acid*, performs many important functions in the body. It helps in the formation and maintenance of *collagen*, a protein that is part of connective tissue. Collagen is the cementing material that holds body cells together. Vitamin C helps make the walls of blood vessels firm, and it helps wounds heal and broken bones mend. It aids in the formation of hemoglobin (a substance in red blood cells) and helps the body fight infections. It also functions as a dietary antioxidant.

Fresh fruits and vegetables are the best sources of vitamin C in the diet. Citrus fruits, strawberries, and cantaloupe are good fruit sources of vitamin C. Leafy green vegetables, green peppers, broccoli, and cabbage are good vegetable sources.

Because vitamin C is a water-soluble vitamin, the body cannot readily store it. Therefore, you need a daily supply. People who smoke face increased oxygen damage in the body and thus need extra vitamin C for its antioxidant effects. Too little vitamin C in the diet can cause poor appetite, weakness, bruising, and soreness in the joints. A prolonged deficiency may result in a disease called **scurvy**. Symptoms of this disease include weakness, bleeding gums, tooth loss, and internal bleeding.

Vitamin C does help the body fight infection. However, scientists do not agree it will prevent or

Fat-Soluble Vitamins		
Nutrient	**Functions**	**Sources**
Vitamin A	Helps keep skin clear and smooth and mucus membranes healthy Helps prevent night blindness Helps promote growth	Butter; Cheddar-type cheese; dark green and orange fruits and vegetables, such as apricots, carrots, and spinach; egg yolk; fortified margarine; liver; whole and fortified milk
Vitamin D	Helps build strong bones and teeth in children Helps maintain bones in adults	Egg yolk; fish liver oils; fortified butter, margarine, and milk; liver; sardines; tuna; the sun
Vitamin E	Acts as an antioxidant that protects cell membranes of cells exposed to high concentrations of oxygen	Eggs, leafy green vegetables, liver and other offal, fats and oils, whole-grain cereals
Vitamin K	Helps blood clot	Cauliflower, leafy green vegetables, and other vegetables; egg yolk; organ meats

Figure 7.2 The fat-soluble vitamins can be stored in the body.

Mini Lab: Titration

Testing Liquids for Vitamin C

This lab will illustrate a scientific procedure called *titration*. This procedure involves adding a substance to an indicator solution to analyze its concentration. In this case, various liquids will be added to the indicator, one drop at a time, to study their concentrations of vitamin C. The indicator solution is made with iodine tincture, which is a poisonous substance. **Do not taste any food items used during this lab experience.** Also use caution when handling iodine tincture, as it will stain clothing and skin.

1. To make the indicator solution, measure ⅔ cup (160 mL) water into a 1-cup (250 mL) glass liquid measuring cup. Using a disposable plastic spoon, stir 2 teaspoons (10 mL) cornstarch into the water.

2. Line a strainer with 2 coffee filters and place it over a 2-cup (500 mL) glass liquid measuring cup. Pour the cornstarch solution through the double-layered filter so it collects in the 2-cup (500 mL) measure.

3. Dispose of the used coffee filters. Wash the 1-cup (250 mL) measure and rinse the strainer. Line the strainer with 2 new coffee filters and place it over the 1-cup (250 mL) measure. Pour the cornstarch solution through the double-layered filter so it collects in the 1-cup (250 mL) measure. At this point, the solution should be clear to translucent, but it should not be opaque white. If necessary, repeat the filtering process one more time. Do not be concerned if the solution is slightly reduced in volume.

4. Using a clean plastic disposable spoon, have one group member constantly stir the solution in the 1-cup (250 mL) measure. At the same time, a second group member should use a clean glass dropper to carefully add iodine tincture, one drop at a time, to the filtered cornstarch solution. Add only enough iodine to turn the solution dark blue. This should take just a few drops. Adding too much iodine will cause the solution to develop a brown color.

5. Obtain 2 tablespoons (30 mL) each of two test liquids, as follows:
   - **Lab group 1**—Orange juice and milk
   - **Lab group 2**—Orange juice and pineapple juice
   - **Lab group 3**—Orange juice and lemon juice
   - **Lab group 4**—Orange juice and lemonade
   - **Lab group 5**—Orange juice and lemon-lime soda
   - **Lab group 6**—Orange juice and green tea with lemon

©iStock.com/Antoine2K

6. Create an observation sheet, listing the liquids your lab group will be testing.

7. For each test liquid, place a clear glass custard cup on a white paper towel. Measure 1 tablespoon (15 mL) of the prepared indicator solution into the custard cup.

8. Using a clean disposable plastic spoon, have one group member constantly stir the indicator solution in the custard cup. At the same time, a second group member should use a clean glass dropper to carefully add the orange juice, one drop at a time, to the indicator solution. Count how many drops of the orange juice are required to change the color of the indicator. When the indicator is colorless, you have completed the titration procedure. The point at which a colorless indicator is obtained is known as the *end point*. On your observation sheet, record the number of drops required to reach the end point.

9. Repeat the procedure with your second test liquid. If time allows, test additional liquids. If you have access to a juice extractor, try testing vegetable juices. Avoid testing red or purple liquids, as it will be difficult to observe the color change of the indicator solution.

10. Carefully dispose of all test liquids and indicator solutions, as directed by your teacher. Place disposable spoons and paper towels in the trash. Place custard cups and measuring equipment in a dishwasher.

11. Compare your observations with those of the other lab groups. Then answer the following questions:
    A. Did all groups have similar results when testing orange juice? If not, explain why.
    B. How did the results of orange juice compare to the other liquids? What does this indicate about the vitamin C concentration of the other liquids?
    C. Which liquid appears to have the highest vitamin C concentration? Which appears to have the lowest vitamin C concentration?
    D. Look at the amount of vitamin C provided by each of the test liquids, as shown on the Nutrition Facts panel. How accurate were your test results?

cure the common cold. Avoid taking vitamin C supplements unless directed to do so by a physician. Excess vitamin C may cause nausea, cramps, and diarrhea.

Thiamin

Thiamin, or vitamin B_1, is part of a larger group of vitamins called the *B-complex vitamins*. All the B-complex vitamins are water-soluble. Each B vitamin has distinct properties. However, they work together in the body.

Thiamin helps the body release energy from food. It forms part of the coenzymes needed for the breakdown of carbohydrates. (*Coenzymes* are chemical substances that work with enzymes to promote enzyme activity.) Thiamin helps promote normal appetite and digestion. It also helps keep the nervous system healthy and prevent irritability.

Nearly all foods except fats, oils, and refined sugars contain some thiamin. However, no single food is particularly high in this vitamin. Wheat germ, pork products, legumes, and whole-grain and enriched cereals are good sources of thiamin.

Symptoms of too little thiamin in the diet are nausea, *apathy* (lack of emotion), and loss of appetite. If untreated, thiamin deficiency can become severe and result in a disease of the nervous system called **beriberi**. It begins with numbness in the feet and ankles followed by cramping pains in the legs. The next stage is leg stiffness. If the deficiency is prolonged, paralysis and potentially fatal heart disturbances may result.

Riboflavin

Riboflavin, or vitamin B_2, is the second member of the B-complex group. Riboflavin forms part of the coenzymes needed for the breakdown of carbohydrates. It helps cells use oxygen and maintains healthy skin, tongue, and lips.

Organ meats, milk and milk products, eggs, and oysters are good sources of riboflavin. Leafy green vegetables and whole-grain and enriched cereal products are good sources, too.

Too little riboflavin in the diet can cause swollen, cracked lips and skin *lesions* (sores). Scaly, greasy areas can form around the mouth and nose. Later symptoms include inflammation of the eyes and twilight blindness.

Niacin

Niacin forms part of two coenzymes involved in complex chemical reactions in the body. It helps keep the nervous system, mouth, skin, tongue, and digestive tract healthy. Niacin also helps the cells use other nutrients.

Exploring Careers

Nutritional Biochemist

Nutritional biochemists study the chemical makeup of nutrients. They look at the ways nutrients exist in food. They also explore how nutrients function in the human body.

Nutritional biochemists may do research for federal agencies. Their studies could be used to shape national nutrition policy. Some of these scientists work for drug companies. They formulate and test dietary supplements. They investigate how drugs can interact with and affect the body's use of and need for nutrients. Nutritional biochemists might also be hired by food manufacturers. Their insight is needed when fortified foods are being developed.

Nutritional biochemists need to be active learners and good readers. They use these abilities as they study the findings of other scientists. They use critical thinking and reasoning as they conduct tests and interpret results. Nutritional biochemists share their results in reports, for which they need strong writing and language skills. They also use listening and speaking skills as they confer with other members of their research teams.

Nutritional biochemistry is not a career for the casual student. Classes in biology, chemistry, and nutrition are at the core of this field. Physiology and pharmacology are also part of this program. Various math and statistics courses are taken as well. Much time is spent doing lab work, and internships are often part of the study requirements. Most nutritional biochemists have advanced degrees.

The most common sources of niacin include muscle meats, poultry, peanuts, and peanut butter. The body can convert *tryptophan*, one of the indispensable amino acids (also known as essential amino acids), into niacin. Milk contains large amounts of tryptophan.

Too little niacin in the diet can cause a disease called **pellagra**. Skin lesions and digestive problems are the first symptoms. Mental disorders and death may follow if the disease goes untreated. Pellagra normally occurs only when the diet is limited to just a few foods that are not good sources of niacin.

Excess niacin from food has not been reported to cause health problems. However, too much niacin from supplements can cause nausea, vomiting, and a red flushing of the face, chest, and arms.

Vitamin B$_6$

Vitamin B$_6$ helps nerve tissues function normally and plays a role in the regeneration of red blood cells. It takes part in the breakdown of proteins, carbohydrates, and fats. Vitamin B$_6$ also plays a role in the reaction that changes tryptophan into niacin.

Vitamin B$_6$ is in many plant and animal foods. The best sources of this vitamin are muscle meats, liver, vegetables, and whole-grain cereals.

Vitamin B$_6$ is in so many foods that a deficiency rarely occurs naturally. In cases of prolonged fasting, however, a B$_6$ deficiency can occur. Skin lesions, soreness of the mouth, and a smooth red tongue can develop. In advanced cases, nausea, vomiting, weight loss, irritability, and convulsive seizures may result.

Folate

Folate is another B-complex vitamin. It helps the body produce normal blood cells. It plays a role in biochemical reactions in cells that convert food into energy. A form of folate called *folic acid* is especially important in the diets of pregnant women and is often given to them as a supplement. Folic acid has been shown to help reduce the risk of congenital disabilities of the brain and spinal cord.

Folate is found in food sources, which include broccoli, asparagus, leafy green vegetables, and dry beans and peas (**Figure 7.3**). Liver, yogurt, strawberries, bananas, oranges, and whole-grain cereals are good sources, too. Folic acid is a **synthetic** (man-made) form of folate that is added to fortified foods and dietary supplements. Folic acid is found in most enriched bread and cereal products, including flour, pasta, and rice.

A poor diet, impaired absorption, or an unusual need by body tissues may cause folate deficiencies. Symptoms include inflammation of the tongue and digestive disorders, such as diarrhea. Folate deficiency can also result in two types of **anemia**. This is a condition that reduces the number of red blood cells in the bloodstream. Fewer red blood cells means a decrease in the amount of oxygen the blood can carry. Symptoms of anemia include weakness and fatigue. People often associate anemia with a deficiency of iron. However, deficiencies of several vitamins and minerals can lead to various types of anemia.

Vitamin B$_{12}$

Vitamin B$_{12}$ promotes normal growth. It also plays a role in the normal functioning of cells in the bone marrow, nervous system, and intestines.

aliasemma/Shutterstock.com

Figure 7.3 Lentils are a good source of folate as well as fiber.

Vitamin B$_{12}$ is in animal protein foods and brewer's yeast. Many cereals and breakfast foods are also fortified with this vitamin. A nutritious diet that includes animal foods should supply enough vitamin B$_{12}$. However, plant foods do not provide vitamin B$_{12}$. Therefore, strict vegetarians need to eat fortified foods or take a supplement to avoid a deficiency (**Figure 7.4**).

In simple cases of vitamin B$_{12}$ deficiency, a sore tongue, weakness, loss of weight, apathy, and nervous disorders may result. In extreme cases, *pernicious anemia* can develop. This is a chronic disease typified by abnormally large red blood cells. It also disturbs the nervous system, causing depression and drowsiness. Pernicious anemia can be fatal unless treated.

Pantothenic Acid

Pantothenic acid is part of the B-complex group of vitamins. Its main function is as a part of coenzyme A. The body needs coenzyme A to use the energy nutrients. Pantothenic acid also promotes growth and helps the body make cholesterol.

Pantothenic acid is in all plant and animal tissues. Organ meats, yeast, egg yolk, bran, wheat germ, and dry beans are among the best sources of pantothenic acid. Milk is also a good source.

Pantothenic acid is in so many foods that deficiencies are rare. In cases where a deficiency does exist, symptoms include vomiting, sleeplessness, and fatigue.

Biotin

Like the other B-complex vitamins, biotin is important in the diet. The body needs biotin for the breakdown of fats, carbohydrates, and proteins. It is also an essential part of several enzymes.

Biotin is in both plant and animal foods. Kidney and liver are the richest sources of biotin. Chicken, eggs, milk, most fresh vegetables, and some fruits are also good sources.

Because biotin is in most foods, deficiencies are rare. Symptoms of a biotin deficiency are scaly skin, mild depression, fatigue, muscular pain, and nausea.

Choline

Choline is an essential nutrient that is often grouped with the B vitamins. It helps the body

Joshua Resnick/Shutterstock.com

Figure 7.4 Fortified cereal and nondairy milk are good sources of vitamin B$_{12}$, especially for people who do not consume food from animal sources.

use fats for energy. It plays a role in the nervous system and is involved in a number of chemical reactions.

Choline can be made in the body by the liver. It is also found in eggs, salmon, beef and chicken liver, peanut butter, and soybeans.

Research data indicate that many people do not get enough choline in their diets. Choline deficiency during pregnancy is linked with an increased incidence of congenital disabilities. Insufficient choline has also been associated with liver damage, especially in older adults.

As with many nutrients, there is little concern that people will get too much choline from the foods they eat. However, consuming excessive amounts of choline from supplements may cause sweating, stomach pain, diarrhea, and vomiting.

The functions and sources of the water-soluble vitamins are summarized in **Figure 7.5**.

Minerals

Carbohydrates, fats, proteins, and water make up about 96 percent of body weight. **Minerals** are inorganic substances that make up the other 4 percent. Minerals become part of

Water-Soluble Vitamins		
Nutrient	**Functions**	**Sources**
Biotin	Helps the body break down the energy nutrients Forms part of several enzymes	Chicken, eggs, fresh vegetables, kidney, liver, milk, some fruits
Choline	This water-soluble nutrient compound serves functions similar to B-complex vitamins: • helps the body use fats for energy • plays a role in the nervous system • involved in a number of chemical reactions	Beef and chicken liver, eggs, peanut butter, salmon, soybeans
Folate	Helps produce normal blood cells Helps convert food into energy Helps prevent damage to the brains and spinal cords of unborn babies	Asparagus, bananas, broccoli, fortified bread and cereal products, leafy green vegetables, legumes, liver, oranges, strawberries, whole-grain cereals, yogurt
Niacin	Helps keep nervous system healthy Helps keep skin, mouth, tongue, and digestive tract healthy Helps cells use other nutrients Forms part of two coenzymes involved in complex chemical reactions in the body	Dried beans and peas, enriched and whole-grain breads and cereals, fish, meat, milk, poultry, peanut butter, peanuts
Pantothenic Acid	Forms part of a coenzyme needed to release energy from carbohydrates, fats, and proteins Promotes growth Helps the body make cholesterol	Bran, dried beans, egg yolk, milk, organ meats, wheat germ, yeast
Riboflavin	Helps cells use oxygen Helps keep skin, tongue, and lips normal Helps prevent scaly, greasy areas around the mouth and nose Forms part of the coenzymes needed for the breakdown of carbohydrates	Cheese, dark green leafy vegetables, eggs, fish, ice cream, liver and other meats, milk, poultry
Thiamin	Helps promote normal appetite and digestion Forms parts of the coenzymes needed for the breakdown of carbohydrates Helps keep nervous system healthy and prevent irritability Helps body release energy from food	Dried beans, eggs, enriched or whole-grain breads and cereals, fish, pork and other meats, poultry
Vitamin B$_6$	Helps nerve tissue function normally Plays a role in the breakdown of proteins, fats, and carbohydrates Plays a role in the reaction in which tryptophan is converted to niacin Plays a role in the regeneration of red blood cells	Liver, muscle meats, vegetables, whole-grain cereals
Vitamin B$_{12}$	Protects against pernicious anemia Plays a role in the normal functioning of cells	Cheese, eggs, fish, liver and other meats, milk
Vitamin C	Promotes healthy gums and tissues Helps wounds heal and broken bones mend Helps body fight infection Helps make cementing materials that hold body cells together	Broccoli, cantaloupe, citrus fruits, green peppers, leafy green vegetables, potatoes and sweet potatoes cooked in the skin, raw cabbage, strawberries, tomatoes

Figure 7.5 The B-complex vitamins and vitamin C are water soluble, so you need to eat sources every day.

the bones, soft tissues, and body fluids. Minerals also help regulate body processes. Scientists have found the body needs at least 21 minerals for good health. However, they do not yet completely understand the roles of some of these minerals.

The body contains larger amounts of some minerals than others. **Macrominerals** are minerals needed in the diet in amounts of 100 or more milligrams each day. Calcium, phosphorus, magnesium, sodium, potassium, and chloride are macrominerals. *Microminerals*, or **trace elements**, are minerals needed in amounts less than 100 milligrams per day. Iron, zinc, iodine, and fluoride are among the trace elements. They are just as important for good health as macrominerals.

Calcium

The body contains more calcium than any other mineral. Most of the calcium is in the bones and teeth. The fluids and soft tissues contain the rest. The body stores a reserve of excess calcium inside long bones.

Calcium combines with phosphorus to build and strengthen bones and teeth. Calcium helps blood clot and keeps the heart and nerves working properly. It also helps regulate the use of other minerals in the body.

Milk and milk products like yogurt and cheese are the best food sources of calcium. Some cereals, fruit juices, and other foods are fortified with calcium. Whole fish, green vegetables, and broccoli also provide some calcium in the diet.

Calcium supplements are available. However, most experts agree food sources supply the most beneficial balance of calcium with other nutrients (like phosphorus and vitamin D).

Children with severe calcium deficiencies may develop malformed bones. However, these bone disorders are most often the result of a vitamin D deficiency. This is because vitamin D affects the body's ability to use calcium.

Many teens and adults in the United States, especially females, do not get the recommended daily intake of calcium. If the diet does not supply enough calcium, the body will take the calcium it needs from the bones. This becomes an increasing problem in old age, when bone mass naturally decreases. Bones weakened further by the draw on their calcium supply become porous and brittle. This is a condition known as **osteoporosis**.

Health and Wellness

Osteoporosis

Osteoporosis afflicts millions of people in the United States. It causes many fractures of hips and other bones. Resulting complications make osteoporosis a leading cause of crippling and death. Women are most often afflicted because they have less bone mass than men. Osteoporosis is also related to hormone changes that take place in older women. Therefore, women who have gone through menopause are at the greatest risk of developing this disease.

Obtaining enough calcium (and phosphorus) can help prevent osteoporosis. This is especially important during the growth years when bones are developing and the body more readily absorbs calcium. Research has shown that being physically active throughout life can also help reduce the risk of osteoporosis. This is because performing weight-bearing activities, such as walking, helps increase bone mass.

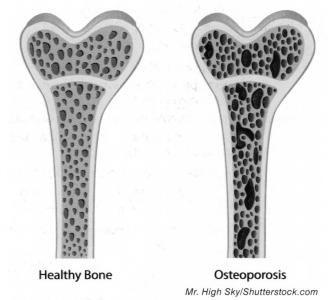

Healthy Bone   **Osteoporosis**

Mr. High Sky/Shutterstock.com

Bones afflicted by osteoporosis have lost calcium, becoming less dense and more likely to break.

Phosphorus

Phosphorus is second only to calcium in the amount found in the body. Like calcium, the body stores a reserve of excess phosphorus in the bones.

Phosphorus works with calcium to give strength to bones and teeth. It aids the body in storing and releasing energy. It helps balance the alkalis and acids in the blood. Phosphorus also helps the body use other nutrients.

Meat, poultry, fish, eggs, and milk and other dairy products are good sources of phosphorus. If you eat enough foods that are high in protein and calcium, you should receive enough phosphorus.

Most people have no trouble getting enough phosphorus in their diets. There are no known symptoms for phosphorus deficiency. On the other hand, too much phosphorus in the diet can cause problems. The ratio of calcium to phosphorus in the diet should be no lower than 1:2. However, people who drink a lot of soft drinks and not much milk may have a lower calcium to phosphorus ratio. This can cause calcium to be pulled from the bones to correct the ratio. As mentioned earlier, depleting the bones' calcium supply can lead to osteoporosis.

Magnesium

About half of the body's magnesium is in the skeleton. The other half is in the soft tissues and body fluids.

Magnesium helps cells use proteins, fats, and carbohydrates to produce energy. It helps regulate the body's temperature and keeps the nervous system working properly. Magnesium also helps muscles contract and improves the balance between alkalis and acids.

Whole grains and grain products are good sources of magnesium. Nuts, beans, meat, and dark green leafy vegetables also supply magnesium.

Healthy people who eat a nutritious diet receive enough magnesium. A deficiency, however, can occur in people with alcohol addictions. People experiencing kidney malfunctions, severe diarrhea, or malnutrition may also form deficiencies. Symptoms include twitching, muscle tremors, an irregular pulse, insomnia, and muscle weakness.

Sodium, Chloride, and Potassium

Like calcium and phosphorus, sodium, chloride, and potassium work as a nutrient team. Blood plasma and other fluids outside the cells contain most of the body's sodium and chloride. In addition, some sodium is in bones, and some chloride is in gastric juices. Most of the body's potassium is within the cells.

Sodium, chloride, and potassium work together to control osmosis. *Osmosis* is the process whereby fluids flow in and out of the cells through the cell walls. These minerals help maintain the acid-alkali balance in the body. They help the nervous system and muscles function properly. They also help the cells absorb nutrients.

Sodium and chloride are found naturally in many foods. Table salt provides added amounts of these minerals. However, processed foods are, by far, the largest source of sodium and chloride in the U.S. diet.

Potassium is widely found in the food supply. It is in some meats, milk products, and many types of seafood. Many vegetables, including sweet and white potatoes, tomato products, beet greens, and legumes, are good sources of potassium. Fruit sources include prune juice, bananas, peaches, and apricots.

Deficiencies of sodium and chloride are rare. People who sweat a lot during heavy work or exercise may lose some sodium. Cases of severe diarrhea, vomiting, and burns can cause losses, too. However, normal eating usually replaces these losses.

Unlike sodium and chloride, potassium intake is low in the diets of many people. People who do not get enough potassium may not have deficiency symptoms. However, they are not getting all the benefits of a diet rich in potassium. Potassium may help people have healthy blood pressure.

Most people consume much more sodium than they need. Normally, you excrete excess sodium through urine. In some cases, however, the body cannot get rid of the sodium, and fluids build up. The resulting swelling is called *edema*.

Research has shown there is a link between sodium and **hypertension**, or high blood pressure. The more salt people consume, the higher their blood pressure will be. Thus, people who have hypertension have a lower limit for sodium.

The functions and sources of the macrominerals are summarized in **Figure 7.6**.

Trace Elements

The body contains very small amounts of trace elements. Experts have determined some of these minerals are vital for good health. Recommended

Macrominerals		
Nutrient	**Functions**	**Sources**
Calcium	Helps build bones and teeth Helps blood clot Helps muscles and nerves work Helps regulate the use of other minerals in the body	Fish eaten with the bones; leafy green vegetables; milk, cheese, and other dairy products
Magnesium	Helps cells use energy nutrients Helps regulate body temperature Helps muscles and nerves work Improves acid-alkali balance in the body	Beans, dark green leafy vegetables, meat, nuts, whole grains
Phosphorus	Helps build strong bones and teeth Helps regulate many internal bodily activities	Protein and calcium food sources
Sodium, Chloride, and Potassium	Work together to control osmosis Help maintain acid-alkali balance in the body Help nervous system and muscles work Help cells absorb nutrients	Sodium: Bread products; condiments; pizza; processed foods, including cured meats, poultry products, and canned soups; salty snacks; sandwiches; table salt Chloride: Table salt Potassium: Bananas, milk products, prune juice, sweet and white potatoes, tomato products

Figure 7.6 You need 100 milligrams or more of each of the macrominerals in your daily diet.

daily intakes have been set for copper, selenium, manganese, and a number of other trace elements besides those discussed here. However, these minerals have not been shown to pose a great concern in the diets of most people in the United States.

Iron

The human body contains about 4 g of iron. Over half of this iron is in the blood, where it combines with a protein to form hemoglobin. *Hemoglobin* is a protein pigment found in red blood cells. It takes oxygen from the lungs and carries it to cells throughout the body.

The body does not excrete iron in any quantity. The body stores iron and reuses it. When iron reserves are low, anemia can result. Loss of appetite, pale skin, and tiredness are common symptoms of anemia.

Women and infants experience anemia more often than other groups of people. Women lose varying amounts of iron each month during menstruation. Women who do not consume enough iron may become anemic. Infants have some iron reserves when they are born. When these reserves are depleted, however, infants must receive iron from foods, such as iron-fortified cereal. Milk is not a good source of iron. Infants kept on a milk-only diet may develop anemia.

Liver, beef, and egg yolks are animal sources of iron. Iron is also found in such plant sources as leafy green vegetables, legumes, and enriched grains. The body absorbs iron from animal sources more easily than iron from plant sources. Eating foods rich in vitamin C with plant sources will enhance iron absorption.

Zinc

Zinc helps a number of enzymes perform their functions. It helps wounds heal and aids the functioning of the immune system. It promotes normal growth and development in children, too. Lack of zinc can stunt the growth and sexual development of children. Zinc deficiency may also result in poor wound healing and impaired taste and night vision. Large doses of zinc supplements can cause fever, nausea, and vomiting. Over time, heart disease and kidney failure can develop. Meat, poultry, seafood, legumes, and whole grains are good sources of zinc.

Health and Wellness

Limiting Dietary Sodium

The best way to reduce sodium in the diet is to limit use of processed foods. Many cured meats, poultry items, canned soups, pizza, and sandwiches are high in sodium. Bread products, salty snacks, and condiments, such as soy sauce, contain a lot of sodium, too. Instead of processed foods, choose fresh fruits and vegetables more often. When you do use processed foods, be sure to read nutrition labels. The amount of sodium can vary widely in similar products. Compare labels and choose those products that are lowest in sodium. Limiting use of salt in cooking and at the table can also help you reduce sodium intake.

Robert Pernell/Shutterstock.com

Iodine

The thyroid gland stores a third of the body's iodine. This small gland is located at the base of the neck. Iodine is an essential part of thyroxine, a hormone produced by the thyroid gland. Thyroxine regulates the rate at which the body uses energy.

If the diet does not contain enough iodine, the cells of the thyroid gland become enlarged. As the gland swells, it forms a lump at the front of the neck. This visible enlargement of the thyroid gland is called a **goiter**.

Insufficient iodine during the prenatal period and early childhood may cause severe intellectual disabilities. Combined with a slowed growth rate, this deficiency can cause swollen facial features and enlarged lips and tongue. Early treatment can reverse some of these characteristics. Seafood, dairy products, and iodized salt are good sources of iodine.

Fluoride

The greatest quantities of fluoride are in the teeth and bones. The teeth need fluoride for maximum resistance to decay. Fluoride is most helpful during the development of teeth, but it serves a protective function for the life of the tooth. Studies have also shown fluoride may be effective in maintaining the health of bones.

Drinking water is the most common source of fluoride, as commonly eaten foods contain very little. Many communities add fluoride to public drinking water. However, it may not be added to bottled water. Most toothpastes also contain fluoride.

The functions and sources of the trace elements are summarized in **Figure 7.7**.

Water

The body must have water to function. People can live more than a month without food. However, they can live only a few days without water.

Between 50 and 75 percent of body weight is water. Age, gender, and body composition affect the percentage of water in the body. Babies have a higher percentage of water than adults. Men typically have a higher percentage of water than women. Muscle tissue contains more water than fat tissue. Therefore, a person with a lean, muscular body will likely have a higher percentage of water than someone who has more body fat.

Functions of Water

Water is found both inside and outside all your cells. Water aids proper digestion as well as cell growth and maintenance. All chemical reactions within the body rely on water. Water also lubricates the joints and body cells and helps regulate body temperature.

Water Intake and Excretion

The body takes the water it needs from the liquids you drink and the foods you eat. About 80 percent of water intake comes from liquids. These liquids include water, milk, broth, coffee, tea, fruit juices, and other beverages. About 20 percent of water intake comes from the food you eat. Different foods contain different amounts of water. For instance, lettuce contains more water than a slice of bread.

Trace Elements		
Nutrient	**Functions**	**Sources**
Fluoride	Helps teeth resist decay Helps maintain bone health	Fluoridated drinking water, toothpaste
Iodine	Promotes normal functioning of the thyroid gland	Dairy products, grains, iodized table salt, saltwater fish and shellfish
Iron	Combines with protein to make hemoglobin Helps cells use oxygen	Dried beans and peas, dried fruits, egg yolk, enriched and whole-grain breads and cereals, leafy green vegetables, lean meats, liver
Zinc	Helps enzymes function Helps wounds heal Aids work of the immune system Promotes normal growth	Legumes, meat, poultry, seafood, whole grains

Figure 7.7 Trace elements are needed by the body in very small amounts; however, they are no less important than any other nutrient in your diet.

The body excretes most of the water it uses through the kidneys as urine. It excretes the remaining water through the skin and lungs and in the feces.

Water Requirements

A popular guideline for meeting water needs is to drink eight 8-ounce glasses (1.9 L) of fluid a day. Most of this fluid should be water. However, other beverages can contribute to your fluid needs as well. You might choose milk and limited amounts of 100 percent fruit juice, which supply nutrients in addition to water. Limit or avoid sugary beverages that supply little more than calories.

Some people need more water. Someone who is in a coma or has a fever or diarrhea has increased water needs. People on high-protein diets and those living in hot climates must also increase their water intake.

Diarrhea, vomiting, excessive sweating, or the unavailability of drinking water can deplete body fluids. Thirst is the first symptom of water loss. If water is not replaced, dryness of the mouth, weakness, increased pulse rate, flushed skin, and fever can result.

Excess water is not a problem for most healthy people. However, the kidneys cannot keep up with rapid intake of extreme amounts of fluids. This level of intake can lead to a rare, but dangerous, condition known as *water intoxication*.

Dietary Supplements

Most health experts agree the best way to get needed nutrients is to eat a varied diet. However, some people have trouble meeting all their nutrient needs from food alone. Doctors may suggest these people take a dietary supplement to help make up for any shortages in their diets. **Dietary supplements** are purified nutrient or nonnutrient substances that are manufactured or extracted from natural sources.

Supplements usually come in tablet, capsule, liquid, or powder form. Some, such as vitamin C tablets, contain single nutrients. Others, like multivitamin capsules, contain a number of nutrients.

Supplements are considered to be neither food nor drugs. Therefore, they are not regulated by the Food and Drug Administration (FDA). No laws require manufacturers to prove their supplement products are safe. Manufacturers are not obliged to prove the claims they make about products are true, either. This does not mean all supplements are harmful. In fact, many products have been safely used for years. However, some products have been taken off the market because they were shown to have harmful effects.

It is wise to seek the advice of a dietitian, physician, or pharmacist before taking any supplements. Some supplements can interact with each other or with certain medications. A healthcare

Learn About...

Bottled Water

Tap water from municipal treatment facilities is safe to drink. However, some people do not care for the taste of tap water. Others are concerned about some of the substances typically found in tap water.

Many people who dislike tap water choose bottled water for taste and convenience. However, there are a few points to consider about this beverage choice. Studies have not shown any health benefit of drinking bottled water over drinking tap water. In fact when tested, some bottled water has been shown to contain contaminants. In addition, there is concern that some of the chemicals in plastic water bottles can leach into the water. Furthermore, a large percentage of plastic water bottles ends up in landfills instead of being recycled. Finally, bottled water costs vastly more than tap water.

However, there is an alternative to bottled water. You can filter tap water and pour it into a reusable water bottle. This is better for the environment, easier on the wallet, and healthier for the body.

There are a number of types of filtering systems available. Many of these, including inexpensive pitchers and faucet-mounted models, use a carbon filter. Reverse osmosis systems are typically mounted under a sink. These systems are more costly, but they filter a larger number of contaminants from a greater amount of water. All systems require some maintenance to remain effective.

When choosing a reusable water bottle, stainless steel and glass are recommended as inert materials. Glass bottles are available with protective frames to reduce the risk of breakage. If you prefer a plastic bottle, look for nonreactive polypropylene. Water bottles and lids should be washed daily with hot soapy water and allowed to air dry completely. Replace bottles that show cracks or signs of damage.

Make sure your hands are clean when opening a water bottle. Once you have started drinking from a water bottle, do not leave the water sitting at room temperature for more than two hours. Taking these measures will prevent bacteria from getting into and building up in the container. This will help keep water the healthy beverage you want it to be.

Consider using reusable metal water bottles to reduce waste.

©iStock.com/bdspn

Know and Apply

1. What do you consider to be the greatest advantage and the greatest disadvantage of buying bottled water?

2. Why is it important to follow use and care guidelines for reusable water bottles?

---

professional can counsel patients about possible side effects and combinations to avoid.

When choosing a dietary supplement, look at the Supplement Facts panel. Avoid supplements that provide large doses—over 300 percent of the Daily Value—of any nutrient.

It is best to take supplements with food. This allows the supplements to work with the nutrients in the food, thus maximizing their benefit for the body.

A source of added nutrients in the diet aside from supplements is **fortified foods**. These are foods to which nutrients are added in amounts greater than what would naturally occur in the food. For instance, orange juice naturally contains very little calcium. However, calcium-fortified orange juice serves as an excellent source of this important mineral. Fortified foods give people additional options for meeting their nutrient needs through food choices.

Nonnutrient Supplements

Not all dietary supplements provide nutrients. Some provide nonnutrient substances. Phytonutrient supplements are one example. **Phytonutrients** are compounds from plants that are active in the human body. These substances are also known as *phytochemicals*. They are found in fruits, vegetables, and whole grains. Nuts, seeds, herbs, spices, and tea are sources of many phytonutrients, too (**Figure 7.8**).

There are thousands of phytonutrients. You may have heard of *carotenoids* and *flavonoids*. These are two phytonutrient groups that have received a lot of attention. **Carotenoids** are pigments that give fruits and vegetables their vibrant colors. These substances function as antioxidants. *Lycopene, lutein,* and *beta-carotene* are just three of the substances in this group. Flavonoids are also antioxidants. *Resveratrol,* which is found in grapes, is in this group.

Researchers have learned some phytonutrients have a preventive effect against heart disease and some types of cancer. They have discovered phytonutrients may also play a role in skin, bone, eye, lung, and joint health. As research continues, more and more potential benefits of these substances are being revealed.

Scientists still have much to learn about the way phytonutrients work and the health benefits they might offer. Strong evidence exists for recommending that people eat a variety of plant foods. A diet based on plant foods will provide you with a number of phytonutrients. However, most health experts recommend caution in the use of phytonutrient supplements until more information is known.

Clockwise from top left: topseller/Shutterstock.com; Alexlukin/Shutterstock.com; photastic/Shutterstock.com; Viktar Malyshchyts/Shutterstock.com; Serhiy Shullye/ Shutterstock.com; Alexander Raths/Shutterstock.com; Roblan/Shutterstock.com; Lizard/Shutterstock.com; M. Unal Ozmen/Shutterstock.com; Madlen/Shutterstock.com

Figure 7.8 Eating a wide variety of plant foods allows the phytonutrients they contain to naturally work together in the body. What are other nutritional advantages of including a broad range of plant foods in the diet?

Chapter 7 Review and Expand

Summary

Individual vitamins and minerals are needed in small amounts to serve specific functions in the body. No one food supplies all the vitamins and minerals. Eating a variety of foods is the best way to meet the body's needs. Health problems arise when there are deficiencies or excesses of these nutrients.

Water is a critical nutrient that plays a number of roles in the body. Water is consumed in nearly all foods and beverages. However, water is continually excreted through breath, sweat, urine, and feces. It is important to make a point of drinking enough fluids each day. It is also necessary to be aware of circumstances that increase water requirements.

Some people have trouble getting enough of certain nutrients from diet alone. Dietary supplements can provide nutrients as well as nonnutrient substances to boost amounts supplied by foods.

Vocabulary Activities

1. **Content Terms**   In teams, play *picture charades* to identify each of the following terms. Write the terms on separate slips of paper and put the slips into a basket. Choose a team member to be the *sketcher*. The sketcher pulls a term from the basket and creates quick drawings or graphics to represent the term until the team guesses the term. Rotate turns as sketcher until the team identifies all terms.

vitamin	mineral
fat-soluble vitamin	macromineral
water-soluble vitamin	trace element
night blindness	osteoporosis
rickets	hypertension
antioxidant	goiter
scurvy	dietary supplement
beriberi	fortified food
pellagra	phytonutrient
anemia	carotenoid

2. **Academic Terms**   Write each of the following terms on a separate sheet of paper. For each term, quickly write a word you think relates to the term. In small groups, exchange papers. Have each person in the group explain a term on the list. Take turns until all terms have been explained.

hemorrhaging	lesion
apathy	synthetic

Review

Write your answers using complete sentences when appropriate.

3. List the fat-soluble vitamins and explain the basic way in which they differ from water-soluble vitamins.
4. What are provitamin A carotenoids?
5. Why is vitamin D sometimes called the "sunshine vitamin"?
6. What is the main function of vitamin E?
7. What health consequence can occur in cases of severe vitamin K deficiency?
8. List four functions of vitamin C.
9. What deficiency disease is associated with thiamin?
10. What substance can the body convert into niacin?
11. What is folic acid and why is it important in the diets of pregnant women?
12. For which of the B vitamins are strict vegetarians at risk of deficiency?
13. Name and describe the calcium deficiency disease that afflicts millions of adults in the United States.
14. What problem can result from consuming a lot of soft drinks and not much milk?
15. What is the process controlled by sodium, potassium, and chloride whereby fluids flow in and out of cells through the cell walls?
16. Where is most of the body's iron found?
17. What is the name for a visible enlargement of the thyroid gland caused by a deficiency of iodine?
18. List three functions of water in the body.
19. How should the Supplement Facts panel be used when choosing a dietary supplement?
20. What are phytonutrients?

Chapter 7 Review and Expand

Core Skills

21. **Research, Reading, Writing** Seek out reliable print or Internet sources to research information about the prevalence of vitamin A deficiency throughout the world. Find out what steps are being taken to address this health concern. Write a two-page report summarizing your findings. Include a table comparing deficiency rates in industrialized nations with those in developing countries. Edit and refine your writing to ensure your ideas are presented in a logical, organized manner.

22. **Science** Observe the effects of vitamins E and C as antioxidants in preventing enzymatic browning. Cut a banana into eight equal pieces. Dip two pieces in water, two pieces in oil expressed from vitamin E capsules, and two pieces in liquid vitamin C. Leave the remaining two pieces untreated. Place the banana pieces on four plates labeled to indicate the treatment methods. After 30 minutes, compare the appearance of the bananas on the four plates and identify the most effective antioxidant treatment.

23. **Reading, Science** Begin your study of minerals by examining a periodic table of the elements. Find the location of nutritionally significant elements in the table.

24. **Reading** Use the Nutrition Facts panel on food products to make a list of 10 foods that provide over 500 milligrams of sodium per serving. For each food, write an alternative food choice that would be lower in sodium.

25. **Science, Writing** Sprinkle six flat-sided ice cubes with salt and stack them one on top of another on a flat plastic plate. Salt, which is made of the minerals sodium and chloride, lowers the freezing point of water. Observe the effects on the ice cubes and then on the salt. Write a report to summarize your observations.

26. **Speaking** As a class, make a list of 10 foods that are enriched or fortified with nutrients. Discuss how the technology used to fortify and enrich foods has affected the quality of the U.S. diet.

27. **Career Readiness Practice** Maintaining a healthy lifestyle has an impact on how you function physically and mentally. Imagine you are developing a campaign to promote drinking more water during the workday. Begin by investigating facts, definitions, regulations, and statistics related to bottled water through the education section of the International Bottled Water Association website. Design a brochure for the campaign.

Critical Thinking and Problem Solving

28. **Evaluate** Read the label of a multivitamin supplement and note the percent Daily Value provided for each vitamin. Evaluate the multivitamin based on what you learned from the chapter about excess fat-soluble and water-soluble vitamins in the body. Present your findings in an oral report to the class.

29. **Create** Write a brochure directed to teenage girls about the importance of iron in the diet. The brochure should mention health concerns associated with iron deficiency and discuss why teen girls are especially at risk. It should also list food sources and include a couple iron-rich recipes that would appeal to teen girls. Edit and refine your writing to ensure your ideas are presented in a logical, organized manner that is clear to the reader. Use page layout software to create an attractive design for the brochure. Import photos and illustrations to add visual interest.

30. **Analyze** Choose a reusable water bottle sold by an online retailer that offers multiple brands and styles of bottles. In addition to the product description, read consumer reviews to help you analyze the pros and cons of the bottle you choose. Write a paper based on your analysis, explaining why you would or would not decide to buy this bottle.

Chapter 8
Making Healthy Choices

SnowWhiteimages /Shutterstock.com

Content Terms ↗

Dietary Reference Intakes (DRIs)
Dietary Guidelines for Americans
dietary pattern
calorie balance
nutrient dense
empty calories
MyPlate
processed food

Academic Terms

curb
outlook
sedentary
modest

Objectives

After studying this chapter, you will be able to

- **name** benefits of making healthy choices;
- **explain** how to use Dietary Reference Intakes (DRIs), the *Dietary Guidelines for Americans*, and the MyPlate food guidance system as diet planning resources to meet daily needs;
- **identify** your recommended daily intake from each food group in MyPlate;
- **list** tips to use when shopping for and preparing foods; and
- **choose** healthy options when eating out.

Reading Prep

Before you begin reading this chapter, consider how the author developed and presented information. How does the information provide the foundation for the next chapter?

Knowing about nutrients gives you an idea of the important roles food can play in health. However, you need to know a bit more to choose foods that will supply adequate amounts of nutrients. Some general guidelines can help you select a nutritious diet. You can use these guidelines when shopping for food, preparing food, and eating out.

Keep in mind that selecting nutritious foods is not the only choice people can make to benefit their health. Making a point of being physically active and getting enough rest are healthy choices. Opting to avoid hazards and take safety measures are wise decisions, too. Of course, factors like heredity and surroundings also have an effect on well-being. Such factors are often beyond control. However, making healthy choices when they can allows people to take an active role in managing their wellness.

Benefits of Healthy Choices

Choosing a diet that provides the body with needed amounts of all the nutrients can benefit people in many ways. This important choice, along with other healthy lifestyle choices, can affect physical health and appearance. It can have social and mental benefits, too (**Figure 8.1**).

Physical Benefits

Many of today's top physical health issues are related to diet and activity. Eating too much and moving too little can lead to obesity. Obesity increases the risks of heart disease, cancer, stroke, and diabetes. Some of these diseases are at the root of disabilities. For instance, diabetes often results in blindness and limb amputations. These diseases are also major causes of death in the United States.

Eat foods within daily calorie needs. Focus on fresh fruits and vegetables and whole grains to get plenty of dietary fiber. Choose low-fat dairy products and lean proteins to *curb* (limit) saturated fats. Select fish, nuts, and seeds to get healthy oils. Limit sugar-sweetened drinks and other sources of added sugars. Get regular physical exercise, too. These choices are part of

the best defense against chief health concerns in today's society.

In addition, make choices that provide an adequate supply of vitamins and minerals. Getting needed nutrients can help people maintain good health and may improve their health. A case in point, carbohydrates provide energy, and B vitamins help the body use carbohydrates. When people get enough of these nutrients, they can avoid deficiency symptoms. They will also have the fuel they need to do daily tasks.

Getting enough nutrients in the diet can benefit appearance as well as health. Vitamin A and the B vitamins promote smooth skin. Fluoride and calcium help form strong teeth. Protein is needed to build well-defined muscles. Nutrients also play a role in keeping hair shiny and nails healthy. Getting needed nutrients helps people look their best.

Social Benefits

Physical benefits of healthy choices can transfer to social areas as well. For instance, by affecting health and appearance, nutritious food choices can promote job performance. People who are in good health will miss less work due to illness. They find it easier to stay focused on tasks and give their best efforts. They are better equipped to manage stress and achieve success.

MBI/Shutterstock.com

Figure 8.1 Healthy lifestyle choices can benefit your performance in school.

Someone who looks his or her best has more confidence to accept new challenges. He or she will be more willing to approach customers to make a sale or to ask supervisors for help.

In similar ways, healthy choices can have benefits in personal life. A nutritious diet, regular exercise, and ample rest can give people strength and energy. This will help them manage all the tasks in their daily schedules. They will have more positive attitudes when interacting with family members and friends.

Mental Benefits

Making healthy choices can help people have a good mental *outlook* (attitude). Along with diet, daily activity choices have a big impact on the way people look and feel. People who choose to be active enjoy greater strength and flexibility. They have an easier time maintaining healthy body weight. These physical benefits help people have more positive attitudes about themselves. They are less likely to become anxious and depressed.

Risks of Unhealthy Lifestyle Habits

Just as making healthy choices can have a number of benefits, making unhealthy choices can have a number of risks. For instance, making too many unhealthy food choices could result in a lack of some nutrients. This could lead to deficiency diseases. Choosing portions that are too large can bring about unhealthy weight gain. Choosing to spend excessive amounts of time in *sedentary* (requiring much sitting) activities can cause a loss of muscle strength and energy (**Figure 8.2**).

Unhealthy choices go beyond decisions about food and activities. Lifestyle choices often become habits. Habits, such as those involving tobacco, carry many health risks. Choosing to use tobacco in any form is hazardous to health. Smoking tobacco is linked with lung and heart diseases and many cancers. It can also weaken bones and damage the digestive tract. Using smokeless tobacco has been shown to cause cancers of the mouth, throat, and tongue. Choosing to be around secondhand smoke (inhaled from nearby smokers) is nearly as dangerous as smoking.

Using alcohol in excess is another lifestyle habit that has a number of health risks. These include liver disease, high blood pressure, and some cancers. Excess alcohol can also contribute to car accidents, suicides, and acts of violence.

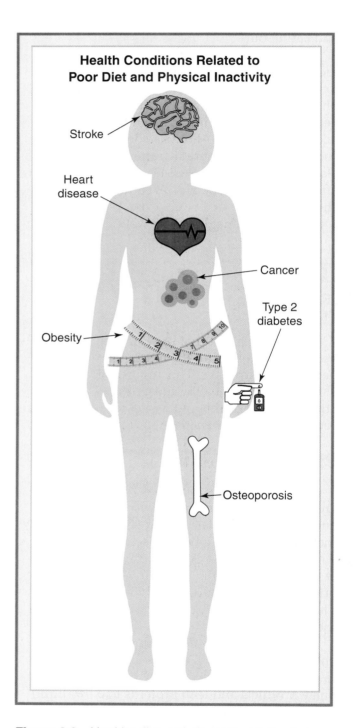

Figure 8.2 Healthy diet and physical activity choices made early in life can decrease or prevent risk factors for these common diseases.

Many diseases caused by unhealthy habits can lead to secondary health risks. For instance, someone who makes the unhealthy choice to smoke tobacco may get cancer. Chemotherapy drugs used to treat the cancer could produce side effects that include nausea and lack of appetite. In response to these symptoms, the patient may be unwilling or unable to eat a healthy diet. This, in turn, will create a secondary health risk for nutrition-related problems.

Resources for Making Healthy Food Choices

Many reports about health issues are linked to nutrients. Supermarkets, health food stores, and pharmacies all have shelves lined with bottles of nutrient supplements. Food packages make claims about the nutrient content of products.

Having some tools can help people sort out all the nutrition information they encounter. Standards are available to help people know how much of each nutrient they should consume each day. General guidelines exist to make it easier to choose a healthy diet. A model has been developed to help plan nutritious meals. Using these resources can assist people in making healthy food choices.

Dietary Reference Intakes

People need a way to tell if they are meeting their nutrient needs. The Institute of Medicine developed a set of values to help. This set of values is called the **Dietary Reference Intakes (DRIs)**. These are estimated nutrient intake levels used for planning and evaluating the diets of healthy people. They are standards against which the nutritional quality of a diet can be measured. The DRIs are designed to help prevent diseases caused by a lack of nutrients. They are also designed to reduce the risk of diseases linked to nutrition. Such diseases include heart disease, some types of cancer, and osteoporosis. **Figure 8.3** shows DRIs for teens for select nutrients.

Dietary Guidelines for Americans

A key resource for planning a healthy diet is the **Dietary Guidelines for Americans**. It is

DRIs for Teens		
Nutrient	**Males 14–18 years**	**Females 14–18 years**
Protein	52 g	46 g
Carbohydrate	130 g	130 g
Fiber	38 g	26 g
Vitamin A	900 µg	700 µg
Vitamin C	75 mg	65 mg
Vitamin D	15 µg	15 µg
Calcium	1,300 mg	1,300 mg
Iron	11 mg	15 mg
Potassium	3,000 mg	2,300 mg

Figure 8.3 Most healthy teens who consume these amounts of nutrients through their daily food choices are eating nutritionally adequate diets.

the federal government's nutritional advice. It is intended to promote health and reduce the risk of *chronic* (long-term) diseases. This resource urges people to adopt dietary patterns and physical activity levels to reach these goals. A **dietary pattern** is a mix of foods and beverages that make up a person's total dietary intake over time. The *Dietary Guidelines* focuses on dietary patterns rather than individual nutrients.

The *Dietary Guidelines* is published by the U.S. Department of Agriculture (USDA) and the U.S. Department of Health and Human Services (HHS). It is based on scientific evidence and is revised every five years to reflect new findings about health and nutrition. The *2020–2025 Dietary Guidelines for Americans* provides the following four guidelines that promote healthy dietary patterns:

- Follow a healthy dietary pattern at every life stage.
- Customize and enjoy nutrient-dense food and beverage choices to reflect personal preferences, cultural traditions, and budgetary considerations.
- Focus on meeting food group needs with nutrient-dense foods and beverages, and stay within calorie limits.
- Limit foods and beverages that are higher in added sugars, saturated fat, and sodium, and limit alcoholic beverages.

Learn About...

Types of DRI Values

Different types of DRI values are set for different nutrients. Values for some nutrients are expressed as *Recommended Dietary Allowances (RDAs)*. Values for other nutrients are expressed as *Adequate Intakes (AIs)*. The difference between these types of values has to do with the amount of research available to nutrition experts. (AIs are used when there is insufficient evidence to establish an RDA.)

What is important to remember is that both types of values can be used as guides to daily nutrient intake. For instance, you might use them to assess whether the latest fad diet provides enough of all the needed nutrients. These values could also help you decide whether a food product promoted to be nutritious really lives up to its advertising claims.

One other type of DRI value is the *Tolerable Upper Intake Level (UL)*. This is the highest level of daily intake of a nutrient that is unlikely to pose risks of adverse health effects. Keep in mind that ULs are not intended to be recommended levels of intake. Health experts have found no advantage to consuming more than the RDA or AI of any nutrient. As intake increases above the UL, the risk of adverse effects increases. People can use ULs to check whether they might be consuming too much of any nutrient. See Appendix A, "Nutritional Goals for Age-Sex Groups."

Know and Apply

1. Use DRI values to explain the concept of nutrient toxicity.

2. Give an example of professionals who are likely to use DRI values in their work and explain how they might use them.

This edition of the *Guidelines* emphasizes the importance of healthy dietary patterns at every life stage and includes recommendations for infants and toddlers for the first time. A basic premise of the *2020–2025 Dietary Guidelines* is that most people, regardless of their health status, can benefit from shifting food and beverage choices to healthy dietary patterns. The sooner changes are made, the sooner positive effects will be enjoyed.

Follow a Healthy Dietary Pattern at Every Life Stage

There is more than one healthy dietary pattern consumers may choose to follow. The *Guidelines* uses the Healthy U.S.-Style Dietary Pattern as an example, but also provides two other healthy dietary patterns: Mediterranean-style and vegetarian. When followed, these dietary patterns provide the nutrients needed for health. Eating healthfully is important at every life stage—infancy, toddlerhood, childhood, adolescence, adulthood, pregnancy, lactation, and older adulthood. The Healthy U.S.-Style Dietary Pattern can be followed by Americans of any age, race, ethnicity, or sex. When healthy dietary patterns are established early and are sustained throughout life, the positive effect on health can be significant. On the other hand, high intakes of foods and beverages that contain much added sugar, saturated fat, and sodium can increase the risk for developing chronic diseases. Fortunately, any efforts to embrace a healthy dietary pattern at any stage of life can improve health.

Regardless which dietary pattern is used, the calorie level must be appropriate. The proper calorie level will help you achieve and maintain a healthy body weight. The total number of calories a person needs depends on the individual's age, sex, height, weight, level of physical activity, and pregnancy or lactation status. The total number of calories needed is also affected by an individual's need to gain, lose, or maintain weight.

In the United States, a main reason for poor health and increased disease risk is overweight. Being overweight is a risk factor for many health conditions, including heart disease and many types of cancer. Following the advice from the *Dietary Guidelines* will help people who have a healthy body weight avoid weight gain. It will help people who are overweight lose excess pounds and improve their weight status.

Body weight is partly due to how many calories people consume through foods and beverages. It is also the result of how many calories are burned through movement and body functions. When calories consumed equal calories burned,

Daily Calorie Needs		
	Sex and Age Group	
Activity Level	Females, 14–18 years	Males, 14–18 years
Sedentary	1,800	2,000–2,400*
Moderately Active	2,000	2,400–2,800*
Active	2,400	2,800–3,200*

*Lower calorie levels within a range are needed by younger teens; higher levels are needed by older teens.

Figure 8.4 Calorie needs are affected by body size as well as age and activity level. These calorie needs are estimates based on median body sizes for 14- to 18-year-old teens.

a person is in **calorie balance**. People who consume more calories than they burn will gain weight.

Activity also has an impact on daily calorie needs. Three levels are used to describe how much movement people include in their lifestyles. Those who are *sedentary* move only as much as needed to do day-to-day tasks. *Moderately active* people add 30 to 60 minutes of extra activity to their daily routines. This activity would require effort equal to brisk walking. People who add more than 60 minutes of extra activity are at the *active* level. Calorie needs for teens at each of these levels are listed in Figure 8.4.

Customize and Enjoy Nutrient-Dense Food and Beverage Choices to Reflect Personal Preferences, Cultural Traditions, and Budgetary Considerations

The *Dietary Guidelines* provides recommendations for food groups and subgroups rather than specific foods and beverages. This strategy allows individuals to customize their dietary patterns by selecting healthy foods, beverages, meals, and snacks that meet their personal and cultural preferences while staying within their budget.

Focus on Meeting Food Group Needs with Nutrient-Dense Foods and Beverages, and Stay Within Calorie Limits

To meet nutrient needs without consuming more calories than needed requires variety.

Health and Wellness

The Physical Activity Side of Calorie Balance

Increasing physical activity goes hand in hand with tracking calorie intake to manage weight. Being physically active does more than burn the calories consumed from foods. It improves muscle tone and strengthens the heart and lungs. It also promotes a sense of mental well-being.

The activities chosen should call for more movement than what is needed for normal daily tasks. Moderate activities include bike riding, brisk walking, and gardening. Jogging, playing soccer, and swimming laps are more vigorous activities. They can be enjoyed instead of or in addition to activities that are less intense. Choosing some muscle-strengthening activities, such as climbing and lifting weights, is also important.

Adults should try to get at least 150 minutes of physical activity per week. Children and teens need at least 60 minutes of activity per day. Spending more time or choosing more intense activities can give added health benefits.

For many people, becoming more active means limiting screen time and other forms of inactivity. Some activity is better than no activity. People who are not already active can begin with short activity periods a few days a week. Choosing fun activities they can enjoy with others will encourage them to stay active. Then they can slowly build up the amount of activity they choose.

©iStock.com/CREATISTA

Dance benefits your health in many ways including improved strength, endurance, balance, flexibility, and bone health.

This means including a diverse assortment of foods and beverages across and within all food groups and subgroups in your daily diet. Eating a variety of foods within the appropriate calorie level is important for good health. An individual's nutrient needs are better met with food rather than with supplements.

While choosing foods within calorie limits, it is important to make choices that are good sources of required nutrients. This means choosing more foods and beverages that are **nutrient dense**. Such choices provide vitamins, minerals, and other health-promoting substances with little or no added sugar, saturated fat, and sodium.

The most nutrient-dense forms of foods also keep nutritional components that occur in them naturally. For instance, unsweetened applesauce is fairly nutrient dense. It is fat free and contains no added sugars. However, a fresh apple is even more nutrient dense than the unsweetened sauce. The whole fruit is a source of dietary fiber, some of which is lost when the fruit is made into sauce (**Figure 8.5**).

Health experts urge people to eat more foods that provide potassium, dietary fiber, calcium, and vitamin D. These nutrients are low in many diets. Many Americans consume less than recommended amounts of fruits and vegetables. Eating more of these foods will help people get many of the nutrients that may be low in their diets. The nutrients supplied by fruits and vegetables vary from one type to another. Choosing

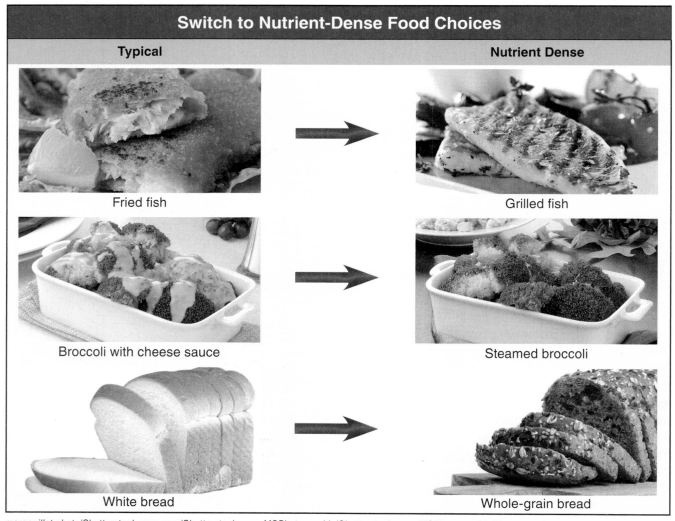

Switch to Nutrient-Dense Food Choices

Typical	Nutrient Dense
Fried fish	Grilled fish
Broccoli with cheese sauce	Steamed broccoli
White bread	Whole-grain bread

Figure 8.5 Over time, small changes in food choices contribute to good health. What other nutrient-dense food choices could you make?

a variety of fruits and vegetables each day will provide a range of nutrients. Studies have shown that diets rich in fruits and vegetables are linked to lower risks of many diseases.

Most fruits and vegetables are naturally low in fat and calories, and high in fiber. Preparing and eating these foods without adding fats and sugars will allow them to remain nutrient dense. Eating more fruits and vegetables can help people eat fewer foods that are higher in calories. This can help people stay within their daily calorie needs.

Healthy dietary patterns include whole grains and limit the amounts of refined grains and products made with refined grains. To include whole-grain foods more often, look for product labels that include the whole grains health claim or the number of grams of whole grain in the product. A product that is 100-percent whole grain will contain 16 grams of whole grains per ounce. Another hint that a food is 100-percent whole grain is if whole-grain ingredients are listed first in the ingredients list.

Similar to fruits and vegetables, dairy products—milk, yogurt, and cheese—are low in many American diets. Increasing intake of these foods will provide needed potassium, calcium, and vitamin D. Fat-free and low-fat milk are the most nutrient-dense forms of dairy products. Flavored yogurt often has added sugars. Whole and reduced fat (2%) milk and cheese contain saturated fats. Replacing higher fat products with those that are lower in fat will reduce calorie intake. People who do not wish to use cows' milk products can use fortified soy beverages or other nondairy milk alternatives instead.

Most American diets include sufficient protein; however, dietary patterns can be improved with slight changes to the choice of proteins. For instance, choosing lean meats and poultry more often, and limiting processed meats and poultry will reduce saturated fats and sodium. Choosing unsalted nuts and seeds will reduce sodium in the diet. Seafood will supply beneficial oils. Beans, peas, and lentils are affordable, low-fat, high-fiber sources of protein.

Oils are important to good health, but are calorie dense. For this reason, oils should replace saturated fats in the diet, rather than be an addition.

Another step many people must take to balance calories is to be mindful of amounts and avoid oversized portions. Unfortunately, large portions are common in many restaurants. Choosing smaller portions from appetizer or lunch menus is one way to address this concern. Splitting a meal with someone and setting aside food to take home are other ways to avoid eating large portions.

When not eating out, be aware of the amounts of food eaten at one time. Read the Nutrition Facts panels on food labels. Check serving sizes listed on labels and compare them with the amounts of food typically eaten. Realize that eating a portion that is double the given serving size will provide twice the number of calories listed. Learn to estimate serving sizes more accurately using your hand as a guide (**Figure 8.6**).

When dishing up foods, serve small amounts. At meals, use small plates to make *modest* (limited in size) food portions look bigger. This will keep you from putting more food on the plate than you really need or want. When eating snacks, put small portions in dishes rather than eating out of packages.

Limit Foods and Beverages That Are Higher in Added Sugars, Saturated Fat, and Sodium, and Limit Alcoholic Beverages

For many people, choosing a dietary pattern means eating less of some foods. These include foods that are higher in added sugars, saturated fat, and sodium. The *Dietary Guidelines* recommends the following limits for a healthy dietary pattern:

- *Added sugars*—less than 10 percent of calories per day starting at age two years; foods and beverages with added sugars should be avoided for those under age two
- *Saturated fat*—less than 10 percent of calories per day starting at age two years
- *Sodium*—less than 2,300 milligrams per day and less for children younger than 14 years old

Some foods, such as sugar-sweetened drinks, candy, and desserts, provide mostly empty calories. **Empty calories** come from saturated fat and added sugars, which offer little nutritional value in foods. Save these foods for occasional treats and choose small portions.

Empty calories are also found in many nutritious foods. For instance, fruit-flavored yogurt

Serving-Size Comparison Chart

FOOD	SYMBOL	COMPARISON	SERVING SIZE
Milk & Milk Products			
Cheese (string cheese)		Pointer finger	1½ ounces
Milk and yogurt (glass of milk)		  One fist	1 cup
Vegetables			
Cooked carrots		  One fist	1 cup
Salad (bowl of salad)		  Two fists	2 cups
Fruits			
Apple		  One fist	1 medium
Canned peaches		  One fist	1 cup
Grains, Breads & Cereals			
Dry cereal (bowl of cereal)		  One fist	1 cup
Noodles, rice, oatmeal (bowl of noodles)		  Handful	½ cup
Slice of whole-wheat bread		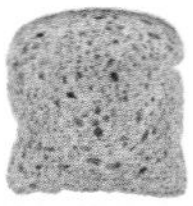  Flat hand	1 slice
Meat, Beans & Nuts			
Chicken, beef, fish, pork (chicken breast)		 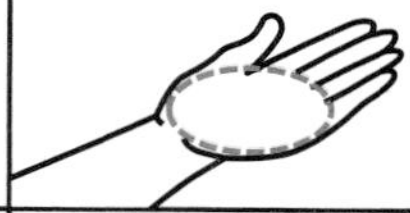 Palm	3 ounces
Peanut butter (spoon of peanut butter)		  Thumb	1 tablespoon

Reprinted with the permission of Dairy Council of California, 2015

Figure 8.6 Your hand can be a useful reference when judging serving sizes and it is always with you no matter where you are eating. Use the images in the Symbol column as practical guidelines to help you judge amounts of food and avoid overeating.

is a good source of calcium and protein, but it contains much added sugar, too. Some fried fish may be high in omega-3 fatty acids, but the batter and frying oil add a number of empty calories from added fat. Plain, fat-free yogurt flavored with fresh fruit and broiled fish would be more nutrient-dense versions of these foods.

In the United States, most people would benefit from consuming fewer foods that are high in sodium. Most of the sodium in the average diet comes from processed foods. Read the Nutrition Facts panel to learn how much sodium foods contain. Compare products and choose those that have lower amounts. Also, limit the amount of salt added to foods during preparation and at the table.

Sodium is a vital nutrient. However, too much salt in the diet can cause high blood pressure. Potassium helps offset some of the effects sodium has on blood pressure. Therefore, along with curbing sodium, make an effort to increase potassium intake. Foods like baked potatoes, tomato products, and yogurt are good sources of this mineral.

Other foods most people need to reduce are those high in added sugars. The largest source of added sugars in American diets is, by far, soda, energy drinks, and sports drinks (**Figure 8.7**). In fact, the average teen consumes about 500 calories a day from added sugars, mostly from drinks. When these calories take the place of calories from foods, vital nutrients may be lacking. When calories from drinks are consumed in addition to foods, weight gain can occur.

Drinking plenty of fluids all through the day is important. This is even more true during periods of increased activity. However, drinking water in place of sugary drinks would greatly reduce added sugars and calories for many people.

Adults of legal drinking age can choose not to drink or to drink alcoholic beverages in moderation. Adult males should limit intake to

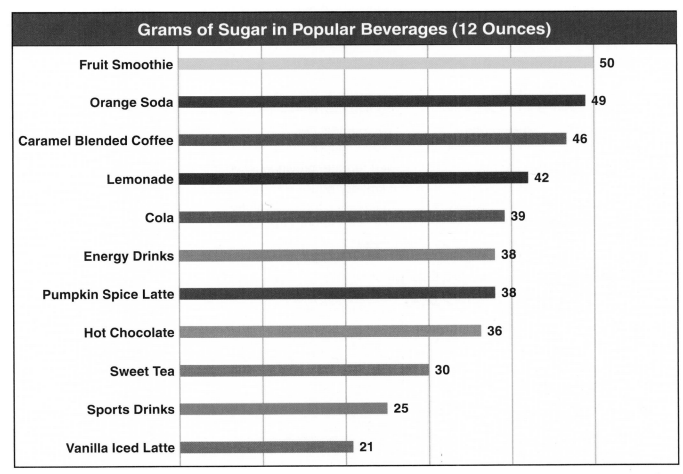

Figure 8.7 Sugary drinks like soda, energy drinks, and sports drinks are the largest source of added sugars in American diets.

Mini Lab: Evaluating Beverage Choices

Looking at the Sugar in Drinks

This lab involves using a kitchen scale to weigh the amounts of sugar in various portions of common beverage choices. If a scale is not available for each lab group, sugar can be measured in teaspoons rather than grams. If using this measurement method, you will need to keep in mind that 1 teaspoon (5 mL) of sugar equals 4 grams.

1. Create an observation sheet identifying your assigned beverage. Make a 5-column table, heading the columns with the following labels: **Portion Size**, **Amount of Sugar**, **Calories**, **Walking Time (minutes)**, **Walking Distance (miles)**.

2. Use a permanent marker to label three small zip-top plastic bags with your lab group's assigned beverage. Also label each of the bags with one of the specified portion sizes for your beverage.

3. Using product information provided by your teacher, calculate the amount of sugar that would be in a 12-ounce (355 mL) serving of your beverage. Record this amount in the appropriate space in your observation table.

4. Set your scale for **grams**. Place a small bowl on the scale and press the **tare** button. This will allow you to measure the weight of the sugar without including the weight of the bowl.

5. Weigh the amount of sugar you calculated in Step 3 and carefully pour it into the bag labeled **12 ounces**.

6. Place the empty bowl back on the scale. Calculate and record the amounts of sugar in the other two specified portion sizes for your beverage. Then weigh those amounts and pour them into the appropriately labeled bags.

7. As a pure carbohydrate, sugar provides 4 calories per gram. Calculate the number of calories provided by the sugar in each portion size of your beverage and record your calculations in the appropriate spaces in your observation table.

8. Place an empty bag on the scale and press the **tare** button. Remove the bag from the scale and weigh the bag of sugar labeled **male**, provided by your teacher. Record this amount on your observation sheet as the recommended daily limit for added sugars for a teen male.

9. Repeat Step 8 with the bag of sugar labeled **female**, provided by your teacher.

10. Walking at a moderate pace (3 miles [4.8 km] per hour), a 150-pound (68 kg) male burns about 4 calories per minute. A 120-pound (54 kg) female burns about 3 calories per minute. Calculate the number of minutes a male and female would need to walk to burn the calories provided by the sugar in each portion size of your assigned beverage. Record your calculations in the appropriate spaces in your observation table, separating the male calculations from the female calculations with a slash (/).

11. Each minute of walking equals a distance of about 0.05 miles. Calculate the distance a male and female would need to walk to burn the calories provided by the sugar in each portion size of your assigned beverage. Record your calculations in the appropriate spaces in your observation table, again separating the male calculations from the female calculations with a slash (/).

12. Compare your observations with those of the other lab groups. Then answer the following questions:

    A. Looking at the amounts of sugar in 12-ounce (355 mL) servings, how did your assigned beverage compare with other beverages?

    B. How did the amounts of sugar in common portions of your beverage compare with the recommended daily limit for added sugars for teen males and females?

    C. What did you find most surprising about the findings in this activity?

    D. What impact will these findings make on your future beverage choices?

two drinks or less per day and adult females should limit intake to one drink or less per day. Some adults should not drink alcohol, such as women who are pregnant.

MyPlate

To help people with their diet choices, the USDA created flexible patterns for healthy eating. These patterns outline daily amounts of foods to eat from five major food groups. The recommended daily intakes are determined by a person's calorie needs. Eating the suggested amounts of foods from each group daily will provide people with required nutrients.

The USDA's food guidance system is called **MyPlate**. The **MyPlate**.gov website offers a variety of information and links to help people make healthy eating choices. A key element of the MyPlate system is its simple visual message. The MyPlate icon helps people visualize how the food groups fit together to build a healthy plate at mealtime (**Figure 8.8**). Choosing nutrient-dense forms of foods from each food group will allow people to stay within their calorie limits.

Grains Group

The grains group includes such foods as breads, cereals, rice, and pasta. These foods are

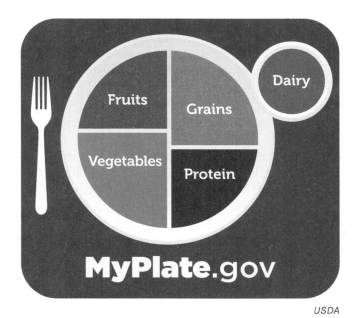

USDA

Figure 8.8 The MyPlate icon shows a place setting to illustrate the proportions of the five food groups that should make up a healthy diet.

Health and Wellness

Make Half Your Grains Whole

Whole grains, such as brown rice, oatmeal, barley, and whole wheat, are good sources of dietary fiber. Getting enough fiber in the diet helps keep bowels working properly. Fiber also helps people feel full after eating, so they may be less likely to overeat.

Refined-grain products do not provide all the nutrients and fiber found in whole grains. Many refined-grain products, such as cakes and cookies, are also high in solid fats and added sugars.

Health experts recommend people get at least half their daily grain needs from whole-grain sources. Look for whole-grain ingredients to appear first on ingredient lists for bread and cereal products. (Be aware that *whole-wheat flour* refers to a whole-grain ingredient but *wheat flour* does not.) Choose a variety of grain foods to receive the most health benefits.

excellent low-fat sources of complex carbohydrates, which supply energy. They are also good sources of B vitamins and iron. Whole-grain foods are high in fiber as well.

Amounts of foods in this group are counted in *ounce-equivalents*. This term refers to a portion size that is equal to a one-ounce (28 g) serving.

MyPlate divides this group into two subgroups—whole grains and refined grains. Whole grains include whole-wheat bread, oatmeal, and brown rice. Refined grains include foods like white bread, enriched pasta, and white rice. People should make at least half their daily grain food choices from the whole-grains subgroup.

Vegetable Group

The vegetable group includes any vegetable or 100-percent vegetable juice. Vegetables may be raw or cooked; canned, frozen, or dried; and may be whole, cut up, or mashed. These foods are good sources of vitamins, minerals, and fiber.

MyPlate divides vegetables into the following five subgroups:
- *dark green vegetables*, such as broccoli, spinach, collard greens, and kale
- *red and orange vegetables*, such as carrots, sweet potatoes, and winter squash
- *beans, peas, and lentils*, such as pinto and navy beans, lentils, and soybean products like tofu
- *starchy vegetables*, such as white potatoes, corn, and green peas
- *other vegetables*, such as tomatoes, lettuce, green beans, and onions

People do not need to choose vegetables from each subgroup every day. However, they should be sure to include foods from all five subgroups in their diets throughout the week.

Fruit Group

The fruit group includes all forms of fruits—fresh, canned, frozen, and dried. Fruits (except avocados) are low-fat, high-fiber sources of vitamins and minerals. Pure fruit juices (not fruit drinks or punches) are part of this group, too. However, they do not provide much fiber. Therefore, choose whole or cut-up fruits most often.

Dairy Group

Foods from the dairy group—such as milk, yogurt, and cheese—are the best sources of calcium. They also provide riboflavin, phosphorus, and protein. Whole- and fortified-milk products provide vitamins A and D as well. Fortified soy milk and yogurt are included in the dairy group.

A number of people avoid foods from this group for health or lifestyle reasons. Yogurt and lactose-free milk may be good alternatives for some people. Increased amounts of calcium-rich foods from other food groups can also help meet calcium needs. Such foods include fortified cereals, tofu, canned salmon with bones, and spinach.

Protein Foods Group

The protein foods group includes meat, poultry, seafood, beans, peas, lentils, eggs, processed soy products, and nuts. These foods are excellent sources of protein. They supply vitamins and minerals, including B vitamins and

iron. Beans, peas, and lentils are also rich in fiber, so choose them often as meat alternates. (Note that beans, peas, and lentils can count toward either protein intake or toward vegetable intake, but not both.) Remember to make seafood the protein on your plate at least twice per week. Like grain foods, protein foods are counted in ounce-equivalents (**Figure 8.9**).

Oils

Oils in the diet come from cooking oil, soft margarines, and salad dressing. They are also found in such foods as fish and nuts. Oils are *not* a food group. However, they are good sources of vitamin E and essential fatty acids. Small amounts are necessary for good health.

Saturated Fats and Added Sugars

Oils are not the only foods that do not fit into the five main groups of MyPlate. Other such foods include butter, jams, jellies, syrups, candies, gravies, and many desserts and snack foods. These foods provide mostly empty calories from saturated fats and/or added sugars. Foods that are high in these components tend to be low in vitamins and minerals.

Most people would nearly reach their daily calorie limits if they chose just nutrient-dense foods to meet their needs from MyPlate. Healthy dietary patterns can allow for only a small number of empty calories from saturated fats and added sugars. One way you might use these calories is to give flavor and variety to nutrient-dense foods. For instance, you could top vegetables with a little butter or drizzle some honey on whole-grain cereal. However, foods such as sugary drinks and candy fit only rarely into most healthy food plans.

MyPlate is flexible. It can help you plan healthy meals at any budget level. MyPlate can also help you plan healthy meals for individuals at most life-cycle stages while accommodating cultural food preferences and special diets. For instance, a vegetarian who enjoys Mexican food might fill a tortilla from the grains group with refried beans from the protein foods group. This could be topped with tomatillos from the vegetable group and cheese from the dairy group. Papaya from the fruit group would complete the meal. People can use their recommended amounts

Food Group Examples		
Food Group	**What Counts?**	**Typical Foods**
Grains Group 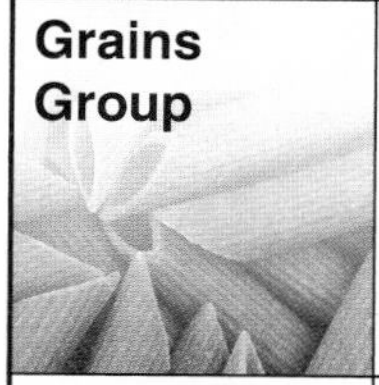	1 ounce-equivalent: • 1 slice bread • 1 cup (250 mL) dry cereal • ½ cup (125 mL) cooked cereal, rice, or pasta	Whole grains: brown rice, bulgur, oatmeal, popcorn, whole-grain barley and corn, whole-grain cereals and crackers, whole-wheat breads, wild rice • Refined grains: enriched cereals, crackers, and pasta; flour and corn tortillas; white breads; white rice
Vegetable Group 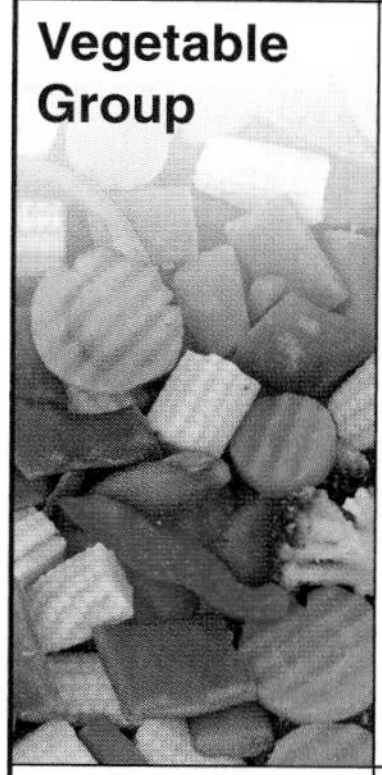	1 cup-equivalent: • 1 cup (250 mL) fresh or cooked cut vegetables • 1 cup (250 mL) vegetable juice • 2 cups (500 mL) raw leafy vegetables	• Dark green vegetables: broccoli; collard, turnip, and mustard greens; romaine; spinach • Red and orange vegetables: carrots, pumpkin, sweet potatoes, winter squash, tomatoes, red peppers, beets • Beans, peas, and lentils: kidney, lima, and navy beans; black-eyed peas; chickpeas; lentils; tofu • Starchy vegetables: corn, green peas, white potatoes • Other vegetables: bok choy, cucumbers, eggplant, green beans, lettuce, okra, onions, pea pods, green bell peppers, summer squash
Fruit Group 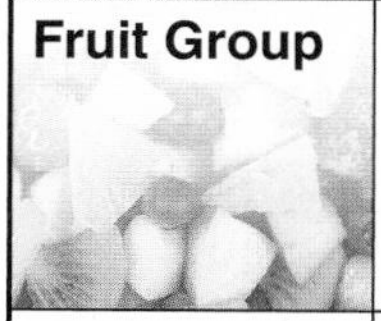	1 cup-equivalent: • 1 cup (250 mL) fresh or canned fruit • 1 cup (250 mL) fruit juice • ½ cup (125 mL) dried fruit	Apples, apricots, bananas, blueberries, cantaloupe, cherries, figs, fruit juice, grapefruit, grapes, kiwifruit, mangoes, oranges, papayas, peaches, pineapple, plums, raisins, strawberries, watermelon
Dairy Group 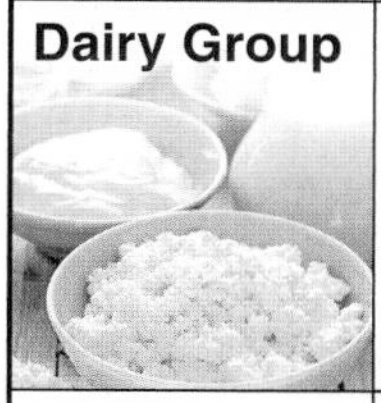	1 cup-equivalent: • 1 cup (250 mL) milk or yogurt • 1½ ounces (43 g) hard cheese • 2 ounces (57 g) process cheese • 2 cups (500 mL) cottage cheese	Buttermilk, calcium-fortified soy milk, cheese, cottage cheese, fat-free milk, frozen yogurt, goat's milk, ice cream, kefir, low-fat milk, whole milk, yogurt
Protein Foods Group 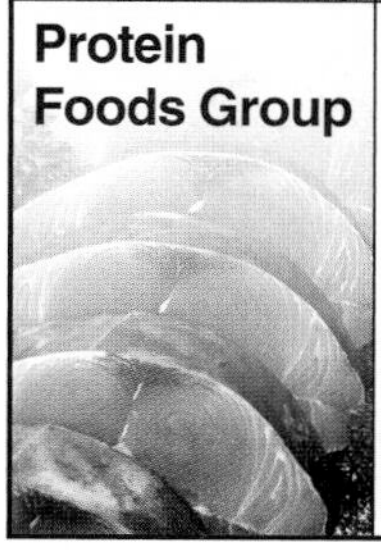	1 ounce-equivalent: • 1 ounce (28 g) cooked lean meat, poultry, or seafood • 1 egg • 1 tablespoon (15 mL) peanut butter • ¼ cup (60 mL) cooked dry beans or tofu • ½ ounce (14 g) nuts or seeds	Beef, beans, peas, chicken, eggs, fish, lamb, lentils, nuts, peanut butter, pork, rabbit, refried beans, seeds, shellfish, tofu, turkey, veal, venison

Top to bottom: ©iStock.com/maggeee; ©iStock.com/JelenaAloskina; ©iStock.com/Boardin1Now; ©iStock.com/letterberry; ©iStock.com/Bignai

Figure 8.9 Choose a variety of foods from each MyPlate food group to get your daily recommended amounts of food.

from each food group to form almost any combination of meals and snacks (**Figure 8.10**).

Meeting Your Daily Needs

How can the various resources be used to help meet daily nutritional needs? An easy way to begin is to plan menus using MyPlate (**Figure 8.11**). Include the recommended number of daily servings in your meals throughout the day. Keep the *Dietary Guidelines for Americans* in mind as you select foods.

You can use the DRIs to help you evaluate your menu plans. These recommended nutrient intakes can show you whether your menus will provide you with all the nutrients you need. Be sure to consider all beverages, condiments, and snack foods as well as meal items.

Recommended Daily Intakes*

	Calorie Level							
	1,800	**2,000**	**2,200**	**2,400**	**2,600**	**2,800**	**3,000**	**3,200**
Grains	6 oz.-eq.	6 oz.-eq.	7 oz.-eq.	8 oz.-eq.	9 oz.-eq.	10 oz.-eq.	10 oz.-eq.	10 oz.-eq.
Vegetables	2.5 c.	2.5 c.	3 c.	3 c.	3.5 c.	3.5 c.	4 c.	4 c.
Fruits	1.5 c.	2 c.	2 c.	2 c.	2 c.	2.5 c.	2.5 c.	2.5 c.
Dairy	3 c.	3 c.	3 c.	3 c.	3 c.	3 c.	3 c.	3 c.
Protein Foods	5 oz.-eq.	5.5 oz.-eq.	6 oz.-eq.	6.5 oz.-eq.	6.5 oz.-eq.	7 oz.-eq.	7 oz.-eq.	7 oz.-eq.
Oils	5 tsp.	6 tsp.	6 tsp.	7 tsp.	7 tsp.	8 tsp.	10 tsp.	11 tsp.

*Food group amounts are shown in cup (c.) or ounce-equivalents (oz. eq.). Oils are shown in teaspoons (tsp.).

Figure 8.10   MyPlate is intended to help each person choose the types and amounts of foods that are right for him or her.

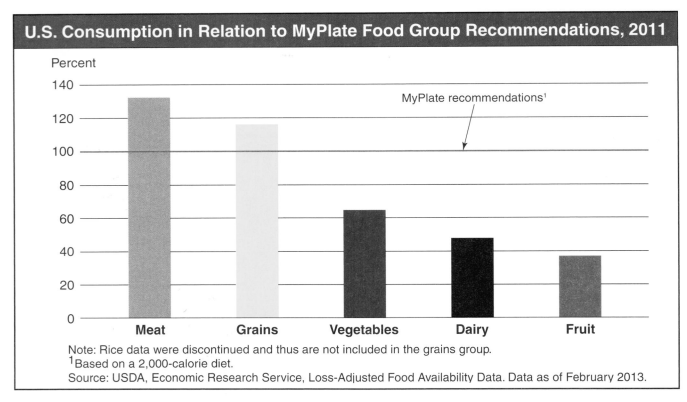

Figure 8.11   This graph shows that U.S. citizens are eating about 133% of the recommended amounts of meat and about 118% of the recommended amounts for grains. According to this graph, roughly what percent of the recommended amounts of vegetables are U.S. citizens consuming?

You can use a computer and a spreadsheet program to perform a nutrient analysis. Alternately, you can make a table on paper to calculate an analysis manually.

Use an online nutrient database to find each food in your menus. Reliable diet analysis websites are also available to help you evaluate menu plans. In either case, note the amounts of nutrients supplied by your menus. Then compare these nutrient totals with the DRIs for your sex and age group.

What if your comparison shows your menu plans are low in some nutrients? You can refer to Chapters 6 and 7 to help you identify food sources of needed nutrients. Then you can add these sources to your menu plans.

Choosing Wisely When Shopping for Food

The foods people choose at the grocery store become the foods they will later choose to eat at home. Plan nutritious menus before going to the store. Then make careful grocery purchases to ensure healthy foods are on hand.

Fresh or Processed?

When shopping for food, one of the decisions you will need to make is when to buy processed foods instead of fresh. **Processed foods** are foods that have undergone some preparation procedure, such as canning, freezing, drying, cooking, or fortification. In most cases, processing adds to the cost of foods. It often decreases the nutritional value of foods as well. For instance, when potatoes are processed into potato chips, they lose nearly all their nutrients. In addition, their fat and sodium contents increase. There are, however, some exceptions to the processing rule. For instance, frozen and canned fruits and vegetables may be as nutritious as fresh fruits and vegetables. When whole milk is processed to remove the fat, it becomes fat-free milk, which is a healthier product.

Fresh foods, such as fresh meat, poultry, eggs, and produce, have not been processed. In general, the closer a food is to its fresh state, the more nutrient dense it is likely to be. However, it is important to note that some nutrients in fresh foods can be lost during storage. Fresh foods can also spoil if they are kept too long. Therefore, fresh foods should be used as soon after purchase as possible.

Some people say they choose processed foods because they do not have time to prepare fresh foods. Keep in mind that many fresh foods require little or no preparation. For instance, snacking on an apple and a glass of milk takes no more time than consuming chips and a can of soda. Not surprisingly, the fresh food snack is lower in calories, saturated fat, added sugars, and sodium. It is also higher in protein, fiber, and many vitamins and minerals (**Figure 8.12**).

Tips for Healthy Shopping

Choose fresh foods as often as possible. Select foods that are high in quality and follow guidelines for storing fresh foods to maintain their nutrients.

When buying canned, frozen, and dried forms of foods, avoid products in packaging that is soiled or damaged. Select package sizes that best suit your needs. Following suggestions about shopping for processed items will help you make healthy choices.

When shopping for processed foods, be aware that some are more nutrient dense than others. For instance, peaches canned in unsweetened fruit juice and peaches canned in syrup are both processed foods. However, the peaches in juice are more nutrient dense because they are lower in added sugars and calories.

Products with labels such as *less sugar, low calorie*, and *reduced fat* can make it easier to fit some foods into a healthy diet. As you consider purchasing these foods, however, be sure to read Nutrition Facts labels carefully. A reduced-fat product could still be high in calories. A low-calorie product might contain a lot of sodium. Reading and comparing package labels can help you choose healthier options.

How Processed Is Your Breakfast?	
Instant Oatmeal Ingredient List	**Home-Cooked Oatmeal Ingredient List**
whole-grain rolled oats, sugar, dehydrated apples (treated with sodium sulfite) natural and artificial flavor, salt, cinnamon, calcium carbonate, citric acid, guar gum, malic acid, niacinamide, reduced iron, vitamin A palmitate, pyridoxine hydrochloride, riboflavin, thiamin mononitrate, folic acid, caramel color	whole-grain rolled oats, diced fresh apples, cinnamon

Figure 8.12 Instant oatmeal requires additional ingredients to make it shelf-stable and convenient. Which of these lists has ingredients with which you are familiar?

Nutritional labeling can also help you compare similar products and different brands of the same product. Suppose you are choosing between three-bean chili and cheese lasagna frozen entrees. Comparing labels can show you which product is lower in calories, saturated fat, sodium, and sugars. Comparing labels can also tell you which product is higher in protein and listed vitamins and minerals. Perhaps you know you want chili, but you cannot decide which brand. Again, comparing labels can help you make a healthy choice.

Choosing Wisely When Preparing Food

Making wise food choices at the grocery store is a good beginning to a healthy diet. However, the way people choose to prepare these foods greatly affects their nutritional quality.

Try to prepare foods from minimally processed ingredients whenever possible. Preparing foods from scratch gives you more control over what goes into them. You can elect how much and what type of fat to use when sautéing vegetables. You can decide when to omit salt or reduce sugar listed in a recipe. You can also choose which seasonings you use to suit your tastes. The ability to make these decisions can help you prepare foods with maximum flavor and nutrition.

Start with the Main Course

Most meal managers plan meals around a main course, which generally includes a source of protein. A few pointers can help people prepare main courses that will get their meals off to a healthy start.

Try increasing the emphasis on plant-based foods. Consider preparing meatless entrees on a regular basis. Legumes, such as dry beans, peas, and lentils, are rich in protein and fiber and low in saturated fat. You can use them to make hearty soups, stews, and casseroles to serve in place of meat dishes.

Another way to include more plant-based foods in the diet is to let side dishes become main dishes. Remember that half the plate should be fruits and vegetables. When seasoning those vegetables, use herbs and lemon juice instead of

Exploring Careers

Nutrition Epidemiologist

Nutrition epidemiologists study how nutritional factors play a role in the cause of some diseases. Through their research, they may find food intake patterns that create health risks. They may also learn about food components that help protect against certain diseases. These findings may then be used to help form public health and nutrition guidelines.

Nutrition epidemiologists may work for government agencies. They may be employed by colleges and universities to teach or carry out research. Drug companies may also hire these professionals.

Nutrition epidemiologists must be willing to take on challenges. They need patience to complete studies that may go on for years. They need leadership skills to be able to take charge of a study and work without close supervision. These professionals also need to be able to get along with fellow researchers. Nutrition epidemiologists use math skills to assess data and statistics. They need attention to detail so they do not overlook factors that could affect study outcomes. They need good communication skills for sharing the results of their studies.

Those interested in working in this area should have a strong background in math and the sciences. Their training will help them learn how to design and conduct scientific studies. Many jobs in this field require a master's degree. Some require a doctorate.

salt and butter. You will add flavor while cutting sodium, saturated fat, and calories.

When the main course does include animal protein foods, limit portion sizes. Remember that meeting protein needs does not require a platter-sized steak or half a chicken. A serving of lean, cooked meat, poultry, or fish is just 2 to 3 ounces (56 to 84 g). A 3-ounce (84 g) portion is about the size of a deck of playing cards. To make a moderate portion look bigger, try slicing it thin and fanning it out on the plate.

Remember to choose seafood in place of meat and poultry for a couple meals each week. When the main course does include meat and poultry, start lean. Trim all visible fat from meat. Remove the skin from poultry. These simple steps will reduce saturated fat and calories.

Use low-fat cooking methods when preparing entrees to keep calories within recommended limits. Instead of frying, choose roasting, broiling, grilling, braising, stewing, stir-frying, and microwaving. Avoid dipping entrees in batters and breading, which add calories. Use a rack when roasting to allow fats to drain. Avoid using cooking sauces that are high in added sugars, fat, or sodium. Use nonstick cooking spray to reduce the need for added fat when stir-frying. Try microwaving to save time as well as fat.

Add herbs to braising and stewing liquids to season them without salt. You may wish to use meat drippings and cooking liquid to make flavorful gravies and stocks. You can use a gravy separator to make it easy to prepare gravies without the fat. You can also chill meat drippings and stocks. Then skim the fat that forms on the top before making gravies and soups.

Add Healthy Side Dishes

After planning the main course, concentrate on other menu items. Choose sensible portions to help balance calories. Make a point of actually measuring out servings of some favorite foods. See what a serving of cereal looks like in one of your bowls. Become familiar with the appearance of a serving of rice or pasta on one of your plates. See how 6 ounces (175 mL) of juice or 8 ounces (250 mL) of milk looks in one of your glasses. Keeping these portion sizes in mind when serving food will help you avoid exceeding calorie needs (**Figure 8.13**).

When preparing pasta for side dishes and casseroles, avoid adding oil or salt to the cooking water. If you are using a packaged pasta mix, cut calories by using only half the amount of butter or margarine suggested. Follow this advice when preparing packaged rice, stuffing, and sauce mixes, too.

When evaluating a menu, do not forget the items served with entrees and side dishes. Toppings and spreads used at the table can affect the nutritional value of foods. Items like sour cream, cream cheese, salad dressings, mayonnaise, and jam add solid fat, sugars, and calories. Use these items

sparingly. Try reduced fat versions, or use plain nonfat yogurt in place of other creamy toppings. Season yogurt with herbs for tasty dressings and dips.

Make Sweets Satisfying

People often like to end a meal with a sweet dessert. Of course, many desserts are loaded with empty calories. However, you can take steps to make desserts more sensible.

Adjust dessert recipes to cut fat, sugar, and calories. One way to do this is to use fat-free or low-fat milk in place of whole milk in recipes. Use fat-free evaporated milk in place of cream, except for whipping. Reducing the number of egg yolks in recipes for baked goods will cut fat and calories. Two egg whites can be used to replace one whole egg. Reduce the amount of sugar listed in recipes for baked goods. Add vanilla or spices, such as cinnamon, ginger, and cloves, to make these recipes seem sweeter. Lightly dust cakes with powdered sugar instead of spreading them with frosting.

Save rich desserts for special occasions. Choose fruit for a dessert that can be enjoyed daily. When a high-calorie dessert is on the menu, serve moderate portions. A single scoop of ice cream, a small dish of pudding, or a slim slice of pie will satisfy the desire for sweets.

Mona Makela/Shutterstock.com

Figure 8.13 Choose whole-grain pasta for a healthier side dish. How many 1 ounce-equivalents from the grains group are in this 1-cup measure? (Hint: see Figure 8.9)

Choosing Wisely When Eating Out

Cooking and eating more meals at home can help people control calorie intake. Studies show that eating out puts people at increased risk of weight gain. Planning ahead by packing healthy meals at home to eat at school or work can help people make better food choices. When people do eat out, they can follow a few tips to make choices that will fit into a healthy diet.

Use Menu Information

Federal requirements make it easier for consumers to choose wisely at some eateries. Menus at many restaurants must show the number of calories in standard food and drink items. These requirements apply at restaurants with 20 or more locations. The ruling includes restaurant-type foods sold at places like grocery stores and movie theaters. Many vending machines are required to post calorie information, too. More detailed nutrition information must be provided if consumers ask for it. Seeing the number of calories in foods before ordering can help people make choices that fit into their daily needs (**Figure 8.14**).

In restaurants that do not post calories, a little knowledge can help consumers choose wisely. The more varied a menu is, the easier it is to find healthy food options when eating out. For instance, a family restaurant is likely to give more choices than a fast-food restaurant. However, even the limited menus at many fast-food restaurants offer some health-oriented foods. Look for menus that list items such as fruits, vegetables, and salads as optional sides.

In any type of restaurant, menu terms can give clues about the food. Many menu items are high in fat, sugars, and sodium. Watch out for buttered vegetables, fish broiled in butter, and pasta with butter sauce. Be aware of items served with cream sauces, gravy, or cheese. Notice items that are breaded, fried, or wrapped in pastry, too. These items are all likely to be high in fat, which adds extra calories. Keep in mind that many soups and sauces are high in sodium. Smoked, pickled, and barbecued foods are also likely to be high-sodium items. In addition, foods prepared by these methods have been shown to contain compounds that may cause cancer.

Order with Care

You can control how restaurants prepare food by ordering items that are made according to your preferences. Keep in mind what you have learned about shopping for and preparing food when ordering. For health-conscious menu selections, choose foods prepared with low-fat cooking methods. Ask to have foods prepared without salt or butter. Request that high-fat sauces and dressings be served on the side. You can add just enough to flavor, rather than smother, your food. Choose whole-grain rolls when they are available. Select a fresh vegetable salad instead of French fries to go with a meal. Go easy on salad dressing and toppings such as bacon bits and cheese. Opt for fresh fruits in place of rich pastries or heavy ice creams for dessert.

Remember, the amount of food eaten affects calorie intake as well as fat, sodium, and sugar consumption. At fast-food restaurants, choose regular rather than large-sized items. At full-service eateries, ask for a petite or half-sized

Andresr/Shutterstock

Figure 8.14 Use nutrition information on the menu to help you with your food choices. Most restaurants must supply this information, so ask waitstaff or the cashier if you do not see it.

portion. Consider ordering an appetizer instead of an entree. Split an entree with a friend. Do not feel you have to consume all the food you are served. You can always ask to have a take-home bag for food you do not finish. You might even want to have half of your entree packed before you begin eating. This will keep you from accidentally eating more than you had intended. These are all ways to help keep calories in balance.

Consider having water with your meal instead of ordering a soft drink. Water is a great thirst quencher, and this choice will save you money as well as calories from added sugars (**Figure 8.15**).

Foods eaten away from home are not always eaten in restaurants, but the same guidelines can be used when choosing foods from vending machines and in the school cafeteria. These guidelines also apply at the snack bar in the mall and the concession stands at ball games and festivals.

Eating out, like shopping for and preparing food, requires thought. Choose the right amounts from the food groups in MyPlate. Be aware of foods that are high in calories, added sugars, saturated fat, and sodium, too. Make healthy eating a lifetime habit.

MAIN DISHES

- Order meat, poultry, or fish that are described as *grilled, steamed, stir-fried, baked, broiled,* or *poached*
- Order meats with *loin* or *round* in the name
- Share an entrée with a friend, order a half-sized portion, or ask for half the entrée to be packaged in a take-home bag before you begin eating
- Avoid sauces and gravies or request they be served on the side
- Select sauces that are tomato based rather than cream based
- Ask for the bread basket to be removed from the table or request whole-grain options

SIDES & VEGETABLES

- Request whole-grain pasta or brown rice
- Ask to substitute steamed vegetables, roasted sweet potatoes, coleslaw, or a green salad for French fries or potato chips
- Select potato salad, coleslaw, or other salads that are dressed with vinaigrette rather than creamy dressings
- Request salad dressings, gravies, or sauces be served on the side so you can control the amount you use
- Order vinegar and oil dressing rather than creamy salad dressings

DRINKS HOT & COLD

- Drink water or seltzer with lime or lemon
- Order unsweetened iced herbal teas
- Skip the sugar and cream in your coffee or tea
- Limit smoothies, they can be very high in calories
- Understand cappuccino, caffe mocha, chai tea, or other sweet hot beverages supply many calories

DESSERTS & ICE CREAM

- Order fresh or poached fruit for dessert
- Share one dessert with a friend

Restaurant MENU of Tips for **Healthy Eating**

Figure 8.15 View the restaurant's menu online before you arrive so you have all the information you need to make a healthy choice. *Can you think of additional tips for making healthy choices when eating away from home?*

Chapter 8 Review and Expand

Summary

Making healthy choices has physical, social, and mental benefits. Choosing a nutritious diet can protect and possibly improve health. An adequate supply of nutrients promotes healthy skin, hair, and teeth. Having a sound body and healthy appearance can, in turn, have positive effects on work and family life. Choosing to be active can lead to a strong, fit body and an optimistic outlook. On the other hand, making unhealthy choices can have a number of risks.

Several resources can help people make healthy choices. They can use Dietary Reference Intakes to evaluate the quality of their diets. Following the *Dietary Guidelines for Americans* will help them form good eating and activity habits. Using the MyPlate food guidance system will assist them in planning menus that meet their daily nutritional needs.

Using these resources, people can make informed choices when shopping for fresh and processed foods. They can also make wise decisions about how they prepare those foods. They can choose sensibly when eating away from home, too.

Vocabulary Activities

1. **Content Terms**   Select three terms from the list of content terms that follow. Explain how these three terms are related to each other. Create a graphic organizer or write a paragraph to explain or illustrate how the terms relate.

   Dietary Reference
     Intakes (DRIs)
   *Dietary Guidelines
     for Americans*
   dietary pattern
   calorie balance
   nutrient dense
   empty calories
   MyPlate
   processed food

2. **Academic Terms**   Individually or with a partner, create a T-chart on a sheet of paper and list each of the following terms in the left column. In the right column, list an *antonym* (a word of opposite meaning) for each term in the left column.

   curb
   outlook
   sedentary
   modest

Review

Write your answers using complete sentences when appropriate.

3. What are four eating habits that can help defend against top physical health issues?

4. Give an example of a health risk associated with a lifestyle habit.

5. What are estimated nutrient intake levels used for planning and evaluating the diets of healthy people called?

6. What does it mean to say that a person is *in calorie balance*?

7. Which food is more nutrient dense, a fresh pear or a pear canned in light syrup? Explain your answer.

8. What mineral helps offset some of the effects sodium has on blood pressure?

9. Name the five main food groups in MyPlate and give your recommended daily intakes from each group.

10. Why do foods like jam and gravy not fit into the main food groups of MyPlate?

11. How does processing affect the nutritional value of foods?

12. When considering two similar processed food products, how can consumers determine which is the healthier option?

13. Name five low-fat cooking methods that can be used to prepare entrees.

14. What are two adjustments that might be made to dessert recipes to reduce fat, sugar, and calories?

15. Which of the following items on a restaurant menu is likely to be the best choice for a side dish that is lower in fat and calories?
    A. Mashed potatoes with gravy.
    B. Steamed broccoli with cheese sauce.
    C. French fries.
    D. Sliced tomatoes sprinkled with fresh herbs.

16. What are two advantages of drinking water with a meal instead of ordering a soft drink in a restaurant?

Chapter 8 Review and Expand

Core Skills

17. **Speaking, Technology**   Choose one general recommendation for making healthy food and activity choices. Set specific goals for improving your adherence to this recommendation and form a plan of action for achieving those goals. Follow your plan for two weeks. Create a video or use presentation software to prepare an oral report describing your progress. Share your report in class along with any tips you found effective for helping you change your eating and/or activity behaviors.

18. **Writing, Technology**   Work in a small group to design a campaign that will inspire teens to make healthier drink choices. Build interest by using facts about the effects of nutritional intake on appearance, health, personal life, and performance at school or work. Choose a slogan for the campaign. Create a campaign poster and a 30-second audio or video public service announcement (PSA) to promote your message. Vote to choose the most creative and effective campaign from among the groups in your class. Then air the PSA from the winning campaign on the school's website and display slogans and posters in the cafeteria.

19. **Technology, Math, Speaking, Listening**   Remember that foods made mostly of saturated fats or sugars do not fit in any of the five main groups of MyPlate. However, foods in all groups can contain saturated fats and added sugars. Use an online nutrient database to compare the calories and nutrients provided by a 1-tablespoon serving of butter with a 1-tablespoon serving of whole milk. Compare a 1-tablespoon serving of jam with a 1-ounce portion of sugar-coated cereal. Discuss your nutrient comparisons and the nutrient density of each of these foods. Also identify where each food fits in MyPlate.

20. **Technology, Math**   Choose a traditional dessert recipe. Then use one or more of the techniques suggested in the chapter to reduce the fat, sugar, and calories in the recipe. Use an online recipe nutrition calculator to determine the differences in nutritive values between the two products. If possible, prepare both versions of the product and compare the appearance, texture, and flavor.

21. **Career Readiness Practice**   Presume you are the human resources director for a small manufacturing company. Recent research shows that employees who have good eating habits and total wellness have a positive impact on productivity. You decide to form a workplace "Wellness Council." Get together with your council members (two or more classmates) and brainstorm a list of several possible ideas for encouraging healthy eating and wellness among employees. Then narrow the list to the three best options. Write a plan describing how you would implement one of these options, encourage employee participation, and measure success.

Critical Thinking and Problem Solving

22. **Analyze**   Use Figure 8.4 to estimate your daily calorie needs. Then use Figure 8.10 to identify the recommended daily intakes from each MyPlate food group for your calorie level. Create a log noting the quantity of all the foods you consume for one 24-hour period. Analyze your log to determine whether you consumed the recommended amounts from each food group. If you did not, make a list of foods you could add to supply the missing amounts.

23. **Evaluate**   Bring in two nutrition labels from similar processed foods, such as frozen entrees or breakfast cereals. Prepare a written evaluation of the nutritional strengths and weaknesses of each product. Based on your evaluation, write a paragraph stating which product you would prefer to buy. Give reasons for your choice.

24. **Create**   Work with a team of classmates to simulate the launch of a new health-oriented menu item for a fast-food restaurant. Each team member should focus on a different aspect of the product launch: nutrition, flavor, packaging, and advertising. Put together a presentation to introduce your menu item to the rest of the class.

Chapter 9
Staying Active and Managing Weight

101akarca/Shutterstock.com

Content Terms ☛

basal metabolism
kilocalorie
physical fitness
cardiorespiratory fitness
*Physical Activity
  Guidelines for
  Americans (PAG)*
aerobic activity
hydrate
dehydration
weight management

body composition
body mass index (BMI)
healthy weight
overweight
underweight
obesity
waist circumference
eating disorder
anorexia nervosa
bulimia nervosa
binge eating disorder

Academic Terms

ambitious
detrimental
regimen
disparate

Objectives

After studying this chapter, you will be able to

- **list** factors that affect your energy needs;
- **describe** the types and amount of physical activity recommended to promote physical fitness for someone in your age group;
- **identify** nutrition concerns of athletes and **suggest** strategies for addressing those concerns;
- **examine** factors that contribute to weight problems and eating disorders; and
- **explain** the philosophy behind weight management.

Reading Prep

Read the chapter title and tell a classmate what you have experienced or already know about the topic. Write a paragraph describing what you would like to learn about the topic. After reading the chapter, share two things you have learned with the classmate.

Weight problems and lack of physical activity are major health concerns in the United States. These concerns have become common among children and teens as well as adults.

Staying active and managing weight are two of the biggest steps people can take to care for and improve their health. People who are already taking these steps need to stay motivated to continue. People who are not taking these steps need to understand the benefits of getting started. It is never too late to begin a program for better health.

Energy Needs

What do you know about your body's energy needs? *Energy*, in one sense, is the power to do work. The human body needs energy to move. It needs energy to produce heat and carry on internal processes. During certain periods of life, the body also needs energy for growth and repair. The body produces energy by *oxidizing* (using oxygen to burn up) the foods you eat.

Basal Metabolism

Basal metabolism is the amount of energy the human body needs to stay alive and carry on vital processes. It can be measured as the amount of heat the body gives off when at physical, digestive, and emotional rest.

Basal metabolism depends on a number of factors. One factor is body size. A person who is overweight will have a higher *basal metabolic rate (BMR)* than someone of the same age who weighs less. Two people who are the same weight and age, however, may have different BMRs if their body shapes differ. A person who is tall has more body surface area than a person who is short. Therefore, the person who is tall has a higher BMR per unit of weight.

The kinds of tissues that make up the body also affect basal metabolism. Men usually have a larger amount of lean muscle tissue than women. This causes them to require more energy per unit of body weight than women (**Figure 9.1**).

Age can affect basal metabolism. Children and adolescents have a higher basal metabolism than adults. This is because basal metabolism is greater during periods of rapid growth. After about age 20, basal metabolism gradually declines.

A person's general health can affect basal metabolism. The basal metabolism of a well-nourished person is higher than that of a malnourished person. An increase in body temperature also increases basal metabolism. For this reason, the basal metabolism of a person with a fever is higher than that of a person with a normal body temperature.

Gland secretions are another factor that can affect basal metabolism. The thyroid gland affects metabolism more than any other gland. Undersecretion of the thyroid gland may lower basal metabolism. Oversecretion can raise it. *Adrenaline*, a hormone secreted by the adrenal glands during times of stress, also increases metabolism.

Physical Activity

When you take part in any *physical activity*, or body movement, your energy needs rise above your basal metabolism. Different activities require different amounts of energy. For instance, it takes more energy to wash dishes than it takes to read a book. It takes still more energy to rake leaves or swim.

Several factors can influence the amount of energy a person needs to perform a physical task. The intensity with which you perform a task can affect energy needs. A person who walks briskly, for example, needs more energy than a person who walks slowly. Body size can affect energy needs. This means a 220-pound (100 kg) student requires more energy to ride a bicycle than a 120-pound (55 kg) student. The temperature of the environment also can affect energy needs. It takes more energy to wash windows when the temperature is 90°F (32°C) than when the temperature is 70°F (21°C).

Meeting Energy Needs with Food

Each food you eat has a particular energy value. Food scientists call the units used to measure the energy value of foods **kilocalories**. Most people refer to these units simply as *calories*.

The three nutrients that provide the body with energy are carbohydrates, fats, and proteins. Carbohydrates and proteins provide the body with 4 calories per gram. Fats provide the body with 9 calories per gram.

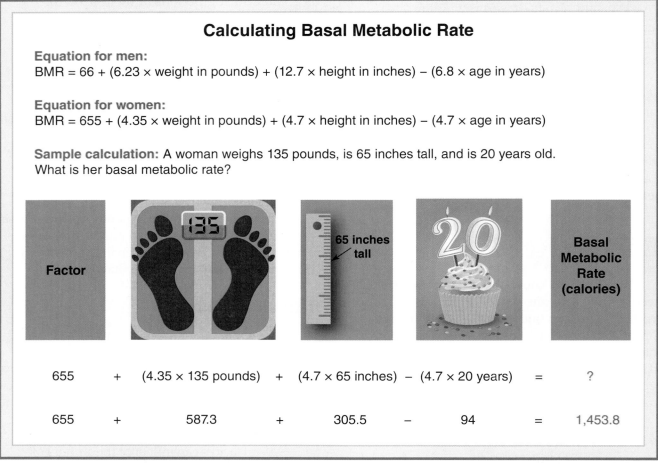

Calculating Basal Metabolic Rate

Equation for men:
BMR = 66 + (6.23 × weight in pounds) + (12.7 × height in inches) − (6.8 × age in years)

Equation for women:
BMR = 655 + (4.35 × weight in pounds) + (4.7 × height in inches) − (4.7 × age in years)

Sample calculation: A woman weighs 135 pounds, is 65 inches tall, and is 20 years old. What is her basal metabolic rate?

Factor		65 inches tall	20	Basal Metabolic Rate (calories)
655	+ (4.35 × 135 pounds)	+ (4.7 × 65 inches)	− (4.7 × 20 years) =	?
655	+ 587.3	+ 305.5	− 94 =	1,453.8

Nemanja Cosovic/Shutterstock.com; A Aleksil/Shutterstock.com; Booka/Shutterstock.com

Figure 9.1   The basal metabolic rate (BMR) is affected by a number of factors. Would the result differ if the sample calculation above was for a man who is the same height, weight, and age as the woman in this example?

Because few of the foods you eat are pure carbohydrates, pure proteins, or pure fats, foods vary widely in their energy values. Foods that are high in fat and low in water have a high energy value. This means a small amount of these foods will provide a lot of energy. Some examples of high energy-value foods are nuts, mayonnaise, cheese, and some meats. Foods that are high in water and fiber and low in fat have a low energy value. A serving of these foods provides only small amounts of energy. Most fresh fruits and vegetables have a low energy value. Lean meats, grain foods, and starchy vegetables have an intermediate energy value.

When the energy (calories) you obtain from food equals the energy you expend, your body weight remains the same. When the energy you obtain from food is less than the energy you expend, your body weight decreases. When the energy you obtain from food is greater than the energy you expend, your body weight increases (**Figure 9.2**). It takes about 3,500 calories to make up 1 pound (0.45 kg) of body weight.

Physical Activity and Physical Fitness

Besides affecting your calorie needs, physical activity can affect your health throughout life. Physical activity promotes **physical fitness**. This is the body's ability to meet the demands of daily life. When you are fit, you have the energy to

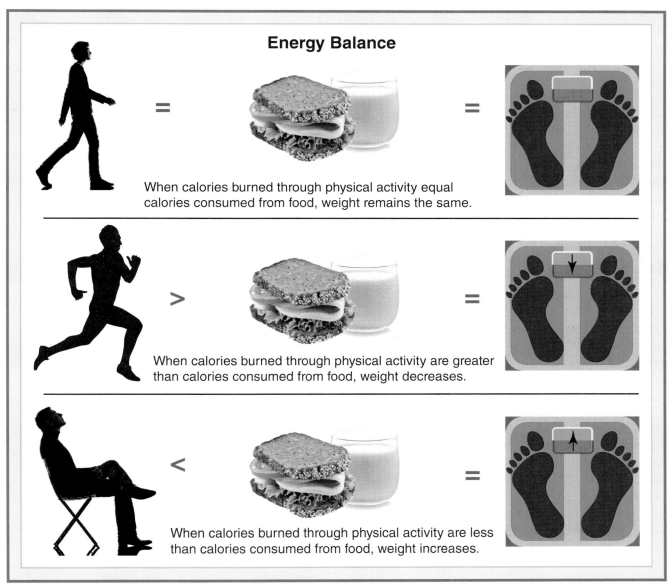

Figure 9.2 Keeping the intake calories from food in balance with calories expended through physical activity is important to maintain a healthy weight. Which section of this illustration do you think best describes the majority of people in the United States?

perform your normal duties with enough energy left to enjoy your free time. You have the strength needed to react to unexpected events that arise, too.

There are several aspects to physical fitness. Being fit means your heart and lungs are strong enough to provide your body with the oxygen needed during physical activity. This is called **cardiorespiratory fitness**. Physical fitness also involves having *endurance* so you can keep going without getting too tired. You need *flexibility*

so you can bend and reach. You need muscle *strength* for lifting. You also need *balance* to keep you steady on your feet.

A key resource to help people stay fit is the ***Physical Activity Guidelines for Americans (PAG).*** The *PAG* was issued by the U.S. Department of Health and Human Services (HHS). It is based on science and complements the *Dietary Guidelines*. In fact, a Key Recommendation of the *Dietary Guidelines* is for Americans of all ages "to meet the *Physical Activity Guidelines*." The *PAG* is designed to help children and adults choose the types and amounts of physical activity needed for good health.

Following the *PAG* will help people do more than stay fit. The levels of activity the *Guidelines* suggests increase metabolism. Keeping active helps people burn calories so they can reach or maintain a healthy weight. Physical activity tones muscles, builds strong bones, and keeps skin healthy. It reduces the risks of heart disease, high blood pressure, diabetes, and some forms of cancer. Physical activity can help reduce symptoms of mood disorders like anxiety and depression. It can provide a fun social outlet, too.

Types of Activity

The *PAG* uses a number of terms for different types of activity. *Baseline activity* refers to routine movements required to do daily tasks. For instance, standing up, bending to tie your shoe, and lifting a carton of milk are part of baseline activity. People who do nothing more than baseline activity are viewed as inactive.

Baseline activity should not be confused with *lifestyle activities*. This term refers to extra movement people purposely include in their daily lives in order to be more active. Climbing stairs instead of taking an elevator would be an example.

The *PAG* is focused on *health-enhancing physical activity*. As the name implies, this type of activity promotes good health. Although baseline activity does not count toward the *Guidelines*, lifestyle activities do.

Aerobic Activity

The *PAG* urges people to do activities that target different aspects of fitness. **Aerobic activity** is suggested to improve cardiorespiratory fitness. This involves rhythmic movement of the arm and leg muscles for a period of time. Cycling, swimming, and jogging are aerobic activities.

The *Guidelines* refers to two levels for aerobic activity: moderate and vigorous. There are a number of ways to describe these two activity levels. The Choose**MyPlate** website offers a simple test to help you gauge your level of intensity. The site suggests you should be able to talk while doing *moderate activities*; however, you should not be able to sing. While doing *vigorous*

Food Science

Energy Value of Foods

Kilocalories is the more accurate term for the units most people call *calories*. One kilocalorie equals the amount of heat needed to raise one kilogram of water one degree Celsius. Food scientists use the term *calorie* spelled with a lowercase *c* to refer to a unit that is 1,000 times smaller than a kilocalorie.

The total energy value of a food depends on that food's chemical composition. Placing a food sample inside a device called a *bomb calorimeter* is one way to determine the food's energy value. The food is placed in a special chamber surrounded by water and ignited. As the food burns, it releases energy as heat. The energy value of the food can then be determined by measuring the temperature change of the water.

Andrei Nekrassov/Shutterstock.com

Burning a food sample in a calorimeter allows food scientists to measure the energy value of the food.

activities, you should not be able to say more than a few words without needing to stop to catch your breath.

Think about the example of walking. Walking from room to room is baseline activity. Walking to the store instead of taking a car is lifestyle activity. Walking involves rhythmically using the large muscles of your legs to take step after step. Therefore, it is an aerobic activity. If you are moving at a pace of three to four miles per hour, you should be able to talk while you walk. At this speed, walking is a moderate aerobic activity. If you are racewalking at a very brisk pace, you would find it hard to talk. At this speed, walking becomes a vigorous activity.

Other Fitness Activity

Along with aerobic activity, the *PAG* advises choosing some activities to help build strong muscles and bones. *Muscle-strengthening activity* requires your muscles to work against a force. For instance, lifting weights is a muscle-strengthening activity. It causes your muscles to work against the force of gravity. Muscles become stronger as the work is repeated and as the force is increased. Therefore, both lifting a weight many times and using a heavier weight will help increase strength.

It is important to choose activities that will target all the major muscle groups in the body. This includes the hips, shoulders, chest, and abdomen as well as arms, legs, and back. Exercises like push-ups and sit-ups help strengthen muscles, as do activities like rock climbing. In addition to weights, you can work out with elastic resistance bands. Even daily activities like lifting groceries, infants, and laundry baskets can help you build strength.

Bone-strengthening activity is designed to build a sturdy skeleton. Such activity causes the legs and hips to carry the body's weight while the feet make forceful contact with the ground. Walking, jogging, and climbing stairs are examples of this type of movement. Targeting this aspect of fitness is most important for children and teens. Strengthening bones while they are still growing can help prevent osteoporosis later in life.

Activities that target each aspect of fitness are listed in **Figure 9.3**. Note that some activities focus on more than one aspect.

Amount of Activity

The minimum amount of activity the *PAG* recommends varies by age group. For children and teens ages 6 to 17, the *Guidelines* recommends at least 60 minutes of physical activity per day. Most of this time should be spent in aerobic activity. Three or more days each week, some activity should be at the vigorous level. Children and teens also need to choose activities that strengthen muscles on at least three days per week. Likewise, they need to choose activities that target strong bones on three or more days each week. The easiest way to meet these goals is to choose a variety of activities and make a point of being active every day.

Health and Wellness

Excessive Exercise

Getting daily physical activity is an important part of taking care of your body. However, getting too much exercise can be harmful to your health. Too much exercise can damage bones and joints. If intense exercise continues, these injuries will not have a chance to heal properly. Long-term problems could result.

Too much exercise can also affect hormone balance in females, causing changes in their menstrual cycles. Excessive exercise causes the body to break down muscle tissue for energy. It can cause weakness and fatigue. It can lead to feelings of depression and low self-image. Overdoing exercise can even strain the heart.

The amount of exercise that is healthy varies from person to person. For instance, most athletes will spend more time working out than most nonathletes. The following signs, however, can indicate that someone is overdoing it and may need professional help:

- feeling guilty or anxious about failing to exercise
- working out when sick or injured or against the advice of health professionals
- skipping other activities in order to exercise
- having undue concern with weight loss, appearance, or physical performance
- combining frequent, intense exercise with unhealthy eating habits

For adults, the *PAG* suggests an amount equal to at least 150 minutes of moderate aerobic activity per week. Note that one minute of vigorous activity is about the same as two minutes of moderate activity. So adults can meet the *Guidelines* in a number of ways. Of course, they could do 150 minutes of moderate activity each week, or they might choose to do 75 minutes of vigorous activity instead. They could also opt for a mix of activities. For instance, 30 minutes of vigorous and 90 minutes of moderate activity per week would meet *PAG* advice. For more health benefits, the *PAG* advises adults to boost moderate activity to equal 300 minutes a week. Adults

Physical Fitness Activities

Aspect of Physical Fitness	Sample Activities
Cardiorespiratory Fitness 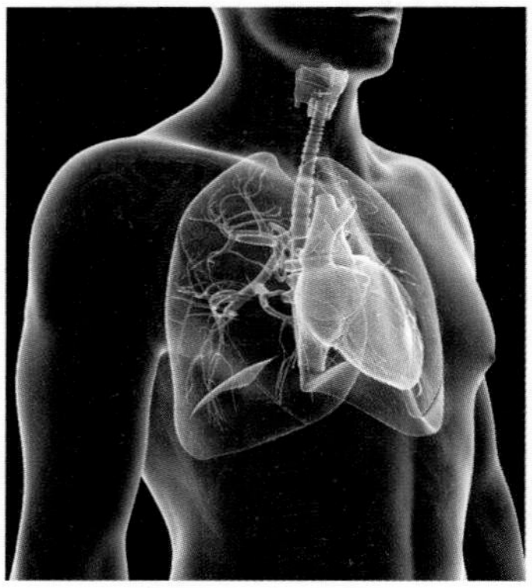	Moderate-intensity aerobic activities: • Active recreation, such as canoeing, cross-country skiing, hiking, rollerblading, and skateboarding • Bicycle riding or brisk walking • Games requiring catching and throwing, such as baseball, basketball, softball, and volleyball • Yardwork and housework, such as sweeping, raking, and pushing a lawn mower Vigorous-intensity aerobic activities: • Active games involving running and chasing, such as flag football and soccer • Bicycle riding • Cheerleading, gymnastics, or vigorous dancing • Jumping rope or running • Martial arts such as karate • Sports such as basketball, ice or field hockey, swimming, and tennis
Strong Muscles 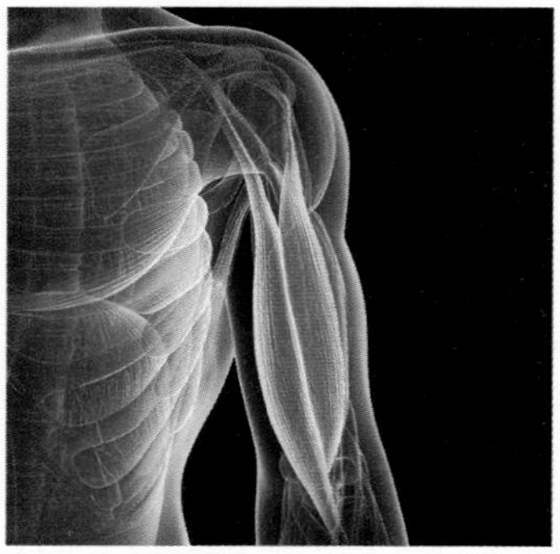	• Cheerleading • Games such as tug-of-war • Gymnastics • Push-ups • Rock climbing • Sit-ups • Lifting weights • Chin-ups • Using elastic exercise bands
Strong Bones 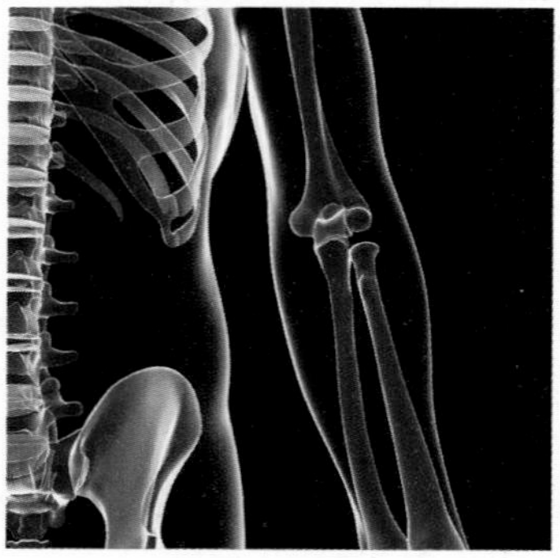	• Hopping, jumping, and skipping • Jumping rope • Running • Sports such as basketball, gymnastics, tennis, and volleyball • Climbing stairs • Tennis • Lifting weights • Push-ups • Chin-ups

Sebastian Kaulitzki/Shutterstock.com; Sebastian Kaulitzki/Shutterstock.com; Sebastian Kaulitzki/Shutterstock.com

Figure 9.3   People can choose from a wide range of activities to target the various aspects of fitness. Which physical fitness activities do you most enjoy?

should include some activities to strengthen their muscles a couple of times a week, too.

Adults need to continue being active as they age. Older adults who are physically active are less likely to have problems with broken bones and weak muscles.

People often think they cannot spare the time required to meet the *PAG*. If this is your

reaction, look at how you currently use your time. How much time do you spend each day watching television or playing video games? How much time do you spend texting and looking at social media? Consider using some of this inactive time to be more active. Instead of watching television or gaming to relax, skate or take a bike ride to unwind after a busy day. Invite friends to join you for a game of tennis or basketball in place of texting them.

You do not have to set aside a block of time to be physically active. Just be sure to be active for at least 10 minutes at a time. You might try using apps, websites, or a wearable fitness tracker. These tools can help you track the type and amount of activity you accumulate throughout the day. For instance, you might ride your bicycle to and from school, pedaling 15 minutes in each direction. Before dinner, you could spend 20 minutes shooting baskets. Then in the evening, you might walk your dog for 10 minutes. By the end of the day, you would have accumulated 60 minutes of activity.

Getting Started

Adding more moderate activity in their lifestyles should not create health concerns for most people. Someone who is starting a new program of vigorous exercise, however, may wish to consult with a healthcare provider first. Talking with a healthcare provider is also suggested for anyone with chronic health problems.

If you have been fairly inactive, you need to begin increasing your activity level slowly. Trying to do too much too soon increases the risk of injury. Setting your initial activity goals too high can also cause you to become discouraged. If you are unable to attain the goals, you are more likely to give up. For instance, starting with a goal to swim, jog, or cycle 60 minutes every day may be too *ambitious* (challenging). Instead, you might begin with a goal to walk 20 minutes a day four days a week. When you reach your initial goal, you can set a new goal that is more challenging.

Adults who have been inactive should keep in mind that some activity is better than no activity. It is best, however, to spread activity throughout the week. Scheduling just one or two lengthy periods of activity per week could increase the risk of injury.

When preparing to be active, be sure to keep safety in mind. Use protective gear, such as pads and helmets, when needed. Also choose environments that are safe. For instance, on a hot day, you might choose to go to an air-conditioned gym instead of an outdoor location. Work out with a friend rather than exercising by yourself.

Making physical activity a regular part of your day is more important than the types of activities you choose. Vary your activities so you do not become bored. Choose activities that are fun and convenient for you to do and that are suited to your level of fitness. Try making physical activity a social outlet by doing it with family members and friends. If you can make physical activity part of your lifestyle, you will enjoy the benefits of fitness for a lifetime.

You can use the decision-making process to help you choose which types of activity to include in your fitness plan. Think about your alternatives. Some of your options may be limited by the equipment and facilities you have available. Consider how your alternatives relate to your fitness goals. Determine which alternatives are acceptable and then choose the ones you will include in your fitness routine. Do not forget to evaluate your decision. You can always adjust your routine if you are not happy with it.

Keep community resources in mind when looking into your activity choices. Many schools and community centers offer activities such as basketball and volleyball in their gyms. Local recreation departments may set up sports leagues for people in various age groups. Many public parks have playground equipment for children. Some also have swimming pools and multiuse trails for walking and bicycling. These facilities provide a range of fitness options and often cost little or nothing to use (**Figure 9.4**).

My Good Images/Shutterstock.com

Figure 9.4 Multiuse trails in public parks are a great free fitness resource for people who enjoy walking, jogging, and bicycling.

Nutrition for Athletes

Being moderately active each day does not create special dietary needs. Most active people can meet their daily nutrient needs by following MyPlate. However, intense physical activity can increase the need for some nutrients. Nutrition also plays a key role in athletic performance. Athletes should be aware of a few specific dietary concerns.

Meeting Fluid Needs

The nutrient that is most likely to affect sports performance is water. Athletes lose much water through sweat when they are training and competing. If an athlete does not **hydrate**, or consume water to restore a proper fluid balance, dehydration can set in quickly (**Figure 9.5**).

Dehydration is an unhealthy lack of water in the body. It can be caused by failure to consume enough fluids. It can also result from loss of too much fluid due to vomiting or diarrhea as well as sweating. Dehydration can cause headache, dizziness, confusion, and a drop in overall performance. In severe cases, it can even result in death.

To prevent dehydration, athletes should begin drinking fluids before an event. They need to continue drinking ½ to 1 cup (125 to 250 mL) of fluids at 15-minute intervals throughout the event. Athletes need to drink more fluids after a competition or workout has ended.

Some athletes choose sports drinks to replace their fluid losses. Sports drinks contain carbohydrates from sugar to help athletes replace some of the fuel they are burning through activity. Many sports drinks also contain sodium to replace sodium lost through sweat. This sodium also helps increase fluid absorption. Sports drinks should not be confused with energy drinks, which contain stimulants, such as caffeine.

For people who engage in lengthy workouts of 90 minutes or more, sports drinks can be helpful. For those who take part in less vigorous activities, however, plain water is a better choice for hydrating the body. Moderately active people do not need the extra sugar and sodium found in sports drinks. Their needs can easily be met

Peter Bernik/Shutterstock.com

Figure 9.5   Drinking water replaces fluids lost during physical activity.

by eating a normal diet. Energy drinks should not be used as fluid replacement for any kind of physical activity. The stimulant ingredients can increase heart rate and raise blood pressure.

Meeting Nutrient Needs

Athletes have some other special nutrient needs besides water. Their high level of activity increases the need for calories. Most of these calories, 55 to 60 percent, should come from complex carbohydrates. Whole-grain breads, cereals, and pasta, and brown rice and starchy vegetables are all excellent sources of complex carbohydrates. Choosing lean meats, poultry, and fish will supply an athlete's slightly increased need for protein. Fat-free and low-fat dairy products provide needed calcium. Fresh fruits and vegetables furnish vitamins, minerals, and fiber (**Figure 9.6**).

If this diet sounds familiar, it's not a coincidence. Like less active people, athletes can meet their nutrient needs by following MyPlate. Athletes should avoid nutrient supplements unless they are being taken on the advice of a dietitian. These costly supplements are not always what they claim to be. Tests have shown some products to be ineffective or even harmful.

Recipe for Good Food

Cranberry Orange DIY Sports Drink

Serves 4

3 cups (750 mL) water
2 green tea teabags
⅛ teaspoon (0.6 mL) salt
1 tablespoon plus 1 teaspoon (20 mL) honey
½ cup (125 mL) pulp-free orange juice with calcium
1 cup (250 mL) cranberry 100% juice

1. In a small saucepan, bring the water to a full boil. Remove the pan from the heat and allow the water to sit for 4 minutes to cool slightly.

2. Place the teabags in a large liquid measuring cup or heatproof pitcher. Pour the slightly cooled water over the teabags. Allow the tea to steep for 3 minutes.

3. Remove the teabags from the tea and discard. Stir the salt and honey into the tea until they are dissolved.

4. Cover the tea and place in the refrigerator for 30 minutes. Then stir in the orange and cranberry juices. Drink is now ready to consume or can be refrigerated for future use.

Per serving: 69 calories. (0% from fat), 0 g protein, 18 g carbohydrate, 0 g fat, 0 mg cholesterol, 0 g fiber, 86 mg sodium.

Detrimental (harmful) effects from these products have included fatigue, upset stomach, joint pain, and irregular heartbeat.

Planning a Pregame Meal

Trainers once thought athletes needed protein for energy. Although athletes do need protein, they need it for growth and repair of muscle tissue—not for energy. A pregame meal can include a small amount of lean protein. The bulk of the meal, however, should be made up of foods like pasta, rice, and potatoes. These foods are packed with complex carbohydrates—an athlete's main energy source. Another reason to choose these foods before a competitive event is that they are low in fat. Fat stays in the stomach longer than carbohydrates. Avoiding fat before a game keeps energy needed to compete from being used for digestion.

The best time to eat a pregame meal is at least three hours before a sports event. An athlete should choose moderate portions so he or she will not feel too full during competition. The athlete should avoid unfamiliar foods, which could cause an upset stomach. He or she should also limit high-fiber foods, such as fruits, vegetables, and whole grains. Although athletes need fiber, they would not want bulk from fiber in their digestive systems while competing. This could make them feel sluggish.

Meeting Weight Goals

Achieving an optimal performance weight is a critical nutrition issue for many athletes. To compete in lower weight classes, some wrestlers use laxatives to speed food through their digestive systems. They also force themselves to vomit

Dirima/Shutterstock.com

Figure 9.6 Fruit makes a healthy snack after practice or a game, providing athletes with needed vitamins, minerals, and fiber.

and avoid drinking fluids. To avoid weight gain, some gymnasts skip meals to restrict their calorie intakes. To increase body mass, some football players go on eating sprees. They consume large quantities of high-calorie, low-nutrient foods. To meet weight goals, some athletes in all sports fields have engaged in such unwise and often dangerous practices. These practices can harm health as well as sports performance.

Athletes who want to lose weight need to do so gradually and well before the start of their sports season. They should not try to lose weight while they are training and competing. They should never restrict fluids, force vomiting, or use laxatives either.

Athletes should not skip meals or restrict calories. The body needs a steady supply of nutrients throughout the day. It needs energy to fuel activity. Teen athletes also need calories to support normal development. Failing to get enough nutrients and calories can stunt growth and make the athlete too weak to compete.

Athletes who want to gain weight need to add moderate amounts of extra calories to their diets from nutrient-rich sources. They also need to follow a *regimen* (systematic plan) of muscle-building exercise. This will ensure that weight gained is due to lean body mass rather than fat.

All athletes wishing to reach weight goals should seek the advice of a registered dietitian nutritionist. Many coaches lack sufficient training in sports nutrition to provide guidance about healthy weight loss, maintenance, and gain.

Weight Management

Of course, athletes are not the only ones who have weight goals. Health professionals suggest every person should have a goal to maintain body weight in a healthy range.

People come in all shapes and sizes. Heredity largely determines bone size and shape. Maintaining a healthy weight, however, depends mostly on lifestyle. **Weight management** means using resources like food choices and physical activity to reach and/or maintain a healthy weight. Weight management is not a short-term program you follow until you lose a few pounds. It becomes part of your way of life.

Exploring Careers

Athletic Trainer

Athletic trainers work on sports teams and in other settings to help athletes avoid injuries. When injuries do occur, athletic trainers may consult with doctors to provide treatment. They then work with the athletes to help restore health and peak function to the injured areas. They also keep coaches updated on the status of injured team members.

These health professionals must have a thorough knowledge of the body. When assessing injuries, they need good listening skills. These skills will allow them to ask the right questions and accurately determine the source and extent of the damage. Their critical thinking skills help them choose the best therapies for each injury. They must be active learners so they can adopt new health information as it becomes available. They also need skills in speaking and instructing to help athletes understand how to care for, strengthen, and protect their injured bodies.

A key personal quality for athletic trainers is a concern for others. They need leadership skills so they can take charge and offer direction in critical situations. They need to be able to work cooperatively with coaches, physicians, and athletes. They must be flexible—willing to try new therapies or adjust treatments that are not proving to be effective. These trainers also need persistence to keep treating injuries that take a long time to heal.

Athletic trainers must have at least a bachelor's degree. Most earn master's degrees. They must pass an exam to become certified athletic trainers and earn the ATC (Athletic Trainer, Certified) credential. They must meet set qualifications and have a license in the state where they practice. Athletic trainers must also take part in continuing education to keep their skills and knowledge current.

Determining Healthy Weight

To maintain a healthy weight, you need to be concerned with more than just the numbers on a scale. You need to know the source of your weight.

Body weight includes the weight of bone, muscle, fat, and other tissues. People have different **body compositions**, or proportions of these types of tissues that make up their body weights. Muscle tissue is denser, taking up less space than an equal weight of fat tissue. These factors explain why two people who appear to be roughly the same size may have *disparate* (markedly different) weights. The person with greater muscle mass will have the higher weight. What concerns health experts most, however, is the amount of weight attributed to fat tissue.

Body Mass Index

Many health professionals assess a person's weight based on his or her **body mass index (BMI)**. This is a calculation involving a person's weight and height measurements. BMI values are calculated the same way for children, adolescents, and adults (**Figure 9.7**). For a table of BMI calculations, see the Appendix D.

According to federal guidelines, **healthy weight** for adults is defined as a BMI of 18.5 to 24.9. **Overweight** is defined as a BMI of 25 to 29.9. A BMI of 30 or more is considered *obesity*. A BMI under 18.5 is considered **underweight**. These BMI cutoffs cannot be used for children and adolescents because their bodies are still growing. For this reason, suggested BMI values for evaluating overweight in these younger age groups vary according to age. **Figure 9.8** shows how BMI cutoffs for weight status vary during adolescence.

Waist Circumference

The use of BMI in assessing weight has limitations because it does not take body composition into account. For example, consider a football player who has a large proportion of muscle tissue compared to fat. Because muscle weighs

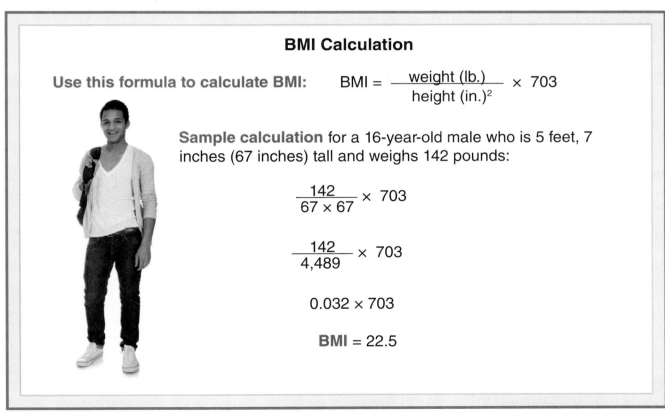

BMI Calculation

Use this formula to calculate BMI:

$$BMI = \frac{weight\ (lb.)}{height\ (in.)^2} \times 703$$

Sample calculation for a 16-year-old male who is 5 feet, 7 inches (67 inches) tall and weighs 142 pounds:

$$\frac{142}{67 \times 67} \times 703$$

$$\frac{142}{4,489} \times 703$$

$$0.032 \times 703$$

$$BMI = 22.5$$

Figure 9.7 Body mass index, a calculation based on body weight and height, is used to evaluate how healthy a person's weight is.

Adolescent Risk for Weight Problems				
Gender	Age	BMI at Risk of Underweight	BMI at Risk of Overweight	BMI at Risk of Obesity
Female	14	15	23	27
	15	16	24	28
	16	16	24	28
	17	17	25	29
	18	17	25	30
Male	14	16	22	26
	15	16	23	26
	16	17	24	27
	17	17	24	28
	18	18	25	28

Figure 9.8 The body mass indexes that identify potential weight problems for an adolescent vary according to age and gender.

more than fat, the player may have a seemingly high weight. His BMI might be in the overweight range. Because his weight is due to muscle, however, it is not a health concern. Therefore, rather than being defined strictly by BMI, **obesity** is a condition characterized by excessive deposits of body fat.

One way to assess whether a high BMI is due to excess fat is to measure **waist circumference**. This is the distance around the natural waistline. For a man with a BMI of 25 or more, a waist circumference of over 40 inches indicates an increased health risk. For a woman with a BMI in this range, such a risk is indicated by a waist measurement of 35 or more inches.

Skinfold Test

A *skinfold test* can help evaluate body composition. This is a measure of a fold of skin using an instrument called a *caliper*. The back of the upper arm, below the shoulder blade, and around the abdomen are common measuring spots. About half the body's fat is located under the skin. Therefore, a skinfold test gives an indication of total body fat (**Figure 9.9**).

An inexact variation of a skinfold test you can do yourself is the *pinch test*. Simply grasp a fold of skin at the back of your upper arm between your thumb and forefinger. A fold that

measures more than an inch (2.5 cm) thick is often a sign of excess fat.

Hazards of Obesity

Obesity is a major health issue in the United States. High blood pressure, diabetes, heart disease, some types of cancer, and other diseases are more common among people who are obese. Studies show people who are obese die at earlier ages than people who are not obese. Some insurance companies view people who are obese as "high risk" and charge them higher rates.

Too much weight puts a strain on the body's bones, muscles, and organs. A thick layer of fat interferes with the body's natural cooling system. People who are overweight use more effort to walk and breathe.

Health concerns are not the only hazard of obesity. Media images of fashion models often promote the idea that being attractive means being thin. Some employers hesitate to hire people who are obese for certain jobs. This social climate can cause people who are obese to face stigma. They may be stereotyped as being too lazy to exercise or too self-indulgent to avoid overeating.

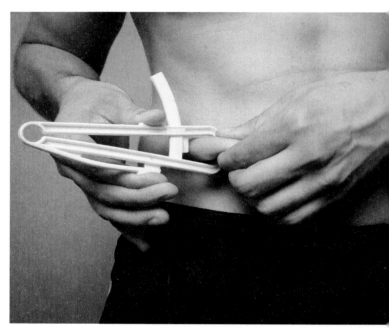

LoloStock/Shutterstock.com

Figure 9.9 Measuring a fold of skin at the abdomen indicates whether excess body weight is due to fat or muscle.

Public education is needed to help counter such inaccurate and unfair views. People need to understand that obesity is a complex problem. Causes go far beyond a lack of willpower.

One of the best techniques people with obesity can use to cope with social pressure is positive self-talk. Focusing on personal strengths can offset negative thoughts. People with obesity can also benefit from the help of family members and friends. With a good outlook and a caring support team, people with obesity are more likely to lose weight and avoid these hazards.

Deciding to Lose Weight

For children and teens who are overweight, health providers most often recommend a plan of increased physical activity. They also emphasize the need to make healthier food choices. They do not generally suggest restricting calories, however. They prefer that children and teens grow into their excess weight rather than try to lose it.

As an adult, you will need to continue to aim for a healthy weight. If your BMI and a skinfold test ever indicate you have excess body fat, you can take steps to lose weight.

To successfully lose weight, you must want to lose weight. You should base a desire to lose weight on more than wanting to fit into a new outfit. Efforts to lose weight are most successful when they are part of a lifelong commitment to maintain good health.

Once you have decided to lose weight, you might want to see a registered dietitian nutritionist. A dietitian can help you design a weight management plan suited to your individual needs (**Figure 9.10**). The dietitian might also recommend a vitamin-mineral supplement.

Most successful weight-loss plans involve three main components: changing poor eating habits, controlling energy intake, and increasing physical activity.

Factors That Contribute to Overeating

People can be overweight for several reasons. Some people inherit a tendency to be overweight. Some people are overweight because of medical problems. Most people, however, are overweight because they eat more calories than they need for basal metabolism and physical activity.

Many people overeat when they do not pay attention to how much they are consuming. They

Razvan Raz/Shutterstock.com

Figure 9.10 A dietitian works with you to create an individualized weight management plan that meets your needs.

fail to notice their bodies' *satiety* (fullness) *signals*. They eat because food is readily available, not because they are hungry.

It is important to understand there are many factors that can distract people from listening to their body signals. Most people are smart enough to know that food has calories, and eating too many calories causes weight gain. Few people eat nonstop from morning to night. The majority of people care about their health and appearance. Therefore, overeating does not occur due to lack of intelligence, self-control, or self-respect.

One factor that can contribute to overeating is social settings. Sharing food is a social activity. When snacking with friends or enjoying a family gathering, people are more focused on others than on food. This may lead them to eat more than they intended.

Food marketing can interfere with satiety signals. Media ads constantly promote foods. Food stores, eateries, and vending machines make food easy to get almost everywhere. Value menus are used as a marketing strategy to encourage people to order foods that appear to be a bargain. This endless exposure to food and food images often spurs people's desire to eat, even when they are not truly hungry (**Figure 9.11**).

bikeriderlondon/Shutterstock.com

Figure 9.11 Watching television is sedentary activity that is often accompanied by distracted eating. Both of these factors contribute to overweight.

Emotions can keep people from noticing their satiety signals. Some people use food as a reward when they are happy. Others use food as a source of comfort when they are angry, frustrated, sad, or bored.

Habits override satiety signals for many people. For instance, some people are in the habit of having a bedtime snack. These people may reach for food in the evening without stopping to discern if they are actually hungry.

In some restaurants, food items such as dinner rolls or chips and salsa are habitually placed on the table. People may eat these items simply because they are in front of them.

When planning menus, certain foods may be served together out of habit. For instance, some families may not even consider healthier options to traditional high-calorie Thanksgiving dishes. These kinds of habits can lead people to consume more calories than they need or even truly want.

Identifying Eating Habits

One of the first steps in losing weight is to keep a *food log*. This is a list of all the foods and beverages you consume. You should also note where you ate, whom you were with, and how you felt when eating. Keep this list for at least a week. Studying it will help you discover some of your eating habits. For instance, you may find you often snack in front of the television. You may also learn you eat when feeling sad, frustrated, or nervous (**Figure 9.12**).

Once you identify some of your eating habits, you can take steps to change them. If you idly snack while watching television, try keeping your hands busy with an activity instead of with food. If you eat when nervous, try taking a brisk walk when you feel full of nervous energy. If you eat when feeling lonely, call a friend when the urge to nibble strikes.

Controlling Energy Intake

There are two key factors in the weight-loss equation. The first factor is controlling energy intake. This means consuming fewer calories than the body burns.

Determining Daily Calorie Need

The first part of the weight-loss equation involves knowing how many calories are needed to maintain present weight. This is called *daily calorie need*. This need must provide enough calories to support basal metabolism as well as energy for activities.

As mentioned, age, sex, and body size all impact basal metabolism. Therefore, these factors also affect daily calorie need. Pound for pound, children and teens need more calories than adults to support growth. Men usually need more calories than women. This is partly because men generally have a higher percentage of muscle tissue than women. Muscle tissue requires more calories to maintain than fat tissue. A large person needs more calories each day than a small person. One reason for this is a larger skin surface area allows more heat to be lost from the body.

Of course, another factor that affects daily calorie need is level of activity. An active person needs more calories to fuel motion than an inactive person.

Meal	Foods	Amount	Time	Location/Activity	People Present	Mood
Breakfast	banana cornflakes fat-free milk orange juice	1 medium 1½ cups ½ cup ¾ cup	7:30 AM	Kitchen	Christopher	Tired
Lunch	veggie burger carrot sticks low-fat milk fruit cup	1 about 8 1 cup ½ cup	12:10 PM	Cafeteria	Tamisha Pilar	Excited
Snack	cookies	4	3:30 PM	Living room Playing video games	No one	Bored

Figure 9.12   Keeping track of what, when, where, and with whom you eat can help you identify patterns in your eating behavior.

With a formula based on your activity level, you can use your BMR to calculate your daily calorie need (**Figure 9.13**). Calorie need calculators can also be found on the Internet. If you enter your age, sex, weight, height, and activity level, these online tools will compute your daily calorie need for you.

Making Calorie Adjustments

To lose weight, a person must consume fewer calories than his or her daily calorie need. Once daily calorie need is known, an adjusted calorie intake for weight loss can be calculated.

One pound (0.45 kg) of fat equals about 3,500 calories. To lose 1 pound (0.45 kg) a week, a person would need to expend 3,500 more calories than he or she consumes. This is roughly 500 calories a day. This adjustment should be made by increasing activity as well as reducing calorie intake.

Losing 1 pound a week will not bring about the quick results some people desire from a weight-loss plan. However, most experts recommend a steady weight loss at the rate of ½ to 1 pound (0.23 to 0.45 kg) per week. Losing weight too quickly can strain body systems. Consuming too few calories may deprive the body of needed nutrients. People also tend to be more successful in maintaining their weight goals if they lose weight slowly.

Choosing a Food Plan

A food plan that will successfully result in weight loss needs to meet several criteria. Of course, it must reduce calorie intake. However, it should also include as many favorite foods as possible. A weight-loss plan should provide a variety of choices. It should be nutritious and fit into the food budget, too.

When choosing a food plan for weight loss, avoid fad diets. These diets often focus on just a few foods or omit certain groups of foods. For instance, some popular diets are very low in carbohydrates. They focus on large intakes of protein. Even if they are nutritionally balanced, such plans lack variety. These diets do not help people form good eating habits, either. People often become bored with fad diets and stop following them. Lost weight is likely to be regained when the diets are discontinued.

It is wise to use MyPlate to evaluate fad diets. A sound diet needs to provide recommended

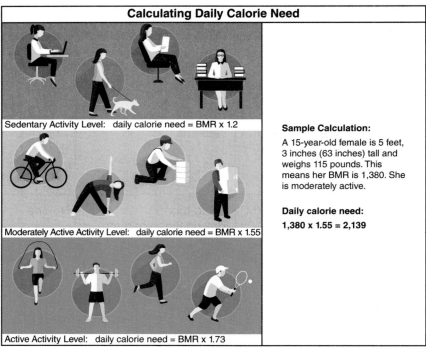

Calculating Daily Calorie Need

Sedentary Activity Level: daily calorie need = BMR x 1.2

Moderately Active Activity Level: daily calorie need = BMR x 1.55

Active Activity Level: daily calorie need = BMR x 1.73

Sample Calculation:
A 15-year-old female is 5 feet, 3 inches (63 inches) tall and weighs 115 pounds. This means her BMR is 1,380. She is moderately active.

Daily calorie need:
1,380 x 1.55 = 2,139

Macrovector/Shutterstock.com

Figure 9.13 Daily calorie need can be calculated using a person's BMR and a formula based on his or her activity level.

amounts from all the food groups. This will assure that needed levels of nutrients are being supplied. A diet that does not meet these standards may not support good health. Along with help for evaluating diets, the Choose**MyPlate** website offers advice and resources for reaching a healthy weight.

When working toward a lower weight goal, some people are tempted to skip meals and avoid snacking to cut calories. Skipping a meal, however, can cause intense hunger. This increases the chances of overeating at the next meal. By keeping hunger at bay, snacking can actually help promote weight loss. The key is choosing healthy snack foods that provide only a modest number of calories to create six small meals each day (**Figure 9.14**). This food plan will increase metabolic rate over a plan made up of three large meals.

When planning meals for weight management, it is important to be aware of the energy value of food choices. Packaged food products and many recipes list the number of calories per serving. Using this information requires taking note of stated serving sizes. People who cannot understand why they are not losing weight often find they are misjudging portion sizes. When

starting a weight-loss plan, it is helpful to measure portions. Soon the look of a one-cup (250 mL), half-cup (125 mL), or tablespoon (15 mL) portion will become familiar. By choosing moderate portions of nutrient-dense foods, adults can stay within calorie limits and meet their goals for weight loss.

Tips for Success

Following a few tips can make it easier to stick with a weight-loss plan and achieve desired results. One tip is to avoid cutting out all favorite high-calorie foods. When trying to lose weight, feeling deprived of all favorites may prompt some people to give up. Instead, they can learn to enjoy their favorites less often and in smaller portions. For instance, they might go out for pizza monthly instead of weekly. They could try settling for 10 French fries instead of a whole order.

Likewise, people following a weight management plan should not feel like they need to avoid social events. Skipping holiday meals or trips to the ice cream shop may help them resist the temptation to eat high-calorie foods. Avoiding fun gatherings, however, can lead to

Sample 1,600 Calorie Menu

Breakfast (328 calories)
1½ cups cereal with ½ cup fat-free milk
1 large banana

Beverage: 1 cup coffee or tea

Snack (154 calories)
½ cup fat-free vanilla yogurt
½ cup canned peaches, juice pack

Lunch (411 calories)
Taco salad:
- 2 cups chopped romaine lettuce
- 2 ounces cooked ground turkey
- ½ cup canned low-sodium black beans
- 2 tablespoons shredded low-fat Cheddar cheese
- 1 ounce tortilla chips
- 2 tablespoons plain fat-free yogurt
- 2 tablespoons salsa

Beverage: 1 cup water, coffee, or tea

Snack (75 calories)
2 tablespoons hummus
8 carrot sticks

Dinner (450 calories)
3 ounces roasted chicken breast
½ cup steamed broccoli with 1 teaspoon margarine spread
¾ cup brown rice with 1 teaspoon margarine spread
Beverage: 1 cup fat-free milk

Snack (175 calories)
¾ cup hot chocolate made with fat-free milk
4 graham crackers

Figure 9.14   This menu includes moderate portions of nutrient-dense foods for breakfast, lunch, dinner, and snacks. It would provide an adult with the recommended amounts from all the food groups for just under 1,600 calories a day.

resentment and rejection of the plan. Rather than steering clear of special occasions, try eating a healthy snack before going. This will make it easier to enjoy the event while reducing the temptation to overeat.

When ordering in restaurants, make sensible food choices. Choose fruit or vegetable juice for an appetizer. Ask to have salad dressings, gravies, and sauces served on the side. Avoid fried menu items and ask to have vegetables served unbuttered. Select fresh fruit for dessert. Put half of the food that is brought to the table into a takeout box before beginning to eat.

Another tip is to try using a smaller plate to make portions look larger. Eating slowly and chewing food thoroughly extends the length of a meal. Using herbs and spices adds flavor to foods. Following these suggestions can make smaller portions of food seem more satisfying (**Figure 9.15**).

Learn About...

Portion Distortion

Portion distortion is another factor that gets in the way of satiety signals. Portion distortion is a mistaken belief about the appropriate amount of food to eat at one time. This problem has arisen because many foods come in portions that are much larger than recommended servings.

Many people do not know these portions are oversized. They think these are the typical amounts of food they should eat. For instance, many people would assume that a bagel is one serving from the grains group. A number of years ago, this was true. At that time, however, a typical bagel was 3 inches in diameter. Today, the typical bagel half is 6 inches across. It equals two servings and provides more than twice the calories of the bagels of the past.

Being aware of what recommended serving sizes look like will help you avoid portion distortion.

Know and Apply
1. What is another example of a food that is typically served in an oversized portion?
2. How can you avoid overeating when faced with portion distortion?

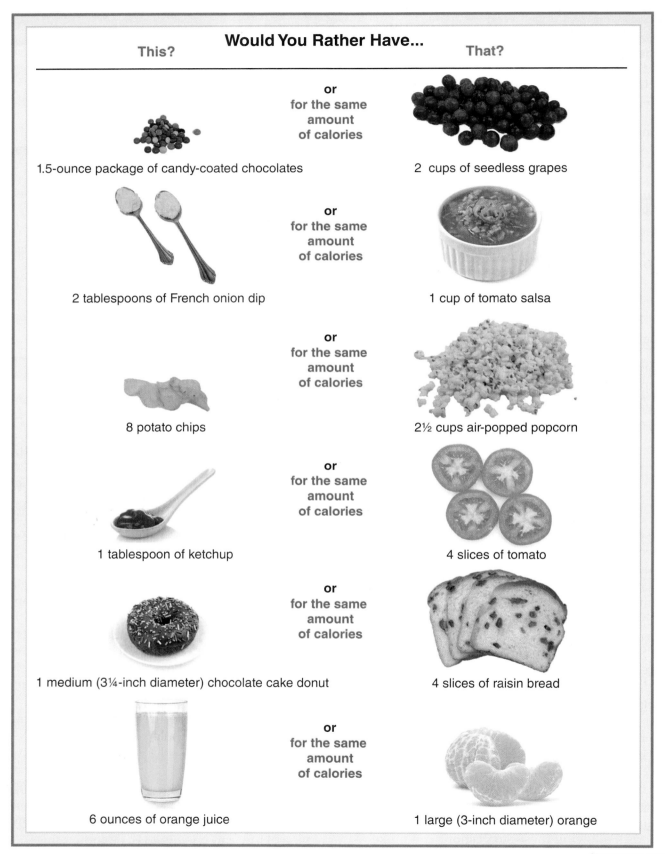

Would You Rather Have...

This? or for the same amount of calories **That?**

1.5-ounce package of candy-coated chocolates

2 cups of seedless grapes

2 tablespoons of French onion dip

1 cup of tomato salsa

8 potato chips

2½ cups air-popped popcorn

1 tablespoon of ketchup

4 slices of tomato

1 medium (3¼-inch diameter) chocolate cake donut

4 slices of raisin bread

6 ounces of orange juice

1 large (3-inch diameter) orange

Shutterstock.com

Figure 9.15 Consider your choices before you eat. Which of these choices would you make?

Avoid stepping on the scale more than once a week. The goal is a gradual weight loss. Checking weight too often may cause feelings of discouragement. When checking weight, realize that weight loss is seldom steady. The first few pounds may come off rather quickly. (This initial loss is usually due to water loss.) On the other hand, plateaus during which little or no progress seems to be made are normal.

Realize that mistakes can happen. A weight-loss plan does not have to be abandoned if a slip-up occurs. Splurging on a rich dessert does not make someone a failure. Everyone makes unwise choices now and then. Turn mistakes into learning experiences. Continuing to keep the food log used to identify eating habits can help avoid repeating mistakes. Think about what might have caused overeating. Then try to avoid that situation in the future.

Set a series of small goals. Instead of focusing on losing 30 pounds, set a goal to lose 5 pounds. Choose a meaningful nonfood reward, such as a trip to the movies, when that small goal is achieved. Then set a new goal to lose another 5 pounds.

Increasing Physical Activity

Watching food intake is only part of a weight management plan. The second key factor in the weight-loss equation is increasing physical activity. As you read earlier, regular activity speeds up metabolism. It also promotes good muscle tone and burns calories. An adult can burn 250 calories with just 30 to 60 minutes of activity. Doing this amount of activity each day uses half of the 3,500 calories needed to lose a pound per week (**Figure 9.16**).

Any type of activity can help burn calories. Adults might choose walking in the neighborhood, playing on a local sports league, or taking a fitness class. The kind of activity is not as important as its regularity.

Extra lifestyle activity can also help burn calories. Taking the stairs instead of using an elevator adds movement to a daily routine. Walking children to school and riding a bike to run nearby errands are ways to include more motion, too.

Calories Burned During Activity			
	Approximate Calories Burned		
Activity	Per Pound of Body Weight per Minute	Per Hour for a Person Weighing	
		125 Pounds	150 Pounds
Basketball, recreational	0.049	370	440
Bicycling, 10 mph	0.043	320	380
Dancing, active	0.045	340	410
Golf, carrying clubs	0.037	280	320
Horseback riding	0.027	200	250
Jogging, 5½ mph	0.067	500	600
Racquetball	0.065	490	590
Roller-skating	0.043	320	380
Running, 8 mph	0.097	730	880
Skiing, cross-country, 4 mph	0.065	490	590
Skiing, downhill	0.049	360	450
Soccer	0.060	450	540
Swimming, crawl, 35 yd./min.	0.049	370	440
Tennis, recreational singles	0.049	370	440
Walking, 4 mph	0.036	270	325

Figure 9.16 If you do not weigh 125 or 150 pounds, you can calculate activities burned performing an activity by selecting the appropriate factor in the second column and multiplying by your weight and the amount of time.

Learn About...

Weight-Loss Aids

Media ads for weight-loss aids are widespread. These aids include special pieces of exercise equipment that promise to slim waists and firm thighs. They extend to pills promoted to make pounds melt away without any changes in current exercise or dietary patterns. They also include diet fads that claim people will lose weight if they simply eat enough of one kind of food and avoid eating another.

The age-old advice to consumers is certainly valid here: If something sounds too good to be true, it probably is. The problem with most diet aids and fad diets is they cannot live up to their claims on a long-term basis. They do not help people develop new lifestyle behaviors. Therefore, as soon as people stop using these products, they go back to their old eating and activity patterns. This causes them to regain the weight.

Another factor consumers must think about when considering weight-loss aids is cost. Prices of weight-loss aids vary, but some can be quite costly. Consumers must decide if the cost is worthwhile for products that may bring disappointment.

A few prescription drugs are designed to help people lose weight. Some surgical procedures, such as gastric banding and gastric bypass, are also available. Like all drugs, weight-loss medications have some side effects and cannot be used by all people. Surgery is generally recommended only for people with obesity who have not had success losing weight with other methods. Surgery always has some risk of complications, too. Those who choose prescriptions or surgery will find they still need to watch their food intake and activity levels. With or without these interventions, the only way a person can lose weight is to consume fewer calories than he or she burns.

Know and Apply

1. Why do you think weight-loss aids are so popular when they often fail to provide lasting results?
2. What lifestyle behaviors are needed to make weight loss a success?

Maintaining Healthy Weight

After reaching weight goals, people should not give up their weight management plans. Remember, weight management is part of a healthy lifestyle. Keeping up this lifestyle will help people enjoy food in a whole new way.

To maintain weight loss, begin eating at, rather than below, daily calorie needs. Use MyPlate to choose food group amounts that match activity level. Remember to select foods that are nutrient dense. Make healthy choices by limiting foods that are high in solid fats, added sugars, and sodium.

Keeping active is a key to maintaining healthy weight. Continuing to engage in 150 to 300 minutes or more of activity per week will help keep weight off. Increasing time and/or intensity offers greater health benefits as well as calorie burning.

Keep in mind that there are alternatives when it comes to food choices, eating habits, and fitness activities. The decision-making process can be used to help choose the options that best relate to goals for maintaining a healthy weight. Do not forget to evaluate choices. Make adjustments as needed to manage weight throughout life.

Underweight

Body weight can be just as much of a problem for people who weigh too little as for people who weigh too much. People who are chronically underweight often experience more infections. They may tire easily. Some people who are underweight feel cold even when the temperature is moderate. They may feel ill at ease when wearing swimsuits and other figure-revealing clothes.

Determining the Cause of Underweight

Underweight may be due to a couple of main causes. A tendency to be underweight can be hereditary. Not eating enough food to meet the body's needs can cause a person to be underweight. Health problems may prevent the body from properly using and storing food energy to maintain healthy weight. A response to a stressful environment can also result in underweight.

Before trying to gain weight, a person who is underweight should see a physician. The physician will investigate if there are any medical reasons the person's body is not using the food it receives. If emotional problems are causing the weight problems, a physician may be able to recommend a therapist.

Following a Weight-Gain Plan

The goal of a weight-gain plan should not be a rapid weight gain. Rapid gains usually are the result of increased fat deposits. Instead, people trying to gain weight need to build up muscle tissue. To do this, they need to carefully follow a twofold plan. First, they need to regularly take part in activities such as weight lifting to strengthen and build muscles. This will ensure that weight gain is not due just to added body fat, which would be unhealthy.

Second, people who are underweight need to consume more calories than their bodies need. They should add 700 to 1,000 calories to their daily diets. This will provide enough energy to fuel the added activity plus allow for a gradual weight gain.

People who are underweight should continue to follow MyPlate. They can choose larger daily amounts from each food group. They can add modest amounts of fats and sweeteners, such as butter and sugar, to some foods. People who are underweight can boost calories by eating small meals every few hours. Nutritious snacks are a good way to add calories, too.

People who are underweight may have trouble eating large quantities of food. Therefore, they need to consume calories in more concentrated forms. They can choose nutritious, calorie-dense foods from each food group. For instance, dried fruit, cheese, and nuts are concentrated sources of calories (**Figure 9.17**).

Other ways to add nutrients and calories without adding bulk include stirring nonfat dry milk into soups, casseroles, and cooked cereals. Choosing starchy vegetables, such as peas, potatoes, and corn will add more calories per serving than nonstarchy vegetables.

While eating more of some foods, people who are trying to gain weight should limit other foods. For instance, they may want to avoid drinking beverages with meals. Consuming liquids can cause feelings of fullness that may lead to an overall reduction in calorie intake. A person who is underweight may do better to consume liquids between meals. For instance, nutritious smoothies made with fruit, yogurt, and nut butters can be used as calorie-dense snacks. Some people find it easier to drink extra calories than to eat them in solid foods.

In the same way, people trying to gain weight may want to avoid eating high-fiber, low-calorie foods like salads with meals. Like beverages, such foods can bring on a feeling of fullness that curbs total calorie consumption. Foods like dried fruits and nuts are more calorie-rich sources of fiber.

Following a weight-gain plan can be just as challenging as following a weight-loss plan. With continued physical activity and careful food choices, weight will gradually increase. Once a weight goal has been reached, a person who is underweight can begin eating at his or her daily calorie need. Making good nutrition and physical activity an ongoing weight management program will help maintain healthy weight.

Eating Disorders

An **eating disorder** is abnormal eating behavior that risks physical and mental health. There are several types of eating disorders. They all involve intense feelings and beliefs about food and weight along with the disturbed behavior.

Gila Photography/Shutterstock.com

Figure 9.17   Calorie-dense snacks like nuts and dried fruits provide nutrients as well as concentrated energy for people who are trying to gain weight.

Eating disorders most often affect young women and teenage girls. People of both genders and all age groups can form eating disorders, however. These conditions affect people of all races and at all social levels, too.

Common Disorders and Their Effects on the Body

Symptoms often point to one of the three most common eating disorders. People who are affected, however, may not exhibit a complete set of symptoms.

Anorexia Nervosa

Anorexia nervosa is an eating disorder characterized by self-starvation. The term *nervosa* indicates the disorder has psychological roots. A person with anorexia has an intense fear of weight gain. He or she also has a distorted body image (**Figure 9.18**). This person may look like skin and bones, yet he or she may complain of being fat. A person with anorexia does not realize he or she has an eating disorder.

Photographee.eu/Shutterstock.com

Figure 9.18   An individual with an eating disorder often has a distorted body image and is ashamed of his or her body.

Starvation causes some body processes to slow down or stop. Blood pressure drops and respiration slows. Hormone secretions become abnormal. This causes women with anorexia to stop menstruating. The body cannot absorb nutrients properly. Body temperature drops and sensitivity to cold increases. The heart cannot function correctly. In some cases, it may stop entirely, resulting in death.

Bulimia Nervosa

Bulimia nervosa is an eating disorder that has two key characteristics. The first is repeated eating *binges*. These are episodes during which the person with bulimia consumes thousands of calories in a short period. The second is an inappropriate behavior to prevent weight gain. For some people with bulimia, this behavior takes the form of *purging*. This means trying to quickly rid the body of the food.

Some people with bulimia purge by forcing themselves to vomit. Others take laxatives or diuretics to speed food and fluids through their bodies. Those who do not purge may fast or exercise excessively to avoid weight gain. The cycle of bingeing and purging or other countering behavior is repeated at least twice a week. This pattern continues for at least three months.

People with bulimia feel a lack of control over their eating behavior. This gives them a sense of guilt and shame. Unlike people with anorexia, however, they know their behavior is abnormal.

Frequent purging upsets the body's chemical balance. This can cause fatigue and heart abnormalities. Repeated vomiting can harm the teeth, gums, esophagus, and stomach.

Binge Eating Disorder

Like bulimia nervosa, **binge eating disorder** involves repeated episodes of uncontrolled eating. People with binge eating disorder consume large amounts of food. However, they do not take part in an opposing behavior to prevent weight gain. Therefore, most people who binge eat are overweight.

People who binge often feel physical discomfort from eating large amounts of food. They may develop health problems linked to obesity, such as diabetes and high blood pressure. They may also feel shame about a lack of self-control (**Figure 9.19**).

Signs of Eating Disorders
• Abnormal weight loss
• Binge eating
• Self-induced vomiting
• Abuse of laxatives and/or diuretics
• Excessive exercise
• Absent or irregular menstrual periods in females
• Depression

Figure 9.19   You should suspect a person has an eating disorder when one or more of these signs are present. Early detection leads to a better chance of recovery.

Causes and Prevention

Doctors do not know what causes eating disorders. A number of factors have been found to contribute to their occurrence, however. These factors include mental issues such as low self-esteem, stress, depression, and anxiety. Being teased about weight and having trouble relating to others can be tied to these complex disorders. Feeling pressure to conform to standards of attractiveness that include a thin, fit body can also be a factor. Researchers even believe genetics may play a role in eating disorders.

To help prevent eating disorders, all people need to be more aware of the factors just mentioned. Everyone can help create a social climate that admires each person's unique qualities. This will reduce the pressure to measure up to an ideal body image promoted by the media.

Being aware of the symptoms of eating disorders is also a key to prevention. Offering support to someone who shows symptoms can help that person get treatment before the problem gets worse.

If you think you know someone who has an eating disorder, you should confront the person with your concerns. Speak to the person privately. Be honest as you express care and support. Describe the behaviors that have caused your concern. Use your knowledge of nutrition and eating disorders to counter any excuses the person may offer. Suggest that the person see a professional about these behaviors. Do not threaten or accuse the person, and avoid making promises you cannot keep.

If the person seems unwilling to seek help, you should talk to a trusted adult about the situation. A parent, teacher, doctor, or counselor should be able to offer advice. The sooner someone with an eating disorder gets help, the better his or her chances of recovery are.

Treatment for Eating Disorders

Early treatment of eating disorders improves the chance of recovery with no severe health problems. These disorders require professional care. Treatment centers first on physical effects of the disorder. A person may need to be hospitalized so doctors can treat symptoms of malnutrition or other damage to the body.

Once a person's physical health has been addressed, he or she must begin psychological counseling. Counselors often urge family members to take part in therapy. Friends as well as family members can form a strong support system for someone with an eating disorder. They can learn to address issues that may have triggered the eating disorder. They can also learn to offer support as the person with an eating disorder works to change his or her behavior. Group therapy may be used to provide peer support to people with eating disorders.

Other specialists are often part of the treatment team for someone with an eating disorder. A registered dietitian nutritionist can help the person learn how to make nutritious food choices. A fitness counselor can aid in setting up a sound program of physical activity. Working as a team, health professionals can help the patient create a plan to manage his or her eating disorder. With patience and care, he or she will learn to form a healthy relationship with food.

Chapter 9 Review and Expand

Summary

Your energy needs are based on your basal metabolism and your activity level. The energy value of the foods you eat depends on the amount of carbohydrate, fat, and protein in the food. The way the energy provided by the foods you eat compares with your energy needs affects your body weight.

The energy you use for physical activity plays a vital role in your body's state of fitness. You need to choose different types of activities and make a point of being active every day. This will help you target all aspects of fitness, which will result in a range of health benefits.

The amount of activity performed by athletes creates some special nutritional needs. Athletes must be sure to drink plenty of fluids to avoid dehydration. They need extra calories to fuel their high level of activity. Food choices, especially for pregame meals, should be nutritious to help athletes compete to the best of their abilities.

Weight management is a lifestyle that will help maintain a healthy weight throughout life. Body mass index, waist circumference, and a skinfold test can help determine whether weight is healthy. Being overweight or obese may lead to a number of health problems. Deciding to lose weight and identifying eating habits are the first steps to reaching healthy weight goals. Weight management involves controlling energy intake and increasing physical activity. After reaching a weight-loss goal, weight management principles are used to maintain a healthy weight. These principles also apply to people who are trying to gain weight.

Weight management is lacking in cases of eating disorders. Anorexia nervosa, bulimia nervosa, and binge eating disorder are three common disorders. These abnormal eating behaviors can damage the body. A number of factors play a role in the development of eating disorders. Treatment requires care of the body and mind to help disordered eaters view food in a healthy way.

Vocabulary Activities

1. **Content Terms**   Write a brief chapter summary to an adult who is interested in entering the nutrition field. In your summary, include each vocabulary term in the list that follows.

basal metabolism   kilocalorie

physical fitness	body mass index (BMI)
cardiorespiratory fitness	healthy weight
Physical Activity Guidelines for Americans (PAG)	overweight
	underweight
aerobic activity	obesity
hydrate	waist circumference
dehydration	eating disorder
weight management	anorexia nervosa
body composition	bulimia nervosa
	binge eating disorder

2. **Academic Terms**   Using a dictionary, look up each academic term listed below. Which terms have additional meanings that vary from the definitions given in the chapter?

ambitious   regimen

detrimental   disparate

Review

Write your answers using complete sentences when appropriate.

3. True or false. Basal metabolism refers to the amount of energy the human body needs just to stay alive and carry on vital life processes.

4. List four factors that affect basal metabolism.

5. What are three factors that can influence the amount of energy a person needs to perform a physical task?

6. How many calories are provided by a gram of each of the following nutrients: carbohydrates, proteins, fats?

7. Explain how adults can use the two levels of aerobic activity to meet the recommendations of the *PAG*.

8. Give three examples of community resources that might be used to promote physical activity and fitness.

9. When should an athlete begin drinking fluids to prevent dehydration?

10. Why should an athlete choose complex carbohydrates rather than fats to make up the bulk of calories in a pregame meal?

11. Explain why the use of body mass index in assessing weight has limitations.

Chapter 9 Review and Expand

12. Describe three factors that can distract people from listening to their bodies' satiety signals.

13. Briefly describe a weight management plan for losing 1 pound (0.45 kg) a week.

14. Give three tips for achieving desired results with a weight-loss plan.

15. How can a weight-gain plan avoid large increases in body fat and why is such a plan recommended?

16. Which common eating disorder involves repeated eating binges followed by inappropriate behavior to prevent weight gain?

17. Identify three health professionals who might be part of a team for treating someone with an eating disorder.

Core Skills

18. **Math** Bring in a Nutrition Facts panel from a food product. Use the panel information to figure the number and percentage of calories in the food product that come from proteins, carbohydrates, and fats.

19. **Research, Technology** Visit the American Council on Exercise (ACE) website to research a specific fitness topic. Prepare an electronic presentation to share your findings with the class.

20. **Math** Calculate the basal metabolic rate for a 32-year-old male who is 5 feet, 11 inches tall and weighs 187 pounds. (Round answer to nearest whole number.)

21. **Technology, Speaking** Visit the Healthy People 2020 website. Review the objectives related to weight status under the topic area of nutrition and weight status. Also review the objectives under the topic area of physical activity. In class, discuss why the federal government sets national health goals.

22. **Writing** Imagine you have a friend who exhibits abnormal eating behaviors. Write a letter to your friend expressing your concern, offering support, and suggesting a possible course of action he or she might take. Reread and revise your letter to be sure your message is expressed with sensitivity and resolve.

23. **Math** Calculate the number of calories burned by a 170-pound person playing recreational basketball for 40 minutes. (See Figure 9.16)

24. **Career Readiness Practice** In addition to performing their work duties, new employees are challenged to keep healthy. Part of this dedication includes taking initiative to maintain a healthy body weight. Imagine you are hosting an event for the workplace such as a walk or jog, volleyball tournament, or skating party. Design a brochure about the benefits of physical activity in weight management to advertise the event.

Critical Thinking and Problem Solving

25. **Create** Plan a pregame meal that would prepare a teenage athlete for an hour of vigorous sports competition. The meal should provide 700 to 800 calories, with 60 to 70 percent of calories from mostly complex carbohydrates, 10 to 20 percent from proteins, and 15 to 25 percent from fats. Use an online nutrient database to help you be sure your menu meets these goals. (Remember that carbohydrates and proteins provide 4 calories per gram and fats provide 9 calories per gram.)

26. **Analyze** Measure your body fat using a scale with a body fat monitor. If possible, have a trained professional measure your body fat using a skinfold caliper. Compare the two measurements to analyze the accuracy of the scale.

27. **Evaluate** Use MyPlate to evaluate a reducing diet suggested online or in a popular magazine. Give an oral report comparing the diet with the weight management principles discussed in this chapter.

Chapter 10
Life-Cycle Nutrition and Fitness

wavebreakmedia/Shutterstock.com

Content Terms ➦

diet
food allergy
food intolerance
cross-contact
growth spurt
vegetarian diet
therapeutic diet
medical nutrition
    therapy (MNT)
food-drug interaction

Academic Terms

foster
augment

Objectives

After studying this chapter, you will be able to

- **describe** health and development concerns that affect the nutritional needs of people in different life-cycle stages;
- **list** meal-planning tips to meet the nutritional needs of people in different life-cycle stages;
- **suggest** appropriate activities to help people at different life-cycle stages maintain physical fitness; and
- **plan** a nutritious diet for yourself.

Reading Prep

After reading each section (separated by main headings), stop and write a three- to four-sentence summary of what you just read. Be sure to paraphrase and use your own words.

A person's **diet** is all the food and drink he or she regularly consumes. Each stage of a person's life is affected by his or her diet. From the prenatal period to older adulthood, each stage is associated with nutritional needs. Poor nutrition in any stage may create health problems, shorten the life span, or both.

Like diet, physical activity is important throughout life. Physical activity helps burn calories and maintain fitness. Remember that flexibility, strength, balance, and endurance are all part of fitness. People who make physical activity a regular part of life can improve or maintain fitness in all these areas.

Pregnancy and Lactation

The human life cycle begins before birth. Therefore, the study of life-cycle nutrition and fitness must start with pregnancy.

Diet during pregnancy affects both the mother and the *fetus*, or developing baby. Good nutrition is especially important during pregnancy. This is because the mother nourishes the fetus through her body. The foods the mother eats must supply the nutrient needs of the fetus (**Figure 10.1**). Otherwise, nutrients for the fetus may be taken from the mother's tissues. This could cause the mother to experience deficiencies.

Nutrient Needs During Pregnancy

A key nutritional need during the first *trimester* (three-month period of pregnancy) is the need for folic acid. Folic acid is the synthetic form of folate found in fortified foods and dietary supplements. Folic acid helps prevent *neural tube* damage in the fetus. This is damage to the brain or spinal cord. It can occur in the early weeks of pregnancy before many women even know they are pregnant. This is why all women of childbearing age should consume 400 micrograms of synthetic folic acid per day in addition to natural food sources of folate. Once pregnancy is confirmed, a woman's doctor may advise her to increase her intake of this vitamin.

wavebreakmedia/Shutterstock.com

Figure 10.1 A healthy diet before and during pregnancy is important for both the mother and baby.

By the beginning of the second trimester, needs for almost all the essential nutrients increase. Some of the extra nutrients are needed to build the child's tissues. Others are needed to protect the mother.

Protein, calcium, and iron are especially important during pregnancy. The mother needs increased amounts of protein to support the growth of the fetus. Most women in the United States eat more than enough protein to meet this increased need.

The fetus requires calcium for well-formed bones and strong teeth. The mother needs to choose foods that supply enough calcium. Otherwise, the needs of the fetus will be taken from the mother's bone tissue. This can increase the mother's risk of developing osteoporosis later in life. Thus, a mother's food choices during pregnancy can have long-term effects.

Iron needs are especially large during the last six months of pregnancy. This is to help the baby build up iron reserves before birth. The baby will need these reserves during the first six months of life. A pregnant woman who does not get enough iron may become anemic as her body works to meet her baby's needs. This is why healthcare providers often advise pregnant women to take an iron supplement.

Exploring Careers

Dietetic Technician

Dietetic technicians work in a range of settings where nutrition topics are a concern. In hospitals and weight management clinics, they might work with clients one-on-one. They may help assess the client's dietary needs for dealing with issues like high blood pressure and obesity. They would help teach clients about how to follow suggested eating plans and would then monitor the clients' progress. In schools and institutions, they would plan menus that meet the nutritional needs of a group of people. In food companies and restaurant chains, they might analyze recipes and test new products. In all of these settings, dietetic technicians would be likely to be working under the direction of registered dietitian nutritionists.

Dietetic technicians need good speaking and listening skills. They need to be able to share information and accurately gather facts. They must give attention to details, be able to work independently, and have a concern for others.

Dietetic technicians may have two-year or four-year degrees. These workers can earn a dietetic technician, registered (DTR) credential. This gives them more credibility with employers. DTRs must pass a national exam. They must also take part in continuing education to keep up the credential.

Special Concerns for Pregnant Teens

Nutrient deficiencies can be a greater problem in the case of teen pregnancies. Teen mothers need high levels of nutrients to support their own growth. Many teen girls do not have good eating habits. Busy schedules may cause them to skip meals. Snacks and fast-food choices eaten on the go are often high in fat and calories. Diets are frequently lacking in vegetables, fruits, and dairy foods. Teen girls are often concerned about weight gain as well. These issues can lead to deficiencies, which could put a teen mother's health as well as her baby's health at risk.

Some teens do not realize they are pregnant until they are nearing the end of the first trimester. By this time, the baby's brain and spinal cord have already begun to form. The organs are developing, and the baby's heart begins to beat.

Good nutrition and healthy lifestyle habits are important right from the very start of pregnancy. Teens who are not following a healthy diet may not be getting the nutrients their babies need. This is especially a concern with folic acid, which is needed to help prevent congenital disabilities of the brain and spinal cord. Teens who smoke or consume alcohol or drugs are exposing their babies to toxic substances. These toxins can stunt normal growth during these critical early stages of a baby's life.

Later in pregnancy, teens who fail to gain enough weight risk early delivery. Premature babies are likely to have a low birth weight. Because they have not had as much time to develop in the womb, these babies have an increased chance of health issues.

Teens are at greater risk of high blood pressure and other health concerns during pregnancy than women who are older. The most important step a teen can take is to see a doctor as soon as she thinks she might be pregnant (**Figure 10.2**). Like all women, a pregnant teen needs prenatal care to oversee the health of her baby. In addition, she needs to eat a good diet; avoid tobacco, alcohol, and drugs; and get moderate exercise and plenty of rest.

Diet During Pregnancy

A pregnant woman should follow a nutritious diet made up of a variety of foods. She can visit ChooseMyPlate.gov and find the recommended daily amounts she should consume for each food group. Recommended amounts are based on a woman's age, body size, and activity level before pregnancy. Calorie needs increase and recommended food group amounts change after the first trimester. If the woman's diet was adequate before pregnancy, a few small additions are all she should need. These additions will meet her increased nutrient needs and help

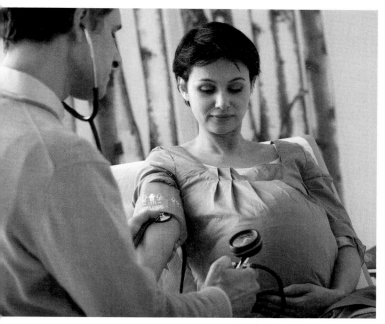

Image Point Fr/Shutterstock.com

Figure 10.2 High blood pressure is more likely to occur during first pregnancies and in women under 20 years of age.

her gain weight at the correct rate. As before pregnancy, she should limit solid fats and added sugars.

During the first trimester, the Dietary Reference Intakes for energy are the same as the mother's prepregnancy energy needs. Energy needs increase roughly 340 calories a day, however, in the second trimester. In the third trimester, a woman should increase her intake by 452 calories over her prepregnancy needs. To meet these increased needs, she must boost a few of her daily food group amounts.

During the second trimester, the woman should add two ounce equivalents from the grains group, a half cup from the vegetables group, one ounce equivalent from the protein foods group, and one teaspoon of oil. In the third trimester, she should add one more ounce equivalent of grain foods and another half cup from the vegetables group. A sample food plan for pregnancy is shown in **Figure 10.3.**

When choosing protein foods, health experts advise pregnant women to consume up to 12 ounces (340 g) of seafood per week. Fish and shellfish provide omega-3 fatty acids and minerals that developing babies need. However, it is important to avoid types that are high in mercury, which could harm a baby. Such types

include swordfish, shark, king mackerel, and tilefish. Seafood that is lower in mercury includes canned light tuna, catfish, clams, cod, salmon, and shrimp.

A pregnant woman should consult with her healthcare provider about a dietary pattern and level of physical activity that is best for herself and her baby. Healthcare providers often prescribe nutrient supplements for pregnant women. These supplements include iron along with vitamins and other minerals. Many women have low iron reserves, and supplements help them meet the increased demands of pregnancy. Pregnant women should never take supplements without consulting their doctors. Too much of some vitamins and minerals can be harmful to pregnant women and their developing babies.

For the well-being of mother and baby, doctors urge women to be at a healthy body weight before becoming pregnant. A woman should ask an obstetrician how much weight to gain during pregnancy.

Health and Wellness

Foodborne Illness and Pregnancy

Some illnesses spread through food pose greater risks during pregnancy. These risks include miscarriage, early delivery, and severe health problems for the baby. Babies can become infected even if the mother does not become sick.

Pregnant women should not eat foods linked with foodborne illnesses. These foods include raw and undercooked meat, poultry, seafood, and egg dishes. Pregnant women should avoid unpasteurized milk and soft cheese made from it. Moms-to-be should also pass up cold hot dogs and luncheon meats and premade deli salads. They should steer clear of raw sprouts and unpasteurized juice and cider, too.

Advice about foods to avoid during pregnancy changes based on new findings. Pregnant women would be wise to check foodsafety.gov to find the most current information. They should also follow safety guidelines when handling foods to help prevent illness.

Sample MyPlate Plan During Pregnancy*

		Grains	Vegetables	Fruits	Dairy	Protein Foods	Oils
Trimester	**1st**	**6 ounces** Choose whole grain and fortified products for folic acid.	**2½ cups** When choosing canned vegetables, avoid added salt.	**2 cups** Choose fresh fruits most often to provide needed fiber.	**3 cups** Choose low-fat and fat-free sources to meet calcium needs.	**5½ ounces** Choose lean sources of protein and include 8 oz. seafood weekly.	**6 tsp.**
	2nd	**8 ounces** (Add 2 oz.)	**3 cups** (Add ½ c.)			**6½ ounces** (Add 1 oz.) 10 oz. seafood weekly	**7 tsp.**
	3rd	**9 ounces** (Add 1 oz.)	**3½ cups** (Add ½ c.)				**8 tsp.**

*Based on 2,000 calories per day prepregnancy needs

Shutterstock.com; ©iStock.com

Figure 10.3   Women are encouraged to follow a healthy diet before becoming pregnant. Then they will only have to make small changes to meet the nutrient needs of pregnancy. What are some specific foods a pregnant woman could add to her food plan to meet her needs in the second and third trimesters?

A common recommendation is a gain of 25 to 35 pounds for women of healthy weight. Doctors also advise women who are overweight not to try to lose weight during pregnancy.

Fitness During Pregnancy

Changing interests and abilities make some activities more suitable than others at each life-cycle stage. The pregnancy stage is no exception. Being physically fit can help a woman have a more comfortable pregnancy and an easier delivery. However, changes in a pregnant woman's body can put her at increased risk of injury. Therefore, it is important to choose moderate rather than vigorous activities at this life stage.

Walking, swimming, and low-impact aerobics are good activities for pregnant women. Many other activities are safe as well. On the other hand, contact sports and activities that involve bouncing, twisting at the waist, or a high risk of falling are not good choices. A pregnant woman should discuss her fitness routine with her healthcare provider. She should listen to her body and stop activity immediately if she feels pain, dizziness, or shortness of breath.

Diet During Lactation

During *lactation* (the production of breast milk), a woman has increased energy, protein, mineral, and vitamin needs. The woman needs these extra nutrients to replace the nutrients secreted in the milk. She also needs them to cover the energy cost of producing the milk and to protect her body.

Like pregnant women, lactating women should make a point of choosing seafood that is lower in mercury a couple of times each week. Nursing mothers will pass the omega-3 fatty acids in the seafood to their babies through breast milk. These fatty acids aid a baby's healthy brain development (**Figure 10.4**).

The diets of a lactating woman and a pregnant woman are similar. However, the lactating woman's needs for some nutrients are greater. Like a pregnant woman, a mother who is breast-feeding can visit **MyPlate**.gov to get a food group plan. Following this plan will help her make sure she is using the right food groups to meet her extra nutrient needs.

Calorie needs may change for a nursing mother six months after her baby is born. A woman's body forms fat stores as she gains weight during pregnancy. During the first six months after delivery, some of the energy needed to produce milk comes from these fat stores. Six months after delivery, the woman is likely to have lost all the weight she gained during pregnancy. At this point, she may need a small amount of extra calories from food to supply the energy she needs to produce milk.

Lactating women need liquids to provide water in breast milk and to meet their own fluid needs. They should drink at least 2 to 3 quarts (2 to 3 L) of fluid each day. Drinking water or another beverage each time she nurses her baby will help a breast-feeding mother get the fluid she needs.

Avoiding Alcohol and Other Drugs

Many drugs can have harmful effects on a developing fetus or nursing baby. Anything a pregnant woman drinks or smokes reaches her baby in the womb. Likewise, anything a lactating mother drinks or smokes reaches her baby through the breast milk. This is why pregnant and lactating women should not use alcohol, tobacco, or drugs.

Alcohol is a drug, and tobacco contains nicotine, which is a drug. During pregnancy, drugs can pass from the mother's body to the baby through the placenta. (The *placenta* is an organ that nourishes the developing child in the mother's womb.) Smoking during pregnancy can cause babies to be born early and have a low birth weight. Babies of smoking moms are at a higher risk of lung problems and Sudden Infant Death Syndrome (SIDS), too. When pregnant women drink alcohol, their babies are more likely to have growth, learning, and behavior problems.

During lactation, drugs can pass to a baby through breast milk. Alcohol and nicotine in breast milk can both affect a baby's sleep patterns. In addition, being around secondhand smoke can cause babies to develop breathing problems.

As a rule, pregnant and lactating women should not take any type of drug unless a doctor approves. Of course, this includes illegal drugs. However, prescriptions should also be avoided except under a doctor's advice. Even

MaraZe/Shutterstock.com   *AnastasiaKopa/Shutterstock.com*   *Robyn Mackenzie/Shutterstock.com*

Figure 10.4 Salmon, trout, and albacore tuna are rich sources of omega-3 fatty acids.

over-the-counter medications, such as aspirin, and herbal products, like ginseng and St. John's wort, need a doctor's okay before use (**Figure 10.5**).

Fitness After Delivery

After having a baby, most women look forward to getting their bodies back in shape. Following a daily fitness routine is a great way to reach this goal. Physical activity can also help lessen feelings of depression that sometimes occur after delivery. A new mother should check with her doctor before beginning a routine. Most women can start moderate exercise as soon as they feel up to it.

Some of the first exercises a new mother may want to do will help her regain balance and strength she lost during pregnancy. Standing on one foot and then the other is one activity that will help improve balance. Doing modified sit-ups and pelvic tilts are among the options for building muscle strength in the back and abdomen.

Walking is a good activity for building endurance during the first weeks after having a baby. A woman can slowly increase her speed and distance as she feels able to keep up with a tougher routine. She can add more intense activities as she feels ready. However, she should avoid activities such as jogging and jumping for the first six to eight weeks after delivery. These activities put stress on joints that have been loosened by pregnancy hormones and can lead to injury.

Pelvic pain, bleeding, shortness of breath, and exhaustion are all signs of trouble for a new mother. A woman who has any of these symptoms should see her doctor before continuing her fitness routine.

Infancy and Early Childhood

Infants and preschool children need good nutrition to grow and develop normally. A healthy diet is more important during the first year of life than at any other time in the life span.

Nutritional Needs of Infants

An infant's requirements for all nutrients are higher per unit of body weight than an adult's. Unlike adults, however, an infant has no nutrient reserves. The exception is iron. A full-term baby should have enough reserve iron to last for the first six months of life. A baby needs iron reserves because he or she consumes only breast milk or infant formula during the first few months. Breast milk is not a rich source of iron. Formula may be fortified with iron, but a baby cannot absorb it well.

Infants generally receive injections of vitamin K at birth. This meets their needs for the vitamin until bacteria in their intestinal tracts develop and begin making it. Some breast-fed infants also receive a supplemental source of vitamin D. This helps prevent *rickets*, the vitamin D deficiency disease that results in malformed bones.

Besides high nutrient needs, an infant has high energy needs to support rapid growth. Growth patterns vary, but an infant's rate of growth is

ksenvitaln/Shutterstock.com

Figure 10.5 The babies of pregnant and lactating women are also exposed to any substances their mothers consume.

fastest during the first few months of life. During the first three months, a normal, healthy infant will gain about two pounds (910 g) a month. The growth rate then slows to about one pound (454 g) a month. As growth slows, an infant's energy needs per unit of body weight decrease slightly. By the end of the first year, the infant's weight has almost tripled. His or her length is one and one-half times the birth length.

Feeding Infants

Newborns usually need to be fed seven or eight times a day. Newborns are just learning to eat, and their small stomachs cannot hold much. Feedings gradually decrease to about five a day by the time the infant is two months old. Although intake varies, most infants will drink about 1 quart (1 L) of breast milk or formula each day.

Breast Milk or Formula

Nutrition experts strongly recommend that mothers breast-feed their infants. Brain development is rapid during the first years of life. Breast milk is recognized as the best food to *foster* (encourage) brain development. Breast milk is easy for a baby to digest. It provides nutrients in ratios that are perfectly designed for babies. It contains immune substances that help a baby resist infection. Breast milk also helps protect the baby from developing allergies (**Figure 10.6**).

Iron-fortified infant formulas are available for mothers who are unable or choose not to breast-feed their infants. Infant formula contains less carbohydrate and fat and more protein than breast milk. Formula also contains more of many vitamins and minerals. However, babies absorb the lower amounts of nutrients in breast milk better than the nutrients in formula. In addition, too much of some nutrients, such as protein and calcium, can place stress on a baby's immature kidneys.

Cow's milk is hard for infants to digest and may cause intestinal bleeding. It should never be given to a baby until a pediatrician gives approval. Cow's milk is not a suitable food for babies under 12 months of age. After a baby's first birthday, a doctor may agree to have whole cow's milk introduced into the baby's diet. Low-fat milk is not recommended for children under 24 months of age because they need fat for normal growth and development.

Marlon Lopez MMG1 Design/Shutterstock.com

Figure 10.6 Breast milk composition changes to meet the changing needs of the infant. What are other benefits of breast-feeding?

Babies get all the fluids they need from breast milk or formula. During hot weather, babies may lose fluids through sweat. In this case, older babies may be offered a small amount of water a couple of times a day. However, babies do not need other beverages and should never be offered sugary drinks like soda and fruit punch whether in a bottle, cup, or any other utensil.

Parents are advised not to offer juice to infants less than 6 months old unless directed by a pediatrician. If juice is offered to older infants, it should be 100 percent juice and be limited to 4 ounces (125 mL) per day. Juice should be offered in a cup, not a bottle. It should be offered with, rather than between, meals. Drinking too much juice can keep babies from consuming breast milk, formula, and nutritious foods. It can also give babies diarrhea and cause them to gain too much weight.

Solid Foods

The introduction of solid foods into a baby's diet should be gradual. Most infants are ready to begin eating solid foods when they can sit in a highchair or infant seat. They should demonstrate good control of their heads and show an interest in foods. These signs of readiness usually appear between four and six months of age (**Figure 10.7**).

AVAVA/Shutterstock.com

Figure 10.7 Starting solids before 4 months of age might result in food entering the airway, too many or too few nutrients, and increased risk for obesity. What signs of readiness indicate a baby is ready to start solid foods?

Parents should check with a baby's doctor about when and how to introduce solid foods. Doctors often suggest iron-fortified oatmeal or rice cereal made for babies as the first food to try. They may advise adding single pureed vegetables and fruits next. These are likely to be followed with strained meats and poultry and then food mixtures. Parents can add finely chopped foods from family meals to a child's diet by his or her first birthday.

Most pediatricians tell parents to start with a small amount of just one new food at a time. Parents should wait at least three days before starting the next new food. This will help the parents identify food allergies. A true **food allergy** involves a response of the body's immune system to a food protein. Medical tests are required to verify food allergies. Allergy symptoms may include diarrhea, vomiting, skin rashes, and runny nose. A severe allergic reaction can be life threatening and requires immediate medical attention. Foods that most commonly cause allergic reactions are milk, eggs, fish, shellfish, tree nuts, peanuts, wheat, and soybeans.

Infants may be sensitive to certain foods without being truly allergic to them. A

Learn About...

Bottle Feeding

Even breast-fed babies are given a bottle from time to time. Bottle feeding allows all family members a chance to bond with a baby. Knowing a few guidelines will help make bottle feeding a safe and happy experience for babies and caregivers.

Do not warm a baby's bottle in a microwave oven. Instead, place the bottle in a bowl of warm water for a few minutes. Milk can heat unevenly in a microwave oven and could accidentally scald the baby. Overheating can also affect the quality of breast milk.

Some people believe putting cereal in a baby's bedtime bottle will help him or her sleep through the night. However, a baby's ability to sleep through the night depends on the maturity of his or her nervous system. Parents should not put cereal in a baby's bottle unless a doctor tells them to do so. Cereal in a bottle can be a choking hazard for a baby and can also cause the baby to consume too many calories. If babies are mature enough to be eating cereal, they should be eating it from a spoon at mealtimes.

Do not put a baby to bed with a bottle. Propping a bottle in a baby's mouth and leaving the baby unattended at any time of day presents a choking risk. It also increases the risk of ear infections for the baby.

In addition, sleeping with a bottle that contains milk, formula, or juice can lead to tooth decay. To protect a baby's gums and teeth, gently wipe them with a soft cloth after feeding and before bedtime. Offering a pacifier can comfort a baby without the concerns of a bottle at bedtime.

Know and Apply

1. How can a caregiver tell if a baby is mature enough to be offered cereal?
2. Why would sleeping with a bottle containing milk, formula, or juice lead to tooth decay?

food intolerance is a negative reaction to a food substance that does not involve the immune system. Symptoms of food intolerance may resemble allergy symptoms. Whether symptoms are due to allergy or intolerance, they should end when parents stop feeding the baby the problem food. Parents may try reintroducing the food a month or two later. Sensitivities often go away as infants mature.

When a child has a food allergy or intolerance, his or her family must help protect the child's health. At restaurants, parents need to look at menus carefully and ask about preparation methods to help keep their child safe. When shopping, parents need to read all labels on every food purchased. Food manufacturers sometimes change the way products are made. Therefore, it is wise to read labels each time a food is purchased rather than to assume it is still safe.

If foods containing allergens are used in the home, family members need to take care to avoid **cross-contact**. This occurs when allergens are transferred from a food source to a person with a food allergy. Allergens can be transferred from one food to another when the two foods touch. Allergens can also be transferred by items such as utensils and cooking oil. It is important to understand that cooking will not eliminate allergens and make foods containing them safe to eat.

Fitness During Infancy

It is never too early to begin a fitness routine. Parents should begin helping their babies exercise from the day they bring them home from the hospital. Of course, babies cannot jog and do sit-ups, but they can enjoy regular "tummy time." Spending time playing on their bellies helps babies develop their muscles and motor skills (**Figure 10.8**). It also keeps them from getting flattened skulls caused by spending too much time on their backs.

Following a few guidelines can help make tummy time safe and enjoyable for babies. Babies should only be placed on their stomachs when they are awake. (It is important to place babies on their backs for sleeping to reduce the risk of SIDS.) Babies should never be left alone when they are on their stomachs. Placing a folded towel or blanket under their chests will help babies lift their heads. Placing toys in front of babies and on both sides will encourage them to reach and turn from side to side.

Babies will also gain from being placed in various positions for daily tasks like feeding and

arek_malang/Shutterstock.com

Figure 10.8 Tummy time encourages babies to develop muscles as they lift their heads to view the world around them.

diapering. Carrying babies in a range of positions and on both sides of the body will help them build different muscles. Holding babies firmly while allowing them to put weight on their feet will strengthen leg muscles they will need for walking. Following these tips throughout the day will help parents make sure their babies develop fitness.

Nutritional Needs of Preschool Children

Growth is slower between the ages of two and six years than it is during the first year of life. However, growth is still quite rapid. The diet should supply enough calories for a weight gain that fits a child's normal rate of development.

Nutrient needs vary from child to child, depending on growth and activity. However, many young children do not get enough potassium, calcium, vitamin D, and fiber in their diets. In fact, these are viewed as nutrients of concern for people at all life stages. Health experts advise people in all age groups to follow MyPlate, which will help them choose more sources of these nutrients. Eating more vegetables, fruits, whole grains, low-fat and fat-free dairy products, and seafood will help people avoid deficiencies (**Figure 10.9**).

Good Sources of Potassium

Baked white[3] and sweet potatoes[3]

Carrot and orange[1,2] juices

Prune juice and stewed prunes[3]

Tomato paste[3], juice, and sauce

White[3], lima[3], pinto[3], and kidney beans[3] and soybeans[3]

Plain yogurt[1,2] and low-fat chocolate milk[1,2], milk[1,2], and buttermilk[1]

Clams, halibut, tuna[2], rockfish[2], cod[2], and trout

Dried peaches and apricots, bananas[3]

[1]Source of calcium (fortified orange juice)
[2]Source of vitamin D (fortified orange juice)
[3]Source of fiber

Shutterstock.com

Figure 10.9 Many sources of potassium also supply other underconsumed nutrients. Which sources of potassium do you think would appeal most to preschoolers?

Meals for Preschoolers

Preschool children can have unpredictable eating habits and are often viewed as picky eaters. Most pediatricians urge parents to be patient and continue offering healthy foods at each meal. Children often need to try a new food a dozen times before they will accept it.

Parents need to set good examples by eating healthy foods themselves. Most experts agree children should not be pressured to eat. Children who do not eat at one meal will often make up for it at another. What matters most is that each day's diet includes all the needed nutrients.

When planning meals for a preschooler, follow MyPlate. Two- and three-year-old children need to consume the equivalent of 2 cups (500 mL)

from the dairy group each day. By the time they are four years old, children need to increase foods from this group to 2½ cups (625 mL) daily.

Following a couple tips when serving foods will often encourage preschoolers to eat. Try offering food choices that are bright colored, mild flavored, soft, and lukewarm. For instance, a child may prefer orange carrots over white potatoes. He or she may enjoy a Mexican dish more if the hot peppers are left out. Soft rolls might be more appealing than crusty French bread. A bowl of soup is likely to be received better if it is just warm rather than piping hot.

Serve foods in a pleasant eating atmosphere. Offer younger children booster seats and smaller utensils to help them feel more comfortable. You may also want to limit the need for utensils, as many children prefer finger foods they can eat with their hands.

Remember, young children have small stomachs and cannot eat large meals. Invite children to serve themselves small portions. Allow them to ask for more if they are still hungry. Offer nutritious snacks, such as whole-grain cereal, fresh or dried fruits, and yogurt smoothies, to help meet daily needs. Try to include choices from at least two food groups in each snack.

Fitness for Preschoolers

Just about any kind of active play can help preschoolers build fitness. The key is that the play is *active*. Children need to move and use their muscles. Running, jumping, riding a tricycle, kicking a ball, and swimming are all great activities for preschoolers. Games such as hide-and-seek and ring-around-a-rosy count as active play, too.

Knowing a few guidelines will help caregivers keep preschoolers active and safe. Limit sitting activities to 60 minutes at a time. Young children should not spend more than 2 hours a day watching television or using electronics. Make sure young children always wear helmets when riding tricycles or bicycles. Instruct children about traffic safety and not playing too close to the street. Keep a close eye on children while they play outdoors, and always supervise children playing in a pool. Set a good example by choosing activities you can do with children, such as playing catch or going for a walk. Children who learn to enjoy being active when they are young will form fitness habits that will last a lifetime.

The Elementary School Years

During the elementary school years, children grow at a fairly steady rate. Between the ages of 6 and 12, children develop many of the food habits they will follow throughout life. Parents can promote healthy attitudes by asking children to help pick out nutritious foods when shopping (**Figure 10.10**). They can invite children to help prepare foods, too. Children are more likely to eat foods if they have been involved in choosing and cooking them. Parents should encourage their children to try new foods. However, they should refrain from using food as a punishment or reward.

Nutritional Needs of School-Age Children

A 6-year-old child does not need as much food as a 12-year-old child. However, both children need the same kinds of food. The amount of food a child needs depends on his or her growth rate and physical activity. Normally, a child's appetite is a fairly reliable indication of energy needs.

Calorie needs increase gradually for children between the ages of 6 and 12. Nutrient needs increase as well, but often at a much greater rate. For instance, at age 9, the recommended calorie intake increases by about 13 percent. However, the recommended calcium intake increases by 30 percent. This is why it is vital for parents to help children make food choices that are nutrient dense. Foods prepared without added solid fats and sugars will help children get the nutrients they need while staying within their daily calorie limits.

School-age children should eat foods from all the food groups to promote growth and development. At age 9, children should increase food choices from the dairy group to the equivalent of 3 cups (750 mL) daily. This will help meet their greater needs for protein, calcium, and potassium.

Andresr/Shutterstock.com

Figure 10.10 Shopping for food can be an opportunity for parents to teach children about healthy food choices.

Planning Meals for School-Age Children

School-age children need to start the day with a nutrient-dense breakfast. Breakfast should supply about one-fourth of the day's total needs. Children who skip this meal do not obtain nutrients when the body needs them most—after a night without food. Studies have shown that eating breakfast helps children do better in school. It also helps them maintain a healthy body weight (**Figure 10.11**).

Children can eat any nutritious food for breakfast. Breakfast does not have to include traditional foods like toast and cereal. Yogurt or a bowl of tomato soup is just as nutritious at breakfast as it is at lunch or dinner.

When planning lunch and dinner, parents often find their school-age children prefer familiar foods that are mild in flavor. Parents should not, however, let these preferences turn them into short-order cooks who prepare different foods for picky eaters. The same foods should be offered to the whole family. When new foods are being served, offer them at the beginning of the meal when children are most hungry. Serve new foods along with familiar favorites so children do not face too many strange flavors at one time. As children mature, their tastes gradually change, and they will begin to enjoy a greater variety of foods.

Many school-age children have trouble eating enough at meals to meet all their nutritional needs. Snack options should be planned to provide added nutrients. Most children like fresh fruit, raw vegetables, low-fat cheese and yogurt, raisins, and whole-grain crackers with peanut butter.

Childhood Overweight and Obesity

Overweight and obesity are common among children. A child is *overweight* if he or she weighs more than what is considered a healthy weight for his or her height. *Obesity* is a condition characterized by excessive deposits of body fat. Children do not have the decision-making skills to make all their own lifestyle choices. Therefore, parents need to help children manage their weight. Otherwise, children are likely to have weight problems as adults.

Failing to make nutrient-dense food choices is one factor that has led to the high rate of overweight and obesity among children. Studies have shown that most of the foods children consume are foods they should be choosing only occasionally. It is no surprise that such foods include sugary beverages, salty snacks, sweets, and desserts. However, children also choose less healthy foods from the five MyPlate groups, such as French fries from the vegetable group.

Figure 10.12 begins as a nutrient-dense meal which includes a tossed salad, glass of milk, chicken breast, broccoli, brown rice, and a peach half. The sources of empty calories that surround the meal illustrate how quickly seemingly minor additions can add calories and few, if any, nutrients. The routine addition of empty calories can place a child at risk for unhealthy weight gain.

One of the best steps parents can take to address children's weight problems is to model healthy eating and activity habits. Parents can urge children to be more active. They can limit the time children spend watching TV and playing video games. Parents can provide healthy snacks to help children avoid high-calorie foods between meals. Parents can help children learn to use hunger signals to guide eating habits. They can encourage children to serve themselves small portions at mealtimes and stop eating when they are full. Parents might also discourage snacking in front of the TV, when children may be too distracted to notice hunger signals. These steps will help slow children's weight gain. In time, their growth will catch up to the excess weight.

Reasons to Eat Breakfast
✓ Faster memory recall
✓ Higher math scores
✓ Fewer behavioral and academic problems
✓ Improved performance on tests

Adapted from Food Research and Action Center's *Breakfast for Learning*

Figure 10.11   Children who eat breakfast perform better in school.

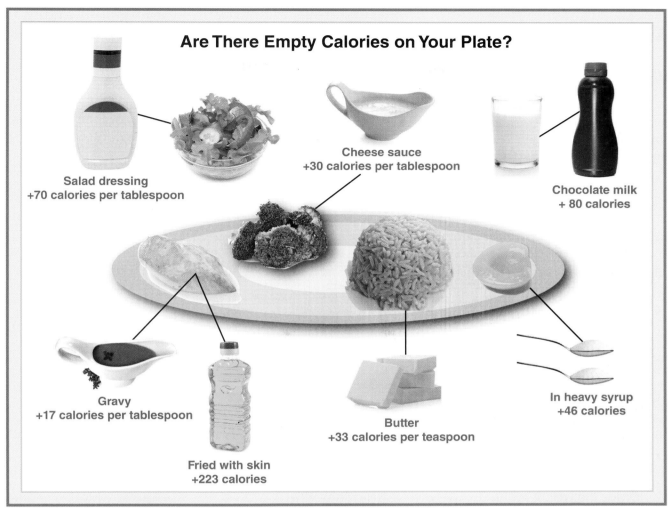

Are There Empty Calories on Your Plate?

Salad dressing
+70 calories per tablespoon

Cheese sauce
+30 calories per tablespoon

Chocolate milk
+ 80 calories

Gravy
+17 calories per tablespoon

Fried with skin
+223 calories

Butter
+33 calories per teaspoon

In heavy syrup
+46 calories

Shutterstock.com

Figure 10.12 Teaching children to make nutrient-dense choices at meals can help them achieve and maintain a healthy body weight.

Parents should consult a registered dietitian nutritionist before making major changes in a child's diet. Children need a nutritious diet to support growth. Restricting foods may result in a lack of important nutrients.

Fitness for School-Age Children

The *Physical Activity Guidelines (PAG)* recommends that children get 60 minutes of physical activity each day. Most schools do not offer physical education classes that meet every day of the week. Therefore, school-age children need to find ways to be active on their own.

The choices of fitness activities for school-age children are almost endless. Swinging and climbing on bars and ladders at the playground will help children get their muscles moving. Playing tag or running an obstacle course in the backyard with friends gives children a chance to be active, too. School-age children enjoy swimming, jumping rope, dancing, and playing soccer. They also like using bicycles, rollerblades, and skateboards but may need to be reminded to wear helmets and other safety gear. In winter weather, sledding, ice skating, and building snow sculptures can help keep children fit. When children cannot go outdoors, they might choose interactive video games that require them to get up and move.

The most important thing caregivers can do to promote fitness is offer a number of activities and the encouragement to do them. This will prompt school-age children to make fitness a part of their daily lives.

Mini Lab: Comparing Food Choices

100-Calorie Snacks

In this activity, you will calculate, weigh, and compare 100-calorie portions of a variety of foods. To calculate how much of a fresh food would provide 100 calories, use the FoodData Central website. To calculate how much of a packaged food would provide 100 calories, use the Nutrition Facts label. Steps for completing these calculations are described in the following examples.

Example I: Fresh apple using FoodData Central website

1. Type **Apples, raw, with skin** in the search field.
2. Select **Apples, raw, with skin** in the food list that appears.
3. Select **1 cup slices, (109 g)** in the portion field.
4. Divide the weight by the energy to calculate the weight of apple that provides 1 calorie: 109 g ÷ 57 cal = 1.9 g/cal.
5. Multiply the weight calculated in Step 4 by 100 to figure the weight of apple that provides 100 calories: 1.9 g/cal × 100 cal = 190 g.

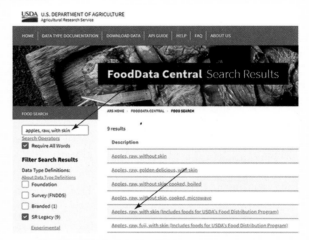

6. Use a kitchen scale to accurately weigh the amount of apple you calculated in Step 5 and put it in a bowl.

Example II: Sweetened applesauce using Nutrition Facts label

1. Note the weight of the serving size (128 g) and calories per serving (110) on the label.
2. Divide the weight by the calories to calculate the weight of applesauce that provides 1 calorie: 128 g ÷ 110 cal = 1.16 g/cal.
3. Multiply the weight calculated in Step 2 by 100 to figure the weight of applesauce that provides 100 calories: 1.16 g/cal × 100 cal = 116 g.
4. Place a small dish on a kitchen scale. Press the **tare** button. Then accurately weigh the amount of applesauce you calculated in Step 3.

Nutrition Facts
5 servings per container
Servings size 1/2 cup (128 g)

Calories **110** per serving

Amount/Serving	%DV*	Amount/Serving	%DV*
Total Fat 0g	0%	**Total Carbohydrate** 27g	10%
Saturated Fat 0g	0%	Fiber 1g	4%
Trans Fat 0g		Total Sugars 25g	
Cholesterol 0mg	0%	Incl. 7g Added Sugars	14%
Sodium 0mg	0%	**Protein** 0g	

Vitamin D 0%   Calcium 0%   Iron 0%   Potassium 2%

With your lab group, follow the examples above to weigh 100-calorie portions of the foods provided by your teacher. Compare the portions and answer the following questions:

A. Which food do you think would be the most filling?

B. Which food would you choose to eat for a snack? Explain your choice.

C. How do the portions of food you weighed in class compare with the portions you typically eat for snacks? What does this indicate about the number of calories in the portions you typically eat?

The Teen Years

All teens undergo a period of rapid growth called a **growth spurt**. The growth spurt varies from teen to teen. However, girls usually experience it at an earlier age than boys.

During the growth spurt, teens of both sexes need more energy. From ages 14 through 18, moderately active teen girls need about 2,000 calories per day. Moderately active teen boys need about 2,600 calories per day. Your needs may be higher or lower, depending on your age, body size, and activity level. Using the USDA MyPlate website can help teens find their daily calorie and food group requirements.

Teens have the freedom to make many of their own food choices. It is important for them to use good judgment and choose foods that promote health. Like younger children, all teens need the equivalent of 3 cups (750 mL) daily from the dairy group. This will provide the calcium and vitamin D needed to support rapid bone growth. Teen boys who are frequently hungry would benefit from eating more whole grains, fruits, and vegetables. These high-fiber foods can promote a feeling of fullness. Teen girls need to be sure to get enough folate and iron in their daily diets. Orange juice, spinach, and enriched-grain products provide folate. Good sources of iron include beef, poultry, seafood, and beans.

Planning Meals for Teens

Eating a healthy breakfast will help teens have the energy they need to start the day. When needed, teens can increase portion sizes of wholesome foods at lunch and dinner to meet energy and nutrient needs.

Snacks often count for one-fourth of a teen's total daily calorie intake. Thus, nutritious snacks are especially important. Baby carrots, apples, low-fat yogurt, popcorn, and unsalted nuts make great snacks that are easy to eat on the go. Reading Nutrition Facts labels will help teens make choices that are lower in sodium (**Figure 10.13**).

When choosing beverages, teens should limit their intake of nondiet soft drinks, which are a major source of added sugars in the diet. Instead, teens should most often choose to drink water and fat-free milk. Juices can be chosen less often and should always be 100 percent juice. Health experts state that energy drinks are not recommended for teens. Other drinks containing caffeine should be avoided as well. Caffeine has been linked to harmful effects on the nervous and cardiovascular systems of young people. In addition, consuming caffeine can keep teens from getting needed sleep.

Adolescent Overweight and Obesity

Rates of overweight and obesity remain high among adolescents, just as they are among children. Unlike children, however, teens have the decision-making skills needed to manage their weight. They can learn to make healthy food choices. They can include physical activity in their daily schedules. They can also learn how to handle situations that might prompt them to overeat.

One way teens can manage their weight is by staying within their limits for empty calories. Most teens have a limit of about 250 to 350 calories per day to use for solid fats and added sugars. Teens need to be aware of food choices that include empty calories. This can help them avoid consuming too many calories and throwing their total intake out of balance.

Many adolescents who have weight problems continue to have weight problems as adults. To break this pattern, a teen who is overweight or obese should talk to a nutrition expert. This professional can check the teen's health and growth status. An expert can help the teen learn weight management skills and develop a healthy eating and activity plan. Such a plan would help the teen learn to choose calorie sources that are rich in nutrients. It would also encourage the teen to adopt an active lifestyle that includes at least 60 minutes of moderate activity daily. Being active is the most important step all teens can take to maintain healthy weight throughout life.

Fitness for Teens

The teen years are a good time to begin including exercise components that help build all areas of fitness. Activities like yoga and tai chi help improve flexibility and balance. Weight training can help build strength. Jogging and biking can increase endurance. However, the type of fitness is not as important as finding something fun. Any type of movement will

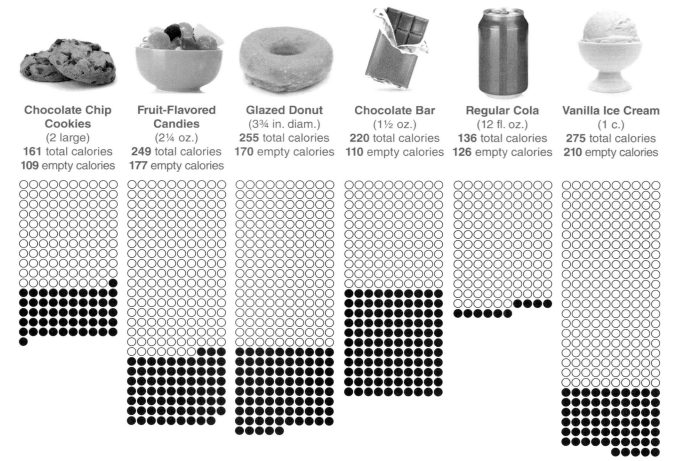

Avoid Snacks with Many Empty Calories

Chocolate Chip Cookies	Fruit-Flavored Candies	Glazed Donut	Chocolate Bar	Regular Cola	Vanilla Ice Cream
(2 large)	(2¼ oz.)	(3¾ in. diam.)	(1½ oz.)	(12 fl. oz.)	(1 c.)
161 total calories	**249** total calories	**255** total calories	**220** total calories	**136** total calories	**275** total calories
109 empty calories	**177** empty calories	**170** empty calories	**110** empty calories	**126** empty calories	**210** empty calories

Nattika/Shutterstock.com; Africa Studio/Shutterstock.com; Hong Vo/SShutterstock.com; Natykach Nataliia/Shutterstock.com;
Evgeny Karandaev/Shutterstock.com; M. Unal Ozmen/Shutterstock.com

Figure 10.13   Snacks make up a significant portion of a teen's diet and should supply needed nutrients not just empty calories. What nutrient-dense alternatives could you substitute for the snacks in this figure?

provide benefits, and teens are most likely to stick with activities they enjoy.

Choosing activities they can do with friends makes fitness fun for many teens. Rock climbing, hiking, and rowing are a few of the many options that can be enjoyed with just one or two friends. For those who prefer a larger group, team sports like soccer and basketball are popular (**Figure 10.14**). No matter what activities teens choose, taking time to warm up before starting will help prevent injuries.

Adulthood

Energy needs begin to decrease for adults in their 20s. Adults who lead active lives require more calories than adults who lead sedentary lives. Even active adults, however, need to consume fewer calories than teens. During this same stage of life, nutrient needs change, with the need for several nutrients increasing.

Although nutrient needs remain fairly constant through age 50, energy needs continue to gradually decrease. For adults over 50, the needs for some nutrients change again.

Vitamin B_{12} is a nutrient of concern for adults over 50. Some adults in this life stage have trouble absorbing vitamin B_{12} from food sources. That is why nutrition experts advise adults in this group to meet vitamin B_{12} needs with fortified foods or supplements.

Adults over 50 need to watch their sodium intake, too. In the United States, many people in all age groups tend to go over their daily sodium needs. Consuming too much sodium increases

Tom Lester/Shutterstock.com

Figure 10.14 Rock climbing builds both confidence as well as muscles, and develops problem-solving skills.

the risk of high blood pressure. The risk of high blood pressure also increases with age. Reading labels and choosing foods lower in sodium would benefit all adults at this life stage.

Like sodium, many people in the United States consume more saturated fats than recommended. A diet high in saturated fat is linked with an increased risk of heart disease. The risk for heart disease also increases with age. Health experts advise adults to replace saturated fats in their diets with healthier mono- and polyunsaturated fats.

Planning Meals for Adults

Jobs, family responsibilities, and other tasks make many demands on adults' schedules. With such busy lives, adults do not always take the time to plan nutritious meals. As a result, many

adults gain unwanted weight. They may also experience vitamin and mineral deficiencies.

With a little planning, adults can improve their meal habits and keep calories in balance. For instance, having foods such as whole-grain English muffins and bananas available can encourage adults to eat a healthy breakfast at home. This will help them resist picking up empty-calorie foods like donuts and sweet rolls on their way to work. Before going to bed, an adult can pack a sandwich and carrot sticks and put them in the refrigerator for tomorrow's lunch. The next day, the lunch will be ready to go without adding to the busy morning routine. This will make it easy to break a lunchtime habit of fast-food burgers and fries. Having some healthy foods on hand will ease dinner preparations at the end of a busy day. Frozen chicken breasts, a jar of pasta sauce, and some whole-grain pasta can quickly become a nutritious entree. Open a bag of salad and a can of peaches or pears, and dinner can be on the table in no time.

Fitness for Adults

Following a daily fitness plan is another step adults can take to keep weight in a healthy range. The *PAG* advises adults to avoid inactivity. Having a fit body can help delay or prevent some of the health issues that often occur as people age (**Figure 10.15**).

Some adults choose to join health clubs to help them stay fit. Others use a treadmill, step machine, or other piece of at-home fitness equipment. Working out with a fitness video is another option. Many adults enjoy leisure activities like golf and tennis to help them stay fit.

During adulthood, it becomes more important to choose a range of activities that address all types of fitness. The *PAG* recommends at least 150 minutes of endurance activities each week. Walking, swimming, and biking are good for this type of fitness. The *PAG* suggests adults choose some activities to strengthen muscles a couple of times a week, too. Lifting weights and using resistance bands will address this goal. Exercises like leg raises that strengthen leg muscles also help improve balance. Stretching movements will build flexibility. Adults who follow a complete fitness routine will be on target for staying fit in their later years.

MBI/Shutterstock.com

Figure 10.15 Physical activity confers both physical and mental health benefits as you age.

The Later Years

Many nutrition and fitness guidelines are the same for adults aged 65 years and older as for younger adults. As adults age, their bodies use less energy to carry on vital processes. This is why calorie needs are lower for older adults than for those who are younger. Unlike energy needs, the needs for most nutrients do not decrease with age. Therefore, foods eaten by people in the later years must be more nutrient dense.

Older adults must keep focusing on the nutrients that were concerns in the earlier adult years. This includes maintaining recommended intakes of vitamin D and calcium. Remember the main role of vitamin D is to help the body use calcium to keep bones strong. A number

of older people experience broken bones and curving of the spine due to osteoporosis. Older women are at the greatest risk of developing this disease. This is because women have less bone mass than men. Earlier in their lives, women are likely to have greater demands made on their calcium stores due to pregnancies. Hormonal changes that take place after menopause also contribute to osteoporosis. Lack of calcium in the diet is a leading cause of osteoporosis. The need for calcium is the same for older adults as it is for adults at age 50. Older adults need to keep consuming the equivalent of 3 cups from the dairy group each day. Choosing calcium-fortified foods will also help older adults meet calcium needs. High calcium intake cannot cure osteoporosis once it has developed. People must meet calcium needs all through life to prevent osteoporosis. However, meeting daily calcium needs in the later years will keep the disease from worsening (**Figure 10.16**).

Planning Meals for Older Adults

A MyPlate meal plan will provide most of the nutrients that are low in the diets of many older adults. However, doctors may recommend supplements for some people over age 65 to help meet needs for vitamins B_{12} and D.

Meals for older adults should consist of well-liked foods. Food likes and dislikes are hard to change. Older people who need encouragement to eat are more likely to eat favorite foods.

Taste buds decrease in number as people age. This can make some foods seem bland and unappealing. Older adults can use more herbs and spices to wake up the flavors of tasteless foods.

Tooth loss and gum disease become problems for some older adults. These problems can make certain foods more difficult to chew. Older adults may need to cut foods into smaller pieces and choose more soft-textured foods to address oral health issues.

Foodborne illnesses pose a greater risk to older adults than to younger adults. Therefore, taking steps to handle, cook, and store food safely is vital when preparing meals for older adults.

Fitness for Older Adults

Many adults remain quite active in their later years. However, people over 65 often begin

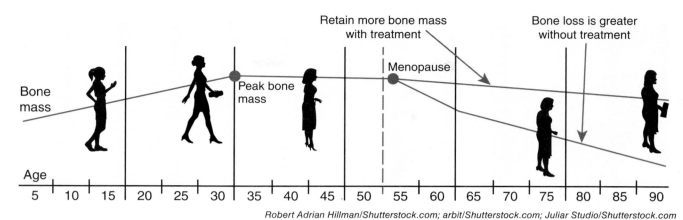

Retain more bone mass
with treatment

Bone loss is greater
without treatment

Menopause

Peak bone
mass

Bone
mass

Age

5   10   15   20   25   30   35   40   45   50   55   60   65   70   75   80   85   90

Robert Adrian Hillman/Shutterstock.com; arbit/Shutterstock.com; Juliar Studio/Shutterstock.com

Figure 10.16   Prevention and treatment typically include adequate amounts of calcium and vitamin D as well as weight bearing physical activity most days.

to have problems with weak muscles and sore joints. In many cases, these discomforts cause older adults to become less active.

Sadly, some older adults do not know that staying active can help lessen many aches and pains. Keeping fit can also help reduce risks of heart disease, some cancers, and diabetes. Weight-bearing exercise can limit the normal loss of bone mass that can lead to osteoporosis. Activity can ease symptoms of depression, too. These benefits of physical activity can help older adults live on their own for many years.

Older people do not need special programs or equipment to stay fit. They can use many routine activities and household items to help them maintain the four types of fitness. Walking, climbing stairs, and gardening help build endurance. Common items like canned goods or bottled water can serve as weights to increase muscle strength. Standing on one foot and walking heel to toe will help improve balance, which is needed to prevent falls. Stretching movements, such as reaching with the arms and pointing the toes, increase flexibility. Many exercises can be done while seated. This allows even adults with limited mobility to receive the benefits of fitness (**Figure 10.17**).

Fitness programs for healthy older adults do not generally require medical supervision. However, people who are starting new routines may want to seek advice from a doctor first. People who have health concerns should also talk to a healthcare provider to find out what types of activities are suitable. Pain, dizziness, and shortness of breath may be signs of problems.

Older adults who have any of these symptoms while exercising should see their doctors before continuing their fitness routines.

Special Diets

Some people choose to follow special diets. Other people follow special diets on their doctors' advice due to allergies or health conditions. A registered dietitian nutritionist can be a resource to help make sure a special diet meets a

wavebreakmedia/Shutterstock.com

Figure 10.17   Exercise balls emphasize balance which is often a concern for older adults.

Learn About...

Easing Meal Preparation

During meal preparation, older people who have limited mobility can save physical energy in many ways. They can use convenience products to save preparation steps. They can sit while preparing some foods. Older adults can store frequently used tools and basic food items on shelves within easy reach. They can install single-handled faucets, which are easy to use with one hand. They can slide heavy objects rather than lift them. If peeling and chopping vegetables is difficult, older people can substitute precut frozen or canned vegetables for fresh. They can make some foods ahead of time to reduce preparation tasks at mealtime. When meal preparation can be made easier, older adults may be more willing to take the time to make nutritious foods.

Know and Apply

1. What nutrient considerations do older adults need to keep in mind when choosing convenience products to save preparation steps?

2. Give an example of how older adults can use appliances to ease meal preparation.

You might think omitting animal foods such as meat, poultry, and fish from the diet would cause a protein deficiency. However, meat alternatives, such as tofu, tempeh, and seitan, are high in protein. Legumes, nuts, grains, and many vegetables are good sources of protein, too. By choosing a variety of these plant foods every day, vegetarians can easily meet their protein needs. The types of amino acids lacking in one food will be provided by another. Lacto-ovo vegetarians can also use dairy foods and eggs to *augment* (add to) the protein value supplied by plant foods. A veggie omlette is an example of a dish that combines dairy, eggs, and various vegetables.

A number of nutrients other than protein can pose concerns for vegetarians, especially vegans. Shortages of vitamins D and B_{12}, calcium, iron, and zinc are common. Many foods high in these nutrients come from animal sources; however, vegetarians might choose from the sources shown in **Figure 10.18** to meet these needs.

Nutrient deficiencies pose greater risks for certain groups of people. Failure to meet nutrient needs can stunt the growth of infants, children, and teens. Nutrient deficiencies can affect the health of pregnant and lactating women and their babies. Vegetarians in these groups are advised to consult with a registered dietitian nutritionist. The dietitian can determine whether nutrient needs are being met. He or she can also recommend nutrient supplements when needed.

person's nutritional needs. Family members can show support by trying new dishes and adopting healthy habits, too. These changes will benefit not only the health of the individual, but also the family's health.

Vegetarian Diets

A **vegetarian diet** is a diet built partly or entirely on plant foods. The types of foods included in vegetarian diets vary. For instance, *lacto-ovo vegetarians* include dairy products and eggs in their diets. *Vegans* eat no animal foods of any kind.

People choose to follow vegetarian diets for a number of reasons. These include religious beliefs, environmental concerns, and animal rights issues. Some people choose vegetarian diets for health reasons.

Meeting Vegetarian Nutrient Concerns	
Nutrient	**Sources**
Vitamin B_{12}	Fortified cereals and soy milk
Vitamin D	Exposure to sunlight, fortified margarine and milk, portobello mushrooms
Calcium	Fortified cereals, orange juice, and soy milk; leafy green vegetables; legumes; tofu
Iron	Leafy green vegetables, legumes, tofu, whole grains (Eat sources of vitamin C, such as citrus fruits, strawberries, tomatoes, and peppers, with iron sources to improve iron absorption.)
Zinc	Dairy products, eggs, legumes, nuts, tofu, whole grains

Figure 10.18 Vegetarians must plan their diets with care to avoid deficiencies of these vitamins and minerals.

Nutrition and Healthcare

The term *therapeutic diet* has been loosely applied to any eating plan used to treat physical, mental, or emotional health. However, a true **therapeutic diet** is an eating plan prescribed by a health professional. Such eating plans may be ordered for patients in hospitals and nursing homes. Doctors often consult with dietitians when ordering therapeutic diets to make sure patients' nutritional needs are met. Patients may be able to choose from menus that are carefully designed with their special health issues in mind. For instance, a doctor may prescribe a therapeutic diet for a hospital patient who had a heart attack. This patient may choose foods from a cardiac menu written by a dietitian.

This patient may also need **medical nutrition therapy (MNT)**. This is a healthcare approach that helps people learn to use their eating habits as part of their treatment. MNT may begin in the hospital when the patient meets with a dietitian to receive counseling about eating habits. MNT is likely to continue, however, as the patient manages his or her health condition after leaving the hospital. Diabetes and food allergies are other conditions for which people might receive MNT (**Figure 10.19**).

MNT is provided by a registered dietitian nutritionist. The dietitian begins by assessing how a client's health condition is affecting his or her body and nutritional needs. The dietitian can then suggest an eating plan that will help the client meet those special needs. The eating plan will take the client's food likes and dislikes into consideration. The dietitian will counsel the client about how to form new eating habits to make following the plan part of his or her lifestyle. This will make it easier for the client to successfully stick with the plan. The dietitian will continue to meet with the client as needed to track his or her progress in following the plan. The dietitian will also decide whether any changes to the plan are needed.

Food and Drug Interactions

Some drugs can affect the way the body uses nutrients from foods. Similarly, some foods can affect the way drugs are absorbed and used in the body. Such reactions between foods and drugs are called **food-drug interactions**.

Anytime you must take prescription or over-the-counter drugs, be sure to read labels carefully. Follow all directions about consuming foods and beverages. Unless your doctor or pharmacist tells you otherwise, take all drugs with water. Water helps most drugs dissolve quickly, and it does not hamper absorption. If you must take drugs for an extended period, you may want to consult a registered dietitian nutritionist. He or she can assess how to best deal with any nutritional problems the drugs might cause.

Food Assistance Programs

Limited income makes it hard for some people to buy nourishing foods. In the United States, help is available to people at all life-cycle stages through various federal food assistance programs. Most of these programs are run by the Food and Nutrition Service, which is an agency of the USDA. Nutrition education is a key part of these programs. The programs are intended to help people learn to make healthy food choices as well as give them access to nutritious foods. In many cases, program benefits go beyond food and nutrition to promote other aspects of wellness.

Federal food assistance funds are provided to agencies in each state. These agencies manage the programs at the state and local levels. They set standards for who is able to receive program benefits. These agencies then provide benefits to those who meet the standards.

In the earliest stages of the life span, food assistance is provided through *Women, Infants, and Children (WIC)*. This program helps women who are pregnant or who have recently had babies. It also assists infants during the first year of life and children up to the age of 5. WIC enables participants to receive foods that will meet the specific needs of people in these life stages. WIC foods include fruits, vegetables, milk, eggs, baby food, and formula. WIC also offers breast-feeding counseling, health screenings, and vaccination referrals.

School-age children and teens can receive food assistance through several programs. The *National School Lunch Program (NSLP)* supplies nutritious lunches for little or no cost through public and some private schools. The *School Breakfast Program (SBP)* provides breakfast for qualified children and

Medical Nutrition Therapy		
Medical Condition	Description	Recommended Nutrition Therapy*
Cancer	Uncontrolled cell multiplication, which interferes with normal functioning of body organs	To cope with nausea and vomiting resulting from cancer treatment and medications • Sip cool, clear liquids to prevent dehydration • Choose bland foods that are easy to digest, such as gelatin, crackers, and dry toast • Avoid strong food odors and greasy and spicy foods
Celiac disease	A genetic autoimmune condition triggered by eating gluten (proteins found in certain grains); affects the intestine and can cause symptoms including gas, diarrhea, and fatigue	Read all food labels carefully to completely avoid gluten, which may be in such ingredients as • Wheat, rye, barley, and triticale • Emulsifiers, stabilizers, and thickeners • Flour, food starch, and hydrolyzed vegetable protein
Diabetes mellitus	Lack of or inability to use the hormone insulin, which results in irregular blood glucose levels and can lead to damage of body tissues	Eat a variety of foods at regularly scheduled meals, spacing calories throughout the day Monitor carbohydrate intake, focusing on whole grains and avoiding added sugars Limit fat intake and choose adequate sources of fiber Maintain healthy body weight
Food allergy	A response of the body's immune system to a food protein, which can cause symptoms such as hives and breathing difficulties	Read all food labels carefully to completely avoid the allergy-causing food or ingredient If an allergic reaction occurs, seek immediate treatment, such as use of medication, an injection, and/or emergency room care
Gastroesophageal reflux disease (GERD)	Recurrent heartburn caused by stomach acid flowing up into the esophagus	Eat small, frequent meals and avoid overeating Drink liquids between meals rather than with meals Avoid spicy and greasy foods Avoid lying down for at least one hour after eating
Heart disease	General term for a variety of diseases affecting the heart muscle and surrounding tissue	Choose a variety of fruits, vegetables, legumes, and whole grains Choose moderate amounts of sources of healthy oils, such as fish and nuts Opt for fat-free and low-fat dairy products and limit red meat to restrict sources of saturated fats
High blood cholesterol	Above average amount of cholesterol in the bloodstream, which is a risk factor for heart disease	Limit sodium Limit sugary beverages and sweets Avoid sources of *trans* fats, such as margarine, snack foods, and commercially fried foods that contain partially hydrogenated oils
HIV/AIDS	A disorder that causes the body's immune system to shut down and is often accompanied by a loss of appetite leading to wasting	When feeling well enough to eat, eat small, frequent meals and choose high-protein, high-calorie foods, such as cheese, eggs, nuts, and liquid meal replacements Limit liquids with meals to keep from feeling full Strictly follow food safety practices
Hypertension	High blood pressure, which is a risk factor for heart disease	Limit sources of sodium, such as processed foods, salty snacks, and table salt Choose sources of potassium, calcium, and magnesium Moderate fat intake and choose adequate sources of fiber
Lactose intolerance	Inability to produce the enzyme lactase, which is needed to digest the sugar in milk; results in symptoms such as gas, cramps, and bloating after consuming milk products	Choose cheese and cultured dairy products, such as yogurt Eat small amounts of dairy products with other foods Choose lactose-reduced dairy products

* This is a partial list of recommended nutrition therapies and is not intended to replace specific advice of a physician or registered dietitian nutritionist.

Figure 10.19 Many patients can help control their medical conditions through diet as well as medication.

Health and Wellness

Nutrition During Illness

Even people who do not have ongoing health problems get sick from time to time. Knowing how minor illnesses can affect your appetite and nutrient needs can help you handle common ailments.

Drinking liquids is a recommended treatment for many everyday health problems. Warm liquids soothe a sore throat. Chilled liquids help cool a fever. Water helps flush bacteria out of your urinary tract to ease the discomfort of an infection. Liquids replace fluids lost through diarrhea and through perspiration caused by fever. They help keep sinus and nasal secretions flowing. This provides relief when you have the flu, a cold, or a sinus infection.

A number of common digestive disorders are related to food habits. Choose sources of sodium and potassium when diarrhea becomes a problem. Also avoid greasy, fried, spicy, and high-fiber foods. On the other hand, you should eat more fiber if you are trying to relieve and prevent constipation.

Nausea, vomiting, and fatigue brought on by illness can often take away your appetite. If a sore throat makes swallowing hard, you may not feel like eating either. However, your body needs nutrients to help the healing process. If you do not feel like eating, try drinking a nutritious beverage instead. Sometimes 100 percent juice or a healthy smoothie made with fruit and yogurt goes down easier than solid food.

to be known as the Food Stamp Program.) Participants in this program receive a plastic card that works much like a bank debit card. Each month, money is made available in the participant's SNAP account. The amount of money is based on the participant's income and household size. Participants can then use the card to make food purchases at authorized food retailers, such as most grocery, drug, and discount stores.

Older adults can receive food assistance through the *Elderly Nutrition Program*. This program is run by the Administration on Aging, which is an agency of the U.S. Department of Health and Human Services (HHS). It provides funds for adults who are homebound to have nutritious meals brought to their homes. It also provides for meals to be served in settings such as senior centers, schools, and places of worship. These meals are called *congregate meals,* and they give older people a chance to socialize as they eat. Nutrition education and health screenings may also be offered as part of this program.

Not all food assistance is provided by the government. Many charities also offer aid to people in need. For instance, *Meals on Wheels* is a charity that brings nutritious meals to homebound older adults. *Feeding America* is an organization that has a network of large food banks. These banks supply food to smaller agencies that pass it out to needy people at the community level. Many local groups also run food pantries, soup kitchens, and shelters that provide food. All these government and private programs share a common goal of ending hunger in the United States.

teens. Schools that take part in these programs are required to have a wellness policy. This policy must include goals for physical activity as well as nutrition education (**Figure 10.20**).

Schools that do not participate in NSLP or SBP may offer milk to children and teens through the *Special Milk Program*. During the summer months, free nutritious meals and snacks may be provided through the *Summer Food Service Program (SFSP)*. This program may operate at sites such as camps and community centers as well as schools.

Low-income households can receive help to buy food through the *Supplemental Nutrition Assistance Program (SNAP)*. (This program used

MBI/Shutterstock.com

Figure 10.20 Over 30 million students participate in the School Lunch Program each day.

Chapter 10 Review and Expand

Summary

Good nutrition is important at all life-cycle stages. During pregnancy, a woman must eat a range of foods to supply her developing baby with the nutrients it needs. For the first few months after birth, infants obtain needed nutrients from breast milk or formula. Most parents slowly begin introducing solid foods into their infants' diets when the infants are about 4 to 6 months old. Preschoolers and school-age children need help to choose foods that will meet their needs. As children become teens, they need more nutrients and calories to support their rapid growth. Adults must select foods carefully to get needed nutrients without getting too many calories. Older adults must make an even greater effort to choose nutrient-dense foods to meet nutrient needs as calorie needs continue to decrease. Throughout life, MyPlate can help people choose foods to meet their nutrient needs.

Fitness goes hand in hand with nutrition to help people stay in good health at all life-cycle stages. Activities that help build endurance, flexibility, strength, and balance make up a complete fitness program. Activity choices may vary from one life stage to another. However, the key factor is getting some form of energetic movement on a daily basis. Being aware of signs of stress and injury will help keep activity safe.

People at any life stage may have special dietary needs. Vegetarians must choose plant foods with care to meet their nutrient needs. People with certain health problems may need to follow specific nutrition advice from a doctor or dietitian. People with limited income can choose to access a range of food assistance programs to help meet their nutritional needs.

Vocabulary Activities

1. **Content Terms**   Reread the text passages that contain each of the following terms. Then write a sentence for each term that explains how the term relates to life-cycle nutrition and fitness.

diet	vegetarian diet
food allergy	therapeutic diet
food intolerance	medical nutrition
cross-contact	therapy (MNT)
growth spurt	food-drug interaction

2. **Academic Terms**   For each of the following terms, draw a cartoon bubble to express the meaning of each term as it relates to the chapter.

foster   augment

Review

Write your answers using complete sentences when appropriate.

3. What could be the long-term effect for a pregnant woman whose food choices failed to meet the calcium needs of the fetus?

4. What are three types of activities that are not good choices for a fitness program during pregnancy?

5. Why should lactating mothers avoid drinking alcohol, using tobacco, and taking medications?

6. What are three reasons nutrition experts strongly recommend that mothers breast-feed their infants?

7. What is the difference between a food allergy and a food intolerance? How might allergies and intolerances impact individual and family health?

8. What types of food choices often encourage preschoolers to eat?

9. What are the benefits for a school-age child of starting the day with a nutrient-dense breakfast?

10. List 10 fitness activities that are appropriate for school-age children.

11. How can a nutrition expert help a teen who is overweight or obese?

12. Why is sodium intake a concern for adults over age 50?

13. Why is it especially important to handle, cook, and store food safely when preparing meals for older adults?

14. What nutrients pose a greater concern than protein for people who choose to follow a vegetarian diet?

15. What is the difference between a therapeutic diet and medical nutrition therapy?

16. What nutrition and wellness services are available through the WIC program?

Chapter 10 Review and Expand

Core Skills

17. **Research, Math** Conduct research to compare the specific nutrient needs of pregnancy with the nutrient needs of lactation. Create a bar graph to illustrate your findings.

18. **Technology, Research, Writing** Visit the Vegetarian Resource Group website. Investigate an aspect of vegetarianism that interests you. Share your findings in a two-page report. Proofread and revise your report as needed for grammar, spelling, and organization.

19. **Research** Choose one health condition that requires medical nutrition therapy. Use reliable print or online resources to conduct research and learn as much as you can about that therapy. Use this information to develop menus for one day that could be followed by someone who has this condition.

20. **Reading, Speaking** Visit the Feeding America website. Investigate stories and statistics about hunger in the United States. Share a fact or anecdote with the class.

21. **Speaking, Listening** As you study nutrient needs and fitness through the life span, identify major events, goals, and concerns of people at each life-cycle stage. Create a table summarizing this information. Discuss in class how meeting nutrient needs and staying fit can help people achieve goals and face concerns in other areas of their lives.

22. **Writing** Write a one-week menu for a pregnant woman in her second trimester. Assume that her prepregnancy nutrition needs were 2,000 calories. Use Figure 10.3 as a guide.

23. **Career Readiness Practice** Before accepting and using new information to make decisions at school and at work, it is important to determine the reliability and validity of research sources. Read more about nutrition during illness from a website that provides medical information for consumers. To determine the reliability of the source, ask the following questions:

    - Information: Is the information current? Is it from a scholarly source, such as an academic institution, trade journal, or professional organization journal? Are assumptions and conclusions supported with evidence?

    - Author: What are the author's credentials, qualifications, and affiliations? What is the author's intent for the research?

    - Bias/Objectivity: Does the research address other points of view? Is the writing style emotional or does it promote a certain viewpoint? Is the article or publication sponsored or endorsed by a special-interest group?

    - Publisher: Is the publisher known as an educational, commercial, or trade publisher of quality or scholarly materials?

    - Quality: Is the information presented in a logical sequence or structure? Can you clearly identify key points that support a main idea?

Critical Thinking and Problem Solving

24. **Create** Interview a group of three to five preschoolers about their interests. Combine their input to design an activity that would encourage children to be more physically active. If possible, have the children try your activity, and discuss their reactions in class.

25. **Create** Work with a small group to plan a health fair booth on childhood obesity. Create a display and a handout with information for parents about preventing and managing this condition in their children. Also design an activity sheet for children that includes fun ideas to help them make healthy food and activity choices.

26. **Analyze** Record your family's typical menu for a day. Imagine one of your family members has been diagnosed with a severe peanut allergy. Analyze the menu and modify it to accommodate the allergy. Write a brief summary about how this might affect your family. Consider the possible effects on the individual's health if your family did not participate in the diet changes.

Unit 3
The Management of Food

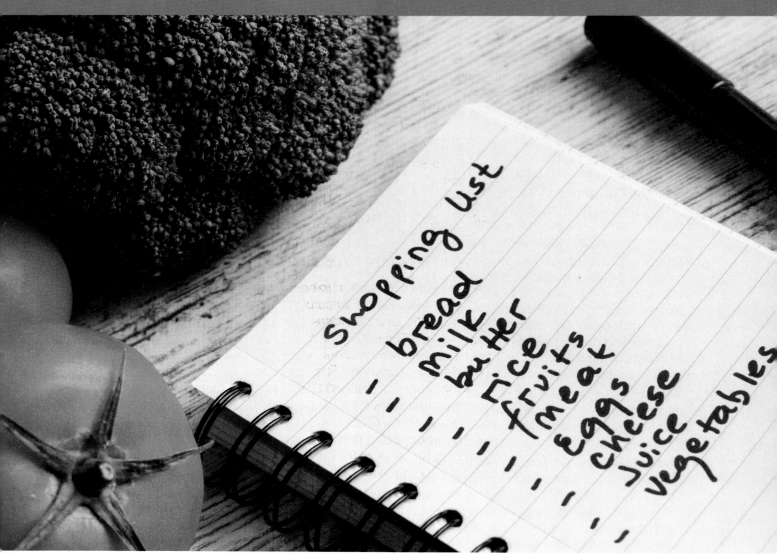

conejota /Shutterstock.com

Essential Questions

- How can the types of appliances and their arrangement affect the function of a kitchen?
- How does the concept of management apply to meal preparation?
- What consumer skills would help a meal manager when shopping for food?

FCCLA: Taking the Lead

Use this section of the text to help your FCCLA chapter create a *Financial Fitness* peer education project. Chapters 11 and 12 describe items needed in a well-equipped kitchen. This could fit into a project for the *Financing Your Future* unit about applying financial skills when furnishing a kitchen in a first apartment. Chapter 13 includes information on planned spending. This material could serve as the basis for a budgeting education project that would relate to the *Cash Control* unit. Chapter 14 covers topics about using money wisely when shopping for food. Teaching these skills to other teens could become a project that would go along with the *Consumer Clout* unit.

While studying, look for the activity icon ⬀ for:
- Content and Academic Terms with e-flash cards, vocabulary games, and matching activities

These activities can be accessed at
www.g-wlearning.com/foodandnutrition/9582

Chapter 11
Kitchen and Dining Areas

MBI/Shutterstock.com

Objectives

After studying this chapter, you will be able to

- **describe** the three major work centers in a kitchen and the six basic kitchen floor plans;
- **explain** considerations in choosing functional surface materials and fixtures for kitchens and dining areas;
- **identify** different kinds of tableware and **list** selection factors applicable to each; and
- **set** a table attractively.

Reading Prep

Before reading this chapter, review the objectives. Based on this information, write down two or three items that you think are important to note while you are reading.

Content Terms

work center
work triangle
universal design
natural light
artificial light
ground
table appointments
dinnerware
flatware
beverageware
tumbler
stemware
holloware
open stock
place setting
table linens
cover

Academic Terms

compact
adequate
functional

The kitchen and dining areas are often the busiest areas of the home. People spend a lot of time in these areas planning, preparing, and eating meals. Therefore, consider the likes, dislikes, and needs of everyone in the home when arranging these areas. Make them comfortable, convenient, and efficient places to work.

Planning the Kitchen and Dining Areas

When planning the arrangement of kitchen and dining areas, you should think about several questions. Are meals eaten in the kitchen, or is a separate dining room needed? How much storage and workspace is needed in these areas? How much time will each person in the home spend in the kitchen and dining areas? What kind of atmosphere do you want these areas to have?

Major Work Centers

Most kitchens have three main **work centers**. A work center is a section in a kitchen that has been designed around a specific activity or activities. Each center focuses on one of the three basic groups of kitchen activities—food preparation and storage, cooking and serving, and cleanup.

The focal point of the *food preparation and storage center* is the refrigerator-freezer. This center requires cabinets for food storage. Cabinets also hold containers and tools used to store and serve frozen and refrigerated foods. Sometimes baked goods are mixed in this center. If so, storage space for mixing tools and workspace for mixing tasks will be needed here.

The *cooking and serving center* focuses on the range and oven. One side of the range should have at least 24 inches (60 cm) of counter space. This counter will hold the ingredients when you cook. Cabinets and drawers in this center store utensils, cookware, and serving pieces.

The *cleanup center* always contains the sink. It may also include a dishwasher and food waste disposer. Work done in this center includes washing dishes; cleaning fresh vegetables, fruits, and fish; and soaking pots and pans. Plenty of counter space and storage space are necessities

Learn About...

Additional Work Centers

If a kitchen is large, it may include additional work centers. A counter between the range and refrigerator can serve as a *mixing center*. It needs to be at least 36 inches (90 cm) wide. An electric mixer, a blender, mixing bowls, measuring tools, and baking utensils need storage space. Baking ingredients, such as flour and sugar, need to be stored, too.

Consider tucking a *planning center* into a corner where it can double as a communications center. This area should have outlets for charging electronics. Use shelves to store items such as cookbooks. A desk or countertop can hold a computer or tablet stand to be used for meal planning. Hang a bulletin board or dry erase board to post messages. Keep recipe cards, note pads, and writing utensils in a drawer.

Some kitchens have a *laundry center*. A laundry facility within the kitchen can save steps. However, be sure to locate it away from food preparation areas.

Know and Apply

1. What kinds of food products might you prepare in a mixing center?
2. Which of these additional work centers would you find most helpful in your kitchen?

in this work center. Keep coffeepots, teapots, dishwashing detergent, dishcloths, towels, and a wastebasket here. Canned goods and vegetables that require no refrigeration might be stored in this center. However, never store food under the sink, where leaking pipes can damage it.

Kitchen Storage Space

As mentioned, space is needed in each kitchen work center to store various items. Two guidelines will help you determine the best place to store each item. First, items should be stored where they will be used. Think about what tasks are likely to be done in each work center.

Mini Lab: Working the Triangle

Toasted Cheese and Tomato Sandwiches

Complete this activity with a partner. If desired, two pairs of students can complete this activity at the same time to further analyze the efficiency of your kitchen when sharing workspace.

1. Identify the floor plan of your lab kitchen and note the three points of the work triangle. If your kitchen does not have a refrigerator, use masking tape to section off an area of counter space. Designate this space as your "refrigerator."

2. Use a tape measure to measure the lengths of the sides of the work triangle. On an observation sheet, record the length of each side as well as the total length. Describe how the size of your work triangle compares with recommended guidelines.

3. Designate a cabinet in your food preparation and storage center to be your "pantry."

4. Store all the ingredients needed for the recipe below in the "refrigerator" or "pantry," as appropriate.

5. **Partner A**—Prepare the recipe below.

   Partner B—Count and record the number of times Partner A walks along each side of the work triangle as he or she prepares the recipe. Note whether equipment used is stored in the most convenient locations.

   Ingredients

   2 100% whole-wheat thin sandwich rolls

   4 ¾-ounce (19 g) slices pepper jack cheese

   ¼ teaspoon (1.25 mL) dried oregano

   1 Roma tomato

   Directions

   A. Open the sandwich rolls and place a slice of cheese on the cut side of all four open halves.

   B. Sprinkle the oregano evenly over all the cheese.

   C. Cut the tomato into ¼-inch (1 cm) slices. Distribute the slices evenly over the two bottom halves of the sandwich rolls. Close the top halves of the rolls over the tomatoes with the cheese inside.

   D. Coat a large nonstick skillet with cooking spray. Heat the skillet over medium heat.

   E. Add the sandwiches to the skillet. Cook 3 minutes per side or until cheese melts and rolls are toasted. Serve.

©iStock.com/robynmac

6. Use your observation sheet to calculate the total distance Partner A walked while preparing the recipe. Analyze his or her motions and suggest ideas for reducing the distance walked. Also suggest ways to work more efficiently when sharing the workspace with others.

Makes 2 sandwiches

Per sandwich: 266 calories (44% from fat), 15 g protein, 23 g carbohydrate, 13 g fat, 23 mg cholesterol, 5 g fiber, 432 mg sodium

Identify all the supplies needed to do each task. For instance, vegetables are chopped in the food preparation and storage center. This task requires knives and a cutting board. Store these items in the drawers and cupboards of that center.

The second point to think about when planning storage space is how often items will be used. Store items used most often in the most convenient places. For instance, saucepans and a double boiler both belong in the cooking and serving center. The saucepans are likely to be used almost daily. However, the double boiler may only be used occasionally. Therefore, store the double boiler in the back of a cupboard. Store the saucepans in the front of the cupboard, which is easier to reach.

Work Triangle

To make a kitchen as efficient as possible, place the focal points of the major work centers at the corners of an imaginary triangle. This triangle is called a **work triangle**.

Ideally, the work triangle follows the normal flow of food preparation. Food is removed from the refrigerator or freezer and taken to the sink for cleaning. From the sink, the food is taken to the oven or range for cooking. After cooking and eating, leftovers are returned to the refrigerator.

Design experts often recommend each side of the work triangle should be 4 to 9 feet (1.2 to 2.7 m) in length. The total length of the three sides should not be less than 13 feet (4.0 m) and should not exceed 26 feet (7.9 m). A triangle that is too small does not offer enough room to work comfortably. A larger work triangle will allow space for people to work together in the kitchen. However, a triangle that is too large will require excess energy and time to move from point to point while preparing foods.

Kitchen Floor Plans

Work centers fit into a variety of kitchen floor plans. The shape of the kitchen depends largely on the size of the room.

The *U-shaped kitchen* represents the most desirable kitchen floor plan because of its *compact* (efficient use of space) work triangle. All the appliances and cabinets are arranged in a continuous line along three adjoining walls.

The *L-shaped kitchen* is popular because it easily adapts to a variety of room arrangements.

Appliances and cabinets form a continuous line along two adjoining walls. In a large room, the open area beyond the work triangle might be used as an eating area.

Appliances and cabinets in a *corridor kitchen* are arranged on two nonadjoining walls. This can be an efficient floor plan if the room is not too long and is closed at one end. However, a long room can create a long work triangle that requires many steps. A room that is open at both ends allows traffic through the kitchen, which can interfere with the work triangle.

The *peninsula kitchen* is most often found in large rooms. In this kitchen, a counter extends into the room, forming a peninsula. The peninsula can serve as storage space or an eating area. It can also hold a sink or a built-in appliance, such as a cooktop.

The *island kitchen* is also found in large rooms. In this kitchen, a counter stands alone in the center of the room. An island and a peninsula serve similar functions. In some kitchens, the island also serves as a mixing center.

The *one-wall kitchen* is found most often in apartments. All the appliances and cabinets are along one wall. This arrangement generally does not give **adequate** (enough) storage or counter space. It also creates a long, narrow work triangle. A folding or sliding door may set off the one-wall kitchen from other rooms. The various kitchen floor plans are illustrated in **Figure 11.1.**

Universal Design in Kitchen and Dining Areas

Well-planned kitchen and dining areas incorporate the principles of universal design. **Universal design** refers to features of rooms, furnishings, and equipment that are usable by as many people as possible. Peninsula, U-shaped, and L-shaped floor plans are examples of universal design. These floor plans provide the fewest restrictions to movement through a kitchen. A floor plan with a compact work triangle also reflects universal design. A compact work triangle prevents household members from using excess energy. This is especially important for people who have limited mobility, such as people who use walkers and crutches.

Work surfaces in a universal design kitchen need to be at a variety of levels. This allows

Kitchen Floor Plans

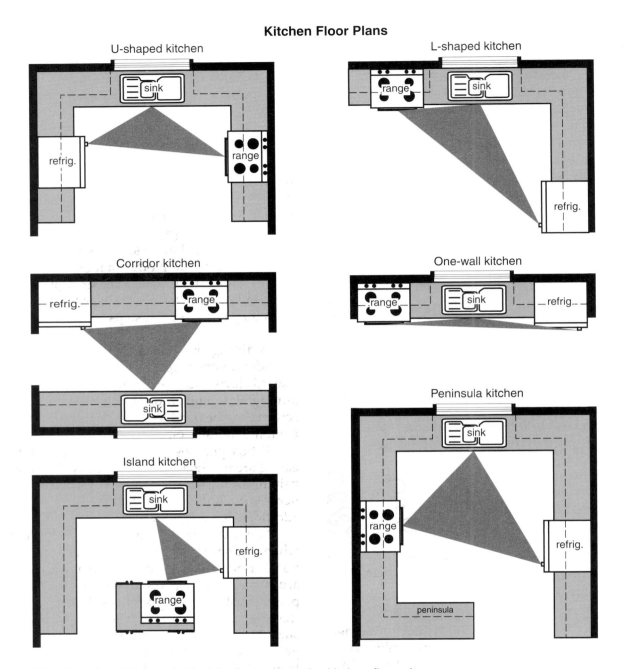

Figure 11.1 The size of the work triangle depends on the kitchen floor plan.

people of all heights to work in the kitchen comfortably. Lower countertops can be reached with ease by children and people seated in wheelchairs. A narrow shelf can be installed above these counters to provide a handy place for items that are used often.

Removing lower cabinets near the sink and cooktop will provide knee space. This will allow someone sitting in a wheelchair or on a stool to move close to these work areas. A shallow sink with a rear drain also allows room for knees

(**Figure 11.2**). Undercoating the sink and insulating the hot water pipes will protect the legs of people working in a seated position. Mounting a lever-type faucet on the side of the sink will make it easy to reach.

Contrasting trim along counters and around doorways is a universal design feature. Contrasting trim makes edges easier to see. Therefore, people will be less likely to bump into them. This feature is especially helpful for people with limited vision.

A counter, a built-in breakfast nook, or a table can serve as a kitchen eating center. Having an eating area in the kitchen saves steps when serving and clearing meals. When planning a counter eating area, provide 18 to 24 inches (45 to 60 cm) of space per person. The counter should be at least 15 inches (38 cm) deep. If a table is serving as an eating area, leave at least 30 inches (75 cm) clearance around it. This provides room to pull out chairs and get seated comfortably. To avoid traffic problems, increase the clearance to 36 inches (90 cm) if the table is in an area where people often walk past it.

Some homes have a separate dining room. A separate dining room offers a more traditional, formal setting. It also provides storage for table-ware and linens. However, a separate dining room may require extra steps to serve and clear meals.

A dining area attached to the living room provides an open, spacious feel. Many people like this layout for family meals and casual entertaining. For cozier, more private dining, however, screens can be used to divide the dining area from the living room.

Patios, porches, and decks may be used as eating areas when weather permits. Trays can help make it easier to transport food and other items outdoors. Carts with wheels can provide additional serving space.

You may want to use a computer for help when arranging kitchen and dining areas. A number of websites and software programs are available to help you draw floor plans and place furniture and appliances. This will spare the effort of moving heavy items until you are sure the arrangement will meet needs. Some programs have a three-dimensional format. This feature lets you feel as though you are walking through rooms. It gives you a more realistic perspective than the overhead view provided by a standard floor plan.

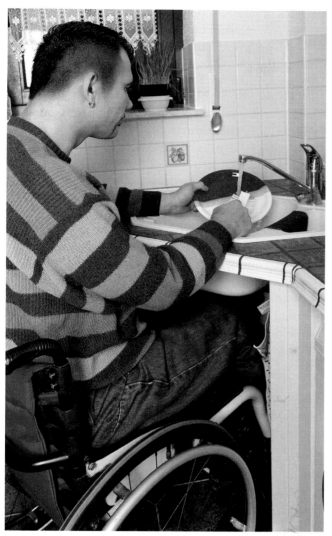

Jenny Sturm/Shutterstock.com

Figure 11.2 This kitchen's cleanup center is an example of universal design.

Universal design can even be used in storage spaces. Loop handles on drawers and cabinets are easier to pull open. Adjustable pantry shelves can be placed at heights that put most-used items within easy reach. Pull-out shelves reduce the need to bend and reach for items stored in the back of lower cabinets. Universal design allows all kitchen and dining areas to better meet the needs of each person in the home.

Planning the Dining Area

The location of the dining area depends on the layout of the home. The number of people in the home and personal preferences affect the dining area, too.

Functional Surfaces and Fixtures

Kitchen and dining areas need to be *functional* (useful). A key factor for reaching this goal is to choose surface materials and fixtures with care.

Exploring Careers

Interior Designer

Interior designers plan the use of space in buildings. They work with clients to select and arrange surface materials, appliances, furniture, and accessories to meet the clients' needs. Some designers specialize in planning space in homes. Others work on commercial buildings. Some designers also focus on certain types of design, such as color design or kitchen design.

Designers must have good listening skills as they find out from clients how the space will be used. They must learn about a client's likes and dislikes in terms of styles and colors, too. Designers must be able to manage money as they help clients set budgets for their projects. Then the designers must be able to stay within those budgets as they present ideas for clients to consider. Interior designers need to know how to read and understand blueprints. They need math skills as they take measurements and plan how to fit furniture and equipment in available space. Interior designers need attention to detail and cooperation skills as they work with architects and builders to get projects completed. They need to be able to manage time to meet project deadlines. Problem-solving skills are also important, as few projects go from start to finish without running into some snags.

Most interior designers have a four-year bachelor's degree. A few years of working with an experienced designer will help a new professional build needed skills. This type of background will help designers acquire status and attract future clients.

Wall and Floor Coverings

Wall coverings in kitchen and dining areas should be smooth and easy to clean. Many wall covering materials are available. Flat finish *paints* are suitable for dining rooms. Satin and semi-gloss finishes are better choices for kitchens. *Glass, ceramic, stone,* and *metal tile* are popular for kitchen walls, especially in the backsplash area behind the sink and range. Other options include *wallpaper* and *paneling* (**Figure 11.3**).

Think about the cost and care requirements when choosing wall coverings. Also, find out how durable the coverings will be when exposed to heat, moisture, and grease from cooking.

Like wall coverings, kitchen and dining area floor coverings must be easy to clean. Floor coverings should also provide walking comfort and be durable. You can choose from several materials. *Solid wood, engineered wood,* and *plastic laminate* all offer the appearance of wood. *Cork flooring* is a warm, comfortable surface that helps absorb sound. *Ceramic* and *stone tile* are durable but offer less walking comfort. *Vinyl sheets* and *tiles* come in a wide range of colors and designs. Although it is available, *carpeting* can be difficult to keep clean in a kitchen. However, a large *rug* under the table can give warmth and definition to a dining area.

The costs of floor covering materials as well as their installation costs vary widely. Resistance to stains, scratches, dents, and other signs of wear varies, too. Be sure to do your research before making a choice.

Countertops and Cabinets

In the kitchen, countertops provide workspace. In dining areas, counter space is used for serving food and holding dishes that have been

Iriana Shiyan/Shutterstock.com

Figure 11.3 A backsplash protects walls and adds visual interest to the kitchen.

cleared from the table. Common countertop materials include *natural stone*, such as granite and marble; *engineered stone*; *laminate*; *solid surface*; and *ceramic tile*. *Wood* counter surfaces are also an option. Use care to protect counter surfaces from damage due to heat, scratches, and moisture.

Cabinets are needed in kitchen and dining areas to store food, appliances, cleaning supplies, cooking utensils, dinnerware, and table decorations. Kitchen cabinets need to be easy to clean.

Cabinets may support countertops or be mounted on walls or suspended from ceilings above countertops and appliances. Tall, free-standing cabinets and special storage features, such as pull-out shelves, are also common in kitchens. *Wood*, *wood veneer*, and *plastic laminates* are popular cabinet materials.

Lighting and Ventilation

In the kitchen, good lighting is needed to prevent eyestrain and accidents while preparing food. In the dining room, there must be enough light to allow diners to see what they are eating.

Lighting can be classified as natural or artificial. **Natural light** comes from the sun. The amount of natural light available during daylight hours depends on the size and placement of windows, doors, and skylights. If there is not enough natural light to perform kitchen and dining tasks, artificial light should be added.

Artificial light generally comes from electrical fixtures. Ceiling fixtures are often hung over dining tables. They may also provide general lighting in kitchens. Extra light fixtures are often installed over ranges and under cabinets to provide *task lighting* in the kitchen **(Figure 11.4)**.

Ventilation is needed in the kitchen to remove steam, heat, and cooking odors. Proper ventilation also helps maintain a comfortable dining atmosphere. If there is not enough natural ventilation, exhaust hood, wall, and ceiling fans will help circulate air.

Electrical Wiring

Another factor that affects the function of kitchen and dining areas is electrical wiring. Kitchens need a large supply of electricity to safely run appliances. In dining areas, electricity is needed mainly for lighting. Power is also needed to operate items such as coffeemakers and warming trays.

When wiring is inadequate, circuits often become overloaded. Be aware of the warning signs of overloaded circuits. Circuit breakers may trip or fuses may blow frequently. Motor-driven appliances, such as mixers, may slow down during operation. Lights may dim when an appliance is being used. Appliances that heat, such as electric skillets, may take a long time to become hot. If any of these signals occurs, call a qualified electrician to check the wiring.

For safety, appliances should be grounded. To **ground** an appliance means to connect it electrically with the earth. If a grounded appliance has a damaged wire, the electric current will flow to the earth instead of through your body. Thus, you will not receive a severe or fatal shock.

Table Appointments

Table appointments are all the items needed at the table to serve and eat a meal. They include dinnerware, flatware, beverageware, holloware, linens, and centerpieces.

Dinnerware

Dinnerware includes plates, cups, saucers, and bowls. The material used to make dinnerware helps determine its durability and cost.

GoodMood/Shutterstock.com

Figure 11.4 Lighting fixtures mounted under these cabinets illuminate the work surface for food preparation tasks. Why is task lighting helpful in the kitchen?

Learn About...

Outlets and Electrical Safety

The *National Electrical Code* is a set of guidelines for electrical safety. The *Code* requires all new homes to have Ground Fault Circuit Interrupters (GFCI) for outlets that are near water sources. This includes outlets that are near kitchen sinks. If the GFCI detects an abnormal flow of electric current through the circuit, it will instantly cut off power to the outlet. This helps prevent shocks and fires. You can recognize an outlet protected by a GFCI by buttons on the outlet used to test and reset the device.

Grounded outlets are another type of outlet that increases electrical safety. These types of outlets have a rounded hole centered beneath two slots. They are designed to accommodate appliances that have three-pronged plugs. The rounded hole is connected to a grounding wire. If a faulty appliance is plugged into the outlet, this wire will send current to the ground. This protects someone holding the appliance from getting a shock.

If the outlets in a home have just two slots, two-pronged adapters will be needed for grounded appliances. An adapter has a metal *grounding tab* or a small wire called a *pigtail* attached to it. The metal screw on the outlet faceplate is supposed to go through the tab or be attached to the pigtail. If the outlet box is grounded, this will ground the appliance. If the outlet box is not grounded, an electrician should replace it with a grounded box to ensure safe use of appliances.

Iasha/Shutterstock.com

Know and Apply

1. Do you have GFCIs and grounded outlets in your home?
2. What are some safety precautions you should take to help prevent electric shocks?

China is the most expensive type of dinnerware, but it is elegant and durable. *Stoneware* is heavier, more casual, and less expensive than china. Like stoneware, *earthenware* is moderately priced. However, it is less durable than stoneware. *Pottery* is the least expensive type of ceramic dinnerware. It is thick and heavy, and it tends to chip and break easily. *Glass-ceramic* is strong and durable. *Plastic* is lightweight, break resistant, and colorful, although it may stain and scratch over time. It is most suitable for very casual meals.

Flatware

Flatware, often called "silverware," includes knives, forks, and spoons. It also includes serving utensils (such as serving spoons) and specialty utensils (such as seafood forks). As with dinnerware, the material helps determine appearance and cost.

Sterling silver and *silver plate* flatware require polishing to remove tarnish caused by exposure to air and certain foods (**Figure 11.5**). *Stainless steel* does not tarnish, but like silver, it can be affected by eggs, vinegar, salt, tea, and coffee. To prevent staining, avoid prolonged contact with these foods and carefully rinse flatware as soon as possible.

When selecting flatware, consider the general shape of each piece, its weight, and the way it feels in your hand. A well-designed piece should feel sturdy and well balanced. Look at the finish. All edges should be smooth. Silver plate should be evenly plated.

Beverageware

Beverageware, which is often called glassware, includes drinking glasses of all shapes and sizes used for a variety of purposes. Beverageware can be made of lead glass, lime glass, or plastic. The two basic shapes of beverageware are tumblers and stemware. **Tumblers** do not have stems. Juice and cooler are common tumbler sizes. **Stemware** has three parts—a bowl, a stem, and a foot. Water goblets, wine glasses, and champagne glasses are popular stemware pieces.

When choosing beverageware, examine the edges to be sure they are smooth and free from

Figure 11.5 Sterling silver flatware will tarnish if not cared for properly.

nicks. Glasses should feel comfortable to hold and be well balanced so they will not tip over when filled or empty. Look to see that the joints between the different parts of stemware are invisible.

Choose pieces that are multipurpose. For instance, you can use some stemware for serving shrimp cocktails, fruit cups, and ice cream sundaes as well as beverages. Consider plastic beverageware for casual dining and when serving young children.

Holloware

Holloware includes bowls and tureens, which are used to serve food, and pitchers and pots, which are used to serve liquids. Holloware may be made of metal, glass, wood, or ceramic. Some holloware pieces have heating elements.

Holloware tends to be expensive, fragile, and difficult to store. You may purchase holloware pieces to match your dinnerware. However, unmatched holloware that complements other table appointments is less expensive and more versatile.

Purchasing Tableware

Dinnerware, flatware, beverageware, and holloware are all referred to as *tableware*. All four types of tableware are available in many patterns and at a variety of prices. When purchasing tableware, you will want to consider your lifestyle and budget. If you enjoy formal entertaining and can afford the expense, you might select china, sterling silver, and lead glass. If you prefer more casual, less expensive tableware, you might choose stoneware, stainless steel, and lime glass for your table.

You can purchase tableware in several ways. You can buy some tableware as **open stock**. This means you can purchase each piece individually. Dinnerware and flatware are often sold in place settings. A **place setting** includes all the pieces used by one person. For instance, a place setting of dinnerware usually includes a dinner plate, salad plate, sauce dish or bread and butter plate, cup, and saucer. A place setting of flatware usually includes a knife, dinner fork, salad fork, teaspoon, and soupspoon. You can also buy some tableware by the set. A box of four water glasses and a set of dinnerware for eight are examples of sets **(Figure 11.6)**.

Caring for Tableware

Proper handling and storage will extend the life of your tableware. Rinse tableware as soon as possible after use. Dried food particles are difficult to remove. You can put most tableware in the dishwasher, but you should check the manufacturer's recommendations.

Store tableware carefully. Handle dinnerware and beverageware with care to prevent chipped, cracked, and broken pieces. Place flatware neatly in a drawer to avoid scratching and bending it.

A

Entrieri/Shutterstock.com

B

Tischenko Irina/Shutterstock

C

Svetlana Lukienko/Shutterstock.com

Figure 11.6 Tableware is sold as (A) open stock, (B) place setting, or (C) by the set to meet a variety of consumer needs. What do you think are the advantages and disadvantages of each of these ways of buying tableware?

Table Linens

The term **table linens** includes both table coverings and napkins. *Tablecloths* protect the surface of the table and provide a background for your table setting. Place mats and table runners are also popular table coverings. *Place mats* come in several shapes and can be used for all but the most formal occasions. *Table runners* are narrower and slightly longer than the table. They are often used with tablecloths or place mats. *Napkins* can match the other table linens or provide a contrast.

The amount of care table linens need depends on the materials used in their construction. Paper tablecloths, place mats, and napkins can simply be thrown away when a meal is finished. Vinyl-coated tablecloths and place mats can be wiped clean with a damp cloth. Most fabric cloths can be machine washed and dried. Linen cloths and napkins must be laundered carefully and then ironed while still damp. Before purchasing table linens, you should consider durability, ease of laundering, colorfastness, and shrinkage (**Figure 11.7**).

Centerpieces

You can buy or make centerpieces to add interest to a dining table. Floral arrangements

Svetlana Lukienko/Shutterstock.com

Figure 11.7 Some people use linen napkins routinely to reduce waste from paper napkins.

are popular centerpieces. However, avoid using potted plants. Soil and food do not mix.

If your centerpiece includes candles, light them and be sure they burn above or below eye level. If open flames are a safety concern, consider using battery-operated flameless candles to add warmth and elegance to your centerpiece. Avoid using candles on the table during the day.

Regardless of the materials used to make your centerpiece, it should be in proportion to the size of the table. Make sure guests will be able to see over the centerpiece while they are seated.

Setting the Table

You should set a table for convenience as well as beauty. There is no "right" way to set a table. The occasion, style of service, size of the table, and menu will help you determine how to set the table.

Begin setting the table with the table linens. A tablecloth should extend evenly on each side of the table. You may lay place mats flush with the edge of the table or 1 to 1½ inches (2.5 to 4 cm) from the table edge. Place runners down the center, along both sides, or around the perimeter of the table.

Handle all tableware without touching the eating surfaces. Start by placing the dinner plate in the center of each cover, 1 inch (2.5 cm) from the edge of the table. A **cover** is the table space that holds all the tableware needed by one person. If using a salad plate, place it to the left of the dinner plate above the napkin. If using a bread and butter plate, place it just above the salad plate, between the salad plate and the dinner plate. Each guest should be able to tell which appointments are his or hers.

Place flatware in the order in which it will be used, working from the outside toward the plate. Forks go to the left of the plate. Therefore, if you are serving salad before the main course, place the salad fork to the left of the dinner fork. Place the napkin to the left of the forks or on the dinner plate.

Knives and spoons go to the right of the plate. This means a soupspoon goes to the right of the teaspoon if you are serving soup before the entree. You can place dessertspoons or forks above the dinner plate. When placing flatware, turn knives so the blades are toward the plates. Place forks and spoons with tines and bowls turned upward. The bottom of each piece of flatware should be in line with the bottom of the dinner plate.

Place the water glass just above the tip of the knife. Place other glasses below and to the right of the water glass. If you are serving a hot beverage, place a cup and saucer to the right of the knife and spoon. The cover for a formal table setting is illustrated in **Figure 11.8.**

Place salt to the right of pepper when placing shakers on the table. Place rolls, butter, and other foods that will be self-served to the right or left of the host's cover. Place serving utensils needed for foods to the right of serving dishes.

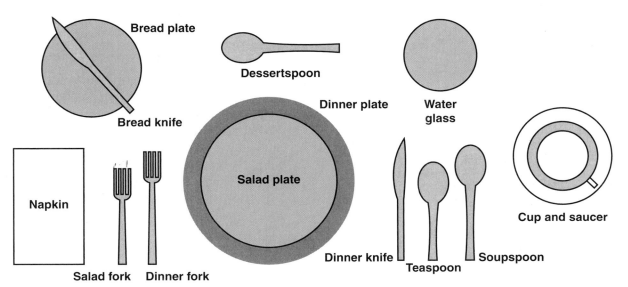

Svetlana Lukienko/Shutterstock.com

Figure 11.8 Place settings will vary based on the menu being served.

Chapter 11 Review and Expand

Summary

Kitchen and dining areas are heavily used spaces in the home. With careful planning, their design will meet the needs of all household members. Three major kitchen work centers focus on the tasks of preparing and storing food, cooking and serving, and cleanup. If space allows, a home may include additional work centers for such tasks as mixing, eating, planning, and doing laundry. Space is needed to store supplies required for the tasks done in each of these work centers. An imaginary line connects the three major work centers to form a work triangle. This triangle takes on different dimensions in different kitchen floor plans. Peninsula, U-shaped, and L-shaped plans reflect universal design, making the kitchen usable by as many people as possible.

Choose surface materials and fixtures that will be functional in kitchen and dining areas. Think about cost, durability, and care when selecting wall coverings, floor coverings, countertops, and cabinets. Plan ample lighting, ventilation, and electrical wiring to safely meet needs.

You will want to select dinnerware, flatware, beverageware, and holloware to suit your lifestyle and budget. Use table linens to provide a backdrop for other table appointments. Choose a centerpiece to add appeal to the dining table. The materials used to make table appointments affect their cost, durability, and care. A few basic guidelines can help you use table appointments to set an attractive table.

Vocabulary Activities

1. **Content Terms**   With a partner, choose two words from the following list to compare. Create a Venn diagram to compare your words and identify differences. Write one term under the left circle and the other term under the right. Where the circles overlap, write three characteristics the terms have in common. For each term, write a difference of the term for each characteristic in its respective outer circle.

work center
work triangle
universal design
natural light
artificial light
ground
table appointments
dinnerware
flatware
beverageware

tumbler
stemware
holloware
open stock
place setting
table linens
cover

2. **Academic Terms**   Write each of the following terms on a separate sheet of paper. For each term, quickly write a word you think relates to the term. In small groups, exchange papers. Have each person in the group explain a term on the list. Take turns until all terms have been explained.

compact
adequate
functional

Review

Write your answers using complete sentences when appropriate.

3. List two items that would be stored in each of the three major kitchen work centers.
4. What two guidelines will help determine the best place to store each item in the kitchen?
5. Why should the total length of the three sides of the work triangle not exceed 26 feet (7.9 m)?
6. What is the most desirable kitchen floor plan?
7. True or false. Work surfaces in a universal design kitchen all need to be at a level that can be easily reached from a seated position.
8. What qualities do floor coverings used in kitchen and dining areas require?
9. Name the two classifications of lighting and give sources of each.
10. What are three warning signs of an overloaded electrical circuit?
11. What type of tableware are plates, cups, and saucers and what factor helps determine their cost and durability?
12. What are three factors to consider when choosing flatware?
13. What are the two basic shapes of beverageware? Give examples of each.
14. Describe the three ways tableware may be purchased.
15. List three types of table linens.
16. Make a drawing that shows how you would set one cover for a family meal in which the salad is eaten before the main dish and water is the only beverage.

Chapter 11 Review and Expand

Core Skills

17. **Research, Speaking, Technology** Use reliable resources to research the National Electrical Code. Use presentation software and images downloaded from the Internet to prepare an oral report on the history, purpose, or content of the Code.

18. **Science** Clean tarnished sterling silver or silver plate flatware by lining the bottom of a sink with aluminum foil. Place tarnished flatware in the sink, making sure each piece touches the foil. Fill the sink with a solution of 1 cup of sodium carbonate washing soda per gallon of hot water. Use enough solution to completely cover the flatware. Observe how quickly the appearance of the flatware improves. Note that tarnish is silver sulfide, formed by a reaction between silver and sulfur in the air. An electrochemical reaction between silver and aluminum causes the tarnish to be transferred from the flatware to the foil.

19. **Writing** Find a picture of a table setting in a magazine or catalog. Attach the picture to your written critique of the table setting based on the guidelines given in this chapter.

20. **Math** Go to a home improvement store that sells flooring, or research online. Choose stone or ceramic tile and a vinyl sheet design that appeal to you for use in a kitchen. Calculate the cost of covering a kitchen floor that measures 10 feet by 14 feet (3.0 m by 4.3 m) with each of these products. Compare the cost of installation as well as materials.

21. **Math** The part of a tablecloth that hangs over the edge of a table is called the *drop*. The drop should be 6 to 8 inches (15 to 20 cm) on all sides of a table for a casual table setting. The drop should be 8 to 10 inches (20 to 25 cm) for a formal table setting. Measure a table in the foods lab and figure what size tablecloth would be needed for casual and formal table settings.

22. **Writing** Visit a restored historic home or living history museum to see a kitchen from a previous century. Note what types of appliances and storage spaces the kitchen contained and how the work centers were arranged. Write a summary describing the biggest difference between the kitchen you visited and your kitchen at home. Edit your writing for grammar, spelling, organization, and clarity.

23. **Career Readiness Practice** Imagine you work for a restaurant, and your manager wants to host a table setting workshop for the staff. Demonstrate how to set tables to correspond to planned menus. Also demonstrate napkin folding techniques and ideas for creating simple, attractive centerpieces.

Critical Thinking and Problem Solving

24. **Analyze** Identify which kitchen floor plan is found in your home kitchen. Survey your family members to find out what, if anything, they would like to change about the arrangement of space and appliances in the kitchen. Analyze their suggestions to determine whether a different kitchen floor plan would better meet their needs. Use online floor plan software to draw a floor plan based on their suggestions.

25. **Create, Evaluate** Work with a partner to design a test to compare the effectiveness of various recommended cleaning products on the countertop material in your foods lab. With permission from your teacher, conduct the test. Compare a traditional cleaning product, a "green" cleaning product, and a homemade cleaning product. Present your findings in class, noting which cleaning product you preferred. Also, give your overall evaluation of the countertop material based on how easy it was to clean.

26. **Evaluate** Make a list of the materials used for the wall coverings, floor coverings, countertops, and cabinets in the dining area of your home. Write an evaluation of the pros and cons of each of these materials. Note which, if any, of these materials you would prefer to replace. State what replacement materials you would choose and give reasons for your choices.

Chapter 12
Kitchen Appliances

Stuart Monk /Shutterstock.com

Content Terms ↗

EnergyGuide label
warranty
service contract
combination oven
convection cooking

Academic Terms

defect
retard

Objectives

After studying this chapter, you will be able to

- **evaluate** energy labeling, safety seals, and warranties to help you make purchase decisions when buying kitchen appliances;
- **describe** functions, styles, and care of major kitchen appliances; and
- **list** points to consider when purchasing portable kitchen appliances.

Reading Prep

As you read the chapter, put sticky notes next to the sections where you have questions. Write your questions on the sticky notes. Discuss the questions with your classmates or teacher.

Today's appliances make food preparation and cleanup easier. Major appliances are available in a range of styles and offer a wide variety of features. Portable appliances perform a multitude of kitchen tasks. Keep in mind that kitchen appliances are an investment. You can spend a lot of money for appliances. You will probably be using the appliances you choose for many years. Therefore, you will want to plan your appliance purchases carefully (**Figure 12.1**).

Safety and Service

Information is available when you buy an appliance to help you know what you can expect from your purchase. Using this information can help you buy safe, efficient products. Energy labeling, safety seals, and warranties can help you get your money's worth when you shop for appliances.

Energy Labeling

The amount of energy appliances require can vary widely from model to model. Consumers must pay for the gas and electricity their appliances use. Energy also has an environmental cost because natural resources are used to produce it. Therefore, it is important to look into how much

Pavel L Photo and Video/Shutterstock.com

Figure 12.1 Before you go to buy a kitchen appliance, you should plan your purchase carefully. This will help you select the best appliance for your needs.

energy appliances will use when making buying decisions.

To help consumers, the Federal Trade Commission (FTC) requires **EnergyGuide labels** on many major appliances. These yellow tags show an estimate of yearly energy use for major appliances. This estimate is shown in kilowatt-hours. An estimate of the yearly operating cost is also given for the model on which the label appears. This cost is based on national average energy costs.

EnergyGuide labels are required on refrigerators, freezers, and dishwashers as well as a number of nonkitchen appliances. You can use these labels when you shop. Compare EnergyGuide labels on appliances of the same size. This will tell you which model is the most energy efficient and least costly to operate (**Figure 12.2**).

Warranties

A **warranty** is a seller's promise that a product will be free of *defects* (flaws) and will perform as specified. A warranty can be full or limited. A *full warranty* states the issuer will repair or replace a faulty product free of charge. The warrantor may also opt to give you a refund for the product. A *limited warranty* states conditions under which the issuer will service, repair, or replace an appliance. For instance, you may have to pay labor costs, or you might have to take the appliance back to the warrantor.

Carefully check the warranty and be sure you understand the terms before you buy an appliance. Both limited and full warranties must state how and where you can fulfill them. Review the warranty to see if it covers the entire item or just parts. Find out if it includes labor costs. Note how long the warranty is in effect. If you have any questions, contact the manufacturer.

Service Contracts

Service contracts are like insurance policies for appliances. You can buy them from appliance dealers. Such contracts may be called *extended warranties* or *protection plans*. A service contract covers the cost of needed repairs for a period after the manufacturer's warranty has expired. However, if your appliance does not need repairs, you receive no service for the money you spent on the contract.

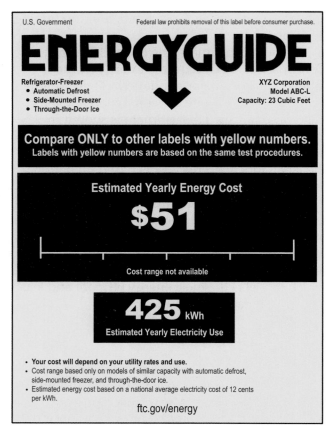

U.S. Government — Federal law prohibits removal of this label before consumer purchase.

ENERGYGUIDE

Refrigerator-Freezer
- Automatic Defrost
- Side-Mounted Freezer
- Through-the-Door Ice

XYZ Corporation
Model ABC-L
Capacity: 23 Cubic Feet

Compare ONLY to other labels with yellow numbers.
Labels with yellow numbers are based on the same test procedures.

Estimated Yearly Energy Cost

$51

Cost range not available

425 kWh
Estimated Yearly Electricity Use

- Your cost will depend on your utility rates and use.
- Cost range based only on models of similar capacity with automatic defrost, side-mounted freezer, and through-the-door ice.
- Estimated energy cost based on a national average electricity cost of 12 cents per kWh.

ftc.gov/energy

U.S. Department of Energy

Figure 12.2 Using energy labeling information can help consumers choose appliances that are less costly to operate and better for the environment. On what type of appliance would this EnergyGuide label appear?

If you are thinking about buying a service contract, be sure you know what you are getting. Read the terms of the contract carefully. Find out if it covers both parts and labor. Ask if the coverage will be good if you sell the appliance or move out of the service area. Check to see if there is a limit to the amount of service you may receive. Be sure you understand all the terms fully before you buy the contract.

Major Kitchen Appliances

Every part of kitchen activity involves major appliances. You use them to cook and store food and to clean up after preparing food. Today's appliances have many convenience features that

reduce the time and effort needed to do these tasks.

When shopping for an appliance, consider how you will use it. You should also think about your space limitations and your budget.

Look for appliances with universal design styles and features. Such appliances will allow all household members to work in the kitchen with ease. For instance, you might choose a side-by-side refrigerator. This style gives wheelchair users and children access to both refrigerated and frozen foods. A built-in oven can be installed in the wall at a level that is easy to reach while seated. Front- or side-mounted appliance controls are a good choice for some households. These controls can assist people who have trouble seeing or reaching rear-mounted controls. An oven with a window and an interior light can help people who have limited vision. Audible signals on appliances can aid those who have trouble seeing. Indicator lights assist users who have difficulty hearing.

Size is an important factor to consider when buying an appliance. The size of appliance you need depends partly on the number of people in the household. For instance, a family of eight will probably need a larger range than a single person. Measure the appliance to find out if it will fit in the area where you want to put it. There must be adequate space for servicing and ventilation. Also measure the doors in your home. They must be wide enough to move the appliance into the room where you plan to install it.

Major appliances require a large financial investment. You must plan the purchase just like any other major household purchase. However, do not buy strictly on the basis of price. Service is also an important consideration. A bargain appliance may not seem to be such a good buy if no one in your area will service it.

Read the use and care manuals that come with your major appliances. Using the information in the manuals will help you get the best service from your kitchen equipment.

Trends and Technology in Major Kitchen Appliances

Each year, manufacturers bring out new appliance models in the hopes of boosting sales.

Learn About...

Safety Seals

Most appliance manufacturers hire independent agencies to test their appliances for safety. These agencies ensure that appliances meet standards of the industry. One such agency that has been testing appliances for years is Underwriters Laboratories (UL). Appliances that pass safety tests carry a safety seal. This seal indicates the appliance has the testing agency's certification of safety.

When shopping for appliances, look for those made by well-known manufacturers. Buy appliances from reputable dealers. Look for safety seals on the appliances. These steps are your best defense against appliances that fail to meet safety standards.

Know and Apply

1. Why would a manufacturer hire an independent agency instead of doing their own safety testing?
2. What are the risks of using an appliance that has not met safety standards?

They tap into the latest technology to build appliances that are easier to use and perform more tasks. For instance, the latest ranges preheat faster and cook more quickly and evenly than older models. They do not just bake and broil foods. They may also have grilling and dehydrating functions. Cooktops have burners that provide intense heat for fast performance. Multi-sized cooking units can be used with a range of cookware pieces. Refrigerators now dispense sparkling and hot water as well as cold water for making a variety of foods and drinks. They also have hands-free sensors that can measure just the amount of water needed (**Figure 12.3**).

Appliances are more flexible to meet changing consumer needs. They have more space inside. This means room for more food in refrigerators and ovens and more dishes in dishwashers. Cooktops have swappable surface units. Grills or griddles can replace regular

burners for different types of cooking. Baking racks in ovens and shelves in refrigerators can be adjusted to hold foods of all sizes. Double ovens make it easier to cook two foods at the same time. Refrigerators have more compartments for storing foods at different ideal temperatures. Consumers in smaller homes can find compact models that conserve space without sacrificing style or function.

Manufacturers also use the latest technology to design equipment that is easier to clean. Cooktops have smooth surfaces for easy wiping. Ovens have steam enhanced cleaning options and oven racks that can withstand the self-cleaning cycle. Refrigerators have shelves that are designed to contain spills.

Some appliances have graphic display screens and/or voice modules. These features allow consumers to program appliances to do specific tasks. They can also show how a selected cycle is progressing and provide use and care information. They can even point out when something is not working right.

One of the most exciting advances is the use of apps to control appliances from smartphones and tablets. This technology allows consumers to check the contents of their refrigerators while they are at the grocery store. They can receive text messages letting them know foods are about to expire. Consumers can also get recipe suggestions for using items they have on hand. Meal

Photo courtesy of GE Appliances

Figure 12.3 New technology allows refrigerators to dispense more than just water.

managers can program oven temperatures and keep an eye on cooking progress when they are out of the kitchen, too.

Today's consumers want appliances that reflect the latest trends in kitchen design. Smooth surfaces and gourmet features create a professional look. Some consumers want their appliances to have an integrated appearance. They can use customized trim kits to make refrigerators and dishwashers mesh with the style of kitchen cabinets. Some appliances also have colored front panels that can be changed to give kitchens a quick facelift.

Cooking Appliances

Before buying cooking appliances, analyze your food preparation needs. You will need a *cooktop* for surface cooking and an *oven* for baking. These can be purchased as separate built-in units or as a single *range*.

Fuel

Whether you choose built-ins or a range, you will need to decide if you wish to use gas or electric fuel. Consider fuel costs, cooking needs, safety issues, appliance performance, and personal preferences when making your choice. Many times, you may decide based on the type of fuel hookups in your home.

Electric cooking appliances require a 240-volt electrical circuit. Electric current flows through coils of wire called *heating elements,* producing heat. Coils can be visible or hidden under a smooth, glass-ceramic top. Some smoothtop electric ranges feature *radiant, halogen,* or *induction* elements. These elements heat much faster than traditional coils.

Gas cooking appliances require both a gas line and a 120-volt electrical circuit. These appliances can use liquid propane (LP) or natural gas to cook food. However, the ignition system, programmable features, timers, clocks, and lights run on electricity.

Dual-fuel ranges and cooktops cook with both gas and electricity. Dual-fuel ranges pair gas surface cooking with electric ovens. Modular cooktops allow consumers to place gas burners and electric elements side by side.

Cooking Appliance Styles

A built-in oven may be mounted into a wall or specially designed cabinet. A built-in

Global Perspective

Energy-Efficient Appliances

The latest appliances are not just better for consumers; they are also better for the environment. Today's appliances are more efficient than ever before. They use fewer resources to do their jobs. Refrigerators have better insulation and door seals. They have sensors that save energy by defrosting only when needed. Multiple doors allow quick access to foods without letting all the cold air out of the appliance. Dishwashers adjust water use to match the amount of cleaning the dishes require. Better filters remove food particles from the water to provide more efficient cleaning. Some appliances are being designed to automatically wait until off-peak hours to perform tasks. This helps avoid draining public power supplies.

Consumers can also do their part for the environment when using appliances. Using the oven to bake more than one food at a time makes the best use of heat energy. Not opening the refrigerator door longer or more often than needed helps limit electricity use. Running full loads in the dishwasher and choosing the no-heat drying option save energy, too. As an added plus, conserving resources cuts utility costs.

cooktop is installed in a countertop. It may be placed along a wall or in an island or peninsula. These separated cooking units offer great flexibility in kitchen design.

Ranges come in three basic styles. *Freestanding ranges* have finished sides. You can place them at the end of a counter or in a cutout between cabinets. Freestanding ranges have backguards that extend above the counter surface, making them taller than other range styles. *Slide-in ranges* sit on the floor. *Drop-in ranges* are shorter and sit on a cabinet base. Both slide-in and drop-in ranges fit snugly between two cabinets. They have a more built-in look with surfaces that are nearly flush with countertops.

Ranges and built-ins may have single or double ovens. Some ovens are **combination ovens**, which can do two types of cooking. Many combination ovens offer a choice of conventional or convection cooking. **Convection cooking** uses a fan to circulate heated air around foods. This saves energy, reduces cooking time, and promotes more even cooking than conventional cooking. In models with double ovens, one oven may be a conventional oven while the other is a convection or microwave oven.

Using and Caring for Cooking Appliances

Always practice good safety habits when using cooking appliances. Place pans on surface units before turning on the units. This will prevent accidents and also save energy. Be sure pan handles do not extend over the front edge of the cooktop to prevent accidental spills. Be careful not to drop heavy objects on the cooktop. Most appliances have finishes that can crack or chip if struck. Wipe up spills immediately with a damp cloth. Do not use cold water when the cooktop is hot. Some appliance surfaces can crack from severe temperature changes.

Wash the surface of appliances regularly. Wash removable parts in warm, soapy water. Then rinse and dry them carefully. Clean the oven regularly. Also, wipe up spills when they occur to keep the oven neat between cleanings.

Microwave Ovens

Microwave ovens can defrost, cook, or reheat food in a fraction of the time required by conventional ovens. Microwave cooking can also save up to 75 percent of the energy used by conventional ovens.

Microwave ovens vary widely in price, size, and features. When buying a microwave oven, consider what best fits your needs. Will the microwave oven be used for full cooking procedures, or will it mainly be used to defrost and reheat prepared foods? Will a compact model be big enough, or do you require a full-size appliance? How many watts of cooking power do you want? (Higher wattage means faster cooking.)

Microwave Oven Styles

Three main styles of microwave ovens are available. *Countertop microwave ovens* can be placed nearly anywhere. With a manufacturer's kit, you can install some models under cabinets or in a wall. *Over-the-range microwaves* have lights

and exhaust vents or fans on the bottom. These models hang over ranges or cooktops in place of standard hoods. *Built-in microwave ovens* are designed to be installed in a wall or cabinet. Trim kits are available to frame these ovens, giving them a more finished look. *Microwave drawers* are a newer version of the built-in style that is often mounted under countertops. Users can easily slide food in and out of the oven as they close and open the drawer (**Figure 12.4**).

All three styles are available as combination microwave/convection ovens. This type of oven allows you to cook with microwaves only, convection heat only, or both methods at the same time.

Using and Caring for Microwave Ovens

Do not plug a microwave oven into an extension cord. Plug it into a 120-volt grounded electrical outlet. You may want the microwave oven to be the only appliance on the electrical circuit. Sharing the circuit with another appliance can reduce the amount of electrical power to the microwave oven. This can affect the cooking time and may harm the oven itself.

Take care not to turn on a microwave oven when it is empty. This could damage the interior.

Dacor Discovery® Microwave-In-A-Drawer™

Figure 12.4 A safety lock can prevent children from accidentally opening a microwave drawer installed beneath a countertop. Would you find a microwave oven installed at this height to be more or less convenient than an over-the-range model?

The door seal on a microwave prevents radiation leakage. Do not let anything become caught between the sealing surfaces. Immediately clean up any food spills to keep the seal intact. If the door or hinges should become damaged, do not use the oven until you have it repaired.

To clean the interior and exterior of the oven, use a damp cloth and mild detergent. Never use an oven cleaner or abrasive cleansers.

Refrigerators

A refrigerator's main job is to keep foods cold and **retard** (delay) food spoilage. Refrigerator space is measured in cubic feet (cubic meters). Fresh food storage compartments should provide about 4 cubic feet (0.11 cubic meters) of space for each adult in a household. If you prepare most of your meals at home, you may need more storage space to keep a variety of fresh ingredients. Freezers should provide about 1.5 cubic feet (0.04 cubic meters) of space per person. If you do not shop often, you may need a larger freezer so you can stock up on items you like to keep on hand.

Refrigerator Styles

Common refrigerator styles are based on the arrangement of the doors and the freezer. *Top-mount refrigerators* have the freezer above the refrigerator. They are the most common and energy efficient style. *French door refrigerators* have the freezer below the refrigerator. The refrigerator has two doors that open from the middle. Some models have a fourth door or a refrigerated drawer compartment. *Side-by-side refrigerators* have the freezer next to the refrigerator. They provide more freezer space, but the narrow compartments may make it hard to store large food items. *Bottom-mount refrigerators* have the freezer below the refrigerator. This style places refrigerated foods at a height that is easier to reach, but fewer models are available. *Compact refrigerators* are small models that are often used in dorm and hotel rooms. Many of these models have a single door with no separate freezer. Instead, there is a small compartment that will allow you to make ice, but it may not keep foods solidly frozen.

Most refrigerator models are *frost free*. This means frost does not accumulate in the freezer. You can save on purchase and operating costs by buying a *manual-defrost* model. To avoid wasting energy, you should defrost the freezer on these models when frost reaches a thickness of ¼ inch (6 mm).

Using and Caring for Refrigerators

For food safety and energy efficiency, keep the fresh food compartment at 37°F to 40°F (3°C to 4°C). Keep the freezer at 0°F to 5°F (–18°C to –15°C). Keep foods covered to hold in moisture and prevent unpleasant odors in the refrigerator. Try to take out all the items you need from the refrigerator at one time. Each time you open the refrigerator door, warm air enters. The refrigerator then has to use more energy to lower the temperature again.

To ensure food safety, keep both the inside and the outside of the refrigerator clean. Refrigerator parts and accessories also need regular cleaning. Wash ice cube trays, door gaskets, drawers, and shelves with warm, soapy water. Rinse and dry carefully.

Dishwashers

Dishwashers have a number of advantages. They can save time and personal energy. Dishes washed in a dishwasher are more sanitary. This is because the water is hotter and the detergent is stronger than the water and detergent used in hand washing. In addition, air drying is more sanitary than drying with a dish towel. Dishwashers offer a choice of wash cycles. Cycles differ in the number and length of washes and rinses, amount of detergent used, and water temperature.

Dishwasher Styles

Two basic types of dishwashers are available. *Built-in* models are the most popular type. They fit under a countertop between two cabinets and load from the front. Built-in dishwashers are permanently connected to a drainpipe, hot water line, and electric circuit. A newer version of built-in is the *drawer dishwasher*. Many drawer dishwashers have two drawers, which can be used separately for smaller loads of dishes. Two drawers also offer the option of running two cycles at the same time. For instance, you might use the normal cycle for plates in the top drawer while using the heavy-duty cycle for pans in the bottom drawer.

Portable dishwashers are designed to be rolled to a sink for use. A portable dishwasher connects to the sink faucet with a hose and drains into the sink. You can convert some portable models to built-ins. One type of portable that is ideal for small kitchens is the *countertop dishwasher*. This appliance is about the size of a microwave oven. It saves water and energy, making it a good choice for households with one or two people (**Figure 12.5**).

Using and Caring for Dishwashers

If you will not be running the wash cycle right away, you should scrape dishes carefully before loading the dishwasher. If food hardens on dishes, it will be harder for the dishwasher to remove. Food left on dishes will also create odors in the dishwasher.

When loading the dishwasher, place dishes so they face the water source and avoid crowding them. Point knives, forks, and spoons down into the flatware basket. Angle pieces with recessed bottoms so water will run off.

To use a dishwasher most efficiently, run it only when there is a full load. Use an automatic dishwasher detergent. If the water in your area is high in some minerals, spots may form on glassware. Using a rinse agent will help reduce spotting.

Danby Products, Ltd.

Figure 12.5 A countertop dishwasher is big enough to wash about six place settings of tableware while using only a few gallons of water.

To maintain water temperature and pressure needed for proper cleaning, you should not use the washing machine while using the dishwasher. You should also avoid watering the lawn and taking a bath or shower.

Periodically empty the drain screen of any food particles that have collected. Occasionally

Exploring Careers

Appliance Sales Manager

Appliance sales managers are in charge of making sure appliances sell. Managers may be responsible for one store or a chain of stores. They must know the needs and desires of consumers in their geographic areas. This will help them stock the types of appliances that are most likely to sell. They may set sales quotas, hold trainings, and conduct job evaluations for salespeople who sell directly to customers. They may help set prices and discount rates, too.

Successful sales managers must show an ability to set and achieve goals. They must be leaders who can handle stress and are not afraid to take control and tackle challenges. Sales managers need to understand why people react the way they do. This will help them know how customers will react to various sales techniques. Good speaking skills are necessary so they can communicate appliance information in employee trainings. They need to be persuasive so they can encourage salespeople to try new ways of approaching customers. Sales managers also need critical thinking skills so they can correct customer issues that reflect problems with sales or service policies.

Most appliance sales managers have four-year bachelor's degrees. These degrees are likely to be in a business field, such as marketing. Many managers begin working as salespeople. Then, after a few years, they use their product knowledge and sales experience to move into management positions.

wipe the outside of the machine with a soapy cloth, then rinse and dry.

Other Major Appliances

Some people choose to buy other major appliances to help in the kitchen. A few examples include *freezers*, which allow consumers to take advantage of discounts and store food for later use. *Warming drawers* are useful for holding prepared foods at serving temperatures for a few hours. *Food waste disposers* use sharp blades to grind food scraps into tiny particles, which wash down the drain.

Before purchasing any of these appliances, consider your needs and the styles and features available. Be sure the appliances will fit in your kitchen without taking away needed storage space. Look at your budget and be sure the benefits you receive from the appliances will be worth their costs.

Portable Kitchen Appliances

Major appliances are needed for basic kitchen functions. However, they cannot do many of the individual preparation tasks meal managers must perform. For these tasks, meal managers often rely on the time and energy savings provided by portable appliances. These small appliances can do many tasks faster and better than you could do them by hand.

Trends and Technology in Portable Kitchen Appliances

Modern portable appliances are designed with smooth, sleek shapes in trim sizes. Most appliances have white, black, or metal finishes. They are neutral enough to blend with any kitchen decor. However, many portable appliances also come in a range of colors to reflect the latest decorating trends. Some consumers want their appliances to have a unified look. For these consumers, manufacturers offer suites of appliances that go together.

Consumers have always wanted appliances that offer quick, safe performance; easy cleaning;

and convenient storage. Manufacturers never stop looking for ways to use technology to meet these demands at higher levels. Today's portables are highly adjustable to allow consumers to get foods just the way they like them. Toasters brown bread to the perfect level of darkness. Coffee grinders grind beans to just the right degree of fineness for every type of bean, brewing method, and beverage. Blenders use the exact amount of power needed, whether crushing ice or pureeing cooked vegetables.

Many of the latest appliances allow a series of functions to be programmed. They can also be programmed for specific food products. In some cases, programming can be done remotely using a smartphone or tablet. This eliminates the need for consumers to keep checking on a food's progress and changing settings. A toaster can be programmed to defrost, toast, and keep warm when a frozen bagel is first dropped into it. Then, a consumer can go take a morning shower and return to have breakfast ready and waiting. Sensors allow appliances to be self-monitoring. The appliances will automatically increase heat or decrease speed as particular food items require.

A growing trend in portables is high-end appliances that perform like machines in commercial kitchens. Top-of-the-line blenders allow home cooks to puree silky smooth soups like the finest restaurants. Professional brewers make drinks in your kitchen that taste like they came from the local coffeehouse. These portables cost as much as some major appliances. However, they are generally well built to provide years of service.

Toasters and Toaster Ovens

Toasters are one of the most common kitchen appliances. You can choose a two- or four-slice model, depending on the number of people who will be using it. Look for a model with extra-wide openings if you like to toast bagels and thick slices of bread.

Toaster ovens bake and broil small food items in addition to toasting bread. These appliances are handy for small apartments and other small quarters. They use less energy and create less heat in the kitchen than full-sized ovens. A toaster oven is shown along with a toaster and a number of other popular portable kitchen appliances in **Figure 12.6.**

Portable Appliances

Toaster

Toaster oven

Stand mixer

Hand mixer

Blender

Hand blender

Food processor

Automatic drip coffeemaker

Single-serving brewing system

Electric can opener

Slow cooker

Multicooker

Shutterstock.com; ©iStock.com

Figure 12.6 What other portable kitchen appliances have you used?

Electric Mixers

Electric mixers are popular among home bakers for blending ingredients, beating egg whites, and whipping cream. These appliances are available in stand and handheld styles. *Stand mixers* leave your hands free. They are also better for heavy-duty mixing jobs. You can remove some stand mixer heads from the stand and use them as hand mixers. The motor on a stand mixer should be strong enough to beat stiff mixtures without overheating. The mixer should provide even, constant mixing at every speed. The beaters should be easy to insert and remove. They should cover the full bowl diameter for thorough mixing of small or large amounts of food.

Hand mixers are smaller, lighter, and less expensive than stand mixers. However, they are not as versatile. You must hold them during the entire mixing operation. They should have stable heel rests or other means of support for standing on the counter when not in use.

Blenders

You might use a blender to blend smoothies, puree soup, or crush ice. Unlike mixers, blenders do not incorporate air into foods.

A blender should have a removable container, molded of heat-resistant glass or plastic. The container should have a wide opening, a handle, a pouring spout, and measurement markings on the side. Also look for a self-sealing vinyl cover that resists odors and stains. A removable center cap makes it easy to add ingredients.

A *hand blender* is handy when blending small batches of foods. It is also great for pureeing soups right in the cooking pot. This small appliance is easier to clean and store than a regular blender. However, it cannot perform some of the same tasks, such as crushing ice. It also must be held the whole time it is being used.

Food Processors

A food processor performs many time-consuming jobs quickly and easily. It blends, purees, grates, chops, and slices. It is especially helpful when you have larger amounts to prepare.

When buying a food processor, look for one that meets your needs for features. A safety interlock switch ensures that you have locked the cover in place before starting the processor.

A dishwasher-safe container and cutting disks or blades will ease cleanup. You may want a food pusher that adapts to processing small or slender foods. Also, make sure the control panel is easy to operate.

Coffeemakers

Several types of appliances are available for brewing coffee. One of the most popular is the *automatic drip coffeemaker*. This appliance has a thermostatic control that heats water without boiling it. The hot water slowly drips down through ground coffee in a filter and into a carafe below. The carafe sits on a warming plate that keeps the brewed coffee at drinking temperature.

A *single-serving brewing system* heats water and forces it through an individual portion of coffee. The brewed coffee pours out of the machine directly into a cup or mug. Single coffee portions can be measured into a reusable filter. They also come in disposable pods or discs designed to fit in specific machines. These throwaway containers come in many coffee flavors as well as tea, cocoa, and other beverages. They avoid the need to measure coffee and clean dirty filter holders. On the other hand, they are much more costly than buying ground coffee or coffee beans. They create excess waste, too. This type of coffeemaker may be a good choice for homes where everyone prefers different beverages. However, many coffee drinkers feel single-serving systems do not provide the same rich taste as drip coffeemakers.

Electric Can Openers

An electric can opener quickly and easily cuts lids off metal cans. A magnet holds the lid for easy removal. Some models adjust to adapt to cans of different heights. Most have removable cutting assemblies for easy cleaning. Many can openers also have a feature that sharpens knives.

Slow Cookers and Multicookers

Slow cookers are designed to cook foods over a period of hours without supervision. You can combine ingredients in a slow cooker in the morning. At the end of the day, you will have a dish that is ready to eat without much additional preparation time.

Multicookers are versatile, time-saving appliances. They can operate as slow cookers, but they also perform a number of other tasks. Common functions include pressure cooker, rice cooker, steamer, yogurt maker, sauté, and warmer.

When choosing these appliances, compare features and functions to find the model that best meets your needs. Look for nonstick cooking vessels for easy cleaning.

Other Portable Kitchen Appliances

In addition to the small appliances discussed, there are many others available on the market. Many of these, such as electric skillets and grills, perform several functions. Others, such as ice cream makers and bread machines, do one basic task. Some single-function appliances are fad items that appear on the market for a while and then fade from popularity. Others meet real consumer needs and become lasting options for appliance buyers.

When choosing a more specialized appliance, consider storage space. Think about how often the appliance will be used. Also, check to see if you have another appliance that will perform the same task. As with all appliances, make selections based on need, available features, quality construction, and ease of use and care.

Purchase Considerations for Portable Appliances

When purchasing small appliances, select those that give the most satisfaction for the money spent. Consider what the appliance does, its limitations, and its special features. Then decide what to buy (**Figure 12.7**).

General Use and Care for Portable Appliances

Before using any portable appliance, be sure to read the manufacturer's use and care booklet. The booklet will give directions for proper use that will help your appliance last for years. It will also include safety guidelines to help avoid mishaps in the kitchen.

The manufacturer's booklet will tell you how to clean the appliance. You should clean most portable appliances after each use. Allow hot appliances to cool. Always unplug portable appliances before cleaning. Wash most removable parts in warm, soapy water. Some parts may be safely cleaned in a dishwasher. Most appliance motor bases and heating elements should not be immersed in water. Instead, wipe them clean with a damp cloth.

Purchase Considerations for Portable Appliances

- Is the appliance made by a reputable manufacturer and sold by a reputable dealer?
- Does the appliance come with a warranty?
- Who provides servicing when the appliance needs repairs?
- Will the appliance be used frequently?
- Does another appliance you already have do the same job?
- Is there adequate, convenient storage space for the appliance?
- Does the appliance have adequate power to perform its intended tasks?
- Does the appliance have a convenient size and shape?
- Is the appliance sturdy and well balanced? (Motor-driven appliances should not tip or "walk" during use.)
- Are parts easy to assemble for operation and easy to disassemble for cleaning?
- Does the appliance have quality construction features?
- Does the appliance have built-in safety features?
- Does the appliance have a safety seal to guarantee that it meets electrical safety standards?

Figure 12.7 Answering these questions before shopping for a portable appliance will help you make a worthwhile purchase.

Mini Lab: Adaptable Appliances

Brewing Up a Banquet

Each lab group will prepare one of the following recipes using a 12-cup automatic drip coffeemaker with a glass carafe. A model with a basket-style filter holder is preferred. Before the lab, follow manufacturer's recommendations for maintenance cleaning with a white vinegar solution. Each recipe yields 4 servings.

Hard-Cooked Eggs

4   large eggs, room temperature

1. Fill the carafe with cold water to the 6-cup mark and pour it into the reservoir of the coffeemaker.
2. Place the eggs in the carafe and place it on the warming plate. Turn on the brew switch. When the water has finished dripping into the carafe, leave the carafe on the warming plate for 30 more minutes.
3. Turn off the coffeemaker and remove the carafe from the warming plate. Use a slotted spoon to remove the eggs from the carafe. Immediately place them in a bowl of ice water for 5 minutes before peeling.

©iStock.com/Issaurinko

Per egg: 77 calories (58% from fat), 6 g protein, 1 g carbohydrate, 5 g fat, 211 mg cholesterol, 0 g fiber, 139 mg sodium.

Pumpkin Spice Oatmeal

1⅓ cups (330 mL) quick oats

1   teaspoon (5 mL) pumpkin pie spice

1   cup (250 mL) canned pumpkin

3   tablespoons (45 mL) maple syrup

1. Fill the carafe with cold water to the 3-cup level and pour it into the reservoir of the coffeemaker.
2. Place oats and pumpkin pie spice in the carafe and stir to combine. Add pumpkin and maple syrup; stir to thoroughly blend.
3. Place the carafe on the warming plate and turn on the brew switch. When the water has finished dripping into the carafe, stir the oatmeal. Leave the carafe on the warming plate for 15 minutes, stirring every 5 minutes.

Per serving: 166 calories (11% from fat), 4 g protein, 32 g carbohydrate, 2 g fat, 0 mg cholesterol, 4 g fiber, 110 mg sodium.

Taiwanese Fruit Tea

⅔   cup (160 mL) orange juice

½   cup (125 mL) Fugi or Gala apple chunks

2   ¼-inch (0.6 cm) orange slices, quartered

1   ¼-inch (0.6 cm) lemon slice, quartered

4   strawberries, stemmed and quartered

1. Fill the carafe with cold water to the 3-cup level and pour it into the reservoir of the coffeemaker.
2. Pour orange juice into the carafe and add all fruit.
3. Place the carafe on the warming plate and turn on the brew switch. Leave the carafe on the warming plate to allow the fruit to infuse for at least 15 minutes before serving. (Longer infusion intensifies fruit flavor.) Sweeten with honey, if desired.

Per serving: 23 calories (0% from fat), 0 g protein, 5 g carbohydrate, 0 g fat, 0 mg cholesterol, 0 g fiber, 1 mg sodium.

Mini Lab: Adaptable Appliances *(Continued)*

Herb-Seasoned Couscous

1⅛	cups (280 mL) whole-wheat couscous	½	teaspoon (2.5 mL) dried basil
2	teaspoons (10 mL) dried parsley flakes	⅛	teaspoon (0.6 mL) garlic powder
¼	teaspoon (1.25 mL) dried minced onion		dash of ground pepper
1	teaspoon (5 mL) low-sodium chicken bouillon granules	2	teaspoons (10 mL) butter

1. Fill the carafe with cold water to the 2-cup mark and pour it into the reservoir of the coffeemaker.
2. Dry the carafe before adding the couscous, parsley, minced onion, bouillon granules, basil, garlic powder, and pepper. Stir to combine. Add butter to the carafe.
3. Place the carafe on the warming plate and turn on the brew switch. When the water has finished dripping into the carafe, stir the couscous. Leave the carafe on the warming plate for 5 minutes. Stir again and serve.

Per serving: 208 calories (13% from fat), 7 g protein, 38 g carbohydrate, 3 g fat, 5 mg cholesterol, 6 g fiber, 27 mg sodium.

Steamed Broccoli and Peppers

1½	cups small broccoli florets	1	clove garlic, quartered
½	cup red bell pepper strips, ¼ × 2 inch (1 × 5 cm)		

1. Fill the carafe with cold water to the 12-cup mark and pour it into the reservoir of the coffeemaker.
2. Place the broccoli florets and red pepper strips into the unlined filter holder. Place the garlic pieces on top of the other vegetables.
3. Place the carafe on the warming plate and turn on the brew switch. When the water has finished dripping into the carafe, carefully remove the filter holder from the coffeemaker. Discard the garlic pieces before serving the other vegetables. If desired, save the vegetable stock collected in the carafe for another use.

Per serving: 15 calories (0% from fat), 1 g protein, 3 g carbohydrate, 0 g fat, 0 mg cholesterol, 1 g fiber, 15 mg sodium.

Iced Tea

4	teabags, tags removed	2	¼-inch (0.6 cm) lemon slices

1. Fill the carafe with cold water to the 8-cup mark and pour it into the reservoir of the coffeemaker.
2. Place lemon slices in the carafe and place it on the warming plate. Put a coffee filter in the filter holder and add the teabags. Place the filter holder in the coffeemaker and turn on the brew switch.
3. When the water has finished dripping into the carafe, turn off the coffeemaker and remove the carafe from the warming plate. Sit the carafe on a pot holder or trivet and carefully open or remove the lid. Allow the tea to cool for 10 minutes. Pour tea into plastic glasses filled with ice and stir. Sweeten as desired.

Calories depend on use of sweetener. Not a significant source of any nutrients.

Chapter 12 Review and Expand

Summary

You can do nearly every kitchen task more easily with the help of appliances. Doing a little research can help you make wise consumer choices. EnergyGuide labels help you choose appliances that are energy efficient. Safety seals assure you appliances have been tested to work safely. Warranties state what you can expect from a manufacturer if an appliance does not perform as intended. Service contracts allow you to extend the coverage of a warranty for an added cost.

Major appliances handle the basic functions of a kitchen. Ranges, built-in ovens and cooktops, and microwave ovens cook foods. Refrigerators store foods and prevent spoilage. Dishwashers ease cleanup.

All major appliances come in several sizes and styles. Different models offer different features. Major appliances are expensive. You must weigh your options carefully to choose the appliances that best meet your needs. Following manufacturers' recommendations for use and care will help appliances work properly and last for a long time.

There are many portable appliances available to help do food preparation tasks. These include toasters, mixers, blenders, food processors, coffeemakers, can openers, and slow cookers. When choosing portable appliances, choose those that are easy to use and store. Look for well-built models that offer the features you desire.

Vocabulary Activities

1. **Content Terms**   On a separate sheet of paper, list words that relate to each of the following terms. Then, work with a partner to explain how these words are related.

   EnergyGuide label   combination oven

   warranty   convection cooking

   service contract

2. **Academic Terms**   Reread the text passages from this chapter that contain each of the following terms. Then write a sentence for each term that explains how the term relates to kitchen appliances. Discuss your sentences as a class to increase understanding.

   defect

   retard

Review

Write your answers, using complete sentences when appropriate.

3. Give two suggestions for buying appliances that have met safety standards.

4. Explain the difference between a full warranty and a limited warranty.

5. Give three examples of universal design features in major appliances that will allow all household members to work in the kitchen with ease.

6. Why do gas cooking appliances require an electrical circuit as well as a gas line?

7. How much energy can cooking foods in a microwave oven save compared with cooking foods in a conventional oven?

8. Which style of refrigerator has the freezer below a refrigerator with two doors that open from the middle?

9. Give three use and care guidelines for dishwashers.

10. List five questions to consider when purchasing portable appliances.

11. Which type of mixer is best for heavy-duty mixing jobs?

12. What are five desirable features of a blender container?

13. What are the advantages and disadvantages of single-serving coffee pods or disks?

14. What are three factors consumers should consider when thinking about buying a specialized portable appliance?

Core Skills

15. **Technology, Writing**   Use reliable resources to find three tips for saving energy and water when using kitchen appliances. Compile your tips with those of your classmates to create a consumer brochure. Edit and refine your writing to ensure your ideas are presented in a logical, organized manner that is clear to the reader. Add illustrations and use page layout software to create an attractive design for the brochure.

16. **Research, Writing**   Use reliable resources to research appliance testing at Underwriters

Chapter 12 Review and Expand

Laboratories or another safety testing agency. Learn what kinds of tests appliances must pass in order to meet safety standards. Write a report summarizing your findings. Edit your writing for style and clarity.

17. **Research, Science** Use reliable print or online resources to investigate how other forms of energy are converted to electrical energy. Also research how electricity flows through household wiring and how circuits are completed when appliances are turned on. Draw a diagram to illustrate one of your findings.

18. **Math, Writing** Investigate what the monthly payment and contract term would be for a major kitchen appliance purchased through a rent-to-own dealer. Compute the total cost of the appliance. Compare this figure to the retail price of the appliance. Use this information to write an opinion paper explaining why you would or would not consider buying a major kitchen appliance through a rent-to-own purchase plan. Review your writing to be sure your points are clear and logical.

19. **Reading, Speaking** Choose a kitchen appliance on which to give an in-service. Locate a user's manual for the appliance either online or from your home file. Read the user's manual before preparing your in-service. Confirm the meaning of any words or concepts that are unfamiliar to you. The in-service should include how to use, clean, store, and maintain the appliance. Be sure to include any safety precautions to take. Use digital media and visual aids to increase understanding and add interest to the presentation. Prepare a few questions to encourage discussion.

20. **Math** The fresh food storage compartment of a refrigerator should provide about 4 cubic feet (0.11 cubic meters) of space for each teen or adult household member. The freezer compartment should provide about 1.5 cubic feet (0.04 cubic meter) of space per teen or adult. Use these guidelines to calculate how many cubic feet of refrigerator and freezer space are needed to store food in your home. Compare these figures with the actual refrigerator and freezer storage space provided by the appliance(s) in your home.

21. **Writing** Research to find an innovation in kitchen appliance technology that interests

you. Write an informative paper for a newspaper or blog describing the innovation. Before you begin writing, be sure you identify and understand your audience. Adjust your level of detail and vocabulary choices as needed for your audience. As you gather information, be sure to keep track of your sources and cite them as necessary. Make sure your introduction captures the reader's attention. Organize your ideas in a logical manner. Be sure to edit and revise your writing.

22. **Practice Career Readiness** Choose a major or portable kitchen appliance and investigate at least one energy-saving tip for using it. Using reliable resources, explain how your tip can have an impact on the environment. Compile the class tips into a handout with color and artwork and make the handouts available at local restaurants.

Critical Thinking and Problem Solving

23. **Evaluate** Use a kitchen appliance with programmable settings, a graphic display, a voice module, and/or an app for a smartphone or tablet. Use your evaluation of these high-tech features as you prepare for and participate in a class debate. Discuss whether these features truly save meal managers time and effort or simply provide a trendy excuse for manufacturers to charge higher prices.

24. **Evaluate** Choose a specific portable kitchen appliance on a sales or manufacturer's website. As you review the information provided, answer each of the questions listed under "Purchase Considerations for Portable Appliances" in this chapter. Use your answers to write a two-page evaluation stating why you would or would not choose to buy this specific appliance. Reread your evaluation and revise as needed for grammar, spelling, and organization.

Chapter 13
Planning Meals

wavebreakmedia/Shutterstock.com

Objectives

After studying this chapter, you will be able to

- **plan** nutritious menus using meal patterns based on MyPlate;
- **prepare** a food budget;
- **develop** menus with an appealing variety of flavors, colors, textures, shapes, sizes, and temperatures; and
- **describe** resources a meal manager can use as alternatives to time and energy.

Reading Prep

Read the chapter title and tell a classmate what you have experienced or already know about the topic. Write a paragraph describing what you would like to learn about the topic. After reading the chapter, share two things you have learned with the classmate.

Content Terms ↱

meal manager
menu
course
convenience food
budget
income
fixed expense
flexible expense
garnish
taste buds
conservation
work simplification
prepreparation

Academic Terms

accommodate
elaborate
economical

People who do not spend much time in the kitchen may not realize what is involved in putting a meal on the table. Of course, beautiful plates of food do not just magically appear. Quality meals take thought, time, and effort. In other words, they require planning.

The Meal Manager

A person who is responsible for planning meals is a meal manager. More specifically, a **meal manager** can be described as someone who uses resources to reach goals related to preparing and serving food. In a home, the person who does most of the cooking would be considered the meal manager. In a restaurant kitchen, the head chef is the meal manager. In a hotel, this role is filled by the food and beverage director.

This chapter focuses on meal managers in a home setting. Meal managers in professional kitchens face many of the same tasks and issues, but their duties are on a much larger scale.

A meal manager's resources include people, money, time, energy, knowledge, skills, and technology. Food and equipment are resources, too. Meal managers must make many decisions based on these resources. They must decide how much time and money they are willing to spend planning and preparing meals. This will affect their decisions about what foods to serve and how to prepare them.

A meal manager will use available resources to reach the following four goals:

- Provide good nutrition to meet the needs of each person eating the meal.
- Use planned spending to make meals fit into a food budget.
- Prepare satisfying meals that look and taste appealing.
- Control the use of time and energy involved in meal preparation.

The meal manager is responsible for seeing these goals are reached. However, he or she may not be the only one working to reach them. Using people as a resource, the meal manager may assign various preparation, serving, and cleanup tasks to others.

Household members need to help the meal manager with planning meals as well as

Exploring Careers

Food and Beverage Director

A food and beverage (F&B) director is in charge of all areas of a hotel's foodservice operations. This includes dining rooms, room service, and catered events served by the hotel's kitchens. The director hires, trains, schedules, and evaluates staff. He or she oversees the preparation of food items and, in smaller hotels, may also do some of the preparation tasks. The F&B director must keep track of food ingredients and order more as needed to have enough supplies on hand. The director is responsible for making sure the kitchens meet standards of safety and sanitation, too.

F&B directors need excellent leadership skills for guiding staff. However, they also require teamwork skills to work alongside their employees. They must be good time managers and pay attention to details to avoid overlooking one of their many duties. They need good communication skills. This includes speaking clearly to instruct staff as well as listening carefully to handle customer needs and complaints. A busy kitchen can be a hectic place. Therefore, F&B directors must be able to deal with stress, adapt to sudden changes, and calmly solve problems.

Getting an associate's degree in a field such as foodservice management is a good way to start on this career path. A few years of work experience in a restaurant may also be required to move into a food and beverage director position.

preparing them. The meal manager requires input to know each person's food preferences when choosing menu items. The meal manager must also be aware of each person's schedule to know who will be eating each meal served. He or she may need to make other plans to *accommodate* (to provide with something needed) household members who will be away at mealtime. Communicating and working together under the guidance of the meal manager will help all household members make sure mealtime goals are met.

Provide Good Nutrition

People tend to eat foods they like. However, foods people like may not always be the foods they require to stay healthy. For good health, the foods people eat must supply their bodies with the right amounts of proteins, carbohydrates, fats, vitamins, minerals, and water. Everyone needs the same nutrients, but not in the same amounts. For instance, pregnant women should have more of some nutrients than other adults. Active people need more of some nutrients than inactive people.

Meal Patterns

Some people might eat a few pieces of pizza and call it "lunch." Others might consume a plate of spaghetti and call it "dinner." Perhaps you realize a meal should be composed of more than just pizza or spaghetti. However, you might not know what else to serve with these food items to make the meals complete.

Meal managers can use a meal pattern to plan meals that provide a variety of foods. A *meal pattern* is an outline of the basic foods normally served at a meal. A meal pattern based on MyPlate can provide all the nutrients needed each day.

A MyPlate meal pattern can be set up for any calorie level. Simply divide the recommended daily amounts of food for each food group by the number of meals needed. This will indicate about how much food from each group is needed at each meal.

This basic pattern works equally well for planning breakfast, lunch, and dinner. The meal manager can use snacks to fill in added food group amounts needed by various individuals. He or she can also add servings to one meal to make up for a shortage in another meal. For instance, some people may want to skip the vegetable group at breakfast. An extra vegetable serving for lunch, dinner, or snack can easily accommodate this preference. A meal pattern with sample food suggestions based on MyPlate is shown in **Figure 13.1**.

In a household, the meal manager must make sure each person eats the recommended amounts from each food group throughout the day. In general, breakfast supplies one-fourth of the day's total nutritional needs. Lunch and dinner each supply one-third. Snacks supply the remaining needs.

Learn About...

The Value of Family Mealtime

Family mealtime provides much more than a chance to consume food. Research shows that families who take the time to regularly eat together have better communication and stronger relationships. This helps children have more self-esteem and a lower risk of depression. These qualities are linked to better grades and lower rates of substance abuse and unplanned pregnancy.

Eating together also helps family members form better food habits. Children are less likely to become obese or develop eating disorders. Helping to prepare meals teaches them important life skills, too.

Many families do not eat together as often as they would like. However, making a commitment to start with just one meal is all it takes to begin seeing the benefits of family mealtime. The point is not to spend hours preparing elaborate dishes. Enjoying a simple meal in a fun, relaxing atmosphere is the goal. Turning off electronics and focusing on meaningful conversation will make the experience more worthwhile. Families can evaluate and make adjustments to create a mealtime routine that works for them.

Know and Apply

1. What do you think is the biggest obstacle to regular family mealtimes?

2. What could you do to maintain or improve regular family mealtimes in your home?

Sample 2,000-Calorie Meal Pattern

Daily Amounts for Each Food Group:

Grains 6 ounce-equivalents (at least half from whole grains)
Vegetables 2½ cups
Fruits 2 cups
Dairy 3 cups
Protein Foods 5½ ounce-equivalents

Meal	Grains	Vegetable	Fruit	Dairy	Protein Foods
Breakfast	**Choose 1 ounce equivalent:** Buckwheat pancakes Grits Oatmeal Toasted oat cereal Whole-wheat bagel	**Choose ½ cup equivalent:** Hash browns Onions, peppers, broccoli, mushrooms in omelet Tomato juice	**Choose ½ cup equivalent:** Grapefruit Melon Orange juice Papaya Mango Strawberries	**Choose 1 cup equivalent:** Low-fat cheese in omelet Hot chocolate Low-fat yogurt Fat-free milk	**Choose 1 ounce equivalent:** Canadian bacon Eggs Ham
Lunch	**Choose 2 ounce equivalent:** Tortilla Whole-grain sandwich bread Whole-wheat pasta in soup or salad	**Choose ½ cup equivalent:** Beans in soup Lettuce and tomato on sandwich Spinach salad Vegetables in soup	**Choose ½ cup equivalent:** Applesauce Bananas Cherries Fruit salad Grapes Plums	**Choose ½ cup equivalent:** Low-fat cheese on sandwich Cottage cheese	**Choose 2 ounce equivalent:** Chicken, tuna, or egg salad Lean luncheon meat Peanut butter Refried beans
Dinner	**Choose 2 ounce equivalent:** Biscuits, cornbread, dumplings Brown rice, pasta Bulgur, kasha, couscous Whole-grain roll	**Choose 1 cup equivalent:** Baked beans, lentils Corn, green beans, winter squash Stir-fried vegetables Sweet potato Green salad	**Choose ½ cup equivalent:** Baked apple Cranberry sauce Grilled pineapple Poached pear Spiced peach	**Choose 1 cup equivalent:** Cheese in casseroles Fat-free milk Pudding	**Choose 2 ounce equivalent:** Beef, lamb, pork, veal Chicken, turkey Fish, shellfish Tofu
Snacks	**Choose 1 ounce equivalent:** Matzos Popcorn Rye crackers	**Choose ½ cup equivalent:** Carrot and celery sticks Cauliflower	**Choose ½ cup equivalent:** Dried figs, dates, and apricots Raisins	**Choose ½ cup equivalent:** Fat-free yogurt Kefir	**Choose ½ ounce equivalent:** Chickpeas Nuts Sunflower seeds

These lists of foods are not all-inclusive. The amounts suggested (in red) at each meal can be either increased or decreased based on personal preference as long as the total daily amount for that food group is equal to the amount stated at the top of the chart.

Shutterstock.com

Figure 13.1 A meal pattern can be created for any calorie level by adjusting the total daily amounts from each food group. If you wanted a two-egg omelet for breakfast, how would you adjust this meal pattern?

Breakfast

Meal managers know eating breakfast will help household members avoid a midmorning slump. When planning this meal, they include a source of complex carbohydrates for energy. Enriched or whole-grain toast and cereals are popular carbohydrate choices for breakfast. Offering berries or bananas to top pancakes or cereal is a good way to add some fruit to the meal. Tossing a handful of nuts on a waffle or a sprinkle of cheese on eggs will provide a small amount of fat. This will keep diners feeling full throughout the morning. Serving low-fat or fat-free milk or yogurt at breakfast can help meet daily needs from the milk group. A meal manager may opt to omit foods from the meat and beans group at breakfast. The 5 to 7 ounce-equivalents (142 to 198 g) needed daily can easily be provided by other meals.

Lunch

Many meal managers make good use of leftovers at lunchtime. Leftovers can be used to prepare nutritious salads, casseroles, and sandwiches. For instance, suppose there is some leftover lean roast beef. People who carry their lunches to work or school could take hearty roast beef sandwiches. Those who eat their lunches at home could add strips of roast beef to a chef's salad (**Figure 13.2**).

stocksolutions/Shutterstock.com

Figure 13.2 Leftover meats can be used to make sandwich wraps for lunch the next day.

In cold weather, hot foods are popular for lunch. Those who must take their lunches can carry soups, stews, and casseroles in wide-mouthed vacuum containers. In warmer weather, the same containers can be used to carry cold fruit or main dish salads.

Dinner

Dinner is often a bigger, more filling meal than lunch. The meal manager can add variety to dinners in many ways. Occasionally serving a new dish is an easy way to add interest to meals. The meal manager can also try serving common foods in new ways. For instance, instead of serving chicken, broccoli, and rice separately, the chicken and broccoli might be combined. Tossing in some red pepper strips and soy sauce and serving this medley over the rice creates a tasty stir-fry.

In hot weather, many people want lighter meals. Meal managers might consider replacing filling, hot entrees with cool, refreshing main dish salads to satisfy smaller appetites. Serving warm whole-grain rolls and a fresh fruit cup would complete the meal.

Varying preparation methods is another way to add variety to meals. For instance, a meal manager who always serves mashed potatoes could try roasted potatoes with herbs for a change of pace.

Snacks

With planning, a meal manager can make sure snacks satisfy nutritional needs as well as hunger. Fresh fruits and vegetables, low-fat cheese and yogurt, whole-grain crackers, and nuts are good snacks. They supplement foods eaten at meals by adding nutrients to the diet.

Planning a Meal

A written menu can be a useful tool in helping a meal manager reach the goal of providing good nutrition. A **menu** is a list of the foods to be served at a meal. Daily menus can help meal managers assess whether they are serving foods from all the groups in MyPlate.

Some menus are planned with several courses. A **course** is a part of a meal made up of all the foods served at one time. At an *elaborate* (fancy) dinner, appetizer, soup, salad, main course, and dessert may each be served as separate courses. At an informal supper, the salad and main dish may be served together. An appetizer, soup, and dessert may be omitted from the menu.

Generally, the best menus center on one food. In the MyPlate meal pattern, grain foods are often the largest portions on the plate. However, plain grain foods have mild flavors that can be seasoned to blend with almost any other food. Therefore, meal managers usually center their menus on a protein food instead. Foods from the meat and beans group often call certain menu combinations to mind. For instance, roast turkey calls to mind stuffing and yams. Baked ham may make some people think of scalloped potatoes and green beans (**Figure 13.3**).

When planning a meal, meal managers may find it easiest to make menu selections in the following order:

1. Choose the main dish of the main course. Keep in mind that the main dish does not have to be from the meat and beans group. Try planning a meal around a vegetable main dish, such as vegetable soup. This can be a great way to help people get recommended amounts of vegetables.

2. Select the grain foods that will accompany the main dish, such as pasta, rice, or barley. Make sure at least half of the choices are from whole-grain sources. Bread or rolls may be served along with or in place of other grain foods. Just make sure the total amount of grain foods served does not exceed daily recommended amounts.

3. Select one or two vegetable side dishes that will complement the main dish. (Vegetables and grain foods may also be part of the main dish rather than side dishes. Casseroles and hearty soups often include vegetables and grains in this way.)

4. Choose the salad. Be sure to go easy on the dressing.

5. Keeping calories in mind, select the dessert and/or first course. Remember to make nutrient-dense choices for these courses, too. Desserts and appetizers are often good places to include a serving from the fruit group in the menu.

6. Plan a beverage to go with the meal. Fat-free milk is often a good beverage choice.

Africa Studio/Shutterstock.com

Figure 13.3 Protein foods such as fish, beans, eggs, or meat are often the focus of a meal.

Serving milk is an easy way to include a food from the milk group in the menu.

Later sections in this chapter will give other points to keep in mind as individual menu items are chosen. Following these guidelines can help meal managers serve meals that are appealing as well as nutritious.

Use Planned Spending

The second goal of meal management is planned spending. Nearly everyone finds a need to establish a spending plan for food. Families in the United States spend, on the average, a little less than 13 percent of their disposable incomes for food. This includes food purchased at restaurants as well as food eaten at home. Meal managers must consider a variety of information when determining the amount of money they can spend for food.

Factors Affecting Food Needs

The activity level, size, sex, and age of each person affect a household's food needs (**Figure 13.4**).

Noam Armonn/Shutterstock.com

Jacob Lund/Shutterstock.com

Figure 13.4   The nutrient needs of a male teen athlete are much greater than those of an older, sedentary woman.

Health and Wellness

Planning for Special Nutritional Needs

Some people have health problems that affect their food needs. For instance, someone with heart disease may be advised to eat a diet low in sodium and saturated fat. When planning meals, a meal manager must consider such special needs.

Initially, the meal manager and the person with unique needs should work with a registered dietitian. The dietitian can offer guidance in meal planning. He or she can also assess whether nutrient needs are being met.

A meal manager could plan separate meals for someone with unique needs. In most cases, however, other household members can adapt their eating habits to follow the special diet. For instance, anyone could follow a diet designed for someone with diabetes mellitus. Such a diet focuses on a moderate intake of carbohydrates and calories spaced through the day.

Adapting eating habits has two key advantages. First, it prevents the person with special needs from feeling isolated. He or she will not feel deprived of foods others are enjoying. Second, it saves the meal manager the time and effort of planning and preparing two sets of meals. Special diets often have a third advantage of being healthier than a typical diet.

It costs more to feed some people than it does to feed others because people's nutrient needs differ. It costs more to feed an athlete, for example, than it does to feed an office worker. It costs more to feed a person who weighs 250 pounds (112 kg) than a person who weighs 110 pounds (49 kg). After the age of 12, it costs more to feed boys than it does to feed girls. It also costs more to feed a teenager than it does to feed a senior citizen.

Health issues also influence food needs. Someone who is allergic to wheat or milk, for example, might require special foods. These special foods are often expensive.

Factors Affecting Food Purchases

You might think all households with similar food needs would spend about the same amount of money for food. However, this is not always true. Similar quantities of nutrients can be acquired at very different costs, depending on the foods purchased.

Think of two baskets of food. One basket contains a beef top sirloin roast, fresh asparagus, fresh raspberries, name brand quinoa, and imported cheese. The other basket contains lean ground beef, fresh carrots, fresh bananas, bulk barley, and domestic cheese. Both baskets provide similar nutrients. However, the second basket will cost quite a bit less (**Figure 13.5**).

The following factors determine the amount of money a meal manager spends for food:

- income
- meal manager's ability to choose foods that are within the food budget

Market Basket Comparison

Market Basket A

1 box @
$6.49/box

1 pint @
$4.99/pint

1.5 pounds @
$12.99/pound

7 ounces @
$13.59/pound

1 pound @
$3.99/pound

Total Basket Cost $40.91

Market Basket B

1.7 pounds @
$.79/pound

1.5 pounds @
$5.29/pound

1 pound @
$.99/pound

.5 pound @
$5.49/pound

1 pound @
$1.69/pound

Total Basket Cost $14.71

Figure 13.5 The cost of food is not an indication of its nutritional value. Which market basket would you rather have? Why?

- meal manager's shopping skills and knowledge of the marketplace
- amount of time the meal manager has to plan and prepare meals
- food preferences of household members
- personal values

Income is a major factor in determining the amount of money a household spends for food. Generally, as income increases, a meal manager spends more money for food. As income increases, the use of dairy products, better cuts of meat, and bakery goods tends to increase. Meanwhile, the use of less expensive staple foods, such as beans and rice, tends to decrease.

Knowing how to choose the tastiest, most nutritious foods for the money spent is an important meal management skill. A meal manager needs to know how similar products differ in quality and nutrition. He or she needs to know when buying a brand name is important. He or she should be able to identify products that contain hidden service costs. A meal manager

also needs to know how to compare prices on a per serving basis. Recognizing seasonal food values and choosing quality meats and produce are other meal management skills.

The meal manager's available time and energy affect the food budget. If these resources are limited, the meal manager will have to spend more money on convenience foods. **Convenience foods** are foods that have had some amount of service added to them. For instance, a meal manager who has ample time and energy could buy ingredients to make homemade lasagna. However, a meal manager who has little time and energy might purchase frozen lasagna instead. The frozen entree cooks quickly and requires no preparation, but it costs more and is more highly processed.

Food likes and dislikes affect spending on food purchases. People who eat steaks and fresh produce will spend more than those who eat casseroles and canned goods.

Value systems affect spending. Some people view food as merely a basic need. They would rather spend their money on other goals. Others enjoy meals as a social activity. People with this outlook are likely to spend more money for food.

Preparing a Food Budget

Most people have a set amount of money that must cover many expenses. To keep from overspending in one area, such as food, they establish a budget. A **budget** is a plan for managing income and expenses. The meal manager has a responsibility to stay within the budget. The following steps will help you prepare a budget:

1. You can get budgeting software or a budgeting app to help you prepare a budget. However a basic spreadsheet program will work, too. The first data you will need to input is your average monthly income. **Income** is money received. You will probably receive most income as wages earned by working. Income also includes money you receive as tips, gifts, and interest on bank accounts. Unless you can count on receiving a set amount from these sources, however, do not include them in your budget. Also, be sure to list only your take-home pay. Money deducted from your paycheck for taxes and other payments is not available for you to use for household expenses.

2. List your monthly fixed expenses and the cost of each. A **fixed expense** is a regularly recurring cost in a set amount. Fixed expenses include rent or mortgage payments, car payments, insurance premiums, and installment loan payments. You should also list savings as a fixed expense. Otherwise, you might end up spending money you intended to save.

3. List your flexible expenses and their estimated monthly costs. **Flexible expenses** are regularly recurring costs that vary in amount. Flexible expenses include food, clothing, healthcare, utility bills, transportation, and entertainment. A sample budget is shown in **Figure 13.6**.

4. Figure the total of your fixed and estimated flexible expenses. Compare this amount with your income. If your income equals your expenses, you will be

Figure 13.6   Creating a budget will help you achieve your spending and saving goals.

able to provide for your needs and meet your financial obligations. If your income is greater than your expenses, you can put the extra money toward future goals. If your expenses are greater than your income, however, you will need to make some adjustments.

Reducing Food Expenses

A budget shortage can be handled in two ways: increasing income and decreasing expenses. Working overtime or getting another job would provide you with extra income. Looking at your current spending patterns will help you see how you can reduce expenses.

Although you cannot do much to change your fixed expenses, you can adjust your flexible expenses, including food. Save your grocery store receipts for a few weeks to see what kinds of foods you are buying.

You already know the cost of food has little bearing on its nutritional value. Each group of MyPlate includes both expensive and inexpensive foods. Protein foods are the most costly, but prices of foods in this group vary widely. T-bone steak, for example, costs more than ground beef. Both, however, provide similar nutrients. Milk, eggs, and cheese are also protein foods. Dried milk costs less than fluid fresh milk. Medium eggs usually cost less than large eggs. Domestic cheeses cost less than imported cheeses. Dried legumes are an inexpensive source of protein that can help stretch food dollars.

The fruit and vegetable groups are the next most costly food groups. However, foods in these groups vary widely in price, too. Before you buy, compare prices of fresh produce with frozen and canned products. Fresh fruits and vegetables are usually *economical* (cost-effective) when they are in season. During off-seasons, however, canned and frozen products usually are cheaper. Grocers often price small pieces of fresh produce lower than larger pieces. Store brand canned and frozen fruits and vegetables cost less than national brands.

When you buy fresh produce, shop with care and buy only what you will use within a few days. Fruits and vegetables are highly perishable and are the types of food that are most often wasted. Throwing away food is like throwing away money. If meal plans change and you will not eat produce before it spoils, freeze it for later use.

The skillful meal manager also knows unsweetened ready-to-eat breakfast cereals usually cost less than presweetened cereals (**Figure 13.7**). Cereals you cook yourself cost even less. Store brand bread usually costs less than brand name bread or bakery bread. Large packages usually are better buys than small packages. However, wise shoppers compare prices on a per serving basis before buying one size over another.

Convenience products and snack foods are often costly. You may be able to save money by preparing more foods from scratch and buying fewer snack foods. Using coupons and taking advantage of store specials will also help you cut costs.

Remember the grocery store is not the only place you buy food. Restaurants, concession stands, and vending machines also take a portion of your food dollar. You will need to evaluate these purchases in relation to your overall budget.

After identifying ways you can reduce food costs, determine a realistic figure for your monthly food budget. If you do your shopping weekly, divide this amount by four. Then keep careful track of your food purchases for a few weeks to see whether you are overspending. Also keep track of any food you throw away to see if you are buying more than you need. Sometimes your records may show you have spent more than your weekly budget. For instance, stocking up on sale items one week may cause you to spend more than your estimated amount. However, this may enable you to spend less money the following week.

Food is only one of the flexible expenses in your budget. You can take similar steps to reduce other spending areas, such as clothing, transportation, and entertainment.

val lawless/Shutterstock.com

MaraZe/Shutterstock.com

Figure 13.7 The presweetened ready-to-eat cereal (A) has been heavily processed and contains over ten ingredients. The oatmeal (B) is minimally processed and contains only one ingredient. Which cereal do you think costs less?

Prepare Satisfying Meals

The third goal of meal management is to prepare satisfying meals. Everyone eating the food should find the meal appealing. This goal can be one of the most difficult to accomplish.

Food Preferences

Studies have shown people like some groups of foods better than others. In the United States, meats are more popular than vegetables. However, there are wide ranges of preferences within each class of foods. For instance, in the meat class, steak is ranked as a most-liked food, while liver is ranked as a least-liked food. When it comes to vegetables, asparagus is preferred over brussels sprouts.

The foods you prefer to eat usually are familiar foods that taste good to you. Many factors affect your food preferences, including sight, smell, and touch. As a result, the color, size, shape, flavor, texture, and temperature of foods help determine how well you like them.

Color

The way food looks can stimulate or squelch a person's appetite before the food is even tasted. Colorful foods appeal to the eyes and whet the appetite. Therefore, try to avoid too many pale foods when planning a menu. Instead, choose foods that provide a variety of colors. However, avoid colors that would clash. For instance, bright red tomatoes would not be pleasing with the purple color of red cabbage.

One way to add color to foods is by garnishing them. **Garnish** means to add edible decorations to foods or serving dishes to make the foods look more appealing. *Garnish* is also the term used to refer to the edible decorations. A dusting of nutmeg on custard or paprika on potatoes adds a touch of color. Meal managers can use tomato wedges, green pepper strips, and carrot curls to add color to a plate. Peach halves, orange twists, and strawberry fans are also simple garnishes (**Figure 13.8**).

When choosing garnishes, make sure they complement the flavors of the foods with which they are served. You can do this by using one of the ingredients in a dish as a garnish. For instance, a shaving of lemon zest would add color to a serving of chicken with lemon sauce. A sprig of cilantro provides a bright contrast on top of a bowl of salsa. A couple chocolate-covered coffee beans might be used to top a mocha cupcake. Besides being attractive, such garnishes help diners identify the flavors in the foods they are about to enjoy.

Size and Shape

The size and shape of food items affect how appetizing they look. Avoid serving several foods made up of small pieces. For instance, spears of broccoli would be a better choice than peas to accompany a chicken and rice casserole.

wavebreakmedia/Shutterstock.com

Figure 13.8 Garnishing foods adds visual appeal with color.

When choosing a salad to serve with the casserole, a lettuce wedge would be more appealing than coleslaw. Choose foods with various shapes and sizes when planning meals.

Flavor

Flavor is a mixture of taste, aroma, and texture. Information about the taste of food is conveyed to the brain by nerves at the base of the taste buds. **Taste buds** are flavor sensors covering the surface of the tongue. The five basic tastes recognized by human taste buds are sweet, sour, salty, bitter, and umami. *Umami* is often described as savory or meaty. It is the taste, other than salty, that is found in soy sauce.

Some foods have one distinct taste. Sugar, for example, is sweet. Other foods have a blend of tastes. Sweet and sour pork has the sweetness of sugar. It also has the sourness of vinegar and the saltiness of pork.

Aroma is closely associated with flavor. When you like a food, it will taste even better to you if it has a good smell. For example, if you like steak, the smell of steak grilling will stimulate your appetite and taste buds.

Mini Lab: Flavor Perception

Impact of Food Color

Work with a partner to complete this lab activity. **Partner A** will keep the identity of the samples and serve the samples. **Partner B** will taste and evaluate the samples.

1. **Partner A**—Label three sets of three disposable cups with the numbers *1*, *2*, and *3*.

   Partner B—Make an observation table with three columns and three rows. Head the columns with the numbers *1*, *2*, and *3*. Label the rows *First tasting*, *Second tasting*, and *Third tasting*.

2. **Partner A**—Choose three flavors of clear sparkling water from the options provided by your teacher. Use one set of cups to pour a sample of each flavor. Record the flavor that corresponds to each cup number. Make sure Partner B does not see the flavors you have chosen.

   Partner B—Taste each of the samples given to you by Partner A. Identify and record each flavor in the appropriate column of the first row of your observation table.

3. **Partner A**—Using the same three flavors of sparkling water, use the second set of cups to pour a sample of each flavor. However, choose different cup numbers to correspond to each flavor than you did for the first tasting. Record the flavor that corresponds to each number for this tasting. Add a drop of an unexpected food coloring to each cup. For instance, you might color grape-flavored water yellow or lemon-flavored water red.

   Partner B—Taste each of the samples given to you by Partner A. Identify and record each flavor in the appropriate column of the second row of your observation table.

4. **Partner A**—Using the same three flavors of sparkling water, use the third set of cups to pour a sample of each flavor. Again, choose different cup numbers to correspond to each flavor than you did for either of the previous tastings. Record the flavor that corresponds to each number for this tasting. Add a drop of an expected food coloring to each cup. For instance, you might color grape-flavored water purple or lemon-flavored water yellow.

   Partner B—Taste each of the samples given to you by Partner A. Identify and record each flavor in the appropriate column of the third row of your observation table.

5. Together, compare the completed observation table with the flavor information recorded by Partner A. Which flavors was Partner B able to correctly identify in each tasting? What does this activity illustrate about the impact of color on flavor perception?

Flavor should be an important consideration when planning meals. Some flavors seem to go together. Turkey and cranberry sauce, peanut butter and jelly, and apples and cinnamon are popular flavor combinations. Other flavors seem to fight one another. For instance, you should not serve rutabagas and brussels sprouts together. Their strong flavors do not complement each other.

When planning meals, do not repeat similar flavors. For instance, avoid serving tomatoes on a salad that will accompany pasta with tomato sauce. Menus should not include all spicy foods or all mild foods. Plan to serve foods with different flavors.

Texture

Texture is the feel of food in the mouth. Familiar food textures are hard, chewy, soft, crisp, smooth, sticky, dry, gritty, and tough. A meal made up of foods that are all soft or all crisp lacks interest. A meal made up of a variety of textures is much more appealing.

Serve foods in combinations that have texture contrasts. Add crisp celery to soft tuna salad, crunchy almonds to tender green beans, and chewy raisins to creamy rice pudding. These simple additions make foods more interesting (**Figure 13.9**).

MSPhotographic/Shutterstock.com

Figure 13.9 Which ingredient supplies texture in this dish?

Learn About...

Food Presentation

Presentation refers to the way food looks when it is brought to the table and presented to a diner. Along with colors, the arrangement of foods on a plate affects their presentation. Some restaurant chefs put much emphasis on the presentation of foods. They carefully fan out meat slices to make a moderate portion look bigger. They artistically sprinkle snipped herbs or grated cheese over pasta. They skillfully drizzle dessert sauces to write words or draw pictures.

If you are preparing a fancy meal, you may want to try some of these creative techniques. For everyday meals, however, two simple guidelines will help you present food attractively. First, avoid heaping foods on top of one another. Place foods side by side and spread them slightly to fill most of the space on the plate. Second, be careful not to smear or splash food on the edge of the plate. If you happen to drip, use a paper towel to wipe the edge of the plate before serving it.

Kondor83/Shutterstock.com

This plate presentation is balanced, colorful, appealing, and simple enough to replicate in your home.

Know and Apply

1. Do you find elaborate food presentations appealing? Why or why not?
2. What food characteristics most affect the appearance of a plate?

When planning meals, work for a balance between soft and solid foods. Be sure to consider chewy versus crunchy, dry versus moist, and smooth versus crisp. Avoid serving two or more chopped, creamed, or mashed dishes together. For instance, mashed sweet potatoes would not be the best choice if you are also serving cranberry sauce. Roasted sweet potatoes would give your meal more texture variation.

Temperature

The temperature of foods can also affect appetite appeal. A cold salad, for example, provides a pleasing temperature contrast to a piping hot entree. A cool dollop of plain yogurt counters the sensation created by steaming chili.

Hot foods should be hot and cold foods should be cold. Imagine a steaming bowl of soup and the same soup barely warm. Picture a cold, crisp tossed salad next to a room temperature salad bowl filled with wilted greens. Foods served lukewarm do not usually stimulate the senses of taste and sight.

Control the Use of Time and Energy

Meal managers use time and energy to plan menus, buy and store food, and prepare and serve meals. They also need time and energy to care for the kitchen and dining area. **Conservation** refers to the planned use of a resource to avoid waste. Meal managers want to conserve all their resources. However, busy schedules may make time and energy seem more valuable than some other resources. That is why some meal managers view controlling the use of time and energy as the most important meal management goal.

Two main factors help determine the amount of time meal managers need to plan and prepare meals. The first factor is the number of people eating. A meal manager will spend more time preparing meals for a large group than for a few people. A meal that provides enough leftovers to feed a small group two meals would feed a large group only once.

Food preferences are the second factor that affects a meal manager's need for time. Preparing complex dishes and five-course dinners takes longer than making simple recipes and one-dish meals.

Alternatives to the Use of Time and Energy

All resources are limited. However, sometimes one resource can be used in place of another. When time and energy are in short supply, meal managers must decide how to use other resources to meet their goals.

Meal managers can use *people* as a resource to help save time and energy. Each household member can play a role in helping with grocery shopping and various preparation tasks. Even young children can take on such responsibilities as setting the table and stirring ingredients. The meal manager can help each person learn how to do assigned jobs as efficiently as possible. This will allow everyone to make the best use of available time and energy.

When *money* is available, meal managers often use it in place of time to buy foods prepared outside the home at restaurants and deli counters. With a little thought, meal managers can choose these foods to meet goals for good nutrition, planned spending, and appealing taste.

Meal-kit delivery services are another time-saving option that typically costs a bit less than eating out. Through a service's website, meal managers choose a delivery plan based on household size and desired number of meals per week. They also select recipes from featured choices. Then meal kits are delivered containing illustrated recipes and all the premeasured ingredients needed to cook the selected dishes at home. Using these services saves planning and shopping time and reduces waste of leftover ingredients.

Meal managers' *knowledge* and *skills* can be alternatives for time and energy. Meal managers may gain some knowledge by studying and asking questions. However, much knowledge and most skills come from experience. Through practice, meal managers find shortcuts and develop speed. For instance, learning the best time, place, and method for buying groceries can save time on a shopping trip. Learning how to correctly clear a table can save energy at the end of a meal.

Technology can be an alternative to time and energy in the kitchen. A computer can be used to help plan menus. Recipe websites and software programs often suggest preplanned menus. These menus can be used as is or adapted to reflect personal preferences. Shopping lists can be printed that go with the menus. Saving menus for favorite meals will reduce planning time in the future.

A meal manager can use *time* itself to save time. Using time to organize the kitchen for efficiency can save time later when preparing meals. Using time to plan menus and write shopping lists can save time later by making shopping more efficient. Make the most of the time spent cooking by preparing double recipes. It takes much less time to prepare one double recipe than to prepare two single recipes. Leftovers can be turned into a different dish to serve on another day or frozen for later use (**Figure 13.10**).

Using Convenience Foods

Most meal managers use convenience foods to reduce food preparation and cooking time at home. Some ready-made foods are so commonly used, people do not think of preparing meals without them. Canned vegetables, bagged salad, and shredded cheese are among the many convenience foods that are staples in some households.

Warren Price Photography/Shutterstock.com

Figure 13.10 Leftovers can be quickly reheated, saving meal managers time and energy in the kitchen. *What is your favorite leftover food?*

You can group convenience foods according to the amount of service they contain. *Finished foods* are convenience foods that are ready for eating either immediately or after simply heating or thawing. Packaged cookies, canned spaghetti, and frozen fruits are examples of finished foods. *Semiprepared foods* are convenience foods that still need to have some service performed. Cake mixes are semiprepared foods. The meal manager beats in eggs and liquid, pours the batter into pans, and bakes it for a specified time.

Some meal managers do not care for the taste of packaged products. Others do not want to give up the pleasure they get from cooking creatively. These meal managers may still enjoy the time savings of convenience products to do *speed-scratch cooking*. This type of cooking might involve adding a few seasonings to a convenience product like prepared pasta sauce to give it a special touch. Speed-scratch cooking also uses convenience products as the basis of recipes. For instance, a meal manager might use a cake mix as the starting point for a batch of homemade cookies.

The cost of convenience depends on the amount of service a product contains. Generally, the more built-in service a product contains, the higher the product's price will be. A product that contains more service reduces the amount of time the meal manager spends measuring, mixing, and cooking. Most convenience foods cost more than their homemade counterparts. However, there are some exceptions. For example, frozen orange juice concentrate and some commercial cake mixes cost less than their homemade counterparts.

The nutritional value of convenience foods varies from product to product. Many highly processed foods provide more calories, fat, added sugars, and sodium and less fiber than homemade foods. Some products also contain a lot of preservatives and other food additives. Meal managers must read Nutrition Facts labels carefully. They need to look at ingredient lists, too. This information will help them evaluate how products meet the goal of providing good nutrition (**Figure 13.11**).

Convenience foods have both advantages and disadvantages. Before buying a convenience product, ask the following questions:

- How does the convenience food help meet daily nutrient needs?

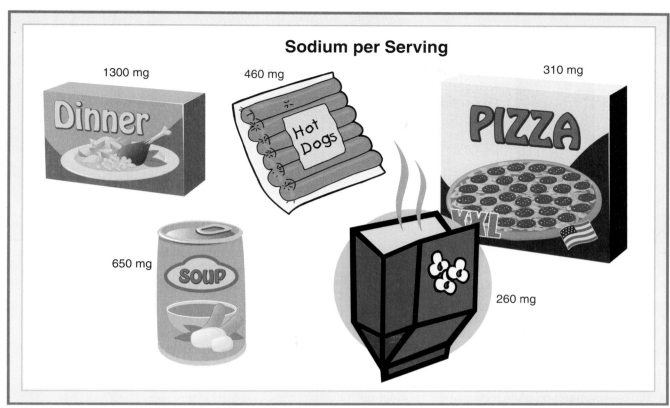

Clockwise from top left: The Turtle Factory/Shutterstock.com; TheBlackRhino/Shutterstock.com; The Turtle Factory/Shutterstock.com; Miguel Angel Salinas Salina/Shutterstock.com; The Turtle Factory/Shutterstock.com

Figure 13.11 The adequate intake (AI) for sodium is 1,500 mg daily. What percent of the AI would a serving of hot dogs supply?

- Does buying convenience foods fit into the food budget? (Is the time saved worth the extra cost?)
- How do the cost and nutritional value of the convenience product compare with those of a homemade product?
- How costly are any additional ingredients that must be added? (Some convenience mixes require the addition of foods such as meat, eggs, or sour cream.)
- How much must be bought? (The cost of a convenience product may seem reasonable if one or two people are being fed. However, it may seem costly if three or more people are being fed.)
- How do the appearance and flavor of the convenience product compare with those of its homemade counterpart? A comparison of the advantages and disadvantages of using convenience foods is shown in **Figure 13.12**.

Work Simplification

Work simplification is the performance of tasks in the simplest way possible to conserve time and energy. Work simplification techniques can help meal managers reach their goal for controlling the use of time. The meal manager can simplify tasks by minimizing hand and body motions. He or she can organize workspace and tools. Changing the product or the method used to prepare the product can also simplify some tasks.

Hand and body motions can be minimized in many ways. Performing a task repeatedly can eventually result in reduced preparation time. This is because the person performing the task develops a skill. A professional cook who chops celery every day soon learns an efficient method for chopping celery.

Another way to minimize motions is to rinse and soak dishes. This simplifies the task of washing dishes.

Convenience Foods

Advantages	Disadvantages
• Time and energy are saved because the meal manager does not have to measure, mix, peel, and slice. • Inexperienced cooks can be confident of product performance. • Many convenience foods have a long shelf life, so they can be kept on hand and used when time is shorter than expected. • Nutrition information is readily available on product packages. • Minimal preparation often means minimal cleanup as well.	• Many mass-produced foods do not taste as good as home-prepared foods. • Frequent use of convenience foods is expensive. • Many convenience foods are high in calories, fat, added sugars, and sodium. • The meal manager has no control over the ingredients, and some products may not be suitable for people with special dietary needs. • Some products are highly processed, containing a number of food additives.

littleny/Shutterstock.com; Karen Culp/Shutterstock.com

Figure 13.12   An alternative to using convenience biscuits is preparing biscuits from scratch.

Saving steps in the kitchen is a method of work simplification, too. Try not to walk back and forth across the kitchen while preparing a meal. Instead, follow the example of professional chefs by practicing *mise en place.* This French phrase, which means "put in place," refers to getting all the equipment ready first before you start to prepare food. It also involves going to the cabinets and then to the refrigerator to get the needed ingredients **(Figure 13.13).** Having all needed items at hand will enable you to work faster and without interruption.

When you are ready to begin preparation, you may find it easier to make several items at once. Work in stages to wash all the fresh produce you will be using. Then do all your cutting tasks, making sure to keep raw meat, poultry, fish, and eggs separate from other foods. Finally, assemble the ingredients and cook, using the oven and multiple cooktop units at the same time. Using this assembly line approach will require less time than making each item individually.

Bruno D'Andrea/Shutterstock.com

Figure 13.13   This mise en place includes all the ingredients needed to prepare chicken curry with vegetables.

Global Perspective

Conserving Resources in the Kitchen

Human energy is not the only type of energy that meal managers need to conserve in the kitchen. They also need to conserve fuel energy, such as gas and electricity. Steps that can be taken to conserve energy include using the oven to cook more than one food at a time. Cover pans on the range to keep in heat. Avoid unnecessarily opening the oven door and letting out heat while using the appliance. Likewise, avoid needlessly opening refrigerator and freezer doors, which lets out cool air.

Water is another resource that should be conserved in the kitchen. Avoid letting the water run while washing dishes. Run the dishwasher only when it is full.

Resources can also be conserved in the kitchen by *recycling*. This means processing a material so it can be used again. Many communities collect paper, cardboard, metal, plastic, and glass packaging for recycling. These materials can be made into new products. Recycling these items keeps them from taking up space in public garbage landfills. It also lessens the need for raw materials to make new products.

One other resource meal managers need to conserve in the kitchen is food. The fact is, a sizable percentage of the food people buy gets wasted. Wasted food not only wastes money, it puts a strain on the environment as well. It squanders the resources used to produce the food. Wasted food also takes up limited space in landfills, where it produces methane, a greenhouse gas that traps heat in the atmosphere. Meal managers can avoid food waste by buying only as much food as they need and storing it properly to prevent spoilage.

Pixavril/Shutterstock.com

Some food waste cannot be avoided. Composting kitchen food waste reduces strain on landfills and produces rich soil for the garden.

An organized kitchen simplifies work. Store tools in the area where they are used most often. For instance, pots and pans can be stored in a cabinet close to the range. Many experienced meal managers buy duplicates of inexpensive tools like spatulas, mixing spoons, and measuring utensils. They store these tools in different parts of the kitchen where the tools will be easy to reach. By using the correct tool for each task, the meal manager can also simplify work. Measuring flour in a dry measure is much more efficient than measuring it in a liquid measure.

Simplify work by changing the food product or the method used to prepare it. For instance, if the meal plan calls for biscuits, but time is short, opt for store-bought bread instead. Making dropped biscuits instead of rolled biscuits would be another way to save time.

Prepreparation is another work simplification technique. **Prepreparation** is any step done in advance to save time when getting a meal ready. Chopping onions and shredding cheese might be prepreparation tasks. After completing these steps, the onions and cheese can be placed in bags in the freezer. When preparing a recipe calling for these ingredients, the needed portion can be quickly measured from the freezer bag. Trimming chicken, peeling oranges, and cooking rice may be other prepreparation tasks that could be done.

Chapter 13 Review and Expand

Summary

Meal managers have four main goals in planning meals. The first goal is to provide good nutrition for everyone eating the meal. Meal managers can use a meal pattern based on MyPlate as a resource to help meet this goal.

The second goal is to use planned spending. A meal manager must consider factors that affect food needs and food purchases when preparing a budget. He or she can use consumer skills to reduce food expenses and stay within the established budget.

The third goal of meal management is to prepare satisfying meals. Meal managers must be mindful of diners' food preferences to achieve this goal. They must also consider flavors, colors, textures, shapes, sizes, and temperatures of foods. This will help them plan menus that are varied and appealing.

The fourth meal management goal is to control the use of time and energy. Meal managers can use a number of resources as alternatives to time and energy. They can use convenience foods and work simplification techniques to reduce the time they spend planning and preparing meals. Meal managers can use appliances efficiently and recycle to conserve fuel energy and other resources in the kitchen.

Vocabulary Activities

1. **Content Terms**   In teams, play *picture charades* to identify each of the following terms. Write the terms on separate slips of paper and put the slips into a basket. Choose a team member to be the *sketcher*. The sketcher pulls a term from the basket and creates quick drawings or graphics to represent the term until the team guesses the term. Rotate turns as sketcher until the team identifies all terms.

meal manager	flexible expense
menu	garnish
course	taste buds
convenience food	conservation
budget	work simplification
income	prepreparation
fixed expense	

2. **Academic Terms**   Individually or with a partner, create a T-chart on a sheet of paper and list each of the following terms in the left column. In the right column, list an *antonym* (a word of opposite meaning) for each term in the left column.

   accommodate   economical

   elaborate

Review

Write your answers using complete sentences when appropriate.

3. Name six resources a meal manager can use to reach goals related to preparing and serving food.

4. What portion of a day's total nutrient intake do breakfast, lunch, dinner, and snacks generally supply?

5. What is usually the first step in planning a menu?

6. True or false. The more nutritious a food is, the more it will cost.

7. List four factors that help determine the amount of money a meal manager spends for food.

8. Describe the steps you would take to estimate the amount of money you could spend for food each week.

9. Which of the following statements about food costs is not true?
   A. Dried milk costs less than fluid fresh milk.
   B. During off-seasons, canned fruits and vegetables cost less than fresh.
   C. Store brands cost less than national brands.
   D. Presweetened breakfast cereals cost less than unsweetened cereals.

10. Define *garnish* and give two examples.

11. What are the five basic tastes recognized by human taste buds?

12. Give an example of two food items that might be served together. Explain how the two foods provide both texture and temperature contrasts.

13. What are the two main factors that help determine the amount of time meal managers need to plan and prepare meals?

14. Give two examples of how a meal manager can use time to save time.

15. What type of convenience food is ready for eating either immediately or after simply heating or thawing?

Chapter 13 Review and Expand

16. Describe three ways a meal manager can simplify tasks.

17. Give three suggestions for conserving resources in the kitchen.

Core Skills

18. **Technology, Math** Search for "USDA food plans cost of food" online and create a food budget for your family based on current year food costs. Develop a one-day menu based on this budget. Submit your menu along with food cost calculations and a grocery list to your instructor.

19. **Reading, Speaking** Find an article from a reliable online source about ways to reduce spending to stay within a food budget. Give an electronic presentation about one or more of the money-saving tips described in the article you read.

20. **Math, Writing** Compare the costs of five foods with built-in convenience with their less convenient counterparts. Examples might include comparing shredded cheese with bulk cheese, instant rice with long-grain rice, and refrigerated juice with frozen concentrate. Also compare the nutritional value and the ingredient lists of the two versions of each product. Write a summary of your comparison, noting any general conclusions you can draw.

21. **Speaking** Visit the school cafeteria, an open kitchen restaurant, or another foodservice operation. Analyze employee's movements as they perform various food preparation tasks. Also study the organization of their workspace and tools. Identify any work simplification techniques you see the employees using. Evaluate ways the employees could make better use of work simplification techniques. Share your findings in a brief oral report to the class.

22. **Listening, Speaking** Survey three students from other classes about some of the alternatives to time and energy used by meal managers in their homes. Ask the following questions:

    A. In an average week, how many meals are prepared at home?

    B. How much time is spent preparing the average meal?

    C. How often does your family eat finished convenience main dishes, such as take-and-bake pizza or frozen entrees?

    D. How often does your family eat ready-made food from a grocery store deli counter?

    E. How often does your family eat takeout food from a restaurant?

    F. How often does your family eat out at a restaurant?

    G. What would you say is the biggest reason your family does not prepare more meals at home?

    Compile your results with those of your classmates. Discuss what, if any, generalizations you can make. Also discuss what suggestions you would offer families who want to prepare more meals at home.

23. **Practice Career Readiness** Presume you are a dietitian. Lilly, your latest client, was recently diagnosed with diabetes. She was instructed to seek nutrition counseling to help deal with her condition. Conduct library and/or online research to investigate the special nutrient needs of someone with this disease. Then write menus that would meet the special nutritional needs you have studied. Cite reliable resources.

Critical Thinking and Problem Solving

24. **Evaluate** Keep track of all the meals you eat for one week. Evaluate the meals according to MyPlate. If each day's meals were not nutritionally balanced, suggest where you could have added or subtracted menu items to provide the recommended daily amounts.

25. **Create** Use a recipe website or software to plan menus for three days. Menus for each day should include breakfast, lunch, dinner, and two snacks.

26. **Analyze** Analyze how the menus created in Activity 25 meet the four goals of meal management.

27. **Create** Choose three recipes for main dishes. Carefully review the list of ingredients in each recipe. Then create an attractive garnish that would be suitable for serving with each dish.

Chapter 14
Shopping Decisions

MBI/Shutterstock.com

Content Terms

produce
comparison shopping
impulse buying
unit pricing
grade
brand name
store brand
national brand

precycling
organic food
food additive
GRAS list
nutrition labeling
Daily Values
Universal Product
  Code (UPC)
open dating

Academic Terms

pesticide
recall

Objectives

After studying this chapter, you will be able to

- **evaluate** store features to decide where to shop for food;
- **identify** factors that affect food costs and comparison shop to decide what foods to buy;
- **use** information on food product labels to make informed decisions about foods to buy; and
- **list** sources of consumer information.

Reading Prep

Before you read the chapter, read all of the table and photo captions. What do you know about the material covered in this chapter just from reading the captions?

To be a smart consumer at the grocery store, you need to know how to read labels and compare prices. You need to be able to choose foods that will give you the most nutrition for your money. You also need to understand basic marketing techniques.

Making wise decisions about where to shop and what to buy takes knowledge and practice. As you develop consumer skills, you will be able to plan appealing, nutritious meals while staying within your budget.

Choosing Where to Shop

Consumers can choose between many kinds of food stores. Some large stores stock thousands of items. Other stores are small and stock just a few specialty items. Some stores sell only food, whereas others also sell drugs, cosmetics, toys, and clothing.

Types of Stores

Being familiar with the different types of stores will help you know what to expect when you shop. You may find one store that meets all your needs, or you may shop in several stores (**Figure 14.1**). The many types of stores at which consumers can buy foods can be grouped into three main categories.

Supermarkets

Supermarkets carry both food and nonfood items. Many large stores have special sections, such as butcher shops, delis, and bakeries. These store areas offer products like cut-to-order meats, catered party foods, and custom cakes. Some stores offer services, such as free child care while you shop and online ordering for in-store pickup. Some supermarkets have in-store pharmacies, health clinics, and banks, too.

Discount supermarkets sell a more limited selection of products, brands, and sizes than larger supermarkets. Many products may be sold under the store's private label. These stores focus on items that offer consumers clear savings over other types of food stores. In order to enjoy these savings, customers may find discount supermarkets to be small with plain decor. Shoppers may also have to bag their own groceries to help keep costs low.

Layland Masuda/Shutterstock.com

Figure 14.1 You may find that several stores or vendors best meet your shopping needs. At this farmers' market, for example, people can shop from several growers in one place. Where does your family usually buy food?

Supercenters

Supercenters are big stores that sell a wide variety of products organized into different areas throughout the store. Home goods, toys, clothing, and electronics are among the departments found in most supercenters. One large section of the store is devoted to selling groceries. Some products may have lower prices than those at supermarkets, though you will need to be aware of product pricing to know when you are truly saving money. The convenience of being able to shop for everything in one place appeals to some consumers. Others find the size of these stores challenging to navigate.

Like supercenters, *wholesale clubs* are very large stores that sell a broad range of products. Wholesale clubs sell a limited selection of foods in bulk quantities. You may be able to buy some items by the case or in restaurant-sized containers. Although you may find reduced prices, be sure you can use the large amounts you buy. Items purchased in bulk may actually cost more if a portion of the product ends up going to waste. Also be aware these stores may not accept coupons, and they often have membership fees.

Small Food Retailers

Many types of stores fit into the general category of small food retailers. Not only are these stores smaller in terms of space, they also

Learn About...

Internet Grocery Stores

More and more purchases are made through online retailers. There is almost no limit to the types of food products available and the vendor websites that sell them. However, for consumers looking to do most of their food shopping online instead of going to a store, the options are more defined.

Internet grocery stores offer service in many regions. They allow consumers to shop from a computer or mobile device through the store's website. Consumers simply choose the brands, sizes, and quantities of products desired from menus on the screen. They can choose to read nutrition, ingredient, and other label information. When they are done shopping, they electronically send the order and arrange for delivery. Professional shoppers fill the order and deliver it to consumers.

Products from Internet grocers tend to cost a bit more than they do from supermarkets. Consumers also pay a delivery fee. However, many people feel avoiding traffic, crowded stores, and heavy shopping bags is worth the cost.

In addition to Internet grocery stores, some supermarkets offer online shopping. A consumer can use a computer or mobile device to choose products and schedule a pickup time. For a small fee, store employees will fill the order and have it ready when the consumer stops by the store at the planned time. This service saves shopping time and effort and reduces the likelihood of making unplanned purchases.

Know and Apply

1. What food products have you purchased from an online retailer?
2. What do you consider to be one advantage and one disadvantage of shopping in a store compared with shopping online for food products?

Most *convenience stores* sell gasoline and are open long hours. These stores may have a fair selection of snacks and drinks as well as some ready-to-eat foods like sandwiches and pizza. They also offer a very limited number of food and nonfood items. Grocery items often cost more at convenience stores. Consumers are willing to pay higher prices when picking up a few products because shopping there is handy.

Specialty stores focus mainly on one specific type of product. Organic and natural food stores, bakeries, and ethnic markets are examples of specialty stores. *Delicatessens* are also a type of specialty store. They sell ready-to-eat foods like cold meats, salads, and rolls. Foods sold in specialty stores are generally high in quality, but they are often high in price, too (**Figure 14.2**).

Outlet stores offer reduced prices on products from individual food manufacturers. Some items in an outlet store may not meet the manufacturer's standards for retail sale. Other items may be excess from supermarkets that did not sell as quickly as expected. Products at outlet stores may be nearing use-by dates printed on labels; however, the foods will be of good quality if used or frozen shortly after purchase.

Food co-ops are owned and operated by groups of consumers. They offer a limited range of products suited to the needs of their members. Co-ops reduce costs by buying foods in bulk, using volunteer labor, and maintaining short hours of operation. Some co-ops are run on a not-for-profit basis. Co-ops may be open to the

aerogondo2/Shutterstock.com

Figure 14.2 Foods sold in delicatessens or other specialty stores are typically high in quality, but also high in price.

offer a more limited range of products. Some of these retailers, such as *dollar stores* and *pharmacies*, focus mainly on other types of goods. They may stock one or two aisles of food items for the convenience of shoppers.

public or to members only. Members may be required to work a certain number of volunteer hours and/or pay a membership fee. In exchange, they receive a discount on product purchases.

During the growing season, growers often bring their fruits and vegetables to sell at *farmers' markets*. Individual growers may operate *roadside stands* near their farms. Homegrown **produce** (fresh fruits and vegetables) is sold at both types of markets. Other locally produced foods, such as meat, poultry, eggs, dairy products, baked goods, and honey, may be available as well. Prices may be lower because food is sold directly from the farm to the consumer. However, production costs and perceived value of fresh, local food may lead some vendors to charge premium prices. To make wise purchases, recognize signs of quality and know retail prices. Also look to be sure vendors are following food safety practices for storing and handling the items they sell.

Store Features

You may shop at a certain food store because it is the only store near you. If you can choose among several stores, however, considering each store's features may help you decide where to shop. You might want to ask yourself the following questions:

- What services does the store offer? (**Figure 14.3**)
- Is the store neat and clean? Are the shelves and cases well stocked?
- Are the store's hours convenient?
- Are the employees courteous and helpful?
- Does the store stock a variety of foods, brands, and sizes?
- Are the prices for both advertised and nonadvertised items comparable to those of other area stores?
- Are the dairy and meat cases cold and clean?
- Is the produce fresh? Is the variety good?
- Does the store also sell nonfood items that I need?

Deciding What to Buy

For consumers who use mobile devices, apps are available to help with almost every aspect of grocery shopping. Apps can be used to find recipes and plan menus. There are apps that will locate sales, download coupons, and create and

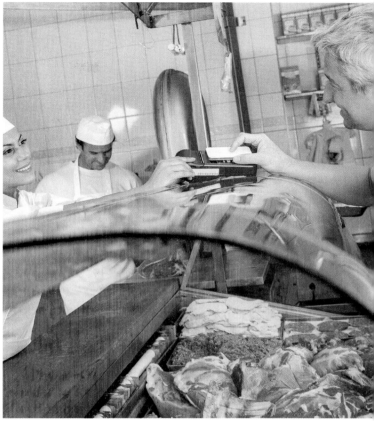

Tyler Olson/Shutterstock.com

Figure 14.3 When choosing a store to visit, consider what services the store offers. Some stores offer special services, such as a butcher shop, pharmacy products, or a bakery section.

organize shopping lists. Apps will compare the nutritional value and cost of food products, too. Using this technology can help consumers save time and money when they shop (**Figure 14.4**).

You can make most of your decisions about what to buy by planning weekly menus before you go shopping. Try to build meals around advertised specials. For example, if ham is a good buy, plan to serve it in several ways during the week. Keep your menus flexible. Suppose you wanted to serve zucchini for one meal, but you find out yellow squash is on sale. You might want to eliminate the zucchini from your menu and add the yellow squash.

Using a Shopping List

A shopping list can help you save time, avoid extra trips for forgotten items, and stick to your food budget. A shopping list can help you meet your nutritional goals, too.

SpeedKingz/Shutterstock.com

Figure 14.4 Apps and other technologies have helped make shopping easier.

You can keep a list handy so you can add items when you find you need them. Before going to the store, check the recipes you plan to prepare during the week. Be sure you have all needed ingredients on hand. Check for staples such as flour, sugar, and milk. Add any needed items to your list.

Also look through sale flyers or visit store websites when making a shopping list. Add advertised specials if you need them and if they really are bargains. Be aware that some stores feature regular prices in their advertisements.

Organize your list according to categories. When adding items under each category, remember to focus on foods that are nutrient dense. In the produce section, you will shop for fresh fruits and vegetables. List lean meats, poultry, and seafood to pick up in the meat department. Add low-fat items to buy from the dairy case. Avoid listing a lot of highly processed foods as well as snacks and drinks that provide nothing but empty calories. Place the categories in the same order as the store aisles.

Global Perspective

Sustainability in Food Marketing

Concern for the condition of planet Earth and those who live here has reshaped the way supermarkets are doing business. Retailers are striving to practice *sustainability* in every facet of food marketing. These efforts show care for the health of people and the environment.

Sustainability begins with how stores are built and maintained. New and remodeled stores require less energy for heating, cooling, and lighting. Stores are being outfitted with equipment that conserves water. Refrigeration systems are using coolants that are environmentally friendly. Landscapes are being designed to resist drought so they will not require watering. Stores are being cleaned with products that contain no harmful chemicals.

Today, stores are taking a look at the products they sell. They are offering more items from local suppliers to reduce the use of fuel for shipping. They are asking manufacturers to use less packaging. Stores are stepping up their efforts to recycle shipping cartons and other materials. They are also donating safely sealed, damaged food packages to food banks to reduce waste and help alleviate hunger.

Education is a key part of sustainable food marketing. Training materials teach store employees where and how to avoid wasting water, energy, and products as they work. Information printed in ads and posted in stores shows consumers how they can make more sustainable choices.

hidesy/Shutterstock.com

Reusable shopping bags help protect the environment by sparing the resources used to make paper and plastic bags.

The use of shopping bags is an example of a simple step each person can take to protect the environment. Stores offer facilities for consumers to recycle plastic shopping bags. They also encourage consumers to choose reusable shopping bags. These efforts save the trees needed to make paper bags and limit the number of plastic bags that end up in landfills.

Carry your shopping list with you and stick to it. You will be less tempted to pick up items you had not intended to buy. Using a shopping list can also help you avoid buying more than you need, which often results in food waste.

Using Unit Pricing

You can get the best buys if you learn to comparison shop and avoid impulse buying. **Comparison shopping** involves evaluating different brands, sizes, and forms of a product before making a purchase decision. **Impulse buying**, on the other hand, is making an unplanned purchase without much thought. Be aware of store displays designed to encourage such purchases. Impulse buying causes excess spending. It can also result in food waste, as impulse purchases are often unusual items that end up getting thrown away.

Many, but not all, grocery stores use unit pricing to help customers comparison shop. **Unit pricing** is a listing of a product's cost per standard unit, weight, or measure. Examples are the cost per dozen, pound, kilogram, quart, or liter. Unit prices generally appear with selling prices on shelf tags underneath products.

With unit pricing, you can compare different brands and package sizes. Unit pricing can also help you compare the cost of different forms of a product quickly and easily. This would tell you whether fruits and vegetables are a better buy in fresh, canned, or frozen form. You could find out if tuna in a can is more or less economical than tuna in a pouch (**Figure 14.5**).

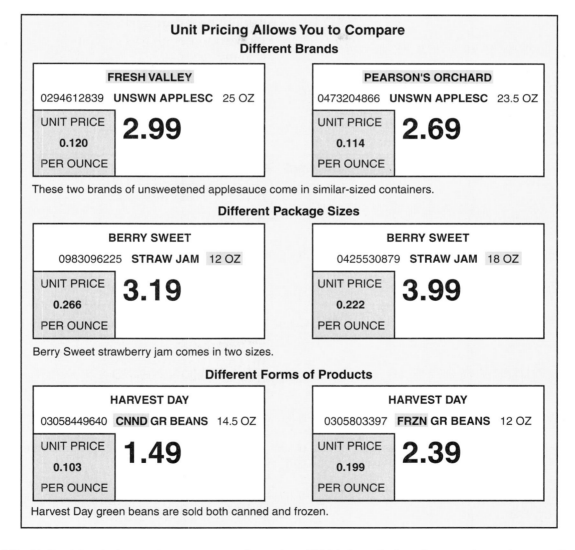

Unit Pricing Allows You to Compare

Different Brands

FRESH VALLEY	
0294612839 **UNSWN APPLESC** 25 OZ	
UNIT PRICE **0.120** PER OUNCE	**2.99**

PEARSON'S ORCHARD	
0473204866 **UNSWN APPLESC** 23.5 OZ	
UNIT PRICE **0.114** PER OUNCE	**2.69**

These two brands of unsweetened applesauce come in similar-sized containers.

Different Package Sizes

BERRY SWEET	
0983096225 **STRAW JAM** 12 OZ	
UNIT PRICE **0.266** PER OUNCE	**3.19**

BERRY SWEET	
0425530879 **STRAW JAM** 18 OZ	
UNIT PRICE **0.222** PER OUNCE	**3.99**

Berry Sweet strawberry jam comes in two sizes.

Different Forms of Products

HARVEST DAY	
03058449640 **CNND GR BEANS** 14.5 OZ	
UNIT PRICE **0.103** PER OUNCE	**1.49**

HARVEST DAY	
0305803397 **FRZN GR BEANS** 12 OZ	
UNIT PRICE **0.199** PER OUNCE	**2.39**

Harvest Day green beans are sold both canned and frozen.

Figure 14.5 Unit pricing helps customers comparison shop. Which brand of applesauce has a lower unit price? Which package size of jam has a lower unit price? Which form of green beans has a lower unit price?

As a smart consumer, you need to be aware that a heavier food might not provide as many servings per container as a lighter food. In this case, the unit cost will not tell you which product is a better buy. Instead, you need to compare prices on a cost-per-serving basis. To find the cost per serving, divide the total product price by the number of servings in each package. You can find the number of servings in a food container by looking at the Nutrition Facts panel on the package (**Figure 14.6**).

Factors That Affect Costs

The cost of food products can determine what fits into a food budget. When food prices are rising, a couple of causes are usually to blame.

One overall influence on food prices is the cost of fuel. Fuel is needed to operate machines used in food production and processing. It is also needed to transport food. Therefore, when fuel costs go up, food prices do, too.

Another issue that puts pressure on food prices is weather. A late frost or a hurricane can destroy a large portion of a crop. This causes prices to increase for the limited share of the crop that remains. A drought can make it difficult and costly for crops to grow. This results in shortages and higher prices.

Even when food prices are generally rising, some factors will cause certain products to cost more than others. These factors include food grades, product brands, and packaging. Understanding these factors can help you be a smart consumer.

Grades

Many food products are given a **grade**, which is an indication of quality. Foods with higher grades usually cost more than those with lower grades. Grades are based on factors that affect the appeal of a food rather than its wholesomeness. For instance, a lower-grade peach may not have a uniform shape or a characteristic color, even though it is nutritious and safe to eat. In many cases, only products with the highest grades are sold in fresh form. Lower-grade products are often used as ingredients in processed foods.

Figure 14.6   Figuring the cost per serving can tell you which product is a better buy.

Learn About...

Coupons and Unit Pricing

Consider the impact of coupons on unit cost. Small packages often have a higher unit cost than large packages of the same product. When using a coupon, however, the small package often becomes the better buy. For instance, suppose a 9-ounce (255 g) box of cereal costs $2.99 and a 12-ounce (340 g) box costs $3.89. The small box would have a unit cost of $0.33 per ounce (28 g). The large box would have a unit cost of $0.32 per ounce (28 g). With a $0.75 coupon, the small box would cost $2.24; the large box would cost $3.14. With the coupon, the unit cost of the small box would be $0.25; the unit cost of the large box would be $0.26.

trekandshoot/Shutterstock.com

Know and Apply

1. How often do you use coupons when you shop for food?
2. Do you consider unit prices or only total product prices when you shop?

Brands

The cost of a product is affected by its **brand name**. This is the name a manufacturer puts on products so people will know what company makes the products. A **store brand**, also called a *house brand*, is a brand sold only by a store or chain of stores. A **national brand** is a brand that is advertised and sold throughout the country. Manufacturers of national brands often package some of their products with store-brand labels. Because the store brands are not promoted with big advertising budgets, they often cost less than national brands. When shopping, compare brands and choose those that best meet your needs.

Packaging

Another factor that affects the cost of food products is the amount and type of packaging material. Packaging affects the environment as well as product costs. As a smart consumer, make a habit of precycling when deciding what to buy. **Precycling** is thinking about how packaging materials can be reused or recycled before buying a product. For instance, you might plan to use a resealable plastic container to store leftovers. You might choose a product in a glass jar instead of a plastic container because you can recycle the glass. You might avoid buying a single-serving product because of the excessive packaging (**Figure 14.7**).

Organic Foods

As you decide what to buy, you may think about choosing some **organic foods**. These are foods produced without the use of synthetic fertilizers, pesticides, or growth stimulants. Genetic engineering methods and ionizing radiation are also banned in the production of organic products.

The United States Department of Agriculture (USDA) has set standards for organic foods. Organic plant foods must be grown on land that has been free of chemical pesticides for at least three years. (*Pesticides* are agents used to kill insects, weeds, and fungi that attack crops.) Organic standards also limit the types of fertilizers farmers can use to help plants grow. Organic meats and poultry must come from animals raised without the use of antibiotics or hormones to promote growth. Drugs may be used only to treat sick animals.

Along with fresh organic foods, you can buy processed foods that have organic ingredients. Look for the exact percentage of organic ingredients in a product to be stated on the label.

Organic foods often cost quite a bit more than nonorganic products. Many consumers are willing to pay higher prices for organic foods. These consumers often say they are concerned about the effects standard farming methods may have on foods or the environment.

Titania/Shutterstock.com

Figure 14.7 If you used the concept of precycling, which of these forms of garlic might you be more inclined to buy?

Much research shows that organic foods are not more nutritious than conventional foods. In blind taste tests, people could not tell the difference between organic and nonorganic products. Note that organic products can have a negative impact on the environment if fuel is used to ship them great distances. When deciding whether to buy organic products, do your own research. Look for unbiased sources to get accurate information (**Figure 14.8**).

Jeffrey B. Banke/Shutterstock.com

Figure 14.8 The USDA organic seal on a food product assures consumers the product meets national standards for organic foods.

Food Additives

Another factor that may affect consumer decisions about what to buy in the supermarket is **food additives**. These are substances that are added to food for a specific purpose. Although over 3,000 additives are in use today, they all fill one of the following four basic purposes:

- add nutrients
- preserve quality
- aid processing or preparation
- enhance flavors or colors

The Food and Drug Administration (FDA) controls the kinds and amounts of additives companies can use in foods. (The Food Safety and Inspection Service [FSIS] of the USDA shares this duty for additives used in meat, poultry, and egg products.) Before the government passed strict food additive laws, about 600 substances were in use. The FDA placed these substances on the "Generally Recognized as Safe" or **GRAS list**. This list includes such common ingredients as salt, sugar, and spices. The FDA has reviewed and evaluated information regarding the substances on this list to make sure they are safe according to today's standards. Food manufacturers can use any additive on the GRAS list without permission.

When a company wants to use a new food additive, it must first receive FDA approval. Before the FDA grants approval, it needs to know the chemical makeup of the additive. The FDA also wants to know the additive's intended purpose and the amount that will be added to food products. The company must submit results of any testing it has done on the additive, too. The FDA carefully reviews all this information. Only after the additive is found to be safe and effective is approval given for its use. The FDA continues to review additive safety based on new findings to decide if approved uses need to be changed.

Shopping Tips

Following a few guidelines will help you get the most value for your money when shopping for food. One way to cut costs is to use coupons for items you need. Coupons are available in newspapers and magazines. Many can be downloaded from websites and printed from your computer. Electronic coupons can be accessed from mobile devices (**Figure 14.9**). They can also be loaded to store loyalty accounts. Discounts will automatically apply when valid products are scanned at the store.

Most coupons have expiration dates. Some require you to buy more than one item. Be sure you have met all the qualifications before you try to redeem coupons. Also, avoid buying a product you do not need just because you have a coupon for it.

Promotions and sales can help you save money on featured products. Still, you should decide whether a promoted product is your best buy. For instance, stores sell some items in multiples, such as three boxes of macaroni and cheese for five dollars. In a case such as this, determine what you would pay for one box. This will help you decide if the multiple price is a good value.

Smart consumers know how to save money without giving up nutrition, quality, or taste when shopping for food. An easy way to save money is to sign up for frequent shopper cards at stores you visit regularly. Present your card when you check out to get special savings and earn rewards open only to cardholders.

Several tips can help you avoid buying food you do not need. Do not take a grocery cart if you plan to buy just one or two items. You will be less tempted to buy extra items if you have to carry them through the store. Shop for groceries just after you have eaten. You will not be as likely to buy unneeded products when you are not hungry. Go grocery shopping by yourself.

Shopping with another person encourages some people to make unplanned purchases. Shop when stores are least crowded—usually this is in the late evening on weekdays. You will be able to do your shopping more quickly and will have less time to get distracted by store displays.

Exploring Careers

Grocery Stock Clerk

Grocery stock clerk is an entry-level job in the food retail industry. A stock clerk's main duty is to refill empty shelf space with products. Stock clerks may set up displays, rearrange shelves, and update product prices as directed by a manager. They may help unpack shipments, checking items against invoices to be sure orders have been filled correctly. They may also scan customer purchases at checkout, bag merchandise, and help customers take items to their vehicles.

To be successful in this job, store clerks need good listening skills so they can follow directions. They must be polite and use speaking skills when answering customer questions. Grocery clerks need to show self-control if they are faced with difficult customers. They must be dependable, doing assigned tasks without close supervision. They also must be able to cooperate with other store employees and accept criticism from managers.

Many stores hire teens with little or no experience to be grocery stock clerks while they are still in high school. Training often comes from coworkers while on the job.

Workers who start as clerks may become interested in food retailing careers. To follow this path, work experience will need to be paired with higher education. A degree in business or marketing will help prepare a former stock clerk for a management post. Store manager, buyer, and food project director are just a few of the options along this career pathway.

Aleksandra Gigowska/Shutterstock.com

Figure 14.9 Electronic coupons can be accessed by a mobile device and can save you money while you shop.

Mini Lab: Brand Comparison

Condensed Tomato Soup

1. Choose a store brand and a national brand of condensed tomato soup, each in a 10¾-ounce (305 g) can. Create a two-column observation sheet. Write the name of the store brand at the top of the left column and the name of the national brand at the top of the right column. Write the price of each product in the appropriate column.

2. Compare the ingredient lists and the Nutrition Facts panels on the two products. Note any differences on your observation sheet.

3. Open both cans. Compare the appearance and smell of the two products. Note any differences on your observation sheet.

4. On two sets of masking tape labels, write *store brand* and *national brand*. Attach one set of labels to two small mixing bowls. Attach the other set of labels to the handles of two small saucepans.

5. Measure ⅓ cup (80 mL) of each condensed soup and pour it into the appropriately labeled mixing bowl for use in preparing two batches of the recipe below.

6. Pour the remaining soup from each can into the appropriately labeled saucepan. Add 1 cup (250 mL) of water to each pan and stir to combine.

7. Place each pan over medium heat and heat until the soup just begins to bubble, stirring occasionally.

8. Sample the two soups, comparing the appearance, texture, and flavor. Note any differences on your observation sheet.

9. Whisk together the following ingredients in each of the labeled mixing bowls to prepare two batches of salad dressing. On your observation sheet, note any differences in the way the condensed soups perform in the recipe preparation.

⅓	cup (80 mL) condensed tomato soup
3	tablespoons (45 mL) vegetable oil
1	tablespoon plus 1½ teaspoons (22.5 mL) sugar
2	tablespoons (30 mL) cider vinegar
¼	teaspoon (1.25 mL) dry mustard
¼	teaspoon (1.25 mL) salt
¼	teaspoon (1.25 mL) celery seed
	dash black pepper
	dash garlic powder

10. Sample the two salad dressings on salad greens, comparing the appearance, texture, and flavor. Note any differences on your observation sheet.

11. Use the information on your observation sheet to answer the following questions:
    A. What did you like about each product?
    B. What did you dislike about each product?
    C. Which product would you choose to buy when making soup? Explain your choice.
    D. Which product would you choose to buy for use as an ingredient in a recipe? Explain your choice.

Salad dressing per tablespoon: 49 calories (73% from fat), 0 g protein, 3 g carbohydrate, 4 g fat, 0 mg cholesterol, 0 g fiber, 105 mg sodium.

Using Food Labeling

When shopping, it is important to read labels carefully so you know exactly what you are buying. Food labels provide a wealth of information that can be helpful to consumers (**Figure 14.10**). Federal law requires the following items on food labels:

- the common name and form of the food
- the volume or weight of the contents, including any liquid in which foods are packed
- the name and address of the manufacturer, packer, or distributor
- a list of ingredients

The Ingredient List

Ingredients on a food label are required to be listed in descending order according to weight. For instance, suppose a label lists "chicken, noodles, and carrots." The product would need to contain, by weight, more chicken than noodles and more noodles than carrots.

Any ingredients that have protein from milk, eggs, fish, shellfish, tree nuts, peanuts, wheat, soybeans, or sesame must be clearly listed. This helps people who are allergic to these foods avoid products that could trouble them.

Consumers can use the ingredient list to analyze advertising claims. For instance, suppose a cereal ad claims that the product is made with whole grain. When you look at the ingredient list, you see *enriched rice flour, sugar, canola oil,* and *whole-grain rice* as the first four ingredients. The appearance of *whole-grain rice* in the list tells you the ad claim is accurate. The fact that this ingredient is listed fourth, however, tells you this cereal is not an excellent source of whole grains. Your analysis shows you this advertising claim is somewhat misleading.

Nutrition Labeling

The FDA requires **nutrition labeling** on almost all food packages. This is a breakdown of how a food product fits in an average diet. You can identify this labeling by the heading "Nutrition Facts."

The first items under the heading are the *servings per containerv* and *serving size*. Serving sizes are stated in both familiar units and metric measures. They are based on amounts people

Figure 14.10 Reading information on food labels helps consumers make informed decisions about the products they buy.

typically consume at one time and should not be viewed as recommended portion sizes. Package size affects the amount normally consumed. Therefore, be sure to check the serving size when comparing different foods. For instance, yogurt products come in several sizes, including 4-ounce (113 g), 5.3-ounce (150 g), and 6-ounce (170 g) cups. These are all considered one-serving containers, but they would obviously differ in the calories and nutrients they provide.

When consuming food from a package that contains multiple servings, remember to compare the listed serving size with what you typically eat. Your portion size is what determines the amounts of calories and nutrients you consume. For example, the label on a large container of yogurt shows the serving size is ¾ cup (170 g). If you eat a 1-cup (226 g) portion, you will be getting one and a third times the amounts of calories and nutrients shown on the Nutrition Facts label. Likewise, eating less than ¾ cup (170 g) would mean you are getting smaller amounts of calories and nutrients than the label shows.

Calories per serving is the next item listed on the Nutrition Facts label. Remember that foods providing 400 calories or more per serving are considered high in calories. Checking these numbers can help you avoid eating more calories than you need each day.

Nutrients with the amounts found in each serving of a food product also appear on the nutrition label. The list must include the amounts of total fat, saturated fat, *trans* fat, cholesterol, and sodium. Total carbohydrate, dietary fiber, total sugars, added sugars, and protein are listed next. Vitamin D, calcium, iron, and potassium are also required. Be sure you consume enough of these nutrients. Besides these required nutrients, manufacturers may opt to list amounts of other nutrients, such as vitamin C and zinc.

Down the right side of the label, you will see a % Daily Value (%DV) for most nutrients. **Daily Values** are reference nutrient amounts that are used for food labeling. The %DV are based on a 2,000-calorie diet. You may need more or less than 2,000 calories per day. Therefore, the percentage of your nutrient needs met by a serving of a food product may be higher or lower than those shown. However, a simple guideline to remember is that 20 percent or more is high and 5 percent or less is low. You can use this guideline to help you limit intakes of saturated fat, sodium, and added sugars. You can also use it to make sure you get enough dietary fiber, vitamin D, calcium, iron, and potassium (**Figure 14.11**).

Health and Nutrient Content Claims

Manufacturers often want to let consumers know what food products will do for their bodies as well as their hunger. To do this, companies may petition the FDA for approval to place health claims on product labels. A *health claim* is a statement that links a food or food component to a health condition. Food products must meet certain requirements to carry these claims. The claims cannot be misleading. They must contain specified phrasing. The FDA classifies different types of claims according to the strength of the scientific evidence on which they are based. An example of one type of health claim is a statement about the

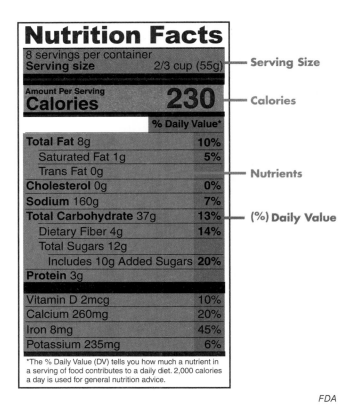

FDA

Figure 14.11 Some food products carry different formats of the Nutrition Facts panel. All nutrition labels provide consumers with valuable information. How many servings does this container provide?

relationship between sodium and hypertension.

Nutrient content claims are another tool companies may use to make consumers aware of the ways food products can affect health. Like health claims, nutrient content claims are regulated by the FDA. These claims may describe the level of a nutrient in a food. For instance, a bottle of fruit juice might have the claim "high in vitamin C." Nutrient content claims may also compare the level of a nutrient in a food with the level in another food. As an example, light mayonnaise may be labeled with the claim "30 percent less fat than regular mayonnaise." The FDA specifies terms that may be used in these claims. FDA regulations spell out the nutrients with which each term can be used. The FDA also identifies acceptable synonyms and specific definitions for each term. Manufacturers must follow FDA guidelines so the claims will be meaningful to consumers. Examples of some

Nutrient Content Claims	
Reduced/Fewer Calories	Contains at least 25% fewer calories per serving than the "full-calorie" version of the food.
Low Calorie	Contains 40 calories or less per serving; 120 calories or less per 100 g for meals and main dishes.
Calorie Free	Contains less than 5 calories per serving.
Good Source	Contains 10% to 19% of the Daily Value of a nutrient. Example: good source of vitamin C.
Healthy	May be used on foods that are not low in total fat, but contain mostly mono- and polyunsaturated fats or provide at least 10% of the Daily Value for vitamin D or potassium.
High	Contains 20% or more of the Daily Value of a nutrient. Example: high in dietary fiber.
Lean	May be used on meat and seafood products that contain limited amounts of fat, saturated fat, and cholesterol.
Light/Lite	Describes a nutritionally altered food product that contains one-third fewer calories or half the fat of the "regular" version of the food. This term can also be used to indicate the sodium of a low-calorie, low-fat food has been reduced by 50%. In addition, labels may state that foods are light (lite) in color or texture.
Reduced/Less	Contains at least 25% less than the amount of a nutrient in the "regular" version of a food. Examples: reduced fat, less sugar.

Figure 14.12 Some common nutrient content claims are listed here. Based on the nutrient content claim for "Good source," does the Nutrition Facts panel in Figure 14.11 describe a food that is a good source of potassium?

commonly used nutrient content claims are shown in **Figure 14.12.**

Health and nutrient content claims can help consumers learn about products and make choices when shopping for food. Keeping all the definitions straight may be confusing. However, following the %DV guideline will help you make wise food choices.

Universal Product Code

Another item found on food labels is the **Universal Product Code**, or **UPC**. This is a series of lines, bars, and numbers that appears on packages of food and nonfood items. This code is used to identify a product, its manufacturer, and its size and form. Grocery checkers pass the UPC on items over a laser beam scanner. As the items pass over the scanner, the store's computer system reads the codes. The correct prices are then rung up on the cash register at the checkout counter. The register prints a description of the items and their prices on the customer's receipt. At the same time, the store's electronic data system tracks changes in product inventory as well as shoppers' buying patterns **(Figure 14.13).**

Monkey Business Images/Shutterstock.com

Figure 14.13 UPC labels and scanners were created to improve the checkout process at food stores, but are now used in many other businesses.

Open Dating

Although dates are printed on many labels, federal law does not require dates on most food products. (Baby formula is an exception.) Certain states have laws ordering dates on some foods. Most dates on food products, however, are determined by manufacturers. Because there are no regulations governing the use of these dates, dates vary from one manufacturer to another.

Some dates on food products are printed in codes, which are used mostly by manufacturers. However, **open dating** uses calendar dates on perishable and semiperishable foods to help retailers know how long to display products. Open dating can help consumers choose products that will maintain quality the longest. These dates also help consumers know which product to use first.

Manufacturers use a few types of dates. Understanding the meanings of the different types is important. Many consumers mistakenly believe dates show when products have expired. This leads them to throw away items that are completely safe, adding to millions of pounds of wasted food each year.

A *sell-by date* is the last day a store should display a product. This type of date is not intended for consumers. Instead, it is designed to help retailers rotate their inventory so they sell oldest products first. You should buy products before they reach this date. However, sell-by dates allow for storage time in consumers' homes. Foods are still safe to eat after the date.

A *best-by date* is a date suggested by the manufacturer for peak quality. You may or may not be able to notice a drop in quality if you buy and use products after this date. However, there is no safety concern with foods that are beyond this date (**Figure 14.14**).

A *use-by date* is the last day a manufacturer recommends consumers should use a product. However, this recommendation is again based on quality, not safety. On meat products, you may see the phrase "use or freeze by." A product that is kept safely frozen can be stored well beyond the date on the package.

Keep in mind that dates refer to the quality of unopened packages. Once a product has been opened, store it properly and use it within the recommended time. Opened products do not necessarily remain safe until dates stamped on packages. For example, an unrefrigerated package of pepperoni may have a sell-by date that is over three months away. You can safely store the unopened product in your pantry until the sell-by date. However, if you open the package, you need to store it in the refrigerator and use the product within three weeks. It will not still be safe to eat on the sell-by date three months from now.

Remember that it is not necessary to throw away a food just because the date on the package has passed. Also remember that proper storage and handling affect food safety. Food that has not been stored correctly may not be safe to eat even if it is within the date on the package. If a product has a use-by date on it, follow that date. For products with other types of dates or no dates, follow reliable food storage guidelines, such as those found throughout this text.

Help with Consumer Problems

From time to time, you may have problems with food products or the businesses that sell them. Many sources of consumer help exist. The source that will best be able to assist you will depend on your particular problem.

Robert Davies/Shutterstock.com

Figure 14.14 Herb and spice containers often have best-by dates to help consumers use seasonings before they lose their peak flavor.

Food stores can help you with a quality problem caused by the way they handled a food product. For instance, you might discover a loaf of bread you just purchased is moldy. If you return the bread, most store managers will refund your money or give you a new loaf.

Product manufacturers can help you with a food quality problem that is due to a processing error. Suppose when you open a package of rice mix, you find the seasoning packet is missing. Look on the package for a website, toll-free telephone number, or address you can use to contact the manufacturer. Keep the package handy so you can refer to it for specific product information the manufacturer might need. Be polite as you make a brief complaint and reasonable request for what action you would like the manufacturer to take. For instance, you might ask for a coupon for a free package of rice mix.

The *Food Safety and Inspection Service (FSIS)* can help you with a food safety problem involving meat, poultry, or egg products. The FSIS is the branch of the USDA that handles product **recalls**, or removal of products from the market. If you found metal shavings in a can of beef stew, the FSIS might contact the manufacturer to recall the product.

The *FDA* is the agency that handles food safety complaints linked to products that do not contain meat or poultry. If you found a piece of glass in a box of cereal, the FDA would handle the investigation. Be prepared to provide detailed product information when you call or complete an online form.

City, county, or *state health departments* address safety problems you might have with food from restaurants **(Figure 14.15).** They inspect facilities, issue warnings and fines, and close businesses when needed.

Better Business Bureaus (BBBs) can help you when you have a problem with the way a food store or restaurant conducts business. BBBs promote honest advertising and selling practices. Imagine the prices at a food store checkout

Speed Kingz/Shutterstock.com

Figure 14.15 Health inspectors periodically perform unannounced inspections at food establishments such as restaurants, convenience stores, bakeries, and supermarkets.

regularly ring up higher than the shelf tags. If the store manager does not give you a satisfactory response, a BBB can contact the store on your behalf. The BBB can also offer to resolve your complaint by other means, if necessary.

These sources of help do more than handle consumer complaints. They can answer questions and provide a variety of consumer information. Some also do testing, grading, and inspecting to ensure the quality and safety of the food supply.

Chapter 14 Review and Expand

Summary

Smart consumers must shop carefully to get the most for their food dollars. They can choose from many types of stores by evaluating store features. Using a shopping list and comparing costs can help consumers know what to buy. Unit pricing makes it easy to compare costs of different brands, forms, and sizes of products. Consumers must evaluate grades, brands, and packaging to choose products that best meet their needs. Thinking about organic foods and food additives will help consumers make purchase decisions, too.

Food labeling provides consumers with information about the foods they buy. Ingredient lists clearly show consumers what is in products. Nutrition labeling helps them get the most nutritional value for the money they spend. Health and nutrient content claims increase awareness of ways foods can affect well-being. The UPC speeds checkout. Open dating helps consumers choose products that will maintain quality the longest.

Various resources can help consumers who have problems with food products. These resources can also provide information and other consumer services.

Vocabulary Activities

1. **Content Terms**   In teams, create categories for the following terms and classify as many of the terms as possible. Then, share your ideas with the remainder of the class.

produce
comparison shopping
impulse buying
unit pricing
grade
brand name
store brand
national brand

precycling
organic food
food additive
GRAS list
nutrition labeling
Daily Values
Universal Product Code (UPC)
open dating

2. **Academic Terms**   Draw a cartoon for one of the following terms. Use the cartoon to express the meaning of the term.

pesticide
recall

Review

Write your answers using complete sentences when appropriate.

3. What type of store sells a wide variety of products organized into different areas as well as having a large section devoted to selling groceries?

4. Describe four types of small food retailers.

5. What are five store features consumers might consider when deciding where to shop?

6. Explain how a shopping list can help a meal manager.

7. What can consumers use to easily compare the cost of different brands, sizes, and forms of the same or similar products?

8. Why do store brand products often cost less than national brands?

9. Compare organic foods with nonorganic foods.

10. What are four basic purposes of food additives?

11. A 14.5-ounce (411 g) can of green beans usually costs $1.79. This week, a large supermarket chain is advertising 3 cans for $5.00. Is this a bargain? Explain.

12. List three tips to help consumers avoid buying food they do not need.

13. A food product label has the following ingredient list: whole-grain oats, roasted almonds, brown rice syrup, canola oil, salt. Does this product contain more rice syrup or canola oil? How do you know?

14. Why is it important to compare the size of portions eaten with serving sizes listed on food products?

15. On a grocery store shelf, the label of one bottle of juice states, "Good source of vitamin A." The bottle next to it is labeled, "High in vitamin A." Which product provides more vitamin A? How do you know?

16. What type of date on a food product is a suggestion by a manufacturer for peak quality?

17. Name four sources of help with consumer problems.

Chapter 14 Review and Expand

Core Skills

18. **Math** Go to a local supermarket and record the prices of three types of fresh fruits and three types of fresh vegetables. Then, visit a farmers' market and record the prices for the same fruits and vegetables. Calculate the percentage price difference for each item. Which location has the best prices overall?

19. **Reading, Speaking** Each student should visit the website for a different supermarket chain. Read about efforts the chain is making to offer more sustainable food choices. Share your findings in a class discussion about the impact of sustainable food choices on society.

20. **Math** Choose a specific product to use for a price comparison study. For example, you might calculate the cost per serving of whole-wheat bread made from scratch using store ingredients, whole-wheat bread made from frozen dough, and bread purchased from the bread aisle and from the in-store bakery. Which supermarket department offers the best value for this product? Compare your findings with those of your classmates to determine if one department consistently offers the best value.

21. **Technology, Speaking** Scan a food label to make a digital image. Use the image to create an electronic slide presentation. Each slide should highlight a different part of the label. As you show your presentation, explain how consumers use each part of the label.

22. **Math** Look at the Nutrition Facts labels on three food products. Figure the percent Daily Values of listed nutrients for people needing 2,800 calories per day and for people needing 1,600 calories per day.

23. **Writing** Write a letter to an appropriate source about a consumer problem with a food product. Be sure to use correct grammar, spelling, organization, and style.

24. **Career Readiness Practice** Evaluate a recent consumer decision you made in terms of its outcome. What could you do differently to yield more successful results? Did you apply *decision tests* such as the following: Is the decision in my best interest? What would happen if my circumstances changed? Would I make the same decision? How might my decision change? After asking yourself such questions, what lesson did you learn to help you improve future decision making?

Critical Thinking and Problem Solving

25. **Evaluate** Visit two supermarkets of comparable size. Using the questions for assessing store features given in the chapter, evaluate each store. Write a report summarizing your findings and identifying your preferred store. Explain your reasoning. Review and revise your writing for clarity and logical organization.

26. **Create** Create a label for a hypothetical food product. Give your product an intriguing name and use color, images, and fonts to make your label eye catching. Your label must include all required information. You can use an online recipe nutrient calculator to analyze the recipe for your product and create the Nutrition Facts label. Assemble a wall display of all the labels created by your class.

27. **Analyze** Find a food label that makes a health or nutrient content claim for the product. What does the claim mean? Analyze how the Nutrition Facts label compares with a similar product that does not make that claim.

28. **Evaluate** Purchase the same food in both organic and nonorganic forms. Compare the two foods and write a summary of your findings.

Unit 4
The Preparation of Food

MBI/Shutterstock.com

Essential Questions

- Why is it important to understand how cooking affects food?
- How can learning about food selection, preparation, and preservations impact your life?
- How might knowledge and skills about entertaining with food benefit you in the future?

FCCLA: Taking the Lead

Use information learned about various food products in this section of the textbook to help you develop a prototype formula for a *Food Innovations* STAR Event. Check the FCCLA national website to find this year's food product scenario for competition.

G-WLEARNING.com

While studying, look for the activity icon ☑ for:
- Content and Academic Terms with e-flash cards, vocabulary games, and matching activities

These activities can be accessed at
www.g-wlearning.com/foodandnutrition/9582

Chapter 15

Heat Transfer and Cooking Methods

Ulga/Shutterstock.com

Objectives

After studying this chapter, you will be able to

- **identify** various methods of heat transfer;
- **differentiate** between dry-heat and moist-heat cooking methods; and
- **demonstrate** correct food preparation techniques, including nutrient retention.

Reading Prep

Before you begin reading this chapter, consider how the author developed and presented information. How does the information provide the foundation for the chapters that follow?

Content Terms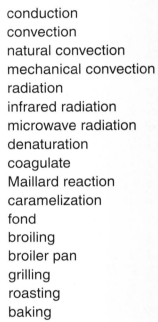

conduction
convection
natural convection
mechanical convection
radiation
infrared radiation
microwave radiation
denaturation
coagulate
Maillard reaction
caramelization
fond
broiling
broiler pan
grilling
roasting
baking

sautéing
smoke point
sweating
stir-frying
wok
panfrying
deep frying
poaching
simmering
boiling
blanching
steaming
en papillote
pressure cooker
braising
stewing
sous vide

Academic Terms

inherent
emit
elicit
viscosity

People cook, or apply heat to, food to prepare it for consumption. Cooking changes food chemically and physically resulting in food that tastes better and is easier to digest. Cooking also makes food safer to eat because the heat kills many microorganisms that cause illness. It alters the protein, as well as affecting the fats, fiber, sugars, and starch present in foods. Appearance, texture, nutritional content, and aroma are transformed as well.

There are a number of cooking methods from which to choose. All these methods apply heat to food, but they differ in how the heat is applied. Some methods are better suited to certain foods than other methods. People who understand and master these methods will have greater success in the kitchen (**Figure 15.1**).

There are three ways in which heat can be transferred to food during cooking. People choose a cooking method based on the desired outcome, the available resources, and their training and skill level. People with a basic knowledge of heat transfer, however, will better understand how different cooking methods affect their food.

Heat Transfer

Cooking involves energy being transferred from a heat source to a food. The three ways heat can transfer are through conduction, convection, or radiation. Most cooking methods use a mixture of these heat transfer forms. For example, when a pan of water is heated over a gas flame, the transfer of heat by the gas flame to the pot is one type of heat transfer. As the water at the bottom of the pot heats and moves up to the top of the pot, this is another method of heat transfer. Next, as the hot water particles move upward, they collide with the cold water particles. During this contact, the hot water particles transfer heat to the cold water particles. This is a third method of heat transfer. After reading this chapter, see if you can identify the forms of heat transfer described in this example.

Conduction

Conduction is the movement of heat from one substance to another by direct contact. For example, when a metal spoon is placed in hot water, the spoon handle becomes hot. Likewise, when you walk barefoot on hot sand or pavement, your feet get hot from direct contact with the walking surface. This is a result of heat being transferred from one substance to another by conduction (**Figure 15.2**).

Figure 15.1   The cooking method and the skill with which it is applied, affect the texture, appearance, aroma, and flavor of the food.

Figure 15.2   In this example of conduction, the warmth from a hand transfers heat to the ice by direct contact, causing the ice to melt. Can you give another example of conduction?

All substances are made up of very small particles. These particles transfer heat to each other as they collide. Substances can be in gas, liquid, or solid form. Some forms are better conductors of heat than others, however. The reason for this is that particles in liquids and gases are much farther apart than those in solids. Because particles in liquids and gases are scarcer, they make contact with other particles less often. The fewer contacts made, the less opportunity there is for one particle to transfer heat to another particle. For this reason, gases and liquids conduct heat less effectively than solids. Additionally, some solids are better conductors than other solids (**Figure 15.3**).

Metal is a great conductor of heat and heats up faster than plastic or wood, which are poor conductors. Furthermore, some metals are better conductors than other metals. Metals that are better conductors heat faster and more evenly, and cool off more quickly. For this reason, it is important to consider what metal pots and pans are made from when selecting cookware.

The cooking process involves conduction on a number of levels—within the cooking utensil, from the utensil to the food, and then from the exterior of the food to the interior of the food. Because conduction relies on direct contact, this form of heat transfer takes longer than other forms. When performed properly, food that is cooked by direct contact develops a desirable crust on the exterior and a tender moist interior.

For example, when cooking a beef roast, the hot air (a gas) in the oven conducts heat to the roasting pan and the roast. Within the pan (solid), the particles are colliding and heating up the pan. Where the roast is in contact with the pan, the pan is conducting heat to the exterior of the roast. At the same time, the hot air in the oven is conducting heat to the exterior of the roast. And lastly, the particles near the exterior of the roast are colliding with cooler particles further inside the roast, and transferring the heat to the roast's interior.

Convection

Convection takes place when heated particles in a gas or liquid flow from a heated area to a cooler area, taking the heat with them.

supirloko89/Shutterstock.com

Figure 15.3 In this image, the flame from the gas burner is conducting heat to the pan. The pan particles closest to the flame are heating up and colliding with cooler particles, conducting the heat through the pan. The heat from the pan then conducts heat to the egg and cooks it.

Learn About...

Induction Cooking

Induction is a type of conduction cooking, however, the heat is transferred with the use of *electromagnetic energy*, instead of a gas flame or electric coil. Magnets cause particles in the cookware to vibrate. The vibration creates heat. Heat is then transferred from the pan to the food through conduction. During this process, the cooktop remains cool to the touch.

Induction cooktops are known for their rapid heating and easy cleanup. Certain types of cookware, such as copper, glass, and aluminum will not work with the magnetic force. Cookware for induction cooktops must have a flat bottom, and be made of a *ferrous* (containing iron) metal such as magnetic stainless steel or cast iron.

People with pacemakers should avoid being near induction cooktops. Induction cooking emits a small amount of noise from an internal cooling fan, and a humming or a buzzing sound can occur. Induction cooktops cost more than traditional cooktops, but can save money in the long run.

Know and Apply

1. List two benefits of induction cooking.

2. Why is the material the cookware is made from important for induction cooking?

Convection is a form of heat transfer that combines conduction with mixing. Convection can be natural or mechanical based on what is generating the flowing movement.

Natural convection occurs when the transfer of heat is caused by the *inherent* (built-in or characteristic) movement of water particles from a warmer area to a cooler one, which creates a circular flow. This flow will continue until the heat source is removed. An example of this is when a pot of water is heated. The water closest to the heat source is hotter than the water near the top. As the liquid heats, it becomes less dense and rises to the top. (Gases also become less dense and rise when they are heated.) This causes the colder water to sink to the bottom of the pot and closer to the heat source where it will become heated and eventually circulate back to the top (**Figure 15.4**).

When cooking soup, this natural convection occurs as the broth heats. Because the consistency of soup is quite liquid, the changes in density move the particles around. For this reason, stirring is not as necessary as with a thicker mixture such as stew. Stews are typically thicker and contain a greater proportion of solids to liquids. As a result, the natural convection is not as effective and cannot be relied on to "stir" the stew.

Mechanical convection uses fans to create the flow that moves the heated particles. *Convection ovens* are an example of this type of heat transfer. Rather than let hot air circulate randomly, a convection oven creates a uniform temperature with an internal fan and heating element. Food in a convection oven is heated as the fan circulates hot air around the oven. Convection ovens save time and energy by cooking food faster than traditional methods. They are known to brown foods more evenly and make meats more tender and juicy. Convection ovens cost more than traditional ovens, however. Additionally, cooking with a convection oven requires adjustments to cook times and temperatures for recipes (**Figure 15.5**).

Radiation

Radiation is the transfer of heat through electromagnetic energy by way of infrared waves and microwaves. The heat source can be gas, infrared, or microwave. Objects with higher temperatures will transfer more radiation heat than objects at lower temperatures. Examples of radiation include the heat *emitted* (given off, released) by the sun or a lightbulb. Radiation does not require direct contact, it works through vibration. It is the energy which has been absorbed by particles, and is then released as waves of energy.

Infrared radiation is invisible waves of energy that act on particles in food. This causes

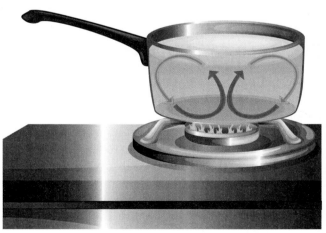

BlueRingMedia/Shutterstock.com

Figure 15.4 Natural convection occurs when the transfer of heat is caused by the movement of water molecules from a warmer area to a cooler one, which creates a circular flow.

Goodheart-Willcox Publisher

Figure 15.5 Convection ovens create a uniform temperature with an internal fan that circulates hot air around the oven.

increased movement of the particles in the food, and this produces heat. Examples of this include the heat transferred from a grill, toaster, or broiler (**Figure 15.6**). It causes the items to brown. Pans with darker surfaces absorb energy better than shiny light-colored pans. As a result, darker pans cook more quickly. Some recipe times may need to be adjusted according to type of pan used.

Microwave radiation transfers energy through short, high-frequency waves, called *electromagnetic radiation*. The waves cause water, fat, and sugar molecules in the food to rub together and vibrate faster, which creates heat. The electromagnetic waves produced by microwave ovens cook faster because they can penetrate the food. As a result, the interior and exterior of the food is heated at the same time. Compare this to conduction which acts on the surface and travels toward the center of the food slowly. For a time, vibrations continue after food is removed from the microwave. This continues to cook the food and must be taken into account when determining preparation time.

Cooking Methods

One of the first steps when learning how to prepare foods is to learn the proper cooking methods. Cooking methods can be divided into two categories, dry heat and moist heat. They are divided into these categories based on the type of heat used. Which method you use will depend on the desired end result.

In some instances, dry- and moist-heat cooking methods *elicit* (bring about) similar changes in foods. For example, both methods can cause protein to denature. **Denaturation** refers to the change in a protein's structure when heat, an alkali, or an acid is applied. The individual protein molecules found in muscle fibers (raw meat) are long strings of amino acids that form into folded shapes. The folds are held in place by bonds. When the protein is heated, the molecules vibrate violently. This causes the weakest bonds to separate and the protein to unfold. The denatured protein molecules then form new bonds, or **coagulate**, causing muscle fibers to change in length and width. This squeezes out moisture and the resulting food product is less liquid and more solid.

The proteins lose their shape and function due to these permanent changes. Denaturation happens quickly and is not visible to the human eye; however, you can observe coagulation. The more firm (well done) the meat is the more denatured it is.

An example of heat causing denaturation can be observed when cooking eggs. Raw egg white is clear and runny. When the egg white is heated, it becomes solid and turns white as it coagulates. This change in color and *viscosity* (resistance to flow, thickness) is due to the protein in the egg becoming denatured and then coagulating as it forms new bonds (**Figure 15.7**).

Dry-Heat Cooking Methods

Dry-heat cooking methods apply heat to foods in the absence of steam, broth, water, or other moisture. Instead, these cooking methods use air or fat to cook foods. Many dry-heat cooking methods expose foods to higher temperatures than other cooking processes.

Foods cooked using dry-heat methods develop a brown color, a crust, and a distinct aroma and flavor due to a chemical process known as the Maillard (pronounced my-YARD) reaction. The **Maillard reaction** occurs when heat is applied to foods containing both amino acids and sugars. It typically occurs when temperatures reach 285°F to 310°F (141°C to

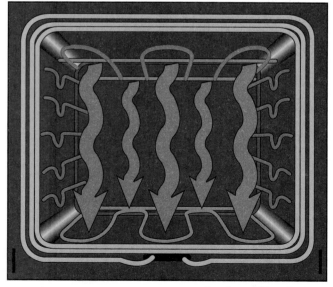

Goodheart-Willcox Publisher

Figure 15.6 The heating coils of a broiler give off waves of radiant heat energy.

Mini Lab: Observing Convection, Conduction, and Radiation

Coffee and Cream

Each student will need:

- a ceramic coffee mug
- approximately 6 ounces (180 mL) of HOT coffee
- 2 tablespoons (30 mL) of liquid creamer

1. Prepare black coffee as directed by your instructor.
2. Pour the HOT black coffee into a ceramic coffee mug.
3. Pour 2 tablespoons (30 mL) of liquid creamer on top of the hot coffee. Do not stir.
4. Observe the hot cup of coffee. When you add the creamer, you will be able to see convection currents as the creamer appears to rise and fall.
5. Place your hand above the coffee mug. You will be able to feel the warmth or heat from the hot air that is rising from the liquid. This is also an example of convection.
6. Touch the coffee cup. You can feel the warmth of the cup in your hand. This is conduction. The hot coffee inside the cup transfers heat to the particles in the cup, and the cup conducts the heat into your hand.
7. To experience radiation, place your hand near (not touching) the side of the coffee cup. You can feel the heat radiating from the cup to your hand. It is heat energy from the hot coffee being emitted.

Fotokostic/Shutterstock.com

Figure 15.7 Coagulation is easy to observe when frying eggs. Can you identify where coagulation has already occurred in this photo?

154°C). This reaction does not occur in foods that are cooked using moist-heat methods.

Browning that occurs when heat is applied to sugar is called **caramelization**. When carbohydrates are exposed to temperatures over 330°F (166°C), caramelization produces rich flavors and attractive browning. Although caramelization and Maillard reaction appear to produce many of the same changes in food, they are different processes. Maillard reaction involves the protein (amino acids) in food, whereas, caramelization involves the carbohydrate (sugars).

Dry-heat methods can be divided into two categories. The first category is food cooked without the addition of fat, such as broiling, grilling, roasting, baking, and griddling. The second category includes foods cooked with fat, such as sautéing, panfrying, stir-frying, shallow frying, and deep frying.

Broiling

There are two types of broiling. One occurs in an oven while the other takes place on a cooktop. Both are low-fat methods of cooking.

Panbroiling—performed on the cooktop—is a dry, high-heat cooking method, achieved without added fat. The heat is set to high, and the pan is placed on the cooktop to preheat. The pan is ready when a drop of water will evaporate the instant it hits the pan. The food is placed in the preheated pan and seared for about two to three minutes per side. Then, the heat is reduced and food is cooked until it reaches the desired temperature. Panbroiling is best for thin steaks, thin chops, and fish fillets.

Panbroiling is a quick and healthy cooking method. Panbroiling often results in bits of food stuck to the bottom of the pan after cooking is complete. These bits are called **fond**. (*Fond* is the French word for "bottom" or "basis.") These brown bits are loaded with flavor and are often used to make a sauce.

Broiling is performed in the oven using a direct heat source located above the food. The oven should maintain a constant temperature during broiling. Broiling is performed at temperatures between 425°F and 550°F (219°C and 288°C). This method works well on thinner cuts of meat, and tender fruits and vegetables (**Figure 15.8**).

To broil, place the oven rack about 3 to 4 inches from the broiler coil or flame. Be sure to use a **broiler pan** (steel slotted pan with stick-resistant finish) so that the grease and fat will drip away from the food. Preheat the broiler pan before placing food on it. This will sear the outside of the food, sealing in moisture and flavor. Flip the food over halfway through the cooking process to promote even cooking.

Grilling

Grilling is similar to broiling; however, the heat source is located below the food when grilling. To grill, food is either placed on a hot *gridiron* (open wire grid) or a *griddle* (flat plate) that is positioned over the heat source.

The high heat used for grilling sears the meat to seal in the flavors. Searing cooks the outside of the meat very quickly to create a thick, flavorful crust. Grilling is usually performed at

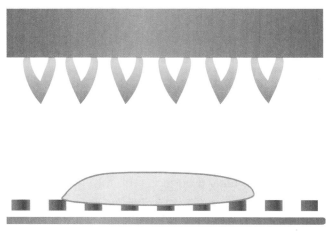

Goodheart-Willcox Publisher

Figure 15.8   Many ranges used in the home have only one temperature setting for broiling. You can control the rate of broiling by increasing or decreasing the distance of the food from the heat source.

temperatures between 425°F and 550°F (219°C and 288°C).

Heat the grill according to manufacturer's directions before adding your food. Foods like meat tend to stick to a cold grill. Grilled foods need to be turned once to ensure even cooking (**Figure 15.9**). Use tongs to turn the meat when grilling to avoid piercing the meat. This helps to prevent the loss of juices and flavor. Various wood chips can be added on top of charcoal to provide additional flavor. Popular choices include mesquite, hickory, pecan, apple, maple, and oak.

Foods that are grilled retain much of their vitamin and mineral content. This method is best for tender cuts of meat.

Goodheart-Willcox Publisher

Figure 15.9   The grate should be preheated before placing food on it. Placing food on a grate that is not hot will cause the food to stick to the grate.

Mini Lab: Amino Acids, Sugar, and Heat

Simulating the Maillard Reaction

The crust on bread, browned onions, and seared meats are all examples of the Maillard reaction. The Maillard reaction is responsible for the browning of foods as well as complex flavors.

High temperature cooking speeds up this reaction due to the high concentration of amino acids and sugars in some foods. The Maillard reaction takes place when both protein (amino acids) and carbohydrate (sugars) are present. When a food comes in direct contact with a hot surface, the water molecules on the surface of the food start to evaporate. Once all the moisture has evaporated, the exterior of the food becomes hot enough to trigger the Maillard reaction in just a few minutes. Many flavors and aromas are achieved when this occurs. This experiment will simulate the Maillard reaction. Each group will need:

- a small skillet
- small bowl
- wooden spoon
- 3 amino acid tablets or capsules (purchase at a health food store)
- 1 tablespoon (15 mL) of corn syrup

Instructions:

1. Crush 3 amino acid tablets to make a fine powder, or break open 3 capsules. (Tablets can be crushed by placing in a plastic bag and rolling over them with a rolling pin.) Pour into a small bowl. Create an observation sheet and write a description of the smell and color of the powder.

2. Preheat skillet over medium-high heat and add 1 tablespoon (15 mL) of corn syrup. Pour the amino acid powder on top of the corn syrup and mix with a wooden spoon.

3. Continue to stir until a light brown color is achieved. The color change is the result of protein molecules (amino acids) reacting with the sugar (corn syrup). Remove the skillet from the heat.

4. Smell the mixture and observe its color. Record your description of the aroma and color on the observation sheet.

Roasting and Baking

Roasting and baking are similar dry-heat cooking methods. The factor that sets the two methods apart is the structure of the food to be cooked. Roasting is performed on foods that have a solid structure before cooking, such as vegetables and meats. Baking involves food that will become solid once baked, such as breads and cakes. Both methods use hot, dry air and cook foods uncovered **(Figure 15.10)**.

Roasting is best for thicker, tender cuts of meat and poultry. Roasting is done in a preheated oven at temperatures between 300°F and 425°F (149°C and 219°C). Roasting involves cooking food in an uncovered pan in the oven. A roasting pan has low sides, which allows more of the oven's heat to make contact with the food. A rack is helpful to suspend food that contains a lot of fat. The fat is able to drip away from the food as it roasts. During roasting, hot air circulates around the meat, cooking all sides evenly, due to the exterior of the food being exposed to the same temperature.

Meat should rest for at least 10 to 20 minutes after it is removed from the oven. This allows

MSPhotographic/Shutterstock.com

Denise Torres/Shutterstock.com

Figure 15.10   Although the cooking methods used to prepare these dishes are similar, the beef is an example of roasting and the lasagna is an example of baking.

the juices to redistribute in the meat, causing it to become moist and tender. The term *pan roast* refers to searing the meat in a skillet, then placing it in the oven to cook.

Baking is virtually the same as roasting, but is the term used for foods that have less solid structure prior to cooking. It is performed at temperatures between 300°F and 425°F (149°C and 219°C). Baking surrounds food with hot air, causing foods to set (such as casseroles) or rise (like breads and muffins.) The hot air causes the sugars in the carbohydrates to caramelize, creating the desirable flavor and golden brown color.

Sautéing, Panfrying, and Deep Frying

Many people think that frying is a moist-heat cooking method because liquid (fat) is used, but it is not. Fat can take a liquid form, but it is the opposite of water. When cooking with oil or fat, you are using a dry-heat method of cooking.

Sautéing is a dry-heat cooking method that cooks food quickly, in a small amount of fat, over high heat. Sautéing is performed at temperatures between 320°F and 450°F (160°C and 232°C). Due to the quick method, foods do not lose their texture and stay crisp. They also produce a rich flavor (**Figure 15.11**).

To sauté, place a pan over medium to medium-high heat. Preheat the pan for about a minute before adding the fat. Only use enough oil or fat to coat the pan. Heat the fat or oil until it is close

to the smoke point. The **smoke point** is a specific temperature at which an oil breaks down and starts to produce a foul smell, bitter taste, or a small amount of smoke. Choose healthier fats, such as peanut or canola oil, which also have a higher smoke point.

When the fat or oil is hot enough, add the food. Stir and toss food to promote even browning and cooking. Food should be cut into uniform pieces. Place only one layer of food in the pan to avoid overcrowding. Overcrowding causes the temperature of the pan to drop. This hinders evaporation, creates steam, and causes the food to stick or become soggy. The unintended result is that the food steams or boils in its own juices.

Sweating is similar to sautéing, but is performed at a much lower temperature. The goal of this cooking method is to soften the food without caramelizing or browning it.

Another cooking method that is similar to sautéing is stir-frying. Unlike sautéing, **stir-frying** uses a very high heat source and

Goodheart-Willcox Publisher

Figure 15.11   Sautéing is performed in a preheated pan with a small amount of fat.

requires the food to be tossed, or moved about the pan, constantly. It is important to cut the food into small bite-sized pieces for fast, uniform cooking.

Typically, a lightly oiled wok is used when stir-frying. A **wok** is a bowl-shaped frying pan with a rounded bottom and deep, slanted sides. Stir-frying cooks the outside of the food quickly, adding a crisp texture and distinct flavor to various foods.

Panfrying and sautéing are very similar. The difference is that panfrying uses more fat than sautéing. Panfrying is performed at temperatures between 325°F and 375°F (163°C and 191°C). When panfrying, enough fat or oil is used to submerge the food nearly halfway (**Figure 15.12**). The goal of both panfrying and sautéing is to sear the food quickly. This keeps vitamin and water loss to a minimum, and improves flavor and color.

Panfrying browns the exterior while cooking the interior, which helps retain moisture. Typically, foods that are panfried are coated with batter, seasoned, or breaded. The result is a flavorful, crisp, brown crust. Panfrying is typically used for larger pieces of tender meats, poultry, or fish.

To panfry, use a skillet or pan with a flat bottom and straight sides. Choose an oil with a neutral flavor, such as peanut oil, or canola oil, and heat the pan to medium or medium-high heat. Make sure not to overcrowd the food so the pan and fat remain hot. For best results, turn only once while cooking. Turning too soon can cause the breading to stick to the pan or fall off.

Deep frying is another dry-heat cooking method that cooks food by submerging it in hot oil. This causes all surfaces of the food to cook at the same time. Temperatures usually range from 325°F to 375°F (163°C and 191°C). If the oil is too hot, it may smoke. If the oil is not hot enough, the oil will absorb into the food causing a greasy taste. When deep frying, cook in small batches to avoid cooling down the fat. Food items that are deep-fried are evenly browned and crispy. The food is finished cooking when it rises to the surface.

Moist-Heat Cooking Methods

Moist-heat cooking methods use steam, water, stock, or other liquids to transfer heat to the food. Moist heat is good for softening tough, fibrous foods, such as meat proteins, legumes, peas, cabbage, and whole grains.

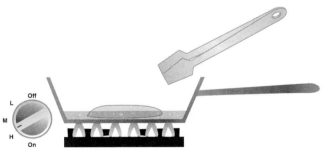

Goodheart-Willcox Publisher

Figure 15.12 Food must be turned during panfrying to ensure even cooking. What types of panfried foods have you eaten?

Learn About...

Rancidity

Rancidity is chemical damage that can occur in fats. Oxygen and light break down fats into fragments that are small and have a strong odor. These fragments provide the telltale smell of fat that has become rancid. Unsaturated fats become rancid quicker than saturated fats. Even though meat is high in saturated fat, it can still become rancid.

Food that is rancid will not necessarily make you sick, but it does not taste or smell pleasant.

Fat oxidation can be delayed by handling meat properly. To protect meat from oxidation, first wrap it in oxygen-impermeable plastic wrap, and then wrap it again in freezer paper or foil. Store the meat in the coldest, darkest part of the refrigerator or freezer.

Oils can be protected from becoming rancid by using proper storage. Oils should be stored in tightly sealed containers in a cool, dark place.

Know and Apply

1. List two factors that contribute to fat becoming rancid.

2. Why do you suppose meats are wrapped first in plastic wrap and again in foil or freezer paper?

Poaching, simmering, and boiling are three different stages of moist-heat cooking. All three involve submerging foods in a liquid, and are considered healthy because they do not use additional fat. The difference between each method is the temperature at which the food is cooked.

Poaching

Poaching refers to cooking food in liquid at a moderate temperature. This method employs the lowest temperature of all the moist-heat methods. The temperature of the liquid should be maintained between 160°F to 180°F (71°C to 82°C).

Poaching is a gentle cooking method that is ideal for cooking delicate foods, such as pears, eggs, and fish. Such foods would be damaged by the vigorous bubbles that accompany higher cooking temperatures. Additionally, the gentle temperature coagulates the proteins in foods without toughening them. The result is foods that are firm, moist, and tender. Poaching also conserves flavor and nutrients.

When small bubbles start to form at the bottom of the pot, gently slip the food into the liquid. If bubbles start to form, reduce the heat under the pot. Do not stir or agitate the food in the liquid (**Figure 15.13**).

Simmering

Simmering is a moist-heat cooking method that is often used for cooking vegetables, soups, stews, and tough meats. The liquid used for simmering is hotter than that used for poaching. Simmering is performed with temperatures ranging from 180°F to 205°F (82°C to 96°C).

Liquid used for simmering needs to remain at a constant temperature to cook foods evenly. This requires a little more attention than boiling. The liquid gives visual clues when it is in the appropriate temperature range for simmering.

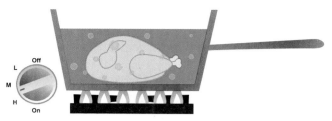

Goodheart-Willcox Publisher

Figure 15.14 Simmering is useful for breaking down connective tissues found in less tender cuts of meat.

You will see bubbles gently rise and break the surface (**Figure 15.14**).

Simmering results in less evaporation than boiling. It is also a slower, gentler cooking method than boiling. Simmered meats are moist and *fork-tender*. Fork-tender refers to meat that shows little resistance when cut with a fork. On the other hand, the same meat would be tough if it were boiled. The higher heat of boiling would cause the proteins in the meat to toughen. Although vitamins and minerals can leach into the cooking liquid, these nutrients can be recaptured if the liquid is used to make a sauce.

Boiling

Boiling employs hotter temperatures than both poaching and simmering. It is an aggressive cooking method, which makes it suitable for hard, dry foods, such as whole grains, beans, and pasta. Boiling liquid reaches temperatures at or above 212°F (100°C). After the water has reached a full boil, gently place your food in the heated liquid to fully cook it for the desired length of time (**Figure 15.15**).

Boiling develops big bubbles, which cause violent agitation of the food being cooked. When liquid achieves a rolling boil, the food is kept

Goodheart-Willcox Publisher

Figure 15.13 Foods are often poached in flavored liquids to add interest to the dish. What liquids would you use for poaching?

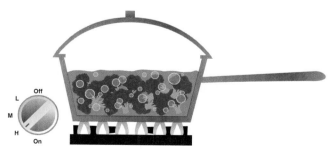

Goodheart-Willcox Publisher

Figure 15.15 Boiling should not be used to cook protein foods. Boiling makes protein foods tough.

in constant motion. This prevents food from sticking together or to the pan, and it cooks the food quickly. Boiling kills most bacteria in food, which is another benefit.

Blanching is a technique that employs boiling. To blanch, place the food into the boiling liquid for approximately one to two minutes. The food is removed from the boiling water and placed in an ice bath. The ice bath stops the cooking process.

Blanching is used to loosen the skin on vegetables and some fruits for easy removal. It also helps stop the enzymatic action that causes foods to deteriorate. Many people blanch foods prior to freezing to maintain freshness and color during storage.

Steaming

When water exceeds the boiling point [212°F (100°C)], water turns into steam. **Steaming** is another moist-heat method. It is gentler than boiling and good for delicate foods, such as vegetables, fish, or seafood (**Figure 15.16**). Because steaming cooks quickly and the food is not sitting in liquid, fewer nutrients are lost than with other methods. It also retains the shape and color of the food.

To steam, water is added to a pot. The water is brought to a boil and a steamer tray is placed in the pot. A steamer tray is a perforated device on which food is placed. The holes in the tray allow steam to circulate around the food. There are also feet on the base to allow the food to sit above the boiling liquid. Food is placed on the tray. The pot is covered to capture the steam so that it surrounds the food. The food is steamed just until tender.

En papillote, is a French cooking technique that uses a pouch made of parchment paper to steam meats, seafood, vegetables, and herbs. This method helps to seal in vitamins, minerals, and flavors (**Figure 15.17**).

Pressure Cooking

A **pressure cooker** is a specialized saucepan or portable kitchen appliance that uses steam and pressure to increase temperatures above the boiling point. It is a sealed pot with a valve that controls the pressure of the heat inside. As the pot is heated, the liquid inside forms steam. Because the steam cannot escape, the pressure inside the pot rises. The increased pressure results in temperatures as high as 250°F (121°C).

The high pressure causes the moisture to penetrate the food, which cooks the food quickly. Typically, cooking times can be reduced to one-third the time of other cooking methods. Foods cooked in pressure cookers also retain more nutrient content than foods cooked with other methods.

Pressure cookers can be dangerous if not handled in the correct way. Failure to release the pressure in the right manner can result in

Goodheart-Willcox Publisher

Figure 15.16 Steaming uses convection to transfer heat from steam to the food being prepared. How do you think steaming food uncovered might affect the cooking process?

Andrey Smirnov/Shutterstock.com

Figure 15.17 En papillote is a cooking technique which encloses food in a pouch made of parchment paper to capture steam. Herbs, vegetables, butter, and sauces are often included to add flavor.

baloon111/Shutterstock.com

Figure 15.18 This pressure cooker must be used on a cooktop, but electric pressure cookers need not.

travellight/Shutterstock.com

Figure 15.19 The hallmarks of braised dishes are moist, tender meat and flavorful sauces.

an explosion or sudden release of hot liquid and scalding steam (**Figure 15.18**).

Combination Cooking Methods

Braising, stewing, and sous vide (pronounced soo VEED) are considered combination cooking methods because more than one method is used to prepare the food.

Braising

Braising is a popular method for large, tougher cuts of meat. It can make an inexpensive cut of meat that is normally tough and chewy, very soft and tender. **Braising** is achieved by using a dry-heat cooking method to sear the meat, followed by a moist-heat cooking method such as simmering. The searing creates rich flavor and brown color. Then, the simmering cooks and tenderizes the meat (**Figure 15.19**).

To braise, first the meat is seared just long enough to achieve the desired color. Next, it is placed in a pot with liquid. The amount of liquid should be enough to cover about one-third to one-half of the meat. The pot is covered to trap the moisture and the food is simmered until tender. Braising can be performed either on a cooktop or in an oven. This method can also be used on poultry and vegetables.

Stewing

Stewing is similar to braising, except for the size of the food being cooked and the amount of liquid used. **Stewing** uses a dry-heat method to sear small pieces of food, which are then cooked using a moist-heat method until tender. Both braising and stewing tenderize the meat and develop nice, rich flavors. The only difference between the two is that stewing uses smaller pieces of meat, and the meat is completely immersed in a liquid. Once the meat is cooked and tender, the liquid can be thickened to create a sauce. The liquid from both braising and stewing contains many of the nutrients that the food loses during cooking. When the liquid is made into sauce, those nutrients are preserved.

Sous Vide Cooking

A third type of combination cooking is called **sous vide** which is French for "under vacuum" (**Figure 15.20**). This is a method of cooking in which food is vacuum sealed in an airtight plastic bag, and then placed in a water bath to heat the food thoroughly. The idea is to cook the item evenly, making sure that the

Guisina/Shutterstock.com

Kondo83/Shutterstock.com

Figure 15.20   In sous vide cooking, the food is (A) vacuum-sealed in plastic, and then placed in a (B) hot water bath to cook. The result is tender, flavorful food.

interior and exterior of the food are properly cooked while retaining moisture, juices, and flavor. Often foods cooked using the sous vide technique need to be browned before or after cooking. This can be accomplished by either grilling or searing. The browning method is done briefly, to avoid overcooking the interior.

Exploring Careers

Farm and Ranch Managers

Farm and ranch managers are responsible for the day to day operations of managing crops, pastures, or animals.

Farm managers oversee the planting, growing, fertilizing, cultivation, spraying, and harvesting of crops. Additional duties include monitoring crops to make sure they are free from insect infestation and disease, and sanitizing and cleaning equipment. They also need to be knowledgeable about current market conditions, available federal programs, irrigation, soil, and weather.

Ranch managers are responsible for monitoring grazing land, feeding animals, maintaining fences, and arranging sales of animals. Additional duties may include breeding, branding, vaccinating, administering medicines, and ensuring animals have water. Ranch managers separate sick animals, assist in birthing, and control the spread of disease and parasites. They need to be knowledgeable about weather conditions, feed prices, and the market value of animals.

Both farm and ranch managers need to have knowledge about farm equipment, financial operations, business management, and computer technology. They also need to understand all aspects of running a business, such as hiring, training, and supervising of employees. Skills required are a strong work ethic, problem solving, decision making, prioritizing, and the ability to organize. Farming and ranching is a year-round job, you rarely get time off and must be available 24 hours a day. Working outside in adverse weather conditions is a must.

Several years of work-related experience is needed. A degree is not required, but most have a bachelor's degree in agriculture and may specialize in ranch operations or agribusiness. College classes include nutritional needs of animals and nutritional retention of crops.

Chapter 15 Review and Expand

Summary

Cooking changes food chemically and physically resulting in food that tastes better and is easier to digest. Cooking also makes food safer to eat. All cooking methods apply heat to food, but they differ in how the heat is applied.

There are three ways in which heat can be transferred to food during cooking. Heat transfer happens through conduction, convection, or radiation. Dry- and moist-heat cooking use a variety of these methods. People choose a cooking method based on the desired outcome, the available resources, and their training and skill level.

Dry-heat cooking prepares food in the absence of moisture. The heat source may be located either directly above or below the food. Dry heat adds flavor, aroma, browning, and crust to foods without added fat. Moist-heat cooking uses steam, water, stock, or other liquids to tenderize tough foods. Combination methods employ both dry- and moist-heat cooking methods.

Vocabulary Activities

1. **Content Terms**   Select three terms from the list of terms that follow. Explain how these three terms are related to each other. Create a graphic organizer or write a paragraph to explain or illustrate how the terms relate.

conduction	sautéing
convection	smoke point
natural convection	sweating
mechanical convection	stir-frying
radiation	wok
infrared radiation	panfrying
microwave radiation	deep frying
denaturation	poaching
coagulate	simmering
Maillard reaction	boiling
caramelization	blanching
fond	steaming
broiling	en papillote
broiler pan	pressure cooker
grilling	braising
roasting	stewing
baking	sous vide

2. **Academic Terms**   Using a dictionary, look up each of the following terms. Which terms have additional meanings that vary from the definitions given in the chapter?

inherent	elicit
emit	viscosity

Review

Write your answers using complete sentences when appropriate.

3. Explain conduction.
4. Name three dry-heat cooking methods and three moist-heat cooking methods.
5. Describe the characteristics that occur in the Maillard reaction and caramelization.
6. Which cooking method are you using when cooking over a direct heat source?
7. Which cooking method are you using when the heat source is from above?
8. List the differences between roasting and baking.
9. Explain the differences between panfrying and sautéing.
10. Describe what water looks like when boiling in comparison to simmering.
11. What is sous vide?

Core Skills

12. **Reading, Writing**   Choose one type of meat or vegetable. Search cookbooks and websites to find four recipes for the meat or vegetable you chose. Each recipe should use a different cooking method. Select two recipes that use dry-heat cooking methods and two recipes that use moist-heat cooking methods. Write a short description of the final product for each recipe based on your understanding of the various cooking methods.

13. **Research, Reading, Speaking**   Investigate heat transfer and the conductivity of different materials used for cookware and bakeware. Incorporate what you learn into a class discussion on the advantages and disadvantages of various materials for cookware and bakeware applications.

Chapter 15 Review and Expand

14. **Science, Research, Technology**   Investigate the pros and cons of induction cooking. Induction cooking heats food by magnetic induction, instead of heat from a flame or heating element. The magnets heat the pan directly, causing the temperature to rise. In order for this type of pot or pan to work, it must be made of a certain type of metal, such as stainless steel or cast iron. Certain types of cookware would not work on this cooktop because nonmagnetic cookware like copper, glass, and aluminum will not interact with the magnetic force. With this in mind, list some pros and cons of induction cooktops.

15. **Math**   Foods cooked in a convection oven cook 25% to 30% faster than foods cooked in a conventional oven. Therefore, cook times based on conventional oven use must be adjusted when using a convection oven. Cook times should be reduced by 25% to 30%. For example, if a recipe says to bake a loaf of bread for an hour and a half (90 minutes), you would adjust the cooking time with the following calculation: $90 - (0.25)90 = 67.5$ minutes or 1 hour and 8 minutes (rounded up). Therefore, you would bake the bread for 1 hour and 8 minutes. Calculate the time you would bake muffins, using this same formula. The muffin recipe says to bake them for 40 minutes. How long would you bake them if you were using 25% less time? What about 30% less time?

16. **Science, Technology, Writing**   Observe heat transfer in action. Heat water until it reaches the boiling point. Place macaroni noodles or red pepper flakes in the boiling water. Observe the effect that is taking place. Is this an example of conduction, convection, radiation, or a combination of methods? Write a lab procedure describing your experiment and your observations.

17. **Science, Technology, Writing**   Use print or online resources to research the greenhouse effect. Explain how conduction, convection, and radiation are used to create this effect. Draw a diagram depicting the greenhouse effect.

18. **Career Readiness Practice**   The director of the food pantry at which you volunteer has asked you to demonstrate a cooking method at the monthly cooking class for clients. The focus should be a healthy cooking method that can be used on low-cost ingredients. She said the food pantry will supply your ingredients. Think about the following as you prepare your demonstration and present it to your classmates:

- What type of cooking equipment do most clients have in their homes?
- What type of cooking equipment is available for your use during the presentation?
- Which healthy, low-cost food will you use for your presentation?
- Which cooking method is healthy and effective with the food you have chosen to prepare?
- How much time does it take to execute this cooking method?
- What food preparation, if any, should you do in advance?

Critical Thinking and Problem Solving

19. **Analyze**   Cook eggs using three different heat methods. Explain the three types of heat transfer used in each method. Make poached eggs, shirred eggs, and fried eggs. Compare the outcomes in each method used. Describe aroma, taste, and visual differences.

20. **Analyze**   Investigate and profile various types of outdoor grills. Assess the features, benefits, and characteristics of each. How do the manufacturers encourage consumers to choose their brand over similar products on the market? List the price points, advantages and disadvantages of each, as well as the materials used to construct them. Grills you may want to investigate are gas, charcoal, electric grills, and Kamado grills.

Chapter 16
Grain Foods

stockcreations/Shutterstock.com

Content Terms

cereal	gluten
kernel	pasta
bran	enriched
endosperm	starch
germ	gelatinization
whole grain	syneresis
refined	al dente

Academic Terms

meal	opaque
elasticity	insoluble
translucent	

Objectives

After studying this chapter, you will be able to

- **list** a variety of cereal products;
- **recall** nutrients found in cereal products;
- **describe** how heat and liquids affect starches; and
- **prepare** cooked breakfast cereals, rice, and pasta.

Reading Prep

After reading each section (separated by main headings), stop and write a three- to four-sentence summary of what you just read. Be sure to paraphrase and use your own words.

Cereals are major staple foods for people throughout the world. This is because they are easy to grow and store. They are also low in cost and have high energy value.

In recent years, the variety of cereal products on supermarket shelves has been increasing. Foods that were once found only in distant lands are making their way around the globe. People are interested in new taste experiences from other cultures. The nutritional value of some of these grain products also adds to their appeal (**Figure 16.1**).

Types of Cereal Products

Cereals are starchy grains that are suitable to use as food. Corn, wheat, rice, oats, barley, and rye are the cereals most often used as food in the United States. They are used to make a wide variety of products, including breakfast foods, flours, *meals* (grain ground into a powder), breads, pasta products, and starches.

Grain Structure

Grains differ in size and shape, but they all have kernels with similar structures. A **kernel** is a whole seed of a cereal. It has three parts: the bran, the endosperm, and the germ.

The **bran** is the outer protective covering of the kernel. It is a good source of vitamins and dietary fiber.

The **endosperm** makes up the largest part of the kernel. It contains most of the starch and the protein of the kernel, but few minerals and little fiber. It holds the food supply the plant uses to grow.

The **germ** is the reproductive part of the plant. It is rich in vitamins, minerals, protein, and fat. It makes up the smallest part of the kernel (**Figure 16.2**).

Whole-grain cereal products contain all three parts of the kernel. **Refined** products have had the bran and germ, along with the nutrients they provide, removed during processing.

Breakfast Foods

Corn, rice, wheat, and oats are made into popular breakfast foods. Breakfast foods can be made from whole grain, enriched refined grain, or a combination of both. They can be presweetened or unsweetened. Some have added ingredients, such as raisins or nuts.

Cereals may be ready-to-eat, or they may require some amount of cooking. *Ready-to-eat*

marekuliasz/Shutterstock.com

Figure 16.1 Cereal products from around the world offer a variety of tastes and nutritional values. What cereal products from different countries have you tried?

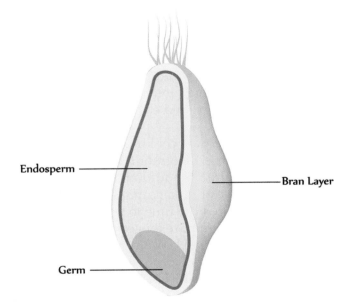

Tefi/Shutterstock.com

Figure 16.2 Each part of a kernel of grain contains different nutrients.

Exploring Careers

Grain Inspector

Grain inspectors collect and assess samples of grains, especially grains that are being exported. They check to see how the samples measure up to specific standards. They test for diseases, infestations, and chemical residues. Then they may issue quality grades based on their evaluations. Inspectors prepare written reports of their findings. They may also guide grain producers to take corrective measures when needed to improve grain quality.

To be successful, grain inspectors must have good communication skills. They should know how to ask the right questions and listen to the answers. They must be able to work independently. Grain inspectors need to be good time managers as they schedule inspection visits at various locations. They also need good analytical skills when looking at test results and making grade assessments.

A grain inspector needs a two-year degree in agriculture. Past farming knowledge and experience is also a plus.

cereals may be puffed, shredded, flaked, granulated, rolled, or formed into shapes. You can pour them into a bowl and eat them without any preparation.

Cereals that require cooking are available in cracked, crushed, granular, and flaked forms. They require the addition of liquid and heat. *Quick-cooking* or *instant cereals* are partially cooked and require little time to prepare. *Raw* or *old-fashioned cereals* require longer cooking times.

Oatmeal is an example of a breakfast food that is available in a variety of forms. *Instant oatmeal* is made simply by pouring hot water over the cereal and giving it a stir. *Quick oats* can be made on the range top with just one minute of cooking. *Old-fashioned oats* take a bit longer, about five

minutes. All three of these products have a flaked texture. However, the flakes in instant and quick oats are cut into small pieces. Therefore, these forms of cooked cereal have a softer texture. A bowl of old-fashioned oats, on the other hand, will have firmer, more distinct cereal grains. *Steel-cut oats* are husked oat kernels that are chopped into pieces. They require 20 to 30 minutes of cooking time and have a firmer, nuggetlike texture (**Figure 16.3**).

Flour

Flour is a finely ground powder made from a plant food. It is the main ingredient in bread products and baked goods. Most flour is made from grain, but a number of other foods are also ground into flour.

Wheat Flours

Any grain can be made into flour. Most consumers use wheat flours for baking because the gluten in wheat flours is superior. **Gluten** is a protein that gives strength and *elasticity* (the ability to yield to pressure and return to original shape) to batters and doughs and structure to baked products.

You can buy many kinds of wheat flour. *All-purpose flour* is popular because it is good for so many uses. It is made from the milled, sifted endosperm of different varieties of wheat. All-purpose flour is available *bleached* and *unbleached*. Bleached flour is whiter than unbleached, but there is no nutritional difference between the two.

All-purpose flour contains about 10 to 12 percent protein, which can be used for most general cooking and baking. People who do a lot of specialized baking, however, may want to keep some other types of flour on hand. The main difference among other flours is their protein content, which depends on the kinds of wheat from which the flours are made. Higher protein content means greater gluten strength. The amount of gluten that is desirable differs among baked products.

Bread flour contains 12 to 14 percent protein. It is listed in some bread recipes to create loaves with a chewier structure. It is also required in many recipes designed for bread machines.

Pastry flour has 8 to 10 percent protein. It is a good choice for making tender baked goods,

Weerameth/Shutterstock.com

David P. Smith/Shutterstock.com

Figure 16.3   Instant oats (A) undergo more processing than steel-cut oats (B). Which form of oats do you think retains more nutrients?

such as pie crust as well as quick breads and cookies (**Figure 16.4**).

Cake flour has only about 6 to 8 percent protein. People use it for making cakes and other baked products with delicate textures.

Instant or *quick-mixing flour* is all-purpose flour that has been specially treated to blend easily with liquids without forming lumps. People use it to make gravies and sauces.

littleny/Shutterstock.com

Figure 16.4   Quick breads, like these scones, often use pastry flour. Some quick breads use whole-wheat pastry flour. What other baked goods might require pastry flour?

Self-rising flour is all-purpose flour with added leavening agents and salt. You will need to adjust the amounts of these ingredients in your recipe when using self-rising flour in place of all-purpose flour.

Whole-wheat flour is made by milling the entire wheat kernel so it contains the bran, germ, and endosperm. Whole-wheat flour is higher in protein, fiber, and many minerals than all-purpose flour. It gives baked products a nutlike flavor and coarser texture than does all-purpose flour.

White whole-wheat flour is also made from the entire wheat kernel, though it is made from a different type of wheat than traditional whole-wheat flour. This gives it a lighter color and milder flavor while retaining the nutritional benefits of whole grain.

Semolina flour is made from a hard variety of wheat called durum wheat. This type of flour is used to make pasta.

Nonwheat Flours

A growing number of nonwheat flours are appearing on supermarket shelves. Cooks choose to use some of these flours for the specific flavors and textures they give foods. Other nonwheat flours are commonly used because they provide alternatives for people who need to avoid gluten. Some of these flours may be found in the health foods section of the supermarket rather than in the baking aisle.

Corn flour is a gluten-free flour made from ground yellow corn. *Masa harina* is made from a different variety of corn that has been specially treated. It is an ingredient in tortillas and other Mexican dishes.

Rice flour is made by milling white rice. It is a white, starchy flour that is popular in Asia and the Far East.

Rye and *pumpernickel flours* are made from ground rye. Both are popular for making breads. Pumpernickel flour is whole grain and produces a darker, coarser loaf. Rye flour may have some or all of the bran and germ removed and produces a lighter loaf.

Many nonwheat flours are made from foods other than grain. *Almond flour* and *coconut flour* are among the flours made from nuts. *Potato flour* is made from cooked potatoes that have been dried and ground. *Soy flour,* which is made from ground soybeans, is one of many flours made from legumes. Even fruits like bananas and plantains are used to make flour.

The flours described here are just a sample of the various types of flour you might find on supermarket shelves. In addition, many other types of flour are available from specialty food stores and online retailers.

Rice

Like other grain foods, the number of varieties of rice on store shelves has been expanding. In the past, when consumers thought of rice, they usually thought of *white rice.* This is the white, starchy endosperm of the rice kernel. With all the options available today, many meal managers keep an array of rice products in their pantries.

Rice can be classified according to grain length. *Long-grain rice* is dry and fluffy when cooked. Many people use it as a side dish. *Jasmine rice* and *basmati rice* are fragrant long-grain varieties. Jasmine rice is often used in Thai and other Southeast Asian cuisines. Basmati rice is commonly found in Indian and Middle Eastern dishes (**Figure 16.5**). *Short-grain rice* is small and sticky when cooked. People often use it in puddings, croquettes, and sushi. *Arborio rice* is a variety of short-grain rice that is used in Italian rice dishes called *risottos.*

Rice is available in a range of colors—brown, black (also known as *purple*), and red. These colorful rice varieties are whole grains that

contain the bran and germ as well as the endosperm. They get their colors as well as many of their nutrients from the bran layer. Whole-grain rice is higher in fiber and in many minerals, compared to white rice.

Parboiled or *converted rice* has been steeped in warm water, drained, steamed, and dried. Parboiling improves the nutritive value and keeping quality of milled rice.

Precooked or *instant rice* has been cooked, rinsed, and dried by a special process before packaging. You can prepare it in a matter of minutes.

Wild rice is not really rice. It is the seed of a grass that grows in the marshes of Minnesota and Canada. It has an appealing, nutlike flavor and is more costly than white rice.

Pasta

Pasta is a dough that may or may not be dried. Macaroni, noodles, and spaghetti are all pastas. Pasta dough is made from *semolina,* which is produced from durum wheat. *Durum wheat* is specially grown for pasta making. It gives pasta products a nutty flavor and firm shape. Noodles are made by adding egg to the pasta dough.

Pasta comes in many shapes and sizes. Commercially, pasta is made by machine. Some

highviews/Shutterstock.com

Figure 16.5   Indian recipes, such as for this biryani dish, often require basmati rice.

people, however, enjoy making homemade pasta either by hand or with a pasta-making appliance (**Figure 16.6**).

Other Grain Products

Cereals are used to make a variety of other products. *Cornmeal* is made from ground white or yellow corn, which is often enriched. It is used to make cornbread, polenta, and a number of other foods.

A

B

Figure 16.6 Pasta can be prepared at home by hand or using a pasta maker.

Hominy, a popular food in the South, is corn minus the hull and germ. When broken into pieces, it is called *hominy grits*.

Cornstarch is the refined starch obtained from the endosperm of corn. People use it as a thickening agent in cooking.

Pearl barley is the whole barley grain minus the hull. It is high in minerals, and people often use it in soups.

Bulgur wheat is whole wheat that has been cooked, dried, partly debranned, and cracked. It is a popular Middle Eastern side dish.

Wheat germ is the germ portion of the wheat kernel separated during milling. Wheat germ is high in vitamins and minerals. You can add it to foods for flavor and nutrition.

Farina is a wheat product made by grinding and sifting wheat that has had the bran and most of the germ removed. People use farina as a thickener and as a cooked breakfast cereal. Cream of Wheat® is a popular brand of farina.

Couscous is granules of precooked, dried semolina, which is the same wheat product used to make pasta. Couscous cooks quickly, so it is a convenient choice for meal managers on a tight schedule. You can use it as a side dish or as a base to top with stews or stir-fried dishes.

Health and Wellness

Choosing Whole Grains

Choosing a variety of cereal products will give you the greatest nutritional value. At least half of your grain food choices should list a whole grain first on the ingredient list. Look for the word *whole* beside any type of grain listed. Brown rice, graham flour, oatmeal, and wild rice are also whole-grain ingredients. Be aware that products labeled *multigrain, stone-ground, 100% wheat,* and *cracked wheat* may not be whole-grain foods. The ingredient list can also help you avoid added sugars in the grain products you choose.

Learn About...
Ancient Grains

The term *ancient grains* does not have a formal definition. However, it generally refers to grains that have remained unchanged by modern plant technology for hundreds of years. Although these grains have existed for centuries, they are experiencing renewed popularity. Many people are drawn to the history and culture associated with these grains. Others are attracted to the taste and texture they add to meals.

Ancient grains offer appealing nutritional profiles. They are high in protein and fiber and rich in minerals, making them an excellent choice in vegetarian diets. Many ancient grains are also gluten free. Like other whole grains, they can be used in breakfast dishes and desserts as well as in soups, casseroles, and side dishes.

A number of ancient grains are turning up on restaurant menus and grocery store shelves. Among them, look for quinoa, amaranth, teff, millet, and sorghum.

Quinoa and amaranth are not true grains. However, they have nutrient, cooking, and flavor characteristics that are similar to grain. In addition to being tasty on its own, *quinoa* can add texture and protein to everything from smoothies to chili. *Amaranth* makes a good substitute for small pasta shapes like orzo and pastina.

Teff is used in Ethiopian cuisine to make a traditional flatbread. It has tiny grains and can be added to breads or cooked like porridge.

Millet has long been grown in India and other parts of Asia. Until recently, millet has mainly been used in the United States as birdseed. Now it is being used in breakfast cereals and side dishes as well as being popped and enjoyed as a snack like popcorn.

Sorghum is a staple grain in parts of Africa, where it can withstand the lack of rain. In the United States, sorghum has commonly been used to feed livestock. However, it is growing in popularity as a replacement for wheat flour in baking.

Know and Apply

1. How does the use of ancient grains in the United States compare with the use of these grains in other parts of the world?

2. What ancient grains are you aware of aside from those discussed here?

Nutritional Value of Cereal Products

Cereal products are in the grains group of MyPlate. Most teens should eat 6 to 10 ounce-equivalents of grain foods each day. One cup (250 mL) ready-to-eat cereal and ½ cup (125 mL) cooked cereal, rice, or pasta each count as 1 ounce-equivalent.

Whole grains provide protein, complex carbohydrates, fiber, B vitamins, iron, magnesium, and selenium (**Figure 16.7**). Federal law requires many refined grain products, including white flour, white rice, pasta, and cereals, to be enriched. **Enriched** products have added nutrients to replace those lost due to processing. Enriched cereals contain added thiamin, niacin, riboflavin, folic acid, and iron.

Fat, sodium, and sugar are added to many breakfast cereals and rice and pasta mixes. Use the Nutrition Facts panel to help you choose products that are lower in these components. The Nutrition Facts panel can also help you choose products that are higher in fiber.

Selecting and Storing Cereal Products

Cereal products are nutritious, economical, and versatile enough to serve at any meal. You

Ami Parikh/Shutterstock.com

Figure 16.7 Whole grains (bottom row) contain more needed nutrients than processed grains (top row). How can you tell whether a grain product is made from whole grain?

can store them for extended periods without refrigeration. Therefore, you will want to keep a variety of cereal products on hand at all times.

Cost of Cereal Products

Cereal products are generally inexpensive, but costs vary according to the type of item. Convenience products and products with added ingredients tend to cost more. Organic and ancient grain products are more costly to produce, so they are likely to have higher prices, too.

Breakfast foods can be costly or economical. Ready-to-eat cereals are more expensive than those that require cooking. Presweetened cereals and cereals with added ingredients cost more than plain cereals. Small boxes often cost more per unit of weight than large boxes. Single-serving boxes cost the most per serving.

All-purpose flour is generally the least expensive type of flour. Specialty flours, such as cake flour, instant flour, and nonwheat flours, are usually higher in price.

Most pasta products, regardless of shape or size, are low in cost. Fresh-made, gourmet pastas are more expensive. Packaged pasta dishes with special sauces and seasonings also cost more.

Long-grain and short-grain rice are the lowest priced rice products. The convenience of converted or instant rice adds to the cost. Wild rice, specialty rice varieties, and seasoned rice mixes also carry higher prices.

Storing Cereal Products

Store flours, breakfast foods, pasta products, and rice in tightly covered containers in a cool, dry place (**Figure 16.8**). Grain products stored uncovered will attract dust and insects. Some may also pick up moisture, which will cause them to lose their characteristic texture. Breakfast foods will keep well for two to three months. Brown and wild rice will keep for six months. White rice and pasta will keep for a year.

Cooking Starches

Starch is a complex carbohydrate stored in plants. Cereal grains contain plant cells that are the sources of starch granules. Wheat flour, cornstarch, and tapioca are starches commonly used in cooking.

villorejo/Shutterstock.com

Figure 16.8 Storing grain products in tightly covered containers will help prevent them from attracting dust or insects. What are some other advantages of storing grain products in tightly covered containers?

(*Tapioca* is not a grain product. It is the starch from cassava, the edible root of a tropical plant.)

Uses of Starch

Cooks use starches primarily as thickening agents. Mixtures thickened with cornstarch or tapioca are *translucent* (see-through), whereas mixtures thickened with flour are *opaque* (not clear). Therefore, cooks use flour to thicken gravies and unsweetened sauces. They use cornstarch and tapioca to thicken puddings and sweet sauces. They also use cornstarch and tapioca to thicken unsweetened sauces in which they want a translucent appearance.

Food Science

Factors Affecting Starch-Thickened Mixtures

The temperature, time, agitation, and mixing method used when cooking with starch can all affect the outcome of the mixture. These factors must be controlled during cooking.

The *temperature* used to cook starch mixtures must be warm enough to make the starch molecules swell uniformly (the same amount). It should not be so hot that it causes uneven swelling or lumping. When lumping occurs, the molecules in the middle of the lump do not swell. They stay small and dry. Cooking starch mixtures in a double boiler or in a heavy pan over moderate heat will help prevent lumping.

The *time* needed for gelatinization to be completed depends on the kind of starch and the cooking temperature. Once gelatinization occurs, cook the starch mixture for a short time longer to thoroughly cook the starch. This will prevent a raw starch flavor in the finished product.

The amount of *agitation* a starch mixture receives can affect its texture. Gentle stirring during cooking will help keep the starch mixture smooth. If you stir the mixture too rapidly or for too long a time, the starch granules may rupture (break down). As a result, the cooked starch mixture will be thinner.

A recipe will usually tell you which *mixing method* to use when adding starch to a hot liquid. If you add starch directly to a hot liquid, the starch granules usually will lump. To prevent lumping, you must separate the starch granules from one another before you add them to the hot liquid. You can separate starch granules by using one of three techniques:

- coating with fat
- combining with sugar
- mixing with a cold liquid to form a paste

Food Science Principles of Cooking Starches

Starches differ in chemical structure and composition. Thus, different starches behave differently. Some starch mixtures form gels; others do not. Some starches form firm gels; others form weak gels. Some cooked starch mixtures are clear; some are semiclear; others are opaque.

Granular starch is completely *insoluble* (unable to dissolve) in cold water. The granules need heat to become soluble. Both dry and moist heat affect starch.

Dry heat causes starch to become slightly soluble and to lose some of its thickening power. This is why gravy made from browned flour is thinner than gravy made from unbrowned flour. Dry heat also causes color and flavor changes. The effect of dry heat on starch causes the browned crust and toasty flavor of baked goods, grilled bread, and some cereals.

Mixing starch granules with water and heating them causes them to become soluble. They absorb water and swell. As starch granules swell, the starch mixture thickens. As heating continues, the starch mixture becomes thicker until it reaches a maximum thickness. This process is called **gelatinization**. It is basic to cooking all starches (**Figure 16.9**).

During cooling, bonds form between the starch molecules. Because of this bonding, most starch mixtures form gels. The spaces of the gel network hold water. If you cut the gel, or if it stands too long, water may leak out. This is called **syneresis**. You may have seen this leakage in a lemon pie filling.

Cooking Cereal Products

The relative low cost and high energy value of cereals make them an important part of the diet. Cereals are popular as breakfast foods. However, you can serve a variety of cereal products at meals throughout the day.

Figure 16.9 The gelatinization of starch is important for thickening products such as gravy and pudding.

Principles of Cooking Cereal Products

Cereal products contain large amounts of starch. Therefore, the principles used in cooking starches also apply to cooking cereal products. Cooking improves both palatability and digestibility of cereal products.

During cooking, the starch granules in cereal products absorb water and swell, causing the products to increase in volume. This swelling causes rice and dried pasta products to soften. It causes cereals to become thicker until they reach a point of maximum thickness (gelatinization).

When cooking cereal products, you must use enough water to permit the starch granules to swell. The amount of water needed will vary depending on the product. You can find correct proportions of cereal products to water along with cooking times on cereal, rice, and pasta packages.

Preparing Cooked Breakfast Cereals

To prepare cooked cereal, bring the recommended amount of water to a boil. The size of the cereal particles and whether the bran layer is present determine the amount of cooking water needed. Whole-grain cereals will cook more quickly if you first soak them to soften the bran. (If you do not soften the bran, it can block the passage of water into the center of the kernel and delay swelling.) If you soak a whole-grain cereal, you should cook it in the soaking liquid, adding more water, if needed.

All the cereal particles must have equal contact with the water and heat so the starch granules can swell uniformly. To prevent lumping, slowly add dry cereal to the boiling water. Wetting the cereal with cold water before adding it to the boiling water will also prevent lumping.

Gently stir the cereal with a fork when you are adding it to the boiling water. This preliminary stirring helps separate the cereal particles and prevent lumping. Stirring throughout the remaining cooking time should be gentle and minimal. Too much stirring will break up the cereal particles, and the cooked product will be gummy.

Cook the cereal until it thickens and absorbs all the water (**Figure 16.10**). Low to moderate heat is best, as temperatures that are too hot can cause lumping and scorching. Like starch mixtures, cereals should be cooked for a short time after gelatinization is complete to prevent a raw starch flavor.

R.legosyn/Shutterstock.com   schankz/Shutterstock.com

Figure 16.10 During cooking, this barley has absorbed all the water. What other liquids could you use to cook barley?

Cooking time will vary depending on the type of cereal and cooking method. Cereals that are finely granulated or precooked will cook faster than cracked or whole-grain cereals. Cereal cooked over direct heat will take less time to cook than cereal prepared in a double boiler.

Cooked cereals should be free of lumps. (Flaked cereals should contain separate and distinct flakes.) Cooked cereals should be thick, but they should flow when poured into a serving bowl.

Preparing Rice

When cooking rice, the goal is to obtain tender kernels that hold their shape. Properly cooked rice is tender and fluffy. The rice kernels should not stick together and form a gummy mass.

Rice may be cooked over direct heat, in a double boiler, or in the oven. The proportion of water to rice varies somewhat. As a rule, white rice requires about twice its volume of water. Milk, bouillon, or another liquid can be substituted for all or part of the cooking water. The rice should absorb all the liquid used in cooking.

The same preparation methods can be used for colored rices that you use for white rice. These varieties, however, will take longer to cook unless they are soaked first. Soaking softens the outer bran layer so the rice will absorb the cooking liquid more quickly. You may also want to soak wild rice before cooking. Follow package directions for soaking and cooking colored and wild rices.

Precooked or instant rice cooks in a very short time. Add the rice to boiling water. Remove the pan from the heat and cover it tightly. When the rice has absorbed all the liquid, it is ready to serve.

Preparing Pasta Products

To cook macaroni, spaghetti, and other kinds of pasta, bring water to a boil in a large pot over high heat. Use at least 1 quart (1 L) of water for each 4 ounces (113 g) of pasta. Pasta requires more water than other cereal products so it can move freely as it cooks.

Add the pasta to the boiling water, keeping the heat high so the water returns to a boil quickly. Stir the pasta occasionally as it cooks to keep it from clumping and sticking to the pot.

As the starch granules absorb water and swell, the pasta becomes tender and doubles in size. Use cooking times recommended on pasta packages only as a guideline. The best way to determine whether pasta is cooked is to taste a piece, being careful of the heat. Properly cooked pasta is described as **al dente**, or slightly firm to the bite (**Figure 16.11**). Use a colander to drain cooked pasta but do not rinse after draining. Water-soluble nutrients can be lost by rinsing.

Microwaving Cereal Products

Cereals, rice, and pasta do not microwave much faster than they cook conventionally. However, these foods are less likely to stick and

Recipe for Good Food

Quinoa Pilaf

Serves 4 to 6

1	cup (250 mL) quinoa
2	tablespoons (30 mL) olive oil
¼	cup (60 mL) chopped onion
1	clove garlic, minced
¼	pound (113 g) mushrooms, chopped
1¾	cups (435 mL) low-sodium chicken broth
3	tablespoons (45 mL) lemon juice
½	teaspoon (2.5 mL) salt
¼	teaspoon (1.25 mL) black pepper
½	teaspoon (2.5 mL) dried thyme
2	tablespoons (30 mL) chopped fresh parsley

1. Place the quinoa in a fine-mesh strainer and rinse under cold water until the water runs clear. Drain well.

2. Heat olive oil in a large skillet over medium-high heat. Add onion and garlic and sauté until vegetables begin to soften, about 2 minutes.

3. Add quinoa to the skillet and stir constantly until it is coated with oil and begins to toast, about 2 minutes.

4. Add the mushrooms and continue to stir until they are tender, about 4 minutes.

5. Stir in the chicken broth and lemon juice; bring to a boil. Reduce heat to low, cover the skillet, and simmer the quinoa 15 to 20 minutes until all the liquid has been absorbed.

6. Remove quinoa from the heat. Season with salt, pepper, and thyme.

7. Sprinkle with chopped parsley to garnish. Serve immediately.

Per serving: 242 calories (37% from fat), 9 g protein, 31 g carbohydrate, 10 g fat, 0 mg cholesterol, 4 g fiber, 335 mg sodium.

Morenovel/Shutterstock.com

Figure 16.11 You can know that pasta is done when it is tender, but still retains its shape.

burn when prepared in a microwave oven. You can also prepare and serve them in the same dish, which saves time on cleanup.

When microwaving cereal products, be sure to use containers that are large enough to prevent boilovers. Cover these foods for microwave cooking.

You can serve pasta immediately after microwaving. Allow rice and cereal to stand a few minutes before serving. Cereals, rice, and pasta can be reheated in a microwave oven without stirring or adding water.

You may wish to use quick-cooking rather than conventional cereal products when making casseroles in a microwave oven. If using conventional products, precook them a bit less than if you were going to serve them immediately.

Chapter 16 Review and Expand

Summary

Grains can be made into a variety of staple food products, including breakfast foods, flours, and pasta. These products are generally nutritious, inexpensive, and easy to store.

Starches obtained from cereals are used chiefly as thickening agents. When mixed with liquid and heated, starches absorb water and swell, causing the mixture to thicken. As they cool, most starch mixtures form gels. Temperature, time, agitation, and mixing method used affect the cooking of starch mixtures.

Cooked breakfast cereals, rice, and pasta all contain large amounts of starch. During cooking, cereal products absorb water and increase in volume. The amount of water needed to make the starch granules in cereal products swell varies depending on the product. Properly cooked cereal products are tender, but they hold their shape and have no raw starch flavor. Microwaving cereal products does not save time, but it may reduce cleanup tasks.

Vocabulary Activities

1. **Content Terms**   Working in small groups, locate a small image online that visually describes or explains each of the following terms. To create flash cards, write each term on a note card and paste the image that describes or explains the term on the opposite side.

   cereal   gluten

   kernel   pasta

   bran   enriched

   endosperm   starch

   germ   gelatinization

   whole grain   syneresis

   refined   al dente

2. **Academic Terms**   For each of the following terms, draw a cartoon bubble to express the meaning of each term as it relates to the chapter.

   meal   opaque

   elasticity   insoluble

   translucent

Review

Write your answers using complete sentences when appropriate.

3. Describe the appearance and nutrients of the three parts of a kernel of grain.

4. How do whole-grain cereals differ from refined cereals?

5. Why do bakers care about the protein content of wheat flour?

6. Give four examples of nonwheat flours.

7. What gives brown, black, and red rice varieties their colors?

8. List three products, other than breakfast food and flour, that come from grain.

9. List five nutrients found in cereal products.

10. Why are many refined grain products enriched?

11. Why do grain products need to be stored tightly covered?

12. What is the name of the process in which starch granules swell when heated in water, causing starch mixtures to thicken?

13. Describe three ways to separate starch granules to prevent lumping.

14. Why should cooked breakfast cereal not be stirred continuously throughout the cooking time?

15. True or false. Rice should absorb all of its cooking liquid.

16. How can pasta be kept from sticking together during cooking?

17. Describe two advantages of microwaving cereal products.

Core Skills

18. **Research, Technology, Speaking**   Choose a country other than the United States. Use reliable resources to research the grains people in that country use as staple foods. (Use the international foods chapters in this textbook as one source of information.) Create an electronic presentation summarizing your findings. Proofread and edit your presentation for grammar, spelling, and organization. Share with the class.

Chapter 16 Review and Expand

19. **Technology, Math** Use an online nutrient database and a spreadsheet program to create a side-by-side comparison of the nutritive values of spaghetti and egg noodles.

20. **Reading** Choose a product from each of five categories: snack foods, bread products, desserts, ready-to-eat breakfast cereals, and frozen entrees. Using product information, make an ingredient list for each. Highlight all the ingredients from grain sources. With your classmates, create a display illustrating the roles grains play in food products.

21. **Math** Choose one of the following types of cereal products: breakfast foods, flours, pastas, or rice products. Visit a grocery store and make a list of 10 products in the group you chose. Make a graph to illustrate and compare the price per serving of all the products you listed.

22. **Science, Writing** Design a science experiment to compare the thickening powers of three types of grain starch, such as wheat flour, rice flour, and cornstarch. Remember to keep amounts of starch and liquid, mixing method, and pan size the same in each sample. The only variable should be the type of starch used. Carefully record your observations and write a brief summary of your experiment, stating your conclusions.

23. **Math** Oatmeal requires twice its volume of water for cooking. The volume of the cooked cereal equals the combined volume of the dry cereal and the water. For example, 1 cup (250 mL) of oatmeal would require 2 cups (500 mL) of water for cooking. This would produce 3 cups (750 mL) of cooked cereal. Figure how much oatmeal and how much water would be needed to make four ½-cup (120 mL) portions of cooked oatmeal.

24. **Career Readiness Practice** What health consequences might teens face later in life due to poor nutritional and fitness choices? With the class, brainstorm a list of consequences. For each consequence, identify two choices a teen could make to avoid the consequence.

Critical Thinking and Problem Solving

25. **Create** Determine the amounts from each MyPlate food group that would be needed by a 35-year-old woman who gets less than 30 minutes of moderate physical activity per day. Plan meals and snacks for one day that provide the appropriate amounts. Attach a written explanation stating how the menus could be modified to provide the additional ounce equivalents from the grains group that would be needed by the woman's active teenage son.

26. **Analyze** Prepare two white sauces. To prepare the first sauce, make a paste with butter and flour. Add the milk slowly, stirring constantly, and cook the sauce until thickened. To prepare the second sauce, warm the milk with the butter. Add the flour all at once. Cook until thickened, stirring constantly. Compare the two sauces. What differences do you notice? What caused them? Which would you rather serve? Why?

27. **Analyze** Prepare two recipes of cherry sauce. Thicken one with cornstarch. Thicken the other with flour. Analyze differences in appearance, texture, and flavor. Which would you rather serve? Why?

28. **Evaluate** Prepare old-fashioned oatmeal, quick-cooking oatmeal, and instant oatmeal. Taste each type of oatmeal. Evaluate how the flavor, texture, and appearance of each product affect your preference.

Chapter 17
Breads

Content Terms ⤷

batter
dough
leavening agent
fermentation

Academic Terms

hydrate
well

Objectives

After studying this chapter, you will be able to

- **recall** nutrients found in baked products;
- **describe** how to select and store baked goods;
- **identify** the functions of ingredients in baked products; and
- **prepare** quick breads and yeast breads.

Reading Prep

As you read the chapter, record any questions that come to mind. Indicate where the answer to each question can be found: within the text, by asking your teacher, in another book, on the Internet, or by reflecting on your own knowledge and experiences. Pursue the answers to your questions.

Quick breads contain leavening agents other than yeast. They are called quick breads because they can be prepared in a short amount of time. Quick breads include biscuits, muffins, popovers, cream puffs, pancakes, and waffles. They also include coffee cakes and breads leavened with baking powder (**Figure 17.1**).

Yeast breads use yeast as a leavening agent. They require more time to prepare than quick breads. Yeast breads include breads, rolls, English muffins, raised doughnuts, and many other yeast-raised products.

Nutritional Value of Baked Products

Baked goods, which are part of the grains group of MyPlate, are an excellent source of complex carbohydrates. They also supply B vitamins and iron. Most teens need 6 to 10 ounce equivalents from the grains group each day, depending on calorie needs. One slice of bread and one small biscuit or muffin each count as one ounce equivalent. Half a sandwich bun or one-fourth of a large bagel also counts as one ounce equivalent.

When buying baked products, be sure to look at the Nutrition Facts label. Many types of bread contain little fat or added sugars and provide less than 100 calories per slice. Biscuits, muffins, and specialty breads, however, are often higher in fat, sugars, and calories. In addition, breads are a major source of sodium, which is an overconsumed nutrient in U.S. diets. Bread frequently contains 150 mg or more of sodium per slice. Someone who eats 6 ounce equivalents per day could easily get 900 mg of sodium just from bread. This is over 39 percent of the 2,300 mg daily recommendation. When added to the sodium consumed from all the other foods in the diet, the daily limit can quickly be exceeded. Look at the dietary fiber listed on the label, too. Whole-grain items provide more of this important component.

Selecting and Storing Baked Products

Quick breads and yeast breads are *baked products*. Cakes, cookies, and pies are baked products, too. Some of the following information applies to *all* baked products. Preparation of cakes, cookies, and pies, however, differs from preparation of breads. Therefore, cakes, cookies, and pies will be discussed further in another chapter.

Baked products can be purchased as freshly baked, partially baked, refrigerated, and frozen. *Freshly baked items* are sold in bakeries, in bakery sections of supermarkets, and on supermarket shelves (**Figure 17.2**). They are ready to serve. *Brown-and-serve baked goods* are partially baked. They need a final browning in the oven before serving.

Refrigerated doughs are ready to bake. They are handy for quickly preparing items like biscuits, turnovers, cookies, and rolls. *Frozen doughs* and *baked goods* require thawing and/or baking. Yeast doughs and cookie doughs are available frozen. Frozen pies, cakes, coffee cakes, and doughnuts can be purchased, too.

Cost of Baked Products

The cost of rolls, cakes, and other bakery products depends a lot on the amount of convenience. Ready-to-serve items usually cost more than items that require some preparation. Bakery yeast rolls, for instance, usually cost more than frozen yeast rolls.

Brent Hofacker/Shutterstock.com

Figure 17.1 Although simple to prepare, biscuits—a popular quick bread product—are a special treat.

Shebeko/Shutterstock.com

Figure 17.2 Freshly baked items are often sold in bakeries. What are the advantages of freshly baked items?

Bread costs depend on size of loaf, extra ingredients, and brand. Large loaves usually cost less per serving than small loaves. Breads with fruit and nuts cost more than plain white or whole-wheat bread. Store brands generally cost less than national brands.

Storing Baked Products

Store freshly baked items at room temperature or in the freezer, tightly wrapped. Freezing bread in hot, humid weather prevents mold growth. Slices of bread can be taken from the freezer as needed to thaw and eat. Refrigerate any baked products with cream, custard, or other perishable fillings or frosting.

Refrigerated doughs should be kept refrigerated until they are baked. Likewise, frozen doughs and baked products should be stored in the freezer until they will be used.

Quick Breads

Quick breads may be made from batters or doughs. Both batters and doughs are mixtures of flour and liquid. **Batters** range in consistency from thin liquids to stiff liquids. Thin batters are called *pour batters*. They have a large amount of liquid

Exploring Careers

Family and Consumer Sciences Teacher

Family and consumer sciences (FCS) teachers help students learn to make informed choices about their health, relationships, and resources. Their goal is to teach principles that will prepare students for careers. They also want to give students the skills they will need to attain a high quality of personal and family life. FCS teachers use a variety of methods, such as lecture, demonstration, and lab activities, to help students learn. They make and evaluate assignments and keep records of student progress. They promote safety and maintain discipline in the classroom, too.

Above all else, the most successful FCS teachers care about students and have a true desire to help them do well. They need to be excellent leaders, time managers, and communicators. FCS teachers need speaking and listening skills to explain concepts, address questions, and clarify misunderstandings. They will use reading skills to study curriculum guides, textbooks, and other resources. They will use writing skills to write lesson plans, assignments, and test questions. FCS teachers need keen observation skills to evaluate students and see when further instruction is required. They must be able to use technology, educational tools, and lab equipment. They also need to be creative, flexible, and persistent.

FCS teachers need a four-year bachelor's degree. This program of study typically includes a number of weeks of student teaching. During this time, future teachers work under the guidance of experienced teachers. This gives them practice working with students in a classroom setting. After graduating, FCS teachers must obtain a teaching certificate to show they have met the requirements for teaching in a given state. Many FCS teachers continue to take classes and go on to get master's degrees.

and a small amount of flour. A pour batter is used to prepare pancakes and popovers. Stiff batters are called *drop batters*. They have a high proportion of flour, and they can be dropped from a spoon. A drop batter is used to prepare drop biscuits and some muffin recipes. **Doughs** have an even higher proportion of flour. They are stiff enough to shape by hand. Soft dough is used to prepare shortcake and rolled biscuits. Stiff dough is used to make rolled cookies and pastry (**Figure 17.3**).

Lucky Business/Shutterstock.com

viennetta/Shutterstock.com

Kitch Bain/Shutterstock.com

Figure 17.3 Quick breads are made from pour batters (A), drop batters (B), and doughs (C). Give an example of a quick bread that falls into each category.

Quick Bread Ingredients

Flour is a basic ingredient in all quick breads. The kinds of ingredients added to the flour are what distinguish one product from another. Leavening agents, liquid, fat, eggs, sugar, and salt are among the other ingredients that may be part of quick breads. Each ingredient serves a specific purpose.

Flour

Flour gives structure to baked products. White wheat flours are most often used for baking. Most quick breads are made with *all-purpose flour*. Some recipes call for *self-rising flour*. This is all-purpose flour with added leavening agents and salt.

Leavening Agents

Leavening agents are ingredients that produce gases in batters and doughs. These gases make baked products rise and become light and porous. Two leavening agents used in quick breads are baking soda and baking powder. Chemical reactions during baking cause these ingredients to release *carbon dioxide* gas.

Two gases other than carbon dioxide that make baked products rise are steam and air. *Steam* is produced when liquid ingredients reach high temperatures during baking. Popovers and cream puffs are leavened almost entirely by steam (**Figure 17.4**).

Air is incorporated into baked products by beating eggs, creaming fat and sugar together, folding doughs, and beating batters. Almost all baked products contain some air.

Liquids

Water, milk, and fruit juices are liquids commonly used in baked products. Eggs and fats are also considered to be liquid ingredients.

Liquids serve several functions. They *hydrate* (cause to absorb water) the protein and starch in flour. Proteins must absorb water to later form gluten. Starches must absorb water to gelatinize during baking.

Another function of liquids is to moisten or dissolve ingredients such as baking powder, salt, and sugar. Liquids also serve as leavening agents when they are converted to steam during baking.

Food Science

Chemical Leaveners

One chemical leavening agent added to many baked products is *baking soda*. Baking soda is sodium bicarbonate, which is an alkali. It is used in quick bread recipes that contain food acid ingredients. When combined with a food acid, baking soda releases carbon dioxide. Acid ingredients also help neutralize the alkaline batter. This prevents a bitter flavor and disagreeable color from forming in the bread. Food acid ingredients include buttermilk, molasses, brown sugar, vinegar, honey, applesauce or other fruit, and citrus juices.

A second chemical leavener often used in baked goods is baking powder. *Baking powders* contain a dry acid or acid salt, baking soda, and starch or flour. Be sure to follow guidelines for using the recommended amount of baking powder. Too much baking powder will produce too much carbon dioxide, and the baked product will collapse. Too little baking powder will not produce enough carbon dioxide, and the product will be small and compact.

Most baking powders are *double-acting baking powders*. They release some of their carbon dioxide when they are moistened. They release most of their carbon dioxide when they are heated.

AS Food studio/Shutterstock.com

Figure 17.4 Cream puffs rely on steam to rise.

Sugar

Sugar gives sweetness to quick breads. It has a tenderizing effect and helps crusts brown, too. Brown sugar gives a distinctive flavor and increased moisture to baked products. Honey and maple syrup are used to sweeten some baked goods; however, these ingredients also function as part of the liquids in a recipe.

Salt

Even though most quick breads do not taste salty, salt is needed for flavor. Along with adding its own flavor, salt helps to enhance the other flavors in baked products. If salt is omitted from a recipe, the resulting food product is likely to be bland.

Adjusting Bread Ingredients

A few simple guidelines can be followed to adjust the ingredients in quick bread recipes to make them more healthful. These suggestions can be applied to yeast breads as well. For instance, fat-free milk can be substituted for whole milk in bread recipes. This change will

Fat

Fat serves primarily as a tenderizing agent in baked products. The fat coats the flour particles and causes the dough structure to separate into layers. Fat also aids leavening. When fat is beaten, air bubbles form. The fat traps these air bubbles and holds them.

Eggs

When beaten, eggs help incorporate air into baked products. They also add color and flavor and contribute to structure. During baking, the egg proteins coagulate. The coagulated proteins give the batter or dough elasticity and form.

reduce fat and calories in each serving of bread products. Also, some recipes call for more baking powder, fat, eggs, sugar, and salt than are really needed. Minimum proportions for these ingredients are shown in **Figure 17.5.** Adjusting recipes to follow these minimums will reduce calories, fat, and sodium without affecting bread quality.

Modifying bread recipes can also help increase the intake of fruits, vegetables, and whole grains. Try adding blueberries or sliced bananas to pancakes to add fruit to the diet. Stir some shredded zucchini or carrots into muffin batter to help meet needs from the vegetable group.

To increase whole grains in the diet, replace half the all-purpose flour in recipes with whole-wheat flour or ground oatmeal. Count these ingredients as flour when figuring proportions of ingredients. Keep in mind, however, that these flours are heavier and may require a little extra baking powder for proper leavening.

Food Science Principles of Preparing Quick Breads

Food science principles can be observed at work in quick breads in the development of gluten. In addition to giving strength and elasticity to batters and doughs, gluten holds in leavening gases. This is what makes quick breads rise. Gluten is created by two proteins found in wheat flour: *gliadin* and *glutenin*. When wheat flour is combined with liquid and stirred or kneaded, the gliadin and glutenin form gluten.

To understand gluten, think of a piece of bubble gum. When you first put gum into your mouth, it is soft and easy to chew. As it is chewed, the gum becomes more elastic, and bubbles can be blown. If you keep chewing, the gum continues to become more elastic. Eventually, the gum gets to be so tough that chewing it makes your jaw ache.

Gluten behaves in a similar way. If a batter or dough is handled too much, the gluten will overdevelop. This can cause a quick bread to be compact and tough. To keep quick breads light and tender, mix them for only a short time and handle them carefully.

Each kind of white wheat flour contains different amounts of gliadin and glutenin. Thus, the strength of the gluten produced by each type of flour differs. Bread flour will give yeast breads a strong gluten structure. Cake flour may be used to give cakes a delicate structure. Most

Minimum Ingredient Proportions per 1 Cup (250 mL) of Flour					
Product	**Fat**	**Eggs**	**Sugar**	**Salt**	**Baking Powder**
Biscuits	2 tablespoons (30 mL)	—	—	¼ teaspoon (1.25 mL)	1¼ teaspoons (6.25 mL)
Muffins	2 tablespoons (30 mL)	½	1 tablespoon (15 mL)	¼ teaspoon (1.25 mL)	1¼ teaspoons (6.25 mL)
Popovers	1 tablespoon (15 mL)	2	—	¼ teaspoon (1.25 mL)	—
Cream Puffs	½ cup (125 mL)	4	—	¼ teaspoon (1.25 mL)	—
Traditional Yeast Breads	1 tablespoon* (15 mL)	½*	1 teaspoon* (5 mL)	¼ teaspoon (1.25 mL)	—
Bread Machine Yeast Breads	2 teaspoons (10 mL)	*	1 tablespoon (15 mL)	½ teaspoon (2.5 mL)	—
*Many traditional yeast breads can be made without any fat or eggs. When recipes for richer breads call for these ingredients, the minimums shown here will produce a suitably rich dough. Sugar is not an essential ingredient in traditional unsweetened yeast breads. However, most recipes call for a small amount to serve as food for the yeast. Fat and sugar are not optional ingredients in yeast breads prepared in bread machines. Adding an egg and decreasing other liquids by ¼ cup (60 mL) will improve structure and volume of whole grain-bread machine recipes.					

Figure 17.5 Following these proportions will reduce the sugar, fat, and sodium in many quick bread and yeast bread recipes.

quick breads are made with all-purpose flour for a texture that falls somewhere in between.

Some recipes are designed to use all whole-grain flour. When replacing all-purpose flour, however, do not replace more than half with whole-grain flour. Otherwise, the product being prepared may not have the right amount of gluten (**Figure 17.6**).

Preparing Biscuits

The method used to mix baked products is another factor that distinguishes one baked product from another. When preparing biscuits, combine the ingredients using the *biscuit method*. This method involves sifting dry ingredients together into a mixing bowl. Use a pastry blender or two knives to cut the fat into the dry mixture. Continue cutting in until the particles are the size of coarse cornmeal. Then add the liquid all at once and stir until the dough forms a ball. This is the same mixing method that is used when making pastry.

The dry ingredients in biscuits are flour, baking powder, and salt. Self-rising flour, which is a mixture of these three ingredients, can also

be used. The liquid in biscuits is usually milk or buttermilk. Drop biscuits contain a higher proportion of liquid than rolled biscuits. When making *drop biscuits*, drop the dough from a spoon onto a greased baking sheet.

When making *rolled biscuits*, gently knead the dough 8 to 10 times and roll or pat it into a circle. Then cut the dough with a biscuit cutter and place the biscuits on an ungreased baking sheet. Bake both types of biscuits in a hot oven until they are golden brown.

A high-quality rolled biscuit has an even shape with a smooth, level top and straight sides. The crust is an even brown. When a biscuit is broken open, the *crumb*, or soft interior, is white to creamy white. It is moist and fluffy and peels off in layers.

Biscuits require gentle handling. An under-mixed biscuit has a low volume and a rounded top with a slightly rough crust. The crumb is tender. An overmixed biscuit also has a low volume and a rounded top, but the top is smooth. The crumb is tough and compact.

Preparing Muffins

When preparing muffins, combine ingredients using the *muffin method*. For this method, measure the dry ingredients into a mixing bowl. Make a *well*, or indentation, in the center of the dry ingredients. In a separate bowl, combine beaten eggs with milk and oil or melted fat. Pour all the liquid mixture into the well in the dry ingredients. For muffins, stir the batter just until the dry ingredients are moistened. This mixing method will also be used when preparing waffles, pancakes, popovers, and some coffee cakes. Batter for some of these baked products may require more stirring than the batter for muffins.

The dry ingredients in muffins are flour, baking powder, salt, and sugar. Fruits, nuts, cheese, and other ingredients may be added to muffin batter for variety. After combining ingredients, drop muffin batter into a greased muffin pan and bake.

A high-quality muffin has a thin, evenly browned crust. The top is symmetrical, but it looks rough. When broken apart, the texture is uniform, and the crumb is tender and light.

An undermixed muffin has a low volume and a flat top. The crumb is coarse. An over-mixed muffin has a peaked top and a pale, slick

Vezzani Photography/Shutterstock.com

Figure 17.6 Replacing some all-purpose flour with whole-wheat flour in a recipe for quick bread can make baked products more healthful.

crust. When broken apart, narrow, open areas called *tunnels* are visible.

Preparing Popovers

Popovers look like golden-brown balloons. They are often eaten with jam or their hollow centers are filled with mixtures of meat, poultry, seafood, and/or vegetables. A variety of sweet fillings, such as ice cream, pudding, fruit, and custard, are also popular in popovers.

Popovers contain flour, salt, eggs, milk, and a small amount of fat. Use the muffin method to combine these ingredients into a thin batter. Pour the batter into greased deep muffin pans or custard cups. Then place popovers in a hot oven for the first part of the baking period. This allows steam to expand the walls of the popovers.

Following this expansion, lower the temperature to prevent overbrowning before the interior has set. Do not open the oven door to check popovers during baking. If the oven door is opened, and they have not set, the steam can condense and cause the popovers to collapse.

A high-quality popover has good volume. The shell is golden brown and crisp, and the interior contains slightly moist (but not raw) strands of dough (**Figure 17.7**).

Insufficient baking is one of the biggest causes of popover failures. If a popover has not baked long enough, it will collapse when it is taken from the oven. The exterior will be soft instead of crisp, and the interior will be doughy.

Preparing Cream Puffs

A cream puff is a golden-brown, hollow shell with crisp walls. Cream puffs can be filled with pudding, custard, ice cream, fruit, or whipped cream and served as a dessert. They can be filled with meat, poultry, or fish in a creamy sauce or gravy and served as a main dish. Small cream puffs can be filled with cream cheese, shrimp salad, or another light filling and served as appetizers. Elongated cream puffs filled with custard are called *éclairs*.

Cream puffs are made from water, fat, flour, and eggs. They require a special mixing method.

Recipe for Good Food

Oat and Honey Muffins

Makes 6 muffins

½	cup (125 mL) quick or old-fashioned oats
½	cup (125 mL) all-purpose flour
¼	cup (60 mL) whole-wheat flour
¼	teaspoon (1.25 mL) baking soda
1	teaspoon (5 mL) baking powder
¼	teaspoon (1.25 mL) salt
	dash cinnamon
2	tablespoons (30 mL) butter
2	tablespoons (30 mL) honey
1	egg
½	cup (125 mL) buttermilk
¼	teaspoon (1.25 mL) vanilla

1. Preheat the oven to 375°F (190°C). Grease a muffin pan or line with paper liners.
2. In a medium mixing bowl, use a fork to stir together oats, all-purpose flour, whole-wheat flour, baking soda, baking powder, salt, and cinnamon. Make a well in the center of the dry ingredients.
3. In a small microwavable bowl, combine the butter and honey. Microwave on 50 percent power for 30 seconds. (Butter does not have to be completely melted.) Whisk the buttermilk, egg, and vanilla into the butter and honey.
4. Pour the liquid ingredients into the well in the center of the dry ingredients. Mix just until blended.
5. Spoon the batter into the muffin pan, filling each depression in the pan about two-thirds full. Bake for 20 to 25 minutes, until a toothpick inserted into the center of the muffins comes out clean.
6. Remove muffins from the pan. Serve warm.

Per serving: 157 calories (29% from fat), 4 g protein, 23 g carbohydrate, 5 g fat, 46 mg cholesterol, 2 g fiber, 265 mg sodium.

©2011 Wisconsin Milk Marketing Board, Inc.

Figure 17.7 High-quality popovers look like golden-brown balloons on the outside with moist strands of dough on the inside.

Begin by bringing the water and fat to a boil. Then add the flour and stir vigorously over low heat until the mixture forms a ball. After removing the mixture from the heat, stir in the eggs until the mixture is smooth. The resulting dough is called *puff paste*.

Drop the puff paste onto an ungreased baking sheet. Begin baking the cream puffs in a hot oven so the steam will cause them to puff (rise). Then reduce the temperature. This will prevent the exteriors of the cream puffs from overbrowning before the interiors have set. Do not open the oven door to check the cream puffs during baking. If the oven door is opened, and the cream puffs have not set, the steam can condense and cause them to collapse.

A properly prepared cream puff has a good volume and a brown, tender crust. When broken apart, the interior of the cream puff is hollow. A few strands of moist, tender dough may be visible.

Cream puff failures usually are the result of underbaking. When an underbaked cream puff is taken from the oven, it will collapse. The interior is moist and filled with strands of dough.

Occasionally, cream puffs will ooze fat during baking. The evaporation of too much liquid can cause this. Evaporation may take place when the water and fat are heated together or when the puff paste is cooked.

Yeast Breads

Homemade yeast bread is decidedly different from commercially prepared sandwich breads. It has a distinctively appealing sweet smell and delicious taste that cannot be matched (**Figure 17.8**).

Yeast Bread Ingredients

All yeast breads must contain flour, liquid, salt, and yeast. Most recipes call for a small amount of sugar, and some include fat and eggs.

Flour

All-purpose flour can be used for making traditional yeast breads. When mixed with liquid

Characteristics of Quality Quick Breads

Biscuit

iStock.com/msheldrake

- even shape with a smooth, level top and straight sides
- uniformly browned crust
- white to creamy white crumb (soft interior)
- moist, fluffy interior that peels off in layers

Muffin

alexsvirid/Shutterstock.com

- thin, evenly browned crust
- symmetrical top with rough appearance
- uniform texture with tender, light crumb

Popover

T.W./Shutterstock.com

- very big volume with thin walls
- golden-brown, crisp shell
- slightly moist (not raw) strands of dough inside

Cream Puff

jiangdi/Shutterstock.com

- good volume with crisp walls
- brown, tender crust
- large, hollow interior with a few strands of moist, tender dough visible

AnjelikaGr/Shutterstock.com

Figure 17.8 The flavor, texture, and aroma of home-made yeast bread create a feast for the senses.

and kneaded, the flour develops gluten to support the carbon dioxide produced by the yeast.

Bread flour contains larger amounts of gliadin and glutenin than all-purpose flour. It produces the strongest and most elastic gluten of all the white wheat flours. Whole-wheat and nonwheat flours, such as rye, soy, corn, and oat, have a lower protein content than all-purpose flour. They will produce a denser loaf than all-purpose or bread flour. Many recipes calling for whole-grain flours also call for an equal amount of all-purpose flour. The all-purpose flour produces more gluten and will help give the bread a better texture.

Food Science

Temperature of Liquids in Yeast Breads

The temperature of the liquids used to make yeast bread affects yeast cells. Liquids used in bread recipes need to be warm to activate the yeast.

In some recipes, the yeast is dissolved in water before other ingredients are added. In this case, the temperature of the water should be 105°F to 115°F (41°C to 46°C). Other recipes require the yeast to be combined directly with flour and other dry ingredients. For these recipes, liquids are heated to 120°F to 130°F (49°C to 54°C) before being added to the dry yeast mixture.

Following a recipe's directions for heating liquids is important. Temperatures that are too high kill the yeast cells. Temperatures that are too low can slow or stop yeast activity.

ChameleonsEye/Shutterstock.com

Yeast is activated in warm water.

Liquid

The liquid used in yeast breads is often plain water or milk. Milk produces a softer crust and helps breads stay fresh longer than water. Other options for liquid ingredients in yeast breads include buttermilk, fruit juices, yogurt, applesauce, and cottage cheese. These options add nutrients and distinctive flavors.

Salt

Salt regulates the action of the yeast and inhibits the action of certain enzymes in the flour. If yeast dough contains no salt, the yeast will produce carbon dioxide too quickly. The bread dough will be sticky and difficult to handle. When baked, the bread may look moth-eaten.

Yeast

Yeast is a microscopic, single-celled plant used as a leavening agent in yeast breads. Two types of yeast are commonly found on supermarket shelves. *Active dry yeast* is made from an active yeast strain that has been dried and made into granules. *Fast-rising yeast* products are highly active yeast strains. The granules of these products are smaller than those of active dry yeast, which allows them to act more quickly. Active dry and fast-rising yeast are both available in small foil packets and glass jars. A third type of yeast, *compressed yeast*, is available in the refrigerated section of stores in some areas (**Figure 17.9**).

Store yeast products in a cool, dry place and refrigerate jars after opening. For fastest action, buy yeast in small quantities and use it promptly.

For best results, use the amount of yeast specified in the recipe. A foil packet typically contains ¼ ounce (7 g), which equals 2¼ teaspoons (11.25 mL) of yeast. This amount of yeast is enough to raise up to 4 cups (1 L) of flour. Using too much yeast will cause the dough to rise too quickly. Excess yeast will also give the

Africa Studio/Shutterstock.com

Figure 17.9 Yeast can be bought either dry or compressed. What are the advantages of using dry versus compressed yeast?

bread an undesirable flavor, texture, and appearance. Using too little yeast will lengthen the rising time.

Sugar

Sugar, brown sugar, honey, and molasses can all be used in yeast bread recipes. These ingredients influence browning, flavor, and texture. They also provide extra food for the yeast so the dough will rise faster. If too much sugar is used, however, the yeast will work more slowly.

Fat

Fat is optional in some yeast bread recipes. When used, its function is to increase tenderness of the bread. Most recipes call for solid fat, but some call for oil.

Eggs

Eggs are considered part of the liquid in yeast bread recipes. Eggs add flavor and richness to breads. They also add color and improve the structure.

Other Ingredients

Other ingredients, such as raisins, nuts, cheese, herbs, and spices, may be added to bread dough. They add flavor and variety (**Figure 17.10**). These ingredients also tend to lengthen the rising time.

Mixing Methods for Yeast Breads

Several methods are used to mix yeast dough. The method used will affect other preparation steps, such as kneading and rising. The recipe will specify which method to use.

Some recipes call for an electric mixer to combine the ingredients. The mixer allows ingredients to blend easily and helps develop gluten. A dough hook attachment can be used to do some or all of the kneading (**Figure 17.11**).

Recipes that require less flour cause the yeast mixture to form a batter rather than a dough. Vigorous stirring, rather than kneading, helps develop the gluten in these recipes. Batter recipes that require two risings rise first in the mixing bowl. Then the batter is spread in a pan for the second rising before baking.

Food Science Principles of Preparing Yeast Breads

Like preparing quick breads, preparing yeast breads requires the development of gluten and the formation of carbon dioxide. During mixing and kneading, the gluten develops. The gluten will form the framework of the bread. It will trap the carbon dioxide produced by the yeast as the

Josef Hanus/Shutterstock.com

Figure 17.10 Other ingredients that can be added to bread dough include nuts, cheese, herbs, spices, and dried fruits.

©iStock.com/OlafSpeier

Figure 17.11 An electric mixer with a dough hook can be used to perform the kneading step.

Kneading Dough

Courtesy ACH Food Companies, Inc.

1. If dough is sticky, sprinkle the surface with a small amount of flour.

Courtesy ACH Food Companies, Inc.

2. Fold dough in half toward your body.

Courtesy ACH Food Companies, Inc.

3. Push against the dough with the heels of your hands.

Courtesy ACH Food Companies, Inc.

4. Turn dough one-quarter turn.

dough rises. As the amount of carbon dioxide increases, the dough will rise, giving volume to the bread.

The preparation of successful yeast bread depends on careful measuring, sufficient kneading, and controlled fermentation temperatures. Correct pan size and baking temperature are also important.

Kneading

After mixing, most yeast dough must be kneaded. Although some of the gluten develops during initial beating, kneading develops most of the gluten. To knead, press the dough with the heels of the hands, fold it, and turn it. This motion must be rhythmically repeated until the dough is smooth and elastic.

Avoid adding too much extra flour when kneading the dough. Too much flour will make the dough stiff. It is also important not to be too rough with the dough. Too much pressure at the beginning of kneading can keep the dough sticky and hard to handle. Too much pressure toward the end of kneading can tear or mat the gluten strands that have already developed.

Fermentation

After kneading, traditional recipes require yeast dough to sit in a warm place for a period of time. During this time, the yeast acts on the sugars in the bread dough to form alcohol and carbon dioxide. This process is called **fermentation**. The alcohol evaporates during baking. The carbon dioxide causes the dough to rise.

Some recipes specify that dough should be covered after kneading and allowed to rest for 10 minutes. This resting period replaces the rising time required in traditional yeast bread recipes.

Courtesy ACH Food Companies, Inc.

Figure 17.12 After letting the dough rise, test for lightness with two fingers.

The dough should at least double in volume during fermentation. To see if dough has doubled in size, gently push two fingers into the dough. If an indentation remains, the dough has risen enough (**Figure 17.12**).

Fermentation time varies depending on the kind and amount of yeast, the temperature of the room, and the kind of flour. Breads made with fast-rising yeast rise up to 50 percent faster than products made with regular yeast. The dough should be kept in a warm place for optimal fermentation.

The temperature range of 80°F to 85°F (27°C to 29°C) is ideal for the production of carbon dioxide by the yeast. Create such a warm environment by placing the bowl of dough over a pan of steaming water. Avoid temperatures that are too warm, which will cause the yeast to work too quickly, causing the dough to rise too fast.

Punching the Dough

When the dough is light (has completed the first rising), it must be punched down to release some of the carbon dioxide. Punch dough down by firmly pushing a fist into the dough (**Figure 17.13**). Then fold the edges of the dough toward the center, and turn the dough over so the smooth side is on top. At this point, some

Courtesy ACH Food Companies, Inc.

Figure 17.13 When dough has doubled in bulk, punch down.

doughs require a second rising time before being shaped. (Doughs made with bread flour need a second rising.)

Shaping

After punching the dough down, use a sharp knife to divide it into portions as the recipe directs. Allow the divided dough to rest about 10 minutes. After resting, the dough will be easier to handle and shape as desired.

To shape yeast dough, first flatten the dough into a rectangle. The width of the dough should be about the length of the bread pan. Using a rolling pin will help to work out any large air bubbles. Fold the ends of the rectangle to the center, overlapping them a little. This should give a smaller rectangle. Use the rolling pin to flatten the rectangle into a square. Roll the dough into a cylinder. Pinch the edge of the dough into the roll to seal it. Seal each end of the roll by pressing down on it with the side of the hand. Fold the ends under.

Place the shaped dough, seam side down, in a greased loaf pan. Brush the top with melted butter, if desired. Cover the loaf with a clean towel, and shape the remaining dough. Let the loaves rise in a warm, draft-free place until they have doubled in bulk (**Figure 17.14**).

Baking

Baking times and temperatures vary somewhat depending on the kind of dough and size of the loaf. Place most yeast breads in a moderately hot oven. During baking, the gas cells formed during fermentation expand. The walls of dough around these cells set and become rigid. During the first few minutes of baking, the dough will

Courtesy ACH Food Companies, Inc.

Figure 17.14 After letting the dough rise a second time, place the loaves in pans.

rise dramatically. This rapid rising is called *oven spring*.

After baking, immediately remove bread from the pans and place it on cooling racks. Cool the bread thoroughly before slicing or storing.

Characteristics of Yeast Bread

A high-quality loaf of yeast bread has a large volume and a smooth, rounded top. The surface is golden brown. When sliced, the texture is fine and uniform. The crumb is tender and elastic, and it springs back when touched (**Figure 17.15**).

If yeast dough has been under- or over-worked, the finished product will have a low volume. This is because carbon dioxide has leaked out of the dough.

©iStock.com/poplasen

Figure 17.15 What characteristics of a high-quality yeast bread can you identify in this bread?

If bread is allowed to rise for too long a time before baking, it may have large, overexpanded cells. The top of the loaf may be sunken with overhanging sides, much like a mushroom. The texture will be coarse, and it may be crumbly.

If bread has not been allowed to rise long enough before baking, it may have large cracks on the sides of the loaf. Its texture will be compact.

Learn About...

Bread Machines

When bread machines first appeared on the market, they were very popular. Like many trendy appliances, their popularity has faded over time. Some consumers, however, still find bread machines help them enjoy fresh, homemade bread more often. Many people also like to use their bread machines to make dough. All a meal manager has to do is measure the ingredients, and the bread machine does the rest. Once the dough is ready, it can be baked in the machine or shaped into items like pizza and rolls and baked in an oven.

Proportions of ingredients vary a bit between traditional yeast breads and those prepared in bread machines. Unlike traditional recipes, fat is not optional in bread machine recipes. Bread machine recipes require more salt and sugar, too.

Bread flour is recommended in bread machine recipes. This is because the actions of a bread machine require stronger gluten. When using whole-grain flour, it is essential to combine it with bread flour. The combination of flours will produce more gluten and help bread rise. Adding an egg to a recipe calling for whole-grain flour will also help improve the structure and volume of the finished product.

Guidelines for recipes and operation vary from model to model. The best way to ensure success when using a bread machine is to follow the manufacturer's directions.

Know and Apply

1. Why do you think you would or would not want to own a bread machine?

2. What characteristic of bread flour allows it to impact gluten strength?

Time-Saving Yeast Bread Techniques

Bread making no longer has to be the all-day task it once was. Blending ingredients with a mixer speeds mixing time and shortens kneading time. Batter bread recipes eliminate kneading entirely. Fast-rising yeast can cut rising time in half. Using recipes that require only one rising after the dough has been shaped saves time, too.

Some recipes allow you to store prepared dough to bake at another time. Recipes for cool-rise, refrigerator, and freezer doughs can be baked when it is most convenient.

Cool-Rise Doughs

Cool-rise doughs are prepared from recipes that are specially designed to rise slowly in the refrigerator. Ingredients are mixed and the dough is kneaded. Then after a brief rest, the dough is shaped and placed in a pan. The dough is covered and stored in the refrigerator. It will rise and be ready to bake at any convenient time from 2 to 24 hours later.

Refrigerator Doughs

Like cool-rise doughs, *refrigerator doughs* are prepared from recipes that are specially designed to rise slowly in the refrigerator. Refrigerator doughs are batter bread recipes. Therefore, they are not kneaded like cool-rise doughs. Refrigerator doughs are shaped after, rather than before, refrigeration. Refrigerator doughs can usually remain in the refrigerator for 2 to 24 hours. Then the dough is shaped, allowed to rise, and baked.

Freezer Doughs

Another type of specially formulated yeast bread recipe is for *freezer doughs*. These recipes allow the dough to be mixed and kneaded. Then the dough is frozen before or after shaping. The dough can be stored in the freezer for up to one month. When it is needed, simply thaw, shape if necessary, let rise, and bake.

Yeast Bread Variations

Add variety to yeast bread by combining white flour with whole-wheat flour, rye flour, or cornmeal. Try adding dried fruits, nuts, herbs, or cheese to the basic dough. Brush the tops of the loaves with butter and sprinkle them with poppy, sesame, or caraway seeds.

Basic bread dough can be shaped into rolls. After punching the dough down, allow it to rest for a short time. Then divide it into equal portions. Weighing the portions on a kitchen scale will help make sure all rolls turn out the same size.

Shaping the dough into round balls will give baked rolls a uniform appearance. Dough can also be shaped into crescent rolls, cloverleaf rolls, and bows for variety. Directions for shaping rolls can be found online and in many cookbooks (**Figure 17.16**).

Marina Grau/Shutterstock.com

Figure 17.16 Shaping yeast dough into dinner rolls is an easy way to make ordinary bread seem extra special. What other special baked products could be made with yeast dough?

Chapter 17 Review and Expand

Summary

Quick breads and yeast breads are baked products. All baked products are available in various forms. Whole-grain varieties are good sources of fiber as well as complex carbohydrates. Convenience tends to affect the cost of bread products. Unless they contain perishable fillings or frostings, most baked products can be kept at room temperature. Use the freezer for longer storage.

Biscuits, muffins, popovers, and cream puffs are four popular types of quick breads. Flour, leavening agents, liquids, fat, eggs, sugar, and salt each serve specific functions in these baked products. Varying proportions and mixing methods result in differences among them.

Most yeast breads require kneading to develop gluten, which forms the structure of the bread. Yeast breads also need time for fermentation. This is the time during which yeast acts on sugars, causing the dough to rise. The dough must be punched down and shaped before baking. Adding ingredients to dough and changing the shape can produce a variety of breads.

Vocabulary Activities

1. **Content Terms**   Work with a partner to write the definitions of the following terms based on your current understanding before reading the chapter. Then pair up with another pair to discuss your definitions and any discrepancies. Finally, discuss the definitions with the class and ask your instructor for necessary correction or clarification.

   batter   leavening agent

   dough   fermentation

2. **Academic Terms**   With a partner, use the Internet to locate photos or graphics that depict the following terms. Print the graphics or use presentation software to show your graphics to the class, describing how they depict the meaning of the term(s).

   hydrate   well

Review

Write your answers using complete sentences when appropriate.

3. List three nutrients found in baked products.
4. Explain the difference between quick breads and yeast breads. Give three examples of each.
5. For which overconsumed nutrient in U.S. diets are breads a major source?
6. What is the advantage of freezing bread in hot, humid weather?
7. What is the difference between a batter and a dough?
8. What are the three gases that make baked products rise?
9. What are three functions of eggs in quick breads?
10. What is the minimum amount of fat, sugar, and salt needed per cup of flour when preparing muffins?
11. Why should no more than half the all-purpose flour be replaced with whole-grain flour when adjusting a recipe?
12. Match the following quick breads with their descriptions:

    _____ May be rolled or dropped.

    _____ Has a peaked top and tunnels when overmixed.

    _____ Leavened almost entirely by steam; baked in muffin pans or custard cups.

    _____ Made with a dough called *puff paste.*

    A. biscuit
    B. cream puff
    C. muffin
    D. pancake
    E. popover

13. Why is following a recipe's directions for heating liquids important?
14. How does fast-rising yeast differ from active dry yeast?
15. What is the function of kneading yeast dough?
16. List three factors that affect the length of fermentation for yeast doughs.
17. What are three types of recipes that are specially formulated to allow prepared yeast dough to be stored and baked at another time?

Chapter 17 Review and Expand

Core Skills

18. **Research, Speaking** Nearly every culture eats some type of bread product as a dietary staple. Research the type or types of bread featured in the cuisine of another culture. Prepare an informative speech to share your findings with the class. Find a bread recipe from this culture to prepare and serve during your speech.

19. **Math, Speaking, Listening** Visit a local grocery store. List the brands, weights, and descriptions of 10 bread products. Then rank them in order according to cost. Share your findings in a class discussion on factors that affect bread costs.

20. **Science, Writing** Design a science experiment to compare the leavening power of baking soda, baking powder, and yeast. Write a step-by-step procedure for your experiment. Follow your procedure to conduct the experiment. Record your observations and write a conclusion. Then revise your written procedure to be sure the steps are clear and complete enough for someone else to follow.

21. **Science, Speaking, Listening** Working in your lab group, have one student place ½ cup (125 mL) of an assigned type of flour in a bowl. One student should stir the flour while another student gradually adds water until the mixture forms a sticky dough. Have lab group members take turns stirring the dough, noting changes in the consistency. As a class, discuss the differences in gluten development among the different types of flour used by the various lab groups.

22. **Writing, Technology** Write a script for a 30-second television commercial advertising homemade wheat bread. Remember that ad copy should persuade consumers to buy the product. Make up a brand name and develop a slogan to include in your commercial. Rehearse the script and then shoot a video of the commercial. Edit the video, adding text, music, and voiceovers, to effectively promote the product. Show the finished commercial in class.

23. **Career Readiness Practice** Research celiac disease and other medical reasons for following a gluten-free diet. Summarize your findings in a brief brochure. Include several gluten-free bread recipes in the brochure. Prepare and distribute samples of the recipes along with the brochures at a local health fair.

Critical Thinking and Problem Solving

24. **Create** Create a poster illustrating the functions of each basic ingredient in baked products. Use color and graphics to make your poster engaging as well as educational.

25. **Analyze** Copy the ingredient list for a traditional muffin recipe. Analyze the list and reference Figure 17.5 to write a revised list that is adjusted to minimum proportions for reducing sugar, fat, and sodium. Also make any other adjustments that might help you increase your intake of fruits, vegetables, and/or whole grains. Use an online nutrient database to prepare a nutrient profile for both versions of the recipe. Compare the two profiles and write a brief analysis describing how your adjustments affected the nutritional value of the muffins.

26. **Analyze** Prepare a plain muffin batter. Drop half of the batter from a large spoon into the depressions of a muffin pan. Place the pan in an oven and bake the muffins as the recipe directs. Continue beating the remaining batter for two more minutes. Drop it into the depressions of another muffin pan and bake as the recipe directs. Analyze the differences in appearance, flavor, and texture of the two products.

27. **Evaluate** Bake a traditional loaf of white bread and a loaf in a bread machine. Evaluate the two loaves along with a loaf of purchased white bread. Rate each product in terms of appearance, texture, flavor, and cost.

Chapter 18
Vegetables

Goran Bogicevic/Shutterstock.com

Objectives

After studying this chapter, you will be able to

- **recall** nutrients found in vegetables;
- **explain** how to properly select and store all forms of vegetables;
- **describe** food science principles of cooking vegetables;
- **identify** methods for cooking vegetables; and
- **prepare** vegetables, preserving their colors, textures, flavors, and nutrients.

Reading Prep

Review the chapter headings and use them to create an outline for taking notes during reading and class discussion. Under each heading, list any term highlighted in yellow. Write two questions that you expect the chapter to answer.

Content Terms 🔗

chlorophyll
carotene
flavones
anthocyanin
crisper
legumes
julienne
crisp-tender

Academic Terms

adversely
retain
spectrum
reconstitute

Most vegetables are fairly low in cost and calories. They can be served raw or cooked to add color, flavor, texture, and nutrients to meals and snacks. Vegetables can be purchased fresh, canned, frozen, and dried.

Nutritional Value of Vegetables

MyPlate sorts vegetables into five subgroups based on the nutrients they provide. *Dark green vegetables* include broccoli, spinach, dark green leafy lettuce, and greens such as collards and kale. Carrots, tomatoes, sweet potatoes, all types of winter squash, and pumpkin are *red and orange vegetables*. *Beans and peas* include lentils and split peas along with beans such as kidney, pinto, garbanzo, black, and soy. White potatoes, corn, green peas, and green lima beans are common *starchy vegetables*. The *other vegetables* subgroup includes onions, green beans, mushrooms, cucumbers, and asparagus.

Including a variety of vegetables in your diet is important because different vegetables provide different nutrients and phytonutrients. Vegetables are low in fat and calories and rich in fiber. They are good sources of folate and vitamins A, C, and E. Vegetables like sweet and white potatoes, tomato products, and beet greens can even help boost your potassium intake. That is why a healthy diet includes plenty of vegetables. Such a diet may reduce your risk for stroke, heart disease, and diabetes. Eating vegetables may also reduce your risk for some forms of cancer.

MyPlate suggests teens eat 2½ to 4 cups (625 to 1,000 mL) per day from the vegetable group. The amount you need depends on your gender and activity level. Cut vegetables and vegetable juice count cup for cup. Two cups (500 mL) of leafy vegetables count as 1 cup (250 mL) from this group.

You do not need to eat vegetables from all five MyPlate subgroups each day to get the nutritional value of vegetables. However, try to get the suggested amount from each subgroup weekly. For many people, this means eating more dark green, and red and orange vegetables as well as more legumes (**Figure 18.1**).

Dark Green Vegetables

Calorie Level	Cups per Week
1,800-2,000	1.5
2,200-2,400	2
2,600-2,800	2.5
3,000-3,200	2.5

Red and Orange Vegetables

Calorie Level	Cups per Week
1,800-2,000	5.5
2,200-2,400	6
2,600-2,800	7
3,000-3,200	7.5

Beans, Peas, and Lentils

Calorie Level	Cups per Week
1,800-2,000	1.5
2,200-2,400	2
2,600-2,800	2.5
3,000-3,200	3

Starchy Vegetables

Calorie Level	Cups per Week
1,800-2,000	5
2,200-2,400	6
2,600-2,800	7
3,000-3,200	8

Other Vegetables

Calorie Level	Cups per Week
1,800-2,000	4
2,200-2,400	5
2,600-2,800	5.5
3,000-3,200	7

Shutterstock.com

Figure 18.1 Get suggested amounts from each vegetable subgroup every week, based on your calorie needs.

Choosing Fresh Vegetables

Many fresh vegetables can be purchased all year long. The cost of fresh vegetables depends a great deal on the time of year. Vegetables cost less when purchased during their peak growing season (**Figure 18.2**). During other seasons, costs vary due to storage, handling, and shipping charges.

Vegetable Classifications

Nutrient content is not the only characteristic used to group vegetables. Vegetables are also grouped according to the part of the plant from which they come. Garlic and onions are *bulbs*. Artichokes, broccoli, and cauliflower are *flowers*. Tomatoes, cucumbers, eggplant, okra, peppers, pumpkins, and squash are *fruits*. Asparagus and celery are *stems*. Brussels sprouts, cabbage, lettuce, and spinach are *leaves*. Peas, corn, and beans are *seeds*. White potatoes and Jerusalem artichokes are *tubers*. Beets, carrots, parsnips, radishes, rutabagas, sweet potatoes, and turnips are *roots*.

Color is another factor used to classify vegetables. Vegetables can be green, orange, white, or red. A vegetable's color depends on the pigments it contains. *Green vegetables*, such as broccoli and spinach, contain the pigment **chlorophyll**. Carrots

Tish1/Shutterstock.com

Figure 18.2 Peak growing seasons vary depending on the vegetable. Carrots are typically harvested in late July for the fresh market.

and sweet potatoes are *orange vegetables*. They contain **carotene**, a source of vitamin A, and they are rich in the group of phytonutrients known as *carotenoids*. *White vegetables*, such as cauliflower and parsnips, contain pigments called **flavones**. Beets and red cabbage are *red vegetables*. They contain a pigment called **anthocyanin**.

Selecting Fresh Vegetables

No matter what their classifications are, fresh vegetables are perishable. The effects of temperature and handling may cause them to deteriorate during shipping. Being familiar with signs of quality will help you choose the best vegetables available when you shop.

In general, look for good color and firmness. Avoid bruised, wilted, decaying, and misshapen vegetables. **Figure 18.3** describes what to look for and what to avoid when buying some specific types of vegetables.

As you shop, the following guidelines will help you get the best value and preserve the quality of what you buy:

- Learn which vegetables are in season at the time you are shopping. These vegetables are usually high in quality and low in price.

- Choose vegetables that are medium in size. Very small vegetables can be immature and lack flavor. Very large vegetables can be overmature and tough.

- Handle vegetables carefully to prevent bruising.

- Buy only what you will use within a short time. Fresh vegetables lose quality and nutrients through prolonged storage.

- Keep fresh vegetables away from raw meat, poultry, and seafood in the shopping cart.

- Buy ready-to-eat vegetables and salads if they fit in your budget. These handy items may prompt you to eat more vegetables.

Storing Fresh Vegetables

Once you buy fresh vegetables, use them as soon as possible for best flavor, appearance, and nutritive value. Most vegetables can be kept fresh in the refrigerator for at least a few days. Place them in plastic bags or containers or in the crisper. A **crisper** is the drawer or

How to Buy Fresh Vegetables		
Vegetable	**Choose**	**Avoid**
Asparagus	Rich, green color; tender stalks; compact tips; rounded spears	Open, moldy, or decayed tips; ribbed spears; excessive sand
Bell Peppers	Bright color, glossy sheen, firm walls, heavy for size	Thin, wilted, cut or punctured walls; decayed spots
Broccoli	Firm, compact clusters of small flower buds; deep green color	Thick, tough stems; open buds; wilted, soft condition; yellow color
Cabbage	Firm heads, heavy for size; bright red or green color; fresh; no blemishes	Wilted, decayed, yellow outer leaves; worm holes
Carrots	Bright color; well-rounded, smooth, firm roots	Flabby, decaying roots; patches of green
Cauliflower	Creamy white to white heads; compact, clean, solid florets	Discolored spots, wilting
Celery	Bright color; smooth, rigid stalks; fresh leaves	Discoloration; flabby or pithy stalks; wilting
Corn	Plump, not overly mature kernels; fresh, green husks	Yellow, wilted, or dried husks; very small, very large, or dark kernels
Cucumbers	Well-shaped, rounded bodies; bright green color; firm	Signs of wilting, large diameter, yellowing
Green Beans	Bright color, tender beans, crisp pods	Thick, tough, or wilted pods, serious blemishes
Green Onions	Fresh, green tops; well-formed, white bulbs	Yellow, wilted, or decayed tops
Lettuce	Crisp leaves for iceberg and romaine, soft texture for leaf lettuce	Very hard heads, poor color, brown or soft spots, irregular heads
Mushrooms	Closed caps that are clean, dry, and firm; firm stems	Pitted or spotted caps; caps that are wide open, showing the gills; mold; soft texture
Onions	Hard, smooth, and firm with small necks; papery outer covering	Wet or soft necks, woody or sprouting areas
Potatoes	Firm, well-shaped, free from blemishes and sunburn	Large cuts, bruises, or green spots; signs of sprouting or shriveling
Radishes	Plump, round, and firm; medium size; bright red color	Large or flabby radishes, decaying tops
Summer Squash	Tender, well-developed, firm body, glossy skin	Dull appearance; hard, tough skin
Sweet Potatoes	Deep orange color; firm, solid roots	Pale color, blemishes
Tomatoes	Well-formed, smooth, free from blemishes, bright red color	Soft spots, moldy areas, growth cracks, bruises

Figure 18.3 Fresh vegetables taste better and retain more of their nutrients.

compartment in the refrigerator designed to keep vegetables firm and fresh. Leafy greens should be thoroughly rinsed and dried before being refrigerated in perforated plastic bags. Washing other vegetables before storage may encourage bacterial growth. Instead, wash vegetables just before you are ready to prepare them. Sweet corn should be stored in the husks and used within two days for best quality.

Cold refrigerator temperatures *adversely* (negatively) affect the flavor and texture of some vegetables. Tomatoes can be ripened at room temperature and kept unrefrigerated for about a week. Onions, potatoes, sweet potatoes, and hard-rind squash are best stored in a cool, dark place. They may keep a month or two if stored at 45°F to 55°F (7°C to 13°C). Air should circulate freely around these vegetables to keep

Plant Scientist

Plant scientists study plants and factors that affect their growth. They may develop new varieties of plants that can resist pests, disease, or drought. They may work to improve the nutritional value of plant foods. They may help farmers increase crop harvests while making the best use of soil and water resources. Some plant scientists try to find new uses for plant products.

To be successful, plant scientists need strong math and science skills. They use critical thinking skills to analyze and solve problems. They must be active learners so they can understand and apply new information. Being able to communicate effectively, through both speech and writing, is important, too. Plant scientists must pay attention to details. They need to be able to work independently as well as with members of a research team. They also need to be willing to stick with a project even when it takes many attempts to achieve a desired outcome.

Taking a variety of math, science, and computer classes can help prepare someone to enter this field. Plant scientists need a bachelor's degree to work as research assistants. However, scientists who wish to direct research projects must have a master's or doctoral degree.

A

Pixeljoy/Shutterstock.com

B

Becky Stares/Shutterstock.com

Figure 18.4   Cool, dry, dark storage locations can slow (A) solanine formation and (B) sprouting in potatoes.

them dry, as moisture can promote spoilage. Storing these vegetables at room temperature shortens keeping time to about a week. Onions and potatoes may begin to sprout. Potatoes that are exposed to light turn green and develop a bitter flavor. This is due to the formation of a substance called *solanine*, which can cause illness if consumed in large amounts. Be sure to trim off and dispose of any green parts on potatoes before preparation (**Figure 18.4**).

Choosing Canned, Frozen, and Dried Vegetables

Most people prefer fresh vegetables for salads and relish trays. For use in recipes or as hot side dishes, however, canned, frozen, and dried vegetables often work just as well.

Canned Vegetables

Canned vegetables can be whole, sliced, or in pieces. Most are canned in water. A few, like baked beans, are canned in sauces. Some are available preseasoned for use in recipes.

Most canned vegetables are packed in cans. A few are available in jars. Choose a container size to meet your needs.

Canned vegetables usually cost less than either frozen or fresh produce. Cost per serving depends on brand, can size, quality, and packing liquid. Choose store brands to save money. Choose cans that are free from dents, bulges, and leaks. Choose the quality that meets your needs and intended use. Store all cans in a cool, dry place. After opening, place unused portions in a covered container and store in the refrigerator (**Figure 18.5**).

Frozen Vegetables

Frozen vegetables *retain* (keep) the appearance and flavor of fresh vegetables better than canned and dried vegetables. However, freezing may alter their texture somewhat. They are available in paper cartons and plastic bags. Some vegetables are frozen in combinations or in sauces.

Frozen vegetables usually cost less than fresh. Green beans are one example. During winter months, frozen green beans are less expensive than fresh green beans. (During the summer months when green beans are in season, fresh beans may cost less than frozen.) Prices will vary according to brand, packaging, size of container, and added ingredients such as butter and sauces.

Choose packages that are clean and solidly frozen. A heavy layer of ice on the package may indicate the food has been thawed and refrozen. Store packages in the coldest part of the freezer.

Dried Vegetables

A few vegetables are dried. Dried **legumes**—peas, beans, and lentils—are the most commonly purchased dried vegetables.

Legumes are high in protein. They are also excellent sources of fiber. They are used in many meatless dishes, making them a staple in most vegetarian diets. When legumes are added to dishes that contain meat, they add volume. This makes meat-based dishes more filling and less costly per serving.

Legumes can be used in a wide variety of recipes. Many people use dried navy beans, lima beans, split peas, and lentils in soups. They use pinto and red beans in chili and many Mexican foods. Black-eyed peas are a popular side dish in the South. Garbanzo beans and kidney beans are tasty in salads. Soybeans are often used in combination with other foods.

Choose legumes that are uniform in size, free of visible defects, and brightly colored. Store them in covered containers in a cool, dry place (**Figure 18.6**).

Jiri Hera/Shutterstock.com

Figure 18.6 Glass jars with tight seals not only keep dried beans fresh, but also make it easy to identify the product.

B Brown/Shutterstock.com

Figure 18.5 Some people preserve vegetables that are in season for use later in the year.

Preparing Vegetables

Vegetables come in a *spectrum* (range) of colors and a variety of flavors. These characteristics, combined with various cooking methods, allow vegetables to be used in countless ways to add interest to meals.

Preparing Raw Vegetables

Eating vegetables raw has a number of advantages. Raw vegetables can provide nearly twice the fiber of cooked vegetables, as heat causes a breakdown of fiber. In addition, raw vegetables are attractive to serve. They are colorful, and their crunchiness adds texture to meals and snacks.

Many vegetables can be eaten raw. You may have eaten raw celery and carrot sticks, pepper strips, and broccoli florets on veggie trays. You might have enjoyed raw lettuce, cucumbers, tomatoes, and cabbage in salads. Raw spinach and kale make great additions to smoothies.

To prepare clean raw vegetables for eating or cooking, trim any bruised areas, wilted leaves, and thick stems. When peeling vegetables, use a peeler rather than a paring knife. Peelers remove a thinner layer of skin, thus preserving as many nutrients as possible.

Cut raw vegetables into appropriate sizes and shapes for their intended use. For a fresh veggie tray, cut pieces that are easy to handle. Sticks, wedges, rings, and florets are good choices. For salads and cooked dishes, vegetables are more often sliced, diced, or **julienned** (cut into thin, matchstick-sized strips). These smaller pieces combine easily with other ingredients and can be picked up on a fork. You can also cut raw vegetables to make colorful garnishes. Carrot curls, celery fans, and radish roses add nutrients and eye appeal to many dishes (**Figure 18.7**).

Raw vegetables taste best when served cold. Place a veggie tray on a bed of ice or arrange vegetables in a bowl lined with ice. Store washed and thoroughly drained vegetables in covered containers in the refrigerator.

Food Science Principles of Cooking Vegetables

When vegetables are cooked, several changes take place. The *cellulose* (fiber) in vegetables

Robyn Mackenzie/Shutterstock.com

Figure 18.7   Firm vegetables like carrots are interesting and attractive when they are julienned. What other vegetables might look appealing when cut this way?

softens to make chewing easier. Starch absorbs water, swells, and becomes easier to digest. Flavors and colors undergo changes, and nutritional value may be affected.

Properly cooked vegetables are colorful and flavorful. They also have a **crisp-tender** texture. This means they are tender, but still slightly firm. They can be pierced with a fork but not too easily. Proper cooking involves using the correct amount of cooking liquid and careful timing.

Amount of Cooking Liquid

Some nutrients in vegetables, including minerals, vitamin C, and the B vitamins, are water-soluble. They will dissolve in cooking liquid. Vegetables cooked with no added water or in a small amount of water retain more of these water-soluble nutrients (**Figure 18.8**).

Cooking Time

In most cases, vegetables should be cooked for a short time. Cooking vegetables too long causes several undesirable changes to take place. Heat-sensitive nutrients, such as thiamin, are lost. Vegetables may develop unpleasant strong or bitter flavors. Overcooking gives vegetables unappealing soft and mushy textures. Too much cooking time can result in dull, discolored vegetables, too. Vegetables cooked for a short time retain more heat-sensitive nutrients, fresh flavors, firm textures, and bright colors.

Effect of Cooking on Vegetable Flavor

Vegetables can have mild, strong, or very strong flavors. Different cooking techniques are suggested to enhance the flavors of vegetables in each of these groups.

Mildly flavored vegetables include green vegetables, such as peas, green beans, and spinach. Yellow vegetables, such as corn; red vegetables, such as beets; and white vegetables, such as parsnips, also have mild flavors. Cook most mildly flavored vegetables for a short time in a small amount of water with the pan covered.

Strongly flavored vegetables, such as cabbage, broccoli, brussels sprouts, yellow turnips, and rutabagas, are exceptions to general cooking rules. Cover these vegetables with water. Cook them in an uncovered pan for a short time. Following these guidelines allows some of the strong flavor substances to escape into the water and air.

Very strongly flavored vegetables, such as onions and leeks, should also be covered with water. Cook them in an uncovered pan for a longer time. As they cook, these vegetables will release strong flavor substances and develop a milder flavor.

Leszek Glasner/Shutterstock.com

Figure 18.8 Cooking vegetables in little or no liquid reduces the loss of their water-soluble nutrients.

Methods of Cooking Vegetables

Vegetables can be cooked by boiling, steaming, pressure-cooking, roasting, frying, stir-frying, broiling, grilling, and microwaving. Regardless of the cooking method, vegetables cooked in their skins retain more nutrients. Consider personal preferences and the other foods in the menu when choosing a cooking method.

Cooking Vegetables in Water

Use a pan with a tight-fitting lid when cooking vegetables in water. Add salt to a small amount of water and bring the water to a boil. Add the vegetables, cover, and quickly bring to a boil again. Then reduce the heat and cook the vegetables at a simmering temperature until they are crisp-tender. Drain and serve the vegetables immediately.

Steaming Vegetables

Young, tender vegetables that cook quickly can be steamed. To steam vegetables, place them

Learn About...

Washing Vegetables

If you have seen a vegetable garden, you know the edible part of most vegetables grows in or near soil. Soil can carry harmful bacteria. Therefore, whether you are preparing fresh vegetables to eat raw or cooked, the first step is to wash them. Careful washing removes dirt, bacteria, and pesticide residues. You should even wash vegetables with rinds and peels that you are going to discard, such as winter squash and onions.

Wash vegetables in cool running water. Use a vegetable brush to remove stubborn dirt from crevices. Do not allow vegetables to soak as you wash them, as this can cause a loss of water-soluble nutrients. After washing, gently dry vegetables with a clean cloth or paper towel. Removing surface moisture helps prevent the growth of bacteria.

Know and Apply

1. Why is it important to wash fresh vegetables?
2. How should fresh vegetables be washed?

Food Science

Effect of Cooking on Vegetable Color

Cooking can affect the color of vegetables. For this reason, cooking times and methods may need adjustment to suit the vegetables being cooked.

Heat affects chlorophyll in green vegetables. Overcooked green vegetables lose their bright green color and look grayish-green. To keep vegetables green, cook them in a small amount of water. Use a short cooking time and keep the pan lid off for the first few minutes of cooking. Then cover the pan for the remainder of the cooking period. (Do not add baking soda to cooking water for green vegetables. Although this weak alkali will produce a bright green color, it can also cause a loss of important nutrients.)

Heat does not destroy carotene in orange vegetables. However, if an orange vegetable is overcooked, the cell structure will break down. This will release the carotene into the cooking liquid. Most orange vegetables should be cooked in a small amount of water with the pan covered.

Flavones in white vegetables are soluble in water. If white vegetables are overcooked, they turn yellow or dark gray. Take care when cooking to avoid these undesirable color changes.

If the cooking water is alkaline, anthocyanins in red vegetables will turn purple. Adding a little vinegar or lemon juice to the water will neutralize the alkali. This will keep red vegetables red. Cook most red vegetables in a small amount of water, with the pan lid on, just until tender.

bitt24/Shutterstock.com

Properly cooked vegetables will retain their bright, appetizing colors.

in a steaming basket over simmering water. Tightly cover the pan and steam the vegetables until they are tender. Shredded cabbage, broccoli, diced root vegetables, celery, sweet corn, and French-style (thinly sliced) green beans can be successfully steamed.

Pressure-Cooking Vegetables

To pressure-cook vegetables, follow the directions that accompany the pressure cooker. The pressure in a pressure cooker produces high temperatures, so foods cook quickly. Time vegetables carefully to prevent overcooking.

Roasting Vegetables

Roasting takes longer than other cooking methods. It uses the dry heat of an oven to cook vegetables. Vegetables can be roasted peeled or in their skins. During the cooking period, natural sugars in the vegetables cause a brown color and slightly sweet flavor to develop. Potatoes, winter squash, and garlic are just a few of the many vegetables that are popular for roasting (**Figure 18.9**).

Roasting is usually done in an open pan. Peeled vegetables can be wrapped in foil before

zkruger/Shutterstock.com

Figure 18.9 The natural sugars in the vegetables are changed during roasting and result in tasty flavors. What is the chemical reaction that produces these flavors? (Hint: see Chapter 15)

placing them in an oven. Peeled vegetables can also be placed in a covered casserole with a small amount of liquid. However, these two methods are not actually roasting, as they use steam rather than oven heat to cook the vegetables.

Frying Vegetables

A couple of methods can be used to fry vegetables. They can be sautéed in a small amount of fat. They can also be dipped in batter and deep-fried.

A third frying method, stir-frying, works well with vegetables that have a high moisture content. To stir-fry vegetables, shred them or cut them into small pieces. Place the vegetables in a heavy skillet or wok. Use a small amount of oil to help prevent sticking. Place the pan over medium-high heat and stir the vegetables constantly, just until tender.

Broiling Vegetables

Tomato halves and eggplant slices are often broiled. To broil vegetables, brush the cut surfaces with oil or melted fat. Place the vegetables under the broiling unit and broil until tender. Because vegetables cook quickly under the broiler, they must be watched carefully.

Grilling Vegetables

When preparing vegetables on a grill, be aware that grilling times will vary. Dense vegetables, like potatoes, take longer to grill than less dense vegetables, like mushrooms and peppers. Whole vegetables also take longer to grill than cut pieces (**Figure 18.10**).

Place vegetables that cook more quickly directly over the heat source on a grill. Grill slower cooking vegetables with indirect heat. Placing vegetables in a grill basket makes it easy to turn them during grilling for more even cooking. Be sure to watch them carefully to avoid charring.

Microwaving Vegetables

Vegetables cooked in a microwave oven retain their shapes, colors, flavors, and nutrients. This is due to the short cooking time and the use of little or no cooking liquid.

Use high power to cook vegetables in a microwave oven. Remember to allow standing time for vegetables to finish cooking. Stir vegetable dishes during the cooking period to redistribute heat. Rearrange whole vegetables during the cooking period to ensure even cooking. Vegetables that have tight skins can explode when cooked in a microwave oven. To prevent this, pierce their skins in several places before microwaving.

Frozen vegetables can be prepared in a microwave oven as easily as fresh vegetables. Slit pouches of vegetables to allow steam to escape. Place vegetables that do not come in pouches in a microwavable casserole for cooking.

MaraZe/Shutterstock.com *photowind/Shutterstock.com*

Figure 18.10 Grilling time will vary depending on the sizes of the vegetable pieces.

Recipe for Good Food

24 Golden Carrots

Serves 4

4   medium carrots, peeled and trimmed
¼   cup (60 mL) orange juice
2   teaspoons (10 mL) sugar
½   teaspoon (2.5 mL) ground cinnamon
1   tablespoon, 1½ teaspoons (22.5 mL) butter
⅓   cup (80 mL) golden raisins

1. Cut each carrot into 24 planks by first cutting it crosswise into thirds. Cut each third in half lengthwise. Lay the flat side of each half on the cutting board and cut it lengthwise into 4 planks.

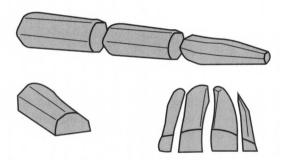

2. Place cut carrots into a medium microwavable bowl and toss with orange juice.
3. Cover the bowl with a vented cover. Microwave on high power for 3 to 4 minutes, until carrots just begin to soften.
4. Stir sugar and cinnamon together in a cup and set aside.
5. Melt butter in a skillet over medium heat. Add the cooked carrots and orange juice.
6. Sprinkle the sugar-cinnamon mixture over the carrots and stir to coat. Continue cooking the carrots until the juice begins to thicken and form a sauce, about 3 minutes.
7. Stir in the golden raisins and cook until heated through, about 3 minutes. Return the carrots to the bowl for serving.

Per serving: 108 calories (33% from fat), 1 g protein, 18 g carbohydrate, 4 g fat, 11 mg cholesterol, 2 g fiber, 65 mg sodium

Selecting Potatoes

Although potatoes are a vegetable, they are treated somewhat differently from other vegetables. Potatoes are classified on the basis of appearance and use. Basic types are russet, white, red, and yellow.

Potatoes in each class have qualities that are well suited to certain preparation methods. *Russet potatoes* have a thick skin and drier texture that make them especially popular for baking. Their mealy flesh allows them to break apart easily, which makes them good for mashing but not for boiling.

White, *red*, and *yellow potatoes* all have thin skins. These kinds of potatoes have a moister texture that is often described as waxy. This quality allows these potatoes to hold their shape well during cooking, making them good choices for potato salad, soups, and stews. All of these kinds of potatoes can be used for mashing and roasting.

One other class of potatoes is *specialty potatoes*, which include blue/purple, fingerling, and petite varieties. These potatoes have thin skins and a moist texture and can be used like other waxy potatoes. The vibrant color of *blue/purple potatoes* will add a twist to any meal. *Fingerling potatoes* are oblong shaped and 2 to 4 inches (5 to 10 cm) long. *Petite potatoes* are small round potatoes. Fingerlings and petite potatoes come in a rainbow of colors. Their small size allows them to cook quickly and create visual interest on a plate (**Figure 18.11**).

Perhaps you have seen a recipe or store display for new potatoes. *New potatoes* are not a variety. They are potatoes that are harvested before they are fully mature.

Types of Potatoes

Russet

White

Red

Yellow

Blue/Purple

Fingerling

Petite

Left to right, top to bottom: Quang Ho/Shutterstock.com; andersphoto/Shutterstock.com; Hong Vo/Shutterstock.com; Viktar Malyshchyts/Shutterstock.com; LogicheCreative.it/Shutterstock.com; Zigzag Mountain Art/Shutterstock.com; Nattika/Shutterstock.com

Figure 18.11 Potatoes should not be stored in the refrigerator. When refrigerated, the potato's starch converts to sugar and results in an unpleasant flavor.

Preparing Potatoes

Four common potato preparations are mashing, frying, baking, and roasting. Before preparing potatoes by any method, be sure to scrub and rinse them gently but thoroughly. Cut away any sprouts and green portions.

To prepare potatoes for mashing, peel and cut them into large, even chunks. Place potatoes in a large pan, cover them with lightly salted water, and simmer until tender. Drain potatoes; then add butter, milk, and salt. Beat the potatoes with an electric mixer or mash them by hand. Be careful not to overbeat potatoes, which causes them to have a sticky texture.

French fries and hash browns are two popular fried potato dishes. Some fried potato dishes are made with raw potatoes, and others are made with boiled potatoes. French fries are made by deep-frying raw potato strips. Hash browns are made from shredded or diced cooked potatoes.

A lower-fat, lower-calorie version of French fries is oven fries. They are less messy to make than French fries, too. To prepare oven fries, cut potatoes into ½-inch (1.25 cm) sticks and place them in a bowl of ice water for about 30 minutes. This helps to remove excess starch and yields crispier fries. Drain potatoes and pat dry with paper towels. Toss potatoes with a tablespoon (15 mL) of oil. Spread in a single layer on a baking sheet covered with parchment paper and sprinkle with desired seasonings. Bake at 450°F (230°C) for about 35 minutes, until golden brown.

To prepare baked potatoes, pierce scrubbed potatoes in several places with a fork. This prevents steam from building up inside the skin, which could cause the potato to explode. Bake potatoes in a 400°F (200°C) oven until they are tender, about 45 to 60 minutes. (Baking time and temperature can be adjusted so potatoes can bake with other foods.) A potato can also be baked in a microwave oven in about 5 minutes.

For roasted potatoes, cut potatoes into large chunks. In a large pan, cover potatoes with seasoned water and simmer for 5 minutes. This step helps give the roasted potatoes a crispy texture outside and a creamy texture inside. Drain potatoes and allow them to dry completely before tossing them with a small amount of oil and desired seasonings (**Figure 18.12**). Spread the potatoes in a single layer in a roasting pan. Roast in a 400°F (200°C) oven for about 30 minutes until golden brown.

Preparing Canned, Frozen, and Dried Vegetables

Canned vegetables have already been cooked. Many vegetables suffer changes in color and texture during canning. Therefore, they

Tomasz Jasiewicz/Shutterstock.com

Figure 18.12 Tossing potatoes with oil and seasonings can add flavor and texture.

Health and Wellness

Using Vegetable Cooking Liquid

After vegetables have cooked, do not throw away the cooking liquid. It contains many valuable nutrients. A small amount of the cooking liquid can be served with the vegetables in a separate dish. If the liquid is not needed right away, freeze it in small amounts. (Ice cube trays work well.) Later, the frozen liquid can be added to sauces, soups, and gravies.

will look and taste better if they are heated no more than necessary before serving.

To prepare canned vegetables, place the vegetables and the liquid from the can in a saucepan. Cook over low heat until the vegetables are heated through. Add seasonings to taste.

Prepare frozen vegetables according to package instructions. Frozen vegetables have already been *blanched* (preheated in boiling water or steam for a short time). Blanching reduces the cooking time needed to about half that needed for fresh vegetables.

Dried legumes need to be rinsed and sorted before cooking (**Figure 18.13**). Remove any debris that may have been packaged with the vegetables. Dried beans must be soaked before cooking so they will absorb water and cook more evenly.

To soak beans, place them in a large pot with plenty of water. Bring the water to a boil for two to three minutes. Cover the pot and remove it from the heat. Allow beans to soak for at least one hour. Discard the soaking water and use fresh water for cooking. This will help reduce the gas-causing properties of beans.

Dried lentils and peas need no soaking. *Reconstitute* (restore to former condition by adding water) other dried vegetables according to package directions.

Steve Lovegrove/Shutterstock.com

Figure 18.13   Rinse legumes before cooking to remove dirt and possible pesticide residues.

Serving Vegetables

Vegetables can be served in many creative and delicious ways. Some people prefer their vegetables served simply, seasoned with herbs or a sprinkling of salt. Others enjoy vegetables topped with a few toasted nuts or a bit of shredded cheese. With just a little extra effort, variety can be added to a vegetable with a low-fat sauce. Light glazes of brown sugar or honey are also popular (**Figure 18.14**).

Yogurt and cottage cheese are tasty, low-fat alternatives to sour cream for fresh vegetable dips and baked potato toppings. Garnish boiled potatoes with fresh chopped parsley or chives. Give ordinary mashed potatoes a new twist by combining them with roasted garlic. Try swirling them with mashed sweet potatoes. Brown small whole potatoes around a roast. Serving vegetables in these different ways adds variety to meals.

Brent Hofacker/Shutterstock.com

Figure 18.14   Bright red pepper strips and crunchy toasted almonds turn ordinary green beans into a special dish. What is your favorite way to serve vegetables?

Chapter 18 Review and Expand

Summary

Vegetables are low in fat and calories, high in fiber, and rich in vitamins and minerals. Eat suggested amounts from each MyPlate subgroup weekly to meet nutrient needs. When buying fresh vegetables, choose items that are in their peak growing season. Select medium-sized, healthy-looking pieces that have good color. Store most vegetables in the refrigerator.

Canned, frozen, and dried vegetables can be a good buy when fresh vegetables are not in season. Choose packages that are intact. Store frozen vegetables in the freezer. Keep canned and dried vegetables in a cool, dry place.

To prepare fresh vegetables, wash and trim them. Cooking affects the pigments in green, yellow, white, and red vegetables. Cook most vegetables for a short time in a small amount of liquid. This will help preserve flavors, textures, colors, and nutrients.

Vegetables can also be steamed, pressure-cooked, roasted, fried, broiled, grilled, and microwaved. Choose a type of potato suited to the desired cooking method. Try new sauces and seasonings when serving vegetables to add interest to meals.

Vocabulary Activities

1. **Content Terms**   Write each of the following terms on a separate sheet of paper. For each term, quickly write a word you think relates to the term. In small groups, have each person in the group explain a term on the list.

   chlorophyll   crisper

   carotene   legumes

   flavones   julienne

   anthocyanin   crisp-tender

2. **Academic Terms**   Review the following terms and identify any that have *roots* and *suffixes* or *prefixes*. Write these terms on a sheet of paper. Beside each term, list the root word and prefix or suffix. How do root words help you understand meaning? suffixes and prefixes?

   adversely   spectrum

   retain   reconstitute

Review

Write your answers using complete sentences when appropriate.

3. List four nutrients found in vegetables.

4. List the five MyPlate vegetable subgroups. Give an example from each subgroup.

5. What are the pigments in white vegetables called?

6. List three guidelines to follow when shopping for fresh vegetables.

7. Why is it important to keep vegetables like onions, potatoes, and hard-rind squash dry during storage?

8. What form of processed vegetables best retains the flavor and appearance of fresh vegetables?

9. What vegetables are most commonly purchased in dried form?

10. How should clean raw vegetables be prepared for eating or cooking?

11. List three changes that take place in vegetables when they are cooked.

12. List the three flavor categories of vegetables and give cooking guidelines for each.

13. List four methods for cooking vegetables. Describe two.

14. Why are white, red, and yellow potatoes good choices for making potato salad, soups, and stews?

15. True or false. Canned vegetables have already been cooked.

16. How can vegetable cooking liquid be used?

Core Skills

17. **Math**   Choose five types of vegetables. Visit a supermarket to find the price of each type of vegetable in fresh, canned, frozen, and dried forms. Calculate the cost per serving of each type and form of vegetable. Illustrate your findings with a bar graph.

Chapter 18 Review and Expand

18. **Science** Place 1 cup (250 mL) of water in each of three medium saucepans. Stir 1 teaspoon (5 mL) baking soda into one pan. Stir 1 tablespoon (15 mL) white vinegar into another pan. Use test strips to test and record the pH of the water in each pan. Heat the water in all three pans to boiling. Add 1 cup (250 mL) shredded red cabbage to each pan. Cover pans and simmer cabbage for 10 minutes. Place a sample of the cooked cabbage from each pan on a separate white plate. Include photos of the samples in a brief written report describing your observations and conclusions.

19. **Research, Reading, Writing** Working in a small team, choose a type of natural disaster or weather condition that occurs in the United States. Identify a region of the country where your chosen condition is likely to occur. Each team member should research one of the following:

    • vegetable crops grown in the region and their economic significance
    • effects of the natural disaster or weather condition on soil quality and future crop yields
    • immediate effects of the natural disaster or weather condition on the quality and supply of vegetables grown in the region
    • effects of diminished quality and supply on vegetable retail prices

    Write a team paper with your findings. As you revise and edit your paper, track changes and add comments electronically to facilitate your collaborative effort. Refine the organization of thoughts and writing style to create a single uniform report. Edit your writing for sentence structure, tense, and spelling. Cite your sources.

20. **Writing** Research the principles behind composting and techniques and procedures for maintaining a compost pile. Find out how vegetable scraps can be used as compost. Summarize your findings in a two-page persuasive report encouraging the reader to compost at home.

21. **Research, Speaking, Technology** Use reliable print or online resources to investigate how ethanol is produced from corn as an alternative to gasoline. Research how the use of this technology affects corn production, prices, and exports in the United States. Present your findings in class using digital media and visual aids.

22. **Career Readiness Practice** Presume you are an early childhood educator at a child care center. With your coworkers (two or more classmates), brainstorm several ideas for encouraging children to eat more vegetables during meals and snacks at the center. Narrow the list to three options. How would you implement one of these options? What criteria would you use to determine how well you are meeting goals? Present your plan to the class. Include a step-by-step summary of the group's work to complete this assignment.

Critical Thinking and Problem Solving

23. **Evaluate** Evaluate the flavor, color, and texture of equal amounts of green beans prepared in each of the following ways:
    A. in a small amount of water for a short time with the pan covered
    B. in a small amount of water for a short time with the pan uncovered for the first few minutes of cooking
    C. in a large amount of water for a long time with the pan covered
    D. in a small amount of water for a short time with baking soda added and the pan covered

    Based on what you've learned in this chapter, identify which cooking technique would result in greater nutrient retention.

24. **Analyze** Prepare two portions of small, whole onions. Use a small amount of water and a covered pan for one portion. Use a large amount of water and an uncovered pan for the other portion. Compare flavor and aroma. Which cooking method would you recommend?

25. **Evaluate** Research vegetables and common preparation methods from an international cuisine. Prepare a vegetable dish from this cuisine. Share your evaluation of the dish in class.

Chapter 19
Fruits

inacio pires/Shutterstock.com

Content Terms

berries
drupes
pomes
citrus fruits
melons
tropical fruits
underripe fruit
immature fruit
enzymatic browning
fritters

Objectives

After studying this chapter, you will be able to
- **recall** nutrients found in fruits;
- **describe** how to properly select and store fruits;
- **identify** the principles and methods of cooking fruit; and
- **prepare** fruits, preserving their colors, textures, flavors, and nutrients.

Reading Prep

Arrange a study session to read the chapter with a classmate. After you read each section independently, stop and tell each other what you think the main points are in the section. Continue with each section until you finish the chapter.

Academic Terms

economy
pliable
palatable

Fresh, canned, frozen, and dried fruits add flavor, color, and texture contrasts to meals. They are generally nutritious and low in calories, so they are good choices for desserts and snacks.

Fruits can be eaten raw or cooked. For example, fresh apples make a great snack and can add a sweet crunch to a salad. They can also be used to make applesauce or a pie (**Figure 19.1**).

Nutritional Value of Fruits

Most fruits are high in vitamins and low in fat. (Avocados are a high-fat exception.) Citrus fruits, and strawberries are excellent sources of vitamin C. Bananas and dried fruits offer potassium. Cantaloupe and apricots are good sources of vitamin A and the phytonutrients known as *beta-carotenes*. Many other fruits provide phytonutrients as well. Watermelon is a good source of lycopene, and berries are high in anthocyanidins. You should eat a variety of fruits to get the full range of nutritional benefits they deliver.

Fruits, especially raw fruits, also supply needed fiber in the diet. It is worth noting that much of the fiber in fruit is found in the pulp. Therefore, pulp-free juices are not good sources of fiber.

Dried fruits are calorie dense because removing water concentrates the natural sugars

found in fresh fruits. In addition, some canned, frozen, and dried fruits contain added sugars. Balance the calories from dried fruits with other food choices and read labels to limit added sugars.

An overall healthy diet that includes plenty of fruits may help prevent heart disease, type 2 diabetes, and some types of cancer. According to MyPlate, teens should eat 1½ to 2½ cups (375 to 625 mL) from the fruit group each day, depending on calorie needs. Most forms of fruit and 100 percent fruit juice count cup for cup. For dried fruit, ½ cup (125 mL) counts as 1 cup (250 mL) from this food group.

Choosing Fresh Fruit

Many varieties of fresh fruit are available year-round. Others are available for only a short time. Knowing how to recognize high-quality fresh fruit will help you make smart choices.

Fruit Classifications

Fruits can be divided into groups according to physical characteristics. **Berries** are small, juicy fruits with thin skins. Blackberries, cranberries, blueberries, red and black raspberries, gooseberries, and strawberries all belong to the berry family. Grapes and currants are also berries. Except for cranberries, all berries are highly perishable.

Drupes have an outer skin covering a soft, fleshy fruit. The fruit surrounds a single, hard seed, which is called a *stone* or *pit*. Cherries, apricots, nectarines, peaches, and plums are all drupes.

Pomes have a central, seed-containing core surrounded by a thick layer of flesh. Apples and pears are pomes.

Citrus fruits have a thick outer rind. A thin membrane separates the flesh into segments. Oranges, tangerines, tangelos, grapefruits, kumquats, lemons, and limes are citrus fruits.

Melons are large, juicy fruits produced by plants in the gourd family. They usually have thick rinds and many seeds. This group of fruits includes cantaloupe, casaba, honeydew, Crenshaw, Persian, and watermelon.

Tropical fruits are grown in warm climates and are considered to be somewhat exotic. Many species of tropical fruits are available throughout the world. Those most commonly available in

freeskyline/Shutterstock.com
Figure 19.1 Add apple slices to sandwiches to provide texture and interest.

the United States include bananas, pineapples, avocados, mangoes, kiwifruit, and pomegranates. Examples of fruits from each of the classifications are shown in **Figure 19.2**.

Selecting Fresh Fruit

Fresh fruits are usually least expensive during their peak growing season. They are also at their best quality during this time. Peak season is a good time to buy large quantities of fruit and freeze or can them for future use.

Ripeness is a guide in judging the quality of fresh fruits. Ripe fruits are those that have reached top eating quality. Test fruit for ripeness by pressing it gently to see if it gives slightly. **Underripe fruits** are fruits that are full-sized but have not yet reached peak eating quality. Some fruits, such as pears and bananas, can be purchased when they are underripe because they will ripen within a few days at room temperature (**Figure 19.3**).

Color and fragrance are guides to ripeness. Most fruits lose their green color as they ripen. For instance, peaches turn from green to deep yellow. Pineapples and melons have a characteristic fruity fragrance when ripe.

Fruit Classifications

Berries   Drupes   Pomes

Citrus Fruits   Melons   Tropical Fruits

Figure 19.2 As a reproductive structure of the plant, the function of fruit is to protect the seed inside and facilitate its distribution.

lightpoet/Shutterstock.com

Figure 19.3 These underripe bananas will ripen within a few days at room temperature.

Maturity is another factor that will help judge the quality of fresh fruits. Do not confuse underripe fruits with immature fruits. **Immature fruits** have not reached full size. They are small and have poor color, flavor, and texture. They will not improve in quality when left at room temperature.

When buying fresh fruit, use the following guidelines:

- Buy just what can be used in a short time.
- Look for signs of freshness and ripeness, as described in **Figure 19.4**.
- Avoid bruised, soft, damaged, or immature fruits.
- Consider needs. For instance, use smaller, blemished apples for stewing and pies. Use fancy apples for fruit trays and other dishes in which appearance is important.

Storing Fresh Fruit

Handle all fruits gently to prevent bruising. Some fruits, including bananas, peaches, plums, pears, nectarines, avocados, and mangoes, are harvested before they are ripe. You should allow them to ripen before storing them in the refrigerator. The best way to do this is to put the fruit in a brown paper bag and leave it at room temperature out of direct sunlight. Natural ethylene gas given off by the fruit will speed ripening within the bag.

Exploring Careers

Agricultural Engineer

Agricultural engineers help solve a wide range of problems related to producing food and other farm products. They might address environmental issues such as irrigation and erosion control. Some work to design and test farm machinery. Others look for ways to increase crop yields. They may also analyze how to better process, pack, and ship farm products.

To be successful, agricultural engineers must have math and science skills. They use reading skills to learn new information. They need critical-thinking skills to approach problems from more than one direction to design solutions that fit each situation. They must be willing to take on challenges and adapt to changes. They also need to be able to take charge, work with little supervision, and pay attention to details.

Most agricultural engineers work with companies that sell products and services to farmers. For instance, they may work for companies that make animal feeds, pesticides, or grain silos.

Agricultural engineers need at least a four-year degree. They take a range of classes. This helps them learn to apply information from a variety of areas to the field of agriculture. Experience working with farm equipment and systems will also help prepare people attracted to this career.

Do not use plastic bags for ripening fruit, as they trap moisture that can lead to mold growth.

Check fruit daily during ripening. When it yields to gentle pressure, it is ripe and ready to be eaten or stored in the refrigerator. Once ripened, most of these fruits will keep in the refrigerator for about three to five days. (Note that refrigerator temperatures may darken banana skins, but the flavor and texture of the fruit will be unharmed.)

How to Buy Fresh Fruits		
Fruit	**Choose**	**Avoid**
Apples	Smooth, firm skin; attached stems	Musky smell; soft, bruised spots
Avocadoes	Firm skin, flesh that yields to gentle pressure when ripe	Soft spots
Bananas	Smooth, firm skin with slightly green color	Bruises, overripe fruit covered with brown spots
Blueberries	Firm, plump berries; dusty blue color; uniform size	Wet, blemished, or moldy berries
Cantaloupe	Creamy or yellow color, fruity smell, heavy for size	Asymmetrical shape, bruised or damaged rind
Cherries	Firm, shiny fruit with stems attached	Soft, shriveled, or blemished fruit
Grapefruit	Heavy for size; smooth rind	Soft, moldy, or concave areas
Grapes	Plump fruit with tight skins, firmly attached to stems	Broken or wrinkled skin, soft fruit, mold around stems
Honeydew Melon	Symmetrical shape, smooth surface, slightly yellow color, heavy for size	Green tint, fuzzy surface
Mandarin Oranges, including Clementines and Tangerines	Unblemished fruit, heavy for size	Soft spots, mold
Mangoes	Firm fruit, sweet aroma	Sticky or wrinkled skin
Nectarines	Firm fruit, smooth skin	Soft or brown spots
Oranges	Bright color; firm, smooth skin	Light for size
Peaches	Yellow coloring beneath red blush; firm, fuzzy skin; fruit yields to gentle pressure	Blemishes, green tint
Pears	Firm fruit, stem end yields to gentle pressure	Bruises, broken skin
Pineapple	Sturdy green leaves, heavy for size, fruity smell	Soft or dark spots, brown or wilted leaves

Figure 19.4 Can you think of additional suggestions when selecting fruits?

Berries, cherries, and grapes will not ripen after purchase. You should store these delicate fruits in the refrigerator in dry, covered containers as soon as you bring them home. Do not wash fruit before storage, as this will cause it to spoil more quickly. Blackberries and strawberries will keep for only two to three days. You can store grapes and cherries a bit longer.

Apples and citrus fruits will not ripen after they have been picked. You can store them for a couple weeks in the refrigerator. Keep apples in a plastic bag to help prevent moisture loss. If you want to place these fruits in a countertop fruit bowl, they will keep for a few days without refrigeration.

In the refrigerator, store fruits in a produce drawer, but keep them separated from vegetables. If you buy precut fruit, you can refrigerate it in the container it comes in from the store.

Choosing and Storing Canned, Frozen, and Dried Fruit

Fruit can be purchased canned, frozen, and dried, as well as fresh (**Figure 19.5**). Fruits are picked at their peak of quality and then preserved so they can be enjoyed all year long.

Kerry V. McQuaid/Shutterstock.com

Carpeira/Shutterstock.com

©iStock.com/bgrier

ruzanna/Shutterstock.com

Figure 19.5 When fresh peaches are not available, preserved forms allow peaches to be enjoyed year round. For what uses would you choose canned, frozen, and dried fruits?

Canned Fruit

Canned fruits are packed in cans or jars. Canned fruits can be whole, halved, sliced, or in pieces. They come packed in juices or in light or heavy syrup. Fruit juices are lower in calories and higher in nutrients than syrups used as packing liquids.

Canned fruits are usually less expensive than frozen or fresh fruits. Costs vary depending on brand, can size, quality, and packing liquid. To receive the greatest *economy* (savings), choose store brands.

When buying canned fruits, choose cans that are free from dents, bulges, and leaks. Choose jars that are free from cracks and chips. Store all cans and jars in a cool, dry place. Cover the fruit after opening and store it in the refrigerator.

Frozen Fruit

Frozen fruits are available sweetened and unsweetened; whole and in pieces. Most frozen fruits come in plastic bags or plastic-coated paper cartons.

Frozen fruits resemble fresh fruits in color and flavor. They may, however, lose some texture qualities during freezing.

The most common frozen fruits are not available in fresh form year-round. When fresh fruits are out of season, frozen fruits are often less expensive than fresh. However, prices of frozen fruits vary according to brand, packaging, and size of container. Be sure to compare price per serving, especially if the fruit is in its peak growing season.

When buying frozen fruits, choose packages that are clean, undamaged, and frozen solid. Store in the coldest part of the freezer. If using only part of a package of frozen fruit, tightly seal the unused portion and return it to the freezer promptly. Once fruit is thawed, store any that is not used in a tightly covered container in the refrigerator. Use as soon as possible. Never refreeze.

Dried Fruits

In the United States, raisins are sold more than any other type of dried fruit. Many other types of fruit are also available in dried form. Dried plums (also known as *prunes*), peaches, pears, apricots, and apples are popular. Dried tropical fruits include figs, dates, pineapple, bananas, mango, and papaya. You will also find dried cherries, cranberries, and blueberries among the dried fruit on supermarket shelves (**Figure 19.6**).

Dried fruits usually come in boxes or plastic bags. Sometimes they are loose, so they can be purchased in any quantity.

Raisins are generally the least expensive type of dried fruit. Remember to compare prices based on cost per serving.

Choose dried fruits that are fairly soft and *pliable* (supple). Read labels to avoid added sweeteners. Store unopened packages and boxes in a cool, dark, dry place. After opening, store unused portions in tightly covered containers. Some package labels recommend storing opened dried fruits in the refrigerator for best keeping quality.

Ozgur Coskun/Shutterstock.com

Figure 19.6 Many types of fruits can be dried for purchase in a supermarket. Do you think there are some types of fruits that cannot be dried? If so, what are they?

Preparing Fruits

Fruits can be served in a variety of ways to add interest to meals and snacks. They can be used raw or cooked, fresh or preserved. Carefully following preparation techniques will help maintain the appealing flavors, colors, textures, and shapes of fruits.

Preparing Raw Fruits

Raw fruits are delicious when eaten out-of-hand. They can also be combined with other foods in appetizers, salads, and desserts.

As with all food, wash your hands thoroughly with warm water and soap before preparing raw fruits for eating. Then wash the fruit carefully under clean running water and dry it with a clean towel. Even fruits that are going to be peeled, such as oranges and melons, need to be washed to remove dirt and microorganisms. Never let fruits soak, as this may cause them to lose flavor and some of their water-soluble nutrients.

Serve raw fruits whole or cut. Cut surfaces on some raw fruits, such as bananas and peaches, darken when exposed to the air. This is called **enzymatic browning**. Dipping these fruits in lemon, orange, grapefruit, or pineapple juice will prevent enzymatic browning and make them look more appealing (**Figure 19.7**).

Use a sharp, thin-bladed knife when peeling raw fruit. Peel as thinly as possible to preserve nutrients found just under the skin.

Principles of Cooking Fruit

Some fruits, like rhubarb, are cooked to make them more *palatable* (fit to be eaten) and easier to digest. Other fruits, like pears, are cooked to give variety to a menu. Cooking allows overripe fruits that are past prime eating quality to be used. For instance, apples that are becoming overripe can be used to make applesauce. Overripe bananas are great in banana bread or muffins.

Overcooked fruits become mushy. They lose their colors, nutrients, natural flavors, and shapes. Correctly cooked fruits can retain these characteristics.

Sometimes it is necessary for a fruit to retain its shape; other times it is not. For instance, if apple slices are being poached for a garnish, the slices should retain their shape. If applesauce is being prepared, however, the apples should lose their shape and form a smooth pulp.

Recipe for Good Food

Peach Salsa and Cinnamon Chips

Serves 4

2   peaches, canned or fresh
10   large green grapes
½   medium Gala or Fuji apple
1½   teaspoons (7.5 mL) lemon juice
1   tablespoon (15 mL) brown sugar
4   whole-wheat soft taco size tortillas
1½   teaspoons (7.5 mL) white sugar
¼   teaspoon (1.25 mL) cinnamon
1½   tablespoons (22.5 mL) butter, melted

1. Preheat oven to 350°F (180°C). Cover a baking sheet with parchment paper or aluminum foil sprayed with nonstick cooking spray.
2. Finely chop peaches, grapes, and apple.
3. In a medium glass mixing bowl, combine chopped fruit with lemon juice and brown sugar to make peach salsa. Toss gently, cover, and refrigerate.
4. Stack tortillas and cut into 8 wedges. Spread wedges in a single layer on prepared baking sheet.
5. Combine white sugar and cinnamon in a custard cup and stir to thoroughly blend.
6. Brush tortilla wedges with melted butter and sprinkle with the cinnamon sugar.
7. Bake tortilla wedges for 10 to 15 minutes, until golden brown and crispy.
8. Allow chips to cool. Serve with peach salsa.

Per serving: 195 calories (23% from fat), 4 g protein, 37 g carbohydrate, 5 g fat, 11 mg cholesterol, 4 g fiber, 205 mg sodium.

Methods of Cooking Fruit

Fruits can be prepared by cooking them in liquid. They can also be baked, broiled, fried, or microwaved.

Darren Pullman/Shutterstock.com

Figure 19.7 Enzymatic browning can make some fruits look unappetizing. Dipping these fruits in lemon, orange, grapefruit, or pineapple juice can help prevent browning.

Cooking Fruit in Liquid

When cooking fruits in liquid, water or sugar syrup can be used. Fruits cooked in sugar syrup will retain their shape. Those cooked in water will not. The intended use of the fruit will determine the cooking method.

When cooking fruits in syrup, use a two-to-one ratio of water to sugar. (Too much sugar will cause the fruit to harden.) Use a low temperature and cook the fruit just until it is tender and translucent. Serve cooked fruit warm or chilled.

When fruits are cooked in water, use as little water as possible. Cook the fruit over low heat until tender, then add sugar as the recipe directs. When sugar is added at the end of cooking, it will thin a fruit sauce. Thus, the amount of cooking water used must be small so the sauce will not be too thin. For a smoother sauce, force the cooked fruit through a sieve or run it through a food mill. Serve cooked fruit sauces warm or chilled.

Baking Fruit

Apples, pears, and bananas are among the fruits that can be baked. Baked fruits should be tender, but they should keep their shape. If fruit is baked in its skin, the skin will hold in

Learn About...

Effects of Cooking on Fruit

During cooking, several changes take place within fruit. Cellulose softens and makes fruit easier to digest. Colors change. Heat-sensitive and water-soluble nutrients may be lost. Flavors become less acidic and more mellow.

Fruits that undergo enzymatic browning will keep their colors if cooked with a small amount of lemon or orange juice. Water-soluble nutrients will be retained if fruit is cooked in a small amount of water just until tender. Natural flavors will be preserved if fruit is not over-cooked. Fruits will hold their shapes if they are cooked in sugar syrup instead of plain water.

keko64/Shutterstock.com

This poached pear retained its shape because it was cooked in sugar syrup.

Know and Apply

1. Do you prefer to eat fruit raw or cooked?
2. How will the desire to have cooked fruit hold its shape impact its nutritional value?

the steam that forms during baking. This steam cooks the interior of the fruit (**Figure 19.8**). If the fruit is skinned before baking, a covered casserole dish will serve the same purpose as the skin. Bake fruits in a small amount of liquid just until they are tender.

Broiling Fruit

Bananas, grapefruit halves, and pineapple slices often are broiled. Sprinkle these fruits with brown sugar or drizzle them with honey before

Julia Sudnitskaya/Shutterstock.com

Figure 19.8 When fruits are cooked in their skins, the steam trapped by the skin helps bake the interior of the fruit.

broiling. Fruits broil quickly, so watch them carefully to prevent overcooking.

Frying Fruit

Some fruits can be fried in a small amount of fat in a skillet. This is called *sautéing*. Fruits can also be dipped into a batter and deep-fried. These deep-fried fruits are called **fritters** (**Figure 19.9**). All fried fruits should be tender, but they should retain their shape.

Microwaving Fruit

Fruits cooked in a microwave oven maintain their flavors and nutrients because they cook quickly using little or no water. When microwaving several pieces of fruit, choose pieces of similar size to ensure even cooking. Pierce fruits covered with a tight skin if they are being microwaved whole.

When microwaving fruit, the type of fruit, its size, and its ripeness will affect cooking time. Fruits with higher moisture content, such as strawberries, will cook more quickly than dense fruits, like rhubarb. Berries and other small pieces of fruit will cook more quickly than larger pieces like apples. Ripe fruit requires less cooking time than firmer, underripe fruit.

padu_foto/Shutterstock.com   *padu_foto/Shutterstock.com*

Figure 19.9 Apples are sliced, dipped in batter, and fried to make apple fritters. Fritters are sprinkled with powdered sugar after they are removed from the oil.

Preparing Preserved Fruits

Canned fruits may be served right from the can. They may be drained or served in the syrup or juice in which they were packed. Canned fruits can be used like fresh or frozen fruits. Unless a recipe says otherwise, drain canned fruits well before using them in baked products such as cakes and muffins.

Frozen fruits make a great addition to smoothies, creating a thick, cold beverage with a boost of fiber and nutrients. In some recipes, thawed frozen fruit can be used in place of fresh or canned fruit. Completely thawing frozen fruits causes them to become soft and mushy. Therefore, when serving a dish of frozen fruits serve them with a few ice crystals remaining.

Dried fruits can be eaten right from the package. They also add an appealing texture contrast to many salads and baked goods (**Figure 19.10**).

Remember that dried fruits are a more concentrated source of calories than fresh fruits. A handful of raisins will provide about four times as many calories as a handful of grapes. Therefore, it is important to be aware of portion sizes when eating dried fruits.

Before cooking or baking, some recipes will direct you to soak dried fruits in liquid. Soaking helps restore the moisture removed during the drying process. In baked goods, this prevents the fruit from becoming dehydrated and hard.

The desired texture of dried fruit in a finished food product may be soft and chewy or tender and plump. Cooking softens the fruit tissues, and dried fruits vary in moisture content. Therefore, to achieve the desired results, it is important to follow recipe directions.

vanillaechoes/Shutterstock.com

Figure 19.10 Chewy dried cranberries combine with tender greens and grapefruit, crisp apples, and crunchy almonds to give this salad a pleasing variety of textures. Why is it important to be aware of portion sizes when serving dried fruits?

Chapter 19 Review and Expand

Summary

Fruits can be grouped into six basic classifications. No matter what their classification is, fruits are high in nutrition. Choose fresh fruits that are mature, ripe, and high in quality. Fresh fruits should be stored promptly in the refrigerator.

Choose canned, frozen, and dried fruits to supplement fresh fruit choices. Look for undented cans and solidly frozen packages. Store canned and dried fruits in a cool, dry place. Store frozen fruits in the freezer.

Wash fresh fruits and cut them as desired for serving raw. If necessary, treat cut fruits to prevent enzymatic browning.

Cooking affects the textures, colors, flavors, and nutrients of fruits. Fruit can be cooked in liquid. It can also be baked, broiled, fried, or microwaved.

Canned and dried fruits can be eaten as is. Frozen fruits should be served with a few ice crystals on them. When using preserved fruits in recipes, canned fruits often need to be drained. Frozen fruits might have to be thawed, and dried fruits may require soaking.

Vocabulary Activities

1. **Content Terms**   On a separate sheet of paper, list words that relate to each of the following terms. Then, work with a partner to explain how these words are related.

    berries   tropical fruits

    drupes   underripe fruit

    pomes   immature fruit

    citrus fruits   enzymatic browning

    melons   fritters

2. **Academic Terms**   For each of the following terms, identify a word or group of words describing a quality of the term—an *attribute*. Pair up with a classmate and discuss your list of attributes.

    economy

    pliable

    palatable

Review

Write your answers using complete sentences when appropriate.

3. List three nutrients found in fruits.
4. List the six fruit classifications and give one example of each.
5. Name two fruits that are excellent sources of vitamin C.
6. When are fresh fruits usually least expensive?
7. What is the best way to ripen fruit before storing it in the refrigerator?
8. In what types of liquids are canned fruits packed?
9. What should consumers look for when buying frozen fruits?
10. After opening dried fruit, how should unused portions be stored?
11. What is the darkening that appears on cut surfaces of some raw fruits when they are exposed to air?
12. Give an example of how overripe fruits that are past prime eating quality might be used in cooking.
13. Describe three changes that take place in fruit during cooking.
14. What function does the skin on fruit serve during baking?
15. What are fruits that are dipped in batter and deep-fried called?
16. How does the size of fruit affect cooking time in a microwave oven?
17. What is the general guideline for using canned fruits in baked products?
18. Why might a recipe for oatmeal raisin cookies require the raisins to be soaked in liquid before adding them to the other ingredients?

Chapter 19 Review and Expand

Core Skills

19. **Research, Technology, Speaking** Divide the class into groups. Each group should choose a different one of the following top fruit-producing states: California, Florida, Washington, Michigan, New York, Oregon, Pennsylvania, or Texas. Identify climatic conditions that make various fruit crops economically important in your chosen state. Prepare a presentation to share your findings with the class. Use photographs or other relevant digital content to add interest to the presentation.

20. **Research, Technology** Use reliable print or digital resources to investigate the production of a particular type of fruit. Create an electronic presentation showing how your chosen fruit goes from farm to table. Include images of planting, harvesting equipment, transportation, wholesale distributors, retailers, and consumers. Provide captions for each image. Show your presentation to the class.

21. **Writing** Look at the different varieties of apples that are available in a local grocery store. Create a pamphlet that includes photos and a brief description of each variety. Use cookbooks or other reliable resources to identify recommended uses for each variety. Then add a recipe that might be prepared with each type of apple. Edit and refine your pamphlet for grammar, spelling, and organization.

22. **Math** Choose five types of fresh fruit and record the price per pound of each. Using a precision scale, weigh each piece of fruit. Remove and weigh the inedible portions, such as peels, cores, and pits. Record both sets of weights. Calculate the percentage of inedible waste in each type of fruit. Then figure the cost per pound of the edible portions.

23. **Science** Slice a banana. Place half the slices on a plate and set aside. Dip the remaining slices in lemon juice, place on a plate, and set aside. Compare slices 30 minutes later. Explain your observations.

24. **Career Readiness Practice** Survey students from your class and other classes to identify their five favorite fruits. Compile your results with those of your classmates. Use reliable Internet or print resources to investigate whether the 10 most popular fruits are good or excellent sources of fiber, folate, potassium, vitamin A, and vitamin C. The Daily Values for these nutrients for a 2,000-calorie diet are as follows:

- fiber—28 grams
- folate—400 mcg DFE
- potassium—4,700 mg
- vitamin A—900 mcg RAE
- vitamin C—90 mg

Remember that good sources are those that contain 10 to 19 percent of the Daily Value per serving. Excellent sources contain 20 percent or more of the Daily Value per serving.

Critical Thinking and Problem Solving

25. **Create** Using the information gathered in Activity 24, make a digital table listing the 10 most popular fruits among students in your school. Complete columns of the table with the number of calories, grams of fiber, micrograms of folate, milligrams of potassium, micrograms of vitamin A, and milligrams of vitamin C provided by a serving of each fruit. Use software tools to make your table colorful and attractive. Sort the table five times in descending order according to the amounts of each of the nutrients. Use the five versions of the table to create a series of posters that encourage people to eat fruits for various nutritional benefits. Give each poster a catchy title and provide a brief description of the body's need for the highlighted nutrient.

26. **Analyze** Sample and compare one type of fruit in all its available forms. For instance, compare fresh peaches with canned peaches, frozen peaches, and dried peaches. Organize your findings into a webbing diagram that describes the differences in flavors, textures, and colors and suggests ways to serve each form.

27. **Analyze** Slice an apple into rings. Cook half the slices in sugar syrup and the other half in plain water until tender. Analyze the differences in appearance, texture, and flavor.

Chapter 20
Dairy Products

bitt24/Shutterstock.com

Objectives

After studying this chapter, you will be able to

- **recall** nutrients found in dairy products;
- **analyze** factors affecting the selection of dairy products;
- **explain** how to store dairy products to maintain quality;
- **describe** guidelines for preventing adverse reactions when cooking with dairy products; and
- **prepare** foods made with milk, cream, cheese, and other dairy products.

Reading Prep

The summary at the end of the chapter highlights the most important concepts. Read the chapter and write a summary in your own words. Then compare your summary to the summary in the text.

Content Terms ↪

pasteurization
ultra-high temperature (UHT) processing
homogenization
milkfat
milk solids
curd
whey
unripened cheese
ripened cheese
processed cheese
scum
curdling
scorching

Academic Terms

synthetic
globules
interchangeably
prior

Dairy products consist of all products made from milk. Cream, butter, cheese, yogurt, and ice cream are all dairy products. Dairy is a widely enjoyed food group in the United States and is produced in every state (**Figure 20.1**). Cheesy casseroles, ice cream and cream pies, and yogurt are just a few types of popular dairy-based foods.

Nutritional Value of Dairy Products

The dairy group of MyPlate consists of foods made from milk that retain their calcium content. Such dairy products include yogurt, cheese, and milk-based desserts. Besides calcium, foods in this group contain high-quality protein, potassium, riboflavin, and vitamins A and D.

Cheese is a concentrated form of milk, so it is an excellent source of complete protein. One pound (450 g) of cheese contains the protein and fat of about 1 gallon (4 L) of whole milk. Cheeses are important sources of calcium and phosphorus. They are fair sources of thiamin and niacin. Whole milk cheeses are excellent sources of vitamin A.

Although foods like cream cheese, cream, and butter are made from milk, they contain little or no calcium. Therefore, they are not considered part of the dairy group. They are, however, discussed in this chapter.

All people ages 9 and older need 3 cups (750 mL) from the dairy group each day. Children ages 2 and 3 need 2 cups (500 mL) daily, and children ages 4 through 8 need 2½ cups (625 mL) each day.

While all dairy products provide calcium, they do not all provide it in the same amounts. When counting foods from the dairy group, count milk and yogurt cup for cup. This means one cup of yogurt or milk counts as one cup in the dairy group. Cottage cheese and ice cream provide about half as much calcium as equal portions of milk or yogurt. Therefore, count each cup of these foods as a half cup from the dairy group. Also, count 1½ ounces (42 g) of natural cheese or 2 ounces (56 g) of processed cheese as 1 cup (250 mL) from the dairy group.

Mirec/Shutterstock.com

Figure 20.1   California, Idaho, Wisconsin, Pennsylvania, and New York are the top five dairy-producing states.

Selecting Dairy Products

Choose dairy products to use fresh or as ingredients in cooking and baking. Numerous creamy sauces, cheesy entrees, smooth drinks, and velvety desserts owe their appeal to dairy ingredients. Dairy products add flavor, texture, and richness as well as nutrients to many foods. They also help baked goods brown.

Milk

Milk, both plain and flavored, is a popular beverage. Milk is also an important ingredient in many foods.

Milk Processing

Milk usually goes through several processes between the dairy farm and the retail store. All milk is tested for traces of antibiotics that may have been used to treat cows. If any antibiotics are detected, the milk is discarded.

Some consumers are concerned about hormones in milk. All cows naturally produce hormones, and small amounts of these hormones are found in all types of milk. Some farmers choose to give their cows *synthetic* (artificially created) hormones to increase milk production. Research has shown no difference in milk from these cows compared with milk from cows who do not receive hormones.

Milk and dairy products sold in the United States are pasteurized. **Pasteurization** is a process by which a food product is heated to destroy harmful bacteria. This process improves the keeping quality as well as the safety of milk. It does not change the nutritional value or the flavor.

Some milk is treated with **ultra-high temperature (UHT) processing**. This preservation method uses higher temperatures than regular pasteurization to increase the shelf life of foods like milk. After heating, UHT processed milk is sealed in presterilized boxes. Unopened UHT milk products can be stored without refrigeration (**Figure 20.2**).

Fresh whole milk is usually homogenized. **Homogenization** is a mechanical process that breaks *globules* (very small drops) of milkfat into tiny particles and spreads them throughout the

©iStock.com/3dsguru

Figure 20.2   Look for UHT processed milk in the center aisles of the grocery store rather than in the refrigerated dairy case. What is an advantage of milk that does not require refrigeration?

milk. This process prevents cream from rising to the surface of milk. Homogenized milk has a richer body and flavor than nonhomogenized milk.

Milk that has not been pasteurized or homogenized is called *raw milk*. Health professionals warn that drinking raw milk can cause illness due to the presence of harmful bacteria.

Milk often goes through a *fortification* process. This is the addition of essential nutrients. Most milk is fortified with vitamin D, which aids the human body in the absorption of calcium. Fat-free, low-fat, and reduced-fat milk are often fortified with vitamin A as well. Vitamin A is added to replace the vitamin A that is removed when the fat content of the milk is reduced.

Types of Milk

Each type of milk must meet specific standards for its composition. *Whole milk* must contain at least 3.25 percent milkfat and 8.25 percent milk solids. **Milkfat** is the fat portion of milk. **Milk solids** contain most of the vitamins, minerals, protein, and sugar found in milk.

All types of milk begin as whole milk. First the milk is pasteurized. Then other types of milk are produced by removing some of the fat. *Reduced-fat milk* has 2 percent milkfat. *Low-fat milk* has 1 percent milkfat. *Fat-free milk*, also known as *skim milk* or *nonfat milk*, has nearly all of the fat removed. The less fat milk has, the fewer calories it provides (**Figure 20.3**). Milk with added flavoring becomes *flavored milk*, such as chocolate milk.

Lactose-reduced milk has been treated with the enzyme lactase to break down lactose—the natural sugar in milk. This type of milk is often used by people with *lactose intolerance*, a condition that results in gas, cramps, and diarrhea after drinking milk. Lactose intolerance is caused by the body's failure to make enough lactase to digest milk sugar.

Organic milk comes from farms that use only organic fertilizers and pesticides. The cows are not given hormones or antibiotics, and they are fed organic diets. The nutrition and safety of organic milk is the same as regular milk.

Cream

Types of cream are defined according to the amount of milkfat they contain. *Heavy whipping cream* has the most fat, followed by *light whipping cream*. Both hold air when whipped, and they are often used in desserts. *Light cream*, or *coffee cream*, has less fat than light whipping cream. It can be used as a table cream and in cooking. *Half-and-half* is made from half milk and half cream. It has the least amount of fat, so it is the lowest in calories.

Yogurt and Other Cultured Dairy Products

A number of dairy products are made from milk to which helpful bacteria have been added. These bacteria are *cultured*, or specially grown for this purpose. Therefore, dairy products to which cultured bacteria are added are called *cultured dairy products*. The bacteria produce lactic acid, which gives these products a thick texture and tangy flavor.

Yogurt is a cultured dairy product. It may contain added nonfat milk solids and flavorings or fruits. An 8-ounce (227 g) serving of yogurt provides a bit more calcium and protein than a cup (250 mL) of milk. The amount of fat in yogurt depends on whether it was made from whole, reduced fat, or fat-free milk. Although yogurt is a nutritious food, fruit-flavored yogurt often contains about 8 teaspoons of added sugar per serving. To limit sugar intake, try stirring fresh fruit and a drizzle of honey into some plain nonfat yogurt.

Greek yogurt has most of the liquid strained out of it, so it is thicker than regular yogurt. Greek yogurt has more protein and less lactose per serving than other yogurt.

Other cultured dairy products include buttermilk and sour cream. People use *cultured buttermilk* for cooking and baking as well as drinking. *Regular sour cream* is made from light cream. *Light* and *reduced fat sour cream* have fewer calories than regular sour cream because they have less fat. These sour cream products can all be used *interchangeably* (in place of the other) in most recipes.

Milkfat and Calories per Milk Type			
Type of Milk	**Milkfat**	**Calories per Cup**	**Calcium (mg) per Cup**
Whole Milk	3.25%	149	276
Reduced-Fat Milk	2%	122	293
Low-Fat Milk	1%	102	305
Fat-Free Milk (skim milk, nonfat milk)	<1%	83	299

Source: Modified from *Dietary Guidelines for American, 2010*, Appendix 14

Figure 20.3 The higher the milkfat content in milk, the higher the amount of calories. What pattern can you identify in the amount of calcium per serving of each milk type?

Learn About...

Dairy Milk Alternatives

A number of consumers look for alternatives to dairy milk. There are several reasons for this trend. Consumers who follow vegan diets want to avoid foods from animal sources. Some people have health issues, such as lactose intolerance or milk allergies. Still others are concerned about the environmental impact of milk production.

To meet the demands of these consumers, there is no shortage of options. Available milk substitutes are made from a variety of foods. These foods include soy, coconut, nuts like almonds and cashews, grains like rice and oats, and seeds like flax and hemp.

When shopping for dairy alternatives, read ingredient labels. Milk alternatives are made from water and plant extracts along with a number of other ingredients. Many dairy alternative products also contain additives not found in dairy milk, such as sweeteners, salts, and gums. These additives give nondairy products a flavor and texture similar to cow's milk.

Be sure to read the Nutrition Facts panel when evaluating dairy alternatives. Some of these products may have more calories per serving than dairy options and less protein. Although milk alternatives may look comparable to cow's milk in terms of calcium, the calcium added to nondairy products is often in a form that is not easily absorbed by the body. For consumers drinking milk substitutes, it is important to find other sources of calcium and protein to compensate.

Know and Apply

1. Why is cow's milk likely to be a better source of calcium than fortified soy milk?
2. Explain why you would or would not be interested in using dairy milk alternatives.

Concentrated Milk Products

Removing water from fluid milk produces concentrated milk products. These products can be canned or dried.

Evaporated milk is whole, reduced-fat, or fat-free milk that has been sterilized and homogenized and has had some of the water removed. When diluted with an equal amount of water, it matches fresh milk in nutritional value. It can then be used in place of fluid fresh milk for drinking and in recipes.

Sweetened condensed milk is whole or fat-free milk with some of the water removed and a sweetener added. It is used most often in cooking and baking (**Figure 20.4**). Sugar affects the flavor and texture of cooked and baked products. Therefore, sweetened condensed milk should be used only in recipes that call for it. Sweetened condensed milk cannot be used interchangeably with evaporated milk. It cannot be diluted for use in place of fluid fresh milk, either.

Removing most of the water and fat from whole milk produces *nonfat dry milk*. Nonfat dry milk can be used to add calcium and protein to many foods. It can also be reconstituted (returned to its original form) and used like fluid milk.

Frozen Dairy Desserts

Ice cream, frozen yogurt, and sherbet are all frozen dairy desserts. The names of these products used on labels indicate fat content. *Light products* must show at least a 50 percent reduction in fat over regular products. *Fat-free products* must contain less than 0.5 grams of fat per serving.

Africa Studio/Shutterstock.com

Figure 20.4 Sweetened condensed milk is denser than fluid milk and has a sweet, creamy taste.

Butter

Churning pasteurized cream produces butter. The churned product may have salt and/or artificial color added. Some cooks prefer *lightly salted butter* for use at the table and in cooking and *unsalted butter* for baking. However, the two products can usually be used interchangeably. *Whipped butter* is butter that has air whipped into it. It cannot be measured accurately for baking, so it is best used as a table spread.

Cheese

Few foods are as versatile as cheese. Its many flavors, textures, and nutrients make it suitable for any meal or snack.

Natural Cheeses

All cheese is made from milk. The milk used can be from cows, goats, or other animals. In simple terms, the milk is *coagulated,* or thickened into a congealed mass. Then the **curd** (solid part) is separated from the **whey** (liquid part). Cheeses made in this way are sometimes called *natural cheeses.*

Adding different ingredients and changing the basic steps of production can produce hundreds of different cheeses. All these cheeses may be classified into two main groups: unripened and ripened.

Unripened cheeses are ready for marketing as soon as the whey has been removed. They are not allowed to ripen or age. Cottage cheese, cream cheese, *queso fresco* (fresh cheese), and ricotta are examples of unripened cheeses. They are mild in flavor.

Controlled amounts of bacteria, mold, yeast, or enzymes are used to make **ripened cheeses**. During ripening, the cheese is stored at a specific temperature to develop texture and flavor. Some cheeses become softer and more tender. Others become hard or crumbly (**Figure 20.5**). Each variety has a distinctive flavor, ranging from mild to strong. Some ripened cheeses require further storage to develop flavor. This process is called *aging*. Cheese is aged anywhere from two weeks to two years, depending on the kind.

Natural cheeses can be made into other products called **processed cheeses**. The cheeses are heated and ingredients called *emulsifiers* are added to prevent the blended mixture from separating. The finished product is smooth and creamy. Processed cheeses are often sold as individually wrapped slices or spreads.

Imitation Cheese

Imitation cheese has a large portion of the milkfat replaced by vegetable oils. Imitation cheese may differ in texture and melting characteristics from real cheese. These differences may affect the outcome of cooked foods made with imitation cheese.

Nondairy Products

A few products that look and perform like dairy products contain no dairy ingredients. *Nondairy products* include *coffee whiteners, whipped toppings,* and *imitation sour cream*. These products do not contain real cream. They get the body and appearance of dairy products from substances

kiboka/Shutterstock.com *Foodio/Shutterstock.com*

Figure 20.5 During the ripening process, brie cheese (A) becomes soft and creamy. Parmesan cheese (B) becomes firm. Both are considered natural cheeses.

Exploring Careers

Cheese Maker

Cheese makers guide milk through a process to turn it into cheese. The process involves carefully controlled timing, temperature settings, and ingredients. These factors vary depending on the type of cheese being made.

Successful cheese makers must be able to operate and maintain equipment. They must have the ability to pay attention to details. They use their attention to detail skill as they monitor dials and gauges to ensure equipment is working correctly. They will also use this skill to measure ingredients exactly. Cheese makers must have strong sensory perception. They use this quality as they evaluate the taste, texture, and smell of samples to determine when cheese is ready for market.

In terms of formal education, cheese makers may need only high school diplomas. Learning the steps of the cheese-making process may take only a few months of training, working with a skilled cheese maker. However, most cheese makers become specialists at making certain kinds of cheese. Masters at this craft may spend years honing their skills to consistently produce the highest quality cheeses.

such as soy protein, emulsifiers, and vegetable fats and gums.

Margarine is another nondairy product. Many people use margarine in place of butter. Compared with butter, full margarine contains the same amount of fat and calories. However, it contains vegetable oil, animal fat, or some of each rather than milkfat. Reduced fat margarine often contains more water and will not perform the same as regular margarine or butter in baking. Most margarine is lower in cholesterol and saturated fat than butter. Stick margarine may provide *trans* fats, however, *trans* fats are being phased out due to health concerns and manufacturers are using them less and less. Tub margarines have little or no *trans* fat.

Cost of Dairy Products

National brand dairy products tend to cost more than local brands. In addition, dairy products differ in cost depending on fat content, form, size of container, and place of purchase. Whole milk usually costs more than fat-free milk. Fluid fat-free milk usually costs more than nonfat dry milk. Ounce for ounce (milliliter for milliliter), milk sold in small containers usually costs more than milk sold in large containers. Milk from a delivery service costs more than milk purchased at a store.

The cost of frozen desserts depends on the amount of fat per container. The kind and amount of extra ingredients, flavorings, and container size also affect cost. Rich ice cream in small containers with many added ingredients costs the most.

The cost of butter and yogurt depends on form. Whipped butter may cost more than regular butter. Margarine costs less than butter, but prices vary depending on packaging and the kind of oil used. Greek yogurt costs twice as much as regular yogurt.

The cost of cheese varies depending on type, weight, and form. Consumers may save money by buying cheese in large pieces rather than purchasing sliced, cubed, shredded, or grated forms. Fully-ripened cheeses often cost more than unripened cheeses or those that ripen for only a short time. Processed cheese costs less than ripened cheese. Plain cheese costs less than cheese with added ingredients like nuts and herbs.

The type of farming used may also impact cost. Organic farming methods are more costly than standard farming methods. Therefore, organic dairy products cost more than nonorganic products.

Making Healthy Dairy Choices

Full-fat dairy products can add a lot of saturated fat and cholesterol to the diet. For good health, choose low-fat and fat-free dairy products most often. These products are lower in cholesterol, and every gram of fat removed cuts 9 calories (**Figure 20.6**).

For example, using plain, nonfat yogurt in place of sour cream can save almost 3 grams of fat per tablespoon (15 mL). This difference may seem small, but it can quickly add up. In a recipe calling for 1 cup (250 mL) of sour cream, 45 grams of fat

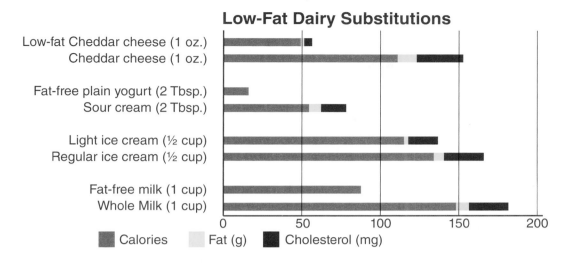

Low-Fat Dairy Substitutions

- Low-fat Cheddar cheese (1 oz.)
- Cheddar cheese (1 oz.)

- Fat-free plain yogurt (2 Tbsp.)
- Sour cream (2 Tbsp.)

- Light ice cream (½ cup)
- Regular ice cream (½ cup)

- Fat-free milk (1 cup)
- Whole Milk (1 cup)

0   50   100   150   200

■ Calories   ▢ Fat (g)   ■ Cholesterol (mg)

Figure 20.6 Compare the differences in cholesterol, fat, and calories when you substitute whole milk with fat-free milk, regular ice cream with light ice cream, sour cream with fat-free plain yogurt, and Cheddar cheese with low-fat Cheddar cheese. Which of these low-fat dairy product(s) contains the least cholesterol? fat? calories?

and 307 calories would be saved. (Larger proportions of carbohydrate and protein in yogurt take up some of the calories saved from fat.) This change would save 115 milligrams of cholesterol, too.

Storing Dairy Products

All dairy products are very perishable. They need careful storage to maintain their flavors and nutrients. Be sure to check the date stamped on product containers when choosing items at the store. Look for products stamped with the latest pull date (**Figure 20.7**).

Store dairy products in their original covered containers in the coldest part of the refrigerator or freezer. Keep containers tightly closed to prevent contamination and off flavors. Pour out just the needed amount of fresh milk and cream and return the rest to the refrigerator. If stored properly, dairy products remain wholesome and can be consumed for a few days past the pull date.

Sealed UHT milk products can be stored unrefrigerated for up to six months. Once opened, refrigerate them and use them like other milk products.

Store dried and canned milk products in a cool, dry place. Reseal opened containers of dried milk carefully. Store reconstituted dry milk like fresh milk. Cover the unused portions of canned milk products and store them in the refrigerator. Use them within a few days.

Unopened yogurt stored in the coldest part of the refrigerator will remain wholesome for a few days after the pull date. Once opened, yogurt should be consumed within about a week for best quality. Discard yogurt if there is any sign of mold, even if it is only on the lid.

Keeping frozen dairy desserts firmly frozen will protect product texture by preventing large ice crystals from forming. For best quality, use these products within a month.

Refrigerate all butter and margarine. Freezing will extend the life of both products. Butter is often sold in one-pound packages. Each package

planet5D LLC/Shutterstock.com

Figure 20.7 Checking dates can help consumers choose dairy products that will maintain quality for the longest time after purchase.

typically contains four sticks of butter. Keeping the package frozen and removing sticks as needed will protect the quality of butter for a prolonged period.

Tightly wrap and refrigerate all cheese to preserve freshness, prevent drying, and keep flavors and odors intact. Strong-flavored cheeses can flavor other foods. Mild-flavored cheeses can pick up flavors from other refrigerated items.

Although hard cheeses keep longer than soft cheeses, both can become moldy if stored improperly or kept too long. A small amount of mold on hard cheese is not harmful. Just cut off the moldy section at least one inch (2.5 cm) into the cheese. Eat the rest of the cheese within a short time. Dispose of hard cheese with large amounts of mold and all moldy soft cheese.

Preparing Dairy-Based Foods

The creamy texture and richness of dairy-based foods have made them favorites for generations. Studying basic preparation techniques will allow you to include these popular foods in your menu planning.

Food Science Principles of Cooking with Milk

When milk is used as an ingredient, it is often heated. Heat affects proteins, and milk is a protein food. Understanding principles for cooking milk will help avoid undesirable reactions.

The same cooking principles that apply to milk also apply to cream. Because cream is richer than milk (it contains more milkfat), heat and acids affect it more quickly than milk. Therefore, extra care should be taken when cooking with cream.

Scum Formation

Scum is a solid layer that often forms on the surface of milk during heating. The scum is made up of milk solids and some fat. Because the scum is rubbery and tough, it should be removed. If the scum is stirred into the milk, it will float in small particles throughout the milk.

Scum formation is difficult to prevent. After scum is removed, another layer will form if heating continues. Stirring the milk during heating or covering the pan will help prevent scum formation.

Beating the milk with a whisk to form a foam layer will also help prevent scum from forming.

Boiling Over

Scum formation is the usual cause of milk boiling over. Pressure builds up beneath the layer of scum. The scum prevents the pressure from being released as steam. The pressure continues to build until the milk finally boils over. Prevent milk from boiling over by using low heat and one of the methods suggested for preventing a scum layer.

Curdling

High temperatures, acids, tannins (acids found mostly in plants), enzymes, and salts can cause milk proteins to coagulate and form clumps. This is called **curdling**, and the clumps are called *curds*. Foods like oranges and tomatoes contain acids. Many fruits and vegetables contain tannins and enzymes. Brown sugar also contains tannins. Cured ham and other meats contain salts. These substances may cause curdling in cream of tomato soup, creamed green beans, scalloped potatoes and ham, and other milk-based foods.

Curdling can be prevented by using low temperatures and fresh milk (**Figure 20.8**). When acid foods are added to milk, either the milk or acid should be thickened first. For example, tomato soup made from milk thickened with starch is less likely to curdle than tomato soup made from unthickened milk. The same is true of tomato soup made from thickened tomato juice.

Figure 20.8 When cooking with milk, use low temperatures and carefully monitor the milk as it heats.

Scorching

Scorching is burning that results in a color change. Scorched milk is slightly brown in color and has an off taste. Milk can scorch because it contains lactose, which is a type of sugar. Like any sugar, lactose can *caramelize*, or change to a brown, bitter substance called *caramel* when it is heated. When milk is heated, the milk proteins coagulate and settle onto the sides and bottom of the pan. If the milk is overheated, the lactose in the coagulated solids caramelizes, thus scorching the milk.

Scorching can be prevented by using low heat. Heating milk in the top of a double boiler will also help avoid scorching.

Microwaving Milk Products

Use lower settings when microwaving milk and milk products. Higher settings can cause milk to curdle. Also, watch milk carefully, as it can boil over quickly in the microwave oven. Fill containers no more than two-thirds full when microwaving milk to help avoid this problem. Stirring during the cooking period to prevent scum formation will also help reduce the risk of boiling over.

Preparing Whipped Cream

For best results when whipping cream, thoroughly chill the bowl, beaters, and cream *prior* to (before) whipping cream. The bowl should be large enough to hold the cream after whipping. (Cream doubles or triples in volume during whipping.)

To whip cream, pour the cream into a chilled bowl. Beat it at medium speed until thickening begins. If the cream is being sweetened, gradually start adding sugar at this point. As the sugar is added, increase the beating speed. Continue whipping the cream until it is stiff. Do not overbeat. Serve whipped cream immediately. (If the whipped cream must be held for a short time, refrigerate it promptly.)

Preparing Puddings

Puddings are thickened milk products usually served as desserts. Pudding can be prepared from an instant mix in a matter of minutes. Although cooked pudding requires more time, it is easy to prepare. It also has a

Food Science

Whipping Properties of Cream

The amount of milkfat in cream affects the volume and stability of whipped cream. Cream must contain at least 25 percent milkfat to whip successfully. However, at least 30 percent milkfat is needed to produce a stable product. More milkfat (up to 40 percent) will produce a product that is even more stable.

When cream is whipped, two changes take place. The first is that air bubbles are incorporated in the cream and a foam forms. The second change is that fat particles in the cream clump together. The clumping of the fat particles produces the stiffness in whipped cream. It is also the first step in churning butter. For this reason, the amount of beating must be carefully controlled. When cream is overbeaten, too much air is incorporated into it. The emulsion around the fat particles breaks, the foam collapses, and the cream turns into butter.

Sugar decreases both the volume and stiffness of whipped cream. It also increases beating time if it is added before the cream has begun to stiffen. If cream is being sweetened, the sugar should be added after the cream has become fairly thick.

Family Business/Shutterstock.com

smoother texture and richer flavor than instant pudding, and it can be enjoyed warm or cold.

Traditional chocolate, vanilla, butterscotch, and banana puddings are cornstarch puddings. You may also have tried tapioca, rice, and bread puddings. All these puddings contain milk and a starch thickening agent. In some pudding recipes, eggs contribute additional thickening as well as protein.

Of all the puddings, cornstarch pudding is the most versatile. It can be served alone or used to make fillings for pies or other desserts.

Follow these steps to prepare a basic cornstarch pudding:

1. Combine sugar, salt, and cornstarch in a heavy saucepan and mix well.
2. Add a small amount of the cold milk and stir to make a smooth paste. (These first steps help separate the starch granules to prevent lumps.)
3. Add the remaining milk, stirring constantly.
4. Cook the pudding over moderate heat, and continue stirring until the pudding boils. Cook for one minute longer to thoroughly cook the starch.
5. Add the flavoring, and pour the pudding into dessert dishes. Chill before serving. A piece of wax paper placed on the surface of the warm pudding will prevent the formation of a skin.

Preparing Ice Cream and Sherbet

Although many people choose to buy ice creams and sherbets, these frozen dairy desserts can be made from a few common ingredients. *Ice cream* contains milk, cream, sugar, and flavoring. You can also make a reduced-fat version of homemade ice cream. Simply substitute fat-free milk for the whole milk and whole milk for the cream found in ice cream recipes. Reduced-fat ice cream is not as rich and smooth as regular ice cream, but it is lower in calories.

Sherbet contains fruit juices, sugar, and milk. It has a lower fat content than ice cream. Its higher sugar content, however, makes it comparable in calories. This composition also gives sherbet less creamy texture than ice cream.

Ice cream products and sherbet must be stirred while they are freezing to achieve a smooth texture. This is because ice crystals form during freezing. Stirring keeps these ice crystals small. Frozen desserts that have small ice crystals taste creamy. Frozen desserts that have large ice crystals taste grainy.

Ice cream products and sherbet can be prepared in an ice cream freezer or in a refrigerator's freezer. In an ice cream freezer, stirring is continuous, so ice crystals remain small. In the refrigerator freezer, stirring is not continuous. Cooked beaten egg whites, whipped cream, whipped evaporated milk, or whipped gelatin

Food Science

Cooking Puddings

All puddings require the use of moderate cooking temperatures to prevent scorching and overcoagulation of the milk and egg proteins. The starch grains must be separated before cooking to prevent lumping. Rice and bread puddings are usually placed in a dish of hot water during baking. This provides further protection against the overcoagulation of proteins.

Some old-fashioned pudding recipes call for scalded milk. *Scalding* means heating to just below the boiling point. In the past, this step was necessary to kill bacteria in unpasteurized milk. Because all commercially purchased milk is now pasteurized, this step can be skipped whenever it is in a recipe.

When eggs are used in pudding, first add a small amount of the hot pudding to the beaten eggs. Then the diluted egg mixture can be added to the rest of the hot pudding. (Eggs added directly to a hot mixture can coagulate into lumps.) Cook the pudding a few minutes longer after adding the eggs to completely cook the egg proteins.

Allyso/Shutterstock.com

may be added to recipes prepared in the refrigerator freezer. These ingredients inhibit the formation of ice crystals.

Preparing Cheese Dishes

Cheese is a concentrated form of milk. Therefore, it is a high-protein food. Like all high-protein foods, heat can adversely affect cheese. If cheese is cooked at too high a temperature or for too long a time, its proteins overcoagulate. As a result, the cheese becomes tough and rubbery and the fat in the cheese may separate.

Recipe for Good Food

Cheddar and Apple Tartines

Serves 4

4   teaspoons (20 mL) light mayonnaise
2   teaspoons (10 mL) spicy brown mustard
2   teaspoons (10 mL) honey
4   slices whole-wheat bread, lightly toasted
1   medium Granny Smith apple
3   ounces (85 g) reduced-fat mild Cheddar
    cheese, shredded

1. Preheat broiler on low.
2. In a small bowl, combine mayonnaise,
   mustard, and honey until thoroughly blended.
3. Place toasted bread on a baking sheet.
   Spread each slice with 2 teaspoons (10 mL)
   of the mustard mixture.
4. Quarter and core the apple, then cut it into
   ⅛-inch (3 mm) thick slices. Cover the bread
   with the apple slices. Top apples on each
   slice of bread with 3 tablespoons (45 mL) of
   shredded cheese.
5. Place the baking sheet under the broiler
   about 5 inches from the heat. Broil 4 to 5
   minutes, until cheese is melted and bubbly.

**Per serving: 176 calories (36% from fat),
10 g protein, 20 g carbohydrate, 7 g fat, 12 mg
cholesterol, 3 g fiber, 352 mg sodium.**

Cheese is often combined with liquids in sauces and soups cooked on a surface unit. Cook these foods over low heat or in the top of a double boiler. The temperature must be hot enough to melt the fat so the cheese will blend smoothly. However, it must be low enough to prevent toughening of the proteins (**Figure 20.9**).

Cheeses that are well ripened blend more easily than less well-ripened cheeses. Well-ripened cheeses also tolerate higher temperatures.

Cheese that is grated, shredded, or cut into small pieces will blend more quickly than cheese cut into large chunks. As a result, a shorter cooking time can be used. Purchasing cheese that is already shredded or cubed can save time in meal preparation. However, these products contain preservatives and ingredients to prevent clumping not found in block cheese. These extra ingredients can affect the melting quality of cheese. Therefore, you may prefer to grate cheese yourself right before cooking.

Processed cheese blends more easily than natural cheese because of the emulsifiers it contains. A cheese sauce made with processed cheese is smooth and less likely to curdle. In comparison, a cheese sauce made with natural Cheddar cheese has a grainier texture, although the cheese flavor is more pronounced.

Cheese dishes prepared in an oven or under a broiler should be cooked just until done. Place cheese-containing foods, such as sandwiches and appetizers, four to five inches (10 to 12 cm) from broiler heat. Watch food carefully while broiling. Remove food from the broiler when the cheese has melted.

Microwaving Cheese

Cheese requires careful timing and the use of low settings when it is being cooked in a microwave oven. Cooking for too long or at too high a power level can cause cheese to separate and become rubbery. All cheeses microwave well, but some cheeses have better melting qualities than others.

bonchan/Shutterstock.com

Figure 20.9   The top layer of cheese on this French onion soup was melted with a low heat.

Chapter 20 Review and Expand

Summary

Dairy products include a wide range of popular foods, such as milk, cream, yogurt, ice cream, butter, and cheese. Many dairy foods are good sources of protein and calcium as well as a number of vitamins and other minerals. The cost of dairy products varies depending on fat content, container size, brand, and place of purchase.

All fresh and frozen dairy products are perishable and require storage in the coldest part of the refrigerator or freezer. Canned products must be stored like fresh products once they have been opened. Dried products should be stored like fresh products after they have been reconstituted.

Cream and whole milk dairy products are high in fat. Choosing reduced-fat and fat-free versions of dairy products can help cut fat and calories.

When cooking with milk, use moderate temperatures and use care to prevent scum formation, boiling over, curdling, and scorching. Also use moderate temperatures when cooking with cheese. This will help keep the cheese from becoming tough and rubbery.

Vocabulary Activities

1. **Content Terms**   Using reliable resources, research the *etymology*, or word origins, of the following terms from this chapter: pasteurization, homogenization, coagulate, and scum. How can studying a term's etymology help you understand a term?

pasteurization	whey
ultra-high temperature (UHT) processing	unripened cheese
	ripened cheese
homogenization	processed cheese
milkfat	scum
milk solids	curdling
curd	scorching

2. **Academic Terms**   Reread the text passages that contain each of the following terms. Then write a sentence for each term that explains how the term relates to dairy products.

synthetic	interchangeably
globules	prior

Review

Write your answers using complete sentences when appropriate.

3. List six nutrients found in dairy products.
4. What is the process of heating milk to destroy harmful bacteria called?
5. Which type of cream has the most milkfat?
6. Name three types of cultured dairy products.
7. Explain why sweetened condensed milk *cannot* be used interchangeably with evaporated milk in recipes.
8. Why is reduced fat margarine not a good choice to use in most recipes for baked goods?
9. Why do organic dairy products cost more than nonorganic dairy products?
10. How long can sealed UHT milk products be stored without refrigeration?
11. Describe the difference between ripened and unripened cheeses.
12. What are the advantages of using low-fat and fat-free dairy products in place of full-fat products?
13. How can you prevent milk from curdling during cooking?
14. If whipped cream is to be sweetened, when should you add the sugar?
15. How can you protect rice and bread puddings against the overcoagulation of milk and egg proteins during baking?
16. Why is it important to stir ice cream products and sherbet during freezing?
17. How does processed cheese compare with natural cheese for use in a cheese sauce?

Core Skills

18. **Research, Reading, Writing**   Use reliable print or online resources to research an animal other than cows that provides milk for some of the world's people. Identify a country in which this animal is used for milk. Write a report describing factors that contribute to the use of milk from this animal instead of or in addition to cow's milk in this country. Revise your report as needed to present your findings in a clear and logical order.

Chapter 20 Review and Expand

19. **Research, Reading, Speaking, Listening** Use reliable print or online resources to research the prevalence of lactose intolerance in a particular population group. Share your findings in class and compare them with classmates who researched other population groups.

20. **Technology, Math, Writing** Choose one of the following four groups of dairy foods: fluid milk, cultured dairy products, frozen dairy desserts, or cheese. Using an online nutritional database, find the calorie, protein, calcium, saturated fat, total fat, and cholesterol content for three products in your chosen group. Select one full-fat product, one reduced-fat product, and one fat-free product. Create bar graphs comparing the three products for each nutrient factor. Then write a brief report explaining what your comparison shows about the nutritional values of dairy options. Edit your report for clarity and style.

21. **Science** Pour 1 cup (250 mL) of whipping cream into a clean plastic jar. Add a clean marble to the jar and cover tightly with a lid. Working in a group, take turns shaking the jar for 30 seconds each and then passing the jar to the next group member. Note when you can no longer hear the clatter of the marble. What does this indicate? Continue shaking your jar past this point until you again hear the clatter of the marble. What does this indicate? What does this activity tell you about preparing whipped cream?

22. **Math** One pound (454 g) of cheese yields 4 cups (1,000 mL) of shredded cheese. Calculate how many ounces of cheese you would need to buy to yield each of the following amounts of shredded cheese:
    - 1½ cups (375 mL)
    - 2¼ cups (560 mL)
    - ¾ cup (185 mL)

    Show your work.

23. **Technology, Research, Speaking** Use reliable online resources to research how ultra-high temperature pasteurization and aseptic packaging are used to extend the shelf life of milk. Download images to include in an electronic presentation illustrating the pasteurization and packaging processes.

24. **Career Readiness Practice** You are a journalist for a local newspaper. Your current assignment is to write a full-page article about the links among calcium, menopause, and osteoporosis. Cite reliable print and online sources as the basis for your article.

Critical Thinking and Problem Solving

25. **Analyze** Compare a dairy milk alternative of your choice with fat-free milk in terms of ingredients, nutritional value, and unit cost. Based on your analysis, state which product you would prefer to buy and why.

26. **Evaluate** Whip heavy cream using the following methods:
    A. Chill bowl and beaters. Whip cream and sugar together until stiff.
    B. Have bowl and beaters at room temperature. Whip cream until it begins to thicken. Add sugar slowly. Continue beating until stiff.
    C. Chill bowl and beaters. Whip cream until it begins to thicken. Add sugar slowly. Continue beating until stiff.

    Evaluate the beating time, appearance, volume, and stability of each sample.

27. **Analyze** Set up a tasting panel. Compare the tastes and mouthfeel of the following types of milk: whole, reduced fat, low-fat, fat-free, lactose-reduced, and organic. Also taste samples of reconstituted evaporated milk and reconstituted nonfat dry milk. Analyze the factors that contribute to the differences in flavors and textures among the products.

Chapter 21
Eggs

Arina P Habich /Shutterstock.com

Objectives

After studying this chapter, you will be able to

- **list** factors affecting the selection of eggs and **explain** how to store eggs safely;
- **describe** the functions eggs serve when they are used as ingredients in food products; and
- **cook** eggs by a variety of methods and **prepare** some classic egg-based dishes.

Reading Prep

Take two-column notes as you read the chapter. Fold a piece of notebook paper in half lengthwise. On the left side of the column, write main ideas. On the right side, write subtopics and detailed information. After reading the chapter, use the notes as a study guide. Fold the paper in half so you only see the main ideas. Quiz yourself on the details and subtopics.

Content Terms ⤢

candling
emulsion
coagulum
omelet
soufflé
meringue
weeping
beading
custard

Academic Terms

allergen
welfare

Eggs are one of the most versatile and nutritious food sources. They can be prepared in a number of ways for use in meal plans throughout the day. Eggs are also used as ingredients in a wide range of food products. Therefore, eggs are a staple many people like to always keep on hand.

Nutritional Value of Eggs

Eggs are one of the best sources of complete protein, and they are in the protein foods group of MyPlate. One egg counts as 1 ounce equivalent from this group. Most teens and adults should consume 5 to 7 ounce equivalents per day, depending on calorie needs. Along with protein, eggs contain a number of vitamins and minerals, and they are especially high in choline.

Some people need to restrict or avoid egg consumption more than others. Egg yolks are high in cholesterol. Doctors advise people with diabetes, high cholesterol, or heart disease to follow a reduced-cholesterol diet. The use of egg yolks and whole eggs must be limited in such a diet. However, egg whites are cholesterol free, so they can be used without restrictions.

Proteins in eggs are a common *allergen* (substance that sets off an immune system response), especially for children. People with egg allergy cannot consume any eggs. They must also read labels carefully to avoid food products containing egg.

Most shoppers in the United States choose white-shelled eggs; however, some people prefer brown eggs. The color of the shell is determined by the breed of the chicken that lays the egg. Shell color does not affect nutritional value, nor does it affect quality or flavor of eggs (**Figure 21.1**).

Selecting and Storing Eggs

As with other food products, consumers have choices to make when buying eggs. Generic and specialty eggs are sold in several sizes and package counts. Eggs are generally inexpensive, but brand and size affect egg prices. Being familiar with available options will allow consumers to choose eggs that best meet their needs.

Egg Grades

Eggs for retail sale are inspected for wholesomeness. In addition, they may be graded for quality. **Candling** is a process by which eggs are quality-graded. The eggs move along rollers over bright lights. The lights illuminate the structure of the eggs. Skilled people can then look at the eggs carefully and remove any that do not meet standards. Many egg packers use mechanized scanning equipment to detect and separate eggs with defects (flaws).

The two grades of eggs available in most supermarkets are Grade AA and Grade A. These grades are given to high-quality eggs that have clean, unbroken shells and small air cells. The egg whites are thick and clear, and the yolks are firm and stand high above the whites.

Some eggs are rated Grade B, but these eggs are rarely seen in food stores. They are usually used in other food products.

Egg Size

Eggs are sized on the basis of an average weight per dozen. For instance, large eggs are bigger and heavier than medium eggs. Therefore,

Frank Chen Photography/Shutterstock.com

Figure 21.1 No matter what the color, eggs look and taste the same when they are cooked. What color of eggs do you prefer?

the average weight of a dozen large eggs is more than the average weight of a dozen medium eggs. Extra large, large, and medium eggs are the most common sizes found in stores.

Although egg size has no relation to quality, it does affect price. Eggs of any size can be Grade AA, A, or B. Extra large eggs cost more than large eggs, and large eggs cost more than medium eggs. Recipes are generally formulated to use large eggs, and this is the size most shoppers buy, regardless of price.

Specialty Eggs

Like most food products, eggs come in several varieties to meet a range of consumer needs. *Nutrient-enhanced eggs* come from chickens fed a diet that improves the nutritional value of the eggs. *Pasteurized eggs* have been treated to kill harmful bacteria that may be present in raw eggs. *Organic eggs* come from hens fed a diet that is free of chemical pesticides and fertilizers. Specialty eggs like these tend to cost more than generic eggs because they are more expensive to produce.

Some consumers are concerned about the *welfare* (well-being) of the hens that produce eggs. They may choose eggs labeled *cage-free* or *free-range*. Hens that produce these eggs are not kept in cages. However, they may live in very confined spaces with minimal access to the outdoors. Contacting an egg producer is the best way to get specific information about how they treat their hens (**Figure 21.2**).

Storing Eggs

Buy eggs only from refrigerated cases. Check to be sure eggs are clean and uncracked before buying them. Cracked eggs can contain harmful bacteria, which can cause foodborne illness. Discard any eggs that become cracked or broken during transportation or storage.

Store eggs in the main compartment of the refrigerator as soon as you bring them home. There is no need to wash eggs before storage. Avoid storing eggs on the refrigerator door, which does not stay as cold.

Eggshells are porous, which allows eggs to pick up odors from other foods in the refrigerator. Storing eggs in their original carton provides a barrier that will help keep them from absorbing food odors.

monticello/Shutterstock.com

Figure 21.2 The best way to learn about how hens are treated by egg producers is to contact the egg producers themselves. Why is the treatment of hens important to egg consumers?

The large end of an egg has an air cell inside the shell. Storing eggs with the large end up holds the air cell in place and helps keep eggs fresh longer. Fresh eggs may be safely stored in the refrigerator for three to five weeks. Their quality, however, will decline somewhat during lengthy storage.

Some recipes call only for egg yolks or egg whites. To store leftover yolks, cover them with cold water and refrigerate in a tightly covered container. Drain yolks before using within two days. Leftover egg whites should also be stored in the refrigerator in a tightly covered container. Use whites within four days.

Eggs as Ingredients

Taking a few precautions when using eggs will help keep foods safe and wholesome. Avoid cracking eggs directly into other ingredients. Instead, crack one egg at a time into a separate small bowl. Check to be sure the egg looks fresh and there are no shell fragments in the bowl. Then you can add the egg to other ingredients and repeat this process with each remaining egg in the recipe. Be sure to wash your hands after you have finished cracking all the eggs before touching other foods or utensils.

Food Science Technician

Food science technicians work with food scientists and technologists. They might help to develop new food products. They may also get involved with food product manufacturing. This work may require testing food products and ingredients to be sure they meet standards for factors like color, texture, and nutrients. It may entail mixing and sampling products to evaluate qualities such as taste and smell. Using and cleaning lab equipment may be part of this job, too.

To be successful, food science technicians need a strong background in math and science. They require good analytical skills to record and assess test results and prepare reports of findings. They must be dependable, so others can count on them to complete their assigned tasks. The abilities to work well with others, deal with stress in the workplace, and accept criticism from supervisors are other needed qualities.

A range of math classes as well as chemistry and biology can help prepare someone for this career area. Knowing how food is grown, harvested, and manufactured is also part of a good foundation for going into this field. Most food science technicians need to earn an associate's degree. However, they will gain much specific knowledge and skill on the job as they work with experienced professionals.

When eggs are used as ingredients in other food products, they contribute a number of qualities. Eggs add important nutrients to many dishes. Eggs lend flavor to foods such as custards. Eggs also give an appealing golden color to light-colored foods.

In addition to these qualities, eggs serve a number of functions as ingredients. For instance, eggs add structure to baked products, such as quick breads and cakes. The heat of the oven *coagulates* (thickens) the egg proteins. This helps create a framework around the air cells that form in baked goods as they rise. Eggs also function as thickeners, binding agents, interfering agents, foaming agents, and emulsifiers.

Thickeners

Heat causes egg proteins to coagulate. Thus, whole eggs and egg yolks can be used as thickening agents. They give foods like sauces and puddings a smooth texture.

Recipes thickened with eggs sometimes require the eggs to be added to a hot mixture. To do this, quickly but gently blend a small amount of the hot mixture into beaten eggs. Then add the warmed eggs to the rest of the hot mixture. Warming the eggs in this way is called *tempering*. Tempering keeps the eggs from coagulating into lumps.

Binding and Interfering Agents

As the heat of cooking sets liquid eggs into a solid state, eggs act as binding agents. They hold together the ingredients in foods such as meatballs (**Figure 21.3**). Eggs also bind crumb coatings to foods like breaded chicken breasts.

As interfering agents, eggs inhibit crystallization. Ice cream stays creamy because the eggs in it act as interfering agents. The eggs inhibit the formation of large ice crystals, which would ruin the texture of ice cream.

Arina P Habich/Shutterstock.com

Figure 21.3 Eggs act as a binding agent to hold the ingredients in meatballs together.

Foaming Agents

Eggs are used as foaming agents to add air to foods. Foams are used to make soft and hard meringues. They are also used to give structure to angel food and sponge cakes, soufflés, and puffy omelets.

Egg foams are prepared by beating air into egg whites, which causes many air cells to form. A thin film of egg white protein surrounds each cell. As beating continues, the cells become smaller and more numerous. The protein film also becomes thinner. As a result, the foam thickens.

Recipes often direct that egg whites are beaten to one of three stages: foamy, soft peak, or stiff peak. Each stage requires increased beating time. Egg whites at the *foamy stage* have bubbles and foam on the surface. Egg whites beaten to the *soft peak stage* form peaks that bend at the tips when the beater is lifted. Egg whites beaten to the *stiff peak stage* form moist peaks that stand up straight when the beater is lifted. If the foam looks dry, the egg whites have been overbeaten.

When using egg foams in recipes, other ingredients are often combined with the foams. To avoid a loss of air, this must be done quickly and gently using a process called *folding*. A flexible spatula is the best tool for folding. Cut down into the mixture, across the bottom, up the opposite side, and across the top. The spatula should remain in the mixture the entire time folding is being done.

Emulsifiers

An **emulsion** is a mixture that forms when liquids are combined that ordinarily do not mix. (Oil and water or a water-based liquid, such as vinegar, are commonly combined to form an emulsion.) To keep the two liquids from separating, an *emulsifying agent* is needed. Egg yolk is an excellent emulsifying agent. The yolk surrounds the oil droplets in an emulsion. It keeps the droplets suspended in the water-based liquid so the two liquids will not separate. Mayonnaise is an example of this type of emulsion.

Methods of Cooking Eggs

Eggs can be fried, scrambled, poached, baked, soft-cooked, or hard-cooked. They can be used to prepare plain and puffy omelets, soufflés, soft and hard meringues, and stirred and baked custards, too.

Food Science

Factors Affecting Egg Foams

Temperature, beating time, fat, acid, and sugar affect the formation of egg white foams. When preparing egg foams, two temperatures are needed. Eggs separate most easily when they are cold. However, egg whites reach maximum volume when they are at room temperature. Use an egg separator to separate whites from yolks when the eggs are taken from the refrigerator. Then let the egg whites stand at room temperature for 30 minutes before beating them. Store leftover yolks.

Avoid both too little and too much beating time when preparing egg foams. Too little beating time produces underbeaten egg whites, which lose volume quickly and do not hold their shape. Too much beating time produces overbeaten egg whites, which also lose volume quickly. In addition, overbeaten egg whites have little elasticity and will break down into curds.

Fat and fat-containing ingredients, such as egg yolk, interfere with the formation of egg white foams. Plastic bowls may hold traces of fat residues. Therefore, use clean glass or metal bowls and beaters when beating egg whites.

Acid makes egg white foams more stable. It also adds whiteness. This is why many recipes that use egg white foams call for a small amount of cream of tartar.

Sugar increases the stability of egg white foam. It also increases beating time. It is usually best to add sugar to the foam after it has reached most of the volume.

Dar1930/Shutterstock.com

Safely cooked eggs have completely set whites and thickened yolks. Yolks do not need to be hard, but they should not be runny. Dishes made with beaten eggs are thoroughly cooked when they no longer contain any visible liquid egg. The most accurate way to test the doneness of casseroles, soufflés, and other egg dishes is with a food thermometer. These dishes should reach the safe internal temperature of 160°F (71°C).

In all methods of cooking eggs, low to moderate temperatures and accurate cooking times are important (**Figure 21.4**). Eggs coagulate when heated during cooking. (Egg white coagulates at a slightly lower temperature than egg yolk. This is why the whites will become set before the yolks during cooking.) Temperature and time affect coagulation. High temperatures and long cooking times can cause egg proteins to lose moisture, shrink, and toughen.

Another factor that affects the coagulation temperature of eggs is the addition of other ingredients. For instance, adding milk to eggs dilutes the egg proteins. This raises the coagulation temperature. That is why eggs scrambled with added milk will take longer to set than eggs scrambled without milk. On the other hand, acid and salt both lower the coagulation temperature of eggs. Therefore, eggs poached in water containing vinegar (an acid) or added salt will set faster than eggs poached in plain water.

When frying or scrambling eggs, use a little fat or a nonstick skillet sprayed with cooking spray. Using a cool pan allows the egg white to spread too far before it sets. Therefore, heat a skillet and any cooking fat over medium heat before placing the eggs in it. The skillet is hot enough if a drop of water sizzles when it hits the surface of the pan. As soon as the eggs are in the skillet, turn the heat down to low. Cooking temperatures that are too high quickly toughen egg proteins.

Frying Eggs

To fry an egg, add the egg to a moderately hot skillet containing vegetable oil spray or a small amount of fat, about 1 teaspoon (5 mL) per egg. A little water may be added to the skillet, too. Cover the skillet and cook the egg until the white is completely set and the yolk begins to thicken. The steam that forms in the covered skillet will cook the upper surface of the egg. The upper surface can also be cooked by gently turning the egg over.

Scrambling Eggs

To scramble eggs, break the eggs into a bowl. Beat the eggs with a fork or whisk until blended. Add about 1 tablespoon (15 mL) of milk or water per egg. Avoid using too much liquid, which will cause the eggs to be watery. For variety, add bits of cooked bacon, shredded cheese, or finely chopped fresh or dried herbs to eggs before scrambling.

Pour the egg mixture into a lightly greased or nonstick heated skillet. When the egg begins to set, draw a bent-edged spatula across the bottom of the skillet. This will allow more of the liquid egg mixture to come in contact with the hot surface of the skillet. The egg will thicken into soft protein clumps, which are called **coagulum**. Gently continue drawing the spatula across the skillet until all the egg mixture has set. Avoid constant stirring. Too much stirring will cause the coagulum to be small (**Figure 21.5**).

Poaching Eggs

To poach eggs, fill a large, deep skillet with 1½ to 2 inches (4 to 5 cm) of liquid. Eggs can be poached in water, milk, broth, or some other liquid. If using water, add a small amount of salt and vinegar. This will cause the proteins to coagulate faster and help keep the egg from spreading. Bring the liquid just to a simmer over medium heat; boiling liquid is too hot for proper poaching.

Fotokostic/Shutterstock.com

Figure 21.4   When cooking eggs, it is important to use a low to moderate temperature.

Recipe for Good Food

Pepper 'n' Egg Sliders

Makes 4

½   medium green or red bell pepper
1   tablespoon (15 mL) olive oil
4   whole-wheat mini buns or dinner rolls
3   eggs
2   tablespoons (30 mL) fat-free milk
1   teaspoon (5 mL) onion powder
3   tablespoons (30 mL) grated Parmesan cheese
       salt and pepper, to taste

1. Preheat broiler.
2. Cut bell pepper into ¼ × 2 inch (1 × 5 cm) strips.
3. Heat olive oil in a skillet over medium heat. Add pepper strips to hot oil and sauté 5 to 7 minutes, until they begin to color.
4. Open buns and place open side up on a baking sheet. Place the baking sheet under the broiler about 5 inches from the heat. Broil 2 to 3 minutes, until buns are lightly toasted.
5. In a medium bowl, whisk together the eggs, milk, onion powder, Parmesan cheese, salt, and pepper.
6. Pour egg mixture into skillet over the pepper strips. When the eggs begin to set, gently begin drawing a bent-edged spatula across the bottom of the skillet to allow more liquid egg mixture to come in contact with the skillet. Avoid constant stirring.
7. When eggs are fully set but still moist, remove the skillet from the heat. Use the spatula to lift a quarter of the pepper and egg mixture onto the bottom half of each toasted bun. Place the top half of the bun on each sandwich and serve.

Per serving: 183 calories (49% from fat), 9 g protein, 17 g carbohydrate, 10 g fat, 162 mg cholesterol, 2 g fiber, 311 mg sodium

---

For the most attractive poached eggs, make sure the eggs are very fresh. Break each cold egg into a separate custard cup. Use the custard cups to quickly slip the eggs, one at a time, into the simmering liquid. Cover the skillet and turn off the heat. Allow the eggs to sit in the hot liquid for five to seven minutes, depending on how firm you prefer your eggs. Do not lift the lid during this time, as that will allow heat to escape from the skillet.

Remove each poached egg from the cooking liquid with a slotted spoon. Use a paper towel to absorb drips from the bottom of the spoon. Then transfer the egg to a plate for serving (**Figure 21.6**).

Baking Eggs

Baked eggs are also called *shirred eggs*. To bake an egg, break the egg into a greased custard cup. Then put the custard cup in a shallow casserole filled with 1 inch (2.5 cm) of warm water. Bake the egg in a 350°F (175°C) oven for 12 to 18 minutes, depending on the firmness desired. Try adding variety to baked eggs by sprinkling them with finely chopped green pepper and onion or grated cheese.

Cooking Eggs in the Shell

Eggs cooked in the shell can be soft-cooked or hard-cooked. Time determines the degree of doneness.

To prepare soft-cooked eggs, place the eggs in a deep pan. Add enough cold water to come 1 inch (2.5 cm) above the eggs. Cover the pan and quickly bring the water to a boil. Immediately

Wiktory/Shutterstock.com

Figure 21.5 Properly scrambled eggs are slightly moist with large, fluffy coagulum. What is your favorite way to eat eggs?

Anna Hoychuk/Shutterstock.com

Figure 21.6 The outsides of the poached egg should be cooked. Poached eggs are often served on bread or with vegetables.

remove the pan from the heat. Let the eggs remain in the water for four to five minutes, depending on the desired degree of doneness.

To prepare hard-cooked eggs, choose eggs that have been stored for a week or two. During storage, the air cell at the wide end of the egg will get larger, making the cooked eggs easier to peel. Use the same method used for soft-cooked eggs, but keep the eggs in the water longer. Large eggs will take about 15 minutes. Medium eggs will take only about 12 minutes. Extra large eggs may take about 18 minutes.

Immediately cool soft- and hard-cooked eggs under cold running water or place them in a bowl of ice water. Rapid cooling stops the eggs from cooking and prevents the formation of greenish rings around the yolks. A chemical reaction between iron in egg yolk and hydrogen sulfide in egg white causes this discoloration in overcooked eggs. The discoloration is harmless, but it looks unappetizing.

When soft-cooked eggs are cool enough to handle, they are ready to eat. A popular way to eat them is to place them in eggcups, small end down. Cut off the large end of the egg and eat the egg out of the shell (**Figure 21.7**).

When hard-cooked eggs are cooled, store them in the refrigerator. They can be kept for up to one week. Do not eat hard-cooked eggs, or any other perishable food, kept at room temperature for over two hours.

Omelets

Omelets are beaten egg mixtures that are cooked without stirring and served folded in half. Omelets can be plain (also called *French*) or puffy. Both types of omelets can be made from eggs, a small amount of liquid (usually milk or water), and seasonings.

An omelet may be served with or without a filling. Savory fillings include all kinds of cheeses and vegetables. A *Western omelet* is filled with diced ham, onions, and bell peppers. Fresh fruit is often used as a sweet filling for omelets.

To make a plain omelet, beat together the eggs, liquid, and seasonings. Pour the mixture into a lightly greased or nonstick heated skillet or omelet pan. The edges of the egg mixture should set immediately. With a wide spatula, gently lift the cooked edges to allow the uncooked egg to run underneath. Tilting the skillet will help. The omelet is ready to fill and serve when the top has set but is still moist.

To make a puffy omelet, beat the egg whites with cream of tartar and water until stiff (but not dry) peaks form. Beat the egg yolks with salt and pepper until they are thick and lemon colored. Gently fold the beaten yolks into the beaten whites. Pour the mixture into a lightly greased ovenproof skillet that is hot enough to sizzle a drop of water. Cook the omelet slowly over medium heat until puffy, about 5 minutes. (The bottom should be lightly brown.) Place the omelet in a preheated 350°F (180°C) oven. Bake it 10 to 12 minutes, or until a knife inserted near the center comes out clean.

Olyina/Shutterstock.com

Figure 21.7 A safely prepared soft-cooked egg has a thickened yolk and a completely set white.

Soufflés

Soufflés are fluffy baked preparations made with a starch-thickened sauce that is folded into stiffly beaten egg whites. Like puffy omelets, soufflés use egg whites for structure. Soufflés can be served as a main dish or for dessert.

To prepare a soufflé, add beaten egg yolks to a basic white sauce. The white sauce may contain chocolate, fruit, cheese, or pureed vegetables or seafood. Gently fold the white sauce mixture into the beaten egg whites. Bake the soufflé in a 350°F (180°C) oven until puffy and golden, about 30 to 40 minutes. Serve the soufflé immediately.

Meringues

Meringues are a fluffy, white mixture of beaten egg whites and sugar. Meringues may be soft or hard. Use soft meringues in fruit whips and as toppings on pies and other baked goods like Baked Alaska. Use hard meringues to make meringue shells, which can be filled and served as desserts. Hard meringues can also be used to make confections, such as meringue cookies (**Figure 21.8**).

Make soft meringues from egg whites, cream of tartar, sugar, and flavoring. Beat the egg whites and cream of tartar to the foamy stage. Add the sugar gradually as the egg whites are beaten to the upper limit of the soft peak stage. Rub a small amount of meringue between thumb and forefinger to detect sugar. When no undissolved sugar is felt, beat in the flavoring.

When using a soft meringue on a pie, spread it over hot pie filling. Carefully seal the meringue to the edge of the pastry. These important steps help minimize weeping and beading. **Weeping** is the layer of moisture that sometimes forms between a meringue and a filling. **Beading** appears as golden droplets on the surface of a meringue. Bake the meringue-topped pie at 350°F (180°C) until lightly browned, about 12 to 15 minutes.

Hard meringues are made from the same ingredients as soft meringues. However, they contain a higher proportion of sugar, and they are beaten to the stiff peak stage. Hard meringues are usually shaped with a spoon and baked on a baking sheet lined with parchment paper. Bake

Learn About...

Egg Substitutes

Egg substitutes provide an option for people who want to limit cholesterol and saturated fat from eggs in their diets. Egg substitutes are pasteurized. Therefore, they can be used in place of raw eggs in recipes that will not be cooked.

Egg substitutes are made largely from real egg whites. They contain no egg yolks. Therefore, these products are cholesterol-free, fat-free, and lower in calories than whole eggs. They compare closely to whole eggs in most other nutrient values. However, they may cost over three times as much as fresh eggs.

Egg substitutes are nearly as versatile as whole eggs. They can be scrambled or used to prepare omelets or quiches. They can also be used in most recipes calling for eggs. Typically, ¼ cup (60 mL) of egg substitute can be used in place of each whole egg or egg yolk. Egg substitutes can even be used to make egg salad and other recipes that call for chopped hard-cooked eggs.

Know and Apply

1. Why would it be a good idea to use an egg substitute in place of raw eggs in a recipe that will not be cooked?

2. How can egg substitutes be cholesterol-free if they are made largely from real egg whites?

Elina Manninen/Shutterstock.com

Figure 21.8   Hard meringues can be cooked to make sweet confections, like these meringue cookies. What other confections involve the use of meringue?

hard meringues at 225°F (110°C) for one to one and a half hours. Then turn off the oven and allow the meringues to stand in the oven with the door closed for another hour. This will produce a meringue with a crisp, dry interior.

Custards

Custards are a mixture of milk (or cream), eggs, sugar, and a flavoring that is cooked until thickened. Custards can be soft (sometimes called *stirred*) or baked. Soft custard may be served as a dessert sauce. It can also be used as the base for desserts like English trifle. Serve baked custard plain or with a topping of caramel, fruit, or toasted coconut. Custard can also be poured into a pastry crust for custard pie or combined with bread cubes to make bread pudding (**Figure 21.9**).

Stir soft custard constantly as it cooks. This breaks up the coagulum as it forms, giving the custard a creamy texture. Be sure to use low heat to prevent *curdling* (the formation of lumps). Soft custard will coat a metal spoon with a thin film when it is fully cooked. Place the pan of cooked custard in a bowl of ice or cold water. Stir the custard for a few minutes to cool it before covering and storing in the refrigerator.

Lack of stirring causes baked custard to become firm enough to hold its shape when removed from the baking dish. Place dishes of

custard in a large baking pan. Place the pan in a preheated oven. Then pour very hot water into the pan around the custard dishes. The water should come within ½ inch (1 cm) of the top of the custard. The water helps prevent the custard from overheating, which can result in *syneresis* (the leakage of liquid from a gel). Overbaked custard will have visible bubbles and leakage. To test baked custard for doneness, insert the tip of a knife near the center. If the knife comes out clean, the custard is baked.

Health and Wellness

Using Raw Eggs

The risk of foodborne illness due to contaminated eggs is small, especially for healthy people. It is safest, however, not to use raw eggs in any dish that is not thoroughly cooked. If a recipe calls for whole eggs, use a pasteurized egg product. A recipe that calls for separated eggs requires some special preparation steps.

Instead of using raw beaten egg whites in an uncooked dish, cook the whites. Using a specific technique, beat the egg whites into a fluffy frosting before adding them to a recipe. Combine the egg whites with the sugar from the recipe in a heavy saucepan or double boiler. (At least 2 tablespoons [30 mL] of sugar are needed per egg white.) Cook the mixture over low heat while beating it to the soft peak stage with an electric mixer.

Instead of adding raw egg yolks to a recipe, cook them as they would be cooked for making stirred custard. Combine the yolks with the liquid from the recipe in a heavy saucepan. (At least 2 tablespoons [30 mL] of liquid are needed per yolk.) Cook the mixture over low heat, stirring constantly until the mixture coats a metal spoon. Cool the mixture quickly and add it to the recipe when the egg yolks would be added.

Another option when preparing uncooked or lightly cooked recipes that call for raw eggs is to use pasteurized shell eggs. These are whole eggs that have been treated using the same heating process used to kill harmful bacteria in milk. This process does not affect the taste or cooking performance of the eggs.

Foodio/Shutterstock.com

Figure 21.9 Custard pies are made by pouring custard into a pastry crust.

Chapter 21 Review and Expand

Summary

When selecting eggs, consumers have a number of options, but all eggs are high in protein. At retail stores, consumers are likely to see Grade AA and A eggs in extra large, large, and medium sizes. These grades and sizes are used for both generic and specialty eggs. All types of eggs are perishable, but they keep well when properly refrigerated.

Eggs serve a number of functions as ingredients in recipes. Eggs add structure to baked goods. They are used to thicken puddings and sauces and to hold ingredients together in foods like meat loaf. They interfere with the formation of ice crystals in frozen desserts. They are used as foams to add air and give structure to foods like meringues and sponge cakes. They are used as emulsifiers to keep oil suspended in water-based liquids.

Eggs require moderate cooking temperatures and carefully monitored cooking times. These principles apply when frying, scrambling, poaching, baking, and cooking eggs in the shell. They should also be followed when preparing egg dishes such as omelets, soufflés, meringues, and custards.

Vocabulary Activities

1. **Content Terms** In teams, create categories for the following terms and classify as many of the terms as possible. Then share your ideas with the remainder of the class.

candling
emulsion
coagulum
omelet
soufflé

meringue
weeping
beading
custard

2. **Academic Terms** Individually or with a partner, create a T-chart on a sheet of paper and list each of the following terms in the left column. In the right column, list an *antonym* (a word of opposite meaning) for each term in the left column.

allergen
welfare

Review

Write your answers using complete sentences when appropriate.

3. In what MyPlate food group do eggs belong?
4. For what size eggs are recipes generally formulated?
5. What type of specialty eggs come from hens fed a diet that is free of chemical pesticides and fertilizers?
6. How long can fresh eggs be safely stored in the refrigerator?
7. How should beaten eggs be added to a hot mixture? Explain why.
8. What are four factors that can affect the formation of egg white foams?
9. How does egg yolk keep the vinegar and oil from separating in mayonnaise?
10. Describe the appearance of safely cooked whole eggs and beaten egg dishes.
11. Why should constant stirring be avoided when making scrambled eggs?
12. What can cause a greenish ring to form around the yolk of a soft- or hard-cooked egg and how can it be prevented?
13. Describe the appearance of a plain omelet that is ready to fill and serve.
14. What are golden droplets that sometimes appear on the surface of a meringue called?
15. What is leakage of liquid from baked custard called?
16. How can a recipe for an uncooked dish calling for whole eggs be safely prepared?

Core Skills

17. **Research, Reading, Speaking, Technology** Seek out reliable print or Internet sources to research a type of bird, other than chickens, that produces eggs eaten by humans. Investigate how these eggs are produced and sold and what cultures most commonly use them. Present your findings in an oral report to the class. Download a photograph of the bird and its eggs from the Internet to use as a visual aid.

Chapter 21 Review and Expand

18. **Science** In a darkened room, hold an egg directly over the lens of a bright flashlight. Describe characteristics of the egg that you cannot see in normal room lighting.

19. **Math** Weigh a dozen medium eggs, a dozen large eggs, and a dozen extra large eggs. Calculate the average weight per egg for each size. Also calculate the percentage weight difference between medium and large and between large and extra large eggs.

20. **Research, Reading, Writing** Seek out reliable print or Internet sources to research information about nutrient-enhanced eggs. Find out how they are produced and what role they play in the consumer egg market. Write a two-page report summarizing your findings. Include tables comparing the nutritional value and retail price of nutrient-enhanced eggs with generic eggs. Edit and refine your writing to ensure your ideas are presented in a logical, organized manner that is clear to the reader.

21. **Science** Pour ½ cup (125 mL) vegetable oil in each of two clear glass bottles. Add 1 tablespoon (15 mL) vinegar to one bottle and 1 tablespoon (15 mL) vinegar thoroughly mixed with one egg yolk to the other bottle. Put the tops on the bottles and shake them vigorously for 30 seconds. Then set the bottles on a counter and do not touch them for 10 minutes. For both bottles, record what you observe immediately after the vinegar is added, after the bottle is shaken, and 10 minutes after shaking has stopped. Use chapter information to explain your observations.

22. **Technology, Reading, Speaking, Listening** Visit the Eggcyclopedia section of the American Egg Board's consumer website. Select a topic to research and share with the class. Conclude the activity by stating something new you learned from listening to your classmates' reports.

23. **Math** In a recent year, the U.S. population numbered 318.9 million. In that same year, people in the United States consumed an average of 256 eggs each. Calculate the total number of eggs consumed. Also calculate how many dozen eggs each person consumed.

24. **Career Readiness Practice** Complete an oral history by interviewing an egg candler. If you are unable to interview someone, read one or more case studies about egg candling from reliable Internet or library resources. How does the information you learned from the interview or reading compare to information presented by the author of your text? Write a detailed summary of your interview or reading.

Critical Thinking and Problem Solving

25. **Create** Seek out reliable print or Internet resources to research the process used to pasteurize eggs in or out of the shell. Then use school-approved software or websites to create an animated presentation to educate consumers about this process. Conclude your presentation with factors consumers may want to keep in mind when they consider buying pasteurized egg products.

26. **Analyze** Beat four egg whites to the stiff peak stage. Before beating, add nothing to the first egg white. Add ⅛ teaspoon (0.6 mL) oil to the second egg white. Add ⅛ teaspoon (0.6 mL) cream of tartar to the third egg white. Add ¼ cup (60 mL) sugar to the fourth egg white. Analyze and compare the volume, appearance, and required beating time of the four samples. Summarize your observations in a brief written report.

27. **Evaluate** Beat three eggs with 3 tablespoons (45 mL) milk. Divide the mixture into three equal portions. Scramble one portion over high heat. Scramble a second portion over low heat, occasionally drawing a bent-edged spatula across the bottom of the skillet. Scramble the third portion over low heat stirring constantly. Evaluate each product on the basis of appearance, tenderness and size of the coagulum, and flavor.

28. **Create** Find a recipe for vanilla custard sauce to use as the basis for creating a new recipe. The new recipe must change the flavor of the basic sauce and/or use the sauce as part of another dish. Name your recipe and format it like recipes in this textbook. Prepare and sample the recipe. Then write a one-page evaluation describing what you did and did not like about the taste, texture, and appearance of the prepared food product. Also describe what, if any, alterations you would make when preparing the recipe again.

Chapter 22
Meat

bonchan/Shutterstock.com

Objectives

After studying this chapter, you will be able to
- **define** terms that refer to various types of meat;
- **analyze** factors affecting the selection of meats;
- **describe** how to properly store meats to maintain their quality;
- **explain** principles of cooking that will result in moist, tender meat; and
- **prepare** meats by dry and moist cooking methods.

Reading Prep

Before reading this chapter, review the highlighted terms within the body. Determine the meaning of each term.

Content Terms 🔗

meat
offal
beef
wholesale cut
retail cut
veal
pork
lamb
marbling
elastin
collagen
cooking losses

Academic Terms

mandatory
constrict
volatile

Many meal managers choose the meat course first when planning menus. Meat dishes should be tender, flavorful, and attractive.

What Is Meat?

Meat is the edible portions of mammals. It contains muscle, fat, bone, connective tissue, and water. The edible parts of the animal other than the muscles are called **offal**, or *variety meats*. Cattle, swine, and sheep are the major meat-producing animals in the United States.

Nutritional Value of Meat

One ounce (28 g) of lean, cooked meat counts as 1 ounce-equivalent from the protein foods group of MyPlate. Most teens and adults need only 5 to 7 ounce-equivalents each day.

All meat and meat products contain proteins essential for building and repairing tissue. Meats are also good sources of B vitamins, iron, and zinc. Some processed meats contain a lot of added salt. Compare labels to choose products that are lower in sodium.

The amount of fat meat contributes to the diet depends on the kind and quality of the meat. Ground meats are generally higher in fat than all other cuts. Although fat gives meat flavor and appeal, it also increases the number of calories meat provides. Experts advise limiting saturated fats and cholesterol in the diet. Diets high in these components can raise cholesterol, increasing the risk of heart disease.

Following a few tips can help people limit fat, cholesterol, and calories and enjoy meat as part of a healthy diet. First, stay within suggested amounts from the protein foods group each day. Choose lean cuts, such as the round and loin sections of beef and the loin and leg sections of pork. Trim all visible fat before cooking (**Figure 22.1**). This prevents fat from melting into the meat during cooking. Use cooking methods like broiling and grilling, which allow fat to drip away during cooking. Use nonstick pans when frying and browning meat to eliminate the need for added fat during cooking. Skim the fat from the surface of chilled meat soups and stocks.

Space Monkey Pics/Shutterstock.com

Figure 22.1 Before cooking this pork chop, trim the thick layer of fat from the left side. Why is it important to cut fat before cooking?

Beef

Beef comes from mature cattle. It has a distinctive flavor and firm texture. Beef is usually bright, cherry red in color with creamy white fat.

Like all animals used for food, beef carcasses are divided into pieces, which are referred to as *cuts*. The carcasses are first cut lengthwise through the backbone into halves. The two halves are called *sides* (**Figure 22.2**). (Veal and lamb carcasses are much smaller than beef and do not require splitting for shipment. Pork carcasses are small enough to be shipped whole, but they are usually split.) Beef sides are cut into *quarters* and then into large pieces, called **wholesale cuts**, for easier handling. Wholesale cuts are shipped to retail grocery stores or meat markets. There, meat cutters divide the wholesale cuts into still smaller pieces, called **retail cuts**, which are sold to consumers.

Beef is also available in ground form. Some people incorrectly call ground beef "hamburger."

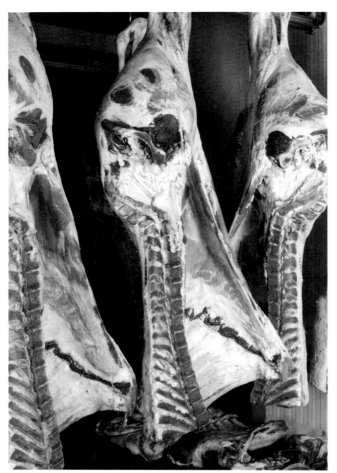

tandem/Shutterstock.com

Figure 22.2 Beef carcasses must be cut into halves for shipping because they are so large.

Ground beef contains only the fat originally attached to the meat before grinding. *Hamburger* can have extra fat added to it during grinding. For the healthiest choice, look for extra lean ground beef. The label should state that it is at least 90 percent lean.

Veal

Veal is meat that comes from young calves. Because the animals are so young, little fat has developed. Thus, most veal is lean. Veal also has quite a bit of connective tissue, but it is still considered to be tender. Veal has a light pink color and a delicate flavor.

Pork

Pork is the meat of hogs. Most pork comes from animals that are 6 to 7 months old. Because

Learn About...

Offal

Liver, heart, kidney, tongue, and *sweetbreads* (thymus glands) are popular types of offal. Other types of offal include beef *tripe* (stomach lining), brains, and *chitterlings* (cleaned intestines). Pork jowls (cheeks), tail, feet, ears, and snout are additional types of offal. Offal is usually inexpensive, and many parts are rich sources of vitamins and minerals. For instance, liver is very high in iron.

The cooking method used for preparing offal depends on the tenderness of each meat. Cook most types of offal using moist heat. However, brains, sweetbreads, and the liver and kidneys of veal and calf are often cooked by dry heat, such as broiling or frying.

Brains and sweetbreads are very delicate meats. To retain their shape, precook them for about 20 minutes in salted, *acidulated* water (water that contains an acid, such as lemon juice). After precooking, they can be fried or broiled.

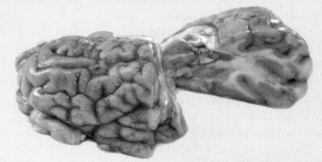

Swapan Photography/Shutterstock.com

It is very important that brains and sweetbreads are fresh and prepared the day they are purchased.

Know and Apply

1. Name five examples of offal.
2. Why do you think offal is not more popular with consumers?

the animals are so young, most pork is tender. The meat is grayish-pink to light rose in color.

Meatpacking plants process many pork products. *Ham* comes from the pork hind leg. It is cured and usually smoked. *Cured* products have salt and spices added to them for flavor and

Recipe for Good Food

Motley Meatballs

Makes about 18 meatballs

1	egg white, lightly beaten
1½	teaspoons (7.5 mL) reduced-sodium soy sauce
1½	teaspoons (7.5 mL) dried parsley
¼	teaspoon (1.25 mL) onion powder
⅛	teaspoon (.6 mL) garlic powder
⅛	teaspoon (.6 mL) fresh ground pepper
¼	cup (60 mL) dry bread crumbs
½	pound (227 g) ground beef, 90% lean

1. Preheat oven to 375°F (190°C). Line a baking sheet with parchment paper.
2. In a medium mixing bowl, combine egg white, soy sauce, dried parsley, onion powder, garlic powder, and pepper. Stir in bread crumbs.
3. Add the ground beef to the mixing bowl and gently fold together until the egg white mixture is completely incorporated into the meat.
4. Shape the meat mixture into 1¼-inch (3 cm) meatballs and place on the prepared baking sheet. Bake in preheated oven until meatballs are browned, about 18 to 20 minutes.
5. While meatballs are in the oven, make desired dipping sauce. Serve meatballs with toothpicks and sauce for dipping.

Dipping Sauces
(Makes about ½ cup each)

Three-Pepper Mayo

½	cup low-fat mayonnaise
⅛	teaspoon garlic powder
1	teaspoon smoked paprika
2	teaspoons red wine vinegar
½	teaspoon hot pepper sauce
	dash cayenne pepper
	Salt and pepper to taste

Chimichurri

½	cup packed fresh flat-leaf parsley
2	cloves garlic
¼	teaspoon salt
¼	teaspoon crushed red pepper
⅛	teaspoon black pepper
2	tablespoons red wine vinegar
¼	cup olive oil

Asian Barbecue Sauce

½	cup ketchup
2	tablespoons low-sodium soy sauce
1	teaspoon ground ginger
¼	teaspoon garlic powder
2	tablespoons packed brown sugar
1	teaspoon hot pepper sauce

1. For three sauces: Combine all ingredients until thoroughly blended. (Use food processor for chimichurri.) Cover and refrigerate until ready to serve.

	Calories	Protein (g)	Carbohydrate (g)	Fat (g)	Cholesterol (mg)	Fiber (g)	Sodium (mg)
Motley Meatball (1 each)	27 (33% from fat)	3	1	1	8	0	36
Three-Pepper Mayo (1 tbsp.)	47 (96% from fat)	0	1	5	0	0	122
Chimichurri (1 tbsp.)	63 (99% from fat)	0	1	7	0	0	75
Asian Barbecue (1 tbsp.)	31 (0% from fat)	1	8	0	0	0	305

preservation (**Figure 22.3**). Ham often has water added to it as well. Most hams are fully cooked and are available fresh boneless or bone-in. Fully cooked canned hams and uncooked fresh hams can also be purchased. *Bacon* is cured, smoked pork belly meat. It can be purchased as precut slices or in slab form. *Canadian bacon* is made from boneless pork loin, which is the back area of the hog. Pork chops, roasts, spareribs, tenderloins, and sausage are other popular pork products.

Lamb

Lamb is the meat of sheep less than one year old. It is tender with a delicate flavor. Fresh lamb is pinkish-red in color with white fat. Older animals are marketed as *yearling lamb* (one to two years of age) and *mutton* (over two years of age). Retail outlets do not sell much mutton. It has a stronger flavor than lamb and is less tender.

Specialty Meats

Specialty meat products are available to suit various consumer needs. *Breed-specific meat* is one type of specialty product. Certain breeds of cattle and hogs are known for producing high-quality meat that is tender and flavorful. Certified Angus Beef and Berkshire Pork are examples. As a rule, these premium meats cost more than other meats.

Organic meats come from animals that are given organic feed and do not receive hormones or antibiotics. Farmers must pay for inspection to be certain organic standards are being met. Higher costs of organic farming and inspection cause organic meats to be more costly for consumers.

Pasture-raised or *grass-fed meat* comes from animals that eat a natural diet of grass and other field plants rather than grain (**Figure 22.4**). Meat from these animals tends to be leaner than grain-fed meat. It is also higher in omega-3 fatty acids and some other nutrients. Because grass-fed animals do not grow as quickly as grain-fed animals, they are more costly to produce. Thus, this meat is more costly for consumers.

Some of these specialty meats may not be available at local grocery stores. However, they can often be found at farmers markets as well as through online retailers.

Selecting Meat

Meats are costly food items. Learning how to judge quality factors and identify meat cuts can help consumers make wise purchases.

Inspection and Grading of Meat

All meat must be *inspected*. This means it is carefully checked to be sure it is *wholesome*, or fit to eat. Meat and meat products shipped across state lines are examined by federal inspectors.

Ekaterina Kondratova/Shutterstock.com

Figure 22.3   Prosciutto and salami are two types of cured meats.

Leena Robinson/Shutterstock.com

Figure 22.4   Pasture-raised cattle require approximately 8 to 15 acres per cow (with calf) if the pasture is native grass.

The inspectors check both live animals and carcasses. They also check processing plants to be sure conditions are sanitary. Meat that is processed and sold within a state is inspected by state inspectors.

While inspection is *mandatory* (required), meat grading is voluntary. *Grading* means evaluating for a level of quality. Higher quality grades go to cuts that are likely to be more tender and flavorful. One factor used to assess quality is **marbling**. This refers to the flecks of fat throughout the lean muscles of meat. Cuts with more marbling are juicier and have more taste appeal.

The most common grades of beef sold in retail stores are Choice and Select. *Choice* beef is high quality with good marbling. *Select* beef is leaner than Choice beef, and it usually costs less. Fine restaurants as well as some grocery stores and butcher shops often sell *Prime* beef. This highest grade is given to beef cuts with the most marbling and finest muscle texture (**Figure 22.5**).

USDA

Figure 22.5 Look for these grade symbols when purchasing beef to determine meat quality.

The standards used for grading veal, pork, and lamb differ somewhat from those used to grade beef. However, the highest grades are given to carcasses that are expected to provide the tastiest meat. The grading program is overseen by the USDA.

Characteristics of the Fat

Color, firmness, and location of fat affect meat quality. Quality meats will have firm to medium-firm creamy white fat. Fat that is yellow and coarse is a sign of poor quality.

Marbling indicates tenderness in a cut of meat. Although more marbling means more tenderness, it also means more total fat, saturated fat, cholesterol, and calories. Cooking can tenderize cuts with less marbling. Therefore, choose leaner cuts most often.

Location of the Meat in the Animal

The location of muscle tissue in an animal indicates the tenderness of the meat cut. Rib and loin muscles are quite tender because they lie along the backbone where they receive little exercise. Leg and shoulder muscles are less tender because the animal uses them more.

The tenderness of a meat cut gives a clue about how to cook it. Tender cuts of meat can be cooked by dry-heat methods, such as broiling or roasting. Sirloin and porterhouse steaks, pork and lamb loin chops, and beef and pork rib roasts are examples of tender cuts of meat. Cook less tender cuts of meat by moist-heat methods, such as stewing or braising. Examples of these cuts include round steak, rump roast, and shoulder steak. The location of various beef cuts and suggested cooking methods are shown in **Figure 22.6**.

How Much Meat to Buy

The amount of meat to buy depends on how many people are being served. It also depends on the cut of meat chosen and whether leftovers are desired.

Meat is sold by the pound (kg). It is necessary to know how many people 1 pound (0.45 kg) of meat will serve. A serving size in a healthy diet is 3 ounces (85 g) of cooked, lean meat. However, the amount of raw meat required to yield this serving size varies from cut to cut. Boneless cuts will serve

Beef Cuts
AND RECOMMENDED COOKING METHODS

Figure 22.6 The part of the animal from which meat comes indicates how tender the meat is and how to cook it. With which cuts of meat are you most familiar?

more people per pound (0.45 kg) than meat with bones. A buying guide based on the weight per serving for cuts with varying amounts of bone is shown in **Figure 22.7.**

To determine how much to buy, multiply the amount of meat per serving by the number of people being served. Then add the amount of leftover meat planned to serve later. For instance, beef back ribs have many bones, so buy ¼ to ¾ pound (225 to 340 g) per serving. If 6 people are being served and enough leftovers to serve 4 are needed, buy 10 servings. This would be between 5 and 7½ pounds (2.25 and 3.40 kg) of ribs.

Cost of Meat per Serving

The cost per serving of meat depends partly on the tenderness of the meat. Usually, tender cuts cost more than less tender cuts. That is why sirloin steak costs more than round steak.

The amount of waste in a meat cut also affects the cost per serving. Meat with bones often is priced lower per pound (0.45 kg) than boneless cuts. For example, a bone-in rump roast usually costs less per pound (0.45 kg) than a boneless rump roast.

Meat extenders like dried beans and rice can stretch meat dollars. For instance, ham will go farther when mixed with nutritious navy beans than when served alone.

Storing Meat

Immediately after bringing fresh meat products home, store them in the refrigerator for use within a few days. Also, refrigerate canned hams until ready for use unless the label says otherwise. Store meats in the meat storage compartment or the coldest part of the refrigerator. The temperature of the refrigerator should be 40°F (4°C) or lower. Refrigerate prepackaged meats in their original wrappers. After cooking meats, store them in tightly covered containers in the refrigerator.

Freeze meats for longer storage. (Canned hams should not be frozen.) The temperature in the freezer should remain at 0°F (–18°C) or colder for maximum keeping quality. Meats can be frozen in their original wrappings for up to two weeks. For extended freezer storage, rewrap meats in moistureproof and vaporproof paper. Tightly sealed heavy-duty foil and freezer bags are also good choices for freezer storage. Label each package with the date and the name and weight of the cut. Be sure to use meats within recommended storage times, as shown in **Figure 22.8.**

Food Science Principles of Cooking Meat

Cooking has several beneficial effects on meat. First, cooking destroys harmful bacteria

Meat Purchasing Guide	
Amount of Bone	**Amount to Buy Per Serving**
Boneless	¼ to ⅓ lb. (115 to 150 g)
Small Bone	⅓ to ½ lb. (150 to 225 g)
Many Bones	½ to ¾ lb. (225 to 340 g)

Figure 22.7 Use this chart as a rough guide when determining how much meat to buy per serving.

Storage Times for Meat		
Type of Meat	**Refrigerator**	**Freezer**
Bacon	7 days	1 month
Chops	3–5 days	4–6 months
Ground Meats	1–2 days	3–4 months
Ham	Whole: 7 days half, slices: 3–4 days	1–2 months
Hot Dogs	Opened: 1 week Unopened: 2 weeks	1–2 months
Leftover Cooked Meats	3–4 days	2–3 months
Luncheon Meats	Opened: 3–5 days Unopened: 2 weeks	1–2 months
Offal	1–2 days	3–4 months
Roasts	3–5 days	4–12 months
Steaks	3–5 days	6–12 months

Figure 22.8 Keep fresh meat safe to eat by cooking or freezing it within a few days of purchase. Date frozen meat and use it within recommended storage times for best quality.

Health and Wellness

Cooking Meat Safely

Meats are often identified as the source of bacteria that cause foodborne illness. Most cases of foodborne illness result from improper food handling. Use care when buying, storing, cooking, serving, and reheating foods to help avoid illness. Review the food handling precautions in Chapter 2. In addition, be aware of the following guidelines when cooking meat:

- Store meats at or below 40°F (4°C).
- Cook or freeze refrigerated meats within recommended time frames (1 to 2 days for ground meats, 3 to 5 days for nonground cuts, 3 to 4 days for leftovers).
- Wash hands for 20 seconds with hot, soapy water before beginning to cook. Wash hands again after handling raw meat.
- Do not wash or rinse raw meat.
- Thoroughly wash cutting boards and utensils used for raw meat before using them to prepare raw vegetables or cooked meat.
- Marinate raw meat in the refrigerator, not at room temperature. Discard marinade after use. If you want to use some marinade to sauce the meat after cooking, set aside a separate portion before placing the raw meat in the marinade.
- Brush sauces only on cooked surfaces of meat.
- Do not set the oven below 325°F (165°C) when cooking meats.
- Use a food thermometer to make sure meat has reached a safe internal temperature. Cook ground meats to an internal temperature of 160°F (71°C). Cook beef, veal, pork, and lamb cuts to at least 145°F (63°C) and include a 3 minute rest time after cooking.
- Reheat leftover meats to an internal temperature of 165°F (74°C).
- Be sure to wash the probe of the meat thermometer in hot, soapy water after each use. Do not reinsert a dirty thermometer into a food or use it to check another food.

that can be present in raw meat. Cooking improves the flavor of meat and makes it easier to digest, too.

Tenderizing Connective Tissue

Another way cooking can benefit meat is by making it more tender. The tenderizing effects of cooking depend on the cooking technique and the amount and types of connective tissue in the meat. *Connective tissue* holds together fibers in the muscle tissues. Meat cuts with a lot of connective tissue are less tender that those with little connective tissue.

Connective tissue in meat contains two main proteins: elastin and collagen. **Elastin** is very tough and elastic, and it cannot be softened by cooking. **Collagen** is strong and flexible. This is the type of connective tissue that can be tenderized by cooking.

Not all cooking methods will tenderize collagen. This protein is water soluble. Therefore, moist-heat methods, such as braising or stewing, are required to break it down. Low heat, a long cooking time, and moisture work together to soften collagen and change it into tender gelatin.

Although elastin cannot be softened by moist heat, it can be broken down mechanically or chemically before cooking. Pounding is sometimes done to round steak. Grinding is done to ground beef. These are two mechanical methods of breaking down elastin as well as collagen. Meat tenderizers contain enzymes that can soften both types of connective tissue chemically. Enzyme tenderizers must not be applied too long before cooking or meat can develop a mushy texture.

Another chemical technique that can help tenderize collagen is marinating. *Marinate* means to soak a food in a flavorful solution called a *marinade*. Marinades contain acid ingredients, such as vinegar or tomato juice. In as little as 15 minutes of soaking, a marinade can enhance the flavor of meat. However, meat needs to stay in a marinade for 6 to 24 hours for the acid to slightly soften collagen. Acid ingredients do not break down elastin. A review of how tenderizing techniques affect collagen and elastin is shown in **Figure 22.9.**

Tenctive	Connective Tissue		

Tenderizing Connective Tissue		
Tenderizing Technique	Collagen	Elastin
Moist-Heat Cooking	✓	
Enzymes (meat tenderizers)	✓	✓
Acids (marinades)	✓	
Mechanically Grinding or Pounding	✓	✓

Figure 22.9 All four tenderizing techniques are effective for softening collagen. Only two techniques—using enzymes and mechanically grinding or pounding the meat—will soften elastin.

Controlling Temperature When Cooking Meat

As meat begins to cook, the proteins in the muscle fibers coagulate. This causes the meat to become firmer. The protein molecules also begin to release water. Much of this water is held within the meat. You see this moisture as juices that come from the meat when you cut into it. As cooking continues, the red or pink color of raw meat changes to the brownish-grey color associated with cooked meat (**Figure 22.10**). If meat reaches the stage of being overcooked, the muscle fibers

begin to *constrict* (become smaller; shrink) and release even more moisture. The result is meat that is tough and dry. Meat cuts that are being cooked in liquid can become stringy at this point.

The fat, water, and other *volatile* (easily vaporized) substances that evaporate from the surface of meat during cooking are called **cooking losses**. Some of these substances are also retained in the pan drippings or cooking liquid. Meat shrinks as these substances are released. Therefore, excessive cooking losses can affect the number of servings meat will provide. For instance, it can be expected that a 6-pound (2.6 kg) bone-in roast will provide about 15 servings. Cooking losses, however, could reduce the number of servings by 2 or more.

Using too high a temperature when cooking meat can increase cooking losses. Meat cooked at too high a temperature can also develop a hard crust. This can make carving and eating difficult.

To avoid undesirable crust and keep cooking losses to a minimum, use moderate temperatures when cooking meat. Meat will be juicier, more flavorful, and easier to carve. Cleanup will be easier because less fat will have spattered on the oven walls or burned onto the pan. Meat, however, should not be cooked at temperatures below 325°F (165°C). Temperatures lower than this may allow bacteria to grow before meat has finished cooking.

Joe Gough/Shutterstock.com

TwilightArtPictures/Shutterstock.com

Figure 22.10 As meat cooks, the internal color changes from red-pink to brown and grey. How does the texture of meat change as it cooks?

Controlling Time When Cooking Meat

The total time a cut of meat is cooked affects its appearance and eating quality just as temperature does. Several factors affect cooking time.

One factor that affects cooking time is cooking temperature. Higher temperatures result in shorter cooking times. Lower temperatures result in longer cooking times. Changing the cooking temperature by just a few degrees can affect cooking time. For instance, suppose a roast is in the oven and the oven door is opened every few minutes to check the roast. Each time the door is opened, cool air enters the oven. This reduces the cooking temperature and will cause the roast to take longer to cook.

The size and shape of the cut of meat are factors that affect cooking time. Large cuts of meat need longer cooking times than small cuts; however, large cuts take fewer minutes *per pound* to cook than small cuts. A rolled rib roast will take longer to cook than a standing rib roast because the meat is more compact (**Figure 22.11**).

The desired degree of doneness is another factor that affects cooking time. The cooking time for medium-rare beef is less than the cooking time for well-done beef. The more well done the meat is to be, the longer it will take to cook.

Methods of Cooking Meat

Consider the tenderness, size, and thickness of a meat cut as well as taste preferences when choosing a cooking method. Roasting, broiling, grilling, pan-broiling, and frying are dry-heat cooking methods. Use them for tender cuts of meat, such as T-bone steaks and rib roasts. Braising and cooking in liquid are moist-heat cooking methods. Use them for less tender cuts of meat, such as chuck roasts and corned beef brisket. Some types of meat, such as ground meat and bacon, can also be successfully prepared in a microwave oven.

Roasting Meat

Roasting is recommended for large, tender cuts of meat. For best results when roasting, place meat with the fat side up on a rack in a large, shallow pan. The fat bastes the meat during cooking, and the rack holds the meat out of the drippings. Season meat with salt and pepper, if desired. Insert a meat thermometer into the thickest part of the muscle, without having the tip touching bone or fat. Roast the meat in a slow oven (325°F to 350°F, 160°C to 180°C), uncovered, until it reaches the desired degree of doneness.

svariophoto/Shutterstock.com

Hannamariah/Shutterstock.com

Figure 22.11   The (A) rolled roast will take longer to cook than the (B) standing rib roast.

(Roast smaller cuts of meat at the higher temperature and larger cuts at the lower temperature.)

Allowing a roast to stand for 10 to 15 minutes after taking it from the oven makes it easier to carve. As the roast stands, it will continue to cook. For this reason, take the roast from the oven when it is about 5°F (3°C) below the desired internal temperature.

Broiling Meat

Tender beefsteaks, lamb and pork chops, ham slices, ground beef, and ground lamb can be broiled. Steaks and chops that are too thin will dry out before they are thoroughly cooked. Therefore, these cuts should be at least ¾ inch (1.9 cm) thick for broiling. Ham slices should be at least ½ inch (1.3 cm) thick.

Broiling is done under a direct flame in gas broilers and under the direct heating element in electric broilers. The closer the meat is to the heat source, the shorter the cooking time will be. Place thick cuts of meat farther away from the heat than thin cuts. Place pork far enough away so the meat will not dry out before it is thoroughly cooked.

For best results when broiling meat, place meat on a cold broiler pan. Adjust the broiler rack to the desired distance from the heat source. Broil the top side of the meat until it is brown. (It should be about half-cooked at this point.) Turn the meat and season if desired. (Do not salt meats before broiling because salt draws juices from the meat. Cured meats should not be salted at all.) Broil the second side until brown.

Time charts can help determine the correct cooking time when broiling. Time charts are available in many basic cookbooks. Use an instant-read thermometer to check the internal temperature of the meat toward the end of the broiling time. This will help evaluate the degree of doneness. It will also assure that the meat has reached a safe internal temperature.

Grilling Meat

The same cuts of meat used for broiling can be successfully grilled. Indirect grilling is recommended as the healthiest grilling method. For indirect grilling, move hot coals to the sides of the grill. To grill meat indirectly on a gas grill, turn off the central gas burners after preheating the grill. Place seasoned meat in the center of the

Learn About...

Degree of Meat Doneness

Be aware of the internal temperature of meat when cooking. The type of meat and the desired degree of doneness determine the correct internal temperature. Overcooked meat is cooked to an internal temperature that is too high. Such meat has more cooking losses than meat cooked to the correct temperature.

The only accurate way to determine the internal temperature of meat is to use a food thermometer. Insert the thermometer into the thickest part of the muscle. Make sure the probe is not touching bone, fat, or gristle. Check the temperature of uneven cuts in several places. Insert the probe horizontally through the side into the center of thin cuts, such as chops and meat patties. Beef and pork cuts like steaks and roasts should be cooked to a minimum internal temperature of 145°F (63°C) and include a 3 minute rest time after cooking. Ground meat, such as burgers and meatloaf, should be cooked to a minimum internal temperature of 160°F (71°C).

People prefer beef steaks and some other cuts to be cooked to different degrees of doneness. For food safety reasons, the USDA does not recommend serving meats at the extra rare or rare stage. Medium rare, medium, and well-done meat cuts are all considered safe. Burgers should be cooked to at least the medium stage. Again, using a meat thermometer is the most accurate way to determine the desired degree of doneness has been reached.

Preventing foodborne illness is also a key reason to be aware of internal temperatures when cooking meat. Thorough cooking kills harmful bacteria. Do not rely on the color of cooked meat as a sign that meat has reached a safe internal temperature.

Determining Meat Doneness	
Medium rare	145°F (63°C)
Medium	160°F (71°C)
Well done	170°F (77°C)

Know and Apply

1. Besides having excess cooking losses, what happens to meat that is overcooked?

2. What is the key reason to be aware of internal cooking temperatures when cooking meat?

grill and cover the grill until the meat is done. Because heat surrounds the meat in the covered grill, there is no need to turn the meat. Grill meat for the correct amount of time needed for the particular cut being cooked. A grilling time chart in a cookbook or the use-and-care manual for the grill will help determine cooking times.

Research suggests the high heat used in grilling and broiling can allow cancer-causing compounds to form on meat. Meat juices that drip onto hot coals and cause smoke and flare-ups increase the formation of cancer-causing agents. Several steps can be taken to keep grilled meats healthier. First, cut any charred surfaces from meat before eating it (**Figure 22.12**). Meat can be marinated before grilling to help reduce the formation of harmful substances. Partially precooking meats in a microwave oven immediately before placing them on the grill will reduce grilling time. Also, try wrapping meats in foil for grilling to avoid exposing them to direct flames.

Pan-Broiling Meat

Meat cuts that can be broiled can also be pan-broiled if they are 1 inch (2.5 cm) thick or less. Pan-broiling is a good method to use when preparing small quantities of meat. It can save energy and cleanup time when cooking just one or two steaks or chops.

gali estrange/Shutterstock.com

Figure 22.12 Before eating grilled foods, such as these grilled lamb kebabs, cut away areas that are charred.

For best results when pan-broiling, place the meat in a heavy skillet or griddle. Do not cover the pan or add fat. (If the meat is very lean, lightly brush the skillet with fat to prevent sticking.) Cook the meat slowly, turning it occasionally to ensure even cooking. Pour off any fat that accumulates. Pan-broiled meats need only about half the cooking time of broiled meats. Insert an

Exploring Careers

Grill Cook

Grill cooks prepare foods in restaurants. The types of cooking and other tasks a grill cook must do depend on the kind of restaurant and the size of the kitchen staff. Tasks may involve everything from grilling meats to frying eggs to cooking soups. Larger restaurants will likely have prep cooks to perform jobs like cleaning and cutting vegetables. Smaller kitchens will rely on the grill cook to handle these duties.

To be successful, grill cooks need good listening skills to hear specifics of food orders that may be called out by managers and wait staff. Grill cooks need reading skills to follow written food orders and recipes. They must have hand-eye coordination when using knives and other utensils. Grill cooks use time-management skills to monitor the progress of multiple food orders being prepared at once. They use sensory evaluation to judge the doneness of foods based on sight, texture, and smell. These workers need to know and follow food safety standards. Grill cooks must be able to work well with other kitchen staff, take direction from managers, and possibly train new coworkers.

Grill cooks usually need a high school diploma. Previous kitchen experience may or may not be required, depending on the restaurant. Skilled grill cooks may be able to move into chef or kitchen manager positions. However, some restaurants will require culinary training for these jobs regardless of experience as a grill cook.

instant-read thermometer horizontally through the side of steaks and chops to be sure they have reached the correct internal temperature.

Frying Meat

Most fried meats are prepared by panfrying, or sautéing. A few can be deep-fried. Panfry meats in a small amount of fat. This fat may be added before cooking, or it may accumulate during cooking. Fairly thin pieces of tender meat, tenderized meat, ground meat patties, or cooked meat slices can be panfried.

For best results when panfrying, brown meat on both sides in a small amount of fat. Season meat after browning or add the seasonings to the breading if the meat is breaded.
Cook the meat uncovered at a moderate temperature, turning occasionally until done. If the temperature is too high, the fat will smoke, and the meat will burn on the outside before the inside is cooked.

A variation of panfrying is *stir-frying*. Stir-fried meats and vegetables are often served together in Asian dishes. Cook thinly sliced meat in a small amount of oil. Use a wok or frying pan. Cook the meat over high heat and stir it constantly until done (**Figure 22.13**).

Joshua Resnick/Shutterstock.com

Figure 22.13 Before stir-frying meat, such as beef or pork, slice the meat into thin slices or cubes. Incorporate a colorful assortment of vegetables to help balance your diet.

Braising Meat

Braising is cooking in a small amount of liquid in a tightly covered pan over low heat. Less tender meat cuts and tender cuts of pork and veal can be braised. Braising can be done in the oven or on the surface unit of a range.

Meat cuts are often seared before braising. *Sear* means to brown the surface of a food very quickly with high heat. This step gives the meat an appealing color and flavor. Preheat a small amount of fat in a pan before adding the meat. (If the meat has sufficient fat, additional fat is not needed.) Make sure the pan is hot enough to make a drop of water sizzle. A hot pan will help the meat brown quickly.

Once the meat is seared, season it and add a small amount of liquid. Use water, broth, tomato juice, or a flavorful sauce as the braising liquid. Cover the pan tightly, and cook the meat slowly until tender. (Gently simmer braised meat. The cooking liquid should never boil.) The juices that accumulate during cooking can be thickened and made into gravy. They contain important vitamins and minerals.

Cooking Meat in Liquid

When cooking meats in liquid, cover them with the cooking liquid. (This method differs from the braising process, in which only a small amount of liquid is used.) Use the cooking method of covering meats in liquid for less tender cuts of meat. When used with whole cuts of meat, this method is called *simmering*. Many people simmer corned beef brisket. When small pieces of meat are cooked in liquid, this method is called *stewing*.

For best results when cooking in liquid, cover the meat entirely with water or stock. This ensures even cooking. Season cooking liquid with salt, pepper, and herbs, if desired. Cover the pot and simmer until the meat is tender. (Cooking time will vary depending on the meat being cooked. When using this method, cook most meat cuts two hours or more.) The cooking liquid should never boil. Boiling can cause meat to shrink and become dry.

If preparing a stew, cut the meat into cubes of uniform size, about 1 to 2 inches (2.5 to 5 cm) (**Figure 22.14**). Sear the cubes in a small amount of fat, if desired. Cover the meat cubes with

Figure 22.14 Stew meat should be uniformly cut for even cooking.

liquid and stew until tender. Vegetables may be added to the meat later, allowing them to cook just long enough to become tender. Before serving, transfer the meat and vegetables to a warm serving platter and thicken the cooking liquid if desired.

Microwaving Meat

Conventional cooking methods are often preferred for preparing cuts such as roasts, steaks, and chops. However, microwaving can be a quick, easy way to prepare meats like bacon, sausage, and ground meat patties. Remember that microwave cooking time increases as the quantity of food increases. Therefore, eight slices of bacon will take longer to cook than four slices.

Covering meats in a microwave oven holds in steam. This keeps meats such as meatballs and ham slices moist and tender and shortens cooking time even further. Cover bacon, hot dogs, and cooked sausages with paper towels to absorb grease and prevent spatters. (Remember to pierce the skin on products like sausage and hot dogs to allow steam to escape and prevent bursting.)

How meats are arranged in a microwave oven affects how evenly the meats are cooked. Arrange uniformly shaped meat, such as meat

patties and sausage links, in a circle. Overlap sliced meats, such as fully cooked ham. Rotating, turning, and rearranging meats during the cooking period will also help them microwave more evenly.

Meatballs, patties, and sausages will not brown in a microwave oven as they do when prepared by conventional methods. Therefore, it might be a good idea to use a sauce or topping to give them a more appealing appearance. Sauces have the added advantage of keeping meat moist in the microwave oven.

Cooking Frozen Meat

Frozen meats can be cooked from the frozen state or defrosted before cooking. Cook prepared frozen meats according to package directions.

For safety, never thaw meat on the kitchen counter. Harmful microorganisms can grow in meat thawed at room temperature, resulting in foodborne illness. Instead, leave meat in its freezer wrapping and thaw it in the refrigerator. Place it on a plate to catch any juices that may drip from the meat as it thaws. Frozen meat can also be safely defrosted in the microwave oven immediately before cooking.

Frozen meat must be cooked longer than thawed meat. A frozen roast will need to cook about 50 percent longer than a thawed roast. Cooking time for frozen steaks and chops will vary depending on size and thickness.

When broiling frozen meats, place meat farther away from the heat source. This will prevent the outside from overcooking before the inside is cooked. To pan-broil frozen meat, use a hot skillet to sear the meat. Then lower the heat and turn meat occasionally to ensure even cooking.

Cooking Meat Alternatives

Even those who follow vegetarian diets often build their main dishes around a protein food. Some of the most popular meat alternatives include tofu, tempeh, and seitan. All three of these products are good low-sodium, cholesterol-free sources of iron as well as protein (**Figure 22.15**). Tofu and seitan also provide calcium. Tempeh is rich in magnesium and vitamin B_6.

Tofu is a mild-flavored custard-like cake made from soybeans. It comes packed in liquid

Figure 22.15 Meat alternatives, such as tofu (A), tempeh (B) and seitan (C), can be cooked in a variety of ways to create protein-rich main dishes. Which of these meat alternatives do you find most appealing?

and should be drained before using. It has little flavor of its own and will take on the flavors of other ingredients used with it. Tofu is available in silken and firm varieties. *Silken tofu* gives a creamy texture to foods like smoothies, soups, and dips when mixed in a blender or food processor. *Firm tofu* can be crumbled and scrambled like eggs. Tofu does not require cooking, but cooking methods can be used to alter its appearance, texture, and flavor. Tofu can be cut into slices, strips, or cubes to fry, bake, or broil. It is often flavored with a marinade before cooking and makes a nutritious addition to soups, casseroles, and stir-fried dishes.

Once opened, unused tofu can be covered with water and refrigerated in a tightly sealed container for up to one week. The water should be changed every day or two to keep the tofu fresh. Cooked tofu can be covered and stored in the refrigerator for up to three days.

Tempeh is a fermented soybean product. It has a firmer texture than tofu and a distinctive, nutty flavor. Tempeh can be marinated and grilled or fried to give it a crispy exterior and a chewy interior. Tempeh prepared this way may be served with side dishes or used in tacos or sandwiches. Like tofu, tempeh takes on the flavors of other ingredients and is often added to sauces for dishes like chili, spaghetti, and curry. Store tempeh in the refrigerator or freeze it for longer storage. Wrap opened tempeh in wax paper or plastic wrap and use within five days.

Seitan is sometimes called *wheat meat*. It is made of wheat gluten and has a chewy texture that is similar to meat. Seitan can be purchased ready-made, but it is also easy to make at home. Prepared seitan can be baked, grilled, or fried. It can be thinly sliced and used like luncheon meat or sliced into thicker cutlets. It can be cut into chunks for threading onto skewers or adding to stews. It can be shaped into logs and seasoned like sausage or made into crumbles that resemble ground meat. Store seitan in the refrigerator wrapped in wax paper or plastic wrap or placed in a tightly covered container in its cooking broth. For longer storage, store seitan and dishes made with it in the freezer.

Chapter 22 Review and Expand

Summary

Beef, veal, pork, and lamb are the most commonly eaten types of meat in the United States. They are all high in protein and are good sources of several vitamins and minerals.

Meat is inspected for wholesomeness and may be graded for quality. Fat appearance is a sign of quality. The part of the animal from which the meat comes indicates tenderness. Boneless cuts yield more servings per pound than bone-in cuts.

Store meats in the coldest part of the refrigerator and use them within a few days. Wrap them well and put them in the freezer for longer storage.

When cooking meats, carefully control temperatures and cooking times to help meats turn out moist and tender. Roasting, broiling, grilling, pan-broiling, and frying generally work best for tender cuts of meat. Braising and stewing are recommended for less tender cuts. A microwave oven can be used to defrost and cook meats. Frozen meats can be cooked from the frozen state or defrosted in the refrigerator before cooking. Meat alternatives can be cooked by many of the same methods.

Vocabulary Activities

1. **Content Terms**   Write a brief chapter summary to a peer who is interested in becoming a chef at a restaurant specializing in meats. In your summary, include each vocabulary term listed below.

meat	pork
offal	lamb
beef	marbling
wholesale cut	elastin
retail cut	collagen
veal	cooking losses

2. **Academic Terms**   Use a dictionary to look up each academic term listed below. Which terms have additional meanings that vary from the definitions given in the chapter?

mandatory	volatile
constrict	

Review

Write your answers using complete sentences when appropriate.

3. Give three tips for selecting and preparing meat to help limit the amount of fat, cholesterol, and calories supplied by meat in the diet.

4. What is the difference between hamburger and ground beef?

5. What are cured pork products?

6. How does the nutritional value of grass-fed meat compare with that of grain-fed meat?

7. What are the most common grades of beef sold in retail stores?

8. How does the location of the meat in the animal affect the tenderness of a cut?

9. Name two factors that affect the cost per serving of meat.

10. Within what time period should refrigerated fresh meat cuts, such as chops, roasts, and steaks, be used?

11. Which type of connective tissue can be tenderized by moist-heat cooking methods?

12. What are three characteristics of meat cooked at moderate temperatures?

13. What are three factors that affect the amount of time required to cook meat?

14. List the dry-heat cooking methods used for meats. What types of cuts are best prepared by these methods?

15. What is searing and why are meat cuts often seared before braising?

16. True or false. Frozen meats must be defrosted before cooking.

17. Name a meat alternative and describe how it can be cooked.

Chapter 22 Review and Expand

Core Skills

18. **Technology, Research, Speaking** Visit the Occupational Safety and Health Administration (OSHA) website. Search for information on the meatpacking industry to get an idea of safety and health hazards in this industry. In class, discuss what you learned about the types of potential hazards that exist for workers in the meatpacking industry. Also discuss why the federal government sets health and safety standards for the meatpacking industry and other industries.

19. **Research, Writing** Using reliable print or online resources, identify the top three states for production of beef, veal, pork, or lamb in the United States. Note what geographic characteristics make these states the leading locations for this type of meat production. Write a brief report summarizing your findings. Include a map highlighting the identified states in your report. Reread and revise your writing for style and clarity.

20. **Technology, Research, Speaking** Visit the Meat Safety website of the American Meat Institute. Research a food safety topic to use as the basis for an oral report to the class. Use presentation software and images to help convey the information and improve understanding.

21. **Writing** Look at the different cuts of meat in the meat case at a grocery store. Compare the appearance of beef, veal, pork, and lamb. Notice what types of offal are available. Compare the appearance of different grades of meat, if available. In a brief written report, summarize how your findings align with chapter information.

22. **Math** Use Figure 22.7 to calculate how much meat you would buy to prepare dinner in each of the following situations:
    - ground beef for six people
    - pork rib chops for four people
    - beef short ribs for five people

23. **Math** Buy a bone-in meat cut. Note the weight, unit cost, and total cost listed on the label. Carefully trim the meat from the bone. Also trim all visible fat from the meat. Then weigh the lean meat. Separately weigh the bone and fat portions. Calculate the percentage of waste in the cut you bought. Then figure the cost of the waste.

24. **Career Readiness Practice** Work as a class to create a pamphlet titled "Lean Is Keen." In the pamphlet, identify the leanest cuts of meat. As a class, brainstorm a list of ideas for incorporating moderate portions of lean cuts of meat into a healthy eating plan. Then narrow the list to five options. Include these options in the pamphlet along with tips for increasing whole grains, vegetables, and fruits. Obtain permission to distribute pamphlets in a local library or community center.

Critical Thinking and Problem Solving

25. **Analyze** Prepare two identical tender cuts of beef, cooking one with high heat and the other with moderate heat. Compare appearance, flavor, and tenderness to help you analyze the effects of high cooking temperatures on meat.

26. **Evaluate** Use two pieces of beef from a less tender cut. Cook one with dry heat and the other with moist heat. Write a description of the cut of beef and two cooking methods used. Describe the appearance, tenderness, and flavor of each cooked cut. Conclude your report with an evaluation explaining which preparation method you prefer for this cut and why. Edit your writing as needed for grammar, spelling, and organization.

27. **Analyze** Investigate the technology used to produce textured vegetable protein (also known as *textured soy protein*) as a meat alternative. Then broil a ground beef patty and a patty made with textured vegetable protein. Compare the two products for appearance, texture, and flavor.

Chapter 23
Poultry

S_Photo/Shutterstock.com

Content Terms ↪

poultry
giblets

Academic Terms

commerce
spokes

Objectives

After studying this chapter, you will be able to

- **analyze** multiple factors to make optimal poultry selection;
- **determine** how to properly store poultry to maintain its quality;
- **describe** the principles and methods for cooking poultry; and
- **prepare** poultry by moist and dry cooking methods.

Reading Prep

Before reading the chapter, skim the photos and their captions. As you read, determine how these concepts contribute to the ideas presented in the text.

The word **poultry** describes any domesticated bird. Chicken, turkey, goose, and duck are the types of poultry most commonly eaten in the United States. At one time, chicken and turkey were eaten only on special occasions, but today they are part of everyday meals.

Nutritional Value of Poultry

Poultry is in the protein foods group of MyPlate. Most teens and adults need only 5 to 7 ounce-equivalents from this group each day, depending on calorie needs. A single chicken breast half is often large enough to provide a full day's requirements from this food group.

All poultry contains high-quality protein and is a good source of phosphorus, iron, and B vitamins. Older birds have more fat than younger birds. Dark meat is higher in fat than light meat (**Figure 23.1**). Poultry labeled as "self-basting" is prepared with a solution that contains added sodium.

Turkey and chicken are lower in total fat, saturated fat, and calories than many cuts of red meat. This is especially true of the light meat portions of poultry. Much of the fat in poultry is located just under the skin. Thus, fat and calories can be reduced simply by removing the skin. Eating the skin or using solid fat when cooking poultry will provide calories that count as empty calories.

Selecting Poultry

Poultry is sold in a variety of forms to meet consumer needs. Poultry can be purchased as fresh, frozen, and in processed poultry products.

Inspection and Grading of Poultry

All poultry sold in interstate *commerce* (the buying and selling of goods and services) must be federally inspected for wholesomeness. Inspection ensures that birds were healthy, processed under sanitary conditions, and labeled correctly.

Alexey Borodin/Shutterstock.com

Jacek Chabraszewski/Shutterstock.com

Figure 23.1 Dark meat from chicken and turkey contains a higher proportion of fat than light meat. For equal portions from the same chicken or turkey, how would the calories in breast meat compare with the calories in thigh meat?

Poultry can be voluntarily graded for quality. A grade shield will appear on the retail package if poultry has been graded. Most poultry sold at the retail level is Grade A (**Figure 23.2**). Grade A birds are full-fleshed and meaty with well-distributed fat. Their skin has few blemishes and pinfeathers. Grade B and C birds are usually used in processed products.

All poultry that is processed and sold as canned poultry is inspected before canning. The quality depends somewhat on the brand.

USDA

Figure 23.2 Poultry that has passed the highest standards of inspection from the U.S. Department of Agriculture receives a Grade A label.

Selecting Fresh and Frozen Poultry

Most fresh and frozen poultry is marketed young. Young birds are tender and suitable for all cooking methods.

Chickens and turkeys have both light and dark meat. Breast meat is light and mildly flavored. The rest of the bird is dark meat, which has a stronger flavor.

Chickens, turkeys, ducks, and geese can be purchased fresh-chilled or frozen. Chickens can be purchased whole, cut into halves, or cut into pieces. Breasts, legs, and thighs are meatier than wings and backs. When deciding what type of pieces to buy, compare prices in terms of servings.

Chicken, like all poultry, contains more bone in proportion to muscle than does red meat. Therefore, when buying chicken with bones, allow about ½ pound (225 g) of meat per serving. Allow a little less per serving if buying meaty pieces like legs and breasts. Allow a little more per serving if buying bony pieces like backs and wings.

Many recipes call for boneless chicken breasts and thighs. Boneless chicken pieces cost more than pieces with bones. Some people can save money by boning chicken themselves. If buying boneless poultry, ¼ pound (115 g) of meat per serving should be adequate.

Whole turkeys are available in many sizes, making them popular for large gatherings. Turkey parts and ground turkey are also available. Allow ⅓ to ½ pound (150 to 225 g) of whole turkey or turkey parts per serving. Allow ¼ pound (115 g) per serving when buying ground turkey. Allow more if leftovers are desired.

Ducks and geese have all dark meat, which is tender and flavorful. Both have more fat than chickens or turkeys. Geese usually have more fat than ducks. Allow ½ pound (225 g) per serving for both duck and goose.

When buying poultry, consider the following guidelines:

- Choose birds with meaty breasts and legs, well-distributed fat, and blemish-free skin.
- Choose the type and amount of poultry that will suit the intended use.
- Look for frozen birds that are solidly frozen.

Recipe for Good Food

Turkey Breakfast Sausage

Makes 4 patties

¼	teaspoon (1.25 mL) salt
½	teaspoon (2.5 mL) rubbed sage
½	teaspoon (2.5 mL) ground thyme
¼	teaspoon (1.25 mL) ground nutmeg
⅛	teaspoon (0.6 mL) ground cayenne
½	pound (227 g) ground turkey, 93% lean

1. In a custard cup, mix together salt, sage, thyme, nutmeg, and cayenne.

2. In a medium mixing bowl, gently but thoroughly combine seasoning blend with ground turkey.
3. Shape turkey mixture into four patties.
4. Lightly coat a skillet with cooking spray. Cook patties over medium heat about 5 to 7 minutes per side until turkey has reached an internal temperature of 165°F (74°C).

Per patty: 64 calories (56% from fat), 8 g protein, 0 g carbohydrate, 4 g fat, 32 mg cholesterol, 0 g fiber, 173 mg sodium.

- Beware of dirty and torn wrappers and freezer burn (pale, dry, frosty areas).

Some fresh poultry carries bacteria that can cause foodborne illness. When buying poultry, put the package in a plastic bag as it is removed from the poultry case. This will keep poultry drippings from getting on other items in the grocery cart and potentially contaminating other foods.

Selecting Processed Poultry Products

Turkey and chicken are available canned. Canned poultry may be whole, cut into pieces, boned, or used in items like chicken chow mein (**Figure 23.3**). Generally, canned poultry items are more expensive than fresh-chilled or frozen poultry.

When buying processed poultry products or food items containing poultry, read labels carefully. The ingredient list may include a poultry part, such as *turkey breast* or *chicken leg*. This indicates the fatty skin, as well as the meat, has been used in the product. However, a listing of *breast meat* or *leg meat* indicates the product contains only lean meat—not skin.

When reading labels, also pay attention to the sodium content on the Nutrition Facts panel. Poultry products are a leading source of sodium

in the U.S. diet. Look for products that provide 100 mg of sodium or less per 4-ounce (113 g) serving.

Storing Poultry

All poultry, except canned, is very perishable. Poultry parts are more perishable than whole birds. Poultry needs proper storage to retard spoilage. Proper storage is also important to inhibit the growth of *Salmonellae*, an illness-causing bacteria often found in poultry.

For refrigerator storage, place poultry in the coldest part of the refrigerator and use within two days. Place poultry on a lower shelf in the refrigerator to keep juices from dripping onto other foods.

For longer storage, place retail poultry packages in freezer bags or wrap them in foil before storing them in the freezer. Poultry that is purchased frozen should be placed in the freezer immediately after purchase. Poultry pieces can be stored in the freezer for nine months. Whole birds can be kept frozen for up to one year. Once poultry is thawed, however, it should be cooked before it is refrozen.

Store all canned poultry products in a cool, dry place. Store all unused portions and cooked poultry in tightly covered containers in the refrigerator. Remove stuffing from cooked poultry and store it separately. Use leftovers within three to four days.

Preparing Poultry

Unlike some types of fish and some premium selections of meat, poultry cannot be eaten raw or undercooked. When preparing poultry, it is important to ensure the internal cooking temperature has reached 165°F (74°C).

Food Science Principles of Cooking Poultry

Like meat, poultry is a protein food. Cooking principles for poultry are similar to those used for other high-protein foods. Low temperatures and careful timing are important. Cooking poultry for too long or at too high a temperature can make it tough, dry, and flavorless.

Thomas Francois/Shutterstock.com

Figure 23.3 Chicken soup is often made with processed chicken products. Which type of processed chicken product would you use to make soup? Why?

Poultry must be cooked to the well-done stage, but it should not be overcooked. Pink flesh does not always mean poultry is undercooked. A chemical reaction causes a pink color in cooked poultry. Gases in the oven combine with substances in the poultry and turn the flesh pink. The pink color is not harmful.

Poultry bones will sometimes turn a dark color during cooking. Blood cells in the bone that have broken down during freezing cause this discoloration. When heated, they turn a dark brown. The color has no effect on flavor, and the meat is safe to eat.

Methods of Cooking Poultry

Poultry can be roasted, broiled, grilled, fried, braised, or stewed. The method chosen will depend mainly on taste preferences.

Do not wash poultry before cooking it. During washing, raw juices can be splashed around the sink area. This increases the risk of cross-contamination.

On the other hand, be sure to thoroughly wash cutting boards, knives, and other utensils after preparing raw poultry. This helps avoid the possibility of cross-contamination, or transferring harmful bacteria that may be in the poultry to other foods.

Roasting Poultry

Roasting is a popular choice for cooking whole birds. When preparing poultry, be sure to remove the neck and the packet of giblets found inside the cavity of the bird. **Giblets** are the edible internal organs of poultry, such as the heart and liver. People often use them in appetizers and to flavor soups and gravies.

Stuffing is often served with roast poultry. Traditionally, it was stuffed into a bird before roasting. However, this practice is not advised for food safety reasons. When stuffing is placed inside a bird, it may not reach a safe temperature fast enough to kill bacteria. For optimum safety, combine wet and dry ingredients just before placing stuffing in a casserole and putting it in an oven. Use a thermometer to be sure the stuffing reaches 165°F (74°C). More guidelines about preparing poultry and stuffing safely are available at foodsafety.gov.

Large birds should be trussed before roasting. A *trussed* bird has its wing tips turned back onto the shoulder and the drumsticks tied to the tail (**Figure 23.4**). Trussing

Figure 23.4   To help ensure even cooking, this chicken has been trussed in preparation for roasting.

Learn About...

Thawing Poultry

Thaw frozen poultry before cooking it. (If the bird is commercially stuffed, cook it without thawing.) To thaw, leave the bird in its original wrapping and let it thaw in the refrigerator. Place a plate under the bird to catch any drips that may form as the bird thaws.

For quicker thawing, wrap frozen poultry in a tightly closed plastic bag. Place it in a sink full of cold water. Change the water about every 30 minutes to keep it cold until the bird defrosts. Once the bird is thawed, cook it immediately.

Know and Apply

1. Why should you avoid thawing a commercially stuffed bird before cooking?

2. Why is it important to catch any drips that may form as a bird thaws in the refrigerator?

Exploring Careers

Fast-Food Counter Attendant

A fast-food counter attendant takes customer orders and enters them into a computerized cash register system. He or she takes payment and gives change. The attendant gathers prepared food items into bags or onto trays. He or she also pours beverages and may fill orders for simple food items, such as ice cream cones and premade salads. Then the attendant ensures food orders are correct before handing them to customers. The counter attendant may also have to do cleaning tasks, such as wiping tables and mopping floors.

Above all, counter attendants must be friendly, polite, and helpful when serving customers. They need good listening skills to understand all the details of customer orders. They must cooperate with coworkers and take direction from managers. Fast-food counter attendants also need math skills to count money. They must function well in a busy work environment. Attendants must know and follow food safety standards, too.

The position of fast-food counter attendant is an entry-level position. Many of these jobs do not require previous work experience or a high school diploma. In addition, many attendants work only part-time. These qualities make counter attendant a good first job for many teen workers.

A counter attendant may move up to become an assistant manager and then a manager of a restaurant. Some managers go on to manage more than one restaurant or move into corporate positions. Background as a counter attendant can be a starting point for a career in culinary arts. Customer service skills learned in this job can apply in almost any career area.

prevents the wing and leg tips from overbrowning. It also makes the bird easier to handle and more attractive to serve.

Place the trussed bird breast side up in a shallow pan. Season the cavity with salt and pepper. Roast the bird in a 325°F (170°C) oven until a meat thermometer reads 165°F (74°C). (For faster roasting, wrap poultry in aluminum foil and cook it in a 450°F (230°C) oven.) If poultry is allowed to stand 10 to 15 minutes after being taken from the oven, it will be easier to carve.

Sometimes the breast of a large bird will brown too quickly during roasting. To prevent overbrowning, make a tent out of aluminum foil. Cover the breast with the foil when the bird is about half-cooked.

Some people prefer to roast poultry in oven cooking bags. Cooking bags shorten cooking time because they use steam to help cook the bird. Because steam is a form of moist heat, this method is not true roasting.

Broiling Poultry

Turkeys and chickens can be broiled. To broil poultry, split the bird into halves or quarters. Place pieces on a broiler pan and brush lightly with cooking oil, if desired. Broil 4 to 5 inches (10 to 12 cm) from the heat source until done. Cooking time depends on the size of the bird. Chicken usually will take about 40 minutes. Turkey will take about 80 to 90 minutes. Thinner pieces will cook faster than thicker pieces. Remove pieces from the broiler when they are cooked and keep them warm until ready to serve.

Grilling Poultry

Grilling is a popular way to cook whole birds and poultry pieces, especially during the summer. Grill poultry with bones using indirect heat. Grill boneless poultry pieces over direct heat. Grilling times depend on the size of pieces.

You can shorten grilling times by partially cooking poultry in a microwave oven immediately before placing it on the grill. Partial cooking also ensures grilled poultry is thoroughly cooked. Use an instant-read thermometer to test the internal temperature of grilled poultry for doneness.

Frying Poultry

Chickens and turkeys can be cut into pieces and fried. To fry poultry, first roll the pieces in flour, egg, and bread crumbs or dip them in a batter (**Figure 23.5**). Then brown the pieces in about ½ inch (1.5 cm) of hot fat. (The fat should not be so hot that it smokes.) Turn poultry pieces with tongs as they brown.

After browning, the bird can finish cooking in the skillet over low heat. Cooking can also be completed in a moderate oven.

Oven-Frying Poultry

Oven-frying is sometimes called *baking*. Oven-frying gives poultry a texture that is similar to frying. However, less fat is used in this preparation method, so the poultry will have less fat and fewer calories when it is eaten.

You can oven-fry chicken pieces by coating them with seasoned flour. Place them on a baking sheet. Cook in a moderate oven until done. Brushing chicken lightly with oil will produce a crisp golden crust.

Braising Poultry

To braise turkey or chicken, brown individual pieces in a small amount of fat. Add a small amount of water to the skillet and cover tightly. Cook the poultry over low heat until tender, about 45 minutes to 1 hour. Poultry can be braised on top of the range or in the oven. For a crisp crust, uncover the pan for the last 10 minutes of cooking.

ffolas/Shutterstock.com

ffolas/Shutterstock.com

ffolas/Shutterstock.com

Figure 23.5 To bread a food for frying or baking, first (A) dredge it in seasoned flour, then (B) dip it in beaten eggs, and lastly (C) coat it with bread crumbs or crushed corn flakes. Can you think of other ingredients with which you coat food for frying or baking?

Stewing Poultry

To stew poultry, put the bird in a large pot and cover it completely with water. Add carrots, celery, and seasonings for flavor. Cover the pot tightly and simmer over low heat until the bird is tender. (Never allow the liquid to boil.) If desired, you can remove cooled stewed meat from the bone for use in soups and casseroles (**Figure 23.6**).

Microwaving Poultry

A microwave oven can be used to defrost or partially cook poultry that is being immediately prepared by another method. Chicken or turkey can also be fully cooked in a microwave oven for poultry that comes out tender and juicy. Poultry generally microwaves in much less time than poultry cooks in a conventional oven. When roasting large birds, however, little or no time may be saved by using a microwave oven. In addition, most microwave ovens are not big enough to hold very large birds.

To ensure even cooking in a microwave oven, arrange poultry pieces with the bony portions to the center of the microwave. Arrange drumsticks like the *spokes* (lines radiating from the center) of a wheel. Place the meaty ends toward the outside of the dish. On whole birds, the breast area and wing and leg tips may cook faster than the rest of the bird.

otnaydur/Shutterstock.com

Figure 23.6 Once stewed, poultry can easily be deboned for use in other dishes.

Learn About...

Testing Poultry for Doneness

A food thermometer is the only accurate way to test poultry for doneness. When testing a whole bird, insert the probe of the thermometer into the thickest part of the thigh. When testing poultry pieces, insert the probe into the thickest area. The probe should not touch bone.

Whole birds and pieces should reach an internal temperature of 165°F (74°C). Due to the uneven shape of whole poultry and poultry pieces, the temperature should be checked in several places.

©iStock.com/CBCK-Christine

The thermometer should be cleaned before and after each use.

Know and Apply

1. Why is it important to be sure poultry is thoroughly cooked?

2. Why might a food thermometer give different readings when testing several areas of a cooked bird?

Chapter 23 Review and Expand

Summary

Poultry, or any type of domesticated bird, belongs to the protein foods group of MyPlate. Poultry is a good source of protein and B vitamins and is lower in fat and calories than many cuts of red meat. Nutritional needs vary, but one-half of a single chicken breast is often enough to meet one day's protein requirements.

When buying poultry, look for meaty birds with well-distributed fat and blemish-free skin. Read labels to make healthier choices when buying processed poultry products.

All poultry is perishable. Store it in the coldest part of the refrigerator and use it within two days. Carefully wrap poultry and place it in the freezer for longer storage.

Always be sure poultry is thoroughly cooked before serving it. However, use moderate cooking temperatures and careful timing to avoid overcooking. Overcooking can result in meat that is tough and dry.

Because most poultry is tender, it is suitable for any cooking method. Poultry can be roasted, broiled, grilled, fried, braised, stewed, or microwaved.

Vocabulary Activities

1. **Content Terms**   For each of the following terms, identify a word or group of words describing a quality of the term—an *attribute*. Pair up with a classmate and discuss your list of attributes. Then, discuss your list with the class.

   poultry

   giblets

2. **Academic Terms**   Review the definition of each term below. Write a simile or metaphor to describe how these two terms can relate to each other. A *metaphor* equates two or more usually nonrelated concepts or objects by likening them to other concepts or objects. A *simile* compares two terms and usually includes the phrases *like*, *similar to*, or *as*.

   commerce

   spokes

Review

Write your answers using complete sentences when appropriate.

3. Name the four kinds of poultry most commonly eaten in the United States.
4. What is a simple way to reduce fat and calories from poultry?
5. What does inspection of poultry for wholesomeness ensure?
6. Why do you need to allow more weight per serving when buying poultry than when buying red meat?
7. What should you look for on the Nutrition Facts panel when buying processed poultry products?
8. Within what time period should refrigerated poultry be used?
9. What causes poultry bones to turn a dark color during cooking? Is the meat safe to eat if this happens?
10. What is the recommended internal temperature for cooked poultry?
11. Why should poultry not be washed before cooking?
12. Why should a large bird be trussed before roasting?
13. What are two advantages of partially cooking poultry in a microwave oven immediately before placing it on a grill?
14. How does the nutritional value of fried poultry compare with that of oven-fried poultry?
15. How should poultry pieces be arranged in a microwave oven to ensure even cooking?

Core Skills

16. **Research, Speaking**   Prepare for and participate in a class debate about poultry production practices in the United States. Half of the class should use poultry industry websites for their research. The other half of the class should use animal welfare websites for their research. Following the debate, discuss possible reasons

Chapter 23 Review and Expand

for differences in the information found by each half of the class. Use your knowledge of evaluating the reliability and validity of resources.

17. **Research, Math, Technology, Writing** Using reliable online resources, research poultry consumption trends in the United States in the last 100 years. Use software tools to make a graph that illustrates your findings. Include your graph in a one-page summary explaining the reasons for any changes in consumption patterns. Be sure to reread and revise your writing for spelling, grammar, and organization.

18. **Math** Compare the price per pound of boneless, skinless chicken breasts with the price per pound of bone-in, skin-on chicken breasts. Calculate the price per ounce of each chicken product. Remove the bone and skin from the bone-in, skin-on breasts. Then weigh the bone and skin on a kitchen scale. Determine the percentage of waste in the bone-in, skin-on product. Then calculate the cost per ounce of the meat portion of this product. How does this new cost compare with the cost of the product sold without bones and skin?

19. **Listening, Writing** Survey three students from other classes about their poultry consumption habits. Ask the following questions:

   A. Which types of poultry—chicken, turkey, goose, or duck—are served in your home?

   B. What, if any, other types of poultry have you ever eaten?

   C. Which forms of poultry does your family buy: fresh, frozen, or canned?

   D. What types of processed poultry products does your family buy?

   E. How many days a week is poultry served in your home?

   F. Is turkey reserved for holiday meals only?

   G. What poultry preparation method is used most often?

   H. What is your favorite poultry dish?

   Compile your results with those of your classmates. Use your findings as the basis for writing a hypothetical post from the perspective of a food blogger. Edit and refine your writing for grammar and spelling and to ensure your ideas are presented in a logical, organized manner that is clear to the reader.

20. **Research, Speaking, Technology** Search print or online resources to investigate the types of poultry dishes that were typically served in colonial America. Research to learn which dishes were served throughout the year and which were served at holiday celebrations. Share your findings in class, using presentation software to add visual interest to your report. Include an example of a historical poultry recipe in your presentation.

21. **Career Readiness Practice** Prepare a brochure about the importance of using a thermometer to check the doneness of poultry at holiday meals. The brochure should also discuss how to properly store and reheat leftovers. Place stacks of the brochures in your local library or community center before an upcoming holiday.

Critical Thinking and Problem Solving

22. **Evaluate** Roast chicken, turkey, duck, and goose. Taste the various types of poultry to compare them in terms of appearance, flavor, and texture. Describe when you would choose to serve each type of poultry and explain your choices.

23. **Create** Find at least three recipes for stuffing. Note what ingredients the recipes have in common and which ingredients are unique to each recipe. Also note the ingredient proportions. Combine components of these recipes to create your own recipe for stuffing. Prepare and sample the recipe. Explain why you would or would not choose to serve it with poultry.

24. **Create** Plan a low-fat dinner menu that provides a maximum of 550 calories. Your menu must feature a chicken entree along with at least one other dish and a beverage. Be sure your menu includes foods from at least four of the five MyPlate food groups. Explain any ingredient substitutions, preparation techniques, and cooking methods you would use to limit fat and calories in your meal.

Chapter 24
Fish and Shellfish

Iryna Melnyk/Shutterstock.com

Content Terms ⮕

finfish
shellfish
lean fish
fat fish
drawn fish
dressed fish
fish steak
fish fillet
crustacean
mollusk

Objectives

After studying this chapter, you will be able to
- **differentiate** between finfish and shellfish;
- **list** factors affecting the selection of fish and shellfish;
- **describe** how to properly store fish to maintain its quality;
- **explain** the principles and methods for cooking fish and shellfish; and
- **prepare** fish by moist and dry cooking methods.

Academic Terms

entrails
vessels
segmented
thorax

Reading Prep

Write the content terms and academic terms on a sheet of paper. Highlight the words that you do not know. Before you begin reading, look up the highlighted words in the glossary and write the definitions.

Commercial fishers in the United States catch several billion fish each year for food (**Figure 24.1**). However, the United States is a small consumer of fish and fish products compared with some other countries.

Choosing Fish and Shellfish

Two kinds of water animals are eaten as food: finfish (often called *fish*) and shellfish. **Finfish** have fins and backbones. **Shellfish** have hard outer shells instead of backbones.

Nutritional Value of Fish and Shellfish

Both fish and shellfish are excellent sources of complete protein. One ounce (28 g) of fish or shellfish counts as 1 ounce equivalent (28 g) from the protein foods group of MyPlate. Most teens and adults need 5 to 7 ounce equivalents (142 to 198 g) from this group each day, depending on calorie needs. Children need 2 to 4 ounce equivalents (57 to 113 g), depending on their age. MyPlate recommends teens and adults choose at least 8 ounce equivalents per week from a variety of cooked seafood. Children should be served smaller amounts based on their calorie needs.

pwrmc/Shutterstock.com

Figure 24.1 Billions of fish are caught each year with commercial fishing boats similar to these.

Most fish have fewer calories and less saturated fat and cholesterol than moderately fat red meat. Eating fish regularly can help increase the intake of mono- and polyunsaturated fats. These types of fats should make up the bulk of fats in the diet.

Exploring Careers

Fish Hatchery Manager

Fish hatchery managers work in facilities that breed and raise fish and shellfish for food, sport fishing, and research. They train, oversee, and help employees in the use of techniques and equipment to fertilize eggs and produce large numbers of young fish. They must monitor the feeding and growth of the fish. Managers check for diseases among the fish and specify treatments, if needed. They determine when fish need to be transferred to different tanks or ponds. They also identify when the fish are ready to be harvested for food or released into the wild.

To be successful, fish hatchery managers need to be good leaders and communicators. They train, schedule, direct, evaluate, and correct workers. They need to make the best use of resources such as equipment, supplies, and money. They use analytical skills as they examine the progress of the fish. Hatchery managers must be problem solvers when concerns arise with the health of the fish or the condition of the facilities. They use math skills as they calculate numbers of fish produced. They also use technology skills to keep records of breeding, shipping, and harvest or release dates.

This career involves some time spent inside doing office work. However, managers must be willing to work outdoors in all types of weather, too. Fish hatchery managers usually need several years of experience and a bachelor's degree in a field such as fishery science.

Seafood is also one of the best sources of omega-3 fatty acids. Some studies show these fatty acids may reduce the risk of heart disease. They have also been shown to promote the development of the nervous system in infants and children. This is why people in all age groups, including pregnant women and children, need to include recommended amounts of seafood in their diets. Salmon, trout, sardines, herring, and oysters are especially good sources of omega-3 fatty acids.

Overall, fish is slightly higher in minerals than red meat. Shellfish have even more minerals than finfish. Fish provide fair amounts of iron. Canned salmon and sardines prepared with their bones are especially good sources of calcium. Saltwater fish are one of the most important sources of iodine.

Fish and shellfish contribute the same vitamins as red meat. Fattier fish provide higher amounts of vitamins A and D.

Forms of Finfish

Finfish can be lean or fatty. **Lean fish** have very little fat in their flesh. Because their flesh is white, they are often called *whitefish*. Haddock and cod are examples of lean fish. **Fat fish** have flesh that is fattier than that of lean fish. Their flesh is usually pink, yellow, or gray. Trout and salmon are fat fish. Lean fish have fewer calories than fat fish. However, fat fish are better sources of omega-3 fatty acids.

Both lean and fat fish can be purchased fresh as whole, drawn, or dressed fish or as steaks or fillets. A *whole (round) fish* is marketed as it comes from the water. It must be cleaned before cooking. A **drawn fish** has the *entrails* (insides) removed. A **dressed fish** has the entrails, head, fins, and scales removed. It is ready for cooking. **Fish steaks** are cross-sectional slices taken from a dressed fish. **Fish fillets** are the sides of the fish cut lengthwise away from the backbone. Fillets have few, if any, bones. The various forms of fresh fish are pictured in **Figure 24.2.**

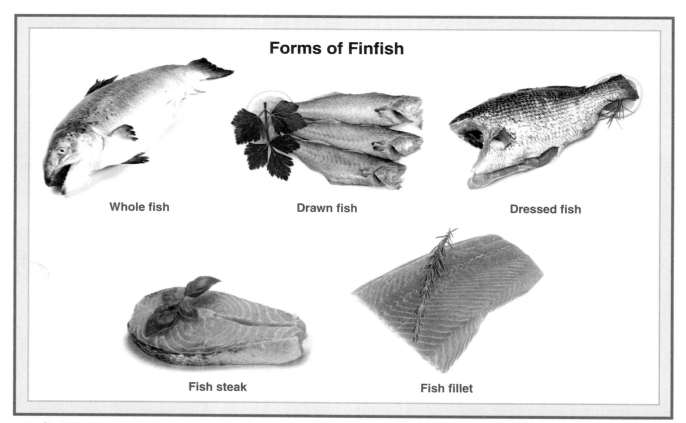

Forms of Finfish

Whole fish   Drawn fish   Dressed fish

Fish steak   Fish fillet

Clockwise from top left: Dmitry Melnikov/Shutterstock.com; Eldred Lim/Shutterstock.com; Eldred Lim/Shutterstock.com; Jessmine/Shutterstock.com; Gregory Gerber/Shutterstock.com

Figure 24.2 Fresh fish can be purchased in several forms. Which forms are the easiest to prepare? Why?

Health and Wellness

Food Safety at the Fish Market

Fresh seafood can be a source of bacteria that cause foodborne illness. To ensure the safety of fish and shellfish, deal only with reputable sellers. Look for the signs of quality described earlier. Be sure the market is clean and the fish is properly stored on beds of ice, preferably under a cover. The employees should be practicing safe food-handling procedures, including wearing disposable gloves when handling seafood.

Mercury in seafood is another food safety issue you need to be aware of when purchasing fish. This chemical element is found in some seafood, and it is toxic. Mercury can damage the nervous systems of babies and cause congenital disabilities (disabilities that exist at birth). Therefore, while you need to eat seafood for its health benefits, you should not eat varieties that are high in mercury.

Tilefish from the Gulf of Mexico, shark, swordfish, and king mackerel are four types of fish to avoid. You should also limit canned "white" tuna (albacore) to less than 6 ounces (170 g) per week. "Light" tuna is lower in mercury and can be eaten in larger amounts. You can choose salmon, flounder, tilapia, trout, pollock, and catfish often, too. These types of fish pose the least mercury risk. This advice is especially important for pregnant and breastfeeding women, women who might become pregnant, and anyone who feeds young children.

If you catch some of the fish you eat, you should make a point of checking local fish advisories. The U.S. Environmental Protection Agency (EPA) posts warnings about the safety of fish from some lakes, rivers, and coastal waters. You should not eat more than one 6-ounce serving per week of fish from water about which you can find no information.

Inspection and Grading of Fish and Shellfish

The National Oceanic and Atmospheric Administration (NOAA) offers an inspection program for the fish industry. The program is voluntary. Participants can pay to have fishing *vessels* (ships) and processing plants inspected to be sure they meet sanitation standards. They can pay to have seafood inspected for wholesomeness, too.

The NOAA also offers a product grading service. Quality grades are based on appearance, odor, flavor, and lack of defects. U.S. Grade A fish are uniform in size and have few defects.

Selecting Fresh Finfish

The cost of seafood depends on the form and the region of the country. Fish fillets generally cost more than whole fish because they require more handling. Money can be saved by buying dressed fish and filleting it at home. Fresh fish purchased where it is taken from the water will be less expensive than fish that must be shipped inland.

When buying fresh fish, look for a stiff body, tight scales, and firm flesh. The gills should be red, and the eyes bright and bulging. A finger pushed into the flesh should leave no indentation. The outside should have little or no slime, and the fish should smell fresh (**Figure 24.3**).

gajdamak/Shutterstock.com

Figure 24.3 When fish is stored on ice, there must be a way for water to drain. Without proper drainage, the fish becomes waterlogged and its texture and flavor deteriorate.

Learn About...

Sustainable Seafood

A growing world population is creating an increased demand for seafood. To meet this demand, the fishing industry is taking more seafood out of the oceans than ever before. Some species are being *overfished*, which means they are being caught faster than they can reproduce. Of course, this unsustainable practice threatens the survival of the overfished species. It also affects other animals that feed on them and destroys the livelihood of the fishers who catch them.

Other unsustainable fishing practices include bycatch and habitat damage. *Bycatch* refers to sea life other than the desired species that gets caught in nets or on hooks. For instance, seabirds often get caught on fishing lines and hooks that are intended for catching halibut. Habitat damage often occurs when nets are dragged across the seafloor. This ruins the fragile environment where many sea creatures live.

With wild seafood populations dwindling, many species are now being produced through *aquaculture*, or fish farming. However, fish farms do not always use sustainable practices, either. Wild fish are sometimes used as feed for farmed fish. Fish farms can also create a lot of pollution and disease that can harm nearby wild fish populations. Fish that escape from fish farms can upset the ecosystem of area waters.

The good news is that sustainable fishing and aquaculture methods do exist. One of the most helpful steps consumers can take is to ask, "Do you sell sustainable seafood?" Asking this question at fish markets and restaurants lets retailers know people care how seafood is produced. The retailers will put pressure on their suppliers. Then the suppliers will put pressure on seafood producers. Through this chain reaction, a healthy balance can be achieved between fish in the ocean and fish on the dinner table.

Know and Apply

1. Why is fish farming not always a good alternative to catching wild fish?

2. How can consumers encourage the use of sustainable fishing and aquaculture practices?

The amount of fish to buy depends on the kind and form. Fish, as a rule, have a large amount of waste. Dressed fish have less waste than whole and drawn fish. Fillets and steaks have even less waste. You will need about ¾ to 1 pound (340 to 454 g) of whole fish per person. If you are buying dressed fish, allow about ½ to ¾ pound (227 to 340 g) per serving. Fish fillets and steaks will yield two to three servings per pound (kg).

Selecting Fresh Shellfish

Shellfish can be divided into two groups: crustaceans and mollusks. **Crustaceans** are covered by firm shells and have *segmented* (divided into sections) bodies. Shrimp, lobsters, and crabs are crustaceans. **Mollusks** have soft bodies that are partially or fully covered by hard shells. Oysters, clams, and scallops are mollusks. Although they do not have outer shells, squid and octopuses are also mollusks.

Most shellfish, except for small oysters, are expensive regardless of location. However, knowing what to look for can help consumers get the most for their money.

Crustaceans

Shrimp are the most eaten shellfish in the United States. Several varieties of shrimp can be purchased. They differ in color and size when they are raw. Shrimp are marketed by sizes such as jumbo, large, medium, and small. Sizes are based on the number needed to weigh 1 pound (0.45 kg).

Most shrimp are sold without the head and *thorax* (middle division of the body). Shrimp labeled as *deveined* have had the intestinal tract removed. (The intestinal tract appears as a dark streak that runs along one side of the shrimp (**Figure 24.4**). When buying fresh shrimp, look for those that are odorless with firmly attached shells.

Lobster shells are dark blue green when removed from the water. They become red when cooked. When buying live lobsters, look for those with legs that are moving. They should also have tails that snap back quickly after being flattened.

The blue crab and Dungeness crab are two common species sold in the United States. They can be bought live in the shell. Fresh king crab legs and claws are popular, too.

Aroy Lim/Shutterstock.com

Figure 24.4 You can save money by deveining shrimp yourself. Use a paring knife to make a ¼-inch deep slit along the back of the shrimp and use the knife's tip to lift out the vein. Be sure to rinse the shrimp under cold water when you are finished.

Mollusks

Several kinds of oysters and clams are eaten in the United States. Oysters are packed according to size. Fresh oysters and clams can be purchased live in the shell or *shucked* (removed from shell). Both should have tightly closed shells or the shells should close when tapped. Shucked oysters and clams should be plump, creamy in color, and odorless.

Tiny bay scallops and larger deep-sea scallops are available on the market. A fresh bay scallop is creamy white or pink. A fresh deep-sea scallop is white. The whole bodies of these mollusks are edible. The large muscle used to close the shell, however, is the only part commonly eaten in the United States. Unlike oysters and clams, fresh scallops are not available in the shell. Common crustaceans and mollusks are pictured in **Figure 24.5.**

Frozen Fish and Shellfish

Frozen seafood is often processed on fishing vessels shortly after being caught, so its quality is close to that of fresh seafood. Drawn and dressed fish, as well as fish steaks and fillets, can be purchased frozen. Frozen fish should be solidly frozen in moistureproof and vaporproof wrapping. There should be no discoloration and little or no odor.

Shrimp, lobster, crab, oysters, clams, and scallops are all available frozen. Uncooked shrimp can

be purchased either peeled or unpeeled. Shrimp is also available cooked and peeled or peeled, cleaned, and breaded. Lobsters and crabs can be purchased cooked whole and as frozen cooked meat. Lobster tails are also available cooked. Frozen oysters, clams, and scallops are sold shucked.

Canned and Cured Fish and Shellfish

Tuna, salmon, sardines, shrimp, crab, lobster, and clams are among the fish and shellfish available in cans and foil pouches. Read labels to be sure of what is being purchased. To reduce fat in the diet, choose tuna packed in water instead of oil. If making shrimp cocktail, choose large, fancy shrimp rather than small shrimp.

Cured fish and shellfish can also be purchased. Fish are cured by drying, smoking, or pickling. These curing methods all use salt to inhibit pathogens in the fish. For this reason, these products contribute more sodium to the diet than other forms of fish. Common examples include dried and salted cod, smoked salmon, and pickled herring.

Storing Fish and Shellfish

Fresh fish is very perishable, so it must be stored with care. Wrap fresh fish tightly in waxed paper or foil. Place it in a tightly covered container in the coldest part of the refrigerator. Use stored fish within a day or two. For freezer storage, wrap fish in moistureproof and vaporproof material. Store it in the coldest part of the freezer. Use frozen fresh fish within about two weeks.

Keep fish bought frozen in its original package. Place it in the freezer as soon as possible after purchase.

Store canned fish in a cool, dry place. Refrigerate any unused portions in a tightly covered container. Use it within a day or two.

Preparing Finfish

Preparing seafood with care can help to avoid foodborne illness. Practice the same precautions when handling seafood that are used when handling meat and poultry:

- Be sure hands are washed thoroughly before and after handling fish and shellfish.

Common Shellfish

Shrimp   Lobster   Crab

Clams   Oyster   Scallop

Figure 24.5   These crustaceans and mollusks are among the most popular types of shellfish.

- Do not thaw frozen products at room temperature.
- Prevent cooked food from touching anything, such as utensils or marinades, that came in contact with raw seafood.
- Use an instant-read thermometer to be sure the internal temperature of cooked seafood has reached 145°F (63°C).
- Refrigerate leftover portions promptly.

Food Science Principles of Cooking Finfish

When a finfish is cooked to the proper degree of doneness, the flesh will be firm, and it will flake easily with a fork. (When the tines of a fork are gently inserted into the flesh and lifted slightly, the flesh will separate into distinct layers.) The flesh of a properly cooked fish will have lost its translucent appearance and will look opaque (solid; not see-through). See **Figure 24.6**.

Methods of Cooking Finfish

All finfish are naturally tender, so both dry and moist heat cooking methods can be used. The fat content of the fish usually determines the cooking method. Generally, fat fish should be cooked by dry heat and lean fish by moist heat.

Fat fish, such as salmon and trout, are delicious when broiled, grilled, or baked. Their fat keeps them from drying out during cooking.

Lean fish, like halibut, flounder, haddock, and red snapper, are usually fried, poached, or steamed. Lean fish can be cooked by dry heat if they are brushed with fat or cooked in a sauce. Likewise, fat fish can be poached or steamed if they are handled gently. (Fat fish can fall apart more easily when cooked in liquid.)

Cooking methods used for fish include broiling, grilling, baking, frying, poaching, and steaming. A general guide can be used to time fish cooked by all these methods, except deep-frying. Measure fish, including stuffed and rolled fish, at

Robcartorres/Shutterstock.com
rvlsoft/Shutterstock.com

Figure 24.6   Properly cooked fish loses its translucent appearance (A) and becomes opaque (B). What other qualities indicate that finfish has been cooked to the proper degree of doneness?

its thickest point. It should be cooked about 10 minutes for every inch (2.5 cm) of thickness. Turn thick pieces of fish once during cooking. Fish that is less than ½ inch (1.25 cm) thick does not need to be turned. If fish is wrapped in foil or covered with a sauce, add 5 extra minutes to the cooking time. Fish cooked from the frozen state will require twice as much time to cook. Test fish for doneness by flaking with a fork.

Broiling Finfish

For broiling, select fish that are at least 1 inch (2.5 cm) thick. Steaks, fillets, and dressed fish can be broiled. Place the fish on a cold broiler pan and brush the fish with oil if it is lean. Broil until the fish flakes easily with a fork. Thinner fish can be cooked closer to the heat source than thicker fish. Thick pieces will need to be turned once during broiling.

Grilling Finfish

The grilling method used for fish depends on the form of fish being prepared. Grill steaks and fillets by placing them directly over hot coals. Turn over thick pieces halfway through the grilling time. Use indirect heat to grill dressed fish. Test steaks and fillets with a fork for doneness. Use an instant-read thermometer to check the internal temperature of dressed fish.

Baking Finfish

For baking, select steaks, fillets, and dressed fish. To prevent fish from drying out, brush the pieces with oil or a sauce. Dressed fish and fillets should be stuffed just before baking. Bake fish at 400°F to 450°F (200°C to 230°C).

Frying Finfish

Finfish can be panfried, oven-fried, or deep-fried. Fillets, steaks, and small dressed fish can be panfried. Coat fish to be panfried with bread crumbs or with a batter. Then fry them in a small amount of fat until browned.

Cut fish to be oven-fried into serving-sized pieces. Dip them in milk and then coat them with crumbs. Drizzle prepared pieces lightly with oil and place them on a greased baking sheet. To get a crispy texture that resembles deep-frying,

Food Science

Cooking Seafood

Finfish contain tender muscle fibers and little connective tissue. For this reason, tenderizing is not a goal when cooking fish as it is when cooking some meats. Finfish need to cook for only a short time. They must be watched carefully to keep them from becoming dry and overcooked.

Fish should neither be undercooked nor overcooked. Undercooked fish can have an unpleasant flavor and may contain harmful bacteria. Overcooked fish is tough and dry. Some varieties become rubbery; others fall apart.

Like finfish, all kinds of shellfish are naturally tender. As a result, they should only be cooked for a short time at moderate temperatures. Overcooking will cause the proteins to overcoagulate and make the shellfish tough.

Recipe for Good Food

Tuna Croquette Small Plates

Serves 4

1	5-ounce (142 g) can chunk light tuna in water, drained
2	tablespoons (30 mL) cold cooked brown rice
1	green onion, finely chopped
1	teaspoon (5 mL) chili powder
⅛	teaspoon (0.6 mL) ground black pepper
1	large egg, beaten
½	cup (125 mL) panko bread crumbs
1	tablespoon (15 mL) cooking oil
2	cups (500 mL) shredded green cabbage or coleslaw blend

Sauce:

3	tablespoons (45 mL) light mayonnaise
1	tablespoon (15 mL) Worcestershire sauce
¼	teaspoon (1.25 mL) onion powder
1	teaspoon (5 mL) lemon juice

1. In a medium mixing bowl, flake tuna with a fork. Add rice, onion, chili powder, pepper, and egg; stir to combine.
2. Shape slightly rounded tablespoonfuls of the mixture into eight balls. Flatten to about ½ inch (1 cm) thickness and place on a parchment-lined tray in the refrigerator for 15 minutes.
3. To prepare sauce, thoroughly combine mayonnaise, Worcestershire sauce, onion powder, and lemon juice in a custard cup until smooth. Cover and place in refrigerator.
4. Place panko bread crumbs in a pie plate. One at a time, gently lift the chilled croquettes from the parchment paper and place them in the pie plate. Press crumbs into both sides and the edges of each croquette. Set the breaded croquettes back on the tray until they are all ready to cook.
5. Heat the oil in a large skillet over medium heat. Gently place croquettes in the skillet and cook until golden brown, about 3 minutes per side. Drain on paper towels.
6. Place ½ cup (125 mL) shredded cabbage on each of four small plates. Top each plate with two croquettes and drizzle with 1 tablespoon (15 mL) of the sauce.

Per serving: 150 calories (42% from fat), 12 g protein, 9 g carbohydrate, 7 g fat, 66 mg cholesterol, 2 g fiber, 283 mg sodium.

bake fish in a 500°F (260°C) oven. At this high temperature, use caution around the oven and watch fish closely as it will cook very quickly. The breading keeps the fish from becoming dry.

Cut fish for deep-frying into serving-sized pieces. Bread them or dip them in batter. Then fry them in 375°F (190°C) fat. If the fat is too hot, the outside of the fish will burn before the inside is cooked. If the fat is too cool, the fish will be soggy and greasy.

Poaching Finfish

Poaching is a gentle cooking method that is ideal for fish. To poach fish, use any tightly covered cookware that is large and deep enough to hold the fish. Add enough liquid to barely cover the fish. Use fish broth or water that is lightly salted and seasoned with spices or herbs as the poaching liquid (**Figure 24.7**). (If a dressed fish is wrapped in cheesecloth or parchment

Figure 24.7   Poaching liquid is often flavored with carrots, celery, and onions to add flavor to the fish as it poaches.

paper or placed on a rack before cooking, it will better retain its shape.) Cover the pan and poach the fish over low heat until it flakes easily with a fork. After the fish is cooked, remove the fish and reduce the volume of the poaching liquid by simmering it in the uncovered pan. Then the reduced liquid can be thickened and served as a sauce.

Steaming Finfish

Steaming differs from poaching only in the amount of liquid used. Less liquid can be used because the steam that forms inside the covered cooking utensil will cook the fish. To steam fish, place dressed fish, steaks, or fillets on a rack over simmering liquid. Cover the pan tightly and steam until the fish flakes easily. (Never allow the water to boil.) Fish can also be steamed in the oven in a covered pan or wrapped in aluminum foil. The cover or foil holds in the steam that forms so the steam can cook the fish.

Cooking Frozen Finfish

Frozen fish can be cooked either frozen or thawed. If fish is thawed, it can be cooked like fresh fish. If fish is not thawed, it must cook at a lower temperature and for a longer time than fresh fish.

Preparing Shellfish

Shellfish can be simmered, baked, broiled, grilled, panfried (sautéed), or deep-fried. The cooking method used depends on the kind of shellfish and whether it is purchased live, frozen, or canned.

People who live in an area where fresh shellfish is available may purchase their shellfish live. Shellfish purchased live in the shell must be alive when cooked. (Fresh, uncooked shellfish deteriorates very rapidly.)

Parboil live lobster, shrimp, and crab by plunging the shellfish into boiling, salted water until it is partially cooked. (Plunge lobster into the water headfirst.) Shellfish then should be simmered, not boiled. After parboiling, shrimp can be broiled, grilled, baked, panfried, or deep-fried. Lobster and crab may be baked or broiled. All three may be combined with other ingredients to make such seafood specialties as lobster

Thermidor, crab Newburg, and shrimp scampi (**Figure 24.8**).

The shells of live oysters and clams should be tightly closed. If they are slightly open, give them a firm tap. Discard oysters and clams that do not close when tapped. When these live mollusks are dropped into simmering water, the shells will open. Throw away any that do not open during cooking, as they may not be safe to eat. The edible part of the shellfish can be removed from the opened shells. After removal, simmer, deep-fry, or sauté oysters and clams. Because fresh scallops are not sold in the shell, they are ready when purchased to be prepared by the desired cooking method.

In inland areas, most of the available shellfish is frozen or canned. Cook uncooked frozen shrimp in salted simmering water until pink. Frozen lobster tails are partially cooked. They may be thawed and broiled, or they may be cooked in simmering liquid like uncooked frozen shrimp. Cooked frozen shrimp, crab, or scallops may be baked, broiled or fried.

Canned shellfish can be served without further cooking. They may also be combined with other foods in salads and main dishes.

Elena Shashkina/Shutterstock.com

Figure 24.8 Shrimp scampi is typically made by broiling shrimp with butter and garlic and serving it over pasta.

Chapter 24 Review and Expand

Summary

Consider choosing fish and shellfish often as a healthful source of protein and omega-3 fatty acids in the diet. Finfish are available whole, drawn, dressed, or as steaks or fillets. The cost of finfish depends on the form and where it is purchased. Knowing signs of quality for both crustaceans and mollusks can help you get good value when buying shellfish. Finfish and shellfish are available frozen and canned as well as fresh. All seafood is quite perishable. It should be stored carefully and used soon after purchase.

Both finfish and shellfish require short cooking periods and moderate temperatures. Properly cooked finfish have an opaque appearance and flake easily with a fork. Appropriate cooking methods include broiling, grilling, baking, frying, poaching, and steaming. However, fat fish are usually best prepared by dry heat and lean fish are usually best prepared by moist heat. The kind of shellfish, and whether it is purchased live, frozen, or canned, will help determine how to cook it.

Vocabulary Activities

1. **Content Terms**   Working in small groups, locate a small image online that visually describes or explains each of the following terms. To create flash cards, write each term on a note card and paste the image that describes or explains the term on the opposite side.

finfish	dressed fish
shellfish	fish steak
lean fish	fish fillet
fat fish	crustacean
drawn fish	mollusk

2. **Academic Terms**   Write each of the following terms on a separate sheet of paper. For each term, quickly write a word you think relates to the term. In small groups, exchange papers. Have each person in the group explain a term on the list. Take turns until all terms have been explained.

entrails	segmented
vessels	thorax

Review

Write your answers using complete sentences when appropriate.

3. How much seafood does MyPlate recommend teens and adults consume?
4. In general, how does the nutritional value of lean fish compare with that of fat fish?
5. Would you need to allow more weight per serving when buying dressed fish or fish fillets? Explain your answer.
6. Give two examples of crustaceans and two examples of mollusks.
7. What are deveined shrimp?
8. List three food safety tips for purchasing seafood.
9. Describe how to prepare fish for refrigerator storage.
10. What is the safe internal temperature for cooked seafood?
11. What type of finfish is usually cooked by dry heat?
12. What can you do to prevent baked fish from drying out?
13. How can you help a dressed fish retain its shape during poaching?
14. What adjustments must be made when cooking frozen fish without thawing?
15. True or false. Shellfish purchased live in the shell must be alive when cooked.

Core Skills

16. **Reading, Writing**   Read three articles from reliable print or online sources about commercial fishing. Then write a paragraph describing why you would or would not be interested in this career. Reread your paragraph to be sure your opinion is clearly and logically stated.

17. **Research, Technology**   Choose a body of water in your area. Identify species of fish and shellfish that live in this body of water that are of interest to commercial or sport fishers. Download images of the fish from online sources to use in creating a poster report illustrating your findings.

Chapter 24 Review and Expand

18. **Research, Speaking** Investigate what varieties of fish and shellfish are available from sources within 300 miles (483 km) of your home. Participate in a class discussion of the advantages and disadvantages of choosing fish from local sources.

19. **Listening, Math** Survey three family meal managers to find out what types and quantities of fish and shellfish they have purchased within the last three months. Compare your findings with those of your classmates to estimate what percentage of people in your area meet the MyPlate recommendation for eating seafood.

20. **Math, Technology** Use an online nutrient database to help you find the calorie, fat, and cholesterol content of the following:
    - Two varieties of lean fish
    - Two varieties of fat fish
    - One type of crustacean
    - One type of mollusk
    - Three cuts of beef or pork

    Use a chart tool to illustrate and compare your data.

21. **Research, Technology, Speaking** Visit Monterey Bay Aquarium's Seafood Watch website. Working with a partner, research a particular fishing or aquaculture method described on the site. Supplement your findings with information from other reliable sources, as needed. Use presentation software to illustrate for the class how the fishing industry uses your chosen method. Your presentation should explain what type of impact the method has on the environment and the sustainability of fish populations. It should also include suggestions for limiting negative impact.

22. **Research, Writing** Research how fish protein concentrate (FPC) is made. Investigate how this product might be used to address protein deficiencies in some population groups. Write a two-page summary of your findings. Edit your writing for accurate spelling, grammar, and organization.

23. **Career Readiness Practice** Imagine you have been hired by a supermarket to help increase sales at the fish counter. Prepare a presentation to educate customers on how to select and prepare fish. Create pamphlets with selection tips and easy fish recipes to distribute at the end of your presentation.

Critical Thinking and Problem Solving

24. **Analyze** Working with your foods lab group, examine an unknown type of fish fillet given to you by your teacher. Predict whether the fish would be best prepared by moist or dry heat. Cut the fillet in half. Prepare one-half by a moist heat method and the other half by a dry heat method. Analyze and compare the flavor and appearance of the two cooked pieces. Write a brief report stating your reasons for your original prediction and an analysis of whether your prediction was accurate.

25. **Evaluate** Panfry, oven-fry, and deep-fry small, dressed fish or fish fillets using both batter and crumb coatings. Prepare a table to evaluate the color, crispness, tenderness, and flavor of the fish prepared by the various methods. Identify which method you prefer to cook and which method you prefer to eat. Explain your preferences.

26. **Create** Write two menus including fish or shellfish. Encourage your family meal manager to use the menus to incorporate seafood in your family's diet at least twice in the coming week. Write a summary of your family's response to the menus.

Chapter 25
Salads, Casseroles, and Soups

Liliya Kandrashevich/Shutterstock.com

Objectives

After studying this chapter, you will be able to

- **distinguish** among herbs, spices, and blends;
- **explain** how to prepare salad ingredients and assemble a salad;
- **describe** how to prepare basic sauces used to assemble casseroles;
- **compare** the preparations of stock soups and cream soups; and
- **prepare** nutritious salads, casseroles, and soups.

Reading Prep

Before reading this chapter, review the objectives. Based on this information, write down two or three items that you think are important to note while you are reading.

Content Terms ⤷

herb
spice
blend
bouquet garni
sachet
gourmet
salad
temporary emulsion
permanent emulsion
casserole
white sauce
roux
slurry
reduction
stock soup
cream soup
bouillon
consommé
bisque
chowder

Academic Terms

temperate
agitate

Salads, casseroles, and soups add versatility to menus. They may be served as the main course or as an accompaniment to a meal. These combination dishes are nutritious as well as economical. They include a variety of ingredients, and preparing them can be a way to use leftovers.

Herbs and Spices

Herbs, spices, and blends can greatly enhance the flavors of any food, including salads, casseroles, soups. **Herbs** are food seasonings made from the leaves of plants usually grown in *temperate* (mild, not extreme) climates. Basil, bay leaf, and mint are examples of herbs. Many herbs can be purchased fresh, but most are sold dried.

Spices are food seasonings made from the dried roots, stems, and seeds of plants grown mainly in the tropics. Cinnamon, allspice, pepper, and ginger are examples of spices. Sometimes people use the word *spice* to mean "hot" or pungent, however, not all spices are hot. Most just give flavor. Spices are sold in whole or ground forms (**Figure 25.1**).

Blends are food seasonings made from combinations of herbs and spices. Poultry seasoning and pumpkin pie spice are examples of blends.

Using Herbs and Spices

The way herbs and spices are used depends on their form. Fresh herbs, such as dill sprigs and basil leaves, make attractive garnishes. Fresh herbs are not as concentrated as dried herbs. You will need to use about three times more fresh herbs to get the same seasoning impact delivered by dried herbs. The fresh herbs, however, will provide a distinct, pure flavor. Unless the recipe says otherwise, use dried herbs when cooking.

Ground spices release their flavor immediately when added to food. Add them toward the end of cooking. Whole spices release their flavor more slowly, so they can be added at the beginning of cooking.

When adding several fresh herbs to a dish, a cook may tie them together into a bundle. This is called a **bouquet garni**. Similarly, dried herbs and whole spices can be put in a cheesecloth bag, which is called a **sachet**. After the herbs and spices have released their flavors, the bundle or bag can be easily removed from the food.

Learn About...

Storing Herbs and Spices

Heat, sunlight, moisture, and air can all cause herbs and spices to deteriorate. Therefore, avoid storing seasonings near or over a range. Instead, store them in a tightly closed container in a cool, dry place away from light.

Buy herbs and spices in small amounts for ordinary cooking. Most spices and herbs will keep their flavor and aroma for about a year when properly stored. However, they lose their strength as they age, so date all containers. Whole spices will last longer than ground spices. To determine if a spice or herb has lost its strength, simply rub a little of it between your hands and smell it. If it has little or no odor, it has been stored too long.

Valentina_G/Shutterstock.com

To enhance the flavor of herbs and spices, use a mortar and pestle to grind whole herbs and spices before adding them to your recipes. Toasting spices in a skillet over medium heat before grinding will yield even stronger flavors.

Know and Apply

1. What herbs and spices do you use most often when cooking?
2. Where are herbs and spices stored in your kitchen? Explain why this is or is not a good storage place for maintaining the quality of your seasonings.

Herbs and spices do more than just flavor foods. They are sources of phytonutrients. They make attractive garnishes. Studies even show that people tend to eat less when food is well seasoned.

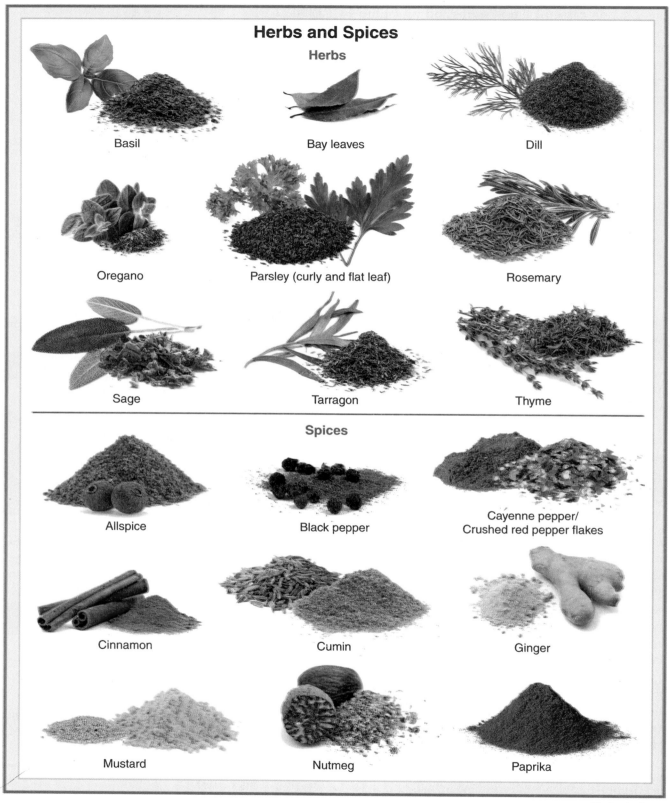

Herbs and Spices

Herbs

Basil

Bay leaves

Dill

Oregano

Parsley (curly and flat leaf)

Rosemary

Sage

Tarragon

Thyme

Spices

Allspice

Black pepper

Cayenne pepper/ Crushed red pepper flakes

Cinnamon

Cumin

Ginger

Mustard

Nutmeg

Paprika

Shutterstock.com

Figure 25.1 From dried oregano on a weekend pizza to cinnamon sprinkled on applesauce, herbs and spices add flavors that can enhance the appeal of almost any dish. What herbs and spices are used to season your favorite foods?

Seasoning and Gourmet Cooking

Gourmets are people who value and enjoy fine food. Some people think gourmet cooking requires hours of work and expensive ingredients that are hard to find. However, this is not necessarily the case. Gourmet food is simply food that is expertly seasoned and prepared. Creative use of herbs and spices can make gourmet dishes out of some of the simplest foods (**Figure 25.2**).

Becoming familiar with a range of herbs and spices can help give foods a gourmet touch.

Recipe for Good Food

Taco Seasoning Blend

Makes about 2 tablespoons plus 1½ teaspoons (37 mL)

1	tablespoon (15 mL) chili powder
½	teaspoon (2.5 mL) garlic powder
¼	teaspoon (1.25 mL) onion powder
¼	teaspoon (1.25 mL) crushed red pepper flakes
½	teaspoon (2.5 mL) oregano
⅛	teaspoon (0.6 mL) cayenne pepper
2	teaspoons (10 mL) cumin
¾	teaspoon (3.75 mL) black pepper

1. Measure chili powder, garlic powder, onion powder, red pepper flakes, oregano, cayenne pepper, cumin, and black pepper into a small bowl. Stir with a fork to combine thoroughly.
2. Store seasoning blend in a tightly covered container in a cool, dark place.
3. To season meat, sprinkle 2 tablespoons plus 1½ teaspoons (37 mL) of the seasoning blend over 1 pound (0.45 kg) of cooked and drained ground or shredded beef, pork, chicken, or turkey. Stir in ½ cup (125 mL) water and simmer over medium heat about 10 minutes, or until very little liquid remains.

Per serving (¼ of recipe): 14 calories (64% from fat), 1 g protein, 2 g carbohydrate, 1 g fat, 0 mg cholesterol, 1 g fiber, 82 mg sodium.

Seasoning Success	
Food Item	**Herbs and Spices**
Beef	Basil, bay leaves, cayenne, cloves, garlic, ginger, oregano, pepper, sage, tarragon, thyme
Lamb	Mint, rosemary
Pork	Cloves, cumin, garlic, ginger, sage
Poultry	Rosemary, sage, tarragon, thyme
Fish	Allspice, cayenne, dill weed, garlic, ginger, mint, paprika, rosemary, sage, thyme
Eggs	Basil, cayenne, chives, oregano, paprika, tarragon
Vegetables	Allspice, basil, bay leaves, cayenne, cloves, dill weed, garlic, ginger, nutmeg, oregano, paprika, rosemary, tarragon, thyme
Fruits	Allspice, cinnamon, cloves, ginger, nutmeg
Breads and Stuffings	Cayenne, cinnamon, dill weed, rosemary, sage, thyme
Desserts	Allspice, cinnamon, cloves, ginger, mint, nutmeg

Figure 25.2 Learning which seasonings complement various food items gives cooks the confidence to be creative when combining ingredients and cooking new dishes.

As cooks work with seasonings, they learn that some herbs and spices go especially well with certain foods. For instance, many recipes for custard call for nutmeg. Rosemary and mint complement the flavor of lamb. People often add cinnamon to apple dishes.

Using herbs and spices well requires practice and skill. When learning to use seasonings, start with small amounts. Ideally, herbs and spices should enhance food, not overpower it.

Salads

What is a salad? A **salad** is a combination of raw and/or cooked ingredients, usually served cold with a dressing. The vegetables, fruits, and protein foods salads contain contribute important nutrients to the diet. Depending on the ingredients, salads can be served as any part of a meal—appetizer, main dish, side dish, or dessert.

Most salads are vegetable salads. They can be made from leafy greens, raw vegetables, or cold, cooked vegetables. Garden salad, coleslaw, and three-bean salad are examples of vegetable salads.

Vegetables are not the only food group that can play the leading role in a salad. Colorful fresh fruits served on a bed of greens or in a hollowed fruit shell make a refreshing fruit salad. Canned, frozen, and dried fruits can be used in salads, too. Protein salads may have small pieces of meat, poultry, seafood, or eggs. Grain-based salads feature pasta, rice, quinoa, or another grain food, usually combined with vegetables (**Figure 25.3**). There are even a few salads built around dairy ingredients like cottage cheese.

Types of Salads

Regardless of the ingredients they include, all salads are one of three main types. Salad types are identified by the way ingredients are combined.

The simplest *tossed salads* are made just from salad greens mixed with a light dressing. More complex tossed salads include any number of other vegetables, such as tomatoes, onions, and cucumbers, along with leafy greens. Dressings may be light or creamy and might be poured over the salad or served on the side.

When making a tossed salad, a combination of three or four types of greens can add flavor, color, and texture variety. Dark leafy greens also provide more nutrients than pale iceberg lettuce. Boston lettuce, watercress, spinach, escarole, endive, and leaf lettuce are some of the many salad greens available. These greens add interest to other types of salads, as well.

Bound salads are made with cooked ingredients that are held, or bound, together with a thick dressing. Chicken, ham, crab, and potato salads are examples of this type. The dressing for a bound salad is often made with mayonnaise, but yogurt or another thick base can also be used.

Composed salads have three key parts—base, body, and dressing—that are attractively arranged rather than being mixed together. The *base* is the foundation on which the main salad ingredients are placed. The *body* is the main part of the salad. The *dressing* is a sauce that adds flavor to a salad. Some composed salads also have a fourth part—the *garnish*.

Preparing Salad Ingredients

Most fruits and vegetables used in salads are very perishable. Preserving their freshness is important to keep colors bright, textures crisp,

Iryna Melnyk/Shutterstock.com

Figure 25.3 This salad combines quinoa, salmon, and a variety of vegetables with a lemon and olive oil dressing. What type of salad is this?

Assembling a Composed Salad

Keeping a few points in mind will help you assemble a composed salad into an attractive arrangement.

Base: Salad greens are often used to make the base of a composed salad. They provide a color contrast with the body of the salad. Greens also keep the serving dish from looking bare. Use care when placing greens to keep the base from extending over the edge of the salad plate or serving dish.

Body: Attractively arrange the salad body on top of the base. If the body is a bound salad, you might want to serve it with an ice cream scoop to give it a uniform appearance. If the body is made up of fruits and vegetables, use their shapes and colors to create eye appeal.

Dressing: The dressing is usually poured over the salad just before serving. Use just enough dressing to complement, not mask, the flavors of the other salad ingredients. Dressings may also be served separately to allow diners to dress their own salads.

Garnish: A garnish can add nutrients as well as sensory appeal. It should complement the other salad ingredients. Try grape tomatoes for color, toasted nuts for crunch, or orange slices for a burst of flavor.

Aaron Amat/Shutterstock.com

and flavors full. Treating salad ingredients carefully will also help protect nutrients.

To prepare salad greens, begin by discarding any wilted outer leaves. Remove the core from head lettuce. Take off fibrous stems and ribs from leaves. Wash greens under clean running water to get rid of soil and microorganisms (**Figure 25.4**). Dry them gently to remove surface moisture.

For convenience, you might choose to use bagged salad greens. Special packaging allows them to stay fresh for an extended time. For best quality, be sure to use bagged greens by the date on the package or within two days after opening.

Like greens, other fruits and vegetables need to be gently washed and dried to prepare them

for use in salads. Trim any bruised or inedible spots. Avoid soaking fresh ingredients to prevent loss of water-soluble nutrients.

The size of pieces of food in a salad should be easy to manage. Tear salad greens into bite-sized pieces. Avoid mincing other salad ingredients to keep them from forming a paste when mixed with the dressing.

Treat fresh cut apples, peaches, bananas, and pears with pineapple or citrus juice. This will prevent enzymatic browning, making the salad look fresher and more attractive.

Many canned fruits and vegetables are already cut into bite-sized pieces. Others, such as peaches and pears, can be served in large pieces because they are easy to cut with a fork. When

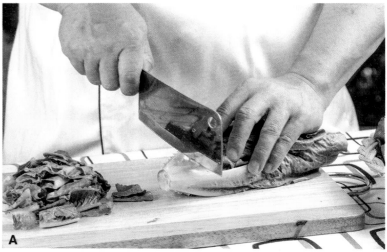

Figure 25.4 Before preparing your salad, (A) remove the core from the lettuce and (B) wash under clean, running water.

using canned fruits and vegetables, be sure to drain liquid. Extra liquid will make salads look and taste watery.

Varying the shapes of pieces will add interest to the appearance of a salad. Citrus fruits will usually need to be sectioned. Tomatoes and hard-cooked eggs might be cut into wedges. Carrots are often sliced or shredded. Meats and poultry are often diced. Fish can be flaked with a fork. Cheese might be crumbled or cut into strips.

Once salad ingredients are prepared and assembled, most salads should be chilled until serving time. A few salads, such as German potato salad, are served hot. If salads include frozen fruits, they should be allowed to soften slightly before serving to give flavors a chance to mellow.

Dressing is generally not added to salad until serving time. For some salads, however, the dressing is added several hours before serving to marinate ingredients and allow flavors to blend.

Preparing Salad Dressings

There are three basic types of salad dressings. All three types are examples of *emulsions*, which are combinations of two liquids that normally will not stay mixed. In the case of salad dressings, these liquids are most often oil and vinegar or some other water-based liquid.

The first basic type of dressing is *vinaigrette*. It is made by combining oil, vinegar, and seasonings. When the dressing is **agitated** (shaken), an emulsion forms. When the agitation is stopped

and the dressing is allowed to stand, the oil and water-based liquid separate, and the emulsion breaks. Therefore, vinaigrette is considered to be a **temporary emulsion**. Vinaigrette must be shaken or stirred to mix it each time it is used (**Figure 25.5**).

Mayonnaise, the second basic dressing, is made from vinegar (or lemon juice), oil,

Figure 25.5 This image shows the temporary emulsion as it begins to separate.

seasonings, and egg yolk. Mayonnaise is an example of a **permanent emulsion**. This type of emulsion will not separate on standing. This is because the egg yolk acts as an *emulsifying agent*. This is an ingredient that surrounds the droplets of oil and keeps them suspended in the liquid (vinegar or lemon juice).

Mayonnaise has a thick, creamy texture and a bland flavor. It makes a good base for other dressings and sauces. For instance, crushed pineapple might be added to create a sweet dressing for a fruit salad. Adding ketchup and pickle relish turns mayonnaise into Thousand Island dressing.

The third type of dressing is *emulsified vinaigrette*. This type of dressing is thickened with an emulsifying agent. Like mayonnaise, it will not separate on standing. It is not as thick, however, and it contains a variety of seasonings to make it more flavorful than mayonnaise.

Casseroles

A **casserole** is a combination of foods prepared in a single dish. Casseroles are quick and easy to prepare. They can help stretch food dollars by using starchy foods and vegetables to extend more costly protein ingredients. Casseroles can help make use of leftovers (**Figure 25.6**). A simple salad and dessert are all

minadezhda/Shutterstock.com

Figure 25.6 This casserole is made from leftover pasta, chicken, and vegetables. Fresh tomatoes, sauce, and grated cheese are added to provide color and richness.

Learn About...

Gelatin Salads

Gelatin salads were once common menu items. Though they are not as popular today, they still appear in some traditional cookbooks. In some regions, gelatin salads are staples on holiday tables and at potluck gatherings, too.

Gelatin salads can be made with commercial fruit-flavored gelatin. Fruit and vegetable juices can also be mixed with unflavored gelatin and sweetened to make a gelatin salad. Almost any fruits, vegetables, and/or protein foods can be added to the gelatin. These ingredients boost nutrition and increase flavor and texture variety.

Gelatin often comes in packets as a dry powder. Fruit-flavored gelatin is typically dissolved in boiling water, and then cold water is added. Unflavored gelatin is usually softened in a small amount of cold liquid before boiling water is added. In either case, it is important to stir the mixture for a few minutes to be sure the gelatin is completely dissolved. Then the mixture is chilled for several hours until it is firm.

A few ingredients can affect the structure of gelatin. Fresh and frozen pineapple contain an enzyme that will keep gelatin from setting. Fresh and frozen kiwifruit, gingerroot, papaya, figs, and guava will prevent gelatin from setting, too. Feel free to use cooked and canned forms of these foods, however. The heat used in cooking and canning deactivates the enzymes that affect gelatin.

When liquid gelatin is poured into a mold, it will take on the shape of that mold once it sets. This characteristic can be used to create attractive salads with unique eye-appeal. Lightly spraying a mold with nonstick cooking spray before filling it with liquid gelatin will make unmolding easier. When the gelatin is firmly set, dip the mold into warm water for about 10 seconds. (Do not keep the mold in the water too long, or the gelatin will lose its shape.) Invert the loosened salad onto a large plate, garnish, and serve.

Know and Apply

1. For what occasions would you consider serving a gelatin salad?
2. What combinations of flavored gelatin and added ingredients would you find most appealing?

Health and Wellness

Keeping Salads Healthy

To prevent nutrient losses, it is best not to clean fresh salad ingredients too far in advance. Wrap cleaned greens loosely in plastic film or a damp cloth or store them in a vegetable keeper. Washed greens can be stored for a few hours in the refrigerator. They will be crisp when ready to serve and will still retain important vitamins and minerals.

Dressing can add a lot of fat and calories to a salad. To avoid this, try using low-fat or fat-free dressing. Low-fat yogurt can be substituted for dressing on many salads. Flavor plain yogurt with herbs and use it on vegetable salads. Vanilla and fruit-flavored yogurts make creamy toppings for fruit salads.

vanillaechoes/Shutterstock.com

Mix plain yogurt with herbs, garlic, pepper, and lemon juice to produce a healthy dressing.

that is needed to accompany most casseroles. They also freeze well, so they can be prepared ahead of time for quick meals on busy days.

Casseroles are a great way to emphasize plant foods in the diet. Casseroles often include a variety of vegetables and grains and only small amounts of meat. Many hearty casseroles can be made without any meat at all. Tasty combinations of rice and legumes or vegetables and pasta can become nutritious entrees.

Sauces

Most casseroles use some kind of sauce to bring the ingredients together. Sauces can also add moisture and flavor enhancement to many other dishes. A casserole sauce can be as simple as a can of seasoned tomato sauce. Learning to make your own sauces, however, allows you to give casseroles and other dishes unique flavor. Making your own sauces also gives you control over components such as fat, calories, and sodium.

Preparing White Sauce

One common type of sauce used in many recipes is **white sauce**. This is a starch-thickened milk product. It is often used as a base for other sauces, such as gravies and cheese sauce.

The proportion of starch to milk determines the thickness of white sauce. Use *thin* sauce as the base of cream soups. Use *medium* sauce in creamy casseroles and *thick* sauce in soufflés. *Very thick* sauce binds the ingredients in croquettes.

Classic white sauce is thickened with a **roux**, which is a cooked paste of equal parts fat and flour. The fat is usually butter. However, pan drippings or oil could be used as well.

To prepare white sauce, melt the fat over low heat. Then whisk in flour and seasonings to form a paste. Whisk milk into the roux. Whisk constantly as the mixture cooks over medium heat until it thickens into a smooth sauce (**Figure 25.7**).

A slurry can be used as the thickening agent in a lower-calorie white sauce that is made without fat. A **slurry** is a liquid mixture of milk and flour blended together until smooth. Combine fat-free milk, flour, and seasonings in a blender container or a small, covered jar. Blend or shake until thoroughly mixed. Cook the slurry in a heavy saucepan over medium heat, whisking gently, until it reaches a boil. Cook the slurry for one minute longer until the sauce is smooth and thickened. (This cooking will also prevent a raw starch flavor.)

When preparing a white sauce, take care to prevent scorching and lumping. Using moderate heat will prevent scorching. Using cold milk and thorough blending will separate the starch granules in the flour. This, along with gentle whisking during cooking, will prevent lumping and produce a smooth-textured sauce.

The principles of preparing white sauce are also used when preparing gravy. Pan drippings from meat or poultry may be used in place of the butter to make a roux. Beef or chicken stock may replace some or all of the milk. These substitutions give gravy color and flavor.

Viktor1/Shutterstock.com   *Viktor1/Shutterstock.com*

Figure 25.7 Flour is added to melted butter and the two are combined and cooked to create a roux.

To reduce fat and calories in gravy, skim the fat from pan juices remaining after cooking meat or poultry. Stir a slurry into the juices. Cook and stir over medium heat until thickened. To thin or extend gravy, add milk or stock as needed. Season to taste with salt and pepper.

Preparing Reduction Sauces

Another type of sauces that are used to add flavor to dishes are **reductions**. These are sauces made by cooking a flavorful liquid until some of the water evaporates. This reduces the volume, intensifies the flavor, and slightly thickens the sauce. Reductions rely on a concentration of flavor rather than a creamy texture like white sauce. They are also generally lower in fat and calories. Reductions are more often served with meat, poultry, and fish dishes than as part of a casserole.

A common way to make a reduction is to cook meat, poultry, or fish in a pan. Set the protein food aside. Remove all but a tablespoon or two (15 to 30 mL) of fat from the pan. Add some minced onion or shallots to the pan. Place it over heat and pour in a small amount of liquid. Chefs often use wine, but liquids like balsamic vinegar and apple juice can be used as well. This liquid is used to *deglaze* the pan, or dissolve the browned bits stuck to the pan from cooking the protein. Use a wooden spoon to scrape all the bits loose and allow the liquid to cook down to half its original volume. Then stir some broth into the pan and again allow it to cook to half volume.

Sprinkle the sauce with some fresh chopped herbs and serve it with the protein (**Figure 25.8**).

Other Casserole Ingredients

The sauce in a casserole is usually added to a combination of protein food, vegetable, and starch. Many casseroles have a topping made of crumbs, cheese, or chopped nuts, too.

One or several foods high in protein can form the basis of a casserole. Turkey, chicken, ground beef, ham, cheese, beans, and seafood make good casserole bases.

Any canned, frozen, or cooked fresh vegetable can be used in a casserole. Try spinach, broccoli, squash, tomatoes, or a combination of vegetables.

Starchy ingredients help make casseroles filling. Use whole-grain ingredients often. Brown rice, barley, and whole-wheat pasta combine easily with most protein foods and vegetables.

Extras can add crunch, color, and flavor to a casserole. Bean sprouts, celery, almonds, and French-fried onion rings add crunch. Tomato wedges, green pepper rings, chopped parsley, and pimiento add color. Horseradish, chili sauce, and chopped onions add flavor.

A topping helps keep a casserole from getting dry. It also adds color, flavor, and texture. Buttered bread crumbs, dumplings, and corn-bread squares are common toppings. For a nutritious change of pace, try a sprinkling of chopped nuts. Crushed unsweetened whole-grain cereals also make healthy casserole toppings.

ruidoblanco/Shutterstock.com   *Foodpictures/Shutterstock.com*   *Josie Grant/Shutterstock.com*

Figure 25.8 To make a reduction sauce to accompany a chicken dish, remove the chicken from the pan once it is cooked, and (A) sauté minced onions or shallots in the remaining fat. (B) The pan is deglazed with stock to dissolve the flavorful browned bits left by the cooked chicken and cooked to reduce its volume. (C) The result is a sauce with intense flavor to serve with the cooked chicken.

Assembling a Casserole

The key to putting a casserole together is combining ingredients that complement each other. Consider personal likes and dislikes. Experience will also help.

Until experience in making casseroles is acquired, it is probably best to choose just one ingredient from each of the protein foods, vegetables, and grains groups. Use seasonings sparingly at first. Also avoid using too many highly seasoned foods at one time.

Be aware of sources of excess fat and sodium in casserole recipes. You can adjust types and amounts of some ingredients to make many casseroles healthier. For instance, use reduced-fat

Recipe for Good Food

Kickin' Chicken and Rice

Serves 6

1 cup (250 mL) long-grain white rice, uncooked
1 cup (250 mL) salsa
1½ cups (375 mL) diced cooked chicken breast meat
1 can (15 ounces, 425 g) low-sodium pinto beans, drained and rinsed
1 tablespoon plus 1½ teaspoons (22.5 mL) taco seasoning blend
1¾ cups (435 mL) low-sodium chicken broth
¾ cup (185 mL) shredded low-fat Colby cheese
3 green onions, sliced
¼ cup plus 2 tablespoons (90 mL) plain fat-free Greek yogurt

1. In a large skillet, stir together the rice, salsa, chicken, pinto beans, taco seasoning, and chicken broth over medium-high heat.
2. Bring mixture to a boil. Then cover the skillet and reduce the heat to low. Simmer for 30 minutes, or until all liquid is absorbed and rice is tender.
3. Remove skillet from the heat. Fluff rice with a fork. Sprinkle with shredded cheese, and then replace lid to allow cheese to melt.
4. Serve topped with sliced green onions and a dollop of Greek yogurt.

Per serving: 273 calories (13% from fat), 23 g protein, 38 g carbohydrate, 4 g fat, 32 mg cholesterol, 4 g fiber, 535 mg sodium.

and low-sodium versions of ingredients like mayonnaise and soy sauce. Try reducing listed amounts of fats and oils. Omit salt from recipes calling for other ingredients that are high in sodium, such as cheese or condensed soup. Increase proportions of vegetables and whole grains for added fiber. Such changes will make casseroles more nutritious without having much effect on flavor (**Figure 25.9**).

Cleanup of baked casseroles will be easier if the casserole is put in a greased dish. Most casseroles are baked in a moderate oven until they are brown and bubbly and reach at least 165°F (74°C). Cooking time will depend on the size of the dish and the starting temperature of the casserole. The topping may begin to brown before the casserole heats through. A piece of aluminum foil placed loosely over the top will prevent it from getting too dark.

Some casseroles can be prepared on top of the range. They are just as quick and easy as oven casseroles. However, they may require some stirring and a bit more attention during the cooking period.

Unlike soufflés and rare roast beef, most casseroles can wait for latecomers. Some casseroles even improve when they are held for a while. This is because their flavors have a chance to blend. When a casserole will not be served right away, cover it tightly and keep it warm in a low oven.

Exploring Careers

Prep Cook

Prep cooks are key members of restaurant kitchen crews. Their work helps ease the tasks of other workers so kitchens run smoothly. Prep cooks prepare foods that will be cooked by chefs. They often wash and chop vegetables and trim meats. They may measure and package ingredients for single servings. This allows chefs to quickly grab just the right amounts to cook for customer orders. Prep cooks may prepare foods like salads and soups. They portion and plate food items such as desserts, making them ready for servers to take to customers. Once foods are prepared, prep cooks store them to maintain safety and quality until they are ready to be used. They may also clean and organize utensils and prep areas.

To be successful, prep cooks need good listening skills and a willingness to follow directions to prepare the correct types and amounts of foods. They need attention to detail to accurately measure ingredients and follow recipes. They must assess what tasks need to be done and take responsibility to complete them. Prep cooks have to cooperate with coworkers. They must also be able to spend long hours on their feet and do some lifting and carrying.

Prep cook is an entry-level position. Some prep cook jobs are open to teens while they are still in high school. Previous foodservice experience is helpful but not required in many restaurants. Most training will take place on the job. Skilled prep cooks may be able to move into other roles on a restaurant kitchen crew. In fact, many chefs begin their culinary careers working as prep cooks.

Timolina/Shutterstock.com

Figure 25.9 Moussaka is a traditional casserole from Greece that includes eggplant, tomatoes, ground lamb, and white sauce.

Soups

People throughout the world serve soup in many forms. It can be hot or cold, hearty or light. It can be an appetizer or a main dish. It can be eaten alone or served with other foods. Soup is most popular in the United States as an appetizer or luncheon dish.

Soup can be made in two ways. **Stock soups** are made with rich-flavored broth in which meat, poultry, or fish bones; vegetables; and seasonings have been cooked. **Cream soups** are made with milk or cream instead of stock.

Preparing Stock Soups

If a *brown stock* is being prepared, begin by roasting meat or poultry bones in the oven until they are brown. Roasted bones give brown stock a darker color and richer flavor. If making a *white stock*, use bones from fish or unroasted meat or poultry bones. To make a stock more flavorful, you need to increase the amount of ingredient surface area exposed to the cooking liquid. Do this by cutting large bones into smaller pieces.

Vegetables, such as onions, celery, and carrots, are included in a stock. Pepper and herbs are added for flavor. All ingredients are covered with water and simmered over low heat for a long time. As flavors are slowly released, stocks become rich and tasty.

Stocks are cooked in large stockpots. During the first stage of cooking, foam will rise to the surface. Periodically skim it from the stock using a wooden spoon or small strainer.

During the final stages of cooking, fat will rise to the surface of the stock. Remove the fat with a baster or fat separator while the stock is hot. Fat can also be removed after it congeals on chilled stock (**Figure 25.10**).

After cooking, strain the stock to remove the solid materials. After the long cooking period, vegetables used to make stock have given up all their flavors. They should be discarded. The stock should be combined with fresh ingredients to turn it into soup. Protein foods, vegetables, rice, noodles or other pasta, and seasonings can be used to create countless recipes.

Clear broth made with more protein and less bone than stock is called **bouillon**. It may be served alone, but it is often used as an ingredient

Figure 25.10   As bones cook, a protein is extracted which contributes body and texture to the stock. When the stock is chilled, it solidifies. This is a sign of a well-made stock.

in other recipes. Clear, rich-flavored soup made from clarified, concentrated stock is called **consommé**.

To make consommé, strained stock is clarified by adding a slightly beaten egg white and a few pieces of eggshell to the boiling broth. As the egg protein coagulates, it traps any solid materials. Then the clarified stock is gently strained again so the egg, solid materials, and eggshell can be removed and discarded. At this point, the strained and clarified stock is simmered for a period of time to reduce the volume. This additional cooking concentrates the stock, making it richer and more flavorful.

Preparing Cream Soups

Milk-based soups, often called *cream soups*, are popular luncheon and supper dishes. The three basic types of cream soups are thickened cream soups, bisques, and chowders. A thin white sauce is often used to make *thickened cream soups*. These soups contain vegetables, meat, poultry, or fish that is pureed or cut into small pieces. Cream of mushroom and cream of tomato soups are popular thickened cream soups.

Bisques are rich, thickened cream soups. Light cream often replaces all or part of the milk in a bisque. Bisques usually contain shellfish that is shredded or cut into small pieces. Lobster bisque is one popular example.

Chowders are cream soups made from unthickened milk. Chowders can contain vegetables, meat, poultry, or fish. (Most chowders contain potatoes, which help add thickness.) (**Figure 25.11**). A few chowders use tomatoes and water instead of milk. Tomatoes form the base for Manhattan clam chowder, whereas milk forms the base for New England clam chowder.

Preparing Thickened Cream Soups

The first step in preparing thickened cream soups and bisques is to cook the added ingredients. Cook the vegetables, meat, poultry, or fish using only a small amount of liquid. This will help preserve as many of the water-soluble nutrients as possible. The cooking liquid may be used later as part of the liquid in the white sauce.

Many cream soup recipes require that vegetables, meat, poultry, or fish be pureed. Use a blender to make the puree as smooth as possible. However, avoid pureeing soups that contain potatoes. The action of a blender can cause the starch in potatoes to become gummy, making the texture of the soup unappealing. Soup ingredients that do not require pureeing should be cut into small pieces.

The second step in making a cream soup is to prepare a soup base that is thickened with a thin white sauce. Add the prepared ingredients to the soup base and season to taste. The soup may be served immediately, or refrigerated and reheated later. Be sure to use low heat when reheating a cream soup to prevent scorching.

Preparing Unthickened Cream Soups

The cooking method used to prepare chowders differs somewhat from the method used to prepare thickened cream soups. Usually, the pieces of vegetables, meat, fish, or poultry are fairly large, and they are cooked in a stock. When they are tender, milk is added to the stock and stirred gently until blended. The milk should be added slowly, and the soup should be heated at a low temperature to prevent curdling.

Foodio/Shutterstock.com

Bochkarev Photography/Shutterstock.com

Figure 25.11 (A) Bisques are smooth and creamy, and (B) chowders are usually thick and chunky.

Chapter 25 Review and Expand

Summary

Herbs, spices, and seasoning blends are important ingredients in many foods. With practice, they can be used to enhance the flavor of almost any dish.

A salad can be served as almost any part of a meal, from appetizer to dessert. There are three main types of salads—tossed, bound, and composed. When preparing salad ingredients, wash, dry, and trim fresh fruits and vegetables and cut foods into bite-sized pieces. Salad dressings may be temporary or permanent emulsions. When assembling a salad, keep flavor, texture, and color in mind to create an appealing dish.

Casseroles are both easy and economical to prepare. They generally contain a protein food, vegetable, starch, sauce, and topping. White sauce is a common base for many casseroles, whereas reductions are more often served with meat, poultry, and fish entrees. Although some casseroles are cooked on the cooktop, most are baked in an oven.

Two main kinds of soups are stock soups and cream soups. Stock soups begin by covering meat, poultry, or fish bones with water and simmering it for a long time. Vegetables and seasonings are added for extra flavor. After cooking, the stock is strained and ready for use in soups and other dishes. Cream soups are made with milk or cream instead of stock. They are often thickened and are richer and heavier than stock soups.

Vocabulary Activities

1. **Content Terms**   Select three terms from the list of key terms at the beginning of this chapter. Explain how these three terms are related to each other. Create a graphic organizer or write a paragraph to explain or illustrate how the terms relate.

herb	permanent emulsion
spice	casserole
blend	white sauce
bouquet garni	roux
sachet	slurry
gourmet	reduction
salad	stock soup
temporary emulsion	cream soup

bouillon	bisque
consommé	chowder

2. **Academic Terms**   For each of the following terms, identify a word or group of words describing a quality of the term—an *attribute*. Pair up with a classmate and discuss your list of attributes. Then, discuss your list of attributes with the whole class to increase understanding.

temperate	agitate

Review

Write your answers using complete sentences when appropriate.

3. List five herbs, five spices, and two seasoning blends.

4. Besides adding flavor, what are two advantages of using herbs and spices when cooking?

5. Name the three main types of salads and give an example of each.

6. Why should fresh salad ingredients not be soaked in water to get rid of soil and microorganisms?

7. What is an emulsifying agent and how is it used in the preparation of salad dressings?

8. List four food products that are made with a white sauce.

9. How would the nutritive value of a white sauce thickened with a roux compare with that of a white sauce thickened with a slurry?

10. How does cooking affect the characteristics of a reduction sauce?

11. List five basic components of most casseroles and give an example of each.

12. Give three tips to follow when assembling casseroles.

13. What is the difference between a brown stock and a white stock?

14. In what type of cream soup might cream be used in place of milk?

Chapter 25 Review and Expand

Core Skills

15. **Research, Speaking**   Research how and why spices are irradiated. Use presentation software to illustrate the irradiation process. Share your research findings and presentation with the class in an oral report.

16. **Research, Writing**   Investigate how Modified Atmosphere Packaging (MAP) is used to keep bagged salads fresh. Summarize your findings in a written report. Proofread and revise your report as needed for grammar, spelling, and organization.

17. **Science**   In your lab group, take turns adding the following ingredients for a vinaigrette dressing to a bottle in the order listed. Add liquid ingredients by pouring slowly. Add solid ingredients by sprinkling. All group members should record their observations after each ingredient is added.

    - ½ cup (125 mL) chilled red wine vinegar
    - ⅓ cup (80 mL) olive oil
    - ¾ teaspoon (3.75 mL) salt
    - ½ teaspoon (2.5 mL) paprika
    - ⅛ teaspoon (0.6 mL) ground black pepper
    - ¼ teaspoon (1.25 mL) dried thyme
    - ⅛ teaspoon (0.6 mL) dried tarragon
    - 1 clove garlic, crushed
    - 1 teaspoon (5 mL) lemon juice

    When all the ingredients have been added, discuss the reasons for your various observations. Cover and shake the bottle vigorously. Observe how long it takes for the liquids to separate. Then add ¾ teaspoon (3.75 mL) ground dry mustard. Cover and shake the bottle again. Note whether there is a difference in how long it takes the liquids to separate. What does this indicate? Sample the dressing on salad greens.

18. **Technology**   Search for soups on a recipe website. Look at the first 10 recipes that appear. Write down the name of each recipe and identify whether it is a stock soup or a cream soup. Compare your findings with those of other students.

19. **Math, Speaking**   Calculate and compare the cost per serving for instant, canned, and homemade bouillon. Taste samples of each and describe when you might choose to use each product in cooking.

20. **Practice Career Readiness**   Organize a canned and packaged food drive for needy people in your community. Place cans of protein foods, vegetables, and cream soups in bags with packages of rice or pasta. Then write recipe suggestions for combining the food items in each bag into a casserole. Distribute the foods through a local relief agency.

Critical Thinking and Problem Solving

21. **Evaluate**   Smell samples of three herbs and three spices. Use the aromas to propose a food item whose flavor would be enhanced by each herb or spice. Sample your proposed flavor combinations and prepare a written evaluation.

22. **Create**   Use input from all lab groups to plan and prepare a class salad buffet. Each lab group should prepare a different variety of salad greens, tossed salad topping, and dressing. Each lab group should also choose a different bound or composed salad recipe to prepare. Coordinate recipe choices with other lab groups to plan for a variety of flavors, textures, colors, sizes, shapes, and temperatures.

23. **Analyze**   Make two sauces—a creamy gravy from a white sauce and a reduction sauce—both using chicken broth. Compare the taste, texture, and appearance of the two sauces. Use your analysis to identify the types of dishes with which you would serve each sauce.

24. **Analyze**   Find a traditional casserole recipe. Analyze the ingredient list and suggest adjustments in amounts and/or types of ingredients to reduce fat, calories, and sodium and increase fiber. Use an online nutrient calculator to compare the nutritive value of a serving of each version of the recipe.

Chapter 26
Cakes, Cookies, Pies, and Candies

shutterdandan/Shutterstock.com

Content Terms [→]

shortened cake
unshortened cake
pastry
crystalline candy
noncrystalline candy
sugar syrup

Academic Terms

porous
optimum
invert
cavity
oblong
conversely
vigorously
novice

Objectives

After studying this chapter, you will be able to

- **determine** the functions of basic ingredients used in cakes;
- **identify** six types of cookies;
- **explain** principles of pastry preparation;
- **compare** characteristics of crystalline and noncrystalline candies; and
- **prepare** cakes, cookies, pies, and candies.

Reading Prep

Read the chapter title and tell a classmate what you have experienced or already know about desserts. Then write a paragraph describing what you would like to learn about desserts. After reading the chapter, share two things you have learned with your classmate.

For many people, a meal is not complete without something sweet. Restaurants are famous for the richness of their cheesecakes. Bakeries pride themselves on their pastries. Candy stores guard their recipes for fudge, peanut brittle, and English toffee.

Cakes, cookies, and pies are three of the most popular desserts (**Figure 26.1**). Candies are not really desserts, but because they are sweet, many people serve them at the end of a meal.

Most desserts are high in calories because they contain large amounts of sugar and fat. Desserts should never replace whole grains, fresh fruits and vegetables, low-fat dairy products, or protein foods in the diet. With moderation, however, desserts can add extra appeal to menu plans.

Cakes

Cakes are a favorite dessert of many people. They add festivity to many special occasions. They can also make a plain meal something special.

Kinds of Cakes

Cakes are classified into two groups: short-ened and unshortened. **Shortened cakes** contain fat. This is why some people call shortened cakes *butter cakes*. Most shortened cakes contain leav-ening agents. Shortened cakes are tender, moist, and velvety.

Unshortened cakes, sometimes called *foam cakes*, contain no fat. They are leavened by air and steam rather than chemical leavening agents. Angel food and sponge cakes are unshortened cakes. The main difference between these two cakes is the egg content. Angel food cakes contain just egg whites. Sponge cakes contain whole eggs. Unshortened cakes are light and fluffy.

Chiffon cakes are a cross between shortened and unshortened cakes. They contain fat like shortened cakes and beaten egg whites like unshortened cakes. They have large volumes, but they are not as light as unshortened cakes.

Cake Ingredients

Cakes contain flour, sugar, eggs, liquid, and salt. All shortened cakes also contain fat, and most cakes contain a leavening agent. Unshortened cakes contain cream of tartar, too.

MSPhotographic/Shutterstock.com

Figure 26.1   Cookies, cakes, and pies are popular dessert items, especially during special events and holidays.

Flour gives structure to a cake. The gluten that develops when flour is moistened and mixed holds the leavening gases that form as cakes bake. Cakes can be made with cake flour or all-purpose flour (**Figure 26.2**). Cakes made with cake flour are more delicate and tender. This is because cake flour has lower protein content, so it yields less gluten. It is also more finely ground than all-purpose flour.

Sugar gives sweetness to cakes. It also tenderizes the gluten and improves the texture of cakes. Recipes may call for either granulated or brown sugar. Both should be free of lumps.

Eggs improve both the flavor and color of cakes. The coagulated egg proteins also add struc-ture to cakes. In angel food and sponge cakes, eggs are important for leavening. Eggs hold the air that is beaten into them, and the evaporation of liquid from the egg whites creates steam.

Liquid provides moisture and helps blend ingredients. Most cake recipes call for fluid fresh milk. However, some call for buttermilk, sour milk, fruit juices, or water instead. In angel food cakes, egg whites are the only source of liquid needed.

Salt provides flavoring. Cakes require a smaller amount of salt than quick breads and yeast breads.

Fat tenderizes the gluten. Shortened cakes may contain butter, margarine, or vegetable

Marie C Fields/Shutterstock.com

Figure 26.2 The type of flour used when baking a cake impacts the texture of the finished cake.

shortening. (For best results in cooking and baking, margarines must contain at least 80 percent oil.) Chiffon cakes contain oil instead of solid fat.

Leavening agents are added to most shortened cakes to make the cakes rise and become *porous* (spongy) and light. Most recipes call for baking powder or baking soda and buttermilk.

Angel food and sponge cake recipes call for *cream of tartar*. Cream of tartar is an acid that makes egg whites whiter and makes the cake grain finer. Cream of tartar also stabilizes the egg white proteins, which increases the volume of the baked cake.

Flavorings are not essential ingredients in cakes, but they help make cakes special. Spices, *extracts* (concentrated flavors), fruits, nuts, poppy seeds, and coconut can be added to cake batters for variety.

Like bread recipes, many dessert recipes call for more of some ingredients than are needed to serve their functions. Try adjusting cake, cookie, and pastry recipes to use less fat, eggs, sugar, salt, and baking powder. The finished products will be lower in calories, fat, sugar, and sodium. Minimum amounts of ingredients needed for good results in common desserts are shown in **Figure 26.3.**

Food Science Principles of Preparing Cakes

Successfully preparing a cake depends on measuring, mixing, and baking. Ingredients must be measured accurately and mixed correctly. The cake batter must be baked in the correct pans at the correct temperature. Baking time must be watched carefully.

Measuring Ingredients

Flour, fat, sugar, liquid, and eggs affect the development of gluten. The correct proportions of each ingredient will produce a cake that is light and tender. Too much or too little of one or more ingredients may affect the finished product.

The optimum amount of flour provides the correct amount of gluten needed for structure. A cake made with too much flour is compact and dry. A cake made with too little flour is coarse, and it may fall.

Optimum (ideal; the best, most appropriate) amounts of fat and sugar tenderize gluten. Too much fat or sugar overtenderizes the gluten and weakens it. A cake made with too much of either ingredient will be heavy and coarse, and it may fall. A cake made with too little of either ingredient will be tough.

Minimum Ingredients Needed per 1 Cup (250 mL) of Flour					
Product	**Fat**	**Eggs**	**Sugar**	**Salt**	**Baking Powder**
Shortened cakes and drop cookies	2 tablespoons (30 mL)	½	½ cup (125 mL)	⅛ teaspoon (0.6 mL)	1 teaspoon (5 mL)
Pastry	¼ cup (60 mL)	—	—	½ teaspoon (2.5 mL)	—

Figure 26.3 For every one cup of flour used in each dessert product, you need at least the amounts of fat, eggs, sugar, salt, and baking powder indicated in this table for successful baking results. If you are making a cookie recipe with two cups of flour, how many of each ingredient will you need at minimum?

The optimum amount of liquid provides the moisture needed for gluten to develop. Too much liquid will make a cake soggy and heavy. Too little liquid will make a cake dry and heavy.

The optimum number of eggs contributes proteins that strengthen the gluten framework. Too many eggs will make a cake rubbery and tough.

Mixing Cakes

The mixing method specified in a recipe is based on the types and amounts of ingredients. It is important to add ingredients in the order listed and mix for the stated length of time. This will produce a smooth batter and a delicate cake.

Cake batters should be neither overmixed nor undermixed. Overmixing will cause the gluten to overdevelop. As a result, the cake will be tough. Undermixing could keep ingredients from being evenly distributed throughout the batter. Failure to beat enough air into the batter through undermixing could result in a cake that is dense rather than light. Overmixing angel food and sponge cakes will cause air to be lost from the beaten egg whites. As a result, the volume of the cake will be smaller.

Baking Cakes

Bake cake batter in pans that are neither too large nor too small. If the pans are too small, the batter will overflow (**Figure 26.4**). If the pans

ninakas/Shutterstock.com

Figure 26.4 When pouring cake batter, leave room at the top to allow the cake to rise in the oven.

are too large, the cake will be too flat and may be dry. The correct pan size will produce a cake with a gently rounded top.

For most shortened cakes, grease the pans and flour them lightly. Grease and flour both the bottoms and sides of the pans or just the bottoms. Do not grease the pans for unshortened cakes. This is because angel food and sponge cake batters must cling to the sides of the pan during baking.

Place cakes in a preheated oven set at the correct temperature and bake them just until they test done. Cakes baked at too high a temperature may burn. Cakes baked too long may be dry.

Preparing a Shortened Cake

Shortened cakes can be mixed by the conventional method or the quick-mix method. For the *conventional method*, cream the fat and sugar together until light and fluffy. Beat the eggs into the creamed fat and sugar. Then add the dry ingredients alternately with the liquid.

The *quick-mix method*, also called the *one-bowl method*, takes less time than the conventional method. Measure the dry ingredients into the mixing bowl. Beat the fat and part of the liquid with the dry ingredients. Add the remaining liquid and unbeaten eggs last.

When baking a shortened cake, pour the batter into prepared pans. Then arrange the pans in the oven so the heat circulates freely around the cake. The pans should not touch each other or any part of the oven. If they do, hot spots may form, and the cake may bake unevenly.

To test a cake for doneness, lightly touch the center with your fingertip. If the cake springs back, it is baked. You can also insert a toothpick or wooden skewer into the center of the cake to test it. If the toothpick or skewer comes out clean, the cake is baked (**Figure 26.5**).

Most recipes say to let cakes cool in the pans for about 10 minutes after removing the pans from the oven. This cooling period makes it easier to remove the cakes from the pans. To remove a cake from the pan, run the tip of a metal spatula around the sides of the cake to loosen it. *Invert* (place upside down) a cooling rack over the top of the pan and gently flip the cooling rack and the pan. The cake should slide out of the pan. Carefully remove the pan and

Vasily Mulyukin/Shutterstock.com

Figure 26.5 Testing for doneness will avoid the dense, gooey interior of an underbaked cake and the dryness of an overbaked cake. If a cake has been baked for the recommended time, what could cause it to be underdone?

place a second cooling rack on top of the cake. Flip the cake and the cooling racks so the cake is right side up. Let cake layers cool thoroughly before frosting them.

Characteristics of a Shortened Cake

A high-quality shortened cake is velvety and light. The interior has small, fine cells with thin walls. The crusts are thin and evenly browned. The top crust is smooth or slightly pebbly and gently rounded. The flavor is mild and pleasing.

Cake Treats

A few common treats are made from shortened cake. Cupcakes can be made from shortened cake batter. The batter is poured into a muffin pan. Paper liners are often placed in the depressions of the pan to make the cupcakes easy to remove and neater to eat. Many people like to serve cupcakes at parties because of their individual portion size.

Cake balls and cake pops are made from shortened cake that is crumbled and mixed with frosting. The mixture is formed into balls, which may be dipped in a coating of icing or melted chocolate. Additional decorations may be added, and cake pops have sticks inserted into the balls to make them easy to eat. These treats are often made from leftover cake or scraps cut from shortened cakes during decorating.

Pound Cakes

Pound cakes are shortened cakes that contain no chemical leavening agents. Pound cakes rely on air and steam for leavening. The fat and sugar must be thoroughly creamed when making pound cake. The eggs are beaten into the creamed mixture until fluffy to incorporate enough air. The dry ingredients and the liquid are then added to the creamed mixture. This mixing method gives pound cakes a closer grain and more compact texture than other shortened cakes.

Preparing an Unshortened Cake

Angel food cake is the most frequently prepared unshortened cake. When preparing an angel food cake, the ingredients should be at room temperature. This will help the egg whites achieve maximum volume when beaten.

Angel food cakes are mixed by a different method from those used for shortened cakes. For an angel food cake, beat the egg whites with some of the sugar until stiff. Carefully fold the flour and remaining sugar into the beaten egg whites.

Carefully pour the batter for an unshortened cake into an ungreased tube pan. Run a spatula through the batter to release large air bubbles and seal the batter against the sides of the pan. Bake the cake in a preheated oven for the recommended time. Test the cake for doneness by gently touching the cracks that have formed in the surface of the cake during baking. The cracks should feel dry and no imprint should remain.

When an unshortened cake is removed from the oven, immediately suspend the pan upside down over the neck of a bottle (**Figure 26.6**). Hanging the cake upside down prevents a loss of volume during cooling. Cool the cake completely before removing it from the pan.

Sponge Cakes

Like angel food cakes, sponge cakes are unshortened. However, sponge cakes contain whole eggs rather than just egg whites. Sponge cakes are made using a variation of the mixing method used for angel food cakes. First, the

Figure 26.6 A tube pan, as shown here, has a hole in the center. When the cake is ready, the pan can be flipped upside down over a bottle to allow the cake to slide out and maintain its shape.

egg yolks are beaten until they are thick and lemon colored. Then the liquid, sugar, and salt are added to the yolks. Beating continues until the mixture is thick. The flour is gently folded into the yolk mixture. Then the stiffly beaten egg whites are folded into the flour-yolk mixture.

Characteristics of an Unshortened Cake

A high-quality angel food or other unshortened cake has a large volume and symmetrical shape. The crust should be thin and golden brown. The top crust has a slightly rough and cracked appearance. The interior has a fine, porous texture with thin cell walls. The cake is tender and moist, but it is not gummy.

Filling and Frosting Cakes

Fillings and frostings can make a simple cake into a really special dessert. Fillings and frostings come in as wide a variety as the cakes they enhance.

Fluffy whipped cream, creamy puddings, and sweet fruits are among the popular fillings for cakes. Fillings can be spread between layers of cake or rolled into the center of a jelly roll. Fillings can also be spooned into a *cavity* (hole) dug into the middle of a cake.

Ganache is a popular filling and frosting for cakes among chocolate lovers. This is a mixture of chocolate and cream that can be poured over

a cake to create a glossy glaze. It can also be whipped to create a rich, creamy filling.

Canned frostings and frosting mixes are available, but frostings can easily be made from scratch. Frostings may be cooked or uncooked.

Cooked frostings use the principles of candy making. They include ingredients that interfere with the formation of crystals in a heated sugar syrup. Then they are often beaten until fluffy. Seven-minute frosting is a commonly used cooked frosting.

Fondant is one type of cooked icing that is commonly used by cake decorators. It can be made at home or purchased premade and ready to use. Rather than the fluffy texture of some cooked frostings, fondant has the consistency of pliable dough. It can be rolled into a thin layer and placed over a cake to give it a smooth surface. Fondant can be painted, dyed, and molded to create almost any type of scene or decoration (**Figure 26.7**).

Uncooked frostings are popular for their creamy texture. They are easily made by beating the ingredients together until they reach a smooth, spreadable consistency. Cream cheese frosting and *buttercream* are well-liked uncooked frostings.

Frostings not only enhance the flavor of cakes, they also enhance the appearance. Cake layers can be cut into pieces and reassembled to form the shapes of animals and objects. Frosting is used as the "glue" to hold the pieces together.

Dulce Rubia/Shutterstock.com

Figure 26.7   Fondant not only gives cakes a perfectly smooth surface, it can also be molded into decorations to create cakes for any theme.

Cookies

Children and adults find it hard to resist a cookie jar filled with fresh homemade cookies. People enjoy chocolate chip, peanut butter, oatmeal, and sugar cookies year-round. At holiday times, many families make special cookies like Swedish pepparkakor, Norwegian krumkake, and Scottish shortbread.

Kinds of Cookies

Cookies are often classified into six basic groups: rolled, drop, bar, refrigerator, pressed, or molded. The ingredients used to make different kinds of cookies are similar. However, the doughs differ in consistency, and they are shaped differently (**Figure 26.8**).

A stiff dough is used to make *rolled cookies.* Roll the dough on a counter to a thickness of ⅛ to ¼ inch (3 to 6 mm). Dust the rolling surface with flour or place the dough between sheets of parchment paper to prevent it from sticking during rolling. Cut the cookies from the dough with a cookie cutter and transfer them to a cookie sheet. Cookie cutters are available in many shapes and sizes. Sugar cookies are popular rolled cookies.

Learn About...

Cake Decorating Tools

A few simple tools can allow you to turn an ordinary cake into a work of art. After covering the cake with a base of frosting on the top and sides, you are ready to begin decorating. The first tool you will need is a decorating bag, which is a cloth, plastic, or paper bag that holds the decorator icing. The icing is piped through decorating tips, which are attached or inserted into the bag. These hollow plastic or metal cones have various notches cut into them. Each tip gives the icing piped through it a different appearance. You can create smooth writing, scalloped borders, and tapered leaves and flower petals among other effects. Decorating tips can be held onto the bag with a two-piece device called a coupler. A coupler is not essential, but it makes it simple to change from one tip to another. If you plan to decorate cakes often, you might also want to get a turntable. This makes it easy to decorate all the way around a cake by just rotating the turntable.

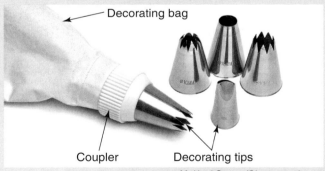

M. Unal Ozmen/Shutterstock.com

Know and Apply

1. Why do decorating tips and bags make decorating a cake easier?
2. Which material—cloth, plastic, or paper bag—would you prefer to work with? Why?

A soft dough is used to make *drop cookies.* Drop or push the dough from a spoon onto cookie sheets. Leave about 2 inches (5 cm) of space between cookies. Drop cookies will spread more than rolled cookies during baking. Chocolate chip cookies are popular drop cookies.

l to r: alisafarov/Shutterstock.com; Brent Hofacker/Shutterstock.com; Marina Shanti/Shutterstock.com; PorNontawat/Shutterstock.com; Tom Grundy/Shutterstock.com; Rojo Images/Shutterstock.com

Figure 26.8   Depending on the type of cookie—rolled, drop, bar, refrigerator, pressed, or molded—the finished good can vary in size, shape, and consistency.

A soft dough is also used to make *bar cookies.* Spread the dough evenly in a jelly roll, square, or *oblong* (elongated) pan and bake it. Depending on the thickness of the dough, bar cookies may be chewy or cakelike. Bar cookies can be cut into different shapes after baking. Brownies are popular bar cookies.

Refrigerator cookies contain a high proportion of fat. Form the stiff dough into a long roll, about two inches (5 cm) in diameter. Wrap the roll in wax paper and refrigerate until firm. Cut the chilled dough into thin slices, and place on lightly greased cookie sheets and bake. Pinwheel cookies are popular refrigerator cookies.

A very rich, stiff dough is used to make *pressed cookies.* Pack the dough into a *cookie press.* This utensil has perforated disks through which the dough is pushed onto cookie sheets. The cookies vary in shape and size, depending on the disk used. Swedish spritz cookies are pressed cookies.

Recipe for Good Food

Chewy Fruit Drops

Makes 12

These cookies can be made with your choice of dried fruit. Each lab group might want to try a different variety. Share and compare cookies with other groups to choose the variation you like best. Suggestions include raisins, dried cranberries, dried blueberries, and chopped dried apricots, dates, or cherries.

2   tablespoons (30 mL) butter, softened
2   tablespoons (30 mL) granulated sugar
3   tablespoons (45 mL) packed brown sugar
¼   cup (60 mL) unsweetened applesauce
½   teaspoon (2.5 mL) vanilla
⅔   cup (160 mL) whole-wheat flour
1   teaspoon (5 mL) baking powder
⅛   teaspoon (0.6 mL) salt
⅔   cup (160 mL) dried fruit

1.   Preheat oven to 375°F (190°C). Cover a cookie sheet with a silicone baking mat or parchment paper.
2.   In a large mixing bowl, combine butter, granulated sugar, brown sugar, applesauce, and vanilla. Stir in whole-wheat flour, baking powder, and salt (dough will be sticky). Stir in dried fruit.
3.   Drop dough by rounded tablespoonfuls about 2 inches apart onto prepared baking sheet. Bake 9 to 11 minutes or until lightly browned around the edges (centers will be soft).
4.   Remove cookies from oven and cool on cookie sheet for 5 minutes. Then remove from cookie sheet and cool on wire rack.

Per cookie: 64 calories (28% from fat), 1 g protein, 11 g carbohydrate, 2 g fat, 5 mg cholesterol, 1 g fiber, 80 mg sodium.

A stiff dough is also used to make *molded cookies*. Small pieces of dough are shaped with the fingers, usually into small balls or crescents. Mexican wedding cookies and almond crescents are two common molded cookies.

Cookie Ingredients

Cookies contain the same basic ingredients used to make cakes. They contain flour, sugar, liquid, fat, salt, egg, and leavening agents. Most cookies contain more fat and sugar and less liquid than cakes. Rolled cookies often contain no liquid. The proportion of ingredients, as well as the way the cookies are shaped, determines if cookies are soft or crisp.

Many cookie recipes call for ingredients such as spices, nuts, coconut, chocolate chips, and dried fruits. Some recipes say to add these ingredients to the dough during mixing. Other recipes say to sprinkle cookies or roll them in colored sugars, coconut, or nuts after baking. Be sure to follow directions specified in your recipe to achieve desired results.

Preparing Cookies

Many cookies are made using the conventional mixing method used for shortened cakes. For this method, blend the sugar and fat until smooth. Then add the eggs, liquid, and flavorings, followed by the dry ingredients. Most cookies are crisp or chewy rather than light and delicate. Therefore, the fat and sugar do not need to be creamed as thoroughly as they are for a cake. Also, in most cases, the flour can be added all at once rather than in parts.

Macaroons, meringues, and kisses contain beaten egg whites (**Figure 26.9**). They are mixed like angel food and sponge cakes. A few cookies, like Scottish shortbread, are mixed using the biscuit method. The recipe will specify which method to use.

Pans for Baking Cookies

Bake drop, rolled, refrigerator, pressed, and molded cookies on flat baking pans or cookie sheets. Cookie sheets should not have high sides, or cookies will bake unevenly. Bake bar cookies in pans with sides.

Baking pans made of bright, shiny aluminum reflect heat. Cookies baked on bright, shiny cookie sheets will have a light, delicate brown color. Dark

Nataliya Hora/Shutterstock.com

Figure 26.9 The delicate structure and texture of macaroons is made possible by careful handling of egg whites. What other types of desserts feature the use of egg whites?

pans absorb heat. Cookies baked on dark cookie sheets will have dark bottoms.

Cookie sheets should be cool when cookies are placed on them for baking. Warm sheets will cause cookies to spread and lose their shape.

It is usually best to bake one pan of cookies at a time on a rack placed in the center of the oven (**Figure 26.10**). If two sheets of cookies are baked at one time, the pans may need to be rotated once in the middle of the baking period. If you are baking on two oven racks, space them evenly in the oven cavity. Switch the placement of the two cookie sheets halfway through the baking period. These steps will help the cookies brown evenly. Baking pans should never touch each other or the sides of the oven.

Alan Poulson Photography/Shutterstock.com

Figure 26.10 For even baking, the sheet pan of cookies should be centered in the oven.

Learn About...

Freshening Stale Cookies

Cookies that have lost their characteristic texture can be freshened. If crisp cookies have become soft or begun to stale, they can be made crisp again. Place cookies on a cookie sheet in a 350°F (180°C) oven for a few minutes. You can also place a small plate of cookies in the microwave for a few seconds. With either method, enjoy the cookies while they are warm, as the stale taste may return as the cookies cool.

If soft cookies have become hard, they can be made soft again. Place a piece of bread in the cookie container. The cookies will soften as they absorb moisture from the bread. Replace the bread every other day.

Know and Apply

1. How can you prevent cookies from becoming stale?
2. What stale foods other than cookies might you be able to freshen using some of these suggestions?

Storing Cookies

Make sure cookies are cooled completely and any frosting is fully set before storing. Then store cookies promptly. Exposure to air will dry out soft cookies, making them hard. *Conversely* (oppositely), crisp cookies tend to pull moisture from the air and lose their crisp texture. Therefore, it is important to store all cookies in air-tight containers. Do not store crisp and soft cookies together because the soft cookies will soften the crisp cookies. Bar cookies can be stored in their baking pan if they are covered with foil. For best quality, all cookies should be eaten within a few days of baking.

For longer storage, freeze cookies. Pack them in sturdy containers with tight-fitting covers. Separate layers of cookies with wax paper. Be sure to date and label containers before placing them in the freezer.

You can also freeze many types of cookie dough. To freeze refrigerator cookie dough, wrap each shaped roll tightly in wax paper and then in aluminum foil. Molded, rolled, and drop cookie doughs can be shaped into large balls and wrapped for freezer storage. Press dough for pressed cookies or drop dough for drop cookies onto cookie sheets and quickly freeze it. The frozen dough can then be removed from the cookie sheet with a spatula and placed in airtight containers or plastic bags. Bar cookie dough can be frozen in the baking pan.

When you are ready to bake frozen cookie dough, thaw until the dough is soft enough to slice and then bake as directed. The dough will need to be thawed before molding, rolling, or dropping it. Cookie dough that is frozen onto cookie sheets and then placed into airtight containers does not need to be thawed before baking. However, you may need to add a minute or two to the baking time. Frozen dough as well as cookies should be used within three months.

Pies

Apple pie is a favorite dessert in the United States. Who can resist the flavor, aroma, and eye appeal of a golden flaky pastry filled with warm, spicy apples? Apple pie and most other types of pie begin with pastry. **Pastry** is the dough used to make piecrusts. Pastry making is not difficult. However, it does require practice and patience.

Uses for Pastry

Pastry can be used in many ways. It is mainly used when making dessert pies. However, pastry can also be used when making main dish pies, such as meat pies and quiche. Small pastry shells can be filled with foods such as creamed tuna or chicken a la king to make potpies. Small pastry shells can be used to make tarts filled with pudding or ice cream. Pastry squares can be folded in half over fruit filling to make turnovers. Pastry can also be used to make appetizers such as cheese sticks.

Kinds of Pies

The four basic kinds of pies are fruit, cream, custard, and chiffon. *Fruit pies* usually are two-crust pies. They may have a solid top crust, or they may have a lattice or other decorative top (**Figure 26.11**).

Figure 26.11 Cherry and berry pies are often topped with a decorative lattice crust, which holds in the juices while still displaying the colorful fruit. What is your favorite kind of pie?

Commercially prepared pie filling or filling made from canned, frozen, dried, or fresh fruit may be used.

Cream pies usually are one-crust pies. The filling for cream pie is a cornstarch-thickened pudding mixture. Cream pies often have a meringue topping.

Custard pies are one-crust pies filled with custard made from milk, eggs, and sugar. The custard may or may not contain other ingredients. Pumpkin pie is a popular custard pie.

Chiffon pies are light and airy. They are one-crust pies filled with a mixture containing gelatin and cooked beaten egg whites. Some chiffon pie fillings also contain whipped cream. Chiffon pies must be chilled until the filling sets.

Pastry Ingredients

Four basic ingredients are used to make pastry—flour, fat, water, and salt. When combined correctly, the four ingredients will produce pastry that is tender and flaky.

Flour gives structure to pastry. Most home bakers use all-purpose flour for pastry making.

Fat makes pastry tender by inhibiting the development of gluten. It contributes to flakiness by separating the layers of gluten. Most bakers use butter, lard, or vegetable shortening. These fats produce tender and flaky pastry. Some pastry recipes call for oil. Oil-based pastry will be tender, but it will be mealy rather than flaky.

Water provides the moisture needed for the development of the gluten and the production of steam. Only a small amount of water is needed. For each 1 cup (250 mL) of flour, 2 tablespoons (30 mL) of water is ample.

Salt contributes flavor to pastry. If salt is eliminated, it will not affect the pastry in any other way.

Food Science Principles of Preparing Pastry

To make pastry that is both tender and flaky, the correct ingredients must be used and measured accurately. The dough must be handled gently and as little as possible, too.

Flour, fat, and liquid all affect the tenderness and flakiness of pastry. If these ingredients are not measured accurately, a poor-quality pastry will result.

Gluten develops when flour is moistened and stirred. The gluten creates a framework that traps air and holds steam formed during baking. This trapped air and steam is what causes pastry to be tender and flaky. Too much flour will make pastry tough.

The fat forms a waterproof coating around the flour particles. This prevents too much water from coming in contact with the proteins of the flour. It also prevents the subsequent development of too much gluten. Layers of fat physically separate the layers of gluten that form. As a result, the pastry is both tender and flaky. Too little fat will make pastry tough; too much fat will make pastry crumbly.

Water hydrates the flour so the gluten will develop. It also produces the steam needed for flakiness. The right amount of liquid will moisten the flour just enough to develop the optimum amount of gluten. Too much liquid will make the pastry tough. Too little liquid will make it crumbly and difficult to roll.

Preparing Pastry

Several methods can be used to mix pastry, but the biscuit method (sometimes called the *pastry method*) is most popular. This method involves combining the flour and salt and then cutting in the fat. You can cut in fat using two knives or a pastry blender. Pulsing the mixture with a food processor is also an easy way to accomplish

Food Science

Handling Pastry Dough

Too much flour, too much liquid, and too little fat can make pastry tough. Too much handling can also make pastry tough. Handling causes gluten to develop. The more the gluten develops, the tougher the pastry will be.

Pastry should be handled gently at all times. It should also be handled as little as possible to prevent overdeveloping the gluten. It is especially important not to

- overmix the dough when adding the liquid;
- use the rolling pin too vigorously when rolling the pastry; or
- stretch the pastry when fitting it into the pie plate.

ffolas/Shutterstock.com

Figure 26.12   Piecrusts that will be filled after baking should be pricked with a fork to prevent the crust from blistering or bubbling.

this step. When the fat is completely cut in, the mixture should look like coarse cornmeal. Then water is added, a tablespoon at a time, just until the mixture is moist enough to form a mass when pressed together. Making sure both the fat and water are very cold keeps the fat from melting before baking, which promotes a flaky crust.

When making a one-crust pie that will be filled after baking, the edges should be fluted. The bottom and sides of the piecrust need to be pricked with a fork to prevent blistering during baking (**Figure 26.12**). Do not prick the bottom or sides of a crust that will be filled before baking.

Characteristics of Pastry

High-quality pastry is both tender and flaky. The amount and distribution of gluten determines tenderness. Flakiness is due to layers of gluten (with embedded starch grains) separated by layers of fat and expanded (puffed up) by steam.

If pastry is tender, it will cut easily with a fork and "melt in the mouth" when eaten. If pastry is flaky, thin layers of dough separated by empty spaces will be visible when the pastry is cut with a fork.

Aside from having pastry that is tender, flaky, and crisp, a pie should be lightly and evenly browned. The filling should have a pleasing flavor and be neither too runny nor too firm.

Candy

People enjoy eating candy throughout the year. At holiday times, however, many people take the time to make candy. Homemade fudge, divinity, peanut brittle, toffee, and caramels are fun to make and give as gifts.

To make good candy, directions must be followed exactly. Candies must be mixed correctly and cooked to the exact temperature specified in the recipe. Otherwise, they are likely to fail.

Kinds of Candy

Many kinds of candy can be made. A few kinds of candies do not need to be cooked, but these require special recipes. Most candies are cooked. Cooked candies are either crystalline or noncrystalline candies.

Crystalline candies contain fine sugar crystals. They are smooth and creamy. Fudge, fondant, and divinity are crystalline candies.

Noncrystalline candies do not contain sugar crystals. They can be chewy or brittle. Caramels, peanut brittle, and toffee are noncrystalline candies.

Learn About...

Types of Chocolate

Chocolate is made from the beans of the cacao tree. The beans are first roasted. Then they are shelled, pressed, and heated until they form a liquid, which is called *chocolate liquor*. At this point, some of the fat, or *cocoa butter*, may be removed. However, high cocoa butter content is a sign of quality in chocolate.

Baking and eating chocolate is made from chocolate liquor. It comes in various degrees of sweetness. *Unsweetened chocolate* contains no sugar. *Bittersweet*, *semisweet*, and *milk chocolate* each contain progressively more sugar. Sweetened chocolates also contain vanilla, and milk chocolate contains milk solids.

Other products related to chocolate include cocoa, white chocolate, and imitation chocolate. *Cocoa* is made from dried chocolate liquor that has been ground to a fine powder. *White chocolate* is made from cocoa butter, sugar, milk solids, and flavorings. Because it contains no chocolate liquor, it is not truly chocolate. *Imitation chocolate* or chocolate-flavored products are made with vegetable oil instead of cocoa butter. Imitation chocolate is less expensive than real chocolate; however, it lacks the creamy smoothness and delicious flavor characteristic of true chocolate.

Know and Apply

1. What is chocolate liquor?
2. Why is white chocolate not considered true chocolate?

Food Science Principles of Candy Making

All cooked candies begin with **sugar syrup**. This is a mixture of sugar and liquid that is cooked to a thick consistency. Successful candy making depends on how this sugar syrup is treated.

When making crystalline candies, the sugar syrup should form crystals. These crystals need to be very small and fine, however. To produce small sugar crystals, the sugar syrup must be heated to a specific temperature. It must then be cooled to a specific temperature and beaten *vigorously* (enthusiastically with strength).

Fudge is one of the most popular crystalline candies. High-quality fudge tastes smooth and creamy because it contains small sugar crystals. It has a deep brown color and a satiny sheen (**Figure 26.13**). Poor-quality fudge tastes grainy because it contains large sugar crystals.

When making noncrystalline candies, the sugar syrup should not form crystals. Crystal formation can be prevented by heating the syrup to a very high temperature. Substances like corn syrup, milk, cream, or butter can be added, which interfere with crystallization. A combination of high temperatures and interfering substances can also be used to prevent crystals from forming.

Peanut brittle is a popular noncrystalline candy. High-quality peanut brittle has a golden color and looks foamy. Cooking the candy to a very high temperature and using interfering substances prevent crystal formation.

Whether making crystalline or noncrystalline candies, temperature is very important. A candy thermometer is the most accurate method of testing the temperature of sugar syrups. Each type of candy requires a specific temperature. The candy thermometer will accurately indicate when sugar syrup reaches the correct temperature.

A heavy saucepan should be used to cook candy. Mixtures that contain large amounts of sugar burn easily. A heavy saucepan will help prevent scorching.

Chocolate

In the minds of some sweet lovers, no candy can match chocolate. The most exquisite chocolates may be best left to professional candy makers. However, even a *novice* (beginner) can melt chocolate to make simple candies. Melted chocolate can be poured into molds. It can be used to make clusters of raisins, nuts, or coconut. Fondant or caramels can also be dipped in a coating of melted chocolate.

To melt chocolate, chop bars into small pieces or use chocolate chips. Place chocolate in the top of a double boiler over hot water and stir constantly. Use care not to get any water in the

Andrea Skjold Mink/Shutterstock.com;

Martin Christopher Parker/Shutterstock.com

Figure 26.13 Traditional fudge can be dark brown and creamy in appearance, as on the top, or contain colorful food dye like the strawberry fudge on the bottom. What type of chocolate do you think is used to make the colorful fudge?

chocolate, as this can cause the chocolate to *seize*, or form grainy clumps. Remove chocolate from heat as soon as it is melted to prevent scorching.

Chocolate can also be melted in a microwave oven. Place the chocolate in a glass bowl. Microwave on high power for 30 seconds at a

Exploring Careers

Candy Maker

Candy making involves a number of steps. A large candy plant hires many machine operators and factory line workers. Each of these workers focuses on a single step, such as shaping, cutting, or wrapping candy. In a small candy business, all candy making tasks may be done by a master candy maker and a few assistants. The candy industry also has a lot of specialization. For instance, some candy makers produce fudge, others make caramels, and others pride themselves in taffy.

Candy factory workers need a basic skill set to be successful in their jobs. They may need only a high school education. They will likely receive on-the-job training in how to run their particular machines. They need good listening and observation skills to follow directions and pay attention to the details of their work. They also need to be able to cooperate with coworkers.

Master candy makers need specialized skills. They may be required to have culinary training, with a focus on confectionery skills. They may also receive training as apprentices under the guidance of skilled candy makers. Master candy makers use reading skills to follow recipes and math skills to figure weights and measurements. They need to understand principles of food science to formulate new recipes. They must be able to evaluate their products for qualities such as taste, texture, and color. Master candy makers also need leadership skills to direct the work of their assistants.

time just until chocolate is melted. Be sure to stir the chocolate after each microwaving period. Be careful not to allow chocolate to overheat, which can also cause seizing.

Chapter 26 Review and Expand

Summary

The two basic types of cakes are shortened, which contain fat, and unshortened, which do not contain fat. All cakes contain the same essential set of ingredients. To make sure cakes bake properly, use correct oven temperatures and baking times.

Rolled, drop, bar, refrigerator, pressed, and molded are six kinds of cookies. Most cookies are mixed by the conventional mixing method. Storing crisp and soft cookies in separate air-tight containers will help cookies stay fresh and retain their textures.

Pastry is the main component of pies. Flour, fat, water, and salt are the basic ingredients in pastry. Carefully measuring these ingredients and gently handling the dough will help produce tender, flaky pie crust.

To make crystalline candies, sugar syrups are heated, cooled, and then beaten to produce fine sugar crystals. For noncrystalline candies, sugar syrups are heated to high temperatures and/or substances are added to keep crystals from forming. Simple candy treats can also be made by stirring or dipping ingredients into melted chocolate.

Vocabulary Activities

1. **Content Terms**   Write a brief chapter summary to a classmate who is interested in working part-time at a bakery. Explain the different kinds of cakes, cookies, pies, and candies. Be sure to include each content term in your summary.

shortened cake	crystalline candy
unshortened cake	noncrystalline candy
pastry	sugar syrup

2. **Academic Terms**   Create a T-chart on a sheet of paper and list each of the following terms in the left column. In the right column, list an antonym for each term in the left column.

porous	oblong
optimum	conversely
invert	vigorously
cavity	novice

Review

Write your answers using complete sentences when appropriate.

3. List the seven basic ingredients of a shortened cake (other than pound cake) and briefly describe a major function of each.

4. What would happen if a cake were made with too much fat?

5. Why do baking pans need to be the correct size when baking a cake?

6. What are the two most common mixing methods for making shortened cakes?

7. How do pound cakes differ from other shortened cakes?

8. How is an unshortened cake handled when it is removed from the oven?

9. What are six basic kinds of cookies?

10. How do proportions of cookie ingredients differ from proportions of cake ingredients?

11. Why should crisp cookies and soft cookies be stored separately?

12. How will pastry be affected if salt is omitted from the recipe?

13. List three reasons pastry might be tough.

14. What two characteristics are used to describe high-quality pastry?

15. How does a crystalline candy differ in texture from a noncrystalline candy?

16. What is the most accurate method of testing the temperature of sugar syrups used in candy making?

17. What happens when chocolate seizes, and what is one cause of seizing?

Chapter 26 Review and Expand

Core Skills

18. **Listening, Writing** Survey three students from other classes about their dessert consumption habits. Ask the following questions:

    A. What is your favorite kind of cake?

    B. At what occasions do you most often eat cake?

    C. What is your favorite kind of cookie?

    D. How often do you eat cookies?

    E. What is your favorite kind of pie?

    F. Who bakes your favorite kind of pie or where do you buy it?

    Compile your results with those of your classmates. Use your findings as the basis for writing a blog post from the perspective of a food blogger. You might choose to write about one type of dessert, or desserts in general. Edit and refine your writing for grammar and spelling and to ensure your ideas are presented in a logical, organized manner that is clear to the reader.

19. **Science** Working in lab groups, slowly pour ¼ cup corn syrup into a liquid measuring cup. Next, slowly pour ¼ cup colored water on top of the corn syrup, followed by ¼ cup vegetable oil. Use care to pour each liquid into the center of the measuring cup to avoid getting the liquids on the sides of the cup. Next, gently drop a chocolate chip, then an ice cube, and then a miniature marshmallow into the measuring cup. Note the respective densities of these common liquid and solid ingredients.

20. **Science, Speaking** Prepare two angel food cakes. In one cake, add cream of tartar to egg whites during beating. Do not add cream of tartar to the egg whites used in the other cake. Discuss the appearance, texture, and volume of the two cakes.

21. **Math** Choose your favorite cookie recipe. Then calculate and record the amount of each ingredient you would need to prepare a double batch. Also note the yield for the double batch.

22. **Writing** Prepare enough pastry for a two-crust pie. Divide the dough in half. Roll half the dough and cut it into 1-inch (2.5-cm) strips. Place the strips on a cookie sheet. Knead the other half of the dough for several minutes. Roll and cut the dough into 1-inch (2.5-cm) strips and place them on a second cookie sheet. Bake both sets of pastry strips. After comparing the appearance and texture of the two samples, write a paragraph explaining why overhandling pastry should be avoided.

23. **Career Readiness Practice** Suppose your class has been asked to develop a signature cookie that will be sold as a school fund-raiser. Use your creativity and innovation, along with online and print resources, to develop a new cookie recipe. In addition to a unique recipe, the cookie should be decorated to appeal to the high school students who will be purchasing the cookies. Develop a recipe and submit it along with a sample to your instructor for evaluation.

Critical Thinking and Problem Solving

24. **Create** Use spreadsheet software to create a formula that will calculate the minimum amounts of fat, eggs, sugar, salt, and baking powder to use in shortened cakes. The formula for each ingredient should immediately show the correct amount when you enter the amount of flour required in a cake recipe. Use the program to compute ingredient proportions that will reduce fat and calories in three recipes.

25. **Evaluate** Prepare two batches of a cake or cookie recipe using an artificial sweetener designed for baking in place of sugar in one batch. Duplicate the recipe using regular sugar in the second batch. Calculate the calorie reduction per serving that resulted from the ingredient substitution. Compare and evaluate the two products in terms of appearance, texture, and taste. State whether you think the calorie savings is worthwhile based on your evaluation of the product made with the artificial sweetener.

26. **Evaluate** Prepare two batches of fudge. Follow directions exactly for the first batch. For the second batch, stir fudge occasionally during cooling. After the fudge has set, evaluate the texture, flavor, and appearance of both samples.

Chapter 27
Food and Entertaining

MBI/Shutterstock.com

Objectives

After studying this chapter, you will be able to

- **plan** a social gathering;
- **wait** on a table correctly;
- **prepare** appetizers;
- **describe** guidelines for safely preparing, transporting, and serving food for outdoor entertaining; and
- **use** appropriate behavior when dining out.

Reading Prep

Skim the Review questions at the end of the chapter first. Use them to help you focus on the most important concepts as you read the chapter.

Content Terms 🠒

RSVP
appetizer
American (family style) service
Russian (continental) service
English service
compromise service
blue plate service
buffet service
manners
etiquette
reservation
entree
a la carte
gratuity
tip

Academic Terms

celebratory
compatible
nibble
designated
inconspicuous
clambake
foliage

Eating food is more enjoyable when others eat it with you. Entertaining and dining out give people chances to renew longstanding relationships and meet new friends.

Planning for Entertaining

Most people enjoy getting together with coworkers, friends, and family members. You might host a formal dinner party, a special birthday celebration, a business gathering, or an impromptu get-together (**Figure 27.1**). No matter what the event is, a little planning will help it go more smoothly.

Social gatherings should allow both guests and hosts to enjoy themselves. Guests may find it hard to relax if their host is running around tending to last-minute details. Hosts may find it hard to have a good time if they have not completed preparations before their guests arrive. Careful planning helps prevent these problems and set a *celebratory* (festive) mood for a party.

Planning a gathering involves money, time, and energy. The kind of gathering you have and the number of guests you invite depend on several important factors, including the ones that follow.

Halfpoint/Shutterstock.com

Figure 27.1 Social gatherings for special events can help you build relationships with your classmates and friends. What is the role of food in a social gathering?

Exploring Careers

Meeting Planner

Meeting planners are in charge of all aspects of setting up meetings for businesses and organizations. They work with their clients to determine goals and a budget for an event. Then they put together an event schedule. They find a meeting location, arrange for food, hire entertainment, and order audio-visual (AV) equipment, as needed. They may contact speakers and arrange for their transportation and lodging. Meeting planners send out details promoting the event. They also have agendas and other materials printed for attendees.

To be successful, meeting planners need outstanding organizational skills. They need good communication skills as they listen to clients and relay information to others. They need to pay attention to details, manage time, and oversee people. They will use math skills to handle budgeting issues. Meeting planners must be able to handle stress and adapt to change. They must be creative problem solvers. They must also be willing to do some traveling and work rather long and irregular hours.

Most meeting planners have four-year degrees. A degree may not be required, but classes in business and communications will help people who want to enter this career. Meeting planners typically start out as part of a staff. At this level, they carry out assignments and follow up to be sure tasks have been done as required. With experience, meeting planners may move into decision-making positions. They may also apply to become Certified Meeting Professionals (CMPs). This certification shows employers that meeting planners have knowledge and background in the field.

The Theme

Social gatherings often have themes. Almost any idea can be turned into a party theme. Sports events and holidays are popular themes. You could plan a gathering with an international theme using information from the international foods chapters in this text.

The theme helps determine what people should wear and what foods might be served. The theme can inspire ideas for decorations and activities, too. For instance, guests could wear traditional Mexican clothes to go with a Mexican fiesta theme. Tacos and enchiladas could be served. You could use cacti, colorful streamers, and a piñata for decorations. Activities could include breaking the piñata and dancing to Latin music.

The Guest List

A guest list is a record of guests you want to invite. When putting together a guest list, keep people's interests and personalities in mind. Common interests will help guests get to know one another. Personalities that are *compatible* (able to coexist without conflict) will help create a setting in which everyone gets along and has a good time.

The number of people invited to a party should reflect how many people can fit comfortably in the amount of space available. The guest list should also fit the host's cooking skills and available equipment. Unless extra help or a large freezer is available, very large parties might not be practical.

The Invitations

Most parties have no rules for invitations. Friends might be invited for a spur-of-the-moment party or casual gathering in person or over the phone. For large parties, e-mail invitations sent through an online service are convenient. A formal event usually requires a printed invitation.

All invitations should include the date, time, and place of the party. Including a map can be helpful for people who might not be familiar with the location. Invitations should specify if a party is to honor a special event, such as a birthday. They should also indicate any need for special clothing, such as swimsuits for a pool party.

You may wish to include the letters **RSVP** on your invitations. This is the abbreviation for a French phrase that means "please respond." Also include your phone number and e-mail address so your guests can let you know if they are coming (**Figure 27.2**).

Keep a list of all replies as you receive them. You will need this list for later planning.

The Menu

Almost any foods can be party foods. Sometimes the kind of gathering will help you plan the menu. Cookies and hot chocolate might be served at a sledding party. Heartier foods, such as sandwiches and pizza, might be served for an after-the-game get-together.

Menu Considerations

A key consideration when planning a menu is the guests' food preferences. Choose foods you think your guests will like. If any of your guests have special dietary needs, try to serve some

Ivan Baranov/Shutterstock.com

Figure 27.2 The abbreviation RSVP comes from the French phrase *Répondez s'il vous plait*. This abbreviation and the host's contact information should be written on formal invitations.

foods and drinks that meet those needs. For instance, offer meatless items for guests who are vegetarians. Also, avoid serving foods to which you know a guest is allergic.

Other factors to consider when planning a party menu include the budget, cooking skills, time schedule, and equipment. Party food can be costly. Preparing food yourself is likely to be less expensive than buying ready-made snacks. You may wish to give a party with friends who can help split the costs. For a casual gathering, you might ask each guest to bring a dish to share.

When you are having guests, choose familiar recipes you know you can prepare successfully. Save new recipes for a trial run later with your family or close friends. Limit the number of dishes that will require your last-minute attention. Choose one or more dishes you can prepare in advance. This gives you more time to enjoy your guests.

Do not finalize the menu until you check your equipment. See if you have all the cookware and serving utensils you will need. For instance, if you do not have a deep, straight-sided dish, do not plan to make a soufflé. Also check to see when you will need to use certain appliances. You may not have enough room to microwave two dishes at the same time. (You may be able to borrow or rent equipment, but check first.)

Appetizers

In a menu, you may want to include appetizers. **Appetizers** are light foods or beverages served to stimulate the appetite. They are often

Recipe for Good Food

Two-Way Roll-ups

Serves 4

Sweet

½ cup (125 mL) part-skim or low-fat ricotta cheese
1 tablespoon (15 mL) strawberry or raspberry preserves
½ teaspoon (2.5 mL) lemon zest
¼ cup (60 mL) finely chopped strawberries
2 whole-wheat soft taco-size tortillas

Savory

½ cup (125 mL) part-skim or low-fat ricotta cheese
½ teaspoon (2.5 mL) garlic powder
½ teaspoon (2.5 mL) dried oregano
1 teaspoon (5 mL) dill weed
⅛ teaspoon (0.6 mL) ground black pepper
¾ teaspoon (3.75 mL) hot pepper sauce
¼ teaspoon (1.25 mL) spicy mustard
2 teaspoons (10 mL) lemon juice
1 tablespoon (15 mL) finely chopped fresh parsley
2 tablespoons (30 mL) shredded carrots
2 tablespoons (30 mL) finely chopped broccoli
2 tablespoons (30 mL) finely chopped red bell pepper
1 green onion, thinly sliced
2 whole-wheat soft taco-size tortillas

1. To make the filling for the desired version, place all the ingredients except the tortillas in a medium mixing bowl. Stir together until thoroughly combined.
2. Place each tortilla on a sheet of wax paper.
3. Spoon half the filling onto each tortilla and spread to evenly cover to within ¼ inch (6 mm) of the edge.
4. Roll each tortilla up tightly and wrap the roll in the wax paper sheet.
5. Place wrapped rolls in the freezer for 10 minutes or refrigerate for 2 hours.
6. Unwrap rolls. Trim off both ends of each roll. Slice trimmed rolls into 6 pieces each.
7. Place pieces on a serving plate with cut sides up to show the colorful pinwheel fillings.

Per savory roll-up: 28 calories (32% from fat), 2 g protein, 4 g carbohydrate, 1 g fat, 3 mg cholesterol, 1 g fiber, 44 mg sodium.

Per sweet roll-up: 31 calories (29% from fat), 2 g protein, 5 g carbohydrate, 1 g fat, 3 mg cholesterol, 0 g fiber, 36 mg sodium.

served at the beginning of a meal. Appetizers are also popular as party foods.

Instead of serving chips and pretzels at your next party, be creative and try making appetizers. Choose appetizers that guests will find easy to *nibble* (eat slowly) while they mingle. Remember to select both hot and cold appetizers, using ingredients with a variety of flavors, colors, and textures (**Figure 27.3**).

A microwave oven might be used to save time when preparing hot appetizers. Mini pizzas, toasted nuts, cocktail sausages, chicken wings, and hot dips are just a few of the tasty appetizers that can be microwaved. Many of these foods can be prepared ahead of time and then microwaved at the last minute.

Appetizers may or may not cost less than serving a full meal. Consider how many appetizers you expect each guest to eat. Also compare costs of ingredients when choosing your menu.

Figure 27.3   When selecting appetizers, aim for variety. What are your favorite appetizers?

The Meal Service

If serving a meal at a gathering, decide how to serve it. Perhaps appetizers may be served in the living room before the meal. This will help eliminate clutter at the table. Likewise, a dessert can be served in the living room after the meal. This will give you a chance to clear the table and start to clean up the kitchen. A serving tray can help you serve courses away from the table more easily.

Meals can be served in several ways. The style of service selected will depend on the formality of the meal, the menu, and the availability of help.

The six major styles of meal service are American or family, Russian or continental, English, compromise, blue plate, and buffet. They

Learn About...

Serving Party Foods

When serving party foods, be sure an appropriate serving utensil accompanies each dish. Use serving spoons for soft foods and serving forks for meats. Tongs work well for serving individual items, such as shrimp and fresh vegetables. When guests will be approaching a buffet table from both sides, place two serving utensils with each dish. You may wish to place bowls of snacks in a few spots so they are accessible in all the areas guests will be.

Throughout the duration of a party, continue to check on the supply of foods and drinks. Refill bowls and trays as they become empty. Refresh melted ice under chilled foods and in pitchers and beverage dispensers. When foods are gone, remove serving pieces. Wipe up spills and crumbs on serving tables to keep party foods safe as well as inviting.

Know and Apply

1. How many guests could you comfortably accommodate in your home if you were serving a meal? How many could you accommodate if you were just serving snacks?

2. What kinds of foods do you like to serve at parties?

differ in the way the guests are served and in the number of courses.

- **American (family style) service** is the style most often used in homes in the United States. In this style of service, the host fills serving dishes in the kitchen and takes them to the table. Diners serve themselves as they pass the serving dishes around the table. After clearing the table, the host may serve dessert at the table or from the kitchen.

- **Russian (continental) service** is the most formal style of meal service. In Russian service, serving dishes are never placed on the table. Instead, waiters serve guests filled plates of food, one course at a time. Plate replaces plate as one course is removed and another is served. This type of service is often used in fine restaurants and at state dinners.

- In **English service**, one of the hosts fills plates at the table and passes them from guest to guest until everyone is served. Because English service requires a lot of passing, it is best for use with small groups.

- **Compromise service** is a compromise between Russian service and English service. The salad or dessert course is often served from the kitchen. For the other courses, one of the hosts fills the plates and passes them around the table. One person acts as waiter to clear one course and bring in the next.

- **Blue plate service** is used in homes when serving small groups of people. It is also used at banquets where waiters are able to serve a crowd quickly. In blue plate service, the host fills plates in the kitchen and carries them to the dining room. The host may offer second helpings at the table or refill plates in the kitchen. One person clears the main course and then brings in the dessert course.

- **Buffet service** is often used for serving large numbers of people. A dining table, a buffet, or another surface may hold the serving dishes and utensils, dinnerware, flatware, and napkins. The guests serve themselves from the buffet.

Depending on the amount of space available, guests may eat at one large table or at several smaller tables. If space is limited, they may eat from plates held in their hands while sitting or standing. If guests will be seated at a table, the host may place napkins, flatware, and beverageware on the table ahead of time.

Buffet service requires careful menu planning. Equipment may be needed to keep hot foods hot and cold foods cold. Precutting foods into individual servings and pouring beverages ahead of time will make serving easier (**Figure 27.4**).

angelo gilardelli/Shutterstock.com

Figure 27.4   Organize the buffet so guests have easy access to foods and are not forced to reach over equipment used to keep food hot. What are some advantages of the buffet style of service?

The Host's Responsibilities

As the host, you have certain responsibilities to your guests. Before your guests arrive, be sure the house is clean and tidy. Put fresh soap and clean towels in the bathroom. Be sure to have a specific place for your guests' coats.

Welcoming Guests

As your guests begin to arrive, make introductions. Introduce a younger person to an older person by giving the older person's name first. Try to say something interesting about each person for a conversation starter. You might say, "Mary Lewis, I would like you to meet LaVarre Johnson. LaVarre worked as a camp counselor last summer."

A planned activity helps people get to know one another. Games, music, and dancing are good ways to break the ice.

Try to participate in your party as much as possible. Circulate from guest to guest instead of spending the evening with just one or two close friends. It is up to you to make all your guests feel welcome.

Waiting on the Table

If your gathering includes a meal, one of your responsibilities as host will be to wait on the table. Rules for waiting on the table are as flexible as rules for setting the table. The style of service and the menu help determine the way in which you clear the table and serve new courses.

Clear the table in a counterclockwise direction, beginning with the person seated to your right. Serve a new course in the same manner. You will use both hands when serving and clearing, but usually at different times. When serving or clearing plates, you should stand at the guest's left and place or remove the plate with your left hand. This avoids a possible collision with the water glass on the right.

Remove beverageware and unused knives and spoons from the guest's right side with your right hand. Place dessert flatware in the same manner, and pour water from the right with the right hand.

When clearing or serving, a cart or large tray can save time and steps. The order for removing and serving a course is listed in **Figure 27.5**.

The Guest's Responsibilities

A good guest also has responsibilities. These begin with the invitation. Always answer an invitation as soon as possible. You may be able to give an immediate response to a telephoned invitation. If not, you should answer

Waiting on the Table	
Removing a Course	
1.	Remove all serving dishes and utensils from the table and take them to the kitchen.
2.	Beginning with the appropriate person, remove the dinner plate from each guest's left with your left hand. Transfer the first plate to your right hand. Place the second plate on top of the first plate. Then remove the third plate with your left hand. Take cleared plates to a serving cart or the kitchen. Continue this process around the table in a counterclockwise direction until you have cleared all covers.
3.	Use a small tray to remove flatware and other items not needed for the next course.
4.	If necessary, refill water glasses from each guest's right, using your right hand. Use a clean napkin to catch drips.
Serving a Course	
1.	Place needed flatware, such as cake forks or dessertspoons, at each cover.
2.	Place cream, sugar, and other needed items on the table.
3.	Place needed dinnerware at each cover.
4.	Place food and/or beverages.

Figure 27.5   Following a standard order for clearing and serving courses makes meal service more efficient.

within a day or two. Formal events require a written response. When responding to an invitation, repeat the time and the date to avoid any misunderstandings.

Arriving as a Guest

Arrive at a party at the *designated* (chosen) time. Guests who arrive too early can disrupt last-minute preparations. Guests who arrive late can be the cause of a ruined meal.

Greet any members of your host's family who happen to be present. Follow house rules and always be courteous.

Offer to assist your host with last-minute details. Most hosts will appreciate your help filling serving dishes or carrying items to the table. Following a meal, you should also offer to help with cleanup tasks, such as clearing plates. If the host refuses your offer, do not insist.

Using Table Manners

When dining in a friend's home, use your best table manners. **Manners** refer to social behavior. Society sets rules of **etiquette**, which outline polite ways of behaving. Knowing proper etiquette will help you relax in unfamiliar settings because you will know how to behave. Those around you will also feel more at ease because your behavior will not be offensive to them.

Use of table manners begins before a meal. If you have a cell phone, silence it and put it away before you approach the table. Wait for your host to indicate where you should sit. Shortly after sitting down, open your napkin to a comfortable size and place it in your lap.

If the meal is served family style, your host will wait until everyone at the table is seated. Then he or she will begin passing serving dishes around the table. All dishes should be passed in a counterclockwise direction. Take an average portion of each food before passing the dish to the diner on your right. If you cannot eat something being served, simply pass the dish without comment. Later in the meal, if you would like more food, do not reach in front of another diner. Ask someone to pass the dish to you.

Once everyone at the table has been served all the dishes, wait for your host to begin eating. During the meal, use your eating utensils in the order in which they have been placed on

the table—from the outside in toward the plate (**Figure 27.6**). Place dirty utensils on the plates with which you used them. For instance, leave the salad fork on the salad plate. Never set a used eating utensil back on the table. If you drop a utensil, do not use it anymore. Your host should give you another one. As you are eating, take care not to place your elbows on the table. Keep your nondominant hand in your lap unless you are using it.

A few guidelines will help you eat certain foods in a proper manner. For instance, you should not take a bite from a whole slice of bread. Tear bread into quarters; tear biscuits and rolls into halves. Put butter on your bread and butter plate with the knife that accompanies the butter. Then use your table knife to spread butter on one piece of bread, biscuit, or roll at a time.

Some foods are considered to be *finger foods*, meaning you generally do not need to use utensils when eating them. Examples include corn on the cob, pizza, and hot dogs. At informal events, you can also pick up fried chicken, French fries, and whole fresh fruits with your fingers. At formal gatherings, however, you should use utensils when eating these foods. Many appetizers may be eaten by using your fingers even at formal events.

If you happen to eat foods such as watermelon and cherries, you can remove seeds and

Africa Studio/Shutterstock.com

Figure 27.6 In this table setting, you would start with the outermost forks and spoons and work your way in for each course. What should you do with utensils once you are done with them?

pits from your mouth with your fingers. You can also use your fingers to remove small fish bones from your mouth, being as *inconspicuous* (unnoticeable) as possible. Place these items on the side of your plate.

Using good manners also means practicing good hygiene. Do not put foods into a bowl of dip after you have had them in your mouth. Use a serving spoon to put a small amount of dip on your plate for dipping chips and vegetables. If you cough or sneeze at the table, use your handkerchief and quietly excuse yourself. If you have a coughing or sneezing spell, quietly excuse yourself and leave the table. Leave your napkin on your chair to indicate that you will be returning to the table.

When you have finished eating, place your knife on the rim of your plate with the sharp edge pointing toward the center. Place your fork parallel to the knife. Lay your napkin casually to the left of the plate. Wait for your host to invite you to leave the table.

Outdoor Entertaining

Outdoor meals are an important part of warm-weather entertaining. An outdoor meal can be as simple as fresh fruit, cheese, and a loaf of bread shared on a park bench. A neighborhood *clambake* (an outdoor gathering where clams and other foods are cooked) on the beach is a more elaborate type of outdoor entertaining.

Picnics are another type of outdoor entertaining. You can prepare picnic foods at home or cook them at the picnic site. Besides traditional hot dogs and hamburgers, consider expanding your picnic menus to include casseroles, salads, and international foods (**Figure 27.7**).

The foods you serve for a picnic and how you carry them depend somewhat on transportation and available facilities. If you plan to bicycle or hike to your picnic site, you will need foods that are compact and easy to carry. Finger foods, such as sandwiches, cut-up vegetables, fresh fruits, and bar cookies, would be good choices.

Picnics on the water usually have some space limitations, though not as many as picnics you reach by bicycle. On small boats, serve foods prepared in advance. On larger boats with cooking facilities, you can finish last-minute

oliveromg/Shutterstock.com

Figure 27.7   Foods that can be prepared ahead of time and are easy to transport are ideal for picnics.

preparations on the boat. Be sure to bring plenty of drinking water to stay hydrated when picnicking on the water.

Grilling

Picnics that include grilled foods are called *cookouts* or *barbecues*. You can cook food over an open fire or on a grill.

Following safety precautions when grilling can help you and others avoid accidents. Always place the grill in the open, away from *foliage* (plants), furniture, and buildings. Wear tight-fitting clothes and a heavy-duty apron. If you have long hair, tie it back away from your face. Do not use gasoline or kerosene to start the fire. Never pour lighter fluid over the coals once the fire has started. Keep all flammable materials away from the fire and have a spray bottle of water handy. Use it to extinguish flare-ups, which can occur when fat drips onto hot coals.

Light the charcoal in a grill about 30 minutes before you want to begin cooking. The time will vary somewhat depending on the wind, the location of the grill, and the kind of charcoal. Coals covered with a gray ash are ready for good heat distribution.

Many foods can be cooked outdoors. Meats, fish, and poultry are probably the most commonly grilled foods. You can put fruits and vegetables on skewers and cook them as kabobs

(**Figure 27.8**). You might also try wrapping them in heavy-duty foil and cooking them over the coals. You can wrap breads and biscuits in foil and warm them on a grill, too.

gkrphoto/Shutterstock.com

Figure 27.8 Kabobs can make healthful and delicious foods for outdoor entertaining. What are some foods that might typically be on a kabob?

Learn About...

Grilling Tools

A grill is an important barbecuing tool. Except for gas and electric grills, all grills use *charcoal briquettes* (pieces of compacted charcoal) for fuel. Place charcoal in the grill's *fire box*. An electric starter or lighter fluid and matches or a lighter will be needed to ignite the charcoal. Put the *grate*, which will hold the food, in place over the charcoal.

In addition to a grill, tongs, a long-handled fork, and a broad turner are useful. A basting brush, fireproof mitts, and heavy-duty foil also come in handy when grilling. A food thermometer is needed so the temperature of the food that is being grilled can be checked.

Lasse Kristensen/Shutterstock.com

A chimney starter is another popular grilling tool. It is used to ignite charcoal without the use of lighter fluid.

Know and Apply

1. Do you prefer to eat foods that have been cooked on a gas, electric, or charcoal grill?

2. What is your favorite grilled food?

Transporting and Serving Foods Outdoors

Hot foods must be kept hot and cold foods must be kept cold when transporting and serving foods for outdoor meals. The general guideline is to leave foods at room temperature for no more than two hours. If temperatures are 90°F (32°C) or higher, however, foods should not be left out for more than one hour. Vacuum containers and insulated picnic coolers can keep foods at proper temperatures during transport. Keep foods for grilling in a cooler until the coals are ready.

When serving foods outdoors, remove foods from coolers in small amounts. Second helpings can always be served. Return all perishable foods to the insulated cooler as soon as possible.

Bring along plenty of aluminum foil to an outdoor gathering. Use it to line grills, shape serving trays, and wrap leftovers. Use plastic containers when possible. They are unbreakable, lighter than glass or metal, and better for the environment than disposable containers.

Keep a supply list inside the picnic basket. Frequently forgotten items include can openers, paring knives, salt and pepper, paper towels, eating utensils, and matches.

Cleaning Up

Litter is unsightly and often illegal. It attracts insects and animals, and it can cause fires. Most parks, forest preserves, and camping grounds have refuse containers available. Be sure to use them to properly dispose of all refuse (**Figure 27.9**).

Also, pack a couple of large plastic bags with the picnic supplies. They will come in handy when picnicking in an area that does not have refuse containers. Use one of the bags to hold trash until a suitable container can be found. Use the other bag to collect cans and bottles to take to a recycling facility.

Before leaving a picnic area, be sure to extinguish all fires, whether in a grill or on the ground. Use plenty of water and stir the coals. Make certain all the embers have stopped smoldering. Place your hand above the ashes. If the ashes still give off warmth, add more water.

Dining Out

When you want to socialize without going to a lot of trouble, dining out is an option for entertaining. Eating in restaurants, however, is not just for social occasions. Many meal managers use eating out as an alternative to preparing food at home.

Dennis Tokarzewski/Shutterstock.com

Figure 27.9 Most parks have refuse containers available for disposing of waste.

The cost of eating out varies according to where you go and what you order. Most of the time, however, eating out costs more than eating at home, even when you consider the cost of labor. The cost difference may be small when you look at the price of a single meal. The difference increases when you figure the price of feeding several people.

Eating out requires time as well as money. You save shopping, preparation, and cleanup time. On the other hand, you tend to spend more time at the table when dining out. You must allow time to be seated, place your order, receive your food, eat, and pay your check. Of course, traveling to and from a restaurant takes time as well.

Restaurant Basics

Regardless of the time and cost factors, dining out is an enjoyable experience. Following some basic guidelines will help you feel comfortable in any restaurant setting.

Being Seated

Before you arrive at a restaurant, you may make a reservation. A **reservation** is a request for a restaurant to hold a table for a guest. Some restaurants do not accept reservations. Others, especially certain small or formal restaurants, require reservations. In busy restaurants, reservations can ensure you will get a table when you arrive. To make a reservation, call the restaurant and request a table for the number of people in your group. Give your name and state the day and time you would like the table.

In some casual restaurants, diners seat themselves. Most restaurants, however, have a host. The host will greet you at the door and ask how many people are in your group. If you have made a reservation, give the host your name. The host will then show you to a table when one is available (**Figure 27.10**).

Ordering from a Menu

As you are seated, you will receive a menu listing the food items that are available. Items will generally be grouped under headings, such as *Appetizers*, *Salads*, *Entrees*, and *Desserts*. (**Entrees** are main courses.) Read the descriptions explaining how foods are prepared. This will allow you to choose items that suit your tastes.

Figure 27.10 A host greets restaurant guests and shows them to a table. What types of restaurants do not have hosts?

When reading a menu, note how items are priced. A fixed-price menu has one price for an entire meal. Usually, this price includes salad, bread, a main course, and side dishes. It may also include an appetizer, soup, dessert, and beverage. **A la carte** pricing means there is a separate price for each menu item.

You will have a few minutes to decide what you want to eat. Then your waiter will come to your table and ask what you wish to order. If you would like an appetizer, order it first. Then tell the waiter what entree you would like. State your preferences for optional items, such as side dishes and salad dressings. On some menus, items are numbered. You can simply order the number of the meal or food item you want.

Restaurants generally serve foods in courses. Your waiter will usually bring out beverages right after you place your order. If you have ordered appetizers, your waiter will serve them first. He or she will then serve soups and salads followed by entrees and side dishes (**Figure 27.11**). The waiter will serve dessert last. You may order dessert with the rest of the meal or after you have finished eating the entree.

Dining in Public

When dining in public, you are a guest of the restaurants to which you go. Your behavior should be that of a well-mannered visitor. Dress appropriately for the setting of the restaurant. Even in casual restaurants, it is important to look neat and clean and use good table manners. Follow the same guidelines you would use when eating in a friend's home.

Occasionally, you may have a problem with the foods or service in a restaurant. Perhaps your food seems unwholesome or is not prepared as you ordered it. Maybe the service is slow or the waiter forgot part of your order. Whatever the problem is, quietly call it to your waiter's attention. Avoid making a scene and disturbing other diners. If the waiter is unwilling or unable to correct the problem, ask to speak to the manager.

Your satisfaction can affect the success of a restaurant. In most cases, restaurant staff members will do their best to make your dining experience a pleasant one.

Paying the Bill

At the end of the meal, the waiter will bring a bill showing how much money you owe. When dining with others, you should know in advance who is going to pay the bill. When someone invites a person to go out for a meal, the person extending the invitation generally pays. When

Figure 27.11 In most restaurants, a waiter will bring out guests' entrees and side dishes.

Learn About...

Restaurant Tipping

Some restaurants automatically include a gratuity on the bill, especially for larger groups. If no gratuity is indicated, leave whatever you feel is proper. For average service, about 15 percent of the total bill is usually appropriate. If a waiter has given you special service, you may want to leave a larger tip.

If the waiter collects payment, you can leave the tip in the folder or on the plate or tray. If you pay the cashier, leave the tip inconspicuously on the table. If you pay with a credit or debit card, you can write the amount of your tip on the receipt. Then add the cost of the meal and the tip. Write the total on the receipt before signing your name.

El Nariz/Shutterstock.com

Great waitstaff are professional, well-groomed, and anticipate the customer's needs.

Know and Apply

1. Calculate the following restaurant tips. Round all answers to the nearest 10.

   A. 15 percent tip for a bill of $15.45

   B. 15 percent tip for a bill of $22.46

   C. 20 percent tip for a bill of $26.76

   D. 20 percent tip for a bill of $32.84

2. Describe the type of service offered by a waiter you would consider worthy of a larger-than-average tip.

---

a group of friends goes out to eat, each person often pays for his or her own meal.

Sometimes it may be easiest to simply split the bill equally among everyone in the group. Other times, each person will pay just for the foods he or she ordered. If you intend to pay this way, ask the waiter when ordering if you can have separate checks. This will make it easy for each person to know how much he or she owes.

Sometimes the bill will be in a folder or on a plate or small tray. Place either cash or a credit or debit card in the folder or on the plate or tray. The waiter will take the payment and bring you your change. (If you are paying with a credit card, your waiter will bring you a receipt to sign.) In casual restaurants, you may pay a cashier on the way out the door. Whether you pay the waiter or a cashier, it is customary to leave a **gratuity**, or **tip**, which is an amount of money paid for service received.

Types of Restaurants

The variety of restaurants is almost limitless. Restaurants offer all cuisines and a range of prices and formality. Some types of restaurants include fast-food restaurants, cafeterias and buffets, family restaurants, formal restaurants, and specialty restaurants.

Fast-Food Restaurants

The foodservice industry refers to fast-food restaurants as *quick-service restaurants* or *QSR*. These restaurants specialize in speedy service. They cater to people who are looking for quick, inexpensive meals.

Most fast-food restaurants have rather limited menus. The menu is usually posted above the counter near the restaurant entrance. All the foods on the menu can be prepared quickly. Many items are fried because frying allows foods to cook rapidly.

Foods at fast-food restaurants are relatively inexpensive. The high sales volume and limited service help keep prices down. Because customers do not receive service from waiters, they do not have to leave tips in fast-food restaurants. This also saves customers money.

Cafeterias and Buffets

Cafeterias have a variety of prepared foods placed along a serving line. Customers carry a tray along the line and select the foods they want. Foods are served in individual portions, and each item is priced separately. Customers pay for the items on their tray when they reach the end of the line (**Figure 27.12**).

Buffets are similar to cafeterias as far as the way the food is served. At buffets, however, customers generally pay a fixed price for the meal. They can serve themselves as much of each food on the buffet line as they like. They can also return to the serving line for more food as many times as they wish.

Neither cafeterias nor buffets have waiters to take customers' food orders at the table, though these servers may take beverage orders, refill coffee, and clear dirty dishes. For these services, leaving a tip of about 10 percent of the food bill is appropriate.

Family Restaurants

Family restaurants offer casual, comfortable dining. These restaurants appeal to people dining out with children. Prices are reasonable, so meals can fit into a family food budget. Family restaurants offer a variety of popular menu items. They generally also have separate menus listing a few items that are typically liked by children. This allows each person to order a different favorite food.

Formal Restaurants

Formal restaurants offer an elegant dining atmosphere. Customers dine on fine foods and receive excellent service. In keeping with the atmosphere, guests in formal restaurants should dress more formally.

Skilled chefs usually prepare the foods served at formal restaurants. They use only the freshest ingredients. In addition to items listed on the menu, your waiter may describe daily specials created by the chef.

The high-quality food and service at formal restaurants often cause them to be rather expensive. Some people also tend to tip a bit more in these restaurants than they would elsewhere. Be prepared for these expenses before you go to a formal restaurant.

Specialty Restaurants

Specialty restaurants focus on a specific type of food. Pizza parlors, steak houses, and restaurants that serve international foods are all specialty restaurants (**Figure 27.13**).

Specialty restaurants come in all price ranges. Some fast-food, family, and formal restaurants are also specialty restaurants.

Figure 27.12 Cafeterias feature foods for purchase in individual portions. How are cafeterias different from buffets?

Figure 27.13 Some specialty restaurants focus on serving one type of food. For example, some restaurants specialize in serving sushi.

Chapter 27 Review and Expand

Summary

Planning a gathering begins with choosing a theme. Then you need to make up a guest list and extend invitations. You need to choose a menu and determine how you will serve it. As a host, you have the responsibility of making your guests feel comfortable. In return, your guests have the responsibility of showing respect and using their best manners.

Almost everyone enjoys picnics and barbecues when the weather is nice. No matter what type of outdoor entertaining you do, you need to transport and serve food carefully to keep it safe. You also need to be sure the outdoor area is clean when your party leaves.

Dining out can be an everyday experience or a special treat. Knowing how to make reservations, order, and tip in a restaurant will help you feel more comfortable when dining out. Your choice of restaurants includes fast-food, cafeteria, buffet, family, formal, and specialty establishments. You should be able to find a menu and a price range to suit any taste.

Vocabulary Activities

1. **Content Terms**   Select 10 terms from the list of key terms at the beginning of this chapter. Reread the sections that introduce each term. Then write down each definition in your own words. Keep your notes to prepare for the exam.

RSVP	buffet service
appetizer	manners
American (family style) service	etiquette
	reservation
Russian (continental) service	entree
	a la carte
English service	gratuity
compromise service	tip
blue plate service	

2. **Academic Terms**   For each of the following terms, draw a cartoon bubble to express the meaning of each term as it relates to the chapter.

celebratory	nibble
compatible	designated

inconspicuous	foliage
clambake	

Review

Write your answers using complete sentences when appropriate.

3. What aspects of planning a party can be influenced by choosing a theme?

4. What information should be included on all invitations?

5. List four factors that should be considered when planning a party menu.

6. What type of meal service is used most often in homes in the United States?

7. In what style of meal service do guests serve themselves from a table that holds the serving dishes and dinnerware?

8. Give three responsibilities of a host.

9. In what direction should a table be cleared?

10. List five examples of table manners.

11. List four important safety precautions you should follow when cooking outdoors.

12. How long can food be safely left out of a cooler at an outdoor event?

13. What factors should a meal manager consider when planning to eat out instead of preparing food at home?

14. In what type of restaurant menu are food items priced individually?

15. What should you do if you have a problem with the food or service in a restaurant?

16. What type of restaurant offers individually priced food items along a serving line?

Core Skills

17. **Research, Reading, Writing**   Choose a culture other than your own. Research the types of events for which people in this culture entertain. Do they have theme parties? What types of foods do they serve? Write an informative paper to share what you learn. Edit and refine your writing to ensure your ideas are presented in a logical, organized manner.

Chapter 27 Review and Expand

18. **Technology** Use card-making software to create and print party invitations. Also, print addresses on the envelopes or make address labels before sending invitations.

19. **Math** Vegetable trays are popular party foods. Compare the cost of purchasing a vegetable tray from the supermarket with the cost of assembling a vegetable tray at home. Consider the cost of labor as well as the costs of all components on the tray.

20. **Writing, Speaking** Write a public service announcement (PSA) to raise awareness about using good table manners. You can focus on a single guideline or on the use of manners in general. Write a slogan and design a poster to summarize your message. Present your poster as you deliver the PSA to the class.

21. **Research, Reading, Writing** Use reliable print or online resources to research food-borne illnesses that can result from improperly handling food. Write a two-page report about how to safely transport and serve picnic and barbecue food in order to avoid illness. Cite your sources in your paper. Reread and revise your report for spelling, grammar, and organization.

22. **Speaking, Listening** Write five daily specials you would offer in a restaurant. Working with a partner, one of you will assume the role of a waiter; the other will assume the role of a restaurant patron. The waiter will read the daily specials he or she created. The patron can ask questions about the specials before ordering. The waiter will answer the patron's questions and then recite the order to be sure he or she heard it correctly. Switch roles and repeat the exercise.

23. **Speaking, Writing** Working in small groups, write a script for and perform a short play demonstrating the responsibilities of both the host and guest at a get-together. The "host" should greet his guests and wait on the table. "Guests" should demonstrate proper etiquette and table manners.

24. **Career Readiness Practice** Research shows that parents tend to make lower-calorie food choices for their children when they have calorie information for menu items. Investigate calorie information for children's menu items at local fast-food restaurants. Compile this information into an organized food guide and distribute the guide to parents. Encourage parents to keep copies of the guide in their cars and refer to them when making trips through fast-food drive-throughs.

Critical Thinking and Problem Solving

25. **Create** Working in a small group, plan a social gathering. Begin by choosing a theme. Then create an invitation, write a menu, and plan appropriate activities.

26. **Analyze** Analyze menus from three casual restaurants and three formal restaurants. Note the number, types, descriptions, and prices of items on each menu. Also look at the layout of the menus. What generalizations can you make about the differences between these two types of restaurants?

27. **Create** Work in a team of four students to write a script for a training video for foodservice workers. The video should demonstrate how to serve meals using one of the styles of meal service discussed in the chapter. Be sure your script includes actions as well as dialogue. Have one team member assume each of the following roles: director, camera operator, actor playing a foodservice worker, and actor playing a restaurant customer. Rehearse the script and then shoot the video. Use editing software to edit the video, adding text, music, and voiceovers as needed to clearly communicate instructions. Show the finished video in class.

Chapter 28
Preserving Foods

Zigzag Mountain Art/Shutterstock.com

Objectives

After studying this chapter, you will be able to
- **determine** factors that cause food spoilage;
- **describe** techniques for home canning and making jellied and pickled products;
- **explain** procedures for freezing and drying foods; and
- **differentiate** among methods of commercial food preservation.

Reading Prep

Arrange a study session to read the chapter aloud with a classmate. Take turns reading each section. Stop at the end of each section to discuss what you think its main points are. Take notes of your study session to share with the class.

Content Terms

mold
yeast
canning
raw pack
hot pack
headspace
processing time
botulism
pectin
pickling

quick-freezing
freezer burn
ascorbic acid
freeze-drying
irradiation
aseptic packaging
retort packaging
vacuum packaging
modified atmosphere
    packaging (MAP)
shelf life

Academic Terms

bountiful
overabundance
concave

corrode
rancid

Even primitive people realized food was subject to spoilage. They understood they needed some form of preservation to keep food from decaying. They learned to preserve food when it was *bountiful* (plentiful) for times of scarcity.

Today's consumers can buy foods in all seasons, but many people still like to preserve food. This is especially true of people who have fruit and vegetable gardens. Three popular methods of food preservation are canning, freezing, and drying.

Food Spoilage

Bacteria, mold, and yeast are all microorganisms related to food preservation. Bacteria can cause foodborne illnesses. Bacteria can also cause chemical reactions in food, some of which lead to spoilage. **Mold** is a growth produced on damp or decaying organic matter or on living organisms. **Yeast** is a microscopic fungus that can cause fermentation in preserved foods, resulting in spoilage.

These microorganisms, along with enzymes, have both good and bad effects on food. (Just as enzymes cause chemical reactions in the body, they can also cause chemical reactions in foods.) Some bacteria are used to make buttermilk and sauerkraut. Certain molds are used in curing some cheeses such as Roquefort and Camembert. Yeast makes breads rise. Enzymes ripen foods and tenderize meats (**Figure 28.1**).

Ozgur Coskun/Shutterstock.com

Figure 28.1 Yogurt gets its thick, creamy texture from the desirable effects of a certain type of bacteria.

The bad effect of microorganisms is food spoilage. Enzymes can cause foods to deteriorate. They can soften the texture, change the color, and impair the flavor of foods. To preserve food, the bacteria, mold, yeast, and enzymes must be inactivated or destroyed.

Canning Foods

Canning is a food preservation process that involves sealing food in airtight containers. The food is heated and held at a high temperature for a period long enough to kill harmful microorganisms.

People can foods at home for many reasons. Many home canners enjoy preserving their own special recipes of items like barbecue or spaghetti sauces. Some people can to avoid wasting an *overabundance* (excess; surplus) of seasonal fruits and vegetables. Others want to avoid the preservatives added to commercially canned foods.

Still another reason for home canning is the low cost. Home canning can reduce food costs if it is done frequently. The equipment is expensive, so it should be purchased only if it will be used for several years. People who can foods may find they are able to save more money if they grow the food themselves.

Canning procedures must be followed carefully to ensure proper preservation of food. Step-by-step directions on home canning may be obtained from manufacturers of canning products and county extension agents.

Canning Jars and Closures

Most foods that are canned at home are put into *glass* jars (**Figure 28.2**). Use only jars especially made for home canning. Do not use jars from commercially canned foods, such as peanut butter or mayonnaise. These will not seal tightly.

The most popular canning jar closures are two-piece vacuum caps. The pieces are a metal screw band and a flat metal lid that has a sealing compound on one side. When using this type of closure, wipe the rim of the filled jar. Put the flat lid on the jar with the sealing compound next to the glass. Then screw the band down tightly over the lid.

A flat metal lid with sealing compound should be used only once. However, canning jars and screw bands can be reused as long as they

Zigzag Mountain Art/Shutterstock.com

Figure 28.2   Glass jars are the most popular type of container used to can foods at home.

are in good condition. Be sure all jars are perfect. Discard jars that have cracks or chips, as these defects prevent airtight seals. Discard metal bands that are dented or rusty.

Preparing Jars and Closures

Wash all canning jars in hot, soapy water and rinse them well before using them. Then heat the jars to help keep them from breaking. When canning foods that are processed less than 10 minutes, such as jellies, the jars need to be sterilized. Leave the jars in the hot environment until they are needed. Then remove and fill them one at a time.

Like the jars, the lids and screw bands need to be washed before using them. After washing in hot, soapy water, dry the screw bands and set them aside. Allow the flat metal lids to heat in very hot (but not boiling) water for at least 10 minutes. Remove them one at a time, as needed.

Filling Canning Jars

Jars can be filled by either the raw pack or hot pack method. For **raw pack**, pack raw fruits or vegetables into containers. Cover with boiling water, juice, or syrup. For **hot pack**, heat food in water, steam, syrup, or juices. Pack loosely in jars and cover with cooking liquid or boiling water.

When filling the jars, leave some headspace. **Headspace** is space between the food and the closure of a food storage container. Follow the canning recipe to determine the correct amount of headspace. Leaving too much or too little headspace may prevent jars from sealing properly (**Figure 28.3**).

Liquid in the canning jars should fill all spaces between food and cover all the food. Food that is not covered tends to darken. Remove air bubbles trapped in the food with a nonmetal spatula to prevent food from darkening.

Pressure Canning

The high temperatures used in canning destroy microorganisms and enzymes. The appropriate temperature varies with the canning method. Since some microorganisms are more heat-resistant than others, the canning method used depends on the type of food being canned.

Use *pressure canning* for green beans and other low-acid vegetables. You can use it for meats, poultry, and fish, too. These foods need a higher temperature than that of boiling water

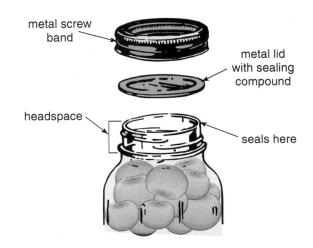

Figure 28.3   The amount of headspace left between food and the two-piece vacuum cap sealing a canning jar depends on the food being canned.

to destroy food-spoiling microorganisms and enzymes.

Pressure canning is done in a *pressure canner*. This type of canner can reach 240°F to 250°F (115°C to 120°C) by building up steam under pressure. Pack low-acid foods into sterilized canning jars. Cover the food with liquid, and cap the jars. Put water in the bottom of the canner, and place the filled jars in the canner on a rack. Lock down the lid of the pressure canner to make the canner steam-tight. After sealing the canner, place it on the range.

A vent in the lid, called a *petcock*, allows air to be exhausted and steam to be released as needed. When the petcock is closed, the temperature and pressure inside the canner rise. A *pressure gauge* measures steam pressure inside the canner. A *safety valve* in the lid prevents explosions. It works only if pressure or temperature inside the canner becomes dangerously high.

When the proper pressure has been reached inside the canner, processing time begins. **Processing time** is the amount of time canned goods remain under heat (or under heat and pressure) in a canner. Processing time varies according to the food being processed.

When processing time is complete, remove the canner from the heat and allow pressure to return to zero. Lift the cover of the canner away from the body to prevent steam burns. Then remove the jars from the canner and allow them to cool.

Boiling Water Canning

Use boiling water canning for high-acid foods, such as acidified tomatoes, fruits, and pickled vegetables. This method of canning is done in a *boiling water canner* (**Figure 28.4**). The temperature of boiling water is enough to destroy the microorganisms and enzymes that cause food spoilage in these foods.

For this method of canning, pack food into clean canning jars, cover it with liquid, and cap the jars. For raw-pack jars, heat water in the canner until it is hot. For hot-pack jars, heat the water to boiling. Set the filled jars on the rack in the canner so water surrounds each one. Add boiling water to bring the water level above the tops of the jars. Cover the canner and allow the water to come to a rolling boil.

When the water comes to a rolling boil, the processing time begins. As with pressure

Food Science

Controlling Microorganisms

Microorganisms need favorable temperatures and moisture to grow on food. By removing either of these conditions, the spoiling action of microorganisms can be stopped and the food can be preserved. Canning removes favorable temperatures by using heat that destroys both microorganisms and enzymes.

Freezing also removes favorable temperatures with cold conditions that prevent microorganisms from growing and retard the action of enzymes. Drying preserves food by removing moisture needed for the growth of microorganisms. To control enzyme activity, fruits and vegetables are treated before drying.

Jenn Huls/Shutterstock.com

Figure 28.4 Boiling water canners are used to process high-acid foods.

canning, processing time varies with the type of food being canned. The water boils steadily throughout the processing time. When processing time is up, quickly remove the jars from the canner and allow them to cool.

Storing Canned Foods

Test the seals on canning jars the day after canning. To do this, press the center of each lid. Make sure it is *concave* (curved inwardly) and does not flex up and down. Then remove the screw band and make sure the lid cannot be lifted off with the fingertips. If the jars pass this inspection, they have formed a good vacuum seal.

If you find a leaky jar, use the food right away. You may also can the food again, treating it as if it were fresh. Check jars and lids carefully for defects before using them again.

When jars are completely cool, carefully remove screw bands. Wash bands and store them in a dry place for future use. Wipe jars clean with a soapy cloth, rinse them well, and dry them thoroughly. Label each jar, listing the type of food and the date (**Figure 28.5**). If more than one lot was canned on the same day, list the lot number, too.

When foods are properly canned and stored in a cool, dry, dark place, they will last as long as a year. A cool temperature helps foods maintain appearance, flavor, and nutrients. Do not allow canned foods to freeze, as this will cause a loss of texture and appeal. Dampness may *corrode* (slowly deteriorate) metal lids and cause leakage. This makes the foods spoil. Heat and light may cause food to lose some of its eating quality after only a few weeks.

Checking for Spoilage

Before eating home-canned foods, take certain safety precautions. When the jars are opened, look for bulging lids, leaks, spurting liquid, off odors, mold, gas bubbles, and unusually soft food. These are signs of broken seals and spoilage. If any of these signs are present, do not taste the food. Dispose of it so neither humans nor animals will eat it. Use a food waste disposer or burn it.

Botulism is a foodborne illness caused by eating foods containing the spore-forming bacteria *Clostridium botulinum*. These bacteria can occur in home-canned foods that were improperly processed. Botulism is the most dangerous

©iStock.com/Clubhouse Arts

Figure 28.5 Always label jars with the contents and the date they were packed. Why is the date important to include?

type of foodborne illness. Even a taste of food containing the toxin produced by these bacteria can be fatal. This is why following only the latest, researched recommendations for canning methods and processing times is so important. Using proper canning methods is especially important for low-acid foods.

The texture of foods spoiled by botulism may be very soft and mushy. The foods may smell like *rancid* (pungent, expired) cheese. Some spoiled foods, however, look and smell normal. If there is any question about the safety of a home-canned food, do not take any chances. Throw it out. If the food looks spoiled, foams, or has an off odor during heating, *destroy it!*

Making Jellied Products

The same canning principles are used in making jellied products. Jellied products include jelly, jam, marmalade, preserves, and conserves.

Jelly is a firm, clear product made from fruit juice. *Jam* is a less firm product made from crushed fruit that is cooked to a fairly even consistency. *Marmalade* is a tender jelly containing small pieces of fruit and fruit rind. It is often made from citrus fruit and it may contain a mixture of fruits. *Preserves* are slightly jellied products that contain whole fruits or large pieces of fruit in thick syrup (**Figure 28.6**). *Conserves* are jams made from a mixture of fruits, usually including citrus fruits and sometimes raisins and nuts. *Fruit butters* are not jellied products. They are spreads made from cooked, pureed fruit.

Ingredients

Four basic ingredients are needed to make jellied products. The first of these is fruit. Fruit gives jellied products their flavors and colors.

Almost any flavorful fruit can be used. Fruit also contributes some or all of two other basic ingredients—pectin and acid.

Pectin is a carbohydrate found in all fruits. It makes fruit juices jell. Some fruits have more pectin than others. If the fruit being used is low in pectin, pectin can be purchased in powdered or liquid form. Either kind can be used with any fruit. Powdered pectin and liquid pectin are not interchangeable, however. Follow the recipe. Use the form and amount of pectin the recipe suggests.

Acid is the third basic ingredient in jellied products. It works with pectin to make the products jell. It also adds flavor. All fruits contain varying amounts of acids. Lemon juice or citric acid can be added to fruits that are low in acid.

Sugar is the fourth basic ingredient. It helps jellied products become firm. It also adds flavor and helps preserve the products. Leaving some

Lilyana Vynogradova/Shutterstock.com; Lilyana Vynogradova/Shutterstock.com

Figure 28.6 Jelly is a clear product made from fruit juice. Jams and preserves contain pieces of the fruit as well as the juice. Which of these products will become jelly?

of the sugar out of a recipe will cause the jellied product to be runny. However, recipes are available for making jellied products with artificial sweeteners for people who want to avoid sugar.

Processing Jellied Products

Jellied products must be processed by the boiling water method. After combining and boiling the ingredients, pour the mixtures into hot, sterilized canning jars. Then seal and process the jars. After cooling, label the products and store them in a dark, dry, cool place.

Uncooked jam is a jellied product that is easy to make and does not require boiling water processing. It can be prepared by adding sugar and commercial pectin to crushed, fully-ripe fruit. Uncooked jams keep up to three weeks in the refrigerator or up to a year in the freezer. However, they spoil quickly at room temperature.

Pickling

Pickles are among the foods that many home canners enjoy preparing. When people hear the term *pickles*, they often think of various types of pickled cucumbers, such as gherkins and dill chips. However, **pickling** is a food preservation technique that involves soaking various foods in a vinegar or salt solution.

A vinegar solution preserves pickled foods because the acid prevents the growth of bacteria that can cause foodborne illness. Bread and butter pickles are a common example of a food preserved with vinegar. You might also see pickled green beans, peppers, okra, watermelon rind, pears, and crabapples. Even foods like eggs, beef, and herring are pickled (**Figure 28.7**).

Soaking foods in a salt solution, or *brine*, causes them to *ferment*. This happens as helpful bacteria naturally found on the surface of foods create lactic acid, which preserves the food. Sauerkraut and many dill pickles are fermented.

The levels of acid and salt used in these processes are important to ensure food safety. Recipes for pickled and fermented products should be followed carefully.

For long-term storage, many pickled foods can be canned in a boiling water canner. But the pickling process alone is enough to preserve most foods for a couple months.

HLPhoto/Shutterstock.com

Figure 28.7 Pickled herring is a popular dish in Scandinavian countries.

Freezing Foods

One of the best ways to preserve the fresh flavor of food is to freeze it. Frozen foods are popular because they offer consumers many advantages. When prepared, frozen foods have the appearance, taste, and nutritive value of fresh foods. They are available at any time of year, and they are easy to prepare. Frozen foods can also help save money. They can be purchased when prices are low and stored for later use.

Many frozen foods that are bought at the grocery store are preserved by **quick-freezing**. Quick-frozen foods are subjected to temperatures between –25°F and –40°F (–32°C and –40°C) for a short time. These extremely low temperatures produce very small ice crystals in foods (**Figure 28.8**). When foods are frozen more slowly, larger ice crystals may form. These large

Figure 28.8 Frozen foods may develop ice crystals.

crystals damage the cell structure of foods and change their textures. After quick-freezing, foods are maintained at a normal freezing temperature of 0°F (–18°C).

Foods frozen at home have the same advantages as commercially frozen foods. Using the right equipment and following recommended procedures will ensure the highest quality in home-frozen foods.

Equipment

A properly operating freezer and suitable containers are needed to freeze foods at home. The key to maintaining quality is to keep moisture in and air out of frozen foods. Therefore, containers used in freezing must be moisture- and vapor-resistant. Foods that have not been wrapped securely may develop off-flavors and lose nutrients, texture, and color. Some foods may develop **freezer burn**, or dry, tough areas. Freezer burn occurs where dry air from the freezer has come in contact with food surfaces, causing dehydration.

Most glass and plastic food storage containers with tight-fitting covers are suitable for freezer use. However, do not freeze foods in glass jars unless they are labeled to be used for freezing. Regular glass jars can break easily at freezer temperatures.

Other choices for packaging foods include freezer bags and heavy-duty aluminum foil.

Plastic-coated paper and clear freezer wraps can also be used. These flexible materials work well when freezing bulky items, such as roasts and cakes.

Freezing Fruits and Vegetables

When selecting fresh produce for freezing, choose ripe, top-quality fruits and young, tender vegetables. Work with small batches. Carefully sort and wash each piece but do not allow them to soak. Pit, trim, and slice fruits and vegetables as desired.

Preparing Fruits and Vegetables for Freezing

Some fruits need treatment with ascorbic acid to prevent darkening. **Ascorbic acid** is a food additive that prevents color and flavor loss. It also adds nutritive value. (*Ascorbic acid* is another name for *vitamin C*.) Ascorbic acid is available in crystalline form or in a mixture with sugar and sometimes citric acid. Follow manufacturer's instructions for use.

Most vegetables must be blanched in boiling water or steam before freezing. This inactivates the enzymes. When blanching is complete, cool vegetables quickly and drain well. Quick cooling prevents vitamin loss and spoilage.

Packing Fruits and Vegetables for Freezing

Pack most vegetables and some fruits using the *dry pack* method. Carefully pour prepared produce into freezer containers. Gently tap containers to pack food closely without crushing. Do not add liquid.

Frozen sweetened fruits usually have a better texture than unsweetened fruits. Therefore, many people use the sugar pack or syrup pack method when freezing fruits. For the *sugar pack* method, place prepared fruit in a shallow pan and add sugar. Turn pieces of fruit gently until the sugar dissolves and forms a syrup (**Figure 28.9**). Carefully pack the fruit into freezer containers. Gently tap each container to exclude air. For the *syrup pack* method, prepare syrup and chill. Place prepared fruit directly into a container. Pour the chilled syrup over the fruit.

For all packing methods, leave 1 inch (2.5 cm) of headspace to allow for expansion. Wipe the top of each container with a clean, damp cloth. Seal tightly and label with the name of the food and the date.

Marzia Giacobbe/Shutterstock.com

Figure 28.9   Preparing fruits in a syrup before freezing them helps the fruit retain its texture. What other benefits are there to using the syrup pack method?

Freeze all foods at 0°F (–18°C) or lower immediately after packing. When food freezes too slowly, a loss in quality or food spoilage may occur. Freeze food in batches, giving each batch a chance to freeze before adding the next batch. This will keep freezer temperature constant. Leave a little space between items in the freezer to allow room for cold air to circulate. Follow the freezer manufacturer's instructions concerning quantity and placement of foods.

Freezing Meat, Poultry, and Fish

Meats and poultry require no special preparation before freezing. Often, however, large meat cuts are trimmed and packaged in serving-sized pieces. Choose only top quality meat cuts for freezing. Poultry may be frozen whole or in pieces.

Meat and poultry can be frozen in their original wrappers for up to two weeks (**Figure 28.10**). For extended freezer storage, add an extra layer of freezer wrap over the original wrapping.

Purchased fish should be rinsed under cold running water and dried well with paper towels before freezing. Then wrap fish securely in plastic wrap. Follow this with a layer of heavy-duty foil.

Freeze meat, poultry, and fish as soon as possible after purchasing them. Be sure to label with product name, weight, and date. Turn the

freezer control to its lowest possible setting for the first 24 to 48 hours. Then maintain the temperature at 0°F (–18°C) as for fruits and vegetables.

Freezing Prepared Foods

Baked pastry, cookies, breads, and cakes all freeze well. Wrap these items carefully in moistureproof and vaporproof wrapping.

Casseroles and stews can be frozen in their baking dishes. To save space, line the baking dish with foil. Fill the lined dish with food, wrap it well, and freeze. The foil liner will allow you to easily remove the frozen block of food from the dish. Then you can rewrap it, label it, and return it to the freezer. The casserole dish can then be used for other foods and the food will take less room in the freezer.

Be sure to label all prepared foods with the name of the product and the date. Freeze promptly and use within the recommended time.

Some foods do not freeze well. These include salad greens, custards, gelatin products, meringues, sour cream, and hard-cooked egg whites. Sandwiches containing salad dressing or mayonnaise do not freeze well, either.

Some foods can be stored longer than others. Beef, whole turkeys, and vegetables, for example, can be stored for up to one year. Soups can be stored for about six months, while cookies and unbaked pies should be used within three months.

©iStock.com/tbaeff

Figure 28.10   If freezing meat, poultry, or fish for a short period of time, use the original packaging to store the frozen food.

Learn About...

Thawing Frozen Foods

Organisms that cause foodborne illnesses multiply quickly at room temperature. Therefore, never thaw foods—especially meat, poultry, and fish—at room temperature. Allow them to thaw overnight in a refrigerator. Use the defrost setting on a microwave oven to thaw foods quickly right before cooking. Foods can also be allowed to thaw during the cooking process.

Some frozen foods, such as vegetables, should be cooked without thawing. Thaw prepared and baked products in their original wrappers to prevent dehydration. Thaw fruits in their original covered containers to prevent *enzymatic browning* (discoloration caused by exposure to air). Fruits have a more appealing texture if served with a few ice crystals remaining.

Meats, poultry, and fish can be cooked either frozen or thawed. Cooking frozen food, however, takes longer than cooking fresh or thawed foods. Consider the extra cooking time when planning meals.

If meat is partially thawed but still firm, it can be refrozen. The meat will have a loss in quality, but it will still be safe to eat. Refreeze it and use it as soon as possible. If the meat is fully thawed but still very cold, refrigerate it and use it immediately. Do not refreeze it.

Know and Apply

1. Why should you never thaw foods at room temperature?
2. What is enzymatic browning?

Drying Foods

Food drying, or dehydrating, is one of the oldest and simplest methods of food preservation. Microorganisms that cause food spoilage need moisture to grow. Drying removes moisture, thus stopping the growth of microorganisms. When drying foods, speed is important. Using a temperature that will dry food without cooking it is important, too.

The many advantages of dried foods make them especially popular with campers, cyclists, and backpackers. Dried foods are lightweight. They take up less space than fresh foods, and they taste good.

Campers are not the only ones who use dried foods. Many people add dried vegetables to soups. A variety of dried mixes are popular convenience products. People enjoy jerky and dried meat sticks as snacks. Dried fruits make good snacks and can be added to salads, desserts, and a variety of other foods.

Fruit leathers are pliable sheets of dried fruit puree. They can be made from almost any fruit. Fruit leathers are nutritious and lightweight for packing in school lunches or taking on camping trips.

Preparing Fruits and Vegetables for Drying

Vegetables must be dried completely to prevent spoilage. Fruits, because of their high sugar content, may retain more moisture than vegetables after drying.

Choose fruits at optimum maturity. Wash, sort, and discard bruised, overripe fruit. Peel and core fruits, if necessary. Berries and other smaller fruits can be dried whole. Larger fruits will dry more evenly and quickly if cut into halves, quarters, or ¼-inch (6 mm) slices.

An ascorbic or citric acid solution can be used to keep fruit from darkening. Ascorbic and citric acid crystals are often sold at drugstores and supermarkets. Follow package directions for mixing a preservative solution. You can also make a solution by using equal parts of water and lemon juice. Soak fruits for 10 minutes and drain well before dehydrating.

Select young, tender vegetables in prime condition. Wash vegetables thoroughly and drain. Trim and cut them into small pieces. Smaller pieces dry more quickly and evenly. Blanch prepared vegetables using steam or boiling water. Drain well and dry with a towel.

Procedure for Drying

Two popular methods of drying fruits and vegetables at home are sun drying and oven drying (**Figure 28.11**). Sun drying is less costly, but it relies on the weather.

Maxsol/Shutterstock.com

Figure 28.11 Sun-dried tomatoes are one of the most popular kinds of sun-dried foods.

Drying in the oven does not depend on the weather, so it can be done at any time. Oven drying can be done in a food dehydrator following manufacturer's instructions. Oven drying can also be done in a conventional oven.

To dry food in a conventional oven, spread food evenly in a single layer on trays. You can make trays by securing a layer of cheesecloth over jelly roll pans, cooling racks, or oven racks. Preheat the oven to 140°F (60°C) or as low as the oven thermostat will allow. Place the lower oven rack at least 3 inches (7.5 cm) from the bottom of the oven. Stack trays evenly, leaving at least 2½ inches (6 cm) of space between trays.

Throughout the drying time, keep the oven door open a few inches to help moisture escape. Use an oven thermometer to be sure the oven maintains a steady temperature. Rotate trays regularly because food on trays near the bottom of the oven will dry more quickly. Stir the food occasionally to ensure more even drying.

Drying time depends on the food being dried. Watch foods carefully to avoid scorching. When dry, vegetables will feel hard and brittle. Fruits will feel leathery but pliable. Cool thoroughly.

Learn About...

Storing and Using Dried Foods

Package dried foods in insectproof and moistureproof containers. Plastic containers and bags, and glass jars are all suitable. Seal, label, and store them in a cool, dark place.

Dried fruits may be eaten in their dry state, or they can be rehydrated. Most dried vegetables are rehydrated before eating. To rehydrate, soak foods for an hour or two. Simmer in the same liquid used for soaking until foods are tender. Do not overcook.

Know and Apply

1. How should you store dried foods?
2. How can you rehydrate dried foods?

Commercial Food Preservation

Of course, canning, freezing, and drying are not just home preservation methods. They are common commercial food preservation methods as well. Advances in food processing have improved the quality of preserved foods available to today's consumers. Commercially preserved foods keep more nutrients than foods preserved at home. Commercial processing is done quickly and very soon after foods are harvested. This allows preserved foods to have nutritional values that are close to fresh foods.

The principles used in commercial food preservation are the same as those used at home. Moisture and temperature conditions are controlled to stop the spoiling action of microorganisms and enzymes.

Freeze-Drying

Food manufacturers preserve foods in a number of ways besides canning, freezing, and drying. One of these ways is freeze-drying.

packaging material forms a tight seal around the food. This reduces the amount of oxygen available to break down the food. See **Figure 28.14**. Vacuum packaging also slows the growth of microorganisms that can cause spoilage. Coffee and nuts are among the foods that often come in vacuum packaging.

Modified atmosphere packaging (MAP) changes the makeup of the gases in the air surrounding a food inside a package. The mix of gases used depends on the food product. The plastic films and other materials used for MAP also depend on the particular food being covered. Using the optimal combination for a specific food helps that food maintain fresh colors, flavors, and nutrients longer. Meats, fresh pasta, and some produce are often packaged this way.

Preservation techniques increase a food's **shelf life**. This is the amount of time a food can be stored and remain wholesome. However, preserved foods cannot be kept forever. Many packaged foods provide information about how long they can be stored. If you are in doubt about how to store a food product, look for information on the manufacturer's website. A range of information including safe storage guidelines is also available at foodsafety.gov.

Svetlana Foote/Shutterstock.com

Figure 28.14 These frozen salmon have been vacuum packaged. How can you tell if a food has been vacuum packaged?

Exploring Careers

Quality Control Microbiologist

Quality control (QC) microbiologists work for food manufacturers. Their job is to help assure products meet company standards. They look for microorganisms that can affect the safety and quality of food. These scientists check samples of water and other ingredients that come into a food plant before they are used in food products. They also check samples of finished products before the products are released to the market. If microbiologists detect contamination, they run tests to find its source. They keep detailed records of when and how samples are collected and all test results. They may have to maintain an inventory of lab supplies. They may also train and supervise lab technicians to assist them.

QC microbiologists must be able to use math skills as they analyze data. They need to be able to handle stress, adapt to change, and quickly deal with problems. These scientists must pay careful attention to details when gathering and testing samples to be sure test results are correct. They use writing skills to prepare reports of their findings. QC microbiologists must know how to do routine lab procedures and use technical equipment. They must know and follow safety and sanitation standards. Although they need to be able to work independently, they also need to cooperate with other lab workers.

QC microbiologists need at least a four-year bachelor's degree. Many of these scientists have advanced degrees. Employers often look for workers who have two or more years of experience working in a lab. Knowledge of food manufacturing processes is also helpful.

Chapter 28 Review and Expand

Summary

Enzymes and microorganisms cause food spoilage. Food, moisture, and favorable temperatures need to be present for spoilage to occur. Removing any one of these factors will help preserve food.

Home-canned foods are stored in jars with two-piece vacuum caps used as closures. Low-acid foods need to be processed in a pressure canner. High-acid foods can be processed in a boiling water canner.

Jellied and pickled products are popular home-canned foods. Sugar is used to help preserve fruit products. Pickled foods are preserved with acid that is either added during the pickling process or formed as the result of fermentation.

Before freezing, some fruits need treatment with ascorbic acid to prevent darkening. Most vegetables need blanching before freezing.

Before drying, vegetables need to be blanched and fruits may need to be treated with ascorbic acid. Foods can be dried in the sun or in a conventional oven. Store dried foods in tightly sealed containers to prevent moisture from affecting them.

Commercial food preservation follows the same principles as home preservation. Freeze-drying, aseptic packaging, retort packaging, and irradiation are all commercial preservation techniques.

Vocabulary Activities

1. **Content Terms** Select three terms from the following list and explain how these terms are related to each other. Create a graphic organizer or write a paragraph to explain or illustrate how the terms relate.

mold	freezer burn
yeast	ascorbic acid
canning	freeze-drying
raw pack	irradiation
hot pack	aseptic packaging
headspace	retort packaging
processing time	vacuum packaging
botulism	modified atmosphere packaging (MAP)
pectin	shelf life
pickling	
quick-freezing	

2. **Academic Terms** Review the following terms and identify any terms that can be divided into smaller parts, having *roots* and *suffixes* or *prefixes*. Write these terms on a sheet of paper. Beside each term, list the root word and prefix or suffix. How do root words help you understand meaning? suffixes and prefixes?

bountiful	corrode
overabundance	rancid
concave	

Review

Write your answers using complete sentences when appropriate.

3. True or false. Bacteria, mold, and yeast can have good effects on food.

4. Describe the most popular type of canning jar closure.

5. What are two foods that must be processed by pressure canning? Explain why.

6. What canning method is used to preserve fruits and pickled vegetables?

7. List three factors that can cause home-canned foods to lose eating quality during storage.

8. What are five signs of spoilage in home-canned foods?

9. What type of jellied product is a tender jelly containing small pieces of fruit and fruit rind?

10. What is the function of each of the four basic ingredients needed to make jellied products?

11. What is brine and how does it help to preserve foods?

12. Describe the advantage quick-frozen foods have over foods frozen more slowly.

13. What can cause foods to develop freezer burn?

14. What are the three packing methods that may be used when freezing fruits?

15. List five foods that do not freeze well.

16. Why should fruits and vegetables be cut in small pieces before drying?

17. What are two methods for drying fruits and vegetables at home?

18. Describe three types of commercial food preservation.

Chapter 28 Review and Expand

Core Skills

19. **Math** A tomato plant produces about 20 pounds (9 kg) of tomatoes. It takes approximately 3 pounds (1.4 kg) of fresh tomatoes to yield 1 quart (1 L) of canned tomatoes. Assume a family uses 75 quarts (75 L) of canned tomatoes per year for pizza, pasta sauce, and salsa. Figure the costs of growing and canning tomatoes, including all equipment and supplies. Compare these costs with buying commercially canned tomatoes. Calculate how much this family would save in the first year by canning tomatoes at home instead of buying commercially canned tomatoes. Calculate how much they would save in subsequent years when they reuse canning supplies.

20. **Research, Technology, Speaking** Prepare an electronic presentation that explains the procedure used to irradiate foods. In an oral report to the class, describe how the food industry uses irradiation to prevent food spoilage from microorganisms and enzymes. Download images from the Internet to help convey the information and improve understanding. Be sure to credit image sources.

21. **Science** Puree three fruits and three vegetables. Then use litmus paper to test the acidity of each puree. Find recommended canning procedures for each of these fruits and vegetables. How does your litmus testing compare with recommendations in terms of whether each of these fruits and vegetables should be treated as high-acid or low-acid foods?

22. **Research, Reading, Writing** Use reliable print or online resources to research the symptoms and treatment of botulism. Also investigate the incidence of outbreaks of botulism associated with home-canned foods. Summarize your findings in a written report. Edit your report for grammar, spelling, and organization.

23. **Research, Reading, Writing** Use reliable online and print resources to research foods that were dried by Native Americans and early settlers in the United States. Also investigate drying procedures that were used. Write an essay detailing this information and cite your sources. Reread and revise your essay to ensure your ideas are presented in a clear and logical manner.

24. **Career Readiness Practice** Prepare a demonstration on how to home can foods safely. Design a brochure about the safe use of home-canned foods. The brochure should describe how to check for spoilage and list types of spoilage of which people should be aware. Explain what to do with spoiled food. Distribute your brochure at a local farmer's market or grocery store.

Critical Thinking and Problem Solving

25. **Analyze** Make two batches of a jellied product. Add commercial pectin to one batch. Do not add pectin to the other batch. Analyze the effects of added pectin on the flavor, consistency, cooking time, yield, and appearance of the jellied product.

26. **Evaluate** Make a batch of cookies. Sample and evaluate the cookies, making notes about their quality characteristics. Package and freeze half of the remaining cookies in a loosely rolled paper bag. Package and freeze the other half of the cookies in a tightly sealed plastic container. After one month, thaw, sample, and evaluate the cookies. Which type of container best preserved the flavor, texture, and appearance of fresh cookies?

27. **Analyze** Choose and sample a product sold in aseptic or retort packaging as well as a similar canned product. Compare the costs, preparation, appearance, and taste of the two products. Write an essay analyzing advantages and disadvantages of the two packaging methods. Edit and refine your paper to ensure your ideas are presented in a logical, organized manner that is clear to the reader.

Africa Studio/Shutterstock.com

Essential Questions

- What types of dishes are typical in various regions of the United States?
- How do geography, climate, and culture affect the development of a country's cuisine?
- How do meal patterns differ in countries throughout the world?

FCCLA: Taking the Lead

Use this section of the text to help you as you create a *Hospitality, Tourism, and Recreation* STAR Event project. Text information would be especially helpful for a project in the culinary focus area. Descriptions of dishes, regional influences, and cooking techniques provide useful details for developing a menu for a restaurant with an international cuisine. Information in Chapter 29 would also be useful for preparing dining and attraction material for a project in the lodging or tourism focus area.

While studying, look for the activity icon for:
- Content and Academic Terms with e-flash cards, vocabulary games, and matching activities These activities can be accessed at www.g-wlearning.com/foodandnutrition/9582

Chapter 29

The United States and Canada

Dan Breckwoldt/Shutterstock.com

Content Terms ⤴

Pennsylvania Dutch
soul food
chitterlings
okra
Creole cuisine
filé
gumbo
jambalaya
Cajun cuisine
potluck
sourdough
luau
imu
Aboriginal

Objectives

After studying this chapter, you will be able to

- **identify** the origins of foods from the seven main regions of the United States;
- **explain** how geography, climate, and culture affected the development of Canadian cuisine; and
- **prepare** foods that are representative of the United States and Canada.

Academic Terms

famine
province
solemn
ingenuity
prospector
enterprising
annexed
array

Reading Prep

Arrange a study session to read the chapter aloud with a classmate. At the end of each section, discuss any words you do not know. Take notes of words you would like to discuss in class.

The food customs of the United States and Canada are as diverse as the inhabitants of these nations. People who live in these two countries have roots that stretch around the world (**Figure 29.1**).

A Historical Overview of the United States

Even before Christopher Columbus set sail for the Americas in 1492, Europeans had been establishing colonies in North America. As history moved forward, more people began leaving their homelands to move to America, which was then known as the "New World." People had many reasons for making this major life change. Some moved to escape debtor's prison. Others sought religious freedom, fame, or fortune. Many fled *famine* (a severe shortage of food) and disease. Some were forced to come as slaves. These early settlers and immigrants began to shape the cuisine associated with the United States today.

The Early Settlers

The British and Spanish were the first permanent colonists in the United States. They established the early settlements of Jamestown and Plymouth (British) and St. Augustine (Spanish). The French

Khwanchai Khattinon/Shutterstock.com

Figure 29.1 These Asian egg rolls are just one example of the international heritage that flavors the cuisines of the United States and Canada. What other dishes represent the international heritage of the United States and Canada?

who settled in the United States established *provinces* (settlements) in Louisiana. A little later, the Dutch arrived and established the New Netherland Colony, which later became New York.

Each group of settlers had to adjust to the climate and geography of the area in which they settled. Many were able to adapt their food customs to take advantage of North American ingredients.

As the colonists' knowledge grew, they added many new dishes to their diets. They used local lobster, crab, and other fish in seafood chowders. They salted pork and preserved beef for use in a variety of meat dishes throughout the winter. They used pumpkin and wild berries to make pies, puddings, and cakes.

The Immigrants

As more and more people came to North America, communities sprang up along the east coast. People also began to settle in more fertile regions farther inland. Many immigrants stayed together in groups and settled in particular regions. For example, many British,

Culture and Social Studies

Native American Influence

Food customs of the United States began with the Native Americans. The Native Americans were excellent farmers. They cultivated many fruits and vegetables. Beans, corn, and squash supplied the basis of their nutritious diets. They hunted wild game, gathered nuts and berries, and fished to supplement these staple foods.

The life of the first colonists was a struggle for survival. The Native Americans contributed to the success of the first colonial settlements in North America. They taught colonists how to hunt, fish, and plant crops. Within a few years, the colonists had cleared land, built small groups of homes, and planted simple gardens. The colonists grew new varieties of vegetables and fruits. They learned to eat animals and fish that had been unfamiliar to them.

Dutch, German, and French people settled in the Northeast. British, French, and Spanish immigrants settled in the Deep South. Other Spanish settlers chose to live in the Southwest. As settlers came to North America, the slave trade came with them, and many Africans were brought to the United States to work on plantations.

During the 1800s, more people came to the United States in search of economic opportunities, land, and freedom. Most of these immigrants settled in areas with climates similar to those of their homelands. Chicago, New York, and other large industrial cities attracted large groups of Polish, Irish, French, and Italian people. Many of these immigrants worked as unskilled laborers. Scandinavians and Germans traveled to Wisconsin and Minnesota to farm. Chinese, Japanese, and other South Asians settled along the Pacific Coast where many of them mined and worked on the railroads.

The new immigrants brought their native food customs with them to North America. They adapted their recipes to the foods that were readily available. Italian immigrants made rich pasta sauces from tomatoes, basil, and onions sold by street vendors in New York. Chinese people used chicken, bamboo shoots, and water chestnuts to make their chow mein. Polish people stuffed cabbage leaves with ground beef and tomato sauce to make their traditional cabbage rolls. These immigrants helped create the cuisine eaten in the United States today.

Holidays in the United States

Immigrants brought their holiday traditions to the United States along with their food customs. As a result, some holidays in the United States are celebrated only in parts of the country where certain regional or cultural groups are found.

One regional holiday in the United States is *Mardi Gras*. It is widely celebrated in some parts of the South, where it was originally introduced by French settlers. *Mardi Gras* is French for "fat Tuesday." Mardi Gras falls on the day before Ash Wednesday, which marks the beginning of Lent in the Christian church. Lent is a 40-day period of prayer and fasting. Mardi Gras began as a last celebration before entering into this *solemn* (serious or somber) time. Mardi Gras festivities often begin the week before the actual holiday and include colorful parades with floats and

marching bands. People wear ornate costumes and masks and attend gala balls and parties.

Cajun favorites featuring locally caught seafood are served at many Mardi Gras parties. A typical menu might include a shrimp mold appetizer, crab bisque, and crawfish stew. The classic Mardi Gras dessert is king cake. This is a ring of cinnamon-filled dough decorated with purple, green, and gold sugar. A tiny plastic baby doll is baked inside the cake. Whoever gets the piece of cake containing the doll is supposed to throw the next Mardi Gras party.

Some holidays are observed mainly by people of certain cultures. *Cinco de Mayo* is a cultural holiday observed by Mexican Americans. The name is Spanish for "Fifth of May," which is a day of celebration. It marks the victory of severely outnumbered Mexican troops over French troops at the Battle of Puebla in 1862. Parades, music, dancing, and carnivals are all part of the celebration (**Figure 29.2**). The day may conclude with Mexican foods, including sweet breads and coffee or hot chocolate flavored with cinnamon.

Another cultural holiday is *Kwanzaa*. This is a family-centered observance of cultural unity

Figure 29.2 Dancing and traditional costumes are part of some Cinco de Mayo celebrations.

among people of African heritage. The name comes from a Swahili word meaning "first fruits." This weeklong celebration occurs between Christmas and New Year's Day. People use this time to think about their ancestry, family, and community. On the next to the last night of Kwanzaa, families hold the *karamu*, which is a ritual feast. Kwanzaa was developed in the United States. This celebration is also becoming popular among people of African descent in other parts of the world.

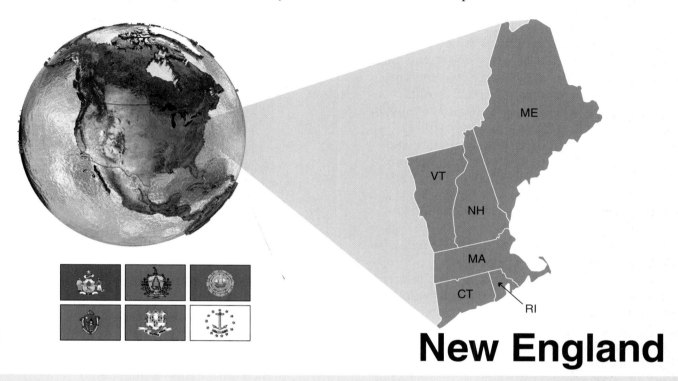

New England

The British were the first people to settle in the area now called *New England*. When these settlers came, much of the New England land was rocky, mountainous, or forested, and winters were long and severe. The early colonists had to work hard to survive.

The character of the people and the land they inhabited shaped the character of New England cooking. Most of the farms that sprang up were isolated and self-sufficient. Seafood and wild game supplemented the foods New Englanders could grow at home. The waters provided lobsters, crabs, clams, and other shellfish, which later became New England specialties. The forests provided wild turkeys, geese, ducks, and pheasants.

Each home had a large fireplace the family used for cooking. New Englanders prepared most foods in iron pots that hung over the fire. They made baked goods in covered Dutch ovens over the coals of the fireplace or in beehive ovens. These baked goods included Indian bread, Sally Lunn, and johnnycakes.

New England cooks used foods that were readily available to create hearty, substantial meals. For instance, they used corn to make corn sticks, Indian pudding, and cornmeal mush. They also used it for *succotash* (a combination of corn and lima beans).

To survive the long, cold winters, the early New Englanders learned to dry and salt foods to preserve them. They commonly dried beans, corn, and apples. Later, they soaked these foods in water and cooked them until tender. Early New Englanders made baked beans in this way by soaking the dried beans overnight. Then cooks would flavor the beans with molasses and salt pork and cook them slowly in big pots.

One-dish meals were popular in New England because they gave the cooks more time to do other tasks. One of the most common one-dish meals of that time, the *New England boiled dinner*, is still popular today. It is a combination of meat (usually corned beef), potatoes, onions, carrots, cabbage, and other available vegetables. The ingredients cook together slowly until they are tender.

The colonists used a variety of meats, seafood, and vegetables to make stews and chowders. Clam chowder was one of the most popular. Many people continue to associate New England cooking with this creamy soup made with potatoes and clams (**Figure 29.3**).

From the sap of New England's sugar maple trees came maple syrup. Native Americans taught the New Englanders how to tap the maple trees. After the colonists boiled down the sap, they used the syrup to make cakes, candies, sauces, and puddings. They also used it to flavor baked beans, squash, and other vegetables.

Blueberries, cranberries, blackberries, and other fruits were another important food source. New England cooks gathered the berries and used them to make a variety of nourishing desserts. Two examples are *blueberry mush* (a steamed pudding) and *blueberry grunt* (berries simmered in a thickened sauce and topped with fluffy dumplings).

New Englanders used leftovers in creative ways. For instance, they would grind the leftovers from a boiled dinner and fry them in a large iron skillet. Beets give this dish a red color, which reminded the New Englanders of red flannel underwear worn during the cold winters. Thus, the dish earned the name *red-flannel hash*.

New England Menu

New England Clam Chowder
Boiled Dinner
Blueberry Muffins
Pumpkin Pie
Tea

New England Clam Chowder
Serves 6

3	slices bacon
2	6.5-ounce cans minced clams
1	large potato, peeled and cubed
1	medium stalk celery, chopped
½	cup finely chopped onion
¼	teaspoon pepper
⅛	teaspoon thyme
2	cups fat-free milk
1½	cups evaporated fat-free milk

1. In large, heavy saucepan, cook bacon until crisp.
2. Remove bacon to a piece of absorbent paper to drain. Pour excess fat from pan.
3. Drain clams, reserving liquid. Set clams aside.
4. In saucepan used to cook bacon, add potato, celery, onion, pepper, and thyme to liquid from clams. Bring to a boil; simmer covered until vegetables are tender (about 10 minutes).
5. Add milk, evaporated milk, and clams and heat almost to the boiling point. Taste to see if additional seasonings are needed. Serve immediately.

Per serving: 198 calories (14% from fat), 18 g protein, 25 g carbohydrate, 3 g fat, 29 mg cholesterol, 2 g fiber, 577 mg sodium.

Foodio/Shutterstock.com

Figure 29.3 Clam chowder is a popular New England food even today. What other foods do you associate with the New England region?

Boiled Dinner
Serves 4

1	pound corned beef brisket
2	cloves garlic
½	teaspoon peppercorns
1	bay leaf
2	medium-sized parsnips, quartered
½	small green cabbage, cut in 4 wedges
2	medium-sized red potatoes, peeled, and cut in half
4	small carrots, quartered
2	small white onions, quartered
	parsley, chopped

1. Trim any fat from corned beef and place it in a large pan with garlic, peppercorns, and bay leaf. Add cold water to cover.
2. Bring to a simmer, cover pan tightly, and reduce heat. Simmer 1¼ to 1½ hours, or until tender.
3. Cook parsnips, cabbage, potatoes, carrots, and onions in salted, simmering water about 30 to 40 minutes, until tender.
4. To serve the dinner, slice the meat and arrange it on a serving platter. Surround meat with vegetables and top with chopped parsley. Serve with horseradish sauce or mustard.
   Note: Vegetables can be added to the corned beef about 30 to 40 minutes before serving as is done in New England. Some people, however, object to the salty flavor the corned beef gives the vegetables.

Per serving: 379 calories (31% from fat), 28 g protein, 38 g carbohydrate, 13 g fat, 73 mg cholesterol, 8 g fiber, 923 mg sodium.

Blueberry Muffins
Makes 6 muffins

1	cup all-purpose flour
1¼	teaspoons baking powder
1½	tablespoons sugar
¼	teaspoon salt
1½	tablespoons butter, melted
1	egg white
½	cup fat-free milk
½	cup blueberries

1. Preheat oven to 400°F.
2. Stir flour, baking powder, sugar, and salt together in mixing bowl.
3. Combine egg white and milk; add melted butter and blend thoroughly.
4. Add liquid ingredients to dry ingredients all at once. Stir only until blended. (Batter will be lumpy.)
5. Gently fold in blueberries.
6. Fill greased muffin pans ⅔ full of batter.
7. Bake muffins 20 to 25 minutes or until brown.

Per muffin: 131 calories (21% from fat), 4 g protein, 22 g carbohydrate, 3 g fat, 8 mg cholesterol, 1 g fiber, 237 mg sodium.

Pumpkin Pie
Makes one 9-inch pie

2	eggs
¾	cup light brown sugar, packed
2	cups canned pumpkin
1½	cups evaporated fat-free milk
1	teaspoon cinnamon
½	teaspoon ground cloves
½	teaspoon ginger
½	teaspoon nutmeg
1	unbaked pastry shell, 9-inch

1. Preheat oven to 450°F.
2. In large mixing bowl, beat eggs slightly; add brown sugar, pumpkin, milk, and spices and mix well.
3. Pour mixture into pastry shell.
4. Bake 10 minutes.
5. Reduce temperature to 300°F and continue baking until knife inserted in center comes out clean, about 40 to 50 minutes.
6. Cool. Serve with whipped cream.

1/8 of pie: 269 calories (27% from fat), 7 g protein, 44 g carbohydrate, 8 g fat, 55 mg cholesterol, 3 g fiber, 277 mg sodium.

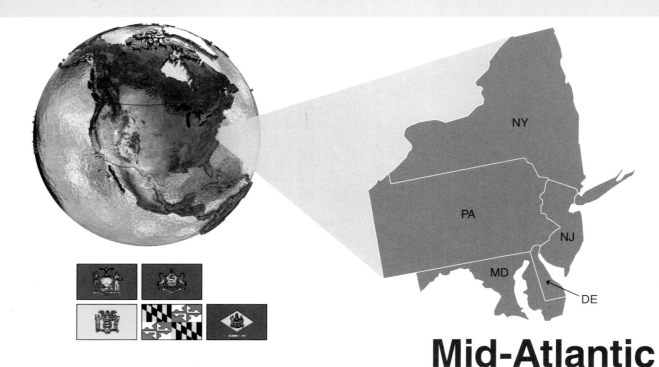

Mid-Atlantic

South of New England, the climate is milder. The land in the mid-Atlantic region is rich and fertile, and farming is profitable. New Jersey is a major center of fresh fruit and vegetable production. New Jersey ships produce including cranberries, bell peppers, spinach, peaches, blueberries, and cucumbers throughout the region.

The mid-Atlantic region was settled by Dutch, German, Swedish, and British immigrants. The Dutch were excellent farmers. They had large vegetable gardens and kept their root cellars well stocked. Many had their own orchards, too.

The Dutch were also excellent bakers. Cookies (*koekjes*), doughnuts (*olykoeks*), molasses cake, and gingerbread figures all have Dutch origins (**Figure 29.4**). The Dutch also introduced waffles, coleslaw, cottage cheese, and griddle cakes.

One group of mid-Atlantic settlers, the Pennsylvania Dutch, deserves special mention. The **Pennsylvania Dutch** were a group of German immigrants who settled in the southeast section of Pennsylvania. (The word *Dutch* comes from the word *Deutsch*, which means "German.") These immigrants came from the Rhine Valley in Germany, where they were farmers. When they came to the United States, they were successful in adapting their farming techniques to the soil in Pennsylvania.

The food customs of the Pennsylvania Dutch were very different from those of their neighbors.

Figure 29.4   Gingerbread figures were brought to the United States by Dutch settlers. What other foods did Dutch settlers bring?

They developed a style of cooking that was rural, hearty, and inventive. They based it on cooking techniques practiced in their homeland. The thrifty *hausfrau* (housewife) canned, pickled, and dried the produce, meat, and poultry raised on the farm. The Pennsylvania Dutch did not waste anything. They used their thriftiness and *ingenuity* (cleverness) to create many new dishes. Examples are pickled pigs' feet, blood pudding, *scrapple* (pork combined with cornmeal), smoked beef tongue, stuffed heart, sausages, and bologna.

Soup was one of the most popular dishes. The Pennsylvania Dutch made it from whatever foods were available. Since they were especially skillful in the production of vegetables and poultry, they served vegetable and chicken soups often. *Chicken corn soup* remains a traditional favorite.

Hearty German foods, such as sauerbraten, sauerkraut, liverwurst, and pork, were mainstays of the Pennsylvania Dutch diet. Noodles, dumplings, potato pancakes, and other filling foods were served as accompaniments (**Figure 29.5**).

Pickled vegetables and fruits, relishes, jams, preserves, and apple butter were often found on the table. Homemakers made all these foods during the summer and stored them in cellars for the winter.

The Pennsylvania Dutch were excellent bakers. Coffee cakes, sticky buns, funnel cakes, and crumb cakes were popular baked goods. *Shoofly pie* (pastry with a filling made of molasses and brown sugar) is another specialty associated with this area.

Several religious groups, including the Amish and the Mennonites, shared a German heritage with the Pennsylvania Dutch. These groups chose to live in isolated communities, which helped preserve their hearty homestyle cooking and native crafts. Some small colonies of Amish and Mennonite peoples still exist throughout the country.

Mid-Atlantic Menu

Stewed Chicken and Dumplings
Buttered Green Beans
Coleslaw
Rye Bread
Shoofly Pie
Coffee

Stewed Chicken and Dumplings
Serves 4

2	skinless chicken breast halves
2	skinless chicken legs and thighs
1	small onion, quartered
2	stalks celery, cut in ½-inch slices
2	carrots, diced
½	teaspoon sage
	salt and pepper
	cold water
2	tablespoons all-purpose flour
½	cup cold fat-free milk

Dumplings:

½	cup plus 2 tablespoons all-purpose flour
⅛	teaspoon salt
1¼	teaspoons baking powder
2	tablespoons shortening
¼	cup fat-free milk

1. Wash chicken and place in a large pot with onion, celery, carrots, sage, and salt and pepper to taste. Add enough cold water to barely cover chicken and vegetables.
2. Cover pot and bring to a boil over high heat.
3. Reduce heat and simmer 30 to 40 minutes, until chicken is tender and has reached 165°F when tested with a food thermometer.

Malivan_Iuliia/Shutterstock.com

Figure 29.5 Potato pancakes are a Pennsylvania Dutch specialty.

4. About 15 minutes after the chicken begins to simmer, start to mix the dumplings. Begin by stirring the flour, salt, and baking powder together into a medium mixing bowl.
5. Cut in shortening with pastry blender or two knives until particles are the size of coarse cornmeal.
6. Add milk and stir with a fork to make a sticky dough.
7. Divide the dough into eighths and drop by spoonfuls onto the chicken (not into the liquid). Allow space between dumplings for them to double in size.
8. Cover the pot and continue to simmer chicken for 15 more minutes without lifting the lid.
9. Lift out the dumplings onto a plate and place the chicken on a serving platter.
10. Shake 2 tablespoons flour with ½ cup cold milk in a small covered container until thoroughly blended.
11. Stir flour mixture into the chicken stock. Heat and stir until stock thickens.
12. Pour thickened stock and vegetables over chicken. Arrange dumplings on top.

Per serving: 331 calories (24% from fat), 31 g protein, 26 g carbohydrate, 9 g fat, 74 mg cholesterol, 2 g fiber, 298 mg sodium.

Buttered Green Beans
Serves 4

1	pound fresh green beans*
½	cup water
⅛	teaspoon salt
1	tablespoon plus 1 teaspoon butter
	salt and pepper, to taste

1. Wash beans under cool running water. Snap off ends; then snap beans in half.
2. Place water and salt in medium saucepan; bring to a boil.
3. Add beans. Return to a boil, then reduce heat and simmer beans gently just until crisp-tender, about 6 to 10 minutes.
4. Drain beans, top with butter, and season with salt and pepper to taste. Serve immediately.
   *One pound of frozen green beans may be substituted for fresh. Follow package directions for cooking.

Per serving: 58 calories (62% from fat), 1 g protein, 5 g carbohydrate, 4 g fat, 11 mg cholesterol, 2 g fiber, 146 mg sodium.

Coleslaw
Serves 4 to 6

½	medium head green cabbage, shredded
1	large carrot, shredded
½	medium green pepper, diced
¼	cup evaporated fat-free milk
½	cup plain nonfat yogurt
½	teaspoon prepared mustard
1	tablespoon plus 1 teaspoon lemon juice
1½	teaspoons sugar
½	teaspoon celery seed
	salt and pepper

1. Combine cabbage, carrots, and green pepper in a medium mixing bowl.
2. In small bowl, beat together the evaporated milk, yogurt, mustard, lemon juice, sugar, celery seed, and salt and pepper.
3. Pour over vegetables, tossing well.
4. Refrigerate 1 hour before serving.

Per serving: 59 calories (0% from fat), 4 g protein, 11 g carbohydrate, 0 g fat, 1 mg cholesterol, 2 g fiber, 118 mg sodium.

Rye Bread
Makes 1 loaf

1	cup all-purpose flour
1	tablespoon plus 1½ teaspoons brown sugar, firmly packed
¾	teaspoon salt
½	teaspoon caraway seeds
¼	teaspoon baking soda
1	package active dry yeast
½	cup buttermilk
2	tablespoons dark molasses
2	tablespoons shortening
½	cup water
2 to 2¼ cups rye flour	

1. In large mixing bowl, combine all-purpose flour, brown sugar, salt, caraway seeds, baking soda, and dry yeast. Mix well.
2. In small saucepan, heat buttermilk, molasses, shortening, and water until very warm (120°F to 130°F).
3. Add milk mixture to dry ingredients blending at lowest speed of electric mixer until moistened. Then beat at medium speed 3 minutes.

4. By hand, stir in enough rye flour to make a stiff dough.
5. Turn dough out onto a lightly floured surface. Knead until smooth and elastic, about 5 minutes.
6. Place dough in a greased bowl, turning once to grease top. Cover with a clean towel; and let rise in a warm place until doubled in bulk, 1 to 1½ hours.
7. Punch dough down and shape into a round loaf.
8. Place loaf on a lightly greased baking sheet. Cover with a clean towel and let rise in a warm place until doubled in bulk, about 1 hour.
9. Bake bread in a preheated 350°F oven for 45 to 50 minutes or until loaf tests done. Cool before slicing.

Per slice: 114 calories (16% from fat), 4 g protein, 21 g carbohydrate, 2 g fat, 0 mg cholesterol, 3 g fiber, 125 mg sodium.

Perry Correll/Shutterstock.com

Made with molasses and brown sugar, this sweet, sticky pie was said to attract many flies that had to be "shooed" away. Thus, it was named *shoofly pie*.

Shoofly Pie
Makes one 9-inch pie

1½	cups all-purpose flour
½	cup butter
1	cup light brown sugar, packed
1	teaspoon baking soda
1	cup boiling water
½	cup molasses
½	cup honey
1	unbaked pastry shell, 9-inch

1. Preheat oven to 375°F.
2. In a large mixing bowl, cut butter into flour with a pastry blender or two knives until mixture resembles small peas.
3. Stir in brown sugar and set aside.
4. Dissolve soda in boiling water. Then add molasses and honey.
5. Pour molasses mixture into pastry-lined pie plate with fluted edge.
6. Sprinkle the flour mixture over the top.
7. Bake pie at 375°F for 10 minutes.
8. Reduce heat to 350°F and continue baking another 25 to 30 minutes or until the filling has set.
9. Cool completely before serving.

1/8 of pie: 507 calories (33% from fat), 4 g protein, 83 g carbohydrate, 19 g fat, 30 mg cholesterol, 1 g fiber, 407 mg sodium.

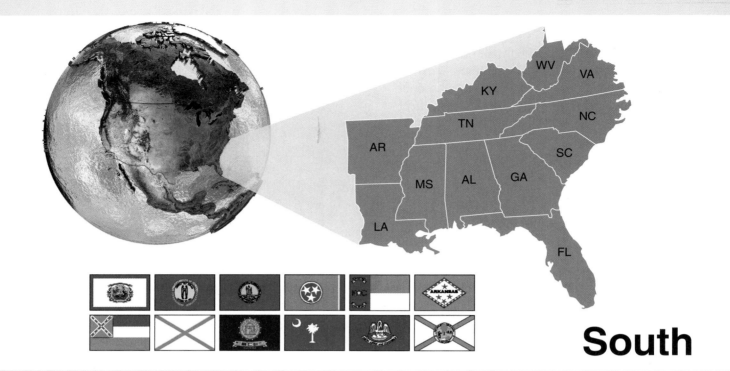

South

Immigrants from France, England, Ireland, Scotland, and Spain settled in the South. Many brought African slaves to the United States. The slaves worked on the large plantations and served in the huge mansions.

The mild climate of the South made year-round production of many crops possible. Sugarcane, rice, and peanuts were the most economically important food crops. Southern farmers also grew fruits and vegetables on a smaller scale.

The waters and forests of the South were important sources of food. Southerners found catfish, bass, trout, and terrapin (turtle) in rivers and streams. They found crabs, crayfish, oysters, and shrimp in the waters of the Gulf of Mexico. Wild game was abundant. Squirrel, goose, and turkey were especially well liked. From these foods evolved the popular *Brunswick stew* (vegetables and game, poultry, or beef cooked together slowly until tender).

Corn is a staple food in the South. Southerners serve it in many ways. At breakfast, they serve corn as hominy or hominy grits. They use cornmeal to make delicious hot breads, such as corn bread and spoon bread. *Spoon bread* is baked in a casserole like a pudding until it is crispy on the outside but still soft in the center.

Two other hot breads, buttermilk biscuits and shortnin' bread, are also Southern specialties. Today, Southern cooks still pride themselves on the tenderness and lightness of their biscuits.

Pigs and chickens were the most common types of livestock in the South. As a result, pork and chicken played an important part in the region's cuisine. Spareribs and cured ham often appeared on Southern tables (**Figure 29.6**). Fried chicken became a Southern specialty.

Christian Jung/Shutterstock.com

Figure 29.6   Cured ham was popular on Southern tables. How is cured ham prepared?

Rice grew abundantly in the Carolinas. Southern cooks used it in many of their dishes. They often combined rice with beans, meat, or seafood to make economical and nutritious dishes.

Aside from corn, popular vegetables included beans, sweet potatoes, and a variety of greens. Southern cooks often prepared turnip and dandelion greens with pork fat for flavor. Black-eyed peas, grits, and nuts were other staple foods used in Southern cooking. *Hoppin' John* (a combination of black-eyed peas and rice) and pecan pie are two popular dishes made from these staple foods.

Soul Food

Soul food is a distinct cuisine that developed in the South. **Soul food** combines the food customs of African slaves with the food customs of Native Americans and European sharecroppers. It developed around those few foods that were readily available to all three groups of people.

Some plantation owners allowed their slaves to have small gardens. Slave families may have been able to keep a few chickens. Although no other domestic animals were allowed, the slaves were permitted to catch and eat catfish. Those slaves who worked in the fields received a small amount of meat at harvest time. Poor sharecroppers and Native Americans hunted game, such as squirrel, deer, and opossum, to supplement garden vegetables.

Slaves used the few foods available to them in many creative ways. They mixed leftovers from the plantation house with rice or beans for nutritious and tasty main dishes. The cooks used the cornmeal portions allotted to each family member to make a variety of hot breads and puddings. Batter bread, hush puppies, corn bread, hoecake, and cracklin' corn bread were a few of the most popular ones.

The slaves used all the parts of hogs and cattle discarded by the plantation owners. They cleaned **chitterlings** (the intestines of the hog) and boiled them with spices or dipped them in batter for deep-frying (**Figure 29.7**). They even used the hogs' feet, tails, snouts, and ears. Slaves often pickled these parts or boiled them to add to stews, soups, beans, or rice.

Nipon Laicharoenchokchai/Shutterstock.com

Figure 29.7 Chitterlings are made from the intestines of a hog. How are chitterlings prepared?

Vegetables used in soul food dishes included corn, squash, black-eyed peas, okra, and greens. Corn and squash had been grown in the South by Native Americans for many years. **Okra** is a green, pod-shaped vegetable that was brought to the United States from Africa. Slaves breaded and fried it or added it to soups and stews. Greens, such as spinach, mustard, sorrel, beet tops, collards, turnip, kale, dock, and dandelion, grew wild and in gardens. When cooked with salt pork, bacon, pork shank, pork jowl, or ham bone, they were nutritious and flavorful.

Sweet potatoes are dark orange tubers that have moist flesh. (They are sometimes mistakenly called *yams*.) Slaves added them to stews, fried them as fritters, and made them into a pudding called *pone*. They also used sweet potatoes to make the popular *sweet potato pie*.

Creole Cuisine

While New Orleans is the home of Creole cuisine, people throughout the South enjoy Creole dishes.

Creole cuisine combines the cooking techniques of the French with ingredients of African, Caribbean, Spanish, and Native American cuisines. The contributions of each group have come together to give Creole foods a character all their own. For instance, the French contributed *bouillabaisse* (a highly seasoned fish stew), court bouillon, and pastries. The Africans contributed okra, which is used as both a vegetable and a thickening agent in soups and stews. The Spanish contributed tomatoes, red and green peppers, and mixtures of rice, seafood, poultry, and meat. The Choctaw Indians were the first to use filé. (**Filé** is a flavoring and thickening agent made from sassafras leaves, which are dried and ground into a powder.) The addition of red beans, rice, and a variety of fish and seafood native to Louisiana resulted in many unusual and delicious dishes.

Gumbo is a soup that reflects the various cultures of Southern Louisiana. Although recipes vary, meats, poultry, seafood, okra, and other vegetables are common ingredients. Cooks may thicken gumbo with roux, okra, or filé. Families often hand their gumbo recipes down from generation to generation.

Jambalaya is a traditional Creole rice dish. It contains rice; seasonings; and shellfish, poultry, and/or sausage. Some cooks also add tomatoes. Creole cooks use a hot pepper sauce to season both gumbo and jambalaya.

Gumbo, jambalaya, and red beans and rice (a main dish made from red beans simmered with a small amount of meat) are economical. Creole cooks often made these dishes from leftovers (**Figure 29.8**).

Other Creole specialties include beignets, café au lait, café brulot, and pralines. *Beignets* are deep-fried squares of bread dough. Small cafés scattered throughout New Orleans serve them hot with a dusting of powdered sugar. Strong coffee flavored with chicory usually is served with them. *Café au lait* is a beverage made from equal portions of this chicory-flavored coffee and hot milk. *Café brulot* is strong coffee flavored with spices, sugar, citrus peel, and brandy. It often is flamed. *Pralines* are a sweet, rich candy made with sugar, pecans, and sometimes milk or buttermilk. They are sold in candy shops all over the South.

Cajun Cuisine

Cajun cuisine is the hearty fare of rural Southern Louisiana. It reflects the foods and cooking methods of the Acadians, French, Native

HG Photography/Shutterstock.com

Figure 29.8 Red beans and rice is a classic Creole dish.

Americans, Africans, and Spanish. (Acadians are French-speaking immigrants from a part of Nova Scotia called *Acadia*.) Like Creole cuisine, jambalayas and gumbos characterize Cajun cuisine. These dishes are seasoned heavily with hot peppers and other spicy seasonings. Cajun dishes are generally prepared from foods that are commonly available in Southern Louisiana. Crawfish, okra, rice, pecans, beans, and *andouille* (smoked pork sausage) frequently appear in Cajun recipes. Many dishes center on locally available game and seafood. They are creative combinations of whatever happens to be on hand and are often prepared from leftovers.

Traditional Cajun dishes include chaudin, rice dressing, and tartes douces. *Chaudin* is braised pig stomach stuffed with ground pork, onions, bell peppers, garlic, and diced sweet potatoes. *Rice dressing* is rice cooked with bits of chicken liver, chicken gizzard, and/or ground pork and seasoned with parsley and onion tops. *Tartes douces* are pies made with a soft, sweet crust and fillings like custard, blackberry, coconut, or sweet potato.

Culture and Social Studies

Floribbean Cuisine

Florida shares much of its cuisine with neighbors in other Southern states. Creole and Cajun dishes, along with country ham and grits, are just as common in Florida as they are in the rest of the South. Florida also has some unique foods. For instance, South Florida is home to a cuisine often known as *Floribbean*.

Floribbean fare is a fusion of flavors. Many dishes reflect influences from Caribbean countries located just a few hundred miles from Florida's southern tip. *Conch fritters*, which are fried cakes of chopped and seasoned sea snail, came to Florida from the Bahamas. The *Cubano*, a pressed, toasted sandwich made with ham, roast pork, cheese, and pickles, was brought to Florida by immigrants from Cuba. Spicy marinated *jerk chicken* from Jamaica is another example of Caribbean inspiration in the southernmost state.

Southern Menu

Southern Fried Chicken
Squash Pudding
Greens with Vinegar and Oil Dressing
Buttermilk Biscuits
Pecan Pie
Chicory Coffee

Southern Fried Chicken
Serves 5

1	3-pound fryer, cut into pieces
½	cup all-purpose flour
1	teaspoon salt
¼	teaspoon pepper
½	cup evaporated fat-free milk
1	egg
	shortening or oil for frying

1. Combine flour, salt, and pepper in a shallow pan.
2. Beat milk and egg together in a pie plate.
3. Dip chicken pieces in seasoned flour, then in milk mixture, then in flour again. Set aside until all pieces are coated.
4. In large, heavy skillet, heat shortening or oil until hot but not smoking.
5. Add chicken pieces, a few at a time. Brown all sides, turning occasionally.
6. When all pieces have been browned, return them to the skillet. Reduce heat, cover tightly, and cook chicken until tender, about 30 minutes. Remove cover the last 10 minutes to crisp chicken.

Per serving: 349 calories (59% from fat), 29 g protein, 6 g carbohydrate, 23 g fat, 135 mg cholesterol, 0 g fiber, 330 mg sodium.

Squash Pudding
Serves 4 to 5

2	cups hot butternut squash, mashed
1	tablespoon plus 1½ teaspoons butter
⅓	cup sugar
⅓	cup fat-free milk
¼	teaspoon salt
1	teaspoon cinnamon
1	teaspoon nutmeg
2	large eggs

1. Preheat oven to 325°F.
2. Add butter to squash; stir until melted.
3. Add sugar, milk, salt, cinnamon, and nutmeg. Beat with a whisk or an electric mixer until blended.
4. Beat eggs; blend in squash mixture.
5. Pour into a greased 1½-quart casserole. Bake until internal temperature reads 160°F on a thermometer, about 30 minutes.

Per serving: 196 calories (32% from fat), 5 g protein, 29 g carbohydrate, 7 g fat, 118 mg cholesterol, 4 g fiber, 222 mg sodium.

Greens with Vinegar and Oil Dressing

Serves 4

2	cups beet greens, chopped
2	cups kale, chopped
2	cups spinach, chopped
2	cups collards, chopped
¼	cup water
4	slices bacon, cooked and crumbled
1	clove garlic, chopped

1. Place greens in a large saucepan with water, bacon, and garlic.
2. Cover and simmer slowly until tender, about 15 minutes.
3. Drain and serve with vinegar and oil.

Per serving: 79 calories (46% from fat), 6 g protein, 7 g carbohydrate, 4 g fat, 9 mg cholesterol, 3 g fiber, 274 mg sodium.

Buttermilk Biscuits

Makes about 8 biscuits

1	cups all-purpose flour
1½	teaspoons baking powder
¼	teaspoon salt
2	tablespoons shortening
⅓	cup low-fat buttermilk

1. Preheat oven to 425°F.
2. In medium mixing bowl, combine flour, baking powder, and salt.
3. Using a pastry blender or two knives, cut in shortening until mixture resembles small peas.
4. Add buttermilk, stirring gently with fork until soft dough forms. If dough seems dry, add another tablespoon of buttermilk.

5. Turn dough out onto a lightly floured surface. Knead 8 to 10 times.
6. Roll dough to ½-inch thickness. Cut into rounds with 2-inch biscuit cutter.
7. Place biscuits close together on an ungreased baking sheet. Bake 10 to 12 minutes or until golden brown. Serve hot.

Per biscuit: 90 calories (30% from fat), 2 g protein, 13 g carbohydrate, 3 g fat, 0 mg cholesterol, 0 g fiber, 177 mg sodium.

Pecan Pie

Makes one 9-inch pie

4	eggs
⅓	cup light brown sugar, packed
¼	cup butter, melted
1¼	cups dark corn syrup
½	teaspoon salt
1½	teaspoons vanilla
1¼	cups chopped pecans
1	unbaked pastry shell, 9-inch

1. Preheat oven to 350°F.
2. In large mixing bowl, beat eggs and brown sugar together until blended.
3. Add melted butter, corn syrup, salt, vanilla, and chopped pecans and mix thoroughly; pour into unbaked pastry shell.
4. Bake until filling is puffed and golden brown, about 35 to 40 minutes.
5. Serve pie slightly warm or cool and top with whipped cream.

1/8 of pie: 426 calories (56% from fat), 6 g protein, 42 g carbohydrate, 28 g fat, 145 mg cholesterol, 2 g fiber, 388 mg sodium.

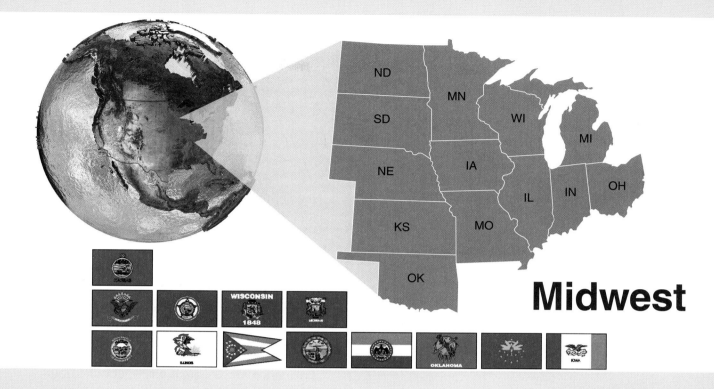

Midwest

People often call the Midwest the "bread-basket" of the nation. Rich soil, good climate, and advanced farming techniques have made the Midwest one of the world's most agriculturally productive regions. Corn, wheat, and soybeans grow in large enough quantities to be exported to many parts of the world.

Beef, pork, lamb, and poultry are produced in large quantities in the Midwest. Lakes and streams in this region provide a variety of fish. People throughout the United States recognize Wisconsin and Minnesota for their dairy products. Small farms throughout the Midwest grow many kinds of fruits and vegetables.

Fairs, festivals, and picnics are popular in the Midwest. Food plays an important part at these gatherings. Homemade breads, cakes, pies, cookies, jams, and jellies are judged at county and state fairs. Cities and towns in many parts of the Midwest hold festivals centered on apples, pumpkins, strawberries, and other fruits and vegetables.

Potlucks are popular social gatherings with religious organizations, clubs, and family groups in the Midwest. A **potluck** is a shared meal to which each person or family brings food for the whole group to eat. These meals get their name from a tradition of hospitality in which a prepared meal would be shared with an unexpected guest. Since the cook did not know the guest was coming, the guest would have to take "the luck of the pot."

Traditional Midwestern cooking is hearty. It features basic preparation methods and simple seasonings. Broiled steak, roast beef, baked and hash brown potatoes, and corn on the cob are staples of the Midwestern diet. Coleslaw, fresh tomatoes from the garden, apple pie, and brownies also belong to the Midwest. Eggs, bacon, pancakes, fruit, and coffee might be served at a filling Midwestern breakfast.

International foods from immigrants who settled in large Midwestern cities have been added to locally grown foods. Swedish meatballs, Greek moussaka, German bratwurst, Polish sausage, and Italian lasagna have become almost as common as steak and potatoes (**Figure 29.9**).

Shebeko/Shutterstock.com

Figure 29.9 Bratwurst, which reflects the German heritage of many Midwesterners, is popular for summer grilling and Oktoberfest celebrations in the fall. What other German foods are popular in the Midwest?

Midwestern Menu

Broiled Steak
Baked Potatoes
Sautéed Zucchini
Sliced Tomatoes
Warm Whole-Wheat Bread
Deep Dish Apple Pie
Milk, Coffee

Broiled Steak
Serves 4

1   boneless top sirloin steak, about 1-inch thick and weighing 1 pound
     garlic powder
     pepper
     salt

1. Preheat the broiler.
2. Trim fat from edges of steak with a sharp knife. Season meat with garlic powder and pepper; place on broiler pan.
3. Broil steak 3 to 4 inches from the heat until brown. Turn and finish broiling. Test doneness with a meat thermometer. Medium rare steaks should reach an internal temperature of 145°F in about 16 minutes. Medium steaks should

reach an internal temperature of 160°F in about 21 minutes.
4. Season with salt, if desired.

Per serving: 132 calories (27% from fat), 23 g protein, 0 g carbohydrate, 4 g fat, 59 mg cholesterol, 0 g fiber, 87 mg sodium.

Baked Potatoes
Serves 4

4   medium baking potatoes
1   tablespoon plus 1 teaspoon butter
¼   teaspoon salt
¼   teaspoon pepper

1. Preheat oven to 400°F.
2. Scrub potatoes under cold running water. Pierce skins in several places with the tines of a fork.
3. Place potatoes on the oven rack and bake until fork pierces potato easily, about 1 hour.
4. Remove the potatoes from the oven. Using pot holders, roll potatoes gently between hands for a minute or two to soften the potato flesh within the skins.
5. Make a slit in the top of each potato and push gently to expose some of the flesh. Top with butter, salt, and pepper. If desired, serve potatoes with shredded reduced fat cheese or plain nonfat yogurt and chives.

Per potato: 200 calories (18% from fat), 4 g protein, 37 g carbohydrate, 4 g fat, 11 mg cholesterol, 5 g fiber, 168 mg sodium.

Sautéed Zucchini
Serves 6

6   small zucchini
2   tablespoons butter
¾   teaspoon dried dill weed

1. Wash zucchini. Trim and discard ends. Cut into ¼-inch slices.
2. Melt butter in a skillet. Add zucchini and sauté until crisp-tender (about 5 to 8 minutes), stirring occasionally.
3. Sprinkle with dill weed. Serve immediately.

Per serving: 61 calories (59% from fat), 2 g protein, 6 g carbohydrate, 4 g fat, 11 mg cholesterol, 2 g fiber, 51 mg sodium.

Whole-Wheat Bread
Makes 1 loaf

2¾ to 3 cups all-purpose flour
1   cup whole-wheat flour
1   tablespoon plus 1½ teaspoons sugar
1   teaspoon salt
1   package active dry yeast
1   cup fat-free milk
¼   cup plus 2 tablespoons water
2   tablespoons softened butter

1. On a large sheet of waxed paper, combine all-purpose and whole-wheat flours.
2. In a large mixing bowl, combine 1¼ cups flour mixture, sugar, salt, and dry yeast.
3. In a small saucepan, combine milk, water, and butter. Heat over low until very warm (120°F to 130°F). Butter does not need to completely melt.
4. Gradually add warm liquids to dry ingredients; beat at medium speed of electric mixer two minutes.
5. Add ½ cup flour mixture and beat on high speed another 2 minutes, scraping bowl occasionally. Stir in enough additional flour mixture to make a stiff dough.
6. Turn dough out onto lightly floured surface. Knead until smooth and elastic, about 8 to 10 minutes.
7. Cover dough with plastic wrap and then a towel. Let rest 20 minutes.
8. Roll dough into a rectangle. Shape into a loaf and place in a greased 9-by-5-inch loaf pan.
9. Brush top of loaf with oil. Cover with plastic wrap and refrigerate 2 to 24 hours.
10. When ready to bake, remove dough from refrigerator; let stand 10 minutes.
11. Using a greased toothpick, prick any bubbles that may have formed on the surface of the loaf.
12. Bake bread at 400°F about 40 minutes or until loaf is golden and sounds hollow when tapped with knuckles.
13. Remove bread from pan and cool thoroughly before storing.

Per slice: 134 calories (12% from fat), 4 g protein, 25 g carbohydrate, 2 g fat, 3 mg cholesterol, 2 g fiber, 159 mg sodium.

Deep Dish Apple Pie
Serves 9

1   cup sugar
½   cup light brown sugar, packed
½   cup all-purpose flour
1   teaspoon cinnamon
¾   teaspoon nutmeg
2   tablespoons lemon juice
12 cups sliced, pared tart apples
2   tablespoons butter, cut into chunks
    pastry for a single-crust, 9-inch pie

1. Preheat oven to 425°F.
2. In a large mixing bowl, combine sugar, brown sugar, flour, cinnamon, and nutmeg; mix well.
3. Sprinkle lemon juice over apples. Toss to coat. Then stir sugar mixture into apples.
4. Pour fruit into ungreased 9-inch square baking dish. Dot with butter.
5. Roll pastry into a 10-inch square and place over top of apple filling. Fold edges of pastry under to fit just inside baking dish. Make steam vents.
6. Bake until juice is bubbly and apples are tender, about 1 hour.

Per serving: 366 calories (22% from fat), 2 g protein, 72 g carbohydrate, 9 g fat, 7 mg cholesterol, 4 g fiber, 165 mg sodium.

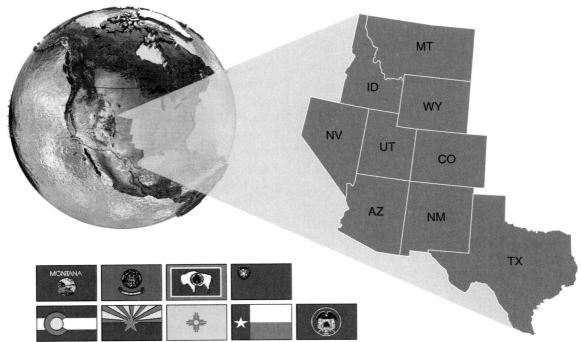

West and Southwest

The western part of the United States is a land of contrasts. Abandoned mining towns, desolate deserts, sprawling ranches, mountains, plateaus, and oil fields make up much of the landscape.

The climate of the Southwest is hot and sunny, so many fruits and vegetables grow year-round. Texas produces large quantities of grapefruit, oranges, and strawberries. Farmers in the Rio Grande valley grow early season melons, lettuce, and other fruits and vegetables. Refrigerated trucks transport this fresh produce to all parts of the United States.

Westerners tend to eat simply. Their diets are based on locally produced meat, game, and farm products. These staples are flavored with ingredients introduced by various groups to create the characteristic cuisine of this region.

Beef plays an important part in Western cooking. Western cooks grill, spit barbecue, and pit barbecue. Depending on the occasion, they might even roast a whole steer at one time.

People in this region often baste their meat with a spicy tomato-based sauce during grilling.

Lamb is also quite popular in some parts of the West. It usually is roasted or stewed. In remote areas, wild game accounts for quite a bit of the meat in the diet. Antelope, rabbit, deer, and pheasant are among the game animals used for meat.

Native Americans, Spanish peoples, and Mexicans shaped the development of Southwestern cuisine. The foods of Native Americans in this region included corn, squash, and beans. To these, the Spanish added cattle, sheep, saffron, olive oil, and anise. The Aztecs of Mexico introduced red and green peppers.

Many foods from across the Rio Grande made their way into Southwestern cuisine. Foods like tortillas, tostadas, tacos, tamales, and sopapillas all have Mexican origins. *Tamales* are a mixture of cornmeal and peppered ground meat that is wrapped in corn husks and steamed. *Sopapillas* are sweet fried pastries (**Figure 29.10**).

Figure 29.10   Sopapillas are sweet fried pastries of Mexican origins.

Southwestern Menu

Nachos
Barbecued Beef Short Ribs
Three Bean Salad
Tossed Greens with Ranch Dressing
Mexican Corn Bread
Sopapillas
Coffee

Nachos
Makes 12 appetizers

	cooking spray
3	corn tortillas
½	cup grated sharp cheddar cheese
1	large jalapeño pepper, sliced
¼	cup light sour cream

1. Preheat oven to 350°F. Coat a baking sheet with cooking spray.
2. Cut tortillas into quarters and spread on prepared baking sheet. Bake for 10 minutes, or until golden and crispy.
3. Remove baking sheet from oven. Sprinkle tortilla wedges with grated cheese and top each with a jalapeño slice.
4. Place pan under broiler and broil just until cheese melts.
5. Top each nacho with a teaspoon of sour cream. Serve immediately.

Per nacho: 36 calories (50% from fat), 2 g protein, 3 g carbohydrate, 2 g fat, 6 mg cholesterol, 0 g fiber, 33 mg sodium.

Barbecued Beef Short Ribs
Serves 6

3	pounds beef short ribs, cut into serving-sized pieces
1½	cups low-sodium tomato sauce
1	teaspoon low-sodium beef bouillon granules
⅓	cup red wine vinegar
¼	cup brown sugar, firmly packed
2	tablespoons Worcestershire sauce
½	teaspoon garlic powder
1½	teaspoons prepared mustard
2	lemons, sliced thinly
1	medium onion, sliced thinly

1. Preheat oven to 350°F.
2. Place short ribs in a deep roasting pan.
3. In a small bowl, combine tomato sauce, bouillon granules, red wine vinegar, brown sugar, Worcestershire sauce, garlic powder, and prepared mustard.
4. Pour sauce over ribs; place lemon and onion slices over sauce.
5. Bake ribs, covered, until tender, 1½ to 2 hours.
6. Serve ribs with sauce.

Per serving: 465 calories (46% from fat), 41 g protein, 19 g carbohydrate, 24 g fat, 119 mg cholesterol, 2 g fiber, 176 mg sodium.

Three Bean Salad
Serves 6

1	cup canned red kidney beans, drained and rinsed
1	cup canned low-sodium green beans, drained and rinsed
1	cup canned chickpeas, drained and rinsed
½	cup finely chopped onion
¼	teaspoon garlic powder
1	tablespoon plus 1½ teaspoons chopped parsley

1	small green pepper, seeded and chopped
½	teaspoon salt
	dash pepper
⅓	cup red wine vinegar
1	teaspoon sugar
3	tablespoons vegetable oil

1. In a large bowl, combine kidney beans, green beans, chickpeas, onion, garlic powder, parsley, green pepper, salt, and pepper; mix well.
2. In small bowl, combine vinegar, sugar, and oil.
3. Pour dressing over beans and toss.
4. Let salad stand in refrigerator for an hour before serving.

Per serving: 164 calories (44% from fat), 6 g protein, 19 g carbohydrate, 8 g fat, 0 mg cholesterol, 5 g fiber, 330 mg sodium.

Tossed Greens with Ranch Dressing
Serves 6

¾	cup plain nonfat yogurt
1½	teaspoons prepared mustard
1½	teaspoons lemon juice
1	tablespoon chopped green onion (tops and bottoms)
1	tablespoon chopped fresh chives
6	cups assorted salad greens

1. In small bowl, combine yogurt, mustard, lemon juice, onion, and chives.
2. Cover and refrigerate dressing until well chilled.
3. Clean salad greens and tear into bite-sized pieces.
4. When ready to serve, place greens in a large salad bowl. Toss with dressing and serve immediately.

Per serving: 33 calories (17% from fat), 3 g protein, 5 g carbohydrate, 1 g fat, 2 mg cholesterol, 1 g fiber, 60 mg sodium.

Mexican Corn Bread
Serves 8

1	cup cornmeal
1	cup all-purpose flour
1	cup buttermilk

¾	teaspoon baking soda
¼	teaspoon salt
½	cup onion, chopped
2	eggs, beaten
2	tablespoons cooking oil
1	can cream-style corn, low-sodium
½	cup green pepper, chopped
¼	pound cheddar cheese, grated

1. Preheat oven to 350°F.
2. In a medium bowl, combine all ingredients except cheese.
3. Pour half the batter in a 2½-quart casserole. Cover with half the grated cheddar cheese.
4. Add the other half of the batter and cover with the remaining cheese.
5. Bake until corn bread is golden brown and tests done, about 40 minutes.

Per serving: 219 calories (41% from fat), 9 g protein, 26 g carbohydrate, 10 g fat, 69 mg cholesterol, 4 g fiber, 334 mg sodium.

Sopapillas
Makes about two dozen pastries

1	cup all-purpose flour
1¼	teaspoons baking powder
¼	teaspoon salt
1½	teaspoons shortening
¼	cup lukewarm water
	shortening or oil for frying

1. In a medium mixing bowl, stir together flour, baking powder, and salt.
2. Cut in shortening until mixture resembles coarse cornmeal.
3. Add water gradually, stirring with a fork until dough clings together.
4. Turn dough out onto lightly floured surface. Knead until smooth. Let rest for 10 minutes.
5. Roll dough into a 10-by-12-inch rectangle, about ⅛-inch thick. Cut into 2-inch squares.
6. In a deep fryer or large saucepan, heat shortening or oil until it reaches 375°F.
7. Add sopapillas, a few at a time. Fry about 30 seconds on each side.
8. Serve warm with butter and honey or sprinkle with confectioner's sugar.

Per sopapilla: 31 calories (41% from fat), 1 g protein, 4 g carbohydrate, 1 g fat, 0 mg cholesterol, 0 g fiber, 39 mg sodium.

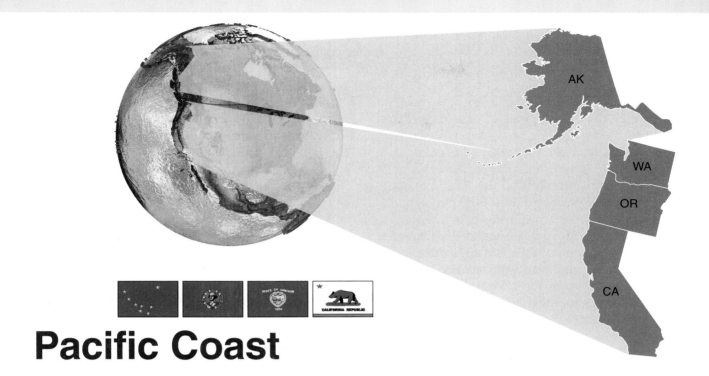

Pacific Coast

The Pacific Coast includes the states of California, Oregon, Washington, and Alaska. These diverse states vary widely in geography, climate, culture, and food customs.

Most parts of California have rich, fertile soil; a warm, sunny climate; and adequate rainfall. Fruits and vegetables of all kinds grow in abundance. Grapes, oranges, and apples are among the state's leading cash crops, as are almonds, walnuts, and rice. Lettuce, tomatoes, cabbage, avocados, strawberries, blueberries, and cantaloupe are also grown in California (**Figure 29.11**).

The ocean and inland lakes provide a bounty of fish and shellfish. Wild-caught seafood includes albacore, lobster, sardines, seabass, shrimp, and sole. In addition, California's fishing industry produces farmed oysters and clams.

Few rules or traditions hamper California-style cuisine. Cooks might simply broil salmon steaks and top them with a fresh dill sauce. More unique combinations, such as crab and artichoke hearts or chicken and anchovies, are also popular. Vegetarian dishes might feature creative uses of tofu, seeds, and nuts.

A lot of the foods that are part of California's cuisine are also available in Oregon and Washington. Many types of berries and tree fruits, such as peaches, apples, and apricots, grow in these states. Other fruits and vegetables are shipped there from California.

Steaks, chops, and other standard fare of the United States make up much of the diet of the Pacific Northwest. These foods are supplemented

Ken Wolter/Shutterstock.com

Figure 29.11 A majority of the salad greens eaten in the United States are grown in California's Salinas Valley.

by wild game, fish, and seafood. Dungeness crabs, butter clams, Columbia River salmon, and Olympia oysters are especially popular.

Cooks in the Pacific states often focus on simple cooking techniques. They take advantage of the natural flavors and colors of the foods (**Figure 29.12**). Cooks usually bake or broil fresh fish and shellfish. They serve vegetables raw in large salads or cooked just until crisp-tender. They often serve fresh fruits for dessert.

The people who settled the Pacific Coast influenced the development of the cuisine. From the Far East came Chinese, Japanese, and Koreans, and from the South Pacific came Polynesians. Many of these immigrants worked as cooks, thus contributing foods and dishes native to their homelands. Chop suey, for example, was supposedly invented in California by a Chinese cook. He named the dish *chop suey*, which means "everything chopped up."

The Mexicans who settled in Southern California brought their cultures' dishes with them. Tacos, tamales, enchiladas, guacamole, chili, and refried beans are all popular in this area of the state. The Spanish brought a type of stew called *cocido* (a mixture of vegetables, beef, lamb, ham, fowl, and a sausage called *chorizo*).

The *prospectors* (explorers who search for mineral deposits) who flocked to the Pacific states in search of gold brought sourdough with them. **Sourdough** is a dough containing active microscopic yeast plants. It is used as a leavening agent. The prospectors made sourdough by mixing together flour, water, and salt. They exposed the mixture to the air to allow it to absorb yeast cells. Then they added the dough to flour, water, and other available ingredients to make a variety of baked products. They always kept a small amount of the dough after each baking to serve as a starter for the next batch. They replenished the starter by adding more flour and water.

Only that part of Alaska that lies within the Arctic region has the long, frigid winters many people associate with the state. Farther south, the climate is more mild, and vegetable, grain, and dairy farms dot the countryside.

Caribou sausage and reindeer steak are Alaskan specialties. Alaskans also enjoy rabbit and bear hunted in the wilderness. The icy, clear waters of the Pacific Ocean provide Alaskan king crab. Glacier-fed lakes and streams provide delicious salmon and trout.

Alaskan cooks use the blueberries, huckleberries, and cranberries that grow wild to make pies and sauces. Other Alaskan specialties include fiddlehead ferns (young leaves of certain ferns eaten as greens), raw rose hips (the ripened false fruit of the rosebush), and cranberry ketchup.

Jacek Chabraszewski/Shutterstock.com

Figure 29.12 Fresh salmon with crisp-tender vegetables and potatoes typifies the use of natural flavors and colors found in Pacific Coast cooking.

Pacific Coast Menu

Spicy Fried Tofu
Cilantro Lime Rice
Avocado Salad
Sourdough Bread
Strawberry Yogurt Dessert
Iced Tea

Spicy Fried Tofu
Serves 4

1   12- to 14-ounce package extra-firm tofu, drained
3   tablespoons light soy sauce
¼   cup cornstarch
⅛   teaspoon cayenne pepper
½   teaspoon cumin
¼   teaspoon garlic powder
2   tablespoons olive oil
¼   cup apricot preserves
2   tablespoons cider vinegar
¼   teaspoon ground ginger
⅛   teaspoon crushed red pepper

1. Cut tofu into ¼-inch thick slices. Place the slices in a single layer on paper towels while preparing the other ingredients.
2. Pour the soy sauce into a pie plate.
3. In a second pie plate, combine the cornstarch, cayenne pepper, cumin, and garlic powder. Stir with a fork until completely blended.
4. Heat the olive oil in a skillet over medium-high heat.
5. Dip the tofu slices in the soy sauce and then in the cornstarch mixture, making sure to coat both sides.
6. Place the coated tofu slices in the hot skillet. Fry until golden brown. Flip and brown the other side.
7. To make the sauce, combine the apricot preserves, vinegar, ginger, and crushed red pepper in a liquid measuring cup, stirring to blend thoroughly. Microwave the sauce for 15 seconds on high power. Stir and serve over fried tofu.

Per serving: 217 calories (46% from fat), 10 g protein, 22 g carbohydrate, 11 g fat, 0 mg cholesterol, 1 g fiber, 216 mg sodium.

Cilantro Lime Rice
Serves 4 to 6

2   cups water
1   cup long-grain rice
¾   teaspoon lime zest
2   tablespoons lime juice
⅓   cup chopped cilantro

1. In a large saucepan, combine water and rice. Bring to a boil over high heat.
2. Reduce heat to low and simmer until rice is tender and all water is absorbed, about 15 minutes.
3. Stir the lime zest, lime juice, and cilantro into the cooked rice.

Per serving: 177 calories (0% from fat), 4 g protein, 38 g carbohydrate, 0 g fat, 0 mg cholesterol, 1 g fiber, 2 mg sodium.

Avocado Salad
Serves 4

½   medium pink grapefruit (or ½ cup canned grapefruit sections)
1   large navel orange
½   cup green grapes
¼   cup pomegranate seeds (optional)
2   cups mixed salad greens
1   avocado, peeled and sliced
2   tablespoons chopped walnuts
¼   cup plus 2 tablespoons low-fat French dressing

1. Section grapefruit and oranges; set aside.
2. In a salad bowl or on individual salad plates, arrange mixed greens.
3. Top greens with orange and grapefruit sections. Arrange avocado slices over citrus fruits.
4. Sprinkle salad with grapes, pomegranate seeds, and walnuts. Serve with French dressing.

Per serving: 167 calories (54% from fat), 5 g protein, 16 g carbohydrate, 11 g fat, 1 mg cholesterol, 3 g fiber, 27 mg sodium.

Sourdough Bread
Makes 1 loaf

Sourdough starter:

3½	cups bread flour
1	tablespoon sugar
1	package active dry yeast
2	cups warm water

Sourdough bread:

2½ to 3 cups all-purpose flour	
1	package active dry yeast
1	tablespoon plus 1½ teaspoons sugar
¾	teaspoon salt
¼	cup plus 2 tablespoons fat-free milk
2	tablespoons water
1	tablespoon butter
¾	cup sourdough starter

1. In large bowl or crock, prepare starter by combining flour, sugar, and yeast. Gradually add warm water, beating until smooth.
2. Cover starter tightly and let stand in a warm place for 2 days.
3. When ready to prepare bread, combine 1¼ cups flour, yeast, sugar, and salt in a large mixing bowl.
4. Heat milk, water, and butter until very warm (120°F to 130°F). Butter does not need to completely melt.
5. Gradually add milk mixture and sourdough starter to dry ingredients. Beat 2 minutes at medium speed, scraping bowl occasionally. Then beat 2 more minutes at high speed, adding enough additional flour to form a stiff dough.
6. Turn dough out onto a lightly floured surface and knead until smooth and elastic, about 8 to 10 minutes.
7. Cover dough with a clean towel and let rise in a warm place until doubled in bulk, about 1 hour.
8. Punch the dough down and shape it into a round loaf. Place the loaf on a lightly greased baking sheet and slash the top with a sharp knife.
9. Cover the loaf with a clean towel and let it rise in a warm place until doubled in bulk, about 1 hour.
10. Bake the bread at 400°F for about 25 minutes or until the loaf sounds hollow when lightly tapped with the knuckles.
11. Remove the loaf from the baking sheet and place it on a cooling rack.

Per slice: 100 calories (8% from fat), 3 g protein, 20 g carbohydrate, 1 g fat, 2 mg cholesterol, 1 g fiber, 85 mg sodium.

Strawberry Yogurt Dessert
Serves 4

2	cups plain fat-free Greek yogurt
¼	cup honey
2	cups strawberries, hulled and quartered
¼	cup slivered almonds, toasted

1. Place ½ cup yogurt in each of four dessert dishes.
2. Top yogurt in each dish with 1 tablespoon of honey. Then add ½ cup of strawberries to each dish.
3. Sprinkle 1 tablespoon of toasted almonds on top of the strawberries in each dish.

Per serving: 206 calories (17% from fat), 15 g protein, 30 g carbohydrate, 4 g fat, 2 mg cholesterol, 3 g fiber, 59 mg sodium.

Hawaiian Islands

The Hawaiian Islands are much more than a tourist's paradise. They have a rich history and colorful culture. They also have beautiful scenery and delicious food.

Historians believe Hawaii's first settlers were Polynesians from other Pacific islands. After their arrival, Hawaii was isolated from the rest of the world for many years. Although no written records exist, the Hawaiians have a rich heritage of songs and stories.

One of the outstanding figures in Hawaiian history is Kamehameha. Kamehameha eventually captured all of the islands and became king. He was able to establish order and peace throughout the islands.

Christian missionaries and European traders came to Hawaii in the 1800s. Some *enterprising* (daring) people came to the Hawaiian Islands and began large sugar plantations. The increasing numbers of Europeans slowly weakened the traditional Hawaiian monarchy. The monarchy finally ended with the death of Kamehameha V. Then, in 1898, the United States *annexed* (added to its own territory) Hawaii. Hawaii became a state in 1959.

In the years since becoming a state, Hawaii has grown rapidly. Today, tourism is Hawaii's biggest industry. Agriculture is also a large part of the state's economy. Hawaii is a leading grower of pineapple and sugarcane. Coffee and macadamia nuts are major crops, too.

The traditional Hawaiian diet was not highly varied. It consisted mainly of *poi*, a smooth paste made from the starchy root of the taro plant (**Figure 29.13**). The Hawaiians also ate *limu*, or seaweed, as a relish. Their main sources of protein were the numerous varieties of fish they harvested from the waters surrounding the islands.

Eric Broder Van Dyke/Shutterstock.com

Figure 29.13 Poi is made from the starchy root of the taro plant. What other foods typify Hawaiian cuisine?

The early Hawaiians had some interesting food customs. Unlike many cultures, in the Hawaiian culture, men typically prepared the food. Men and women were not permitted to eat at the same table. Their foods were not allowed to be prepared in the same oven, either.

Today, Hawaiian meal patterns are similar to those in other regions of the United States. Breakfast may consist of fruit, cereal, eggs, and coffee. Lunch and dinner may incorporate some traditional Hawaiian foods. Poi, fish, and seaweed may be a typical noon meal. These foods may also be served for dinner, along with a vegetable and a dessert, such as baked bananas.

Throughout history, various groups of people who came to Hawaii each contributed different foods. The first Polynesians are thought to have brought coconuts and *breadfruit* (a round, starchy fruit). European traders are believed to have introduced chicken and pork. The missionaries brought the stews, chowders, and corn dishes of their native New England. Curries reflect Indian influence.

Sugar plantation owners brought large groups of Chinese workers to labor in the fields. The Chinese brought rice, bean sprouts, Chinese cabbage, soybeans, snow peas, and bamboo shoots. They also introduced the stir-fry technique for cooking foods quickly over high heat.

A number of Japanese immigrated to the Hawaiian Islands. They brought with them a variety of rice and fish dishes and pickled foods.

Contributions from all these groups led to the amazing variety visitors find in Hawaiian markets today. Water chestnuts, watercress, squash, and lotus root are just a few of the many vegetables sold. Papayas, mangoes, and pineapples are among the many locally grown fruits. Lobsters, crabs, opihi (a clamlike mollusk), oysters, shrimp, tuna, snapper, and salmon come from the bounty of the surrounding waters. Other popular items are fresh tofu, soybean cakes, Japanese fish cake, Korean kim chee, and persimmon tea.

The native Hawaiians held lavish feasts on special occasions. **Luaus** are elaborate outdoor feasts that are still popular in the islands today. At these feasts, *kalua puaa* is often served as a main course. This is a whole, young pig that is dressed, stuffed, and cooked in a pit called an **imu**. The imu is lined with hot rocks covered with banana leaves. The dressed pig is stuffed with hot rocks and placed on a wire rack. More leaves are placed over the top of the imu followed by more hot rocks and earth. Bananas, sweet potatoes, and meat or seafood dishes wrapped in leaves may be roasted with the pig. After several hours, the pig and other foods are dug from the pit and are ready to serve.

No traditional Hawaiian meal would be complete without poi. Other Hawaiian foods that may be served at a luau include *kamano lomi*. This is salted salmon that is mashed with tomatoes and green onions. *Haupia* is a pudding made of milk, sugar, cornstarch, and grated fresh coconut. A variety of fresh fruits, macadamia nuts, and kukui nuts may be served along with the haupia for dessert (**Figure 29.14**).

Musical entertainment, singing, and dancing usually accompany a luau. Guests often join in the festivities.

g215/Shutterstock.com

Figure 29.14 Macadamia nuts are often served with haupia at Hawaiian gatherings.

Hawaiian Menu

Shrimp Curry
Rice
Spinach with Evaporated Milk
Banana Biscuits
Tropical Fruit Medley
Coffee

Shrimp Curry
Serves 4

¾   pound peeled, deveined shrimp*
1½   teaspoons butter
1   finely chopped green onion
½   teaspoon grated fresh ginger root*
1   tablespoon plus 1½ teaspoons flour
½   cup cold fat-free milk
¾   cup coconut milk
¼   teaspoon salt
1 to 1½ teaspoons curry powder
3   cups cooked brown rice

1. Melt butter in a skillet over medium-high heat. Add onion and ginger root. Sauté 2 to 3 minutes until onion is tender.
2. Shake flour and milk in a small, tightly covered container until thoroughly blended.
3. Add the flour mixture to the skillet and reduce heat to low. Cook sauce, stirring constantly, until smooth and bubbly.
4. When sauce begins to thicken, stir in coconut milk, salt, and curry powder. Cover and allow mixture to simmer over low heat for 10 minutes.
5. Add shrimp. Continue simmering just until shrimp are cooked through, about 5 minutes.
6. Serve over rice. Pass small dishes of several of the following accompaniments: shredded coconut, finely chopped green pepper, finely chopped green onion, pineapple chutney, and/ or orange marmalade.

*You can substitute ¾ pound cooked boneless, skinless chicken breast cut into bite-sized pieces for the shrimp. You can use 1½ teaspoons ground ginger in place of the fresh ginger root.

Per serving: 369 calories (32% from fat), 24 g protein, 39 g carbohydrate, 13 g fat, 171 mg cholesterol, 3 g fiber, 383 mg sodium.

Spinach with Evaporated Milk
Serves 4

1   pound fresh spinach
¼   teaspoon salt
1½   teaspoons butter
2   tablespoons water
2   tablespoons fat-free evaporated milk

1. Wash spinach thoroughly and remove stems.
2. Place spinach, salt, butter, water, and evaporated milk in a large nonstick saucepan. Cover and cook over medium heat until the spinach begins to wilt.
3. Uncover and cook until spinach is tender, stirring frequently. Serve immediately.

Per serving: 43 calories (42% from fat), 4 g protein, 5 g carbohydrate, 2 g fat, 4 mg cholesterol, 3 g fiber, 255 mg sodium.

Banana Biscuits
Makes about 8 biscuits

¾   cup all-purpose flour
1   teaspoon baking powder
1   teaspoon sugar
¼   teaspoon salt
½   cup mashed bananas
1   tablespoon plus 1½ teaspoons shortening
2   tablespoons fat-free milk
1   large egg white, lightly beaten

1. Preheat oven to 425°F.
2. In a medium mixing bowl, combine flour, baking powder, sugar, and salt.
3. In a smaller bowl, thoroughly combine mashed bananas with shortening.
4. Add banana mixture to flour mixture. Using a pastry blender or two knives, cut in bananas until mixture resembles small peas.
5. Combine milk with beaten egg white. Gently stir liquids into flour mixture with a fork until a soft dough forms.
6. Turn dough out onto lightly floured surface. Knead 8 to 10 times.
7. Roll dough ½ inch thick. Cut into rounds with a 2-inch biscuit cutter.
8. Place biscuits close together on an ungreased baking sheet. Bake 12 to 15 minutes or until golden brown. Serve hot.

Per biscuit: 82 calories (33% from fat), 2 g protein, 13 g carbohydrate, 3 g fat, 0 mg cholesterol, 1 g fiber, 143 mg sodium.

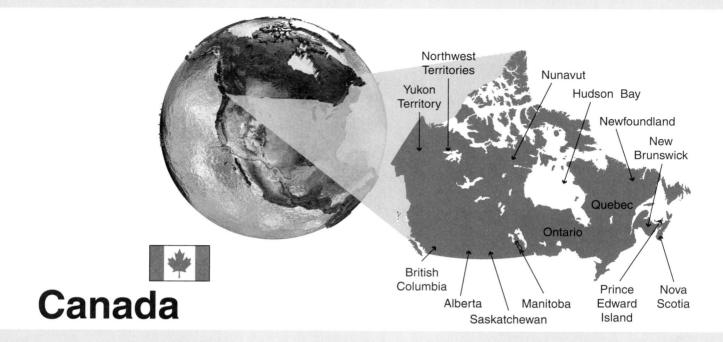

Canada

In terms of land mass, Canada is the second largest country in the world; however, it has a population smaller than the state of California. The majority of Canadians live within a few hundred miles of the country's southern border. Over half the people live in the area around the Great Lakes and the St. Lawrence River.

Like the United States, Canada is a land that was settled by immigrants from many nations. These settlers combined their cultures with those of native peoples. Their food customs were major influences on Canadian cuisine.

Geography and Climate of Canada

Canada is divided into 10 provinces and 3 territories. Diverse geography partly accounts for the country's varied climate. Canada boasts the world's longest coastline. On the Atlantic side, air currents from over the ocean bring high annual levels of rain and snow. Along the Pacific coast, ocean airstreams give British Columbia the warmest average temperatures throughout the year. Just off the mainland, Vancouver Island's tremendous annual rainfall combines with the warm air to create a rain forest climate. The Arctic Ocean to the north surrounds many islands. It borders a region with long, dark winters. Temperatures here stay below freezing all but a few weeks of the year.

Several mountain ranges break up the landscape and shape the climate of Canada's interior regions. Rain and snow are common in the mountain areas. The valleys, by contrast, are often described as desertlike.

The key geographical feature of central and eastern Canada is a rocky, U-shaped region called the *Canadian Shield*. This area, which encircles Hudson Bay, is made up mostly of low hills and lakes. The soil in this region is not very suitable for farming.

Between the Rocky Mountains and the Canadian Shield lie the vast Interior Plains. The southern part of this region is home to some of the most productive grain fields in the world. This region reports some of the lowest levels of annual rainfall in Canada. Much of the rain that falls comes in the spring, preparing the fields for planting. The summers in this area are hot, but the winters bring some of the lowest temperatures south of the Arctic.

Canadian Agriculture

Food products play a large role in the Canadian economy. Much of Canada's land is well suited for agriculture. Wheat, barley, apples, berries, and potatoes are among the economically important crops grown by Canadian farmers. Dairy products and livestock are significant, too. Fishing is an important industry in coastal regions. Cod, flounder, lobster, and salmon are among the most valuable catches brought in by Canadian fishers.

Canadian Culture

By European standards, Canada is a young country. Despite its youth, Canada has developed into one of the world's leading nations. It is strengthened by a rich history and a diversity of cultures.

Influences on Canadian Culture

The **Aboriginals**, or first inhabitants of the land, influenced Canadian culture and food customs. Canadian Aboriginals form two groups—*First Nations* and *Inuit*. First Nations lived throughout Canada. Some were farmers; others were fishers or nomadic hunters. Inuit (once known as Eskimo) lived in the far northern regions where the land was not suitable for cultivation. Therefore, Inuit hunted inland game animals or marine mammals (**Figure 29.15**).

redfrisbee/Shutterstock.com

Figure 29.15 Stone figures called *inukshuk* were built by the Inuit people to mark the land for such purposes as travel routes, food supplies, and ancestral memorials.

In the early 1600s, British and French fur trappers and traders began establishing settlements in Canada. The British settled primarily along the Atlantic coast and in the Hudson Bay area. The French explorers claimed a vast territory along the St. Lawrence River and the Great Lakes. This territory became known as New France. The Inuit had little contact with these early settlers. The First Nations, however, helped the settlers learn how to hunt, fish, and plant crops.

A series of wars between the French and English colonists in Canada took place between 1689 and 1763. As a result, most of New France came under British rule and was renamed Quebec. Through the Quebec Act in 1774, Britain granted the French-speaking citizens in this area political, religious, and linguistic rights.

The following year, the Revolutionary War broke out in the American colonies. Thousands of colonists who chose to remain loyal to the British crown moved north into Canada. This led Britain to split Quebec into two colonies. They were later reunited as the Province of Canada. In 1867, this colony was joined with Nova Scotia and New Brunswick to form a new country—the Dominion of Canada. Each of the former colonies became a province in the new country.

Exploration and settlement of western Canada had been increasing since the first half of the early 1800s. Within four years of the formation of the Dominion of Canada, two more provinces were added. By 1949, a total of 10 provinces had joined the Dominion.

Modern Canadian Culture

Today, Canada is a federal state with a democratic parliament. The Parliament is modeled after the British government system. It is made up of a Senate and a House of Commons.

Canada has a multicultural society. Most of Canada's people have a British or French background. Many Canadians also claim ties to other European countries. Others have an Asian heritage. In addition, three to four percent of Canada's people are of native descent.

Canada has two national languages. English is the primary language of the majority of Canadians. French is also the main language of a sizable percentage of the people. The largest segment of the French-speaking population lives in the province of Quebec.

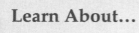

Learn About...

Canadian Holidays

As in all countries, holidays are an important part of the lifestyle in Canada. Many of these events involve the sharing of traditional foods.

Spring and summer holidays include Easter and Canada Day. Spring vegetables, such as asparagus and fiddlehead ferns, are often served with ham for Easter dinner. Canada Day, which is observed on July 1, honors Canada's freedom from British rule. Strawberry festivals are often held at the time of this holiday. Picnics, fireworks, parades, and concerts are also part of the festivities.

The fall and winter months bring a number of holidays in Canada. Thanksgiving is observed on the second Monday in October. A turkey dinner ended with hot pumpkin pie is the typical feast. A traditional Christmas dinner reflects the British heritage of many Canadians. This meal is likely to include roast goose with plum pudding. Shortbread and fruitcake are also common holiday treats.

Know and Apply

1. What holiday in the United States is similar to Canada Day?
2. What is your favorite food associated with a holiday?

Canadian Cuisine

The typical Canadian diet is nutritious. It includes a variety of foods and features a bounty of fruits, vegetables, and grain products. Meat and dairy products also play key roles in Canadian cuisine.

Health experts in Canada encourage people to read labels to make wise choices from the *array* (large amount) of available foods. They want people to limit calories, fat, sugar, and salt in the foods they eat. They promote the use of whole grains, lean meats, and lower-fat dairy products. Canadian health experts also encourage people to be active to maintain healthy body weight and help reduce disease risk.

Canada's diverse climate and geography have caused available foods to vary from one part of the country to another. Different native and immigrant influences also affected each area. Like the United States, therefore, Canada has a regional cuisine.

Traditional Canadian foods were based largely on native ingredients. Canadian cooks could not obtain these ingredients all year long. Therefore, classic Canadian cuisine was seasonal in nature. The distinctive qualities of what was once standard Canadian fare have become less striking in recent years. Food products are made by large manufacturers instead of small-scale entrepreneurs. Busy lifestyles have led to widespread use of processed foods. Modern transportation has brought cooks a broad range of foods that are not produced in Canada. It has also allowed year-round availability of foods that were once seasonal. These factors have worked together to remove some of the unique character from everyday menus in Canada. Traditional dishes do still appear at holidays and other special occasions.

In the past, food was central to many Canadian social events, such as teas, church suppers, and quilting bees. It was the main focus of parties celebrating the harvest of such foods as strawberries, smelts, apples, and maple sugar. Food also played a key role at weddings, funerals, picnics, and other family gatherings. At these functions, cooks proudly displayed their pickles, preserves, and baked goods for all to enjoy.

Immigrant Influence on Canadian Cuisine

British, Scottish, Irish, French, and German settlers all had an effect on the development of Canadian cuisine. British influence can be seen in the popularity of such dishes as steak and kidney pie. *Yorkshire pudding* is a British food that appears in some Canadian cookbooks. It is a quick bread flavored with drippings from beef roast (**Figure 29.16**). Tea (both the drink and the light afternoon meal) are also signs of British influence on Canadian cuisine. Scones, custards, and baked and steamed puddings are other British favorites that have become part of Canadian fare.

Two traditional entrees served in Canada for Christmas and New Year's dinners are Irish in

Joe Gough/Shutterstock.com

Figure 29.16 Yorkshire pudding can be found in many Canadian cookbooks. What other British foods do Canadians often prepare and eat?

origin. Spiced beef and stuffed pork tenderloins are often the center of winter holiday meals.

Provincial French influence is most prominent in the cuisine of Quebec. It also plays a role in the foods of the East Coast provinces. Hollandaise sauce and oil and vinegar salad dressings flavored with garlic are examples of French influence.

German influence is seen in foods brought to Canada by groups of Mennonite and Amish settlers. One example is dandelion salad with bacon and sour cream dressing. German influence is also seen in the quality baked goods that are popular in areas with large Amish and Mennonite populations.

Even the United States influenced the cuisine of Canada. Many people from New England moved north and settled along the east coast of Canada. Their effect is seen in such dishes as seafood chowders, baked beans, and steamed brown bread. People from the mid-Atlantic states settled in Ontario. Pancakes, gingersnap cookies, and hearty soups may be among the Canadian foods that reflect their influence. Another example of the United States' influence is in the traditional foods served for Thanksgiving in Canada—turkey, cranberries, and pumpkin pie.

Canadian Main Dishes

Main dishes in Canada generally include meat, poultry, or fish. Not surprisingly, menus in the coastal provinces often feature seafood (**Figure 29.17**). The East Coast is known for cod, flounder, lobster, crab, and oysters. In this part

Maurizio De Mattei/Shutterstock.com

Figure 29.17 Fishing is important to the economy in Canada's coastal areas, and fish is important to the cuisine in these areas, too.

of Canada, seafood chowders, boiled lobster, oyster dressing, and fish salads are popular dishes. Salmon is the primary catch in the West Coast province of British Columbia. Canadians enjoy salmon poached, smoked, broiled, and grilled. Inland lakes and streams, especially in the northern provinces, provide freshwater fish including trout, pickerel, and whitefish. Commercial ice fishing makes these fish widely available during the winter months. Panfrying and baking with stuffing are two popular preparation methods.

Canadian people eat beef more than any other meat. Throughout Canada, people enjoy grilled steaks, roast prime rib, and beef sandwiches. Spiced beef, which is preserved with a mixture of salt, cloves, nutmeg, and allspice, is a Canadian Christmas specialty.

Pork was once the most commonly eaten meat in some parts of Canada, and it is still quite popular. In Canada's early days, hogs were raised on almost every farm. Butchering and sausage making were annual fall events. Most pork cuts were salted to preserve them for use throughout the winter. Better cuts, such as the hams, were cured in brine and smoked. This extra processing inspired many people to save hams for special occasions, such as Easter dinner.

Poultry is also common as a Canadian main dish. Chicken is most popular, and it is served in a variety of ways. Roasted chicken, grilled chicken, and chicken salads are favorite entrees. Canadians enjoy other types of poultry, too, especially at holiday times. Turkey is the traditional entree for Thanksgiving in Canada. Goose is often the bird of choice for Christmas dinner.

Game meats are not unusual on the menus of people living in rural northern regions. Bear, caribou, and moose are abundant in these wilderness areas (**Figure 29.18**). In other parts of Canada, rabbit is a more likely game entree. Stewing and roasting are two favorite cooking methods.

Canadian Fruits and Vegetables

The soil and climate in Southern Canada are suitable for growing a wide variety of fruits and vegetables. Apples are probably the most popular fruit in Canada. Different species are available from midsummer to late fall. Canadians use apples to make cider, apple butter, and a number of desserts and condiments.

GoodMood Photo/Shutterstock.com

Figure 29.18 Caribou meat is lean and nutritious because caribou feed on grasses and plants.

Gooseberries, strawberries, and rhubarb are available in Canada in the spring. Blueberries, raspberries, and blackberries are part of the harvest of summer fruits. Plums, peaches, and cherries are among the tree fruits grown in this region. With this range of fruits, few would wonder why fruit pies are such popular desserts in Canada. Canadians also have a long tradition of putting up their bounty of native fruits in jams, jellies, and other preserves.

Canadian vegetables are just as varied as the fruits. Asparagus and watercress are often the first vegetables ready for picking in the spring. Peas, leaf lettuce, radishes, tomatoes, cucumbers, and corn follow in the summer. Canadians enjoy vegetables in soups, salads, and side dishes.

Canadian Grain Products

Canada has an abundant wheat crop, and bread products are part of most meals. Breakfasts may include buckwheat pancakes or muffins, which are sometimes called *gems*. Lunches and teas are likely to feature sandwiches on hearty yeast breads. Yeast rolls or quick breads flavored with fruits are popular accompaniments to dinner entrees.

Baked goods such as cakes, cookies, and pies are also Canadian standards. Early Canadian cookbooks included a wealth of recipes for these treats, which were the pride of many cooks. Many of these traditional recipes were sweetened with maple sugar or maple syrup, which was made locally every spring.

Classic Canadian menus seldom include pasta products. Wild rice, however, may appear as a side dish or in a stuffing. Wild rice grows in shallow Canadian lakes and streams. It must be harvested by hand from canoes and then dried. The labor-intensive harvesting process causes wild rice to be fairly costly (**Figure 29.19**).

Canadian Dairy Products

Large herds of dairy cows make dairy products popular in Canada. A variety of flavorful cheeses are produced throughout the country. Cheddar may be the most commonly produced cheese, but Oka, Ermite blue, and St. Benoit are uniquely Canadian.

The use of dairy products is prominent throughout traditional Canadian recipes. Oysters may be poached in milk. Cream is added to various soups, which are a filling first course in many winter menus. In the summer, homemade ice cream is a classic dessert.

Dionisvera/Shutterstock.com

Figure 29.19 Wild rice, with its long, dark grains, adds a firm texture and nutty flavor to some Canadian side dishes.

Canadian Menu

Cheddar Cheese Soup
Harvest Pork Roast
Spicy Lemon Squash
Wild Rice Medley
Watercress and Mushroom Salad
Nova Scotia Oatcakes with Maple Butter
Cranberry-Orange Sorbet
Apple Cider

Cheddar Cheese Soup
Serves 6

⅓	cup minced onion
1	tablespoon butter
2½	cups low-sodium chicken broth
½	cup fat-free milk
2	tablespoons flour
1½	cups evaporated fat-free milk
1½	cups shredded reduced-fat cheddar cheese
½	teaspoon dry mustard
⅛	teaspoon cayenne pepper

1. In a large nonstick saucepan, sauté onion in butter over medium heat until tender.
2. Stir in chicken broth, reduce heat to low, and simmer for 15 minutes.
3. Combine milk and flour in a small, tightly covered container. Shake vigorously to mix thoroughly.
4. Slowly pour flour mixture into broth, stirring constantly. Continue stirring gently until soup begins to thicken.
5. Add evaporated milk, cheese, dry mustard, and cayenne pepper. Continue stirring gently until cheese is melted and soup is heated through. Do not allow soup to boil.

Per serving: 177 calories (41% from fat), 15 g protein, 12 g carbohydrate, 8 g fat, 23 mg cholesterol, 0 g fiber, 376 mg sodium.

Harvest Pork Roast
Serves 6

1	2-pound boneless pork loin roast
1	tablespoon vegetable oil
½	cup apple cider
½	teaspoon dried thyme
¼	teaspoon dried marjoram
1	tablespoon dried parsley

1. Trim exterior fat from pork loin.
2. Combine oil and apple cider in a blender. Blend for 15 seconds.
3. Generously brush cider mixture over the pork loin. Sprinkle moist surface with thyme, marjoram, and parsley.
4. Place pork loin on a rack in a shallow roasting pan. Place roasting pan in 350°F oven and roast for 45 minutes to an hour, until internal temperature measures 145°F on a meat thermometer.
5. Remove pork loin from oven. Let it stand for 10 minutes before slicing.

Per serving: 176 calories (41% from fat), 24 g protein, 2 g carbohydrate, 8 g fat, 67 mg cholesterol, 0 g fiber, 58 mg sodium.

Spicy Lemon Squash
Serves 6

1	teaspoon grated lemon peel
¼	cup brown sugar
½	teaspoon ground ginger
½	teaspoon ground cinnamon
¼	teaspoon ground nutmeg
3	tablespoons butter, melted
1	teaspoon rum extract
3	acorn squash

1. In a small bowl, combine lemon peel, brown sugar, ginger, cinnamon, and nutmeg. Stir in butter and rum extract.
2. Wash squash. Cut in half and remove seeds.
3. Sprinkle the insides of the squash with the spice mixture.
4. Place squash halves, cut sides up, in a shallow baking dish. Add ¼ inch of water to the dish.

5. Cover the dish with aluminum foil and bake at 400°F for 30 minutes, or until tender.

Per serving: 128 calories (42% from fat), 1 g protein, 18 g carbohydrate, 6 g fat, 16 mg cholesterol, 3 g fiber, 63 mg sodium.

Wild Rice Medley
Serves 6

¼	cup chopped onion
¼	cup minced celery
1	tablespoon butter
½	cup wild rice
2¾	cups low-sodium chicken broth
¼	teaspoon salt
½	cup brown rice
1	tablespoon chopped fresh parsley

1. In a medium saucepan, sauté onion and celery.
2. Add wild rice, chicken broth, and salt. Increase heat to high and bring to a boil.
3. Cover, reduce heat to low, and simmer for 15 minutes.
4. Add brown rice, cover, and simmer an additional 30 minutes.
5. Remove pan from heat. Drain any unabsorbed liquid. Sprinkle rice with parsley.

Per serving: 133 calories (20% from fat), 5 g protein, 23 g carbohydrate, 3 g fiber, 5 mg cholesterol, 2 g fiber, 197 mg sodium.

Nova Scotia Oatcakes
Makes 16

½	cup all-purpose flour
3	tablespoons brown sugar
½	teaspoon salt
¼	teaspoon baking soda
1½	cups oatmeal, quick or old fashioned, uncooked
¼	cup shortening
¼	cup cold water

1. Preheat oven to 425°F.
2. In a medium mixing bowl, combine flour, brown sugar, salt, baking soda, and oats.
3. Cut in the shortening with a pastry blender or two knives until the mixture resembles coarse crumbs.

4. With a fork, add water a tablespoon at a time until dough will hold together but is not sticky.
5. Press dough into a greased 9-inch square pan. Cut dough into 16 squares; do not separate.
6. Bake in preheated oven for 15 minutes, or until browned.
7. Separate squares into a napkin-lined basket. Serve warm with maple butter.

Per oatcake: 81 calories (44% from fat), 1 g protein, 11 g carbohydrate, 4 g fat, 0 mg cholesterol, 1 g fiber, 94 mg sodium.

Maple Butter
Makes ¾ cup

⅓   cup butter, softened
3   tablespoons brown sugar
¼   cup maple syrup
⅛   teaspoon cinnamon

1. In a small mixer bowl, beat butter until light and fluffy.
2. Beat in brown sugar, maple syrup, and cinnamon.

Per teaspoon: 25 calories (72% from fat), 1 g protein, 3 g carbohydrate, 2 g fat, 5 mg cholesterol, 0 g fiber, 18 mg sodium.

Watercress and Mushroom Salad
Serves 6

¼   pound mushrooms, sliced
1   tablespoon chopped fresh parsley
1   tablespoon chopped fresh chives
¼   cup vegetable oil
1   tablespoon lemon juice
½   teaspoon dry mustard
¼   teaspoon pepper
¼   teaspoon salt
2   bunches watercress

1. Place mushrooms, parsley, and chives in a large bowl.
2. Combine the oil, lemon juice, dry mustard, pepper, and salt and pour over mushroom mixture. Stir gently, cover, and refrigerate for 15 minutes.

3. Meanwhile, wash the watercress and pat dry with paper towels.
4. Add the watercress to the mushroom mixture. Toss well to blend. Serve immediately.

Per serving: 75 calories (84% from fat), 1 g protein, 2 g carbohydrate, 7 g fat, 0 mg cholesterol, 1 g fiber, 108 mg sodium.

Cranberry-Orange Sorbet
Serves 6

2   cups fresh or frozen cranberries
1¾   cups water, divided
¾   cup sugar
½   cup orange juice concentrate

1. In a small saucepan, combine the cranberries and 3/4 cup water. Cook over medium heat until cranberries are tender, about 10 minutes. Remove from heat and set aside to cool.
2. In a separate saucepan, bring sugar and remaining 1 cup water to a boil, stirring to dissolve sugar. Boil for 5 minutes. Set aside to cool slightly.
3. Press cooled cranberry mixture through a large strainer to collect juice in a mixing bowl.
4. Stir orange juice concentrate and cooled sugar syrup into cranberry juice. Cover mixture and chill.
5. Pour the chilled mixture into the canister of a 1-quart ice cream freezer and freeze according to the manufacturer's directions.

Per serving: 150 calories (0% from fat), 1 g protein, 38 g carbohydrate, 0 g fat, 0 mg cholesterol, 2 g fiber, 4 mg sodium.

Chapter 29 Review and Expand

Summary

Immigrants from certain countries tended to settle together in the United States. Therefore, the cuisine of the United States has some regional characteristics. Hearty one-dish meals and foods made with locally produced maple syrup are popular in New England. German foods can be found in the mid-Atlantic region. The South is known for fried chicken and buttermilk biscuits. Soul food and Creole and Cajun cuisines also originated in the South. In the Midwest, where much of the nation's grain is grown, meat and potatoes are standard fare.

Native Americans, Mexicans, and Spanish peoples influenced the foods of the West and Southwest. Chili and barbecued meats are favorites in this region. Sourdough bread, Alaskan seafood, and fresh fruits and vegetables are typical of the Pacific Coast. Tropical fruits and vegetables, often prepared with an Asian flair, are common in Hawaii.

Seasonal and regional distinctions are less apparent in Canadian cuisine today than in previous years. In coastal regions, main dishes often feature seafood. Beef and pork are more standard in inland areas. Canadian meals feature a broad range of fruits and vegetables, baked goods, and dairy products.

Vocabulary Activities

1. **Content Terms**   Work with a partner to write the definitions of the following terms based on your current understanding before reading the chapter. Then pair up with another pair to discuss your definitions and any discrepancies. Finally, discuss the definitions with the class and ask your instructor for necessary correction or clarification.

Pennsylvania Dutch	jambalaya
soul food	Cajun cuisine
chitterlings	potluck
okra	sourdough
Creole cuisine	luau
filé	imu
gumbo	Aboriginal

2. **Academic Terms**   Read the text passages that contain each of the following terms. Then write the definitions of each term in your own words. Double-check your definitions by rereading the text and using the text glossary.

famine	prospector
province	enterprising
solemn	annexed
ingenuity	array

Review

Write your answers using complete sentences when appropriate.

3. Name three reasons immigrants came to North America.

4. What regional holiday is celebrated in some parts of the South before the beginning of Lent?

5. How did New Englanders preserve foods for winter?

6. Name three foods associated with the Pennsylvania Dutch.

7. Name five types of greens used in soul food dishes.

8. What city is closely associated with Creole cuisine?

9. Name six agricultural products of the Midwest.

10. What three groups of people had the most influence on cooking in the Southwest?

11. How did the prospectors make and use sourdough?

12. Identify three groups that influenced Hawaiian cuisine and give an example of a food contributed by each group.

13. For each of the following foods, identify the regions of the United States with which they are associated: poi, baked beans, salmon, tamales, gumbo, and shoofly pie.

14. Describe the two groups of Canadian Aboriginals who influenced Canadian culture and food customs.

15. How did people in the United States influence the cuisine of Canada?

16. What is the most commonly eaten meat in Canada?

17. True or false. Pasta is a common side dish on Canadian menus.

Chapter 29 Review and Expand

Core Skills

18. **Technology, Speaking** Use presentation software to give an illustrated talk identifying the regions of the United States and Canada that were colonized by various groups of Europeans. Discuss ways the influence of these European groups can still be found in these regions today.

19. **Research, Writing** Use reliable print or online resources to research the first Thanksgiving in the United States or Canada. Write a report about the foods that were served. Note how many of these foods are still served today. Reread and revise your report for organization and style.

20. **Math** Use reliable print or online resources to find the total area of the United States in square miles. Then find the area of one of the regions discussed in this chapter. Calculate the percentage of the total United States area occupied by your chosen region.

21. **Research, Speaking, Listening** As a class, brainstorm dishes you think best represent your region. Vote to identify two dishes the class thinks are most representative. Choose one of the final dishes and research its cultural origins, evolution, classic ingredients, and reasons it became popular. Use your findings to participate in a class debate to determine the ultimate regional dish.

22. **Technology** Visit a trip planner website. Use this resource to plan a travel route from your school to a United States or Canadian destination. Investigate tourist attractions and identify restaurants at which you would stop.

23. **Research, Speaking, Listening** Prepare for and participate in a class debate about the statement "Mass production, convenience foods, and modern transportation have improved the Canadian diet." Cite reliable print or online resources you use to find information supporting your agreement or disagreement with the statement.

24. **Technology, Writing** Download a travel app and take it with you on a trip. Use it to create an electronic journal, writing entries and organizing photos of places you visit, foods you eat, and special memories each day.

25. **Career Readiness Practice** Your employer asks you to spearhead a team of employees in planning a Hawaiian luau fund-raiser. Divide into groups for food, decorations, music, games, program, and promotion. Each group should conduct research to come up with ideas for their part of the event. Combine input from all the groups to finalize the details, assign tasks, and create a preparation schedule.

Critical Thinking and Problem Solving

26. **Analyze** Choose one of the immigrant groups that helped settle a particular region of the United States. Find two regional recipes that reflect the influence of your chosen group. Then find two recipes for similar foods that are from your group's homeland. Compare the pairs of recipes, analyzing them for similarities and differences. Share with the class your conclusions about how and why the original recipes were adapted when they were brought to the United States.

27. **Create** Prepare a time line illustrating important dates in Canada's history.

Chapter 30
Latin America

Tati Nova photo Mexico/Shutterstock.com

Content Terms ⤷

Latin America	manioc
national dish	cassava
tortilla	arepa
frijoles refritos	ceviche
chile	ají
guacamole	gaucho
mole	empanada
plantain	dendê oil
comida	feijoada completa

Academic Terms

proximity	lush
arid	meteorologist
plateau	intermingled
rustic	nomadic

Objectives

After studying this chapter, you will be able to

- **identify** geographic and climatic factors that have influenced the characteristic foods of Mexico and South American countries;
- **describe** cultural factors that have affected the food customs of Mexico and South America; and
- **prepare** foods native to Latin America.

Reading Prep

As you read the chapter, record any questions that come to mind. Indicate where the answer to each question can be found: within the text, by asking your teacher, in another book, online, or by reflecting on your own knowledge and experiences. Pursue the answers to your questions.

The landmass that stretches southward from the Rio Grande to the tip of South America is known as **Latin America**. It is called Latin America because the official language of most of the countries is either Spanish or Portuguese, both of which are based on Latin.

Latin America was first explored and settled by the Spanish. Later, other Europeans established settlements. A large number of Portuguese settled along the eastern shores of South America in what is today Brazil.

Extremes are the rule rather than the exception in Latin America. Dense, tropical rain forests are as common as snow-capped mountains. Large, modern cities may not be far away from wild jungles.

The food customs of Latin America are rich and varied. They reflect the culture, climate, and geography of each country. The Aztecs and the Spanish conquistadores influenced Mexico. The foods of Peru reflect the ancient Inca civilization. The foods of Argentina are a mixture of European influences and native foods grown in the rich soil. The foods of Brazil reflect strong African and Portuguese heritage.

For the most part, the cuisines of Latin America are healthful. They include large amounts of fruits and vegetables and daily portions of grains and beans (**Figure 30.1**). In many regions, meat and poultry are costly, so people use them in limited amounts. Experts believe this plant-based diet is partly the reason for the low cancer rates in many Latin American countries. One aspect of Latin American cuisine that is a health concern is the frequent use of animal fats in cooking. The popularity of pickled, smoked, and salted foods in some regions is a nutritional concern, too. These factors have been linked with increased cancer risk.

This chapter focuses on Mexico and South America. However, the countries of Central America are also part of this region. Each country has its own cuisine and national dishes. (A **national dish** is a food that is associated with a certain country and is very popular among the nation's people.) For instance, Guatemala is known for *pepian*, a spicy, filling meat and vegetable stew that is thickened with pumpkin seeds. El Salvador's national dish is *pupusa*, which is a thick tortilla filled with cheese, ground pork, and refried beans. *Gallo pinto* is a fried mixture of rice and beans that is served in both Nicaragua and Costa Rica.

Iakov Filimonov/Shutterstock.com

Figure 30.1 Fruits and vegetables are essential to Mexican cuisine. Which foods can you identify from this market?

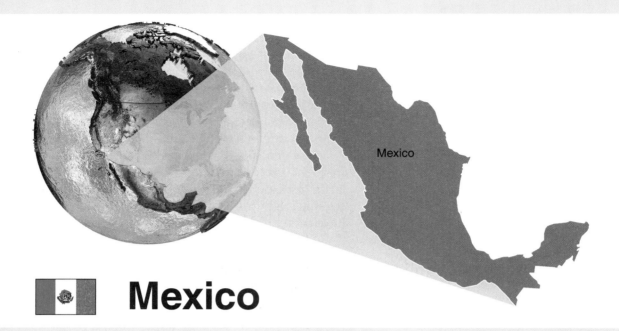

![Mexico]

Mexico

Of all the Latin American countries, Mexico is most familiar to the majority of people in the United States. The close *proximity* (physical closeness) of Mexico has made a rich cultural exchange possible.

Thousands of United States tourists visit Mexico each year. Mexican foods, such as tacos, enchiladas, and refried beans, are popular in the Southwest and throughout the United States.

Geography and Climate of Mexico

Mexico is a land of deserts, mountains, grasslands, woodlands, and tropical rain forests. The Rio Grande separates Mexico from Texas. The Pacific Ocean, Gulf of California, Caribbean Sea, and Gulf of Mexico form Mexico's coastlines. Much of Mexico is mountainous, with valleys separating the different ranges (**Figure 30.2**). Although the climate in a few regions is wet and humid, nearly half of Mexico is *arid* (dry) or semiarid.

Both geography and climate have affected food customs in Mexico. In those sections of the country bordered by water, fish is an important part of the cuisine. The areas that border the United States have land that is too dry for large-scale crop production. However, it is suitable for

raising cattle. As a result, beef is a staple food in these areas. A variety of tropical fruits and vegetables grow along the southern Gulf Coast where rainfall is adequate. In the central *plateau* (flat area that is higher in elevation than surrounding land), the level land, adequate moisture, and cool temperatures make the production of crops like corn and beans profitable.

Svetlana Bykova/Shutterstock.com

Figure 30.2 Many regions in Mexico have mountainous landscapes. How does landscape affect a region's food customs?

Mexican Culture

A region's geography and climate influence a region's culture. Family life and homes, marketplaces, and holidays are among additional contributors to Mexican culture.

Family Life and Marketplaces

Mexican culture is centered on family life. In many homes, family members have clearly defined roles. Women are generally responsible for caring for children and the home. Men are the primary decision makers. Members of the extended family commonly live near one another. Families often work and socialize together, as well.

Big cities in Mexico are filled with modern buildings and businesses. However, rural areas are likely to have more modest homes and a central market area. Homes are typically constructed with cement walls and tile floors. Walls are often painted with vibrant colors like bright blue, orange, or yellow. Traditional homes have *rustic* (rural or country-like) wooden furniture. Accent pieces, like lamps and mirrors, may be crafted from metal or clay.

Local markets have stalls or booths operated by different vendors. Some markets feature locally made arts and crafts. Others sell clothes, shoes, jewelry, books, and seasonal products. Vendors at food markets sell specific types of foods. Some offer fresh produce, meat, fish, or spices. Others sell cooked foods like takeout restaurants.

Mexican Holidays

Most Mexicans are Roman Catholic. Many holidays throughout the year focus on religious celebrations.

Food plays a role in some Mexican holidays. The Feast of Epiphany on January 6 falls at the end of a 22-day Christmas celebration. This day celebrates the coming of three kings to see the infant Jesus. People get together and share a special supper, which includes a ring-shaped cake with a tiny plastic baby baked inside. The person who gets the piece of cake with the baby hosts a tamales party for all who are present. This party is held on February 2, which is Candlemas Day. This day is recognized as the day Jesus' parents took him to the temple in Jerusalem.

Global Perspective

Mexican Agriculture

A little more than half of Mexico's people are farmers. Because good, rich soil is scarce, farming is difficult. Many farmers cannot afford modern machinery or fertilizers. As a result, they are challenged to produce good crop yields. In recent years, government irrigation projects and credit to farmers have helped improve yields.

Corn is Mexico's major crop. Bean production is second. Other important crops include sugarcane, coffee, tomatoes, green peppers, peas, melons, citrus fruits, strawberries, and cacao beans. Wheat is grown in the North as are smaller amounts of barley, rice, and oats. Cattle graze on northern pastures.

Coastal waters provide a variety of seafood. Large quantities of shrimp are caught and exported. Sardines, tuna, turtles, and mackerel are also important.

The observance of the Day of the Dead (*Dia de los Muertos*) also involves a food tradition. According to this tradition, some believe dead souls return to visit the living between October 31 and November 2. During this time, many families set up altars in the corners of their homes. They set these altars with candles, photos, and favorite foods and drinks of dead loved ones (**Figure 30.3**).

Mexican Cuisine

In addition to the influence of Mexico's geography, climate, and culture, Mexican cuisine is also influenced by historical factors. Different regions in Mexico also show variations in cuisine.

Historical Influences

The *Aztecs* were the original inhabitants of Mexico. In 1520, Hernando Cortes and the *conquistadores* (conquerors) explored Mexico

AGCuesta/Shutterstock.com

Figure 30.3 Pan de muerto (bread of the dead) is a symbolic Mexican bread shaped to resemble bones and teardrops for Dia de los Muertos.

and took control of the land for Spain. Both the Aztecs and the Spaniards made many contributions to Mexican cuisine.

The Aztecs contributed chocolate, vanilla, corn, peppers, peanuts, tomatoes, avocados, squash, beans, sweet potatoes, pineapples, and papayas. The Aztecs boiled, broiled, or steamed their food or ate it raw. Their more elaborate dishes were similar to modern stews.

The Spanish added oil, wine, cinnamon, cloves, rice, wheat, peaches, apricots, beef, and chicken. With the introduction of oil, many of the early Aztec foods could be fried. Today, frying is an important part of Mexican cooking. Mexican cooks fry foods in deep fat or on lightly greased griddles.

Another contribution to Mexican cuisine was made by Emperor Maximilian of Austria. He was asked to come to Mexico in 1864 to set up a monarchy. One of his goals was to help bring stability to life after a period of war. During his short reign, he introduced dishes from his homeland. His chefs also brought refined French and Italian dishes to Mexico. One example is the *bolillo*. This Mexican roll, which is often used to make sandwiches, is a variation of crusty French bread.

Characteristic Foods of Mexico

Corn, beans, and peppers are staple ingredients in Mexican cuisine. Mexican cooks use a variety of other locally grown vegetables and

fruits, too. Flavorful sauces and stews, as well as some distinctive desserts and beverages, are also typical foods of Mexico.

Corn

Corn has formed the basis of Mexican cuisine since the days of the Aztec civilization. Mexican cooks use corn in many ways, but its most important use is in the production of tortillas. A **tortilla** is a flat, unleavened bread made from cornmeal or wheat flour and water. The dough is shaped into a thin pancake in a tortilla press. Then it is cooked on a lightly greased griddle called a *comal*.

Many popular dishes are made from tortillas. Mexican cooks fill tortillas with a mixture of shredded meat or sliced chicken, onions, garlic, and chiles to make *enchiladas*. Then they bake and serve the enchiladas with cheese and a red or green tomato sauce. Cooks also fry tortillas until crisp and garnish them with chopped onions, chiles, beans, shredded lettuce, meat, and cheese to make *tostadas*. *Quesadillas* are toasted turnovers made of tortillas filled with meat, sauce, cheese, beans, or vegetables. Tortillas wrapped around a meat or bean filling are called *burritos*. Crisp, fried tortillas filled with meat or cactus, beans, shredded lettuce, and cheese and seasoned with chiles are called *tacos*.

Mexican cooks never waste corn. They do not even discard the husks. They use the husks to make *tamales*. The cooks stuff small amounts of corn dough with meat and beans and tuck it into the corn husks. They fold the husks into small parcels and steam them or roast them over an open fire (**Figure 30.4**).

Beans

Like corn, beans are a staple food in Mexico. Local farmers grow many varieties of beans. Sometimes people boil the beans and serve them from the pot as was done during Aztec times. Often they cook the beans until they are soft and then mash the beans and fry them slowly. This dish is called **frijoles refritos** (refried beans) and is frequently served with grated cheese.

Peppers

People throughout Latin America use peppers, but they are especially important in Mexico. Many types of peppers are sold in local markets throughout the country.

Brent Hofacker/Shutterstock.com

Figure 30.4 Corn is the main ingredient in traditional tamales.

Over 30 varieties of peppers are used in Mexican cuisines. The peppers range in size and color. They can be sweet, pungent, or burning hot. Generally, the mild peppers are called *sweet peppers*, and the hot ones are called **chiles**.

The peppers used most often in cooking can be divided into two groups according to color—red and green. Mexican cooks use red peppers dried, except for ripe red bell peppers and pimientos. They often use green peppers fresh.

Fruits and Other Vegetables

Farmers in Mexico grow a variety of vegetables. Vegetables are usually not eaten plain. Instead, cooks often add them to casseroles and use them as garnishes for other dishes.

Mexican-grown vegetables that are common in the United States include zucchini, artichokes, white potatoes, spinach, chard, lettuce, beets, cauliflower, and carrots. Less common are *huazontle* (wild broccoli), *jicama* (a large, gray root), *nopales* (tender cactus leaves), and *chayotes* (a tropical squash).

Many fruits grow in Mexico. Avocados have a bland flavor and are often added to other foods. **Guacamole**, for example, is a spread made from mashed avocado, tomato, and onion. It may be served with tortillas or crisp corn chips. Bananas, pineapples, guavas, papayas, and prickly pears are other tropical fruits that are popular in Mexico. The fruits are often served alone or in syrup as a light, refreshing dessert.

Sauces and Stews

Mexican cooks often use thick sauces. They pour some sauces over other foods. Other sauces contain pieces of meat, vegetables, tortillas, or beans and are served as main dishes.

Very simple sauces are made from chiles and/or sweet peppers mixed with finely chopped onions and tomatoes. More complex sauces are called **moles** (pronounced MO-leys). The word *mole* is derived from the Aztec word *molli*, which means a chile-flavored sauce. Cooks make one type of mole from a variety of chiles, almonds, raisins, garlic, sesame seeds, onions, tomatoes, cinnamon, cloves, coriander seeds, and anise seeds. They finely chop these ingredients and add them to chicken stock. They add the final ingredient—unsweetened chocolate—just before serving. This type of mole is part of turkey mole, which is a traditional dish.

Mexican stews are as unique as moles. Stews begin with a sauce. Cooks grind dried peppers and mix them with ground spices and vegetables. They add some meat or poultry stock to the ground mixture to make a thick paste. Then they fry the paste, thin it, and add it to cooked meat or poultry.

Long, slow cooking gives stews their characteristic flavors. Because of the high altitude, the boiling point in many parts of Mexico is lower. As a result, stews can be simmered for many hours to develop flavor without becoming overcooked.

Mexican Desserts

Other than fresh fruits and sweet tamales, the Aztecs had few desserts. Catholic convents begun by the Spaniards developed many of the desserts and sweets eaten in Mexico today. Early Spanish and Portuguese cooks influenced those desserts that use large amounts of egg and sugar, such as *flan* (a caramel custard). *Churros* (fried pastry dough) were introduced by the conquistadors.

Mexican Regional Cuisine

Although many foods are common throughout Mexico, regional differences exist. These occur mainly as a result of geographic and climatic conditions.

In the climate of northern Mexico, farmers can grow wheat and raise cattle. Therefore, tortillas in

Learn About...

Mexican Beverages

Mexican markets sell a variety of tropical fruit juices and soft drinks. Fruits are also main ingredients in many cold drink recipes. *Agua fresca*, for instance, is a strained, sweetened puree of fresh fruit and water with a squeeze of lemon or lime juice. Agua fresca may be made with almost any kind of fruit. Pineapple, cantaloupe, watermelon, strawberries, papaya, and even cucumbers are popular. *Horchata*, another popular cold drink, is made from a pureed mixture of rice, water, and cinnamon.

Chocolate drinks and coffee are popular Mexican beverages. The cacao bean, known since the days of the Aztecs, is toasted and ground into cocoa or made into chocolate. Mexican chocolate is similar to the hot chocolate drink served in the United States. However, it is flavored with cinnamon and a pinch of cayenne pepper. A type of wooden whisk called a *molinillo* is used to beat the chocolate into a foam before serving. At breakfast, people often enjoy coffee served with milk, which is called *café con leche*. *Café de olla* is dark roasted coffee served with a type of brown sugar and, sometimes, a stick of cinnamon.

Know and Apply

1. Which type of fruit would you choose for making agua fresca?

2. Which of the beverages described do you think sounds most appealing?

this area are made from wheat flour rather than corn. People commonly eat beef, which they may dry or cook with onions, peppers, and tomatoes and serve with beans. Cheese is also popular in several northern states. In Chihuahua, for example, people fry beans in lard and then carefully heat them with cheese. In Sonora, cooks cover a potato soup with a thick layer of melted cheese.

Finfish and shellfish are important protein sources for people living in coastal areas. People in these regions use seafood in appetizers, soups, and main dishes. Cooks near the Gulf Coast make a popular dish from plantains. **Plantains** are green, starchy fruits that have a bland flavor

and look much like large bananas. The cooks fry the plantains with onions and tomatoes and serve the mixture with shrimp (or other seafood) and chili sauce (**Figure 30.5**). *Paella*, derived from the Spanish dish with the same name, contains seafood, chicken, and peas cooked in chicken broth and served with rice.

Wild duck is popular in eastern Mexico. Turkey is one of the most important foods of the Yucatán (peninsula that forms Mexico's southern tip).

Squash blossoms and sea chestnuts (a type of crustacean) are popular in southern Mexico. Because banana trees are abundant, tamales in this region are wrapped in fresh banana leaves rather than corn husks.

Mexican Meals

Mexican meal patterns differ somewhat from those of the United States. Families with ample incomes may eat four meals a day.

The first meal of the day is *desayuno*, or breakfast. This may be a simple meal of sweet rolls and coffee or chocolate. Desayuno can also be more substantial. The menu might include fruit, bread, and *huevos rancheros* (eggs prepared with chiles and served on tortillas).

Comida is a leisurely meal served in the middle of the day between two and four o'clock. It is the main meal of the day and is likely to include several courses. These may consist of an appetizer, a soup, a main course, beans, dessert, and coffee. Tortillas are traditionally served, but bread sometimes is substituted.

©iStock.com/lanabyko

Figure 30.5 Fried plantains are golden yellow in color and have a sweet taste similar to bananas.

A light snack, *merienda*, is served around five or six o'clock. It includes chocolate or coffee, fruit, and *pan dulce* (sweet breads) (**Figure 30.6**).

Cena, or supper, is often eaten between eight and ten o'clock. Cena is similar to comida, but smaller and lighter. (Many Mexican families combine merienda and cena and eat one meal in the early evening.)

Figure 30.6 The Mexican meal pattern often includes a light snack, such as coffee and sweet breads, served around five or six o'clock in the evening.

Mexican Menu

Enchiladas Verdes de Pollo
(Chicken-Filled Tortillas with Green Sauce)

Tacos

Ensalada de Zanahoria
(Carrot Salad)

Frijoles Refritos
(Refried Beans)

Rodajas de Piña
(Pineapple Slices)

Polverones
(Mexican Wedding Cookies)

Zumo Granada
(Pomegranate Juice)

Tortillas
(Flat Cornbread)
Makes 12

2¼ cups instant masa harina (corn flour)
1 teaspoon salt
1⅓ cups cold water

1. In a medium mixing bowl, combine corn flour and salt. Gradually add all but 3 tablespoons of the water.
2. Knead the mixture with your hands, adding more water (1 tablespoon at a time) until dough no longer sticks to the fingers.
3. Divide the dough in half. With a rolling pin, roll half the dough between sheets of wax paper to a thickness of ¹⁄₁₆ inch. Repeat with the other half of the dough.
4. Using a 6-inch plate as a pattern, cut the dough around the plate with a sharp knife or pastry wheel. Place rounds of dough between pieces of wax paper.
5. Preheat oven to 250°F.
6. Heat a heavy 7- to 8-inch skillet over moderate heat.
7. Cook tortillas one at a time on each side. When lightly browned (about 2 minutes on each side), transfer to foil and keep warm in the oven. Fill as desired.
    Note: Tortillas may be made ahead and refrigerated lightly covered. To rewarm tortillas, brush both sides with water and heat a few minutes in a skillet, one at a time.

Per tortilla: 94 calories (4% from fat), 2 g protein, 20 g carbohydrate, 0 g fat, 0 mg cholesterol, 2 g fiber, 178 mg sodium.

Enchiladas Verdes de Pollo
(Chicken-Filled Tortillas with Green Sauce)
Makes 6

3 green bell peppers
1 whole boneless, skinless chicken breast
½ cup chicken stock
3 ounces Neufchâtel cheese
1 cup evaporated fat-free milk, divided
⅓ cup finely chopped onions
⅓ cup canned Mexican green tomatoes, drained
1 hot chile (canned) drained, rinsed, and finely chopped
2½ teaspoons chopped fresh cilantro

1   egg
      dash pepper
4½   teaspoons shortening
6   tortillas
3   tablespoons grated Parmesan cheese

1. Preheat broiler. Cut peppers in half. Remove stems and seeds. Place peppers, skin side up, on a foil-lined baking sheet. Broil peppers 4 to 6 inches from the heat until they are evenly blackened and blistered, about 5 to 10 minutes. Wrap the foil from the baking sheet around the blackened peppers and seal. Allow the peppers to rest for 15 minutes. Then peel the skins with a sharp knife and set aside.
2. Place the chicken breast in a small skillet. Pour stock over chicken breast and cover; simmer until chicken is tender, about 20 minutes. Remove chicken to a plate and reserve stock. When chicken is cool enough to handle, shred meat and set it aside.
3. In a small mixing bowl, beat Neufchâtel cheese until smooth. Add ½ cup evaporated milk, a little at a time. Then add onions and shredded chicken, stirring with a wooden spoon or flexible spatula. Set aside.
4. Coarsely chop the skinned peppers and place them in a blender container. Add green tomatoes, hot chile, cilantro, and ¼ cup reserved stock. Blend on high speed until smooth. Add remaining ½ cup of evaporated milk, egg, and pepper. Blend 10 more seconds; pour into a bowl.
5. Preheat oven to 350°F. Grease a small baking dish or 8-inch square pan.
6. Melt shortening in a small skillet.
7. Fry tortillas one at a time; filling each before frying the next. To fill tortillas, place ¼ cup filling in center of tortilla. Fold one side to center; roll tortilla up completely to form a cylinder. Place filled tortillas side by side in baking dish.
8. When all the tortillas have been filled, pour sauce over them and sprinkle with Parmesan cheese. Bake about 15 minutes or until cheese has melted. Serve immediately.

Per enchilada: 253 calories (36% from fat), 19 g protein, 24 g carbohydrate, 10 g fat, 81 mg cholesterol, 2 g fiber, 280 mg sodium.

Tacos
Makes 6

¾   pound lean ground beef
1   tablespoon chili powder
½   teaspoon garlic powder
¼   teaspoon onion powder
¼   teaspoon crushed red pepper flakes
½   teaspoon oregano
⅛   teaspoon cayenne pepper
2   teaspoons cumin
¾   teaspoon black pepper
¾   cup tomato juice
6   tortillas
1   tablespoon softened butter
      shredded lettuce
      shredded Monterey Jack cheese
      coarsely chopped tomatoes
      salsa

1. In a large skillet, brown ground beef, pouring off fat as it accumulates.
2. When meat is browned, add seasonings and tomato juice. Stir well. Simmer covered, about 10 minutes; stir occasionally.
3. Arrange tortillas on a greased baking sheet; brush with butter. Bake at 400°F for 10 to 15 minutes. (Tortillas should begin to set, but they should still be flexible.)
4. Remove tortillas from the baking sheet and fold in half to form shells.
5. To serve tacos, set out individual bowls of meat mixture, lettuce, cheese, and tomatoes. Each person can prepare his or her own taco and top with salsa, if desired.

Per taco: 282 calories (50% from fat), 17 g protein, 19 g carbohydrate, 16 g fat, 57 mg cholesterol, 1 g fiber, 440 mg sodium.

Ensalada de Zanahoria
(Carrot Salad)
Serves 4 to 6

1	pound carrots, peeled and shredded
1	jalapeño pepper, minced
3	green onions, finely chopped
3	tablespoons olive oil
2	tablespoons lime juice
¼	teaspoon salt
¼	teaspoon pepper
2	tablespoons chopped cilantro

1. In a serving bowl, combine carrots, jalapeño pepper, and green onions.
2. In a small covered jar, combine olive oil, lime juice, salt, and pepper. Shake to blend thoroughly. Pour the dressing over the vegetables and toss to coat.
3. Sprinkle cilantro on top of salad.

Per serving: 138 calories (65% from fat), 1 g protein, 11 g carbohydrate, 10 g fat, 0 mg cholesterol, 3 g fiber, 217 mg sodium.

Frijoles Refritos
(Refried Beans)
Serves 6

2	15-ounce cans low-sodium pinto beans, drained and rinsed
2	tablespoons olive oil
1	medium onion, finely chopped
2	medium tomatoes, seeded and finely chopped
¼	cup canned chopped green chiles
¾	cup low-sodium chicken broth
	salt
	pepper
½	cup low-fat Monterey Jack or Cheddar cheese, shredded

1. In a large bowl, mash beans with a potato masher or the back of a wooden spoon.
2. In a large, heavy skillet, heat oil. Add onions and cook until lightly browned.
3. Add tomatoes and chiles to the skillet; cook, stirring frequently, for 5 minutes.
4. Stir in mashed beans, ½ cup broth, and salt and pepper to taste. Cook, stirring occasionally. Add more broth if beans seem dry.
5. When beans are hot and have reached the desired consistency, sprinkle with cheese. Allow cheese to begin to melt, then remove beans from the heat and serve immediately.

Per serving: 162 calories (39% from fat), 8 g protein, 17 g carbohydrate, 7 g fat, 6 mg cholesterol, 5 g fiber, 258 mg sodium.

Polverones
(Mexican Wedding Cookies)
Makes 2 dozen cookies

½	cup butter
½	teaspoon vanilla
½	cup confectioner's sugar, divided
1	cup all-purpose flour
6	tablespoons finely chopped walnuts

1. Preheat oven to 425°F.
2. In a medium mixing bowl, cream butter and vanilla until fluffy.
3. Mix ¼ cup confectioner's sugar, flour, and nuts together; add to creamed mixture, stirring to form a soft dough.
4. Shape dough into small balls and place on an ungreased baking sheet. Bake cookies about 10 minutes or until lightly brown.
5. Roll warm cookies in remaining confectioner's sugar.

Per cookie: 75 calories (84% from fat), 1 g protein, 7 g carbohydrate, 6 g fat, 10 mg cholesterol, 0 g fiber, 1 mg sodium.

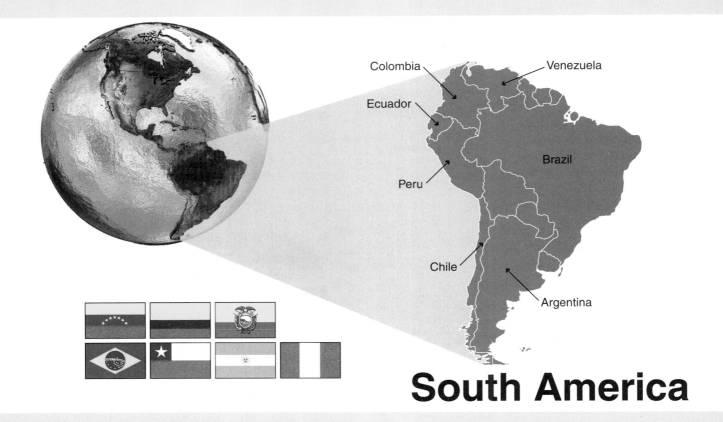

South America

The Atlantic and Pacific Oceans and the Caribbean Sea form the boundaries of South America. South America is nearly twice the size of the United States. It is a land of contrasts— dense rain forests and snowcapped mountains; deserts and *lush* (plentiful in healthy growth) farmland; large, modern cities and untamed jungles.

Geography and Climate of South America

The geography in South America is varied. Mountains, grasslands, jungles, forests, plateaus, and deserts divide the continent. The Andes Mountains form the longest and second highest mountain chain in the world (**Figure 30.7**). These mountains and dense jungles have made travel nearly impossible in many parts of the continent. As a result, each country has developed independently and has preserved a unique culture.

You can find nearly every kind of climate in South America. In parts of Chile, *meteorologists* (professionals who study weather and atmosphere)

have never recorded any rainfall. The area is an arid wasteland. However, rain falls daily in the tropical rain forests of Brazil. Snow and high winds bring bitter cold to the peaks of the Andes, yet the jungles below are hot and humid.

Filipe Frazao/Shutterstock.com

Figure 30.7 The Andes Mountains extend along the western side of South America.

South American Culture

A number of peoples influenced the development of South American culture. These include ancient native tribes like the *Inca*. Spanish and Portuguese explorers left their marks on this land. African slaves brought to work on Brazilian sugar plantations made contributions as well. The influences of all these groups can still be seen in the lifestyle of South America.

Today, Brasília, Rio de Janeiro, Caracas, and Buenos Aires are among the major cities of the world. These cities feature modern architecture and transportation systems. *Intermingled* (mixed in) with modern buildings are churches that date back to the Spanish conquistadores and the Inca. These churches are preserves that indicate the rich history in these areas.

Many festivals in South America are blends of Christian celebrations and other beliefs. In Brazil, many holidays combine traditions of African religions with days honoring saints in the Catholic Church. In Peru, ancient Incan beliefs are mixed with church holy days.

Many South American festivals last for several days. They are public celebrations with processions through village streets. Music, dancing, parades, and colorful costumes are part of many of these celebrations. Vendors often sell food to the crowds of people who gather to celebrate.

The most elaborate of the South American festivals is *Carnival*. This is the Brazilian festival that parallels the Mardi Gras festival celebrated in the southern United States. Carnival is held the six days before Ash Wednesday, which is the beginning of Lent in the Christian church. All year, people plan the floats, costumes, and exotic masks that will be part of this celebration.

South American Cuisine

South American cuisine combines influences of native tribes with those of the Spanish, Portuguese, and Africans. Many staple foods, such as corn, potatoes, and manioc, are found throughout the continent. (**Manioc**, known as

Global Perspective

South American Economy

Much of South America's economy is based in its mineral resources. Iron and steel are produced in Brazil. Gold, coal, and emeralds are mined in Colombia. Copper is a major product in Chile.

Other chief industries in South America include textiles and chemicals. Food processing and motor vehicle assembly play large roles in the economy, too.

South America exports a number of agricultural products. Coffee and cacao are important crops, as are corn and soybeans. Brazil and Argentina export beef, and Chile is a major exporter of shrimp. Lumber, paper pulp, and wool from sheep and llamas are also key economic products.

South America's economy is strong. However, there is much inequality in the economic condition of the people. The members of the upper classes enjoy the best foods, entertainment, and housing. At the same time, the lower classes are hindered by unemployment and lack of education and health care. South American governments are working to reduce the gap between the wealthy and the poor.

cassava in some regions, is a starchy root plant eaten as a side dish and used in flour form in cooking and baking (**Figure 30.8**). However, most food customs have developed on a regional basis because of geographic isolation. Each region reflects cultural influences as well as geographic and climatic ones. The following discussion will give you an overview of some of the unique dishes typical of some South American countries.

Venezuela

The Spanish who explored Venezuela found rich, fertile soil and a temperate climate in the valleys formed by the Andes. The cuisine of this

AN NGUYEN/Shutterstock.com

Figure 30.8   Manioc, also called *cassava*, can be used as is or as a ground flour.

country reflects these two factors. It also reflects the tropical climate found in the jungle lowlands just south of the valleys and the food customs of the Spanish explorers.

Much of Venezuela is inhabited by families who do small-scale farming. **Arepa**, a corn pancake similar to a tortilla, is a traditional Venezuelan bread. It forms the basis of the farmer's diet. Cooks make arepa by mixing corn flour with water and salt. They shape the stiff dough into balls or patties and toast it on a lightly greased griddle. Although people often eat arepa plain, they also use it to make more elaborate dishes. *Bollos pelones*, for example, are balls of arepa dough stuffed with a meat mixture. These dumplings are then deep-fried or simmered in soup or sauce.

People living in the tropical lowlands make good use of the banana, plantain, and coconut. Bananas and plantains are boiled, fried, baked, and added to stews and soups. Plantains, thinly sliced and fried until crisp, are a popular Venezuelan snack. Banana leaves are used to wrap *hallacas*, Venezuela's national dish, which is cornmeal dough filled with other foods. Coconuts are a primary ingredient in candies, puddings, and cakes. Coconut and coconut milk are also added to stewed meats. A sponge-type cake moistened with rum-flavored syrup and covered with coconut cream is a famous Venezuelan dessert called *Bien Me Sabe*.

Colombia

Potatoes, which are grown high in the mountains, are especially important in the diets of northern Colombians. Farther south, cassavas are used instead of potatoes.

Meat is popular in the Colombian diet. However, some Colombians cannot afford to eat much meat. They may base meals on stews and thick soups instead. Cooks make one soup, *ajiaco*, with potatoes, chicken, corn, and cassava.

Colombia is an important coffee-producing country. The coffee trees thrive on the cool slopes of the Andes Mountains. The coffee served in Colombia is much stronger than that served in the United States; however, Colombians do not drink as much coffee as people in the United States.

Ecuador

Because Ecuador is a large producer of bananas, local dishes often feature bananas. Ecuadorian people make bananas into flour, which they use to make breads and pastries. They cut firm green bananas and plantains into chips and deep-fry them. The simplest and most common banana dessert is made by slowly frying ripe bananas in butter. As the slices begin to brown, sugar is added little by little until the bananas are brown on both sides. Before serving, the sautéed banana slices are splashed with brandy and dusted with powdered sugar.

Peru

The descendants of the Inca still live in Peru. They have retained many of the customs of their ancestors. Their cuisine reflects both Incan and Spanish traditions.

Peruvians often make *cuy* (guinea pig) into a stew. They also brush cuy with olive oil and garlic and roast it. Vendors on Peruvian streets sell another popular meat dish called *anticuchos*. They marinate small strips of beef heart overnight and thread them on skewers. Then they baste the meat with a sauce and grill it over hot coals.

Peruvians who live along the coast eat a variety of seafood. Shrimp is especially popular in both appetizers and main dishes. *Chupe*, a thick soup made from milk, vegetables, and shellfish, is served as a main dish.

Peruvians invented **ceviche**, a marinated raw fish dish. However, people throughout Latin America enjoy it. Cooks usually make ceviche from *corvinas* (a type of whitefish found off the Peruvian coast), but they can use other types of whitefish (**Figure 30.9**). Peruvian cooks cut the fish into small cubes. Then they cover it with a marinade made of lime juice, lemon juice, salt, pepper, garlic, onion, and ají. **Ají** is the Peruvian and Chilean term for chiles. After the fish has marinated for several hours, its texture becomes similar to that of cooked fish. The ceviche is then ready to eat. Peruvians often serve ceviche with corn and sweet potatoes. People in other Latin American countries often serve ceviche as an appetizer.

Peruvian tamales contain a variety of foods including meat, chicken, sausage, eggs, peanuts, raisins, and olives. Unlike Mexican tamales, they often are somewhat sweet.

Chile

Chile is a long, thin country. The upper third of Chile is arid desert, and the lower third is mountainous. The central region has fertile valleys, irrigated fields, and forests.

Because the land is not suitable for raising cattle or sheep, Chileans eat little meat. Instead, seafood, beans, and small amounts of meat are combined with vegetables in many delicious stews. *Porotos granados*, for example, contains cranberry beans, corn, squash, garlic, and onion.

Another popular dish in Chile is *pastel de choclo*. It is a meat pie made with a sugar-coated topping of ground fresh corn. Beef, or a combination of beef and chicken, usually is used in the filling. Raisins and olives may be added. Some cooks also add pepper or ají; however, most Chilean dishes are not peppery.

Of all the South Americans, Chileans probably eat the most seafood. Chile's long coastline makes seafood both plentiful and inexpensive.

Learn About...

Peruvian Potatoes

Since the days of the Inca, the *papa* (potato) has been the staple food of the Peruvian people. The Inca developed over 100 potato varieties. To preserve their potatoes, they freeze-dried them. The cold night air of the Andes quickly froze the potatoes. When the sun came out, the potatoes thawed. The moisture that formed evaporated. At night, the potatoes froze once again. Soon the potatoes became hard as stone but very lightweight. The Inca could then store the potatoes indefinitely.

The poorest people of Peru eat boiled potatoes alone or with a few local herbs or ají. Those who can afford other ingredients prepare potatoes in many unique and tasty ways. One popular potato dish is made by pouring a thick sauce made of cheese, milk, ají, and spices over boiled potatoes. Another flavorful potato dish of Incan origin is *causa a la limeña*. A mixture of stiff mashed potatoes, olive oil, lemon juice, salt, pepper, chopped onions, and ají is pressed into small molds. The unmolded dish is garnished with hard-cooked eggs, cheese, sweet potatoes, *prawns* (a shrimplike crustacean), and olives.

Know and Apply

1. Identify the MyPlate food groups in which each ingredient and garnish in causa a la limeña belongs.

2. How would you rate the nutritional value of this dish?

Cameron Whitman/Shutterstock.com

Figure 30.9 Although ceviche is often made with corvinas, it can also be prepared with other types of seafood, such as lobster and shrimp. Why are lemons and limes important in ceviche preparation?

Shellfish are particularly popular. Crabs, lobsters, clams, scallops, and sea urchins are used in many dishes. *Chupe de marisco* (scallop stew) is baked in a deep dish. A creamy cheese sauce flavored with paprika, nutmeg, pepper, and onion complements the flavors of scallops and rice.

Argentina

The Pampas (plains) are the richest lands in South America. They cover the southeastern part of the continent and reach into the countries of Argentina and Uruguay. Here, large herds of cattle and sheep graze until they are ready for market.

Because it is so readily available, the people of Argentina eat large amounts of meat. Much of the meat is roasted in the style of the gauchos. The **gauchos** were *nomadic* (wandering; travelling) herders of the Pampas during the eighteenth and nineteenth centuries. They put meat from freshly slaughtered cattle on large stakes placed at an angle around a fire. (This prevented the juices from dripping into the coals.) A peppery herb and parsley sauce called *chimichurri* accompanied the freshly roasted meat.

Argentine cooks also prepare meat in other ways. They make the popular dish, *matambre*, by layering spinach, hard-cooked eggs, carrots, and onions on top of a marinated flank steak. Then they roll the matambre, tie it, and either poach it or roast it until tender.

Argentine appetizers are called **empanadas**. They are small turnovers filled with chopped meat, olives, raisins, and onions. Empanadas (sometimes called *empanadillas*) can contain a variety of fillings and are popular throughout Latin America, Spain, and Portugal (**Figure 30.10**).

Although most of the foods of Argentina have a strong flavor, mild-flavored squashes and pumpkins have been popular for centuries. Cooks use squash to make fritters, soups, and puddings. They sometimes thicken and decorate stews with squash. *Carbonada criolla*, a colorful stew, contains pieces of beef, squash, tomatoes, corn on the cob, and fresh peaches. It sometimes is served in a squash or pumpkin shell.

Humitas are similar to Mexican tamales. Unripe kernels of corn are mixed with onions, tomatoes, salt, pepper, sugar, and cinnamon. Sometimes cheese is also added. Humitas may be cooked with milk until tender and served plain.

They may also be rolled into corn husks, tied, and boiled or steamed.

Brazil

Brazilian culture is a mixture of Native South American, Portuguese, and African cultures. The native inhabitants of Brazil did not practice agriculture on a wide scale. However, they did produce manioc, which is still a staple food in Brazil.

In 1500, explorers from Portugal landed in the area that is now Brazil. The Portuguese stayed in the area and built large plantations where they grew sugarcane. Today, Portuguese is the official language of Brazil.

The Portuguese brought Africans to Brazil as slaves to work in the sugar fields. African women were skilled cooks and worked in the kitchens of the Portuguese. The Africans made a great impact on Brazilian cuisine. They raised crops of foods from their homeland, including bananas, yams, and coconuts. These ingredients are now used in many Brazilian dishes. African cooks also introduced the use of red pepper and **dendê oil** (palm oil that gives Brazilian dishes a bright yellow-orange color).

The African women made use of the readily available shrimp and fish. *Vatapa*, for example, is a delicious stew made of pieces of shrimp and fish cooked with coconut milk, palm oil, and pieces of bread. Vatapa is usually served over rice.

HLPhoto/Shutterstock.com

Figure 30.10   Empanadas may be savory or sweet.

The Brazilians serve rice, a second staple food, in a variety of ways. One popular dish is a casserole made of layers of rice, shrimp, ham, chicken, cheese, and tomato. A popular Afro-Brazilian coconut pudding also contains rice.

Beans, a third staple food, are as important to Brazilian cooking as they are to Mexican cooking. Brazilians prefer shiny black beans they can cook to a paste (**Figure 30.11**). They use these beans to make **feijoada completa**, Brazil's national dish. Feijoada completa is made with meat and beans. It can be simple or elaborate depending on the ingredients used. Traditional feijoada completa includes dried beef and smoked tongue. Other meats, such as fresh beef, pork, bacon, sausage, and pigs' feet, can also be added. The meats are cooked until tender and then arranged on a large platter. The black beans, cooked to a pulp, are served in a separate pot. Bowls of hot sauces, cooked rice, manioc meal, shredded kale or collard greens, and orange slices accompany the beans and meat.

A Brazilian version of the tamale, called *abara*, is African in origin. Abara is a mixture of cowpeas, shrimp, pepper, and dendê oil rolled into banana leaves and cooked over an open fire.

Cuscuz, a steamed grain dish, is either Arabian or North African in origin. The Brazilians adopted it and developed two different forms of it. One kind of cuscuz is sweet and is served as a dessert. Cooks mix tapioca, freshly grated coconut, coconut milk, sugar, and water together with boiling water. They pour the mixture into a mold and refrigerate it. Later, they slice and serve the chilled cuscuz. The other type of cuscuz, often called *cuscuz paulista*, is served as a main dish. Cuscuz paulista is made with specially prepared cornmeal mixed with shredded vegetables and meat and a small amount of fat. The mixture is steamed and garnished decoratively.

South American Menu

Empanadas
(Turnovers)

Carbonada Criolla
(Beef Stew)

Couve à Mineira
(Shredded Kale)

Tortillas de Maiz
(Corn Pancakes)

Plàtanos Tumulto
(Broiled Bananas)

Bolinhos de Coco Brasileiros
(Brazilian Coconut Cookies)

Café
(Coffee)

Gayvoronskaya_Yana/Shutterstock.com

Figure 30.11 Black beans are one of the most popular types of beans used in Brazilian cuisine.

Empanadas
(Turnovers)
Makes about 12

Filling:
½   pound lean ground beef
½   cup finely chopped onion
½   clove garlic, chopped
1   medium tomato, finely chopped
4   large green olives, chopped
¼   cup raisins
     salt
     pepper

1. In a large, heavy skillet, brown ground beef with onions and garlic.
2. Add tomato, olives, raisins, and salt and pepper to taste. Simmer mixture uncovered until cooked, about 20 minutes.

3. Remove from heat and refrigerate until you are ready to fill the empanadas.

Pastry:

1　cup all-purpose flour
¼　teaspoon salt
½　teaspoon baking powder
¼　cup shortening
3　tablespoons ice water

1. Preheat oven to 450°F.
2. In a medium mixing bowl, use a fork to stir together flour, salt, and baking powder.
3. With pastry blender or two knives, cut shortening into dry ingredients until particles are the size of coarse cornmeal.
4. Add ice water, one tablespoon at a time, stirring gently with a fork until dough forms a ball.
5. On a lightly floured surface, roll out dough about ⅛ inch thick. Using a 2-inch biscuit cutter, cut dough into circles.
6. Place about 1 tablespoon of filling in the center of each circle. Fold dough over filling and seal edges well with a little cold water.
7. Place empanadas on a baking sheet and bake until lightly browned, about 10 to 15 minutes. (For a more authentic dish, empanadas can be fried, a few at a time, in 375°F oil until golden brown.)

Per serving: 126 calories (50% from fat), 5 g protein, 11 g carbohydrate, 7 g fat, 11 mg cholesterol, 1 g fiber, 95 mg sodium.

Carbonada Criolla
(Beef Stew)
Serves 5

1　tablespoon vegetable oil
1¼　pounds boneless beef chuck, cut into 1-inch cubes
½　cup coarsely chopped onions
¼　cup coarsely chopped green pepper
½　teaspoon finely chopped garlic
2¼　cups low-sodium beef broth
2　medium tomatoes, seeded and chopped
½　teaspoon oregano
1　bay leaf
¾　teaspoon salt
¼　teaspoon pepper
2¼　cups sweet potatoes, peeled and diced (about 1 pound)

2¼　cups white potatoes, peeled and diced (about 1½ pounds)
½　pound zucchini, cubed
2　small ears sweet corn, shucked and cut into rounds, 1 inch wide
3　canned peach halves, rinsed in cold water

1. Heat oil in a large Dutch oven. Add meat and brown.
2. Transfer browned meat to a platter and set aside. Then add onions, green peppers, and garlic to the Dutch oven and cook until lightly browned.
3. Add beef stock and bring to a boil.
4. Return meat to the Dutch oven and add tomatoes, oregano, bay leaf, salt, and pepper. Cover Dutch oven and reduce heat to low. Simmer stew for 15 minutes.
5. Remove cover and add sweet potatoes and white potatoes. Simmer for 15 minutes more.
6. Remove cover and add zucchini. Cover and cook 10 minutes more.
7. Remove cover and add corn and peach halves. Cover and cook 5 minutes more.

Per serving: 376 calories (22% from fat), 31 g protein, 45 g carbohydrate, 9 g fat, 71 mg cholesterol, 6 g fiber, 420 mg sodium.

Couve à Mineira
(Shredded Kale)
Serves 6

1½　pounds kale*
2　tablespoons bacon drippings
1　cup water
½　teaspoon salt
　　dash pepper

1. Under running water, carefully wash kale. With a sharp knife, remove any bruised spots and cut tender leaves from tough stems. Discard stems. Shred kale into strips about ½ inch wide.
2. In a large, heavy skillet, melt bacon drippings. Add kale and cook, turning with tongs, until it begins to wilt, about 1 minute. Then add water and simmer until kale is crisp-tender, about 6 to 10 minutes.
3. Drain any remaining water off kale. Add salt and pepper and serve immediately.

*Collard greens may be substituted for kale.

Per serving: 58 calories (62% from fat), 1 g protein, 4 g carbohydrate, 4 g fat, 8 mg cholesterol, 3 g fiber, 193 mg sodium.

Tortillas de Maiz
(Corn Pancakes)
Makes 8 pancakes

1   cup frozen corn kernels, thawed
1   egg
2   tablespoons all-purpose flour
¼   teaspoon salt
3   tablespoons plus 1 teaspoon butter
½   cup plain nonfat yogurt
4   teaspoons chopped fresh parsley

1. Preheat oven to 225°F.
2. Using paper towels, pat corn completely dry.
3. Heat a large, heavy skillet, sprayed with nonstick cooking spray. Add corn and cook until lightly browned. Remove browned corn to a plate lined with paper towels.
4. In a large mixing bowl, beat egg until foamy. Add flour, salt, and corn.
5. In a small skillet or crepe pan, heat 1 tablespoon butter until it foams. Use a low heat. Pour in ⅛ cup batter. As the tortilla cooks, gently lift edges to allow uncooked batter to flow underneath.
6. When tortilla is brown on the bottom, flip with spatula and cook the other side 1 minute. Slide cooked tortilla onto a heated platter and keep warm in the oven.
7. Continue making tortillas, adding a teaspoon of butter before frying each one.
8. Serve tortillas topped with 1 tablespoon of yogurt and chopped parsley.

Per tortilla: 79 calories (55% from fat), 2 g protein, 7 g carbohydrate, 5 g fat, 48 mg cholesterol, 1 g fiber, 137 mg sodium.

Plàtanos Tumulto
(Broiled Bananas)
Serves 6

6   firm, small bananas
1   tablespoon lemon juice
2   tablespoons light brown sugar, packed
¾   teaspoon cinnamon
2   tablespoons butter

1. Preheat broiler.
2. Peel bananas and slice in half lengthwise. Place banana halves cut side up on the broiler pan; sprinkle with lemon juice.
3. Combine brown sugar and cinnamon in a small bowl; cut in butter until mixture resembles large peas. Sprinkle over banana halves.
4. Place bananas 2 inches from heat and broil until sugar has melted. (Watch carefully.) Serve immediately.

Per serving: 143 calories (29% from fat), 1 g protein, 28 g carbohydrate, 4 g fat, 10 mg cholesterol, 3 g fiber, 3 mg sodium.

Bolinhos de Coco Brasileiros
(Brazilian Coconut Cookies)
Makes about 24

½   cup butter, softened
½   cup sugar
1   large egg
¼   cup cream of coconut
1½ teaspoons vanilla extract
¼   teaspoon salt
¾   cup cornstarch
1   cup shredded unsweetened coconut
1½ cups all-purpose flour

1. In a mixing bowl, use an electric mixer to cream the butter and sugar until light and fluffy. Add the egg and mix well. Then add the cream of coconut and vanilla extract and mix again.
2. With the mixer on low speed, add the salt; then gradually add the cornstarch until it is all incorporated. Blend in the coconut, mixing well.
3. Mix in 1 cup of flour. Add remaining flour, a tablespoon at a time, until the dough is soft but not sticky.
4. Cover the mixing bowl with plastic wrap and let the dough rest for 30 minutes. Meanwhile, preheat the oven to 350°F and line two cookie sheets with parchment paper.
5. Roll dough into 1-inch balls and place on cookie sheets. Gently flatten the balls of dough with the tines of a fork. Bake cookies until they just start to brown around the edges, about 15 minutes.
6. Allow cookies to cool on cookie sheet for 5 minutes before transferring to a cooling rack.

Per cookie: 115 calories (47% from fat), 1 g protein, 15 g carbohydrate, 6 g fat, 19 mg cholesterol, 1 g fiber, 30 mg sodium.

Chapter 30 Review and Expand

Summary

Latin America is the term used to refer to the landmass that stretches southward from the Rio Grande to the tip of South America. Types of cuisine vary according to historical influences, culture, climate, and geographical region.

The Aztecs and the Spanish conquistadores played an influential role in Mexico's history. They also contributed to Mexico's cuisine. The corn and beans farmers grow are important to the economy. These foods are important ingredients in Mexican cuisine, too. Mexican cooks also make much use of peppers, fruits, and vegetables in their cooking. They prepare a variety of flavorful sauces and stews and unique desserts and beverages. Many of these dishes have evolved on a regional basis due to Mexico's varied climate and geography.

Spanish, Portuguese, and African influences are blended with foods of native tribes to form South American cuisine. Throughout the continent, corn, potatoes, and manioc are used as staple foods. However, geographic isolation is the reason the use of these foods varies from region to region.

Vocabulary Activities

1. **Content Terms**   Review the following terms and their definitions. How do these terms relate to each other? Write a brief paragraph explaining your vocabulary connections.

Latin America	manioc
national dish	cassava
tortilla	arepa
frijoles refritos	ceviche
chile	ají
guacamole	gaucho
mole	empanada
plantain	dendé oil
comida	feijoada completa

2. **Academic Terms**   In teams, play *picture charades* to identify as many of the following terms as possible. Write the terms on separate slips of paper and put the slips into a basket. Choose a team member to be the *sketcher*. The sketcher pulls a term from the basket and creates quick drawings or graphics to represent the term until the team guesses the term. Rotate turns as sketcher until the team identifies all terms.

proximity	lush
arid	meteorologist
plateau	intermingled
rustic	nomadic

Review

Write your answers using complete sentences when appropriate.

3. Name two Central American countries and give an example of a national dish for each country.
4. How have climate and geography affected Mexican food customs?
5. Describe a food tradition associated with a Mexican holiday.
6. The Aztecs and the Spaniards made many contributions to Mexican cuisine. Name four contributions of each.
7. What is a tortilla and how is it made? Describe three Mexican foods made from tortillas.
8. What are the colors of peppers used in Mexican cooking and how are they used?
9. Describe one type of mole.
10. How and why do tortillas in northern Mexico differ from those served in other regions?
11. What is Mexico's main meal of the day called? What foods are usually served at this meal?
12. What are three staple foods found throughout South America?
13. What is the name of the traditional Venezuelan bread that is similar to a tortilla?
14. Describe two ways Ecuadorian people use bananas.
15. How is ceviche prepared in Peru?
16. Why don't Chileans eat much meat?
17. What is chimichurri and how is it used in Argentina?
18. Brazilian culture is a mixture of three cultures. Name them.

Chapter 30 Review and Expand

Core Skills

19. **Technology, Listening, Speaking** Type the highlighted and italicized Spanish terms in this chapter into an online translator tool. Listen to the pronunciations of the terms and practice saying them.

20. **Research, Writing** Use reliable print or online resources to research the lifestyle and conquest of the Mexican Aztec civilization. Also research the lifestyle and conquest of the South American Incan Empire. Write a report comparing the ends of these two cultures, citing your sources. Reread and revise your report for grammar, spelling, and organization.

21. **Reading, Speaking, Listening** Investigate how the celebration of Mardi Gras in the United States compares with the celebration of Carnival in Brazil. Share your findings in a class discussion.

22. **Math, Technology** Make a list of 10 ingredients you might opt to include in a Mexican entree such as a taco or burrito. Be sure to specify the quantity of each ingredient you would use. For instance, you might use 2 ounces (56 g) of cooked chicken breast. Use an online nutrient database to find nutrition information for each ingredient. Then use a chart tool to illustrate the calorie, protein, carbohydrate, total fat, cholesterol, fiber, and sodium content of each ingredient. Use the charts to create nutritional profiles of various combinations of ingredients. Note how adding or eliminating certain ingredients affects the nutritional value of Mexican entrees.

23. **Technology, Speaking** Choose a Latin American destination and hypothetical travel dates. Use a travel website to find available flights to your chosen destination from your nearest airport. Identify top tourist attractions of your destination. Then, search for restaurants in this location and identify three to four traditional foods served. Evaluate whether these foods sound or look appealing to you. Share your findings in class and explain why you would or would not want to take this trip.

24. **Career Readiness Practice** The ability to gather and analyze information with cultural relevance is an important workplace skill. Consider the following problem: As foodservice director for a multinational corporation, it has come to your attention that foods served in the company cafeteria are not meeting cultural needs of all employees. Most offices in the United States have many employees from Latin American cultures. You and your culinary team need to make changes in some types of foods served, but need more information. With your team members, create a plan to gather and analyze the information you need with culture in mind. List culturally sensitive questions you need to ask about food needs and potential sources of reliable information.

Critical Thinking and Problem Solving

25. **Analyze** On a map of Mexico, identify areas in which fish would play a main part in the diet and areas in which beef would be more prevalent. Analyze geographic features that have resulted in these dietary distinctions.

26. **Create** Visit a Mexican tourism website. Navigate the site and related links to find information about the Mexican tourist destination of your choice. Investigate lodging, tours, restaurants, and activities in your chosen city to plan a four-day, three-night vacation. Compile your findings into the form of a travel itinerary.

27. **Create** Create a new dish made with tortillas. Give your dish a name and write a recipe. Prepare a sample. Describe your dish to the class and share your creation.

28. **Evaluate** Some South American baked goods are made with cassava flour instead of wheat flour. Research the nutritional value of cassava flour compared with the nutritional value of white wheat all-purpose flour. Evaluate the nutritional impact on a typical U.S. diet that would result if cassava flour were used in place of wheat flour. Share your findings in class.

Chapter 31
Europe

pamuk/Shutterstock.com

Objectives

After studying this chapter, you will be able to
- **identify** food customs of the British Isles, France, Germany, and the Scandinavian countries;
- **explain** how and why these customs have evolved; and
- **prepare** foods native to each of these countries.

Reading Prep

As you read the chapter, put sticky notes next to the sections where you have questions. Write your questions on the sticky notes. Discuss the questions with your classmates or teacher. You may also create a separate document to keep track of your questions.

Content Terms

cockle
fish and chips
pudding basin
tea
haggis
colcannon
haute cuisine
provincial cuisine
nouvelle cuisine
hollandaise sauce
fines herbes
hors d'oeuvre
croissant
crêpe
truffle
bouillabaisse

escargot
quiche
braten
bratwurst
hasenpfeffer
kartoffelpuffer
sauerkraut
spätzle
strudel
crayfish
smørrebrød
lutefisk
smörgåsbord
husmankost
lingonberry
sauna

Academic Terms

wellspring
emblem
rivaling
peasant
wharf

commodity
nobility
herald
lowland
prosperous

Europe is the second smallest continent in terms of land area. Despite its small size, it is one of the most heavily populated continents. Nearly one-fifth of the world's population lives in Europe. Europe has been a cultural, political, and economic leader for centuries. Its history is rich and varied. Although many countries are part of Europe, this chapter will focus on the British Isles, France, Germany, and Scandinavia. Spain, Italy, and Greece are discussed in another chapter.

Each European country has a unique cuisine, but some common diet patterns emerge. The diets of the British Isles, France, Germany, and Scandinavia include a variety of fruits, vegetables, and breads. Meals in these countries also tend to center around meat, fish, poultry, or game. Dairy products also play an important role in many Northern and Western European cuisines. Rich desserts are popular in these cuisines, too. Together, these food patterns describe a diet that tends to be fairly high in fat.

To include Northern and Western European foods in a healthy diet, choose generous portions of vegetables and whole-grain dishes. Limit portion sizes of meat and opt for low-fat or fat-free dairy foods. Select fruits for dessert often. Enjoy rich desserts only occasionally.

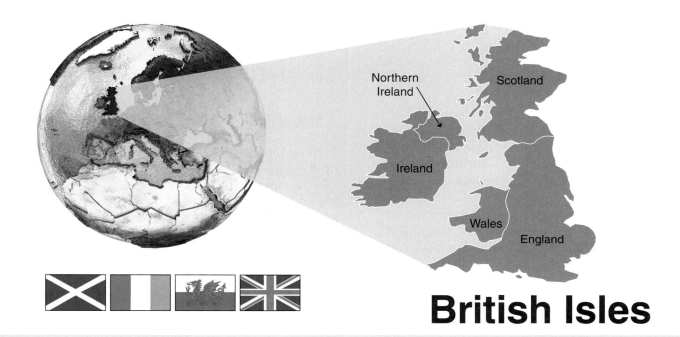

British Isles

The British Isles are a group of two large islands and several small islands. They are located northwest of mainland Europe. The largest island, Great Britain, includes England, Scotland, and Wales. The second largest island, Ireland, is politically divided between two countries. Northern Ireland is joined with England, Scotland, and Wales to form the United Kingdom of Great Britain and Northern Ireland. The United Kingdom has four political divisions united under a single government. The southern part of the island of Ireland is the country of Ireland, which is an independent nation with its own government.

The people of the British Isles share a common ancestry and culture. Due to geographic isolation, however, each region of the British Isles has separate customs and traditions.

Geography and Climate of the British Isles

The Atlantic Ocean, North Sea, Irish Sea, Celtic Sea, and English Channel are the bodies of water that surround the British Isles. Much of England is composed of fertile farmlands. The

Pennine Chain is a mountain range that runs northward through the center of England to the Scottish border. Southern Scotland is made up of rolling hills. The central lowland region is the location of most of Scotland's population, industry, and farmland. Northern Scotland is a rugged, mountainous area known as the Highlands. Wales can be divided into two parts. North Wales is mountainous country. South Wales is marked by valleys and coastal plains. Much of Ireland is covered with rolling hills and windswept plains. The landscape of Northern Ireland rises into low mountains along the northeast coast.

The weather changes in Britain from hour to hour and from village to village. Fog along the coasts is common, and the air is often raw and bone-chilling.

Agriculture of the British Isles

Much of the land on the British Isles is suitable for growing crops and raising livestock (**Figure 31.1**). Wheat, oats, and barley are the key grains grown in the British Isles. Potatoes are also an important crop throughout this area. Ireland has always been known for its excellent cattle, and Irish pedigree bulls are traded all over the world. Chickens, hogs, and dairy cattle are important sources of food. Sheep are raised for their wool as well as their meat.

David Crosbie/Shutterstock.com

Figure 31.1 The English countryside is dotted with farms that produce grain and livestock.

Because water surrounds the British Isles, fishing is an important industry. Cod, haddock, and mackerel are among the most important catches. Along the Welsh coast, a type of mussel called **cockles** has flourished for hundreds of years. Licensed pickers still make their livings harvesting cockles out of the sand to sell in nearby markets.

Culture of the British Isles

The British Isles have a long and colorful history. For centuries, this was the center of one of the world's greatest empires. It was a *wellspring* (significant source) of contributions in the areas of art, architecture, and literature. The United Kingdom is still one of the most influential nations on earth.

British History

A number of groups of people shaped the culture of the British Isles. These included the Celts, Romans, Germanic tribes, and Normans. The Celts lived on the British Isles from about 500 BC until the Romans invaded some 600 years later.

The Jutes, Angles, and Saxons were Germanic tribes that invaded England from mainland Europe in the 400s AD. Eventually, the Angles and Saxons set up kingdoms throughout England. (The name *England* comes from "land of the Angles.") In 1066, William the Conqueror led a Norman army into England. (The Normans were a group of Scandinavian Vikings who had settled in northern France.) Through a military victory, William became the new king of England. Under William's reign, Norman influence spread throughout the British Isles.

The English language developed from the Germanic and Norman languages. English is the official language used throughout the United Kingdom. Welsh is a second official language in Wales. Many people in Scotland and Northern Ireland speak a form of an ancient Celtic language called *Gaelic*. Gaelic and English are both official languages in Ireland.

British Government

Wales was united with England in 1536 under King Henry VIII. In 1707, Scotland was united with England and Wales to form the

Global Perspective

Ireland

Most of the people on the island of Ireland had been Roman Catholic for centuries. During the early 1600s, land on the northern part of the island was given to Protestants. Ongoing conflict existed between the Protestants in the north and the Catholics in the south. In 1921, the British Parliament agreed to the formation of the Irish Free State in southern Ireland. In 1937, this state adopted a new constitution and changed its name to Ireland, or *Eire* in Gaelic. In 1949, Ireland severed all connections with the United Kingdom and became an independent nation. Northern Ireland remains part of the United Kingdom.

Kingdom of Great Britain. Ireland became joined with Great Britain in 1801 to form the United Kingdom of Great Britain and Ireland.

London is the capital of the United Kingdom. It is the home of the Houses of Parliament, where British laws are made. The House of Lords and the House of Commons are the two bodies that make up Parliament. The monarchy has no real power. Instead, the head of government is the prime minister. The prime minister is usually the political party leader with the most members in the House of Commons.

Recreation in the British Isles

The people of the British Isles enjoy outdoor activities and sporting events throughout the year. Golf, hiking, mountain climbing, horseback riding, cycling, fishing, and tennis are well-liked activities when the weather is warm. In colder weather, skiing and curling are favorite pastimes. Popular sporting events in the British Isles include soccer, rugby, cricket, and hurling.

In Scotland, the Highland games are an annual recreational event. They are held in different areas throughout the spring, summer, and fall. The games include a variety of events, similar to a track meet.

Throughout the British Isles, a favorite social activity is relaxing with friends in a local public

house, or *pub*. People gather to enjoy a glass of beer, play darts, and talk.

British Holidays

Festivals and holiday traditions are reflections of culture among the people of the British Isles. In Scotland, New Year's Eve is called *Hogmanay*. It is celebrated with bonfires and feasts. A Scottish tradition centers on the first person to enter a family's home after midnight. This person is called the *first-footer*. The Scots look for the first-footer to carry bread, coal, and money. They believe this means the family will not be hungry, cold, or poor in the coming year. The Scots drink a New Year's toast of sweet or spiced ale from a *wassail bowl*. This name comes from "Waes hael," which is Gaelic for "Be well."

An annual Welsh festival is *St. David's Day*, which honors the patron saint of Wales. This celebration takes place on March 1. Welsh people pin daffodils (a spring flower) or leeks (a winter vegetable) to their clothes. This symbolizes the passing of winter into spring. St. David's Day feasts feature traditional Welsh foods, such as leek soup, lamb, and Welsh wines and cheeses.

St. Patrick's Day is a national celebration held in honor of Ireland's patron saint. People often dress in green and display shamrocks to observe St. Patrick's Day (**Figure 31.2**). Green represents the color of Ireland's countryside. Shamrocks are Ireland's national **emblem** (symbol). This day is

Figure 31.2 Shamrocks are globally recognized as the national symbol for Ireland.

celebrated by Irish people throughout the world with food, folk music, and parades. In Ireland, however, St. Patrick's Day is an important religious holiday spent quietly with family and friends.

November 5 is a distinctly English holiday—*Guy Fawkes Night.* This celebration is named for a man who tried to blow up the Houses of Parliament in 1605, but was caught in his plot to do so. The British gather for fireworks and bonfires to celebrate his failed plot. The bonfires are topped with figures made of paper or straw stuffed into old clothes to represent Guy Fawkes.

Cuisine of the British Isles

The cuisine of the British Isles is hearty and filling. Cooks use many locally grown foods. They prepare them in a variety of ways to create dishes that are substantial yet simple and economical.

British Cuisine

The bread, meat, cheese, pies, and puddings of the Anglo-Saxons are still staples of the British diet today. For centuries, England has specialized in a variety of dishes based on these staple foods. Steamed puddings and pickled meats are among the many foods for which British cooks are famous. Savory and sweet pies, crumpets, and a slightly sweet yeast bread called Sally Lunn are also popular British foods.

British Main Dishes

The British enjoy beef, pork, lamb, mutton, and wild game. The British perfected the art of roasting centuries ago, and roasting is still popular.

Rivaling (competing with) the British love of meat is the love of fish. The British eat fresh mackerel, whiting, cod, haddock, Dover sole, halibut, salmon, and many other varieties. They often prepare these fish by baking or poaching. *Kippers* (split and salted herring) are popular smoked fish.

Shops selling fish and chips are scattered throughout England. **Fish and chips** are

Culture and Social Studies

Development of British Cuisine

The early Anglo-Saxons hunted, fished, and gathered nuts and berries for food. They eventually made small gardens and grew grain along the edges of the forests.

Using techniques they had brought from their homelands, the Anglo-Saxons brewed ale from barley. They ground grain for use in baking bread. They made the milk of sheep and cattle into butter and cheese. The Anglo-Saxons also grew apple trees for cider and kept bees for honey. They either roasted the meat from freshly caught game or cooked it in large iron pots. By the eleventh century, the Anglo-Saxons had added puddings and pies to their cuisine.

Several other contributions to British cuisine were made during the reign of William the Conqueror. The Normans prepared delicious breads and pastries. They made some creative dishes, such as *tripe* (stomach tissue of cattle and oxen). They also used spices and herbs in large quantities.

Norman meals had several courses. Normans served their meat course on *trenchers* (wooden or metal platters or large slices of bread). This was an example of the more refined manners the Normans used.

battered, deep-fried fish fillets served with the British version of french fries. The type of fish that vendors use often depends on the particular day's catch. Cod, haddock, and sole are the most popular types.

Creative British cooks turn leftovers into a number of popular dishes. *Bubble and squeak* is the name for a dish made from leftover beef and potatoes. Cold cooked beef and potatoes are mixed with either raw cabbage or brussels sprouts and cooked until crisp. *Shepherd's pie* is a mixture of finely chopped meat and leftover vegetables topped with mashed potatoes and baked (**Figure 31.3**). *Toad in the hole* is made by

British Pies and Puddings

A discussion of British foods would not be complete without mentioning pies and puddings. Both can be either desserts or main dishes. *Steak and kidney pie* is one of the best known British main dish pies. Cooks combine diced kidney with cubes of beef and a savory gravy and cover it with a pastry crust. A popular dessert pie is a plum pie dusted with sugar.

The British serve hundreds of sweet puddings. British puddings are nothing like the creamy cornstarch pudding served in the United States. Instead, they are similar to cakes and breads in texture and appearance. British puddings all begin with the same basic ingredients—milk, sugar, eggs, flour, and butter. Extra ingredients, such as dried fruit, spices, and lemon juice, make each pudding unique.

Most puddings are steamed in a **pudding basin**. The traditional basin is a deep, thick-rimmed bowl. A cook pours the pudding mixture into the basin and covers it with a clean cloth. Then the basin goes into a large kettle that is partially filled with water to steam the pudding. Cooks make boiled puddings by wrapping the dough in a piece of floured cloth. Then they tie the cloth at the top and immerse the pudding in a kettle of boiling water.

A *summer pudding* is neither boiled nor steamed. A basin is lined with slices of bread. The lined mold is then filled to the top with sweetened, fresh berries, covered with more bread, weighted, and chilled. During chilling, the bread soaks up the fruit juices. The unmolded pudding often is served with heavy cream.

The *trifle* is another popular British dessert. You might call it a pudding-cake. A mold or serving dish is lined with slices of pound cake spread with a fruit jam. The cake is soaked with sherry. The mold is then filled with layers of custard, fresh fruit, whipped cream, and slivered almonds.

British Meals

Traditional British breakfasts are hearty. They can include eggs, bacon, baked beans, fried bread served with marmalade, and tea. People in many parts of England also eat fruits, main dish pies, ham, smoked fish, and porridge as breakfast foods.

During the week, lunch often is little more than a hearty meat or cheese sandwich and tea.

Michael C. Gray/Shutterstock.com

Figure 31.3 Hearty shepherd's pie is a filling British main dish that can be made from leftovers. How can leftovers be inspiration for creating new dishes?

pouring a thick batter over pieces of leftover meat and baking the mixture.

British Fruits and Vegetables

Apples have grown in England for centuries, and British cooks use apples in many simple but creative ways. Baked apples, apple charlotte, apple crumble, apple pudding, and apple sponge are popular desserts. Other fruits are popular, too. Fresh strawberries are served with rich, thick cream. The British also use a variety of berries as well as apples, plums, and other fruits to make jams, jellies, and preserves.

Carrots, spinach, parsnips, peas, beans, cabbage, cauliflower, onions, and potatoes grow well in British gardens. Sauces appear occasionally, but the British usually serve vegetables right from the garden cooked with just butter and simple seasonings.

On Sunday, however, lunch is the main meal of the day.

People in all the countries of the British Isles serve tea throughout the day as a beverage. The term **tea** also refers to a light meal. In rural areas, for example, the evening meal is called tea. In the cities, where people usually serve dinner in the evening, tea is a snack in the afternoon.

The British serve many foods for tea. A simple tea may consist of tea and a few cookies or a piece of cake. More elaborate teas may include a variety of sandwiches, sausages, cheeses, breads, cakes, and cookies. In England, people often serve crumpets with butter and homemade jam. *Crumpets* are a bread product similar to the English muffin served in the United States.

Scottish Cuisine

Oats and barley grow well in Scotland. Both grains have long been staple foods. Cooks often use them to make breads and porridges. Cooks also use oats to prepare the traditional Scottish holiday dish called haggis. **Haggis** is a pudding made from oatmeal, seasonings, and a sheep's organs boiled in a sheep's stomach (**Figure 31.4**). Barley is basic to the production of ales and liquors, many of which are exported. Fine Scotch whiskey, for example, is known throughout the world.

Scottish cooks are known for the good, simple, wholesome foods they prepare. Many Scottish dishes contain locally produced beef, lamb, or mutton. Others contain fish caught in coastal waters. Fresh fruits and vegetables, cereal products made of oats and barley, and dairy products may be added to meat- or fish-based dishes. For example, a hearty broth made from meat bones and vegetables often forms the basis for soup. Scotch broth and cock-a-leekie are two traditional Scottish soups. *Scotch broth* is made with lamb and barley; *cock-a-leekie* is made from chicken broth and leeks.

Fishing is an important industry in Scotland. As a result, the Scots eat fish often. Kippers and *finnan haddie* (split and smoked haddock) are especially popular in Scotland.

The Scots eat even heartier breakfasts than the British. Scottish breakfasts may include large amounts of porridge with *baps* (soft breakfast rolls), kippers, and many steaming cups of tea. Dundee is the birthplace of marmalade, which is eaten throughout the British Isles. Aberdeen is the birthplace of the breakfast sausage.

Scottish cooks consider baking to be one of their greatest skills. Their baking skills are most apparent at high tea, which they serve at around six o'clock. Scottish specialties served at high tea include scones, shortbread, Dundee cake, and black bun. *Scones* are rich, triangle-shaped biscuits. They are usually split in half and spread with butter and marmalade. *Shortbread* is a rich, buttery cookie made from flour, sugar, and butter. *Dundee cake* is a rich fruitcake sprinkled with almonds. *Black bun* is a fruitcake covered with pastry. Gingerbread cakes, oatcakes, and brown and white rolls are other favorites.

Welsh Cuisine

Welsh food is similar to the foods of England and Scotland in its simplicity. The Welsh use homegrown foods to prepare dishes that are substantial yet plain and economical.

The rugged hills found in much of Wales are suitable for sheep production. The finest spring lambs in the British Isles graze on the grasses in the Brecon Beacons of Wales. Understandably, lamb and mutton are prominent in the Welsh diet. For example, *cawl* is a hearty soup made from mutton and leeks and other vegetables.

Besides lamb, the Welsh diet includes beef, pork, veal, and seafood. The Welsh often serve ham boiled. They eat cockles with a dash of vinegar (**Figure 31.5**).

Paul Cowan/Shutterstock.com

Figure 31.4   Haggis is the national dish of Scotland.

Irish Cuisine

Though the island of Ireland is divided politically, the people share a culinary heritage. Local dishes are still prepared with recipes that have been handed down from generation to generation.

Irish Vegetables

Potatoes have been the mainstay of the Irish diet for centuries. Their importance can best be seen in the results of the 1847 potato crop failure. Thousands of Irish people died, and over a million fled to the United States to escape the "black famine."

In many Irish homes, potatoes are still part of the daily diet. The Irish cook potatoes in a small amount of salted water and serve them with butter. They also use potatoes in soups, stews, breads, rolls, and cakes. Crisp, fried cakes made from grated raw potatoes, flour, salt, and milk are called *boxty*. Potatoes mashed with finely chopped scallions and milk and served with melted butter are called *champ*. Mashed potatoes mixed with chopped scallions, shredded cooked cabbage, and melted butter are called **colcannon** (**Figure 31.6**).

A variety of other vegetables are also grown in small gardens across Ireland. Cabbage, onions, carrots, cauliflower, parsnips, turnips, and peas are plentiful. The Irish may serve these vegetables creamed, baked, or cooked in water. Mushrooms gathered from the fields are sautéed in butter or added to soups and stews. Garlic and parsley add both color and flavor to meats, poultry, soups, and stews.

Irish Main Dishes

The excellent beef cattle produced in Ireland account for the popularity of *corned beef and cabbage.* This Irish dish is economical because it is made with the beef brisket. The Irish also use beef for roasting, braising, and adding to stews. The Irish steak and kidney stew is similar to the steak and kidney pie served in England.

Sheep thrive in the mountainous areas of Ireland where the land is too poor for farming. The Irish serve the first lamb of the year on Easter Sunday to mark the beginning of spring. They usually roast the leg of lamb. Less tender parts of the animal are often used to make Irish

D. Pimborough/Shutterstock.com

Figure 31.5 Cockles gathered along the coast of Wales are a popular seafood item in Welsh cuisine.

The Welsh grow potatoes, carrots, and other vegetables in local gardens and add them to soups and stews. *Tatws slaw* (potatoes mashed with buttermilk) frequently accompanies ham.

The Welsh serve tea in late afternoon or early evening. Various baked goods accompany cups of steaming tea. *Crempog* (buttermilk cakes) and *bara ceirch* (oatcakes spread with butter and eaten with buttermilk) are especially popular. Sponge cake and *bara brith* (a bread filled with currants) are enjoyed as well.

Familiar to many people in the United States is Welsh rabbit (or rarebit). *Welsh rabbit* is toast covered with a rich cheese sauce. One story says this dish got its name because Welsh **peasants** (people who do not have much money and have low social status) were too poor to buy meat, even rabbit meat. The closest dish they could afford was this cheese dish, which they nick-named "Welsh rabbit."

Brent Hofacker/Shutterstock.com

Figure 31.6 This variety of colcannon includes bacon. Why are many Irish dishes made with potatoes?

stew. *Irish stew* is pieces of lamb and potatoes in hearty gravy.

The Irish eat pork both fresh and cured, but Ireland is best known for its boiled hams. Traditionally, the Irish covered a whole boiled ham with sugar and bread crumbs and studded it with cloves.

The Irish who live close to the sea carry home buckets of seafood from fishing boats on the *wharf* (dock). Most kinds of seafood are inexpensive because they are readily available. Favorites include crabs, mussels, prawns, and scallops.

Irish Baked Goods

Many people consider Irish breads to be some of the best in the world. Some Irish farm families still bake *soda bread* and *brown bread* every day.

Baking is most important at tea. The Irish sometimes serve eggs, cold meats, and salads at tea. However, they always serve a variety of breads and cakes. They thickly spread butter on soda bread, brown bread, oatcakes, and scones. *Barmbrack*, a light fruitcake served with butter, is one of the most popular Irish cakes. On All Hallows' Eve (October 31), the family baker adds a wedding ring wrapped in paper to the batter before baking. Legend says the person who receives the slice of barmbrack with the ring will

marry before the year ends. Two other favorite desserts served for tea are sponge cake and Irish whiskey cake.

Irish Meals

In Ireland, as in other parts of the British Isles, the day begins with a hearty breakfast. Breakfast commonly includes porridge, eggs, bread, butter, and tea. The Irish serve dinner in the middle of the day. It is the main meal for many people, especially those who live in rural areas. The Irish serve tea at about six o'clock in the evening.

British Isles Menu

Welsh Rabbit
Corned Beef and Cabbage
Parsley-Buttered Potatoes
Carrots
Scones and Marmalade
English Trifle
Tea

Welsh Rabbit
Serves 6

2 tablespoons all-purpose flour
¾ cup fat-free milk
⅛ teaspoon pepper
¼ teaspoon dry mustard
½ teaspoon Worcestershire sauce
1 cup shredded Cheddar cheese
6 slices toast, cut diagonally into quarters

1. Combine flour and milk in a small, tightly covered container. Shake until thoroughly blended.
2. Pour flour mixture into a small saucepan. Blend in pepper, mustard, and Worcestershire sauce, stirring until mixture is smooth. Cook over medium heat, stirring constantly, until sauce comes to a boil. Cook and stir for one additional minute until sauce is thick and smooth.
3. Remove sauce from heat and add cheese, stirring constantly until the cheese is melted. Serve over toast pieces. Garnish with hard-boiled egg wedges, parsley, or paprika.

Per serving: 164 calories (38% from fat), 9 g protein, 16 g carbohydrate, 7 g fat, 20 mg cholesterol, 0 g fiber, 274 mg sodium.

Corned Beef and Cabbage
Serves 4

1	pound corned beef
1	sprig thyme
1	small onion studded with 4 cloves
¼	teaspoon pepper
1	bay leaf
1	carrot, cut into 8 sticks
	cold water
½	small head cabbage, cut into 4 wedges

1. Place beef, thyme, studded onion, pepper, and bay leaf in a large pot. Cover with cold water. Bring to a simmer, cover pan tightly, and reduce heat. Simmer 1 hour and 15 minutes.
2. Remove thyme sprig and bay leaf and add carrot and cabbage. Simmer for another 10 to 15 minutes or until the cabbage and carrot are crisp-tender.
3. Remove corned beef to heated serving platter. Surround with cabbage wedges, carrot sticks, and onion.

Per serving: 240 calories (49% from fat), 24 g protein, 6 g carbohydrate, 13 g fat, 73 mg cholesterol, 2 g fiber, 877 mg sodium.

Parsley Buttered Potatoes
Serves 6

2	pounds small new potatoes*
2	tablespoons butter
1	tablespoon fresh parsley, coarsely chopped

1. Carefully scrub potatoes. Remove one strip of peel around the center of each potato.
2. Place potatoes in a large pan filled with cold water. Bring to a boil. Gently simmer 35 to 40 minutes or until potatoes are tender.
3. Drain potatoes well. Add butter and parsley; stir gently until potatoes are coated. Serve immediately.

*Red potatoes may be substituted for the new potatoes.

Per serving: 140 calories (26% from fat), 2 g protein, 25 g carbohydrate, 4 g fat, 10 mg cholesterol, 2 g fiber, 7 mg sodium.

Carrots
Serves 6

1½	pounds carrots, sliced
1	tablespoon plus 1 teaspoon butter
	salt and pepper

1. Bring a small amount of lightly salted water to a boil in a saucepan; add carrots.
2. Bring water to a boil again. Then reduce heat, cover pan, and let carrots gently simmer until crisp-tender, about 7 to 9 minutes.
3. Drain carrots well and toss with butter. Season with salt and pepper to taste. Serve immediately.

Per serving: 65 calories (42% from fat), 1 g protein, 10 g carbohydrate, 3 g fat, 7 mg cholesterol, 3 g fiber, 95 mg sodium.

Scones
Makes 8 scones

2½	cups all-purpose flour
2½	teaspoons baking powder
½	teaspoon salt
1	tablespoon sugar
3	tablespoons butter
1	egg
1	cup fat-free milk

1. Preheat oven to 400°F. Grease a baking sheet and set aside.
2. In a large bowl, combine flour, baking powder, salt, and sugar. Cut in butter until mixture resembles coarse cornmeal.
3. In a separate bowl, beat the egg until frothy, reserving 1 tablespoon.
4. Add the milk to the beaten egg and pour into the flour mixture. Stir dough lightly with a fork until it forms a soft ball.
5. On a floured surface, roll the dough into a square ½-inch thick. With a sharp knife, cut the square into quarters. Then cut each quarter diagonally into a triangle.
6. Place the triangles about 1 inch apart on the baking sheet; brush the tops with the reserved beaten egg. Bake scones for 15 minutes or until light brown. Serve at once.

Per scone: 207 calories (23% from fat), 6 g protein, 33 g carbohydrate, 6 g fat, 46 mg cholesterol, 1 g fiber, 306 mg sodium.

English Trifle
Serves 6

4   slices reduced-fat pound cake
2   tablespoons raspberry jam
½   cup blanched almonds, halved
1   cup fresh raspberries or 1 package frozen raspberries, 10 ounces
1   cup soft custard (homemade or prepared vanilla pudding)
1   cup heavy cream
1   tablespoon confectioner's sugar

1. Coat two slices of pound cake with jam. Cut them diagonally and arrange them, jam side up, in the bottom of a glass bowl.
2. Cut the remaining pound cake into cubes and scatter them over the jam-covered slices.
3. Reserve a small portion of almonds to use as garnish. Then sprinkle the remaining ½ cup of the almonds over the cake.
4. Reserve 12 of the best raspberries. (Drain juice from frozen berries.) Sprinkle the remaining berries over the cake.
5. Using a flexible spatula, gently spread the custard over the fruit.
6. In a small, chilled bowl, whip the cream until slightly thick. Add sugar gradually, beating until cream forms soft peaks.
7. Spread half the whipped cream over the custard.
8. Using a pastry bag, pipe the remaining whipped cream decoratively around the edge of the trifle. Garnish with reserved berries and almonds.

Per serving: 352 calories (59% from fat), 8 g protein, 32 g carbohydrate, 23 g fat, 87 mg cholesterol, 3 g fiber, 172 mg sodium.

Losangela/Shutterstock.com

Trifle can be prepared in a large trifle bowl or in individual dessert glasses.

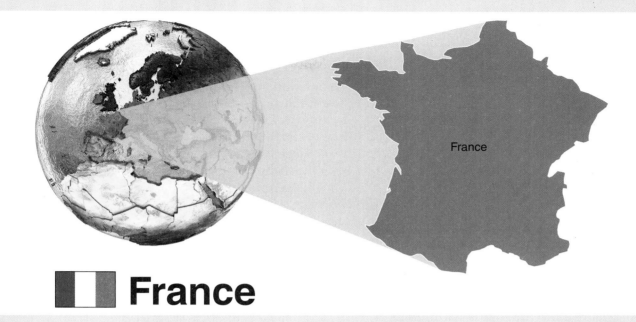

France

Geography and Climate of France

France is the largest country in Western Europe. France is also the oldest unified nation in Europe. It has been an important world power for centuries. The French have had an impact on the development of the entire Western civilization. They have made many contributions in art, science, government, and philosophy.

The Atlantic Ocean, the Mediterranean Sea, and the English Channel border France. Belgium, Luxembourg, Germany, Switzerland, Italy, and Spain also border France. All these nations have influenced the development of French culture.

The eastern and southwestern areas of France are mountainous. The northern and western parts of the country are rolling plains. Both highlands and lowlands are found in the central provinces.

The climate of France is moderate. In the higher elevations, snow falls during the winter. However, most of the country has cool, rainy weather instead of snow. Throughout much of France, spring is humid, summer is moderate, and autumn is long and sunny. These climatic conditions are especially favorable for the production of the grapes used to make famous French wines (**Figure 31.7**).

Volfoni/Shutterstock.com

Figure 31.7 Wines made from French grapes are regarded as some of the finest in the world.

French Agriculture

Fishing and agricultural industries are important to France. Fishers catch large amounts of cod, crab, herring, lobster, mackerel, oysters, sardines, shrimp, and tuna along the French coastlines. Grapes grow throughout much of the southern part of the country. Cattle provide meat and dairy products. Wheat, corn, oats, and barley are important grain crops. Sugar beets, fruits, vegetables, flax, flowers, and other livestock are also important agricultural *commodities* (important economic goods).

French Culture

The French are a mixture of many different peoples who originally came to France from areas throughout Europe. Each group settled in a different part of the country.

In the Middle Ages, France was divided into areas called *domains*. A member of the *nobility* (highest social class) ruled each domain and peasants worked the land. During the Renaissance, France became a unified country. However, many of the people of France did not think of themselves as French citizens. Instead, they considered themselves citizens of the regions in which they lived, such as Brittany and Burgundy. Today, regional ties continue to be strong in many parts of France, especially in rural areas.

Today, France is a republic headed by a president. Paris, France's largest city and capital, is a marketing and distribution center as well as the seat of government. The official language is French. The greatest percentage of the population is Roman Catholic.

Joan of Arc Day is a national holiday in France, which is observed on the second Sunday in May. This day is named for a 17-year-old girl who became a French national heroine and a Catholic saint. French people celebrate the holiday held in her honor by decorating the streets with statues and pictures of Joan.

France's national independence day, Bastille Day, is July 14. On this date in 1789, a crowd of French citizens captured a Paris prison called the Bastille. This volatile event signaled the start of the French Revolution. The French celebrate this holiday with parades, parties, dancing, and fireworks.

Many other celebrations throughout the year in France are church holidays. On January 6, the eve of Epiphany, children lay fruit and cake on the church altar for the Christ child. *Mardi Gras heralds* (welcomes enthusiastically) the beginning of Lent with parades of flower-covered floats. *Pâques*, the French name for Easter, comes from the name of the Jewish Passover. On this day, children receive colored candy eggs and chocolate chickens. Corpus Christi is a festival in early June honoring the bread and wine used for Holy Communion. The bread and wine are taken from church altars in gold and silver bowls and carried through the streets. Small altars covered with boughs and flowers are set up at village crossroads. *Noël*, or Christmas, is a time for family reunions, carol singing, and gifts for the children.

French Cuisine

In France, good food and wine are an important part of daily life. In many parts of France, cooks buy food fresh each day, and they take great care in selecting it. The French usually shop in small specialty shops rather than in large supermarkets.

French cooking can be divided into three main classes: haute cuisine, provincial cuisine, and nouvelle cuisine. **Haute cuisine** is characterized by elaborate preparations, fancy garnishes, and rich sauces. Chefs make lavish use of eggs, cream, and butter in this style of French cooking. Haute cuisine is seen most often in leading restaurants and hotels.

Provincial cuisine is the style of cooking practiced by most French families. Provincial cooks make fewer fancy sauces and lavish creations. Instead, the flavors of locally grown foods are enhanced by simple cooking methods. Many provincial dishes were once regional specialties.

Nouvelle cuisine emphasizes lightness and natural taste in foods. Flavor, color, texture, and presentation are as important in nouvelle cuisine as they are in haute cuisine. However, nouvelle cooks believe the richness and heaviness of haute cuisine spoil the natural flavors of food. The idea behind nouvelle cuisine is to preserve the nutrients and natural taste of foods. Nouvelle cuisine appeals to people who love French food but are concerned about fat and calories (**Figure 31.8**).

Visionsi/Shutterstock.com   Carlos Rondon/Shutterstock.com

Figure 31.8   Nouvelle cuisine uses high standards of presentation for plating. What characteristics do these two dishes have in common?

Nouvelle cooks serve less butter, cream, and other high-calorie foods. They use fewer starches and sauces. When they do serve a sauce, they do not thicken it with flour. Instead, nouvelle cooks use vegetable purees to thicken sauces. Nouvelle cuisine includes more fresh fruits and vegetables. (The vegetables are served nearly raw.) Meat, fish, and poultry are often broiled or poached.

Foundations of French Cooking

Two basic points form the secret of good French cooking. First, the ingredients used must be of top quality. Bread, for example, is baked twice a day in French bakeries to ensure its freshness. Second, successful cooks are very patient. Patience can make the difference between a dish that is good and one that is excellent. Cooks may simmer some sauces for hours to develop the flavors of all their ingredients.

French Sauces

The French use a variety of sauces. A sauce can be used as the basis for a dish or as a finishing touch.

A *roux* is a mixture of butter (or other fat) and flour. It forms the base of all white sauces. When milk is added to a roux, the mixture becomes a *béchamel* sauce. If chicken, veal, or fish stock is added to a roux, the mixture becomes a *velouté* sauce. Many variations of these sauces can be made by adding extra ingredients like mustard or cheese.

The classic French brown sauce is called a *demi-glace* sauce. Cooks make it from a slightly thickened stock-based sauce they have simmered for a long time. They add additional stock and flavorings to this basic sauce. They may or may not use a thickening agent, such as a roux.

Hollandaise sauce contains egg yolks, lemon juice, and butter. The cook must warm and gently thicken the beaten egg yolks to prevent curdling. Then the butter must be added slowly to keep the sauce from separating. Hollandaise sauce often accompanies green vegetables such as asparagus (**Figure 31.9**).

Vinaigrettes are made by combining wine vinegar, oil, and seasonings. Many variations are possible. Vinaigrettes are commonly used as dressings on green salads and as marinades for vegetables.

Butter sauces include *cold flavored butters*, *white butter sauce*, and *brown butter sauce*. Cooks use them when baking and broiling seafood, when preparing vegetables and poultry, and when making other sauces.

French Seasonings

Herbs are just as important to French cooking as sauces. **Fines herbes** is a mixture of fresh chives, parsley, tarragon, and chervil. Many French chefs use this combination of herbs to flavor soups and stews. Marjoram, rosemary,

Glenn Price/Shutterstock.com

Figure 31.9 Hollandaise sauce is commonly served with eggs Benedict.

basil, saffron, oregano, fennel, bay leaves, thyme, and savory are also common in French cooking.

Cooks add herbs directly to some dishes. For other dishes, such as stews, they tie herbs in a cheesecloth bag and add it to the liquid. (They remove the bag before serving.)

French Appetizers and Soups

A substantial French meal always begins with hors d'oeuvres. **Hors d'oeuvres** are small dishes designed to stimulate the appetite. They may be hot or cold, but chefs always plan for them to complement the other menu items.

Soup often follows hors d'oeuvres. French soups fall into four basic categories: consommés, puree soups, cream soups, and velouté soups. *Consommés* have a meat stock base. They are rich and clear and may be served hot or cold. Puree soups are made from meat, poultry, fish, or vegetables that have been cooked in liquid and pureed. Cream soups generally use a béchamel sauce as a base. Pureed meat, fish, poultry, or vegetables are added to the béchamel sauce along with cream. *Velouté soups* are similar to cream soups. Meat, fish, poultry, or vegetables are added to a velouté sauce. Egg yolks, butter, and cream thicken the soup.

French Main Dishes

Seafood and poultry form the basis of many French main dishes. As a rule, the French eat red meat less often than people in the United States.

Many types of freshwater and saltwater foods are popular in France. Frog legs, crabs, scallops, and mussels are especially popular. Poaching is the preparation technique used most often for fish fillets and whole fish.

The French eat all types of poultry. They often truss and roast chicken, duck, and goose whole with or without a stuffing. They also add chicken to stews, such as *chicken fricassee*. This dish is made by cutting chicken into pieces that are stewed and served with a white sauce. French cooks finely chop and season the meat of game birds, such as pigeons, to make a spread called *pâté* (**Figure 31.10**).

The French usually broil beef steaks and serve them with a sauce. They often braise other beef and veal cuts and use some of them in stews. Lamb is particularly popular in the spring. The French consider organ meats of all kinds to be delicacies.

French Vegetables and Salads

Vegetables are an important part of a French meal. The French often serve two or more fresh vegetables with a main dish. They cook vegetables just to the crisp-tender stage and then serve them immediately to preserve their textures.

The French often serve vegetables with just butter and seasonings. Vegetables can also be creamed, braised, glazed, or served with a cheese

Ekaterina Kondratova/Shutterstock.com

Figure 31.10 Different types of pâté, such as this chicken liver pâté, may be served as a spread and eaten as an appetizer.

or hollandaise sauce. Some vegetables, such as spinach, adapt particularly well to soufflés.

The French usually serve a green salad after the main course but before dessert. They often dress it with a vinaigrette sauce. Other salads, such as potato salads and meat salads, are popular additions to lighter and more casual meals. One of the best-known salads of this type is *salade nicoise*. This popular salad is a colorful combination of potatoes, green beans, and tomatoes, served with a vinaigrette sauce.

France is famous for its cheeses, and cheese is an important part of meals. The French serve cheese and fresh fruit after the green salad and before the sweet dessert in a large meal. Many simpler meals include only cheese, sausage, bread, fresh fruit, and wine.

French Baked Goods

The French serve bread at every meal. *Baguette* is the most popular. It contains only yeast, flour, salt, and water. People buy the long, crusty loaves daily from local bakers. Other breads are popular, too. *Brioche* is a rich yeast roll that contain eggs and sugar. **Croissants** are flaky, buttery yeast rolls shaped into crescents.

The dessert course may be simple or elaborate. Some of the most elegant desserts in the world originated in France. *Napoleons* are layers of puff pastry separated by creamy fillings. *Éclairs* are slender pastry shells filled with custard or a cream filling and iced. *Baba au rhum* is a yeast cake soaked in a rum syrup. Chocolate, vanilla, liqueur, or fruit-based soufflés are popular choices. Tarts filled with fruit, custard, or other sweet filling are also favorite desserts.

Regional Nature of French Cuisine

French cuisine is regional in nature. A visitor can travel throughout the country and never eat the same dish prepared in the same way twice. A traveler can even identify certain regions by their local dishes.

Normandy is located in the northwestern corner of France. Cattle graze in the fertile green pastures, and apple orchards dot the countryside. Normandy is known for tender veal, rich cream and butter, and apples. *Calvados*, a liquor made from apple cider, is produced locally for export around the world.

Brittany is Normandy's neighbor to the southwest. Much of the land is rocky and wooded. The fishing industry is an important part of the economy in this region. Brittany is also known for producing beef, pork, poultry, milk, and vegetables. The cabbage, artichokes, and spinach grown here are reported to be the best in France. Brittany's agricultural products are featured in many local dishes. Brittany is also known for its crêpes. **Crêpes** are thin, delicate pancakes usually rolled around a filling (**Figure 31.11**).

To the southwest in the *Aquitaine* region, the finest pâté is produced. It is made from expensive goose liver and truffles. **Truffles** are a rare type of fungi that grow underground near oak trees. This region is also known for its poultry, veal, and pork.

Cassoulet is a traditional stew of the *Languedoc-Roussillon* region located in southern France. It is made with white beans, goose or chicken, pork, bacon, and herbs.

Provence is a rich agricultural region in southeastern France. Fresh vegetables are used in many colorful dishes. One of the most popular vegetable dishes is *ratatouille*. It is a vegetable casserole containing tomatoes, eggplant, green pepper, zucchini, onions, and seasonings. The olive trees that grow on the sunny slopes along the Mediterranean Sea provide the oil needed to make aioli. (*Aioli* is a regional sauce made from

135pixels/Shutterstock.com

Figure 31.11 Crêpes may be savory or sweet, such as these strawberry crêpes drizzled with chocolate glaze. How do crêpes differ from pancakes?

Learn About...

French Meals

Most French people eat three meals a day. *Le petit dejeuner* (breakfast) usually is light. The French often have *café au lait* (hot milk and coffee) and brioche or crusty bread with butter and jam.

Traditionally, *le dejeuner* (the midday meal) was the main meal of the day. People ate it leisurely. In many parts of France, this is still the case. People in the major cities, however, often eat the heavier meal in the evening. A traditional midday meal might include hot or cold hors d'oeuvres, soup, and a main dish. A vegetable, a green salad, bread and butter, dessert, and wine would also be served. If the main dish contained vegetables, a separate vegetable usually would be eliminated.

In France, bread usually remains on the table through the end of the meal. The salad usually is served after the main course, and coffee usually accompanies dessert.

The traditional evening meal is light. Soup, an omelet, bread and butter, fruit, and a beverage are typical supper dishes. City dwellers, however, may eat a more substantial evening meal. Business hours are later in France than they are in the United States. Therefore, the evening meal usually is not served before eight o'clock.

Know and Apply

1. What is the difference between le petit dejeuner and le dejeuner?
2. Why is dinner in France usually served after eight o'clock?

For centuries, the people of the *Rhône-Alpes* region have based their diets on local foods. Potatoes grow in the hilly land. The cows that graze on mountain grasses provide milk and cheese. Many Alpine dishes combine these three staple foods.

German and French culture has influenced the foods of the *Alsace* and *Lorraine* regions. Sausages and smoked hams are popular throughout these regions, as are fruit pies and tarts. Fine white wines are produced in Alsace. **Quiche**, a custard tart served in many variations as an appetizer and a main dish, originated in Lorraine. The most famous type of quiche is called *Quiche Lorraine*. It contains grated Swiss cheese, crumbled bacon, and diced onions along with eggs and cream.

French Menu

Soupe à l'Oignon
(Onion Soup)

Poulet au Citron
(Chicken with Lemon)

Ratatouille
(Vegetable Casserole)

Salade Verte
(Green Salad)

Pain
(French Bread)

Mousse au Chocolat
(Chocolate Mousse)

Café
(Coffee)

Soupe à l'Oignon (Onion Soup)
Serves 6

5	medium onions, sliced thin
2	tablespoons butter
	dash pepper
6	cups low-sodium beef broth
6	thick slices French bread, toasted
3	tablespoons grated Parmesan cheese
¾	cup shredded Swiss cheese

1. In a large, heavy skillet, melt butter. Add onions and pepper and sauté until onions are

olive oil and garlic.) **Bouillabaisse** (seafood stew), leg of lamb, grilled fish, and chicken are equally popular. Many of the dishes of Provence are flavored with locally grown herbs.

Burgundy, located in central France, is famous for its vineyards and the wines they produce. Many Burgundy dishes are flavored with the local wines. *Boeuf à la Bourguignonne* (beef Burgundy) is one of the most famous of these dishes. **Escargots** (snails eaten as food) are another Burgundy specialty. They often are served in their shells with garlic butter.

golden brown and transparent (about 10 minutes).

2. Slowly stir in beef broth. Bring soup to a boil, reduce heat, and simmer for 30 minutes.
3. Preheat broiler.
4. Place one piece of toasted bread in each of six ovenproof soup bowls or use one large tureen. Sprinkle bread with Parmesan cheese.
5. Pour soup over bread. Sprinkle Swiss cheese on top.
6. Place soup bowls under broiler and broil until cheese is light brown. Serve soup immediately.

Per serving: 192 calories (42% from fat), 9 g protein, 18 g carbohydrate, 9 g fat, 21 mg cholesterol, 2 g fiber, 407 mg sodium.

Poulet au Citron (Chicken with Lemon)
Serves 4

2 teaspoons butter
2 teaspoons vegetable oil
1 cut-up chicken, skin removed
½ teaspoon salt
pepper to taste
1 tablespoon finely chopped parsley
1½ teaspoons minced chives
½ teaspoon marjoram
1 teaspoon paprika
1½ teaspoons lemon zest
1 tablespoon lemon juice
½ cup low-sodium chicken broth
1 tablespoon cornstarch
2 tablespoons cold water

1. Preheat oven to 400°F.
2. Heat butter and oil together in a large nonstick skillet. Sear chicken pieces.
3. Place chicken in a large casserole or baking pan. Season with salt and pepper, parsley, chives, marjoram, and paprika. Sprinkle with lemon zest and juice.
4. Cover pan tightly, and bake chicken until tender, about 20 to 30 minutes. Use a meat thermometer to be sure chicken pieces have reached an internal temperature of 165°F. Remove chicken to a heated platter.
5. Pour juices into a small saucepan. Add chicken

broth and bring to a boil. Quickly whisk in cornstarch dissolved in cold water. Simmer sauce until thickened, about 2 minutes. Serve with chicken.

Per serving: 244 calories (41% from fat), 31 g protein, 3 g carbohydrate, 11 g fat, 135 mg cholesterol, 0 g fiber, 404 mg sodium.

Ratatouille (Vegetable Casserole)
Serves 4 to 6

½ medium eggplant, peeled and cubed
1 teaspoon salt, divided
1 tablespoon vegetable oil
1 medium onion, cut into rings
1 clove garlic, crushed
1 medium green pepper, cut into strips
1 medium zucchini, sliced
1 medium tomato, cut into wedges
1 bay leaf
½ teaspoon thyme
pepper to taste

1. Place eggplant cubes in a colander. Sprinkle with ¾ teaspoon salt and toss to coat. Place the colander over a bowl, and let it stand for 30 minutes while preparing the remaining ingredients.
2. In a large skillet, heat oil. Sauté onions and garlic until golden, about 10 minutes.
3. Add green pepper strips and cook for 2 minutes.
4. Rinse the eggplant and pat it dry with paper towels. Add the eggplant to the skillet and cook for 3 minutes, stirring constantly.
5. Add zucchini and continue stirring and cooking another 3 minutes.
6. Add tomato, bay leaf, thyme, remaining ¼ teaspoon salt, and pepper. Simmer uncovered for 10 minutes or until vegetables are tender.
7. Remove bay leaf. Ratatouille can be served immediately or refrigerated and reheated later.

Per serving: 75 calories (48% from fat), 2 g protein, 10 g carbohydrate, 4 g fat, 0 mg cholesterol, 4 g fiber, 445 mg sodium.

Salade Verte
(Green Salad)
Serves 6

6	cups assorted salad greens
1	tablespoon lemon juice
1	tablespoon white wine vinegar
	salt
	pepper
⅓	cup olive oil

1. Wash salad greens and tear into bite-sized pieces.
2. To make the salad dressing, whisk together lemon juice, wine vinegar, and salt and pepper to taste in a small bowl.
3. Add oil, a few drops at a time, while beating with a whisk. Continue to beat dressing until all of the oil has been added.
4. Toss greens together in a salad bowl with the dressing. (If dressing has separated, shake well before using.)

Per serving: 119 calories (91% from fat), 1 g protein, 2 g carbohydrate, 12 g fat, 0 mg cholesterol, 1 g fiber, 105 mg sodium.

Pain
(French Bread)
Makes 1 loaf

1	cup plus 2 tablespoons water
3¼	cups all-purpose flour
1	package active dry yeast
1	teaspoon salt
	cornmeal
	vegetable oil
	cold water

1. In a small saucepan, heat water to 120°F.
2. In a large mixer bowl, combine 1½ cups flour, yeast, and salt. Add warm water and mix by hand or on medium speed of electric mixer for 3 minutes. Gradually add enough remaining flour to form a stiff dough.
3. Turn dough out onto lightly floured surface; knead until smooth and satiny, about 8 to 10 minutes.
4. Place dough in a greased bowl, turning once to grease top. Cover and let rise in a warm place for 30 minutes.
5. Punch dough down and roll into a 15-by-8-inch rectangle on a lightly floured surface.

6. Beginning with the long side, roll dough up tightly, sealing edges and ends well. Place loaf seam side down, diagonally, on a lightly greased baking sheet that has been sprinkled with cornmeal. Brush loaf with oil, cover. Refrigerate 2 to 24 hours.
7. When ready to bake, preheat oven to 400°F.
8. Remove bread from refrigerator, uncover and let stand 10 minutes. Then brush bread with water and slash top of loaf diagonally at 2-inch intervals.
9. Bake 35 to 40 minutes. Cool on wire rack.

Per slice: 98 calories (6% from fat), 3 g protein, 20 g carbohydrate, 1 g fat, 0 mg cholesterol, 1 g fiber, 134 mg sodium.

Mousse au Chocolat
(Chocolate Mousse)
Serves 6

1½	cups miniature marshmallows
4	tablespoons butter, softened
1½	cups semisweet chocolate chips
¼	cup hot water
1	cup heavy cream
¾	teaspoon orange or vanilla extract
6	strips orange peel

1. In a heavy saucepan, combine the marshmallows, butter, chocolate chips, and water. Place over low heat and stir constantly until marshmallows and chocolate are melted and mixture is smooth. Remove from heat.
2. Using a chilled bowl and beaters, beat the cream at medium speed until it begins to thicken. Add the extract and increase the beating speed. Continue whipping the cream until it is stiff, being careful not to overbeat it.
3. Using a flexible spatula, gently fold the whipped cream into the cooled chocolate mixture, folding until no streaks of white are visible. (Chocolate does not need to be completely cooled.)
4. Pour mousse into a pretty bowl or individual serving dishes and refrigerate until ready to serve. Garnish mousse with strips of orange peel.

Per serving: 445 calories (71% from fat), 3 g protein, 37 g carbohydrate, 35 g fat, 75 mg cholesterol, 3 g fiber, 30 mg sodium.

Germany

Germany is in the heart of Western Europe. Germany's boundaries have changed several times over the years. Many of these border changes were the result of wars.

German culture and cuisine developed with more unity than German politics. Common heritage and ingredients have led to the origin of dishes that are liked throughout Germany. Germany also has many regional dishes.

Geography and Climate of Germany

To the north of Germany are the Baltic and North Seas. The Rhine and the Elbe are the most important rivers in Germany. *Lowlands* (flat, sandy plains) make up much of the northern part of the country. Highlands are in the central and southern regions. Two other important geographical regions, the Bavarian Alps and the Black Forest, are in southern Germany (**Figure 31.12**).

Germany's climate is generally moderate. However, the Baltic region has extremes of temperature. Also, the higher elevations in the southern mountains receive large amounts of snow.

German Agriculture

The northern lowlands and southern highlands of Germany are primarily agricultural. Potatoes and sugar beets are the main crops of

a9photo/Shutterstock.com

Figure 31.12 The Black Forest region of Germany gets its name from the dense growth of pine trees, which block out daylight in the forest.

the northern lowlands. In addition, farmers grow some rye, oats, wheat, and barley and raise some cattle. The southern highlands are known for their cattle, wheat, and dairy products. Grapes and other fruits grow in the west and southwest regions. Hops grow in Bavaria, the center of the German brewing industry.

German Culture

After the collapse of the Roman Empire, a series of empires rose and fell. Each one brought new peoples to Germany. Many of these peoples came from modern-day Poland, Denmark, Switzerland, Austria, and France.

Until the last half of the nineteenth century, Germany was a loose mixture of states, kingdoms, duchies (areas controlled by a duke or duchess), and principalities (areas ruled by a prince). Following the unification of these territories, Germany became involved in the two World Wars. Both wars left much of Germany devastated. World War II resulted in the split of the country. West Germany had a democratic government. East Germany had a communistic government.

For years, the people of both German nations longed to live under a common flag. In 1989, they tore down the Berlin Wall—a symbol of the political division between the countries. In the following year, the two nations were reunited under a single democratic government.

The Germans celebrate many church holidays with traditional foods. One of these holidays is St. Martin's Day, which is a harvest festival held on November 11. Roast goose and breads baked in symbolic shapes are among the foods typically served on St. Martin's Day. At dusk, children sing and parade with paper lanterns.

During Advent, the four-week period leading to Christmas, German bakers prepare holiday cakes, cookies, and breads. On December 6, children receive candy and fruit from St. Nicholas. Children also go door to door receiving candy and money from friends and neighbors. Advent ends on Christmas Eve, which is a bigger celebration than Christmas Day. German parents decorate Christmas trees as a surprise for their children. Family members exchange gifts and enjoy a festive meal. The traditional Christmas meal was carp because the church forbade the eating of meat. Today, however, roast turkey, goose, or duck is more common. The Germans also observe 12 Days of Christmas, which last until January 6. On this date, German boys dress up in celebration of the kings who visited the infant Jesus.

German Cuisine

German cuisine is characterized by roasted meats, filling side dishes, and delicious baked goods. World-famous beers and fine white wines are also typical German fare.

German Main Dishes

Meat has been the foundation of German cuisine for centuries. The **braten** (roast) is Germany's national dish. A variety of traditional German dishes contain pork, beef, veal, and game.

Pork, both fresh and cured, is the most popular of all meats. Hams are roasted, marinated in wine, or cut in slices and then fried and served with a sauce. One of the most popular pork dishes is called *kasseler rippenspeer*. It is a whole smoked pork loin that is roasted. It is served with sauerkraut, apples or chestnuts, peas, white beans, mushrooms, and browned potatoes. Pork is also the main ingredient of **bratwurst**, a type of sausage served grilled or panfried throughout Germany (**Figure 31.13**).

Boiled beef served with a horseradish sauce is one of the most popular beef dishes. *Sauerbraten*, a sweet-sour marinated beef roast, is popular, too. The ingredients used in the marinade vary from one region to another. One method uses red wine, wine vinegar, onion, peppercorns, juniper berries, and bay leaves. Sauerbraten gravy may be thickened and flavored with crushed gingersnaps and raisins.

Hasenpfeffer is rabbit that is first marinated in wine, vinegar, onions, and spices. Then the meat is stewed in the marinade. Sour cream is often added to the stew for thickening and flavor.

Many German meat dishes have regional origins. One such dish is schnitzel. *Schnitzel* is a breaded, sautéed veal cutlet. Schnitzel originated in Holstein, where it is served with a fried egg. Richly flavored, smoked uncooked *Westphalian ham* originated in Westphalia, but it is served throughout Germany.

Figure 31.13 German cuisine is well known for its sauerkraut and many varieties of bratwurst.

The German people use leftovers to make hearty soups and one-dish meals. Filling lentil soups and *eintopf*, a popular stew, are both made with leftover meats.

In northern regions of Germany, seafood is especially popular. Open-air fish markets scattered throughout northern Germany sell a variety of seafood obtained from the North and Baltic Seas. Smoked eel, enjoyed by many northern Germans, is inexpensive. Herring is prepared in a variety of ways. Salty, sharp, pickled Bismarck herring bears the name of a chancellor who helped unify the German territories.

German Side Dishes

Germans usually serve fruit accompaniments with pork and game dishes. Apples, prunes, raisins, and apricots accompany pork. Tart fruits like currants and *preiselbeeren* (small, cranberry-like fruits) accompany game.

At least one meal a day in Germany includes potatoes. Potatoes cooked in salted water, drained, and steamed until dry are known as *salzkartoffeln*. Salzkartoffeln are served most often as a side dish with melted butter, parsley, and bits of bacon. *Kartoffelsalat* is hot or cold potato salad made with a vinegar dressing and bits of cooked bacon. **Kartoffelpuffer** are the famous potato pancakes enjoyed throughout Germany.

Learn About...

German Sausages

A discussion of German meat dishes would not be complete without mentioning *wurst*, or sausages. Sausages are mixtures of meat, seasonings, and other ingredients stuffed into a casing. The Germans produce hundreds of types of sausages. Some are ready-to-eat. Others must be grilled, boiled, or fried. Sausages may be firm enough to slice or soft enough to spread. Some sausages are smoked, and a few are pickled.

Sausages often bear the names of the cities where they were first produced. *Braunschweiger*, for example, is a type of liver sausage. It was first produced in Braunschweig. The long, thin *frankfurter* originated in the German city of Frankfurt.

Other well-known types of German sausages include *blutwurst*, which is blood sausage. *Leberwurst* is a spreadable sausage made with liver. *Knockwurst* is a boiled sausage best eaten warm. *Schinkenwurst* is a ready-to-eat pork sausage that contains pieces of ham. *Bratwurst* refers to a group of sausages that may be raw or precooked. Each region of Germany produces its own variety of bratwurst.

Know and Apply

1. When are German sausages often served in the United States?
2. How are the names of some sausages determined?

They are served with mixed stewed fruit or applesauce. *Kartoffelklösse* are potato dumplings.

Sauerkraut, another German specialty, is fermented or pickled cabbage. German cooks usually flavor sauerkraut with caraway, apple, onion, or juniper berries and serve it hot. Sauerkraut is often served with pig's knuckles, spareribs, pork chops, and pork roasts.

German cooks may serve vegetables as side dishes or add them to stews. Cabbage and root vegetables are especially popular during winter months. Asparagus and mushrooms are spring delicacies. Cooks use fresh greens to make delicious salads, which they often serve with a vinegar dressing flavored with bacon.

Spätzle (small dumplings made from wheat flour) are another popular side dish. Cheese spätzle and liver spätzle are just two of the many kinds of spätzle eaten in Germany.

German Baked Goods

The German people serve bread at nearly every meal. Many breads and rolls are produced all over the country, while others are strictly regional. Some breads are baked in round or oblong rolls. Others are made into fanciful shapes and called *gebildbrote* (picture breads) (**Figure 31.14**).

Rye, pumpernickel, and other dark breads are favorites. Bakers make *pumpernickel* bread from unsifted rye flour. They let it rise and bake for long periods. This allows the natural sugars in the rye to sweeten the bread evenly.

Sweet baked goods are also popular in Germany. Sweet rolls, breads, and coffee cakes are served at coffee time. Snail-shaped *schnecken*, streusel-topped coffee cakes, and *apfelkuchen* (apple cake) are served throughout Germany. *Stollen* is a rich yeast bread filled with almonds, raisins, and candied fruit. It usually is served at Christmastime.

German bakers have traditionally made cakes with honey or honey and spices. *Lebkuchen*, one of Germany's best known honey-spice cakes, has a long history. For centuries, the Germans have used decorated lebkuchen to celebrate weddings, birthdays, and anniversaries. Sometimes young men and women have given lebkuchen to their sweethearts as gifts.

Glamorous *torten* (tortes) are made of layers of cake separated by sweet fillings. The most famous German torten is the *Schwarzwälder Kirschtorte* (Black Forest cherry cake). Bakers make this rich dessert with three layers of chocolate sponge cake. They moisten the cake with *Kirschwasser*, which is brandy made from a special variety of cherry. They spread kirsch-flavored whipped cream and cherries between the cake layers. They then decorate the torten with tart cherries, chocolate curls, and more whipped cream.

Another popular German dessert with a regional origin is strudel. **Strudel** is paper-thin layers of pastry filled with plums, apples, cherries, or poppy seeds. It usually is sprinkled with confectioners' sugar and served warm. (People in some parts of Germany also make strudel with a protein-based filling and serve it as a main dish.)

German Beverages

Beer drinking is one of Germany's oldest customs. Germans drink beer by itself and with meals. Beer halls are familiar sights in all German cities and towns.

Many wine experts agree the finest table wines are produced in France and Germany. They also agree the best German wines are white wines. Most of the grapes used to make Germany's white wines grow in the valleys bordering the Rhine and Moselle Rivers.

The Germans serve table wines with meals and snacks. Both wine and beer festivals are common in many parts of the country.

German Meals

Traditionally, Germans who could afford to do so ate five meals a day. Some Germans still follow this custom.

Frühstück (breakfast) is hearty. The Germans serve eggs with dark bread and freshly baked crisp rolls. They eat butter and jams with the

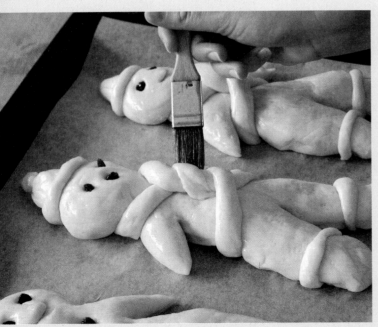

Ina Ts/Shutterstock.com

Figure 31.14 These doll-shaped breads are being made in preparation for St. Nicholas Day.

breads, and serve their coffee with milk. People in northern Germany often serve ham, sausage, and cheese with the eggs.

The Germans eat *zweites frühstück* (second breakfast) during midmorning. Office workers may eat thick sandwiches made of sausage and cheese. Other Germans leave their morning's work for a snack of beer and sausage at a beer hall. Still others prefer fresh pastries at the *bäckerei* (bakery) or cheese sandwiches at the *mölkerei* (dairy).

Mittagessen is the main meal of the day for those Germans who are able to go home at noon. A typical mittagessen might include soup, eintopf, dumplings, and a simple dessert like rote grutze. *Rote grutze* is a pudding made of raspberry, cherry, or red currant juice thickened with cornstarch.

The Germans eat *kaffee* (a sociable snack) in late afternoon. They serve coffee and a variety of small sandwiches, cakes, and rich pastries. Kaffee is important to the Germans, for it is a time to talk with friends.

The Germans usually serve *abendbrot* (light supper) in the early evening. Traditionally, abendbrot is nothing more than buttered breads served with a variety of cold meats, sausages, and cheeses. For those who cannot eat a hearty meal at noon, however, abendbrot is the main meal of the day. An appetizer, soup, main dish, vegetable, bread, and dessert are typical.

German Menu

Sauerbraten
(Marinated Beef in Sweet-Sour Sauce)

Kartoffelpuffer mit Apfelmus
(Potato Pancakes with Applesauce)

Rotkohl
(Red Cabbage)

Grün Salat mit Heisser Specksosse
(Green Salad with Hot Bacon Dressing)

Pumpernickel
(Rye Bread from Westphalia)

Pflaumenkuchen
(Plum Cake)

Kaffee
(Coffee)

Sauerbraten
(Marinated Beef in Sweet-Sour Sauce)
Serves 4

½	cup water
½	cup vinegar
¼	cup packed brown sugar, divided
½	teaspoon salt
½	teaspoon peppercorns
¼	teaspoon pepper
2	bay leaves
½	medium onion, sliced
1	pound boneless beef rump roast
1	tablespoon vegetable oil
2	tablespoons raisins
3	gingersnaps, broken
½	cup plain nonfat yogurt

1. In a large saucepan, combine water, vinegar, 2 tablespoons brown sugar, salt, peppercorns, pepper, bay leaves, and onion and bring to a boil. Then remove marinade from heat and let cool to room temperature.
2. Place roast in a deep crock or stainless steel pot. Pour the cooled marinade over the meat. Cover the pan tightly and refrigerate for 24 to 48 hours, turning meat occasionally.
3. Remove meat from marinade and pat dry with paper towels.
4. Heat oil in a large Dutch oven. Add meat and sear on all sides. Then add marinade and cover. Simmer meat until tender, about 1½ hours.
5. Take meat from Dutch oven and slice; keep warm.
6. Meanwhile, strain marinade. Add 2 table-spoons brown sugar to Dutch oven. Add strained marinade gradually and stir until sugar dissolves. Add raisins and gingersnaps. Cook sauce until smooth and thick, about 5 minutes, stirring constantly.
7. Blend yogurt into sauce and heat through but do not let sauce boil. Serve sauce over sliced meat.

Per serving: 276 calories (28% from fat), 21 g protein, 27 g carbohydrate, 10 g fat, 58 mg cholesterol, 1 g fiber, 384 mg sodium.

Kartoffelpuffer mit Apfelmus
(Potato Pancakes with Applesauce)
Makes about 6

1½	cups shredded potatoes (1½ medium potatoes)
1	tablespoon all-purpose flour
½	teaspoon salt
¼	teaspoon sugar
⅛	teaspoon baking powder
	dash pepper
1	large egg, well beaten
1½	teaspoons grated onion
1½	teaspoons minced parsley
¾	cup applesauce

1. Drain shredded potatoes thoroughly. Press potatoes against the sides and bottom of a sieve with spoon to remove excess moisture.
2. In a medium mixing bowl, stir together flour, salt, sugar, baking powder, and pepper with a fork.
3. Combine egg, onion, and parsley; add to sifted ingredients. Stir in shredded potatoes. Mix thoroughly.
4. Spray heavy nonstick skillet with no-stick cooking spray and place over medium heat. For each pancake, drop about ¼ cup of potato mixture into the hot skillet and spread with the back of the spoon to make a 3-inch round.
5. Fry pancakes until crisp and golden brown. Turn carefully and brown other side.
6. Drain on paper toweling. Serve with applesauce.

Per pancake: 62 calories (15% from fat), 2 g protein, 12 g carbohydrate, 1 g fat, 44 mg cholesterol, 1 g fiber, 231 mg sodium.

Rotkohl
(Red Cabbage)
Serves 4

1½	cups water
½	head red cabbage, coarsely shredded
2	tablespoons light brown sugar
1	tablespoon plus 1½ teaspoons vinegar
1	tablespoon plus 1½ teaspoons bacon drippings
¼	teaspoon salt
1	teaspoon all-purpose flour
	dash allspice
2	whole cloves
	dash pepper

1. Put water into large saucepan and bring to a boil. Add cabbage, cover, and bring water again to a boil. Reduce heat and gently simmer cabbage until tender, about 10 minutes. Drain cabbage well.
2. In a separate bowl, combine brown sugar, vinegar, bacon drippings, salt, flour, allspice, cloves, and pepper. Pour sauce over cabbage; toss well and serve.

Per serving: 110 calories (52% from fat), 1 g protein, 13 g carbohydrate, 7 g fat, 6 mg cholesterol, 2 g fiber, 252 mg sodium.

Pumpernickel
(Rye Bread from Westphalia)
Makes 1 loaf

3	cups all-purpose flour
1	cup rye flour
1	teaspoon salt
⅓	cup whole bran cereal
¼	cup yellow cornmeal
1	package active dry yeast
1	cup plus 2 tablespoons water
1	tablespoon plus 1½ teaspoons dark molasses
½	ounce unsweetened chocolate
1¼	teaspoons softened butter
⅔	cup mashed potatoes (at room temperature)
¾	teaspoon caraway seeds

1. Combine all-purpose and rye flours.
2. In a large mixing bowl, combine ¾ cup of flour mixture, salt, bran cereal, cornmeal, and dry yeast; mix well.
3. In a large saucepan, combine water, molasses, chocolate, and butter. Heat over low heat until liquid is very warm (120°F to 130°F). (The butter and chocolate do not have to be completely melted.)
4. Gradually add liquid ingredients to dry ingredients and beat 2 minutes with an electric mixer, at medium speed, scraping bowl occasionally.
5. Add mashed potatoes and ½ cup flour mixture. Beat at high speed 2 minutes, scraping bowl occasionally. Stir in caraway seeds and enough additional flour mixture to make a soft dough.

6. Turn dough out onto lightly floured surface. Knead until smooth and elastic, about 15 minutes.
7. Place dough in greased bowl, turning once to grease top. Cover with a clean towel and let rise in a warm place until doubled in bulk, about 1 hour.
8. Punch dough down and let rise again for 30 minutes.
9. Punch dough down, and turn out onto lightly floured surface. Shape dough into a round ball. Place shaped dough in an 8- or 9-inch greased round cake pan. Cover with a clean towel and let rise in a warm place until doubled in bulk, about 45 minutes.
10. Bake bread at 350°F about 50 minutes or until loaf sounds hollow when tapped with the knuckles. Remove bread from pan and cool on rack.

Per serving: 140 calories (8% from fat), 4 g protein, 29 g carbohydrate, 1 g fat, 0 mg cholesterol, 3 g fiber, 186 mg sodium.

Grün Salat Specksosse mit Heisser
(Green Salad with Hot Bacon Dressing)
Serves 4

1 cup fresh spinach
1 cup iceberg lettuce
1 cup red leaf lettuce
1 cup escarole
½ medium sweet onion, cut into rings
5 slices bacon, finely diced (about ¾ cup)
¼ cup finely chopped onions
2 tablespoons cider vinegar
2 tablespoons water
¼ teaspoon salt
⅛ teaspoon pepper

1. Place greens in a large salad bowl and add onion rings.
2. In a heavy skillet, cook bacon over moderate heat until crisp. Remove bacon from skillet and place on paper towels.
3. Add chopped onions to bacon fat remaining in skillet. Cook onions until soft and transparent, stirring constantly, about 5 minutes.
4. Add vinegar, water, salt, and pepper to skillet; cook, stirring constantly for a minute or so. Then stir in bacon.

5. Pour hot dressing over salad greens. Serve immediately. Dressing also may be served alongside the greens, if desired.

Per serving: 85 calories (43% from fat), 5 g protein, 7 g carbohydrate, 4 g fat, 7 mg cholesterol, 4 g fiber, 289 mg sodium.

Pflaumenkuchen (Plum Cake)
Serves 8

Topping:
1½ tablespoons all-purpose flour
¾ cup sugar
½ teaspoon cinnamon
2 tablespoons butter
Cake:
1¼ cups all-purpose flour
1 teaspoon sugar
1 teaspoon baking powder
½ teaspoon salt
¼ cup butter
1 tablespoon fat-free milk
1 egg
3 cups purple plum halves

1. Prepare topping by combining flour, sugar, and cinnamon in a small mixing bowl. With pastry blender or two knives, cut in butter until mixture resembles coarse crumbs. Set aside.
2. Preheat oven to 350°F.
3. Prepare cake by sifting flour, sugar, baking powder, and salt onto a large piece of waxed paper; set aside.
4. In a large mixing bowl, cream butter until fluffy. Add dry ingredients and mix well.
5. Gently beat milk and egg together until combined; add to flour mixture.
6. Press dough into a greased 8-inch square pan.
7. Overlap plum halves in neat rows on top of dough; sprinkle with topping.
8. Bake for about 45 to 50 minutes or until cake tests done.
9. Serve warm or at room temperature with ice cream or whipped cream.

Per serving: 287 calories (28% from fat), 3 g protein, 49 g carbohydrate, 9 g fat, 57 mg cholesterol, 3 g fiber, 280 mg sodium.

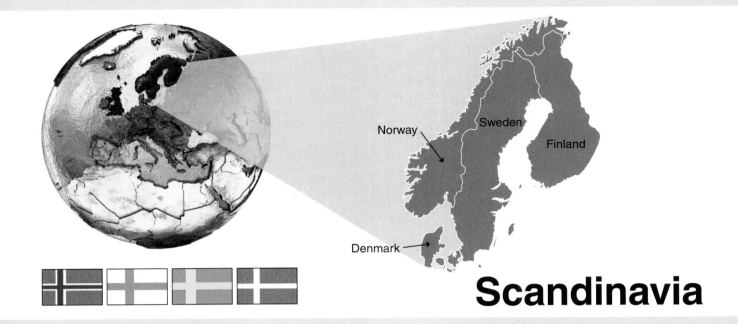

Scandinavia

Scandinavia is a land of rugged wilderness and breathtaking beauty. Lakes made centuries ago by glaciers are crystal clear. Dense forests, snowcapped mountains, and lush valleys dot the landscape once ruled by Vikings.

Geography and Climate of Scandinavia

Scandinavia includes the countries of Denmark, Norway, Sweden, and Finland. Norway, Sweden, and Finland are part of a large peninsula that extends above the Arctic Circle. In the northern sections of these three countries, winters are long and severe. Summers are short and cool, thus making the growing season short. Above the Arctic Circle, however, the sun does not set for about two months during the summer. For this reason, the Scandinavian regions above the Arctic Circle are often called the "Land of the Midnight Sun."

Norway is a long, narrow country. Its rocky, mountainous coast makes up much of its land area. Norway is known for its *fjords*, which are slender, deep bays that cut deeply into the land. Norway's greatest wealth is in timber and seafood.

Mountains separate Sweden from Norway, and forests cover much of the northern part of Sweden. The most fertile areas are located in the southern tip of the peninsula.

Glaciers have left much of Finland stony, rough, and dotted with over 60,000 lakes. The glaciers also formed large marshy areas. These areas give the country its Finnish name, *Swomi*, which means swamp. Forests cover much of the rest of the land.

Of the four Scandinavian nations, Denmark has the most moderate climate and the least rugged geography. Forests fringe the eastern shore, and the occasional hill cuts through the central part of the country. The climate is mild with plenty of rainfall. The average winter temperature is 32°F (0°C), which is considerably warmer than the rest of Scandinavia.

Scandinavian Agriculture

Many Scandinavians make their living in the large fishing industries found in all four countries. They catch herring, cod, haddock, salmon, and a variety of other fish and shellfish. They sell some fish locally, but they export much of their catch (**Figure 31.15**).

All the Scandinavian countries obtain as many agricultural products as possible from the land. Denmark's climate and geography help make it the most agriculturally **prosperous** (economically successful). In Denmark, the climate is mild and about 60 percent of the land can be farmed.

Grigorev Mikhail/Shutterstock.com

Figure 31.15 Fishing is a major industry in regions of Scandinavia. What is another major industry in Scandinavian countries?

(Only 8 percent of the land in Finland and in Sweden can be farmed.) Denmark's main wealth is in pigs, cows, and chickens. These animals provide bacon, dairy products, and eggs, which the Danes export. Danish farmers grow grain and other crops for home use and to feed livestock.

Grain and livestock (including dairy cattle) are the main agricultural products of the other Scandinavian countries. Norway also produces large quantities of potatoes.

Scandinavian Culture

The *Vikings* are the ancestors of the Scandinavian peoples. (The Finns' origins are found in the Central Asian steppes, but Viking influence is present.) The Vikings were both industrious and warlike. They sailed to all parts of the known world during the eighth, ninth, and tenth centuries.

As the Viking Age was ending, the people of Norway, Sweden, Denmark, and Finland began a series of governments. Some of these were joint governments; others were single. These governments lasted into the nineteenth century.

Today, governments in Sweden, Norway, and Denmark differ in form but are similar in effect. Denmark and Norway have constitutional monarchies, and Sweden has a limited monarchy. Finland has a representative government headed by a president. All four nations are peace-loving, and all are known for their advanced forms of social welfare.

Scandinavians, for the most part, have the height, light hair, and blue eyes of their Viking forebears. They are industrious, hard-working people with deep family ties. Scandinavians enjoy singing, dancing, and a variety of sports. They like to ski and ice skate in the winter. They enjoy swimming, sailing, and hiking in the summer.

Throughout the year, festivals and holidays are times for merrymaking in Scandinavia. One annual event celebrated in Denmark is

Learn About...

Factors Affecting Scandinavian Cuisine

Three major factors have affected the development of Scandinavian cuisine. The first of these is geography. The geography of Scandinavia has made it hard to produce food. (Denmark is an exception.) Scandinavians have had to work to gain enough food from the water, forests, and tillable (farmable) land.

Human isolation is the second factor affecting Scandinavian cuisine. Mountains and seas have separated the Scandinavian countries from most of Europe. As a result, other European countries have had little impact on Scandinavian cuisine. Geography has also kept the Scandinavian people apart from one another. Therefore, many local and regional dishes vary.

The third factor affecting Scandinavian cuisine is climate. The Scandinavian climate includes long winters. The growing seasons are short. Therefore, much effort has to be put into preserving food. Pickled, dried, and salted foods are common.

Know and Apply

1. How does Denmark's geography differ from that of other Scandinavian countries, and how does this difference impact food production?

2. How might modern technology impact the development of regional cuisine?

not Danish at all. It is the July 4 celebration of Independence Day in the United States. Like U.S. citizens, Danes enjoy this day by singing, dancing, eating, listening to speeches, and watching fireworks. This event promotes international unity. It also honors values Denmark shares with the United States.

In Norway, as in other Scandinavian countries, Midsummer's Eve is a time to celebrate. This festival, which is held on June 23, really falls at the beginning of summer in Scandinavia. In the part of Norway that lies above the Arctic Circle, the sun never sets at this time of year. Norwegians welcome the sunshine and warm weather by dancing around a maypole. New potatoes with dill are a traditional food at Midsummer celebrations. Fresh strawberries are a classic Midsummer dessert.

A traditional Swedish festival is Lucia Day, which is December 13. Before dawn, young girls dress in long white robes with red sashes. Wearing crowns of candles on their heads, they awaken their families with a traditional song. They serve hot coffee, saffron buns called *lussekatter*, and gingerbread biscuits called *pepparkakor* (**Figure 31.16**).

In Finland, July 21 marks the beginning of an annual tradition—the crayfish party. **Crayfish** are crustaceans related to the lobster. The Finns drop the crayfish one by one into a pot of boiling water flavored with fresh dill. As they cook, the crayfish turn bright red. The Finns serve them with toast, butter, schnapps, and beer. The atmosphere at these parties is casual and fun as guests feast on this summer treat.

Scandinavian Cuisine

The basic diets of the Danes, Norwegians, Swedes, and Finns are hearty. Preparation and serving methods for each region differ.

Danish Food

Of all Scandinavian foods, Danish foods are the richest. The Danes use butter, cream, cheese, eggs, pork, and chicken in large quantities. Fish is not nearly as popular in Denmark as it is in the other Scandinavian countries.

The Danes are famous for their smørrebrød, which is literally translated as *buttered bread*. **Smørrebrød** are open-faced sandwiches usually made with thin, sour rye bread spread thickly with butter. (Soft white bread is used for smørrebrød with shellfish toppings.) Toppings can be nearly any type of meat, fish, cheese, or vegetable (**Figure 31.17**). Danish blue cheese with raw egg yolk is a typical topping. (Consumption of raw eggs can cause foodborne illness and is not

©iStock.com/ezoom

Figure 31.16 *Lussekatter* are popular baked breads served on Lucia Day in Sweden.

jps/Shutterstock.com

Figure 31.17 Types of smørrebrød can include nearly any topping. This type includes ham, lettuce, and cucumbers with fresh herbs.

recommended.) Sliced roast pork garnished with dried fruit and smoked salmon and scrambled eggs garnished with chives are also popular toppings.

The Danes frequently accompany their smørrebrød with glasses of chilled aquavit. *Aquavit* is a clean, potent spirit distilled from grain and potatoes and flavored with caraway seeds. It is served throughout Denmark, Sweden, and Norway.

Danish cheeses are exported and used in Danish homes to make smørrebrød. Tybo, Danbo, Danish brie, havarti, Danish blue, and Danish Camembert are particularly well known.

Danes eat a great deal of pork. They often stuff pork roasts with dried fruits. They mix ground pork with ground veal to make *frikadeller* (meat patties). The Danes use pork liver to make liver paste, which is an important part of the Danish cold table. This cold table, which is a buffet similar to the Swedish smörgåsbord, is called *koldtbord*.

Many Danes love desserts. Fruit pudding, apple cake, rum pudding, and pancakes wrapped around ice cream are favorites.

The Danes often begin their day with a substantial breakfast. This meal consists of several dairy products, such as yogurt, sour milk served with cereal, and ymer. *Ymer* is a high-protein milk product. This may be followed with cheese, bread, a boiled egg, juice, milk, strong coffee, and weinerbrød. *Weinerbrød* are layers of buttery pastry filled with fruit or custard and sprinkled with sugar or nuts. The famous smørrebrød are eaten for lunch. Dinner may include a roast, vegetables, bread, and a rich fruit-and-cream dessert.

Norwegian Food

Norwegians begin the day with a big breakfast. They may eat herring, eggs, bacon, potatoes, cereals, breads, pastries, fruit, juice, buttermilk, and coffee.

The Norwegians work from early in the morning to midafternoon. Norwegians enjoy foods that are quick to prepare, yet filling and nourishing. Such foods include hearty soups like Bergen fish soup and rich desserts like sour cream waffles. *Lefse*, a thin potato pancake, is also a traditional Norwegian food.

Because of their nearness to the sea, Norwegians have relied on seafood as a staple in their diets. Herring (smoked, pickled, and fresh),

halibut, cod, and salmon are all popular (**Figure 31.18**). The Norwegians often poach fish or add it to nourishing stews and soups. **Lutefisk** (dried cod that have been soaked in a lye solution before cooking) is a traditional Norwegian fish dish.

The Norwegians raise goats and sheep on their mountainous land. They use goats' milk to make cheese. They use lamb and mutton in a variety of dishes. The Norwegians make a stew called *får i kål* from mutton and cabbage. One of the most popular smoked meat dishes is *fenalår*, which the Norwegians make from smoked mutton.

Danish cooks use sweet and whipped cream, but Norwegian cooks traditionally use sour cream. Soups, sauces, salads, and meat dishes are all likely to contain sour cream. Sour cream spread on bread or crackers is a popular snack.

Norwegians take great pride in their baked goods. They serve many traditional cookies and cakes at Christmastime. *Krumkaker* are thin,

Shebeko/Shutterstock.com

Figure 31.18 Pickled herring, often garnished with dill and paired with onions, are a favorite dish in Norway. Why is pickling a popular form of food preparation?

delicate cookies baked on a special iron and rolled around a wooden spoon while still warm. The cooled cookies are eaten plain or filled with whipped cream and fruit. *Rosettes* are light and airy cookies cooked on the ends of special irons in hot fat. *Fattigman*, diamond-shaped cookies, are also fried in fat. *Kringla* are rich with sour cream or buttermilk and tied in figure eights or knots.

Swedish Food

The famous smörgåsbord originated in Sweden, where it is served in private homes as well as in restaurants. A **smörgåsbord** is a buffet that includes a wide variety of hot and cold dishes. The word *smörgåsbord* means "bread and butter table." However, smörgåsbords can be elegant and may include 30 or more dishes, depending on the occasion. Typical smörgåsbord dishes include herring dishes; cold fish, meats, and salads; hot meats, eggs, or fish; breads; cheeses; and desserts (**Figure 31.19**). Diners return to the smörgåsbord several times to partake of the different courses.

Generally, people save the smörgåsbord for large gatherings and special occasions. The traditional, everyday style of cooking, called **husmankost**, is very simple. Visitors in Swedish homes are likely to see rich yellow pea soup and salt pork served for supper. Traditionally, these foods are followed by Swedish pancakes and **lingonberries** (tart, red berries) for dessert.

Baked brown beans, herring and sour cream, fried pork sausages, pickled beets, and fruit soups are other traditional Swedish foods. *Nyponsoppa* is a fruit soup made with rose hips (the orange seed capsules of the rose). It is served with whipped cream and almonds and is a Swedish specialty.

Reindeer is not exclusively Swedish, for reindeer herds roam the northern sections of Norway and Finland as well as Sweden. Reindeer flesh has a mild, wild flavor. Shaving reindeer meat into hot fat and frizzling it is one popular preparation method.

Some Swedes consider dessert to be the best part of a meal. Ostkaka and spettekaka are two of their favorites. They make *ostkaka*, a rich pudding-like cake, from milk, heavy cream, eggs, sugar, rennet, and flour. Strawberries, lingonberries, or raspberries are common accompaniments. *Spettekaka* is a delicate cake made of eggs, sugar, and flour. Swedish bakers slowly pour the batter onto a cone-shaped spit placed in front of a fire. As they rotate the cone, the batter dries in layers and forms a pattern.

Finnish Food

In Finland, forests are everywhere. The Finns gather raspberries, strawberries, lingonberries, arctic cloudberries, Finnish cranberries, and mesimarja from the forests. (Finnish cranberries are smaller than those grown in the United States. *Mesimarja* are small, delicate fruits similar to raspberries.) The Finns use berries to make liqueurs, puddings, tarts, and snows (light puddings containing beaten egg whites). One popular fruit pudding is called *vatkattu marjapuuro*. Finnish cooks make it by whipping fruit juice, sugar, and a cereal product similar to farina until light and fluffy.

Finnish foods are hearty, often in a primitive way. *Vorshmack*, which is ground mutton, salt herring, and beef combined with onions and garlic, is a traditional Finnish dish. Pork gravy, black sour rye bread, and rutabagas and other root vegetables help warm the Finns during the bitter winters. The Finns add mushrooms to soups, sauces, salads, gravies, and stews. They

Figure 31.19   Smörgåsbords include a colorful array of foods.

make porridges and gruels from whole grains, just as their ancestors did centuries ago. *Mämmi* is a pudding made of molasses, bitter orange peel, rye flour, and rye malt. The Finns serve it at Easter with sweet cream.

At one time, the Finns lived under Russian rule. As a result, some Russian foods have become part of Finnish cuisine. Two of the most popular Finnish dishes with Russian origins are pasha and piirakka. *Pasha* is a type of cheesecake, and *piirakka* are pastries or pies. The Finns fill piirakka with meat, fish, vegetables, and fruits. They serve the piirakka as appetizers, side dishes, or desserts.

A Finnish tradition is the sauna. The **sauna** is a steam bath in which water is poured on hot stones to create steam. Finns follow the heat of the sauna with a quick dip in a chilly lake or swimming pool. They serve snacks during the sauna. They often serve salty fish to help replace the salt lost through sweat during the sauna. After the sauna, the Finns eat a light meal. Grilled sausages, piirakka, poached salmon, salads, and Finnish rye bread are popular after-sauna supper dishes. The Finns may serve chilled vodka or beer with the meal.

Scandinavian Menu

Sill med Kremsaus
(Herring in Cream Sauce)

Kesäkeitto
(Summer Soup)

Frikadeller
(Danish Meat Patties)

Brunede Kartofler
(Caramelized Potatoes)

Syltede Rødbeder
(Pickled Beets)

Limpa
(Swedish Rye Bread)

Kringla
(Double-Ring Twist Biscuits)

Kaffe
(Coffee)

Sill med Kremsaus
(Herring in Cream Sauce)
Serves 6

1½	cups coarsely chopped herring (salt, pickled, or Bismarck herring)
2	tablespoons finely chopped onion
2	tablespoons fresh dill, divided
	dash pepper
3	tablespoons white wine vinegar, divided
2	chilled hard-cooked egg yolks
1	teaspoon prepared mustard
1	tablespoon vegetable oil
3½	tablespoons evaporated fat-free milk

1. In a small mixing bowl, combine herring, onion, 1 tablespoon dill, pepper, and 1 tablespoon plus 1½ teaspoons white wine vinegar; set aside.
2. In another bowl, mash egg yolks with a wooden spoon. Add mustard, remaining 1 tablespoon plus 1½ teaspoons vinegar, and oil, beating until smooth. Gradually add evaporated fat-free milk, beating constantly, until sauce is the thickness of heavy cream.
3. Pour sauce over herring mixture and refrigerate, covered, at least two hours.
4. Garnish with remaining fresh dill just before serving.

Per serving: 168 calories (73% from fat), 16 g protein, 2 g carbohydrate, 11 g fat, 114 mg cholesterol, 0 g fiber, 108 mg sodium.

Kesäkeitto
(Summer Soup)
Serves 4 to 6

½	cup fresh green peas*
1½	cups cauliflower florets
3	small carrots, diced
1	small potato, diced
1	cup fresh string beans, cut into narrow strips*
2	cups cold water
1	cup fresh spinach, finely chopped*
2¼	cups reduced-fat (2%) milk
2	tablespoons all-purpose flour
	salt and white pepper to taste
	chopped parsley

1. In a large saucepan, combine peas, cauliflower, carrots, potato, and string beans. Cover with cold water and simmer until just tender, about 5 minutes.

2. Add spinach and cook another 5 minutes.
3. Remove vegetables from heat. Strain liquid into a bowl; set aside. Place vegetables in a second bowl.
4. Pour milk into the saucepan used for the vegetables. Whisk in flour until smooth. Cook over medium heat, stirring constantly until sauce comes to a boil. Cook and stir for one additional minute until sauce is thickened and smooth. Add hot vegetable stock slowly, stirring constantly.
5. Add vegetables and bring soup to a simmer. Simmer uncovered over low heat for 3 to 5 minutes. Taste and add salt and pepper as needed.
6. Pour into a tureen and garnish with chopped parsley.
   *If fresh peas, string beans, or spinach are not available, substitute frozen June peas, French-style green beans, and chopped spinach. Adjust cooking time accordingly.

Per serving: 168 calories (16% from fat), 9 g protein, 28 g carbohydrate, 3 g fat, 11 mg cholesterol, 5 g fiber, 200 mg sodium.

Frikadeller
(Danish Meat Patties)
Makes about 15 meat patties

½ pound ground pork shoulder or fresh ham
½ pound ground shoulder of veal
½ cup flour
2 eggs
1 large onion, chopped
salt and pepper to taste
⅔ cup fat-free milk
butter for frying

1. In a large bowl, mix the meats with the flour, eggs, onion, salt, and pepper. Add milk gradually and mix thoroughly. Let the mixture stand 15 minutes to allow the flour to absorb the milk.
2. Shape the mixture into small meat patties.
3. Melt butter in a skillet over medium heat. Fry patties about 5 minutes on each side. Use a meat thermometer to be sure the internal temperature has reached 160°F.
4. Drain on paper towels.

Per meat patty: 98 calories (50% from fat), 7 g protein, 5 g carbohydrate, 5 g fat, 62 mg cholesterol, 0 g fiber, 40 mg sodium.

Brunede Kartofler
(Caramelized Potatoes)
Serves 6

2 pounds small red potatoes
¼ cup sugar
2 tablespoons melted butter

1. Scrub potatoes carefully. Do not remove skins.
2. Fill a large, heavy saucepan with water and bring it to a boil. Add the potatoes and simmer 15 to 20 minutes or until potatoes are tender.
3. Cool potatoes slightly; slip off skins.
4. In a large, heavy skillet, melt sugar. Use a low heat and stir sugar constantly until it turns into light brown syrup. (Heat must be low or sugar will scorch.) Add melted butter.
5. Add the potatoes to the skillet, a few at a time, shaking the pan to coat all sides of the potatoes with syrup. Serve immediately.

Per serving: 216 calories (17% from fat), 3 g protein, 43 g carbohydrate, 4 g fat, 10 mg cholesterol, 3 g fiber, 54 mg sodium.

Syltede Rødbeder
(Pickled Beets)
Makes 2 ½ cups

¼ cup cider vinegar
¼ cup white vinegar
½ cup sugar
½ teaspoon salt
dash pepper
2½ cups thinly sliced canned beets

1. In a medium stainless steel saucepan, combine all ingredients except beets. Boil briskly for 2 minutes.
2. While marinade boils, place beets in a deep stainless steel or glass bowl. Pour hot marinade over beets; let cool for 20 minutes, uncovered.
3. Cover bowl and refrigerate at least 12 hours, stirring occasionally.

Per ½-cup serving: 105 calories (0% from fat), 1 g protein, 28 g carbohydrate, 0 g fat, 0 mg cholesterol, 2 g fiber, 466 mg sodium.

Limpa
(Swedish Rye Bread)
Makes 1 loaf

1	package active dry yeast
⅞	cup warm water (105°F to 115°F)
¼	cup light brown sugar, packed
¼	cup light molasses
¾	teaspoon salt
1	tablespoon shortening
1½	teaspoons grated orange peel
¼	cup raisins
1¼	cups rye flour
1¾ to 2 cups all-purpose flour	

1. In a large bowl, dissolve yeast in warm water. Add brown sugar, molasses, salt, shortening, orange peel, raisins, and rye flour; beat well. Add enough all-purpose flour to make a soft dough.
2. Turn dough out onto a lightly floured surface. Cover; let rest 10 minutes.
3. Knead dough until smooth and elastic, about 10 minutes.
4. Place dough in a lightly greased bowl, turning once to grease surface. Cover with a towel. Let dough rise in a warm place until doubled in bulk (about 1½ to 2 hours).
5. Punch dough down. Turn dough out on lightly floured surface and shape into a ball; cover, let rest 10 minutes.
6. Pat ball of dough into a round loaf and place on a greased baking sheet. Cover loaf and let rise in a warm place until doubled (about 1½ to 2 hours).
7. Bake loaf at 375°F for 25 to 30 minutes.
8. Remove bread from pan to cooling rack. For a soft crust, butter top of loaf while hot.

Per slice: 119 calories (8% from fat), 3 g protein, 25 g carbohydrate, 1 g fat, 0 mg cholesterol, 2 g fiber, 107 mg sodium.

Kringla
(Double-Ring Twist Biscuits)
Makes about 24 cookies

1	cup sugar
1	cup plain nonfat yogurt
1	cup fat-free sour milk
1	egg
1	teaspoon baking soda
	pinch salt
½	teaspoon cinnamon
1½ to 2 cups all-purpose flour	

1. Preheat oven to 375°F.
2. Combine sugar, yogurt, sour milk, egg, baking soda, salt, and cinnamon in a large bowl. Add enough flour to make a fairly stiff dough.
3. Roll dough between palms of hands to form pencil-sized rolls; shape rolls into figure eights.
4. Place cookies on a lightly greased baking sheet and bake until lightly browned, about 10 to 12 minutes.

Per cookie: 92 calories (4% from fat), 2 g protein, 20 g carbohydrate, 0 g fat, 12 mg cholesterol, 0 g fiber, 51 mg sodium.

Chapter 31 Review and Expand

Summary

The British Isles include England, Scotland, Wales, Northern Ireland, and Ireland. Roasted meats, baked apples, main-dish pies, and steamed puddings are popular foods in England. Simple, wholesome foods in Scotland often include oats, barley, lamb, and fish. The hearty fare of Wales is similar to that of its neighbors. Potatoes are the staple of the Irish diet.

The French may prepare foods in the style of haute cuisine, provincial cuisine, or nouvelle cuisine. Cooks use the finest ingredients and have the patience to develop flavors. A variety of sauces and delicate seasonings characterize French cooking.

German cuisine includes roasted meats and a variety of sausages. Potatoes, sauerkraut, and dumplings are popular as hearty side dishes. Delicious breads, sweet rolls, and cakes are the pride of German bakers.

Denmark, Norway, Sweden, and Finland are part of Scandinavia. Danish foods tend to be rich, often containing butter, cream, cheese, eggs, and pork. The Norwegians eat much fish and use sour cream in many recipes. Special occasions in Sweden often feature a smörgåsbord, but chefs use husmankost for everyday, simpler cooking. Many Finnish dishes include berries, mushrooms, and potatoes.

Vocabulary Activities

1. **Content Terms** For each of the following terms, identify a word or group of words describing a quality of the term—an *attribute*. Pair up with a classmate and discuss your list of attributes. Then, discuss your list of attributes with the whole class to increase understanding.

cockle	croissant
fish and chips	crêpe
pudding basin	truffle
tea	bouillabaisse
haggis	escargot
colcannon	quiche
haute cuisine	braten
provincial cuisine	bratwurst
nouvelle cuisine	hasenpfeffer
hollandaise sauce	kartoffelpuffer
fines herbes	sauerkraut
hors d'oeuvre	spätzle
strudel	smörgåsbord
crayfish	husmankost
smørrebrød	lingonberry
lutefisk	sauna

2. **Academic Terms** In teams, create categories for the following terms and classify as many of the terms as possible. Then, share your ideas with the remainder of the class.

wellspring	commodity
emblem	nobility
rivaling	herald
peasant	lowland
wharf	prosperous

Review

Write your answers using complete sentences when appropriate.

3. What annual festival is celebrated in Wales on March 1, and what foods are traditionally served on this day?
4. What are four staples of the British diet that were introduced by the Anglo-Saxons?
5. What foods might be served for a traditional breakfast in England?
6. True or false. Haggis is an Irish porridge made with potatoes and cabbage.
7. Describe characteristics of haute cuisine, provincial cuisine, and nouvelle cuisine.
8. Name and describe three types of French sauces.
9. When do the French serve salad?
10. Name three foods that are eaten in the Provence region of France.
11. What is Germany's national dish?
12. Describe three popular German potato dishes.
13. What sweetener is traditionally used to make German cakes such as lebkuchen?
14. How do German meal patterns differ from those in the United States?
15. What are two specific toppings commonly eaten on Danish smørrebrød?
16. Describe three kinds of Norwegian cookies.
17. What dishes are typically included at a smörgåsbord?
18. What do Finns often snack on during a sauna and why?

Chapter 31 Review and Expand

Core Skills

19. **Technology, Math, Speaking** As a class, create a list identifying a major city in each of the countries discussed in this chapter. Type the list in a word processing program and sort it so the cities are listed in alphabetical order. Using the class master list, give a printout of the list to five friends, asking them to rank the cities according to their interest in visiting each city. Tally your results and enter them into the data fields of a chart tool to illustrate and compare relative interest in the various cities as tourist destinations. Then share your charts in class, discussing similarities and differences with classmates.

20. **Research** Use reliable print or online resources to investigate how widely used the English language is in the world today. Create a map identifying countries in which English is a primary language.

21. **Research, Reading, Writing** Write a research paper exploring how the monarchy in Great Britain differs from the presidency in the United States. Cite your resources and review your writing for clarity and accuracy.

22. **Research, Reading, Technology, Speaking** Research the celebration of a holiday of your choice from one of the countries mentioned in this chapter. Use presentation software to illustrate information about traditional customs, decorations, and foods in a brief oral report. Include images in your presentation.

23. **Technology, Speaking, Listening** Working in a small group, visit a tourism website to find information about one of the Scandinavian countries discussed in this chapter. With your group, give a report on your assigned country. Reports should include information about the country's geography, history, government, economy, and lifestyle. Each group member should be responsible for presenting a different aspect of the report.

24. **Math** Europeans use the metric system of measurement. List the metric equivalents for each ingredient in the British, French, German, or Scandinavian recipes found in this chapter.

25. **Career Readiness Practice** Parliamentary procedure is a set of rules for conducting meetings that began in the British Parliament in the 16th century. Volunteer to lead a group in your school or community in learning how to conduct a successful meeting using parliamentary procedure. *Robert's Rules of Order Newly Revised (11th Edition)*—an orderly system of conducting business that protects the rights of group members and keeps discussions focused—is the foundation for using parliamentary procedure. Discuss the impact of following or not following this procedure on the effectiveness of an organization. How can using parliamentary procedure help individuals consistently act in ways that align to personal and community-help ideals and principles? How might failure to use parliamentary procedure impact making decisions?

Critical Thinking and Problem Solving

26. **Create** Create a dish using leftovers from another meal. Give your dish an interesting name, like those coined by British cooks. Prepare a form to help your classmates evaluate your dish for appearance, texture, and flavor. Your evaluation form should also invite your classmates to offer suggestions for improving the dish.

27. **Analyze** Find recipes for two varieties of French sauces. Compare the ingredients, preparation techniques, and nutritional profiles of the two sauces. Based on your analysis, identify the types of meals and food items with which you would serve each sauce. Also identify which sauce you would prefer to prepare and explain your choice.

Chapter 32
Mediterranean Countries

Samot/Shutterstock.com

Objectives

After studying this chapter, you will be able to

- **describe** the food customs of Spain, Italy, and Greece;
- **discuss** how geography, climate, and culture have influenced these customs; and
- **prepare** foods that are native to each of these countries.

Reading Prep

Skim the chapter by reading the first sentence of each paragraph. Use this information to create an outline for the chapter before you read it.

Content Terms

del pueblo
tapas
gazpacho
chorizo
paella
risotto
minestrone
antipasto
taverna
avgolemono
phyllo
baklava
mezedhes

Academic Terms

balmy
marvel
amicability
amateur
hock
mariner

Chapter 32 Mediterranean Countries

The Mediterranean Sea is a warm, salty body of water that lies south of Europe. The Mediterranean region supports crops like citrus fruits, olives, grapes, wheat, barley, peaches, and apricots. The sea itself harbors an abundance of sea salt, as well as a variety of fish, sponges, and coral. For ages, people living in the Mediterranean region have harvested these products to earn a living.

The Mediterranean climate is *balmy* (warm) with plenty of sunshine throughout the year. The winters are mild with average rainfall. The summers are hot and dry. This weather makes the Mediterranean a popular vacation area.

Spain, Italy, and Greece lie along the Mediterranean Sea. Because of these countries' similar climates and resources, their cuisines resemble one another. Vegetables like tomatoes, eggplants, and green peppers are used in many Spanish, Italian, and Greek dishes. (*Eggplant* is a fleshy, oval-shaped vegetable with a deep purple skin.) Seafood is also common in each of these cuisines (**Figure 32.1**).

martiapunts/Shutterstock.com

Figure 32.1 Paella is a Mediterranean dish containing rice and seafood. It is a dish commonly associated with Spain. Name two of Spain's primary crops.

Health and Wellness

Mediterranean Dietary Patterns

Nutrition experts have continued to recognize the health benefits of traditional Mediterranean-style dietary patterns. Such dietary patterns are linked to lower rates of cancer and heart disease.

Mediterranean dietary patterns have a number of healthy features. The most notable feature is the broad use of plant foods. Tomatoes, eggplants, peppers, legumes, onions, and garlic form the basis of many dishes. Pasta, rice, and/ or breads are staples at most meals. Many of the grain foods served are whole grains. Nuts—a good source of omega-3 fatty acids—are also commonly included in Mediterranean dishes. Fruits such as grapes, oranges, figs, and melons grow well in the warm Mediterranean climate. These fruits, in place of rich desserts, are often served at the end of Mediterranean meals. Another healthy feature in Mediterranean eating is the wide use of olive oil for cooking. Olive oil has no cholesterol and is high in monounsaturated fats.

People in the Mediterranean region use only limited amounts of full-fat dairy products. They also tend to eat limited portions of red meat. Instead, their diets include much seafood, which is another good source of omega-3 fatty acids. These characteristics define dietary patterns that are fairly low in fat. Mediterranean dishes also provide good sources of vitamins, minerals, fiber, and phytonutrients.

As you read about Spain, Italy, and Greece, you will recognize how their food customs are similar. You will also note unique aspects of each cuisine.

Copyright Goodheart-Willcox Co., Inc.

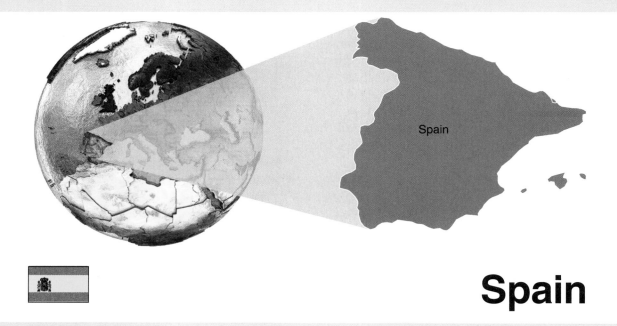

Spain

Between the Mediterranean Sea and the Atlantic Ocean lies the Iberian Peninsula, a landmass that forms the southwestern corner of Europe. Spain and Portugal share this peninsula. Spain occupies the largest part.

Geography and Climate of Spain

The two main geographic features of the Iberian Peninsula are the surrounding water and several mountain ranges that crisscross the land. Most Spaniards live along the coast of either the Bay of Biscay or the Mediterranean Sea. There the land is fertile and agriculture is prosperous.

To the North, the Pyrenees Mountains separate Spain from France and the rest of Europe. Four other mountain ranges divide the rest of Spain into isolated units. Within the circle formed by these mountain ranges is the *Meseta*, a large plateau that occupies more than half of the total area of Spain.

Spain has a surprising range of climates for a country that is relatively small. Much of Spain has a typical Mediterranean climate with hot, dry summers, mild winters, and light rainfall. Northern Spain has cool summers with mild, damp winters. The Meseta of Central Spain has the most severe climate with extremes of both heat and cold. The southernmost tip of Spain is a semidesert with virtually no winter.

Spanish Agriculture

Many Spaniards make their living fishing or farming. There are some large landowners in Spain; however, most people live on their own small farms (**Figure 32.2**). Wheat, olives, barley,

Noradoa/Shutterstock.com

Figure 32.2 Most people in Spain live on small farms and vineyards, where they grow numerous crops.

oats, rye, potatoes, rice, beans, grapes, and honey are Spain's primary crops. Valencian oranges grown in Spain are among the best oranges in the world. Farmers raise sheep on the Meseta and in mountainous areas. They raise some cattle in grassy areas.

The land along the southeastern Mediterranean coast is the "gardenland" of Spain. Extensive irrigation systems built in this once arid land have allowed a variety of crops to thrive. Today, almonds, oranges, lemons, figs, dates, melons, pomegranates, and sugarcane grow in this region. Spain's two most popular wines are also produced there.

Spanish Culture

Spain has a rich cultural heritage. This heritage has influenced life in the country today. Those who visit Spain enjoy the inviting climate and beautiful scenery. Tourists *marvel* (show awe, appreciation, and wonder) at all that Spain has to offer in terms of music, art, and architecture. The *amicability* (friendliness) of the Spanish people is also a key factor that makes visitors feel welcome.

Family life is a very important part of Spanish culture. Although friendships are highly valued, people see family as a main source of social support. Men are typically viewed as the heads of families, and members of the extended family often live and work near one another.

One aspect of Spanish life that visitors are sure to notice is the later business hours. For many Spanish people, the workday starts at 10 o'clock in the morning and lasts until 7 o'clock at night. Many offices and shops also close for a couple of hours in the middle of the day for a late afternoon lunch break. Traditionally, a *siesta* (rest period) follows this meal. Although this custom is fading, it is still observed in many parts of Spain.

Annual Spanish celebrations include some unique traditions. In one New Year's Eve custom, a person pops a grape into his or her mouth each time the clock strikes at midnight. Twelve grapes represent twelve months of good luck.

Bullfights are part of the festivities during the annual feast day observed for the patron saint of

Culture and Social Studies

History of Spanish Cuisine

Spanish cuisine began centuries ago with the Romans, who ruled Spain for a period of six centuries beginning in the 200s BC. The Romans contributed olive oil and garlic. Spanish cooks still use these two ingredients in many dishes.

In AD 711, the *Moors*, Muslim people from northern Africa, crossed into Spain and started taking control. The Moors brought citrus fruits, peaches, and figs. They introduced the cultivation of rice. They also grew a number of spices, including saffron, pepper, nutmeg, and anise. The Romans knew of almonds; however, it was the Moors who planted large almond groves and often used almonds in cooking.

In the fifteenth century, during the reign of Ferdinand and Isabella, Spanish explorers journeyed to the Americas, then known as the *New World*. These explorers claimed land for Spain. Spain's colonies in the Americas provided tomatoes, chocolate, potatoes, and sweet and hot peppers.

Invasion by various enemy groups and Spain's rugged terrain further affected the development of food customs. These two factors helped divide the country into distinct culinary regions.

each town. Besides bullfighting, feast days are celebrated with parades, bonfires, and beauty contests.

A well-known Spanish festival is *Fiesta de San Fermín*, which is held in Pamplona each July. As part of this celebration, a herd of bulls is set loose to run through the streets of the town. Young men run ahead of the bulls to a bullring, where they take part in *amateur* (untrained) bullfights.

Spanish Cuisine

Spanish cuisine can best be described as **del pueblo**, or the "food of the people." It is simple for the most part. Its goodness relies on fresh ingredients and basic preparation methods.

Characteristics of Spanish Cuisine

Today, each of Spain's regions still clings to its style of cooking. Still, cooks throughout the country use similar ingredients and cooking methods.

Spanish cuisine differs in several ways from Mexican cuisine. Spaniards made many contributions to Mexican cuisine; however, Spanish cooking differs from the spicy cooking of Mexico. Throughout Spain, tomatoes, onions, and garlic form the base of many sauces. Garlic, pepper, and paprika flavor many main dishes, soups, and salads. Olive oil replaces butter in most recipes. Parsley serves as more than a garnish. In *salsa verde*, for example, large amounts of parsley add flavor as well as color. Spaniards eat raw almonds as appetizers. They use toasted almonds in sauces, cookies, cakes, pastries, and appetizers.

A traditional Spanish cooking method is to slowly simmer foods in earthenware pots. Cooks gently move the pots back and forth across a flame as they slowly stir the food inside. Cooks often use natural juices from cooking meat, fish, or poultry as the base for a sauce. They add other ingredients only to heighten the natural flavors of these juices.

Spanish cooks like to mix two or more food flavors in a single dish. They prepare mixtures of meat and fish; fish and vegetables; and meat, fish, and rice. One of the best examples of this method of mixing flavors is the *cocido*. Vegetables, beef, lamb, ham, poultry, and a spicy sausage cook together in a large pot. Spaniards first eat the thick soup in large bowls. Then they follow with the tender meats, poultry, and vegetables as a separate course.

Spanish Appetizers

Spanish meals often begin with **tapas**, or appetizers. Tapas are also enjoyed as snacks when friends visit together at sidewalk cafés. Tapas may be as simple as a few olives or toasted almonds. Other tapas that are simple to prepare include scallops, prawns, pickled herring, ham, marinated mushrooms, and anchovies. Other tapas are fancier and require hours to prepare. Fancier tapas include *buñuelitos*, which are small fritters. They are prepared by deep-frying small pieces of vegetables, meat, poultry, or fish that have been coated with a batter. *Empanadillas* are small pastries filled with chopped meat, fish, or poultry. They can be eaten hot or cold. *Banderillas* are colorful tapas served on long toothpicks (**Figure 32.3**). *Pinchos* are grilled foods.

Spanish Salads and Soups

A salad often follows the tapas. Sometimes a salad may be little more than lettuce and tomato with a simple oil and vinegar dressing. Other times, it may be an attractive arrangement of raw vegetables on a plate.

Soups are popular throughout Spain. One of the heartiest soups is a fish soup called *sopa al cuarto de hora*, or "15-minute soup." It is made with mussels, prawns, whitefish, rice, peas, hard-cooked eggs, saffron, salt, pepper, and meat broth. All the ingredients cook together for 15 minutes—just long enough to blend the flavors.

Robcartorres/Shutterstock.com

Figure 32.3   Banderillas are tapas served on toothpicks. They often include pickled vegetables, such as olives, cucumbers, onions, and red peppers. What other foods could be served on toothpicks like banderillas?

People throughout Spain enjoy garlic soup. One simple version of garlic soup is prepared by slowly sautéing two cloves of garlic in olive oil. Once the garlic browns, a few slices of bread, salt, pepper, and water are added. Then the soup cooks for just a few minutes. Other versions include a small amount of minced ham and tomatoes.

Another popular Spanish soup is **gazpacho**. This soup is often made with coarsely pureed tomatoes, onions, garlic, cucumbers, and green peppers; olive oil; and vinegar. It can be thick or thin, served icy cold or at room temperature.

Spanish Main Dishes

Most culinary experts agree that few cooks can prepare seafood as well as the Spaniards. Mussels, shrimp, and crab are popular shellfish in Spain. Tuna, hake, sole, squid, and cod are also caught off Spain's coasts. Cooks bake, fry, and poach fish and shellfish. In some parts of Spain, they serve seafood with *aioli* (garlic mayonnaise).

Although methods for cooking meat are not as refined as those for seafood, Spain produces some excellent meat dishes. Veal, lamb, and pork are the most popular meats. The lean, dark Spanish pig is used in many ways. Raw ham, which is air-cured high in the mountains, is a specialty. Filet of cured pork is sliced thinly and served as an appetizer. The best known Spanish pork product is **chorizo**, a dark sausage with a spicy, smoky flavor.

People throughout Spain eat poultry. Although Spaniards eat pigeon, pheasant, and partridge, chicken is by far the most popular type of poultry. Cooks stew and roast chicken. They also use it in the famous Spanish dish called paella. **Paella** is a Spanish rice dish that has many variations. The version most often seen in the United States contains chicken, shrimp, mussels, whitefish, peas, and rice. It is flavored with saffron, salt, pepper, and pimiento.

Spanish Accompaniments

The Spanish serve bread with soups, salads, and main dishes. A variety of breads are popular. *Pan de Santa Teresa* (fried cinnamon bread) is a sweet bread similar to French toast. *Picatostes* (fried sugar breads) are more like pastries. They are served as an afternoon snack with coffee.

Tortilla española (Spanish omelet) may be served as a separate course or as an accompaniment. Spanish cooks use a variety of fillings for tortillas. Potato, onion, white bean, and eggplant are the most popular (**Figure 32.4**). Sometimes cooks pile several tortillas with different fillings on top of one another. They serve them the way people serve pancakes in the United States.

Spaniards generally serve vegetables as a separate course, though potatoes or grilled tomatoes may sometimes accompany a main dish. Vegetables served alone are often cooked in a tomato sauce or coated with a batter and deep-fried. Two or more vegetables are often combined and cooked in liquid. Many Spanish vegetable dishes contain artichokes, cauliflowers, and eggplants. Spaniards also enjoy dried beans, lentils, and chickpeas, which they call *pulses*. Dried beans often appear in one-dish meals with meat, poultry, and fish.

Spanish Desserts

Simple desserts like fresh fruit, dried figs, cheese, or almonds often follow a meal. Spaniards usually save fancy cakes, cookies, pastries, and other rich desserts for guests. They may also serve these desserts as afternoon snacks. Rice pudding, sponge cake, and *flan* (caramel custard) are especially popular.

Pat_Hastings/Shutterstock.com

Figure 32.4 Potatoes make a hearty filling for Spanish tortillas. How are Spanish tortillas different from Mexican tortillas?

Spanish cakes and pastries contain very little baking powder or butter. Instead, they contain many eggs and powdered almonds. They are flavored with cinnamon, anise, and orange and lemon peel. Spaniards fry rather than bake many cakes and pastries. This is because most Spanish homes did not have ovens until recent years.

Spanish Meals

Spanish meals are similar to Mexican meals and share the same names. The people of Spain begin each day with *desayuno* (breakfast). They may just have coffee or a chocolate drink. Sometimes they have bread and jam or a sweet roll. *Churro*, a thin pastry fried in deep fat, is especially popular at breakfast.

People who have slept late or workers who find themselves hungry around 11 o'clock eat a second morning meal, *almuerzo*. Almuerzo is more substantial than desayuno. This meal varies depending on locale and personal taste. It may include an omelet, grilled sausage, fried squid, open-faced sandwiches, fish, or lamb chops.

The *comida* is the main meal of the day. Spaniards eat this meal in the middle of the afternoon, around two or three o'clock. Most businesses close during this time, and workers go home to eat. A main course of fish, poultry, or meat usually follows salad or soup. Fruit or another light dessert ends the meal.

Spaniards serve *merienda* around six o'clock. It usually is a light snack of cakes and cookies or bread and jam. If a family has visitors, however, the meal may be more substantial.

Dusk is a pleasant time of day in Spain. The sidewalk cafés fill with people, and the odors of the tapas drift out to the streets. Around nine or ten o'clock, people enjoy the last meal of the day, *cena* (supper). Cena may be a light meal, similar to almuerzo, or a full meal with a salad, main course, and other dishes.

Wine is Spain's national drink, and both the rich and poor serve it with every meal. Two popular Spanish wines are Malaga and sherry. *Malaga* has a brown color and a sweet taste. *Sherry* has a characteristic nutlike flavor. Restaurants and taverns throughout Spain serve *sangria*, a wine-based punch. There are many versions of the punch, but they all include red wine, fruit juice, and sparkling water (**Figure 32.5**).

iuliia_n/Shutterstock.com

Figure 32.5 Mock sangria, a fruity punch, can be made without alcohol.

Spanish Menu

Empanadillas de Pollo
(Chicken Turnovers)

Gazpacho
(Cold Vegetable Soup)

Paella de Mariscos y Pollo
(Saffron Rice with Seafood and Chicken)

Ensalada Catalana
(Catalan Salad)

Sangria Falsa
(Mock Red Wine Punch)

Flan
(Caramel Custard)

Empanadillas de Pollo (Chicken Turnovers)

Makes about 20

Pastry:

1½	cups all-purpose flour
½	teaspoon salt
¼	cup olive oil
¼	cup cold water

Filling:

1 tablespoon olive oil
1 small onion, chopped
1 small tomato, peeled and chopped
¼ teaspoon minced garlic
1 hard-cooked egg
⅜ cup diced, cooked chicken
1 egg, beaten (optional)

1. To make the pastry, mix the flour and salt together in a large mixing bowl. Add ¼ cup olive oil and ¼ cup water. With fingers, mix dough until it forms a ball. Let dough rest while preparing the filling.
2. To prepare the filling, heat 1 tablespoon oil in a skillet until very hot (but not smoking). Add onion and sauté until golden. Add tomato and garlic and continue cooking vegetables until the liquid has evaporated.
3. In a small bowl, mash the hard-cooked egg. Add mashed egg and cooked chicken to the skillet. Cook mixture 2 to 3 minutes, stirring occasionally; remove from heat. Taste filling and add salt and pepper, if needed.
4. Preheat oven to 425°F.
5. On a lightly floured surface, roll pastry to a thickness of ⅛ inch. Cut circles from pastry with a 3-inch biscuit cutter.
6. Place a rounded teaspoon of filling on one-half of each circle. Fold the other half of the dough over the filling and press edges together with a fork to seal.
7. Place turnovers on a lightly greased baking sheet and brush surface with beaten egg, if desired. Bake turnovers until brown and crisp, about 25 minutes.

Per turnover: 77 calories (47% from fat), 2 g protein, 8 g carbohydrate, 4 g fat, 16 mg cholesterol, 0 g fiber, 60 mg sodium.

Gazpacho
(Cold Vegetable Soup)
Serves 4

Soup:

2 cups low-sodium chicken broth
2 medium tomatoes, chopped
1 cucumber, peeled and chopped
1 medium onion, sliced
¼ cup chopped green pepper
1 cup bread cubes
1 tablespoon wine vinegar
¼ teaspoon minced garlic
½ teaspoon sugar
dash cayenne

Garnish:

½ cup bread cubes (¼ inch)
2 tablespoons chopped onion
¼ cup chopped green peppers
¼ cup peeled and chopped tomato

1. In a large bowl, combine chicken broth, tomatoes, cucumber, onion, green pepper, bread cubes, vinegar, garlic, sugar, and cayenne.
2. Puree mixture in a blender, 2 cups at a time.
3. Chill thoroughly.
4. Just before serving, stir soup lightly. Pour into a tureen or individual soup bowls. Pass garnishes separately.

Per serving: 85 calories (11% from fat), 4 g protein, 16 g carbohydrate, 1 g fat, 0 mg cholesterol, 3 g fiber, 169 mg sodium.

Paella de Camarones y Pollo
(Saffron Rice with Shrimp and Chicken)
Serves 5

½ pound garlic-seasoned smoked pork sausage
1 pound cut-up chicken pieces, skin removed
½ teaspoon garlic salt
1 dash pepper
¼ cup olive oil
¼ cup chopped onion
1 medium green pepper, chopped
1 medium tomato, peeled and finely chopped
1 clove garlic, crushed
1 cup uncooked long-grain rice
⅛ teaspoon ground saffron
2 cups boiling water
6 medium-sized shrimp, peeled and deveined
½ cup frozen peas, thoroughly defrosted

1. Prick sausage in several places with a fork. Place in a large, ovenproof skillet and cover with cold water. Bring water to a boil, then reduce heat to low. Simmer sausage uncovered for 5 minutes. Drain sausage well and slice into rounds about ¼ inch thick; set aside.
2. Season chicken with garlic salt and pepper.

3. Heat 2 tablespoons olive oil in the skillet until very hot but not smoking. Add chicken pieces, two at a time, and fry until golden brown. Remove browned pieces to a plate lined with paper towels and continue cooking the rest of the chicken.

4. Add sausage slices to the skillet and quickly brown; transfer to a plate lined with paper towels and drain.

5. Remove oil from the skillet and wipe the skillet with paper towels. Add 2 tablespoons fresh olive oil and heat until hot but not smoking. Add onion, green pepper, tomato, and garlic. Cook vegetables, stirring constantly, until most of the liquid has evaporated. (This is called a *sofrito*.)

6. Preheat oven to 400°F.

7. Add the rice and saffron to the skillet with the sofrito. Pour boiling water into the skillet. Bring the mixture to a boil, stirring constantly. Then remove from heat immediately and taste for seasonings.

8. Arrange shrimp, sausage, and chicken over the top of the rice. Sprinkle peas over meats and seafood.

9. Cover the skillet and place it on the bottom rack in the oven. Bake for 25 to 30 minutes or until the liquid has been absorbed. (Do not stir the paella.)

10. When paella is cooked, remove it from oven and let it rest about 5 minutes. Serve immediately.

Note: All of the ingredients can be prepared a short time ahead. The oven should be preheated one-half hour before paella is to be served.

Per serving: 471 calories (42% from fat), 30 g protein, 37 g carbohydrate, 22 g fat, 101 mg cholesterol, 2 g fiber, 648 mg sodium.

Ensalada Catalana
(Catalan Salad)
Serves 6

½   head romaine lettuce
3   medium tomatoes
1   large sweet onion
1   green pepper
1   red pepper
¼   cup green olives
¼   cup pitted black olives
     olive oil
     wine vinegar

1. Clean romaine lettuce under cool running water. Separate and dry leaves. Break into bite-sized pieces.

2. Wash tomatoes; slice into wedges.

3. Peel onion; cut into rings.

4. Wash and clean green and red peppers; cut into thin rings.

5. Set six chilled salad plates on a tray. Make a bed of romaine on each plate. Attractively arrange the rest of the ingredients on the top of the lettuce.

6. Serve salads with olive oil and wine vinegar.

Per serving: 107 calories (71% from fat), 2 g protein, 7 g carbohydrate, 9 g fat, 0 mg cholesterol, 3 g fiber, 145 mg sodium.

Sangria Falsa
(Mock Red Wine Punch)
Serves 4

4   lemon slices
4   orange slices
4   lime slices
4   cups red grape juice, well chilled
2   cups club soda, well chilled
     ice cubes

1. In large pitcher, combine fruits and grape juice. Refrigerate until ready to serve.

2. Just before serving, add club soda. Serve sangria immediately over ice.

Per serving: 152 calories (0% from fat), 1 g protein, 37 g carbohydrate, 0 g fat, 0 mg cholesterol, 1 g fiber, 13 mg sodium.

Flan
(Caramel Custard)
Serves 4

⅝   cup sugar, divided
1   tablespoon water
1   cup fat-free milk
1   cup evaporated fat-free milk
3   eggs
1   pinch salt
¾   teaspoon vanilla extract

1. Warm four custard cups by placing them in hot water.
2. In a small, heavy saucepan combine ¼ cup sugar and water. Cook over moderate heat, stirring constantly, until the sugar melts and turns a golden brown.
3. To caramelize custard cups, quickly pour some of the syrup into each of the warmed cups. Turn the custard cups in all directions so the syrup coats the bottoms and sides. Set aside.
4. In a medium saucepan, combine milk and evaporated milk; heat to just below boiling. Remove from heat and cool slightly.
5. Preheat oven to 350°F.
6. In a mixer bowl, beat eggs and salt slightly. Add remaining ¼ cup plus 2 tablespoons of sugar gradually as you continue beating. Add combined milks slowly, beating constantly, then add vanilla extract.
7. Pour the custard mixture into the caramelized custard cups. Place the cups in a cake pan; fill the pan with very hot water to about ½ inch from the tops of the cups. Bake about 25 to 30 minutes, until a knife inserted near the center of each cup comes out clean.
8. Cool custard 10 minutes, then refrigerate until well chilled.
9. To unmold, run a knife between the custard and cup. Place a serving dish on top of the cup and invert. The custard should slide out.

Per serving: 254 calories (14% from fat), 12 g protein, 42 g carbohydrate, 4 g fat, 164 mg cholesterol, 0 g fiber, 193 mg sodium.

Ramon Espelt/Shutterstock.com

Flan is a popular dessert served throughout Spain.

Italy

The warm, sunny climate and awesome scenery of Italy make it a popular vacation spot. Italy's remarkable art, architecture, and history appeal to culture lovers. In addition, Italy boasts a variety of delicious foods.

Geography and Climate of Italy

Italy is a rather small country composed of many islands and a boot-shaped peninsula that juts into the Mediterranean Sea. Italy's expansive coastline makes seafood important in Italian cuisine.

Much of Italy is mountainous. The rugged Italian Alps form a semicircular barrier in the North, shutting out neighboring countries. The Apennines run in a bow shape, dividing the Italian peninsula in half. Between the Alps and the Apennines lies the Po Valley, which is a rich agricultural area. Narrow coastal plains that border both sides of the peninsula are also suitable for agriculture. Farming can take place in small valleys formed by the mountains, too.

Italy has three distinct geographic regions. Northern Italy has great beauty and rich land. The fertile Po River basin makes the Po Valley the most productive farming area in the country.

Central Italy is mountainous and hilly. Grain, grapes, and olives grow on the terraced hillsides (**Figure 32.6**). Southern Italy has fewer natural resources, but olives, tomatoes, and mozzarella

Mostovyi Sergii Igorevich/Shutterstock.com

Figure 32.6 With terrace farming, Italian farmers can grow crops even on hilly or mountainous landscapes. Explain the concept of terrace farming.

cheese are still important agricultural products of this region.

Italy's climate is as variable as its geography. Much of Italy has a Mediterranean climate. Summers are sunny and dry with most of the rainfall occurring in the winter. In Northern Italy, however, temperatures are cooler, and rain can come during any season. As a result, Italy has a range of vegetation. Pine trees grow in the North. Citrus fruits grow in the South.

Italian Agriculture

Agriculture is vital to Italy's economy. About one-half of the nation's land is used for farming. In some areas, the terrain is too steep for farmers to use machines to do farm work. Therefore, they must do it by hand.

The richest farmland is located in Northern Italy in the Po River Valley. Leading crops are wheat, corn, rice, sugar beets, and flax. The many dairy herds make this region the largest cheese-producing region in the country. Olive trees thrive in Southern Italy. Farmers grow vegetables and fruits for local use and for export to other European countries.

Vineyards are scattered throughout the country. They supply grapes for Italy's large wine industry. Italian wine makers produce a variety of red, white, and sparkling wines for domestic use and export.

Italian Culture

Italy has been the site of many major historical and cultural events. The city of Rome was once the head of a mighty empire. Rome's rule and cultural influence reached through Europe, northern Africa, and western Asia. With the fall of the Roman Empire, which began in AD 330, the Roman Catholic Church slowly gained power. The Church met people's needs for leadership and became a center of learning.

As the Roman Catholic Church became more governmental, it continued to be a shaping force in Italian culture. Centuries after Rome fell, the Church and some wealthy Italian families encouraged the development of the arts in Italy. This led to the start of the *Renaissance*, a time of a

great rebirth in art and learning. The movement spread all through Europe. The Renaissance spanned the fourteenth to the seventeenth centuries. During this time, literature and science flourished along with the arts.

Almost all Italians are Roman Catholic. Many Italian holidays celebrate events in the Church. *Pasqua*, or Easter, is one important holiday. A number of foods are used to celebrate this holiday that ushers in spring. Cakes and breads made with fruits and nuts are baked in shapes such as doves (**Figure 32.7**). People serve lamb as a symbol of spring. Eggs symbolize life, and wheat symbolizes the resurrection of Christ.

Italians hold harvest festivals in the late summer and early fall. These events celebrate the gathering of important foods. At an olive festival, farmers and workers who have brought in the olive crop sit at a long outdoor table. They feast on a meal of pasta, olives, and wine. At fishing festivals held in coastal towns, people enjoy eating seafood barbecued along the shore.

On November 2, Italians celebrate *Festa Dei Morti*, or All Souls' Day. On this day, they pay respect to dead relatives by visiting cemeteries to place flowers and candles on the graves. People may also leave buns, fruit-shaped candies, and lentils in their kitchens at night. They believe the souls of their relatives will enter the home through an open window and enjoy the food.

Christmas is a special time of celebration in Italy. Some people travel to Rome to hear the

©iStock.com/lev1977

Figure 32.7 Bread shaped like a dove is one of the traditional foods that are part of the Easter celebration in Italy.

Pope deliver a Christmas sermon. Many families decorate trees and display nativity scenes depicting the birth of Christ. Children receive gifts from *Babbo Natale,* or Father Christmas.

A number of food traditions are part of the Christmas celebration. Italians refrain from eating meat on Christmas Eve, so a meal of fish is often served instead. In Southern Italy, Christmas Eve is celebrated with the *Feast of the Seven Fishes.* Families serve a symbolic number of types of fish at this special meal. Though the actual number of varieties served may be more or fewer than seven, the meaning is always tied to the Biblical Christmas story. On Christmas Day, families dine for hours at an elaborate lunch, which is served using the finest dinnerware and table linens. Another big, but somewhat less fancy, meal is served on December 26 in honor of St. Stephen's Day.

Italian Cuisine

During the Renaissance, Italian cooking came to be known as the "mother cuisine." It gained this name because it is the source of many Western cuisines.

History of Italian Cuisine

Italian cuisine began with the Greeks, who colonized Southern Italy and the island of Sicily around 1000 BC. During the time of the Roman Empire, Rome was known for its elaborate feasts. Romans paid high prices for Greek chefs because good food was a status symbol (**Figure 32.8**).

Cooking declined somewhat after the fall of the Roman Empire, but experienced a rebirth during the Renaissance. Many people say the French have the greatest Western cuisine; however, even the French grudgingly give Italy credit for laying the foundation for haute cuisine.

Catherine de Medici, an Italian of noble birth who was married at a young age to the future French king Henry II, is credited with playing important culinary and political roles in France. When she moved to France, she is reported to have brought her Italian cooks with her. They are said to have introduced new foods to the French, including olive oil, white beans, artichokes, and parsley. Catherine also brought the use of forks and the practice of table etiquette with her from

Waj/Shutterstock.com

Figure 32.8   Symbols such as good food and magnificent architecture expressed status for ancient civilizations. The effects of these symbols in the Roman Empire can still be felt today. Are good food and architecture still expressions of status for cultures today?

Italy. Her influence as queen led the French people to adopt these customs.

Characteristics of Italian Cuisine

Italian food, as a whole, is lively, interesting, colorful, and varied, yet it is basically simple. The Italians believe in keeping the natural flavors of food, and they insist on fresh, high-quality ingredients. Many Italian cooks shop daily so foods will be as fresh as possible. They do not indulge in convenience foods. If a particular food is too costly or out of season, an Italian cook substitutes whatever is available.

Italian cooks use many kinds of herbs, spices, and other seasonings. They stock their kitchens with parsley, marjoram, sweet basil, thyme, sage, rosemary, tarragon, bay leaves, oregano, and mint. Other commonly used flavorings include cloves, saffron, coriander, celery, onions, shallots, garlic, vinegar, olives, and lemon juice.

Fresh fruits and vegetables are as important to the Italian kitchen as herbs and spices are. Those who live in the country grow many of the fruits and vegetables they use. City dwellers make trips to the local market each day (**Figure 32.9**).

Dieter Hawlan/Shutterstock.com

Figure 32.9 The freshness of ingredients is prized in Italian culture. Italian cooks visit local markets to buy fresh produce for their meals.

There, they select the ripest and freshest tomatoes, artichokes, peas, beans, and other produce.

Italian cooks prepare many dishes on top of the range, either by simmering or frying. Because fuel is relatively expensive, Italian cooks use the oven as little as possible.

Italian Staple Foods

Italy has a number of characteristic staple foods. Throughout Italy, many people eat pasta. *Pasta* refers to any paste made from wheat flour that is dried in various shapes. Pasta may be made from just flour and water or may have added ingredients like eggs. It may be made at home or commercially.

Italians serve pasta in many ways, but they always serve it cooked *al dente* (slightly resistant to the bite). They may serve it with butter, a sprinkling of cheese, or a variety of sauces. They may add it to soups or stews or stuff it with meat, poultry, vegetables, or cheese.

After pasta, Italy's most important staple food is seafood. Every locale with a coastline has developed unique methods of preparing and serving fish. Sole, sea bass, anchovies, sardines, mackerel, tuna, eel, squid, and octopus are some of the varieties of seafood caught. Equally popular are shellfish, including oysters, clams,

mussels, spiny lobsters, shrimp, and crayfish (**Figure 32.10**).

Rice is both an important agricultural product and a staple food. Italians cook rice so the grains remain separate with a slight firmness.

Pork, lamb, veal, and beef are also produced and eaten in Italy. Sausage, wild game, and poultry are equally popular. Meat is relatively expensive, so many Italian dishes rely on meat extenders. The sauces for many pasta dishes contain little meat. If large cuts of meat are served, they usually are roasted.

Italian Dairy Products

Italy is known for producing exquisite dairy products, including cheeses and ice cream. Among the best-known Italian cheeses sold in the United States are Parmesan, mozzarella, Romano, ricotta, provolone, and Gorgonzola. Some varieties of cheese are named after their places of origin. For instance, *Parmesan cheese* is named for its origins in the Italian regions of Parma and Reggio Emilia.

The Italians also introduced ice cream to the rest of Europe. There are two basic varieties of Italian ice cream. *Granita* is a light sherbet made with powdery ice and coffee or fruit-flavored syrup. *Gelato* is made with milk and resembles the vanilla and chocolate ice creams familiar to people in the United States.

svariophoto/Shutterstock.com

Figure 32.10 This seafood dish contains the Italian staple ingredients of pasta and clams.

Culture and Social Studies

An Italian Culinary Division

Geography and climate create a culinary division between the North and South in Italy. Northern Italy has more resources than Southern Italy. In the North, meat is easier to obtain and less expensive, and dairy products are more common. Foods in the North are not as heavily spiced as they are in the South, and cooks in the South use delicate sauces instead of heavier tomato sauces.

Most of the farming and grazing land in Southern Italy is of poor quality. This region is rather sparsely populated and many of its people have lower incomes. Meat is expensive and eaten in small amounts. Dairy products, except for cheese, are rare. Most foods are hearty, filling, and economical. Southern Italian cooking is the cooking with which most people in the United States are familiar. This is because most Italian restaurants in the United States are *Neapolitan* (characteristic of Naples), and Naples is the heart of Southern Italian cooking.

Cooking fats and pasta varieties also differ between the North and the South. Northern Italy is too cold to raise olive trees, but has excellent grazing land for dairy cattle. Southern Italy is warm enough for olive trees, but has poor grazing land. Therefore, butter is the favored cooking fat in the North. In the South, cooks prefer olive oil.

Northern Italy is the home of the fat, ribbon-shaped groups of pastas called *pasta bolognese*. These pastas usually are made at home and contain eggs. Southern Italy is the home of the tubular groups of pastas called *pasta napoletana*. These pastas are usually produced commercially. They do not contain eggs and they have a longer shelf life.

Italian Beverages

Characteristic Italian beverages include coffee and wine. *Caffè espresso* is a rich, dark, flavorful coffee served throughout Italy. It is made in a special type of coffeemaker called a *caffettiera*. Darkly roasted, finely ground coffee beans must be used. This type of coffee is often called *French roast* in stores in the United States.

Even more important to the Italians than caffè espresso is *vino* (wine). Even children drink wine. Mild burgundy wine or Chianti wine usually replaces water at Italian meals.

Regional Italian Specialties

Thanks to modern transportation, people throughout Italy can now buy foods that were once strictly regional. Pizza, for example, originated in Naples. Today, it is eaten all over Italy and in much of the rest of the world as well. Despite this, Italian cooking is still regional cooking. Most culinary experts agree that the best regional foods are still found within their home regions.

Specialties of Northern Italy

The specialties of Northern Italy include the simple *minestra* (soups) of the Friuli-Venezia Giulia region. The elegant stuffed pastas and rich meat sauces of the city of Bologna are also part of this fare.

The North is known for its sausages and other pork products. Bologna's *mortadella* is one of the best-known Italian sausages in the United States. It is made with beef and pork and is seasoned with pepper and garlic. Delicately flavored *Parma ham* is a popular appetizer in the North.

In the North, people often serve risottos, gnocchi, and polenta instead of pasta. **Risottos** are rice dishes made with butter, chopped onion, stock or wine, and Parmesan cheese. They may have meats or seafood and vegetables added. Because many of the northern regions lie along the sea, risottos in this area often contain seafood. *Gnocchi* are dumplings. They may be made of potatoes or wheat flour (**Figure 32.11**). *Polenta* is a porridge made of cornmeal. It sometimes is combined with butter and cheese and served as a filling side dish. In several of the northeastern regions, Austrian influences on Italian cuisine are

Stepanek Photography/Shutterstock.com

Figure 32.11 Potato gnocchi provides a delicious and filling alternative to pasta in Northern Italy. What ingredients are used to make gnocchi?

evident. Foods such as *apfelstrudel* (apple strudel) and *crauti* (sauerkraut) are served.

Other Northern Italian specialties popular in the United States are chicken cacciatore, minestrone soup, and ossobuco. *Pollo alla cacciatora* (chicken hunter-style) is prepared by simmering pieces of chicken with tomatoes and mushrooms. **Minestrone** is a satisfying soup made with onions, carrots, zucchini, celery, cabbage, rice or pasta, and seasonings. It is served with Parmesan cheese. *Ossobuco* is the portion of a calf's leg between the knee and **hock** (hind joint). It is served with the marrow that fills the center of the bone. The flavorful marrow is eaten with rice.

Famous Northern Italian sweets include zabaglione and panettone. *Zabaglione* is fluffy egg custard flavored with Marsala wine. *Panettone* is a sweet cake filled with fruit and nuts. It is often served for breakfast.

Specialties of Central Italy

Several of Central Italy's specialties have Roman origins. Roman cooks serve spaghetti in at least 25 ways. Of these, people in the United States may be most familiar with the spaghetti dish called *spaghetti alla carbonara*. The sauce for this dish contains eggs, pork, pepper, and cheese.

Of all meats, Romans enjoy lamb the most. Cooks rub young lambs with garlic, rosemary, pepper, and salt. Then they cover the lambs with rosemary and roast them until tender.

The Romans must be given credit for inventing cheesecake. The early Romans made their *crostata di ricotta* (cheese pie) without any sweetening. It contained flour, cheese, and eggs. Today's cooks sweeten crostata di ricotta with sugar and flavor it with candied fruits, almonds, and vanilla.

In the rich countryside of Tuscany, home-grown vegetables, beans, and charcoal-grilled meats are specialties. Tuscan cooks add beans to minestra. They also cook beans with garlic and tomatoes or flavor them with sage and cheese. They prepare beans *nel fiasco* by cooking them with garlic, water, and olive oil in an empty wine flask. Tuscan cooks grill large beefsteaks on gridirons. The steaks are sprinkled with coarse salt and pepper to make *bistecca alla fiorentina*.

Cenci and panforte are sweets with Central Italian origins. *Cenci* are deep-fried pastry strips shaped like bows. *Panforte* is a honey cake flavored with cinnamon and cloves (**Figure 32.12**).

Specialties of Southern Italy

Southern Italian cooks serve pasta with rich tomato sauces. They may flavor the sauces with meat, seafood, or vegetables. Spaghetti and lasagne are the southern pastas with which people in the United States are most familiar. Southern Italian cooks do not limit themselves to just these varieties, however. *Fusilli* (pulled-out spirals), *orecchiette* (little ears), and *ricci di donna* (ladies' curls) are equally popular. Large, tubular pastas like cannelloni and rigatoni are used as well.

With pasta, the Southern Italians love rich tomato sauces. The traditional Neapolitan tomato sauce is simple. Cooks combine fresh tomatoes with fried onions, larded filet of beef, and a sprig of basil. The mixture simmers in an earthenware pot for several hours to bring out all the flavors.

One popular Neapolitan dish is *stuffed lasagne*. Long, wide noodles are layered with cheeses and meats. Cheeses include ricotta, mozzarella, and grated Parmesan. The filling may contain pieces of sausage, minced pork, strips of ham, and hard-cooked egg slices. A thick tomato sauce is poured over the mixture, and the lasagne is baked until bubbly.

Quanthem/Shutterstock.com

Figure 32.12   Panforte is often served during Italian holidays.

Tomatoes and mozzarella cheese are two of Southern Italy's major agricultural products. They are also key ingredients in the popular Neapolitan dish called *pizza*. The Italians make many kinds of pizza. Most pizzas contain tomato sauce, cheese, and a crust made from yeast dough. Sausage, anchovies, mushrooms, green peppers, olives, and other ingredients are optional.

Other Southern Italian specialties feature vegetables. *Soffritti* are lightly fried onions and other vegetables mixed with a small amount of meat. *Eggplant Napoli* is eggplant layered with tomato sauce and cheese. *Zucchini Parmesan* is sliced zucchini and cubed tomatoes tossed with Parmesan cheese.

Italian Meals

Like many Europeans, Italians typically eat a light breakfast and a hearty noon meal. The noon meal is the largest meal of the day, and people usually eat it at home.

The well-known **antipasto** is an appetizer course that often begins the meal. Foods in an antipasto may include salami, Parma ham, anchovies, and hard-cooked eggs. Celery, radishes, pickled beets, black olives, marinated red peppers, and stuffed tomatoes are popular antipasto foods, too. Regardless of the selection of foods, the tray must have both color and taste appeal.

Minestra may follow or replace the antipasto at the start of a meal. Each region has its favorite soups. One common soup is *pasta in brodo*, which is a simple broth with pasta.

A main course of a meat, poultry, or fish dish usually follows the soup. Italians often roast their meat, and lamb is particularly popular when roasted. Poultry often is served in a sauce, whereas fish is baked or broiled. (If meat is too costly, a large serving of pasta may replace the main dish. Pasta is usually served with a sauce containing small pieces of meat or fish.) A vegetable or salad usually accompanies the main dish. Salads always contain tomatoes and other vegetables. Fruit and cheese end a typical meal. Italians reserve fancier desserts for special occasions.

The evening meal usually is light. Soup, omelets, and risottos are popular supper dishes. Bread, wine, and a simple fruit dessert complete the meal.

Italian Menu

Antipasto
(Appetizers)

Minestrone
(Vegetable Soup)

Pollo alla Cacciatora
(Chicken Hunter-Style)

Fettuccine Verde
(Green Noodles)

Panne
(Italian Bread)

Spumoni
(Three-Flavored Ice Cream)

Caffe Espresso
(Rich Coffee)

Antipasto
(Appetizers)

Many different foods can appear in an antipasto. Regardless of the number of types of foods chosen, however, all antipasto ingredients should be attractively arranged on the serving platter. The following foods frequently are part of an antipasto:

anchovy fillets
artichoke hearts
black olives
celery hearts
finocchio (Italian celery)
pepperoncini (small green peppers pickled in
     vinegar)
prosciutto (smoky-flavored Italian ham)
provolone cheese
radishes
salami
sautéed cold mushrooms marinated in vinegar and oil
sliced hard-cooked eggs
sliced tomatoes
sweet red peppers

Minestrone
(Vegetable Soup)
Serves 4

1	tablespoon olive oil
½	cup chopped onion
1	clove garlic, minced
½	teaspoon oregano
⅛	teaspoon pepper
1	cup canned low-sodium Italian peeled tomatoes
1	rib celery, cut into 1-inch pieces
2	tablespoons chopped parsley, plus additional for garnish
1	cup canned chickpeas, drained and rinsed
½	cup cubed zucchini
½	cup fresh or thoroughly defrosted frozen peas
½	cup diced carrots
½	cup chopped cabbage
4	cups low-sodium chicken broth
¼	cup uncooked white rice or orzo pasta
¼	cup grated Parmesan cheese

1. Heat olive oil in a large pot. Add onion and garlic and sauté until vegetables are translucent, stirring occasionally. Add oregano and pepper; sauté another 30 seconds.
2. Add tomatoes, onion, celery, 2 tablespoons parsley, chickpeas, zucchini, peas, carrots, cabbage, broth, and rice or pasta; simmer 20 to 25 minutes or until vegetables and rice or pasta are tender.

3. Before serving, taste soup and adjust seasonings if needed. Pour soup into large tureen or individual soup bowls. Pass bowls of grated Parmesan cheese and chopped parsley separately.

Per serving: 256 calories (28% from fat), 14 g protein, 35 g carbohydrate, 8 g fat, 4 mg cholesterol, 7 g fiber, 289 mg sodium.

Pollo alla Cacciatora
(Chicken Hunter-Style)
Serves 4

½	cup all-purpose flour
½	teaspoon salt
¼	teaspoon pepper
1	cut-up chicken, skin removed
2	tablespoons olive oil
1	medium onion, chopped
1	clove garlic, finely minced
1	cup canned whole tomatoes, low sodium
1	cup sliced green pepper
1½	cups sliced mushrooms

1. Combine flour, salt, and pepper. Coat chicken pieces with seasoned flour.
2. In a large skillet, heat oil over medium-high heat until hot but not smoking. Add chicken pieces a few at a time; fry until golden brown, about 3 or 4 minutes per side.
3. Add onions, garlic, tomatoes, green peppers, and mushrooms to skillet. Cover skillet and simmer chicken slowly until tender, about 20 to 25 minutes.
4. Use a food thermometer to be sure the chicken pieces have reached an internal temperature of 165°F. Taste; add additional seasonings if needed. Serve immediately.

Per serving: 295 calories (40% from fat), 30 g protein, 13 g carbohydrate, 13 g fat, 124 mg cholesterol, 2 g fiber, 251 mg sodium.

Fettuccine Verde
(Green Noodles)
Serves 4

1	package frozen chopped spinach, 10 ounces
1	egg
1	cup all-purpose flour
¼	teaspoon salt
4 to 6	quarts water
1	tablespoon butter, softened

1. In a medium saucepan, cook spinach in a small amount of simmering salted water until tender. Drain well and squeeze as dry as possible.
2. Process spinach in a food processor until finely chopped but not liquefied. Add egg to the food processor and process until combined. Then add flour and salt and process until dough begins to come together, about 20 seconds.
3. Turn dough out onto a floured surface and knead until smooth and no longer sticky, adding additional flour if needed.
4. Roll dough into a rectangle about ⅛ inch thick. Cover with a damp towel and let rest for 30 minutes.
5. Starting at the narrow end closest to you, fold dough over and over until it is about 3 inches wide. Using a sharp knife, cut folded dough into very thin strips, about ¼ inch wide.
6. Unroll strips on a cooling rack and allow to dry. If cooking immediately, dry noodles until no longer sticky, about 20 to 30 minutes. If noodles will be stored before cooking, dry 2 to 3 hours or overnight until completely dry. (For faster drying, dry on a tray in a 200°F oven.)
7. When ready to cook, bring water to a boil in a large pot. Add noodles and simmer until tender, about 5 to 7 minutes. Drain well. Toss with butter and serve immediately.

Per serving: 174 calories (26% from fat), 7 g protein, 27 g carbohydrate, 5 g fat, 61 mg cholesterol, 3 g fiber, 242 mg sodium.

Panne
(Italian Bread)
Makes 1 loaf

2¼ to 2¾	cups all-purpose flour
1½	teaspoons sugar
¾	teaspoon salt
1	envelope active dry yeast
1½	teaspoons softened butter
⅞	cup very warm water (120°F to 130°F)
	cornmeal
	olive oil
1	egg white
1	tablespoon cold water

1. In a large mixing bowl, combine ¾ cup flour, sugar, salt, and dry yeast on low speed of electric mixer. Work in butter. Then gradually add warm water and beat 2 minutes on medium speed, scraping bowl occasionally.
2. Add ½ cup flour and beat 2 more minutes on high speed. Stir in enough additional flour to make a stiff dough.
3. Turn dough out onto a lightly floured surface. Knead until smooth and elastic, about 8 to 10 minutes.
4. Place dough in a greased bowl and turn once to grease top. Cover with plastic wrap and a clean towel and let rest 20 minutes.
5. Using a rolling pin, roll dough into an oblong. Beginning at a wide end, tightly roll dough by hand like a jelly roll and seal edges well to shape it into a long loaf.
6. Place the loaf on a lightly greased baking sheet that has been sprinkled with cornmeal. Brush the loaf lightly with olive oil and cover it with plastic wrap. Refrigerate dough 2 to 24 hours.
7. When ready to bake, remove dough from refrigerator. Uncover dough carefully and let stand at room temperature for 10 minutes. Meanwhile, preheat oven to 425°F.
8. Slash loaf diagonally 4 to 5 times with a sharp knife. Bake for 20 minutes.
9. Remove bread from the oven and brush it with beaten egg white mixed with water.
10. Return bread to the oven and bake an additional 5 to 10 minutes or until loaf is golden brown and sounds hollow when tapped with the knuckles. Remove to cooling rack.

Per slice: 73 calories (8% from fat), 2 g protein, 14 g carbohydrate, 1 g fat, 1 mg cholesterol, 1 g fiber, 106 mg sodium.

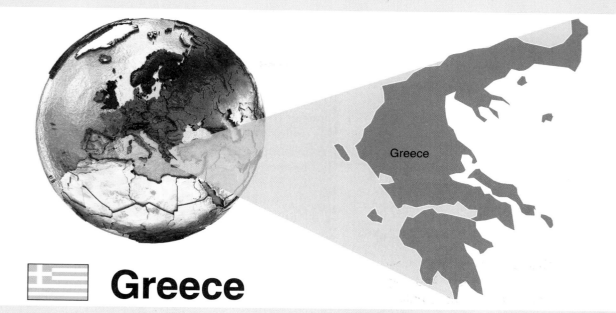

Greece

Greece is a land of terraced gardens, busy seaports, and ancient temples. In this sunny land, the art, literature, science, and philosophy that form the basis of Western civilization began. Parts of Greek culture, such as some Greek foods, have their roots in the older civilizations of the Middle East. The foods moussaka and baklava are examples.

Geography and Climate of Greece

Greece forms the southern tip of Europe's Balkan Peninsula. The country is made up of one large landmass and many islands.

The geography of Greece is varied. Mountain ridges form the jagged coastline. To the east lie Mount Olympus and another strip of mountains separated by fertile valleys. The mountainous land with its stony, dry soil makes farming difficult. Olive trees and grapevines, with their deep roots, can be cultivated in this terrain, however. Sheep also thrive on the short grasses of the more mountainous areas (**Figure 32.13**).

Greece has mild winters and warm, sunny summers. Rainfall rarely exceeds 20 inches (50 centimeters) per year, and most of the rain falls in the winter. Because Greece has little or no frost, subtropical fruits and flowers can be grown.

Greek Agriculture

Nearly three-fourths of the Greek population lives in urban areas. The people of Greece share a common language, Greek, and a common religion. The majority of Greeks belong to the Greek Orthodox Church.

Greece does not have a wealth of natural resources, and the country has faced a number of economic struggles. Despite the lack of fertile

Paul Cowan/Shutterstock.com

Figure 32.13 Greece's terrain is suitable for raising sheep, making lamb the country's favorite meat. What are some Greek dishes that use lamb?

farmland, however, Greek farmers grow wheat and corn on small acreages. They raise vegetables in terraced gardens. Grapes, olives, and citrus fruits grow in more fertile areas. Goats and sheep, which graze in the mountains, provide milk, cheese, and meat. The Greek government has encouraged agricultural development; however, agriculture makes up only a small part of Greece's economy.

Greek Culture

The Greek people are skilled *mariners* (seafarers), and Greek ships carry cargo to ports all

Culture and Social Studies

Ancient Greece

Greek history spans centuries. The period between 800 and 330 BC saw the flourishing of the civilization known as *Ancient Greece*. Ancient Greece, sometimes called *Classical Greece*, was marked by significant achievements in art, literature, science, and philosophy. The philosophers Socrates, Aristotle, and Plato and the jurist Solon were products of Ancient Greece. The playwrights Sophocles, Aristophanes, and Euripides and the scientist Hippocrates were from this culture, too. This is also the era that produced examples of classical architecture, such as the Parthenon in Athens.

Ancient Greece was divided into *city-states*. These were self-governing political units that each consisted of a city and surrounding territory. Although Ancient Greece never became unified, two of the city-states, Athens and Sparta, became seats of power. Athens was democratic, and the Athenians originated the basic concepts of Western law. Sparta, on the other hand, was not democratic. Spartans lived a strict, military life with stern laws. The Spartan ideal was individual sacrifice for community welfare.

These city-states eventually fell to the Roman Empire. After the seat of the Roman government moved to Constantinople, Greece became less of a world power.

over the world. Fishing is an important industry on the islands and in coastal areas. Much of the seafood that is caught is eaten in Greece. Some is also exported along with olive oil and raisins.

In small communities, **tavernas** are cafés that serve as public meeting places. Guests who gather in tavernas often order glasses of retsina or ouzo. (*Retsina* is a resin-flavored wine. *Ouzo* is a strong spirit with the flavor of anise.) Often, someone will play a mandolin-like instrument called a *bouzoukia* while the other guests talk, play games, or dance.

Religious holidays hold great importance in Greece. People devote much time and energy to their celebration. Many of these celebrations involve special food traditions (**Figure 32.14**).

The year of Greek celebrations begins with Saint Basil's Day, which is also New Year's Day. On this day (rather than on Christmas), Greek people exchange gifts. Children receive a Saint Basil's cake, which is covered with almonds and walnuts and has a coin baked inside. Eating something sweet on New Year's Day is believed to bring a sweet year.

Easter is the most important religious holiday in Greece. A seven-week fast characterizes the Lenten season that precedes Easter. The

Anastasios71/Shutterstock.com

Figure 32.14 One traditional Greek holiday food is the *melamakarono*, a dessert made with olive oil, flour, and honey.

fast is broken on Holy Saturday (the day before Easter) with a dish called *mayeritsa*. This is the internal organs of a lamb cooked in a seasoned broth. After midnight on Holy Saturday, people watch displays of fireworks. Then early the next morning, the rest of the lamb is roasted whole and served for Easter dinner.

Each village and town in Greece has a patron saint. The feast day for the local patron saint is a holiday. On the feast day and the evening before, people go to a church service. Then the feast day is celebrated with food, wine, singing, and dancing. Some people wear traditional Greek clothes for the celebration.

Many Greek towns also hold annual harvest festivals. For example, the town of Megara has a fish festival in the spring.

Greek Cuisine

For thousands of years, the Greeks have been developing their cuisine. Early records show that the Greeks cooked foods while the rest of the world ate raw foods. Early Greek foods included roast lamb with capers, wild rice with saffron, and honey cakes. As Greek civilization spread throughout the Mediterranean, so did Greek cuisine. The Greeks taught the Romans how to cook, and a Greek named Hesiod wrote one of the first cookbooks.

Greek cooking has a rich, varied past. A pre-Greek people living in the Stone Age brought foods like lamb and beans to Greece. Other foods, like olives, grapes, and seafood, are native to the area. Invading groups of peoples added their food customs to these native foods. The many Greek pasta dishes, for example, are Italian in origin. Layers of pasta, ground lamb, and cheese covered with a rich custard and baked is called *pastitsio*. Kebabs, yogurt, Greek coffee, and rich sweet pastries are Turkish in origin. (*Kebabs* are pieces of meat, poultry, fish, vegetables, or fruits threaded onto skewers and broiled.)

Greek Staple Foods

A number of foods are basic to Greek cooking. Greek cooks make liberal use of lemon juice, tomatoes, and green peppers. **Avgolemono**, one of the most popular Greek sauces, is a

mixture of egg yolks and lemon juice. The Greeks use it to flavor soups and stews. They serve it with vegetables and fish, too. Greek cooks stuff tomatoes and green peppers with meat and other vegetables. They also thread meat and vegetables on skewers, broil them, and add them to soups and stews. Tomato sauces are used with both meat and fish dishes.

Greek cooks use many herbs and spices to bring out the natural flavors of lamb, fish, and vegetables. The most widely used herbs and spices include cinnamon, basil, dill, bay leaves, garlic, and oregano.

The Greeks serve eggplant as a side dish or add it to main dishes. Cooks prepare *moussaka* by layering slices of eggplant, ground lamb, and cheese. (They often cook the lamb with tomato paste, wine, cinnamon, and onion.) They pour a rich cream sauce over the meat, vegetable, and cheese mixture before baking.

Learn About...

Greek Olives

Olives grow in abundance in Greece. Their many sizes, shapes, and colors often amaze people from the United States. Olives are naturally bitter and must be cured to make their flavors more appealing.

People throughout Greece eat olives as appetizers and snacks or add them to other dishes. Olives marinated with oregano, garlic, and lemon juice are a simple appetizer. *Pasta elias* is a delicious spread made from olives blended with olive oil, vinegar, and garlic; it is usually served with bread. The popular *horiatiki salata* is a salad that contains olives, a variety of greens, tomatoes, and feta cheese.

Olive oil is produced by crushing olives into a pulp and then squeezing the oil out of them. The flavor of olive oil dominates Greek cuisine. It is used as a cooking oil and as an ingredient that adds distinctive flavor to dressings, marinades, and other foods.

Know and Apply

1. What varieties of olives have you tasted?
2. What type of oil do you choose most often for cooking?

Lamb

Sheep have been raised in Greece since prehistoric times. Greek cooks roast lamb whole or thread it onto skewers and broil it. They also grind and layer it with other ingredients in casseroles. They use lamb as a filling for vegetables and add it to soups and stews, too.

Seafood

Because of Greece's location, seafood is an important part of the Greek diet. Fishers catch red mullet, crawfish, cuttlefish, sea bass, red snapper, swordfish, squid, and shrimp in the Mediterranean Sea.

Greek cooks prepare freshly caught seafood simply, usually by baking or broiling. They often bake fresh vegetables, such as tomatoes and zucchini, with the fish. Squid is particularly popular. Fresh squid stuffed with rice, onions, nuts, and seasonings is poached and served as a favorite main dish. Raw squid, served with raw green beans or artichokes, is eaten as an appetizer. Another popular appetizer or snack is *taramasalata*, a pâté made from fish roe (eggs). See **Figure 32.15**.

Honey

Greek honey is world famous. In Ancient Greece, people used honey to make *melamakarona* (honey cakes), which they offered as gifts to the gods. Today, Greek bakers prepare the same honey cakes to celebrate the New Year. Honey is the basic sweetener used in the preparation of many Greek desserts, pastries, and cakes.

Although the Greeks enjoy sweets, they usually serve sweets only on special occasions. The Greeks make many of their desserts with **phyllo**, a paper-thin pastry made with flour and water. Some Greek cooks still make phyllo; others prefer to buy sheets of phyllo ready-made. **Baklava**, a traditional Greek dessert, is made of thin layers of phyllo that are filled with nuts and soaked with a honey syrup. *Galaktoboureko* is phyllo layered with rich custard and honey. *Kopenhai* is a nut cake with phyllo.

Other popular sweets contain flour, eggs, and oil rather than phyllo. These sweets are deep-fried and are similar to fritters. *Diples*, for example, are small thin sheets of dough that are rolled with two forks as they are fried. They may be coated with a honey and nut syrup that is flavored with cinnamon.

Greek Meals

The Greeks appreciate simple pleasures. Their meals reflect this simplicity. Breakfast is often no more than a slice of dry bread and a cup of warm milk. Sometimes, eggs or cheese accompany the bread. Both lunch and dinner are hot meals. The Greeks eat lunch at noon and dinner late in the evening.

Early evening is generally the most pleasant and enjoyable time of day. Many Greek families go for an evening walk. Some choose to sit at small outdoor cafés and enjoy a variety of appetizers called **mezedhes**. Olives, feta cheese, pistachio nuts, garlic-flavored sausage, shrimp, and hard-cooked eggs are popular mezedhes (**Figure 32.16**). (*Feta cheese* is a slightly salty, crumbly, white cheese made from goat's milk.) Ouzo and conversation accompany this early snack.

Later, families gather at home for the evening meal. This meal might include either baked or broiled fish, a vegetable, and bread. Fresh fruit would complete the meal.

Studiovd/Shutterstock.com

Figure 32.15 Taramasalata is made from salted and cured fish eggs, combined with lemon juice, olive oil, potatoes or bread, and sometimes almonds.

Christian Jung/Shutterstock.com

Figure 32.16 Pistachios might be enjoyed as an evening snack by patrons of a local café in a Greek village. How do Greek meal patterns differ from meal patterns in the United States?

1. In a large saucepan, bring chicken broth and rice to a boil. Reduce heat, cover, and simmer until rice is tender, about 15 minutes.
2. Pour the contents of the saucepan through a strainer, catching excess broth in a large liquid measuring cup. Set rice and broth aside.
3. Put eggs and lemon juice into a blender container. Cover and blend at high speed until frothy. Then remove the center cap from the blender cover and slowly pour the hot broth into the egg mixture while blending at low speed.
4. Pour the soup into the saucepan; add the cooked rice. Cook over low heat until thoroughly heated and slightly thickened. Do not allow soup to boil.
5. Season soup with salt and pepper. Serve immediately garnished with parsley.

Per serving: 174 calories (31% from fat), 12 g protein, 19 g carbohydrate, 6 g fat, 110 mg cholesterol, 0 g fiber, 144 mg sodium.

Greek Menu

Soupa Avgolemono
(Egg-Lemon Soup)

Moussaka
(Baked Eggplant and Lamb with Cream Sauce)

Horiatiki Salata
(Greek Salad)

Psomi
(Greek Bread)

Yiaourti me Meli
(Greek Yogurt with Honey)

Kafés
(Greek Coffee)

Soupa Avgolemono
(Egg-Lemon Soup)

Serves 4 to 6

6	cups low-sodium chicken broth
⅓	cup uncooked white rice
2	eggs
2	tablespoons lemon juice
	salt
	pepper
	finely chopped parsley

Moussaka
(Baked Eggplant and Lamb with Cream Sauce)

Serves 6

1½	medium eggplants, peeled and sliced
1¾	teaspoons salt, divided
1	pound ground lamb
1	cup chopped onion
1	tablespoon tomato paste
¼	cup tomato sauce
2	tablespoons chopped parsley
1	dash pepper
¼	cup water
1	dash cinnamon
⅜	cup grated Parmesan cheese, divided
¼	cup bread crumbs, divided
1½	tablespoons all-purpose flour
1½	cups fat-free milk
1	dash nutmeg
2	egg yolks, lightly beaten
1	tablespoon olive oil

1. Use 1½ teaspoons salt to sprinkle both sides of eggplant slices. Place salted slices in a colander while browning meat and making sauce.

2. In a large skillet, sauté ground lamb and onion until meat is browned. Add tomato paste, tomato sauce, parsley, ¼ teaspoon salt, pepper, and water. Simmer until liquid is absorbed; cool.

3. Stir cinnamon, ¼ cup Parmesan cheese, and 2 tablespoons of the bread crumbs into meat mixture. Set aside.

4. Combine flour and milk in a covered jar or blender container. Shake or blend until smooth. Pour milk mixture into a heavy saucepan. Cook over medium heat, stirring constantly until sauce comes to a boil. Cook and stir for one additional minute until sauce is thick and smooth; add nutmeg.

5. Stir a little of the hot sauce into beaten egg yolks, then stir egg mixture back into the sauce and cook over very low heat for 2 minutes, stirring constantly. Set aside.

6. Preheat oven to 375°F.

7. Rinse the eggplant slices and pat dry with paper towels.

8. In a large skillet, heat oil. Brown the eggplant slices on both sides.

9. Grease an 8-inch square pan and sprinkle the bottom with the remaining 2 tablespoons of bread crumbs. Cover with a layer of eggplant slices. Spread the meat mixture over the eggplant. Place another layer of eggplant slices on top of the meat.

10. Pour the sauce over the eggplant and meat; sprinkle with remaining 2 tablespoons of grated cheese. Bake until hot and bubbly, about 25 to 30 minutes.

Per serving: 300 calories (48% from fat), 21 g protein, 18 g carbohydrate, 16 g fat, 126 mg cholesterol, 4 g fiber, 273 mg sodium.

Horiatiki Salata (Greek Salad)

Serves 6

6	cups assorted salad greens
3	medium tomatoes, washed and cut into wedges
½	medium red onion, sliced into rings
1	medium cucumber, washed and sliced thinly
⅓	cup olive oil
2	tablespoons lemon juice or red wine vinegar
	few dashes salt and pepper

1½	ounces feta cheese, crumbled
6	whole pitted ripe olives, preferably Kalamata dried oregano

1. Wash greens and pat dry.

2. In a large salad bowl, combine greens with tomatoes, onions, and cucumber.

3. In a small bowl, whisk together olive oil, lemon juice or wine vinegar, and salt and pepper to taste. Toss dressing with greens mixture.

4. Sprinkle crumbled cheese over salad in a ring. Arrange olives inside the ring of cheese. Sprinkle oregano over salad and serve.

Per serving: 178 calories (76% from fat), 4 g protein, 9 g carbohydrate, 15 g fat, 10 mg cholesterol, 3 g fiber, 474 mg sodium.

B.and E. Dudzinscy/Shutterstock.com

The Greek salad is a colorful representation of healthy Mediterranean eating.

Psomi
(Greek Bread)
Makes 1 loaf

1¾ to 2¼ cups all-purpose flour
1   package active dry yeast
⅔   cup fat-free milk
1   tablespoon honey
2   teaspoons shortening
¾   teaspoon salt
1   tablespoon butter, melted
1   tablespoon sesame seeds

1. In a large mixing bowl, combine ¾ cup flour and yeast.
2. Combine milk, honey, shortening, and salt in a saucepan and heat until very warm (120°F to 130°F). (Shortening does not need to be completely melted.)
3. Add warm milk mixture to yeast and flour. Beat on low speed of electric mixer 30 seconds, scraping the sides of the bowl often. Beat an additional 3 minutes at high speed. Add enough additional flour to make a soft dough.
4. Turn dough out onto lightly floured surface and knead until smooth and elastic (about 8 to 10 minutes).
5. Place dough in a lightly greased bowl, turning once to grease top. Cover with a clean towel and let rise in a warm place until doubled in bulk (about 1½ hours).
6. Punch dough down and shape into a round loaf. Place the loaf on a lightly greased baking sheet. Brush the top with melted butter and sprinkle with sesame seeds. Cover with a clean towel and let rise in a warm place until almost doubled in bulk (about 1 hour).
7. Bake loaf at 375°F until it is golden brown and sounds hollow when gently tapped with the knuckles. Remove bread to a cooling rack and cool thoroughly before storing.

Per slice: 72 calories (13% from fat), 2 g protein, 12 g carbohydrate, 1 g fat, 2 mg cholesterol, 1 g fiber, 102 mg sodium.

Yiaourti me Meli
(Greek Yogurt with Honey)
Serves 4

¼   cup coarsely chopped walnuts
½   teaspoon vegetable oil
½   teaspoon vanilla extract
2   cups plain Greek nonfat yogurt
¼   cup honey
¼   teaspoon cinnamon

1. Spread chopped walnuts in a glass pie plate. Drizzle the nuts with vegetable oil and toss with a fork to coat.
2. Microwave the walnuts for 1 minute on high power; stir with the fork. Continue microwaving the walnuts on high power, stirring every 30 seconds, until they are toasted, about 3 minutes total. Set aside to cool.
3. Stir vanilla extract into Greek yogurt.
4. Spoon ½ cup yogurt into each of four dessert dishes. Drizzle 1 tablespoon of honey over the yogurt in each dish. Top each dish with 1 tablespoon of toasted walnuts and a sprinkle of cinnamon.

Per serving: 193 calories (28% from fat), 14 g protein, 24 g carbohydrate, 6 g fat, 2 mg cholesterol, 1 g fiber, 59 mg sodium.

Chapter 32 Review and Expand

Summary

The mild climate of the Mediterranean is favorable for the growth of fruits and vegetables. These foods, along with fish from the sea, appear in a variety of dishes throughout Spain, Italy, and Greece.

Spanish cuisine is simple and colorful, focusing on natural flavors. Spaniards enjoy tapas, and attractive salads and flavorful soups are popular throughout Spain. Main dishes such as cocido and paella include a variety of ingredients cooked together.

Italy was the center of the Roman Empire, and the foods of Italy are as notable as its cultural heritage. Italian cuisine focuses on fresh fruits and vegetables, seasonings, and range-top cooking methods. The cuisines of Italy have distinct features. In Northern Italy, foods are cooked in butter, and homemade, ribbon-shaped pastas are popular. Central Italy is known for roasted lamb, cheese-cake, grilled meats, and bean dishes. In Southern Italy, cooks use olive oil and tubular pastas.

Greek cuisine has been evolving for centuries. Staple foods of the Greek diet include lamb, seafood, olives, and honey. Lemon juice, tomatoes, green peppers, garlic, and eggplant also appear in many Greek dishes.

Vocabulary Activities

1. **Content Terms**   With a partner, choose two words from the following list to compare. Create a Venn diagram to compare your words and identify differences. Write one term under the left circle and the other term under the right. Where the circles overlap, write three characteristics the terms have in common. For each term, write a difference of the term for each characteristic in its respective outer circle.

   del pueblo   antipasto
   tapas   taverna
   gazpacho   avgolemono
   chorizo   phyllo
   paella   baklava
   risotto   mezedhes
   minestrone

2. **Academic Terms**   Read the text passages that contain each of the following terms. Then write the definitions of each term in your own words. Double-check your definitions by re-reading the text and using the text glossary.

   balmy   amateur
   marvel   hock
   amicability   mariner

Review

Write your answers using complete sentences when appropriate.

3. What are three healthy characteristics of Mediterranean dietary patterns?

4. Name three culinary advances the Moors made to Spanish cuisine.

5. What do Spaniards call the appetizers they often serve at the beginning of a meal?

6. What is the best known pork product from Spain?

7. What is the first meal of the day in Spain?

8. Identify two agricultural products for each of Italy's three geographic regions.

9. Why is Italian cuisine known as the "mother cuisine"?

10. Describe three ways Italians may serve pasta.

11. What is the preferred cooking fat of Southern Italian cooks?

12. List the courses that would make up a typical noon meal in Italy. Give an example of a food that might be served for each course.

13. What holiday do Greek people celebrate on January 1st, and what food tradition is associated with this day?

14. Name four of the most widely used herbs and spices in Greek cuisine.

15. What is the basic sweetener used in the preparation of many Greek desserts, pastries, and cakes?

Chapter 32 Review and Expand

Core Skills

16. **Research, Technology, Speaking** Go to a weather information website to find average high and low temperatures for each month for a specific Mediterranean location. Use software to create a line chart of your data. Share your chart in class.

17. **Research, Reading, Writing** Use reliable print or online resources to research the similarities and differences between Spanish and Mexican cuisines. Summarize your findings in a two-page written report. Cite your resources and edit your report for spelling, grammar, and organization.

18. **Research, Speaking** Conduct research to prepare a time line illustrating major events in Italian history from the rise of the Roman Empire to the present. Explain to the class why one of the events was significant in shaping future events in Italy. Also describe any international impact the event may have had.

19. **Math** Suppose a school organization wants to hold a spaghetti dinner as a fund-raiser. Find a spaghetti-sauce recipe and calculate the amounts of ingredients that would be needed to serve 250 people. Visit a grocery store or go online to get prices for all the ingredients. Calculate the cost of preparing the sauce for the fund-raiser. Assume the sauce accounts for 15 percent of the total cost of the dinner. Calculate what the ticket price for the event should be in order to allow the organization to generate 100-percent profit.

20. **Career Readiness Practice** Suppose that you and your work team are in charge of the monthly *Health & Wellness Lunch and Learn* meeting for your employer. The focus of this month's meeting will be on the Mediterranean dietary pattern. Assign each of your team members to research one of the following food groups in Mediterranean eating: fruits, vegetables, grains, protein foods (including nuts), and dairy. Also research healthful oils and fats common to Mediterranean dietary patterns. Have each team member research and compare typical daily intakes of his or her assigned food group for a Mediterra-nean dietary pattern and for a typical dietary pattern in the United States. Each should also compare the health benefits of the Mediterranean levels of intake over levels in the United States for his or her food group. As team leader, your responsibility will be to locate images of healthful examples of foods for each food group. Use presentation software to combine the information in an illustrated report for the *Lunch and Learn* meeting. Prepare an illustrated fact sheet based on your presentation to give to the meeting attendees.

Critical Thinking and Problem Solving

21. **Analyze** Working in lab groups, research and prepare a regional version of paella. Each group should choose a different version. Serve all the paellas buffet-style. Analyze the major differences that are apparent among the dishes.

22. **Create** Make a map of Italy showing the three main culinary regions. Use icons to illustrate the chief agricultural products of each region. Be sure to include a key identifying the meaning of each icon. Attach a recipe for an Italian regional specialty dish to your map. Highlight the use of locally produced ingredients in the recipe.

23. **Create** Divide the class into four groups and turn your classroom into a Greek taverna. One group should find appropriate music and learn a traditional Greek dance to teach the rest of the class. One group should be responsible for decorations. One group should learn a few Greek games to teach the rest of the class. The fourth group should choose a menu of Greek appetizers and find recipes to distribute. Each group should prepare one of the appetizer recipes.

Chapter 33
Middle East and Africa

James Michael Dorsey/Shutterstock.com

Content Terms

haram	shohet
halal	milchig
pita bread	fleishig
bulgur	pareve
mazza	falafel
chelo kebab	cacao
kibbutz	injera
matzo	teff
kashrut	wat
kosher	

Objectives

After studying this chapter, you will be able to

- **describe** the food customs of the Middle East, Israel, and Africa;
- **discuss** how geography, climate, and culture have influenced these customs; and
- **prepare** foods that are native to each of these countries or regions.

Academic Terms

dialect	taboo
barren	cloven
bazaar	savanna
abstain	humus
caravan	illiterate

Reading Prep

Skim the Review questions at the end of the chapter first. Use them to help you focus on the most important concepts as you read the chapter.

The Middle East and Africa are regions that cover a large area. These regions are home to several races and many nationalities of people who speak a number of major languages and hundreds of *dialects* (forms of a language spoken in different areas). Geographical features in the Middle East and Africa vary widely. In Egypt, a hot, dry, sandy desert stretches for miles. In Eastern Africa, rugged, snowcapped mountains rise above the arid plains. Along the equator, tropical rain forests boast lush vegetation.

Middle Eastern and African climates limit the types of foods that are available in each country. Strict religious doctrines also restrict the foods that many Middle Eastern and African people can eat. These factors have caused a number of distinct cuisines to emerge in these regions.

As a whole, cooking styles in the Middle East and Africa vary. There are, however, some similarities in foods from this part of the world. For instance, many foods eaten in Israel originated in other Middle Eastern countries and in parts of Africa (**Figure 33.1**). The cuisines of the Middle East and Africa are also generally nutritious. Cooks in the Middle East and Africa use only limited amounts of meat. Instead, a starchy food, such as cassava, rice, plantains, or some type of bread, accompanies every meal. Meals also include a wide variety of vegetables and fruits. These mealtime staples are rich in complex carbohydrates, vitamins, minerals, and fiber. Because frying is a favored cooking method, some dishes can be high in fat; however, many foods are prepared by low-fat cooking methods, such as broiling and stewing. By practicing balance when planning menus, all Middle Eastern and African foods can fit into a healthy diet.

As you read about these regions, you will become more familiar with their cultures, climates, and customs. You will begin to identify differences and similarities in their cuisines.

Learn About...

Religion in the Middle East

More than 90 percent of people living in the Middle East practice the same religion. This religion is *Islam*, and those people who follow it are called *Muslims*. Islam is based on the teachings of the prophet Muhammad. Islam greatly affects the lifestyles and food choices of Muslim people.

Muslims read and follow a book of sacred Islamic writings known as the *Koran*. The Koran specifies foods Muslims should and should not eat. It forbids the eating of animals that have died from disease, strangulation, or beating. Only animals that have been slaughtered by a proper ritual are considered edible. The Koran also forbids Muslims from eating pork and drinking wine and other alcoholic beverages.

Know and Apply

1. What is the term used to identify foods that are permitted according to the Islamic religion?

2. Give an example of a dietary restriction associated with another religion.

Figure 33.1 Shakshuka, an Israeli dish with eggs and tomatoes, has North African origins.

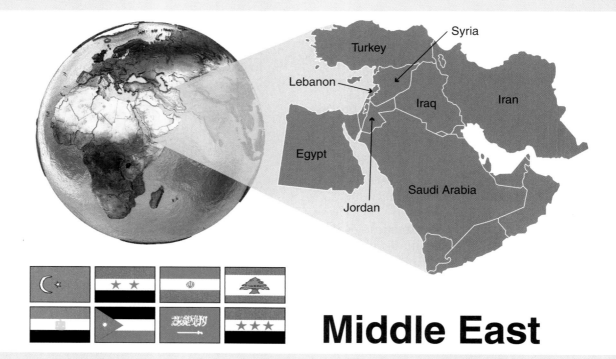

Middle East

The Middle East is a horseshoe-shaped region that spans from the eastern edge of the Mediterranean Sea to North Africa. This land is sometimes known as the "cradle of civilization." Christianity, Judaism, and Islam all began in this region. The Middle East is also where the Byzantine, Persian, Arab, and Ottoman Empires flourished.

The exact boundaries of the Middle East are sometimes disputed, but the countries of Iran, Iraq, Syria, Lebanon, Jordan, Egypt, and Saudi Arabia form the region's center. (Israel is also part of the Middle East, but because its cuisine has unique qualities, Israel will be discussed separately.) Turkey, which lies just to the north and east, shares some culinary characteristics with its Middle Eastern neighbors.

Geography and Climate of the Middle East

Mountains, high plateaus, and deserts are important geographical features of the Middle East. Much land in the Middle East is arid and *barren* (not agriculturally productive); however, fertile oases are scattered throughout the region.

Seven major bodies of water border the nations that form the core of the Middle East.

Three of the world's most famous rivers—the Nile, Tigris, and Euphrates—are in this region. The lands along the banks of these rivers are among the world's most fertile. Coastal lands and inland mountain valleys are also excellent farming areas.

Rainfall varies in the Middle East. Areas in Southern Egypt may not have rain for 10 to 20 years. On the other hand, some coastal regions may have 20 to 30 inches (50 to 70 centimeters) of rain during one season. As a whole, much of the Middle East is hot and dry. As a result, irrigation is essential (**Figure 33.2**). When rain does fall, it is often so heavy that flooding occurs.

The climates in Middle Eastern regions along the Mediterranean coast are subtropical with warm, dry summers and mild, rainy winters. Mountain valleys have hot, dry summers and cool winters. Desert areas can have daytime temperatures above 100°F (38°C) and little, if any, rain.

Middle Eastern Agriculture

Today, many Middle Easterners make their living as farmers or herders. Sheep, goats, and camels graze on the short, stubby grasses of the arid regions. These cattle supply meat, milk (used

Ryan Ihle/Shutterstock.com

Figure 33.2 Irrigation, or the process of artificially supplying water, is vital to agriculture in barren Middle Eastern regions or regions without reliable rainfall. What irrigation methods are available today?

to make yogurt and cheese), and hides. Camels also serve as pack animals, helping Middle Easterners travel distances.

A variety of crops grow in areas where there are irrigation systems or where there is enough rain. Wheat and barley are the major grain crops. Corn also grows in some areas. Citrus fruits, Persian melons, olives, bananas, figs, grapes, and other fruits grow in the subtropical climate of the coastal regions. Other important food crops include sugar beets and rice. Many families also grow vegetables for home use on small plots of land.

Middle Eastern Culture

Visitors to the Middle East are often struck by the history of this region. Many cities in the Middle East have existed for thousands of years. Travelers are awed by ancient temples and ornate palaces, as well as by modern museums, hotels, and office buildings.

Walking the streets of a Middle Eastern city is a treat for the senses. *Bazaars*, or Middle Eastern marketplaces, are filled with colorful wares and fragrant spices. Tasting regional dishes from restaurants and cafés is not to be missed.

Tourists in the Middle East find the local people to be warm and friendly. Family is highly valued in this society. In fact, family contacts are often used to aid business dealings. Traditional aspects of life in the Middle East abound. It is

common, however, to see Western influence on consumer goods, housing, and fashion.

Ancient Empires of the Middle East

Much history in the Middle East centers around large empires that rose to power, weakened, and fell. The earliest of these was the highly advanced civilization of Ancient Egypt. As early as 3400 BC, the ancient Egyptians had an orderly government and a written language. They traded with other parts of the world and built great structures of stone (**Figure 33.3**).

Four more great Middle Eastern empires shaped the development of this region, beginning with the Persian Empire in 550 BC. Today, the country of Iran is all that remains of the once-mighty Persian Empire. The Byzantine Empire, which was formed when the Roman Empire split into East and West, also shaped the Middle East. The Byzantine Empire's headquarters were in Constantinople, which later became the capital of the Ottoman Empire. The third empire to shape the Middle East was the Arab Empire, which was formed by the followers of the prophet Muhammad. People in Middle Eastern countries where Islam is the primary faith still speak the Arabic language. Eventually, the Ottoman

Martin M303/Shutterstock.com

Figure 33.3 Magnificent stone structures and a complex system of written hieroglyphics are legacies of Ancient Egypt.

Turks combined parts of the Persian, Byzantine, and Arab empires to form the fourth empire that significantly shaped the Middle East—the Ottoman Empire. As a result of this empire, Turkish foods and customs are evident in many parts of the Middle East.

Middle Eastern Holidays

With a large Muslim population, it is not surprising that many Middle Eastern celebrations are Muslim holidays. Each country in the Middle East may have different names for and ways of celebrating these holidays.

The first month of the Muslim year is called *Muharram*. This is also the name given to the 10-day Muslim New Year Festival. The last day of this festival is another Muslim holiday called *Ashura*. This day commemorates the death of the Muslim martyr Husain, who was the grandson of the prophet Muhammad. It also celebrates the safe landing of Noah's Ark as described in Biblical and Koranic texts. On Ashura, Muslim people eat a pudding known as *Ashure* or *Noah's Pudding*. This pudding is made with dates, raisins, figs, and nuts and is modeled after the legendary pudding made by Noah's wife (**Figure 33.4**).

Another Muslim observance is the *Fast of Ramadan*. Ramadan is the ninth month of the Muslim calendar, and the fast lasts the entire month. Muslims are to **abstain** from (refrain from consuming) food and drink throughout the day. Each night they may break the fast. In some regions, the fast is broken with a light meal; in other areas, people feast during the night. *Eid al-Fitr* is a three-day celebration that marks the end of the Fast of Ramadan.

Another Muslim holiday is *Mawlid an-Nabi*. This is a nine-day celebration of the prophet Muhammad's birthday. Fairs, parades, and community feasting may be part of the observance.

Middle Eastern Cuisine

Middle Eastern cuisine, which is sometimes called *Eastern Mediterranean cuisine*, has been developing for centuries. It has been influenced by traders who crossed Middle Eastern deserts and by groups of people who conquered one

Feyyaz Alacam/Shutterstock.com

Figure 33.4 Recipes for Ashure vary by region and by family. This recipe for Ashure includes pomegranate seeds. Does your family have unique recipes for specific dishes?

another, exchanging and modifying recipes. As a result, it is often difficult to determine the exact origins of a particular Middle Eastern dish. Middle Eastern cuisine can be discussed in terms of foods found throughout the Middle East, Turkish foods, foods of the Arab States, and Iranian foods.

Foods Found Throughout the Middle East

Basic to all Middle Eastern cuisines are five ingredients: garlic, lemon, green pepper, eggplant, and tomato. These ingredients appear again and again in dishes served throughout the area. Both olives and olive oil are also common in Middle Eastern cuisine. Olives come in a variety of shapes, sizes, and colors. People eat them as appetizers and snacks and use olive oil in place of butter or lard for cooking. Fresh olive oil gives a distinct flavor to Middle Eastern foods.

Spice **caravans** (groups of travelers who sell goods) were once a common sight in the Middle East. Therefore, it is only natural that Middle Eastern cooks use spices liberally. Middle Eastern foods are not spicy hot. Instead, spices and herbs add delicate flavors to foods.

Middle Eastern Meats and Yogurt

Throughout the Middle East, there is a *taboo* (prohibition) against eating pork. Both Judaism and Islam forbid their followers to eat the meat of swine. Pork and other foods that are forbidden according to Islam are called **haram**. Foods considered lawful according to Islam are called **halal**.

In the Middle East, lamb is the staple meat. It is often roasted whole. Chunks of lamb may also be threaded on skewers and served as *shish kebabs* or added to hearty stews. Ground lamb is used to make dolmas. *Dolmas* are mixtures of ground meat and seasonings wrapped in grape leaves or stuffed into vegetables (**Figure 33.5**).

Middle Eastern yogurt is curdled milk with a tangy flavor. It is not at all like the yogurt eaten in the United States. People throughout the Middle East eat yogurt as a side dish, snack, and dessert. They also use it to make cakes and hot and cold soups. In some areas, people serve diluted yogurt as a beverage.

Middle Eastern Grains and Legumes

Wheat, rice, beans, lentils, and chickpeas are the staple grains and legumes of the Middle East. Middle Easterners use wheat flour to make bread. They serve bread at every meal and often buy it from the village baker twice a day. **Pita bread** is one type of bread found throughout the Middle East, as well as in Africa. It is a flat, round, hollow bread. When cut in half, each half of the bread opens like a pocket and can be filled with meat or vegetables.

Middle Eastern people also serve wheat as bulgur. **Bulgur** is a grain product made from whole wheat that has been cooked, dried, partly debranned, and cracked. Middle Easterners add bulgur to soups, stews, stuffings, and salads. They also serve it as a side dish with ground lamb.

Rice is as popular as bulgur; in Iran, it is even more popular. People in the Middle East often serve rice plain. They may also cook rice with tomato juice or saffron and make it into a seasoned rice dish called *pilav* (**Figure 33.6**).

Middle Eastern Desserts and Coffee

Middle Eastern people, as a group, enjoy sweets and rich desserts. They usually eat these foods as snacks or serve them on special holidays. They eat fruits at the end of most meals. Quince, pomegranates, figs, and melons are particularly popular.

People throughout most of the Middle East drink coffee. (Iran is an exception. There, tea is the main beverage.) All Middle Eastern coffees are strong, but coffee can be prepared in several ways. People who make *khave* (Turkish-style

Ramilya Bogens/Shutterstock.com

Figure 33.5 Dolmas are a common Middle Eastern dish or appetizer.

HLPhoto/Shutterstock.com

Figure 33.6 This rice has been seasoned with saffron, giving it a distinct gold color. Where does saffron come from?

coffee) use a long-handled pot with a wide bottom and thin neck. They combine and heat water, coffee, and sugar until the mixture just begins to foam. Then they quickly remove the pot from the heat and return the pot to the heat once or twice to again build up the foam. Finally, they pour the foaming liquid into small cups and top them with the remaining coffee, grounds and all. More sugar can be added if desired. *Arab-style coffee*, on the other hand, rarely contains sugar. People who make this type of coffee bring it to a boil only once. They pour the coffee into a second pot to get rid of the grounds and sediment. They may add cloves and cardamom seeds before serving.

Turkish Foods

Many people do not regard Turkey as part of the Middle East. Turkey does, however, lie next to three Middle Eastern countries; and the influence of Turkish cuisine can be found throughout the Middle East. Any discussion of Middle Eastern cuisine, therefore, would be lacking if it did not include information about Turkish foods.

The waters that border Turkey on three sides provide a variety of fish and shellfish. Thus, Turkish cooks use much seafood in their dishes. Seafood vendors in Istanbul sell lobster, salty red caviar, jumbo shrimp, mussels, haddock, bass, and mackerel. Throughout Turkey, lamb is the most readily available and most popular meat. Lamb cubes marinated in a mixture of olive oil, lemon juice, and onions are threaded onto skewers and charbroiled. Rice, sliced tomatoes, and bread often accompany this dish, which is called *shish kebab*. Another type of kebab, the *döner kebab*, is a large cone made of thin pieces of lamb. As the cone rotates over a bed of charcoal, the outside slices of meat become crisp and flavorful. Turkish cooks slice these crisp pieces from the cone with large knives. They then serve the meat with a salad, rings of onion, cucumbers, and tomato slices. By the time they serve one helping, the next layer of meat has become crisp (**Figure 33.7**).

Stuffed vegetables, cacik, and pilav are other common Turkish foods. *Cacik* is slices of cucumber in a yogurt sauce flavored with mint. Turkish cooks may serve pilav plain or mix it with currants, nuts, and tomato sauce.

Snacking is popular in Turkey. Nuts, pumpkin seeds, and toasted chickpeas are favorite snack foods. Vendors in the streets of Istanbul sell crisp rings of bread, called *simit*, from carts. Other vendors have special presses for squeezing fresh pomegranate juice, which is a popular beverage.

Sweets are popular in Turkey. *Halva* is a candylike sweet made from farina or semolina and sugar. *Kurabiye* is a rich butter cookie. *Rahat lokum* (Turkish delight) is a candylike sweet made from grape jelly coated with powdered sugar. Turkish people also enjoy baklava like their Greek neighbors to the west. Other sweets have even more creative names. The "vizier's finger" is a sweet roll fried in olive oil until crisp. A "lady's navel" is a deep-fried fritter with a depression in the center. "Sweetheart's lips" are rounds of dough filled with nuts and folded in a way that resembles human lips.

Foods of the Arab States

The countries of Lebanon, Iraq, Jordan, Syria, Saudi Arabia, and Egypt are often called the *Arab States*. The Arab States include the area once called the *Fertile Crescent*, where people first learned to grow crops.

People can buy a variety of spices at bazaars throughout the Arab world. Vendors scoop cinnamon, cumin, ginger, coriander, allspice, and hot peppers onto pieces of paper, which they

Figure 33.7 Döner kebab cooks as the dish is served, ensuring that each helping is flavorful and crisp.

roll into cones. Arab cooks add spices to many dishes. They use rose water and orange-flower water to flavor their sweets (**Figure 33.8**).

No Arab meal is complete without **mazza** (appetizers). *Arak,* an anise-flavored liqueur, is usually served with mazza. One kind of mazza, called *tabbouleh,* is actually a salad. It is made of chopped tomatoes, radishes, green and white onions, parsley, mint, and bulgur. People break off pieces of *shrak* (a flat bread) and use them to scoop up the tabbouleh.

Islamic law forbids the eating of pork, but Arabs enjoy both camel and lamb meats. Camel is served as a delicacy at special occasions. Lamb is more likely to appear at daily meals. *Kibbi* (called *kibbi* in Syria, *kobba* in Jordan, and *kubba* in Iraq) is a popular Arab lamb dish. Arab cooks pound raw lamb and bulgur into a paste and shape it into flat patties or hollow balls. They fry the patties. If the lamb and bulgur are shaped into hollow balls, Arab cooks stuff the balls with ground lamb, pine nuts, rice, or vegetables and either bake or broil them.

Arab cooks love color and pattern, and they use both lavishly. For example, they often

Maksym Poriechkin/Shutterstock.com

Figure 33.8 Middle Eastern sweets, such as this croissant, are often flavored with rose water. Rose water is made by steeping rose petals in water. What other sweets are made with rose water?

garnish hummus with red pepper, green parsley, and brown cumin. *Hummus* is a mixture of chick-peas and sesame paste. Arab cooks serve torshi the way people serve pickle relish in the United States. *Torshi* is a mixture of pickled turnips, onions, peppers, eggplant, cucumbers, and occasionally beets. Arab cooks use saffron to give a bright gold color to a variety of dishes.

Along the eastern Mediterranean coastline of the Middle East, fishers catch a variety of fish daily. Cooks quickly clean mullet, sea bass, turbot, swordfish, cod, sardines, and other fish. Then they bake or poach the fish or cook them over charcoal. Restaurants that line the river-banks of the Tigris serve smoked *shabait* (a kind of trout).

Iranian Foods

The Persians (predecessors of the present-day Iranians) laid the foundation for Middle Eastern cooking. Scholars believe that wine, cheese, sherbet, and ice cream were first made in Persia. The Persians were also the first to extract the essence of roses and combine exotic herbs and spices with foods.

For centuries, rice has been the staple food of the Iranians. Iranian people serve many kinds of rice dishes. All these dishes belong to one of two groups: chelo or polo. *Chelo* is plain, boiled, buttered rice served with *khoresh* (a topping made of varied sauces, vegetables, fruits, and meats). *Polo* is similar to pilav in that all the accompaniments cook with the rice.

Iran's national dish is called **chelo kebab**. The kebab consists of thin slices of marinated, charcoal-broiled lamb (**Figure 33.9**). Diners combine three accompaniments with the chelo: a pat of butter, a raw egg, and a bowl of *sumac* (a tart-flavored spice).

Iranians use yogurt to make a variety of hot and cold soups. One popular soup contains grated cucumber and is served with a topping of raisins and fresh mint leaves. When combined with plain or carbonated water, yogurt becomes a refreshing drink.

Iranians are not quite as fond of rich pastries as other Middle Easterners are. Iranians eat fresh fruits instead. Iran produces some of the finest Persian melons, watermelons, peaches, pomegranates, apricots, quinces, dates, pears, and grapes. Iranians often eat these fruits plain.

Matyas Rehak/Shutterstock.com

Figure 33.9   To make kebab, slices of lamb are charbroiled. Kebab is often served with flat bread.

Sometimes they may also slice and sweeten the fruits and serve them with crushed ice or make them into sherbets.

Middle Eastern Menu

Shish Kebabs
(Chunks of Meat Threaded on Skewers)
Pilav
(Seasoned Rice)
Mast va Khiar
(Cucumber and Yogurt Salad)
Pita Bread
(Pocket Bread)
Baklava
(Layered Pastry with Walnuts and Honey Syrup)
Khave
(Turkish Coffee)

Shish Kebabs
(Chunks of Meat Threaded on Skewers)
Serves 4

2	tablespoons olive oil
¼	cup lemon juice
½	teaspoon salt
¼	teaspoon pepper
¼	teaspoon garlic powder
1	pound lean, boneless lamb cut into 1-inch cubes
1	medium red onion, cut into 1½-inch pieces
2	large tomatoes, quartered
2	large green peppers, cut into chunks
2	tablespoons evaporated fat-free milk

1. In a medium bowl, thoroughly combine oil, lemon juice, salt, pepper, and garlic powder. Add lamb cubes and onion to marinade, tossing to coat well. Cover the pan and place in refrigerator for at least 20 minutes, turning lamb occasionally.
2. Preheat broiler. Oil the broiler pan.
3. Alternate threading lamb cubes and onion pieces on four long skewers so there is a piece of onion between each cube of lamb. Thread tomato quarters and green pepper chunks on two more skewers.
4. Place skewers of meat and onion side by side along the length of a broiler pan. Brush the meat with evaporated milk. Then add vegetable skewers to the broiler pan.
5. Broil 4 inches from the heat for 6 to 8 minutes, turning all skewers halfway through cooking period. Test meat with an instant-read thermometer to be sure lamb has reached an internal temperature of 145°F. Watch vegetables carefully and remove when tender and golden. Serve lamb with broiled vegetables and pilav.

Per serving: 157 calories (42% from fat), 16 g protein, 7 g carbohydrate, 7 g fat, 50 mg cholesterol, 2 g fiber, 133 mg sodium.

Pilav
(Seasoned Rice)
Serves 4 to 6

1	tablespoon olive oil
½	cup chopped onion
1	clove garlic, minced

1   cup uncooked white rice
2   cups low-sodium chicken broth
     salt
     pepper
2   teaspoons butter

1. Heat oil in a heavy saucepan. Add onion and garlic and sauté until vegetables are tender and just beginning to turn golden. Then add rice and stir for several minutes to evenly coat rice with fat. (Do not let rice brown.)
2. Add chicken broth and salt and pepper to taste. Bring mixture to a boil, stirring constantly.
3. Cover pan, reduce heat, and simmer rice slowly for 15 minutes or until all the liquid has been absorbed.
4. Add butter and stir with a fork. Let rice stand, covered, for 5 minutes before serving.

Per serving: 251 calories (25% from fat), 6 g protein, 41 g carbohydrate, 7 g fat, 5 mg cholesterol, 1 g fiber, 116 mg sodium.

Mast va Khiar
(Cucumber and Yogurt Salad)
Serves 4

1   medium cucumber, peeled
2   tablespoons finely chopped green pepper
1   green onion, finely chopped
1   tablespoon dried tarragon or dill
½   teaspoon lime juice
¼   teaspoon salt
1   cup plain nonfat yogurt

1. Slice each cucumber in half lengthwise. Scoop out seeds and chop cucumber coarsely.
2. Put cucumber in a serving bowl and add green pepper, green onion, tarragon or dill, lime juice, and salt. Mix well. Add yogurt and stir to coat vegetables.
3. Chill salad until ready to serve, preferably at least one hour.

Per serving: 40 calories (4% from fat), 4 g protein, 6 g carbohydrate, 0 g fat, 1 mg cholesterol, 0 g fiber, 178 mg sodium.

Pita Bread
(Pocket Bread)
Makes 8

2½ to 3 cups all-purpose flour
1   package active dry yeast
1   cup water
1   tablespoon sugar
¾   teaspoon salt

1. In a large mixing bowl, stir together 1 cup flour and yeast.
2. Heat water, sugar, and salt over low heat until very warm (120°F to 130°F), stirring to blend.
3. Add liquid ingredients to flour mixture and beat until smooth, about 2 minutes on medium speed of electric mixer. Add ½ cup flour and beat 1 minute more. Stir in enough additional flour to make a moderately stiff dough.
4. Turn dough out onto a lightly floured surface and knead until smooth and satiny, about 8 to 10 minutes.
5. Divide dough into 8 portions. Roll each into a 3-inch circle. Place circles on a lightly greased baking sheet. Cover with a clean towel and let rise in warm place until doubled, about 45 minutes.
6. Bake on middle rack of preheated 450°F oven, 10 to 12 minutes or until lightly browned. Cool.

Per pita: 150 calories (0% from fat), 4 g protein, 32 g carbohydrate, 0 g fat, 0 mg cholesterol, 1 g fiber, 219 mg sodium.

Baklava
(Layered Pastry with Walnuts and Honey Syrup)
Makes about 18 pieces

2   cups walnuts, finely chopped
⅝   cup sugar, divided
½   teaspoon ground cinnamon
     dash ground cloves
     nonstick cooking spray
½   pound *phyllo* (about 12 sheets), or Greek pastry dough
½   cup water
1½   teaspoons lemon juice
¼   cup honey
2   thin slices lemon

1   3-inch cinnamon stick, broken

1   teaspoon vanilla extract

1. In a mixing bowl, combine walnuts, 2 tablespoons sugar, ground cinnamon, and cloves; set aside.
2. Preheat oven to 350°F. Spray an 8-inch square pan with cooking spray.
3. Unfold the room-temperature stack of phyllo sheets. Cut the whole stack in half to fit in the prepared pan. Cover the phyllo with a slightly damp dish towel. Keep the stack covered as you work.
4. Place one sheet of cut phyllo in the pan. Spray it lightly with cooking spray. Place another sheet of phyllo on top of the first sheet and spray it with cooking spray. Continue layering phyllo sheets and spraying them with cooking spray until 6 sheets have been used.
5. Sprinkle ⅔ cup of the nut mixture over the phyllo in the pan. Place 6 more sheets of phyllo over the nut layer, spraying each with cooking spray. Repeat this step two more times, using all the nut mixture and ending with 6 sheets of sprayed phyllo.
6. With a very sharp knife, cut the baklava diagonally into diamond-shaped pieces.
7. Bake baklava until golden and crisp, about 45 minutes.
8. While baklava is baking, prepare syrup. In a small saucepan, combine remaining ½ cup sugar, water, lemon juice, honey, lemon slices, and cinnamon stick. Bring to a boil, stirring until sugar is dissolved. Simmer syrup uncovered for 10 minutes.
9. Remove lemon slices and cinnamon stick from the syrup. Add vanilla extract. Set syrup aside to cool.
10. As soon as the baklava comes out of the oven, pour the syrup over the hot pastry. Allow the pastry to set for several hours before serving.

Per piece: 167 calories (49% from fat), 3 g protein, 21 g carbohydrate, 9 g fat, 0 mg cholesterol, 1 g fiber, 38 mg sodium.

The origin of baklava is believed to date back many centuries.

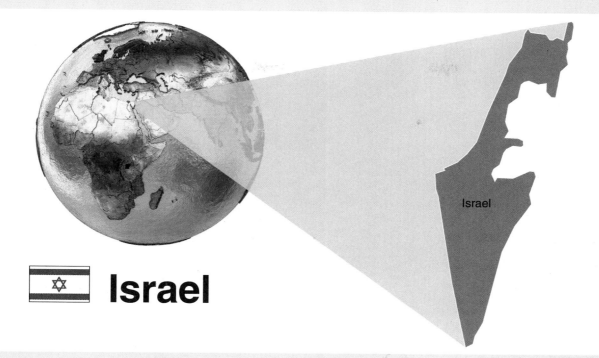

Israel

Israel

Israel is a distinct part of the Middle East. The state of Israel was established in 1948. Since that time, Israel has grown at a rapid rate. This country is known for its agricultural production and for the heavy industry that flourishes in Haifa, the nation's largest seaport. As the home of many talented writers, artists, and musicians, Israel is also rich in cultural assets.

Israel is a religious center. Israel's capital city of Jerusalem has been an important place to people of many races and religions for centuries. Jerusalem is called the "Holy City" by Christians, Jews, and Muslims alike (**Figure 33.10**).

Geography and Climate of Israel

The Mediterranean Sea forms Israel's western border. The northern part of the country borders Syria and Lebanon. There, the land rises from a fertile coastal plain to the hills of Galilee. Galilee's scattered green valleys are suitable for agriculture. To the east is the Jordan River, which separates Israel from Jordan. To the south lies the triangular Negev Desert, bordered by Egypt and the Red Sea.

Israel has four climatic regions. Along the Mediterranean Sea, summers are warm, and winters are mild with occasional rain. In the central highlands, summers are again warm and dry, but the winters are cold and wet. The Negev Desert is hot and dry in the summer and cool and dry in the winter. The Jordan Valley has hot, dry summers and mild winters.

Israeli Agriculture

Almost no rain falls in Israel from May to October. This makes irrigation necessary for the production of most crops. In Israel, most farms are operated by communities. Almost all the fruits and vegetables eaten in Israel are grown there. Guavas, citrus fruits, mangoes, dates, bananas, avocados, and melons are some of the most popular fruits. Cattle, sheep, poultry, and fish are also available from local sources. Cattle breeds that are suitable for the semiarid land are raised. Fresh fish and ducks are scientifically raised on farm ponds.

Israeli Culture

Many of Israel's citizens live in collective communities, which are called **kibbutzim**. Members of a kibbutz own their property collectively and live together in a cluster of dwellings. They receive no wages for their work, but all

Figure 33.10   Jerusalem is a city rich with history, heritage, and meaning. Why is Jerusalem important to Muslims, Jews, and Christians?

their needs are met. Food, clothing, medical care, and entertainment are supplied. Children who live in a kibbutz are educated communally according to age. A kibbutz may have anywhere from 30 to 2,000 members and may or may not have a few small industries.

Holidays are an important part of the culture in Israel. About three-fourths of Israel's citizens are Jewish, so most holidays revolve around Judaism, the Jewish faith. These celebrations always begin and end at sunset. Many of them involve special food traditions. For instance, the holiday *Rosh Hashanah* begins a period called the *Ten Days of Repentance*. This holiday celebrates the Jewish New Year. On this day, Jews in Israel eat sweet foods, such as sliced apples, honey cookies, and sweet potato pudding. They hope eating these foods will bring a new year that is sweet and happy. The last day of the Ten Days of Repentance is called *Yom Kippur*. This is the holiest day of the year. Jewish people spend the day at the synagogue fasting, praying, and reading.

Hanukkah is a festival in December that lasts for eight days. It celebrates a victory when Jews regained control of the Temple in Jerusalem. It also honors a miracle when one day's supply of oil burned in the Temple for eight days. During this holiday, families light candles in a nine-branched candleholder called a *menorah*. Traditional

Hanukkah foods include *latkes* (potato pancakes) and *sufganiyah* (doughnuts). These foods are cooked in oil to commemorate the miracle.

Pesakh, or Passover, is celebrated for eight days in the spring. It commemorates the Jews' freedom from slavery in Egypt thousands of years ago. On the first evening of Passover, families share the *Seder*. This is a traditional meal of specific foods, each with a symbolic meaning (**Figure 33.11**). Bitter herbs, such as horseradish, are eaten as a symbol of the bitterness of slavery. Parsley represents the coming of spring. **Matzo**, an unleavened bread, reminds the Jews that their ancestors had no time to let bread rise when they were fleeing Egypt. A roasted egg and a shank of lamb symbolize beasts given to God as sacrifices. A dish of saltwater stands for the tears of the Hebrew slaves. *Charoset*, a mixture of nuts, apples, and wine, represents the cement the slaves used to build cities for the Egyptians.

Israeli Cuisine

When Jews and other peoples immigrated to Israel, they came from many parts of the world. People from over 70 nations added their foods to the Israeli area's native Middle Eastern cuisine. Some of these dishes were adapted to use readily

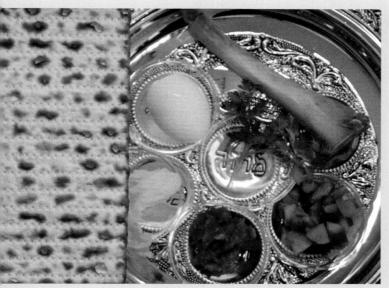

©iStock.com/chameleonseye

Figure 33.11 Each food in the traditional Passover meal invites reflection and acknowledgment of an aspect of the Jews' liberation from Egypt.

available ingredients. Thus, Israeli cuisine is multinational. An Israeli cookbook might list Russian soups, German side dishes, and North African entrees along with dishes of local origin.

Jewish Dietary Laws

People in many Israeli homes and restaurants observe the Jewish **kashrut**, which are religious dietary laws set out by Judaism. Foods prepared according to the dietary laws are considered **kosher**.

The first of these religious dietary laws concerns foods that are suitable for eating. Only animals that have *cloven* (split) hoofs and that chew their cud are considered fit to eat. Therefore, Jews who follow the kashrut cannot eat pigs because pigs do not chew their cud. Fish must have both scales and fins, so Jews who follow the kashrut cannot eat shellfish. Jewish people who follow the kashrut can eat domesticated fowl, but not wild fowl. Cooks must carefully check vegetables and cereals to be sure they are free of insects. They must break eggs into a separate dish and inspect them for blood spots before using them. Manufactured products must not contain any nonkosher ingredients.

Other religious dietary laws describe the proper methods of slaughter. According to these laws, a **shohet** (licensed slaughterer) must slaughter all animals and fowl.

Global Perspective

A Land of Jewish Heritage

The state of Israel was founded on a land that had been called *Palestine* for centuries. This land was the birthplace of the Jews; however, throughout history, the Jewish population dwindled as a result of revolts, invasions, and periods of foreign rule. Some Jews were killed or sold into slavery. Some fled to nearby Middle Eastern countries and to other countries around the world.

Before the establishment of Israel, Jews were physically separated from their homeland and from one another. Even so, they kept their identity and religion. Jews around the world waited for the time when they could return.

In the late 1800s, Jews started to move back into Palestine. In the years leading up to World War II, many Jews moved to Palestine to escape rising oppression in Europe. Jews suffered during World War II, as six million Jews were murdered in the Holocaust by the Nazis in Germany. It was three years after the end of World War II, on May 14, 1948, that the state of Israel was declared. This date marked the first time in more than 2,000 years that Jews were able to govern themselves. Hundreds of thousands of Holocaust survivors and other Jews then flocked to the new country.

The resulting boost in population was needed to support the young nation of Israel; however, the rapid growth put a strain on the country's economy. Through a treaty, West Germany agreed to pay reparations to Israel. This was seen as a way to compensate the Jews for property stolen from them by the Nazis. These reparations were made in the form of resources rather than cash. Israel used these resources to build much-needed infrastructure and to promote the development of industry. These efforts laid the foundation for a stronger economy, which the country needed to thrive.

Israel has continued to grow and prosper. Today, Israel is recognized as a leader among the world's nations and is home to millions of Jewish people.

In a kosher kitchen, there are distinctions between what is considered *milchig* and what is considered *fleishig*. **Milchig** describes foods made with milk and the utensils that are used to prepare, serve, and eat them. **Fleishig** describes foods made with meat or poultry as well as utensils and dishes used with these foods. Jews who follow the kashrut cannot cook or eat milchig and fleishig foods together. For this reason, kosher kitchens contain two complete sets of eating, serving, and food preparation utensils. Cooks use one set for milchig foods. They use the other set for fleishig foods. The two sets of utensils must be washed and stored separately. Jewish people who follow the kashrut may eat fleishig foods after milchig foods, but only if they thoroughly cleanse their mouths first. They must wait a period of time after eating fleishig foods before eating milchig foods.

Foods and utensils that are neither milchig nor fleishig are described as *pareve*. **Pareve** foods include eggs, fruits, vegetables, cereals, fish, and baked goods made with vegetable shortening (**Figure 33.12**). Except for fish, pareve foods can be prepared and eaten with either milk or meat dishes.

ChameleonsEye/Shutterstock.com

Figure 33.12 Baked goods, like this challah, are considered pareve foods if they are made with vegetable margarine instead of butter. How could you tell whether a food from the grocery store is made with vegetable margarine or butter?

Ashkenazi Jewish Dishes

Jews of Central or Eastern European descent are known as *Ashkenazi* Jews. When discussing Jewish fare, Ashkenazi dishes are what come to mind for many people. Some of these foods are served in Israel; however, they are not mainstays of Israeli cuisine.

A few Israeli restaurants specialize in Ashkenazi dishes. Foods that are hot, filling, and inexpensive are an important part of the diet in Eastern Europe. Therefore, chicken soup is a classic menu item in an eatery that features this cuisine. The soup is often served with *matzo balls*, which are dumplings made from matzo meal (ground-up matzo). Another frequent addition to chicken soup is *kreplach*. These are squares of noodle dough stuffed with a filling made of meat, cheese, potato, chicken, or chicken liver.

Kugel is an Eastern European dish that resembles pudding. The traditional version may contain vegetables, fruits, noodles, rice, or fish. A kugel may be a separate course or a side dish. Sweet kugels are often served for dessert. An Israeli adaptation of this dish is the *Jerusalem kugel*, which is made with caramelized noodles and black pepper.

Tzimmes are sweetened combinations of meats, vegetables, and fruits. They are usually served as stews or casseroles. Although the cook's imagination determines the choice of ingredients, long, slow cooking improves the flavor of all tzimmes.

Blintzes and challah have been Ashkenazi Jewish specialties for centuries. *Blintzes* are thin pancakes similar to French crêpes. They are browned on one side only and folded like a napkin with the browned side up after a filling is added. Sweet fillings are made with cheese or fruit. Savory fillings include potatoes, meat, and salty cheese. *Challah* is a braided, rich egg bread. Jewish people eat it on the weekly Sabbath and serve it at holiday meals.

Middle Eastern Israeli Foods

Many of the foods found in Israel originated in other Middle Eastern countries. One of these foods, falafel, has become one of Israel's national dishes. **Falafel** is a mixture of ground chickpeas, bulgur, and spices that is formed into balls and deep-fried. Street vendors sell warm falafel tucked inside a piece of pita bread. It may also be served folded in *laffa*, a soft, chewy flatbread. Sauce made with *tahini*, a sesame seed paste, is a typical condiment on falafel. Hummus, another Middle Eastern food, is another common accompaniment (**Figure 33.13**).

Baba ghanoush is sometimes known as *eggplant salad* in Israel; however, it is really more of a dip. It is made with roasted eggplant, tahini, and garlic along with a variety of seasonings.

With Israel's abundance of fresh fruits and vegetables, salads are very popular. Israelis serve *salat katzutz* (chopped salad) at nearly every meal, including breakfast. This salad developed from a Turkish salad. It is commonly made with diced cucumbers and tomatoes with a dressing of lemon juice and olive oil. *Gezer hai* (living carrots) is a salad made with grated carrots tossed with orange juice.

Malabi is a popular dessert in Israel with Middle Eastern origins. It is a custard made with milk and flavored with rose water (**Figure 33.14**). Unlike custard in the United States, it does not contain any egg.

Some Israeli dishes have North African origins. *Shakshuka* is a spicy dish made with eggs and tomatoes that may be served for breakfast. *Leben* is a type of cheese made from sour milk. Israeli people often serve it for breakfast or with crackers as an appetizer.

Israeli Additions

While many foods in Israeli cuisine are local variations of dishes from other lands, a few foods are uniquely Israeli. One of these foods is *ptitim*, which is also known as *Israeli couscous*. This is a pasta product shaped like rice or little balls. It was developed in the early days of the nation when economic hardships made rice hard to get. In Israel, ptitim is often considered a dish for children. It may be eaten plain or cooked with onions and spices.

Over a century before Israel became an independent state, *Tzfat cheeses* were being produced in the region. *Tzfat* is the Hebrew name for Safed, the city where the cheeses were first made and are still made today. These cheeses are made from sheep's milk and are known for their salty flavor and smooth texture.

hadasit/Shutterstock.com

Figure 33.14 Malabi is an Israeli custard that makes use of rose water, a common ingredient in Middle Eastern desserts. What other Israeli dishes are Middle Eastern in origin?

Teodora D/Shutterstock.com

Figure 33.13 Falafel is an Israeli national dish. It is often accompanied by hummus.

Israeli Menu

Falafel

Gezer Hai
(Carrot Salad)

Hummus

Laffa Bread

Malabi
(Milk Custard)

Limonana
(Lemonade with Mint)

Falafel
Makes 12 patties

2	cups canned low-sodium chickpeas, drained
½	cup chopped onion
3	tablespoons finely chopped fresh parsley
3	tablespoons finely chopped fresh cilantro
½	teaspoon salt
¼	teaspoon cayenne pepper
2	cloves garlic, minced
1	teaspoon cumin
1	large egg
1	tablespoon lemon juice
1¼	teaspoons baking powder
½	cup all-purpose flour, divided

1. Place the chickpeas, onion, parsley, cilantro, salt, cayenne pepper, garlic, cumin, egg, and lemon juice in a food processor. Pulse until blended but not pureed. Add the baking powder and ¼ cup flour and pulse to combine.
2. Turn mixture into a bowl and place in the freezer for 15 minutes.
3. Remove the mixture from the freezer. Preheat the oven to 375°F. Line a baking sheet with parchment paper. Spread remaining ¼ cup flour on a small plate.
4. Gather about 3 tablespoons of the chickpea mixture and roll into a ball. Roll the ball in the flour and place it on the prepared baking sheet, flattening the ball into a small patty. Repeat with remaining mixture to make 11 more patties.
5. Bake for 20 to 30 minutes, flipping patties halfway through cooking period. Serve hot from the oven or allow to cool.

Per patty: 50 calories (18% from fat), 2 g protein, 8 g carbohydrate, 1 g fat, 18 mg cholesterol, 2 g fiber, 201 mg sodium.

Gezer Hai
(Carrot Salad)
Serves 4

3	tablespoons fresh orange juice
⅛	teaspoon ground ginger
⅛	teaspoon salt
1	tablespoon lemon juice
2	tablespoons honey
2	cups coarsely grated carrots
4	cups salad greens
1	navel orange, peeled and sectioned

1. In a small bowl, mix together orange juice, ginger, salt, lemon juice, and honey. Pour over carrots, cover, and refrigerate until serving time, preferably for at least 1 hour.
2. When ready to serve, line 4 small salad plates with salad greens. Top greens with grated carrots. Garnish with orange sections. Serve at once.

Per serving: 87 calories (0% from fat), 2 g protein, 21 g carbohydrate, 0 g fat, 0 mg cholesterol, 3 g fiber, 132 mg sodium.

Hummus
Makes 1 cup

1	cup canned low-sodium chickpeas, drained and rinsed
2	tablespoons tahini paste
1	clove garlic, minced
4½	teaspoons lemon juice
2	teaspoons olive oil, divided
½	teaspoon cumin
	dash salt
	dash cayenne pepper
1	teaspoon chopped fresh parsley
	dash paprika

1. Place chickpeas, tahini, garlic, lemon juice, 1 teaspoon olive oil, cumin, salt, and cayenne in a food processor. Process until almost smooth.
2. Use a flexible spatula to spread the hummus on a small plate. Drizzle with remaining 1 teaspoon olive oil. Sprinkle with parsley and paprika. Serve.

Per 2 tablespoon serving: 52 calories (69% from fat), 2 g protein, 4 g carbohydrate, 4 g fat, 0 mg cholesterol, 1 g fiber, 51 mg sodium.

Laffa Bread
Makes 8 loaves

2 to 2½ cups bread flour
1   package rapid-rise yeast
2   teaspoons sugar
½   teaspoon salt
1   cup warm water, 120°F to 130°F
1   tablespoon plus 1 teaspoon olive oil

1. In a large mixing bowl, stir together 1 cup flour, yeast, sugar, and salt. Add warm water and olive oil, and mix until well blended. Add enough remaining flour to form a soft dough.
2. Turn dough out onto a floured surface. Knead about 6 minutes until dough is smooth and elastic, adding more flour if needed.
3. Place dough in an oiled bowl, turning to coat dough with oil. Cover the bowl with plastic wrap and allow dough to rise until doubled in bulk, about 15 to 20 minutes.
4. Punch the dough down and divide it into 8 equal portions. Shape each portion into a ball and place it on an oiled baking sheet. Cover the dough and let it rest for 10 minutes.
5. Roll each ball of dough into a circle about 8 to 9 inches in diameter.*
6. Brush a griddle or large, heavy skillet with olive oil and heat over medium heat. Place one circle of dough on the hot surface and cook for 1 to 2 minutes. Bread is ready to flip when bubbles appear on the top surface and the bottom begins to brown. Use tongs to flip the bread and flatten it to be sure it has good contact with the cooking surface. Cook the second side 1 to 2 minutes, until the bubbles start to brown.
7. Remove laffa from the pan and place between clean kitchen towels to cool for a minute. Then transfer to an airtight container and seal. This allows the steam to make the bread more soft and pliable.
8. Repeat the cooking process with remaining pieces of dough, brushing more oil on the pan as needed. Serve warm.

*Traditional laffa bread is about 12 inches in diameter. The size specified here is a bit easier to handle and yields a less filling serving size.

Per loaf: 151 calories (12% from fat), 5 g protein, 26 g carbohydrate, 2 g fat, 0 mg cholesterol, 1 g fiber, 146 mg sodium.

Malabi
(Milk Custard)
Serves 4

2   cups reduced-fat (2%) milk, divided
1½   teaspoons rose water (or ½ teaspoon almond extract)
¼   cup cornstarch
3   tablespoons sugar
½   teaspoon vanilla extract
2   tablespoons strawberry syrup
2   tablespoons chopped pistachios

1. In a small bowl, whisk together ½ cup milk, rose water, and cornstarch until thoroughly blended. (If using almond extract in place of rose water, do not add it at this point.)
2. In a medium saucepan, heat remaining 1½ cups milk with the sugar over medium heat. Stir constantly until the sugar dissolves and the mixture is simmering.
3. Lower the heat and stir in the cornstarch mixture. Cook, stirring constantly, until the custard begins to thicken.
4. Remove pan from heat and stir in vanilla extract. (If you are using almond extract, stir it in as well.) Pour custard into 4 dessert dishes. Allow to cool 20 minutes, then cover dishes with plastic wrap and refrigerate for at least 4 hours.
5. Top each dish with 1½ teaspoons strawberry syrup and 1½ teaspoons chopped pistachios before serving.

Per serving: 198 calories (27% from fat), 6 g protein, 32 g carbohydrate, 6 g fat, 10 mg cholesterol, 1 g fiber, 61 mg sodium.

Limonana
(Lemonade with Mint)
Serves 4

¾   cup fresh-squeezed lemon juice (about 5 lemons)
⅜   cup sugar (or more, to taste)
¼   cup mint leaves
3   cups ice

1. Place lemon juice, sugar, mint leaves, and ice in a blender. Blend until smooth and slushy.
2. Pour into four small glasses. Serve garnished with additional mint leaves.

Per serving: 86 calories (0% from fat), 0 g protein, 23 g carbohydrate, 0 g fat, 0 mg cholesterol, 0 g fiber, 1 mg sodium.

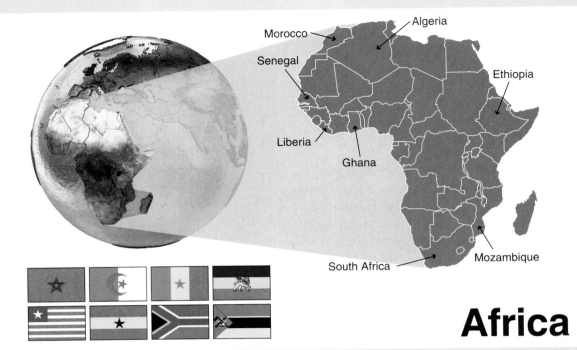

Africa

Africa is the second largest continent, next only to Asia, and is made up of over 50 nations. These two factors make Africa a land of great diversity. There are many types of climates and a broad range of geographic features in Africa. Africa is home to thousands of animal species and countless varieties of plants.

The people of Africa are as diverse as the lands in which they live. Each nation has unique culture, history, and languages. Therefore, Africa does not have one typical cuisine. Each African nation has its own foods and food customs.

Climate and Geography of Africa

In North Africa, much of the land is covered by the Sahara Desert. There are areas where irrigation makes crop production possible; however, extreme heat is typical during most of the year. The Sahara is not the only desert in Africa. About 25 percent of the continent receives less than 10 inches of rain annually, including the Kalahari Desert in Southern Africa. In the African deserts, there are places called *oases* where water is available. *Nomadic tribes* move from one oasis to another, herding sheep, goats, and camels like their ancestors did.

In contrast, along the equator in Central and Western Africa, the climate is tropical. Warm temperatures are fairly constant throughout the year. Some of this area is covered by rainforests and sees frequent, heavy rainfall. Broad areas above and below the equatorial belt are tropical *savannas*, or grasslands. These areas receive less precipitation and have greater temperature ranges (**Figure 33.15**).

Some areas of the continent have rainy seasons and dry seasons each year. Other areas, such as the country of South Africa, have distinct seasons of spring, summer, autumn, and winter. Winter weather includes snow in some places.

A number of mountain systems are found throughout Africa. The country of Tanzania in East Africa is the location of Mount Kilimanjaro, the tallest freestanding mountain in the world.

African Agriculture

Because of Africa's diversity in climate, agriculture varies widely throughout the continent. Desert areas, such as the Sahara Desert, require extensive irrigation for crops to grow.

In tropical, humid regions, root crops and vegetables are grown. Other products grown in these areas include palm oil, groundnuts (peanuts), bananas, dates, figs, plantains, citrus

Figure 33.15 The African savannas are home to many types of wildlife.

fruits, sugarcane, coffee, and cacao. **Cacao** is a plant that produces beans that are ground into cocoa or made into chocolate.

In grassland areas, raising crops is difficult and unprofitable because the soil is poor. The soil has little *humus,* a substance formed by decayed matter. Humus holds water near the ground surface, within reach of plant roots.

African Culture

Native Africans make up the majority of Africa's population; however, millions of people of European descent also live in Africa. Some African nations have large urban centers, but the majority of people in Africa live in rural areas. More than 800 languages are spoken in Africa. Most Africans speak a local language in their home village. They also speak an interchange language to communicate with people outside their village.

Much of Africa is in a state of political, economic, and cultural development. Many of the people in Africa have not had an opportunity to attend school. As a result, a number of Africans are *illiterate* (unable to read or write). Efforts are being made to improve literacy rates. Studies show this will help reduce poverty and improve health among the people. This will benefit communities and nations as well.

Many of the holidays in African countries are religious festivals. Therefore, holidays vary from region to region, depending on the main form of religion. Muslims in Africa observe such events as the Fast of Ramadan. Christmas and Easter are celebrated by African Christians. Besides these holy days, New Year festivals are popular in Africa, and many areas hold harvest festivals in the autumn. Independence Day celebrations are also common in Africa. People celebrate the days their nations gained freedom from the European countries that colonized them. These festivals often involve parades, speeches, parties, and fireworks. Music, dancing, and the wearing of masks are part of many African festivals, too.

African Cuisine

Each African country has unique dishes. Some ingredients are found in numerous places throughout the continent.

Grains serve as the base of the diet in many African cuisines. *Sorghum* and *millet* both grow fairly well even in poor soil and dry climates, so they have become staple African foods (**Figure 33.16**). These grains are commonly used

Figure 33.16 Grains that grow well in unfavorable conditions are valued in African cuisine. Sorghum is one of these hardy grains. Why does African cuisine rely on hardy grains?

to make porridges as well as breads. *Maize*, or corn, is grown in several regions and ground into flour. Rice is a staple food in some African cuisines, though much of Africa is too dry to cultivate rice.

A wide variety of fruits and vegetables grow in Africa. Bananas are an important crop in many African nations. Coconuts grow in tropical areas and are used in a number of African dishes. Other fruits and vegetables grown in Africa include papayas, mangoes, plantains, cassava, and okra. *Papayas* are small, melonlike fruits with many seeds. *Mangoes* have sweet, juicy flesh and a large stone in the center of the fruit. *Plantains* are like bananas, but they are much larger and have a bland flavor. *Cassava* is a starchy root vegetable much like a sweet potato. It is a major source of carbohydrates, especially for people in the tropical regions of Africa. *Okra*, which also grows in the United States, is a native African vegetable. Yams and sweet potatoes, which are two distinct types of vegetables, are widely used in African diets, too. This is just a small sample of the fresh produce available for African cooks to use in many delicious and creative ways.

Several herbs and spices play key roles in African cuisine. Cinnamon, cloves, coriander, cumin, garlic, ginger, nutmeg, and parsley are used to flavor many dishes.

Most African homes do not have refrigerators. Cooks who live in cities are likely to take daily trips to the market to buy fresh ingredients (**Figure 33.17**). Those who live in rural areas often grow the fruits and vegetables they need.

North Africa

Though each African country has unique dishes, African countries in various regions of the continent have some foods in common. The dishes described here offer a small glimpse into the cuisine of the major regions of this large continent.

Among the countries of North Africa, French influence is seen in regional foods, especially in Algeria and Morocco. In the nineteenth century, the French invaded these countries and brought their European customs to the region.

A common meat in Algeria is lamb. It is usually grilled or stewed. *Mechoui* is lamb that has smoldered and cooked over a fire for many

MickyWiswedel/Shutterstock.com

Figure 33.17 The lack of refrigeration in African countries makes buying fresh ingredients especially important.

hours. The smoked head of a sheep is considered a delicacy in this country. *Kesra* is an unleavened Algerian bread. It is cooked on a griddle or pan rather than being baked in an oven.

In Morocco, meats like chicken and lamb are often cooked in a *tajine*. This is a cone-shaped earthenware pot that is placed over hot coals. Foods cook long and slow with a variety of seasonings to develop flavors like a stew. *Couscous* is also a common dish in Morocco as well as in other North African countries. It is a steamed grain topped with stewed meat and/or vegetables.

East Africa

One of the oldest countries in Africa is Ethiopia, which is located in East Africa. Christianity is the predominant religion in Ethiopia. As a result, Ethiopian cuisine is not bound by the many religious dietary restrictions found in neighboring Muslim countries. Ethiopia's main dish is **injera**, which is a large, sourdough-like pancake made from teff. **Teff** is a milletlike grain grown only in Africa and the Middle East. Injera is served with **wat**, a spicy sauce or stew. Diners tear the injera into pieces, roll it around in the wat, and eat it with their fingers (**Figure 33.18**).

Another East African country is Kenya. *Ugali* is the national dish of Kenya. It is a mixture of maize, millet, or sorghum flour and water cooked until it

Dereje/Shutterstock.com

Figure 33.18 Ethiopian injera is made from teff and is used to scoop sauces and other foods. Why do many African cuisines include foods that can be used for scooping or soaking up other foods?

has the texture of dough. Kenyans roll small pieces of the dough into a ball and use it to scoop up other foods. Collards or kale simmered with tomatoes, a dish called *sukuma wiki*, are often served with ugali.

Southern Africa

Portuguese influence can be seen in the foods of Mozambique, a country in Southeastern Africa. Chicken is cooked the Portuguese way with tomatoes and wine. It is typically served with spicy *piri piri sauce*. In fact, this sauce accompanies many entrees, including seafood from Mozambique's coastal areas.

Off the southeastern coast of the main continent is the large island nation of Madagascar. A popular dish in this country is *romazava*. It is a meat stew made with various leafy greens grown on the island. The meat often used for this dish in Madagascar is *zebu*, a type of cattle with humps on their shoulders.

The country of South Africa is located at the very southern tip of the continent. It is a country with many contrasts. Dutch, French, German, and British colonists brought foods to South Africa from their home nations. These European foods have been blended with native foods over the years. *Bobotie* is a national dish in South Africa with Dutch origins. It is a seasoned meat mixture baked with eggs to form a type of casserole.

West Africa

Akla is a popular snack food in Ghana, a country in Western Africa. It is made of cowpeas, which are cooked, mashed, formed into balls, and fried. This dish, known by many other names, is also found in other West African countries.

Ghana is located on the coast of the African continent. This has made seafood an important ingredient in many of the spicy soups and stews served in this country. These main dishes are usually served with a starchy side dish, such as boiled yams, cassava, or plantains. These starchy vegetables may also be boiled and pounded into a dish called *fufu*, which is similar to dumplings.

Another country along the western coast is Liberia, which was founded by freed slaves from the United States. Some of the foods of Liberia are similar to soul food in the United States. Liberian cuisine is a combination of American and African cooking. *Jollof rice* is also popular in Liberia, as it is in other West African countries. This dish is made with rice, tomato paste, onions, and hot pepper along with chicken and beef. Other meats and vegetables may be added, too.

One of the breads in the West African region is *puff puff*. This Nigerian bread is deep-fried by dropping wheat batter into hot oil.

Central Africa

Central Africa is also known as *Middle Africa*. The country of Angola did not gain its independence from Portugal until late in the twentieth century. Therefore, Portuguese influences are seen in the cuisine. *Caruru* is a dish that originated in Brazil, another nation colonized by the Portuguese. It is made with okra, shrimp, manioc meal, onion, and garlic (**Figure 33.19**). The country's national dish is *moamba de galinha*, which is chicken stewed in palm oil. It may be served with rice, ugali, or fufu.

The national dish of Cameroon is a stew known as *ndole*. It is made with a locally grown vegetable called *bitter leaf*. It also contains peanuts, shrimp, fish, and beef. It is often served with boiled or fried plantains. Cameroonians enjoy a variety of tropical fruits. Mangoes, bananas, and citrus fruits are especially popular.

Paul_Brighton/Shutterstock.com

Figure 33.19 Caruru is a Central African dish that is made with okra.

African Meals

In urban areas of Africa, some people follow a daily meal pattern that includes breakfast, lunch, and dinner. Most people in rural areas, however, are more likely to follow the traditional pattern of eating just two meals a day. Both meals, the first at midday and the second in the evening, are quite similar. They typically consist of a main dish soup or stew and a starchy accompaniment, such as rice or bread.

Snacking is popular in Africa. In city streets, vendors sell such foods as fried plantains and broiled meat to satisfy hunger between meals.

African Menu

Meat on a Stick
(East Africa)

Spinach Stew
(West Africa)

Rice

Salatat Fijl wa Latsheen
(Radish and Orange Salad—North Africa)

Melktert
(Milk Pie—South Africa)

Coffee

Culture and Social Studies

African Meal Traditions

Africans often serve meals on low tables, where pillows, folded carpets, or the floor serve as seats. Food is often served in the brass or earthenware vessels in which it was cooked. The food is usually arranged on one large tray and placed in the center of the table. Then each household member takes his or her individual share. Although diners do not use knives and forks, they may use spoons. They use the fingers of their right hands to eat most foods. They may also use flat breads and thick, starchy side dishes to sop up the stews and sauces.

Meat on a Stick
Serves 4

¼   teaspoon cayenne pepper
½   teaspoon garlic salt
½   pound round steak, cut into 1-inch cubes
½   medium onion, cut into 1-inch chunks

1. Place 8 12-inch bamboo skewers in a 13-by-9-inch oblong pan. Cover with water and allow to soak for 30 minutes.
2. Combine cayenne pepper and garlic salt in a resealable plastic bag.
3. Toss steak cubes, a few at a time, into the bag with the seasonings. Seal and shake to coat. Remove coated cubes from the bag and set aside while repeating coating process with remaining cubes.
4. Alternately thread steak cubes and onion chunks onto skewers.
5. Place skewers under broiler. Broil 4 to 5 minutes. Turn; broil another 4 to 5 minutes until meat is cooked and onions are browned.

Per serving: 72 calories (38% from fat), 11 g protein, 1 g carbohydrate, 3 g fat, 28 mg cholesterol, 0 g fiber, 168 mg sodium.

Spinach Stew
Serves 6

1	medium onion, chopped
2	tablespoons peanut oil
1	medium tomato, cubed
⅜	cup tomato paste, unsalted
1	10-ounce package frozen chopped spinach, thawed
2	cups canned corned beef hash
½	teaspoon cayenne pepper
4½	cups hot, cooked rice

1. In a large, nonstick skillet, sauté onion in peanut oil over medium heat until tender.
2. Add tomatoes and tomato paste. Cook, stirring gently, until tomatoes are tender, about 5 minutes.
3. Add spinach, corned beef hash, and cayenne pepper. Reduce heat to low, cover, and cook for 30 minutes.
4. Serve over rice.

Per serving: 416 calories (30% from fat), 21 g protein, 51 g carbohydrate, 14 g fat, 48 mg cholesterol, 2 g fiber, 615 mg sodium.

Salatat Fijl wa Latsheen
(Radish and Orange Salad)
Serves 6

⅓	cup lemon juice
3	tablespoons sugar
¼	teaspoon salt
6	seedless oranges, peeled and sectioned
12	small red radishes, coarsely grated
¼	teaspoon cinnamon

1. In a large bowl, whisk together lemon juice, sugar, and salt until sugar and salt are dissolved.
2. Add orange sections and radishes and toss to combine. Sprinkle with cinnamon and serve immediately.

Per serving: 89 calories (0% from fat), 1 g protein, 23 g carbohydrate, 0 g fat, 0 mg cholesterol, 3 g fiber, 101 mg sodium.

Melktert
(Milk Pie)
Serves 6

2	cups fat-free milk, divided
1	tablespoon butter
1	cinnamon stick
1	small orange, peeled and cut into pieces
4½	tablespoons sugar, divided
⅓	cup flour
2	eggs, beaten
	pastry for one single-crust, 9-inch pie
¼	teaspoon ground cinnamon

1. In a 2-quart heavy saucepan, combine 1¾ cups milk, butter, cinnamon stick, and orange pieces. Bring to a boil.
2. Remove from heat. Remove cinnamon stick and orange pieces with a slotted spoon.
3. Combine ¼ cup sugar with the flour. Add remaining ¼ cup milk and stir until smooth.
4. Stir the flour mixture into the milk in the saucepan. Place over low heat and cook, stirring constantly, until thickened.
5. Remove from the heat. Stir a small amount of the hot liquid into the beaten eggs. Then add the eggs to the hot mixture, mixing well.
6. Pour the pudding into a pastry-lined pie plate. Bake at 450°F for 20 minutes.
7. Reduce heat to 350°F and bake for another 10 minutes.
8. Combine remaining 1½ teaspoons sugar with the ground cinnamon and sprinkle over the top of the pie. Serve warm.

Per serving: 303 calories (39% from fat), 8 g protein, 40 g carbohydrate, 13 g fat, 78 mg cholesterol, 1 g fiber, 283 mg sodium.

Chapter 33 Review and Expand

Summary

The climate throughout much of the Middle East and Africa is hot and dry. Religion is an important part of culture in this part of the world. Religious laws and climate have an impact on the foods of this region.

A number of ingredients and foods are common throughout the Middle East. Lamb is the staple meat of this region, and bulgur and rice are often served as side dishes. Fish is popular in coastal countries. Fruits and rich pastries are common desserts. Coffee is a favorite beverage.

Israel has a rather eclectic cuisine. Jewish people from many parts of the world have made contributions to the cuisine. The neighboring Middle Eastern and African countries have had an influence, too. Of course, Jewish dietary laws also affect many foods.

European countries that colonized Africa left their marks on African cuisines. Although each African country has unique dishes, some foods are common all over the continent. Such foods include staple grains, fruits and vegetables, and seasonings.

Vocabulary Activities

1. **Content Terms** Choose one of the terms on the following list. Then use the Internet to locate photos that visually show the meaning of the term you chose. Share the photo and meaning of the term in class. Ask for clarification if necessary.

haram	shohet
halal	milchig
pita bread	fleishig
bulgur	pareve
mazza	falafel
chelo kebab	cacao
kibbutz	injera
matzo	teff
kashrut	wat
kosher	

2. **Academic Terms** Reread the text passages that contain each of the following terms. Then write a sentence for each term that explains how the term relates to Middle Eastern and African foods.

dialect	taboo
barren	cloven
bazaar	savanna
abstain	humus
caravan	illiterate

Review

Write your answers using complete sentences when appropriate.

3. What low-fat cooking methods are commonly used in the Middle East and Africa?

4. How do Muslims observe the Fast of Ramadan?

5. List the five ingredients basic to all Middle Eastern cooking.

6. What food do both Islam and Judaism forbid their followers to eat?

7. What is the round, flat, hollow bread found throughout the Middle East and Africa that opens like a pocket?

8. Describe three Turkish sweets.

9. Name and describe the two groups of rice dishes served in Iran.

10. Explain the symbolism of five foods eaten as part of the Seder.

11. Explain the meanings of the following terms: *fleishig*, *halal*, *kosher*, *milchig*, *pareve*, and *shohet*.

12. With what group of people are Ashkenazi dishes associated?

13. What Middle Eastern food has become one of Israel's national dishes?

14. What are three staple grains widely found throughout Africa?

15. What is injera? How is it served and eaten?

16. What region of Africa is associated with fufu, puff puff, and jollof rice?

Chapter 33 Review and Expand

Core Skills

17. **Research, Technology, Speaking** Use reliable print or online resources to research the Islamic (Hijri), Jewish, and Gregorian calendars. Compare the current year as well as the names and dates of the months among the three calendars. Also identify three holidays associated with each calendar. In a class discussion, share an interesting fact you learned.

18. **Technology** Use a map of the Middle East and presentation software to create a slide display about the geography of the region. Label the core nations discussed in the chapter. Locate and identify the seven bodies of water that border the core nations. Highlight the Nile, Tigris, and Euphrates. Use color coding to designate deserts, mountains, and agricultural regions. Use transitions, animations, and audio clips to increase the appeal of your presentation.

19. **Research, Reading, Technology, Speaking** In a small group, research life on a kibbutz. Each group member should be responsible for a different aspect of the research. Give a group presentation using digital media and visual displays.

20. **Reading, Writing** Use print or online resources to read about the establishment of a particular African nation. Summarize your findings in a two-page written report. Proofread your report for grammar, spelling, and organization.

21. **Research, Math, Speaking** Choose an African country. Research the following statistics for your chosen country and for the United States: male and female literacy rates, male and female life expectancies, under age-five mortality rate, per capita gross domestic product, percentage of urban and rural population using improved drinking water sources, and percentage of urban and rural population using adequate sanitation facilities. Create a presentation using charts to compare these statistics. Present your findings in class.

22. **Career Readiness Practice** Presume you are the head teacher at an early childhood center. You are getting ready to take your class of five-year-olds on a trip to a zoo. Before the trip, you want to teach the children about African culture and foods. In preparation, create a short digital presentation with images showing a variety of elements from African culture. Prepare African snacks for children to try, and prepare to help the children identify all the animals that are native to Africa.

Critical Thinking and Problem Solving

23. **Analyze** Find a report about a recent event in the Middle East at each of two news websites. Search the two reports for the same three key terms, highlighting each term in a different color. Make color printouts of the two highlighted reports. Use the highlighting to compare the angles and emphases of the two reports. Share your findings in class, suggesting possible reasons for any differences.

24. **Create** Choose an African nation not discussed in this chapter. Work in a small group to trace the origins of some specific foods and food customs in this country. Use visual aids to make a presentation about the ingredients, cooking methods, eating habits, and meal patterns. Following the group presentations, each group should prepare a dish typical of their country.

Chapter 34
Asia

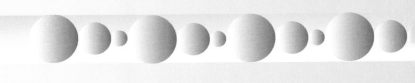

Atosan/Shutterstock.com

Objectives

After studying this chapter, you will be able to

- **describe** how geography, climate, and culture have influenced the food customs of Russia, India, China, and Japan;
- **name** foods that are native to each of these countries; and
- **use** recipes to prepare foods that are native to each of these countries.

Reading Prep

Examine the figures in the chapter before you read it. Write down questions you have about them. Try and answer the caption questions as you read.

Content Terms

kimchi	chapati
kasha	tandoori
zakuska	congee
caviar	chopsticks
schi	gohan
borscht	soybean
beef stroganov	tofu
paskha	sushi
kulich	sukiyaki
caste system	tsukemono
curry	kaiseka
masala	nihon-cha
ghee	

Academic Terms

crude	glutinous
monsoon	picturesque
caste	typhoon
commune	tillable

Asia is the largest continent in the world, covering nearly one-third of the earth's total land surface. Asia is also home to over three-fifths of the world's population. Deserts, jungles, swamps, and mountains cover much of Asia. Most of the population in Asia is concentrated in areas that can best support crops.

In early history, people in much of the world were making *crude* (simple) tools. At the same time, people in Asia were becoming highly advanced. Asian art, architecture, and technology paved the way for later progress in the Western world.

This chapter focuses on Russia, India, China, and Japan—four countries dominate Asia in area and population. (The largest portion of Russia lies in Asia. The smaller portion lies in Europe.) Many other countries are also located in this vast continent. Each country has its own culture, traditions, and foods.

Many Asian cuisines are becoming increasingly popular in Western restaurants, especially Thai, Korean, and Vietnamese cuisines. Examples of these cuisines include *pad thai*, a dish that is commonly available from street carts in Thailand. It is made with rice noodles that are stir-fried with tofu and vegetables. Pad thai is served with a number of garnishes to add color, flavor, and texture. **Kimchi** (also spelled *kimchee*) is a national dish served with nearly every meal in Korea. It is salted cabbage fermented with spicy red pepper. Each Korean family has their own kimchi recipe. Families typically make huge batches of kimchi in the fall, which they then store outdoors in large earthenware pots through the winter. A national dish in Vietnam is *pho bo*, which is soup made with a spicy beef broth and rice noodles. Vietnamese people often eat pho bo for breakfast.

As you read about Russia, India, China, and Japan, you will learn how geography and climate have affected the foods available in each country. You will also gain an understanding of how culture helps shape the ways these foods are used. A growing Western influence can be seen throughout Asian regions; however, foods and food customs are one facet of life in which traditions have been preserved.

Russia

Inside Russia's borders are vast natural resources. Forests provide timber. Thousands of rivers provide power, food, water, and transportation. A large population representing a range of cultures has added to the diversity of Russian cuisine.

Geography and Climate of Russia

Russia is the largest country in the world, almost twice the size of the United States. Most of Russia is a vast lowland, but mountains cover some areas of the country. The Ural Mountains divide Russia between Europe and Asia. The other important mountain ranges in Russia form a large arc along the southern and southwestern borders. The rivers of Russia are important transportation arteries. Because many of the rivers run north and south, canals have been built to improve east-west transportation.

The climate in a large portion of Russia is marked by short, cool summers; long, severe winters; and light precipitation. Much of the European part of Russia (including Moscow) has short, mild summers. The winters are long and cold, and precipitation is moderate. In the northern Arctic regions, summers are short and chilly, and winters are long and bitterly cold. Temperatures of -90°F (-68°C) have been recorded in northeastern Siberia. In the far southeastern portion of the country, the Pacific Ocean brings **monsoons** (storms with high winds and heavy rains).

Russian Agriculture

Wheat is Russia's major grain crop, followed by barley, oats, and rye. Other important crops include sunflower seeds and potatoes. Fruit and vegetable crops are not as varied as they are in the United States, but hardy fruits and vegetables, such as apples and cabbage, grow where climate and soil are suitable.

Russian Culture

Russian history and cultural influences date back for centuries. For hundreds of years, Russia was ruled by an imperial government. In this imperial government, the ruler was known as a *czar*. The czar ruled much like the monarchs of other European countries and built many extravagant palaces throughout Russia. In 1917, Russian Bolsheviks overthrew the imperial government and formed the Russian Socialist Federative Soviet Republic. Then, in 1922, Russia became part of the Union of Soviet Socialist Republics (also known as the *U.S.S.R.* or the *Soviet Union*). The U.S.S.R. was ruled by a Communist dictatorship, or a government in which absolute power is held by one person or *dictator*. In 1991, the Communist Party was dissolved. The Soviet Union was broken up into 15 independent countries, one of which is current-day Russia.

Many traditional Russian holidays are linked to the Russian Orthodox Church (**Figure 34.1**). During the years of Communist rule in the U.S.S.R., the government closed churches and discouraged the celebration of religious holidays. With the fall of Communism, however, churches reopened. Religious holidays, such as Christmas and Easter, regained importance in the lives of the Russian people.

Two of Russia's winter festivals involve some special food traditions. Most Russian people consider New Year to be the best holiday. Children receive candy and gifts from Grandfather Frost and the Snow Maiden, who arrive in a horse-drawn sled. Families get together to enjoy a meal that includes borscht, beef stroganov, pickled tomatoes, and salads. The *Festival of Winter* is a period of several weeks during which parks are decorated with lights

Reidl/Shutterstock.com

Figure 34.1 Religious holidays linked to the Russian Orthodox Church are important in Russia.

and Christmas trees. People stroll through the parks and enjoy blinis and tea purchased from vendors. *Blinis* are pancakes made from buckwheat flour. Russians fry them in butter and serve them with butter and sour cream, caviar, smoked fish, or jam. Their round shapes symbolize the sun and the coming of spring.

Russian Cuisine

Russian cuisine is, for the most part, hearty and filling. The Russian diet is also nutritious, with bread and other grain products forming the foundation. Vegetables frequently appear in healthful soups and side dishes. Russians make more liberal use of meat and dairy products than many of their Asian neighbors. Although these foods add a balance of nutrients, they also increase the amount of fat in the diet. Serving moderate portions is important to help keep fat amounts under control. Smoked and pickled foods, which are linked with certain types of cancer, should be enjoyed in limited amounts, too.

Staple Foods of Russian Peasants

During the imperial rule of the czars, most people living in Russia were *peasants*, or poor farmers with low social status. Russian peasants ate foods they could grow themselves or obtain from the forests and rivers. Some peasant families had enough money to maintain small vegetable gardens and some livestock. Their gardens supplied potatoes, cabbage, cucumbers, beets, carrots, and turnips. Cows provided milk and milk products. Chickens gave eggs, and hogs and cattle provided meat.

Bread, kasha, and soup formed the basis of the diet for Russian peasants. These foods are still important in Russian cuisine today. Peasant bread was dark, nourishing, and filling. Peasants usually made it from rye flour because they could grow rye in the short, cool growing season. Kasha was another staple food. Russian peasants usually made **kasha** from buckwheat, but they also used other grains. To make kasha, they first fried the raw grain, then simmered it until tender. The peasants could eat the kasha alone,

Culture and Social Studies

Contributions to Russian Cuisine

Much Russian cuisine has Slavic origins. Thousands of years ago, the *Slavs* were a group of people who lived in the land that is now Russia. The first Slavs depended on the forests, mountains, and waters for most of their food. Cream sauces and the queen cake are examples of foods contributed by these early people. (*Queen cake* is apples and cherries baked between layers of sweet pastry and topped with meringue.)

The next major contributor to Russian cuisine was the Mongols, who invaded Russia in the thirteenth century. The Mongols taught the Slavs how to broil meat and how to make sauerkraut, yogurt, kumys, and curd cheese. (*Kumys* is a mild alcoholic beverage.) The Mongols also introduced tea drinking and the *samovar* (a special piece of equipment used to make Russian tea).

In 1547, Ivan the Terrible became the first in a line of Russian czars. (The word *czar* means "ruler.") The czars influenced Russian cuisine by staging elaborate banquets and introducing European foods. For instance, Peter the Great brought French soups and Dutch cheeses to the Russian court. He also introduced the custom of serving fruit preserves with meat.

but those who could afford to do so added vegetables, meat, eggs, or fish. The third staple food of the Russian peasants was soup. Cabbage, beet, and fish soups were the most common.

Modern Russian Cuisine

The Russian cuisine of today combines native Russian foods with foods of neighboring European and Asian countries. Russian appetizers and soups, main dishes, side dishes, and desserts reflect this variety.

Russian Appetizers and Soups

Zakuska (appetizers), such as smoked salmon, pickled herring, fish in aspic, and sliced cold meats, begin many Russian meals. Pâtés, salads, cheese, pickles, and breads are also among the many foods that appear on a zakuska table. The star of the table, however, is always caviar.

Caviar is the processed, salted roe (eggs) of large fish. The roe of the sturgeon fish are used most often. Russians serve their fine, black caviar on small pieces of white bread (**Figure 34.2**).

Soup usually follows the zakuska. **Schi** (cabbage soup) is one of the most popular Russian soups. Cooks obtain different flavors by varying the vegetables and broth. **Borscht** (beet soup) can be thin and clear or thick with chunks of beets and other vegetables. Russians often top borscht with a dollop of sour cream. Popular soups also include *ukha*, which is a clear fish broth. *Rassolnik* is a soup of vegetables garnished with chopped veal or lamb kidneys. *Solianka* is a soup containing meat or fish and salted cucumber.

Russian Main Dishes

Many Russian main dishes have regional origins. *Shashlik* (cubes of marinated lamb grilled on skewers), for example, developed in Georgia (a country that borders Turkey).

One of the best-known Russian main dishes was created for a Russian count of the late nineteenth century. **Beef stroganov** is made with tender strips of beef, mushrooms, and a seasoned sour cream sauce.

Other Russian main dishes are made with chicken. *Chakhokhbili* is stewed chicken with tomato sauce, onions, vinegar, wine, peppers, and olives. *Kurnik* is a chicken and rice pie, and *kotmis satsivi* is roasted chicken with walnut sauce. *Kotlety po-kyivskomu* (chicken Kiev) is pounded chicken breasts wrapped around pieces of sweet butter. The rolls of chicken are then breaded and deep-fried until golden brown. When a fork pierces the golden coating, the butter spurts out and serves as a sauce.

More than 100 types of fish live in the waters that border Russia. Sturgeon, pike, carp, bream, salmon, and trout were favorites of the Russian czars. A branch of Russian cuisine developed around these and other varieties of fish. In one region, sturgeon and swordfish are prepared on skewers. White-fleshed fish are served in aspic, and crisp fish cakes are eaten with a mustard sauce (**Figure 34.3**).

Russian Side Dishes

Russian side dishes include vegetable dishes, cereals, and milk and milk products. Russian vegetable dishes have always changed with the

comeirrez/Shutterstock.com

Figure 34.2 Traditional Russian caviar is black and is served on pieces of white bread. What other types of caviar are served throughout the world?

Perednankina/Shutterstock.com

Figure 34.3 Fish in aspic is a common Russian dish. Aspic is a jelly made with meat stock.

seasons. During the cold winters, rutabagas and other root vegetables, potatoes, pickles, dried mushrooms, and sauerkraut are eaten. During the summers, asparagus, peas, and fresh cabbage are more common.

Cereals are available year-round. Because they are both filling and inexpensive, they serve as staples in the Russian diet. Russian cooks use cereals to make dark breads, white breads, and sweet breads. They use cereals to make kasha, which is still popular in Russia. Russians may serve kasha plain or add it to soups. They may combine it with other foods and serve it as a side dish or as a puddinglike dessert. Russian cooks use flour doughs to make noodles, dumplings, and pirozhki. *Pirozhki* are pastries filled with protein-based or sweet fillings.

Milk and milk products are an important part of Russian cooking. Russian cooks use *smetana* (sour cream) on top of borscht and in cakes, pastries, salads, sauces, and main dishes. They also use *prostokvasa* (sour milk), *kefir* (a type of yogurt), and *koumys* (sour mare's milk).

Russian Desserts

Russian desserts have varied origins. Some Russian desserts, like *charlotte russe* (ladyfinger mold with cream filling) and fruit tarts, were favorites of the czars. Other desserts, like *kisel* (pureed fruit), were eaten by the peasants. Many desserts are strictly regional in origin. These include *samsa* (sweet walnut fritters) and *medivnyk* (honey cake).

Two of the most popular Russian desserts are part of the Easter celebrations of the Russian Orthodox Church. **Paskha** is a rich cheesecake that is molded into a pyramid and decorated with the letters *XB* (**Figure 34.4**). These are the initials of the Greek phrase *Christos voskres*, meaning "Christ has risen." **Kulich** is a tall, cylindrical yeast cake filled with fruits and nuts. Russians always serve kulich by first removing the top half of the cake and placing it on a serving plate. Then they slice the rest of the cake and arrange the slices around the mushroom-shaped top.

Figure 34.4 The paskha cake is symbolic of the Russian Orthodox Church's Easter celebrations. How do Easter celebrations in Russia compare to Easter celebrations in other countries?

Russian Meals

The average Russian family eats three meals a day. Breakfast generally is simple. Kasha with milk, bread, butter, jam, hot tea, and an occasional egg are typical.

Lunches may be eaten wherever workers find themselves in the middle of the day, such as in factory cafeterias or farm fields. Lunch may consist of a hearty soup, thick slices of bread with a little cheese or sausage, and tea. In wealthier families, a fish or meat course and vegetables may follow the soup.

Dinner is the main meal of the day. Russians serve a small assortment of zakuska with glasses of vodka or *kvas* (similar to European beers). They often follow zakuska with soup. Then they serve the main course of meat, poultry, or fish. Potatoes, vegetables, and bread usually accompany the main course. A simple dessert, such as kisel and hot tea, follows.

Russian Menu

Borscht
(Beet Soup)
Chernyi Hleb
(Black Bread)
Tvorog
(Cottage Cheese)
Cranberry Kisel
Tchai
(Tea)

4. Meanwhile, drain beets over a bowl to reserve liquid. Pulse beets in a food processor to chop coarsely.
5. When the vegetables are tender, add the chopped beets, beet liquid, sugar, vinegar, and beef to the pot. Increase heat to medium and cook, stirring often, until heated through.
6. Add dill. Taste to adjust seasonings. Serve, topping each bowl with 1 tablespoon of sour cream.

Per serving: 218 calories (37% from fat), 17 g protein, 19 g carbohydrate, 9 g fat, 35 mg cholesterol, 3 g fiber, 323 mg sodium.

Borscht
(Beet Soup)
Serves 6

2	tablespoons vegetable oil, divided
¾	pound sirloin steak, trimmed and cut into ¾-inch cubes
½	teaspoon pepper, divided
1	medium onion, chopped
2	medium carrots, shredded
2	cups shredded green cabbage
2	medium tomatoes, coarsely chopped
4	cups low-sodium beef broth
½	teaspoon salt
4	cups canned low-sodium sliced beets
2	teaspoons sugar
2	teaspoons cider vinegar
1½	teaspoons dried dill weed
⅜	cup low-fat sour cream

1. In a large Dutch oven, heat 1 tablespoon of oil over medium heat. Sprinkle steak with ¼ teaspoon pepper and add to the pot. Cook, stirring often, until the meat is browned on all sides, about 2 minutes. Transfer to a bowl.
2. Add the remaining 1 tablespoon of oil to the pot and increase the heat to medium-high. Add the onion. Cook, stirring occasionally, until the onion becomes translucent, about 2 minutes. Add the carrot and cabbage; cook for 2 more minutes. Add the tomatoes; cook 1 more minute.
3. Add beef broth, salt, and pepper to the pot. Increase heat to high, cooking until broth begins to simmer. Stir, cover, reduce heat to low, and cook until vegetables are tender, about 15 minutes.

Chernyi Hleb
(Black Bread)
Makes 1 loaf

2	cups rye flour
1½	cups all-purpose flour
½	teaspoon sugar
1	teaspoon salt
1	cup whole-bran cereal
2¼	teaspoons caraway seeds, crushed
1	teaspoon instant coffee
½	teaspoon onion powder
¼	teaspoon fennel seed, crushed
1	package active dry yeast
1¼	cups water
2	tablespoons vinegar
2	tablespoons molasses
4½	teaspoons cocoa
2	tablespoons butter
1	egg white
2	teaspoons cold water

1. In a medium bowl, combine rye flour and all-purpose flour.
2. In a large mixer bowl, combine 1 cup mixed flour, sugar, salt, bran cereal, caraway seeds, instant coffee, onion powder, fennel seed, and dry yeast.
3. In medium saucepan, combine 1¼ cups water, vinegar, molasses, cocoa, and butter. Heat over low heat, stirring occasionally, until very warm (120°F to 130°F). (Butter does not need to melt.)
4. Gradually add warm liquids to the dry ingredients in the mixer bowl and beat on medium speed of electric mixer 2 minutes,

scraping bowl occasionally. Add ½ cup of mixed flour and beat on high speed 2 minutes. Add enough remaining mixed flour to form a soft dough.

5. Turn dough out onto a lightly floured surface. Cover with a clean towel and let rest 15 minutes.
6. Knead dough until smooth and elastic, about 10 to 12 minutes. (Dough may still be a little sticky.)
7. Place dough in a greased bowl, turning to grease the top. Cover with a clean towel and let rise in a warm place until doubled in bulk, about 1 hour.
8. Punch dough down; turn out onto a lightly floured surface. Shape the dough into a ball about 5 inches in diameter. Place the ball in a greased 8-inch round cake pan. Cover with a clean towel and let it rise in a warm place until doubled in bulk, about 1 hour.
9. Brush the top of the loaf with egg white that has been mixed with 2 teaspoons of water. Bake at 350°F for 45 to 50 minutes or until loaf sounds hollow when gently tapped with knuckles. Remove bread to a cooling rack.

Per slice: 126 calories (16% from fat), 4 g protein, 26 g carbohydrate, 3 g fat, 3 mg cholesterol, 5 g fiber, 206 mg sodium.

Cranberry Kisel
Serves 4

2	cups fresh cranberries
1½	cups cold water, divided
⅔	cup sugar
3	tablespoons cornstarch

1. Wash cranberries and put them in a medium saucepan with 1¼ cups of cold water. Place cranberries over medium heat and bring to a boil. Reduce heat and simmer for 5 to 10 minutes, until cranberries pop.
2. Remove cranberries from heat and allow to cool for 10 minutes. Then puree the cranberries in a blender or food processor until smooth.
3. Return the puree to the saucepan. Stir in sugar.
4. Combine cornstarch with the remaining ¼ cup of cold water; stir until smooth.
5. Add cornstarch mixture to cranberry puree. Place over medium heat. Bring mixture to a boil; reduce heat and simmer for 1 minute, stirring constantly. Remove from heat.
6. Pour kisel into a bowl or serving dishes and chill. Serve with whipped cream, if desired.

Per serving: 175 calories (0% from fat), 0 g protein, 45 g carbohydrate, 0 g fat, 0 mg cholesterol, 2 g fiber, 1 mg sodium.

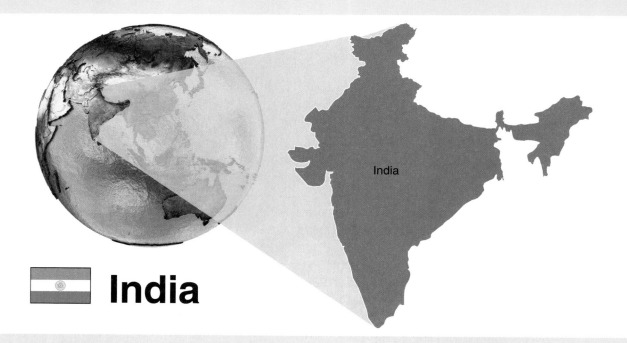

India

Geography and Climate of India

Called *Bharat* by those local to its lands, India is the seventh largest country in the world. It is a beautiful country with mountains, jungles, rich valleys, and miles of coastline.

India is located on a peninsula of southern Asia. The country can be divided into three distinct geographical areas.

The Himalayan Mountains form one of the three geographical areas in India. These mountains create a natural barrier from the rest of Asia (**Figure 34.5**). The hilly regions beneath the mountains include forests or grazing lands.

The plains formed by the Indus, Ganges, and Brahmaputra rivers are the second geographical area. The rich, deep soil of the Ganges River basin allows farmers to plant two crops each year.

The third geographical area lies to the south of the fertile river plains. It is a large plateau, called the *Deccan*, which covers most of the peninsula. Agriculture is possible in level areas of the Deccan, where rainfall or irrigation systems provide enough moisture.

India has a tropical climate. Cool weather lasts only from about December to March. The monsoon season lasts from June until the end of

f9photos/Shutterstock.com

Figure 34.5 The Himalayan Mountains separate India from the rest of Asia.

September. The monsoon rains provide needed moisture for the dry earth. In just a short time, however, they can force rivers to flood their banks.

Indian Agriculture

Nearly one-half of India's workers are farmers. Rice is India's major crop. Wheat, corn, millet, and *pulses* (legumes) are also grown for food. Sugarcane, tea, coffee, and coconut are raised to sell for income.

Indians raise more cattle than they do any other type of livestock. Cows provide some milk, but Indians primarily use cattle as work animals. They also raise smaller numbers of goats, hogs, sheep, and water buffalo and export the hides and skins.

Indian Culture

The people of India belong to a number of races. Indians speak over 700 languages and dialects. This variety is the result of foreign invasions that lasted many centuries.

Religion plays an important role in the culture of India's people. Most Indians are Hindus. Muslims are the next largest group. Small groups of Christians, Sikhs, Jains, Buddhists, and Parsees also live in India.

One influence of religion on Indian culture is the observance of the **caste system**. This ancient social system, which evolved from Hinduism, divided people into *castes*, or groups that are based largely on occupation and have a ranked order. For instance, priests and teachers are in a higher caste than unskilled laborers. Today, many of the old caste restrictions have been relaxed; however, caste divisions are still observed in some aspects of Indian life. As one example, people do not generally marry outside their castes.

Another way religion influences Indian culture is in the celebration of holidays. Three popular festivals honor Hindu gods in India. The *Pongal Harvest Festival* is a time of thanksgiving for the winter harvest of rice, an important crop in India. It honors Surya, the sun god, for helping to ripen the rice. Hindu families offer a special

rice pudding to Surya before eating it themselves (**Figure 34.6**). *Janmashtami* celebrates the birthday of one of the most popular Hindu gods, Krishna. The traditions of this holiday include going to the temple and bathing a statue of Krishna. The statue is bathed with clarified butter mixed with milk, sugar, and honey. The people in the temple then eat the sweet mixture with which they washed the statue. The *Ganesha Festival* is named for an elephant-headed god, Ganesha. Hindu people ask Ganesha to bring them success when they start new projects. During the festival, people place statues of Ganesha in their homes and present offerings of candy and fruit to it.

Indian Cuisine

Indian cuisine is known for being very nutritious. Many Indian dishes are vegetarian, and even those dishes that include meat generally do so in small amounts. This plant-based diet, which centers on grains, vegetables, and legumes, is high in fiber. Indian cuisine includes a variety of seasonings, which researchers believe may offer health benefits. The Indian diet is also rich in vitamins, minerals, and many other nutrients, although the fat content of some Indian dishes can be high due to the liberal use of fat in cooking.

GreenTree/Shutterstock.com

Figure 34.6 At the Pongal Harvest Festival, Indian people serve a rice pudding known as *pongal*.

Culture and Social Studies

Influence of Religion on Indian Cuisine

In addition to geography and climate, religion has been a third major influence on the development of Indian cuisine. Most Indian people are either Hindu or Muslim. Therefore, the dietary restrictions of these two religions have had the greatest impact.

Many Hindu taboos concern food. Hindus cannot eat beef because they consider the cow to be sacred. Most Hindus are vegetarian, although some Hindus eat mutton, poultry, goat, and fish. In addition, Hindus cannot eat food that has been organically altered. (Artificial color and chemical processes used as preservatives are allowed.)

Although Muslims cannot eat pork, they do eat beef, mutton, lamb, fish, and poultry. These animal foods are more common in Northern India, where most Indian Muslims live.

Geography and climate have influenced India's cuisine. Geographically, Indian cuisines are most different in the North and the South. Invading groups of people, especially the Mongols in the thirteenth century, influenced Northern India. The Mongols brought the meat-based cuisine of their Central Asian home. This cuisine developed in royal kitchens and became characterized by foods that are rich and heavily seasoned. Other groups of people had less influence on Southern India. Thus, foods in Southern India are hotter and not as subtle or refined as those in the North.

Climate has also played a large part in the development of the two styles of Indian cooking. The heavy rainfall of the South allows large crops of rice, fruits, and vegetables to grow. In the drier North, where wheat grows, bread sometimes replaces rice.

Indian Vegetable Dishes

Vegetable dishes are common in Indian cooking. This is especially true in the South, where many people are vegetarian. There, pulses are an important source of protein.

Many Indian cooks prepare pulses by combining them with other vegetables in filling stews. They also serve pulses by mashing or pureeing them with spices to make *dal*. Dal may be thinned and eaten as soup. It may also be poured over rice or served as a dipping sauce for bread.

Indian cooks prepare many vegetable dishes by frying vegetables with spices. They shape mashed vegetables into balls, deep-fry them, and serve them with a sauce. Indian cooks may also grill vegetables. In preparing eggplant, they may flavor it with oil, pepper, and lemon and then grill it. Vegetables are also used in cool dishes. *Raita*, a salad made of yogurt, vegetables, and seasonings, is a cool accompaniment to spicy dishes. *Rayata*, a potato salad flavored with yogurt, cucumber, tomatoes, cumin, and paprika, is served as a main dish.

Indian Main Dishes

Rice is a staple food throughout much of India. Rice often is served as a side dish; however, it sometimes is used in a variety of main dishes and desserts. Rice is also served as part of a group of dishes called *curries*.

Literally, **curry** is a variation of a word meaning "sauce." It describes a type of stew. Curry can be prepared in many ways, depending on the region. All curries are made with a mixture of spices called **masala**. One common curry is prepared by adding the masala to pickled fruit. This mixture is cooked with sugar and vinegar. The curry may be combined with vegetables, meat, poultry, or fish and accompanied by a variety of condiments (**Figure 34.7**).

India's many miles of coastline provide a variety of fish. Fish are dried, marinated, and smoked. One Indian specialty is a marinated fish prepared by layering fillets of fish with spices, salt, and tamarind pulp. *Bombil*, a small, nearly transparent fish, is caught in large quantities. When dried, it can be stored for long periods. *Pomfret* often is stuffed with a mixture of spices. It is then wrapped in a banana leaf and steamed, baked, or fried.

Joe Gough/Shutterstock.com

Figure 34.7   Many types of curry are found throughout India. What types of Indian curry have you tried?

Shellfish are also widely available in India. Shrimp and prawns are baked, grilled, or used in curries. Cooks often coat these crustaceans with a spicy batter and deep-fry them. Crabs and lobsters are shredded; mixed with coconut milk, eggs, and spices; and fried in butter.

Most Indian meat dishes are made with goat or mutton. Few Indians eat pork, and beef is both scarce and expensive. Indians prepare meat in many ways. Meat braised in yogurt, cream, or a mixture of the two is called *korma*. *Bhona* is meat that is first sautéed and then baked. Kebabs are made from mutton that has been spiced, minced, and grilled. *Koftas* are spicy meatballs.

Chicken dishes are also popular in parts of India. People in the North marinate chicken in a mixture of yogurt and spices and then roast it on a spit. People in the South add chicken to a spicy, coconut-flavored curry.

Indians cook many dishes in oil or fat. **Ghee** (Indian clarified butter) is the preferred cooking fat. Ghee is prepared by simmering butter and then straining it to remove solids that could cause rancidity during storage.

Indian Breads

Indians eat several kinds of *roti*, or bread. Most Indian breads are made from wheat, are

Learn About...
Indian Seasonings

The essence of Indian cooking lies in the art of using spices. For example, to prepare a curry, Indian cooks must be able to make an excellent masala. The combinations of spices in masalas can vary. To be an excellent masala, however, each ingredient in the masala must retain its identity without overpowering the other flavors.

The spicy dishes of coastal Southern India use *wet masalas*. These are prepared by mixing spices with vinegar, coconut milk, or water. Wet masalas must be used immediately. Northern Indians use dry masalas. *Dry masalas* contain no liquid, and cooks can prepare them ahead and store them for a short time.

Saffron, fenugreek, cumin seed, coriander seed, turmeric, and fennel seed are basic to Indian cooking. Other seasonings essential to Indian cooking are garlic, onions, and hot chili peppers. Spices add color as well as flavor to Indian dishes. Saffron and turmeric give rice and potato dishes a bright yellow color. Red and green chilies add vivid color to curries.

Fresh herbs also add flavor to Indian foods. They are used to make sauces and *chutneys* (condiments containing fruits, onions, spices, and herbs). Coriander leaves, mint, and sweet basil are the most popular fresh herbs.

Know and Apply
1. What is the key to an excellent masala?
2. Which seasonings used in Indian cuisine are used to flavor foods you enjoy?

unleavened, and are round. The most common Indian bread is **chapati**, a flat bread. *Poori* is an unleavened fried bread. Indian bakers also make *paratha*, which they roll and fold several times so layers form when the bread bakes. Indians often stuff paratha with a meat or vegetable mixture.

Indian Sweets

Indians make many of their sweets from milk. Cooks simmer the milk into a thickened mass called *mawa*. They cook the mawa with sugar and add flavorings, such as almonds and coconut.

Another group of Indian confections is made from semolina, chickpea flour, wheat flour, or corn flour. *Halva*, one type of flour-based sweet, is made from semolina.

Indian Cooking Techniques

Many Indian foods are prepared using common cooking methods, such as frying, baking, boiling, and steaming. Some cooking techniques, however, characterize specific Indian dishes. These techniques may involve the way certain ingredients are used, as well as the cooking method employed.

Tandoori is among the techniques that are unique to Indian cuisine. This simple cooking technique involves baking foods in a clay oven called a *tandoor*. This method is used most often in Northern India. Tandoori chicken, lamb on skewers, and a type of bread called *naan* are three traditional foods prepared by this method (**Figure 34.8**). In another technique known as *korma*, foods are braised, usually in yogurt. Lamb traditionally is prepared in this way. Dishes prepared in the *vindaloo* way have a hot, slightly sour flavor created by combining vinegar with spices.

Indian Meals

During Indian meals, all dishes are served at one time, sometimes on a thali. A *thali* is a large, round platter placed in the center of the table. (In some parts of India, a banana leaf is used as a thali.) Rice generally is placed in the center of the thali. Small bowls of chutneys, pickles, yogurt, and other condiments are placed around the rice. Diners help themselves to the food by using their fingers.

In middle-class Indian homes, the main meal of the day usually includes a meat or fish dish. (Vegetarian families would omit this dish.) Several vegetable dishes, rice, or lentils and breads are also included. Occasionally, appetizers may be served. One popular appetizer is *samosas*, which are small pastries stuffed with vegetables, fish, or meat. If sweets are served, Indians eat them with the meal rather than afterward.

Family etiquette requires that Indian diners wash their hands and rinse their mouths following a meal. Indian people frequently follow this ritual with paan. *Paan* is a betel leaf spread with lime paste and wrapped around chopped betel nuts. As people chew it, it acts as a mouth freshener and digestive aid.

Maksim Denisenko/Shutterstock.com

Figure 34.8 The use of a tandoor is unique to Indian cooking. How does a tandoor differ from an oven in the United States?

Indian Menu

Ghee
(Clarified Butter)

Garam Masala
(Indian Spice Mixture)

Samosas
(Savory Stuffed Pastries)

Chatni
(Mixed Fruit Chutney)

Raita
(Yogurt with Vegetables)

Dal
(Lentil Puree)

Chapatis
(Unleavened Bread)

Pongal Rice
(Rice Pudding)

Tea

Ghee
(Clarified Butter)
Makes about ¾ cup

½ pound sweet butter

1. In a heavy saucepan, melt butter over low heat. When the butter has completely liquefied, increase heat to medium-low to bring the butter to a boil.
2. Reduce heat back to low to keep the butter at a simmer. With a slotted spoon, skim off any foam that rises to the surface of the butter. Continue simmering the butter for 5 to 10 more minutes.
3. The ghee is done when no more foam forms and the liquid butter is transparent and golden. The milk solids that have collected on the bottom of the pan should be slightly brown.
4. Line a funnel with 3 or 4 thicknesses of cheesecloth. Carefully strain the clear liquid ghee through the cheesecloth into a heatproof glass jar. Make sure none of the solids in the bottom of the pan go through the cheesecloth.
5. Tightly cover the jar and store ghee in a cool place. It does not require refrigeration.

Per tablespoon: 100 calories (100% from fat), 0 g protein, 0 g carbohydrate, 11 g fat, 31 mg cholesterol, 0 g fiber, 2 mg sodium.

Garam Masala
(Indian Spice Mixture)
Makes ¼ cup

1½ teaspoons ground cardamom
3¾ teaspoons ground coriander
1 tablespoon ground cumin
1½ teaspoons ground black pepper
¾ teaspoon ground cloves
¾ teaspoon ground cinnamon
¾ teaspoon ground nutmeg

1. In a small bowl, use a fork to stir together cardamom, coriander, cumin, pepper, cloves, cinnamon, and nutmeg until thoroughly combined.
2. Transfer mixture to an airtight container and store in a cool, dark place.

Samosas
(Savory Stuffed Pastries)
Makes about 15

Pastry:
¾ cup all-purpose flour
1½ teaspoons vegetable oil
¼ teaspoon salt
¼ cup warm water

1. In a medium mixer bowl, blend flour, oil, salt, and water until a soft dough forms.
2. Turn dough out onto a lightly floured surface. Knead until dough is smooth and elastic, about 10 minutes.
3. Cover and set aside while preparing filling.

Filling:
1½ teaspoons ghee
¼ teaspoon minced garlic
½ teaspoon chopped ginger root
⅓ cup chopped onion
¾ cup mashed potatoes
¼ cup cooked peas
½ teaspoon garam masala
1½ teaspoons fresh coriander or mint
vegetable oil for frying

1. In a medium skillet, heat ghee over medium heat. Add garlic, ginger root, and onion. Sauté until vegetables are tender.
2. Remove from heat. Stir in mashed potatoes and peas. Season with garam masala and coriander or mint.
3. Using fingers, shape tablespoons of pastry dough into small balls. Roll each ball into a flat circle about 6 inches in diameter. Cut each circle in half.
4. Place 1 teaspoon of filling on one side of each half circle. Moisten the edge of the pastry with water. Fold dough over to form a triangle and press edges together to seal.
5. In a deep saucepan, heat 2 to 3 inches of vegetable oil to 375°F. Fry samosas a few at a time until golden brown.
6. Drain on absorbent paper. Serve immediately.

Per samosa: 50 calories (36% from fat), 1 g protein, 7 g carbohydrate, 2 g fat, 1 mg cholesterol, 1 g fiber, 90 mg sodium.

Chatni
(Mixed Fruit Chutney)
Serves 4

1 medium plum
1 medium cooking apple
1 small pear or 2 medium apricots
¼ teaspoon minced garlic
1 teaspoon minced fresh ginger root
1 teaspoon garam masala
½ teaspoon caraway seeds
½ teaspoon salt
1 tablespoon raisins
¾ teaspoon chili powder
¼ cup brown sugar
½ cup vinegar

1. Peel fruit, core or pit, and cut into small pieces.
2. Put fruit, garlic, and ginger root in a medium saucepan. Add garam masala, caraway seeds, salt, raisins, and chili powder. Bring mixture to a boil over medium heat. Reduce heat and simmer for 15 to 20 minutes, stirring frequently, until fruit is very tender.
3. Remove from heat, stir in sugar and vinegar, and cool. Serve cold as an accompaniment.

Per serving: 106 calories (4% from fat), 1 g protein, 29 g carbohydrate, 1 g fat, 0 mg cholesterol, 2 g fiber, 278 mg sodium.

Raita
(Yogurt with Vegetables)
Serves 4 to 6

2 medium cucumbers
2 tablespoons chopped onion
¾ teaspoon salt
2 medium firm ripe tomatoes
2 tablespoons chopped coriander
2 cups plain nonfat yogurt
2 teaspoons cumin

1. Peel cucumbers. Slice them lengthwise into halves. Scoop out the seeds. Make lengthwise slices about ⅛ inch thick. Then cut slices crosswise into ½-inch pieces.
2. In a medium mixing bowl, combine cucumbers, onion, and salt and mix thoroughly. Let rest at room temperature for 5 minutes.
3. Squeeze cucumbers and onions gently to remove the excess liquid and transfer to a clean bowl.
4. Add the tomatoes and coriander and toss together thoroughly.
5. Combine the yogurt and cumin. Pour over the vegetables. Refrigerate until ready to serve.

Per serving: 93 calories (10% from fat), 7 g protein, 14 g carbohydrate, 1 g fat, 2 mg cholesterol, 1 g fiber, 434 mg sodium.

Dal
(Lentil Puree)
Serves 6

1½ cups dried lentils, washed and sorted
3 cups water
2 tablespoons ghee or butter
3 cloves garlic, crushed
½ teaspoon ground ginger
1 teaspoon coriander seeds
¾ teaspoon salt
½ teaspoon cayenne pepper

1. Place lentils and water in a large saucepan. Bring to a boil over medium-high heat.
2. Reduce heat, cover, and simmer until lentils are very tender, about 20 minutes.
3. In a large skillet, heat ghee or melt butter. Add the garlic, ginger, and coriander seeds. Stir over medium heat for about 3 minutes.
4. Add lentils and any remaining cooking water to the skillet. Mash lentils until smooth as you stir them into the seasonings. Add water as needed to reach desired consistency for dipping. Then stir in salt and cayenne pepper.
5. Serve hot with chapatis for dipping.

Per serving: 152 calories (24% from fat), 9 g protein, 21 g carbohydrate, 4 g fat, 10 mg cholesterol, 8 g fiber, 294 mg sodium.

Chapatis
(Unleavened Bread)
Makes 4

1	cup whole-wheat flour
¼	teaspoon salt
2	tablespoons butter
⅜	cup water
1½	teaspoons ghee

1. Mix flour and salt together in a mixing bowl. With pastry blender, two knives, or fingers, cut butter into dry ingredients until particles are the size of small peas.
2. Add 2 tablespoons water all at once. Mix with fingers, gradually adding enough additional water to form a soft dough.
3. Turn dough out onto a lightly floured surface. Knead dough until smooth and elastic, about 10 minutes.
4. Place dough in a bowl, cover, and let stand at room temperature 30 minutes.
5. Turn dough out onto a floured surface. Divide into 4 pieces. Roll each piece into a thin circle about 5 inches in diameter.
6. Meanwhile, heat a heavy skillet over moderate heat.
7. Put chapatis, one at a time, in the skillet. When small blisters appear on the surface, turn and cook the other side until golden.
8. Remove bread from the skillet. Brush with ghee and keep warm in a 200°F oven until all chapatis are cooked. Serve warm.

Per piece: 163 calories (40% from fat), 4 g protein, 21 g carbohydrate, 8 g fat, 4 mg cholesterol, 6 g fiber, 201 mg sodium.

Pongal Rice
(Rice Pudding)
Serves 4 to 6

1½	cups cooked rice
1¾	cups fat-free milk
1	tablespoon ghee
3	tablespoons raisins
3	tablespoons slivered, blanched almonds
⅓	cup brown sugar
¼	teaspoon cardamom
¼	teaspoon cinnamon

1. In a medium heavy saucepan, combine rice and milk. Cook over medium-low heat, stirring often until thickened, about 20 minutes.
2. In a small skillet, heat ghee over medium heat. Add raisins and almonds. Cook 2 to 3 minutes until raisins are plump and almonds are toasted.
3. Stir raisin and almond mixture, brown sugar, cardamom, and cinnamon into pudding in the saucepan. Cook and stir until sugar is dissolved.
4. Serve warm or cooled.

Per serving: 265 calories (20% from fat), 6 g protein, 47 g carbohydrate, 6 g fat, 10 mg cholesterol, 2 g fiber, 52 mg sodium.

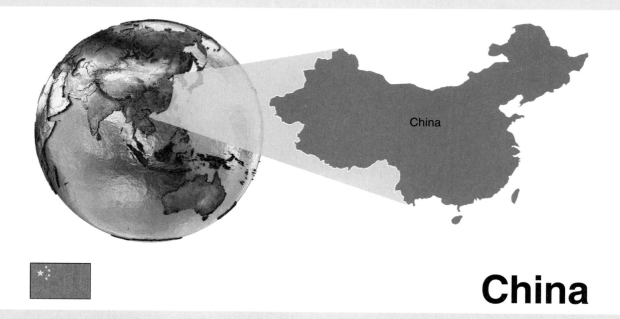

China

The People's Republic of China (commonly called *China*) is the home of one of the oldest civilizations in the world. In modern history, China has gone through many changes. Some of these changes have affected the nation's diet; however, the roots of Chinese cuisine date back centuries.

Geography and Climate of China

China is the third largest country in the world, occupying nearly one-fourth of Asia. Geographical features have kept China isolated for much of its history.

The Pacific Ocean and the South China Sea form China's coastlines. Western China is mountainous. The Himalayan and Tien Shan Mountains are most familiar to the Western world. Much of Western and Southwestern China is barren. The mountains are too high and rugged and the valleys too cold and dry for food production.

Eastern China is more suitable for human life. The mountains and hills are lower, and the rolling plains are fairly level. The wide valleys formed by China's great rivers have rich soil. Historically, most of China's people have crowded within this geographic area.

Because China's borders extend so far north and south, some Chinese lands have extreme climates. In China's northernmost regions, the ground stays frozen two-thirds of the year. Subarctic conditions keep temperatures below zero for months at a time, and rainfall is scarce. In the southernmost provinces, the climate is subtropical with ample rainfall (**Figure 34.9**).

Monsoons that come off the Pacific Ocean bring dust storms to Northern China. They also bring undependable rainfall to much of the eastern third of the country. In these regions, both drought and flooding are common.

Chinese Agriculture

Today, about one-third of China's people are employed in agriculture. On small family farms, nearly all the work is done by hand or with the help of animals. The Chinese government controls other farms and operates them as *communes* (groups of people who share living areas, resources, and tasks).

China's chief agricultural product is rice. Other important crops include wheat, oil seeds (used to make cooking oil), and tea. Cabbage, celery, peas, beans, lettuce, leeks, and onions are important vegetable crops. Leading fruits in China are apples, pears, peaches, and grapes.

The Chinese raise few beef or dairy cattle. Instead, they raise pigs, chickens, ducks, geese, and other small animals that can eat scraps. A few sheep and goats graze in mountainous and grassy areas. China's waters provide an abundance of fish.

aphotostory/Shutterstock.com

Figure 34.9 In contrast to the subarctic conditions of China's northernmost regions, the southernmost regions have plentiful rainfall and are rich in agriculture.

Chinese Culture

China has a population larger than that of any other nation. Many notable achievements have been made in China throughout the ages. The Chinese are credited with numerous inventions, including paper, gunpowder, and the magnetic compass. They built the Great Wall of China, which stretches about 4,000 miles through Northern China (**Figure 34.10**). The Chinese also created beautiful works of art and made important contributions in literature.

The People's Republic of China was established in 1949 under Communist rule. In pre-Communist days, most Chinese were Buddhists, Taoists, or Confucianists. Smaller groups of Chinese Christians and Muslims lived in scattered groups. Today, most people do not openly practice religion in China.

The most widely celebrated festival in China is the *Spring Festival*, which recognizes the New Year. The Chinese zodiac follows a 12-year cycle, in which each year is named for a different animal. Each new year is welcomed with a

Hung Chung Chih/Shutterstock.com

Figure 34.10 The Great Wall of China is a collection of Chinese walls built over several centuries. The majority of the wall that survives today was built by the Ming Dynasty. Why was the Great Wall of China built?

Learn About...

Chinese Ingredients

In the past, many Chinese ingredients were difficult to obtain in the United States. Today, however, many large cities have specialty shops that stock Chinese foods. Chinese items can also be found in international sections of most supermarkets.

The ingredients described in the following list often appear in Chinese recipes. Besides these ingredients, Chinese cooks use many seasonings. Important seasonings include ginger root, scallions, garlic, bean paste, and fermented black bean. Hot pepper, sesame seed oil, star anise, Chinese peppercorns, and five-spice powder are also common.

Basic ingredients used in Chinese cooking include:

- **Bamboo shoots**: Cream-colored vegetable that adds a crisp, chewy texture to foods.
- **Bean curd**: Gelatinous, cream-colored cake made from soybeans that is a major source of protein in the Chinese diet.
- **Bean sprouts**: Sprouts of mung beans.
- **Bean threads (cellophane noodles)**: Thin, smooth, and translucent noodles.
- **Black mushrooms**: Very dark mushrooms that are sold dried.
- **Chinese cabbage (bok choy)**: Type of cabbage with a white, celerylike stalk topped with green leaves; is used for cooking and stewing.
- **Chinese pea pods**: Tender, crisp, green, pod-shaped vegetable.
- **Golden needles**: Parts of the tiger lily plant that look like brown, shriveled stems.
- **Hoisin sauce**: Dark, thick sauce made from beans, salt, spices, and sugar; is used in cooking and at the table.
- **Oyster sauce**: Dark brown sauce that is made from oysters and seasonings; is used with dark-colored dishes and as a dipping sauce.
- **Soy sauce**: Brown sauce made from soybeans, wheat, flour, salt, and water.
- **Water chestnuts**: Round, cream-colored vegetables that can be purchased canned or fresh.
- **Winter melon**: Large melon with pale green skin and white flesh; is cooked with vegetables and meat or added to soup.
- **Wood ears**: Type of brown fungus that grows on trees.

Know and Apply

1. What common characteristics do you notice among many of the ingredients listed in the table?
2. With which of the listed basic ingredients are you most familiar?

---

special dinner of festive foods, including candied fruits and dumplings.

The *Dragon Boat Festival* falls in midsummer. During this festival, people used to throw rice cakes into the river to appease a mythical dragon. Now, Chinese people recognize this occasion by holding boat races and eating rice cakes that have been wrapped in bamboo leaves.

The *Moon Festival* comes in midautumn. The Chinese celebrate this festival by eating *moon cakes*, which are pastries filled with bean paste or lotus seeds. Adults sit outside and enjoy the full moon while children parade through the streets with lanterns.

Chinese Cuisine

The Chinese enjoy a nutritious cuisine. Their meals include large amounts of rice and vegetables, but only small amounts of meat. They stir-fry, steam, or simmer many of their dishes. This combination of healthful ingredients and light cooking methods makes Chinese cuisine fairly low in fat, but high in vitamins, minerals, and fiber. One nutritional drawback of the Chinese diet is the high sodium levels that result from liberal use of soy sauce.

Besides nourishing the body, Chinese cuisine delights the senses. An old Chinese proverb describes a well-prepared dish as one that smells appealing as it is brought to the table. The dish must stimulate the appetite by its harmonious color combinations. The food must taste delicious and sound pleasing as it is being chewed. Today, the best Chinese dishes still live up to these high standards.

Chinese Cooking Utensils

Of all Chinese cooking utensils, the wok is the most versatile. A wok looks like a metal bowl with sloping sides. Some woks have covers. A metal ring makes it possible to use a wok on a gas or electric range.

Woks are ideal for stir-frying because they conduct heat evenly and rapidly. (A heavy, smooth skillet can also be used for this type of cooking.) There are few foods that cannot be cooked in a wok. Other cooking methods, such as deep-frying, can be done in a wok, too.

A second piece of Chinese cooking equipment is the *steamer*. A steamer looks like a round, shallow basket with openings. Steamers often are sold in sets so several foods can steam at the same time (**Figure 34.11**). Most Chinese steamers are made from bamboo, but in the United States, metal steamers are more common.

A third cooking tool is the *cleaver*. Because the Chinese eat with chopsticks, cooks must cut all the ingredients in a dish into pieces that diners can handle easily. Small pieces of food also cook more evenly and rapidly. Chinese cooks use cleavers to perform all cutting tasks, as well as crushing and pounding tasks. They use the wide, flat sides of cleaver blades to scoop and transfer food.

nioloxs/Shutterstock.com

Figure 34.11 Sets of bamboo steamers are common in China.

A number of other tools will come in handy when preparing Chinese foods. A *curved spatula* that fits the shape of a pan is ideal for stirring and turning foods in a wok. *Long chopsticks* are useful for loosening and mixing food. A *wire-mesh strainer* helps lift deep-fried foods out of hot oil. A *ladle* can be used to serve foods and spoon liquids over ingredients in a wok. A *bamboo brush* is helpful for cleaning the wok.

Chinese Cooking Methods

Because most Chinese dishes cook so quickly, cooks must assemble all the ingredients in advance. In fact, the Chinese spend more time preparing food to be cooked than they spend cooking.

Much of the preparation time for cooking Chinese dishes involves slicing, chopping, shredding, dicing, and mincing vegetables and meats. Many ingredients can be prepared hours or even days in advance and refrigerated until needed.

Once the ingredients are prepared, the Chinese may use one of four main cooking methods: stir-frying, steaming, deep-frying, or simmering. Less often, they might choose roasting as the cooking method.

Stir-Frying

Stir-frying is the most common Chinese cooking method. Meat, poultry, fish, and vegetables can be stir-fried. All ingredients must be cut into uniform pieces so they will cook evenly.

To stir-fry foods, heat a small amount of oil in a wok. When the oil becomes hot, add the ingredients that need the longest cooking time. Then add the ingredients that cook more quickly. Stir continuously throughout the cooking period. When the vegetables are crisp-tender, the dish is ready to serve. (Sometimes, a little stock or water and seasonings might be added to form a sauce.)

Stir-fried foods cook rapidly, so they must be watched carefully. Stir-fried foods retain their color, texture, flavor, and nutrients. They must be served immediately, however, or they will lose their texture and flavor. Never overfill a wok. If more than a few people are being served, several batches of the same dish will need to be prepared.

Steaming

Steaming is the second most common cooking method in China. Because many Chinese people do not have ovens, steaming often replaces baking. Meats, poultry, dumplings, bread, and rice can be steamed. The kettle used for steaming must be large enough that the steam circulates freely around the food. (The water should never touch the food.) Like stir-frying, steaming is economical. Because several dishes can be steamed at the same time, energy is saved.

Deep-Frying

Deep-frying seals in juices and gives foods a crisp coating. Meat, poultry, egg rolls, and wontons are often deep-fried (**Figure 34.12**).

Foods to be deep-fried are first cut into cubes. The cubes can be coated with cornstarch or dipped in a flour and egg batter. (Sometimes the cubes might be marinated before being coated.) To deep-fry, plunge the coated food into hot fat a few pieces at a time. Drain all deep-fried foods on absorbent paper.

Simmering

Chinese soups and large pieces of meat may be prepared by *simmering*. In this method of cooking, the ingredients are cooked in simmering liquid over low heat. If a clear liquid, such as chicken broth, is used, this method is called *clear-simmering*.

Roasting

The Chinese occasionally use several other cooking methods. Of these methods, *roasting* is most popular. The Chinese sometimes roast pork and poultry. They first rub the meat or bird with oil and/or marinate it. A quick searing over an open flame makes the skin crisp. Then they place the meat or bird on a rack or hang it on a hook to roast slowly. Of all roasted dishes, *Peking duck* is the best known. The Chinese roll slices of the crisp duck skin and tender flesh inside thin pancakes with scallions and hoisin sauce. (*Hoisin sauce* is a soy-based barbecue-type sauce.)

Traditional Chinese Foods

From basic ingredients and cooking methods, the Chinese prepare a variety of traditional foods, including grain products, vegetables, main dishes, soups, desserts, and tea.

Chinese Grain Products

For centuries, rice has been the backbone of the Southern Chinese diet. This is mainly because rice is both inexpensive and filling.

The Chinese use *glutinous* (gluelike), short-grain rice to make rice flour and translucent rice noodles. They also use rice flour to make pastries and dumplings. Chinese people serve long-grain rice as a side dish and use it to make a main dish called *fried rice*. For this dish, Chinese cooks mix rice with meat, poultry, or fish; eggs; vegetables; and seasonings (**Figure 34.13**). The Chinese prepare most rice by steaming. When ready to serve, the rice should be fluffy with firm, distinct grains.

In some parts of China, noodles or flat pancakes made from wheat flour are used in place

manasapat/Shutterstock.com

Figure 34.12 Egg rolls are a common Chinese deep-fried food. What are typical ingredients in an egg roll?

Karissaa/Shutterstock.com

Figure 34.13 Fried rice is made of long-grain rice and a mixture of meat, vegetables, and seasonings.

of rice. One type of noodle is called *lo mein*. It is made from flour and eggs and resembles spaghetti.

The Chinese also use wheat flour to make the skins or wrappers for *wontons* (dumplings) and *egg rolls*. The dough for both contains wheat flour and eggs. The Chinese usually fill egg rolls and wontons with a mixture of minced vegetables and meat, poultry, or shellfish. They prepare wontons by steaming, deep-frying, or boiling them in soups. Egg rolls usually are deep-fried.

Chinese Vegetables

Vegetables are used to a greater extent than meat in the Chinese diet. The Chinese grow many varieties of vegetables. These include Chinese cabbage, broccoli, spinach, pea pods, radishes, mushrooms, and cauliflower. The Chinese eat vegetables alone, in salads, and in soups. They also use vegetables to stretch small amounts of meat, fish, and poultry. Vegetables help make Chinese cooking economical and nutritious.

Chinese Main Dishes

Although the Chinese eat chicken and duck, they eat little beef. This is partly because beef in China is scarce and not very good. Also, some religions forbid the eating of beef. Religions may forbid the eating of pork as well. *Sweet and sour pork* is a popular dish among those Chinese who are allowed to eat pork. Sweet and sour pork is a mixture of deep-fried pork cubes, pineapple, and vegetables in a sweet-sour sauce.

Fish are more important to the Chinese diet than meat. Many kinds of fresh- and saltwater fish and shellfish are available. The Chinese preserve some fish by drying, which allows them to transport the fish inland or store them for times of need.

The Chinese also like eggs, which they consider a sign of good luck. The Chinese eat both chicken eggs and duck eggs, but they prefer chicken eggs. They use eggs in soups, such as *egg drop soup* (seasoned chicken broth containing beaten eggs). They also use eggs in main dishes, such as fried rice and *egg foo yung* (the Chinese version of an omelet). The Chinese scramble, steam, and smoke eggs, too.

Chinese Soups

Soups are popular throughout China. Some soups, such as *Chinese noodle soup*, are very light. Others, such as *velvet-corn soup*, are heavier. In some parts of China, soup is served inside of dumplings as a snack.

Most Chinese soups are accompaniments rather than filling main dishes. Soup is the only dish the Chinese eat without chopsticks. They use spoons instead.

Chinese Desserts

Chinese cooks use few dairy products. Chinese recipes rarely call for milk, cheese, butter, or cream; although some Chinese people now eat ice cream and serve Peking dust at banquets. *Peking dust* is a dessert made of whipped cream covered with chestnut puree and garnished with nuts.

Sweet desserts are much less common in China than in other Asian countries. The Chinese reserve sweet desserts for banquets. Then they serve the desserts in the middle of the meal rather than at the end. Fresh or preserved fruits, almond cookies, almond float, and eight-treasure rice pudding are popular desserts (**Figure 34.14**). *Almond float* is cubes of almond-flavored gelatin garnished with fruit. *Eight-treasure rice pudding* is a molded rice pudding made with candied or dried fruits.

Chinese Tea

Tea is China's national drink. The Chinese serve black teas, oolong teas, and green teas. (In China, black tea is called *red tea* because black is considered to be an unlucky color.) Some teas are scented with fragrant blossoms. The Chinese never add cream, lemon, or sugar to their tea. They usually serve tea at the end of meals. They also offer tea to arriving and departing guests as a sign of hospitality.

Chinese Meals

The Chinese eat three meals a day. Breakfast may be just a bowl of **congee** (a thick porridge made from rice or barley), rice, or boiled noodles. More well-to-do families often serve the congee with several salty side dishes. They may also serve hot sesame muffins, Chinese doughnuts, or pastries bought from a nearby street vendor.

Lunch and dinner are similar. At both meals, all the dishes are served at once. The soup is placed in the center of the table. Four other dishes of pork, chicken, or fish, with or without vegetables, and one vegetable dish surround the soup. Rice always accompanies the main dishes.

Andrea Skjold Mink/Shutterstock.com

Figure 34.14 Chinese almond cookies are a popular dessert. What are some other Chinese desserts?

Although the Chinese eat few sweets, they do enjoy snacks. *Dim sum* (steamed dumplings) are delicate pastries filled with meat, fish, vegetables, or occasionally a sweet fruit. Most are steamed, but a few are deep-fried.

At a Chinese table, each person's cover is set with a rice bowl, soup spoon, and shallow soup bowl. A shallow sauce dish, a larger dish for entrees, and a tea cup are also placed at each cover. The Chinese use **chopsticks** as their eating utensils for all dishes except soup and finger foods.

Chinese Menu

Ch'un-Chuan
(Egg Rolls)
Tan-Hau-T'ang
(Egg Drop Soup)
T'ien-Suan-Ku-Lao-Jou
(Sweet and Sour Pork)
Chao-Hsueh-Tou
(Stir-Fried Snow Peas with Chinese Mushrooms and Bamboo Shoots)
Pai-Fan
(Steamed Rice)
Preserved Kumquats
Hsing-Jen-Ping
(Almond Cookies)
Ch'a
(Tea)

Ch'un-Chuan
(Egg Rolls)
Makes 8 to 10 egg rolls

½ pound lean ground pork
  dash pepper
1 cup shredded cabbage
1 cup raw bean sprouts, washed and drained
¼ cup shredded carrots
2 green onions, finely chopped
½ teaspoon ground ginger
1½ teaspoons light brown sugar
1½ teaspoons cornstarch
1 tablespoon low-sodium soy sauce
1 tablespoon cold water
8 to 10 egg roll wrappers
1 tablespoon olive oil

1. Heat a skillet or wok over medium-high heat. Stir-fry the pork until it is lightly browned, about 2 to 3 minutes. Stir in the pepper. Then add the cabbage, bean sprouts, carrots, and green onion. Cook 2 minutes until vegetables just begin to soften.
2. Blend together the ginger, brown sugar, and cornstarch in a small bowl. Whisk in the soy sauce and cold water. Add the sauce to the skillet. Cook and stir to allow the sauce to thicken and glaze the meat and vegetables evenly.
3. Transfer the filling mixture to a shallow pan. Cover and refrigerate until cool enough to handle, about 15 minutes.
4. Preheat oven to 400°F. Cover a baking sheet with parchment paper.
5. Place one egg roll wrapper diagonally on the surface in front of you. Place about 2 tablespoons of cooled filling in the center of the wrapper. Fold the bottom corner of the wrapper over the filling. Fold the two side corners toward the center like an envelope. Brush a little water on the top corner. Then roll the egg roll tightly toward the top corner and seal well. Repeat this step with the remaining wrappers and filling.
6. Place filled egg rolls on the prepared baking sheet. Brush the egg rolls with olive oil and bake until golden brown, about 10 to 12 minutes. Serve immediately.

Per egg roll: 151 calories (36% from fat), 8 g protein, 16 g carbohydrate, 6 g fat, 23 mg cholesterol, 1 g fiber, 296 mg sodium.

Tan-Hau-T'ang
(Egg Drop Soup)
Serves 5 to 6

5 cups low-fat chicken broth
¾ cup minced, cooked chicken
1 tablespoon cornstarch
3 tablespoons cold water
2 eggs, lightly beaten
2 scallions, finely chopped

1. In a large saucepan, bring chicken broth to a boil. Reduce heat to medium and add chicken. Simmer 5 minutes.
2. Mix cornstarch with cold water. Add to soup, stirring until soup thickens and becomes clear.
3. Slowly pour beaten eggs into soup and stir once, gently. Turn off the heat.
4. Transfer soup to a heated tureen and garnish with chopped scallions.

Per serving: 60 calories (45% from fat), 6 g protein, 3 g carbohydrate, 3 g fat, 87 mg cholesterol, 0 g fiber, 188 mg sodium.

T'ien-Suan-Ku-Lao-Jou
(Sweet and Sour Pork)
Serves 5 to 6

Pork:
2 eggs, lightly beaten
1 teaspoon low-sodium soy sauce
½ cup cornstarch
½ cup flour
½ cup low-fat chicken broth
1 pound lean pork, trimmed and cut into 1-inch cubes
3 cups vegetable oil for frying

Sauce:
2 tablespoons vegetable oil
3 green onions, finely chopped
3 medium green peppers, cleaned, seeded, and cut into strips
2 cups canned pineapple chunks, drained (reserve juice)
3 tablespoons brown sugar
½ teaspoon ground ginger
¾ cup reserved pineapple juice
4 tablespoons cider vinegar
2 tablespoons red wine vinegar
3 tablespoons reduced-sodium soy sauce

4½ teaspoons cornstarch
2 tablespoons cold water

1. In large bowl, prepare coating batter by combining eggs, 1 teaspoon soy sauce, ½ cup cornstarch, flour, and chicken broth. Set aside while you prepare and assemble all other ingredients.
2. Just before cooking, add pork cubes to the coating batter. With a fork or chopsticks, stir to coat cubes evenly.
3. Preheat oven to 250°F.
4. Put 3 cups oil into wok or very large skillet. Over high heat, heat oil to 375°F.
5. Add pork cubes, a few at a time, and fry until crisp and golden. Remove pork to paper towel-lined baking pan to drain. Then, put pork in a baking dish and keep warm in the oven.
6. Pour remaining oil from wok or skillet. Add 2 tablespoons fresh oil and heat over high heat for 30 seconds.
7. Add green onions and green peppers to wok or skillet. Stir-fry about 2 to 3 minutes. Add pineapple and stir-fry an additional minute.
8. Add brown sugar, ginger, pineapple juice, cider vinegar, red wine vinegar, and soy sauce. Cook until bubbly.
9. Dissolve 4½ teaspoons cornstarch in cold water and add it to the sauce. Cook, stirring constantly, until sauce thickens and becomes clear. Pour sauce over fried pork cubes and serve immediately.

Per serving: 494 calories (42% from fat), 18 g protein, 60 g carbohydrate, 23 g fat, 121 mg cholesterol, 2 g fiber, 477 mg sodium.

Chao-Hsueh-Tou
(Stir-Fried Snow Peas with Chinese Mushrooms and Bamboo Shoots)
Serves 6

⅔ cup dried Chinese mushrooms
½ cup boiling water
1½ pounds fresh snow peas (or thoroughly defrosted frozen snow peas)
2 tablespoons vegetable oil
1 cup canned sliced bamboo shoots, drained and rinsed
2 teaspoons sugar
4½ teaspoons low-sodium soy sauce

1. In a small bowl, combine mushrooms with boiling water. Let soak 15 minutes.
2. Drain, squeezing excess water from mushrooms with fingers. (Reserve soaking liquid.) Cut off stems and cut mushrooms into quarters.
3. Remove tips from fresh snow peas and string from pods.
4. In a wok or heavy skillet, heat the oil over high heat. Add the mushrooms and bamboo shoots and stir-fry for 2 minutes.
5. Add the snow peas, sugar, 2 tablespoons of the reserved soaking liquid, and soy sauce. Cook over high heat, stirring constantly, until water evaporates, about 2 to 3 minutes.
6. Transfer contents of wok to a serving dish and serve immediately.

Per serving: 92 calories (49% from fat), 3 g protein, 8 g carbohydrate, 5 g fat, 0 mg cholesterol, 2 g fiber, 262 mg sodium.

Pai-Fan
(Steamed Rice)
Serves 6

1   cup uncooked long-grain rice
2   cups cold water

1. Put rice and cold water in a heavy saucepan and bring to a boil. Stir once or twice. Cover the pan, reduce heat to low, and simmer 15 minutes.
2. Remove the pan from the heat and let rest 5 minutes. (Do not uncover pan.)
3. Remove cover and fluff rice with chopsticks or a fork. Serve immediately.

Per serving: 112 calories (1% from fat), 2 g protein, 25 g carbohydrate, 0 g fat, 0 mg cholesterol, 1 g fiber, 2 mg sodium.

Hsing-Jen-Ping
(Almond Cookies)
Makes 20 cookies

1⅓   cups all-purpose flour
½   cup sugar
¼   teaspoon baking powder
¼   teaspoon salt
⅓   cup shortening
1   egg, separated
1   teaspoon water
½   teaspoon almond extract
20   blanched whole almonds
2   tablespoons fat-free milk

1. Preheat oven to 375°F.
2. In a medium mixing bowl, combine flour, sugar, baking powder, and salt. With pastry blender or two knives, cut in shortening until particles are the size of small peas.
3. In small bowl, whisk together egg white, water, and almond extract. Add to flour mixture all at once and mix well.
4. Knead dough in the bowl for 1 minute.
5. Roll dough into small balls. Place them 2 inches apart on ungreased baking sheets. Flatten dough balls to about ⅜-inch thickness.
6. Top each cookie with a blanched almond and brush with an egg glaze made by combining the egg yolk with milk.
7. Bake cookies until lightly browned, about 12 minutes.

Per cookie: 93 calories (46% from fat), 1 g protein, 11 g carbohydrate, 5 g fat, 9 mg cholesterol, 1 g fiber, 40 mg sodium.

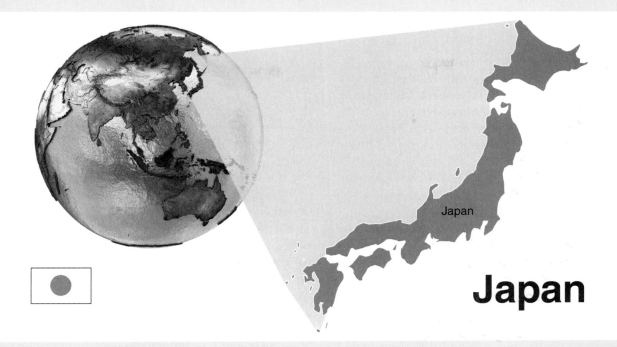

Japan

The Asian country of Japan has adapted to many Western ways without losing its sense of identity. Despite Western influence, Japan's traditional values are still alive today. These values include respect for family, love of nature, and belief in hard work. The Japanese word *sappari* means "clean, light, and sparkling with honesty." Sappari still describes the Japanese people, their country, and their cuisine.

Geography and Climate of Japan

Japan is a nation of islands. Three-fourths of Japan's total land area is mountainous or hilly. These mountains have made farming difficult and have caused crowded living conditions in the few lowlands (**Figure 34.15**).

Swift-flowing rivers and crystal clear lakes dot Japan's landscape. Many of the rivers end in *picturesque* (beautiful) waterfalls; others bring in water needed to irrigate rice fields. A few provide hydroelectric power.

Because the Japanese islands cover such a vast latitude, Japan has a variety of climates. The southern part of the country is subtropical with hot, humid summers and mild winters. The bulk of the Japanese population lives in this area, and their housing, clothing, and farming methods are suited to the warm climate.

Hokkaido, Japan's northernmost island, has cold winters. Temperatures fall below freezing for at least four months during the winter, and snowfall is heavy.

Overall, Japan receives more than adequate moisture. Seasonal monsoons bring rain in the summer and snow in the winter. During September, severe storms called *typhoons* bring heavy rains and damaging winds.

Sean Pavone/Shutterstock.com

Figure 34.15 Crowded living conditions typify many of Japan's best agricultural areas. One such area is the Kanto region, where the city of Tokyo is located.

Japanese Agriculture

Rice is Japan's most important crop. Over one-half the *tillable* (farmable) land is used for rice production. In the far south, Japanese farmers can grow two crops each year. Other important crops include sweet potatoes, wheat, and sugar beets.

The Japanese raise tea bushes on terraced hillsides (**Figure 34.16**). They grow mandarin oranges and strawberries in the South. They grow peaches, pears, persimmons, cherries, apples, and other hearty fruits in the North. The Japanese also grow beans, large radishes, cucumbers, lettuce, onions, cabbage, turnips, carrots, and spinach. They grow many varieties of peas, squash, and pumpkins, too.

The teachings of Buddhism, which are practiced by a large number of Japanese people, forbid the eating of meat. In addition, land has always been scarce in Japan; therefore, the Japanese have traditionally raised little livestock. In recent years, however, livestock production has increased. This is partly due to growing abandonment of Buddhist dietary laws. Also, a taste for eggs, milk, meat, and poultry has been developing among the Japanese people.

Seafood provides most of the protein in the Japanese diet. In fact, Japan's fishing industry is one of the world's largest. Sardines, salmon, herring, cuttlefish, yellowtail, and other kinds of fish, as well as seaweed, live in coastal waters. The Japanese freeze or can some of the seafood catch for export.

Japanese Culture

Although Japan has a modern society, the Japanese are proud of their heritage. They still practice some customs that began centuries ago.

Respect for others is very important in Japanese culture. People greet one another by bowing as a sign of respect. Older adults are held in especially high regard.

The Japanese people also place a high value on education. This is a key reason they have become leaders in technological innovations. The Japanese have made advances in the areas of science and medicine. They are also known for their contributions in art and entertainment. Today, Japan plays a major role in world affairs.

Holidays are an important part of Japanese culture, and foods are an important part of many holidays. The biggest celebration in Japan is the New Year festival. The Japanese eat long noodles on New Year's Eve as a symbol for living a long life. They also make offerings of rice cakes to the New Year god (**Figure 34.17**).

Soybeans play a symbolic role in a second Japanese New Year celebration, which is called *Setsubun*. This holiday takes place in early February—the time of the new year according to Japan's archaic lunar calendar. Japanese people still celebrate this event by eating one soybean for each year they have lived. They also throw handfuls of roasted soybeans in and around their homes to chase away demons. Celebrities stand near shrines

akiyoko/Shutterstock.com

Figure 34.16   These women are harvesting green tea leaves from bushes grown on terraced hillsides.

mitchii/Shutterstock.com

Figure 34.17   To celebrate the New Year, Japanese people eat a group of dishes known as *osechi*. Osechi can include fish cakes, sweet black soybeans, and boiled seaweed. What other dishes may be included in osechi?

and throw soybeans into crowds of people. People who catch the beans are believed to be blessed with good fortune throughout the following year.

A third annual tradition in Japan is the welcoming of spring with Cherry Blossom celebrations. The cherry blossom is Japan's national flower. Families enjoy picnicking under the blooming trees. People also recognize this time of year by eating cherry blossom cakes. These cakes are made of cooked, sweetened azuki beans wrapped in a pounded rice mixture to look like cherry blossoms (**Figure 34.18**).

Japanese Cuisine

Japan's staple foods can be easily obtained from the sea and from the country's limited land resources. Rice, which forms the basis of the Japanese diet, is rich in complex carbohydrates. Soybeans and fish are the main sources of protein. These foods keep the cuisine lower in fat, saturated fat, and cholesterol than a cuisine based on meat. Vegetables, fruits, and seaweed supply vitamins, minerals, and fiber. Light cooking methods help retain the nutritional value of Japanese staple foods; however, the Japanese diet is rather high in sodium due to the popularity of soy sauce as a flavoring agent.

An important element of Japanese cuisine is subtlety of taste. Cooks achieve this subtlety through the careful selection of ingredients and cooking methods.

Arancio/Shutterstock.com

Figure 34.18 Cherry blossom cakes are eaten to celebrate the coming of spring.

Another important element is aesthetic appearance. Japanese cooks place great emphasis on the color, shape, and arrangement of food on a serving dish. Many times, an arrangement may suggest a particular season or mood. For instance, a cook might arrange ingredients to represent the mountains, rivers, trees, and flowers of a Japanese spring. Such a dish might be served at the spring fish festival.

Basic Japanese Ingredients

Ingredients commonly used in Japanese cooking include sesame oil, mild rice vinegar, and mushrooms. Kanpyo and shirataki are common ingredients, too. *Kanpyo* is strips of dried gourd. *Shirataki* is a type of noodle made from a yamlike tuber. The Japanese also use salt, pepper, sugar, chives, onions, mustard, scallions, and other familiar seasonings. Four ingredients are basic to most Japanese cookery: rice, soybeans, fish, and seaweed.

Rice

Rice is so important to the Japanese diet that the Japanese word for *meal* is **gohan**, which means "rice." Japanese rice is a short-grain variety. Cooks usually steam it and serve it plain. Sometimes they cook rice with other ingredients or serve it with a sauce. Two other products, *sake* (Japanese rice wine) and *mirin* (sweet wine), are obtained from rice.

Soybeans

The Chinese introduced the soybean to the Japanese. The **soybean** is a legume with seeds that are rich in protein and oil. The Japanese use soybeans in many forms.

Miso is a fermented soybean paste. The Japanese use miso in a soup they serve for breakfast. It may also be an ingredient in a marinade used to prepare fish and vegetables.

Tofu is a custardlike cake made from soybeans and has a very mild flavor. The Japanese may roll tofu in cornstarch and deep-fry it. They may scramble it with eggs. They may also sauté, boil, or broil it. Sometimes, they add tofu to soups. *Sumashi* (clear broth with tofu and shrimp) is an example.

Shoyu, Japanese soy sauce, contains wheat or barley, salt, water, and malt along with soybeans. Shoyu is an all-purpose seasoning in the Japanese kitchen. (Chinese soy sauce is heavier and does not make a suitable substitute.)

Fish

Tuna, bass, flounder, cod, mackerel, *ayu* (sweet fish), carp, and squid are popular in Japan. The Japanese also eat many varieties of shellfish and more unusual subtropical species. *Katsuo* (dried bonito) is an essential ingredient of *dashi*, a Japanese fish stock. *Fugu* (blowfish) is a Japanese delicacy. Fugu contains a lethal toxin that can kill a diner unless the fish has been properly cleaned. Licensed fugu chefs perform this task.

Japanese cooks demand that all fish and shellfish must be fresh. Therefore, they do not kill shellfish until minutes before cooking. They keep freshwater varieties that will be eaten raw alive until serving time.

Two of the most popular Japanese fish dishes are sashimi and sushi. *Sashimi* are raw fillets of fish eaten alone or with a sauce (**Figure 34.19**). **Sushi** are balls of cooked rice flavored with vinegar. They are served with strips of raw or cooked fish, eggs, vegetables, or seaweed. Sashimi and sushi restaurants and snack bars are found throughout Japan.

Seaweed

The Japanese use seaweed from the surrounding oceans in both fresh and dried forms. They roll *nori*, a dried variety of seaweed, around fish or rice. They also use it as a garnish. The Japanese use *konbu* (dried kelp) in dashi. They use other varieties of seaweed as flavorings, garnishes, and vegetables in soups.

Japanese Vegetables and Fruits

Japanese farmers grow many vegetables. Traditional Japanese vegetables include *daikon*, which is a giant white radish. *Negi* is a thin Japanese leek. *Wasabi* is Japanese horseradish, and *bakusai* is Chinese cabbage. *Gobo* is burdock root, a vegetable that grows up to two feet long. Lotus roots and shoots, edible chrysanthemum leaves, spinach, ginger root, and bamboo shoots are also popular. Many types of peas, beans, ferns, and mushrooms are common, too.

Japanese cooks often mix vegetables together in salads. Japan has two kinds of salads: *aemono* (mixed foods) and *sunomono* (vinegared foods). Aemono salads contain several raw or cooked vegetables in a thick dressing. Sunomono salads contain crisp, raw vegetables and cold, cooked fish or shellfish. They are served with a thin dressing made of rice vinegar, sugar, and soy

abc7/Shutterstock.com

Figure 34.19 This sashimi dish consists of raw fish fillets. How do Japanese cooks ensure the safety of eating raw fish?

sauce. *Namusu* (vegetables in a vinegar dressing) is an example of a sunomono salad.

Japanese fruits are plentiful. Persimmons and many types of oranges grow in Japan. One of the best-known oranges is the *mikan*, or mandarin orange. Apples, pears, cherries, strawberries, plums, and melons also grow well.

Japanese Main Dishes

Meat traditionally was not part of the Japanese diet. Today, however, meat appears on many Japanese tables. Because it is costly, the Japanese usually serve meat in small amounts with other foods.

Although the Japanese eat both pork and beef, their beef is famous. The tenderness of the meat results in part from the treatment the cattle receive. Japanese farmers feed the animals bran, beans, rice, and beer. They massage each steer daily with *shochu* (Japanese gin).

Poultry production in Japan has grown in recent years. Chickens are less costly to raise, so they appear more often in Japanese recipes than meat. Eggs are becoming more popular, too. *Tamago dashimaki* is the Japanese version of an omelet.

Japanese Cooking Methods

In Japan, cooks always cut food into small pieces before cooking. This makes the food easy to pick up with chopsticks. (The Japanese use knives only for food preparation. They do not place knives on the table.)

Japanese cooks boil a variety of foods, including meat, poultry, seafood, and vegetables. The cooking liquid may be a strongly flavored stock or a mild broth. Foods cooked in boiling liquid are called *nimono*. Examples of nimono are *kimini* (sake-seasoned shrimp with egg yolk glaze) and *kiriboshi daikon*. Kiriboshi daikon is chicken simmered with white radish threads (**Figure 34.20**).

Steaming is the simplest of all cooking methods. *Mushimono* (steamed foods) retain their fresh flavors, colors, and nutrients. Japanese cooks use two steaming methods to make mushi and chawan mushi foods. *Mushi* foods are foods cooked on a plate suspended over boiling water. *Chawan mushi* foods are foods steamed in an egg custard. Mushi foods are mild in flavor, so the Japanese usually serve them with a dipping sauce. Chawan mushi foods are richer in flavor and usually are served without a sauce.

The Japanese use frying to prepare *tempura*. Japanese cooks prepare tempura by coating vegetables, meat, poultry, and seafood in a light batter. Then they quickly fry the coated pieces in oil. Other Japanese *agemono* (fried foods) are deep-fried in oil. All Japanese agemono are light and delicate. They are never greasy or heavy.

The Japanese usually use broiling for meat, poultry, and fish. One popular *yakimono* (broiled food) is beefsteak. It is dipped in a mixture of soy sauce and mirin and grilled over charcoal. Beef teriyaki and yakitori are two types of yakimono popular in the United States. *Beef teriyaki* is slices of beef glazed with a special sauce. *Yakitori* is chicken, scallions, and chicken livers broiled on a skewer.

Japanese cooks prepare many dishes at the table. They use one or a combination of the above cooking methods. **Sukiyaki** is a popular Japanese dish that combines two cooking methods—nimono and *nabemono* (dishes cooked at the table). Sukiyaki is made of thinly sliced meat, bean curd, and vegetables cooked in a sauce. Cooks prepare all the raw ingredients in the kitchen. Then they cook the beef and vegetables with their accompanying sauce in a skillet at the table. Another method of preparing food at the table uses the hibachi. A *hibachi* is a small grill that can be freestanding or built into the center of the table.

jreika/Shutterstock.com

Figure 34.20 Kiriboshi daikon is an example of nimono.

Culture and Social Studies

Japanese Eating Customs

The Japanese have several eating customs unique to their culture. The Japanese do not use napkins. Instead, they use small, soft towels, called *oshibori*, that are brought to the table at the beginnings and ends of meals. The oshibori are warm, damp, and fragrant. The Japanese use them to wipe their faces and hands.

In a Japanese meal, hot foods in bowls are served covered. Diners usually remove the cover of the individual rice bowl first. This indicates that rice is Japan's most honored food. The Japanese do not eat the rice all at once. Instead, they eat it with the other foods in much the same way people in the United States eat bread. The Japanese must use both hands to place a rice bowl on a tray for refilling. To use one hand is a breach of courtesy.

The Japanese drink soup from a cup rather than spooning it from a bowl. They remove the cup from the table and hold it in the left hand. Then they hold their chopsticks in the right hand to secure the food. The oldest guest always picks up his or her chopsticks first as a token of respect. After use, diners return their chopsticks to the chopstick rest.

To show appreciation for the cook's skill, it is quite proper to smack the lips or make sucking sounds. Guests often exchange sake cups with their host as a sign of respect.

Japanese Meals

Japanese meals are made up of many light dishes. The quantities served are much smaller than those served in Western cultures.

In the morning, some Japanese people eat eggs and other breakfast foods popular in the United States. In many parts of Japan, however, people eat more traditional breakfast foods. Such foods include umeboshi and miroshiru. *Umeboshi* is a tiny, red, pickled plum. *Miroshiru* is a hearty soup made of dashi, miso, and rice. Japanese breakfast foods also include rice, which is often sprinkled with nori.

Japanese families may serve a carefully prepared lunch if family members come home at noon or if they are expecting guests. Otherwise, Japanese cooks usually prepare simple lunches. The morning rice is reheated and served with leftover vegetables and meat or a simple sauce.

The evening meal is much more elaborate. Because businesses stay open later in Japan than in the United States, the meal usually is served later. The young children eat their meal first. The Japanese prepare children's versions of many popular foods. An example is *kushizashi* (meats, fowl, and vegetables grilled on a skewer). Cooks make kushizashi with hot peppers for adults, but they use milder scallions when preparing the dish for children.

The Japanese serve all the dishes in the main meal together. They usually serve broiled or fried meat, poultry, or fish as a main course. Although the main course can vary, rice, soup, and tsukemono are also usually served. **Tsukemono** (pickled foods) are lightly pickled pieces of daikon, cucumber, melon, eggplant, and other vegetables. The Japanese eat these with rice near the end of the meal (**Figure 34.21**).

The Japanese rarely eat sweet desserts. They reserve sweets for special occasions. Instead, most meals end with fresh fruit.

Another meal enjoyed by the Japanese is **kaiseka**. This is a delicate meal that may be served after a tea ceremony. Tea is Japan's national drink, although the Japanese people also enjoy coffee. The Japanese serve green teas, which they call **nihon-cha**. The Japanese perform the tea ceremony just as their ancestors did hundreds of years ago. Each step of the ceremony is done according to established rules. Each movement the host makes is designed to bring pleasure to the guest. Harmony must exist

kazoka/Shutterstock.com

Figure 34.21 Tsukemono can be bought at the store, but many Japanese people make their own tsukemono. How are tsukemono made?

among all the elements of the ceremony and among all the people present. Simple tea ceremonies may last just 40 minutes. Those that include kaiseka may last as long as four hours.

Japanese Menu

Sumashi Wan
(Clear Broth with Tofu and Shrimp)

Sukiyaki
(Beef and Vegetables Cooked in Seasoned Liquid)

Namasu
(Vegetables in a Vinegar Dressing)

Gohan
(Steamed Rice)

Mikan
(Mandarin Oranges)

Nihon-Cha
(Green Tea)

Sumashi Wan
(Clear Broth with Tofu and Shrimp)
Serves 6

3	cups water, divided
6	ounces firm tofu, cut into 6 equal squares
1	dash salt
7	spinach leaves (or ½ package frozen leaf spinach thoroughly defrosted and separated into leaves)

4 cups clam broth
2 cups low-fat chicken broth
6 small canned shrimp

1. In a small saucepan, bring 2 cups of water to a boil. Add tofu and let water return to a simmer. Remove from heat immediately and cover. Set aside until ready to serve soup.
2. In a second saucepan, bring the remaining 1 cup water to a boil with a dash of salt. Add spinach and cook just until tender.
3. Drain spinach immediately and rinse under cold running water. Remove excess moisture with paper towels and set aside.
4. In a clean saucepan, combine the clam broth and chicken broth and bring to a boil.
5. Meanwhile, set six soup bowls on a tray. Place a spinach leaf, a shrimp, and a cube of tofu in the bottom of each bowl. Pour the heated broth into the bowls, filling each bowl about ¾ full and being careful not to disturb the garnish. (Pour broth down the sides of the bowls.) Serve immediately.

Per serving: 50 calories (41% from fat), 5 g protein, 2 g carbohydrate, 2 g fat, 7 mg cholesterol, 0 g fiber, 169 mg sodium.

Sukiyaki
(Beef and Vegetables Cooked in Seasoned Liquid)
Serves 4 to 6

1 pound beef tenderloin or sirloin steak
1 cup water
8 ounces *shirataki* (long noodlelike threads) or cooked vermicelli
2 medium onions, sliced crosswise
5 leeks, split lengthwise and cut in 1½-inch lengths
¾ pound fresh mushrooms, washed and sliced
5 stalks celery, cut diagonally into ¼-inch slices
1 pound fresh spinach, cleaned (or 1 package frozen leaf spinach, thoroughly defrosted)
½ pound tofu, cut into cubes
½ cup low-sodium soy sauce
2 tablespoons sugar
1½ cups low-sodium beef broth
¼ cup margarine

1. Slice beef cross-grained into paper-thin slices, 1 by 2 inches. (Slightly frozen meat is easier to slice.) Trim fat. Arrange slices attractively on a plate, cover with plastic wrap, and refrigerate.
2. Bring one cup of water to a boil. Add shirataki and return water to a boil. Drain and slice shirataki into thirds.

---

3. Arrange shirataki, onions, leeks, mushrooms, celery, spinach, and tofu attractively on a serving platter, cover with plastic wrap, and refrigerate.
4. Combine soy sauce, sugar, and beef broth in a small bowl. Cover and refrigerate.
5. To cook sukiyaki, heat two tablespoons margarine in a wok over moderately high heat or in an electric skillet preheated to 425°F. Add half of the beef slices and cook until meat loses its pink color. Push meat to the side.
6. Add half of the onions and leeks and cook until transparent and lightly browned. (Turn meat as needed.) Push vegetables to the side.
7. Add half of the mushrooms and half of the celery in two groups. Stir-fry 2 to 3 minutes.
8. Add half of the sauce and simmer about 5 minutes. Turn all foods occasionally.
9. Add half of the spinach and cook 1 minute.
10. Add half of the noodles or vermicelli and tofu. (These will absorb the broth.) Serve immediately or keep warm in a 225°F oven while you cook the remaining half of the ingredients.

Per serving: 474 calories (23% from fat), 28 g protein, 66 g carbohydrate, 12 g fat, 26 mg cholesterol, 7 g fiber, 992 mg sodium.

Namasu
(Vegetables in a Vinegar Dressing)
Serves 6

½ pound daikon or white turnip, peeled and shredded
1 medium carrot, scraped and shredded
1 teaspoon salt
1 cup cold water
¼ cup preflaked, dried bonito
1 tablespoon white vinegar
2 teaspoons sugar

1. In a small bowl, combine daikon, carrot, salt, and water. Stir to mix and let stand 30 minutes.
2. Put dried bonito in a small pan and heat over low heat for 3 to 4 minutes to dry further. Then transfer the bonito to a blender container and grind it into a fine powder.
3. Drain daikon and carrot mixture. Squeeze the vegetables dry and put them in a mixing bowl.
4. Add vinegar and sugar. Mix well and add powdered bonito. Serve at room temperature.

Per serving: 38 calories (5% from fat), 5 g protein, 4 g carbohydrate, 0 g fat, 8 mg cholesterol, 1 g fiber, 451 mg sodium.

Chapter 34 Review and Expand

Summary

Russia, India, China, and Japan have cuisines that differ greatly from one another.

Russian cuisine was influenced by the Slavs and Mongols. The staple foods of Russian peasants remain basic components of the Russian diet. Russian meals often begin with zakuska. A hearty soup and a meat, fish, or poultry dish would follow.

Religious dietary restrictions play a major role in Indian cuisine. Different climates and influences have created distinctions between the cuisines of Northern and Southern India. Specific cooking techniques are used to prepare some Indian dishes.

Chinese foods contain some unique ingredients. Most Chinese foods are prepared by stir-frying, steaming, deep-frying, or simmering. Rice is a staple of the Chinese diet.

Four ingredients are basic to Japanese cuisine: rice, soybeans, fish, and seaweed. The Japanese often boil, steam, fry, or broil their foods. The aesthetic appearance of foods is an important aspect of Japanese cuisine.

Vocabulary Activities

1. **Content Terms**   Working in pairs, locate a small image online that visually describes or explains each of the following terms. Create flash cards by writing each term on a note card. Then paste the image that describes or explains the term on the opposite side.

kimchi	chapati
kasha	tandoori
zakuska	congee
caviar	chopsticks
schi	gohan
borscht	soybean
beef stroganov	tofu
paskha	sushi
kulich	sukiyaki
caste system	tsukemono
curry	kaiseka
masala	nihon-cha
ghee	

2. **Academic Terms**   With a partner, create a T-chart. Write each of the following terms in the left column. Write a synonym for each term in the right column. Discuss your synonyms with the class.

crude	glutinous
monsoon	picturesque
caste	typhoon
commune	tillable

Review

Write your answers using complete sentences when appropriate.

3. Name five Russian agricultural products.
4. What are four contributions the Mongols made to Russian cuisine?
5. Name and describe two Russian soups.
6. What is the name for Russian sweet walnut fritters?
7. How does the cuisine of Northern India differ from the cuisine of Southern India?
8. What is the preferred cooking fat in India, and how is it made?
9. What Indian cooking technique involves braising foods in yogurt?
10. What is a *thali* and how is it used at Indian meals?
11. What is China's chief agricultural product?
12. What is the most versatile of all Chinese cooking utensils?
13. What is the most common Chinese cooking method?
14. Name and describe three traditional Chinese dishes.
15. Why have the Japanese traditionally raised little livestock?
16. Name and describe three food products made from soybeans in Japan.
17. Name two Japanese cooking methods and a dish prepared by each method.
18. Describe two Japanese eating customs.

Chapter 34 Review and Expand

Core Skills

19. **Research, Technology, Speaking** Use reliable Internet resources to research the cuisine of an Asian country not covered in this chapter. Use photos in preparing an electronic presentation for the class.

20. **Research, Technology, Speaking** Divide the class into four teams. Each team will research trade between the United States and one country discussed in this chapter. Identify top products exported to and imported from the country. Determine dollar values of imports and exports for the five most recent years for which data is available. Note the trade deficit or surplus each year. Give a group presentation to the class using digital media and visual displays.

21. **Research, Reading, Writing** Use reliable resources to research one Russian czar. Write a two-page biographical report about the czar and one notable event during his reign. Revise your report for grammar, spelling, and organization.

22. **Research, Reading, Speaking** According to archaeologists, the region that is now India was a highly developed society as early as 3000 BC. Advances of this society included sewers; brick houses; irrigation ditches; and systems of counting, measuring, weighing, and writing. Research one advance and create an illustration to show during an oral report to the class.

23. **Research, Reading, Speaking** Research one of the provinces of China. Point out your chosen province on a map of China and share an interesting fact about the province with your classmates.

24. **Math** Identify the basic units and subunits of currency in Russia, India, China, and Japan. Using current exchange rates, calculate 100 dollars in each currency.

25. **Career Readiness Practice** The preschool education team you chair will be introducing children to foods of Asia. Choose one country from this chapter and write lesson plans for two activities focusing on the country. Be sure to clearly define your objectives for each activity, list needed supplies and detailed steps for conducting the activities, and state how you will assess preschoolers' learning. Submit the lesson plans to the preschool director (your instructor) and ask for feedback.

Critical Thinking and Problem Solving

26. **Analyze** Prepare ghee. Dice 4 cups (1 L) of potatoes. Fry 1 cup (250 mL) of potatoes in 1 tablespoon (15 mL) of each of four types of fat: lard, vegetable shortening, margarine, and ghee. Analyze the differences in browning and flavor.

27. **Evaluate** Design an evaluation form for various sensory characteristics of tea. Then complete the form as you taste and evaluate three varieties of tea popular in China.

28. **Create** Work as part of a team to research the traditional Japanese tea ceremony. Pool your ideas to prepare a demonstration for the class. Each member of the team should be responsible for demonstrating a different aspect of the ceremony.

Unit 6
Food, Nutrition, and Careers

©iStock.com/Wavebreakmedia

Essential Questions

- How can career planning improve your quality of life?
- How are family, community, and work interrelated?

FCCLA: Taking the Lead

Use this section of the text to plan and carry out a project for the *Career Connection* FCCLA national program. Chapter 35 provides information to help you understand work for the *Plug In* unit. This chapter will also help you link interests, skills, and goals to career clusters for a project in the *Sign On* unit. Chapter 36 discusses habits and behaviors workers need to be productive and promotable. This information could help you develop a project for the *Access Skills* unit. Chapter 36 focuses on managing the interconnected roles in families, careers, and communities for the *Integrate* unit, too. Both chapters include topics that relate to the *Program* unit.

While studying, look for the activity icon for:
- Content and Academic Terms with e-flash cards, vocabulary games, and matching activities
These activities can be accessed at
www.g-wlearning.com/foodandnutrition/9582

Chapter 35
Investigating Careers

Kaspars Grinvalds/Shutterstock.com

Objectives

After studying this chapter, you will be able to

- **summarize** how career clusters and pathways can help you choose a career;
- **explain** how to make a career plan;
- **evaluate** important factors involved in considering careers;
- **demonstrate** how to use sources of career information; and
- **investigate** entrepreneurship opportunities.

Reading Prep

Read the chapter title and tell a classmate what you have experienced or already know about the topic. Write a paragraph describing what you would like to learn about the topic. After reading the chapter, share two things you have learned with the classmate.

Content Terms ⤤

career
occupation
career clusters
lifelong learning
transferable skills
aptitude
abilities
entrepreneur
profit

Academic Terms

dexterity
fraud
incentive

The actions you take now lay the groundwork for your future career. Preparing for your career may seem overwhelming at first, but doing a step at a time will make the process easier. What would you like to do for a living? Whether your future lies in the nutrition field, food industry, or some other area, this chapter presents guidelines that are useful for planning your career.

Career Planning

Do not be fooled into thinking the right job will simply "come along." In today's highly competitive workplace, that is most unlikely. People who make no career plans usually find themselves left with jobs no one else wants.

Having a career means you will hold several occupations related by a common skill, purpose, or interest over your lifetime. A **career** is a series of related occupations that show progression in a field of work. The term *job* is commonly used to mean *occupation*. Strictly speaking, a *job* is a task, while an **occupation** is paid employment that involves related skills and experience.

Career Clusters and Pathways

Career clusters are 16 groups of occupations or career specialties that are similar or related to one another (**Figure 35.1**). The occupations within a cluster require a set of common knowledge and skills for career success. These are called *essential knowledge and skills.*

If one or two job titles in a career cluster appeal to you, it is likely that others will, too. This is because the jobs grouped together share certain similarities. To help you narrow down your options, each career cluster is further divided into *career pathways*. These subgroups often require more specialized knowledge and skills.

Knowing the relationship between careers in a given pathway is helpful when researching facts about careers. The skills required for related jobs in a career field are similar. Preparing for more than one career in a related field allows more flexibility when you are searching for employment. If you cannot find the exact position you desire, your skills will be needed by other occupations in the same pathway.

Programs of Study

Since occupations in a career pathway require similar knowledge and skills, they also require similar programs of study. A *program of study* is the sequence of instruction used to prepare students for occupations in a given career pathway. The program includes classroom instruction, cocurricular activities such as student organizations, and other learning experiences including work-site learning.

Customizing a program of study for an individual learner results in a *personal plan of study* that helps prepare you for the career direction you choose. You start by taking the appropriate classes and participating in related student organizations. One organization you may want to think about joining is Family, Career and Community Leaders of America (FCCLA). FCCLA prepares young men and women for future roles at home and in the workplace. FCCLA chapters are organized through Family and Consumer Sciences courses.

Once you have laid this foundation, seek out programs that address your career interest. You may even find that some high school classes can count toward college credit. Your plan of study does not expire with high school. Students should update their plans at least yearly, but more often if plans change.

Understand Your Values

Your family, friends, and life experiences shape your *values*, or beliefs that are important to you. What you value will determine the career you choose and shape the way you live your life. People who value independence, for example, desire flexibility in their work hours. People who value education want a job that pays for job-related degrees they earn while employed. A person who values family life avoids employment options that require constant travel. Carefully considering your values will point you to the job that best suits you.

Setting Goals

Preparing for a career involves setting goals. A *goal* is an aim you try to reach. Goals are the endpoints of your efforts. When you decide what career you would like to have, you are setting a career goal. Because this goal will take a number of years to achieve, it is a *long-term goal*. You can set short-term goals that will help you reach your

Common Occupational Categories

Category	Job Emphasis
Agriculture, Food, and Natural Resources	Develop, process, market, distribute, and finance agricultural products and resources such as food, fiber, wood products, and other plant and animal products/resources.
Architecture and Construction	Design, plan, construct, manage, and maintain building structures.
Arts, A/V Technology, and Communications	Design, direct, exhibit, write, perform, and produce multimedia, fashion, visual and performing arts, journalism, and entertainment.
Business Management and Administration	Plan, organize, direct, and evaluate business functions for efficiency and productivity.
Education and Training	Teach and train in various learning environments; provide administrative and professional support services.
Finance	Provide services for financial planning and management, banking, and insurance.
Government and Public Administration	Plan and execute government functions at the local, state, and national levels.
Health Science	Plan and provide therapeutic, diagnostic, and health support services.
Hospitality and Tourism	Address family and human needs in restaurant and food/beverage services, lodging, travel, tourism, recreation, and attractions.
Human Services	Provide child care, adult care, and other personal care services; address family and human needs in early childhood development, counseling and mental health, community services, and consumer services.
Information Technology	Design, develop, and manage hardware, software, multimedia, and integrated communication systems.
Law, Public Safety, Corrections, and Security	Provide protective services and public and workplace safety.
Manufacturing	Source and process materials into intermediate or final products; provide related professional and technical support activities.
Marketing	Sell goods and services; perform market research and forecasting; advertise, merchandise, and communicate the brand and sales item.
Science, Technology, Engineering, and Mathematics	Provide scientific research, testing services, and product development.
Transportation, Distribution, and Logistics	Move people, materials, and goods by road, pipeline, air, rail, and water; manage infrastructure and maintain facilities.

Figure 35.1 The career clusters can help you determine your career area of interest. How are occupations within a cluster similar?

long-term goal. *Short-term goals* can be achieved in a matter of weeks or months. Successfully completing a high school class and getting a part-time job related to your career are short-term goals.

The classes you take in high school can help you prepare for a career. If you think you would like a career in a particular field, take courses related to that field. For instance, some family and consumer sciences classes would help you prepare for a career in the food and nutrition industry (**Figure 35.2**).

Syda Productions/Shutterstock.com

Figure 35.2 Family and consumer sciences courses, such as this high school foods course, can help prepare you for a career in the food and nutrition industry.

Lifelong Learning

No matter what career you enter, you will be expected to keep pace with the changes in your field. Continually updating your knowledge and skills is known as **lifelong learning**. The term implies that your need for learning will never end. You cannot assume that the skills you have will be all you ever need in life. Technology and other advances mean you must continue to learn so you can keep up with changes in the field. Employers usually provide some training; however, employees are often expected to use time outside the job to stay up-to-date in their field of expertise. People who enjoy their work will view lifelong learning as an exciting challenge.

Possessing transferable skills helps you succeed in whatever job you choose. The **transferable skills** useful in all jobs include accurate reading, writing, speaking, and math skills (**Figure 35.3**). Also included are common computer skills.

Transferable skills are basic skills, while the essential knowledge and skills for a given career cluster are more advanced. An example of an essential skill for a career cluster is "to identify the uses of new technologies and their impact on agricultural systems." Careers within the Agriculture, Food and Natural Resources cluster need this skill.

Learn About...

Developing Goals

The ability to set and achieve goals is key to success. Well-defined goals meet certain criteria. They must be specific (S), measurable (M), attainable (A), realistic (R), and timely (T). Use the acronym SMART to remember how to create effective goals.

A specific goal is expressed in an unambiguous way. It should describe precisely what you intend to achieve. To develop a specific goal, be sure it answers the questions who, what, when, where, why, and how.

A goal that is measurable allows you to track your progress. For instance, setting target dates for completing various stages is one way to measure your progress.

An attainable goal is one that you can achieve. Nearly any goal can be achieved with enough thought, planning, and effort. For example, if you lack certain skills necessary to achieve the goal, part of your goal must include a plan for acquiring those skills.

Realistic goals are practical. An unrealistic goal may simply require further development. For instance, a goal to become employed as a registered dietitian nutritionist after graduating from high school is not realistic. This goal needs to be expanded into more incremental goals such as acquiring a bachelor's in dietetics from an accredited program, completing a post-graduate internship, and passing the registration exam.

A timely goal will have an appropriate time frame for completion. Using the previous example, a timely goal might be to acquire a bachelor's in dietetics in four years.

Know and Apply

1. Write one short-term and one long-term goal that are specific, measurable, attainable, realistic, and timely.

2. Use callouts to show where each of the SMART criteria is met in your goal statement.

Many people may change career directions at some point and pursue other interests. In that case, they may need additional training or education to succeed in a new career area.

wavebreakmedia/Shutterstock.com

Figure 35.3 Many jobs involve using math. What kind of skill is math?

Considering Career Options

Before you can set career goals, you need to consider your values and explore the real you. You also need to identify your interests, aptitudes, and abilities.

Once you decide which careers interest you, begin to evaluate other important factors. Among these are the kind of wages you might earn and the education or training you would need. Knowing the job duties and responsibilities will also impact your decision.

Career Interests, Aptitudes, and Abilities

Few teens know exactly what career they want. Sometimes adults who have prepared for one career decide they want to pursue another. As you grow older, you may notice that your interests change. This is perfectly normal. Active people are constantly developing new interests. By reviewing your likes and dislikes, you will get a better picture of the tasks you would enjoy in a career.

Career planning cannot take place until you know what you can do well. What are your aptitudes? An **aptitude**, or natural talent, is an ability to learn something quickly and easily. Are some of your subjects in school much easier than others? You may not be aware of all of your aptitudes if you have never been challenged to use them. A school counselor can give you an aptitude test to help reveal your strengths (**Figure 35.4**).

Abilities are skills you develop with practice. As you prepare to handle a new responsibility, you will learn that it requires certain skills. Can you develop those skills with practice? For example, can a person who is afraid of heights become a good roofer? Can someone lacking finger *dexterity* (skill and ease in use) learn to manipulate precision tools? It is impossible to excel at every skill, so discover what you can do well.

Earning Levels

You will want to check average earnings before choosing a career. What is the average beginning pay? What does it take to achieve higher earnings? Are additional degrees or training generally required? When checking pay levels for various careers, you can expect professional positions to get higher pay.

MBI/Shutterstock.com

Figure 35.4 Working with a career counselor can help you to identify your aptitudes and develop a program of study for your future career.

When investigating earning levels, research those of other careers in the same career pathway. You may discover another occupation in the pathway that suits you, yet earns higher pay.

Education and Training Requirements

Some employment opportunities in food- or nutrition-related careers require completion of a postsecondary program. Some require occupational training and others require college and advanced degrees. When planning your career, you will need to decide how much education you need and want. There are a number of ways to acquire the education and training you need.

Work-Based Learning Programs

Work-based learning programs offer students an opportunity for job placement while still taking classes. A program coordinator works with students and the work sites to make these work experiences successful. Participating in such work-based learning programs can help ease the transition from school to career. Here are some program options to explore.

- *Cooperative programs (co-ops).* High school work-based learning programs are often called *cooperative programs.* The program coordinators place students in part-time positions. Students generally attend school for at least half the day and then work the remainder of the day. The program coordinators and workplace supervisors evaluate student performance on the job. This gives students a realistic view of job realities and responsibilities.

- *Internships.* Work-based learning opportunities at the postsecondary or college level are called *internships.* Such internships offer paid or unpaid practical work experience that is supervised. Students enroll in internship programs much like they enroll in courses. They may work several days per week with a reduced class load or during the summer. Students generally receive college credit for internships while gaining valuable work skills.

Occupational Training

Occupational training is available through apprenticeship programs, technical schools, and trade schools.

Apprenticeship programs offer students the opportunity to learn a trade or skill on-the-job under the direction of a skilled worker. Apprenticeships may last several months or many years. Requirements for entering these programs vary from state to state and one trade to another.

Technical schools offer job training at both secondary and postsecondary levels. Students who attend classes at technical schools during high school often receive a certificate for a specific job skill with their high school diplomas. Postsecondary programs at technical schools may offer a two-year degree or a certificate (**Figure 35.5**).

Trade schools provide job-specific training at the postsecondary level. Programs at trade schools may take one to three years to complete. Successful completion of these programs may result in a certificate or possibly an associate's degree.

Wavebreak Media Ltd./Wavebreak Media/Thinkstock

Figure 35.5 Many postsecondary culinary programs at technical schools offer both degree and certificate options for students. Why might one option be preferable to the other?

Colleges and Universities

Careers that require a high skill level and have great potential for advancement are highly competitive. A college degree is generally needed for such positions. You can obtain degrees from community or junior colleges, four-year colleges, and universities.

Attending a community or junior (two-year) college leads to earning an *associate's degree*. Completing a program at a four-year college or university results in a *bachelor's degree*. For careers that require a higher level of education, students can earn a *master's degree*. It usually takes another one to two years of study to obtain a master's. Other professional occupations, such as research scientists, require a *doctorate*, or *Ph.D*. Doctoral degrees often require three to six years of study beyond a master's degree (**Figure 35.6**).

Talk with your school guidance counselor to find out about schools that offer the education and training you desire. You may also want to explore schools of interest on the Internet.

Certification and Licensing

People who work in jobs that deal with people's lives, health, or safety often have certification or a license. Doctors, dietitians, and teachers are examples of such professions. Many jobs in the food industry have these requirements, too.

Meeting certification and licensing requirements means a person has a clear grasp of the science involved in his or her career field. It also means the person has proven ability to apply scientific principles correctly with each client or patient. These extra requirements keep unqualified people from holding important jobs. The requirements also help prevent physical harm that may result from bad advice.

Certification is a special standing within a profession as a result of meeting specific requirements. A *license* is a work requirement set by a government agency. Licensing requirements are similar or identical to the certification requirements. The one main difference is license requirements carry the force of law. The government controls the performance standards of licensed professionals.

Certification and licensing usually require the following:

- completion of an approved program of study
- acceptable level of education or degree(s)
- completion of an internship and/or on-the-job experience
- acceptable grade or score on a national exam
- continuing education

Those who meet the requirements receive a certificate or license. Many professionals display these documents at their workplaces. This allows clients to know they are dealing with qualified professionals.

Certificates and licenses usually have expiration dates. If the person takes the suggested courses and/or attends a required number of

Education and Careers	
Education Levels	**Possible Careers**
High School Diploma*	Baker, Cook, Diet clerk, Food service worker, Food and nutrition tech, Food inspector, Home health aid, Restaurant server
Associate's (2 years)*	Dietetic technician, Food meal supervisor, Food and drug inspector, Lactation consultant, Personal chef
Bachelor's (4+ years)*	Clinical dietitian, USDA Extension Specialist, Food and drug inspector, Food bank director, Food writer/editor, Food purchasing agent, Food scientist, Food technologist, Health and safety sanitarian, Journalist, Media spokesperson, Registered dietitian, Sports nutrition consultant
Master's (Bachelor's+)*	Research dietitian, Research food scientist
Doctorate (Master's+)*	Research dietitian, Research food scientist

*May require a combination of apprenticeship, internship, licensing, and/or certification.

Figure 35.6 Different careers require different levels of education.

approved meetings, renewal is granted. Having regular renewal requirements helps ensure professionals keep their knowledge and skills up-to-date.

The use of certain initials after a person's name often indicates certification. A certified dietitian is called a *registered dietitian nutritionist*. He or she uses the initials *RDN* (**Figure 35.7**). A certified fitness director uses the initials *ACSM*. This indicates the American College of Sports Medicine. A certified family and consumer sciences professional uses the initials *CFCS*. Examples include a teacher or a youth services counselor.

When a license is a job requirement, the government controls the use of related titles and initials. For example, a person who uses the initials *LDN* or the title *Licensed Dietitian Nutritionist* must

Alliance/Shutterstock.com

Figure 35.7 Some registered dietitian nutritionists (RDN) hold additional certifications in specialty practice areas such as sports nutrition, pediatrics, and diabetes education.

have the qualifications to do so. If not, fines or penalties may result.

Many states have licensing requirements for dietitians. The licensing process for nutrition and fitness professionals in general is expanding due to increasing consumer complaints. Consumers are concerned about deceitful people who give harmful nutrition or exercise advice. Such *frauds* (fakes) lack proper training and are primarily interested in selling a product or service.

Professional associations are also expanding their certification efforts to cover more job categories. Jobs that direct, counsel, or treat people are their main focus. Their goal is to keep unqualified people from spreading wrong information.

Job Responsibilities and Rewards

It is important to find out exactly what a job entails. Remember, you will be fulfilling these duties every day for many years. If they do not sound appealing now, it is unlikely that you will enjoy them in a few years' time.

When exploring different occupations, look carefully at what each involves and what is expected of the jobholder. Also study the qualifications for entering that field.

People have different ideas about what constitutes a "reward." For example, does the occupation involve frequent travel? Adventurous people would consider this job factor a reward. On the other hand, people who like to stay at home would be annoyed, perhaps irritated and angry, at so much traveling. Each job situation presents certain conditions that involve personal preferences (**Figure 35.8**).

Personality Traits

Some people have personality traits that are in conflict with the requirements of certain occupations. Choosing one of these occupations would not lead to career satisfaction or success. For instance, if you prefer a quiet working environment, you may not enjoy working in a noisy setting. If you prefer a routine, you may resent a job that involves constant change. Think carefully about your personality while you are exploring career choices and keep your preferences in mind.

wavebreakmedia/Shutterstock.com

erwinova/Shutterstock.com

Figure 35.8 When choosing a career, consider what aspects would be a reward for you. For example, would you prefer to work in a laboratory or in a kitchen? Would you prefer to work regular or irregular hours?

Desired Lifestyle

The career you choose affects your lifestyle in many ways. It affects your income, which determines how much you can spend on housing, clothing, food, and luxury items. Your career choice may also affect where you live. You will want to locate where the work is plentiful. If you prefer not to live in a large city, you should be sure to choose work that is available in other areas.

Your friendships are affected by your career choice, too. You are likely to become friends with some of your work associates. You may meet other friends through the people you know from work. Your leisure time is affected by the hours and vacation policies of your job. If you prefer to work weekdays from 9 to 5, you should avoid jobs that require overtime, late shifts, or working weekends.

Employment Outlook

In 10 years, will the need for a certain career increase, stay the same, or decrease compared to average employment trends? Are too many people flocking to a field that is not growing? If the employment outlook for a career is poor, you will have fewer employment choices. It is best to focus on career areas that are growing. They will offer you greater employment options when you are ready to begin your career. You can research job trends when investigating other career information.

Sources of Career Information

You can obtain career information from many sources. Talk to your school counselor, teachers, and parents. Find people in your community involved in various careers and ask them questions. If you know the career of your choice requires further education, research colleges that have the curriculum you will need. Many high school libraries have college catalogs and career manuals.

One of the best ways to research careers is using the Internet (**Figure 35.9**). You can start at the U.S. Department of Labor's website to search the following helpful sources:

- The *Occupational Outlook Handbook* describes the major U.S. jobs and their working conditions, requirements, average salaries, and future outlooks. This publication is available in most libraries, too.

- The *O*NET* (the *Occupational Information Network*) website replaces the *Dictionary of Occupational Titles* and is the most complete online resource available. It provides tools for exploring careers, examining job trends, and assessing personal abilities and interests.

- The *CareerOneStop* website has components for exploring careers, salaries, benefits, education, training, and other resources.

michaeljung/Shutterstock.com

Figure 35.9 Using the Internet, you can research a variety of interesting careers.

- One part of CareerOneStop is the Toolkit. You can use these resources for exploring careers, including industry trends, wage information, and state resources.

Considering Entrepreneurship

Some people do not want to work for an employer. They prefer to find opportunities, make decisions, and set schedules on their own. In other words, they prefer to be self-employed. These people are often called entrepreneurs. **Entrepreneurs** are people who start and run their own business.

Many people in food-related businesses are entrepreneurs. Farmers are frequently self-employed. Grocers, butchers, and bakers often own their stores. Many restaurateurs and caterers operate their own businesses. Food stylists may work alone to set up contracts with clients (**Figure 35.10**).

There are many opportunities for entrepreneurship in the nutrition field as well. For instance, some dietitians experience entrepreneurial success providing nutrition consultations in private practice settings. Others author

Exploring Careers

Caterer

Caterers play an essential role in celebrating special occasions and successful corporate events. They work closely with private customers and event planners to design menus for a variety of functions. Some caterers may specialize in a certain kind of cuisine or type of event. Others work with a wide range of foods in a wide variety of venues. Some caterers are one-person entrepreneurs, while others work for large companies.

Caterers must be skilled in food preparation and service, cleanup, and sales and marketing. They must be able to prepare large quantities of food and serve it creatively. They must have good customer service and communication skills. Good business skills are essential to calculate budgets and pricing when planning menus. Caterers also need to know how and where to order high-quality ingredients at affordable prices.

Artistry and efficiency are both important in the catering business. Sometimes knowledge of specialty foods and décor is required. For instance, a client may request a one-of-a-kind birthday cake for a circus-themed child's birthday party. Industrial caterers must provide appetizing menus and prompt service.

The work can be physically tiring. It involves transporting and setting up equipment, carrying heavy food trays, and standing for many hours. Caterers can expect to work nights, weekends, and holidays. They need the ability to work well under pressure.

Training to become a caterer varies. There are several ways to learn the business. Some people learn on the job, beginning as kitchen helpers, advancing to the position of cook or chef, and then starting their own catering service. Others learn cooking in technical or trade schools or by joining a family business. Many two-year colleges offer training in food service. Another way to prepare for a catering career is by earning a family and consumer sciences degree or a restaurant management degree from a four-year college or university. Many states require caterers to be licensed. State and local inspectors visit caterers periodically to check on cleanliness and safe food handling procedures.

Jupiterimages/Stockbyte/Thinkstock

Figure 35.10   An entrepreneur can face many challenges and rewards. What personal traits would help an entrepreneur face challenges?

nutrition-related books, magazine articles, or blogs. Dietitian-entrepreneurs have built successful businesses that provide services such as implementing employee nutrition and wellness programs, designing nutrition software, working with media, or speaking professionally on nutrition and wellness topics.

Entrepreneurship holds great appeal for some people. Being their own bosses makes them feel independent. They achieve a sense of satisfaction from setting and reaching business goals.

Entrepreneurship involves risks as well as rewards. Starting a business takes money. The amount depends on the type of business. However, every business has some operating costs and requires the purchase of some equipment and supplies.

Starting a business requires responsibility and organization. If a customer is unhappy, an entrepreneur must fix the problem. Entrepreneurs must keep orderly records of the money they take in and pay out. They must also keep track of meetings, customer orders, employee files, and taxes.

If entrepreneurship interests you, you should first consider several factors. Think about what kind of business you would like to start. Find out how much need there is for a business of this nature. Be sure it is something you can manage.

Advantages and Disadvantages

Many people become entrepreneurs so they can be their own boss. They enjoy being able to make all the decisions and work whatever hours they choose.

Some people start a business for the satisfaction of working with subjects they understand or enjoy. Starting a business may also provide a sense of accomplishment. It is likely that an entrepreneur will value profit. **Profit** is any money that remains after a business has paid its expenses. Profit is the compensation or pay entrepreneurs receive for their efforts. Entrepreneurs are not guaranteed a salary or wages as employees are; rather, they are paid only if the business makes a profit. The profit motive is a big *incentive* (reason) for starting a business. The success of a business is based on its ability to maintain or increase its profits and grow.

Chief among the disadvantages to becoming an entrepreneur is the hard work. At first, you may work nonstop just to get the business started. During this period, very little money—if any—is coming in. You may have to put most of your savings into the business since affordable loans for an unproven business are rare. If the business fails, you could lose everything. According to the Small Business Administration Office of Advocacy, about half of new businesses remain open five years or more. About one-third of these start-ups remain in business 10 years or longer. All these factors add to a heightened sense of stress. Too much stress could even affect your health. To cope with these challenges, entrepreneurs need several characteristics.

Common Characteristics of Entrepreneurs

First, entrepreneurs must be optimistic. They have to believe their business will succeed. Entrepreneurs must be self-starters who can recognize when they need to initiate action. They should be hard workers who are willing to put extreme effort into the business. They must have interesting new ideas about doing or providing something that is not available anywhere else. Usually, a business succeeds by fulfilling a consumer need. A smart entrepreneur will be able to recognize a need that could become a money-making opportunity (**Figure 35.11**).

Learn About...

Managing Business Basics

An entrepreneur must manage the company's finances for the business to survive and thrive long-term. This includes managing revenues and expenses. *Revenue* is the amount of money coming in to a business from the sale of its product or service. *Expenses* are the costs experienced as a result of doing business. If an entrepreneur neglects to manage revenues and expenses, even a business providing a great, innovative product or service will fail.

Consider a dietitian-entrepreneur who implements employee nutrition and wellness programs for other companies. The dietitian charges the companies a fee for her services. These fees are her revenues. However, the dietitian also generates expenses. For instance, she may have costs due to travel such as air fare or gasoline. She may have to purchase nutrition analysis software and client education brochures. These revenues and expenses must be carefully recorded and tracked to determine whether the business is making a profit or losing money.

Whether a business is operating at a profit or loss is determined using the following formula:

Revenue–Expense=Profit (Loss)

When revenues are greater than expenses, the business makes a profit. If revenues are less than expenses, however, the business experiences a loss. A business operating at a loss cannot survive long-term. To increase profits, a business must increase revenues, decrease expenses, or both.

Know and Apply

1. Use problem-solving techniques to identify two strategies the dietitian-entrepreneur could use to increase her revenues.

2. In the month of October, this business had revenues of $4,250 and expenses totaling $3,975. Did the business experience a profit or loss in October? How much?

Monkey Business Images/Shutterstock.com

Figure 35.11 Seeing a need led this entrepreneur to open a successful coffee shop where people in the community can gather.

More than just optimism and an interesting idea are necessary for a business to grow and be profitable. An entrepreneur must have an understanding of the financial aspects of sustaining and growing a business.

An entrepreneur needs to be committed to the business. This involves using his or her personal money, time, and other resources to make the business succeed. Entrepreneurs must be energetic and in good health to handle long workdays. An entrepreneur must also be willing to take risks. It is a huge risk to give up a steady paycheck for a business that may not succeed.

Importance of Entrepreneurship

Over 95 percent of businesses in the U.S. are considered small businesses. These businesses each have less than 500 employees. About half the people employed in the United States work for small businesses. Of the people who do not work in government jobs, more than half are employed by small businesses.

Small businesses help create jobs. More jobs help keep the economy strong. A strong economy creates more demand for goods and services, which raises the standard of living. This, in turn, spurs the growth of small businesses that offer the goods and services desired.

Because small businesses usually produce highly specialized products, they may fulfill a focused need (**Figure 35.12**). However, to fill this need, they may require employees who are highly trained or experienced in one specialty. Many small businesses employ workers who are just starting their careers. This helps workers gain employment experience.

erwinova/Shutterstock.com

Figure 35.12 Small businesses often fulfill a specific, focused need. As a result, training for employment in these businesses may be highly specialized.

Learn About...

Questions for Entrepreneurs

According to the Small Business Administration, entrepreneurs should ask themselves the following questions:

- Why am I starting a business? What kind of business do I want? Am I prepared to spend the time, money, and resources needed to get my business started? How will I market my business?

- What products/services will my business provide? What is my target market? Who is my competition? What is unique about my business idea and the products/services I will provide? How long will it take before my products/services are available?

- How much money do I need to get my business set up? Will I need to get a loan? How long must I finance the company until I start making a profit? How will I price my product compared to my competition?

- How will I set up the legal structure of my business? What do I need to ensure I am paying my taxes correctly? How will I manage my business?

- Where will I house my business? How many employees will I need? What types of supplies will I need? What kind of insurance do I need?

Imagine you are going to start your own business and then answer the following questions.

Know and Apply

1. What service or product would you provide?
2. Where would you open your business?
3. What existing business, if any, would be your competition?

Getting Started

Consider working for someone else before starting a business of your own. This will give you work experience and show you what is involved in operating a business.

Once you have thought through your business idea, you need to write a detailed business plan. This will include a complete description of any product or service you will sell. The plan should explain everything you must do to get the business started and keep it going.

It is unlikely that you are an expert in all areas of entrepreneurship. Where can you go for support?

First, consult the Small Business Administration. Its website has helpful answers to many common questions. It also links to the state Departments of Commerce. Many of the regulations that affect small businesses are set by the states. You would be wise to investigate these regulations before starting a business. Your local chamber of commerce may also be able to check for local regulations. These sources may be free or require a small fee.

From time to time, you will also need support in specialized business areas. A lawyer will make sure you fulfill all legal requirements. An accountant can handle or check your bookkeeping and tax-related records. An insurance agent will determine the amount and types of insurance you need. These professionals can be expensive, but they limit your business risk and provide peace of mind.

With your business plan in hand, the sky is your limit. Teen entrepreneurs have started such food-related ventures as party planning, pizza delivering, and cookie baking. If you are ambitious, you too can be successful in starting a business (**Figure 35.13**).

Gines Romero/Shutterstock.com *Dean Drobot/Shutterstock.com*

Figure 35.13 A passion for food and nutrition can be the foundation for a successful business as a food photographer or blogger.

Chapter 35 Review and Expand

Summary

Studying the career clusters can make choosing a career less overwhelming. Within each career cluster are career pathways that are grouped by similar knowledge and skills. Programs of study can help you plan now how to get the education and training you need for the job you want.

Staying skilled and knowledgeable is important for career success and advancement. Understanding your interests, abilities, and aptitudes is the first step in choosing a career. Sources such as O*NET and CareerOneStop can help you thoroughly research career details.

There are advantages and disadvantages to becoming an entrepreneur. Being committed to your business and having a well-prepared business plan will help you succeed.

Vocabulary Activities

1. **Content Terms**   For each of the following terms, identify a word or group of words describing a quality of the term—an *attribute*. Pair up with a classmate and discuss your list of attributes. Then, discuss your list of attributes with the entire class to increase understanding.

career	aptitude
occupation	abilities
career clusters	entrepreneur
lifelong learning	profit
transferable skills	

2. **Academic Terms**   With a partner, create a T-chart. Write each of the following academic terms in the left column. Write a *synonym* (a word that has the same or similar meaning) for each term in the right column. Discuss your synonyms with the class.

dexterity	incentive
fraud	

Review

Write your answers using complete sentences when appropriate.

3. What is the difference between a career and an occupation?
4. True or false. Career clusters are 16 groups of occupations or career specialties that are similar or related to one another.
5. How can knowing the relationship between careers in a given pathway be helpful when researching information about careers?
6. Describe a program of study.
7. Continually updating your knowledge and skills is known as _____.
8. Why are transferable skills important?
9. What is the difference between an aptitude and ability?
10. Give two examples of work-based learning programs.
11. What is the difference between a certification and a license?
12. Name three sources of career information.
13. _____ are people who start and run their own businesses.
14. Explain why you should consider working for someone else before starting a business of your own.

Core Skills

15. **Reading**   Read a newspaper or journal article about various occupations in your area. Based on your research, what is the predominate occupation in your community? How does this occupation affect the standard of living among members of the community?

Chapter 35 Review and Expand

16. **Speaking, Research** Gather information to compare the education or training needed for two nutrition-related careers that interest you. For each career, research the specific certification or degree required, identify leading programs or colleges for these certifications or degrees, and determine admission requirements, estimated costs, and so on. Give a digital presentation of your findings in class. Share how this exercise influenced your career plans.

17. **Listening** As your classmates present their findings from the previous activity, listen closely to each presentation. Take notes on anything you find particularly interesting, or write any questions you think of during each presentation. Identify any techniques each speaker used that made the delivery of the message more or less effective. After each classmate finishes presenting, participate when appropriate by asking a question or expanding on the presenter's idea. Do this for all of the presentations in your class.

18. **Writing, Technology** Use the O*NET website or other reliable source to further research the careers you identified in Activity 16. Focus your research on the knowledge, skills, abilities, and interests required to do the work. Use such online self-assessments as the Abilities Profiler, Interest Profiler, or Work Importance Locator on the O*NET website or the Interest Assessment, Skills Assessment, or Skills Matcher on the CareerOneStop website to help you analyze whether your personal interests, skills, and abilities are a logical fit with one or both careers. Write a summary explaining why you think you are well suited for either career.

19. **Listening, Research** Interview an entrepreneur in the nutrition field to learn more about entrepreneurial opportunities in nutrition. Prepare for the interview by creating a list of questions. Practice active listening by focusing on the speaker's responses and seeking further clarification when appropriate. During the interview, focus on the speaker's word choice, tone, stance, and points of emphasis.

20. **Math** Investigate the salary potential for the careers in Activity 16. A rule of thumb often used to budget for rent expense is to spend no more than 25 percent of your pretax income. For each career, calculate how much you could spend on rent. Research the type of housing that amount of rent buys in the area you desire to live.

21. **Career Readiness Practice** Based on your findings from Activity 16, establish personal short-term and long-term career goals. Write a paper outlining these goals. Organize your paper so that it is logical and sequential.

Critical Thinking and Problem Solving

22. **Analyze** What type of job environment do you think best suits your abilities and interests? Do you think you would be more successful as a member of a team in an established company or as an entrepreneur? Compare and contrast the benefits and challenges each choice offers.

23. **Draw conclusions** After reviewing this chapter and one or more career websites, draw conclusions about which careers appear to have excellent job outlooks. Why? Report your conclusions and your reasoning to the class.

24. **Evaluate** Suppose a classmate posted untrue, negative remarks about you on a social networking site. You are in the process of submitting college applications and waiting for acceptance. You know that your first-choice college examines social networking sites looking for information about their applicants. Predict the potential consequences of these remarks on your pending college acceptance. How could these remarks impact future employment opportunities? What are some ways you can safely deal with cyberbullying?

Chapter 36

Career and Job Success

michaeljung/Shutterstock.com

Content Terms ↱

reference
résumé
cover letter
portfolio
networking
ethical behavior
punctual
self-motivation
attitude
verbal communication
nonverbal communication
team
negotiation
leadership
service learning

Academic Terms

consent
persevere
sporadic
verbatim
insufficient

Objectives

After studying this chapter, you will be able to

- **produce** materials needed for a job search;
- **carry out** a job search;
- **identify** the skills, attitudes, and behaviors important for maintaining a job and attaining career success;
- **demonstrate** appropriate communication skills to use in the workplace;
- **summarize** the procedure for leaving a job; and
- **give examples** of how to effectively balance family, community, and work.

Reading Prep

Before you read the chapter, interview someone in the workforce (your supervisor, a parent, relative, or friend). Ask the person what skills are important for success in the workplace. Take notes during the interview. As you read the chapter, highlight the items from your notes that are discussed in the chapter.

If a career in the food and nutrition industry interests you, you can start getting job experience now. Many entry-level jobs are available in restaurants, grocery stores, hospital nutrition departments, and other related businesses. Getting experience while you are still in high school will prepare you for higher-level positions in the future.

Career and job success depend on many factors. Your skills, attitudes, and behaviors are critical in keeping a job and succeeding in a career. Effectively balancing your family, community, and work responsibilities can help you to achieve the lifestyle you desire.

Prepare for the Job Search

Prior to beginning your job search, there are a few tasks you should complete. You will leave a favorable impression on potential employers if it is apparent you are prepared. Before you begin your job search, you should acquire a list of references, write your résumé, and create your portfolio.

Acquire References

Potential employers frequently request a list of references when you interview for a job. **References** are individuals who can speak to your work history and personal qualities. A possible reference might be a previous employer, teacher, or coach. Family members should not be used for this purpose. Contact potential references to seek their *consent* (permission) before adding them to your list. Be sure to ask for their work title, phone number, and address. Once you find a job, keep this list for future use and update it on a regular basis.

Write a Résumé

Applicants are often asked to submit a résumé during the job search process. A **résumé** is a document that lists your education and work experience. This document forms the employer's initial impression of you and is instrumental in the decision whether to interview you.

Consider using a résumé template to create your résumé. There are many free templates available on the Internet. The résumé should be designed so that the reader can easily find key information. Many employers scan résumés quickly when deciding which candidates to interview. Select a template that has sufficient white space and margins, headings that are larger than the body text, and that is relatively straightforward. Most importantly, the résumé should be well written and free of errors. Try to identify key words used in job listings that interest you and use them in your résumé (**Figure 36.1**).

Save your résumé as an electronic file on your computer for use when applying to jobs online. You may be asked to either upload your résumé to the company's website or e-mail it to the hiring manager. Be sure to bring hard copies of your résumé with you to an interview even if you already submitted the résumé electronically.

Write a Cover Letter

In addition to a résumé, you will probably be asked to submit a cover letter during the job search process. A **cover letter** is a letter or e-mail message that invites potential employers to review your résumé. In your cover letter, you will introduce yourself and summarize the reason you are applying for the position without repeating your attached résumé.

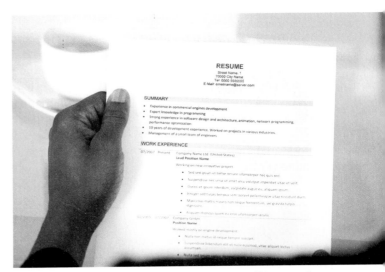

Andrey_Popov/Shutterstock.com

Figure 36.1 Résumés must be easy to read because hiring managers often scan them quickly. Which of the elements discussed in this chapter can you see in this résumé?

A good cover letter is brief, positive, and to the point. Cover letters can make a lasting impression. Make sure your letter is neat and follows standard business format. Be sure to check the spelling and punctuation. Consider having several people proofread your letter and offer advice on improvements.

Create Your Portfolio

A **portfolio** is a collection of materials that you assemble and organize to showcase your qualifications, skills, and talents. Materials may include samples of your writing, letters of reference, awards or certifications, videos of presentations you gave, or even photos of dishes you prepared. Update your portfolio regularly with new accomplishments, work experiences, or other relevant information. When shared with potential employers, your portfolio will provide concrete examples of your qualifications and experience.

The Job Search

Armed with a list of references, your résumé, and portfolio, you are now ready to begin your job search. Locating a job opportunity is the first step.

Locate Job Opportunities

When you are ready to find employment, you can locate opportunities through a variety of sources. Start your search at the placement office of your school. Usually school counselors and teachers can direct you to helpful job information. You can check newspaper want ads and job fairs. Good information is also available in libraries. The professional journals in your career field and the leading professional organizations often announce job openings (**Figure 36.2**). Family members and neighbors can provide help, too.

There are many websites that post open positions, and many sites also offer tips for job hunting. For instance, the *O*NET* (the *Occupational Information Network*) website includes options for finding jobs within a career cluster or searching for jobs related to specific skills. *Find Local Help*, a component of CareerOneStop, helps users find jobs and job-related resources in their local area. One-Stop Career Centers offer assistance in job-seeking skills, such as résumé writing. They also offer help with various types of job training. Many companies post openings for full-time positions on their own websites.

Organizations for Professionals in the Nutrition and Food Industry		
Organization	**Website**	**Functions**
Academy of Nutrition and Dietetics	eatright.org	Serves food and nutrition professionals. It is committed to improving the nation's health and advancing the profession of dietetics through research, education, and advocacy.
American Association of Family and Consumer Sciences (AAFCS)	aafcs.org	Serves family and consumer sciences professionals. Works to provide leadership and support for professionals whose work assists individuals, families, and communities in making informed decisions about their well-being, relationships, and resources to achieve optimal quality of life.
Food Marketing Institute (FMI)	fmi.org	Serves grocery retailers and wholesalers. It provides leadership to retailers and wholesalers of food and consumer products, as well as to their supplier partners, by fostering their growth and promoting their role in feeding families and enriching the lives of their customers.
Institute of Food Technologists (IFT)	ift.org	Serves technical personnel in food industries, production, product development, research, and product quality. Its function is to advance the science of food and to promote the application of science and engineering to the evaluation, production, processing, packaging, distribution, preparation, and utilization of foods.
National Restaurant Association (NRA)	restaurant.org	Serves personnel in all areas of the foodservice industry. It supports foodservice education and research.

Figure 36.2 Professional organizations often post job opportunities on their websites or in their publications.

Many people find employment through networking. **Networking** is the exchange of information or services among individuals or groups. As a newcomer to the career field, the goal of your networking is to learn about possible job leads.

Social networking sites have become popular places to find information on companies and their available positions. Many companies network on these sites because these sites are an additional source of advertising for them. Users find that these sites expand their job search possibilities. In addition, these sites allow a personal exchange between users and company representatives.

Apply

When you hear of a job that interests you, contact the employer to express your interest. Depending on the job and the employer's requirements for application, you may make this contact by e-mail, letter, telephone, or in person.

If the job is still available, the next step is to fill out an application. Many employers now require potential job candidates to complete their applications online (**Figure 36.3**). When filling out online applications, it is extremely important to use the key words from the employer's job listing to describe your abilities as they relate to the job. Online applications are screened for such key words, which help employers sort through the applications. If you are filling out a form in person, be sure to bring a pen. Be prepared to provide all information an application is likely to request. Your résumé should contain most of the information required and can serve as your resource for completing the application.

When completing an application, you will need to provide your name, address, phone number, and possibly an e-mail address. The application form may also ask you to state the position for which you are applying, your expected wages, and when you can start working. You will need to list the names and locations of schools attended and provide information about any current or previous jobs held. Be ready to provide a list of references as well.

Employers may not request your Social Security number until they are interested in hiring you. All workers need a Social Security number for tax and identification purposes.

Interview

A neat, well-written résumé and a completed application can lead to an interview. An interview is a chance for an employer and a job applicant to discuss the job and the applicant's qualifications.

To make a good impression at an interview, you should be well groomed and neatly dressed. Speak in a clear voice and have a positive attitude. Be prepared to answer a variety of questions about your skills, interests, and work experiences (**Figure 36.4**). In addition, do your homework—know some background information about the employer. This will help you ask more specific questions about the company and the job.

If the interview goes well, the employer may decide to offer you the job. In many cases, however, the employer is interviewing other applicants for the same job. At the interview, ask the employer when you can expect to hear his or her decision.

After the interview, be sure to write a short *thank-you message* to the person or persons with whom you interviewed. The purpose of this message is to thank the interviewer for his or her time and reinforce your interest in the position. By sending a thank-you message, you will stand out as someone who has good manners and a genuine interest in the position.

Rawpixel.com/Shutterstock.com

Figure 36.3 Many companies offer online applications. What are some benefits and drawbacks of applying online?

Common Interview Questions

In what position are you interested?

Would you be interested in any other position(s)?

What other jobs have you had?

How many hours a week can you work?

Are you involved in other activities that could cause time conflicts with your work schedule?

What kinds of classes do you take in school?

What class do you like best?

Would you have transportation to and from work?

How much do you expect to earn?

How well do you work with others?

Why should we hire you?

Figure 36.4 Be prepared not only to answer questions during a job interview, but also to get your questions about the job answered. *What questions would you ask during a job interview?*

Handling an Offer or a Rejection

When you receive an offer, let the employer know as soon as possible if you will accept the job. Ask when you should report to work. Find out any necessary information regarding items such as uniforms and training sessions.

If the employer does not offer you the job, ask yourself the following questions:

- Was my application accurate and neat?
- Did I arrive for the interview on time and appropriately dressed?
- Did I show interest in the job and willingness to work?
- Did I appear friendly and cooperative?
- Did I answer all questions accurately?

Answering *no* to a question may give you a clue about why you did not receive a job offer. This will help you improve for your next interview.

Succeeding in the Workplace

After securing employment, adjusting to your new duties and responsibilities will occupy your first few weeks. Your supervisor and coworkers

Learn About...

Managing Your Online Presence

If future employers searched the Internet for information about you, what would they find? This is called your *online presence*. Many employers also use the Internet to check job applicants as well as employees.

A first step in managing your online presence is to identify what is currently posted about you. Plug your name into one or more search engines and examine what comes up. Delete anything you wouldn't want a prospective employer to see. However, since you cannot control the flow of information online, be prepared to answer questions employers may ask. Here are some additional pointers.

- Do not say or do anything that is unethical or illegal.
- Do not take photos or videos that show you in a bad light. Images that depict drinking, drugs, gang signs, firearms, and lewd behavior have created problems for those pictured.
- Do not say anything negative about current or former employers, jobs, or coworkers. Negative comments and anything profane, sexist, or racist can result in the rejection of a job application or being named in a lawsuit.

Remember that cybercriminals are searching the Internet for victims. They collect and piece together data that they use to commit crimes. Avoid posting personal information, especially your address, date of birth, and phone number. Revealing your future whereabouts is also risky.

Know and Apply

1. Some people believe that having no online presence is the best solution for avoiding a negative one. How would you evaluate this strategy?

2. In addition to avoiding a negative online presence, creating a positive presence is desirable. What are two ways you could enhance your online presence?

will help you learn the routine. An introduction to company policies and procedures as well as the special safety rules that all employees must know is common for new employees.

While your coworkers will be watching what you do, they will also pay attention to "how you work." How to behave in the workplace is an important lesson all employees should learn. Making an effort to do your best will help you succeed.

Professionalism

Demonstrating professionalism is essential to job success. Professionalism is having the competence to perform your job. More than just technical know-how, it is also the respect with which you treat your boss, coworkers, and yourself. Professionals assume responsibility and *persevere* (press on) despite problems or setbacks (**Figure 36.5**).

Part of behaving professionally is responding appropriately to *constructive criticism*. Every employee, no matter how knowledgeable or experienced, can improve his or her performance. If you receive criticism from a supervisor or coworker, do not be offended. Instead, use the feedback to improve yourself. The more you improve, the more successful you will be in your work.

Ethical Workplace Behavior

Ethical behavior on the job means conforming to accepted standards of fairness and good conduct. A person's sense of right and wrong is the basis for his or her behavior. Individuals and society as a whole regard ethical behavior as highly important. Integrity, confidentiality, and honesty are crucial aspects of ethical workplace behavior. *Integrity* is firmly following your moral values.

Unfortunately, employee theft is a major problem at some companies. The theft can range from carrying office supplies home to stealing money or expensive equipment. Company policies are in place to address these concerns. In cases of criminal or serious behavior, people may lose their jobs. If proven, the charge of criminal behavior stays on the employee's record. Such an employee will have a difficult time finding another job.

Work Habits

Employers want employees who are punctual, dependable, and responsible. They want their employees to be capable of taking initiative and working independently. Other desirable employee qualities include organization, accuracy, and efficiency.

A **punctual** employee is always prompt and on time. He or she is on time not only when the workday starts, but also when returning from breaks and lunches (**Figure 36.6**). Being

nandyphotos/iStock/Thinkstock

Figure 36.5 Be sure you understand your profession's dress code and follow it. Avoid strong fragrances and jewelry that makes noise or is excessive.

Lucky Business/Shutterstock.com

Figure 36.6 A punctual employee returns from coffee and lunch breaks on time.

dependable means that people can rely on you to fulfill your word and meet your deadlines. If you are not well, you should inform your employer as soon as possible. If there are reasons you cannot be at work, discuss this with your employer and work out an alternate arrangement. Many people have lost jobs by not checking with their supervisor about time off.

Taking *initiative* means that you start activities on your own without being told. When you finish one task, you do not wait to hear what to do next. Individuals who take initiative need much less supervision. They have **self-motivation**, or an inner desire to perform well. Generally, this motivation will drive you to set goals and accomplish them. All of these qualities together show that you are capable of working *independently* (**Figure 36.7**).

You are expected to be as accurate and error-free as possible in all that you do. This is why you were hired. Complete your work with precision and double-check it to assure accuracy. Your coworkers depend on the careful completion of your tasks.

lightwavemedia/Shutterstock.com

Figure 36.7 Employers value employees who work independently and stay focused on their work.

Time Management

A good employee knows how to manage time wisely. This includes the ability to prioritize assignments and complete them in a timely fashion. It also involves not wasting time. Time-wasting behaviors include visiting with coworkers, making personal phone calls, texting, sending e-mails, or doing other nonwork activities during work hours.

While it is important to complete all your work thoroughly, you must also be able to gauge which assignments are most important. Avoid putting excessive efforts into minor assignments when crucial matters require your attention. Even though you are still accomplishing work, this is another way to waste time.

Attitude on the Job

Your attitude can often determine the success you have on your job. Your **attitude** is your outlook on life. It is reflected in your reactions to the events and people around you. A smile and courteous behavior can make customers and fellow employees feel good about themselves and you. Clients and customers prefer to do business in friendly environments. Being friendly may take some effort on your part, but it does pay off.

Enthusiasm spreads easily from one person to another. Usually, enthusiasm means a person enjoys what he or she is doing. In a sales environment, enthusiasm increases sales. In an office, enthusiasm builds a team spirit for working together.

People who do a good job feel pride in their work. They feel a sense of accomplishment and a desire to achieve more. This attitude can inspire others as well (**Figure 36.8**).

Health and Hygiene

As an employee, you are a representative of your company. Therefore, your employer expects you to be neat and clean on the job. Taking care of yourself gives the impression that you want people to view you as a professional.

Employers expect workers to dress appropriately. Many places of work have a dress code. If your workplace does not, use common sense and avoid extremes. Refrain from wearing garments

Rob Marmion/Shutterstock.com

Figure 36.8 Your attitude toward your work greatly affects your success on the job as in life. Identify someone you believe is successful either in life or career. How would you describe his or her attitude?

that are revealing or have inappropriate pictures or sayings. Some employers have rules requiring that tattoos or piercings beyond pierced ears remain covered. Good appearance is especially important for employees who have frequent face-to-face contact with customers.

Safety Consciousness

Safety on the job is everyone's responsibility. Many workplace accidents occur because of careless behavior. Often poor attitudes can cause unsafe behavior, too. Common causes of accidents include the following:

- taking chances
- forgetting safety details
- disobeying company rules
- daydreaming
- losing your temper
- falling asleep

Practicing good safety habits is essential for preventing accidents and injuries on the job. A healthy worker is more alert and less likely to make accident-prone mistakes. Knowing how to use machines and tools properly is the responsibility of both the employer and employees. Wearing protective clothing and using safety equipment correctly helps keep workers safe (**Figure 36.9**). Your employer will emphasize the

Learn About...

OSHA for Young Workers

Work-related injuries claim the lives of 60–70 young workers each year, while about 200,000 young workers seek emergency medical treatment. All employees, including young workers, have a right to a safe, healthy workplace. They also have a responsibility to be safe.

As a young worker, you have the following responsibilities:

- Trust your instincts about dangerous situations.
- Follow all safety rules.
- Wear proper safety equipment.
- Ask questions about potentially dangerous situations or equipment.
- Tell your supervisor or parent if you suspect unsafe conditions.
- Be aware of your work environment.
- Work safely.
- Stay sober and drug-free.
- Know your workplace rights.

Employers have the following responsibilities:

- Provide a workplace free from serious recognized hazards and follow all OSHA safety and health standards.
- Provide training about workplace hazards and required safety gear.*
- Tell you where to get answers to your safety or health questions.
- Tell you what to do if you get hurt on the job.

Employers must pay for most types of safety gear.

Know and Apply

Visit the OSHA Young Workers website at www.osha.gov/youngworkers. Find your state's wage and child labor laws. Search to discover the following:

1. What, if any, occupations are prohibited for your age group by your state?
2. What are the minimum paid rest requirements in your state?

MBI/Shutterstock.com

Figure 36.9 Employers must identify and provide appropriate personal protection equipment for employees. It is the employees' responsibility to wear personal protection equipment properly.

safety practices that employees must follow in your workplace.

The government agency that promotes safety in the workplace is the Occupational Safety and Health Administration (OSHA). You will be required to follow the specific OSHA regulations that apply to your workplace.

Decision Making and Problem Solving

Employers value workers who have the ability to make sound decisions and solve problems. This process applies in the workplace as well as to other aspects of life. Having the ability to solve problems on the job shows an employer that you are able to handle more responsibility. Solving problems as a group can help employees feel more pride in their work.

The ability to make decisions and solve problems requires *critical-thinking skills*. These are higher-level skills that enable you to think beyond the obvious. You learn to interpret information and make judgments. Supervisors appreciate employees who can analyze problems and think of practical solutions (**Figure 36.10**).

Problem-Solving Process

1. Identify the problem.
2. Analyze and define the problem causes.
3. List potential solutions.
4. Select solution and develop action plan.
5. Implement the action plan.
6. Evaluate the effectiveness of the solution.

Figure 36.10   Many people make the mistake of skipping the final step in the problem-solving process. Why is the final step important?

Communication Skills

Communicating effectively with others is important for job success. Being a good communicator means that you can share information well with others. It also means you are a good listener.

Good communication is central to a smooth operation of any business. Communication is the process of exchanging ideas, thoughts, or information. Poor communication is costly to an employer, as when time is lost because an order was entered incorrectly. Poor communication can result in lost customers, too.

The primary forms of communications are verbal and nonverbal. **Verbal communication** involves the use of words to send or receive a message. For instance, speaking, listening, writing, and reading are all forms of verbal communication. **Nonverbal communication** is the sending and receiving of messages without the use of words. It involves *body language*, which includes the expression on your face and your body posture.

Listening is an important part of communication. If you do not understand, be sure to ask questions. Also, give feedback to let others know you understand them and are interested in what they have to say. Leaning forward while a person is talking indicates interest and keen listening (**Figure 36.11**). Slouching back in a chair and yawning give the opposite signal—that you are bored and uninterested.

The message you convey in telephone communication involves your promptness, tone of voice, and attitude. Answering the phone

Dragon Images/Shutterstock.com

Figure 36.11 Nonverbal communication can be as effective as verbal communication for delivering a message. What nonverbal cues can you see in this photo?

quickly with a pleasant voice conveys a positive image for the company. Learning to obtain accurate information from the caller without interrupting that person's message is important.

Communication tools have advanced with the development of new technologies. To be an effective employee, you need to know how to communicate well with the common tools of your workplace. For example, when sending e-mail communications, remember to think through each message as you would before sending a postal letter. Often messages are sent quickly without

Global Perspective

International Business

Increasingly, more business is transacted internationally. Even within the United States, dealing with people from different cultures is common. Make a point of learning about the culture of your business associates. This will allow you to be sensitive to their cultural differences. Your consideration will enhance communication as well as have a positive impact on your success in the workplace.

thought of how the recipient may interpret them. The same is true of voicemail.

The development of good communication skills is an ongoing process. Attending communication workshops and applying what you learn can keep your skills sharp. You should periodically give yourself a communications checkup by asking your supervisor to suggest areas that need improvement.

Presentation Skills

Giving presentations is a task common to many jobs. Some jobs may require frequent, formal presentations to large groups. Others may involve only *sporadic* (infrequent), informal presentations to a few people. Regardless of what type of presentation you are giving, planning is necessary for it to be successful. Use the following guidelines when planning a presentation:

- *Identify the purpose.* Are you trying to inform, persuade, make a request, or give instructions? Answering this question will help focus your presentation.

- *Understand your audience.* Is the audience knowledgeable in the topic being discussed or unfamiliar with the subject? This understanding should guide your level of detail and vocabulary choices.

- *Know your time limit.* Prioritize and adjust the amount and type of information you share to fit the allotted time. Consider providing supporting details or facts in the form of handouts or visual aids.

- *Gather information.* Determine and obtain the information needed to support the purpose of the presentation. Be sure to cite sources where appropriate.

- *Choose a delivery method.* If you plan to use technology to enrich your presentation, be sure the necessary equipment will be available and that you know how to use it.

Effective presenters avoid reading their presentations *verbatim* (word for word) from notes or slides. They inject humor where appropriate to establish a rapport with their audience. Visual aids are used to increase understanding and add interest to the presentation. Most importantly, presenters practice until they are comfortable with the presentation (**Figure 36.12**).

MBI/Shutterstock.com

Figure 36.12 This presenter is using a visual aid to increase understanding. Recall a recent formal or informal presentation you attended. Was it effective? Why?

Interpersonal Skills

Interpersonal skills involve interacting with others. Some workplace activities that involve these skills include teaching others, leading, negotiating, working as a member of a team, and interacting with customers. Getting along well with others can require great effort on your part, but it is essential for accomplishing your employer's goals.

Teamwork

Employers seek employees who can effectively serve as good team members. Due to the nature of most work today, teamwork and collaboration is necessary. A **team** is a small group of people working together for a common purpose. Often cooperation requires flexibility and willingness to try new ways to get things done. If someone is uncooperative, it takes longer to accomplish the tasks. When people do not get along, strained relationships develop and get in the way of finishing the tasks.

A big advantage of a team is its ability to develop plans and complete work faster than individuals working alone. Team members need some time before they become comfortable with one another and function as a unit. Team development goes through various stages. In the beginning,

Exploring Careers

Grocery Store Manager

Grocery store managers oversee the work of employees, such as produce managers, cashiers, customer service representatives, and stock clerks. They are responsible for interviewing, hiring, and training employees. Grocery store managers ensure that customers receive satisfactory service and quality goods. They also answer customers' inquiries, deal with complaints, and sometimes handle purchasing, budgeting, and accounting responsibilities. They organize shelves, displays, and inventories. Grocery store managers inspect merchandise to ensure that products are not outdated. They develop merchandising techniques and coordinate sales promotions. In addition, they may greet and assist customers and promote sales and good public relations.

Grocery store managers must possess good communication skills and get along with everyone. They need initiative, self-discipline, good judgment, and decisiveness. They also must be able to motivate, organize, and direct the work of their employees. They need good math and business skills as well as strong customer service and public relations skills.

Grocery store managers usually gain knowledge of management principles and practices through work experience. Many supervisors begin their careers as salespersons, cashiers, or customer service representatives. There is no standard educational requirement for grocery store managers. For some jobs, a college degree is required. Grocery store managers who have college degrees often hold associate or bachelor's degrees in liberal arts, social sciences, business, or management. Regardless of education level or major area of study, several high school or college courses are recommended. These include those related to business, such as accounting, marketing, management, and sales, as well as those related to social science, such as psychology, sociology, and communication.

people are excited about being on a team. Later, disagreements may replace harmony. The good result of this is people express themselves and learn to trust the other team members. Eventually leaders emerge and the team develops a unique way to interact and achieve goals. Finally, the team becomes very productive and performs at its highest level. It takes time and a genuine desire to work together to build a strong team.

Creative ideas often develop from building on another person's idea. Honesty and openness are essential. Also, trying to understand the ideas of others before trying to get others to understand your ideas is an effective skill to develop.

Negotiation

Often, employees and employers must negotiate on a task or work-related issue. **Negotiation** is the process of agreeing to an issue that requires all parties to give and take. The goal is a "win-win" solution in which both parties get some or all of what they are seeking.

Negotiation begins with trying to understand the other party's interests. Possible solutions that meet their mutual concerns can be developed. Often the best solution becomes clear when both parties have ample time to explain what they are trying to accomplish.

Leadership

All careers require leadership skills. **Leadership** is the ability to guide and motivate others to complete tasks or achieve goals. It involves communicating well with others, accepting responsibility, and making decisions with confidence. Those employees with leadership skills are most likely to be promoted to higher levels.

Leaders often seem to carry the most responsibility of a group. Other group members look to them for answers and direction. The most important role of leaders is to keep the team advancing toward its goal. Leaders do this by inspiring their groups and providing the motivation to keep everyone working together (**Figure 36.13**).

Good leaders encourage teamwork, because a team that is working together well is more likely to reach goals. They listen to the opinions of others and make sure all team members are included in projects. Leaders also want to

Fuse/Fuse/Thinkstock

Figure 36.13 Effective leaders get along well with their coworkers and inspire them to perform better as a team.

set a good example by doing a fair share of the work. In these ways, leaders cultivate a sense of harmony in the group.

Customer Relations

Working with customers requires good interpersonal skills. The most important aspect of customer relations is always remaining courteous. This may also require patience in some situations. When customers visit your business, you want them to have the best possible service and to leave happy. Remember that your behavior and skills at handling customers can determine if the customer will return to your business. The customer may spread the word about his or her experience to other potential customers. Make sure your customers know you appreciate their business.

Customer relations may also involve problem solving and negotiation. If a customer needs help, you must provide answers as quickly and accurately as possible while remaining pleasant and polite. When a situation becomes stressful, you must be able to control your own level of stress without letting it affect your performance. At the same time, you must be able to lessen the customer's stress and attempt to eliminate its source.

Learn About...

Protecting the Planet

Regardless of what type of career you choose, be a good citizen by taking steps to care for the earth's environment. Small efforts made by you and your coworkers can make a big difference. Consider the following ideas:

- Carpool to your job or use public transportation.
- Use a reusable lunch bag to carry your lunch to work.
- Keep a ceramic mug in your workplace so you will not have to use disposable cups.
- Recycle office paper and cardboard cartons.
- Reuse manila envelopes.

Know and Apply

1. List additional ways you could make a difference.
2. Consider how a business's attitude about supporting efforts to care for the earth's environment might affect its employees.

Develop Your Skills

Leading others may not be easy for some people, but everyone can improve their leadership skills with practice. Becoming involved in a school club or organization can help. Taking a role as an officer or a committee chair will give you even more practice.

Belonging to an organization can also help you develop your teamwork skills. You will learn how to work well in a group as you plan events, create projects, and accomplish goals together.

Leaving a Job

More money, more responsibility, and better benefits are some of the reasons for leaving a job. There are others, too, but all job departures need to be handled in a way that is considerate of the employer. You should try not to leave your job with noticeable anger and hostility. Employers

know that employees will not stay forever; however, they dislike *insufficient* (not enough) notice, especially during a busy season.

When you make the decision to leave your job, let the employer know in writing by giving at least a two-week notice. It would be helpful to give a longer notice if you can. A letter of resignation should state your reason for leaving and the date you expect to leave. The letter allows the employer to begin looking for your replacement. Perhaps there will be enough time to hire someone who can work with you during your final days. Many people have found that a past employer became their greatest ally when they needed a good reference for a future position (**Figure 36.14**).

Balancing Family, Community, and Work

Your success in a career will affect your satisfaction with your personal and family life. Likewise, your roles and responsibilities related to home and community life will affect your career. Balancing career with home and community life is important in any lifestyle.

Dragon Images/Shutterstock.com

Figure 36.14 Leaving your previous job well can help you get your new job off to a good start.

Belonging to a family involves roles and responsibilities. As a son or daughter, your responsibilities at home may involve watching younger siblings, helping with family meals, and keeping your clothes and room clean. Usually these tasks do not interfere with your responsibilities to attend school and perform well. Adding a part-time job can complicate matters, however, and force you to manage your time more carefully.

The roles of spouse, parent, homemaker, and employee are much more demanding and may conflict at times. People with *multiple roles* must balance their responsibilities to fully meet them all. Sometimes family responsibilities will dictate the career decisions you make.

Parents may adjust work responsibilities so they can spend more time with the family. These adjustments might include telecommuting, working less overtime, taking a part-time job, or starting a home-based business. If both parents work away from the home, they must provide *substitute care* for young children.

Belonging to a community also involves roles and responsibilities. As a citizen of a community, you may choose to volunteer to help others. You may choose to volunteer because you want to be a good citizen or because you care about a cause. Volunteers are not paid for their services; however, volunteering can be rewarding and may provide valuable experiences that may help you in a future career (**Figure 36.15**).

Examples of ways to volunteer in your community may include the following suggestions:

- work with a recycling program
- help at an animal shelter
- take part in organizations such as Special Olympics, Habitat for Humanity, or Toys for Tots
- assist campaigns against drunk driving or drug abuse
- work at a food bank
- raise money for a homeless shelter or veterans' group
- work as an aide at a hospital or retirement home

Catherine Yeulet/iStock/Thinkstock

Figure 36.15   Volunteering to pick up litter is one way to contribute to your community.

- help the park department in planting flowers or trees or in cleanup efforts

Many communities benefit from service learning projects. Using what you learn in the classroom to meet a need in the community is called **service learning**. If your school does not have a service learning program, consider starting one. Involvement in service learning projects will help make your community a better place to live.

Chapter 36 Review and Expand

Summary

Preparation for the job search includes gathering references, writing a résumé, and creating a portfolio. Resources to locate job opportunities are available at your school, online, or through networking. The quality of your application and how you represent yourself during the interview are important to a successful job search.

Workplace success requires demonstrating professionalism, ethical behavior, good work habits, effective time management, and a positive attitude. Developing your decision-making, communication, presentation, and interpersonal skills can help you succeed. Staying safety conscious will help you prevent workplace accidents.

Terminating the job has procedures to follow, too, including notifying the employer in writing. Leaving a job properly improves your chances for receiving good references in the future.

Having a family and a career involves balancing multiple roles and responsibilities. Being a good citizen of a community also involves responsibilities and provides opportunities for volunteering and service learning.

Vocabulary Activities

1. **Content Terms** Write each of the following terms on a separate sheet of paper. For each term, quickly write a word you think relates to the term. In small groups, exchange papers. Have each person in the group explain a term on the list. Take turns until all terms have been explained.

reference	attitude
résumé	verbal communication
cover letter	nonverbal
portfolio	communication
networking	team
ethical behavior	negotiation
punctual	leadership
self-motivation	service learning

2. **Academic Terms** Individually or with a partner, create a T-chart on a sheet of paper and list each of the following terms in the left column. In the right column, list an *antonym* (a word of opposite meaning) for each term in the left column.

consent	verbatim
persevere	insufficient
sporadic	

Review

Write your answers using complete sentences when appropriate.

3. Explain why it is important that your résumé is easy to read and error-free.
4. Compare and contrast a résumé and a portfolio.
5. List seven resources for locating job opportunities.
6. Name a public figure whom you believe displays positive work ethics and professionalism. Give examples to support your choice.
7. True or false. Having initiative means that you must be constantly supervised to accomplish tasks.
8. What is the difference between verbal and nonverbal communication?
9. Describe the stages through which a team progresses.
10. Explain the proper procedure for leaving a job.
11. Give an example of how you would balance family, community, and a career.
12. Using what you learn in the classroom to meet a need in the community is called _____.

Core Skills

13. **Writing, Technology** Using a résumé template based on the recommendations in this chapter, write your résumé, as well as an accompanying cover letter. Have a family member or classmate critique your résumé and cover letter. Use the critique to revise and edit. Upload your résumé and cover letter to your portfolio.

Chapter 36 Review and Expand

14. **Technology** Research various online resources for locating job opportunities. Based on your findings, develop a strategy to employ in your next job search. First, determine the job you will be searching for. Create a document outlining your strategy. The document should identify specific websites and technologies, and how you will use them.

15. **Research, Speaking** Team up with a classmate to role-play an interview for a job. First, identify the job for which you will be interviewing. Research to learn what this type of job usually pays, the education requirements, and so on. Take turns assuming the role of interviewer and interviewee. Create questions specific to the job based on your research.

16. **Writing** Working in small teams, develop a brief evaluation form to use to assess the effectiveness of team members. The form should evaluate cooperation/collaboration, time management, willingness to assume responsibility, communication skills, professionalism, and completion of assigned tasks. Include instructions encouraging evaluators to provide constructive criticism.

17. **Reading, Speaking, Technology** Obtain a copy of a career-search book (such as the latest edition of *What Color Is Your Parachute?*). Read the book. Employing the presentation skills discussed in this chapter, give a class presentation identifying the important guidelines the author suggests for finding meaningful employment. Use technology to add interest to your presentation.

18. **Listening, Speaking, Writing** Working in small teams, use the problem-solving process in Figure 36.10 to identify a solution to a sustainability problem in an imaginary food business. The solution must maintain or increase profits and/or organizational health. Assign roles and responsibilities to each team member. Write a paper that documents the team's work as it progresses through each step of the process. If a step has not been completed due to time constraints, document this with details regarding when and how the step would be completed. Finally, complete an evaluation form such as the one developed in Activity 16 for each member of the team. Submit the evaluations along with the paper to the instructor for review. The instructor can then sort and distribute the evaluations to the appropriate team members.

19. **Writing, Research** Research to learn about time and energy management. Evaluate your findings and write a short paper examining the importance of time and energy management to success in the workplace. Cite your sources.

20. **Career Readiness Practice** Suppose you are interested in a career in the Restaurants & Food/Beverage Services career pathway. You have done your research in regard to educational requirements for such careers and think this fits with your personal goals and career goals. However, you feel you are missing the firsthand experiential knowledge necessary to commit to such a career. Locate a person with a local company or organization who is an expert in your career of interest. Make arrangements to job shadow or work with this individual as a mentor as you pursue your career. How can you benefit by having such a mentor in your life?

Critical Thinking and Problem Solving

21. **Determine** Review the evaluations from Activity 18. Based on your analysis of your team's feedback, identify three actions you will take to improve your performance as a team member.

22. **Draw conclusions** Have you ever had an informal communication experience in which you felt totally misunderstood? How could such experiences impact workplace communication? Draw conclusions about ways to prevent such misunderstandings.

23. **Analyze** In teams, brainstorm a list of ethical behaviors you have observed in real life. What characteristics help you and your team members recognize these behaviors as ethical? How do ethical behaviors in nonwork situations transfer to workplace behaviors?

24. **Analyze** Form teams to identify and solve a problem. Use leadership skills to guide the team as it performs. After the exercise, write an analysis of the leadership skills you used and their effectiveness.

Appendix A

Nutritional Goals for Age-Sex Groups

Based on Dietary Reference Intakes and *Dietary Guidelines* Recommendations

	Source of goal[a]	Child 1–3	Female 4–8	Male 4–8	Female 9–13	Male 9–13	Female 14–18	Male 14–18	Female 19–30	Male 19–30	Female 31–50	Male 31–50	Female 51+	Male 51+
Calorie level(s) assessed		1,000	1,200	1,400, 1,600	1,600	1,800	1,800	2,200, 2,800, 3,200	2,000	2,400, 2,600, 3,000	1,800	2,200	1,600	2,000
Macronutrients														
Protein, g	RDA	13	19	19	34	34	46	52	46	56	46	56	46	56
Protein, % calories	AMDR	5–20	10–30	10–30	10–30	10–30	10–30	10–30	10–35	10–35	10–35	10–35	10–35	10–35
Carbohydrate, g	RDA	130	130	130	130	130	130	130	130	130	130	130	130	130
Carbohydrate, % calories	AMDR	45–65	45–65	45–65	45–65	45–65	45–65	45–65	45–65	45–65	45–65	45–65	45–65	45–65
Dietary fiber, g	14g/ 1,000 calories	14	16.8	19.6	22.4	25.2	25.2	30.8	28	33.6	25.2	30.8	22.4	28
Added sugars, % calories	DGA	<10%	<10%	<10%	<10%	<10%	<10%	<10%	<10%	<10%	<10%	<10%	<10%	<10%
Total fat, % calories	AMDR	30–40	25–35	25–35	25–35	25–35	25–35	25–35	20–35	20–35	20–35	20–35	20–35	20–35
Saturated fat, % calories	DGA	<10%	<10%	<10%	<10%	<10%	<10%	<10%	<10%	<10%	<10%	<10%	<10%	<10%
Linoleic acid, g	AI	7	10	10	10	12	11	16	12	17	12	17	11	14
Linolenic acid, g	AI	0.7	0.9	0.9	1.0	1.2	1.1	1.6	1.1	1.6	1.1	1.6	1.1	1.6
Minerals														
Calcium, mg	RDA	700	1,000	1,000	1,300	1,300	1,300	1,300	1,000	1,000	1,000	1,000	1,200	1,000[b]
Iron, mg	RDA	7	10	10	8	8	15	11	18	8	18	8	8	8
Magnesium, mg	RDA	80	130	130	240	240	360	410	310	400	320	420	320	420
Phosphorus, mg	RDA	460	500	500	1,250	1,250	1,250	1,250	700	700	700	700	700	700
Potassium, mg	AI	2,000	2,300	2,300	2,300	2,500	2,300	3,000	2,600	3,400	2,600	3,400	2,600	3,400
Sodium, mg	AI	800	1,000	1,000	1,200	1,200	1,500	1,500	1,500	1,500	1,500	1,500	1,500	1,500
Zinc, mg	RDA	3	5	5	8	8	9	11	8	11	8	11	8	11
Copper, mcg	RDA	340	440	440	700	700	890	890	900	900	900	900	900	900
Manganese, mg	AI	1.2	1.5	1.5	1.6	1.9	1.6	2.2	1.8	2.3	1.8	2.3	1.8	2.3
Selenium, mcg	RDA	20	30	30	40	40	55	55	55	55	55	55	55	55

	Source of goal[a]	Child 1–3	Female 4–8	Male 4–8	Female 9–13	Male 9–13	Female 14–18	Male 14–18	Female 19–30	Male 19–30	Female 31–50	Male 31–50	Female 51+	Male 51+
Vitamins														
Vitamin A, mcg RAE	RDA	300	400	400	600	600	700	900	700	900	700	900	700	900
Vitamin E, mg AT	RDA	6	7	7	11	11	15	15	15	15	15	15	15	15
Vitamin D, IU	RDA	600	600	600	600	600	600	600	600	600	600	600	600[c]	600[c]
Vitamin C, mg	RDA	15	25	25	45	45	65	75	75	90	75	90	75	90
Thiamin, mg	RDA	0.5	0.6	0.6	0.9	0.9	1.0	1.2	1.1	1.2	1.1	1.2	1.1	1.2
Riboflavin, mg	RDA	0.5	0.6	0.6	0.9	0.9	1.0	1.3	1.1	1.3	1.1	1.3	1.1	1.3
Niacin, mg	RDA	6	8	8	12	12	14	16	14	16	14	16	14	16
Vitamin B_6, mg	RDA	0.5	0.6	0.6	1.0	1.0	1.2	1.3	1.3	1.3	1.3	1.3	1.5	1.7
Vitamin B_{12}, mcg	RDA	0.9	1.2	1.2	1.8	1.8	2.4	2.4	2.4	2.4	2.4	2.4	2.4	2.4
Choline, mg	AI	200	250	250	375	375	400	550	425	550	425	550	425	550
Vitamin K, mcg	AI	30	55	55	60	60	75	75	90	120	90	120	90	120
Folate, mcg DFE	RDA	150	200	200	300	300	400	400	400	400	400	400	400	400

[a] RDA = Recommended Dietary Allowance, AI = Adequate Intake, AMDR = Acceptable Macronutrient Distribution Range, DGA = *2015–2020 Dietary Guidelines* recommended limit; 14 g fiber per 1,000 kcal = basis for AI for fiber.

[b] Calcium RDA for males ages 71+ years is 1,200 mg.

[c] Vitamin D RDA for males and females ages 71+ years is 800 IU.

CFG: Snapshot

Canada's food guide

Eat well. Live well.

Healthy eating is more than the foods you eat

Be mindful of your eating habits

Cook more often

Enjoy your food

Eat meals with others

Use food labels

Limit foods high in sodium, sugars or saturated fat

Be aware of food marketing

Discover your food guide at
Canada.ca/FoodGuide

Health Canada   Santé Canada

Canada

CFG: Snapshot

Appendix C

Nutritive Values of Foods

(Tr indicates nutrient present in trace amount.)

Item	Approximate Measures (edible portion)		Nutrients in Indicated Quantity								
			Food Energy	Protein	Fat	Saturated Fat	Carbo-hydrate	Dietary Fiber	Calcium	Iron	Vitamin A
		Grams	Calories	Grams	Grams	Grams	Grams	Grams	Milli-grams	Milli-grams	Micro-grams
BEVERAGES											
Club soda	12 fl. oz.	355	0	0	0	0.0	0	0	18	Tr	0
Cola, regular	12 fl. oz.	369	160	0	0	0.0	41	0	11	0.2	0
Coffee, brewed	6 fl. oz.	180	Tr	Tr	Tr	0.0	Tr	0	4	Tr	0
Fruit punch drink	6 fl. oz.	190	85	Tr	0	0.0	22	0	15	0.4	2
DAIRY PRODUCTS											
Cheese:											
Cheddar, cut pieces	1 oz.	28	115	7	9	0.6	Tr	0	204	0.2	86
Cottage, low-fat (2%)	1 cup	226	205	31	4	2.8	8	0	155	0.4	45
Mozzarella, whole milk	1 oz.	28	80	6	6	3.7	1	0	147	0.1	68
Mozzarella, part skim milk	1 oz.	28	80	8	5	3.1	1	0	207	0.1	54
Parmesan, grated	1 tbsp.	5	25	2	2	1.0	Tr	0	69	Tr	9
Pasteurized process cheese, American	1 oz.	28	95	6	7	4.4	2	0	163	0.2	62
Milk, fluid:											
Whole (3.3% fat)	1 cup	244	150	8	8	5.1	11	0	291	0.1	76
Low-fat (2%)	1 cup	244	120	8	5	2.9	12	0	297	0.1	139
Low-fat (1%)	1 cup	244	100	8	3	1.6	12	0	300	0.1	144
Nonfat (skim)	1 cup	245	85	8	Tr	0.3	12	0	302	0.1	149
Buttermilk	1 cup	245	100	8	2	1.3	12	0	285	0.1	20
Milk beverages:											
Chocolate milk, low-fat (2%)	1 cup	250	180	8	5	3.1	26	3	284	0.6	143
Shakes, thick, chocolate	10-oz. container	283	335	9	8	6.5	60	Tr	374	0.9	59
Milk desserts, frozen:											
Ice cream, vanilla, regular (about 11% fat)	1 cup	133	270	5	14	9.0	32	Tr	176	0.1	133

Item	Approximate Measures (edible portion)		Food Energy	Protein	Fat	Saturated Fat	Carbo-hydrate	Dietary Fiber	Calcium	Iron	Vitamin A
		Grams	Calories	Grams	Grams	Grams	Grams	Grams	Milli-grams	Milli-grams	Micro-grams
Sherbet (about 2% fat)	1 cup	193	270	2	4	2.2	59	0	103	0.3	39
Yogurt, low-fat, fruit-flavored	8-oz. container	227	230	10	2	1.6	43	1	345	0.2	25
Yogurt, low-fat, plain	8-oz. container	227	145	12	4	2.3	16	0	415	0.2	36
EGGS											
Eggs, large (24 oz. per dozen):											
Fried in butter	1 egg	46	95	6	7	1.9	1	0	29	1.1	94
Hard-cooked, shell removed	1 egg	50	80	6	6	1.6	1	0	28	1.0	78
Scrambled (milk added) in butter; also omelet	1 egg	64	110	7	8	2.2	2	0	54	1.0	102
FATS AND OILS											
Butter (4 sticks per lb.)	1 tbsp.	14	100	Tr	11	7.1	Tr	0	3	Tr	106
Margarine, imitation (about 40% fat), soft	1 tbsp.	14	50	Tr	5	0.9	Tr	0	2	0.0	139
Corn oil	1 cup	218	1,925	0	218	29.4	0	0	0	0.0	0
Salad dressings, commercial:											
French, low calorie	1 tbsp.	16	25	Tr	2	0.1	2	Tr	6	Tr	Tr
Italian, regular	1 tbsp.	15	80	Tr	9	1.0	1	Tr	1	Tr	3
Thousand Island, regular	1 tbsp.	16	60	Tr	6	1.0	2	Tr	2	0.1	15
FISH AND SHELLFISH											
Fish sticks (stick, 4×1×½-in.)	1 fish stick	28	70	6	3	0.9	4	Tr	11	0.3	5
Shrimp, French fried (7 medium)	3 oz.	85	200	16	10	3.8	11	Tr	61	2.0	26
Tuna, canned, drained, water pack, solid white	3 oz.	85	135	30	1	0.2	0	0	17	0.6	32
FRUITS AND FRUIT JUICES											
Apples, raw, unpeeled, 2¾-in. diam.	1 apple	138	80	Tr	Tr	0.1	21	3	10	0.2	7
Apple juice, bottled or canned	1 cup	248	115	Tr	Tr	Tr	29	Tr	17	0.9	Tr
Applesauce, canned, unsweetened	1 cup	244	105	Tr	Tr	Tr	28	3	7	0.3	7
Avocados, raw (about 2 per lb.)	1 avocado	173	305	4	30	4.5	12	6	19	2.0	106
Bananas, raw (about 2½ per lb.)	1 banana	114	105	1	1	0.2	27	2	7	0.4	9

Item	Approximate Measures (edible portion)		Food Energy	Protein	Fat	Saturated Fat	Carbo-hydrate	Dietary Fiber	Calcium	Iron	Vitamin A
		Grams	Calories	Grams	Grams	Grams	Grams	Grams	Milli-grams	Milli-grams	Micro-grams
Cherries, sweet, raw	10 cherries	68	50	1	1	0.1	11	Tr	10	0.3	15
Fruit cocktail, canned, juice pack	1 cup	248	115	1	Tr	Tr	29	3	20	0.5	76
Grapefruit, raw, 3¾-in. diam.	½ grapefruit	120	40	1	Tr	Tr	10	1	14	0.1	1
Grapes, raw, Thompson seedless	10 grapes	50	35	Tr	Tr	0.1	9	Tr	6	0.1	4
Grape juice, canned or bottled	1 cup	253	155	1	Tr	0.1	38	2	23	0.6	2
Melons, raw, canta-loupe, 5-in. diam.	½ melon	267	95	2	1	0.1	22	2	29	0.6	861
Nectarines, raw (about 3 per lb.)	1 nectarine	136	65	1	1	0.1	16	2	7	0.2	100
Oranges, raw, whole, 2⅝-in. diam.	1 orange	131	60	1	Tr	Tr	15	3	52	0.1	27
Orange juice, frozen concentrate, diluted per directions	1 cup	249	110	2	Tr	Tr	27	Tr	22	0.2	19
Peaches, raw, 2½-in. diam.	1 peach	87	35	1	Tr	Tr	10	2	4	0.1	47
Peaches, canned, juice pack	1 cup	248	110	2	Tr	Tr	29	4	15	0.7	94
Pears, raw with skin, Bartlett, 2½-in. diam.	1 pear	166	100	1	1	Tr	25	4	18	0.4	3
Pineapple, raw, diced	1 cup	155	75	1	1	Tr	19	2	11	0.6	4
Pineapple, canned, juice pack, chunks or tidbits	1 cup	250	150	1	Tr	Tr	39	2	35	0.7	10
Plums, raw, 2⅛-in. diam.	1 plum	66	35	1	Tr	Tr	9	1	3	0.1	21
Raisins, seedless	1 cup	145	435	5	1	0.2	115	5	71	3.0	1
Raspberries, raw	1 cup	123	60	1	1	Tr	14	5	27	0.7	16
Strawberries, raw	1 cup	149	45	1	1	Tr	10	2	21	0.6	4
Watermelon, raw, piece (4×8-in. wedge)	1 piece	482	155	3	2	0.6	35	1	39	0.8	176
GRAIN PRODUCTS											
Bagels, plain, enriched, 3½-in. diam.	1 bagel	68	200	7	2	0.1	38	2	29	1.8	0
Breads:											
Italian bread, enriched, slice, 4½×3¼×¾-in.	1 slice	30	85	3	Tr	0.3	17	1	5	0.8	0
Pita bread, enriched, white, 6½-in. diam.	1 pita	60	165	6	1	0.1	33	1	49	1.4	0

Item	Approximate Measures (edible portion)		Food Energy	Protein	Fat	Saturated Fat	Carbo-hydrate	Dietary Fiber	Calcium	Iron	Vitamin A
		Grams	Calories	Grams	Grams	Grams	Grams	Grams	Milli-grams	Milli-grams	Micro-grams
Raisin bread, enriched (18 slices/loaf)	1 slice	25	65	2	1	0.3	13	1	25	0.8	Tr
White bread, enriched (18 slices/loaf)	1 slice	25	65	2	1	0.2	12	1	32	0.7	Tr
Whole-wheat bread (16 slices/loaf)	1 slice	28	70	3	1	0.3	13	2	20	1.0	Tr
Breakfast cereals:											
Corn (hominy) grits, regular and quick, enriched	1 cup	242	145	3	Tr	0.1	31	5	0	1.5	0
Oatmeal, regular, quick and instant, nonfortified	1 cup	234	145	6	2	0.4	25	4	19	1.6	4
Oatmeal, instant, fortified, plain	1 pkt.	177	105	4	2	0.3	18	3	163	6.3	453
Cap'n Crunch® (about ¾ cup)	1 oz.	28	120	1	3	2.2	23	1	5	7.5	4
Cheerios® (about 1¼ cup)	1 oz.	28	110	4	2	0.3	20	2	48	4.5	375
Froot Loops® (about 1 cup)	1 oz.	28	110	2	1	0.2	25	1	3	4.5	375
Grape-Nuts® (about ¼ cup)	1 oz.	28	100	3	Tr	Tr	23	3	11	1.2	375
Honey Nut Cheerios® (about ¾ cup)	1 oz.	28	105	3	1	0.1	23	1	20	4.5	375
Nature Valley® Granola (about ⅓ cup)	1 oz.	28	125	3	5	5.0	19	2	18	0.9	2
Rice Krispies® (about 1 cup)	1 oz.	28	110	2	Tr	Tr	25	Tr	4	1.8	375
Shredded Wheat (about ⅔ cup)	1 oz.	28	100	3	1	0.2	23	4	11	1.2	0
Frosted Flakes® (about ¾ cup)	1 oz.	28	110	1	Tr	Tr	26	1	1	1.8	375
Cakes prepared from cake mixes with enriched flour:											
Angel food, 1/12 of cake	1 piece	53	125	3	Tr	0.1	29	1	44	0.2	0
Coffeecake, crumb, 1/6 of cake	1 piece	72	230	5	7	1.3	38	1	44	1.2	32
Devil's food with chocolate frosting, 1/16 of cake	1 piece	69	235	3	8	3.2	40	2	41	1.4	31

Item	Approximate Measures (edible portion)		Food Energy	Protein	Fat	Saturated Fat	Carbo-hydrate	Dietary Fiber	Calcium	Iron	Vitamin A
		Grams	Calories	Grams	Grams	Grams	Grams	Grams	Milli-grams	Milli-grams	Micro-grams
Devil's food with chocolate frosting, cupcake, 2½-in. diam.	1 cupcake	35	120	2	4	1.9	20	1	21	0.7	16
Carrot with cream cheese frosting, ¹⁄₁₆ of cake	1 piece	96	385	4	21	5.5	48	1	44	1.3	15
Cookies made with enriched flour:											
Brownies with nuts, commercial, with frosting, 1½×1¾×⅞-in.	1 brownie	25	100	1	4	1.1	16	1	13	0.6	18
Chocolate chip, commercial, 2¼-in. diam., ⅜-in. thick	4 cookies	42	180	2	9	3.1	28	1	13	0.8	15
Oatmeal with raisins, 2⅝-in. diam., ¼-in. thick	4 cookies	52	245	3	10	1.7	36	2	18	1.1	12
Sandwich type (chocolate or vanilla), 1¾-in. diam., ⅝-in. thick	4 cookies	40	195	2	8	1.7	29	1	12	1.4	0
Crackers:											
Cheese, plain, 1-in. square	10 crackers	10	50	1	3	0.9	6	Tr	11	0.3	5
Graham, plain, 2½-in. square	2 crackers	14	60	1	1	0.4	11	Tr	6	0.4	0
Saltines	4 crackers	12	50	1	1	0.3	9	Tr	3	0.5	0
Wheat, thin	4 crackers	8	35	1	1	0.7	5	1	3	0.3	Tr
Doughnuts made with enriched flour:											
Cake type, plain, 3¼-in. diam.	1 doughnut	50	210	3	12	1.9	24	1	22	1.0	5
Yeast-leavened, glazed, 3¾-in. diam.	1 doughnut	60	235	4	13	3.5	26	1	17	1.4	Tr
English muffins, plain, enriched	1 muffin	57	140	5	1	0.1	27	2	96	1.7	0
French toast, from home recipe	1 slice	65	155	6	7	2.0	17	Tr	72	1.3	32
Macaroni, enriched, cooked	1 cup	130	190	7	1	0.1	39	2	14	2.1	0
Muffins, 2½-in. diam., from commercial mix:											
Blueberry	1 muffin	45	140	3	5	0.7	22	1	15	0.9	11
Bran	1 muffin	45	140	3	4	1.1	24	4	27	1.7	14
Corn	1 muffin	45	145	3	6	1.3	22	2	30	1.3	16

Item	Approximate Measures (edible portion)		Food Energy	Protein	Fat	Saturated Fat	Carbo-hydrate	Dietary Fiber	Calcium	Iron	Vitamin A
		Grams	Calories	Grams	Grams	Grams	Grams	Grams	Milli-grams	Milli-grams	Micro-grams
Noodles (egg noodles), enriched, cooked	1 cup	160	200	7	2	0.5	37	2	16	2.6	34
Pancakes, 4-in. diam., plain, from mix (egg, milk, and oil added)	1 pancake	27	60	2	2	0.1	8	Tr	36	0.7	7
Piecrust, home recipe, 9-in. diam.	1 pie shell	180	900	11	60	15.5	79	3	25	4.5	0
Pies:											
Apple, piece, ⅙ of pie	1 piece	158	405	3	18	3.3	60	3	13	1.6	5
Cream, piece, ⅙ of pie	1 piece	152	455	3	23	7.4	59	0	46	1.1	65
Pecan, piece, ⅙ of pie	1 piece	138	575	7	32	5.2	71	5	65	4.6	54
Snacks:											
Corn chips	1-oz. package	28	155	2	9	1.3	16	1	35	0.5	11
Popcorn, air-popped, unsalted	1 cup	8	30	1	Tr	Tr	6	1	1	0.2	1
Popcorn, popped in vegetable oil, salted	1 cup	11	55	1	3	0.5	6	1	3	0.3	2
Pretzels, twisted, thin, 3¼×2¼×¼-in.	10 pretzels	60	240	6	2	0.4	48	2	16	1.2	0
Rice:											
Brown, cooked	1 cup	195	230	5	1	0.4	50	4	23	1.0	0
White, enriched, cooked	1 cup	205	225	4	Tr	0.2	50	1	21	1.8	0
White, enriched, instant, ready-to-serve	1 cup	165	180	4	0	0.1	40	1	5	1.3	0
Rolls, commercial, enriched:											
Dinner, 2½-in. diam.	1 roll	28	85	2	2	0.7	14	1	33	0.8	Tr
Frankfurter and ham-burger (8 per pkg.)	1 roll	40	115	3	2	0.5	20	1	54	1.2	Tr
Hard, 3¾-in. diam.	1 roll	50	155	5	2	0.3	30	1	24	1.4	0
Spaghetti, enriched, cooked	1 cup	130	190	7	1	0.1	39	2	14	2.0	0
Tortillas, corn	1 tortilla	30	65	2	1	0.1	13	2	42	0.6	8
Wheat flours:											
All-purpose or family flour, enriched, sifted	1 cup	115	420	12	1	0.2	88	3	18	5.1	0
Cake or pastry flour, enriched, sifted	1 cup	96	350	7	1	0.1	76	2	16	4.2	0
Whole-wheat, from hard wheat, stirred	1 cup	120	400	16	2	0.4	85	15	49	5.2	0

Item	Approximate Measures (edible portion)		Food Energy	Protein	Fat	Saturated Fat	Carbo-hydrate	Dietary Fiber	Calcium	Iron	Vitamin A
		Grams	Calories	Grams	Grams	Grams	Grams	Grams	Milli-grams	Milli-grams	Micro-grams
LEGUMES, NUTS, AND SEEDS											
Almonds, shelled, slivered	1 cup	135	795	27	70	6.7	28	13	359	4.9	0
Black-eyed peas, dry, cooked	1 cup	250	190	13	1	0.2	35	12	43	3.3	3
Chickpeas, cooked, drained	1 cup	163	270	15	4	0.4	45	8	80	4.9	Tr
Lentils, dry, cooked	1 cup	200	215	16	1	0.1	38	5	50	4.2	4
Peanuts, roasted in oil, salted	1 cup	145	840	39	71	9.8	27	10	125	2.8	0
Peanut butter	1 tbsp.	16	95	5	8	1.5	3	1	5	0.3	0
Peas, split, dry, cooked	1 cup	200	230	16	1	0.2	42	6	22	3.4	8
Pistachio nuts, dried, shelled	1 oz.	28	165	6	14	1.7	7	3	38	1.9	7
Refried beans, canned	1 cup	290	295	18	3	1.0	51	14	141	5.1	0
Sesame seeds, dry, hulled	1 tbsp.	8	45	2	4	2.9	1	3	11	0.6	1
Tofu, piece, 2½×2¾×1-in.	1 piece	120	85	9	5	0.9	3	1	108	2.3	0
Sunflower seeds, dry, hulled	1 oz.	28	160	6	14	1.9	5	2	33	1.9	1
Walnuts, English or Persian, pieces or chips	1 cup	120	770	17	74	6.7	22	5	113	2.9	15
MEAT AND MEAT PRODUCTS											
Beef, cooked:											
Cuts braised, sim-mered, or pot roast-ed, such as chuck blade, 2½×2½×¾-in.	3 oz.	85	325	22	26	11.6	0	0	11	2.5	Tr
Cuts braised, sim-mered, or pot roast-ed, such as bottom round, 4⅛×2¼×½-in.	3 oz.	85	220	25	13	3.6	0	0	5	2.8	Tr
Ground beef, broiled, patty, 3×⅝-in., regular	3 oz.	85	245	20	18	7.9	0	0	9	2.1	Tr
Roast, such as eye of round, 2 pieces, 2½×2½×⅜-in.	3 oz.	85	205	23	12	6.2	0	0	5	1.6	Tr
Steak, sirloin, broiled, 2½×2½×¾-in.	3 oz.	85	240	23	15	8.7	0	0	9	2.6	Tr
Lamb, cooked:											
Chops	2.2 oz.	63	220	20	15	3.5	0	0	16	1.5	Tr

Item	Approximate Measures (edible portion)		Food Energy	Protein	Fat	Saturated Fat	Carbo-hydrate	Dietary Fiber	Calcium	Iron	Vitamin A
		Grams	Calories	Grams	Grams	Grams	Grams	Grams	Milli-grams	Milli-grams	Micro-grams
Pork, cured, cooked:											
Bacon, regular	3 medium slices	19	110	6	9	3.3	Tr	0	2	0.3	0
Ham, light cure, roasted, 2 pieces, 4⅛×2¼×¼-in.	3 oz.	85	205	18	14	6.8	0	0	6	0.7	0
Luncheon meat, ham (1-oz. slice), regular	2 slices	57	105	10	6	1.9	2	0	4	0.6	0
Pork, fresh, cooked:											
Chop, loin, broiled	3.1 oz.	87	275	24	19	4.6	0	0	3	0.7	3
Rib, roasted, piece, 2½×¾-in.	3 oz.	85	270	21	20	6.7	0	0	9	0.8	3
Sausages:											
Bologna (1-oz. slice)	2 slices	57	180	7	16	3.2	2	0	7	0.9	0
Brown and serve	1 link	13	50	2	5	1.7	Tr	0	1	0.1	0
Frankfurter	1 frankfurter	45	145	5	13	4.9	1	0	5	0.5	0
Salami, dry type	2 slices	20	85	5	7	2.5	1	0	2	0.3	0
MIXED DISHES AND FAST FOODS											
Mixed dishes:											
Beef and vegetable stew, from home recipe	1 cup	245	220	16	11	4.9	15	2	29	2.9	568
Chicken chow mein, canned	1 cup	250	95	7	Tr	0.0	18	2	45	1.3	28
Chili con carne with beans, canned	1 cup	255	340	19	16	3.4	31	4	82	4.3	15
Macaroni (enriched) and cheese, from home recipe	1 cup	200	430	17	22	8.9	40	1	362	1.8	232
Spaghetti (enriched) with meatballs and tomato sauce, canned	1 cup	250	260	12	10	2.1	29	6	53	3.3	100
Fast-food entrees:											
Cheeseburger, 4-oz. patty	1 sandwich	194	525	30	31	10.2	40	0	236	4.5	128
Enchilada	1 enchilada	230	235	20	16	15.0	24	0	322	11.0	352
English muffin, egg, cheese, and bacon	1 sandwich	138	360	18	18	8.6	31	1	197	3.1	160
Fish sandwich, regular, with cheese	1 sandwich	140	420	16	23	6.2	39	Tr	132	1.8	25
Hamburger, 4-oz. patty	1 sandwich	174	445	25	21	9.7	38	0	75	4.8	28

Item	Approximate Measures (edible portion)		Food Energy	Protein	Fat	Saturated Fat	Carbo- hydrate	Dietary Fiber	Calcium	Iron	Vitamin A
		Grams	Calories	Grams	Grams	Grams	Grams	Grams	Milli- grams	Milli- grams	Micro- grams
Pizza, cheese, ⅛ of 15-in. diam. pizza	1 slice	120	290	15	9	2.9	39	2	220	1.6	106
Taco	1 taco	81	195	9	11	4.6	15	1	109	1.2	57
POULTRY AND POUL- TRY PRODUCTS											
Chicken:											
Fried, batter dipped, breast, (5.6-oz. with bones)	4.9 oz.	140	365	35	18	4.9	13	Tr	28	1.8	28
Fried, batter dipped, drumstick	2.5 oz.	72	195	16	11	3.0	6	Tr	12	1.0	19
Roasted, flesh only, breast, (4.2-oz. with bones and skin)	3 oz.	86	140	27	3	0.9	0	0	13	0.9	5
Turkey, roasted, flesh only, dark meat, piece, 2½×1⅝×¼-in.	4 pieces	85	160	24	6	4.0	0	0	27	2.0	0
Turkey, roasted, flesh only, light meat, piece, 4×2×¼-in.	2 pieces	85	135	25	3	2.7	0	0	16	1.1	0
SOUPS, SAUCES, AND GRAVIES											
Soups, canned, condensed:											
Prepared with equal volume of milk, cream of chicken	1 cup	248	190	7	11	4.6	15	Tr	181	0.7	94
Prepared with equal volume of milk, tomato	1 cup	248	160	6	6	2.9	22	1	159	1.8	109
Prepared with equal volume of water, beef broth, bouillon, consommé	1 cup	240	15	3	1	0.3	Tr	0	14	0.4	0
Prepared with equal volume of water, chicken noodle	1 cup	241	75	4	2	0.7	9	1	17	0.8	71
Prepared with equal volume of water, green pea	1 cup	250	165	9	3	1.8	27	5	28	2.0	20
Prepared with equal volume of water, vegetable beef	1 cup	244	80	6	2	0.9	10	Tr	17	1.1	189
Sauces:											
From home recipe, white sauce, medium	1 cup	250	395	10	30	6.4	24	Tr	292	0.9	340

Item	Approximate Measures (edible portion)		Food Energy	Protein	Fat	Saturated Fat	Carbo- hydrate	Dietary Fiber	Calcium	Iron	Vitamin A
		Grams	Calories	Grams	Grams	Grams	Grams	Grams	Milli- grams	Milli- grams	Micro- grams
Ready to serve, barbecue	1 tbsp.	16	10	Tr	Tr	Tr	2	Tr	3	0.1	14
Ready to serve, soy	1 tbsp.	18	10	2	0	Tr	2	0	3	0.5	0
Gravies:											
Canned, beef	1 cup	233	125	9	5	2.7	11	1	14	1.6	0
From dry mix, chicken	1 cup	260	85	3	2	0.5	14	Tr	39	0.3	0
SUGARS AND SWEETS											
Candy:											
Chocolate, milk, plain	1 oz.	28	145	2	9	5.2	16	1	50	0.4	10
Chocolate, milk, with peanuts	1 oz.	28	155	4	11	3.4	13	2	49	0.4	8
Fudge, chocolate, plain	1 oz.	28	115	1	3	1.5	21	Tr	22	0.3	Tr
Gum drops	1 oz.	28	100	Tr	Tr	0.0	25	0	2	0.1	0
Jelly beans	1 oz.	28	105	Tr	Tr	0.0	26	0	1	0.3	0
Marshmallows	1 oz.	28	90	1	0	0.0	23	Tr	1	0.5	0
Gelatin dessert prepared with powder and water	½ cup	120	70	2	0	0.0	17	0	2	Tr	0
Honey	1 cup	339	1,030	1	0	0.0	279	Tr	17	1.7	0
Jams and preserves	1 tbsp.	20	55	Tr	Tr	0.0	14	Tr	4	0.2	Tr
Popsicle, 3-fl.-oz. size	1 popsicle	95	70	0	0	0.0	18	0	0	Tr	0
Pudding, canned, chocolate	5-oz. can	142	205	3	11	1.0	30	1	74	1.2	31
Sugar, brown, packed	1 cup	220	820	0	0	0.0	212	0	3	0.1	0
White, granulated	1 tbsp.	12	45	0	0	0.0	12	0	Tr	Tr	0
Syrup, chocolate- flavored syrup or topping, thin type	2 tbsp.	38	85	1	Tr	0.2	21	1	38	0.5	13
Syrup, table syrup (maple)	2 tbsp.	42	122	0	0	0.0	30	0	26	0.4	0
VEGETABLES AND VEGETABLE PRODUCTS											
Asparagus, green, cooked and drained, cuts and tips	1 cup	180	45	5	1	0.2	8	4	43	1.2	149
Beans, snap, cooked, drained, from frozen (cut)	1 cup	135	35	2	Tr	Tr	8	4	61	1.1	71
Broccoli, cooked, chopped	1 cup	185	50	6	Tr	Tr	10	5	94	1.1	350

Item	Approximate Measures (edible portion)		Food Energy	Protein	Fat	Saturated Fat	Carbo-hydrate	Dietary Fiber	Calcium	Iron	Vitamin A
		Grams	Calories	Grams	Grams	Grams	Grams	Grams	Milli-grams	Milli-grams	Micro-grams
Cabbage, raw, shredded or sliced	1 cup	70	15	1	Tr	Tr	4	1	33	0.4	9
Carrots, raw, whole, 7½×1⅛-in.	1 carrot	72	30	1	Tr	Tr	7	2	19	0.4	2,025
Carrots, cooked, sliced	1 cup	146	55	2	Tr	Tr	12	6	41	0.7	2,585
Cauliflower, cooked	1 cup	180	35	3	Tr	Tr	7	4	31	0.7	4
Celery, pascal type, raw, stalk, large outer, 8×1½-in. (at root end)	1 stalk	40	5	Tr	Tr	Tr	1	1	14	0.2	5
Collards, cooked	1 cup	170	60	5	1	0.2	12	6	357	1.9	1,017
Corn, sweet, cooked, ear, 5×1¾	1 ear	77	85	3	1	0.2	19	2	2	0.5	17
Corn, sweet, cooked, kernels	1 cup	165	135	5	Tr	Tr	34	4	3	0.5	41
Cucumber, with peel, slices, ⅛-in. thick	8 small slices	28	5	Tr	Tr	Tr	1	Tr	4	0.1	1
Kale, cooked, chopped	1 cup	130	40	4	1	Tr	7	2	179	1.2	826
Lettuce, raw, iceberg, wedge, ¼ of head	1 wedge	135	20	1	Tr	Tr	3	1	26	0.7	45
Mushrooms, raw, sliced or chopped	1 cup	70	20	1	Tr	Tr	3	Tr	4	0.9	0
Onions, raw, chopped	1 cup	160	55	2	Tr	Tr	12	3	40	0.6	0
Peas, green, canned, drained solids	1 cup	170	115	8	1	0.2	21	6	34	1.6	131
Peas, green, frozen, cooked, drained	1 cup	160	125	8	Tr	Tr	23	8	38	2.5	107
Peppers, hot chile, raw	1 pepper	45	20	1	Tr	Tr	4	1	8	0.5	484
Potatoes, cooked:											
Baked (about 2 per lb., raw), with skin	1 potato	202	220	5	Tr	0.1	51	5	20	2.7	0
Boiled (about 3 per lb., raw), peeled after boiling	1 potato	136	120	3	Tr	Tr	27	2	7	0.4	0
French fried, strip, 2 to 3½ in. long, frozen, oven heated	10 strips	50	110	2	4	3.8	17	1	5	0.7	0
French fried, strip, 2 to 3½ in. long, frozen, fried in vegetable oil	10 strips	50	160	2	8	2.5	20	2	10	0.4	0
Mashed, milk and margarine added	1 cup	210	225	4	9	2.2	35	4	55	0.5	42
Potato chips	10 chips	20	105	1	7	3.1	10	1	5	0.2	0
Spinach, cooked	1 cup	190	55	6	Tr	Tr	10	4	277	2.9	1,479
Sweet potatoes, (raw about 2½ per lb.), baked in skin, peeled	1 potato	114	115	2	Tr	Tr	28	4	32	0.5	2,488

Item	Approximate Measures (edible portion)		Food Energy	Protein	Fat	Saturated Fat	Carbo-hydrate	Dietary Fiber	Calcium	Iron	Vitamin A
		Grams	Calories	Grams	Grams	Grams	Grams	Grams	Milli-grams	Milli-grams	Micro-grams
Tomatoes, raw, 2⅖-in. diam.	1 tomato	123	25	1	Tr	0.1	5	1	9	0.6	139
Tomatoes, canned, solids and liquids	1 cup	240	50	2	1	0.1	10	2	62	1.5	145
Tomato products, canned, paste	1 cup	262	220	10	2	0.3	49	11	92	7.8	647
Tomato products, canned, sauce	1 cup	245	75	3	Tr	Tr	18	3	34	1.9	240
Vegetables, mixed, frozen, cooked	1 cup	182	105	5	Tr	Tr	24	5	46	1.5	778

Appendix D

Body Mass Index

								Weight in Pounds																
		90	95	100	105	110	115	120	125	130	135	140	145	150	155	160	165	170	175	180	185	190	195	200	205
Height in feet and inches	4'11"	18	19	20	21	22	23	24	25	26	27	28	29	30	31	32	33	34	35	36	37	38	39	41	42
	5'0"	18	19	20	21	22	23	23	24	25	26	27	28	29	30	31	32	33	34	35	36	37	38	39	40
	5'1"	17	18	19	20	21	22	23	24	25	26	26	27	28	29	30	31	32	33	34	35	36	37	38	39
	5'2"	17	17	18	19	20	21	22	23	24	25	26	27	28	28	29	30	31	32	33	34	35	36	37	37
	5'3"	16	17	18	19	20	20	21	22	23	24	25	26	27	28	28	29	30	31	32	33	34	35	36	36
	5'4"	15	16	17	18	19	20	21	22	22	23	24	25	26	27	28	28	29	30	31	32	33	34	34	35
	5'5"	15	16	17	18	18	19	20	21	22	22	23	24	25	26	27	28	28	29	30	31	32	33	33	34
	5'6"	15	15	16	17	18	19	19	20	21	22	23	24	24	25	26	27	28	28	29	30	31	32	32	33
	5'7"	14	15	16	17	17	18	19	20	20	21	22	23	24	24	25	26	27	28	28	29	30	31	31	32
	5'8"	14	14	15	16	17	18	18	19	20	21	21	22	23	24	24	25	26	27	27	28	29	30	31	31
	5'9"	13	14	15	16	16	17	18	19	19	20	21	22	22	23	24	24	25	26	27	27	28	29	30	30
	5'10"	13	14	14	15	16	17	17	18	19	19	20	21	22	22	23	24	24	25	26	27	27	28	29	30
	5'11"	13	13	14	15	15	16	17	18	18	19	20	20	21	22	22	23	24	25	25	26	26	27	28	29
	6'0"	12	13	14	14	15	16	16	17	18	18	19	20	20	21	22	22	23	24	25	25	26	26	27	28
	6'1"	12	13	13	14	15	15	16	17	17	18	19	19	20	21	21	22	23	23	24	25	25	26	26	27
	6'2"	12	12	13	14	14	15	15	16	17	17	18	19	19	20	21	21	22	23	23	24	24	25	26	26

Photo Credits

Recurring Images Food Science–Nixx Photography/ Shutterstock.com; Global Perspectives–Markus Pfaff/ Shutterstock.com; Health and Wellness–©iStock.com/ donskarpo; Culture and Social Studies–Africa Studio/ Shutterstock.com; Exploring Careers features (see chapter-specific images under specific chapter entry)–wavebreakmedia/Shutterstock.com; Photo by Stephen Ausmus, ARS/ USDA; Air Images/Shutterstock.com; Monkey Business Images/Shutterstock.com; Dmitry Kalinovsky/Shutterstock. com; Photo by Peggy Greb, ARS/USDA; Robert Kneschke/ Shutterstock.com; Naphat_Jorjee/Shutterstock.com; U.S. Department of Agriculture; Mini Labs–StepanPopov/Shutterstock.com; Recipe for Good Food–SunnySideUp/Shutterstock.com; All Foods of the World region/country/continent features (see Chs. 29–34), photo credit for globes–Harvepino/Shutterstock.com; **Chapter 1** Learn About–marekuliasz/ Shutterstock.com; Exploring Careers–Alliance/Shutterstock.com; **Chapter 2** Learn About (governing)–Alexander Raths/ Shutterstock.com; Learn About (temp danger zone)–Kateryna Kon/Shutterstock.com; Exploring Careers–Schweinepriester/ Shutterstock.com; **Chapter 3** Learn About–ContantinosZ/ Shutterstock.com; Exploring Careers–SpeedKingz/Shutterstock.com; **Chapter 4** Learn About–NinaB/Shutterstock.com; Exploring Careers–wavebreakmedia/Shutterstock.com; **Chapter 5** Learn About–Lukas Gojda/Shutterstock.com; Exploring Careers–Monkey Business Images/Shutterstock. com; **Chapter 6** Learn About–Jacob Hamblin/Shutterstock. com; Exploring Careers–Keith Weller, ARS/USDA; **Chapter 7** Learn About–OlegDoroshin/Shutterstock.com; Exploring Careers–Photo by Peggy Greb, ARS/USDA; **Chapter 8** Learn About–Syaheir Azizan/Shutterstock.com; Exploring Careers– Photo by Stephen Ausmus, ARS/USDA; Figure 8.2 top to bottom: eveleen/Shutterstock.com; eveleen/Shutterstock.com; eveleen/Shutterstock.com; St22/Shutterstock.com; Viktoria/ Shutterstock.com; HelgaMariah/Shutterstock.com; eveleen/ Shutterstock.com; **Chapter 9** Exploring Careers–Aspen Photo/Shutterstock.com; Learn About (portion distortion)– bestv/Shutterstock.com; Learn About (weight loss aids)–iQoncept/Shutterstock.com; Figure 9.2 top row: ostill/Shutterstock. com; Maria Komar/Shutterstock.com; artphotoclub/Shutterstock.com; Nemanja Cosovic/Shutterstock.com; middle row: aarrows/Shutterstock.com; Maria Komar/Shutterstock.com; artphotoclub/Shutterstock.com; Nemanja Cosovic/Shutterstock.com; bottom row: ostill/Shutterstock.com; Maria Komar/ Shutterstock.com; artphotoclub/Shutterstock.com; Nemanja Cosovic/Shutterstock.com; Figure 9.14 top row: Goodheart-Willcox Publisher; Goodheart-Willcox Publisher; 2nd row: Goodheart-Willcox Publisher; Timolina/Shutterstock. com; 3rd row: Goodheart-Willcox Publisher; Goodheart-Willcox Publisher; 4th row: Melica/Shutterstock.com; Hong Vo/Shutterstock.com; 5th row: spaxiax/Shutterstock.com; AN NGUYEN/Shutterstock.com; bottom row: Iuliia Azarova/ Shutterstock.com; EM Arts/Shutterstock.com; **Chapter 10** Learn About (bottle feeding)–BlueSkyImage/Shutterstock. com; Learn About (easing meal preparation)–Iakov Filimonov/Shutterstock.com; Exploring Careers–Photo by Stephen Ausmus, ARS/USDA; Figure 10.3 grains top to bottom: Kongsak/Shutterstock.com; Johann Helgason/Shutterstock. com; Eleor/Shutterstock.com; vegetables top to bottom: alexvav/Shutterstock.com; Alexeysun/Shutterstock.com; photogal/Shutterstock.com; fruits top to bottom: Cheryl E. Davis/Shutterstock.com; risha green/Shutterstock.com; dairy top to bottom: Artbox/Shutterstock.com; Volosina/Shutterstock. com; donatas/Shutterstock.com; protein foods top to bottom: Gregory Gerber/Shutterstock.com; Binh Thanh Bui/Shutterstock.com; Garsya/Shutterstock.com; oils ©iStock.com/ Afromeev; Figure 10.9 top row, l to r: Joe Gough/Shutterstock. com; julie deshaies/Shutterstock.com; Africa Studio/Shutterstock.com; Digital Genetics/Shutterstock.com; mama_mia/ Shutterstock.com; Foodpictures/Shutterstock.com; Volosina/ Shutterstock.com; Nattika/Shutterstock.com; bottom row, l to r: Andrey Starostin/Shutterstock.com; Elena Elisseeva/Shutterstock.com; Svetlana Foote/Shutterstock.com; Yulia Davidovich/Shutterstock.com; Louella938/Shutterstock.com; Africa Studio/Shutterstock.com; Olga Popova/Shutterstock.com; Iurii Kachkovskyi/Shutterstock.com; Figure 10.12 Top row: Jamie Duplass/Shutterstock.com; Meelena/Shutterstock.com; Angorius/Shutterstock.com; Yuri Samsonov/Shutterstock.com; fotostokers/Shutterstock.com; 2nd row: Tobik/Shutterstock. com; BrunoRosa/Shutterstock.com; narunza/Shutterstock. com; jiangdi/Shutterstock.com; bottom row: Robyn Mackenzie/ Shutterstock.com; Andrey Eremin/Shutterstock.com; Pairoj Sroyngern/Shutterstock.com; rangizzz/Shutterstock.com; rangizzz/Shutterstock.com; **Chapter 11** Learn About (additional work centers)–Joy Rector/Shutterstock.com; Learn About (outlets and electrical safety)–Iriana Shiyan/Shutterstock.com; Exploring Careers–Naphat_Jorjee/Shutterstock. com; **Chapter 12** Exploring Careers–Dmitry Kalinovsky/ Shutterstock.com; Figure 12.6 top row, l to r: Voronina Svetlana/Shutterstock.com; f9photos/Shutterstock.com; Steve Bower/Shutterstock.com; second row, l to r: PhotoBalance/ Shutterstock.com; nito/Shutterstock.com; aperturesound/Shutterstock.com; third row, l to r: bonchan/Shutterstock.com; Alexandru Nika/Shutterstock.com; ©iStock.com/Aero17; bottom row, l to r: gvictoria/Shutterstock.com; Robyn Mackenzie/Shutterstock.com; Guzel Studio/Shutterstock.com; **Chapter 13** Learn About–Anna_Pustynnikova/Shutterstock. com; Exploring Careers–wavebreakmedia/Shutterstock.com; Figure 13.1 top to bottom: moonkin/Shutterstock.com; moonkin/Shutterstock.com; moonkin/Shutterstock.com; Anna. abella/Shutterstock.com; Anna.abella/Shutterstock.com; Anna.abella/Shutterstock.com; Kolopach/Shutterstock.com; Kolopach/Shutterstock.com; Kolopach/Shutterstock.com; moonkin/Shutterstock.com; moonkin/Shutterstock.com; Figure

Glossary

A

abdominal thrust: A technique that exerts pressure on a choking victim's abdomen and causes a trapped object to be expelled from his or her airway. (2)

ability: A skill developed with practice. (35)

Aboriginal: A member of the first group of inhabitants of a land. (29)

absorption: The process of taking in nutrients and making them part of the body. (6)

abstain: To refrain from consuming. (33)

accommodate: To provide with something needed. (13)

adequate: Enough. (11)

adversely: Negatively. (18)

aerobic activity: An activity targeting cardiorespiratory fitness. (9)

agitate: To shake. (25)

agriculture: The use of knowledge and skill to tend soil, grow crops, and raise livestock. (1)

ají: Chiles. (30)

a la carte: A pricing system in which there is a separate price for each menu item. (27)

al dente: Slightly firm to the bite. (316)

allergen: A substance that sets off an immune system response. (21)

alloy: A mixture. (3)

alternative: One of the various options you might choose. (1)

amateur: Untrained. (32)

ambitious: Challenging. (9)

American (family style) service: The style most often used in homes in the United States. (27)

amicability: Friendliness. (32)

amino acid: A small unit that makes up protein. (6)

anemia: A condition of a reduced number of red blood cells in the bloodstream. (7)

annexed: Added to a country's own territory. (29)

anorexia nervosa: An eating disorder characterized by self-starvation. (9)

anthocyanin: A pigment found in red vegetables, such as beets and red cabbage. (18)

antibody: A specific type of protein that helps fight infection. (6)

The numbers in parentheses following definitions represent the chapter in which the terms appear.

antioxidant: A substance that prevents or slows damage caused by chemical reactions involving oxygen. (7)

antipasto: An appetizer course often beginning the Italian meal. (32)

apathy: A lack of emotion. (7)

appetite: A psychological desire to eat. (1)

appetizer: A light food or beverage served to stimulate the appetite. (27)

aptitude: A natural talent. (35)

aquaculture: Farming to raise animals or plants that live in water. (1)

arcing: Sparking that occurs in a microwave oven when metal comes in contact with the oven walls. (4)

arepa: A corn pancake similar to a tortilla. (30)

arid: Dry. (30)

array: A large amount. (29)

artificial light: Light that comes from electrical fixtures. (11)

artificial sweetener: A product that sweetens foods with fewer calories and less carbohydrates than sugar; also known as a *nonnutritive sweetener*. (6)

ascorbic acid: A food additive that prevents color and flavor loss and adds nutritive value. (28)

aseptic packaging: A type of commercial packaging that involves separately sterilizing a food and its container and then packing the food in the container in a sterile chamber. (28)

attitude: A person's outlook on life. (36)

augment: To add to. (10)

avgolemono: A mixture of egg yolks and lemon juice used to flavor soups and stews. (32)

B

bacterium: A single-celled microorganism. (2)

baking: A dry-heat cooking method performed in an oven at temperatures between 300°F and 425°F (149°C and 219°C). It involves foods with less solid structures prior to cooking. (15)

baklava: A traditional Greek dessert made of thin layers of phyllo filled with nuts and soaked with a honey syrup. (32)

balmy: Warm. (32)

barren: Not agriculturally productive. (33)

basal metabolism: The amount of energy the human body needs to stay alive and carry on vital processes. (9)

batter: A mixture of flour and liquid that ranges in consistency from thin liquids to stiff liquids. (17)

bazaar: A Middle Eastern marketplace. (33)

beading: The golden droplets that appear on the surface of a meringue. (21)

beef: The meat that comes from mature cattle. (22)

beef stroganov: A Russian main dish made with tender strips of beef, mushrooms, and a seasoned sour cream sauce. (34)

beriberi: A disease caused by thiamin deficiency that results in limb numbness, cramping, stiffness, and possibly death. (7)

berry: A small, juicy fruit with a thin skin. (19)

beverage: A drinkable liquid. (5)

beverageware: Drinking glasses of all shapes and sizes used for a variety of purposes; also called *glassware*. (11)

binge eating disorder: An eating disorder characterized by repeated episodes of uncontrolled eating. (9)

bisque: A rich, thickened cream soup. (25)

blanching: A technique that employs boiling food for approximately one to two minutes and then removing the food from the boiling water and placing it in an ice bath. (15)

blend: A food seasoning made from a combination of herbs and spices. (25)

blue plate service: A style of meal service in which the host fills plates in the kitchen and carries them to the dining room. (27)

body composition: The proportion of tissues, such as bone, muscle, and fat, making up a person's body weight. (9)

body mass index (BMI): A calculation involving a person's weight and height measurements. (9)

boiling: An aggressive moist-heat cooking method using hotter temperatures than both poaching and simmering. (15)

borscht: Beet soup. (34)

botulism: A foodborne illness caused by eating foods containing the spore-forming bacterium *Clostridium botulinum*. (28)

bouillabaisse: Seafood stew. (31)

bouillon: Clear broth made with more protein and less bone than stock. (25)

bountiful: Plentiful. (28)

bouquet garni: Several fresh herbs tied together into a bundle. (25)

braising: A combination cooking method achieved by using a dry-heat cooking method to sear the food, followed by a moist-heat cooking method. (15)

bran: The outer protective covering of a kernel. (16)

brand name: The name a manufacturer puts on products so people will know what company makes the products. (14)

braten: A roast. (31)

bratwurst: A type of sausage served grilled or panfried throughout Germany. (31)

broiler pan: A steel, slotted pan with a stick-resistant finish. (15)

broiling: A dry-heat cooking method performed in the oven using a direct heat source located above the food. (15)

budget: A plan for managing income and expenses. (13)

buffet service: A style of meal service in which guests serve themselves from a table, a buffet, or another surface where the serving dishes, dinnerware, and flatware are held. (27)

bulgur: A grain product made from whole wheat that has been cooked, dried, partly debranned, and cracked. (33)

bulimia nervosa: An eating disorder characterized by repeated eating binges and an inappropriate behavior to prevent weight gain. (9)

C

cacao: A plant that produces beans that are ground into cocoa or made into chocolate. (33)

caffeine: A naturally occurring compound in coffee and some other plant products that acts as a stimulant. (5)

Cajun cuisine: The hearty fare of rural Southern Louisiana, reflecting the foods and cooking methods of the Acadians, French, Native Americans, Africans, and Spanish. (29)

calorie: The unit used to measure the energy value of foods. (6)

calorie balance: The state in which a person's calories consumed equal the person's calories burned. (8)

candling: A process by which eggs are quality-graded. Bright lights are used to illuminate the egg's structure for inspection by skilled workers. (21)

canning: A food preservation process that involves sealing food in airtight containers. (28)

caramelization: Browning that occurs when heat is applied to sugar. (15)

caravan: A group of travelers who sell goods. (33)

carbohydrate: The nutrient that is the body's chief source of energy; also known as a *carb*. (6)

cardiorespiratory fitness: The ability of the heart and lungs to provide the body with the oxygen needed during physical activity. (9)

career: A series of related occupations that show progression in a field of work. (35)

career clusters: The 16 groups of occupations or career specialties that are similar or related to one another. (35)

carotene: A pigment found in orange vegetables, such as carrots and sweet potatoes; also a source of vitamin A. (18)

carotenoid: A pigment that gives fruits and vegetables their vibrant colors. (7)

cassava: A starchy root plant eaten as a side dish and used in flour form in cooking and baking; also known as *manioc*. (30)

casserole: A baking dish with high sides made of glass, glass-ceramic, or earthenware; some casseroles are designed for freezer-to-oven use (3); a combination of foods prepared in a single dish. (25)

caste: A group of people based largely on occupation that has a ranked order among other groups. (34)

caste system: An ancient social system still observed by the Indian culture, in which people are divided into groups based largely on occupation and have a ranked order. (34)

caviar: The processed, salted roe of large fish. (34)

cavity: A hole. (26)

celebratory: Festive. (27)

cereal: A starchy grain suitable to use as food. (16)

ceviche: A marinated raw fish dish. (30)

chapati: A flat, Indian bread. (34)

chef's knife: A versatile kitchen knife with a long, smooth blade for slicing, dicing, and mincing fresh fruits, vegetables, and herbs; also known as a *French knife*. (3)

chelo kebab: Iran's national dish, consisting of thin slices of marinated, charcoal-broiled lamb. (33)

chile: A hot pepper. (30)

chitterlings: The intestines of a hog. (29)

chlorophyll: A pigment found in green vegetables, such as broccoli and spinach. (18)

cholesterol: A fatlike substance that is present in skin tissue, aids in the transport of fatty acids in the body, and is needed to produce hormones. (6)

chopsticks: The eating utensils Chinese people use for all dishes except soup and finger foods. (34)

chorizo: A dark sausage with a spicy, smoky flavor. (32)

chowder: A cream soup made from unthickened milk. (25)

citrus fruit: A fruit with a thick outer rind and a thin membrane that separates the flesh into segments. (19)

clambake: An outdoor gathering at which clams and other foods are cooked. (27)

cloven: Split. (33)

coagulate: When denatured protein molecules form new bonds, causing muscle fibers to change in length and width. This squeezes out moisture, and the resulting food product is less liquid and more solid. (15)

coagulum: The soft protein clumps that form when a liquid egg mixture comes in contact with a hot surface. (21)

cockle: A type of mussel flourishing along the Welsh coast. (31)

coffee blend: A mixture of several varieties of coffee beans. (5)

colander: A perforated bowl used to drain fruits, vegetables, and pasta. (3)

colcannon: Mashed potatoes mixed with chopped scallions, shredded cooked cabbage, and melted butter. (31)

collagen: A protein in connective tissue that is strong and flexible and can be tenderized by cooking. (22)

combination oven: An oven that can do two types of cooking. (12)

comida: The main meal of the day served in the middle of the day. It is a leisurely meal likely to include several courses; also means *food*. (30)

commerce: The buying and selling of goods and services. (23)

commodity: An important economic good. (31)

commune: A group of people who share a living area, resources, and tasks. (34)

compact: Efficient use of space. (11)

comparison shopping: Evaluating different brands, sizes, and forms of a product before making a purchase decision. (14)

compatible: Able to coexist without conflict. (27)

complement: To complete or make better. (5)

compromise service: A compromise between Russian service and English service. (27)

concave: Curved inwardly. (28)

conduction: The movement of heat from one substance to another by direct contact. (15)

congee: A thick porridge made from rice or barley. (34)

consent: Permission. (36)

conservation: The planned use of a resource to avoid waste. (13)

consommé: Clear, rich-flavored soup made from clarified, concentrated stock. (25)

constrict: To become smaller; to shrink. (22)

contaminant: A potentially harmful substance that has accidentally been introduced to food. (2)

convection: A form of heat transfer that takes place when heated particles in a gas or liquid flow from a heated area to a cooler area, taking the heat with them. (15)

convection cooking: Cooking in an oven that uses a fan to circulate heated air around foods. (12)

convenience food: A food that has had some amount of service added to it. (13)

conversely: Oppositely. (26)

cooking losses: The fat, water, and other volatile substances that evaporate from the surface of meat during cooking. (22)

cooking time: The total amount of time food is exposed to energy; when preparing food in a microwave oven, it is the total amount of time food is exposed to microwave energy. (4)

corrode: To slowly deteriorate. (28)

course: A part of a meal made up of all the foods served at one time. (13)

cover: The table space holding all the tableware needed by one person. (11)

cover letter: A letter or an e-mail message inviting potential employers to review a person's résumé. (36)

crayfish: A crustacean related to the lobster. (31)

cream soup: A soup made with milk or cream instead of stock. (25)

Creole cuisine: A cuisine combining the cooking techniques of the French with ingredients of African, Caribbean, Spanish, and Native American cuisines. (29)

crêpe: A thin, delicate pancake usually rolled around a filling. (31)

crisper: The drawer or compartment in the refrigerator designed to keep vegetables firm and fresh. (18)

crisp-tender: Tender, but still slightly firm. (18)

croissant: A flaky, buttery yeast roll shaped into a crescent. (31)

cross-contact: The transfer of an allergen from a food source to a person with a food allergy. (10)

cross-contamination: The transfer of harmful bacteria from one food or surface to another food. (2)

crude: Simple. (34)

crustacean: A shellfish that is covered by a firm shell and has a segmented body, such as a shrimp, lobster, or crab. (24)

crystalline candy: Candy that contains fine sugar crystals. (26)

culture: The traditions and beliefs of a racial, religious, or social group. (1)

curb: To limit. (8)

curd: The solid part of coagulated milk. (20)

curdling: The formation of clumps or curds that can happen when milk is overheated or exposed to acids, tannins, enzymes, or salts. (20)

curry: A type of stew made with a mixture of spices. (34)

custard: A mixture of milk (or cream), eggs, sugar, and a flavoring that is cooked until thickened. (21)

custom: A typical way of behaving. (1)

customary: Usual. (4)

D

Daily Value: A reference amount of a nutrient that is used for food labeling. (14)

decaffeinated: Having had most of the caffeine removed. (5)

decision-making process: A method for thinking about possible options and outcomes before making a choice. (1)

deep frying: A dry-heat cooking method that cooks food by submerging it in hot oil. (15)

defect: A flaw. (12)

deficiency disease: An illness caused by the lack of a sufficient amount of a nutrient. (6)

dehydration: The removal of water from foods or other items (4); an unhealthy lack of water in the body. (9)

del pueblo: The food of the people. (32)

denaturation: The change in a protein's structure when heat, an alkali, or an acid is applied. (15)

dendê oil: Palm oil that gives Brazilian dishes a bright yellow-orange color. (30)

designated: Chosen. (27)

deterrent: An obstacle. (5)

detrimental: Harmful. (9)

dexterity: Skill and ease in use. (35)

diabetes: A common disease caused by the body's failure to produce or use insulin, resulting in an inability to keep blood sugar at normal levels. (6)

dialect: A form of a language spoken in a certain area. (33)

diet: All the food and drink a person regularly consumes. (10)

dietary fiber: A form of complex carbohydrates from plants that humans cannot digest. (6)

Dietary Guidelines for Americans: The federal government's nutritional advice. (8)

dietary pattern: The mix of foods and beverages making up a person's total dietary intake over time. (8)

Dietary Reference Intake (DRI): The estimated nutrient intake level used for planning and evaluating the diet of a healthy person. (8)

dietary supplement: A purified nutrient or non-nutrient substance that is manufactured or extracted from natural sources. (7)

digestion: The bodily process of breaking food down into simpler compounds the body can use. (6)

dinnerware: Plates, cups, saucers, and bowls. (11)

discerning: Showing good judgment. (5)

disparate: Markedly different. (9)

distinctive: Unique. (4)

double boiler: A small pan that fits into a larger pan containing simmering water. Food is placed in the smaller pan for gentle cooking. (3)

dough: A mixture containing liquid and a high proportion of flour that is stiff enough to be shaped by hand. (17)

dovetail: To overlap tasks to use time more efficiently. (4)

drawn fish: A fish that has the entrails removed. (24)

dressed fish: A fish that has the entrails, head, fins, and scales removed. (24)

drupe: A soft, fleshy fruit with an outer skin. The fruit surrounds a single, hard seed, which is called a *stone* or *pit*. (19)

E

eating disorder: An abnormal eating behavior that risks physical and mental health. (9)

economical: Cost-effective. (13)

economy: Savings. (19)

elaborate: Fancy. (13)

elasticity: The ability to yield to pressure and return to original shape. (16)

elastin: A protein in connective tissue that is very tough and elastic and cannot be softened by cooking. (22)

elicit: To bring about. (15)

emblem: A symbol. (31)

emit: To give off or release. (15)

empanada: A small turnover filled with any of a variety of fillings. (30)

empty calories: Calories obtained from solid fats and added sugars, which offer little nutritional value. (8)

emulsion: A mixture that forms when liquids are combined that ordinarily do not mix. (21)

endosperm: The largest part of a kernel. (16)

EnergyGuide label: A yellow tag that shows an estimate of yearly energy use for a major appliance. (12)

English service: The style of meal service in which one of the hosts fills plates at the table and passes them from guest to guest until everyone is served. (27)

en papillote: A French cooking technique using a pouch made of parchment paper to steam meats, seafood, vegetables, and herbs. (15)

enriched: Having added nutrients to replace those lost due to processing. (16)

enterprising: Daring. (29)

entice: To tempt. (1)

entrails: The insides. (24)

entree: A main course. (27)

entrepreneur: A person who starts and runs his or her own business. (35)

environment: Interrelated factors, such as air, water, soil, mineral resources, plants, and animals, that ultimately affect the survival of life on Earth. (1)

enzymatic browning: The darkening of fruit caused by exposure to the air. (19)

enzyme: A complex protein produced by living cells that causes a specific chemical reaction. (6)

escargot: A snail eaten as food. (31)

ethical behavior: Behavior conforming to accepted standards of fairness and good conduct. (36)

etiquette: The rules outlining polite ways of behaving. (27)

expel: To force out. (2)

F

fad: A practice that is very popular for a short time. (1)

fair trade product: An environmentally sustainably-produced good for which farmers and workers are paid a reasonable wage, workers are assured safe working conditions, and practices such as child and slave labor are prohibited. (1)

falafel: A mixture of ground chickpeas, bulgur, and spices formed into balls and deep-fried. (33)

fallacy: A mistaken belief. (1)

famine: A severe shortage of food. (29)

fasting: Denying oneself food. (1)

fat: An important nutrient that provides energy to and insulates the body. (6)

fat fish: A fish that has fattier flesh than that of a lean fish. (24)

fat-soluble vitamin: A vitamin that dissolves in fat. (7)

fatty acid: A chemical chain that contains carbon, hydrogen, and oxygen atoms that occur in lipids. (6)

feijoada completa: Brazil's national dish made with meat and black beans. (30)

fermentation: The process of yeast acting on the sugars in bread dough to form alcohol and carbon dioxide. (17)

filé: A flavoring and thickening agent made from sassafras leaves, which are dried and ground into a powder. (29)

fines herbes: A mixture of fresh chives, parsley, tarragon, and chervil. (31)

finfish: A fish that has fins and a backbone. (24)

fish and chips: Battered, deep-fried fish fillets served with the British version of french fries. (31)

fish fillet: The side of a fish cut lengthwise away from the backbone. (24)

fish steak: A cross-sectional slice taken from a dressed fish. (24)

fixed expense: A regularly recurring cost in a set amount. (13)

flatbread: Flat, thin bread. (5)

flatware: Knives, forks, spoons, serving utensils, and specialty utensils; also called *silverware*. (11)

flavone: A pigment found in white vegetables, such as cauliflower and parsnips. (18)

fleishig: Foods made with meat or poultry, as well as the utensils and dishes used with these foods. (33)

flexible expense: A regularly recurring cost that varies in amount. (13)

foliage: Plants. (27)

fond: The bits of food stuck on the bottom of the pan after cooking is complete. (15)

food additive: A substance added to food for a specific purpose. (14)

food allergy: A response of the body's immune system to a food protein. (10)

Food and Drug Administration (FDA): The government sector that ensures the health and safety of all foods other than meat, poultry, and eggs. (1)

foodborne illness: A disease transmitted by food. (2)

food-drug interaction: A reaction between a food and a drug that can affect how the body uses nutrients from the food or the way the drug is absorbed and used in the body. (10)

food intolerance: A negative reaction to a food substance that does not involve the immune system. (10)

fortified food: A food to which nutrients are added in amounts greater than what would naturally occur in the food. (7)

foster: To encourage. (10)

fraud: A fake. (35)

freeze-drying: A commercial food preservation technique that involves the removal of water vapor from frozen foods. (28)

freezer burn: A dry, tough area on food that results from freezer air coming into contact with a food surface and causing dehydration. (28)

frijoles refritos: Refried beans. (30)

fritter: A fruit dipped in batter and deep fried. (19)

functional: Useful. (11)

functional food: A food that provides health benefits beyond the nutrients it contains. (1)

fused: Joined. (3)

G

garnish: To add edible decorations to foods or serving dishes to make the foods look more appealing. (13)

gaucho: A nomadic herder of the Pampas during the eighteenth and nineteenth centuries. (30)

gazpacho: A popular Spanish soup often made with coarsely pureed tomatoes, onions, garlic, cucumbers, and green peppers; olive oil; and vinegar. (32)

gelatinization: The process in which starch granules are mixed with water and heated so they absorb water and swell, and the mixture thickens. (16)

genetically modified organism (GMO): A plant or an animal whose DNA has been changed in a way that does not happen in nature. (1)

germ: The reproductive part of a plant. (16)

ghee: Indian clarified butter. (34)

giblets. The edible internal organs of poultry, such as the heart and liver. (23)

globule: A very small drop. (20)

glucose: The form of sugar carried in the bloodstream for energy use throughout the body. (6)

gluten: A protein that gives strength and elasticity to batters and doughs and structure to baked products. (16)

glutinous: Gluelike. (34)

goal: An aim you try to reach. (1)

gohan: The Japanese word for *meal*; rice. (34)

goiter: The visible enlargement of the thyroid gland caused by iodine deficiency. (7)

gourmet: A person who values and enjoys fine food. (25)

grade: An indication of quality. (14)

GRAS list: The list of substances the FDA has ruled "Generally Recognized as Safe." (14)

gratuity: An amount of money paid for service received. (27)

grilling: A dry-heat cooking method in which the direct heat source is located below the food. (15)

ground: To connect an appliance electrically with the earth. (11)

growth spurt: A period of rapid growth. (10)

guacamole: A spread made from mashed avocado, tomato, and onion. (30)

gumbo: A soup reflecting the various cultures of Southern Louisiana. (29)

H

haggis: A pudding made from oatmeal, seasonings, and a sheep's organs boiled in a sheep's stomach. (31)

halal: Foods considered lawful according to Islam. (33)

haram: Foods that are forbidden according to Islam. (33)

hasenpfeffer: Rabbit that is first marinated in wine, vinegar, onions, and spices and then stewed in the marinade. (31)

haute cuisine: A class of French cuisine characterized by elaborate preparations, fancy garnishes, and rich sauces. (31)

headspace: The space between food and the closure of a food storage container. (28)

healthy weight: A BMI of 18.5 to 24.9. (9)

hemorrhaging: Bleeding. (7)

herald: To welcome enthusiastically. (31)

herb: A food seasoning made from the leaves of plants usually grown in temperate climates. (25)

hock: The hind joint. (32)

hollandaise sauce: A sauce containing egg yolks, lemon juice, and butter. (31)

holloware: Bowls and tureens, which are used to serve food, and pitchers and pots, which are used to serve liquids. (11)

homogenization: A mechanical process that breaks globules of milkfat into tiny particles and spreads them throughout the milk. (20)

hormone: A chemical that controls a certain body function or process. (6)

hors d'oeuvre: A small dish designed to stimulate the appetite. (31)

hot pack: A canning method in which food is heated in water, steam, syrup, or juices; packed loosely in jars; and covered with cooking liquid or boiling water. (28)

humus: A substance formed by decayed matter. (33)

hunger: The physical need for food. (1)

husmankost: The traditional, everyday, simple style of cooking in Sweden. (31)

hydrate: To consume water to restore a proper fluid balance (9); to cause to absorb water. (17)

hydrogenation: The process of adding hydrogen atoms to unsaturated fatty acids in liquid oils. (6)

hydroponic farming: Growing plants in a nutrient-rich liquid, rather than in soil. (1)

hypertension: High blood pressure. (7)

I

illiterate: Unable to read or write. (33)

immature fruit: A fruit that has not reached full size. (19)

impaired: Damaged. (2)

impulse buying: Making an unplanned purchase without much thought. (14)

imu: A pit lined with hot rocks covered with banana leaves. (29)

incentive: A reason. (35)

inclement: Harsh. (1)

income: Money that is received. (13)

inconspicuous: Unnoticeable. (27)

infrared radiation: Invisible waves of energy that act on particles in food. (15)

ingenuity: Cleverness. (29)

inherent: Built-in or characteristic. (15)

injera: A large, sourdoughlike pancake made from teff. (33)

insoluble: Unable to dissolve. (16)

insufficient: Not enough. (36)

interchangeably: In place of the other. (20)

intermingled: Mixed in. (30)

invert: To place upside down. (26)

irradiation: A commercial food preservation technique that exposes food to controlled doses of gamma rays, electron beams, or X-rays. (28)

J

jambalaya: A traditional Creole rice dish containing rice; seasonings; and shellfish, poultry, and/or sausage. (29)

julienne: To cut into thin, matchstick-sized strips. (18)

K

kaiseka: A delicate meal enjoyed by Japanese people that can be served after a tea ceremony. (34)

kartoffelpuffer: Potato pancakes enjoyed throughout Germany. (31)

kasha: A staple food for Russian peasants usually made from buckwheat. The raw grain is fried and then simmered until tender. (34)

kashrut: The religious dietary laws set out by Judaism. (33)

kernel: A whole seed of a cereal. (16)

kibbutz: A collective community in which many of Israel's citizens live. (33)

kilocalorie: The unit used to measure the energy value of foods. (9)

kimchi: A national dish served with nearly every meal in Korea. It is salted cabbage fermented with spicy red pepper. (34)

kosher: Prepared according to the Jewish dietary laws. (33)

kulich: A tall, cylindrical yeast cake filled with fruits and nuts. (34)

L

lamb: The meat of sheep less than one year old. (22)

Latin America: The landmass stretching southward from the Rio Grande to the tip of South America. (30)

leaching: Seeping. (4)

leadership: The ability to guide and motivate others to complete tasks or achieve goals. (36)

lean fish: A fish that has very little fat in its flesh. (24)

leavening agent: An ingredient that produces gases in batters and doughs. (17)

legumes: Beans, peas, and lentils that are commonly sold in dry form. (18)

lesion: A sore. (7)

lifelong learning: Continually updating one's knowledge and skills. (35)

lifestyle: The way a person usually lives. (1)

lingonberry: A tart, red berry. (31)

lowland: A flat, sandy plain. (31)

luau: An elaborate outdoor feast that is still popular in the Hawaiian Islands today. (29)

lush: Plentiful in healthy growth. (30)

lutefisk: Dried cod that has been soaked in a lye solution before cooking. (31)

M

macromineral: A mineral needed in the diet in amounts of 100 milligrams or more each day. (7)

Maillard reaction: A chemical process that occurs when heat is applied to foods containing both amino acids and sugars, producing a distinct flavor and aroma. (15)

malnutrition: A lack of the right proportions of nutrients over an extended period. (6)

mandatory: Required. (22)

manioc: A starchy root plant eaten as a side dish and used in flour form in cooking and baking; also known as *cassava*. (30)

manners: Social behavior. (27)

marbling: Flecks of fat throughout the lean muscles of meat. (22)

mariner: A seafarer. (32)

marvel: To show awe, appreciation, and wonder. (32)

masala: A mixture of spices used to make curries. (34)

matzo: An unleavened bread. (33)

mazza: Appetizers at an Arab meal. (33)

meal: Grain ground into a powder. (16)

meal manager: Someone who uses resources to reach goals related to preparing and serving food. (13)

meat: The edible portions of mammals, which contain muscle, fat, bone, connective tissue, and water. (22)

mechanical convection: A type of heat transfer in which fans are used to create the flow moving the heated particles. (15)

medical nutrition therapy (MNT): A healthcare approach that helps people learn to use their eating habits as part of their treatment. (10)

melon: A large, juicy fruit produced by any of several plants in the gourd family. (19)

menu: A list of the foods to be served at a meal. (13)

meringue: A fluffy, white mixture of beaten egg whites and sugar. (21)

metabolism: The chemical processes that take place in the cells after the body absorbs nutrients. (6)

meteorologist: A professional who studies weather and atmosphere. (30)

mezedhes: Greek appetizers such as olives, feta cheese, pistachio nuts, garlic-flavored sausage, shrimp, and hard-cooked eggs. (32)

microorganism: A living substance so small it can be seen only under a microscope. (2)

microwave radiation: A type of radiation in which energy is transferred through short, high-frequency waves. (15)

milchig: Foods made with milk and the utensils used to prepare, serve, and eat them. (33)

milkfat: The fat portion of milk. (20)

milk solids: Substances that contain most of the vitamins, minerals, protein, and sugar found in milk. (20)

mineral: An inorganic substance that helps regulate body processes and becomes part of bones, soft tissues, and body fluids. (7)

minestrone: A satisfying soup made with onions, carrots, zucchini, celery, cabbage, rice or pasta, and seasonings. (32)

modest: Limited in size. (8)

modified atmosphere packaging (MAP): A commercial packaging technique that changes the makeup of the gases in the air surrounding a food inside a package. (28)

mold: A growth produced on damp or decaying organic matter or on living organisms. (28)

mole: A complex, chile-flavored sauce. (30)

mollusk: A shellfish that has a soft body partially or fully covered by a hard shell. Oysters, clams, and scallops are examples. (24)

monsoon: A storm with high winds and heavy rains. (34)

MyPlate: The USDA's food guidance system. (8)

N

national brand: A brand that is advertised and sold throughout the country. (14)

national dish: A food associated with a certain country and very popular among the nation's people. (30)

natural convection: A type of convection occurring when the transfer of heat is caused by the inherent movement of water particles from a warmer area to a cooler one, which creates a circular flow. (15)

natural light: Light that comes from the sun. (11)

negotiation: The process of agreeing on an issue that requires all parties to give and take. (36)

networking: The exchange of information or services among individuals or groups. (36)

nibble: To eat slowly. (27)

night blindness: A reduced ability to see in dim light. (7)

nihon-cha: Green teas. (34)

nobility: The highest social class. (31)

nomadic: Wandering; traveling. (30)

noncrystalline candy: Candy that does not contain sugar crystals. (26)

nonstick finish: A coating applied to both the inside and outside of cookware and bakeware that prevents foods from sticking. (3)

nonverbal communication: The sending and receiving of messages without the use of words. (36)

nouvelle cuisine: A class of French cuisine emphasizing lightness and natural taste in foods. (31)

novice: A beginner. (26)

nutrient: A chemical substance from food that the body needs to live. (6)

nutrient dense: Providing vitamins, minerals, and other health-promoting substances with little or no added sugar, saturated fat, and sodium. (8)

nutrition: The study of how the body uses the nutrients in the foods that are eaten. (6)

nutrition labeling: A breakdown of how a food product fits in an average diet. (14)

O

obesity: A condition characterized by excessive deposits of body fat. (9)

oblong: Elongated. (26)

occupation: Paid employment involving related skills and experience. (35)

offal: The edible parts of an animal, other than the muscles; also known as *variety meats*. (22)

okra: A green, pod-shaped vegetable brought to the United States from Africa. (29)

omelet: A beaten egg mixture that is cooked without stirring and served folded in half. (21)

opaque: Not clear or see-through; solid. (16)

open dating: The use of calendar dates on perishable and semiperishable foods to help retailers know how long to display products. It can help consumers choose products that will maintain quality the longest. (14)

open stock: A supply of tableware in which each piece is available for purchase individually. (11)

optimum: Ideal; the best, most appropriate. (26)

organic food: A food produced without the use of synthetic fertilizers, pesticides, or growth stimulants. (14)

osteoporosis: A condition caused by calcium deficiency that results in bone weakness, porousness, and brittleness. (7)

outlook: Attitude. (8)

overabundance: An excess; a surplus. (28)

overweight: Having a BMI of 25 to 29.9. (9)

P

paella: A Spanish rice dish with many variations. (32)

palatable: Fit to be eaten. (19)

panfrying: A dry-heat cooking method very similar to sautéing, but using more fat. (15)

parasite: A microorganism that needs another organism, called a *host*, to live. (2)

pareve: Foods and utensils that are neither milchig nor fleishig. (33)

paskha: A rich cheesecake molded into a pyramid and decorated with the letters *XB*. (34)

pasta: A dough that may or may not be dried. (16)

pasteurization: A process by which a food product is heated to destroy harmful bacteria. (20)

pastry: The dough used to make piecrusts. (26)

pathogen: A microorganism that causes disease. (2)

peasant: A person who does not have much money and has a low social status. (31)

pectin: A carbohydrate found in all fruits that makes fruit juices jell. (28)

peer pressure: The influence that comes from people in a person's social group. (1)

pellagra: A disease caused by niacin deficiency that results in skin lesions, digestive problems, mental disorders, and possibly death. (7)

Pennsylvania Dutch: A group of German immigrants who settled in the southeast section of Pennsylvania. (29)

perishable: Likely to spoil. (5)

peristalsis: Waves of contractions with which muscles push food through the digestive tract. (6)

permanent emulsion: A type of mixture that will not separate on standing. (25)

persevere: To press on. (36)

pesticide: An agent used to kill insects, weeds, and fungi that attack crops. (14)

phyllo: A paper-thin pastry made with flour and water. (32)

Physical Activity Guidelines for Americans (PAG): A key resource issued by the U.S. Department of Health and Human Services (HHS) to help people stay fit. (9)

physical fitness: The body's ability to meet the demands of daily life. (9)

phytonutrient: A compound from plants that is active in the human body. (7)

pickling: A food preservation technique that involves soaking foods in a vinegar or salt solution. (28)

picturesque: Beautiful. (34)

pita bread: A flat, round, hollow bread found throughout the Middle East, as well as in Africa. (33)

pitting: A marking with tiny indentations. (3)

pizza: A dish with Italian origins. It is typically made of flattened dough, spread with flavorful sauce, covered with toppings, and baked. (5)

place setting: All the tableware pieces used by one person. (11)

plantain: A green, starchy fruit that has a bland flavor and looks much like a large banana. (30)

plateau: A flat area that is higher in elevation than the surrounding land. (30)

pliable: Supple. (19)

poaching: Cooking food in liquid at a moderate temperature between 160°F to 180°F (71°C to 82°C). (15)

pome: A fruit with a central, seed-containing core surrounded by a thick layer of flesh. (19)

pork: The meat of hogs. (22)

porous: Spongy. (26)

portfolio: A collection of materials assembled and organized to showcase a person's qualifications, skills, and talents. (36)

pot: A piece of cookware with two handles used for cooking foods in liquid over direct heat. (3)

potluck: A shared meal to which each person or family brings food for the whole group to eat. (29)

poultry: Any domesticated bird. (23)

precycling: Thinking about how packaging materials can be reused or recycled before buying a product. (14)

prepreparation: Any step done in advance to save time when getting a meal ready. (13)

pressure cooker: A specialized saucepan or portable kitchen appliance that uses steam and pressure to shorten cooking time by increasing temperatures above the boiling point. (15)

prior: Before. (20)

processed cheese: A cheese made when a natural cheese is heated and emulsifiers are added to prevent the blended mixture from separating. (20)

processed food: A food that has undergone some preparation procedure, such as canning, freezing, drying, cooking, or fortification. (8)

processing time: The amount of time canned goods remain under heat (or under heat and pressure) in a canner. (28)

produce: Fresh fruits and vegetables. (14)

profit: Any money remaining after a business has paid its expenses. (35)

promote: To encourage. (4)

prospector: An explorer who searches for mineral deposits. (29)

prosperous: Economically successful. (31)

protein: A chemical compound that provides energy to the body and aids in the formation of enzymes, some hormones, and antibodies. Also known as a *macronutrient* or an *energy nutrient*. (6)

protein-energy malnutrition (PEM): A condition that results from a diet not containing enough protein and calories. PEM causes fatigue and weight loss in adults. (6)

province: A settlement. (29)

provincial cuisine: The style of cooking practiced by most French families that includes the flavors of locally grown foods enhanced by simple cooking methods. (31)

proximity: Physical closeness. (30)

pudding basin: A deep, thick-rimmed bowl used for steaming British pudding. (31)

punctual: Always prompt and on time. (36)

Q

quiche: A custard tart served in many variations as an appetizer and a main dish. (31)

quick-freezing: A food preservation method in which foods are subjected to temperatures between −25°F and −40°F (−32°C and −40°C) for a short time. (28)

R

radiation: The transfer of heat through electro-magnetic energy by way of infrared waves and microwaves. (15)

rancid: Pungent, expired. (28)

raw pack: A method of canning in which raw fruits or vegetables are packed into containers. (28)

recall: The removal of a product from the market. (14)

recipe: A set of instructions for preparing a specific food. (4)

reconstitute: To restore to a former condition by adding water. (18)

reduction: A sauce made by cooking a flavorful liquid until some of the water evaporates and the liquid thickens. (25)

reference: An individual who can speak to your work history and personal qualities. (36)

refined: Having had the bran and germ, along with the nutrients they provide, removed during processing. (16)

regimen: A systematic plan. (9)

regulate: To control. (6)

reservation: A request for a restaurant to hold a table for a guest. (27)

residue: The remains. (2)

résumé: A document listing your education and work experience. (36)

retail cut: A smaller piece of meat than a wholesale cut that is sold to consumers. (22)

retain: To keep. (18)

retard: To delay. (12)

retort packaging: A type of commercial packaging in which food is sealed in a foil pouch and then sterilized in a steam-pressure vessel known as a *retort*. (28)

rickets: A disease caused by vitamin D deficiency that results in bone abnormalities. (7)

ripened cheese: A cheese made with controlled amounts of bacteria, mold, yeast, or enzymes. (20)

risotto: A rice dish made with butter, chopped onion, stock or wine, and Parmesan cheese. (32)

rivaling: Competing with. (31)

roasting: A dry-heat cooking method performed with food in an uncovered pan in a preheated oven at temperatures between 300°F and 425°F (149°C and 219°C). It involves foods with solid structures prior to cooking. (15)

roux: A cooked paste of equal parts fat and flour. (25)

RSVP: The abbreviation for a French phrase that means "please respond." (27)

Russian (continental) service: The most formal style of meal service, in which waiters serve guests filled plates of food, one course at a time. (27)

rustic: Rural or country-like. (30)

S

sachet: A cheesecloth bag of dried herbs and whole spices. (25)

salad: A combination of raw and/or cooked ingredients, usually served cold with a dressing. (25)

saliva: A mucus- and enzyme-containing liquid secreted by the mouth that moistens food particles. (6)

sandwich: A food item in which ingredients are placed on, in, or between bread. (5)

sanitation: Maintaining conditions to prevent disease and promote good health. (2)

saucepan: A piece of cookware with one handle used for cooking foods in liquid over direct heat. (3)

sauerkraut: Fermented or pickled cabbage. (31)

sauna: A steam bath in which water is poured on hot stones to create steam. (31)

sautéing: A dry-heat cooking method that cooks food quickly, in a small amount of fat, over high heat. (15)

savanna: A grassland. (33)

schi: Cabbage soup. (34)

scorching: Burning that results in a color change. (20)

scum: The solid layer that often forms on the surface of milk during heating. (20)

scurvy: A disease caused by vitamin C deficiency that results in weakness, bleeding gums, tooth loss, and internal bleeding. (7)

sedentary: Requiring much sitting. (8)

segmented: Divided into sections. (24)

self-motivation: An inner desire to perform well. (36)

serrated blade: A knife blade with a sawtooth edge. (3)

service contract: A contract that covers the cost of needed repairs for an appliance for a period after the manufacturer's warranty has expired. (12)

service learning: Using what is learned in the class-room to meet a need in the community. (36)

shelf life: The amount of time a food can be stored and remain wholesome. (28)

shellfish: A fish that has a hard outer shell instead of a backbone. (24)

shohet: A licensed slaughterer. (33)

shortened cake: A cake containing fat. (26)

simmering: A moist-heat cooking method using hotter liquid than used in poaching, with temperatures ranging from 180°F to 205°F (82°C to 96°C). (15)

slurry: A liquid mixture of milk and flour blended together until smooth; used to thicken sauces. (25)

smoke point: A specific temperature at which an oil breaks down and starts to produce a foul smell, bitter taste, or small amount of smoke. (15)

smörgåsbord: A buffet including a wide variety of hot and cold dishes. (31)

smørrebrød: Open-faced sandwiches usually made with thin, sour rye bread spread thickly with butter. (31)

snack: A light meal. (5)

solemn: Serious or somber. (29)

soufflé: A fluffy baked preparation made with a starch-thickened sauce that is folded into stiffly beaten egg whites. (21)

soul food: A distinct cuisine developed in the South, combining the food customs of African slaves with the food customs of Native Americans and European sharecroppers. (29)

sourdough: A dough containing active microscopic yeast plants. (29)

sous vide: A combination cooking method in which food is vacuum sealed in an airtight plastic bag and then placed in a water bath to heat the food thoroughly. (15)

soybean: A legume with seeds rich in protein and oil. (34)

spätzle: Small dumplings made from wheat flour. (31)

spectrum: A range. (18)

spice: A food seasoning made from the dried roots, stems, or seeds of plants grown mainly in the tropics. (25)

spokes: Lines radiating from the center. (23)

sporadic: Infrequent. (36)

springform pan: A round cake pan with a removable bottom and sides that hook together with a latch or spring. This pan is used for making cheesecakes, tortes, and other desserts that are delicate and difficult to remove from the pan. (3)

standing time: The time during which foods finish cooking by internal heat after being removed from a microwave or traditional oven. (4)

starch: A complex carbohydrate stored in plants. (16)

steaming: A moist-heat cooking method that is gentler than boiling and good for delicate foods, such as vegetables, fish, and seafood. (15)

stemware: A type of beverageware that has three parts—a bowl, a stem, and a foot. (11)

stewing: A combination cooking method achieved by using a dry-heat cooking method to sear small pieces of food, which are then cooked using a moist-heat cooking method until tender. (15)

stir-frying: A dry-heat cooking method similar to sautéing, but performed with a very high heat source and requiring the food to be tossed constantly. (15)

stock soup: A soup made with rich-flavored broth in which meat, poultry, or fish bones; vegetables; and seasonings have been cooked. (25)

store brand: A brand sold only by a store or chain of stores. (14)

stress: Mental and physical tension caused by change. (1)

strudel: Paper-thin layers of pastry filled with plums, apples, cherries, or poppy seeds. (31)

sugar syrup: A mixture of sugar and liquid that is cooked to a thick consistency. (26)

sukiyaki: A popular Japanese dish that combines two cooking methods—nimono and nabemono. It is made of thinly sliced meat, bean curd, and vegetables cooked in a sauce. (34)

surmise: To assume. (1)

sushi: Balls of cooked rice flavored with vinegar and served with strips of raw or cooked fish, eggs, vegetables, or seaweed. (34)

sustainability: Practices that either preserve or improve societal, environmental, and economic conditions for future generations. (1)

sweating: A dry-heat cooking method similar to sautéing, but performed at a much lower temperature. (15)

syneresis: The leakage of water from the gel formed by starch mixtures. (16)

synthetic: Man-made; artificially created. (7, 20)

T

table appointments: All the items needed at the table to serve and eat a meal. (11)

table linens: Table coverings and napkins. (11)

taboo: A prohibition. (33)

tandoori: A simple cooking technique unique to Indian cuisine that involves baking foods in a clay oven. (34)

tapas: Appetizers often beginning Spanish meals. (32)

taste buds: Flavor sensors that cover the surface of the tongue. (13)

taverna: A café serving as a public meeting place. (32)

tea: The leaves of a small tropical evergreen used to make a beverage (5); a light meal. (31)

team: A small group of people working together for a common purpose. (36)

technology: The use of knowledge to develop improved methods for doing tasks. (1)

teff: A milletlike grain grown only in Africa and the Middle East. (33)

temperate: Mild, not extreme. (25)

temporary emulsion: A substance that must be shaken before each use due to the separation of the oil and water-based liquids when at rest. (25)

therapeutic diet: An eating plan prescribed by a health professional. (10)

thorax: The middle division of the body. (24)

tillable: Farmable. (34)

time-work schedule: A written plan that lists times for doing specific tasks to prepare a meal or food product. (4)

tip: An amount of money paid for service received. (27)

tofu: A custardlike cake made from soybeans that has a very mild flavor. (34)

tortilla: A flat, unleavened bread made from cornmeal or wheat flour and water. (30)

toxic: Poisonous. (3)

toxicity: Poisoning. (6)

toxin: A poison. (2)

trace element: A mineral needed in amounts less than 100 milligrams per day. (7)

trans **fatty acid:** A fatty acid with an odd molecular shape that increases the risk of heart disease; also known as a *trans fat*. (6)

transferable skills: The skills, such as accurate reading, writing, speaking, math, and computer skills, that are useful in all jobs. (35)

translucent: See-through. (16)

transmission: Spread. (2)

tropical fruit: A fruit grown in a warm climate and considered to be somewhat exotic. (19)

truffle: A rare type of fungi that grows underground near oak trees. (31)

tsukemono: Pickled foods. (34)

tumbler: A type of beverageware that does not have a stem. (11)

typhoon: A severe storm bringing heavy rains and damaging winds. (34)

U

ultra-high temperature (UHT) processing: A preservation method that uses higher temperatures than regular pasteurization to increase the shelf life of foods such as milk. (20)

underripe fruit: A full-sized fruit that has not yet reached peak eating quality. (19)

underweight: Having a BMI under 18.5. (9)

United States Department of Agriculture (USDA): The government sector that promotes farm production that feeds people in the United States. (1)

unit pricing: A listing of a product's cost per standard unit, weight, or measure. (14)

universal design: The features of rooms, furnishings, and equipment that are usable by as many people as possible. (11)

Universal Product Code (UPC): A series of lines, bars, and numbers appearing on packages of food and nonfood items used to identify a product, its manufacturer, its size, and its form. (14)

unripened cheese: A cheese ready for marketing as soon as the whey has been removed. This cheese is not allowed to ripen or age. (20)

unshortened cake: A cake containing no fat; also called *foam cake*. (26)

V

vacuum packaging: A commercial packaging technique that removes most of the air so the packaging material forms a tight seal around the food. (28)

value: An item or idea that a person or group considers important. (1)

veal: The meat that comes from young calves. (22)

vegetarian diet: A diet built partly or entirely on plant foods. (10)

verbal communication: Communication involving the use of words to send or receive a message. (36)

verbatim: Word for word. (36)

vessel: A ship. (24)

vigorously: Enthusiastically, with strength. (26)

viscosity: The resistance to flow; thickness. (15)

vitamin: A complex organic substance that the body needs in small amounts for normal growth, maintenance, and reproduction. (7)

volatile: Easily vaporized. (22)

W

waist circumference: The distance around the natural waistline. (9)

warranty: A seller's promise that a product will be free of defects and will perform as specified. (12)

wat: A spicy sauce or stew popular in Ethiopia. (33)

water-soluble vitamin: A vitamin that dissolves in water. (7)

watt: A unit of power; the cooking power of microwave ovens is measured and expressed in watts. (4)

weeping: The layer of moisture that sometimes forms between a meringue and a filling. (21)

weight management: Using resources, such as food choices and physical activity, to reach and/or maintain a healthy weight. (9)

welfare: Well-being. (21)

well: An indentation. (17)

wellness: The state of being in overall good health. (1)

wellspring: A significant source. (31)

wharf: A dock. (31)

whey: The liquid part of coagulated milk. (20)

whisk: A mixing tool made of loops of wire attached to a handle, used to incorporate air into foods. (3)

white sauce: A starch-thickened milk product often used as a base for other sauces. (25)

whole grain: Containing all three parts of the kernel. (16)

wholesale cut: A large cut of meat for use at a retail grocery store or meat market. (22)

wok: A metal, bowl-shaped frying pan with a rounded bottom and deep, slanted sides used in Chinese cooking. (15)

work center: A section in a kitchen that has been designed around a specific activity or specific activities. (11)

work simplification: The performance of tasks in the simplest way possible to conserve time and energy. (13)

work triangle: An imaginary triangle with focal points at the major work centers that follows the normal flow of food preparation. (11)

wrap: A filling rolled in some type of flatbread. (5)

Y

yeast: A microscopic fungus that can cause fermentation in preserved foods, resulting in spoilage. (28)

yield: The average amount or number of servings a recipe makes. (4)

Z

zakuska: Russian appetizers. (34)

Index

H

Recipe Index